Nineteenth-Century Literature Criticism

Topics Volume

Guide to Gale Literary Criticism Series

When you need to review criticism of literary works, these are the Gale series to use:

If the author's death date is:	You should turn to:

After Dec. 31, 1959 (or author is still living)

CONTEMPORARY LITERARY CRITICISM

for example: Jorge Luis Borges, Anthony Burgess, William Faulkner, Mary Gordon, Ernest Hemingway, Iris Murdoch

1900 through 1959

TWENTIETH-CENTURY LITERARY CRITICISM

for example: Willa Cather, F. Scott Fitzgerald, Henry James, Mark Twain, Virginia Woolf

1800 through 1899

NINETEENTH-CENTURY LITERATURE CRITICISM

for example: Fyodor Dostoevsky, Nathaniel Hawthorne, George Sand, William Wordsworth

1400 through 1799

LITERATURE CRITICISM FROM 1400 TO 1800 (excluding Shakespeare)

for example: Anne Bradstreet, Daniel Defoe, Alexander Pope, François Rabelais, Jonathan Swift, Phillis Wheatley

SHAKESPEAREAN CRITICISM

Shakespeare's plays and poetry

Antiquity through 1399

CLASSICAL AND MEDIEVAL LITERATURE CRITICISM

for example: Dante, Homer, Plato, Sophocles, Vergil, the Beowulf Poet

Gale also publishes related criticism series:

BLACK LITERATURE CRITICISM

This three-volume series presents criticism of works by major black writers of the past two hundred years.

CHILDREN'S LITERATURE REVIEW

This series covers authors of all eras who have written for the preschool through high school audience.

DRAMA CRITICISM

This series covers playwrights of all nationalities and periods of literary history.

POETRY CRITICISM

This series covers poets of all nationalities and periods of literary history.

SHORT STORY CRITICISM

This series covers the major short fiction writers of all nationalities and periods of literary history.

ISSN 0732-1864

Volume 36

Nineteenth-Century Literature Criticism

Excerpts from Criticism of the
Works of Novelists, Poets, Playwrights,
Short Story Writers, Philosophers, and Other
Creative Writers Who Died between 1800
and 1899, from the First Published Critical
Appraisals to Current Evaluations

Joann Cerrito

Editor

**Alan Hedblad
Jelena O. Krstović
James E. Person, Jr.
Mark Swartz**

Associate Editors

Gale Research Inc. · DETROIT · LONDON

Since this page cannot legibly accommodate all copyright notices, the acknowledgments constitute an extension of the copyright notice.

While every effort has been made to ensure the reliability of the information presented in this publication, Gale Research Inc. neither guarantees the accuracy of the data contained herein nor assumes any responsibility for errors, omissions, or discrepancies. Gale accepts no payment for listing; and inclusion in the publication of any organization, agency, institution, publication, service, or individual does not imply endorsement of the editors or publisher. Errors brought to the attention of the publisher and verified to the satisfaction of the publisher will be corrected in future editions.

The paper used in this publication meets the minimum requirements of American National Standard for Information Sciences—Permanence Paper for Printed Library Materials, ANSI Z39.48-1984. ∞™

Library of Congress Catalog Card Number 76-46132
ISBN 0-8103-5836-0
ISSN 0732-1864

Printed in the United States of America

Published simultaneously in the United Kingdom
by Gale Research International Limited
(An affiliated company of Gale Research Inc.)

10 9 8 7 6 5 4 3 2 1

Contents

Preface

Since its inception in 1981, *Nineteenth-Century Literature Criticism* has been a valuable resource for students and librarians seeking critical commentary on writers of this transitional period in world history. Designated an "Outstanding Reference Source" by the American Library Association with the publication of its first volume, *NCLC* has since been purchased by over 6,000 school, public, and university libraries. The series has covered more than 300 authors representing 26 nationalities and over 15,000 titles. No other reference source has surveyed the critical reaction to nineteenth-century authors and literature as thoroughly as *NCLC*.

Scope of the Series

NCLC is designed to serve as an introduction for students and advanced readers to the authors of the nineteenth century, and to the most significant interpretations of these authors' works. The great poets, novelists, short story writers, dramatists, and philosophers of this period are frequently studied in high school and college literature courses. By organizing and reprinting the enormous amount of commentary written on these authors, *NCLC* helps students develop valuable insight into literary history, promotes a better understanding of the texts, and sparks ideas for papers and assignments. Each entry in *NCLC* presents a comprehensive survey of an author's career or an individual work of literature and provides the user with a multiplicity of interpretations and assessments. Such variety allows students to pursue their own interests; furthermore, it fosters an awareness that literature is dynamic and responsive to many different opinions.

Every fourth volume of *NCLC* is devoted to literary topics that cannot be covered under the author approach used in the rest of the series. Such topics include literary movements, prominent themes in nineteenth-century literature, literary reaction to political and historical events, significant eras in literary history, prominent literary anniversaries, and the literatures of cultures that are often overlooked by English-speaking readers.

NCLC continues the survey of criticism of world literature begun by Gale's *Contemporary Literary Criticism (CLC)* and *Twentieth-Century Literary Criticism (TCLC)*, both of which excerpt and reprint commentary on authors of the twentieth century. For additional information about *TCLC, CLC,* and Gale's other criticism series, users should consult the Guide to Gale Literary Criticism Series preceding the title page in this volume.

Coverage

Each volume of *NCLC* is carefully compiled to present:

- criticism of authors, or literary topics, representing a variety of genres and nationalities
- both major and lesser-known writers and literary works of the period
- 7-10 authors or 4-6 topics per volume
- individual entries that survey critical response to each author's work or each topic in literary history, including early criticism to reflect initial reactions; later criticism to represent any rise or decline in reputation; and current retrospective analyses.

Organization of This Book

An author entry consists of the following elements: author heading, biographical and critical introduction, list of principal works, excerpts of criticism (each preceded by an annotation and followed by a bibliographic citation), and a bibliography of further reading.

- The **author heading** consists of the name under which the author most commonly wrote, followed by birth and death dates. If an author wrote consistently under a pseudonym, the pseudonym will be listed in the author heading and the real name given in parentheses on the first line of the biographical and critical introduction. Also located at the beginning of the introduction to the author entry are any name variations under which an author wrote, including transliterated forms for authors whose languages use nonroman alphabets.

- The **biographical and critical introduction** outlines the author's life and career, as well as the critical issues surrounding his or her work. References are provided to past volumes of *NCLC* and to other biographical and critical reference series published by Gale, including *Children's Literature Review, Contemporary Authors, Dictionary of Literary Biography, Drama Criticism, Poetry Criticism, Short Story Criticism,* and *Something about the Author.*

• Most *NCLC* entries include **portraits** of the author. Many entries also contain reproductions of materials pertinent to an author's career, including manuscript pages, title pages, dust jackets, letters, and drawings, as well as photographs of important people, places, and events in an author's life.

• The list of **principal works** is chronological by date of first book publication and identifies the genre of each work. In the case of foreign authors with both foreign-language publications and English translations, the title and date of the first English-language edition are given in brackets. Unless otherwise indicated, dramas are dated by first performance, not first publication.

• **Criticism** is arranged chronologically in each author entry to provide a perspective on changes in critical evaluation over the years. All titles of works by the author featured in the entry are printed in boldface type to enable the user to easily locate discussion of particular works. Also for purposes of easier identification, the critic's name and the publication date of the essay are given at the beginning of each piece of criticism. Unsigned criticism is preceded by the title of the journal in which it appeared. Publication information (such as publisher names and book prices) and parenthetical numerical references (such as footnotes or page and line references to specific editions of works) have been deleted at the editors' discretion to provide smoother reading of the text.

• Critical excerpts are prefaced by **annotations** providing the reader with information about both the critic and the criticism that follows. Included are the critic's reputation, individual approach to literary criticism, and particular expertise in an author's works. Also noted are the relative importance of a work of criticism, the scope of the excerpt, and the growth of critical controversy or changes in critical trends regarding an author. In some cases, these annotations cross-reference excerpts by critics who discuss each other's commentary.

• A complete **bibliographic citation** designed to facilitate location of the original essay or book follows each piece of criticism.

• An annotated list of **further reading** appearing at the end of each author entry suggests secondary sources on the author. In some cases it includes essays for which the editors could not obtain reprint rights.

Cumulative Indexes

• Each volume of *NCLC* contains a cumulative **author index** listing all authors who have appeared in Gale's Literary Criticism Series, along with cross-references to such biographical series as *Contemporary Authors* and *Dictionary of Literary Biography.* Useful for locating authors within the various series, this index is particularly valuable for those authors who are identified by a certain period but who, because of their death dates, are placed in another, or for those authors whose careers span two periods. For example, Fyodor Dostoevsky is found in *NCLC,* yet Leo Tolstoy, another major nineteenth-century Russian novelist, is found in *TCLC* because he died after 1899.

• Each *NCLC* volume includes a cumulative **nationality index** which lists all authors who have appeared in *NCLC,* arranged alphabetically under their respective nationalities, as well as Topics volume entries devoted to particular national literatures.

• Each new volume in Gale's Literary Criticism Series includes a cumulative **topic index,** which lists all literary topics treated in *NCLC, TCLC, LC 1400-1800,* and the *CLC* Yearbook.

• Each new volume of *NCLC,* with the exception of the Topics volumes, contains a **title index** listing the titles of all literary works discussed in the volume. The first volume of *NCLC* published each year contains an index listing all titles discussed in the series since its inception. Titles discussed in the Topics volume entries are not included in the *NCLC* cumulative index.

A Note to the Reader

When writing papers, students who quote directly from any volume in Gale's Literary Criticism Series may use the following general forms to footnote reprinted criticism. The first example pertains to material drawn from periodicals, the second to material reprinted from books.

[1] T. S. Eliot, "John Donne," *The Nation and the Athenaeum,* 33 (9 June 1923), 321-32; excerpted and reprinted in *Literature Criticism from 1400 to 1800,* Vol. 10, ed. James E. Person, Jr. (Detroit: Gale Research, 1989), pp. 28-9.

[2] Clara G. Stillman, *Samuel Butler: A Mid-Victorian Modern* (Viking Press, 1932); excerpted and reprinted in *Twentieth-Century Literary Criticism,* Vol. 33, ed. Paula Kepos (Detroit: Gale Research, 1989), pp. 43-5.

Suggestions Are Welcome

In response to suggestions, several features have been added to *NCLC* since the series began, including annotations to excerpted criticism, a cumulative index to authors in all Gale literary criticism series, entries devoted to criticism on a single work by a major author, more extensive illustrations, and a title index listing all literary works discussed in the series since its inception.

Readers who wish to suggest authors or topics to appear in future volumes, or who have other suggestions, are cordially invited to write the editors.

ACKNOWLEDGMENTS

The editors wish to thank the copyright holders of the excerpted criticism included in this volume, the permissions managers of many book and magazine publishing companies for assisting us in securing reprint rights, and Anthony Bogucki for assistance with copyright research. We are also grateful to the staffs of the Detroit Public Library Complex, and University of Michigan Libraries for making their resources available to us. Following is a list of copyright holders who have granted us permission to reprint material in this volume of *NCLC*. Every effort has been made to trace copyright, but if omissions have been made, please let us know.

COPYRIGHTED EXCERPTS IN *NCLC,* VOLUME 36, WERE REPRINTED FROM THE FOLLOWING PERIODICALS:

Comparative Literature Studies, v. XV, March, 1978. Copyright © 1978 by The Pennsylvania State University. Reproduced by permission of The Pennsylvania State University Press.—*The Drama Review,* v. 13, Winter, 1968 for "Naturalism in Context" by Martin Esslin. Copyright © 1968, *The Drama Review.* Reprinted by permission of The MIT Press, Cambridge, MA and the author.—*Journal of Popular Culture,* v. 1, Winter, 1967. Copyright © 1967 by Ray B. Browne. Reprinted by permission of the publisher.—*South Atlantic Bulletin,* v. XLII, November, 1977. Copyright © 1977 by South Atlantic Modern Language Association. Reprinted by permission of the publisher.—*Studia Neophilologica,* v. L, 1978. Reprinted by permission of the publisher.

COPYRIGHTED EXCERPTS IN *NCLC,* VOLUME 36, WERE REPRINTED FROM THE FOLLOWING BOOKS:

Alewyn, Richard. From "The Origin of the Detective Novel," translated by Glenn W. Most, in *The Poetics of Murder: Detective Fiction and Literary Theory.* Edited by Glenn W. Most and William W. Stowe. Harcourt Brace Jovanovich, 1983. Originally published as *Probleme und Gestalten.* Insel Verlag, 1974. Copyright © 1983 by Glenn W. Most and William W. Stowe. © Insel Verlag Frankfurt am Main 1974. Reprinted by permission of Insel Verlag and the editors.—Barrett, James Wyman. From *Joseph Pulitzer and His World.* Vanguard Press, 1941. Copyright, 1941, by The Vanguard Press, Inc. Renewed 1969 by James Wyman Barrett.—Barzun, Jacques. From *Classic, Romantic and Modern.* Revised edition. Little, Brown, 1961. Copyright 1943, 1961, © renewed 1989 by Jacques Barzun. All rights reserved. Reprinted by permission of Little, Brown and Company in association with The Atlantic Monthly Press.—Behler, Ernst. From "The Theory of Irony in German Romanticism," in *Romantic Irony.* Edited by Frederick Garber. Akadèmiai Kiadò, 1988. © Coordinating Committee of A Comparative History of Literatures in European Languages 1988. Reprinted by permission of the author.—Bishop, Lloyd. From *The Romantic Hero and His Heirs in French Literature.* Lang, 1984. © Peter Lang Publishing, Inc., 1984. All rights reserved. Reprinted by permission of the publisher.—Block, Haskell M. From *Naturalistic Triptych: The Fictive and the Real in Zola, Mann, and Dreiser.* Random House, 1970. Copyright © 1970 by Random House, Inc. All rights reserved. Reproduced with permission of McGraw-Hill, Inc.—Brewer, Elisabeth. From "The Pre-Raphaelites: Morris and Swinburne," in *The Return of King Arthur: British and American Arthurian Literature Since 1800.* By Beverly Taylor and Elisabeth Brewer. D. S. Brewer, 1983. © Beverly Taylor and Elisabeth Brewer 1983. Reprinted by permission of the publisher.—Brombert, Victor. From *The Romantic Prison: The French Tradition.* Princeton University Press, 1978. Copyright © 1978 by Princeton University Press. All rights reserved. Reprinted by permission of the publisher.—Brophy, Brigid. From *Don't Never Forget: Collected Views and Reviews.* Jonathan Cape, 1966. Copyright © 1966 by Brigid Brophy. Reprinted by permission of the author.—Brown, Charles H. From *The Correspondents' War: Journalists in the Spanish-American War.* Charles Scribner's Sons, 1967. Copyright © 1967 Charles H. Brown. All rights reserved. Reprinted with the permission of Charles Scribner's Sons, an imprint of Macmillan Publishing Company.—Brown, Marshall. From *The Shape of German Romanticism.* Cornell University Press, 1979. Copyright © 1979 by Cornell University. Used by permission of the publisher, Cornell University Press.—Buckler, William E. From *Man and His Myths: Tennyson's "Idylls of the King" in Critical Context.* New York University Press, 1984. Copyright © 1984 by New York University. All rights reserved. Reprinted by permission of the publisher.—Buckley, Jerome Hamilton. From *Tennyson: The Growth of a Poet.* Cambridge, Mass.: Harvard University Press, 1960. Copyright © 1960 by the President and Fellows of Harvard College. Renewed 1988 by Jerome Hamilton Buckley. All rights reserved. Excerpted by permission of the publishers and the author.—Cargill, Oscar. From *Intellectual America: Ideas on the March.* Macmillan, 1941. Copyright 1941 by Macmillan Publishing Company. Renewed © 1968 by Oscar Cargill. All rights reserved. Reprinted with the permission of Macmillan Publishing Company.—Eggers, J. Philip. From *King Arthur's Laureate: A Study of Tennyson's "Idylls of the King."* New York University Press, 1971. Copyright © 1971 by New York University. Reprinted by permission

PHOTOGRAPHS AND ILLUSTRATIONS APPEARING IN *NCLC,* VOLUME 36, WERE RECEIVED FROM THE FOLLOWING SOURCES:

Culver Pictures, New York: **p. 348;** Courtesy of W. W. Norton: **p. 363.**

The Arthurian Revival

INTRODUCTION

The legends surrounding King Arthur, the knights of the Round Table, and the kingdom of Camelot have occupied a central place in English literature since the Middle Ages, reaching a climax with the first printing of Sir Thomas Malory's enormously popular *Morte Darthur* in 1485. Interest in Arthuriana declined over the following three centuries, however, until writers and artists in the nineteenth century brought about a revival of appreciation for and curiosity about the story of the legendary English monarch and his entourage. The literature of this resurgence, epitomized by Alfred, Lord Tennyson's epic poem *Idylls of the King* (1859-85), was remarkable both for its quality and its quantity. Victorian poems and, to a lesser extent, novels concerning the Arthurian legend provided escape for their readers from the difficulties and social upheavals engendered by industrialization. The transition from an agricultural to an industrial economy, from a ruling aristocracy to a democratic government, and from relatively secure religious faith to increasing skepticism sparked a need for a reemphasis of traditional values and ideals. As Beverly Taylor writes, "in the midst of increasingly sombre surroundings, the quaint, remote world of the Middle Ages offered colour, elegance, ritual, and pageantry." The world of Arthur as illustrated in the works of the Arthurian revival authors also offered an ideal and imitable economic, political, and social order.

Early in the nineteenth century, British scholars began rediscovering the contributions of the medieval period to English culture, particularly in the areas of literature and art. Such literary antiquarians as Thomas Percy and Sir Walter Scott restored the texts of medieval romances, making them available to large numbers of readers in new, inexpensive editions. The appearance of Malory's *Morte Darthur* in four separate editions in just over forty years, beginning in 1816, helped to popularize the Arthurian legend among Victorian audiences. Artists such as Edward Burne-Jones, William Morris, and Dante Gabriel Rossetti began to look to medieval models for their compositions; known as the Pre-Raphaelite Brotherhood, these painters (many of whom were also writers) helped to shape a new aesthetic, incorporating elements from the Middle Ages and depicting Arthurian characters and scenes. By mid-century, the revival of Arthuriana in literature had become even more pronounced. Charlotte M. Yonge's novel *The Heir of Redclyffe* (1853), William Morris's *The Defence of Guenevere, and Other Poems* (1858), and Algernon Charles Swinburne's *Tristram of Lyonesse, and Other Poems* (1882), exemplify the prominent place the legend held in the poetry and fiction of the day. Some modern critics have divided Victorian writers' approaches to the legend into two groups: the moralists, associated with Tennyson and his *Idylls,* who saw in the relationship

of Arthur and his knights an ideal society worthy of emulation in contemporary life; and the romantics, associated with the Pre-Raphaelite movement, who were inspired by the vividness of the stories—the chivalry, the quests, the battles, the romance, and the pageantry—rather than by their didactic possibilities.

While acknowledging the contributions of other writers, critics nevertheless regard Tennyson as the central figure in the Arthurian Revival. In the *Idylls,* he examines the rise and fall of an ideal society, focusing on his concern for what he considered to be a growing tendency toward hedonism in modern culture and an attendant rejection of spiritual values. *Idylls of the King* expresses Tennyson's vision of the British empire as an exemplar of moral and social order: the "Table Round / A glorious company" would "serve as a model for the mighty world." In Tennyson's view, this perfect world is undermined by individual acts of betrayal and corruption like the adultery committed by Arthur's wife, Guinevere, and his favored knight, Lancelot, which destroy the harmony of the Round Table and symbolize the effects of moral decay on society. Some nineteenth-century critics regarded the *Idylls* as self-indulgent and irrelevant to modern England, while others praised Tennyson's depiction of Camelot, claiming that his creative retelling of the legend helped to define its universal appeal. Despite its mixed critical reception, commentators have come to view Tennyson's *Idylls* as the most influential work of the Arthurian revival. Following Tennyson's example, the writers and artists who led the reawakening of interest in Malory's tales offered escape into the vibrant world of Arthur and his knights, along with commentary on the rapidly shifting values of Victorian society. As Taylor points out, "stories of King Arthur and the Round Table appealed to Victorian poets because, for all their remoteness and quaintness, they deal with ethical, moral, and emotional problems that transcend custom, place, or time."

REPRESENTATIVE WORKS

Arnold, Matthew
  Tristram and Iseult (poem) 1852; published in
    Empedocles on Etna and Other Poems
Heber, Reginald
  "Morte D'Arthur" (poem) 1812
  "The Masque of Gwendolen" (poem) 1826
Morris, William
  The Defence of Guenevere, and Other Poems
    (poetry) 1858
  Sir Galahad: A Christmas Mystery (poem) 1858
Peacock, Thomas Love
  The Misfortunes of Elphin (novel) 1829
Scott, Sir Walter
  Marmion (poem) 1808
  The Bridal of Triermain; or, The Vale of St. John
    (poem) 1813
Swinburne, Algernon Charles
  Tristram of Lyonesse, and Other Poems (poetry)
    1882
  The Tale of Balen (poem) 1896
Tennyson, Alfred, Lord
  Idylls of the King (poetry) 1859-85
Wordsworth, William
  *The Egyptian Maid; or, The Romance of the Water
    Lily* (poem) 1835; published in *Yarrow
    Revisited, and Other Poems*
Yonge, Charlotte M.
  The Heir of Redclyffe (novel) 1853

OVERVIEWS

Beverly Taylor

[*Taylor is an American educator and critic and the author of several works on Victorian literature. In the following excerpt, she explores the reasons behind the Victorian resurrection of the Arthurian legend.*]

In the final pages of Sir Thomas Malory's late fifteenth-century *Morte Darthur*, King Arthur bids farewell to Sir Bedivere—and to English medieval romance—as he is carried from the battlefield to a barge destined for Avalon, where he may be healed of his wounds. Although Malory records that the king died and was buried at Glastonbury, he also narrates the alternative legend that Arthur survived and awaits return—the once and future king. After three centuries of banishment from literature truly Arthurian in focus and inspiration, Arthur reappeared in England early in the nineteenth century, and he must certainly have felt himself to have chosen an unlikely time and place for his second coming. Industrialisation, urbanisation, utilitarianism, democratisation, along with modern science and rational skepticism, seemed to be extirpating all traces of the world familiar to Arthur or to the writers who celebrated him throughout the Middle Ages. The environmental change is succinctly sketched in Gerard Manley Hopkins' description of the once gracefully medieval Oxford, wearing in the nineteenth century 'a base and brickish skirt' ('Duns Scotus's Oxford', 1879). Long before Hopkins' observation, brickish factories dominated landscapes, and man found himself inhabiting not only a different physical world, but a new and frequently bewildering spiritual realm as well. Hence Matthew Arnold compared modern man to an inexperienced child, shorn of the secure religious faith represented by the Middle Ages, yet lingering fearfully in the shade of the medieval monastery in which he could no longer dwell ('Stanzas from the Grande Chartreuse', 1855).

Despite an external and internal landscape apparently hostile to romance, Arthur returned to English literature after more than three hundred years with an intensity remarkable for both the quality and the quantity of works produced. Even those who avoided specifically Arthurian subjects—Robert Browning, for example—were influenced by Arthurian concepts such as the quest and the chivalric code. From Alfred Tennyson's early Arthurian poems published in the 1830s and 1840s, through William Morris' *Defence of Guenevere* volume published after midcentury, to Algernon Charles Swinburne's *Tristram of Lyonesse* and *The Tale of Balen* appearing in the last two decades of the century, Arthurian materials fascinated important writers throughout the Victorian era. The major literary work achieved by Arthur's return, Tennyson's *Idylls of the King* (1859-85), occupied the poet for more than fifty years and came closer than any other work of the age to being an epic and a national poem.

This Victorian enthusiasm, contrasting sharply with the preceding century's general lack of interest in the Middle Ages (Voltaire acerbically judged the life of medieval men to be of no greater interest than the activities of bears and wolves), vividly signalled Arthur's second coming. Although between Malory's romance, printed in 1485, and Tennyson's publication in 1832, Arthurian works had appeared in England in an inconstant but unbroken flow, these works generally had little connection with medieval tradition other than names or occasional episodes familiar from the Middle Ages. By and large these Renaissance and Enlightenment works, such as Spenser's epic *Faerie Queene*, Dryden's dramatic opera *King Arthur*, or Fielding's play *Tom Thumb,* simply wove Arthur or his famous knights into a tapestry of situations and events remote from Arthurian stories and concerns. Malory's romance, the major collection of Arthurian legends available in English, having appeared frequently between Caxton's edition in 1485 and Stansby's corrupt version of Caxton in 1634, thereafter remained unpublished and was mainly known only to antiquarians until the nineteenth century.

The resurrection of Malory, and of Arthurian legend in general, may be largely credited to the work of such antiquarians as Richard Hurd, Thomas Percy, Thomas Warton, George Ellis, Sir Walter Scott, and the more scholarly Joseph Ritson. Their painstaking labours recovered medieval romance from obscurity and brought it to a large body of cultured readers. While their editing and other studies may be said to have stimulated the first serious historical and linguistic interest in the literary documents of the Middle Ages, they also focused attention on medieval romance as distinguished literature which had influenced the giants—Chaucer, Shakespeare, Milton, and Spenser. Moreover, the eighteenth-century antiquarians made modern writers aware of models other than the classics, thereby expanding the subject matter and stimulating the inventiveness of contemporary literature. Renewed interest in Malory, specifically, may be traced to Thomas Warton's *Observations on the Faerie Queene* (1754, revised 1762), which described Spenser's indebtedness to the *Morte Darthur,* among other medieval romances, for much of the imaginative richness of his epic.

As a result of the antiquarian zeal of the eighteenth century, Malory was rediscovered with such enthusiasm that the *Morte Darthur* appeared in two separate editions in 1816, another in 1817, and a fourth in 1858. Though the printing of 1817, introduced by Robert Southey, was rather expensive, the editions of 1816 were relatively inexpensive and aimed at a popular audience. The effect of these publications was to take Malory beyond the domain of antiquarians, into the hands of poets such as Tennyson and Morris, thus effectively transporting Arthur back from Avalon and restoring him to prominence in English letters.

This revival of interest in Arthur was in Britain the most concentrated literary aspect of the pervasive phenomenon of nineteenth-century medievalism, which registered in the work of linguists and editors, historians, architects, painters, and writers throughout Europe, and to a lesser extent even in America. While the efforts to retrieve the past through studying folklore and literature and emulating medieval plastic arts may be seen as a self-conscious historicism—and even, in the case of Germany, as an attempt to recreate a nationalistic heritage—the broad medievalism of the Romantic period began as varied reactions against neo-classical symmetry, decorum, and order. Ironically, although eighteenth-century novelists, for example, had used medieval (or pseudo-medieval) machinery to intrigue their readers with the exotic or unfamiliar—stimulating terror with dungeons, ancient curses, and haunted castles—aspects of the Middle Ages became increasingly popular and meaningful to the nineteenth-

century as they became more familiar, as the influence of medieval architecture visibly testified. Beginning in such eccentricity as Horace Walpole's Strawberry Hill—a plain Georgian house fantastically remodelled after 1750 with battlements, twisted chimneys, and quatrefoil windows—nineteenth-century architectural medievalism soon domesticated the strange Gothic-style banks and railway stations. (pp. 15-17)

[Scott's] immensely popular metrical romances and 'medieval' novels (more than a half dozen, from *Ivanhoe* in 1819 to his last work, *Castle Dangerous* in 1832), may in part be credited with stimulating the medieval interests of the century, but they must also be seen as his shrewd efforts to tap currents originating elsewhere. To a great extent the popularity of Scott's medieval works grew out of nostalgia—both his and his readers'—a desire to freeze, if only in literature, an essentially familiar way of life which was rapidly changing in the face of shifts from rural to urban dwelling, from agriculture and cottage crafts to mechanised industry, from secure religious faith to profoundly unsettling skepticism, from government centred in the hands of aristocracy and gentry to democracy. Scott's medieval novels memorialise a relatively static society with a defined set of values, which if imperfect, was also a known quantity attractive to nervous skeptics of change because it had survived for centuries. Admittedly, Scott's version of the Middle Ages offered fancy and local colour more than history. As A. O. J. Cockshut has observed [in *The Achievement of Walter Scott,* 1969], Scott 'was writing for a public ready to be entertained and bewitched by an unreal middle age, a public that had emancipated itself from the stock Augustan prejudices about medieval barbarism, and was now ready to adopt different misconceptions, and to be deceived in new ways.'

Yet Scott's depictions, regardless of historical misrepresentations, were not escapist literature. While some of his characters represent ideals of chivalry—a concept which Scott defined for his age in the *Encyclopedia Britannica* (1818) as an individual's altruistic devotion to his society and religion—others criticised the excesses and misapplications of the chivalric code, as, for example, when Rose in *The Betrothed* questions a knight's automatically claiming marriage to a damsel he has saved. In *Count Robert of Paris* Scott shows the decay of chivalric idealism into jaded pretension. In such a work as *The Antiquary,* where he focuses on a relatively modern period, he criticises his contemporaries' superficial and warped view of the past (by showing, for instance, the discrepancy between Oldbuck's daydreams and actuality), suggesting simultaneously that in some ways the past was superior to the present and that man can probably never fully understand former ages. His depictions of changing society also show the foolish vulnerability of characters (like Arthur Philipson and his father in *Anne of Geierstein*) who fail to adapt to changes or to understand contemporary man and moment. But at the same time, Scott suggests that the past age is in many ways more engaging than the present, not only more picturesque but more noble. In his medieval world, ideals of chivalry and honour thrive, though only in rare individuals. While his romanticised past scarcely reflects the brutal actualities of life in the Middle Ages, it focuses on ideals which from the distance of centuries could be distilled from the adulterating mass of petty details of daily living.

Besides representing the ideals popularised by Scott—chivalrous individual behaviour and a comfortably traditional society—the Middle Ages for other nineteenth-century writers illustrated an ideal social, economic, and political order. Although the actualities of feudalism would scarcely have suited a society which increasingly recognised the evils of slavery and the worth of democracy, the medieval relationship between lord and vassal was easily sentimentalised as a familial bond. The worker who fulfilled his obligations with dignity was in turn succoured by a paternal lord. This envisioned relationship surely contrasted attractively with the contemporary chasm between rapacious captains of industry and exploited workers. In addition to offering the idealised notion of society organised in a secure, hierarchical economic family, the Middle Ages for such figures as John Ruskin and William Morris represented an economy desirably built upon individual craftsmanship and accomplishment rather than on mechanised uniformity, and also built upon the fellowship of trade guilds rather than on cut-throat competition. All of these economic and social notions appealed to Thomas Carlyle, who in *Past and Present* (1842) cites the medieval monastic society of Bury St. Edmunds as an instructive contrast to his age. In his view the monastic order reflected vigorous spirituality and a communal co-operation sacrificed by his own materialistic, competitive society. At the same time, the heroic leadership of the medieval Bishop Samson illustrated the merit of organising a hierarchy behind a strong, enlightened leader. Thus Carlyle's work illustrates the nineteenth-century sense that the Middle Ages could not only represent noble ideals but also offer practical lessons and patterns for modern economic and social organisation.

Many of Carlyle's contemporaries, on the other hand, saw that medieval life was not always noble, practical, or organised. At least one nineteenth-century poet described the Middle Ages not as a more civilised time, but as an age of violence. If order existed, it grew from conflicts between individual desires and visions of right. William Morris's poems based on Froissart's *Chronicle* focus on militaristic values and bloodshed. In 'The Judgment of God' (1858), for example, a knight recalls his father's instructions to slash at his foe's head 'When you catch his eyes through the helmet-slit / . . . And the Lord God give you joy of it!' To cite but one other instance, in 'The Haystack in the Floods' (1858) a damsel watches her jealous lord slay her lover: 'Right backward the knight Robert fell, / And moan'd as dogs do, being half dead, / . . . so then / Godmar turn'd grinning to his men, / Who ran, some five or six, and beat / His head to pieces at their feet.' By portraying such scenes so graphically, Morris in one sense refrained from idealising the Middle Ages. But in another sense, the very coarseness of his portrait idealised the vitality of medieval man. In contrast to Englishmen of the present age—when, Arnold declared, 'The kings of modern thought are dumb; / . . . . They have the grief men had of yore, / But they contend and cry no more' ('Stanzas from the Grande Chartreuse')—the warriors of Morris'

Middle Ages acted—fiercely, violently, but more important, dynamically. And even in this vibrant, brutal world, Morris portrayed subtle psychological and emotional states.

Other writers eschewed a sentimental view of the Middle Ages for purposes of satire. Peacock, for example, was one of many who satirised the medieval enthusiasms of his age. *Nightmare Abbey* (1818), like Jane Austen's *Northanger Abbey* (1817), mocks Gothic architecture and the conventions of the Gothic novel; it also mocks the taste of Romantic writers for remote ages and quaint, exotic customs. Far more frequently, however, the medieval period served as a vehicle for satirising the present. Peacock himself seriously studied Welsh language and lore and in his novels translated or emulated medieval ballads and romances to provide aesthetic contrasts to the modern emphasis on fact and figures. In *Crochet Castle* (1831), although Peacock satirises his protagonist's excessively sentimental enthusiasm for the weapons, dress, and customs of the Middle Ages, he also allows this Mr. Chainmail (who may be seen as a parody of Scott) to condemn the commercialism of the modern world by praising the earlier era. In a central episode, characters debate whether the present state of society is inferior or superior to that of the twelfth century. Ultimately the novel resolves this issue by showing modern perspectives, whether pragmatic or transcendental, to be inadequate equipment for coping with growing materialism. Whereas contemporary currents—derisively termed 'the march of the mind'—promote greed, corruption, and loveless marriages, the medieval values of Mr. Chainmail underlie his affectionate, familial relationship with his domestics and allow him to achieve genuine love and even a measure of valour.

Mr. Chainmail's delight in battle-axes, coats of mail, and other physical trappings of medieval custom, though comic in its excess, suggests another level on which the Middle Ages appealed to the nineteenth century. In the midst of increasingly sombre surroundings, the quaint, remote world of the Middle Ages offered colour, elegance, ritual, and pageantry. While such ritual doubtless appealed to man's desire for order and stability, it also satisfied purely aesthetic hungers. Medieval stained glass windows and illuminated manuscripts could hardly fail to attract artists like Dante Gabriel Rossetti who painted under skies being darkened by industry. The extreme example of the Eglinton Tournament suggests the delight in pageantry and colour afforded by medieval practices. When the coronation of Queen Victoria was modernised and divested of much of its medieval pomp, the disappointed Earl of Eglinton sponsored a chivalric extravaganza complete with a formal procession, medieval costumes, jousting, a Queen of Beauty, and thousands of participants. The event was not just a frolic for the idle rich, for it attracted a crowd of spectators numbering between sixty and eighty thousand, and press coverage—which ranged from mockery to measured admiration—by its volume alone suggests the cultural significance of the tournament. For an age of mass production, urban dwelling, and the consequent blighting of nature's brightness and of human individuality—likewise an age of utilitarianism and sober social customs which prescribed the frock coat and iron corset—the flamboyance of prancing chargers and glinting armour, fluttering pennons and colourful pavilions exerted great attraction. The notion of English gentlemen in 1839 reviving the lapsed customs of the tourney is on one level ludicrous. Trollope satirised such a plan in *Barchester Towers* (1857), where one gentleman eschews tilting at a flour sack to preserve his clothing, while another trips his horse with the unwieldy twelve-foot lance. Yet the very fact that so many participants lavished so much money on accoutrements and so much time in preparing, to be watched by so many spectators who could share the experience only vicariously, testifies that the Eglinton tournament addressed significant needs arising from what Matthew Arnold later termed the deficiency of the 'poetical' in 'the age and all one's surroundings.' To him nineteenth-century England was 'not unprofound, not ungrand, not unmoving:—but *unpoetical*' [from *The Letters of Matthew Arnold to Arthur Hugh Clough,* 1932]. (pp. 18-21)

While the Middle Ages might awaken the imagination and supply pleasing colours and tones, artists clearly had to face modern technical matters related to their media. In literature this issue received extensive attention from critics who insisted that poets address timely concerns in modern forms and language. In her verse novel *Aurora Leigh* (1857), which dealt with current issues such as materialism, illegitimacy, and prostitution, Elizabeth Barrett Browning stated the argument for contemporaneity. Medieval works tended to exaggerate events and figures of the past, and more important, to diminish awareness of the grandeur of one's own age:

> All actual heroes are essential men,
> And all men possible heroes; every age,
> Heroic in proportion . . .
> . . . Ay but every age
> Appears to souls who live in't (ask Carlyle)
> Most unheroic. . . .
> . . .That's wrong thinking, to my mind,
> And wrong thoughts make poor poems . . .
> Nay if there's room for poets in the world . . .
> Their sole work is to represent the age,
> Their age, not Charlemagne's . . .
> [That] spends more passion, more heroic heat,
> Betwixt the mirrors of its drawing rooms,
> Than Roland with his knights at Roncesvalles
> . . . King Arthur's self
> Was commonplace to Lady Guenever,
> And Camelot to minstrels seemed as flat
> As Fleet Street to our poets.

Similarly, Robert Browning's 'Tray' (1879) disparaged modern celebrations of knights written in the archaic style of medieval romances. Such tedious, artificial poems, 'Tray' implies, are decidedly inferior to a realistic story about a heroic dog (concluding with a topical protest against vivisection) recounted in contemporary language.

In a critical climate encouraging modernity and 'relevance', Tennyson's Arthurian poems drew fire for being irrelevant and artificial, in both style and subject matter. As one critic admonished, 'The old epics will probably never be surpassed, any more than the old coats of mail; and for the same reason; nobody wants the article; . . .

> **What is most significant about readers' and writers' increasing awareness of multiple versions of Arthurian legend is that nineteenth-century Arthurian poets recognised that they were writing in a tradition, that they were selecting tales from various versions and were consciously deleting, adding, and rearranging details, motifs, and themes.**
>
> **—Beverly Taylor**

they are become mere curiosities' [William J. Fox, *Westminster Review,* 14 (January 1831)]. Even Ruskin, who was so much attracted to the creative economic example of the Middle Ages, felt that the 'treasures of wisdom' and incomparable 'word-painting' of Tennyson's *Idylls of the King* were squandered: 'it seems to me that so great power ought not to be spent on visions of things past but on the living present. For one hearer capable of feeling the depth of this poem I believe ten would feel a depth quite as great if the stream flowed through things nearer the hearer' [quoted in *Alfred Lord Tennyson: A Memoir,* 1897]. Although most critics celebrated Tennyson's felicitous language and imagery, they generally concurred that 'to bewitch us with our own daily realities, and not with their unreal opposites, is a still higher task' [John Sterling, *Quarterly Review,* 70 (September, 1842)]. In part such objections arose from critics' sense that modern treatments of the Middle Ages distorted actuality. Sentimental views of the past obscured not only distant history, but also the relative merits of the present. Yet many critics conversely recognised that creative distortion of fact could illuminate essential truth. [Walter Bagehot, in *National Review,* 9 (October 1859)] argued, for example, that 'the events of the chivalric legend are better adapted to sustained and prolonged poetry than the events of . . . the present day . . . because they abound much less in dangerous detail, . . . give us a sort of large-hand copy of life which it is comparatively easy to understand.' Unfettered by petty facts, literature based on medieval matter could reflect universal concerns.

Other critics defended works set in the Middle Ages on grounds that they allowed aesthetic pleasure and free play of the imagination. Despite his own argument for contemporary relevance, Ruskin also recognised an aesthetic appeal inherent in the medieval world but not in his own: 'On the whole, these are much *sadder* ages than the early ones; not sadder in a noble and deep way, but in a dim wearied way,—the way of ennui, and jaded intellect. . . . The Middle Ages had their wars and agonies, but also intense delights. Their gold was dashed with blood; but ours is sprinkled with dust' [*The Works of John Ruskin,* V, E. T. Cook and Alexander Wedderburn, 1904]. Arnold echoed these sentiments when he declared [in a letter to Frances Arnold dated 17 December 1860] that although the Middle Ages were marked by 'a strong sense of . . .

irrationality', they exerted a 'peculiar charm and aroma', 'poetically the greatest charm and refreshment possible for me.'

Though such critics recognised the value of aesthetic escape from pressing contemporary issues and a comparatively drab environment, the important Arthurian works of the nineteenth century do not merely afford temporary diversion or aesthetic relief. While Tennyson, for example, acknowledged the romantic value of remoteness—'it is the distance that charms me in the landscape, the picture and the past, and not the immediate to-day in which I move' [quoted in James Knowles, "Aspects of Tennyson, II: A Personal Reminiscence," *The Nineteenth Century,* 33 (1893)]—he also insisted that his was not escapist art; it was essentially didactic and aimed at modern problems. He adopted medieval setting and story in part because he felt that men would accept lessons couched in myth and romance.

Ironically, Tennyson, who was criticised for writing about the past rather than the present, was also criticised for not being sufficiently medieval. Reviewers argued that he had merely depicted Victorian characters and concerns in the garb of the early era. Thus Gerard Manley Hopkins [in a letter to Richard Watson Dixon dated 27 February 1879] termed the *Idylls* 'Charades from the Middle Ages' in which picturesque effects—like 'real lace and good silks and real jewelry' used in a blatantly artificial tableau—never disguised the Victorian presence.

The pressure of this critical debate over setting poetry in the Middle Ages probably prompted Tennyson to frame his early medieval narratives within contemporary scenes. In *The Princess* (1847), for example, a modern episode introduces the timely issue of higher education for women. The subject then develops in a romance vaguely set in the medieval period. This rather daring blend of old and new struck many readers as merely absurd. When Browning heard of the scheme—a female university to be described in a 'fairy-tale'—he declared [in a letter to Elizabeth Barrett dated 31 January 1846] such anachronistic treatment to be unsuitable for a world in which 'locomotives . . . must keep the very ghosts of [fairies] away.' Although some critics echoed Browning's judgment and held that the medieval ambience and the contemporary concerns blurred each other, Tennyson by pursuing what he termed a 'strange diagonal' between romance and realism, medieval and modern, succeeded in treating the controversial 'woman question' with humour, sensitivity, and detachment. Approaching the contemporary issue through medieval fiction allowed him to convey a complex attitude, to champion the cause of university training for women and to oppose male domination, while simultaneously defending the values of traditional female roles rejected by his educationally ambitious heroine, Princess Ida. In addition, throughout the medieval tale he subtly employed references to modern scientific thought in order to suggest that traditional attitudes must adapt to a new sense of mankind and the world.

Tennyson similarly used a modern frame for the earliest published portion of his Arthurian *Idylls,* embedding the narrative of Arthur's death within 'The Epic' (1842), an English idyl which illustrates customs among the nineteenth-century gentry. The modern frame raises the topic of prevailing critical debate—the value of old literary forms and subject matter for the present century. In the introduction, the host of a Christmas party reads the salvaged fragment of an Arthurian epic which its author had years before cast into the fireplace. The poet had destroyed most of the work because he decided that 'truth / Looks freshest in the fashion of the day' and that the epic form is outmoded—'why should any man / Remodel models?' Moreover, the subject matter—the Round Table society—is extinct, and 'nature brings not back the Mastodon, / Nor we those [heroic] times.' Yet the rescued poetic fragment proves to be no mastodon of verse, for it affects the listeners, particularly the narrator. Stirred by the reading, he dreams of Arthur's returning to nineteenth-century England, freshly dressed—like truth—in the fashion of the day, as 'a modern gentleman / Of stateliest port.' When the narrator awakens to the sound of Christmas bells memorialising another ideal figure who promised a second coming, we fully see the applications of the medieval tale to the modern world described in the frame. This contemporary world has been characterised by one speaker, Parson Holmes, as a declining society: 'all the old honour had from Christmas gone'; schism, geology, and debates over church procedure have rendered a 'general decay of faith / Right through the world.' This modern complaint is echoed in the medieval narrative by Sir Bedivere, who laments Arthur's defeat and the failure of the Round Table order: 'For now I see the true old times are dead, / When every morning brought a noble chance, / And every chance brought out a noble knight.' Bedivere himself links the early promise of Camelot to the birth of Christ: 'Such times have been not since the light that led / The holy Elders with the gift of myrrh.' Thus the culmination of the modern coda, linking the envisioned reappearance of Arthur in the modern world with the tolling of Christmas bells, signals an opportunity for the ideals of Christianity and of medieval chivalry to be restored to the world Parson Holmes has declared moribund. In effect we see that, as King Arthur comments, 'The old order changeth, yielding place to new, / And God fulfills Himself in many ways, / Lest one good custom should corrupt the world.' Each day—even in the nineteenth century—brings a noble chance, and each chance can bring forth a noble knight—although chance, knight, and nobility can be clothed (like Arthur in the narrator's dream) in the fashion of the new order and the new day.

In 'The Epic' Tennyson joins the medieval narrative and its modern frame to suggest two important principles about nineteenth-century medieval works. The first arises from a cyclical concept of history and implies that man may learn from the examples of the past. After suggesting that the Arthurian order recaptured the ideals of early Christianity, the conclusion, which depicts a symbolic second coming of Arthur and memorialises the birth of Christ, implies that the modern world can, despite Parson Holmes' harangue, recapitulate the ideals common to Christian and Arthurian society. As the Round Table order attempted to remodel the model of Christ, the Victorian world may profit from the patterns of the past. The second important principle suggested by the combined modern frame and the framed medieval narrative is that for the contemporary world, literature will provide the enlightened leadership supplied in earlier periods by messiahs and kings, or in more recent time by ministers. In declaring that there is 'no anchor, none, / To hold by,' the Parson in effect betrays his responsibility to represent just such an anchor. The modern parallel to King Arthur—or to the Parson—as a spiritual leader of men is the diffident poet Everard Hall, whose epic fragment inspires the narrator to dream of Arthur and the ideals of Camelot restored to the present age. Whereas Tennyson's combining medieval and modern elements in *The Princess* distances a volatile contemporary issue and permits him simultaneously to commend and to caution against feminist attitudes, the similar combination in 'The Epic' and the 'Morte d'Arthur' establishes the contemporaneity of a superficially remote Arthurian narrative. Throughout the century poets used medieval materials both to focus on modern concerns through the objectifying distance permitted by a medieval setting or myth and to discern in traditional tales emblems meaningful, even instructive, to the present. (pp. 22-6)

What is most significant about readers' and writers' increasing awareness of multiple versions of Arthurian legend is that nineteenth-century Arthurian poets recognised that they were writing in a tradition, that they were selecting tales from various versions and were consciously deleting, adding, and rearranging details, motifs, and themes. They were consciously crafting new expressions in an already rich and manifold body of literature. This awareness contrasts markedly with the approaches of writers between Malory and Tennyson, who by and large appropriated characters and motifs to works which otherwise had little kinship to Arthurian tradition. In many instances, the nineteenth-century writer measured his own innovations against medieval treatments to emphasise his contribution and either his fidelity to tradition or the independence of his vision. While Tennyson, for example, cited suggestions in Joseph of Exeter, Albéric des Trois-Fontaines, and the *Brut ab Arthur* to justify his portrait of Arthur, he also liked to emphasise the individuality of his Lancelot, his 'own great imaginative knight' [*The Poems of Tennyson,* 1969]. Tennyson specifically proposed to modernise the tales and to show their special relevance to his age. As Hallam Tennyson explained about his father's treatment of Arthurian legends, he 'infused into them a spirit of modern thought and an ethical significance, . . . as indeed otherwise these archaic stories would not have appealed to the modern world at large' [*Alfred Lord Tennyson: A Memoir,* 1897]. When Tennyson read the suggestion that his Grail narrative echoed medieval treatments, he demurred: 'I can't conceive how the Grail . . . can well be treated by a poet of the 13th century from a similiar point of view to mine, who write in the 19th, but, if so, I am rather sorry for it, as I rather piqued myself on my originality of treatment.' Although medieval literature provided the fabric from which the *Idylls* were fashioned, the cut and style were to Tennyson's mind his own.

But while Tennyson intended to do something new and contemporary, he also aimed to partake of the rich literary heritage. He based his *Idylls* primarily on Malory's *Morte Darthur* and the *Mabinogion.* Justly noted for the quantity and eclecticism of his reading, however, he also informed his sense of the Middle Ages by investigating not only medieval romance and songs, but also studies of medieval literature, history, and folklore—and some of the material he probably read in Welsh. Swinburne likewise conducted 'research' of sorts for his Arthurian poetry. Before reshaping the Tristram legend, he read all available extant medieval versions of the story, including Malory, Scott's edition of *Sir Tristrem,* and Francisque Michel's *Tristan: Recueil de ce qui reste des poèmes relatifs à ses aventures, composés en français, en anglo-normand, et en grec dans les XII. et XIII. siècles* (1835-39), which includes Béroul and Thomas.

Swinburne may have known Wagner's opera *Tristan und Isolde* (based on Gottfried von Strassburg), the libretto for which was begun in 1857 and finished in 1859, although the opera was not actually performed until 1865. This point raises the issue of Wagner's possible influence on Victorian Arthurians. Tennyson expressed little interest in Wagner's operatic treatment of Arthurian legend. When one enthusiast recommended the subject of his opera on the son of Perceval, the Swan Knight Lohengrin, for a poem, the Laureate brushed the suggestion aside by noting 'what a remarkably sharp nose you've got' [as quoted in Charles Tennyson's *Alfred Tennyson,* 1949]. Arnold, who found Wagner's Tristram story interesting although the music was not, felt his own version of the legend, which antedated the opera, to be superior. Swinburne seems to have been alone among Victorian Arthurians in his enthusiasm for the German composer. Discussing his projected *Tristram of Lyonesse,* he wrote [in a letter to Edward Burne–Jones dated 4 November 1869] that 'Wagner's music ought to abash but does stimulate me.' Although Wagner's operatic reshaping of the Tristram legend represented, in effect, the overwhelming love tragedy of the age, it does not seem to have affected English poets as it did German audiences. Wagner's other Arthurian opera, *Parsifal,* based largely on the *Parzival* of Wolfram von Eschenbach, was his last opera, not performed until 1882 although the libretto was apparently written by 1877, eight years after Tennyson completed the major nineteenth-century version of the Grail story in English.

Swinburne purposefully consulted medieval versions of the Tristram story because he intended to work within established tradition, to create a new poem 'acceptable for its orthodoxy and fidelity to the dear old story'. Although he could not include 'a tithe of the various incidents given in the different old versions', he meant to include 'everything *pretty* that is of any importance, and is in keeping with the tone and spirit of the story'. He also planned to portray the legend more authentically than his contemporaries had: Arnold had 'transformed and recast the old legend, and Tennyson—as usual, if I may be permitted to say so—has degraded and debased it' [in a letter to R. H. Horne dated 13 February 1882]. We need not agree with Swinburne that Tennyson's 'Morte d'Albert' dressed Victorians in medieval costume and actually represented the modern 'divorce-court' more than a courtly past ('Under the Microscope') in order to recognise that such debate marked a serious interest among Victorian poets in the place of their works in Arthurian tradition.

Clearly not all nineteenth-century writers were so much concerned with literary antecedents. After Arnold read the Tristram story in the *Revue de Paris,* he turned to Malory but found that his own poem 'was in the main formed, and I could not well disturb it' [in a letter to Herbert Hill dated 5 November 1852]. Except for echoing the summary of the thirteenth-century French Vulgate *Ystoire de Merlin* which prefaces Southey's edition of Malory, and echoing the *Morte Darthur* in the haunting last line, Arnold's *Tristram and Iseult* distinctly resists many traditional elements of the legend. Also countering the general concern with tradition were writers like William Morris, who may be said to have subscribed unconsciously to Scott's theory that 'tradition, generally speaking, is a sort of perverted alchemy which converts gold into lead' [Sir Walter Scott, *Quarterly Review,* 1 (1809)]. Far from rehashing events in earlier works, Morris, once inspired by Malory, freely invented details and formulated radically independent conceptions of characters.

Yet even the poems of Arnold and Morris fall well within Arthurian tradition. Romancers of the Middle Ages, who used basic legends again and again, frequently altered plot, recombining narrative details and familiar motifs to create many different versions of a single legend. Variety in plot, literary form, and style have always marked Arthurian literature, as versions of the Tristram legend ranging from Béroul's twelfth-century poem to Malory's late fifteenth-century prose attest. Whether a writer—like Gottfried and Swinburne—linked Tristram's death to the classical motif of the black and white sails; or—like Malory and Tennyson—described Mark's ignoble stroke; or—like Arnold—adapted no medieval version, the legend allowed a variety of archetypal and symbolic effects. What Arnold, Morris, Tennyson, and Swinburne shared with medieval writers, whether or not they followed narrative details, was recognition of the expressive, didactic, and symbolic potential of Arthurian legends. Even the earliest medieval versions are set in the distant past or the long-ago of fairy tale and myth. That they may initially have derived from historical events and actual customs notwithstanding, the tales became in medieval romances meaningful emblems rather than slices of life. The most encompassing symbolic potential lies in the idea of Camelot as an ideal order. The concept of the Round Table inextricably combines social, political, ethical, and religious ideals in a society which flourished yet ultimately failed. Thus Arthurian story provided for nineteenth-century writers a broad canvas and crowded palette with which to delineate significant contemporary concerns and to paint either brightly optimistic pictures of human potential or darker possibilities.

As the key which unlocked the treasury of Arthurian legend for the nineteenth century, Malory's *Morte Darthur* can scarcely be emphasised sufficiently. His style—curiously diffuse for modern readers—was not always admired. Scott, celebrating the 'high tone of chivalry', nevertheless described the work as 'extracted at hazard, and without much art or combination' (preface to *Sir Tristrem*). Tennyson thought the *Morte Darthur* 'much

the best' of chivalric romances. Even though it contained 'very fine things', however, they were 'all strung together without Art' [*Alfred Lord Tennyson: A Memoir,* 1897]. Yet in these 'very fine things' distilled from Malory's voluptuous presentation, Tennyson found the heady essence for his own greatest work. This essence, curiously, is conflict. The *Morte Darthur* depicts a world of conflict ranging from the physical encounters of international battles and civil wars, tournaments, and the almost incessant jousting of individual knights; to the emotional clashes of illicit love, adultery, and jealousy; to the spiritual conflict of religious faith belied by action, the hope of eternal salvation jeopardised by awareness of immediate sin. Stories of King Arthur and the Round Table appealed to Victorian poets because, for all their remoteness and quaintness, they deal with ethical, moral, and emotional problems that transcend custom, place, or time. (pp. 30-3)

> *Beverly Taylor, "The Return of Arthur: Nineteenth-Century British Medievalism and Arthurian Tradition," in* The Return of King Arthur: British and American Arthurian Literature Since 1800 *by Beverly Taylor and Elisabeth Brewer, D. S. Brewer, 1983, pp. 15-33.*

Mark Girouard

[*In the following excerpt, Girouard discusses the division of nineteenth-century attitudes toward the Arthurian legend into two groups: the romantics, or those who "read Malory and were deeply moved and excited by the vividness of his stories of love, quests, fighting, and marvels," and the moralists, or those who "saw Arthur and his knights as epitomizing (at their best) virtues which were still valid as a source of moral lessons for contemporary life."*]

Roughly speaking, attitudes to the Arthurian story in the mid-nineteenth century divide into two groups, one moral and the other romantic. The romantics read Malory and were deeply moved and excited by the vividness of his stories of love, quests, fighting and marvels. The moralists saw Arthur and his knights as epitomizing (at their best) virtues which were still valid as a source of moral lessons for contemporary life. The moral school might be described as Tennysonian, and the romantic as Pre-Raphaelite, except that Tennyson's approach in his four early Arthurian poems of 1832-4 was largely a romantic one.

Although there are moral elements in both 'Sir Galahad' and the 'Morte d'Arthur' they are chiefly memorable as a series of vivid images. Purity, and indeed virginity, were popular subjects of discussion in the 1830s; it was at this time, for instance, that Richard Hurrell Froude was urging 'the severe idea of virginity' on his friends in the Oxford Movement [as noted by John Henry Newman in his *Apologia pro Vita Sua,* 1864]. But Tennyson gives the impression of being attracted to Sir Galahad's purity less for its moral implications than as one extreme of knight-errantry, the other being represented by Lancelot's passion for Guenevere. The passion is as exciting to him as the purity. Tennyson's poem about Lancelot and Guenevere came much nearer completion than the fragment which was published in 1842 suggests. According to his friend J. M. Kemble, a substantial part of it was written in June 1833, when Tennyson read or showed it to him. Kemble was excited by its description of how 'in the Spring, Queen Guinevere and Sir Lancelot rode through the forest green, fayre and amorous: and such a queen! such a knight!' He copied out the song which Lancelot sang—to quote one verse:

> Bathe with me in the fiery flood
> And mingle kisses, tears and sighs
> Life of the Life within my blood,
> Light of the Light within mine eyes.

He sent the song to his friend W. B. Donne with the warning, 'for the sake of my future clerical views and Alfred's and Sir L's character, I must request that it be kept as quiet as possible'. It was, he confessed, 'but a loose song', sung, apparently, as Lancelot took Guenevere to live with him at Joyous Gard, having rescued her from being burnt as an adulteress [*The Poems of Tennyson,* edited by Christopher Ricks, 1969].

Kemble's comments make clear how stringent the moral climate had already grown by the 1830s; to appear to condone, or even describe, an adulterous relationship was likely to cause a fuss. It was perhaps for this reason that Tennyson only published a portion of the poem in his 1842 volume, and that this did not include the song.

Sir Lancelot and Queen Guinevere, *James Archer, 1864, oil on canvas.*

The problem of how to treat the Arthurian story surfaced again with Dyce's commission for the Queen's Robing Room in 1847. On 20 July 1848 he wrote to the Fine Art Commissioners suggesting two possible approaches. One was a chronological series of pictures telling the main story of the *Morte d'Arthur,* from Guenevere's infidelity to Arthur's final disappearance in the barge, Guenevere's remorse and Lancelot's conversion. The other was to 'consider the Companions of the Round Table as personifications of certain moral qualities, and select for representation such adventures of Arthur and his Knights as best exemplified the courage, magnanimity, courtesy, temperance, fidelity, devoutness and other qualities which make up the ancient idea of chivalric greatness'.

It is not surprising that the Commission opted for the moral qualities; Guenevere presented problems for proper Victorians, even if she did repent in the end—and was perhaps considered especially unsuitable for a room to be used by a woman. The subjects finally decided on were mercy, hospitality, generosity, religion, courtesy, fidelity and courage. Dyce started on the frescoes in 1849, but *Hospitality* was not quite finished at the time of his death in 1864, and *Fidelity* and *Courage* were never started. Eight small compartments under the big ones were filled in 1867-70 with wood sculptures by H. H. Armstead showing other episodes in the Arthurian story.

In spite of their mediaeval trimmings, the Arthurian 'moral qualities' which the pictures express are clearly being presented for admiration and imitation by the monarch and aristocracy of Britain. All are entirely appropriate for a Victorian gentleman. *Hospitality* (Plate XVI), for instance, in fact depicts 'The Admission of Sir Tristram to the Fellowship of the Round Table', that is to say to the Arthurian equivalent of an officers' mess; the word 'fellowship', frequently used in Malory, was to become powerfully emotive in Victorian England. *Mercy* and *Courtesy* stress the obligation on gentlemen to be courteous to women and to come to their protection. In *Generosity* Sir Lancelot spares his opponent King Arthur when he is unhorsed and at his mercy; all Victorian gentlemen knew that one did not hit a man when he was down.

In 1855, when Tennyson finally took up the Arthurian story again, his approach was much closer to Dyce's than to that of his poems of the 1830s. In the twenty or so intervening years he had married and become a national figure. He had never been in the least sexually promiscuous, and after marriage became increasingly disapproving of sexual adventures; moreover his wife Emily, in spite of her deliberately self-effacing image, was a powerful personality completely wedded to conventional Victorian morality. In the *Idylls of the King* not only has adultery become shameful rather than glamorous; but the main theme is how Arthur's achievements as king are brought to nothing as a result of Guenevere's guilty love for Lancelot, and everything that flows from it. Arthur himself hammers this home in the celebrated scene in 'Guinevere' where, like a grim but sorrowful god, he speaks to the Queen as she grovels at his feet:

> Then came thy shameful sin with Lancelot;
> Then came the sin of Tristram and Isolt;

Then others, till the loathsome opposite
That all my heart had destined did obtain,
And all thro' thee.

['Guinevere']

'Guinevere' was one of the first four *Idylls,* all published in 1859. The title which it was first intended to publish them under, 'The False and the True', sums up their theme; false as against true womanhood. Enid unquestioningly follows and serves her husband, even though he humiliates her owing to his groundless belief that she has been unfaithful to him. Elaine, 'delicately pure and marvellously fair', dies of grief owing to her innocent but overwhelming love for Lancelot ['Lancelot and Elaine'], who would have done much better to marry her than to carry on with Guenevere. In contrast the lissom and snake-like Vivien, who is incapable of believing that anyone is not, under the surface, as rotten as herself, successfully seduces Merlin, whose wisdom is not proof against his lust; and Guenevere betrays her husband, and repents too late.

Between 1859 and 1873 Tennyson wrote six more *Idylls,* and adapted his 'Morte d'Arthur' to make a final one, so as to produce something resembling a logical and chronological sequence, carefully designed to underline and expand on the moral of the original four. In the process he worked out symbolisms which he may not have fully envisaged in the 1850s: Arthur, for instance, represents 'the Ideal Soul of Man coming into contact with the warring elements of the flesh' [*Idylls of the King*]. The whole sequence forms a powerful and extremely depressing account of the decay and defeat of an ideal; the only consolation lies in the possibility of the ultimate return of Arthur, carried away wounded but still alive on the barge of the three queens.

The ideal for which Arthur stands is expressed in the oath sworn to him by his knights [in 'Guinevere'] (and later applied by Tennyson to the Prince Consort, in shortened and slightly altered form):

I made them lay their hands on mine and swear
To reverence the King, as if he were
Their conscience, and their conscience as their
   King,
To break the heathen and uphold the Christ,
To ride abroad redressing human wrongs,
To speak no slander, no, nor listen to it,
To honour his own word as if his God's,
To lead sweet lives in purest chastity,
To love one only, cleave to her
And worship her by years of noble deeds,
Until they won her; for indeed I knew
Of no more subtle master under heaven
Than is the maiden passion for a maid,
Not only to keep down the base in man,
But teach high thoughts and amiable words,
And courtliness, the desire of fame,
And love of truth, and all that makes a man.

['Guinevere']

Literary historians disagree as to Malory's own views. Did he or did he not fashion his *Morte d'Arthur* out of earlier romances in order to point a moral not dissimilar to Tennyson's? Tennyson himself seems to have thought not. His

own Arthur, he wrote in 1872, was 'ideal manhood closed in real man', in contrast to

. . . him of Malleor's, one
Touched by the adulterous finger of a time
That hovered between war and wantonness.
[*Idylls of the King* 'To the Queen']

In his presentation of the Arthurian story he consciously and deliberately bowdlerised Malory in many particulars. Malory can say of Guenevere 'that while she lived she was a true lover, and therefore she had a good end'. His Arthur, far from being a loving but deceived husband, shows little interest in Guenevere and is much more concerned about the quarrel with Lancelot and his followers than the loss of his wife: 'for queens I might have enow, but such a fellowship of good knights shall never be together in no company.' Tennyson's Arthur tells Guenevere that 'I was ever virgin save for thee', but in Malory the false Sir Mordred who finally betrays Arthur is in fact his illegitimate son. Malory's Nimue (from whom Tennyson's Vivien derives) is a benevolent rather than baneful sorceress, and her enchantment of Merlin is considered a feather in her cap rather than a foul deed.

Tennyson was, as a result, criticised both at the time and later for turning Malory's king and knights into pattern Victorian gentlemen. But he did so out of intention rather than ineptness; his Arthur was deliberately designed to be an inspiration to modern members of the ruling class, just as Gareth in 'Gareth and Lynette' ('the young knight who can endure and conquer', as Edward FitzGerald described him) was taken as model for modern public-school boys; hence his appearance in stained glass on the main stairs at Glenalmond.

To many thousands of Tennyson's readers Arthur, 'selfless man and stainless gentleman', was 'the great pillar of the moral order, and the resplendent top of human excellence', as Gladstone described him. To others he seemed a cold cuckold, whose forgiveness of Guenevere

Lo, I forgive thee, as Eternal God
Forgives . . .

was self-satisfied rather than moving. George Meredith thought that he sounded like a 'crowned curate'. To them Lancelot, like Milton's Satan, stole the show in spite of the author.

The great and guilty love he bare the Queen,
In battle with the love he bare his lord,
Had marr'd his face, and mark'd it ere his
   time . . .

His mood was often like a fiend, and rose
And drove him into wastes and solitudes
For agony, who was yet a living soul.
Marr'd as he was, he seemed the goodliest man
That ever among ladies ate in hall.
['Lancelot and Elaine']

The *Idylls of the King* were designed as a warning. Their pessimism reflected Tennyson's own belief that the age was getting worse, and would continue to do so until the English were to live up to the moral standards necessary for members of an imperial nation. His worries were, by his own standards, justified, at any rate as far as concerned sexual morals. A different attitude to that of the *Idylls* had already begun to make its appearance before the first *Idylls* were published, and grew steadily more prevalent during the 1860s and 1870s.

In 1852 Matthew Arnold published a volume of poems which included 'Tristram and Iseult', a poem mainly written in 1849-50 under the influence of a frustrated love affair in Switzerland and his subsequent marriage to Frances Lucy Wightman. In Tennyson's 'Guinevere' Arthur condemned the adulterous 'sin of Tristram and Isolt', but there is no hint of condemnation in Arnold's poem. It depicts an emotional triangle—Iseult of Cornwall in love with Tristram but married to Mark, Tristram in love with Iseult of Cornwall but married to Iseult of Brittany, Iseult of Brittany in love with Tristram—without praise or blame, just as something tragic which happened. The poem centres round Tristram on his deathbed in Brittany, yearning for Iseult of Cornwall, and the tragedy is summed up in the couplet:

> TRISTRAM Soft—who is that, stands by the dying fire?
> PAGE Iseult.
> TRISTRAM Ah! not the Iseult I desire.
>
> ['Tristram and Iseult' II 7–8]

The action takes place many years after Tristram's love affair with his lost Iseult, and this time-gap throws a veil of wistful melancholy over the whole poem. The poems in Morris's *Defence of Guenevere,* published in 1858, treat a similar situation with much more immediacy. (pp. 180-85)

The poems in *The Defence of Guenevere* are essays in bringing Malory to life for modern readers by using the techniques of direct broken verse evolved by Browning. Such an analysis can give no idea of the power and originality of these remarkable poems. With the exception of two poems on Galahad their themes are sex and violence. The sex seldom leads to happiness; it is either frustrated or interrupted by violence. Sudden openings and awkward hesitating rhythms give the reader an extraordinary feeling of being present in person, of actually feeling physical surfaces and sensing physical contacts. There is no moralising. Guenevere is not shown as a guilty wife lying at the feet of her husband, but as a splendid and sensuous woman, defying her accusers, celebrating her love (though denying that it went as far as adultery), and minimising her marriage:

> ' . . . for a little word
> Scarce ever meant at all, must I now prove
> Stone cold for ever?' . . .
>
> 'I scarce dare talk of the remembered bliss
> When both our mouths went wandering one way
> And aching sorely, met among the leaves.'
>
> (p. 186)

The Defence of Guenevere was too direct for most Victorians. One achievement of Morris's later poems, and the later pictures of Burne-Jones and Rossetti, was to make sex acceptable in Victorian drawing-rooms. They achieved this by calling it Love, and all Victorians knew that Love was superior to sex. Sex could come in under its skirts,

however; many Victorians found the dreamy rhythms of Morris's poems, or the far-away beauty of Burne-Jones's women extremely suggestive. They helped inaugurate a new form of love affair, conducted on a high plane, excitingly spiced with guilt or frustration, involving much talk of the 'passion of the soul' and a total absence of erotic language or even mention of sex, but always moving towards the final act and sometimes getting there. (pp. 188-193)

[The Pre-Raphaelites' brand of idealized but sensual and often adulterous love] has carried the story a long way from Tennyson's 'love one only, cleave to her', with marriage as the end, or indeed from his own long and unruffled marriage to Emily Selwood; but perhaps it has brought it a little closer to mediaeval courtly love. Courtly love *à la* Pre-Raphaelite did indeed provide an alternate model of chivalry to Tennyson. The innumerable Arthurian paintings of the period tend to divide themselves between the two, with one school (to which, for instance, Arthur Hughes, Noel Paton and the artists of the Royal Tapestry Works at Windsor belong) favouring Arthur, Galahad, Enid, Elaine, and purity vanquishing the Wicked Woman, the other (of which Aubrey Beardsley is an extreme example) preferring Lancelot, Tristram, Guenevere, Iseult, and sorceresses deliciously triumphant.

It was Tennyson's version of chivalry, 'Live pure, speak true, right wrong, follow the King', which provided what might be called the establishment ethic of chivalry, approved of by the public schools and, not surprisingly, by the Queen. One result of Tennyson's great prestige and popularity was a spate of books retelling Malory for children: the first of them, J. T. Knowles's *Story of King Arthur* (1862) was actually dedicated to Tennyson. The versions were all written in pseudo-mediaeval language, but they inevitably involved a good deal of cutting and also careful editing. The object (as U. W. Cutler put it in 1905, in his *Stories of King Arthur and his Knights*) was to remove whatever was 'so crude in taste and morals as to seem unworthy of the really high-minded author of five hundred years ago'.

Lancelot and Guenevere clearly presented problems. Lancelot, in particular, was so powerful and attractive a character that even if given the moral treatment of the *Idylls* there was a danger that he might set boys off on the wrong path. The solution was to bowdlerise him, on lines in fact suggested by Tennyson. According to a 'minstrel of Caerleon' in the *Idylls,* it was 'out of naked knightlike purity' that

> Sir Lancelot worshipped no unmarried girl
> But the great Queen herself.
>
> ['Vivien']

As treated by Tennyson this was, indeed, the way in which the relationship started, but it soon went much further. In Cutler's *Stories of King Arthur,* it stays at its starting point; Mordred's accusations are baseless; Guenevere's supposed adultery is a put-up job; Lancelot remains a pure and honourable gentleman throughout. Not surprisingly, this was the version recommended by Baden-Powell to his Boy Scouts. Sidney Lanier's *Tales from King Arthur* (1880) went even further. Adultery is never even hinted at; in the final drama Lancelot and Guenevere are accused of a mysterious 'treason', the nature of which is never explained.

Of course Victorians were not attracted to the Arthurian story solely by its morals or lack of them. To many its chief claim was simply that it provided an escape into a magical world—or rather a series of magical worlds, varying from Malory's own to Burne-Jones's. Walter Crane [in his *An Artist's Remembrances,* 1907] described the effect of paintings by Burne-Jones on young men coming across them for the first time. 'The curtain had been lifted and we had a glimpse into . . . a twilight world of dark mysterious woodland, haunted streams, meads of dark green starred with burning flowers, veiled in a dim and mystic light, and stained with low-toned crimson and gold.' (pp. 194-96)

> Mark Girouard, "The Return of Arthur," in his The Return to Camelot: Chivalry and the English Gentleman, *Yale University Press, 1981, pp. 177-96.*

TENNYSON AND HIS INFLUENCE

J. Philip Eggers

[*Eggers is an American educator and critic who writes on Victorian literature. In the following excerpt, he compares Tennyson's* Idylls *with Malory's* Morte Darthur, *concluding that while Malory uses the Round Table as "an example for readers of his day to admire and emulate," Tennyson focuses on the relationship between Lancelot and Guinevere in the* Idylls *as "an example of misconduct, and he makes the story more a warning than a pattern for imitation."*]

The ethic of weeding our gardens is not the most important ideal of the *Idylls,* for Arthur's reliance upon that principle seems in the light of the tragedy he is to encounter to be like putting a ship in order while letting it blindly drift toward disaster. Even the ideal behind the king's wise advice to the grail knights after their return—that the king must tend his fields and not follow wandering fires—ignores the fact that the realm seems lost beyond recovery; tilling the fields would, to borrow Morris' language, be useless toil rather than useful work. More important to Tennyson than laboring in the moment is the difficult work of finding directions and ideals. The warning against taking true for false and false for true concerns the large danger of a whole society pursuing destructive goals. Working industriously on immediate tasks—following the Victorian ethic of work—would in such a context do little to prevent a social calamity.

Malory's greatness as a tragedian differs from Tennyson's, and the difference is reflected in their styles. Malory's prose—direct, pellucid, moving—suits well the story of an Order brought to its end by fate and conflicting desires. What could equal the simplicity of Galahad's last prayer:

"Lord, I thank thee, for now I see that
which hath been my desire many a day;
now blessed Lord would I no longer live,
if it might please thee good Lord."
    [quotes from Malory are taken from *The*
    History of the Renowned Prince Arthur,
    1816]

Eugene Vinaver finds this passage one of the most deeply religious moments in any version of the grail quest. Malory's Galahad follows his desire to see the grail, much as all of the knights live by impulse and a charming freedom from hard ethical choices. Tennyson does not give most of the knights in the *Idylls* this sort of innocence; in fact he stresses their ethical perplexities. In "The Holy Grail" Tennyson has Sir Percivale describe Galahad's disappearance:

A thousand piers ran into the great Sea.
And Galahad fled along them bridge by bridge,
And every bridge as quickly as he crost
Sprang into fire and vanish'd, tho' I yearn'd
To follow; and thrice above him all the heavens
Open'd and blazed with thunder such as seem'd
Shoutings of all the sons of God. And first
At once I saw him far on the great Sea,
In silver-shining armor starry-clear;
And o'er his head the Holy Vessel hung
Clothed in white samite or a luminous cloud.
                    (lines 503-513)

The description is as religious as Malory's passage but in the manner of a Victorian recessional; it has the brilliant silver notes of a cathedral organ's state trumpets. The difference is more than one of period styles. Malory's Galahad in the twelfth book of the *Morte Darthur* simply dies, and the angels bear his soul to heaven. Tennyson instead conceives of Galahad's disappearance as an apotheosis parallel to Arthur's passing at the conclusion of the *Idylls.* Arthur and Galahad are set apart by their ethical perfection from the corruption of the Round Table and are received by celestial hosts in an Order befitting their characters. Everyone is included in Malory's version of the tragedy; all are imperfect, but Tennyson sees the possibility of a hero's transcending human failure. For Malory there is one world—human society; for Tennyson two spheres of being conflict with each other—the ideal, or the world of spirit, and the social, or the world of the senses.

Launcelot is Malory's hero, whose failure to live the life of purity the author—himself a knight who had spent time in prison—no doubt felt to be his own fate and mankind's. Tennyson's hero is the king himself, whose quixotic perfection he felt to be a needed example for modern man. Malory's Launcelot epitomizes the simultaneous strength and weakness of the chivalric code: he fails in love, in religion, and in chivalry because of his relationship with Guinevere. The ideals of chivalry are tested against his humanity; the absence of chivalric perfection seems to increase the humanity of the whole order of knights. Tennyson's morally impeccable king has no parallel in Malory's; the blameless king epitomizes not the Order but the consciences or spiritual ideals of the Round Table—their mystery as to origin, their sublimity, and their vulnerability to antisocial forces.

Malory's vision is humanistic; Tennyson, living in a society in which humanism is only one of many contending philosophies, sees the complexities caused by diverse intellectual positions and yet upholds the transcending moral responsibility of which Arthur's code is symbolic. Deviations from the code in the *Idylls* are not just the result of natural weaknesses of human beings, as in Malory, but the self-assertions of men who feel that their rights have been impinged upon and their ideas contradicted. Arthur blames Guinevere for her betrayal; he calls Bedivere traitor-hearted; and he finally sees that "all whereon I lean'd in wife and friend / Is traitor to my peace. . . . " ("The Passing of Arthur," lines 24-25). Guinevere, Vivien, Balin, Tristram, and the Red Knight (Pelleas) all blame Arthur for the strictness or hypocrisy of his vows and consider him a fool.

Malory's king is a human member of a society in which the chivalric code has grown organically; Arthur brings together the Order of the Round Table but is not the founder of a whole way of life, as he is in the *Idylls*. In "Gareth and Lynette" Tennyson adds to Malory's story of Beaumains a passage describing the change Arthur has brought to his society. Lynette says that the four evil knights guarding Lyonors are

> . . . of the foolish fashion, O Sir King,
> The fashion of that old knight-errantry
> Who ride abroad, and do but what they will;
> Courteous or bestial from the moment, such
> As have nor law nor king. . . .
>
> (lines 613-617)

Arthur has created a code of values at a time before which barbarism had existed. Throughout the *Idylls* a self-conscious tone of Victorian social concern sets the story apart from Malory; the separation widens into Tennyson's repudiation of the *Morte Darthur* as "Touched by the adulterous finger of a time/That hovered between war and wantonness" (Epilogue, lines 43-44) in its portrait of the king. Tennyson seems to imply that Malory portrays the style of old knight-errantry condemned in "Gareth and Lynette."

In a period when the French Revolution was still almost a living memory and one reform bill was to be followed by another, Tennyson not surprisingly portrays King Arthur as a leader who creates, not inherits, the order of chivalry, and whose failure is a warning to those who would take for granted the delicate equilibrium necessary to keep sudden social gains from becoming setbacks. Malory has King Arthur preside over a tradition of chivalry in which he and his knights strive to live by ideals inherited from the past. Camelot, according to Malory, is merely Winchester, but it is a major symbol for Tennyson. The two significant descriptions of Camelot occur in "Gareth and Lynette" and "The Holy Grail"; neither is based upon Malory. Both descriptions suggest the paradox of Victorian time—the simultaneous feeling of rapid change and gradually evolving tradition. Tennyson does not eliminate the past from his Camelot: it is "a city of shadowy palaces/And stately, rich in emblem and the work/Of ancient kings who did their days in stone. . . . " ("Gareth and Lynette," lines 296-298). Merlin's hand has, by its

touch, "made it spire to heaven" (line 302). Although Tennyson explained this as "Symbolizing the divine", Victorian readers no doubt caught the allusion to the Tower of Babel: "Let us build us a city and a tower, whose top may reach unto heaven" (Genesis 11:4). Pelleas later groans, "Black nest of rats, . . . ye build too high" ("Pelleas and Ettarre," line 544), and Arthur himself fears that the tower may fall ("The Holy Grail," line 341). Camelot is in fact a symbol of man's civilization. For Tennyson the action of the poem represented figuratively "a whole cycle of generations" [as quoted in Hallam Lord Tennyson's *Alfred Lord Tennyson: A Memoir by His Son,* 1897]. Tennyson is portraying the tragic truth of history underlying short-term gains made with spectacular success in his own society.

The zones of Camelot in "The Holy Grail" also betoken the advance of civilization:

> And four great zones of sculpture, set betwixt
> With a mystic symbol, gird the hall;
> And in the lowest beasts are slaying men,
> And in the second men are slaying beasts,
> And on the third are warriors, perfect men,
> And on the fourth are men with growing wings.
>
> (lines 233-238)

The evolutionary overtones of the images are evident enough; it is not, however, clear whether the movement upward from beast to man to angel is to be immediate or gradual. In a sense King Arthur brings about a momentary telescoping of the evolutionary process. Tennyson, like Huxley, is too acute to follow the line of crude social Darwinism that argues in favor of a society patterned on the survival of the fittest and a gradual emergence of a superior human species.

Tennyson also suggests that utopian plans for the sudden transformation of institutions, with the pattern of the French Revolution in mind, seemed unlikely to offer the realization of Camelot's ideals. The *Idylls* does not indicate man's easiest route to social perfection, but it does show how men might revert to barbarism. King Arthur's endeavors are not the way to utopia but prove only that "one good custom" alone might "corrupt the world." His King Arthur is capable of facing social change with equanimity, but the descent into cynicism and betrayal by the knights and ladies, Tennyson believes, cannot be justified by the casting off of an outworn belief.

Because Tennyson portrays a social tragedy rather than an individual one, King Arthur is not a tragic hero in quite the same sense that Oedipus is, for the blindness he suffers is part of the larger blindness of a limited society. Slanderers like Vivien are no less myopic in their moral judgment; she sees wickedness in everything, even where there is none. Being only part of the larger tragic entity, Arthur cannot undergo a purification through suffering. He cannot be purified, being pure; he cannot gain humility, being humble; and he cannot gain humanity, being perfect in a scale of values beyond the human. Tennyson heightens the social tragedy inherent in Malory by viewing the fall of the Order as a widening separation between the King and his followers. The real tragedy is the fall of the Order. Arthur and Guinevere are left looking forward to meeting in heaven and finding perfect love there, but the Round Table "Reels back into the beast, and is no more" ("The Passing of Arthur," line 26). Tennyson consciously refers to the "coming" and "passing" of the king, whereas Malory portrays his actual birth and death, to distinguish Arthur from the evanescent humanity of his Order (except Galahad, who also vanishes into light).

Malory sees the king as a poignant human figure, but Tennyson makes him a Christ figure. Arthur's failure in the *Idylls* is Tennyson's way of warning his society against rejecting its own spiritual conscience. Reflected in the knights' desertion of Arthur one can see the Victorians abandoning the Christian basis of their ethical tradition. To make the analogy more explicit, Tennyson draws a close parallel between Arthur and Christ, just as he shows similarities between the knights and his Victorian contemporaries. Like Christ, King Arthur brings to society a new ideal, founded upon absolute vows and a vision of perfect human relationships. He succeeds in living according to the vows himself but in the end falls victim to an extreme violation of his code—so extreme that he momentarily utters words of despair: Arthur echoes Christ, "My God, thou has forgotten me in my death!" ("The Passing of Arthur," line 27). But he forgives even the worst transgression, for he knows that his soul belongs to another realm: "Nay—God my Christ—I pass but shall not die" ("The Passing of Arthur," line 28). By thus placing the king in a symbolic role beyond tragedy, Tennyson sharpens the effect of the social tragedy. King Arthur, as the Order declines, becomes less and less a part of its society, whereas Malory's king remains an active participant in the plot.

Tennyson surrounds Arthur's origin in mystery, but Malory gives an unequivocal, down-to-earth account:

> So after the death of the duke, king Uther lay with Igraine more than three hours after his death, and begat on her Arthur the same night.

Such particularity would be destructive to Tennyson's purpose of suggesting that ideals themselves are attributed by men to different origins—nature, God, social tradition, etc. The separation of the king from the knighthood marks the dying of the Order; since there can be no Round Table without the ideal represented by the king, the *Idylls* ends abruptly with his disappearance, the Order having ceased to exist. Malory relates the events that take place after Arthur's death. For Tennyson the king is the informing spirit and supporting energy of the Order; for Malory he is the leader of great knights, of whom Launcelot, who lives six years as a monk after the king's death, is the greatest.

In portraying the Round Table rather than the king, Tennyson reverses his method of changing Malory's story. Malory leaves the origin of the table uncertain, but Tennyson describes its creation. Malory emphasizes the separate adventures of the knights; for him the Round Table serves as a convenient setting. The stories themselves derive from various sources and are not arranged in a clear structure. Tennyson, however, brings his stories together in an intricate curve analogous to the Round Table itself, as an "image of the mighty world." Parallels between the beginning and ending of the story, along with seasonal imagery suggesting the condition of the realm at the time each story occurs, convey the impression of historical cycles. The tragic hero for Tennyson is not Arthur, or even Lancelot, as for Malory, but the Order itself, to whose larger story the separate legends are subordinated.

Both Malory and Tennyson depict the failure of an ideal society—or rather the failure of a real society to attain utopia. But Malory's world is "golden" in a different sense from Tennyson's. For Malory the Order is primarily a "fellowship"; its greatness derives from communal spirit as much as heroic action. The king laments the dissolution of this comradery:

> ". . . and therefore wit you well that my heart was never so heavy as it is now; and much more greater sorrow for my good knights' loss, than for the loss of my queen; for queens I might have enough, but such a fellowship of good knights shall never be together in no company."

"Golden," in mythical language, denotes love and friendship. In the *Morte Darthur* the Order remains golden to the end, for despite the human failures and split loyalties, the knights still feel the emotional bond that has made their Order glorious. The fall of chivalry in the *Idylls,* however, is due to a loss of purity and slackening of moral resolve—a failure to maintain Victorian standards.

There are not many instances of fellowship in the *Idylls,* except for the ironic closeness of Arthur and Lancelot in "The Coming of Arthur" and "Gareth and Lynette," which is undermined by the growing relationship between Lancelot and the queen. Otherwise, Balin and Balan stand fast together against Arthur; the Red Knight and his followers revel together in the mock Round Table in the North. The spiritual fellowship the knights achieved at the moment of Arthur's coronation disintegrates into spiritual discord by the time of the "The Holy Grail," in which each knight seems to have his separate and isolated experience. When Sir Bors tries to communicate with Lancelot on the grail quest, Lancelot vanishes wildly with madness in his eyes. Tennyson's world of Camelot is golden, as far as fellowship is concerned, only for a brief moment, if at all.

Tennyson works quite freely, rearranging, adding, dropping, and retelling events in the eight idylls of the Round Table series that he derived from Malory. He makes of Malory's individual romances a single social tragedy, one story told through many episodes, with the Round Table as its tragic protagonist. He ranges from a near retelling of Malory's Pelleas story to almost complete invention in "Guinevere." Sometimes he reduces a famous legend—like the Tristram story—from its prominence in Arthurian tradition to the level of parallel example. It is a subordination necessary to the larger scheme. He reduces the grail quest, the other most popular legend of the century, to a foolish mistake. He makes Lancelot, Malory's hero, a good man, troubled and human, but less important in the story than King Arthur, to whom Tennyson gives enormous importance. Tennyson also makes some characters into bad men. Malory portrays King Mark as rather admirable; Tennyson makes him villainous. He creates entirely new characters, such as Vivien (if not the story of Merlin's imprisonment). The nearest corresponding character Malory wrote of would be Morgan le Fay. Tennyson also changes the fates of some characters: Pelleas, who in Malory rejects Ettarde and marries Nimuë, the Lady of the Lake, under the influence of her love potion, is left by Tennyson in lovesick despair and returns in the next idyll as the Red Knight (who is mentioned in Malory's Gareth story instead). Tennyson changes the essential characteristics of some figures. Malory portrayed Sir Dagonet as the clownish object of ridicule. Tennyson makes him the center of intelligence in "The Last Tournament."

Some of the changes were based on the many other Arthurian works Tennyson knew, but it is a mistake to regard the *Idylls* as a pastiche of fragments from many sources. Many were the result of coincidental similarities, some conscious, some half-conscious, some forgotten. Tennyson's reshaping of Malory's tragedy, nevertheless, can be attributed in large part to conscious craftsmanship.

Tennyson of course sometimes follows Malory very closely, and is often at his best in such passages. Malory's account of Arthur's end is a memorable passage in the *Morte Darthur:*

> "Now put me in the barge," said the king. And so he did so softly, and there received him three queens with great mourning; and so these three queens sat them down, and in one of their laps king Arthur laid his head. And then that queen said, "Ah! dear brother, why have ye tarried so long from me? Alas, this wound on your head hath taken overmuch cold." And so they rowed from the land; and sir Bedivere beheld all those ladies go from him. Then sir Bedivere cried, "Ah! my lord Arthur, what shall become of me now ye go from me, and leave me here alone among mine enemies?"—"Comfort thyself," said king Arthur, "and do as well as thou mayest; for in me is no trust for to trust in; for I will into the vale of Avilion, for to heal me of my grievous wound; and, if thou never hear more of me, pray for my soul." But evermore the queens and the ladies wept and shrieked, that it was pitiful for to hear them: and, as soon as Sir Bedivere had lost the sight of the barge, he wept and wailed, and so took the forest, and so he went all the night; and, in the morning, he was aware, between two hills, of a chapel and a hermitage.

Tennyson, although he interpolates short passages to bring out the uncertainty of Arthur's destiny and to include in the picture a vision of social change, gives nearly the same account:

> Then murmur'd Arthur, "Place me in the
>   barge."
> So to the barge they came. There those three
>   queens
> Put forth their hands, and took the King, and
>   wept.
> But she that rose the tallest of them all
> And fairest laid his head upon her lap, ...
> Then loudly cried the bold Sir Bedivere:
> Ah! my Lord Arthur, whither shall I go?
> Where shall I hide my forehead and my eyes?
> And slowly answer'd Arthur from the barge:
> "The old order changeth, yielding place to new,
> And God fulfills himself in many ways,

> Lest one good custom should corrupt the world.
> Comfort thyself; what comfort is in me?
> I have lived my life, and that which I have done
> May He within himself make pure! but thou,
> If thou shouldst never see my face again,
> Pray for my soul. More things are wrought by
>   prayer
> Than this world dreams of. . . .
> But now farewell. I am going a long way
> With those thou seest—if indeed I go—
> To the island-valley of Avilion; . . .
> Where I will heal me of my grievous wound."
>
>   . . .
>
>   Long stood Sir Bedivere
> Revolving many memories, till the hull
> Look'd one black dot against the verge of dawn,
> And on the mere the wailing died away.
>   ("The Passing of Arthur," lines 373-440)

Malory glorifies a past heroic age to the denigration of the fallen present; for him the love of Launcelot and the queen is an example of virtuous devotion that renders honor to God:

> But nowadays, men cannot love, may not endure by reason; for where they be soon accorded, and hastily heat soon cooleth; right so fareth love now-a-days, soon hot, soon cold. This is no stability, but the old love was not so. Men and women could love together seven years, and no licorous lusts were between them; and there was truth and faithfulness. And so in likewise was love used in king Arthur's days. . . .

For Malory, that is, the story of the Round Table is primarily (although not entirely) an example for readers of his day to admire and emulate. For Tennyson, the relationship of Lancelot and Guinevere is an example of misconduct, and he makes the story more a warning than a pattern for imitation. The difference is one of central focus, if not of tragic conception. As Caxton, the first publisher of the *Morte Darthur,* says in his preface, through Malory "noble men may see and read the noble acts of chivalry, the gentle and virtuous deeds that some knights used in those days. . . . " Tennyson's reader, in days of grave social crises, is to see and avoid "the darkness of that battle in the west / Where all of high and holy dies away." (pp. 36-49)

J. Philip Eggers, in his King Arthur's Laureate: A Study of Tennyson's "Idylls of the King," *New York University Press, 1971, 274 p.*

Roger Simpson

[In the following excerpt, Simpson considers literary influences and aspects of allegory in two of Tennyson's Idylls of the King: *"The Lady of Shalott" and "Sir Launcelot and Queen Guinevere."]*

Written by about May 1832, the initial version of 'The Lady of Shalott' is Tennyson's first poem to be wholly engaged with Arthurian material. Comparison of the poem with medieval treatments of the Elaine legend reveals that in Malory's *Le Morte Darthur,* in the Stanzaic *Le Morte*

Arthur and in the Italian novella that was Tennyson's most probable source, there is no introduction of a supernatural element: Elaine's misery and death are attributed solely to her unrequited human love. However, the early nineteenth century preoccupation with faerie is evident in the two analogues which derive from the same novella source as does Tennyson's poem. Although these two analogues have been almost wholly overlooked by twentieth century critics, the poems provide a valuable basis for a comparison both between Tennyson's source and his completed poem, and between Tennyson's verse and that of two of his contemporaries.

In the first of these, Louisa Stuart Costello's 'The Funeral Boat', two such fairy allusions are of only slight import. The damsel's 'lonely bark' (40) is fairy-like: 'Frail as the shell whose fairy sail / Sinks before the summer gale' (48-49); and Lancelot later vows to make her a grave where 'fairies paint their nightly rings' (183). Both references, however, indicate not only a conventionally rendered prettiness, but also the suggestion that the heroine's physical and emotional feminine delicacy is associated with the sheltering ambience of faerie, in retreat from a harsh everyday world. Much more significant, though, is the song that preludes the bark's arrival among the knights and ladies of the Arthurian court. Here the actual source of the song is left deliberately mysterious—

> Was it the moan of waves . . .
> Was it the sea-bird's mournful cry . . .
> Where is the minstrel . . . ? (120-27)

However, despite its indeterminate origin, the song's message is unambiguously directed in reproof of Lancelot's flirtatious song to the 'lovely bands' of ladies (96):

> Ah! hush that lute's persuasive tone,
>   By thee too sweetly taught to feign:
> Its melody is sound alone,
>   And truth avoids the fatal strain.
> One who has known thy scorn too well,
>   Thy lays of falsehood would reprove;
> Even from the grave she comes to tell
>   How harsh a foe thou art to Love! (130-37)

Thus, Lancelot is morally castigated for being a 'worthless traitor' (178) to the damsel who had died for him; and the supernatural song is employed by Costello as a means whereby moral obloquy is apportioned and publicly announced with greater authority than if spoken by the narrator. The novella had described the contents of an explanatory letter borne by the damsel: this 'scroll' is adopted by Costello, and its message amplified to include the damsel's request to Lancelot for 'One only boon . . . a grave' (174). But whereas the novella concludes upon the last line of the damsel's letter ('fallen a victim only for loving too true'), Costello's narrative continues with an admission by Lancelot of his responsibility for the death, and his promise of twelve months' penance spent away from the court and the camp. Costello's characters are wholly human, the narrative is described in terms of a psychologically naturalistic development, and the faerie is largely confined to inessential décor or to the device of a choric song for the full expression of the poem's unambiguous moral attitudes.

A second analogue to Tennyson's poem is Letitia Elizabeth Landon's 'A Legend of Tintagel Castle', which appeared in October 1832, a month before 'The Lady of Shalott'. Here, once more, the concept of faerie is used as a routine simile for an attractively crowded scene: 'There was many a fair dame, and many a knight, / Made the banks of the river like fairy-land bright' (41-42). Nevertheless, in contrast with Costello's naturalistically human heroine, Landon's is a 'wood-nymph' who retires with Lancelot to an 'odorous cave, / Where the emerald spars shone like stars on the wave, / And the green moss and violets crowded beneath' (25-27). The poem's imagery associates her with the 'flowers of the forest' which are 'crushed at each step' by the 'proud' feet of Lancelot's courser (5-6). That Lancelot first catches sight of her by means of her reflection in a stream suggests her role as nature-spirit; and, appropriately for this context, her funeral bark which sets sail for Tintagel is towed by two white swans. However, despite her occupancy of a similar elfin grot, she has not the same eerie and destructive potency as Keats's La Belle Dame sans Merci. Rather, she shares the common misfortune of generously imprudent womanhood: she 'was left as aye woman will be, / Who trusts her whole being, oh false love to thee' (35-36). Furthermore, Landon's sentimental moralising represents the 'lady' as a conventionally pathetic heroine whose disaster is typical of the human condition:

> And these are love's records; a vow and a dream,
> And the sweet shadow passes away from life's
>   stream:
> Too late we awake to regret—but what tears
> Can bring back the waste to our hearts and our
>   years! (57-60)

Like Landon, Tennyson presents an inversion of the Fairy Bride legend: for, in this altered form, the fairy is destroyed by the human. But in Tennyson's poem the role of faerie has far greater obliquity. As for the Lady's nature, it is on the whisper of a reaper that she is described as 'the *fairy* / Lady of Shalott' (35-36). The attribution of her fairy nature is thereby credibly contextualised within the countryman's belief in fairies. Moreover, the 'curse' is similarly internalised and presented only from the Lady's own viewpoint: she has heard 'a whisper' say, and she says it herself when she first looks down to Camelot (116). This Tennysonian distancing of himself from an explicit avowal may also be seen at the end of the poem where the knights 'crossed themselves for fear' (166): an action which hints at their terror of a sinister fairy presence, but does not actually assert either that the Lady was a fairy or that their fears were justified. Again, being compared to a 'bold seër in a trance' (128) endows her with a quasi-prophetic role, but the device of comparison ('Like') renders the assertion merely tentative. What might have been treated as purely magical properties—the mirror, the web and the boat—are all given a mundane plausibility. The boat, for instance, is found convincingly moored beneath a willow, and, to embark, the Lady has first to loosen a 'chain': moreover, earlier references to the river ('willow-veiled' with its barges and shallops) have prepared us for the appearance of the Lady's vessel. Tennyson's addition of a mirror to the Lady's bower brings with it some of the enchantment which had originally surrounded one of its main sources—the mirror in which Britomart had first espied Sir Artegall (*Faerie Queene* III. ii. 18-26). This wondrous 'myrrhour', constructed by Merlin in the shape of a 'glassie globe', had enjoyed a revived celebrity in the Romantic period. Besides Moultrie's introduction of it into *La Belle Tryamour,* and Coleridge's image in 'The Pang More Sharp Than All' . . . , Thomas Pringle had used a relevant quotation from Spenser to preface an extensive series of historical scenes viewed in a magical elfin mirror in 'A Dream of FairyLand'. Tennyson, however, does not invest his mirror with extravagantly magical properties: it has, in fact, a workaday practicality, as [Arthur Waugh, in his *Alfred, Lord Tennyson,* (1902)] first showed, by being a necessary instrument for the weaver to see the back of the tapestry. The 'magic' of its 'sights' may be interpreted as the colourful and emotional pull of the exterior world, and if these sights are woven into the web, what wonder that the web itself be magic? (38). Yet, these naturalistically presented aspects are balanced by a contrasting fairy quality, less in minor detail than in overall effect. The reflection of Landon's wood-nymph in the stream may be deemed as 'bright as a *vision,* and fair as a *dream*' (17) but the event remains on the level of sober diurnal occurrence, whereas in Tennyson the image of Lancelot flashing into the 'crystal mirror' has an unexpected and compelling effect, creating a magical and dramatic response from the Lady and the mirror. Much of Tennyson's effect here is achieved through a reduction of an orthodox story line. In both other contemporary versions, the Lady's death is directly attributable to her unreturned love for Lancelot, and her final voyage is made with the express aim of confronting him with her corpse. Tennyson's poem lacks such explicit outline: mystery hangs over the web, the mirror, the curse, her death, her voyage, or even Lancelot's awareness of his own role in what has befallen. Moreover, in Malory, Camelot is explicitly stated to be Winchester, and his unlocated romance venues of Carbonek and Lonazep jostle with a recognisable London, Dover, Humber and Salisbury. By contrast, there is in Tennyson a systematic reduction in topographical reference, for whereas Malory's 'Astolat, that is Gylford' (= Guildford, XVIII. ix), lies on Lancelot's direct route from Winchester to London, and the Lady is later carried 'in a charyot unto the next place where Temse (= Thames) is' before being placed in a barge that floats her to Westminster (XVIII. xix), Tennyson chose to follow the *Cento Novelle Antiche* version, which mentions only an unlocated Camelot. His modification of the novella's place-name 'Scalott' to his own 'Shalott' was made, he claimed, for reasons of euphony; an additional clue to the fact that a naturalistic topography lay outside Tennyson's concern. His deliberate suppression of narrative thread presents the action in a staccato series of tableaux: the Lady at her loom, the arrival of Lancelot, the cracking of the mirror, her setting sail, then arrival in Camelot. And Tennyson's 1842 version decreases the exoteric by depriving the Lady even of her parchment which had 'puzzled more than all the rest' by its gnomic terseness:

'The web was woven curiously,
The charm is broken utterly,
Draw near and fear not—this is I,

The Lady of Shalott.' (1832 version)

If 'The Funeral Boat' and 'A Legend of Tintagel Castle' may be regarded as sentimental and didactic narrative, the absence of outwardly cogent narrative in 'The Lady of Shalott' has considerably broadened the poem's scope and application. That the poem has a secondary significance has been widely canvassed: the exact nature of that significance, however, remains the subject of acute disagreement. The claims of allegory have been strongly advanced, and have divided claimants into three main camps. The first of these has read the poem as illustrating a tragic failure to pursue the lofty demands of Art, through the Artist's succumbing to the attractions of Love and the World. A much larger party has made an exactly opposite interpretation. This sees the poem as heroic rather than tragic, in that it is believed to illustrate the duty of the Artist, *qua* human being, to love and thereby to enter life fully. Neither viewpoint may easily be maintained. As for the former, it runs clean counter to Tennyson's later recorded dictum that:

The new-born love for something, for some one
in the wide world from which she has been so
long secluded, takes her out of the region of
shadows into that of realities.

There is here no indication that she suffers a moral or aesthetic decline on entry into the world. It is difficult to refute this dictum by invoking the intentionalist fallacy, because the poem itself speaks of the 'shadows of the world' (48) that appear in her mirror, and of these shadows the Lady is 'half sick' (71). The cracking of the mirror suggests an end to mirror- or shadow-gazing, and thus impels a direct confrontation with reality rather than its avoidance through an over-isolated art. On the other hand, those who claim that the Lady makes a wholly justifiable decision and that she achieves a moral victory in choosing love and the wide world do not give due weight to the pathos with which her death is represented, in which there is a greater sense of loss and waste than of positive achievement. Additionally, as the Lady is compared to a seer who can foresee his own 'mischance', the mischance would seem to apply also to her own fate, which she has twice previously described as a 'curse'. Nor can Edgar F. Shannon's claim [in 'Poetry as Vision: Sight and Insight in "The Lady of Shalott"', *Victorian Poetry,* 19 (1981)] be supported that her aesthetic triumph is signified by the term 'carolled':

Although mixed with sadness, befitting a lament
for imminent death, it is a carol, a hymn of joy
and praise, which is traditionally associated with
the birth of Christ—the representation of hope
and eternal life.

But, in Tennyson's poem, the context is that the listeners

Heard a carol, mournful, holy,
Chanted loudly, chanted lowly,
Till her blood was frozen slowly,
And her eyes were darkened wholly (145-48)

The immediate proximity of the adjective 'mournful' does not suggest 'hope and eternal life', and the subsequent description is that of decline rather than rebirth. 'Carol' is used here without its Christian connotations but with a neutral sense of 'song'. Such a suggestion may be justified by an appeal to a very similar use of the term occurring in 'Mariana in the South', another poem in the 1832 collection:

> 'Ave Mary', made she moan,
> And 'Ave Mary', night and morn,
> And 'Ah', she sang, 'to be all alone,
> To live forgotten and love forlorn'.
> She, as her *carol* sadder grew . . . (9-13)

The difficulty involved in maintaining the two above-mentioned allegorical interpretations has encouraged the widespread adoption of a third: that the poem contrasts the claims of Life and Art, a conflict the resolution of which is held in abeyance: as human being in need of human interests and affection, the artist is impelled to abandon isolation, but ironically the 'world' brings loss of love, tragedy and death. Critics who relate literature closely to biographical origins have accepted this third interpretation as an allegorical account of Tennyson's life in the early 1830s, and have contended that the poem reveals both Tennyson's desire to develop a broader human concern in his verse, and his fear that he might spoil his art in so doing. However, whilst this third ironic viewpoint is considerably more defensible than the two previous, it should not be awarded the canonical accolade, because the poem ultimately resists interpretation at an allegorical level. In the light of the fact that most early critics found the poem difficult or warned against the needless unravelling of a message, one ought to be intensely wary of a completely codified explication. This is not to imply that poetry necessarily defies analysis, merely that analysis of this poem rests uneasily on continually shifting bases. At even the most superficial level, the poem is not as clear as it might seem. The crowd, for example, read her 'name' round the 'prow', but it is not her name that they see, only her title—the Lady of Shalott. Again, there is rich ambiguity in a crucial statement: she is merely '*half* sick of shadows'. The elliptical narrative induces mystery, and there is tension between the narrative lacunae and the clarity of the visually apprehended surface, a tension which achieves a distinctively dream-like effect. Just as the Lady cannot be definitively categorised as human or fairy, so the action falls midway between psychological drama and fairytale. The complex interweaving of imagery (the funeral has 'plumes', as does the sun-like Lancelot); the 'conclusion' of the poem upon an inconclusive note of prayerful adjuration; and the taut balance between song and silence, between the refrain of Camelot and Shalott, unite to form a richly allusive work. To select, as an instance, one bright image from the poem—the shield of Lancelot in which a 'red-cross knight for ever kneeled / To a lady' (78-79)—is to encounter an essential ambivalence: does the lady represent Guenevere (and therefore Courtly Love or Adulterous Liaison?) or is she the Virgin Mary, whose image Arthur had traditionally borne? Or does the image foreshadow Lancelot's final homage to the dead Lady of Shalott ('God in His mercy lend her grace')? Does it have any relevance to the human actors in the poem? The rich labyrinthine mystery at the heart of the work invites speculative interpretation, and the poem has

never lacked for self-appointed guides, but the allusiveness which ripples out from the poem cannot be confined within a strict allegorical schema, as can Lytton's 'The Fairy Bride'. Tennyson's defence of his poetry against 'Dark-brow'd sophist[s]' who would impose such a schema may be seen in another early poem, 'The Poet's Mind' (1830), which treats of the sophist's attempts at understanding as merely a murderous frost that blights poetic growth. Although some later critics have spoken correctly of 'a kind of allegory', 'allegorical pointers' and 'parabolic drift', the claims for widely conflicting, and mutually exclusive, allegorical reductions would indicate that the poem lacks such a clearly enunciated schema and cannot therefore be defined as allegory. In its ability to suggest multiple meanings, none of which can finally and adequately epitomise the poem, it should more accurately be regarded as symbolist, as a precursor of a mode later distinguished from allegory by Yeats [in his *Essays and Introductions*, 1961], who contrasted allegory, which 'said things which could be said as well, or better, in another way, and needed a right knowledge for its understanding', with symbolism, which 'said things which could not be said so perfectly in any other way, and needed but a right instinct for its understanding'.

The fragment of 'Sir Launcelot and Queen Guinevere' was the only portion published by Tennyson of his projected 'The Ballad of Sir Launcelot', which had had many allegorical overtones. In this schema, Galahad (the type of Chastity), Merlin (Worldly Prudence) and three knights (Worldly Force) are ranged against the lovers. That the knights should be physically, and allegorically, defeated is unremarkable in that their vanquisher (Launcelot) is traditionally of martial prowess, but it is noteworthy that Merlin should be 'miserably floored' by Launcelot's verbal ripostes since Tennyson had no literary precedent for such a confrontation between the two, and his own later portrait of Merlin in *Idylls of the King* treats him more sympathetically. Tennyson's invention of a meeting between Sir Galahad and the lovers indicates that a dramatic conflict was intended between such differing types; and, despite the omission of Galahad and Merlin from the published fragment, an inherent polarity remains at many levels within the poem. Natural scenery is, for example, presented in its most contrasting aspects, as in 'a sun-lit fall of rain' (4) or 'sun and shade' (37). The birds are either innocently melodious songbirds ('the linnet piped his song', 'the throstle whistled strong', 10-11) or, like the sparhawk, are the predatory cause of the ominous hush that stills the groves. The verse is redolent of other comparisons ('*Like* souls that . . . with full*er* sound . . . the *perfect* fan . . . and fleet*er* now') that create a tautly strained tissue of contraries, which is reinforced by the tensions of the rhyme scheme, which demands three or four successively rhyming line ends. Again, Guinevere paradoxically 'swayed / The rein with dainty finger-tips' (40-41); and the 'maiden Spring' (3) is matched by 'the boyhood of the year' (19). The perspective strains into the distance: 'far, in forest-deeps' (7) to the 'topmost' elm-tree (8). The visual delineation is sometimes very precise: for example,

> Now on some twisted ivy-net,

> Now by some tinkling rivulet,
> In mosses mixt with violet
> Her cream-white mule his pastern set (28-31)

Despite this there is an opposite tendency towards the general and idealised. Thus, the poem opens with a simile hovering on the verge of personification ('Like souls that balance joy and pain') and it closes with a general statement ('A man had given all other bliss'). Emotions within the poem are heightened and intense, whether 'tears', 'fear', 'smiles', 'laughed', 'blissful', 'bliss', 'happy' or 'joyous'. These oppositions are complemented by the tension between movement and restraint: as in the birdsong hushed by fear, the rein swayed with finger-tips, or the ringlet blown from the braid.

Clyde de L. Ryals has shown that the imagery has a role far greater than inessential adjunct in that 'it tells in miniature the entire story of the two lovers', with the images of fecundity ('teeming ground', 'chestnut-buds') counterpointing the sexual love of the two protagonists. However, Ryals drives his original and valuable insight too far by attempting to press almost every word of the poem into an explicit schema. This entails some over-ingenious Freudian readings: he claims, for example, that 'treble' (in 'With blissful treble ringing clear', 22) suggests 'three, the masculine number', and that it thus indicates the 'impossible' triple relationship linking Launcelot, Guinevere and Arthur. Moreover, too fixed an insistence on the subordination of every phrase to an Arthurian, and presumably Malorian, framework, limits the relevance of Tennyson's work, in which the purely Arthurian element in the plot had been reduced by the author. In 1842 the poem was, in fact, grouped not with other Arthurian poems but was preceded and followed by a number of love poems ('Lady Clare', 'The Lord of Burleigh', and 'The Beggar Maid'), all of which share a celebration of the power and value of love, and which are all structured by a dramatisation of the social constraints that impede, but may be transcended by, lovers.

What marks the language of 'Sir Launcelot and Queen Guinevere' is the extent to which it draws on Malorian elements. In, for example, Malory's account of Launcelot's love for the Queen (XVIII. i,ii) there occur the words 'perfectyon', 'draughtes', 'maydens', 'joye', and 'payne', all of which become a cluster of key terms in Tennyson's poem. Other words in the poem, such as 'gown', 'waste', and 'bliss' are also distinctively Malorian, whose own lovers ride through woods and meadows in the month of May, all 'clothed in grene outher in sylke outher in clothe' until all are 'bedasshed with herbys, mosses and floures' (XIX. i,ii). But Tennyson avoids producing a servilely limp imitation, by combining an idiom which remains close to Malory with that of language which is evidently of later date, such as the adjectival precision of 'twisted ivy-net' or the details of early nineteenth century fashionable coiffure: 'Blowing the ringlet from the braid' (39), such ringlets forming the subject of frequent attention in other early Tennyson poems based both on legendary and contemporary subjects. Moreover, despite taking up a few verbal cues from Malory, Tennyson removes the 'fragment' from the original narrative and allegorical setting of his draft, and omits all specific reference to placenames, or to a com-

mencement and conclusion of the lovers' ride. Rhythmically, the insistent onward impetus transforms the ride into a quintessential lovers' journey; the movement is without commencement or terminus, and thus assumes the quality of an arrested stasis. Nor is characterisation within the poem accommodated solely to a Malorian canon. When Guinevere is compared to her

> whose elfin prancer springs
> By night to eery warblings,
> When all the glimmering moorland rings
> With jingling bridle-reins (33-36)

the Queen acquires by proximity affinities with the Fairy Bride. Indeed, Scott's edition of the ballad of 'Thomas the Rhymer' is a probable major source for this passage. His 'Queen of fair Elfland' wore a 'shirt' of 'grass-green silk', whilst on her horse's mane hung 'fifty siller bells and nine' so that the bridle rang. She rode a 'milk-white steed' which flew faster than the wind, and when the Rhymer kissed her lips and rode off with her, he surrendered himself totally to her power, and left this world. In Tennyson, Guinevere rides 'a cream-white mule' and wears a 'gown of grass-green silk'. Green being the fairies' colour, she also wears a 'light-green tuft of plumes', thereby reinforcing these elfin allusions, besides associating her with the 'green' of the 'topmost elm-tree' and the 'grassy capes', just as the lovers' 'blissful treble ringing clear' echoes the song of linnet and throstle; whilst Guinevere's 'golden clasps' recall the 'yellowing' river, or the 'perfect fan' of the chestnut preludes her labial excellence. Seeming 'a part of joyous Spring', she, in turn embodies the beauty, youthfulness and vigour of the landscape. The presentation of the Queen thus gains in rich allusiveness. It also endows her with the amorality of a nature goddess, rather than with the immorality of the sinful queen.

A major result of Tennyson's freeing his fragment from the projected 'Ballad of Sir Launcelot' was that he evaded the implications that a longer poem would have induced him to confront, namely the relationship between Launcelot and the Queen, and the manner in which this relationship was regarded by other personae (for example, Merlin and Galahad) within the poem. As jokingly expressed by Kemble's letter, the theme was potentially risqué:

> I can only offer you Sir L.'s song, though for the sake of my future clerical views and Aelfred's and Sir L.'s character, I must request that it be kept as quiet as possible.

The poetical treatment of an avowed adultery could have deeply offended contemporary moral sensibility, particularly as the draft gives the impression that Tennyson was portraying the lovers sympathetically, Worldly Prudence being floored, and Galahad made to look sheepish. To a limited extent, Tennyson could escape the stricter moral categories by presenting the material as mythic. Certainly, greater moral latitude was accorded Olympian deities or romance enchantresses than would have been tolerated in a modern setting. But, even so, many aspects of the mythical or historical past were felt to require sanitising. The *Morte*'s reputation still suffered for being, in Roger Ascham's phrase, an account of 'open manslaughter and plain bawdry'. This was a charge to which much of Arthurian romance was subject. In a review of Scott's edition of *Sir Tristrem* [in *Critical Review,* 3 (September 1804)], William Taylor of Norwich ventured a prophecy on 'this favourite story of our ancestors':

> It will not recover its ancient popularity: our correcter notions of the importance and duty of conjugal fidelity will prevent Essylt . . . from ever becoming a favourite heroine.

Great uneasiness was later expressed by William Dyce when undertaking research in 1848 for his frescoes in the Palace of Westminster, for 'the chief part' of *Morte Darthur,* he considered,

> turns on incidents which, if they are not undesirable for representation under any circumstances, are at least scarcely appropriate in such an apartment.

Accordingly, had Tennyson chosen to complete and publish his poem as originally drafted, it would have signified a remarkable departure from conventional mores since all other early nineteenth century references to the Launcelot and Guinevere affair were muted, satirical or disapproving. Common to many reworkings of Malory was a constant amelioration of the original characters' immoral sexual behaviour. With Hogg, for example, Launcelot is made the Queen's knight but this homage remains chaste; neither does the drug-induced love of Tristram and Isonde lead to a consummated adultery: Isonde remains a 'faultless queen', her fame 'spotless'. In contrast with Hogg, both Heber and Riethmuller create a slightly darker moral climate: Arthur seems peremptory in both, and in Riethmuller is made the father of an illegitimate Mordred by Morgan le Fay, who is ambiguously described as being close to Arthur in 'birth and blood'. The Launcelot-Gwenever relationship is strictly muted: in both works, Launcelot and Gwenever had met and fallen in love before her arranged marriage to Arthur: they had thus established a mitigating prior claim on each other's affections. Whilst Heber abandoned his poem before the reintroduction of Launcelot and the expected liaison with the Queen, in Riethmuller their reunion is chaste, and it is only Morgan's malevolence which traps Launcelot into visiting the Queen's bower. Thus, neither work represents an actually adulterous liaison: such were the ways in which early nineteenth century writers attempted to accommodate the 'plain bawdry' of much Malorian material.

In comparable fashion, Tennyson removed from an original draft of his poem those lines which probably appeared too overtly sexual:

> Each clasp, a point of brightest light
> Was made, a Lady and a Knight:
> And when the clasp was buckled tight
> The Lady seemed to fold the Knight.

And a slender lyric could, of course, avoid a direct reference to the adultery theme. Tennyson deliberately blurs, by the removal of the poem from its initial context, a distinct moral perspective from which to judge the Launcelot-Guinevere relationship. Accordingly, the fragment includes no biographical detail of Guinevere, but represents the situation obliquely. That she is already married to Ar-

thur is suggested by her title of 'Queen', but Tennyson's poem makes no specific reference to her husband or to the exact nature of the connection between Launcelot and Guinevere. Whilst the story was sufficiently well-known for a reader of the time to have been aware that the pair represented an adulterous love affair, Tennyson concentrates his poem explicitly on the spring-time ride. Although, as Ryals suggests, the imagery may provide an undertow of ominous allusion, a tragic outcome is not allowed to dominate the poem's mood. About succeeding events, the verse is delicately ambiguous:

> A man had given all other bliss,
> And all his wordly worth for this,
> To waste his whole heart in one kiss
> Upon her perfect lips. (42-45)

The suggestiveness is densely organised: 'a man' could mean Launcelot but it also implies 'every man'; and, if every man would do this, it mitigates the heinousness of Launcelot's surrender to passion. Conversely, 'had' has the force of 'would have', and this conditional tense implies that the surrender has not yet taken place, perhaps never will. Furthermore, the placing of 'perfect lips' at the end of the poem gives the phrase a climactic quality, and, in comparison with the dimly adumbrated foreshadowings of woe, the poem's realisation of present joy and beauty is so intense that one must, on balance, see the poem as a celebration of the love affair. But, as the polarities within the poem convey, the ultimate significance of the work remains qualified and oblique. The situation has widened in scope beyond the Malorian context, the characters appear to be moving towards the archetypal, but an exact determining of their roles proves elusive, for if one may be certain that Galahad represents Chastity and Moral Purity, Launcelot and Guinevere are not quite so easily reducible: they certainly typify a Romantic Love, but it is not clear whether this is to be regarded favourably, pejoratively or as a mixed blessing. On account of this ambiguity, the poem cannot finally be classified as an allegory. (pp. 195-207)

[The] Arthurian legend was adopted as a literary subject much more frequently than has been assumed by recent literary historians concerned with the early nineteenth century. This resurgence of interest in Arthur is notable not only for its plenitude but also for its diversity, because the Arthurian Revival derived from richly complex sources, which we are now in a position to summarise.

Of prime importance in this Revival was the recovery of a hero who would, like Alfred or Richard I, impart a historical grandeur to the national pantheon. As putative hero, Arthur enjoyed considerable advantages, for his legend is characterised by its special power of attracting originally discrete elements. This essential adaptability is demonstrated by his dual function in war, wherein he may act as an imperial Continental conqueror, or take the role of partisan leader against a Germanic invader. Yet, contrasting with these feats of arms is his pacific role as a just and benevolent ruler in a golden age: and the nature of his rule appeals both to royalist sentiment and also, by means of the distinctive institution of the Round Table, achieves a measure of egalitarian fraternity, whereby the ancient code of chivalry is upheld against a materialist and selfishly anarchic utilitarianism. In contrast, the cult of Robin Hood, though potent in this period, could never match the range and rich dualisms of Arthur's role. Although retaining his power to symbolise Welsh patriotism, Arthur might represent not only this minority culture but also a Great Britain which saw itself as a harmonious union of Celt and Saxon. Most importantly—and this was a major reason for his supplanting other comparable national heroes—his mythological aura endows him with the Messianic attribute of a promised return: he therefore remains imminent, and of perpetual modern relevance; and his second coming—itself an apt metaphor for the Medieval Revival or Celtic Renaissance—may be constantly reinterpreted to adapt to new meliorist prescriptions. Although he has a slenderly outlined historical career, its indeterminacy provides great scope for controversial theory or for imaginative invention. Moreover, his mythological base is neither too abstract nor confined to one precise geographical area, since local legend clung to widely ranging loci: from major sites in the Eildon Hills, Penrith, Caerleon, Glastonbury, Tintagel and Winchester, to the innumerable other spots where a slender association persisted. A powerful adjunct, too, in the legend's ability to assimilate other material is that the concept of a Round Table brotherhood of knights continually encourages the enlistment of additional heroes, such as Lancelot, Tristram, Galahad, Launfal and later men, whose *gestes* are then inter-related with the core legend, and their love affairs and religious quests then provide a varied texture of human concern. Arthurian literature could thus accommodate a wide variety of type and interest, and was able to engraft most kinds of event. Given, moreover, that the period was especially concerned with supernatural agency, together with a perception of the imaginative and irrational aspects of man, these concerns found a convenient focus in the deeply ambivalent nature of Merlin, a figure who was already the most prominent amongst the personae associated with Arthur. Another contributory factor in the Revival was that contemporary literature was not required to construct a mythology totally afresh, for the gradual recovery of medieval texts revealed a vast international literature on the Matter of Britain, providing an inexhaustible source of theme, character and adventure; and the massive Arthurian context of medieval literature almost entirely eclipsed the potential rivalry of any other potential British hero. Finally, the resilience of the Arthurian myth is shown by the fact that even derisive detraction of it was integrated with the persistent comic elements within the literature to form a vigorous English burlesque tradition, and therefore, paradoxically, helped to ensure the survival of a residue of the original myth. (pp. 220-21)

[If we take into account] the large amount of Arthurian scholarship and literary creation within the early nineteenth century, we may no longer regard Tennyson as a pioneer of the subject. On the contrary, he often appears quite distinct from many contemporary Arthurian currents. In subject, the early published verse of Tennyson avoided certain Arthurian areas that had already attracted the attention of many of his contemporaries. Working outside the traditional concern with a historical Arthur, Tennyson displays no interest in any of the topographical sites commonly associated with Arthur's birth (e.g. Tintagel) or his tomb (e.g. Glastonbury) or the location of his court (e.g. Carlisle or Winchester). Nor does he describe Arthur's role as a sixth century *dux bellorum* achieving twelve victories over foreign invaders. Neither is Arthur presented as a Celtic or, more particularly, as a Welsh figure. Tennyson thus appears very clearly separate from scholarly historians, topographers or participants in the Welsh Revival. What is more, besides moving away from burlesque, Tennyson rejects also some favoured areas of the romance literary tradition, such as Launfal, Morgan le Fay and the Loathly Lady. The fairy elements are thus curtailed, and the opportunity for bawdy burlesque removed. One may indicate the extent of comparative isolation from received tradition, by noting that Tennyson moves sharply away, too, from the post-Renaissance convention of fancifully free adaptation of legendary material. (p. 223)

[Tennyson's] poetic development led him away from the powerful literary conventions of fancifully free adaptations of Arthurian legend—and in doing so, Tennyson distanced his work from that of Spenser, Dryden, Blackmore or Richard Hole—and returned, instead, to what had once been regarded as a quasi-canonical romance summary of Arthurian legend: Malory's *Le Morte Darthur*. That Tennyson was well apprised of rival handlings of the material is shown by the existence, in the Trinity MS, of 'The Ballad of Sir Launcelot', and by the prose drafts of the early 1830s which include many non-Malorian concepts, such as the Sacred Mount of Camelot; the three Guineveres; Merlin Emrys, who marries his daughter to Modred; Merlin's oak tomb; and Guinevere's throwing the presented diamonds into the river. Tennyson's progression away from the above, and towards the use of Malory as his major source, is an important development in the course of the Arthurian Revival. As has been shown, Tennyson added almost as much as he derived from Malory; nonetheless, he was largely instrumental in altering popular attitudes towards Malory, and the focal centre of Arthurian study would thereby be shifted from Geoffrey of Monmouth, Spenser, Drayton or Warton; and the resonances of this adjustment are to be heard plainly throughout the Pre-Raphaelite movement. This shift towards Malory was latently important in that it would bring into central prominence the 'guilty love' of Launcelot and Guinevere, the quest of the Sangraal, and the incestuous descent of Mordred. In many respects, a more tragic doom-laden atmosphere would prevail; but these later developments were not yet apparent in the 1840s. At that point, the contribution wrought by Tennyson was less evident. He had certainly neglected much material that was commonly treated, although in 'The Lady of Shalott' he had taken a story that was popularly current. If he had given a novel prominence to the role of Galahad as Grail hero, had lent an unusual glamour to the morally ambivalent love of Launcelot and Guinevere, and had established an unlocated Camelot as the Arthurian capital, he had remained more orthodox in his moral idealisation of Arthur, and in the promulgation of the political myth of the need for the chivalrous hero's return in modern guise. (pp. 225-26)

Roger Simpson, "Tennyson and the Arthurian

Revival," in his Camelot Regained: The Arthurian Revival and Tennyson, 1800-1849,
D. S. Brewer, 1990, pp. 190-254.

John D. Rosenberg

[*An American educator and critic, Rosenberg is the author of several works on nineteenth-century English literature, including* The Fall of Camelot: A Study of
Tennyson's "Idylls of the King." *In the following excerpt from that work, he considers the form Tennyson
chose for his* Idylls, *noting that the poet achieved both
structural and thematic complexity through his use of
antitheses and symbolist techniques.*]

A clue to Tennyson's earliest intentions [in *The Idylls of
the King*] appears in the introductory verses to the "Morte
d'Arthur," where we learn that the poet has burnt his epic
on "King Arthur, some twelve books," for they were
mere "faint Homeric echoes, nothing-worth." Only the
"Morte" was plucked from the flames in the conviction
that "its use will come." The imaginary burning of the
books is more than a device for introducing, in medias res,
the isolated fragment on Arthur's passing. It symbolizes
Tennyson's rejection, sometime between the drafting of
the "Morte" in 1833 and its publication nine years later,
of an epic model for the *Idylls.* "At twenty-four I meant
to write an epic or drama of King Arthur," he remarked
after the *Idylls* was nearly completed: "I said I should do
it in twenty years; but the Reviews stopped me." Hyper-
sensitive to criticism, Tennyson was doubtless distressed
by the mixed reviews of the "Morte"; if they in fact
stopped him, one can only be grateful. Eleven more books
in the ostensibly epic form of the "Morte" might indeed
have produced "Homeric echoes, nothing-worth." As is,
he began with that part of the Arthurian cycle which, together with "The Coming of Arthur," most lends itself to
epic treatment: the national hero who creates a kingdom
and dies in single combat in its defense. Tennyson himself
pointed out that the form and style of these two frame
poems are "purposely more archaic" than the ten Round
Table idylls which they enclose. Once the final design
completed itself in his mind, he turned the initial disparity
to aesthetic advantage. He added to the original epic fragment the great opening lines of "The Passing" (1-169) that
draw together all the dominant symbols of the *Idylls,*
thereby binding the "Morte" to all that precedes it. And
by setting off from the Round Table idylls the paired
poems which mark Arthur's coming into the mutable
world and passing into another, Tennyson incorporates
into the very structure of the *Idylls* its cyclic themes of
change and permanence, of time and eternity.

Despite its evident excellence, one detects a certain un-
evenness in the "Morte." Its most moving moments are
elegiac rather than epic, pictorial rather than narrative,
such as Arthur's eulogy to his fallen knights or Bedivere's
lament as he watches the barge vanish, knowing that he
must

> . . . go forth companionless,
> And the days darken round me, and the years,
> Among new men, strange faces, other minds.
> ("The Passing of Arthur," 404-406)

One suspects that Tennyson's abandoned prose sketch, in
which absolutely nothing happens but everything is seen
with fixed intensity, was in fact closer to his essential genius than the more conventionally epic portions of the
"Morte." Yet the Arthurian story to which he had committed himself was crowded with actions of all kinds,
some suited to epic treatment, such as Arthur's last battle,
some to the highly mannered conventions of romance,
such as the tale of Lancelot and Elaine, some to a more
allegorical handling, such as the story of Merlin and Vivi-
en, which Tennyson recast as a medieval debate of body
and soul. The reviewers doubtless slowed his progress, but
the seventeen-year hiatus between the publication of the
"Morte" and that of the first four idylls of 1859 was due
far more to Tennyson's uncertain quest for a form that
would encompass the inherent diversity of his subject.

In addition to the prose sketch for an Arthurian work,
Tennyson considered two other schemes, both fortunately
abandoned. One was for a drama or masque in five acts;
the scenario, with its projected "Chorus of Ladies of the
Lake," disastrously suggests a sort of Christmas panto-
mime set to music. The second, more fragmentary outline
calls for an allegorical rendering in which Arthur is to
stand for "Religious Faith," Merlin for "Science," and the
Round Table for "liberal institutions."

Although Tennyson very soon gave up the idea of structuring the *Idylls* as a strict allegory, his commentators persisted in interpreting the poem as such, provoking him to
remark: "They have taken my hobby, and ridden it too
hard, and have explained some things too allegorically, although there is an allegorical or perhaps rather a parabolic
drift in the poem." Tennyson appears to have been both
flattered by the finding of allegorical significances in the
Idylls and deeply apprehensive that such readings were reductive of his whole intention. Hence his revealingly ambiguous reply to those who asked whether or not the Three
Queens who appear at Arthur's coronation stand for
Faith, Hope, and Charity: "They are right, and they are
not right. They mean that and they do not. They are three
of the noblest of women. They are also those three Graces,
but they are much more. I hate to be tied down to say,
'This means *that,'* because the thought within the image
is much more than any one interpretation." By "parabolic
drift" and "thought within the image," Tennyson means
precisely what we mean by *symbol,* the antithesis of the reductive, this-for-that equivalence which his commentators
have found in the *Idylls.* The point is not that allegory is
simplistic—a patent absurdity—but that the *Idylls* is not
an allegory and that those who so read it are forced into
simplistic conclusions.

Yet in a curiously conspiratorial way Tennyson encouraged such misreadings: "By King Arthur I always meant
the soul, and by the Round Table the passions and capacities of a man." But if, as Tennyson writes in the Epilogue,
the *Idylls* is about "Sense at war with Soul," why is the
"sinful" Lancelot, usurper of the Soul's bed, the secular
hero of the poem? The answer lies in a confusion of intention in Tennyson and of perception in his critics. An allegorical residue remains embedded in the overall symbolic
structure of the poem, although only once—when Arthur

The Lady of Shalott, *John William Waterhouse, 1888, oil on canvas.*

("Soul") denounces Guinevere ("Sense")—does the mixture of modes jar on the reader. Elsewhere, this residue results in a certain deficiency of realization, as with the Lady of the Lake or those

> three fair queens,
> Who stood in silence near his throne, the friends
> Of Arthur, gazing on him, tall, with bright
> Sweet faces, who will help him at his need.
> ("The Coming of Arthur," 275-278)

The difficulty with the trio is that they have no narrative function and no real connection with the poem's central characters or symbols, and so they stand in idle silence. They are simply part of the magical donné of Arthurian legend, to which Tennyson remains perhaps too diffidently faithful. His awareness of this dilemma always shows itself in a failure in his craft as a poet: the verse either becomes portentous or, as in the cited passage, lapses into the *contrivedly* prosaic (unlike Wordsworth, Tennyson is incapable of being unwittingly prosaic).

At the other extreme from an abstraction such as the Lady of the Lake ("The Church") are those characters who so richly embody the poem's moral and psychological complexities that any attempt to tag them with allegorical labels at once breaks down. Lancelot, for example, is larger than any didactic formula we might devise to contain him, and it is his greatness as a character that he compels us, in our attempts at explanation, to enlarge our terms of moral definition. His love for his king is as absolute as his love for his queen, and it is his tragedy that loyalty to one must be disloyalty to the other:

> The great and guilty love he bare the Queen,
> In battle with the love he bare his lord,
> Had marred his face, and marked it ere his time.
> (["Lancelot and Elaine,"] 244-246)

The whole force of this passage lies in the juxtaposed "great *and* guilty": the guilt of the love is indisputable, but so too is its greatness, by which Tennyson means not only intensity but nobility. Indeed, the guilt is a function of the nobility; were it not for Lancelot's nobility, he would feel no guilt, and without the guilt, there would be less greatness. The paradox of the adultery of Lancelot and Guinevere is that it not only "mars" them (and the kingdom) but ultimately ennobles them (and the kingdom), as Tennyson emphasizes by contrast with another adulterous triangle—the guiltless, peculiarly modern and joyless affair of Tristram and Isolt.

Yet in a recent book on the *Idylls* [Ryals, *From the Great Deep*] we read that Lancelot's guilty love of Guinevere "has coarsened not only his moral sensibilities but also his appearance." Nothing could more starkly illustrate the pitfalls consequent upon reading the *Idylls* as a war of Sense versus Soul, in which certain characters represent the vices of the first and others the virtues of the second. The warfare, as James D. Merriman has brilliantly shown, "is not between individuals, but rather within individuals, and the various characters in the *Idylls* illustrate at any given time some stage of victory or defeat in that inner struggle." Gawain's losing inner battle exactly parallels the outer struggle of the kingdom. His progressive degeneration from idyll to idyll is so beautifully integrated with that of the realm, from its founding in the spring to its barren end in the winter, that we scarcely notice him, for the changes in the character's moral foliation all but merge with those of the kingdom. Lancelot's far more tempestuous struggle moves in the opposite direction, toward salvation, and even those characters at the moral extremes of humanity—the harlot Vivien, for example—have an energy and solidity that elude any reductive personification such as "The Flesh." Only Galahad stands outside the arena of moral combat, and his victory over the flesh, as Merriman points out, "comes at the expense of simply abandoning the world, the real battleground of the war between Sense and Soul."

The *Idylls* dramatizes on all levels the only conflict that can engage the mature moral imagination—the clash not of right versus wrong but of right versus right. Allegorical interpretations of the *Idylls* obscure this distinction and substitute didactic solutions for the moral dilemmas it poses. Thus one critic assures us that the *Idylls* represents the triumph of "the high soul of man" over the passions, while another describes the poem as an allegory of the collapse which "must follow the rejection of spiritual values." Yet the moral of the *Idylls* is not that men must abide by spiritual values, any more than the moral of *Othello* is that wives should look to their linen. In this sense, the poem is totally without a moral but explores instead the ambiguous results of man's quest for such values, and the disastrous effects of abandoning them. In "Lancelot and Elaine" *denial* of the flesh proves fatal, and as "The Holy Grail" makes clear, spiritual values can drive men as mad as sexual obsession. Tennyson suggests a possible connection between the two: the color red, which throughout the *Idylls* symbolizes sexuality, is also associated with the Grail itself, first seen as "rose-red" by a nun in a condition of erotic ecstasy, then as "blood-red" by Galahad—as is fitting for the vessel that bore Christ's blood.

Even of this simplest of the poem's thematic antitheses—white as purity, red as passion—we cannot say *"this means that."* The lily maid of Astolat, white in purity, is at first glance a personification of Virgin Innocence; but her dreams are insistently sexual and the sleeve she gives Lancelot is scarlet, for her purity, like the nun's, is profoundly passionate. Because the lily maid is not a conventional figure in an allegory, our impulse is to distort her into a modern simplism of our own: seeming purity masking a libidinous reality. Yet like the symbols associated with her, she is neither this nor that, but both pure *and*

passionate, sexual *and* innocent, embodying the same intense conjunction of contrary elements that draws her instantly—and fatally—to Lancelot.

In 1859, when "Lancelot and Elaine" was published, Tennyson for the first time grouped his new series of Arthurian poems under the general title *Idylls of the King.* An idyll is a "little picture" of a character or mood colored by a single, dominant emotion. Tennyson's choice of the plural *idylls* stresses his intention, as Jerome Buckley points out, to portray "not a single unified narrative but a group of chivalric tableaux selected from a great mass of available legend . . . Each of the Idylls moves through a series of sharply visualized vignettes toward its pictured climax, its moment of revelation." Yet true as this is, one's experience of the *Idylls* is less static than it suggests. The sharply visualized vignettes which characterize so much of the poem—Lancelot kneeling before Guinevere in the vine-clad oriel window, Balin and Balan "sitting statue-like" by the fountain—are not simply pictures but *actions,* or rather their pictorial intensity is so great that we experience them as actions. The very early "Mariana" consists entirely of this hypercharged description. Imprisoned in her moated grange, Mariana is an animate extension of the setting, the setting a symbolic embodiment of her mental entrapment. The *Idylls* is filled with such moments of fixed intensity in which the energy of outward action turns in upon itself and narration becomes a kind of dramatized vision. The first critic to perceive this quality in Tennyson's verse was Arthur Hallam, and there is a certain ghostly aptness in summoning Hallam to illuminate the poetry in which he later figures so largely. Reviewing the volume in which "Mariana" first appeared, Hallam remarks on Tennyson's

> power of embodying himself in . . . moods of character, with such extreme accuracy of adjustment, that the circumstances of the narration seem to have a natural correspondence with the predominant feeling, and, as it were, to be evolved from it by assimilative force . . . These expressions of character are brief and coherent: nothing extraneous to the dominant fact is admitted, nothing illustrative of it, and, as it were, growing out of it, is rejected. They are like summaries of mighty dramas . . . We contend that it is a new species of poetry, a graft of the lyric on the dramatic.

Although the phrase was not in Hallam's vocabulary, he comes astonishingly close to saying in 1831 what we are only now recognizing in the 1970's: Tennyson is essentially a symbolist poet. Donald Smalley has noted the anomalous fact that while on one side of the Channel middle-class Victorians were finding the *Idylls* congenial to their taste, on the opposite shore the poem was being appreciated by an audience that "the Laureate would scarcely have anticipated or been likely to welcome—the French Symbolists." The influence of Tennyson on Poe ("I regard him as the noblest poet who ever lived") and, through Poe, on Baudelaire and Mallarmé constitutes one of the vital currents flowing into the poetry of our century. Mallarmé translated "Mariana," Baudelaire borrowed from Tennyson, and Yeats, who read Hallam's essay in the 1890's, found it indispensable to an understanding of the French Symbolists.

The symbolist technique that Hallam recognized in "Mariana" reaches its furthest development in the *Idylls.* The solitary Elaine in her tower, dreaming of Lancelot and stripping the silken case from his naked shield, is a more complex version of Mariana in her moated grange. Tennyson's whole problem in structuring the *Idylls* consisted in getting Elaine, as it were, down from her tower and onto the poem's field of action. A long narrative poem made up of separate vignettes, however sharply visualized, would collapse of its own static weight. Tennyson solved the problem by incorporating individual characters into the larger landscape of the *Idylls;* as in "Mariana," he obliterates the gap between self and scene and frees himself from bondage to conventional narrative. Building on the techniques of the classical idyll, with its intensification of mood, its highly allusive texture, its startling juxtapositions, flashbacks, and deliberate discontinuities, Tennyson creates an inclusive psychological landscape in which all the separate consciousness in the poem participate and in which each action is bound to all others through symbol, prophecy, or retrospect.

Seen from this perspective, the first lines Tennyson composed for the *Idylls* take on a singular significance. The "Morte" begins with the simplest and apparently slightest of alterations from Malory:

> So all day long the noise of battle rolled
> Among the mountains by the *winter* sea . . .

Tennyson's shift in the setting of Arthur's death from summer to winter suggests that from the start he had in mind the symbolic season in whose cycle of florescence and decline every scene and character in the *Idylls* is enmeshed. It is impossible to exaggerate the fullness of consequence this single alteration bears. Throughout Malory, with the exception of the closing chapters, one feels the suspension of time characteristic of romance. In such a world everything is possible, coincidence abounds, and spring is eternal. Only in "Gareth and Lynette," the first of the Round Table idylls, does Tennyson allow his reader this primal fantasy of romance. By linking the separate idylls to the cycle of seasons, Tennyson transposes the dominant mode of Arthurian myth from romance to tragedy, in which the only release from time is death.

The symbolic season, then, enabled Tennyson to control the random, timeless sequence of events in Malory. In the *Morte d'Arthur,* for example, the tragedy of Balin and Balan precedes the romance of Gareth and Lynette. Tennyson reverses the order of the two tales, as elsewhere he compresses the more diffuse episodes in Malory or cuts them altogether. What remains of this distillation from the *Morte d'Arthur* Tennyson orders along a strict narrative sequence in which the clock of Arthur's fall ticks at a steadily accelerating rate. Yet this *linear* movement through time, while it lends a propulsive thrust to the narrative, tends to make of each idyll a separate episode spaced out along the temporal chain. And so Tennyson superimposes upon this strict chronological sequence a much more fluid temporal movement in which events that are narratively sequential appear to take place simulta-

neously in the reader's mind. Thus although "Balin and Balan" comes quite early in the chronological sequence and is set in the time of the lady-fern and the lily, we are made to feel a sudden acceleration of the symbolic season, in consonance with this first of the idylls that ends tragically. By implying early in "Balin and Balan" that Arthur's youth has passed, Tennyson ages his hero and the kingdom in a single line:

> Early, one fair dawn,
> The light-winged spirit of his youth
> *returned* . . .
> (18-19, italics added)

The very brevity and symmetry of "Balin and Balan"—it is less than half as long as "Gareth and Lynette," one third as long as the Geraint idylls that precede it—reinforce this sense of propulsive doom.

Tennyson's manipulation of time in the *Idylls* produces an effect akin to that of syncopation in music or, closer to his medium, to departures from regular meter in a line of verse. When the stress falls unexpectedly, it falls with twice the weight. The annual Tournament of Diamonds, spaced over nine years, establishes the normal temporal rhythm of the poem. But in "The Holy Grail," when the knights seek violent escape from the diurnal world to the world of eternity, Tennyson causes time to run amok: the narrative is deliberately discontinuous and kaleidoscopic; lightning and darkness, droughts and floods, replace any recognizable moment of day or year; apocalyptic time—in which all times are simultaneously present—displaces chronological time.

Throughout the *Idylls* leitmotifs of all kinds cut across the linear narrative and connect past and future. "Merlin and Vivien" opens with an impending storm that finally bursts in the closing lines; recurrent images of tempests and waves gather to a climax the storm of warring passions internalized in Merlin and externalized in nature. Before Vivien seduces him, indeed before the "present" in which the idyll is narrated, Merlin has

> walked with dreams and darkness, and he found
> A doom that ever poised itself to fall,
> An ever-moaning battle in the mist,
> World-war of dying flesh against the life.
> (188-191)

The wave poised to break symbolizes the seer's prevision of his own doom, but his fall is both a cause and prophecy of the larger fall of the kingdom. And so the dreams and darkness through which he walked later become the clouds of self-doubt that enshroud Arthur at the end; the moaning struggle in the mist foreshadows the last dim battle in the West, when the "wave" of heathen at last engulfs the kingdom, and it reverberates back to the founding, when Arthur pushed back the heathen wave and "made a realm and reigned" (CA, 518).

Like each of the idylls, "Merlin and Vivien" tells a self-contained story that is also interwoven into the central story of Arthur's coming and passing. Through dreams, prophecy, and retrospect, through recurrent symbols, characters, settings, and verbal echoes, any part of the poem implies all other parts. Guinevere's marriage vow to Arthur, itself ironic—"King and my lord, I love thee to the death!" (CA, 469)—is ironically echoed much later by the vow of Tristram to Isolt:

> Come, I am hungered and half-angered—meat,
> Wine, wine—and I will love thee to the death—
> ("The Last Tournament," 713-714)

a lie made true by Tristram's murder the instant after it is sworn, as Guinevere's lie is finally proven true by her repentance in the convent of Almesbury.

The major characters reappear from idyll to idyll, forming a "human chain of kinship" whose linkages serve the same unifying function as the poem's clusters of symbols. Minor characters who appear only once, or rarely, are in turn incorporated into the larger story by a kind of analogical patterning through which one character reenacts the role previously played by another. The early idylls present special problems of narrative continuity, for happy endings are by definition self-contained, as the tag-phrase "they lived happily ever after" makes clear. "Gareth and Lynette" has just such an ending: Gareth's fearsome adversaries prove to be mock-monsters in disguise, and the novice knight wins the scornful lady. "Pelleas and Ettarre" tells the same story in reverse, the later idyll retrospectively enriching the earlier. Fair appearance conceals a hideous reality, and the sadistic Ettarre drives the young Pelleas impotent and mad. Gareth tests and finds himself at a time when the integrity of the kingdom and his own naive idealism are in perfect accord. Pelleas is Gareth reborn in decadent times; the clash between his idealism and the corruption of the kingdom destroys him, for he can find no supporting matrix for his fledgling identity. "What name hast thou?" Lancelot asks as Pelleas bears down upon him in blind rage. "No name, no name," he shouts, "I am wrath and shame and hate and evil fame" (551-556).

As certain characters seem to exchange identities, so certain settings recur throughout the *Idylls.* Early in "Balin and Balan," for example, Balin observes a meeting between Lancelot and Guinevere in a garden of roses and lilies. The queen walks down the path of roses toward Lancelot but he pauses in his greeting, for he has dreamed the previous night of "That maiden Saint who stands with lily in hand / In yonder shrine" (256-257), and the dream restrains him, just as his praise of the perfect purity of the lilies chills Guinevere:

> "Sweeter to me," she said, "this garden rose
> Deep-hued and many-folded! sweeter still
> The wild-wood hyacinth and the bloom of May.
> Prince, we have ridden before among the flowers
> In those fair days—not as cool as these,
> Though season-earlier."
>
> (264-268)

Guinevere nowhere more richly expresses the sensuousness which first drew Lancelot to her than in these lines, "deep-hued and many-folded." The consequences of that first, fatally joyous meeting reverberate throughout the poem, as here, when the sight of the lovers shocks Balin into his former "violences," and he rides off from the orderly garden into the wilderness where he meets his death. The garden scene works perfectly within the narrative of "Balin and Balan" at the same time that it takes us back, through Guinevere's reminiscence, to the time before the founding of the Round Table and forward to "Lancelot and Elaine." The scene opens out to become the entire settling of the later idyll, in which Lancelot again must walk the same divided path and choose between the rose of Guinevere and the lily-maid of Astolat.

In the light of such subtle architectonics one is at a loss to understand much of the twentieth-century criticism of the *Idylls:* "Utterly wanting in unity and coherence of structure . . . strikingly uneven . . . a collection of episodes . . . Tennyson could not tell a story at all . . . he failed signally to bring out the underlying, archetypical significance of the ancient mythological symbols he was employing." Tennyson could of course tell a story perfectly well. He handles the conventional narrative devices with virtuosity, ranging from the first-person monologue of Percivale in "The Holy Grail" to the omniscient narrator in "Lancelot and Elaine," from the simple plot of "Merlin and Vivien" to the complex interweavings of the two adulterous triangles in "The Last Tournament." Yet however skillfully he might retell the tales in Malory or the *Mabinogion,* he would end where he began, with "a collection of episodes." And so he developed, in Hallam's phrase, "a new species of poetry" in order to convey his

---

Geoffrey Ashe on the Arthurian Revival:

The *Idylls of the King* were read—genuinely read and by millions, not merely praised. They were translated into other media. They inspired playwrights and painters, and even a photographer, who broke new ground by illustrating the stories with painstakingly posed stills. Arthur's Britain played an appreciable part in refurbishing that royal glamour which the four Georges, and Victoria's dismal widowhood, had almost effaced. It helped to foster that latter-day English state of mind in which medieval ritual and feudal titles could coexist with democracy. No continental monarchy found a Tennyson, and no continental monarchy managed to keep such a halo.

So, for some years, the visionary kingdom flourished again; and the results were to persist. One aspect of its revival was very much Tennyson's. By making the Round Table sexually respectable, he helped to associate royalty with a virtue which, after the Georges, it stood in need of. His Arthur was a 'blameless king'. . . . Respectability had awkward artistic consequences. The love-stories with which the Matter of Britain had once been almost synonymous could no longer be dwelt upon. Guinevere's infidelity was the turning-point of Tennyson's own plot, yet he avoided giving any outright account of it. Nor could he trace Tristram's affairs in any detail. He circled round these topics, he alluded to them, but he never got near enough to provoke a blush. . . . As shaped by Tennyson, the legend could only decline into children's books, romantic little societies, the gift-shops and pastiche Hall of Chivalry at Tintagel.

Geoffrey Ashe, in his The Quest for Arthur's Britain, *edited by Geoffrey Ashe, Frederick A. Praeger, 1968.*

vision of Arthurian myth to the contemporary world. Like every great long poem, the *Idylls* draws on traditional forms and is itself a new genre. Shakespeare had Seneca and Marlowe; Milton had Homer; but tragedy and epic radically redefine themselves in their works. Tennyson bears this same innovative relation to tradition, but we have yet to assimilate into our literature this poem which is at once epic and lyric, narrative and drama, tragedy and romance. Our difficulty with Tennyson's "medieval charade" is not its derivativeness but its novelty. (pp. 19-33)

> *John D. Rosenberg, "Evolving the Form," in his* The Fall of Camelot: A Study of Tennyson's "Idylls of the King," *Cambridge, Mass.: The Belknap Press of Harvard University Press, 1973, 182 p.*

William E. Buckler

[*In the following excerpt, Buckler explores the degree to which Tennyson succeeded in developing an original construction of the character of Arthur in his* Idylls.]

The wasting of heroes and the rehabilitation of villains has been a favorite exercise among popular moralists for some time, and Arthur has certainly had his share of detractors. Insulated against the corrective of the poet's declared purposes by the critical disrepute into which the "intentional fallacy" had fallen, they often made quick work of one of literature's grand fallible heroes and, with a wry inconsistency, even began to claim that Tennyson intended conclusions that they could not possibly have reached except by declaring inadmissible, or by implicitly faulting, the poet's own declarations of intention.

More critically ironic yet is the apparently unredacted assumption that one can demote or even demolish Arthur— "the greatest of all poetical subjects," "the central dominant figure" upon which the integrity of the poem depends, *"the King"* whose *"Idylls"* these are—and still make extraordinary critical claims for the poem. Thus Clyde de L. Ryals makes the "co-existence and interplay" of "many layers of meaning" the basis for claiming that *"Idylls of the King* [is] a poem of which one never tires" even though, by his analysis, Arthur "learns" chiefly "that the world is impregnable to morality" and "stands, finally, in moral terms, as both the hero and the villain of the *Idylls of the King"* [*From the Great Deep,* 1967]. Gerhard Joseph easily concedes "the inconsistencies of the conceptual scheme," finds *our* (as distinct from *his*) admiration for Arthur "either as ideal representative of soul or as long-suffering husband" undermined by Guinevere's "weakness," and, citing Tennyson's failure in the most crucial test of his powers as a dramatic poet, asserts that even "the most sympathetic reader *must* concede a priggishness that has been the scorn of those who see in Tennyson's Arthurian pageant little more than a representatively obnoxious document of Victorian male chauvinism" [*Tennysonian Love: The Strange Diagonal,* 1969]. John Rosenberg, the most rhetorically intense advocate of the poem in this century, seems to find erosion of Arthur's character positively high-minded. He speaks of its "inevitable duality," calls it both a substantive and an aesthetic "dilemma" of the poet, sees Arthur as being always in

"double jeopardy," and characterizes Arthur's final speech to Guinevere with such words as "ferocity," "onslaught," "chilling," "shocking," making the Queen writhe "in bestial abasement" and leaving us "as breathless as the man who boasts of his own humility" [in his *The Fall of Camelot,* 1973]. He says that *Vivien* has taught us not to "uncritically accept Arthur's judgment in his own case"; that he is by no means "blameless," "although his faults are the defects of his virtues"; and that both Vivien and Dagonet are "right and wrong" to "call him a fool." As conclusive evidence of "how heavily Tennyson has hedged his King in ambiguity," he cites the failure of Arthur's purposes and then goes on to say that Arthur's indictment of Guinevere (" 'And all through thee!' " ["Guinevere," 490]) is not only "cruel" but "simplistic" and that the "very profusion and variety of evil" in the poem "belie" it. According to Rosenberg, Arthur is "destroyed . . . for the vulnerability of his virtues," and the essence of his tragedy is that his punishment "vastly and inexplicably exceeds" his "crime" of "noble delusion." Despite Arthur's assertion that his "last hope" is that

> "We two may meet before high God, and thou
> Wilt spring to me, and claim me thine, and know
> I am thine husband . . . "
>
> (G, 561-563)

and the fact that Guinevere finds redemption by clinging to that hope, Rosenberg dismisses their marriage as impersonal and says that what Arthur cannot "survive" is "the loss of 'the goodliest fellowship of famous knights/Whereof this world holds record' " ("The Passing of Arthur," 183-184). Arthur emerges, finally, as a "noble" but deluded fool whose judgment of himself, his Queen, and his world cannot be trusted and who is deprived even of the tragic recognition and redemption tendered to Lancelot and Guinevere.

Arthur has also had his defenders, of course, though the general tendency has been to assume that Tennyson faltered rather egregiously in the multifaceted challenge of Arthur. William Brashear escapes the issue by seeing Arthur and the other dramatis personae as "vitalistic" rather than symbolic ["Tennyson's Tragic Vitalism: *Idylls of the King,*" *Victorian Poetry,* 6 (1968)]. Robert Pattison sees Arthur's freedom "from the psychic turmoil born of divided will that surrounds him" as both defining his heroism and rebutting, in part, the charge that he is "a self-righteous prig" [*Tennyson and Tradition,* 1979]. By comparing Arthur's and Guinevere's moral situation with that of Adam and Eve in Book IX of *Paradise Lost,* Donald Hair seeks to establish that Arthur succeeds in an austere moral duty in which Adam had failed [*Domestic and Heroic in Tennyson's Poetry,* 1981].

J. M. Gray has mounted the most elaborate defense of Arthur of any recent commentator [*Thro' the Vision of the Night: A Study of Source, Evolution and Structure in Tennyson's "Idylls of the King,"* 1980]. But however acceptable one may find Gray's detailed list of Arthur's credits, one is still faced with the critical problem on which Browning focused at the end of *The Ring and the Book:*

> Why take the artistic way to prove so much?

Because, it is the glory and the good of Art,
That Art remains the one way possible
Of speaking truth, to mouths like mine at least.
How look a brother in the face and say,
"Thy right is wrong, eyes hast thou yet art blind;
Thine ears are stuffed and stopped, despite their
    length:
And, oh, the foolishness thou countest faith!"
Say this as silverly as tongue can troll—
The anger of the man may be endured,
The shrug, the disappointed eyes of him
Are not so bad to bear—but here's the plague
That all this trouble comes of telling truth,
Which truth, by when it reaches him, looks false,
Seems to be just the thing it would supplant,
Nor recognizable by whom it left;
While falsehood would have done the work of
    truth.
But Art,—wherein man nowise speaks to men,
Only to mankind,—Art may tell a truth
Obliquely, do the thing shall breed the thought,
Nor wrong the thought, missing the mediate
    word.
So may you paint your picture, twice show
    truth,
Beyond mere imagery on the wall—
So, note by note, bring music from your mind,
Deeper than ever e'en Beethoven dived,—
So write a book shall mean beyond the facts,
Suffice the eye and save the soul beside.

Gray has so conceived his defense that he asserts his admiration for an Arthur whom others dislike without apparently perceiving that, for many persons on both sides of the issue, it may be essentially the same Arthur.

Whether one personally likes or dislikes this Arthur is, in and of itself, only tangentially relevant; whether one is *right* in liking or disliking him is the primary literary question. That is the question that challenges the reader who would be critically just to take as circumspect and sympathetic a view of the controlling intuition of the poem as its direct, internal evidence requires and to see the parts in relation to a whole that is shaped by that intuition. He may still find fault with the intuition itself or with its poetic construction, including both the overall architecture and the thousands of individual decisions that, in a poem of epic-like ambition, the poet attempts to make in a manner that will satisfy the most capable of his sympathetic readers. But he will enjoy the positive pleasures of critical conscientiousness in the knowledge that, however fallible his judgment may be, he has not subjected the work of a serious and gifted poet to the caprice of critical peremptoriness or critical neglect.

This subject is a large one: the critical premise and the particular case of Arthur could each be profitably developed at monograph length. All that will be attempted here, however, is a highly selective demonstration of the implications of the critical premise for a judgment of *the artist's Arthur*—that is, the Arthur whom Tennyson has suspended in idea and form, imaginative intuition and imaginative construction.

Above all else, it must be recognized that Arthur's fallibility is not such an elusive perception as to justify hammering his "faults" home with the lawyer-like overkill that

has marked some of the commentary. It is the organizing assumption of the poem seeded in Arthur's initial epiphanic dilation over Guinevere—magnificent in its ego-strength and generosity and terrifying in its tragic promise—that leads him in his youthful idealism and inexperience to dream the impossible dream. He can, perhaps, will his will, work his work, and become " 'Victor and lord' " in his own " 'realm' "—that is, achieve, at a seemingly ideal level, self-conquest. But to extrapolate this conversion of self into an ideal conversion of community, drawing from the intensity of his love-magnification and the sublimity of his ideal of union the "pure, generous, tender, brave, human-hearted" [*The Works of Alfred Lord Tennyson,* 1908] idea that therefore he can " 'Have power on this dark land to lighten it,/And power on this dead world to make it live' " ("The Coming of Arthur" 92-93), makes either sentimentality or tragedy inevitable. Every person who has experienced a first love of any grandeur can identify with the young King's feelings of hieratic ardor, but if he has lived long enough, he has gradually learned that, even if he himself has remained faithful, the human community ultimately resists such magic, however glamorous it may have seemed initially, and puts an infinity of obstacles in its way.

From a poet like Tennyson, stern of mind and learned in the best epic and dramatic traditions, we know that matters will work themselves through many literary-experiential variations to their severest tragic conclusion and that only so much of a remnant hope will be saved as classical tragedy allows. What we may not be quite so alert to is Tennyson's keen sensitivity to the sentimental alternative to tragedy which, in the less imaginatively ordered world of daily living, the overwhelming majority opt for and even writers and readers tend to prefer if they possibly can. As a result, tragedy and sentimentality are so persistently played against each other throughout *Idylls of the King* that the tension between them is one of the literary ground tones of the poem, the sentimental alternative to tragic realization being one of the "wandering [emotional] fires" that lead character after character into a precarious or fatal quagmire.

The quest for the Holy Grail is a sentimental journey. Merlin capitulates to sentimentality. Lancelot's romantic search for anonymity, undertaken on the advice of Guinevere, brings him to the verge of death physically and, spiritually, to the temptation of Elaine's fatal pathos that, had he succumbed to it, would have drowned all possibility of salvation in an ocean of sentimentality. Guinevere wraps herself in sentimentality so long and so successfully that it dyes her very sense of self and makes her recognition and redemption at the final hour inextricably dependent on Arthur's austere truth-telling in their last scene together.

In *Lancelot and Elaine,* Tennyson had made the crucial choice between pathos and the tragic vision difficult by presenting "the lily maid of Astolat" in such an ingratiating way that the reader must overcome his habitual inclinations toward sentimentality to hold steady in the morally bracing truth of tragedy. In *Guinevere,* he reverses the reader's challenge by making the very relentlessness with which Arthur perseveres in his moral duty—the equivalent of Oedipus's putting out of his eyes—almost more than the residual sentimentality of the reader can tolerate. Indeed, the *ad hominem* scoffing of many commentators may be a cry of moral pain, like that of the reader who laughs at Little Father Time's genocide-suicide in *Jude the Obscure* because he is unprepared to accept the terrifying truth of the boy's actions or their explanation. But when one fairly considers the alternative—a potentially magnificent woman, "the fairest of all flesh on earth," going to her death tortured to distraction by her inability to find the peace of tragic recognition and acceptance, the grandeur that Arthur has always known to be her birthright pathetically wasted in moral blindness—then one may be driven by poetic necessity, not personally to like the scene or to claim perfection for the two fallible principals who enact it, but to acknowledge that Tennyson, like other poets of the first order, has saved something cathartic and therefore precious from the catastrophe and has spared the reader the horror of hopelessness. Both the poet and his king would thus merit, not vituperation, but the sympathy that understanding brings: the sad wisdom that literary necessity brings is suffered by them as well as by the reader.

There is obviously a contradiction between this insistence on Arthur's fundamental fallibility and the customary notion that he is an "ideal" figure in some superhuman or God-like sense. Obviously, too, such contradictory perceptions lead their respective adherents to reach quite different conclusions on Tennyson's poetic handling of his hero.

According to Jerome Buckley [in his *The Growth of a Poet*, 1960], "Arthur is presented as an ideal figure of supernatural origin and destination, as the emissary of God, and not as a realistic and therefore fallible hero," and this leads Buckley to perceive Arthur as "conspicuously ineffective" in the drama of the poem—"woodenly imperceptive" toward Guinevere, positively obtuse toward Lancelot, "recessive," "a shadowy background presence." Ryals, too, is uncompromising in his stress on the "ideal" at the expense of the "real." Arthur, he says, "is *exactly* what Tennyson says he is: an ideal man. . . ." Reed characterizes himself as Buckley's propagandist: his goal, he says, is "to promote" Buckley's "views," which he finds "quite sound" [*Perception and Design in Tennyson's "Idylls of the King,"* 1969]. By seeing Arthur as "perfect in a scale of values beyond the human," Philip Eggers, who also takes Buckley as his guide, deprives him of any exemplary role in the struggle with the fatality of human experience. In Arthur, "Tennyson sees the possibility of the hero's transcending human failure" [*King Arthur's Laureate*, 1971]. Fleshing out his argument, Eggers says that Tennyson makes Arthur "a Christ figure." By this, he means that Arthur is Tennyson's fictional and metaphoric equivalent of Christ, so idealized in his perfection that he is "beyond tragedy," and Eggers allows for none of the meticulous and delicate care with which the poet puts a crucial distance between the Christian God-Man and the "Ideal manhood closed in real man" of *Idylls of the King*.

Tennyson was too fine a poet to be heavy-handed on either side of this crucial issue, but even while insisting on the symbolic import of the poem's ingredients, he asserted that "there is no single fact or incident in the *Idylls*, however seemingly mystical, which cannot be explained as without any mystery or allegory whatever" [*The Works of Alfred Lord Tennyson,* 1908]. In other words, though the imaginative vitality of *Idylls of the King* is clearly dependent on the richness of its metaphoric or symbolic texture, with each image, incident, and character having meanings that, in Browning's phrase, reach "beyond the facts," it is not necessary to rush to mystical or inflatedly allegorical ("too allegorical") explanations of those meanings. Indeed, the clear implication is that, despite his profound disinclination to place restrictions on any insight that a capable and sympathetic reader might find in his poem, Tennyson felt that some of the perceptions that he himself prized most highly were being deflected or obfuscated by this too-mystical, too-allegorical tendency. A misunderstanding of the central revelation embodied in Arthur would certainly fall into that category.

Two basic questions thus emerge: (1) Are Tennyson's extra-textual characterizations of Arthur—"shadowing Sense at war with Soul,/Ideal manhood closed in real man," ("To the Queen"); "I intended Arthur to represent the Ideal Soul of Man coming into contact with the warring elements of the flesh" [*The Works of Alfred Lord Tennyson,* 1908]; "By King Arthur I always meant the soul, and by the Round Table the passions and capacities of a man" [quoted in James T. Knowles's "Aspects of Tennyson," *Nineteenth Century,* 33 (January 1893)]—reasonably susceptible to a critical turning that is "without any mystery or allegory whatever"? And (2) What difference does such a critical turning make to our assessment of the character of Arthur and the imaginative integrity of Tennyson's poem?

An affirmative answer to the first question requires that one establish a nonmystical, nonallegorical meaning for the variant phrases with which Tennyson commented on his intent in the portrayal of Arthur. That task is made relatively easy through the poet's own artistic circumspection. In the tradition of Shakespeare, he has planted in the text a translation that carries the authority of the person most qualified by rank and experience to enunciate it:

> "now I see thee what thou art,
> Thou art the highest and most human too,
> Not Lancelot, nor another."
> ("Guinevere," 643-645)

Not an infallible "emissary of God" in any extraordinary sense; certainly not "perfect in a scale of values beyond the human"; but "the highest" human being on a comparative scale of human beings that an illumined Guinevere has ever known. "Ideal manhood closed in real man" has as its only authoritative textual translation " 'the highest and most human too.' " According to this translation, when we speak of Arthur as an "ideal figure," we should mean simply that he symbolizes the finest idea of the fallen but redeemable creature called man that the conscientious secular imagination of this poet could conceive of—fallible and ever-changing because human, but still very, very fine.

But what of his "supernatural origin and destination"? To assert this as a fact or even as a peculiarly Arthurian possibility is to assert what the poem does not and to literalize in this story one of the universal subjects of man's perpetually unrequited longings. We know as little about the "unfacts" of man's birthing or even of our own births as is known about Arthur's. But there is nothing incredible or even unusual about associating with the event the four elements of fire, air, water, and earth or perceiving it as a strange new beginning, just as there is nothing incredible or even unusual about associating death with a double-pointing myth of the return or perceiving the event as muffled in strange talk of rest, journeying, unearthly wailing, solitariness, rigorous cold, and eventual rebirth. As Matthew Arnold pointed out in *Literature and Dogma,* even Plato was unequal to a really satisfactory idea of immortality, but if one is willing to leave the idea as open as the text of *Idylls of the King* essentially demands, then Tennyson's nonimperious, nondoctrinal representation of man's myth of a hopeful passing, his myth of an eventual return, is a marvelously evocative fusion of aesthetic and hieratic intimations.

The more genuinely human the reader allows Arthur to be—*both* fallible *and* admirable—the more realistic and dramatic he becomes. Like everyone's, Arthur's initial social problem is that of establishing a public role that will enable him to realize a life mission that is inherent in who he knows he is. In seeking a life-companion, he, like many idealistic young men, mythicizes and hence, in the short term, misperceives his choice, just as she, also in the short term, mythicizes and misperceives both him and Lancelot, and the horrid shows, agonies, and "long-drawn days of blight" that ensue are rooted in these identity misperceptions—both his and hers—and their progeny is a whole symbolic generation of identity misperceptions. At the end of life, they finally discover, through catastrophic challenges, who they really are, she a misguided Queen, he a misguided King. They have been misguided about different things, however—she about him and hence about herself, he about the world and the lasting effect he could have on it. But, significantly, he was not misguided about her; though it took catastrophe to prove it, catastrophe proved him right, not wrong, about her. Proof came too late in this cycle of time to reverse the present tragedy, and *this* Arthur and *this* Guinevere must pass into *historical* oblivion. But the *myth* has been born and confirmed by the reconstruction of the only records history has left us. The Arthur and Guinevere *idea* has been reborn and proved viable, and that can never die. So in the cycles of time, the Arthur and Guinevere of corrected vision (the poet's gift to history) may very well have their "new year," and who knows what they then may make of this "fair world"? It is only a hope, of course, but a profoundly educated hope and as dependable as man's endlessly reasserted faith in himself.

We may also begin to discover an alternative explanation of Arthur's so-called recessiveness—his obliviousness to Guinevere's and Lancelot's infidelity, the blankness with which he reacts to Vivien's seductive ploys—and on the basis of it we can perhaps see his "dramatic relation" to the other characters as simply distinctive rather than "conspicuously ineffective."

Arthur is, for a long time, a prisoner of his own gloriously misguided dream. It does have a "fair beginning"—a delusive "false dawn"—and this further fixes in his mind the unrealistic idea (itself a wholly realistic poetic insight) that the impossible dream is in fact possible, that the evanescent appearance is the perfect reality when only a fleeting glimpse of perfection is momentarily imaged there. Like Karshish's Lazarus in Browning's *An Epistle,* Arthur is a man possessed by a heavenly insight, and, like Lazarus, his responses do not follow the quotidian pattern of those not so possessed. He has sworn a deathless love for both Lancelot and Guinevere, and fidelity not only to vows but to vows inextricably interwoven with his aspirations for the world hold him aloof from even that shadow of infidelity, suspicion. In the celebrated incident with Vivien, Arthur is like the unsoiled innocent in many a ribald tale, his blankness to her seductive overture being a source of cynical amusement to the worldly, but ultimately a proof of the innocent's innocence. If it mirrors an aspect of his fallibility and hence his tragedy, it is a token of his worthiness and hence of his triumph too. This is itself a keenly dramatic concept of character, and the poet is to be praised rather than censured for not invalidating Arthur in order to conform to less faithful notions of dramatic propriety.

Tennyson was too shrewd a poet-observer not to realize that Arthur would have his plausible detractors. In fact, he built Arthur's most effective detractors into the poem itself and not only made them in degree credible, but also put the rebuttals to those detractions into curiously faulted hands—Balin growling at Garlon on the eve of stamping the royal crown into defacement and Merlin the seducer in the very act of being seduced. Of course, it might be argued that one of Tennyson's great strategic errors in the conception and execution of *Idylls of the King* was not to be sufficiently forthcoming on the issue of Arthur's foolish innocence in the manner, say, of Dostoevsky's *The Idiot.* His theme allows it, and Arthur's great recognition scene in *The Passing of Arthur* (9-28) frankly says it, " 'For I, being simple. . . .' " But that would perhaps have been too great a violation of the tragic traditions of poetry in a poem that very finely measures grades of tragedy, too flippant a divorce from the examples of Homer, Virgil, Spenser, Shakespeare, and Milton. Moreover, the softening of Arthur's character in that way might have seemed to Tennyson a creative coup at the risk of a creative collapse. *That is not this artist's Arthur,* who is every inch a King—talks like one, acts like one, thinks like one, even loves, hurts, grieves, and forgives like one—and one example of impeccable kingliness is not more than the literature of the modern world can bear. Moreover, the very mystique of kingliness, its infinite possibilities for good, is the source of Arthur's "simple" reading of the paradox of human life and the motive equally of his grandeur, his error, the catastrophe to which it leads, the recognition that he reaches, and the hope with which he faces *both* death *and* the future.

To most sympathetic readers, the style of *Idylls of the King* is faultless but not intimidating, the overall simplicity of its manner of discourse challenging any expectation of poetic style that they may have learned from, say, Spenser, Shakespeare, Donne, Dryden, Blake, Keats, and Browning. It is a style that announces that language is going to provide full facility of access, that language is going to be a clear transparency through which to look at the poet's subject. That, of course, is poetry's ultimate illusion, and the pleasure of the illusion combined with the recognition that it is a most delicate and deceptive illusion is a source of one of the first and most sustained aesthetic responses that the poem incites; it announces that, however conspicuously or inconspicuously referential *Idylls of the King* may be in the working out of its art and ideas, it is self-referential in its style and therefore to a degree self-referential, too, in *its way* with art and ideas since their imaginative truth subsists in the poem's style. Tennyson carried the art of concealing his art to a point of rare finish, just as he carried the idea of concealing his ideas in metaphors that do not disclose their inner meaning until one has looked through the apparent substance at the thing signified by it beyond our usual sense of imaginative evasiveness. And until critics of the poem root their conclusions in the artistic soil to which the art and ideas are native and without which they have only an abstract and somewhat unreal existence, readers should look upon them as not only highly provisional, but in many cases perhaps as not what Tennyson meant at all. (pp. 341-53)

William E. Buckler, "In Defense of Arthur: The Moral Imperatives of Artistic Form," in his Man and His Myths: Tennyson's "Idylls of the King" in Critical Context, *New York University Press, 1984, pp. 341-53.*

Jerome Hamilton Buckley

[*Buckley is a Canadian-born American educator and critic and the author of numerous works on Victorian literature, including* The Victorian Temper *(1951) and* Season of Youth *(1974). In the following excerpt from his* Tennyson: The Growth of a Poet, *he explores Tennyson's use of theme, imagery, and atmosphere in his* Idylls of the King, *suggesting that these three elements are the main unifying forces in the poem.*]

When Tennyson at last took up the Grail theme, he composed with great speed and assurance. The complete first draft of "The Holy Grail" came, [as Emily Tennyson recorded in her journal], "like a breath of inspiration"; it was written in less than a week in September 1868, and thereafter required little revision. A literal belief in the legend no longer seemed essential to its execution; for the poet, working in a symbolic mode, felt unconstrained by the standards of "realism" that had prevailed in the *Enoch Arden* volume. With a firm aesthetic control he boldly adapted his materials to his own vision, now sharp and coherent, of the Arthurian world. In its context the Grail quest was to prove no sacred mission, but to all except the prepared and dedicated Galahad a quite unholy mistake, the symptom and the contributing cause of a social decadence.

Though satisfied with the Idyll as a unit, Tennyson decided to withhold it until he had established its relation to the whole sequence. "I shall write three or four more of the 'Idylls,'" he told Palgrave [in a letter dated 24 December 1868], "and link them together as well as I may." At the end of 1869, however, before he had fashioned most of the necessary links, he published "The Holy Grail" along with two other new poems, "The Coming of Arthur" and "Pelleas and Ettarre," and one old one, the "Morte D'Arthur" of thirty-five years before, now expanded as "The Passing of Arthur." Then, so that his public might associate these four pieces with the four parts of the *Idylls of the King* issued in 1859, he added a prefatory note to the volume explaining the order in which "the whole series should be read." But not until 1872, by which time he had written the tale of Gareth (to come in second place) and "The Last Tournament," a fine bitter version of the story of Tristram and Isolt (to be inserted near the end), did he print the *Idylls* in proper sequence and append the epilogue "To the Queen," wherein he distinguished his purpose throughout from that of Malory or of Geoffrey. And even then he had many changes still to make and several significant additions. "Balin and Balan" first appeared in 1885; and it was yet another three years before "Enid" was divided as "The Marriage of Geraint" and "Geraint and Enid" and the *Idylls* could finally be published "In Twelve Books."

The product of such long deliberation, the finished poem (or series of poems) was, not surprisingly, the poet's longest work, the most elaborately wrought, the most ambitious in scope. Yet many critics have complained that the whole, perhaps because of the protracted and intermittent composition, lacks both structural and stylistic unity. The fact that the early "Morte D'Arthur" first appeared in a modern framework as "The Epic" may suggest that Tennyson originally planned a tightly knit Arthuriad celebrating the epical exploits of the King himself rather than the trials and quests of his knights. And the title-page description "In Twelve Books" may seem to imply that the completed *Idylls* aspires to an epic status. Yet Tennyson was far too familiar with the traditional genres ever to confuse the idyl and the epic; and he must in any case have expected his title *Idylls*—in the plural—to designate not a single unified narrative but a group of chivalric tableaux selected from a great mass of available legend. The "idyl" is strictly a picture of mood, character, or gesture; and each of the Idylls moves through a series of sharply visualized vignettes toward its pictured climax, its moment of revelation. Though a few of the characters recur as links between some of the idyls, the unity of the sequence lies not in action or plot but in theme, imagery, and atmosphere.

In effect, the ten poems that constitute "The Round Table" stand as separate panels arranged in orderly progression and framed on the one side by "The Coming of Arthur" and on the other by "The Passing of Arthur." The frame defines the beginning and the end of Arthurian society, and each of the panels marks a stage in its growth or decline. Each of the parts is given an appropriate seasonal setting so that the colors of the background may accent the prevailing temper of the protagonists in the foreground and symbolize the moral condition of the realm itself. The sequence accordingly follows the cycle of the year from the fresh springtime of Arthur's marriage and Gareth's arrival at an uncorrupted Camelot, through a long summer of intense idealisms and hot destructive passions, on to the decadent October of the Last Tournament, the bleak November of Guinevere's repentance, and the winter wasteland of Arthur's defeat. Far from being consistently epical or heroic, the style from idyl to idyl is as variable as the weather. The blank verse is carefully adapted in tone to the shifting subject matter, and there is an intentional difference in texture between the frame and the pictures it encloses: " 'The Coming and the Passing of Arthur,' " Tennyson explained, "are simpler and more severe in style, as dealing with the awfulness of Birth and Death." The form of the *Idylls of the King* is, in short, essentially a new one which is neither to be measured nor understood by the standards of the epic. (pp. 171-73)

[The] image of a musical harmony recurs throughout the *Idylls* betokening the faith in which alone a society may prosper. At the inception of Arthur's order the knights chant in unison before the King, and "for a space" he and they are "all one will." A peal of music greets young Gareth as he approaches Camelot, and at the gate the "riddling" Merlin explains the provenance of the enchanted city:

> "For an ye heard a music, like enow
> They are building still, seeing the city is built
> To music, therefore never built at all,
> And therefore built forever."

When Arthur receives Balin returning from banishment, he bids him once again "move / To music with thine Order and the King," and as Balin for the moment accepts the challenge of self-control, then

> all the world
> Made music, and he felt his being move
> In music with his Order and the King.

Vivien, however, from her first appearance is the siren of discord, and as she comes to destroy Balin's last hope of peace, the litany of hell she sings silences "the wholesome music of the wood." Later with ill-concealed irony she reminds Merlin of the truth in Lancelot's song:

> It is the little rift within the lute,
> That by and by will make the music mute,
> And ever widening slowly silence all.

By the time of the Last Tournament the Arthurian harmony has been altogether disrupted, and Dagonet the wise fool may appropriately rebuke Tristram, who has broken the music of his own life, as a source of the dissonance: "And so thou breakest Arthur's music too." In the final battle the King hears no echo of the first resolute knightly chorus but instead the jarring scream of confusion and defeat,

> And shouts of heathen and the traitor knights,
> Oaths, insult, filth, and monstrous blasphemies,
> Sweat, writhings, anguish, labouring of the lungs
> In that close mist, and cryings for the light,
> Moans of the dying, and voices of the dead.

The only music possible now must come from beyond life itself; the black-stoled figures on the funeral barge lift "as it were one voice" of lament and then, as the barge bears Arthur to his rest—

> Then from the dawn it seem'd there came, but faint
> As from beyond the limit of the world,
> Like the last echo born of a great cry,
> Sounds, as if some fair city were one voice
> Around a king returning from his wars.

Within the confines of the earthly kingdom, Arthur exacts rigorous vows of his knights but scarcely expects them to achieve the perfect or superhuman concord. He asks only that each desire it and work toward it according to his best capacity and through the common instruments of everyday experience,

> For every fiery prophet of old times,
> And all the sacred madness of the bard,
> When God made music thro' them, could but speak
> His music by the framework and the chord.

Yet "Arthur's music," his will for the good of his little world, is clearly in tune with the moral order of creation. The "score" is, ideally, to be accepted as given, not amended to suit the convenience or weakness of the individual performers. The king's authority, in other words, must be credited; it cannot be explained or proven. For Arthur is presented as an ideal figure of supernatural origin and destination, as the emissary of God, and not as a realistic and therefore fallible hero. Tennyson's last change in his text, made not long before his death, was the addition to the epilogue of the line "Ideal manhood closed in real man," a description intended to clarify the design of the *Idylls* by further distinguishing the nominal protagonist from

> that gray king whose name, a ghost,
> Streams like a cloud, man-shaped, from mountain peak,
> And cleaves to cairn and cromlech still; or him
> Of Geoffrey's book, or him of Malleor's, one
> Touch'd by the adulterous finger of a time
> That hover'd between war and wantonness,
> And crownings and dethronements.

His Arthur, he wrote on the completion of "The Holy Grail," was, in short, "mystic and no mere British Prince."

Despite Swinburne's complaint [in his *Under the Microscope*, 1909]—echoed by many others—that such a conception had done violence to the Arthurian sources, Tennyson found at least some medieval warrant for the idealization of his subject. He liked to cite a passage from Albéric des Trois-Fontaines to the effect that Arthur's character was stainless, and he drew the epigraph for the finished sequence from Joseph of Exeter: *"Flos Regum Arthurus."* But whatever precedent he was following, he gave increasing attention as his poem developed to the "ideal manhood" at the expense of the "real man." In the "Guinevere" of 1859 he had allowed Arthur to speak of Modred as his nephew; but in later editions he felt it necessary to have Arthur deny any kinship whatsoever with the traitor knight said by Malory to have been the child of an incestuous union between Arthur and his sister Margawse. "The Coming of Arthur" shrouds the king's unnatural birth in myth and mystery, and the late *Idylls* make all questioning of Arthur's absolute probity the measure of social disintegration. Pelleas in bitter disillusion asks, "Have any of our Round Table held their vows? . . . Is the King true?" And Tristram, openly mocking Arthur and his code, confesses to Dagonet that he has never espoused any ideal beyond self-interest:

> "Fool, I came late, the heathen wars were o'er,
> The life had flown, we sware but by the shell."

Though Tennyson resisted a rigid allegorical reading of his poem, he admitted "a parabolic drift"—which is to say a symbolism—in his argument. Arthur may be intended as something more than the simple personification of conscience. Yet he acts only from ethical commitment, and his behavior consciously sets the standard by which the conduct of his whole realm is to be governed or, wanting that control, judged. In the war of Sense and Soul, which is the declared theme of the *Idylls,* he bears the banner of the Soul.

But despite his ideal manhood, or perhaps because of it, Arthur is conspicuously ineffective when brought into dramatic relation with the real men of the Round Table and the complex tumultuous woman who is his Queen. In his encounters with the marred goodly Lancelot, he seems almost wilfully naive; unwavering in his own faith, he is all trustfulness; he cannot bring himself to believe his best and strongest knight capable of deception, and he thus cannot begin to understand the meaning or even the intensity of Lancelot's recurrent dark "moods" or the "madness" that blurs his vision of the Grail. Likewise in his treatment of Guinevere he seems woodenly imperceptive. Throughout their last interview his avowed charity scarcely matches his self-approving inflexible regard for moral justice. As a man of perfect principle, he may indeed be ready to forgive "as Eternal God / Forgives," but as injured husband, he should hardly make the equation with divine mercy so explicit, and he certainly need not rehearse in detail the wrongs done to him and to his order by the wife cringing at his feet in a remorse which achieves strange dignity. Fortunately, however, he is seldom called upon to engage directly in the dramatic action of the *Idylls.* His major role is essentially recessive; as King, he is a shadowy background presence, a legendary hero off fighting the heathen, or at his own court an aloof voice of command and judgment, always a rather remote yet available standard of reference. Even in "The Coming of Arthur" he is more talked of than actually seen; he is known by his work as the bringer of civilization to a barbarous people, but his personality is no less a mystery than his origin. Not until the end does he appear at the center of a single Idyll; but there, in "The Passing of Arthur," he is more completely himself than he could ever be among real men, a ghostly figure now, "whiter than the mist that all day long / Had held the field of battle" and unsure of his physical identity as he approaches his ideal death:

> "Hearest thou this great voice that shakes the world,
> And wastes the narrow realm whereon we move,
> And beats upon the faces of the dead,
> My dead, as tho' they had not died for me?—
> O Bedivere, for on my heart hath fallen
> Confusion, till I know not what I am,

> Nor whence I am, nor whether I be king;
> Behold I seem but king among the dead."

First and last Arthur's vitality is of the spirit, whereas the drama of the *Idylls* arises from the demands of passion which he can neither experience nor fully understand. His own conduct in life and beyond it is entirely commensurate with his vision.

But in the actual society of the Arthurian realm, with which the body of the poem is concerned, appearance and reality seldom coincide. As the great and greatly human exemplars of the Order, Guinevere and Lancelot seem all beauty and all courage; but the adulterous love between them, the more culpable because necessarily furtive, partakes of ugliness, suspicion, and cowardice; and the gradual discovery of their guilt destroys the idealism of others and ultimately offers a sanction for the deliberate hypocrisies of the whole culture. In the beginning, when faith is in the ascendant, evil may prove but illusion; the reality may be fairer than the appearance. Thus Gareth—followed at a distance by the protective Lancelot, who is his hero—challenges and easily overcomes the foolish knights of the river before the Castle Perilous and at length confronts their brother the fearsome Death, who is really just "a blooming boy" in grim masquerade. Geraint, on the other hand, disturbed by a vague rumor of the Queen's "guilty love for Lancelot," questions the apparent reticence of his own Enid but learns, after needless agonies, to recognize in her a real devotion utterly beyond his deserving. So central to the theme of the *Idylls* is the problem of misapprehension that Tennyson allowed a rare intrusion of direct moral commentary to preface the narrative of Geraint's excursion into the wilderness of error:

> O purblind race of miserable men,
> How many among us at this very hour
> Do forge a lifelong trouble for ourselves,
> By taking true for false, or false for true;
> Here, thro' the feeble twilight of this world
> Groping, how many, until we pass and reach
> That other where we see as we are seen.

In taking true for false, Geraint anticipates the skeptics reluctant to believe in the actual repentance of Edyrn, the villain whose reform Geraint himself has effected; and these in turn foreshadow the cynics who will not credit even the King's goodness. Yet Geraint, living in a society still relatively pure, at least escapes the darker delusion of imputing truth to falsehood. As Arthur's Order advances in time, however, the fair appearance more and more frequently glosses over the evil reality, and the young knights who accept the fairness at face value meet an increasingly bitter disillusion. Balin, arriving at court, yearns to emulate the chivalry of Lancelot and chooses the Queen's crown as the device for his shield, the "golden earnest of a gentler life." But when he comes inadvertently upon a clandestine tryst of Lancelot and Guinevere, he cannot but feel that his old madness has returned:

> "Queen? subject? but I see not what I see.
> Damsel and lover? hear not what I hear.
> My father hath begotten me in his wrath.
> I suffer from the things before me, know,
> Learn nothing; am not worthy to be knight—
> A churl, a clown!"

In final effect, then, the *Idylls,* which traces the rise of a purposeful order and the gradual catastrophic betrayal of its sustaining idealism, stands as an oblique warning, if not a direct ultimatum, to nineteenth-century England.

—*Jerome Hamilton Buckley*

Later, when Vivien confirms the truth of his worst suspicions, he yields, "horror-stricken," to a brutish violence and unwittingly fells his own brother Balan; but before both die, "either lock'd in either's arm," Balan convinces him that Vivien alone is false, while "Pure as our own true mother is our Queen." Balin's fair illusion is thus ironically restored; like Elaine, who has "lived in fantasy," he dies deluded. For the young Pelleas, on the contrary, there can be no recovery in life or death from a complete and shattering disenchantment. Convinced like Gareth of the world's goodness, Pelleas seeks for himself a maiden "fair . . . and pure as Guinevere." His quest leads him to the proud Ettarre, "a great lady in her land," whose apparent fairness belies her essential cruelty:

> The beauty of her flesh abash'd the boy,
> As tho' it were the beauty of her soul;
> For as the base man, judging of the good,
> Puts his own baseness in him by default
> Of will and nature, so did Pelleas lend
> All the young beauty of his own soul to hers.

But though he wins the prize for her at the Tournament of Youth, Ettarre, "affronted by his fulsome innocence," rebuffs his attentions. Rejected, Pelleas accepts the offer of Gawain to plead for him with the lady, much as Gareth once accepted the help of Lancelot. Yet whereas Gareth proved the validity of his confident idealism, Pelleas must learn the reality of evil. His initiation is similar to Balin's but far more decisive. In the hot still night he discovers Gawain sleeping with Ettarre, and in cold despair he leaves his "naked sword athwart their naked throats." Utterly bewildered in mind, he experiences to his own disgust the intense frustration of the body; as he rides off, he "crushes the saddle with his thighs, and clenches his hands, and maddens with himself." He now imputes hypocrisy to the whole Round Table, blames the King for having made "fools and liars" of all his subjects, and charges himself with self-deception and blind sensuality: "I never loved her, I but lusted for her." At the last Lancelot suffers his contempt, and Guinevere quails before his pathetic fierce complaint, "I have no sword." In the madness of Pelleas, the lovers foresee "the dolorous day to be." Tristram, whose adventure immediately follows, has no illusions to lose; with a cynical "realism" he is able to exploit the now hollow conventions of a corrupt society. For by the time of Tristram only Arthur can believe in the correspondence of the fair appearance and the true reality, and even he must endure the taunt of the Red Knight, who boasts of honest evil:

> "Tell thou the King and all his liars that I
> Have founded my Round Table in the North,
> And whatsoever his own knights have sworn
> My knights have sworn the counter to it—and
>   say
> My tower is full of harlots, like his court,
> But mine are worthier, seeing they profess
> To be none other than themselves—and say
> My knights are all adulterers like his own,
> But mine are truer, seeing they profess
> To be none other."

If the mock Round Table, so described, is founded on the defiant recognition of selfish lust, the true Round Table is destroyed by its concealed sensuality. In each of the ten Idylls within the frame, desire—usually sexual desire—determines the central action. Even in "The Holy Grail," where the quest demands complete disinterest, none but Galahad is willing to lose himself that he may find himself; Lancelot cannot wholly renounce his sin; and Gawain is easily persuaded by a bevy of "merry maidens" in a silk pavilion that an erotic satisfaction is quite sufficient. Only in the tale of Gareth does desire fully accord with duty; by persisting in the tasks assigned to him, Gareth justifies his innocent and overt love of Lynette. Elsewhere reason contends, for the most part vainly, with physical passion. Merlin's yielding to the seductive wiles of Vivien is merely the grossest example of the abject surrender of the intellect to the flesh. Lancelot refuses to accept Elaine as his paramour less from high principle than because of his physical commitment to the Queen, his "faith unfaithful" which keeps him "falsely true," and Elaine herself betrays her own purity, and indeed her life, by desperately offering her whole being on any terms to Love or else to Death— "O Love, if death be sweeter, let me die." Both Balin and Pelleas cling so intensely to the ideal of passion that no regard for the calmer way of reason remains to save them from madness when they suspect or discover that the ideal has been sullied. Tristram has achieved a modus vivendi, but only by the deliberate perversion of reason toward the rationalizing of passionate appetite. None of these characters practices or clearly recognizes the cardinal Tennysonian virtues of "self-reverence, self-knowledge, self-control." Yet the great argument of the *Idylls* as a whole is simply that, without such virtues and the faith which sanctions them, neither the individual nor the state can attain rational order or spiritual health.

In depicting the war of Sense and Soul, of passion and purity, Tennyson freely invokes the familiar color symbolism of red and white. At the outset the Lady of the Lake, "Clothed in white samite, mystic, wonderful," entrusts the sword Excalibur to Arthur; the knights, arrayed "in stainless white," attend the King's marriage; and all "the world is white with May." Soon Gareth comes in a "silver-misty morn" to a Camelot still starry-white in honor. Later he departs through "the weird white gate" to meet his adversaries, the brothers of Death: Morning-Star from whose ornate pavilion flutters a slender crimson banner; Noonday Sun, mounted "on a huge red horse"; and Evening-Star, suffused "All in a rose-red from the west." Enid, whose love will remain innocent, seems from the first "like a blossom vermeil-white." Elaine is appropriately "the lily maid of Astolat," and in death she holds the white flower against her white robe; but the passion which destroys her is clearly represented by a scarlet sleeve that Lancelot carries to the tourney as her token. Lancelot himself, as he paces the "long white walk of lilies" in the palace garden, muses rather sadly on these "perfect-pure" emblems of the spirit; but Guinevere, who has come to meet him, declares her preference for the "garden rose / Deep-hued and many-folded." Pelleas, vexed by a song he once heard sung to the Queen, "A worm within the rose," stumbles by night through Ettarre's garden of "roses red and white," symbols of his own confused emotion, until he discovers the perfidy of Gawain. On the Grail quest the pure Galahad reaches the resolution of all contraries, when he perceives the holy vessel "Clothed in white samite or a luminous cloud" yet in itself "Redder than any rose"; but the troubled Lancelot has only a momentary glimpse of the Grail "All pall'd in crimson." The Last Tournament, which begins as "one white day of Innocence," ends with the white banners besmirched and the watching ladies eager to shed "the simple white" that they may glow in "kindlier colors." Tristram, who has won the red prize, a ruby carcanet, receives it in avariciously red hands, and carrying it to the Irish Isolt, dreams of the white-handed Breton wife he has deserted:

> He seem'd to pace the strand of Brittany
> Between Isolt of Britain and his bride,
> And show'd them both the ruby-chain, and both
> Began to struggle for it, till his queen
> Graspt it so hard that all her hand was red.
> Then cried the Breton, "Look, her hand is red!
> These be no rubies, this is frozen blood,
> And melts within her hand—her hand is hot
> With ill desires, but this I gave thee, look,
> Is all as cool and white as any flower."

Meanwhile, Arthur vanquishes the Red Knight in "blood-red armour," but the violence that ensues, the massacre and arson, "red-pulsing" up to the stars, brings but a foretaste of the madness in which his own kingdom must perish. Before long he must upbraid Guinevere as the mother of "sword and fire, / Red ruin, and the breaking up of laws." And ultimately the white abides only in the mists that shroud his retreating figure from the Queen's view or—beyond earthly things altogether—in the arm "Clothed in white samite, mystic, wonderful" that retrieves Excalibur from the reluctant Bedivere. (pp. 173-84)

Each of the Idylls reshapes rather than reproduces the Arthurian legends; but "Guinevere" owes less than any of the others to Tennyson's printed sources and correspondingly more to his own creative imagination. If Arthur reflects his mystical apprehension, Guinevere partakes of his deepest aesthetic sensibility. She shares the poet's cherished yet mistrusted delight in the shapes and colors of material objects. Even in her defeat she confesses to a nostalgia for the sensuous past, despite the fact that her pleasure has been her guilt; still "half-guilty in her thoughts," she comes reluctantly to understand that true repentance must mean

> Not even in inmost thought to think again
> The sins that made the past so pleasant to us.

Yet she has known also the familiar Tennysonian burden of personality, and in parting from Lancelot she has cried, "Would God that thou couldst hide me from myself!" Like Princess Ida, whose sadness "blacken'd all her world in secret" and made it all seem "blank and waste . . . and vain," she is troubled by the nightmare of her own image stretching across a surrealistic wasteland to distant ruined towers—she dreams

> An awful dream, for then she seem'd to stand
> On some vast plain before a setting sun,
> And from the sun there swiftly made at her
> A ghastly something, and its shadow flew
> Before it till it touch'd her, and she turn'd—
> When lo! her own, that broadening from her
>   feet,
> And blackening, swallow'd all the land, and in
>   it
> Far cities burnt.

Like the Soul in "The Palace of Art," whom God "plagued" with merciful despair, she is to be saved only by the awakening conscience:

> Henceforward too, the Powers that tend the
>   soul,
> To help it from the death that cannot die,
> And save it even in extremes, began
> To vex and plague her.

And like both of these, she ultimately recognizes her sin as pride—though hers, as she describes it, is a "false voluptuous pride, that took / Full easily all impressions from below." Guinevere is, of course, first and last a distinct individual, the most vivid and dramatic figure in the *Idylls*. But insofar as she may also be considered a symbol of beauty which must eventually come to terms with moral truth, she may (once again like the Soul and the Princess) represent the anima, the essential aesthetic self of the poet. As a woman she fully indulges her selfish passions, yet seeks final atonement in a life of service; to the nuns at Almesbury she offers the example of the selfless dedication that Arthur vainly hoped she would bring to his kingdom. As a counterpart of Tennyson's own poetic struggle, she suggests not only his attraction to a sensuous art for art's sake but also, by her last gesture, his mature demand for a moral aesthetic.

By the end of the sixties Tennyson had made the ethical intent of the *Idylls* sufficiently clear to alienate the new Aesthetes. Yet within a few years the young Henry James, who had no quarrel with moral concern, declared the meaning of the poems less significant than the fastidious workmanship [in *Views and Reviews,* 1908] "If one surrenders one's sense to their perfect picturesqueness," James wrote, "it is the most charming poetry in the world. . . . It appeals to a highly cultivated sense, but what enjoyment is so keen as that of the cultivated sense when its finer nerve is really touched?" Such a judgment recalls Ruskin's more troubled approach to the four Idylls of 1859, and it anticipates the censure of many later critics less disposed than either Ruskin or James to admire the picturesque in poetry. The *Idylls* have all too frequently been dismissed—often by those who have not read them—as an elaborate exercise in rhetoric, an ornate escape from the realities of experience; and the relevance of their central themes both to Victorian England and to the modern world has been accordingly for the most part ignored.

The objection that the sequence as a whole misrepresents medieval life and manners is hardly pertinent, for the city built to music belongs to no society in time. The poet's method is not the way of literary realism, and the philosophy that informs his poem is itself a protest against the tyranny of fact that enslaves the realist. Though the epilogue (no doubt to the amusement of the English Aesthetes) denounced an "Art with poisonous honey stolen from France," the French Symbolists, who were most consistent in their devotion to Tennyson, immediately and quite properly recognized the *Idylls* as an antidote to the positivistic spirit that had invaded nineteenth-century poetry. In the reconstructed Arthurian mythology they found a welcome and spacious release for the poetic imagination from the narrowed materialisms of their own age.

Tennyson, however, sought freedom from the momentary pressures of the time, the immediate social and economic concern, in order to interpret rather than to escape the larger spiritual crisis of his culture. By avoiding the homely local color that had sentimentalized "Enoch Arden" and the direct emotional involvement that had made his political verses of the fifties merely shrill and ephemeral, he hoped in the *Idylls* to give his vision of modern society perspective, objectivity, and dramatic substance. There are in the poem a few possible reflections of his impatience with some particular Victorian practices or attitudes. The description, for instance, of King Pellam's chapel, rich in reliquaries and thronged with plaster saints, may indicate his distaste for certain aspects of the new Anglo-Catholic ritualism; and the rough treatment of the foppish Sir

Sir Galahad, *Dante Gabriel Rossetti, 1857.*

Morning-Star, attended by bare-footed, bare-headed damsels in "gilt and rosy raiment," may testify to his scorn of the new dandified Aesthetes, some of whom were affecting Pre-Raphaelite gestures. But such specific parallels are neither frequent nor essential to the action. The central narratives have few contemporary referents; King Arthur is not Prince Albert, Lancelot is neither Gladstone nor Disraeli, and Guinevere is assuredly not Victoria. Yet the epilogue "To the Queen" spells out the general modern relevance in no uncertain terms:

> Take withal
> Thy poet's blessing, and his trust that Heaven
> Will blow the tempest in the distance back
> From thine and ours; for some are scared, who mark,
> Or wisely or unwisely, signs of storm,
> Waverings of every vane with every wind,
> And wordy trucklings to the transient hour,
> And fierce or careless looseners of the faith, . . .
> And that which knows, but careful for itself,
> And that which knows not, ruling that which knows
> To its own harm. The goal of this great world
> Lies beyond sight; yet—if our slowly-grown
> And crown'd Republic's crowning common-sense,
> That saved her many times, not fail—their fears
> Are morning shadows huger than the shapes
> That cast them, not those gloomier which forego
> The darkness of that battle in the west
> Where all of high and holy dies away.

Here the trust that the tempest may be averted and that the crowned Republic may so be spared such a last great battle in the west as destroyed the realm of Arthur seems faint and ineffectual beside the strong forebodings of social disaster that accompany it. In final effect, then, the *Idylls,* which traces the rise of a purposeful order and the gradual catastrophic betrayal of its sustaining idealism, stands as an oblique warning, if not a direct ultimatum, to nineteenth-century England.

It may have been his interest in the problem and the threat of cultural decadence that led Tennyson to regard the bitter *Troilus and Cressida* as "perhaps Shakespeare's finest play." At any rate, the *Idylls,* read in proper sequence, builds somewhat like *Troilus* to a tragic denouement, which the temper of a whole civilization rather than the sin of any one individual makes inevitable. The poem no longer presupposes the early-Victorian idea of progress, which rang through "Locksley Hall," but a later and gloomier cyclical view of history. Could Arthur's kingdom remain true to its first principles, could it rise in time of crisis to what Arnold Toynbee would call the moral challenge, it might learn to control its successes and turn to social good its manifold selfish energies. But increasingly committed as it is to the values of expediency, sensuality, and self-interest, it must face its certain doom; there can be no renewal, except in another milieu altogether, for by the fundamental law of being "The old order changeth, yielding place to new." Though few of the Victorians could see the pertinence of the analogy to their own age, Tennyson by the time of "The Holy Grail" and all the later Idylls was wholly persuaded of the soundness of his somber vision and able to write with a deeply felt urgency. His finished poem, itself a city built to music, attains its most compelling resonance in the overtones of his conviction. (pp. 189-94)

> *Jerome Hamilton Buckley, "The City Built to Music: 'Idylls of the King',"* in his *Tennyson: The Growth of a Poet, Cambridge, Mass.: Harvard University Press, 1960, pp. 171-94.*

Jonathan Freedman

[*In the following excerpt, Freedman discusses the difficulties Tennyson and Morris encountered in attempting to adapt the Arthurian legend in their poetry. He concludes that Tennyson's* Idylls *displays "lingering guilt and [a] sense of inauthenticity," while Morris's* Defence of Guenevere *plays with both medieval and Victorian conventions.*]

To discuss the endurance of Arthur is obviously to perform an act of cultural preservation and redemption, to pay tribute to the power of the past and seek to make that past a palpable presence in the present. But it is also to participate in that process of remodeling the past which lies guiltily at the heart of any effort of commemoration. The history of the nineteenth-century Arthurian revival reinforces this lesson, for the revival brought with it a reinvention of the Arthurian. Men and women, acting out of different motives and responding to different needs, rearranged the bundle of narratives that compose the Arthurian cycle to mirror their own images, to resemble their own desires and fears. Thus Arthurianism entered Victorian culture as many things at one and the same time: for Rossetti and the Pre-Raphaelites, it embodied an exoticism at once native and strange; for Tennyson, it provided a parable of ideal imperial order and an image of that order's decadence; for Morris, it represented a haven of intense, vital experience in a world which seemed bereft of such experience, and a reflection of the cruelty and violence intrinsic to the exercise of social authority.

What is most striking about this list is its resolute doubleness. To each of these poets or painters, the Arthurian legend itself was deeply contradictory. Thus for Tennyson, the Arthurian cycle was simultaneously a narrative of creation and dissolution, of an ideal community whose very principles of organization undermined it, of an imperialism which brought order without but fell to a greater chaos within. For Rossetti, its legends provided at once images of restraint and indulgence, passion and destruction, sexual freedom and chaste purity. And for Morris, Arthurianism conjured forth a romance-world whose authenticity, intensity, and vitality stood in vivid contrast to the industrial ugliness of Victorian England, and at the same time evoked a privileged heterocosm whose squalor and violence ironically mirrored that of his contemporary world.

A phenomenon such as this—the revival of a set of narratives to serve similar, but contradictory, ends—calls for a cultural as well as a formal analysis. One can easily imagine the lines on which such an analysis would be conducted. A structural anthropologist, for example, would want to speak of the ways that the Arthurian narratives served the classic function of myth—mediating cultural conflict, recounting and thus reconciling the antinomies of experience: the conflict between civilization and violence on the one hand and ordered and destructive sexual passion on the other. Indeed, we could hypothesize that in a good Lévi-Straussian manner the two sets of antinomies speak to, and release the tensions created by, each other. Thus the contradiction of a violence intrinsic to the civilization which conquers violence is displaced into the epic's erotic plot—it is the violence unleashed by sexual betrayal which brings down Camelot. Similarly, the fear of sexuality inherent in the Guenevere plot and enhanced by the Galahad plot upon which Victorians fixated with particular fervor is released by the demonization of the bestial heathen that the Arthurian knights battle and (intermittently) conquer.

Alternatively, one could imagine an ideological critique of this doubleness. The Arthurian revival, one could say, provided a way of criticizing the dominant presuppositions of the contemporary order—imperialism, capitalism, patriarchy—but also provided a way of managing those criticisms: it safely suffused them with the musty odor of nostalgia, the aura of loss and regret, in order to forestall their transformation into principles of belief and incitements to action.

Both of these approaches seem to me to be reasonable and cogent. But I want to take another approach to this phenomenon. I want to suggest that the battlegrounds of Arthurian romance served not only as the field upon which competing ideologies clashed by night, but also as the locus of a deeper, more intense (if equally ideological) struggle: the struggle to shape the random collocation of narratives that compose our experience of the past into an order—any order at all. The desire and the difficulty of doing so, I want to suggest, is the story these Victorian narratives tell, and the narrative we participate in as we speak about them.

As we all know, the Arthur cycle, lying as dormant as the enchanted Merlin for most of the eighteenth century, was revived in the early nineteenth century as part of the general renewal of romance that accompanied the rise of British romanticism. "Let us have the old Poets and robin Hood," cried Keats, and Arthurian romance provided both the archaic poetic diction and the native British subject-matter Keats demanded. But from the first, discovering the correct formal vehicle for the Arthurian proved problematic. Trying to write verse-romance in a disenchanted age proved difficult enough for Spenser, for whom it meant a turn to conscious archaism. The difficulty could only multiply exponentially in an age for which the quest-romance had been transformed into mock-epic on the one hand and low-mimetic, realistic narrative on the other. Many of the first Arthurian efforts of the nineteenth century reflect this difficulty. The initial efforts of Victorian Arthurianism are formally awkward; the material does not fit easily into even the most flexible formal structures. Arnold's *Tristram and Iseult* (1853), for example, giddily alternates between poetic forms: at once poetic drama, dramatic monologue, and philosophical lyric, the poem seeks to pour itself into one formal vessel or another, but can never wholly do so. "If I republish that poem," Arnold wrote his friend Arthur Clough [*The Letters of Matthew Arnold to Arthur Hugh Clough,* 1933], "I shall try to make it more intelligible. . . . The whole affair is by no means thoroughly successful." Arnold to the contrary, however, the result is far from displeasing. The formal difficulties of the poem testify to the power of the narrative it inscribes; the incommensurability between the love of Tristram and Iseult and the social conventions or forms that fail to contain or restrain that love is reflected in the very awkwardness of Arnold's verse.

Similar problems are posed by Tennyson's first efforts in the Arthurian mode. Indeed, the elaborate framework within which he felt it necessary to enclose the "Morte D'Arthur" in his 1842 *Poems* vividly demonstrates the problems Victorian poets faced when translating these narratives into a contemporary idiom: the difficulties, that is, of finding an appropriate way to appropriate the Arthurian. The relation between frame and poem is one of carefully wrought echo. In the frame, a group of young men a few years out of college, having sent the women off to bed ("The game of forfeits done—the girls all kiss'd / Beneath the sacred bush and past away" [*The Poems of Tennyson,* edited by Christopher Ricks, 1969. Further citations in the text refer to this edition.]), gather round the wassail bowl to hear one of their number, "the poet Everard Hall," read the eleventh book of his Arthuriad, which his friend Francis had saved from the fire. The scene represents, in other words, a diminished parody of the Arthurian scene, here tidily enclosed within a domestic framework: it is no coincidence that two of the characters have the domestic monickers of "Holmes" and "Hall." These young modern knights, well on their way to becoming old fogeys (they listen to the parson denouncing modernity— the Higher Criticism, geology, the Oxford Movement) gather to celebrate a rite analogous to the rite of the Round Table, a rite of male bonding which here centers on the experience of art, not warfare.

What is most interesting about this faintly comic scene, however, is the hesitancy with which Hall (like Tennyson himself, who felt compelled to erect this elaborate scaffolding) adverts to the Arthurian. Hall burned his epic, he tells his audience, out of a certain anxiety about the decorousness of his attempt to rework the matter of Arthur:

> "Why take the style of those heroic times?
> For nature brings not back the mastodon,
> Nor we those times; and why should any man
> Remodel models?" [35-38]

These lines express two somewhat contradictory notions about the heroic narratives of the past, and therefore the past itself. On the one hand, there is the sense that the heroic is no longer efficacious or possible in the modern world—that it represents a previous stage of evolutionary development which, like the mastodon, has been surpassed in a world tidily enclosed and domestically ordered. But on the other hand, the attempt to import the heroic idiom into a contemporary venue is seen as transgressive; to attempt to "remodel models" is to display

one's own inauthenticity vis-à-vis those models—as a poet, doubtless, but also as a human being.

And this anxiety is not groundless. The frame-poem never fully encloses the "Morte d'Arthur"; the Arthurian epic disrupts the elaborate setting in which it is placed. For at the very end of the poem, we hear the reactions of all the members of its audience; all but one are, in their way, inadequate to it. (That one, I should say here, is Everard Hall himself, who lets his poem speak for him.) The parson, fast asleep during the performance, wakes himself amidst silence to utter "Good," as if to reembed the poem in a moral framework which is also the moral equivalent of deafness. Francis, the host, "mutters, like a man illused, / 'There now—that's nothing,' " as if speaking to a child waking from a bad dream; yet the bad dream is the poem he has just heard, and the child he is speaking to is himself (285). The narrator finds a richer revery. He falls into a troubled sleep and dreams of "King Arthur, like a modern gentleman / Of stateliest port . . . ," sailing down the river, hailed by throngs of Englishmen, to whom he promises peace on earth, good will to men (294-95). He awakes to the tune of Christmas bells in the distance.

This final response is obviously intended to triumph, yet it remains, to my eye, the most inadequate of all. This dream-vision of Arthur seems to accommodate the past, and all that it embodies for Tennyson—social order, peace, stable criteria of value—into a contemporary world by means of the imagination. But such a project is self-defeating. Tennyson's language here performs at one and the same time two contradictory acts: it translates Arthur and the Arthurian into a contemporary idiom yet suggests the inadequacy of that idiom in comparision to the historical wholeness it is measured against—and therefore calls into question the possibility of performing the very act of integration between past and present that Tennyson has attempted. Tennyson accomplishes this complicated work because, like Milton, he makes us hear the echoes of language past in the language of the present. Underneath the word "gentleman" chimes the notion of "gentle-man," of the participant in and subscriber to the code of gentilesse; underneath "stately" echoes first, perhaps, "state," then its etymon "estate," with its associations of proper social order and hierarchy. But although they resonate, these terms ring hollow, serving only to suggest the gap between the code of gentilesse and the code of the Victorian gentleman, between a world of hierarchical estates and one of "stately port"—a term which, wittingly or not, has the unfortunate effect of making this Victorian Arthur sound something like a well-fed banker. These lines seek to resurrect the image of Arthur for the Victorian audience; they succeed merely in measuring the fullness of his loss.

It might be argued that Tennyson himself eventually wrote his way out of these difficulties, especially in *Idylls of the King* in which, as Henry Kozicki has suggested [in his *Tennyson and Clio: History in the Major Poems,* 1979], he found in Hegelian dialectic a solution to his problems. My own view is that the *Idylls* fail to relate past and present even dialectically. Even at those moments in which Tennyson sought to do so—in the vague gestures toward a progressivist dialectic launched within the cyclical theory of history the poem affirms, and in the embarrassing compliment to Prince Albert, which evades but therefore reminds us of the fact that Albert played a manifestly unheroic role, played in fact a more complacent Guenevere to Queen Victoria's Arthur—his attempt to integrate past and present remains incomplete. The Arthurian past remains for Tennyson either embedded in a mythic past or an equally mythic apocalyptic future; when it enters the present it does so with a resounding thud.

I must confess here a certain ambivalence about this failure; perhaps inadvertently, it pays a tribute to the pastness of the past, to its resolute difference from the historical situation of those experiencing it in the present. Perhaps Everard Hall's sense of transgressiveness of "remodeling models" is ultimately justified. But I want to turn now to a work in which this work of historical translation is performed with a certain amount of giddy abandon—William Morris' "Defence of Guenevere," published in 1859, the same year that Tennyson's first *Idylls* were published. I want to look at what happens when the model is remodeled without the lingering guilt and sense of inauthenticity Tennyson displays. For here that model is reconstituted as a site of otherness itself: Guenevere stands in the same relation to her accusers as does the past to the present in Tennyson's poem. She does so because she stands the relation one might have assumed between subject and audience on its head; she accuses her accusers, both in the immediate context of the poem, and in the larger, extended context of the Victorian public to which it is addressed. And in doing so, she provides an entirely different model of relating past to present, historical myth to the realities of the moment.

Morris' remodeling of models here is dual. On the one hand, he remakes or reimagines the account he is given in Malory; on the other hand, however, he simultaneously adopts but subverts the conventions of the Victorian dramatic monologue. Beginning with the latter act of subversion will allow us to note the true audacity of the former. For Morris is particularly interested, I think, in the ways the monologue interacts with its audience—the audience within the poem and the audience beyond, for whom that inner audience stands. In most dramatic monologues, the audience within the poem remains silent. In the classic examples of the form, we have no way of knowing what the audience's response might be, nor do the characters within the dramatic monologue always know what the object of their address thinks of them. Yet—like the silence of a rigorous psychoanalyst—the very lack of response and participation from these implicit audiences challenges the speakers. It forces them into revelations of memories or of aspects of their experience they wish to hide. And beyond this implicit audience stands the actual audience, ready (as Robert Langbaum has shown [in his *The Poetry of Experience: The Dramatic Monologue in Modern Literary Tradition,* 1963]) to approve and to reject, to judge these characters or to sympathize with them. By so revealing themselves to implicit others, Browning's characters also reveal themselves to those who exist beyond the imaginative life of the poem—that is, to its readers, who, isolated from yet drawn into contact with these self-revealing *personae,* form opinions and judgments about them.

Morris enters into this tradition as he enters into all traditions: to demonstrate and then demolish from within its hidden assumptions. Like Browning's monologists, Guenevere presents a series of specious casuistries. She offers in her own defense a dizzying series of arguments, ranging from threats (Lancelot killed Mellyagraunce, her last accuser; he may do the same to you) to blandishments, an appeal to what she calls the "gracious proof" (I.241) of her own beauty, to manifestly false analogies, to direct appeals to the pity of her audience [*The Defence of Guenevere and Other Poems,* 1858]. But unlike Browning's monologists, in doing so Guenevere does not open herself up to the "sympathy" and "judgment" of her audience. Rather, she turns that audience's desire to judge her back upon themselves. Guenevere challenges the very terms her audience applies to her—not only those of the fictive historical audience to whom she speaks directly, but more powerfully and more importantly, those of the contemporary Victorian audience that stands behind Arthur's court. Like a good lawyer, she performs this transvaluation by shifting the very ground on which judgment is to be passed. Although it is true that Arthur is at best an inadequate helpmeet—

> "bought
> By Arthur's great name and his little love
> . . . . .
> . . . for a little word
> Scarce ever meant at all, must I now prove
> Stone cold for ever?"
>
> [82-83; 86-88]

she asks—although it is true that she loves Lancelot, and he at least defends her honor; although it is true that it was his blood that was found on her bed; although it is true that he was found in her bedchamber, with Guenevere's head resting on Lancelot's breast; though all these things be true, nevertheless, she insists, theirs was what Henry James would call a virtuous attachment:

> "Nevertheless you, O Sir Gauwaine, lie,
> Whatever may have happen'd these long years,
> God knows I speak truth, saying that you lie!"
>
> [283-88]

Guenevere's assertion here is enormously complex, and well worth pondering. It has usually been taken to be an outrageous prevarication. Her claim is frequently understood to be that she and Lancelot have not committed adultery, or if they have, have done so only in spirit, in which case she is indeed lying. But this is not, of course, what she says. "Whatever may have happen'd during those long years," Gauwaine cannot tell the truth about it: such is the substance of her claim. And on those terms, her assertion is clearly true: Gauwaine does not, cannot pierce the mystery of the love she and Lancelot share. In that sense, her assertion is perfectly correct; God knows she speaks the truth—but only when she says that Gauwaine lies.

This is a brilliant equivocation, yet one also feels, at least in dramatic context, that it is a fundamentally irrelevant one. As a legal defense, even in a medieval court, it is flimsy at best; and as an emotional defense, in front of Arthur's own knights, it is less than politic. How then can it be said to constitute a "defense" at all, at least under the criteria Guenevere's audience brings to the process of judgment? The answer lies at the end of the poem. Guenevere turns sideways from her accuser, "listening, like a man who hears / His brother's trumpet sounding through the wood / Of his foe's lances" and, at that moment, Lancelot arrives "at good need" to carry her off (288-90). We now recognize that Guenevere's performance here is to be taken as a defense in a different sense: a knightly defense, a parrying, by the use of language, of the thrusts of her accusers—a holding action, while she awaits the intervention of Lancelot.

Guenevere's language, then, evades the categories that her immediate audience—and the audience beyond the poem for whom they stand—bring to the task of judgment. Truth, like the "troth" Guenevere has pledged in the "little words" of the marriage ceremony, is extraneous to the language she employs. Her language is tactical: it is to be judged by the canons of rhetoric rather than by those of empirical verification or logic. That is, her arguments, her analogies, her threats, her use of evidence, are to be evaluated not on the basis of their truth and falsity, but rather for their effectiveness. Her words are her weapons. And as such, they serve to challenge the notion of judgment on the basis of truth and troth alike—the notion that language has an objective grounding in an overarching "reality" which lies behind it, the notion that this reality is embedded in a larger network of values (being true to one's vows, one's word) which lies behind and authenticates that reality. Guenevere's defense issues a challenge to both the fallible epistemology and moral assumptions of *all* the audiences she faces.

There are many things to say about this dimension of Morris' poem, for it helps to place Morris in the context of literary theory as well as literary history. What I want to point to here, however, is the way that Guenevere's redefinition of the possibilities of language alters the ways that Morris can deploy the matter of Arthur. I suggested earlier that Morris' Guenevere explicitly stands to the judging court just as Tennyson's sense of the Arthurian past implicitly stands to his sense of the present. I want to conclude by suggesting that Morris' Guenevere also stands in the resonant relation to her author that Tennyson erects his elaborate framework to escape. As Guenevere rewrites her own history in the trial, so Morris rewrites the character and legend that is Guenevere (indeed, he creates the entire scene, which is never mentioned in Malory). As she conceives of language as a weapon, as an instrument analogous to, indeed allied with, Lancelot's arms, so too Morris seizes upon the narrative of Guenevere for a polemical purpose—in this case, to make full subversive use of the Arthurian legend in an indirect but nevertheless powerful statement to his contemporary audience.

In Morris' hands, what Guenevere reminds the Victorian audience—and a twentieth-century one as well—is this: that narratives such as Guenevere's are always written from the point of view of Gauwaine; that history is not a value-neutral set of facts or even a privileged set of myths expressing universal human truths, but a trial, a contesta-

tion, a clash of interpretations which the more socially powerful always wins; that from the point of view of the present, all narratives, even (especially) the privileged narratives which speak of and come to represent the past, are ideologically determined; that rich and resonant as they may be, they represent history only as it is experienced from the point of view of a censorious court. Morris' point here is not, however, to bemoan this fact, but to reappropriate, remake, rework, and respeak the Arthurian, a respeaking which is analogous to his character's more effective form of speaking because it is, actually or potentially, a weapon in his arsenal of power.

Let me conclude ambivalently. Each of these models for deploying the Arthurian possesses an attraction for the twentieth-century critic, particularly at the historical moment of a turn—or return—to historical criticism. Although the Arthurian cycle is notoriously more "myth" than "history," Tennyson's and Morris' attempts to embed the narratives of the past in the context of the present possess a clear relevance to the concerns of an historicist criticism. Although he may reach it by a circuitous and ideologically suspect route, Tennyson's sense of the otherness of the past, his invocation of the past as the site of difference itself, is one that many historically-minded scholars and critics aspire to—even if, like Tennyson himself, they inevitably reveal their interests, their fears, and their desires in the very terms by which they image that difference. Morris' gleefully ideological appropriation of the narratives of the past serves as a corrective to this view. For Morris reminds us of the tactical and political dimensions of these narratives and, more importantly, of the political nature of the acts of judgment we inevitably perform as we encounter them and transform them into narratives of our moment. Morris thus effects, in the words of Jean Howard (writing of the failures of Stephen Greenblatt and Louis Montrose to politicize their historicist criticism [in "The New Historicism in Renaissance Studies," *English Literary Renaissance,* 16 (1986)]), "a move into history [as] an *intervention,* an attempt to reach from the present moment into the past in order to rescue both from meaningless banality."

But in doing so Morris also forcefully demonstrates the problematics of a fully *engagé* historicism of the sort Howard advocates. For the historical "intervention" performed by Morris is too easy and too powerful—and, finally, too ahistorical. Morris' reworking of the matter of Arthur, unlike Tennyson's recountings of Arthurian legends, swallows these narratives up with dizzying ease; one finds no acknowledgment of the possibility that these narratives can resist his "interventions," can fail in any way to conform themselves to the expectations and judgments he brings to them. In this sense, Morris is not to be identified with Guenevere, as he probably would have wished, or even with Lancelot, whose rescue-mission might also have served as an acceptable model for his historical poetics, but rather with the kangaroo court Guenevere addresses. And in *this* judgment, to follow the allegory through, the Arthurian narrative has no defense against its accusers. It can only stand humbly before its audience and respond to their charges with silence.

Neither Tennyson's nor Morris' deployment of Arthurian narratives is finally satisfactory, then, for both lead to positions that prove, by their own logic, untenable. Tennyson's evocation of the pastness of the past conduces to an utter detachment of past from present—a detachment which denies the very impulse that had impelled this turn to the historical. The impulse of Everard Hall—and the Everard Hall side of Tennyson—to find in the past a locus of value has the paradoxical effect of blocking any avenue of communication between historical narratives and contemporary concerns. The former recede into pure myth, and the latter empty themselves of any sense of historical connection or meaning. Morris' ideological appropriation of the Arthurian narratives reestablishes the network of communication between past and present that Tennyson had disrupted, but the fervor with which he accomplishes this task reduces the narratives themselves to silence. Guenevere herself may be given full voice by Morris' subversive text, it is true; but as she speaks, the difference between the narrative which encloses her and Morris' own is effaced, stilled. And past and present alike may thereby be rescued from (in Howard's phrase) "meaningless banality," but only at the cost of eliminating the gap between the two, only at the price of eliding the sheer otherness of Arthurian narrative. It is true that one could easily seek to unify these strategies and say that Tennyson's vision of the past demands Morris' and Morris' Tennyson's, and that both, when taken together, provide a satisfactory way of bringing the narratives of the past to the consciousness of the present. But rather than perform this tactical maneuver, I remain content to let these two visions clash with each other on the ideological battleground we all inhabit as we reexperience and reimagine the Arthurian. (pp. 235-46)

> *Jonathan Freedman, "Ideological Battle-ground: Tennyson, Morris, and the Pastness of the Past," in* The Passing of Arthur: New Essays in Arthurian Tradition, *edited by Christopher Baswell and William Sharpe, Garland Publishing, Inc., 1988, pp. 235-48.*

David Staines

[*Staines is a Canadian educator and critic who writes on Canadian literature and poetry in general. In the following excerpt, he considers the influence of Tennyson's poem on other nineteenth-century artists and authors who created their own versions of the Arthurian legend.*]

The second half of the nineteenth century saw the emergence of unprecedented interest in the stories of King Arthur and the Round Table. Painters, writers, and literary scholars turned to the medieval world of Camelot with intense dedication. Tennyson's poetry did not stand behind all the Arthurian art and literature of Victorian England, but it did serve to raise the subject-matter to a new level of literary respectability. The neglect and abuse of the Arthurian legends which characterized the romantic and early Victorian attitudes gave way to the literary eminence of the world of Camelot by the end of the nineteenth century. Though a complete analysis of the Arthurian art and literature of the period remains outside the realm of this study, a survey of the major Arthurian works does reveal the pervasive influence of Tennyson.

In the world of painting, Dante Gabriel Rossetti and his Pre-Raphaelite associates often turned to the Middle Ages for their subject-matter. Rossetti found in Malory incidents which would serve as objective correlatives for his own feelings. His Arthurian paintings usually present two episodes from the legends: the relationship of Lancelot and Guinevere or the quest of the Holy Grail. For Rossetti, the earthly and the spiritual were opposing forces vying for man's soul. In Lancelot's love for the Queen, he saw his own passion for womanly beauty; in the Grail quest, he saw the mystical experience that he and Lancelot would never attain.

Though it is impossible to date Rossetti's first encounter with Malory, his admiration of Tennyson's early poetry may have been his first introduction to Arthurian stories. The Pre-Raphaelite Brotherhood was aware of Tennyson's plan to write an Arthurian epic a decade before the appearance of the first volume of the *Idylls.* When Rossetti turned to Malory in the early eighteen-fifties, he knew that Tennyson, now Poet Laureate, had established the literary stature of the Arthurian legends.

Tennyson provided Rossetti with his first extended employment of Arthurian material. For the 1857 illustrated edition of Tennyson's *Poems,* Rossetti contributed five illustrations; three of them depicted Arthurian episodes. The Arthurian trio did not prompt Rossetti to consult Malory; indeed, he used Tennyson's poetry only as a suggestion for the illustrations.

In 1858 Rossetti began *God's Graal,* his only attempt to write an Arthurian poem. He was unable to complete it at that time. The publication of Tennyson's *The Holy Grail* prompted Rossetti's return to his unfinished poem. In 1870, however, his understanding of the polarity of the earthly and the spiritual was changing so that Lancelot's quest became an example of the superiority of the earthly. To re-create Malory so that Lancelot's failure was not essentially tragic perplexed Rossetti and the poem remained incomplete.

Tennyson's early Arthurian poetry may have fostered Rossetti's initial interest in the Arthurian legends; his later poetry did prompt Rossetti to return to his only effort at an Arthurian poem. And the *Idylls* may have caused Rossetti's increasing hesitation to employ Arthurian themes. When the 1859 volume of the *Idylls of the King* appeared, Rossetti read about an Arthurian world which bore little relationship to his more passionate Camelot. The moral tone of Tennyson's account of the Grail story influenced his decision to attempt a different version, yet the popularity of Tennyson's Arthurian poetry may have been the final factor in his inability to create his own Arthurian world.

Rossetti's associates showed similar fascination with Arthurian themes, and they too entered the world of Camelot through the guidance of Tennyson. Their Arthurian paintings were either illustrations of Tennyson's poems or depictions of incidents which originated in Tennyson's Arthurian world. As a consequence, Tennyson became the source of their understanding of the legends. Their medievalism owed more to Tennyson than to the medieval world and the *Idylls of the King* came to hold the inspirational force that Malory occupied for Tennyson.

Among the Pre-Raphaelite associates, Edward Burne-Jones was the most devoted disciple of the Arthurian legends. When he first read Malory in 1855, he discovered a world that would become his natural and perpetual haunt; like Tennyson he made his artistic career an attempt to re-create the beauty and the power of the legends. Yet his endless re-creation of the medieval world found its initial inspiration in Tennyson. Burne-Jones first encountered Arthurian characters in Tennyson's early poetry. He never realized his early plan to form a "small conventual society," but his plan emphasized his admiration for Tennyson and especially for his early Arthurian poetry. When he discovered Malory, he found further inspiration, "reading the Morte d'Arthur, the chapters about the death of Percival's sister and the Shalott lady." His first Arthurian painting, *Sir Galahad,* was his entrance into the world of Camelot and his unconscious acknowledgement of his debt to Tennyson. For Burne-Jones and his Pre-Raphaelite associates, Tennyson opened the door to the wealth of the Arthurian legends.

Tennyson's re-creation of the Arthurian legends precipitated an abundance of literary treatments of the story of Camelot. The three major literary figures who also employed Arthurian material shared both an interest in the subject-matter and a dislike of Tennyson's re-creation. Despite their criticism and their own Arthurian works, Tennyson's poetry continued to exert enormous influence in Victorian England.

Matthew Arnold did not approve of Tennyson's medieval characters [as shown in his letter to Miss Arnold, 17 December 1860]:

> The fault I find with Tennyson in his *Idylls of the King* is that the peculiar charm and aroma of the Middle Age he does not give in them. There is something magical about it, and I will do something with it before I have done. The real truth is that Tennyson, with all his temperament and artistic skill, is deficient in intellectual power; and no modern poet can make very much of his business unless he is pre-eminently strong in this.

Arnold's only Arthurian poem, *Tristram and Iseult* [1852], never satisfied its author; his revisions and additions only served to emphasize his artistic failure. As an Arthurian work his poem became isolated in its own time. The fact that no other writer followed his originality in the depiction of the second Iseult as a mother of two children is final proof of the curious unimportance of the first modern English treatment of the Tristram story in the history of Arthurian literature. Despite his criticism of Tenny-

son's Arthurian poetry and his vow to "do something with it before I have done," Arnold never returned to the Arthurian legends.

William Morris shared Arnold's appreciation of the Middle Ages and his dislike of Tennyson's treatment of the legends. His first volume of poetry, *The Defence of Guenevere and Other Poems,* begins with four Arthurian poems [including *The Defence of Guenevere, King Arthur's Tomb, Sir Galahad: A Christmas Mystery,* and *The Chapel in Lyoness*]; each of them is a distinct, dramatic, and vividly realized incident borrowed from Malory with varying degrees of fidelity. Morris employs personal names, the basic structure of certain incidents, and the general portrait of the *Morte d'Arthur,* but closer examination reveals the dissimilarities, the distinctly Pre-Raphaelite intensity of depiction and the sense of heightened passion which he imposed upon basic beginnings offered to him by Malory. Morris continued to study the medieval Arthurian world, but later years found him increasingly suspicious of his own ability to employ that world effectively. He disapproved of "the transfusion of modern sentiment into an ancient story," which he observed in the *Idylls of the King* [quoted in *The Life of William Morris,* by J. W. Mackail, I, 1899]; he did not attempt, however, to realize his original plan of an Arthurian cycle. His early idolatry of Malory and the popularity of Tennyson's achievement seemed to unite in preventing him from employing Malory in his own literary efforts.

Like Morris, Swinburne turned to the Arthurian world and recreated Malory according to the Pre-Raphaelite devotion to pictorial intensity. His earliest Arthurian poem, *Queen Yseult,* is an unsatisfying combination of medieval narrative romance and Pre-Raphaelite detailed depiction. His other early Arthurian efforts are further attempts to create some kind of Arthurian cycle. His rejection of the Pre-Raphaelite creed marked the end of Morris' influence upon his treatment of Malory, yet he never abandoned his interest in the legends. *Tristram of Lyonesse* and *The Tale of Balen,* his major Arthurian poems, are deliberate reactions against Tennyson's Arthurian world. In each he tries to retell the medieval story without any embellishments. *Tristram of Lyonesse* is more than a retelling; it is a re-creation that becomes a celebration of love. In *The Tale of Balen* Swinburne observes such close fidelity to Malory that the poem is his most unoriginal Arthurian work; it is little more than a dramatic paraphrase. His explicit denunciations of Tennyson's treatment of the legends make him adhere closely to his source; such adherence dictates the form of his final employment of Arthurian material. It is ironic that *The Tale of Balen* employs the stanza of *The Lady of Shalott* and achieves a degree of structural and verbal fidelity to Malory that Tennyson never sought after his early *Morte d'Arthur.* Swinburne's rejection of Tennyson's method of handling the legends led him to a method of retelling them that is both a direct criticism of Tennyson's method and an acknowledgement of the influence and popularity of Tennyson's poetry.

The final testimony of Tennyson's importance to the development of interest in the Arthurian legends is the sudden emergence in the latter half of the nineteenth century of scholarly commitment to Malory. Whereas the first half of the century saw the publication of three editions of Malory which were not reprinted, the second half witnessed the appearance of several new editions. More significantly, in 1862 James Knowles compiled *The Story of King Arthur and His Knights of the Round Table*, the first modernization of Malory and a volume destined to pass through seven separate editions before 1900. Knowles dedicated his book to Tennyson: "This attempt at a popular version of the Arthur legends is by his permission dedicated, as a tribute of the sincerest and warmest respect." Five more modernizations appeared before the end of the century and each of them noted the importance of Tennyson in the steadily growing interest in Arthurian stories.

By the beginning of the twentieth century the Arthurian legends attained the literary stature they had commanded in the Middle Ages and in the Renaissance. The story of Camelot inspired many artists in Victorian England. Behind this revival of interest in the material stood the august figure of the Poet Laureate, who first employed the legends when they seemed to lack proper respectability for artistic consideration. At the same time that his lifelong commitment to the material created the *Idylls of the King,* which, "regarded as a whole, gives his innermost being more fully, though not more truly, than 'In Memoriam',," his Arthurian poetry created the Arthurian renaissance of the nineteenth century. The *Idylls* presented Victorian England with an avenue into the medieval accounts of Camelot. Some contemporaries employed Tennyson's poetry as a medieval document and failed to study the original legends. Others turned to Malory as a rebuttal of Tennyson's treatment of the material. In any event, Tennyson's pervasive presence and influence are evident.

Tennyson never answered Coleridge's question about King Arthur: "What have *we* to do with him?" He recreated the medieval legends to present a "mundane" rather than "national" poem. At the same time the *Idylls of the King* raised Arthur to a stature which made him assume epic dimensions within English literary tradition. Tennyson brought the Arthurian legends to the consciousness of the English people; his poetry re-established their literary eminence. Though Tennyson made no attempt to answer Coleridge's question, many of his contemporaries would agree with Edward Strachey's assertion: "it was well that the old order should yield place to the new, or at least make room for it at its side. And such are the thoughts and sentiments with which the lover of the old Morte Arthur will, if he be also a student of the growth of our national character, read the new *Idylls of the King.*" Tennyson recreated the medieval legends according to his own idealistic philosophy so that the Arthurian world of his creation stands both after and beside the Arthurian world of medieval England. (pp. 156-163)

David Staines, "Epilogue: Alfred Tennyson and Victorian Arthuriana," in his Tennyson's Camelot: The Idylls of the King and Its Medieval Sources, *Wilfrid Laurier University Press, 1982, pp. 156-63.*

OTHER LEADING FIGURES

Elisabeth Brewer

[*Brewer is an English educator and critic who writes on medieval English literature and its revival in the nineteenth century. In the following excerpt, she examines how two Pre-Raphaelite poets, William Morris in his* The Defence of Guenevere *and Algernon Charles Swinburne in his* Tristram of Lyonesse, *chose to adapt the Arthurian legend in their work.*]

Interest in the Arthurian legend appears to have arisen independently among the young artists and writers who belonged to or were associated with the Pre-Raphaelite movement. D. G. Rossetti had discovered Malory some time before Morris and Burne-Jones first met him, and later, with some older colleagues, contributed woodcut illustrations to the Arthurian poems in Edward Moxon's 1857 edition of Tennyson's poems. Morris and Burne-Jones, while undergraduates at Oxford, spent much time reading and discussing the copy of *Le Morte Darthur* which Morris had bought for them both, because the impecunious Burne-Jones could not afford it. Swinburne, meanwhile, had become familiar with the story of Tristram and Iseult in childhood, and indeed claimed that in so far as a child could understand it, the story had been his delight before he was ten years old. Their fascination with the Arthurian legend was of course part of the wider interest in the Middle Ages which these young men shared, and which was becoming an important trend in the mid-nineteenth century. But though D. G. Rossetti was well read in medieval Italian literature and Morris in English and French, both found Malory a more fruitful source of subjects for new creative work than other medieval writers, just as the imagination of other artists and authors was fired by various aspects of the Arthurian legend very much more than by any other medieval romance or topic. It was to *Le Morte Darthur* that Rossetti and his friends naturally turned for subjects for the decoration of the Oxford Union, in their corporate endeavour in the Long Vacation of 1857. By 1858, it was possible for Richard Garnett, reviewing Morris's poem, 'The Defence of Guenevere' in *The Literary Gazette* [6 March 1858], to remark that the Pre-Raphaelite poets and painters had 'made the Arthurian cyclus their own', and for another critic [in the *Saturday Review* (20 November 1858)] to assert that 'pre-Raffaelitism' had taken *Morte d'Arthur* under its special protection.

The Pre-Raphaelites' enthusiasm for the past was comprehensive: it included not merely the literature, the art and the architecture, but also the crafts, the social structures and to some extent the religious practices of the Middle Ages. Out of it they constructed an image of medieval times that was of course highly selective and romanticised, but not necessarily the worse for that. The Arthurian legend offered them a symbolic system for the poignant and dramatic presentation of those inward dramas of the soul which in their view were the stuff of poetry and of art. It allowed truth to nature in the depiction of scene and background to be combined with the stylisation appropriate to the age of chivalry. Their attraction to the Middle Ages was neither mere escapism nor simply nostalgia because it was closely connected with their active need to find a mythology—or mythologies—to give outward form to inner experience. While other myths also provided them with symbols, Arthurian legend offered greater possibilities than other stories for the expression of the human passions. What could not be directly treated in a modern setting could be presented as a tragic occurrence in remoter, perhaps more primitive times: the story of Tristram, for example, gave Swinburne more freedom to write about illicit love than a contemporary story would have afforded him. Overwhelming passion and its moments of ecstasy and torment, as well as relationships condemned by society, could thus find expression; and at the same time the writer or artist could use the story as a medium for the expression of his own inner experience. The subjectivity no longer acceptable to contemporary literary taste could be avoided through the use of symbolism, as the Arthurian legend provided an outlet for introspective tendencies.

Though the image of the Middle Ages which the Pre-Raphaelites created was in some respects a romanticised one, their Arthurian world was one in which suffering was acknowledged and confronted, not ignored or magically dispelled. Their shared vision enabled them to interpret Malory with a consistency of tone and value, expressed through pictorial detail of an equal consistency, and to construct an imaginary world that was self-contained and autonomous. It has sometimes been suggested that Morris's 'Defence of Guenevere' poems are little more than a series of vividly realised pictures strung together, but in fact the verbal pictures also provide a psychological counterpart to the events of the poems. Morris's imagery suggests a desolate and frightening, at times almost surrealistic world in which inner experience takes on concrete form. In 'King Arthur's Tomb', for example, as the Queen is waiting for Launcelot's last visit after Arthur's death, and looking back over her past life, Morris says that beyond her window, 'the grey downs bare / Grew into lumps of sin to Guenevere'. Here and in his other Arthurian poems, Morris depicts a world which knows depths of suffering undreamed of in most other Arthurian texts of the nineteenth century. His vision is a sombre one, but its subtlety seems to have been little appreciated. It does not depend upon a facile correspondence between emotion and atmospheric effects; it does not idealise the Middle Ages, though emblematic images often give a romantic surface patterning. For although the Pre-Raphaelites, and perhaps Morris most of all, could see in the Middle Ages much that they felt to be attractive and even to be desired in modern life, the Arthurian legends did not furnish for them a fantasy that could be re-worked into an ideal dream-world.

The shared experience of the Arthurian legend, the extraordinary homogeneity which is perhaps the most striking aspect of the Pre-Raphaelites' embodiment of it, whether in painting or in poetry, may perhaps be attributed to no small extent to Tennyson's influence. Tennyson's poetic techniques indicated ways in which Arthurian themes could be given pictorial settings, either in poetry or in painting, as well as ways in which some aspects of the medieval world could be conceptualised and imagina-

tively reconstructed in art and literature. When Rossetti, together with Millais, Holman Hunt and Maclise, undertook to provide the woodblock illustrations for Moxon's 1857 edition of Tennyson's poems, Rossetti commented [in a letter to William Allingham dated 23 January 1855] that he had undertaken the work of illustration because it was possible in doing it 'to allegorise on one's own hook . . . without killing, for oneself and everyone, a distinct idea of the poet's.' It was the influence of Rossetti's pictures, however, even more than Tennyson's poems, that affected William Morris. Rossetti had illustrated 'The Lady of Shalott', 'Sir Galahad' and 'Morte D'Arthur', as well as offering an Arthurian subject, 'King Arthur and the Weeping Queens', as an illustration for 'The Palace of Art'. His 'Sir Galahad at the Ruined Chapel', like his earlier water-colour of 'Arthur's Tomb: the Last Meeting of Launcelot and Guenevere' (1855), gives an indication of the interchange of ideas between Rossetti and Morris. The latter's poems, 'King Arthur's Tomb' and 'Sir Galahad: A Christmas Mystery', are close in spirit and visual imagery to Rossetti's illustrations, while Morris's poem, 'The Defence of Guenevere', may be seen as the inspiration of Rossetti's 'Launcelot in the Queen's Chamber'.

Generally speaking, however, Tennyson's influence on the artists of his time was enormous: he had 'invented a new poetry' which suggested not only subjects that they were eager to paint, but also a way of looking at them and representing them that was consonant with current artistic theory. Later, his moral attitude to some aspects of the Arthurian stories also had its effect, which could be counterproductive, but which could not be ignored.

The stories of Tristram and Iseult, of the Grail quest and of Lancelot and Guenevere were those which held the strongest appeal for the Pre-Raphaelites, partly because they lent themselves most readily to a psychological approach, and partly because they allowed artist or writer to focus on a moment of dramatic confrontation or discovery. Though Malory's straightforward narrative usually formed the basis of their reinterpretation, the symbolical use of detail gives a new resonance to the stories. It is frequently a dark, mysterious world that the Pre-Raphaelites depict, and the dim interiors of the pictures often suggest the nature of the inner experience with which they are concerned. (pp. 129-31)

The preference, until the later decades of the [nineteenth] century, for poetry that dealt with the more common and familiar aspects of life often lent itself to triviality. However, the developing interest in psychology (indicated by, among other things, the popularity of such pseudo-sciences as phrenology and mesmerism) and a gradual broadening of attitudes led to a greater readiness on the part of reviewers and readers to encounter more complex and less conventional characters and situations, such as the poetry of Robert Browning continued to offer them. The influence of Browning on other writers was also of great significance: his Dramatic Monologues suggested to the young William Morris the possibility of a psychological approach to the Arthurian themes, and enabled him to see that the exploration of states of mind and emotion might be an appropriate task for poetry. The reader of

Malory's *Le Morte Darthur* must deduce what he can about the workings of the protagonists' minds from their words and actions: it was scarcely possible for the medieval writer to see his characters as individuals whose idiosyncrasies and inmost thoughts and motives it was his business to delineate. Traditional tales do not call for detailed individual characterisation; their protagonists are necessarily types. But for the nineteenth-century writer, or artist, it was possible to stop the story, as it were, and to take a given moment or incident or situation and explore the thoughts and emotions of the participants in it. Morris, meditating on Guenevere and Galahad, could investigate what might have been going on in their minds, and give expression to it in poetry or painting. Morris's 'The Defence of Guenevere' laid him open to censure by presenting the Queen as defiant, finally triumphant and uncondemned, but it also made it apparent that the story could be treated in different ways, and that the Arthurian legend could extend as well as enlarge the reader's sympathies. Though stern moral disapproval might be the immediate reaction to the sinful Queen, her pleading suggested that other responses might also be appropriate, whatever the final verdict might be. In the same way, the Pre-Raphaelite fascination with the Grail legend, finding expression in the art of Burne-Jones and others, and in the poems of Morris, pointed the way to a deeper understanding of a certain kind of religious experience. Such experience might not be shared by many, but it could be better understood and evaluated by those who did not share it, through the mediation of Pre-Raphaelite art. The reader's sympathies are both enlarged and extended by Morris's 'Sir Galahad', confronting the demands of his religious vocation in solitariness and deprivation. The possibility of analysing and dramatising the Arthurian stories from a psychological point of view was one of the great discoveries of the nineteenth-century writers on these themes. They detected a lack in the medieval versions of the stories, and were quick to supply what was felt to be a deficiency in characterisation. (pp. 133-34)

The revival of interest in the figure of Arthur did not ultimately lead to the great national epic that the age felt it should have, but it made it increasingly possible for 'living poetry' with its roots firmly embedded in the past, to provide a medium for the expression of contemporary thought. As it became increasingly apparent that the Arthurian legend was more than legend, was in fact the great national fount of myth and symbol, poets became increasingly able to draw on it more extensively. Poets and artists found that it could easily be used figuratively, could be related to modern problems, and so could be directly relevant to contemporary society rather than merely romantic or escapist.

It has been suggested that Rossetti, Morris, Burne-Jones and others of the Pre-Raphaelites found in the Arthurian legend subjects which allowed them to give expression to, and indeed also to analyse, states of mind and emotion. Their work did not always conform with the preconceptions about art and poetry of their contemporaries, partly because the imaginary world which they shared could not be an idealised one, concerned as it was less with the ecstasies of passionate love than with more complex and often more painful states of mind that were equally inherent in the traditional stories. Although they did not treat the subjects allegorically, through their subtle use of symbolic imagery and their poignant evocations of thought and emotion, they expanded the horizons of the nineteenth-century mind both through their art and through their poetry. (p. 135)

Although Morris's introduction to Malory did not come until he was an undergraduate at Oxford, his interest in the Middle Ages originated in early childhood and prepared the soil for his later devotion to *Le Morte Darthur* and other medieval literature. He is said to have read all Scott's Waverley Novels by the age of seven; as a small boy he used to ride through Epping Forest in a little suit of armour. His interest in medieval architecture dates at least from his school-boy years at Marlborough, when he was able on holidays to make expeditions into the neighbouring countryside to look at churches. Thus, when he and Burne-Jones discovered Malory, it gave a new dimension to his interest in the past. It is not surprising that a boy whose imaginative life was so encouraged and fostered should have later made use of Arthurian themes for the expression of his more adult fantasies, but perhaps the most interesting thing is that despite his devotion to and close familiarity with Malory, he wrote only six Arthurian poems, of which 'The Defence of Guenevere', 'King Arthur's Tomb' and 'Sir Galahad: a Christmas Mystery' are the most important, published in 1858 when he was twenty-four. He never returned to Arthurian topics in any later writing.

'My work is the embodiment of dreams in one form or another', wrote Morris to his friend Cormell Price in 1856, and this early formulation was to hold good in one way or another throughout his life. But the 'embodiment of dreams' suggests the need to create imaginary worlds, and it seems likely that the Arthurian theme imposed its own conditions on Morris and forced him to move into territory where he could give his imagination a freer rein. Morris's Arthurian poems probably come closer than any other nineteenth-century interpretation to the spirit of Malory, although he makes some minor changes in the stories that he uses as basis for his own work. In his poems he attempts to enter into the experiences and events that Malory records, to examine crucial moments within the story from the point of view of the protagonists, and so to suggest how Guenevere might have reacted to a public accusation of adultery, what the thoughts of Launcelot and Guenevere might have been just before and during their last meeting, and how Galahad felt about his commitment to the Grail quest. The poems are close to Malory in their uncritical acceptance of the lovers' situation, and avant-garde in their uncensorious treatment of the relationship. The influence of Browning is apparent in the psychological approach, the influence of Rossetti in the sharply realised visual detail, and in both respects Morris is, as it were, supplying Malory's deficiencies. Morris's protagonists are seen against a background which is often stylised and symbolic with its towers and gardens, bright heraldic colours and flowers, and its Pre-Raphaelite figures with their long throats and flowing hair. Morris's medieval world is not Malory's: his medieval settings re-create the

Middle Ages, yet relate to *Le Morte Darthur* more closely than the poems of Arnold, Swinburne and Tennyson do. Morris's poems thus supplement Malory, providing new insights into the traditional stories, without completely re-interpreting them, or using them freely as myths. Morris takes a particular point in the narrative and explores it in psychological terms, and his identification with the protagonists gave his interpretations an authenticity that reviewers found lacking in the Arthurian poems of Bulwer Lytton and Tennyson. As they speak or meditate, Morris's characters evoke their past lives, and their memories build up images of the life of Camelot or Glastonbury. For all its beauty, Morris's medieval world is no Earthly Paradise: the characters are caught in a moment of suffering or weakness: Guenevere confronts death, or the realisation of her guilt, or a final separation from Launcelot; Galahad speaks in a moment of self-pitying despair, Launcelot in sleepless confusion or in incredulous horror at Guenevere's rejection of him. The reader sees an unexpected aspect of the familiar, heroic figure.

At the same time, there is a strong sense that the poems mean more than they seem to say. Each one involves the topic of choice or vocation, or a static moment before a change of state. It seems probable that the topics and incidents that he chose had a special importance and a symbolic significance for Morris, only apparent upon close examination of the poems in the context of his life at the period when he was writing them.

May Morris records her father as saying—of course many years after the publication of *The Defence of Guenevere* poems—that the best way to retell an old romance was to 'read it through, then shut the book and write it out again as a new story for yourself', and these Arthurian poems suggest that this is, at least in part, what Morris has done.

In the first poem, 'The Defence of Guenevere', Morris presents a scene, not to be found in Malory, in which Gawain is Guenevere's accuser, and she defends herself against his accusation, unstated in the poem. Malory portrays Guenevere as a woman both petulant and querulous, yet capable of unselfish courage and noble feeling, a character who through dialogue and action, emerges from the last books of the story as increasingly vivid and credible, and whose maddening capriciousness enhances the reader's sense of her appeal, for her beauty must indeed be great to retain Launcelot's devotion to her despite her cruelty to him. Morris gives Guenevere the spirit with which Malory had endowed her, but it takes a different form, as she justifies her past life with desperate but queenly eloquence. Cancelling an earlier, explanatory opening, Morris plunges into the scene without introduction:

> But knowing now that they would have her
>   speak,
> She threw her wet hair backward from her brow,
> Her hand close to her mouth touching her cheek

The complex mixture of defiance, shame and contempt for the listening lords leads in to her first attempt to gain their sympathy by recounting the choice that she had been forced to make, in ignorance, long before, between Arthur and Launcelot. In symbolical terms, she describes how she first found herself obliged to choose, not simply between Arthur and Launcelot, but between two ways of life, one way apparently sterile and deadening, the other enriching. At the moment of choice, she did not realise that the first was the way of salvation, the second of damnation. She tells her hearers how, when she was 'quite alone and very weak', indeed actually confronting death, 'A great God's angel' had stood at the foot of her bed holding on wands two 'choosing cloths', one 'blue, / wavy and long', the other 'cut short and red'. 'Heaven's colour, the blue', she decides; but the blue cloth symbolises not heaven, but hell. Appealing to the sympathy of her audience, she continues:

> Perhaps you then would roll upon your bed,
> And cry to all good men that loved you well
> 'Ah Christ! if only I had known, known, known.'

She returns to the story of Launcelot's coming to court at Christmas, his splendour suggested by the acclaim of heralds and the pealing of bells, after she had been 'bought / By Arthur's great name and his little love'. The court listens in silence as she describes the slow but irresistible growth of her love for Launcelot, in terms of the cycle of the year, and through an image of gradual slipping down a path into the sea. The moment of final yielding to temptation takes place in a 'quiet garden walled round every way', like the enclosed gardens of medieval romance carrying suggestions of the Garden of Eden, but also symbolising inner experience.

Morris, in making Guenevere repudiate Gawain's accusation, makes her an enigmatic figure. 'God knows I speak truth, saying that you lie' she declares to Gawain, asserting that she could not weep if she were evil enough to be guilty. Morris's imaginative insight represents her as caught up in a tumult of emotions, well aware of her status as a great queen, but also of her position as an accused woman facing a terrible death, isolated and to all appearances guilty, with no defence but her beauty. She is brought to bay at last, with no champion to rescue her, and the impassioned courage of her confrontation of her enemies contrasts with the weakness which had caused her to yield to Launcelot's love. She appeals to Gawain's sympathy and better feelings, she attempts to frighten him with the threat that she will haunt him. Undaunted by his turning away, she returns to her story with renewed determination: 'See me hew down your proofs'. She reminds her listeners of what had happened to Mellyagraunce after he had dared to accuse her of adultery with one of her wounded knights in his castle after he had carried her off. In a dramatic evocation of the scene, she recalls how she had been chained by the waist to the stake to be burnt, and how Launcelot had fought Mellyagraunce, until suddenly Launcelot had struck the sword from his antagonist's hand:

> Caught it, and swung it; that was all the fight
> Except a spout of blood on the hot land;
> For it was hottest summer; and I know
> I wonder'd how the fire, while I should stand,
> And burn, against the heat, would quiver so,
> Yards above my head; thus these matters went.

The startlingly vivid recollection reminds her hearers of what they have in mind to do to the Queen. The pictorial imagery, moving from blood to fire, increases the psychological realism by suggesting the horror of the experience as well as its potential, in the Queen's eyes, as a means of shocking her accusers into revulsion against the act of burning her.

She pauses to remind the audience of her beauty, which they would destroy, and that the truth of what she has said may be seen in her face. She moves on to the attack of Mordred and Agravaine, when she and Launcelot were alone together, and repudiates the suggestion that she and her lover were other than innocent, for 'When a queen says with gentle queenly sound: / "O true as steel come now and talk with me" ', what good knight would refuse? Though Guenevere speaks of the moment of terror when the bawling and stone-throwing of Mordred and his party began, she does not mention Launcelot's heroic fight against his enemies, and Morris does not allow her or Launcelot the noble words that Malory gives them in that tense, dramatic scene. Instead she admits to her own weakness and fear:

> The stones they threw up rattled o'er my head,
> And made me dizzier; till within a while
> My maids were all about me, and my head
> On Launcelot's breast was being soothed away
> From its white chattering.

In the end, her defence proves nothing, for there is only her word against Gawain's and no other character speaks but the Queen. She insists again:

> God knows I speak truth, saying that you lie!
> All I have said is truth, by Christ's dear tears.

Her tale is done, but at that moment, her knight Launcelot appears 'at need'. Does she truly believe throughout her defence that she is innocent, or does she merely assert it in the hope that her beauty will persuade her hearers to agree? The uncertainty adds to the subtlety of the portrayal.

Morris has altered the story as he found it in Malory at this point, where after Mordred's attack, Arthur is obliged to condemn Guenevere to the stake:

> So then there was made great ordinance in this heat, that the queen must be judged to the death. And the law was such in those days that whatsomever they were, of what estate or degree, if they were found guilty of treason, there should be none other remedy but death; and either the men or the taking with the deed should be causer of their hasty judgment. And right so was it ordained for Queen Guenever, by cause Sir Mordred was escaped sore wounded, and the death of thirteen knights of the Round Table. These proofs and experiences caused King Arthur to command the queen to the fire there to be brent. Then spake Sir Gawaine and said: My lord Arthur, I would counsel you not to be over-hasty, but that ye would put it in respite, this judgment of my lady the queen, for many causes. (XX, vii)

It is in fact Gawaine's continuing speech (in which he tries to restrain Arthur) that is Guenevere's defence in Malory: 'For I dare say, said Sir Gawaine, my lady, your queen, is to you both good and true.' Morris knew Malory so well

that it is very unlikely that he was confused about the details and events at this crucial point in the story.

His changes allowed Guenevere to tell her own story, in making her own defence, and to appear in her queenly splendour; but there are other elements in Morris's version that are less easy to account for, for example the introduction of the strange choosing-cloths, and Guenevere's own emphasis on her beauty.

The phrase 'choosing-cloths' seems to have been coined by Morris himself: the visual image that lies behind the term is that of banners. Guenevere's choice is between the long wavy pennon which in medieval heraldry was assigned to a young knight, and the short pennon of a proven warrior. Morris and Burne-Jones were both at this time reading Froissart, and their edition contained many illustrations of scenes in which just such banners were depicted. Burne-Jones had a sketch-book devoted solely to these two types of banners; and Morris often mentions banners in his early poems. He also, as the choosing-cloths indicate, had a keen sense of medieval colour-symbolism: blue is conventionally indeed 'heaven's colour', as also the colour of true and faithful love, while red often symbolises passion. His interest in heraldry would probably have suggested to him the appropriateness of the blue and red choosing-cloths as devices for Launcelot and Arthur; blue for the long and faithful love of Launcelot, red for the royal standard of Arthur, whose 'little love' had originally caused him to marry Guenevere against the advice of Merlin. Her choice of the 'heaven' of Launcelot's love threatens final damnation for her, while she rejects the choice that would have made life hell but promised heaven after it.

The invention of the choosing-cloths emphasises the originality of Morris's treatment of his material, and points to the inner significance of the poem. For Guenevere has no choice in Malory: her role is almost entirely passive; in Morris's poem, she must make a choice which is not only significant and frightening, but also very difficult and conclusive—'Now choose one cloth for ever'. The addition of this episode seems to suggest that it had a special importance for Morris. He had had to make significant choices himself in the years in which he was absorbing Malory, and the *Defence of Guenevere* poems were written at that stage in his life when he had finally decided to abandon his long-standing intention of entering into Holy Orders, to the acute disappointment of his family. Such an intention can hardly have been set aside without inner conflict and a sense of guilt, while to go against the fondest wishes of a Victorian mother was no easy undertaking, as a letter of explanation [quoted by J. W. Mackail in *The Life of William Morris,* 1899] written in November 1855 suggests. Not only did Morris give up what had always been thought of as his vocation when he joined Street to begin training as an architect in 1856, but he was to stoop still lower (in terms of upper middle-class assumptions) in later abandoning this profession, under D. G. Rossetti's influence, at the end of 1856 in the hopes of becoming a painter. Morris's biographer remarks upon the adverse reaction of Morris's family, adding that 'It had always been taken for granted that he was to enter the Church. . . . To be a painter was barely respectable . . . Mrs Morris

Queen Guenevere, *William Morris, 1858, oil on canvas.*

at first hardly credited the project announced to her.' On Morris himself, he continues, 'the resolution had an unsettling, and for a time, almost a disastrous effect'; for the two years during which he was trying to become a painter, he was moody and irritable, brooded much by himself, 'and lost for the time a good deal of his old sweetness'.

The close identification with Guenevere in the poem, which enabled him to produce her 'defence', is in itself surprising in a young man in his early twenties, and can perhaps be seen as relating to his own dilemma when confronted with the choice between the commitment made in ignorance of its implications, and now seen as life-denying, and the alternative which allows fuller scope for growth and fulfilment. It is not difficult to see that Guenevere may have symbolised the creative side of his nature, allowed to find expression in liberating union with the practical, represented by Launcelot, the 'mighty man of his hands' as Malory constantly describes him. Unconventional and unacceptable in terms of contemporary attitudes, such a union calls forth the 'defence' of William Morris, too, as his creativity seeks a means of expression through art and rejects the choice, made in ignorance, of a career in the Church.

Thus in 'The Defence of Guenevere' Morris makes use of an Arthurian theme to give expression to inner conflict, and to express what contemporary literary conventions

would otherwise have found too subjective. Its unconventionality as regards moral attitudes, indicated by Morris's implicit championing of the adulterous queen, contrasts with Tennyson's censorious attitude to her, as well as with Ludlow's, quoted earlier, but as in other respects, the poem is closer in its tolerance and sympathy to Malory's presentation. (pp. 135-41)

Morris is not concerned with the great contemporary topics that find expression in much nineteenth-century Arthurian literature—the problems of the loveless marriage and love outside marriage—but with the externalisation and resolving of his own tensions and doubts. He neither glorifies romantic love nor explicitly censures adultery; indeed in his first two poems, Launcelot's and Guenevere's love becomes the symbol of a different kind of union which need not, indeed cannot be judged in terms of conventional morality, for 'The Defence of Guenevere' is a defence of the creative vocation and its source of inspiration. Assurance gives place to doubt in 'Arthur's Tomb', while the Galahad poems approach the problem of vocation from another angle.

The undercurrent of bitter frustration which plays so important a part in all the poems arises not merely from Morris's need in his early twenties for an outlet for his enormous creative energies, but also from a consciously or unconsciously suppressed desire for sexual satisfaction, too. The poems are full of sexual imagery, but the secondary symbols of hair, lips and hands predominate. The lips of lovers strain to meet, hands reach out for brief and tenuous contact, insentient tresses link Launcelot and Guenevere, Ozana and his love. The stylised or emblematic nature of much of the imagery distracts attention from its physicality, as for example in these lines:

> And she would let me wind
> Her hair around my neck, so that it fell
> Upon my red robe, strange in the twilight
> With many unnamed colours, till the bell
> Of her mouth on my cheek sent a delight
> Through all my ways of being . . .

Here, the red robe, the twilight and the bell-image give an impression of the setting, and so mask the sensuous feeling with which the lines are really concerned. This sensuousness, absent in Malory, together with the psychological approach which Morris adopted in the first three of his Arthurian poems is one of the main innovations that he brought to Arthurian legend in the nineteenth century. In addition, his powerful evocation of the Arthurian world, brilliant in its colour, haunting in its images, and alive with passion, can still capture the imagination. In giving the old stories a private and personal, rather than a merely public and general meaning, he made the symbolic potential of the traditional material more accessible to later writers. That he wrote no more Arthurian poems after 1858 perhaps suggests that when the difficult period with which the subjects were associated was left behind, he had no wish to revisit Camelot.

Morris's poems lack Malory's cosmic optimism: the cold breath of Calvinism which seems to have given a new exclusiveness to heaven in the nineteenth century can be felt even here, threatening eternal punishment to those who have sinned. Nor could Morris share Malory's predominant interest in the institution of the Round Table itself, or in the code of chivalry and the noble ideal on which the institution was based. But as with many other nineteenth-century writers, that aspect of the story with which Malory was perhaps least concerned proved the most fruitful point of entry for Morris. While Malory is little concerned with love, except as a potentially disruptive force in society, for Morris the love of Launcelot and Guenevere was of wider symbolic significance, and led him to the psychological realism which would have been impossible for a medieval writer. (pp. 146-47)

Swinburne, as has already been indicated, was early fascinated by the Arthurian legend, and seems to have written a poem on the theme of Tristram while still a schoolboy. Later, at Oxford, he came under the influence of William Morris, and his earliest attempts at Arthurian poems to survive, 'Queen Yseult', 'Lancelot' and 'Joyeuse Garde' are full of echoes of Morris's *Defence of Guenevere* poems. Queen Yseult is a Pre-Raphaelite beauty:

> And no gems the maiden had,
> But with tresses golden-glad
> Was her perfect body clad.

Again and again phrases reminiscent of Morris occur—'her dear face', 'hot and bitter drouth', 'the happy garden land'—and there is, if anything, even more flowing, glowing golden hair, more locks and tresses and deep streams of dropping hair than anywhere else in the work of the Pre-Raphaelites. The form of the story that Swinburne tells is certainly a strange one: Yseult comes to collect Tristram on a winter night and carries him on her back through the snow, with bare feet, so that no-one will know that they have been together. Many stanzas are given to Tristram's bridal night with Yseult of Brittany, 'sleeping in her maidenhood', in which the full poignance of the situation of both characters is brought out. 'Lancelot', too, is in form and cadence strongly reminiscent of Morris's early poems, in particular of 'Sir Galahad: A Christmas Mystery.'

> Always sate I, watching her
> By her carven gilded chair,
> Full of wonder and great fear
> If one long lock of her hair
> In the soft wind sink or stir,
> Fallen to her knee.

The poem, which deals allusively with the conflict in Lancelot's soul as a result of his love for Guenevere, which holds him back in the quest for the Grail, ends inconclusively. In 'Joyeuse Garde' Swinburne attempts something different, an evocation of the situation and atmosphere at Joyeuse Garde, from the point of view of Yseult. It suggests a preliminary sketch for *Tristram of Lyonesse.*

It was not until the publication of Tennyson's 'The Holy Grail' in 1869 that Swinburne set to work in earnest on the theme of Tristram and Iseult. He wrote to Rossetti [in a letter dated 22 December 1869]: 'I fell tooth and nail upon "Tristram and Iseult" and wrote an overture of the poem projected, all yesterday. My first attempt at a poetic narrative may not be as good as "Gudrun", but if it doesn't lick the Morte d'Albert, I hope I may not die without extreme unction.' It was not Tennyson's version of the story of Tristram in 'The Last Tournament', since it was not published until 1871, that prompted him to return to the theme in the first instance; but the enthusiasm with which he began upon the project did not result in its early completion, for the poem did not appear until 1882.

By 1869, Swinburne no longer associated himself with the Pre-Raphaelites as far as his work was concerned, and had freed himself from Morris's early influence. He adopted a new mode, modelling his verse, as he explained in the letter to D. G. Rossetti quoted above, 'not after the Chaucerian cadence of Jason, but after my own scheme of movement and modulation in Anactoria, which I consider original in structure and combination'. He studied the medieval versions of the story as related by Thomas, Béroul and Malory, though he seems not to have made direct use of Eilhart or Gottfried. Sir Walter Scott's edition of the Middle English 'Sir Tristrem' was a primary source. Though the author claimed that Wagner was a major influence (as Stoddard Martin points out in his study of Wagner's influence on English literature [*Wagner to the Waste Land: A Study of the Relationship of Wagner to English Literature,* 1982]) it is very unlikely that Swinburne could have known his music at all when he wrote 'Queen Yseult'; as also that he could have known *Tristan und Isolde,* except perhaps as piano music, when he wrote his *Tristram.* Martin further maintains that Swinburne's aesthetic was derived from Shelley and the Romantic tradition rather than from Wagner, and adds that though his poetry 'has moments of clear contact with Wagner—in favoured images such as the sea, themes such as the association of love with death, style which was equally passionate and prolonged, and subjects from the rediscovered body of partially pagan north European myths', they are coincidental rather than the result of direct influence, and indeed are characteristics shared with other contemporary writers.

Swinburne's intention, as he expressed it in the Dedicatory Epistle to the poem, was to present his story straightforwardly, 'as it was known to the age of Dante . . . mainly through a succession of dramatic scenes or pictures with descriptive settings or backgrounds.' This dignified aim may be contrasted with some of Swinburne's other comments: he intended, he said, to show Guenevere, long afterwards at Camelot, in 'a tête-a-tête with Iseult, when they exchange confidences about their husbands and lovers'; and in his letter to Rossetti of February 1870, he said that he hoped 'to make the copulative passages of the poem more warm . . . than anything my chaste Muse has yet attempted.' Their warmth, in the end, though rather tepid by present-day standards, caused Watts-Dunton some nervousness about the poem's reception, and *Tristram of Lyonesse* was published with a padding of miscellaneous verse accompanying it to deaden the impact.

The old story enabled Swinburne to analyse the lovers' experience and its implications, to discuss at least indirectly the problem of such situations, and to give expression to the emotional intensity of frustrated sexual desire. The retelling of the legend gave him a freedom less available to the nineteenth-century novelist of contemporary life, and the romanticised world of the Middle Ages provided the ideal setting. Critics complained of the incongruity of allowing Tristram, the medieval knight, to express modern sentiments, but that the poem should have some sort of contemporary relevance, since its theme is Love, was obviously a large part of its point. There is, in fact, very little in the work that suggests the Middle Ages.

His story enabled Swinburne to create a setting in which natural imagery could provide the symbols of both emotion and sexual experience. He begins with the voyage, with 'the fair ship stoutly sailing' (as does Wagner) to take Iseult to her bridegroom King Mark in Cornwall, only summarising briefly, in introducing Tristram, the earlier part of the traditional story which deals with his birth and upbringing, and the adventures which take him to Iseult's home in Ireland. Swinburne is not much interested in Tristram as paragon of chivalry and courtesy, but only in the experience of passionate love. On the other hand, he does not immediately introduce the love-potion as Wagner does, because he has other things to do first. He creates a glitteringly beautiful, idealised picture of ship, sea and sky as a setting for Iseult's beauty, which, blended with the splendour of the morning, suggests her innocence and youth. She is still childlike, 'as if a rose's blood Beat in the live heart of a lily-bud.' She questions Tristram about Arthur's court, and hears the old story of Morgause and Arthur, of the terrible consequences of their love: 'Blind to him blind his sister brought forth seed,' followed by the prophecy of the doom to come from 'the sin they knew not.' In Tristram and Iseult alone on the ship, against an elemental background, and far from the dark world of past sin and future retribution, Swinburne creates an image of high romance to offset the other aspects of the unhappy story—its deception, frustration and despair—and to glorify the power of irresistible passion.

The poem is in many ways a late offshoot of the Romantic tradition, and Swinburne's admiration for Shelley is very much apparent in his adoption of some aspects of his techniques. Like Shelley in 'Epipsychidion', Swinburne through natural images and the suggestion of scene and atmospheric conditions builds up an erotic atmosphere and suggests intense emotional experience. When Shelley imagines his beloved,

> The glory of her being, issuing hence,
> Stains the dead, blank, cold air with a warm shade
> Of unentangled intermixture, made
> By Love, of light and motion: one intense
> Diffusion, one serene Omnipresence,
> Whose flowing outlines mingle in their flowing,
> Around her cheeks and utmost fingers glowing
> With the unintermitted blood, which there
> Quivers, (as in a fleece of snow-like air
> The crimson pulse of living morning quiver,)
> Continuously prolonged, and ending never,
> Till they are lost, and in that Beauty furled
> Which penetrates and clasps and fills the world.

Swinburne's description of Iseult in the early morning is even more sensuous and suggestive:

> And her heart sprang in Iseult, and she drew
> With all her spirit and life the sunrise through
> ......

> And as the august great blossom of the dawn
> Burst, and the full sun scarce from sea withdrawn
> Seemed on the fiery water a flower afloat,
> So as a fire the mighty morning smote
> Throughout her, and incensed with the influent hour
> Her whole soul's one great mystical red flower
> Burst, and the bud of her sweet spirit broke
> Rose-fashion, and the strong spring at a stroke
> Thrilled, and was cloven, and from the full sheath came
> The whole rose of the woman red as flame.

After this, Swinburne's later 'copulative passages' come as rather an anticlimax.

Childhood is left behind with Iseult's experience of the sunrise, but before the love-potion is consumed, Swinburne changes the mood of ecstasy by once again introducing the threat of evil. He returns to Merlin's sinister origins and to Mordred and Agravane, and images of the Waste Land remind the reader of the wider context of the lovers' story. Then a squall strikes the ship, and Tristram goes to the help of the crew; when the danger is past, he is thirsty and Iseult fetches the love-draught. They drink

> And all their life changed in them, for they quaffed Death.

Shuddering with terror, not knowing what they have done, they are drawn together until 'their four lips became one burning mouth.'

The poem is not simply about the experience of ungovernable passion, unacceptable to society, but about the cruelty of life, of the chance happening that leads to inescapable disaster or entanglement. It further enabled Swinburne to raise questions about guilt and responsibility; as well as about death and judgement, which were still controversial topics even towards the end of the century. Through it he was able to romanticise and idealise a situation with which much nineteenth-century literature is concerned, the mismatch, the meeting that comes too late, the life-long commitment that can bring no happiness. Here it is presented in its most powerful imaginative form, for both Tristram and Iseult are entirely guiltless and unaware of the possible implications of their action. Though there is a hint of the story of the Fall in the 'serpentine desire' that Tristram feels, he could not know that what he did would be disastrous. Swinburne's dramatic presentation of this moment, fraught with horrified realisation, brings out the psychological significance of the experience. Both the lovers have only just emerged from childhood; the ship and their voyage represent the state of transition from childhood to adulthood when, alone together, both are vulnerable and defenceless. They are the victims not only of a natural experience, but also of the well-meant intentions of their elders to arrange their lives for them. The symbol of the love-draught, like Eve's apple, is resonant with the hidden implications of a perpetually re-enacted natural experience. That Swinburne follows the earlier versions of the story that make the draught the sole cause of their love (instead of as in Thomas's version, allowing them to fall in love before they drink it) enhances their innocence and the dramatic quality of the episode, though, through the natural imagery of sun and flower, he has already linked them symbolically in an innocent organic union.

The compelling force of their love is the subject of the next section, which deals with the arrival at King Mark's court and the wedding night. Swinburne manages the substitution of Brangwain for Iseult with considerable delicacy, while not losing any of the ironies inherent in the situation. He makes Mark, awaiting the arrival of Iseult, a convincing figure of latent passion:

> and his face was as the face of one
> Long time athirst and hungering for the sun . . .
> A swart lean man but kinglike, still of guise,
> With black streaked beard and cold unquiet eyes
> Close-mouthed, gaunt-cheeked, wan as a morn-
>   ing moon.

In due course,

> Soft like a bride came Brangwain to King Mark,
> And to the queen came Tristram.

But when Mark wakes he sees Iseult and

> all that strange hair shed
> Across the tissued pillows, fold on fold,
> Innumerable, incomparable, all gold . . .
>   so shone its flowering crown above
> The brows enwound with that imperial wreath,
> And framed with fragrant radiance round the
>   face beneath
> And the king marvelled . . . and said out of his
>   heart
> 'What have I done of good for God to bless
> That all this he should give me, tress on
>   tress . . . '

The superbly Pre-Raphaelite picture is underlaid by the irony that it is only Iseult's hair that has been 'given' him. To the modern reader, unshocked by the situation, it is a successfully handled episode which avoids the unromantic explicitness of the medieval versions without bowdlerising, but it is scarcely as sensational now as it must have been meant to be. Swinburne reserved his greatest powers of erotic suggestion for later passages, such as the lovers' meetings in the forest bower, where with natural imagery as earlier in the poem, he builds up an impression of feverish love-making; as Tristram embraces Iseult, she is merged with flower images as he

> strained her to him till all her faint breath
>   sank
> And her bright limbs palpitated and shrank
> And rose and fluctuated as flowers in rain
> That bends them and they tremble and rise again
> And heave and straighten and quiver all through
>   with bliss
> And turn afresh their mouths as for a kiss . . .

The sea-imagery, used thematically throughout the poem, ends the idyllic episode with equal voluptuousness:

> Her lips for love's sake bade love's will be done
> And all the sea lay subject to the sun.

So, as in the Haidée episode in Byron's *Don Juan,* a sense of joy and fulfilment in a beautiful world is created; but the bower in which the lovers lie together summer-long, reminiscent of Keats' vision of Cupid and Psyche, suggests

the extent of the fantasy that is being created. Juan and Haidée have to eat; she becomes pregnant, and her furious father tears the lovers apart: Byron makes sure that realism surrounds his idyll of young love. Swinburne's lovers here, however, as later in Joyous Gard, are lotus-eaters upon whom reality never impinges. They want nothing but love, they do nothing but make love without weariness or satiety. Their bower, far away from court and castle, almost out of time, emphasises the self-enclosed, sterile nature of their love, excessive and disproportioned as it is. The fantasy of the all-sufficiency of love has something regressive about it, for, denied the creative complementariness of adult love, Tristram and Iseult together inhabit and can only find satisfaction in a womb-like, isolated world of their own. It is, however, a fantasy in which we the more eagerly indulge because of the attraction of its other aspects: the fantasy of the first love that retains its intensity and faithfulness through life, in an equal balance of devotion.

Tristram's banishment at the end of this episode leads to his exile in Brittany, where the King's daughter is also called Iseult. She, too, is young, virginal and doomed to love him; the intensity of her passion for him is significant, for her frustration when Tristram marries her and is unable to consummate the marriage, is an important theme in the poem. Swinburne makes a convincing study of Iseult's patient expectation turning to bitterness and eventually poisoning her love and her nature. Tristram's inability to fulfil his obligation to his bride directs attention to another significant aspect of the story. There is a deeper level of meaning, as Anne Wilson has pointed out in *Traditional Romance and Tale,* in her very interesting discussion in Freudian terms of the implications of the story. She suggests that 'The story of Tristan appears to be the story of the eternal sadness associated with the hero's having to renounce his maternal first love. Indeed, he has been unable to renounce the sexual side of his love for her in his mind and therefore embarks on a search for her which can never be satisfied in his lifetime. Anne Wilson draws attention, in an earlier discussion, to the fact that there are three Iseults, the first a mother-figure to whom Tristram goes for healing of a wound in his thigh. He later arranges a marriage between King Mark, a father-figure, and Queen Iseult's daughter Iseult because he cannot dissociate Iseult the daughter from Iseult the mother, so that for him, she is taboo. In his mind he possesses Iseult, though she belongs to another man; he cannot consummate his marriage with the third Iseult, because of his association of her with the first. Such an interpretation makes sense of some very puzzling aspects of the story (particularly in the earlier episodes which Swinburne did not include in his version), suggests an additional reason for what we feel to be the power of the story, and indicates why it is this story which was so important to Swinburne (whose psychological make-up remained unhappy throughout his life) rather than, for example, the story of Lancelot and Guenevere, or of the Grail.

Though one may see, at the deepest level, and beneath conscious intention, such a meaning as giving power to the story, like other symbolic stories it can provide a medium for other meanings, too, and for the deliberate discussion of serious issues. In 'Iseult at Tintagel', which is the climax of the poem, Iseult of Ireland, separated from the now-banished Tristram, is considering her own situation and the degree of guilt to be ascribed to her. Alone on a night of storm, she meditates on the paradox of her sinful love, and weighs her love for God against her guilty love for Tristram, the purity of Christ against her own uncleanness. Can love of such intensity for a mere mortal be itself acceptable to God, and is repentance possible? she asks herself. She does not blame fate or God for the love that came from drinking the love-draught; rather she claims that she has chosen to love Tristram more than God. The conflict in her mind, as she struggles to renounce Tristram so that he will not be damned, is echoed by the fierce storm outside:

> And swordlike was the sound of the iron wind,
> And as a breaking battle was the sea.

The scene rises to a climax as she pleads with God for mercy, and implores Christ to have pity on their sufferings, and the storm becomes more fearful:

> And as man's anguish clamouring cried the
>   wind
> And as God's anger answering rang the sea.

As she prays to bear the weight of all their guilt, Tristram's as well as hers, the storm begins to die down. The intensity of the scene is increased by the irony that at the very moment that Iseult offers herself for Tristram's redemption, he has married Iseult in Brittany, and by the contrast of the harsh and merciless anger of God with the faithful love of Tristram's hound at her side.

Though Swinburne makes use of rather obvious devices such as the storm and the faithful hound to intensify the effect of this section, it contrasts well with the earlier ones and brings into the poem serious matters for consideration which give it a metaphysical dimension that it would otherwise have lacked. To the modern reader the topics under discussion may seem rather academic, but for many of Swinburne's contemporaries they were highly relevant to their own lives. Iseult takes her spiritual situation seriously, and her debate raises her love from the level of mere carnal desire to that of noble and self-sacrificing devotion. Swinburne suggests, not that love of such irresistible force must be morally justifiable, but that love so prepared to sacrifice itself for the sake of another must be a sufficient atonement. In this respect, he is perhaps closer to the medieval trust in the mercy of God, through which in Malory Guenevere and Lancelot are finally saved, than is Tennyson, whose moral indignation is so apparent in both his Tristram and his Lancelot and Guenevere stories. Iseult is so far a Victorian as to see herself as 'unclean till the day I die', but the 'fallen woman' aspect of her story is not stressed.

The poet was reproved by a reviewer for making Tristram talk like a modern young man, instead of like a medieval knight, an accusation which left Swinburne unrepentant, since it had never been his intention to produce a medieval pastiche. The whole argument about responsibility, guilt and atonement presents an interesting example of how Swinburne modernised his story, and attempted to give it

new meaning and relevance for his own age. For—contrary perhaps to expectations—anxiety about guilt and future punishment does not feature in the medieval versions of the story, and in *Tristram of Lyonesse* it is an addition of the nineteenth-century author to meet the tastes of his contemporaries. He further updates the story by stressing Tristram's guilt in terms of a breach of the Ten Commandments instead of a breach of chivalry, or a betrayal of loyalty.

At the very end of the poem, however, Swinburne suggests that the lovers have won forgiveness and peace, for Tristram has put himself in the hands of God. The ending, taken from Thomas's version, is dramatically managed in a way that intensifies the total meaning of the poem. As Iseult of Ireland draws near to the coast of Brittany in the white-sailed ship, Iseult of the White Hands declares to Tristram that the sails are black, and grief kills him before Queen Iseult can land and reach him. We have seen the sweet and loving nature of Iseult of Brittany embittered by the humiliation and frustration of Tristram's refusal to consummate their marriage and his desertion of her; as a consequence, she cannot resist the temptation to revenge herself by deceiving him and thwarting her rival, in the full knowledge of what she is doing. With dreadful irony, as she deceives Tristram at the last, she says to herself, 'I am death.' Iseult of Ireland comes too late, but her identification with Tristram, in death as in life, is proved at once, when 'she felt his death upon her,' and 'their four lips became one silent mouth.' The hatred of Iseult of Brittany has hastened Tristram's death, but the love of Iseult of Ireland unites them in death, in a passage reminiscent of Shelley's *Adonais*:

>   nor might now
> Fear and desire bid soar their souls or bow.
> Lift up their hearts or break them, dread nor disbelief
> Touch them with shadowy cold or fiery
>   sting . . .
> And round the sleep that fell around them then
> Earth lies not wrapped, nor records wrought of
>   men . . .
> But all time long the might of all the main
> Spread round them as round earth soft heaven
>   is spread,
> And peace more strong than death round all the
>   dead.

They are made one with nature, 'And over them, while death and life shall be, The light and sound and darkness of the sea.'

Swinburne's poem is a fine re-creation of the old story, very much more than a mere re-telling of the tale, for it releases from it new meanings. Charles Williams, writing of Arthurian matters [in "Malory and the Grail Legend," *The Dublin Review* (April 1944)], says that, of nineteenth-century writers, Swinburne 'gets nearest to the tone of Myth.' Swinburne's skilful handling of his source material eliminates what for the modern reader might be considered irrelevant detail, and so is able to focus attention on the main theme, the topic of romantic love and the subsidiary topic of sexual fulfilment. The medieval versions of the story are much concerned with the 'enfances' of Tristram, with his noble origins, his upbringing, his courtly and chivalric accomplishments and adventures, and in the depiction of the heroic society to which he belonged. Though the medieval audience was deeply interested in stories of the power of love, their interest was of a different kind from that of the modern reader, just as the experience of love had a different context, social and spiritual. For Swinburne's contemporaries, the psychological aspects were of greater importance because of their greater awareness of the complexity of the individual's response to experience. Swinburne's treatment of the story eliminates many of the incidents by which medieval authors gave a sense of what was going on in the minds of their protagonists, in order to explore in greater detail through dialogue and soliloquy, their thoughts and emotions, and to give a sense of inner experience through atmospheric imagery, as when, before his battle with his namesake's enemy, Tristram bathes in the sea. Here, images of sea and sun keep the love-theme in the reader's mind:

> but with a cry of love that rang
> As from a trumpet golden mouthed, he sprang,
> As toward a mother's where his head might rest
> Her child rejoicing, toward the strong sea's
> breast . . .

> . . . and against the tide
> Struck strongly forth with amorous arms made
> wide
> To take the bright breast of the wave to his
> And on his lips the sharp sweet minute's kiss
> Given of the wave's lip for a breath's space
> curled
> And pure as at the daydawn of the world.

Here sea-images, earlier in the poem used to suggest Iseult, help to indicate Tristram's longing for her, while the whole episode suggests his virility. At the same time, bride and mother images overlap significantly.

Such a passage would have been impossible for a medieval author. The medieval sources suggested Tristram's manly powers through the details of his upbringing, and through his various martial exploits; the intensity of his love is indicated by his becoming mad. Swinburne is careful to eliminate unromantic as well as extraneous details from his version: the intriguing and plotting of the jealous courtiers, for example, and Tristram's unappealing disguises. By doing so, he focuses attention on the two main characters; even Mark and Brangwain play a very minor part. Swinburne thus achieves and maintains a quintessentially romantic tone.

The setting for the medieval versions of the story is a recognisably medieval world, where battles, hunting, feasting and courtly entertainments of various kinds take place. The world of the lovers in Swinburne literally suffers a sea-change, with striking effect and immensely increased symbolic power. The image of the sea dominates the poem as the scene of or background to the action, but also as a symbol for Iseult, as sundering flood and sea of life, as echo of inner conflict and symbol of fluctuating emotion. It not only unifies the poem, but it also gathers up and gives expression to all the romanticism associated with the story: the wild yearning, the overwhelming passion, the calm joy

of the moments of fulfilment, the agony of separation, the longing for the ship bearing Iseult at the end. The poem thus establishes its own imaginary world. Perfectly synthesised in imagery and feeling, it draws together past and present in a form that is highly wrought and richly varied. (pp. 149-59)

Art knows nothing of time in *Tristram of Lyonesse,* and what for many readers must be the dry bones of the medieval versions of the story are triumphantly brought to new life in Swinburne's vibrant re-interpretation. Like William Morris, but liberated from his constricting influence, Swinburne found new forms for the old stories and gave them a new validity. Like the Pre-Raphaelite painters in another medium, he gave expression to the vision of romantic love characteristic of his time, and by so doing, charted for later periods an important aspect of human experience. (p. 161)

> *Elisabeth Brewer, "The Pre-Raphaelites: Morris and Swinburne," in* The Return of King Arthur: British and American Arthurian Literature Since 1800 *by Beverly Taylor and Elisabeth Brewer, D. S. Brewer, 1983, pp. 129-61.*

Howard Maynadier

> [*In the following excerpt, Maynadier discusses Morris's* The Defence of Guenevere *and Swinburne's* Tristram of Lyonesse, *characterizing the former as having "too little substance" and the latter as rightly focusing on the theme of love.*]

Of literature . . . it may be said, despite Scott's romances and Keats's *Eve of St. Agnes,* that the mediæval tendency of romanticism was strongest after the first quarter of the nineteenth century. At any rate, it was not until then, after the tentative efforts of Warton, Scott, and Heber at original Arthurian composition, that interest in the old legends caused that great production of new Arthurian material which has continued to the present time. It began with Peacock's *Elphin* in 1829, which was followed the next year by Wordsworth's *Egyptian Maid,* when already the greatest Arthurian poet of the century was making his rough draft of *The Lady of Shalott* and planning his *Idylls.* Within ten years appeared Lady Charlotte Guest's *Mabinogion . . .* and new editions of romances and ballads. . . . In 1842 Tennyson published his *Morte d'Arthur;* and in the fifties he wrote the four *Idylls* which, with this, have remained the most popular. In these same years, on the Continent, Wagner composed his *Lohengrin* and his *Tristan und Isolde.* Lowell in America had been inspired by the Grail legend to write his pretty sermon of *Sir Launfal.* And in the fifties began the Præ-Raphaelite treatment of Arthurian themes. The tide of mediævalism flowing in so strongly so long was at last at the full. Since then, either the tide-gates have been shut, or another Joshua has made the moon stand still, for it bids fair to be long before the flats of unpoetic fact are laid bare again, as they were in the eighteenth century.

Præ-Raphaelitism was the manifestation of mediævalism in two of the fine arts, poetry and painting. It grew up in a coterie of four painters and sculptors, the so-called

Præ-Raphaelite Brotherhood, who enlarged their number to seven, and then to eight, of whom the world has looked on Dante Gabriel Rossetti as the leader. Their object in painting was not unlike that of the reformers of Oxford in religion. Like them, the Præ-Raphaelites sought the zealous sincerity of an earlier time, and its picturesque beauty. By 1851 they had attracted so much attention that Ruskin, who sympathised with them, and whose *Modern Painters* had helped inspire them, wrote in explanation of the motives of the new painters [in his *Pre–Raphaelitism*, 1851]:—

> They have opposed themselves . . . to the entire feeling of the Renaissance schools. . . . If they . . . paint nature as it is around them, with the help of modern science, with the earnestness of the men of the thirteenth and fourteenth centuries, they will . . . found a new and noble school in England. If their sympathies . . . lead them into mediævalism . . . , they will . . . come to nothing. But I believe there is no danger of this, at least for the strongest among them.

Ruskin's hopes have not been entirely realised. The consensus of opinion is that the Præ-Raphaelites made a mistake in rejecting all the teaching of the Renaissance; they did become too mediæval; they fell into mannerisms. A peculiar type of feminine beauty came to be recognised as their favorite: a woman always graceful, but always large-boned, long-limbed, long-necked, with long and more or less dishevelled hair. This figure they often placed before an ornate mediæval background. Nor did they stop with painting. The fact that Rossetti and two or three others of the Brotherhood were poets as well as painters led to the growth of a Præ-Raphaelite school of poets, who, like the Præ-Raphaelite painters, sought their inspiration in mediæval times. They tried to put into words such pictures as they had been painting on canvas, and so they have told us stories, chiefly mystical and mediæval, suited to such pictures, with the characters in the brilliant, picturesque garb of the Middle Ages, amid highly pictorial, brilliant surroundings.

One would naturally have expected Rossetti to write a notable Arthurian poem, for his illustrations for Moxon's quarto edition of the *Poems of Tennyson,* in 1857, show that he was appreciative of the pictorial beauties of Arthurian story. So do the frescoes for the Oxford Union, which were partly his work. The fact remains, nevertheless, that he produced no such poem, but left the first Præ-Raphaelite treatment of Arthurian themes in verse to William Morris, born in 1834 and dead in 1896, who never felt truer poetic inspiration than while under the influence of Malory and other mediæval romancers. True, the strongest mediæval influence he felt was the Scandinavian, as his translations and adaptations from the Norse show; and critics may regard *Sigurd, the Volsung,* published in 1877, as his principal work. Then, too, *The Life and Death of Jason,* various stories in *The Earthly Paradise,* and his translations of Homer and Virgil show that Morris was not blind to the beauty of classic poetry. But he sang most spontaneously as a lyric poet in that volume of verse which was his first, *The Defence of Guenevere and Other Poems,* published in 1858, when Morris was only twenty-four years old. Though but four poems in this volume are Arthurian, they are the poems which have the place of honor, standing first in the book, *The Defence of Guenevere,* which gives the volume its name; *King Arthur's Tomb; Sir Galahad, A Christmas Mystery;* and *The Chapel in Lyoness.*

In *The Defence of Guenevere,* the Queen seems to be pleading her cause before various judges, who have been chosen from Arthur's lords, waiting, as she talks, for Lancelot to come and fight in her behalf. The story is so faithful to the *Morte Darthur* that, to understand it, you need a knowledge of Malory. There is reference, for instance, to Mellyagraunce and his abduction of Guinevere—the incident related first as we know it by Chrétien de Troies—which would be almost incomprehensible without knowledge of the old story. Yet in one respect Morris has made a change. According to Malory and the romancers before him, when the guilt of Lancelot and Guinevere was discovered, Gawain was their steadfast friend. He would hear nothing of the scandal regarding them; and when Sir Agravaine said that he would disclose their guilt to the King, Gawain replied, "Ye must remember how ofttimes Sir Launcelot hath rescued the king and the queen, and the best of us all had been full cold at the heart-root, had not Sir Launcelot been better than we; and that hath he proved himself full oft. And as for my part, said Sir Gawaine, I will never be against Sir Launcelot, for one day's deed, when he rescued me from king Carados of the dolorous tower, and slew him, and saved my life. Also, brother Sir Agravaine, and Sir Mordred, in likewise Sir Launcelot rescued you both, and threescore and two, from Sir Turquin. Methinketh, brother, such deeds and kindness should be remembered." Nor would Gawain's younger brothers, Gareth and Gaheris, take any more part than he with Agravaine and Mordred, but all three departed, unwilling to hear another word against the Queen or Lancelot. For some reason, however, Morris saw fit to make Gawain the Queen's chief accuser; and she says to him three times in the course of the poem:—

> "Nevertheless, you, O Sir Gauwaine, lie,
> Whatever may have happened through these years,
> God knows I speak truth, saying that you lie."

In making Guinevere answer the charge brought against her, Morris shows something, though not so much as Heber and Tennyson, of the nineteenth-century inclination to excuse her conduct. Till she meets Lancelot, Guinevere has never found such love as she wishes; and that is why she falls. She says herself that she was bought by Arthur's great name and little love. Moreover, she struggles courageously against her growing affection for Lancelot. She meets him first at Christmas. The winter passes, and spring, summer, autumn, and winter again, and a second spring has come, before she grants the knight his first kiss. Whether she ever grants him much more, Morris does not say certainly in this poem. Were it not for *King Arthur's Tomb* which follows, and which may be taken as a sequel to *The Defence of Guenevere,* the Queen's guilt would not be indubitable.

In his characterisation of Guinevere, Morris has tried, no

doubt, to present the great tragic, epic queen of Malory and the other old romancers. To my mind he has not succeeded. Morris's Guinevere is a woman at bay, with her nerves all unstrung, not an unreal woman by any means, but hardly the Guinevere whom Malory presents. She, like Tennyson's, could forget herself utterly in a storm of passion, and she does so at times in private, but not often, if ever, in public. Before the court she can assume queenly composure; and probably she would on such an occasion as this which Morris is describing. It seems to be a trial for which she has had some chance to prepare; she is not taken unawares. Under the circumstances, she would hardly charge the judges, in defending herself:—

> "say no rash word
> Against me, being so beautiful . . .
>
>   . . . see my breast rise,
> Like waves of purple sea, as here I stand;
> And how my arms are moved in wonderful wise,
> Yea also at my full heart's strong command,
> See through my long throat how the words go
>   up
> In ripples to my mouth; how in my hand
> The shadow lies like wine within a cup
> Of marvellously colour'd gold; yea, now
> This little wind is rising, look you up,
> And wonder how the light is falling so
> Within my moving tresses . . . "

With Guinevere talking like this, and with Morris leaving it uncertain whether he intended her to be guilty of adultery or not, you cannot help thinking that a dash of clear eighteenth-century reason would have made his poetry, as it would that of the other Præ-Raphaelites, a stronger thing than it is.

In *King Arthur's Tomb,* Morris tells the tale of Guinevere's last meeting with Lancelot, transferred for dramatic effect from the nunnery at Almesbury, where Malory puts it, to Arthur's tomb at Glastonbury. Otherwise there is little change, except that the quaint, conventional dignity of Malory's narrative has given place to a peculiarly Præ-Raphaelite passion. There is reality in each, but not of the same kind. "Lady," says Malory's Lancelot, "I insure you faithfully I will ever take me to penance, and pray while my life lasteth." Here is Morris's:—

> "Guenevere!
> Do you not know me, are you gone mad? fling
> Your arms and hair about me, lest I fear
> You are not Guenevere, but some other thing."

And when the Queen refuses Lancelot even the parting kiss which he asks for, he falls in a swoon, according to Morris, and she cries out:—

> "Alas! Alas! I know not what to do;
> If I run fast it is perchance that I
> May fall and stun myself, much better so,
> Never, never again! not even when I die."

But Malory: "Nay, said the queen, that shall I never do, but abstain you from such works. And they departed."

In his third Arthurian poem, *Sir Galahad,* Morris is more inventive. He imagines Sir Galahad's musings on

> "the longest night in all the year,

> Near on the day when the Lord Christ was
>   born,"

as the young knight ponders over the love which makes joyous the men he knows. With a pang of regret he remembers that for himself is, after all, only the quest of the Grail. Then two angels enter in white, with scarlet wings, and four ladies in red and green, who are saints. When they have passed, Galahad's earthly longings are stilled; he is at peace. And then there enter Sir Bors, Sir Percival, and Percival's sister, who tell that the knights who sought the Grail have either met with death or come back wounded and sick, "foil'd from the great quest." But we know that to Galahad sight of the Grail is to be granted. On the whole, the poem presents a Galahad who, with all the purity of the mediæval knight, is more human.

Morris is more inventive yet in *The Chapel in Lyoness,* a fragmentary story of a knight, Sir Ozana le Cure Hardy, whose name Malory gives us, but nothing else. Sir Ozana himself tell us,—

> "All day long and every day,
> From Christmas-Eve to Whit-Sunday,
> Within that Chapel-aisle I lay,
> And no man came a-near."

There he lay with the truncheon of a spear in his breast, no meat ever passing his lips, speechless, trance-like, and yet not sleeping; and there Sir Galahad watched him day by day, till at last, by plucking a faint wild rose and laying it across Ozana's mouth, he brought the wounded knight out of the waking, half-mad trance. Then Sir Ozana died in peace; and Sir Bors, who stood by, looking at Sir Galahad's great blue eyes which stared dreamily, as if they saw what mortal man may not often behold, heard Sir Galahad:—

> "Ozana, shall I pray for thee?
> Her cheek is laid to thine;
> No long time hence, also I see
> Thy wasted fingers twine
>
> Within the tresses of her hair
> That shineth gloriously,
> Thinly outspread in the clear air
> Against the jasper sea."

This is the sum of William Morris's Arthurian poetry. In all of it, there is nothing modern except the careful workmanship of his verse and his subjective, analytical method of portraying characters. Like the other poems in his first volume, these four have a singing fascination, and they are full of vivid, highly colored mediæval pictures; they transport you, whether their intangibility irritates or pleases you, into a remote, poetical Middle Age, which for the time being, unreal as it is, you accept as real. You may never be quite satisfied with these poems, because of their too little substance and their too much length and color and imagery; but their spontaneity must rouse your wonder. They seem to have come from Morris's pen as naturally as if this man of the nineteenth century, who deplored the sky-polluting smoke of its factories and the roar and clatter of its steam engines, had lived in the earlier ages of which he wrote. No one has shown more clearly their power to inspire poets of later times—the power which Chatterton felt, and then Scott and Keats and Coleridge, but none so intensely and steadily as Morris and the other Præ-Raphaelites. (pp. 354-63)

Mr. Swinburne, scarcely less mediæval in his Arthurian poems than Morris . . . , wrote his *Tristram of Lyonesse* and his *Tale of Balen* at a time when the Præ-Raphaelite spirit had really waned. Unlike Morris, whose junior he was by only three years, Mr. Swinburne found his earlier inspiration in classical story or mediæval history rather than in romance. But later, when Morris had become less mediæval, Mr. Swinburne felt strongly the charm of Arthurian legend. And so, in 1882, he brought out his *Tristram,* and fourteen years later, his *Balen.*

In the former, Mr. Swinburne follows the mediæval *Tristram* stories with a good deal of fidelity. Though indebted most to Malory, he does not take his material entirely from any one romance, but seems to have been familiar with several, and with both versions of the *Tristram* legend. In his title, for instance, he follows the Baeroul version, which makes Lyonesse Tristram's native land; and this he is following, too, when he makes Tristram and Iseult guests of Lancelot, at his castle of Joyous Gard. In giving the love potion lasting power, however, Mr. Swinburne follows the Thomas version, and so he does in making Tristram receive his mortal wound while rendering service to his namesake, a Tristram of Brittany. To either version Mr. Swinburne may be indebted for his conclusion of the story, for both, we have seen, were substantially agreed as to that, till the later French romancers, and Malory after them, changed the more poetic account of Tristram's death—the sail reported black when it was white, and Tristram's consequent despair—to that which made him treacherously slain by Mark. Mr. MacCallum has suggested that Tennyson's choice of the less poetic conclusion, and his general debasing of the Tristram story in his *Last Tournament,* may be the reason why Mr. Swinburne, so late as 1882, was moved to write an Arthurian narrative of the length of *Tristram of Lyonesse.* By that time the success of the *Idylls* had made the treatment of Arthurian themes on a large scale so peculiarly Tennyson's own, that no contemporary could hope to equal him, except in telling a story which, for some reason, Tennyson had not chosen to tell, or to which he had not done justice. Perhaps for this reason, thinking that he could give to the great romantic love story the beauty which Tennyson had failed to give it, Mr. Swinburne decided to write his *Tristram.* Since he wished especially to emphasise the love in it, Mr. Swinburne omitted the early part of the story—the hero's birth, childhood, arrival in Cornwall, fight with the Irish champion, his torturing wound, and his final healing at the hands of the Queen of Ireland and her daughter. Of all these we have no circumstantial account, but only occasional allusions to them.

The story begins on that fateful day when Tristram and Iseult, sailing by the Cornish coast, drank from the flask which Brangwain had carefully guarded. Straightway—

> "Their heads neared, and their hands were drawn in one,
> And they saw dark, though still the unsunken sun

> Far through fine rain shot fire into the south;
> And their four lips became one burning mouth."

Henceforth, through danger and disgrace, the two are held in the chains of love till death.

In depicting this love, Mr. Swinburne is not essentially different in spirit from Gottfried von Strassburg and the other mediæval romancers. Each of his lovers, like theirs, is ready for self-sacrifice, so the other be helped, as Iseult shows in her prayer when she keeps lonely vigil at Tintagel, not knowing that that very night her lover has been married, almost unwittingly, to another Iseult beyond the sea in Brittany.

> "Nay, Lord, I pray thee let him love not me,
> Love me not any more, nor like me die,
> And be no more than such a thing as I.
> Turn his heart from me, lest my love too lose
> Thee as I lose thee, and his fair soul refuse
> For my sake thy fair heaven, and as I fell
> Fall, and be mixed with my soul and with hell.
> Let me die rather, and only; let me be
> Hated of him so he be loved of thee,
> Lord: for I would not have him with me there
> Out of thy light and love in the unlit air,
> Out of thy sight in the unseen hell where I
> Go gladly, going alone, so thou on high
> Lift up his soul and love him."

But almost directly comes the passion, that in Mr. Swinburne's presentation of the story is more emphasised than the unselfishness of the lovers. None of his mediæval masters made it stronger.

> "Yea, since I surely loved him, and he sinned
> Surely, though not as my sin his be black,
> God, give him to me—God, God, give him back!
> For now how should we live in twain or die?
> I am he indeed, thou knowest, and he is I.
> Not man and woman several as we were,
> But one thing with one life and death to bear.
> How should one love his own soul overmuch?
> And time is long since last I felt the touch,
> The sweet touch of my lover, hand and breath,
> In such delight as puts delight to death,
> Burn my soul through, till spirit and soul and sense,
> In the sharp grasp of the hour, with violence
> Died, and again through pangs of violent birth
> Lived, and laughed out with refluent might of mirth;
> Laughed each on other and shuddered into one,
> As a cloud shuddering dies into the sun.
> Ah, sense is that or spirit, soul or flesh,
> That only love lulls or awakes afresh?
> Ah, sweet is that or bitter, evil or good,
> That very love allays not as he would?
> Nay, truth is this or vanity, that gives
> No love assurance when love dies or lives?
> This that my spirit is wrung withal, and yet
> No surelier knows if haply thine forget,
> Thou that my spirit is wrung for, nor can say
> Love is not in thee dead as yesterday?
> Dost thou feel, thou, this heartbeat whence my heart
> Would send thee word what life is mine apart,
> And know by keen response what life is thine?
> Dost thou not hear one cry of all of mine?

O Tristram's heart, have I no part in thee?"

Mediæval thus, Mr. Swinburne yet has his modern side, as we should expect of an author of the nineteenth century. Like Morris, he tries far more than mediæval writers to get at the motives of his characters; he is of his own time in laying bare the thoughts and emotions which their great love inspires. Indeed, he analyses this love too much. And he is of his own time, too, in his marvellous technique, in the easy, steady flow of his beautiful verse. This fluency and his fondness for analysis and mediæval pictures become faults. They give ground to Mr. Andrew Lang's criticism that "Mr. Swinburne's poem of 'Tristram of Lyonesse' merely showed that among Mr. Swinburne's many gifts the gift of narrative is not one. The story was clogged and covered out of sight by the heavy splendour of the style. Events and characters were lost in vast digressions of description." This criticism, however, is over-severe. Mr. Swinburne's purpose, evidently, was not to give the adventures of Tristram and Iseult in consecutive narrative. It was rather to give the most significant scenes in their history; and the nine which Mr. Swinburne has chosen for the nine books of his poem are well chosen. Often, too, his pictures are appropriate ornaments to the narrative, as in the opening lines of the poem:—

> "About the middle music of the spring
> Came from the castled shore of Ireland's king
> A fair ship stoutly sailing, eastward bound
> And south by Wales and all its wonders round
> To the loud rocks and ringing reaches home
> That take the wild wrath of the Cornish foam,
> Past Lyonesse unswallowed of the tides
> And high Carlion that now the steep sea hides
> To the wind-hollowed heights and gusty bays
> Of sheer Tintagel, fair with famous days."

At other times, however, you feel that Mr. Lang's criticism is justified. Mr. Swinburne's tendency to digression and to over-elaboration is too great; in his pictures you frequently do lose his story. In the eighth book, *The Last Pilgrimage,* there is an especially long digression. Tristram of Lyonesse, accompanying the other Tristram, has been camping over night by the sea; and as the summer day dawns, he feels the natural desire of a healthy young man for a swim in the shining water. But for a healthy young man, he moves slowly; it takes him two pages from waking to casting off his clothes. Once he touches the waves, their shock seems to accelerate his motions, but only slightly. The narrative has been held up in all for four pages before Tristram gets his clothes on again, and even then Mr. Swinburne stops us for another page to tell how refreshed his hero felt after the bath. Well, there are few goodlier sights than a graceful, strong-limbed young man, stripped for his plunge in lake or river or sea; but a few lines may suggest the picture as well as five pages, perhaps better. Though we feel at times that the divine afflatus came to no man in the nineteenth century more certainly than to Mr. Swinburne, such digressions as this, however beautiful, make us wish that he had had less fluency.

Yet he can be rapid when he wishes, as at the end of *Tristram of Lyonesse,* when things move quickly enough. In less than one page from Tristram's wondering on his bed of fever if Iseult of Ireland will come to him, his wife has given him the false information about the sail, and he and his Irish Iseult are dead.

> "And high from heaven suddenly rang the lark,
> Triumphant; and the far first refluent ray
> Filled all the hollow darkness full with day.
> And on the deep sky's verge a fluctuant light
> Gleamed, grew, shone, strengthened into perfect
> sight,
> As bowed and dipped and rose again the sail's
> clear white.
> And swift and steadfast as a sea-mew's wing
> It neared before the wind, as fain to bring
> Comfort, and shorten yet its narrowing track.
> And she that saw looked hardly toward him
> back,
> Saying, 'Ay, the ship comes surely; but her sail
> is black.'
> And fain he would have sprung upright, and
> seen,
> And spoken: but strong death struck sheer be-
> tween,
> And darkness closed as iron round his head:
> And smitten through the heart lay Tristram
> dead.
> And scarce the word had flown abroad, and
> wail
> Risen, ere to shoreward came the snowbright
> sail,
> And lightly forth leapt Ganhardine on land,
> And led from ship with swift and reverent hand
> Iseult: and round them up from all the crowd
> Broke the great wail for Tristram out aloud.
> And ere her ear might hear her heart had heard,
> Nor sought she sign for witness of the word;
> But came and stood above him newly dead,
> And felt his death upon her: and her head
> Bowed, as to reach the spring that slakes all
> drouth;
> And their four lips became one silent mouth."

The Tale of Balen is better narrative than *Tristram of Lyonesse,* because less digressive, though inferior in poetic imagery, and in itself a story less calculated to rouse human interest. Like all verse from Mr. Swinburne's pen, it is most musical. Of a manlier tone than *Tristram, The Tale of Balen* at the end attains almost equal power. From the fatal mistaken fight of the two brothers of Northumberland, it is genuinely moving. After both lay dying,—

> "Balan rose on hands and knees
> And crawled by childlike dim degrees
> Up toward his brother, as a breeze
> Creeps wingless over sluggard seas
>   When all the wind's heart fails it: so
> Beneath their mother's eyes had he,
> A babe that laughed with joy to be,
> Made toward him standing by her knee
>   For love's sake long ago."

Then came the explanation of Balen's bearing another shield than his own. And Balan and Balen died,—

> "And there with morning Merlin came,
> And on the tomb that told their fame
> He wrote by Balan's Balen's name,
>   And gazed thereon, and wept."

This story of the two brothers and their mutual slaughter,

neither recognising the other, is one of the best in Malory's *Morte Darthur,* and Mr. Swinburne has done wisely to modernise it but little. In consequence, his version is better than Tennyson's in the *Idylls.* Tennyson puts too much moral into the old tale; he makes Balin (as he spells the name) bring misfortune on himself almost entirely by his own violent nature. Now the quick anger of the knight has something to do with his sad fate both in Malory's story and in Mr. Swinburne's; in both he is called, or rather, as Balan says, miscalled the Wild. But there is greater tragedy in their version, which makes Balen persistently the victim of fate, than in Tennyson's story with a moral. (pp. 369-77)

> Howard Maynadier, "The High Tide of Mediaevalism," in his The Arthur of the English Poets, *Houghton, Mifflin and Company, 1907, pp. 344-77.*

David Staines

[*In the following excerpt, Staines explores the extent to which Swinburne's* Tristram of Lyonesse, *"the most famous treatment of the Tristram story in the English language," both closely follows the structure of its source and allows the poet to fully exercise his imagination.*]

Of all the Victorian writers who turned to the Arthurian legends for artistic inspiration, only Alfred Tennyson made a larger contribution than Swinburne to the Arthurian renaissance. Though the *Idylls of the King* justifiably receives much critical attention, Swinburne's Arthurian poetry is often relegated to passing references in studies of Arthurian legends or extended minor commentaries in studies of Swinburne's career. His contributions to the Arthurian renaissance demand further study because they occupy a central position within the development of the legends, a position in direct opposition to Tennyson's recreation of the world of Camelot. In addition, his Arthurian poetry has an important place within his poetic development because Camelot often summoned his attention throughout his career.

Unlike Tennyson who was raised on Malory's medieval world, Swinburne turned to the medieval legends, not because of any particular interest in the material, but because of the Pre-Raphaelite fascination with the Arthurian stories and, in particular, the early Arthurian poetry of William Morris. Unlike Morris, however, who found a natural home in the legends, Swinburne never felt a complete poetic ease in the medieval domain. He initially lacked the personal commitment to the material that characterized the interest of his contemporaries. Yet after he was introduced to the legends, he soon became a devoted disciple of Camelot, especially of Tristram and Iseult, which haunted his imagination for nearly three decades. When he completed his early Pre-Raphaelite poems of the Arthurian world, his anger at Tennyson's free adaptation of the legends prompted him to present an Arthurian world which aimed to recapture, not recreate, the medieval world. His *Tristram of Lyonesse* is an attempt to respond directly to the world of the *Idylls* with a faithful depiction of the medieval lovers, and his later *Tale of Balen*

is a deliberate contrast to Tennyson's *Balin and Balan.* Yet despite its role as an answer to Tennyson, Swinburne's Arthurian poetry is an exciting and original realm fused with his own special poetic fervor and intensity.

Swinburne's contributions to the development of the Arthurian legends fall naturally and conveniently into three phases of his career: the early Arthuriana, those poems written under the direct influence of William Morris; *Tristram of Lyonesse,* his supreme achievement in the Arthurian realm; *The Tale of Balen,* his homage to Northumbria and a final answer to Tennyson. (pp. 53-4)

Swinburne's interest in the story of Tristram and Yseult [haunted] his poetic imagination. In the mid-sixties he was working on another poetic version of the legend, yet no finished poem appeared. Only the appearance of Tennyson's second quartet of *Idylls of the King* in 1869 prompted him to employ the Arthurian world again in his own work [as he wrote in a letter to D.G. Rossetti dated 22 December 1869]:

> I am impelled to write on the instant to say how delighted I am to find the Tennysonian seed ('if seed it may be called that seed has none—distinguishable in member, joint or limb') bearing the same fruit in your mind as in mine. Having read a few pages of the 'Grail' I fell at once tooth and nail upon Tristram and Iseult and wrote out an overture of the poem projected, all yesterday. My first sustained attempt at a poetic narrative may not be as good as Gudrun—but if it doesn't lick the Morte d'Albert I hope I may not die without extreme unction.

The overture, a long prelude published in 1871, is a lyrical rhapsody on love's power. In an elaborate and contrived conceit, Swinburne creates a calendar in which a classical love-heroine becomes a monthly astrological sign. Apart from Iseult's presence in April, "a light blossom and beam and shower, / My singing sign that makes the song-tree flower," the prelude is not significantly related to the narrative of the final poem; it is an extravagant and independent litany to love.

Tristram of Lyonesse, Swinburne's finest Arthurian work, first appeared in 1882. Turning again to the medieval romance of *Sir Tristrem,* the poet ignored the story of Tristram's parentage and his early childhood in order to concentrate on the development of Tristram's love, his subsequent sufferings, his marriage, and his tragic death; he seemed to have no need of the early material already employed in *Queen Yseult. Tristram of Lyonesse* is neither an epic nor a continuous narrative romance, but a detailed description of significant moments in the growth of the love of Tristram and Iseult. Swinburne described his poem's structure [in a letter to Edward Burne-Jones dated 22 July 1882]: "I have tried to make it a harmonious narrative throughout with as little manipulation as was possible of the different versions of the story—having found in each something too good to lose." Later he rescinded his description of the poem as "a harmonious narrative" by explaining his intention [in *Swinburne Replies,* ed. C. K. Ryder, 1966]:

> My aim was simply to present that story ("the

deathless legend of Tristram"), not diluted and debased as it had been in our own time by other hands, but undefaced by improvement and undeformed by transformation, as it was known to the age of Dante wherever the chronicles of romance found hearing, from Ercildoune to Florence; and not in the epic or romantic form of sustained or continuous narrative, but mainly through a succession of dramatic scenes or pictures with descriptive settings or backgrounds: the scenes being of the simplest construction, duologue or monologue, without so much as the classically permissible intervention of a third or fourth person.

Tristram of Lyonesse is "a succession of dramatic scenes or pictures with descriptive settings or backgrounds," which become concrete illustrations of the abstract attributes of love enumerated in the prelude.

Having outgrown his youthful Pre-Raphaelite temperament that dictated the form of his early Arthurian poetry, Swinburne now created his own Arthurian world, a world closely defined by the medieval legends yet simultaneously liberated from them by the poet's imagination. He conceived *Tristram of Lyonesse* as a distinct and deliberate contrast to Tennyson's *The Last Tournament* and Arnold's *Tristram and Iseult* [as he wrote in a letter to R. H. Horne dated 13 February 1882]:

> I am working just as hard as ever I worked towards the completion of a poem in nine parts on the story of Tristram, which is and was always in my eyes the loveliest of mediaeval legends. I do not forget that two eminent contemporaries have been before me in the field, but Arnold has transformed and recast the old legend, and Tennyson—as usual, if I may be permitted to say so—has degraded and debased it.

He chose to make his poem not a recreation, but a retelling of the legend [as he explains in a letter to Matthew Arnold dated 19 July 1882]:

> But the only possible excuse for an English poet who has ventured, after you [Arnold], to re-handle the story of Tristram and Iseult must be that which I offer—namely, that the old legend was so radically altered in its main points by your conception and treatment of that subject, and especially of the circumstances which bring about the catastrophe in all the old French forms of the romance, that the field was really open to a new writer who might wish to work on the old lines.

The consequences of his desire "to work on the old lines" is a poetic celebration of love through an exalted reproduction of the structure of the medieval legend.

Swinburne's poem follows the narrative structure of *Sir Tristrem,* though it reduces the narrative to a series of selected episodes. Seizing the center of the medieval legend, the fatal passion of the two lovers, Swinburne chooses the lyrical moments of the medieval romance which he can refashion with his own lyrical grandeur. Fidelity to his medieval sources is fidelity to the narrative outline of the plot; though he does not violate the outline, he embellishes the

episodes he employs so that the final retelling is Swinburne's own creation. A direct comparison of *Tristram of Lyonesse* and its source only emphasizes the fact that no comparison is finally valid or helpful to our study. Without altering the basic structure of his source, Swinburne embroiders his own vision of the fatal grandeur of human love.

Tristram of Lyonesse opens with Tristram returning to Cornwall with Iseult, soon to be Mark's bride. No account is offered of Tristram's birth or parentage; such background material is dismissed with brevity: "And nothing save his name he had of grief, / The name his mother, dying as he was born, / Made out of sorrow in very sorrow's scorn, / And set it on him smiling in her sight, / Tristram." From the opening canto with its depiction of the return and their drinking of the potion to the final canto and its presentation of the death of the two lovers, the poem follows the outline of the romance and introduces all the characters of the medieval account, including Brangwain, Iseult's attendant and Mark's bed-companion, Ganhardine, Tristram's new brother-in-law, and even Palamede, the minstrel who demands Mark's queen. All the characters and all the incidents have a direct correspondence to the world of medieval romance.

Tristram of Lyonesse is ultimately a celebration of sexual love realized in all its beauty and tragedy. Following the pattern established in *Queen Yseult,* Swinburne does cast the story in an Arthurian framework, yet the focus of the poem rests firmly and solely on the love affair with a relentless intensity unparalleled except in Wagner's treatment of the legend. Such focus determines the degree of structural fidelity Swinburne observes; an extensive and telling series of omissions removes details not central to the love story. No longer present is the account of Tristram's parentage and his arrival in Cornwall; the story of his slaying of Iseult's brother is also absent. The episode with Palamede is remarkably brief, especially in contrast to Malory's detailed account. The poem contains none of the marvels and picturesque embellishments which were part of the medieval romance tradition. And Tristram's adventures during his third visit to Ireland and Iseult's lengthy ordeal by fire have no place in the poem. Through the use of dialogue and monologue, Swinburne makes the legend an inner drama rather than an external adventure; the poem has an intensity of focus, a lyrical grandeur, and a degree of characterization foreign to the world of medieval romance.

Tristram and Iseult are characters of passionate love and equally passionate actions; they bear a correspondence to their medieval counterparts in their actions, but not in the intensity of their behavior and in their frequent displays of affection. At the same time, the lovers now exist within a world that is circumscribed by an omnipresent sense of fate, "that of all things save the soul of man / Is lord and God since body and soul began". Swinburne makes the lovers the victims of his conception of fate so that the poem ends as a balance to the prelude's concentration on love; the conclusion is tragic in that their love meets its earthly termination, yet it is also happy since the natural power of fate offers the lovers "deliverance to perpetual rest."

Swinburne's employment of the legend as a celebration of love necessitates one major change from the medieval romance. He creates a new version of Mark, not solely the evil king overcome by his wife's love for Tristram, but also, at the end, an understanding widower who repents of his hostility towards the couple. Rejecting the more common depiction of a thoroughly blackened Mark, he makes the king's repentance final testimony to the quality of the love of Tristram and Iseult and their position as the natural victims of fate:

> And when the long sealed springs of fate were
>   known,
> The blind bright innocence of lips that quaffed
> Love, and the marvel of the mastering draught,
> And all the fraught age of the fateful bark,
> Loud like a child upon them wept King Mark,
> . . . and his heart
> Was molten in him, wailing as he kissed
> Each with the kiss of kinship—'Had I wist,
> Ye had never sinned nor died thus, nor had I
> Borne in this doom that bade you sin and die
> So sore a part of sorrow.' And the king
> Built for their tomb a chapel bright like spring
> With flower-soft wealth of branching tracery
>   made
> Fair as the frondage each fleet year sees fade,
> That should not fall till many a year were done.

Though every character and incident of the poem have some foundation in the medieval Tristram legends and though the narrative structure of the poem does follow the outline of *Sir Tristrem, Tristram of Lyonesse* is more than an embellished retelling; it is a recreation which becomes Swinburne's celebration of love and his understanding and acceptance of the power of fate.

Tristram of Lyonesse shows a more marked fidelity to the structure of its source than any of the earlier Arthurian poems display. Without the omnipresent influence of Morris forcing him into a degree of imitation unsuitable to his own poetic temperament, Swinburne created a poem whose degree of indebtedness to sources displeased Morris [as quoted in J. W. Mackail's *The Life of William Morris,* 1899]:

> As to the poem, I have made two or three attempts to read it, but have failed, not being in the mood I suppose: nothing would lay hold of me at all. This is doubtless my own fault, since it certainly did seem very fine. But, to confess and be hanged, you know I never could really sympathize with Swinburne's work; it always seemed to me to be founded on literature, not on nature.

Morris failed to see that Swinburne utilized his Arthurian sources to express his own vision of the power of love and the influence of fate. Though perceiving the increasing indebtedness to sources, he did not realize that such indebtedness has become a disciplining force on Swinburne's imagination. The Pre-Raphaelite Arthurian poems find their origin in some incident in a medieval story, but their chief inspiration is Morris whose influence seemed to force

Swinburne into imitation, not creation. *Tristram of Lyonesse* finds its incidents and its basic narrative structure in medieval accounts of the Tristram legend, yet its chief indebtedness is to the poet's imagination and his understanding of life. Inspired and also controlled by the medieval legends, Swinburne creates a version of the Tristram story which, while remaining faithful to the structural outline of his major source, *Sir Tristrem,* is a vital representation of his own view of life. (pp. 59-64)

It is impossible to define simply Swinburne's Arthurian world. Whereas Tennyson's *Idylls of the King* is one particular Arthurian world, Swinburne's Arthurian poems are separate worlds, often complete in themselves. One can define, however, the particular nature of the three phases of his Arthurian career.

Swinburne's fascination with the Arthurian legends, created by Morris, led to the composition of a series of short poems filled with a Pre-Raphaelite intensity of graphic delineation. Though there are some remote medieval sources for these poems, their source is always Morris whose Arthurian poetry dominated Swinburne's poetic imagination; indeed his early efforts at creating an Arthurian world amount to little more than a disciple's imitations of his master. When he divested himself of this degree of dependence upon Morris, he turned again to the legends to create *Tristram of Lyonesse,* the most famous treatment of the Tristram story in the English language. His success in this work is the consequence of his new independence from Morris and his anger at Tennyson's Arthurian poetry; in the Tristram story he found a vehicle that would allow him to reproduce the medieval world while offering a poetic celebration of his own understanding of the human condition. The increasing fidelity to medieval sources, evident in *Tristram*'s dependence upon the structural outline of *Sir Tristrem,* does not diminish the achievement; *Tristram of Lyonesse* is a happy union of originality and fidelity, an artistic creation that captures both the medieval legend and Swinburne's own vision of life. (p. 69)

Swinburne's Arthurian poetry stands as a fascinating commentary on the poet's need for imitation of other literary achievements, an interesting example of a contempo-

---

Alfred, Lord Tennyson on the spirit of chivalry:

All ages are ages of transition, but this is an awful moment of transition. It seems to me as if there were much less of the old reverence and chivalrous feeling in the world than there used to be. I am old and I may be wrong, for this generation has assuredly some spirit of chivalry. We see it in acts of heroism by land and sea, in fights against the slave trade, in our Arctic voyages, in philanthropy, etc. The truth is that the wave advances and recedes. I tried in my "Idylls" to teach men these things, and the need of the Ideal.

Alfred, Lord Tennyson, Quoted in Walter E. Houghton's The Victorian Frame of Mind 1830–1870, *Yale University Press, 1957.*

rary's reaction to the increasing popularity of Tennyson's Arthurian world, and yet another example of the importance of the Arthurian legends in the world of Victorian poetry. (p. 70)

> David Staines, "Swinburne's Arthurian World," in Studia Neophilologica, Vol. L, 1978, pp. 53-70.

Margaret J. C. Reid

[*In the following excerpt, Reid examines two versions of the Tristram and Iseult legends—one by Tennyson ("The Last Tournament"), and one by Swinburne (Tristram of Lyonesse).*]

"The Last Tournament," published in 1872, is one of the latest of the *Idylls of the King*. Tennyson found in his source a conventional enough Tristram [Tennyson makes use of this form of name] to be fitted in with his other chivalric tales and his general plan. His Tristram is not the sea-faring hero of the epic, strong and vigorous, torn between loyalty to his feudal lord and a fatal and passionate love. The poet substitutes a moralising half-scornful, world-weary knight who thinks the best way to regain the favour of his lady-love is to excite her jealousy of Guinevere and then to placate her by clasping a necklace around her neck. The reunion is an ignoble scene. Isolt's [Tennyson makes use of this form of name] mind is so full of hatred of Mark that, like a noxious weed, it has smothered her once noble love for Tristram. The talk of the lovers is not elevating. It is of former pleasures in the grotto and of Mark's weaknesses, his crafts and "legs of crane." And a curious *revanche!* Tristram seems to have become the advocate of free love—not a love free to expend itself passionately on one chosen object, but free to wander from one to another. Tennyson here wishes to depict the general slackening of the ideal of love in the court, an ideal which was his own idea of marriage sanctity rather than the ideal of chivalry.

The chivalric ideal was a romantic one rather than a moral one. The knight must have some one to inspire his heroic deeds and he must worship the lady-love chosen for this and be faithful to her in spirit. Often, however, she was far removed from him in station and he had lighter loves for his less lofty moments. Tristan is not a typical chivalric hero, his love is too primitive and passionate. He belongs to the earlier heroic rather than the chivalric age. So the poet's choice of Tristan to expound a Victorian poet's moral ideals is unfortunate.

For excuse, it must be said that Tennyson was a student of Malory. He had not the heroic conception of Tristram on which to work. He found in Malory a Tristram who was just one of Arthur's knights, a rival to Lancelot in knightly prowess and love, a rival who must not be shown to eclipse Lancelot, the romantic lover. In Malory, King Mark is also vilified. Tennyson had but to heap a few extra scornful insults upon him. The "horses' ears" of the early fairy-tale have become curiously "cranes' legs."

Tennyson devised an incident—the tale of the jewels—and made Tristram the chief figure. This ingenious story does not add much to the dramatic significance of Tristram. It serves as a centre round which to paint a scene, which shows the failure and degeneration of Arthur's court through the sin of Lancelot. All the poet's art is used. He has suborned Nature to add her testimony to declare how a high ideal has been ruined by unlawful love. Every leaf that breaks off a bough and falls to the earth sighs in sympathy for the moral hopes frustrated. The languorous, half-mocking spirit is skilfully impersonated by Dagonet the Fool, who dances in and out "like a withered leaf before the hall." Lancelot, the arbiter of the tournament sits aloft in Arthur's dragon-chair, but does not bestir himself even to prevent the laws of the tournament being broken.

The tournament is sarcastically called "The Tournament of the Dead Innocence." The ladies wear white in irony. Within, is heard the mocking laughter of the fool, and without, the coarser laughter of the brutal world which has never professed any ideals. Tristram visits Isolt and is slain treacherously by his uncle, the King. The deed only adds to the general futility and meanness of everything.

There are fine passages of description, of a falling wave, flowery meadows. But these have not much dramatic relation to the story. One of these shows that Tennyson has not realised Tristram as a wanderer or seafarer. Queen Isolt looks out of her casement at Tintagel and in the beauty of the sea forgets her lover:

> "Here in the never-ended afternoon,
> O sweeter than all memories of thee,
> Deeper than any yearnings after thee
> Seemed these far-rolling westward smiling seas
> Watched from this tower."

A musical description! But surely the sight of the sea would have made Isolt remember Tristram, at least the Tristan of the older legend. The unknown Tristan was brought first, to her shores in a drifting boat, a sick man and then, a second time with definite purpose, as King Mark's messenger. The love-drama had taken place to the sound of the wild, lawless waves. It was the sea which had borne her lover away to his simple white-handed bride, Iseult. Swinburne recognised and immortalised the salient fact of this legend. But to Tennyson, as to Malory, Tristram is a knight of the green wood "arrayed all in finest green."

Wagner had produced his *Tristan* Opera at Munich seven years before Tennyson published "The Last Tournament" in his third instalment of the *Idylls of the King,* but the actual plan of these had been conceived much earlier. Thus Wagner seems to have had no direct influence on the poet. But the dissemination of his Operas throughout Europe must have aroused interest in the public mind in his version, summarised on the programmes, often in a translation. Scholars also had been slowly preparing the ground for the more creative products. Sir Walter Scott had edited and concluded *Sir Tristrem* in 1804. In 1835, Frances Michel had also edited the romance of Tristan, giving excerpts from Béroul and Thomas. It remained for Swinburne to add his great poetical contribution in *Tristram of Lyonesse* in 1830 in order to make this form of the story familiar in literary form.

In studying *Tristram of Lyonesse* and in trying to deter-

The Beguiling of Merlin, *Edward Burne-Jones, 1874-76, oil on canvas.*

mine its literary and historical value, we must always keep in mind the poet's purpose as clearly stated by himself. Much of the derogatory criticism of this poem is discounted if the true aim of the poet is realised.

Swinburne writes that in undertaking to "rehandle the deathless legend of Tristram," his aim was "simply to present that story not diluted and debased, as it has been in our own time by other hands, but undefaced by improvement, and undeformed by transformation, as it was known to the age of Dante, wherever the chronicles of romance found hearing from Ercildoune to Florence; and not in the epic or romantic form of sustained and continuous narrative, but mainly through a succession of dramatic scenes of pictures with descriptive settings or backgrounds."

Let us first examine his claim to have set forth the story as known in chronicles of romance from Ercildoune to Florence. Lafourcade, in *La Jeunesse de Swinburne,* supplies and comments on data which fortunately enables us to trace the early stages of the poet's effort through imitation, and also the poet's knowledge and use of his sources.

The first canto of "Queen Yseult" was published in 1857 in the *Undergraduate Papers.* Afterwards, five other cantos were found among a number of College papers, making six complete cantos in all. An introduction by the poet himself gives the plan and scope of the unfinished work, originally meant to be an epic in ten cantos. This preliminary sketch also supplies us with a knowledge of Swinburne's reading at the time. As his biographer points out, it included the old romances of Béroul and Thomas, parts of which were given in Michel's text, which Swinburne knew. From the names employed of Tristram's father and mother, Roland and Blancheflour and other details, it can be deduced that Swinburne also was acquainted with Sir Walter Scott's *Sir Tristrem.* In the early poem the influence of Malory is not so much seen as in the later, and his version of the story is rejected as inferior. "Queen Yseult" was written in 1857 immediately after Swinburne had met William Morris at the Pre-Raphaelite gathering in Church Street at Oxford and had heard him read "The Defence of Guenevere." Like Morris in this poem, Swinburne strives to regain the simplicity and *naïveté* of the mediæval romances and ballads. "Queen Yseult" is directly modelled either on Morris's "Blanche" or the "Willow," which are also written in a trochaic metre of three lines with triple rhymes, and he copies the effect which Morris uses so often of the monotone. Morris at the time generously praised it, considering it superior to his own. Swinburne himself did not, in his later years, think highly of these youthful efforts nor did he include them in *Poems and Ballads.* The metrical form is evidently crippling to a poet who was to show himself master of such a range of complicated metres. In Swinburne's poem the hero and heroine are cut out in the accustomed Pre-Raphaelite pattern; the heroine possesses gold corn-ripe hair, an arrow hand, wears an embroidered blue robe and so on. Like Aubrey Beardsley's illustrations of Malory's *Morte Darthur* the composition is stronger in design than in likeness to life. For example, the description of the "Lady Yseult aux Blanches Mains" (the second Yseult) in Canto Five may be taken, which describes Tristram's wife entering the bridal chamber:

> And the singing maidens there
> Led the bride with tresses bare,
> Singing bridal songs of her.
>
> Purple flowers, blue and red,
> On the rushes round the bed,
> Strewed they for her feet to tread.
>
> But about the bed they set
> Long white blossoms white and wet,
> Crowns the fairest they could get.
>
> Her blue robe along the hem
> Coloured like a lily's stem,
> She put off and gave to them,
>
> And she bade the fairest girl
> All her soft hair comb and curl
> With a comb of jet and pearl.
>
> By the mirrored steel she stood
> Thinking gently as she could
> Sweet new thoughts of womanhood.

These lines suggest the ballad rather than the epic. The poem continues with an innocent frankness of detail also copies from the older romances. The more passionate element is excluded. In *Tristram of Lyonesse* this passion in the young wife who is spurned is turned into bitterness, which makes for itself the excuse of righteous wrath. But in the earlier poem the gentle maiden shows no resentment, though it must be remembered the poem is unfinished.

As far as the narrative is concerned, in the six completed cantos there is simplicity and directness of action. In Canto One the story of Roland and Blancheflour, his death, the birth of Tristram and his mother's death, the youth of Tristram, his appearance at court and his fight with Moronde are told dramatically. The tale is not overweighted with wealth of simile and ornament as in the more elaborate later poem.

Adaptation of tradition is shown in the incident in which Yseult (Mark's wife) sends Tristram leaves of melilote as a sign to come to her. He had sent to beseech her to have pity on his love-longing. This is her answer, those leaves of sweet-smelling clover:

> But when snows were thick about
> Yseult sent for Tristram out
> Soft dry leaves of melilote.
>
> That was for a sign to stand
> That he came to take her hand
> In the happy garden land.
>
> So that when his love had got
> Those dry leaves of melilote
> He the pain remembered not.
>
> But he saw not where to go
> Lest his feet some man should know,
> For the ways were marred with snow.
>
> So his bitter doubt he wrote,
> And she sent him for his doubt
> The same leaves of melilote.

She comes to meet him through the snow and with bare and bleeding feet carries him on her back through the court to her own chamber, where the floor is strewn with rushes. Thus the danger of detection through the discovery of footsteps is obviated. The incident corresponds no doubt with that in the early romances in which Tristan sent to the Queen the piece of bark which floated down the stream which ran through Iseult's chamber. The snow is probably a reminiscence of the flour spread by Mark's dwarf between the two beds of the lovers. Swinburne may have changed the incident partly to bring in the tuneful word "melilote" in which he evidently delighted.

When Swinburne came to write his poem in 1882, he used the same sources as in 1857, with one important difference. In 1882 he was much more under the influence of Malory. It is true that in the main essentials of the story he had rejected his version, but in his description of *Joyous Gard* and Tristram's fight with Palamede, traces of the knowledge of that great prose stylist are found. For Swinburne, a past-master himself in the art of words, could not have failed to appreciate and fall under the glamour of Malory's style, which like a fairy-like mist enhances much which broad daylight would reveal as commonplace.

But the poet's scholarly instincts and wide knowledge of early French romance told him that the older tales of Béroul and Thomas (and *Sir Tristrem*) contained finer material for his poem than Malory. Also, writing as he did after Tennyson, he was fully conscious that he had a rival to surpass. His wider scholarship here stood him in good stead.

Lafourcade points out that Swinburne used *Sir Tristrem* as a source in his early Tristan poem. In his later *Tristram of Lyonesse* its influence makes itself felt. The *Sir Tristrem* is a translation of the French Thomas, who was confused with "Thomas of Ercildoune, the Rhymer," to whom the poem was wrongly ascribed. It differs in certain details from Thomas. For instance, it mentions the curious circumstance that Tristram's faithful dog Hodain also drank the love-potion, a detail to be found again in the Italian romances. It is written in an irregular rhymed stanza of four lines, the first and the third, the second and the fourth, rhyming. Swinburne made use of it, but transformed its dry clipped style into a lyrical form, enriched by simile and enchanting to the ear, with its full-throated melody.

For example, in *Sir Tristrem* the lines run:

> They rowed, those knights so true,
> Tristrem, an oar took he
> E'en as his turn fell due,
> Nor one against the three
> From toil would shrink,
> Ysonde the maiden free
> Bade Brengwain give them drink.

In lieu of these bare cold facts, Swinburne describes glowingly the manly Tristram at the oar and how Iseult looked upon him:

> Then Tristram girt him for an oarsman's place
> And took his oar and smote, and toiled with might
> In the east wind's full face and the strong sea's spite
> Labouring; and all the rowers rowed hard, but he
> More mightily than any wearier three.
> And Iseult watched him rowing with sinless eyes
> That loved him but in holy girlish wise
> For noble joy in his fair manliness
> And trust and tender wonder; none the less
> She thought if God had given her grace to be
> Man, and make war on danger of earth and sea,
> Even such a man she would be; for his stroke
> Was mightiest as the mightier water broke,
> And in sheer measure like strong music drave
> Clean through the wet weight of the wallowing wave;
> And, as a tune before a great king played
> For triumph was the tune their strong strokes made,
> And sped the ship through with smooth strife of oars
> Over the mid seas's grey foam-paven floors,
> For all the loud breach of the waves at will.
> So for an hour they fought the storm out still.
> [quotations of Swinburne's poetry are taken from his *Collected Poems*]

And so on, simile after simile succeeds the other as wave succeeds wave, till the inward eye and the ear are sated with magnificence. In the same elaborate style, the poet describes how Tristram naturally became thirsty when the storm abated, and asked drink from Iseult. Iseult went downstairs and spied the fatal flask in Brangwain's bosom. From a loving desire not to waken the sleeping maid, "half-dead with fear and pain" of the past storm, Iseult took it by stealth away. Then she returned to the deck and innocently gave Tristram to drink and drank it herself. Thus Swinburne translates the seven bald lines of the ballad into a hundred or more.

Yet, as in *Sir Tristrem* and Thomas, Swinburne follows the primary conception of Tristan as a sea-hero. Tennyson makes him a knight of the woods, following Malory. This latter conception also appears in early tradition, though less stressed than the sea-hero one. It is found in an old thirteenth-century poem "Donnei des Amanz" when Tristan is found imitating the song of the birds. One of the chief differences between the version of Thomas and that of Béroul is that in Béroul the Tristan story is connected with Arthur. Swinburne follows him in this (and, of course, Malory) and describes the court and tournaments in all their splendour. The lovers, Tristram and Iseult, also discuss the beauty of Guinevere, and relate the story of Merlin and Nimue. King Arthur is pictured by the poet thus:

> King Arthur, yet unwarred upon by fate,
> Held high in hall at Camelot, like one
> Whose lordly life was as the mounting sun
> That climbs and pauses on the point of noon,
> Sovereign: how royal ran the tourney's tune
> Through Tristram's three days' triumph, spear
>   to spear.

Swinburne's description of the grotto reminds us rather of Thomas than Béroul. In Thomas, as in Swinburne, Nature smiles on the lovers and the beauties of the scene are painted in glowing colours. In Béroul, the lovers are in real danger of their lives and take refuge in a cave, where they have to bear the hardships of rough weather, fortified only by their love.

Thus the lovers' dwelling is described by Swinburne:

> There was a bower, beyond man's eye more fair
> Than ever summer dews and sunniest air
> Fed full with rest and radiance till the boughs
> Had wrought a roof as for a holier house
> Than aught save love might breathe in: . . .
>   . . . . . .
> And thither, ere sweet night had slain sweet day,
> Iseult and Tristram took their wandering way,
> And rested, and refreshed their hearts with
>   cheer
> In hunters' fashion of the woods; and here
> More sweet it seemed, while this might be, to
>   dwell
> And take of all world's weariness farewell . . .
> Than reign of all world's lordship queen and
>   king.

Béroul's description appeals more to the heart, Thomas, and after him Swinburne, to the eye and ear. Swinburne follows Béroul in his dramatic description of Tristram's

escape to the chapel and his plunge into the sea. This gives the poet an opportunity of using all the wealth of words at his command to describe Tristram swimming, a sport the poet himself rejoiced in in his youth. A second description, to be compared with it, is given when Tristram has his last encounter with the sea, before he meets the enemy who is to give him his death-wound (Canto VIII).

Swinburne follows closely his source Thomas, in the story of Tristram's last days and the incident of the black and white sail. Tristram's famous henchman is called Ganhardine, no doubt a poetical form of Kaherdin, Iseult's brother, mentioned in Thomas.

The character of the second Iseult, who resembles at first the lily maid Elaine, who died of loving Lancelot, is strongly yet subtly drawn. Her sweet and innocent love for Tristram becomes soured, as hope gradually dies out, and turns to bitter and revengeful hate. Hate, to Swinburne, was no negative quality but as positive as love. It blows like a bleak, devastating wind through what was once the fair garden of Iseult's soul, withering all the opening flowers. She is no hesitating liar, lying out of a jealous spasm and then repenting. Outwardly, she is as gentle and yielding as ever, but inwardly, she nurses with firm resolution the desire for revenge, what she considers a just revenge:

> And as a soil that cleaves in twain for drouth
> [She] thirsted for judgment given of God's own
>   mouth
> Against them, till the strength of dark desire
> Was in her as a flame of hell's own fire.
> Nor seemed the wrath which held her spirit in
>   stress
> Aught else or worse than passionate holiness,
> Nor the ardent hate, which called on judgment's
>   rod,
> More hateful than the righteousness of God.

When the dying Tristram asks her as a last behest to tell him whether a ship is coming towards him on the sea, and what colour its sail is, she is strong enough to hide the bitterness that is consuming her, and promises to obey.

> Then seemed her face a pale funereal flame,
> That burns down slow by midnight, as she said;
> "Speak, and albeit thy bidding spake me dead,
> God's love renounce me, if it were not done."

On beholding the ship, with its white sail, riding the breast of the waves, she replies unhesitatingly that the sail is black. The lie performs its fatal work:

> And fain he would have sprung upright, and
>   seen,
> And spoken; but strong death struck sheer be-
>   tween,
> And darkness closed as iron round his head,
> And smitten through the heart lay Tristram,
>   dead.

Out of the ship which, alas! has arrived too late, steps Iseult, led by Ganhardine. She hears the wailing, and instinctively realises it is for Tristram her lover.

Swinburne, when he likes to, can use words sparingly, with swift dramatic effect. The reader could almost wish the poem had ended here.

These passages are sufficient to show how Swinburne uses his sources. In the main he follows the facts without change, but he often simplifies incident and suppresses names and details which would spoil the harmony and beauty of his description. Wagner employs the same device in his Operas, but for a different reason, for the sake of dramatic unity. For example, the early life and exploits of Tristram given in the somewhat conflicting versions of Thomas and Béroul, are summed up by Swinburne in a flowing description, which just mentions enough facts to justify Iseult's youthful admiration of her hero. Tristram's prowess as a harper and a fighter, set on fire maidens' hearts in secret and his youth "gave his fame flower-like fragrance and soft growth." Again, no detail of Tristram's fight with the dragon and dreadful wound is told, which wound was the real cause why he set out in a boat with only his harp as company. Finally his little bark drifted on to Ireland's shore. All is generalised in our modern poet:

> And in mid change of time and fight and song
> Chance cast him westward on the low sweet
>   strand
> Where songs are sung of the old green Irish land
> And the sky loves it, and the sea loves best,
> And as a bird is taken to man's breast
> The sweet-souled land where sorrow sweetest
>   sings
> Is wrapt round with them as with hands and
>   wings
> And takes to the sea's heart as a flower.

No one with any sense of poetic rhythm and metre could deny that Swinburne in this poem has enriched by his descriptive power the story of Tristan. But the question of the valuation of his poem as a whole and its definite contribution to the Tristan legend is a more difficult one.

This poem has many adverse critics, the chief of whom is Edmund Gosse. In his life of Swinburne, he pronounces the poem a failure. Others, including Sturge Moore, complain that Swinburne cannot tell a story. In a fine essay in the *Criterion* [vol. 1], Sturge Moore writes: "There is a wind which blows and blows the tale out of the mind." One of the weakest points in the tale, he continues, is the nightly substitution of Brangwain.

But in judging any work of Art, it is only fair to consider the original purpose of its creator. Swinburne does not claim to write a unified drama or to tell a story. To repeat his own words, he rehandled the legend "not in the epic or romantic form of sustained and continuous narrative, but mainly through a succession of dramatic scenes or pictures with descriptive settings or backgrounds." The incidents for the scenes, such as the substitution of Brangwain for Iseult on the marriage night, he takes as he found them. The relations of Mark and Iseult are left purposely vague. We have to afford the poet a "poetic licence" on this account which is not given in prose.

It must be admitted that Swinburne has fulfilled the aim he set before him. It might have been a greater triumph still, if he could have created a swiftly moving drama like *Atalanta,* with one central theme. But he did not set this task before himself, and we cannot judge his work on this basis.

True it is that the poem of Tristram and Iseult is not perfect, but can any long poem be perfect? Often Swinburne does not leave enough to the imagination. For example, in describing Iseult, he is not content to give a general description but enumerates nearly all the parts of her body. Some poets give us one apt simile which, like a flash of lightning in the night, lights up the darkened country behind it. But Swinburne's similes are often heaped up one on the other till the reader is somewhat dazed, and pleased to let the active mind be lulled to sleep by euphonious sound.

Sometimes these quick-changing similes are used with fine effect, as when he speaks in the Prelude of Lovers, whose lives are "inlaid with hopes and fears, spun fine as fire and jewelled thick with tears." These are really four telescoped similes. At other times, simile follows simile, and we are left with enchanting musical sound in our ears but with blurred images in our mind.

Again, the description of the lovers and their amorous joys (in Canto II) becomes wearisome. Like the babes in the wood they become buried, but it is under words, not leaves.

But if there are some passages which are over-luscious, on the other hand there are many perfect descriptive and dramatic passages. One may be referred to here in Canto II, one which combines both elements, the scene where King Mark, "a swart lean man, but kinglike," "close-mouthed" and "gaunt-cheeked" receives his new bride, Iseult. The castle built on its summit of jagged rocks, "a wave-walled palace with its eastern gate, full of the sunrise," is pictured in a vivid and clear manner.

What seem often a greater weakness of the poem than over-luxuriance are the passages of reflection and moralising. Swinburne is at no time a deep or subtle thinker. Also, his pantheistic philosophy and impersonal view of Fate and the gods has been adequately given in the Prelude in fine poetical expression. As the Prelude is in the form of an Invocation or Epitaph, the personal expression of the poet's philosophy or belief is fitting as it is fitting in Shelley's *Adonais.* But the long appeal to Fate at the beginning of Canto IX is too long drawn out and a needless repetition. It does not add either to the lyrical or dramatic excellence of the poem.

Iseult's appeal to God is also, in my opinion, an error of judgment on the part of the poet. For he has taken a hero and heroine, representative of no especial age or nation, but belonging to an early and vigorous epoch. He has drawn them in large outlines, as the first man or woman might be drawn, magnificent in their bodily perfection and youthful prowess, against a background of sea and sun and sky. They had drunk a magic draught and had been, in spite of barriers of circumstance, drawn irresistibly to each other. So far, so good. But with Iseult's appeal to God, the factor of morality is brought in and the limiting time-element. What laws of morality are the lovers subject to, that of the early Celtic age of the fifth or sixth century, or that of the feudal and religious conception of the twelfth century? Iseult, in her passionate, unlawful but self-forgetting love, is nobler than the God she appeals to, with His fixed relentless condemnation of it. Surely this is Swinburne's revolt against the narrow conception of his own day, not Iseult's!

Swinburne has prefaced his poem by a magnificent Prelude. In it he has enumerated a zodiac of famous women-lovers, in which each is depicted as a star in the firmament, ruling over her especial month. The history of each is told in a pregnant phrase or two, of Juliet, Dido, Cleopatra, Guinevere and others. Dido's betrayal by Æneas is aptly phrased:

> . . .—and for June,
> Flares like an angered and storm-reddening moon
> Her signal sphere, whose Carthaginian pyre,
> Shadowed her traitor's flying sail with fire.

Iseult, the poet's chosen heroine, reigns aloft amidst her compeers.

This Invocation to Lovers ranks as one of the most beautiful English poems on the subject of Love, and may be compared with Shelley's *Epipsychidion*. It shines resplendent with fire and light, and ranges from the trumpet-tones of Milton to the ethereal music of Shelley. In the description of the Valley of the Shades where the dead lovers wander, there are touches reminiscent of the pitying humanity of Virgil in the sixth book of the *Æneid,* when he also visits these nether regions. Yet it is not a mere pastiche, it is characteristically Swinburnian, full of splendid images and of volume, swift and sure. The poet had learned from the Greeks to personify the forces of Nature, giving them body and motion. The image of the Sun-god, who reigns supreme, is a Titanic figure:

> These are the signs wherethrough the year sees move,
> Full of the sun, the sun-god which is love,
> A fiery body, blood-red from the heart,
> Outward, with fire-white wings made wide apart,
> That close not and unclose not, but upright
> Steered without wind by their own light and might
> Sweep through the flameless fire of air that rings
> From heaven to heaven with thunder of wheels and wings
> And antiphones of motion-moulded rhyme
> Through spaces out of space and timeless time.

The Invocation to the Lovers is also an epitaph and, as in Shelley's *Adonais,* the poet gives expression to his pantheistic philosophy. Swinburne can promise his lovers no individual existence in the future, no fuller life where their aspirations will be fulfilled:

> They have the night, who had like us the day,
> We, whom day binds, shall have the night as they,
> We from the fetters of the light unbound,
> Healed of our wound of living, shall sleep sound.

The most they can hope for is to be resolved into the elements and be at peace. One gift alone the poet can make

them; he can blow the "living breath between dead lips and immortalize in words these lives." (pp. 204-19)

Margaret J. C. Reid, "Tristan: Tennyson and Swinburne," in her The Arthurian Legend: Comparison of Treatment in Modern and Mediæval Literature, a Study in the Literary Value of Myth and Legend, *Oliver and Boyd, 1938, pp. 204-19.*

Audrey Shaw Bledsoe

[*In the following excerpt, Bledsoe explores the seasonal-cyclical imagery linking the four Arthurian poems of William Morris's* The Defence of Guenevere, *suggesting that "as the four poems progress seasonally from summer through fall and winter to spring, then, the Arthurian cycle progresses from comedy through tragedy and irony and back to romance."*]

The question that critics have found most interesting about William Morris' four Arthurian poems in *The Defence of Guenevere* (1859) is whether or not Guenevere is "guilty" and, if so, of what. Other than that, the poems have received little critical attention. Recently, however, there has been a growing interest in the poems' relationships with one another, leading to the conclusion that "The Defence of Guenevere" and "King Arthur's Tomb" are pendants and that similarly "Sir Galahad: A Christmas Mystery" and "The Chapel in Lyoness" are a kind of diptych. Meredith B. Raymond, asserting that the entire group is a "spiritual drama—a unit with a certain observable structure," tries to show the relationship between the two pairs. However, by stressing that in the first pair "the haughty and defiant Guenevere progresses toward . . . a recognition of her own guilt and weakness" and that in the second pair "the self centered Galahad progresses toward his role of savior," Raymond emphasizes a parallel rather than a unified structure ["The Arthurian Group in *The Defence of Guenevere and Other Poems,*" *Victorian Poetry* 4 (1960)]. I believe that the four poems can be read as a continuous whole and that each poem is dependent on all of the other three for its full resonance; that the four form a thematic whole in which Morris retells and redramatizes the romance-tragedy of the Arthurian cycle. The links between the poems are the seasonal-cyclical imagery; Morris' conflation of themes from Malory, particularly the tragedy of Lancelot and Guenevere and the quest of the Holy Grail; and the continued emphasis on Lancelot throughout the poems.

Seasonally, "The Defence of Guenevere" represents summer, "King Arthur's Tomb" represents autumn, "Sir Galahad: A Christmas Mystery" represents winter, and "The Chapel in Lyoness" represents spring. This representation is literal as well as imagistic: the seasonal time of each is stated. Not only is the time of Guenevere's defence implicitly summer (the blue sky, the green hopes), but twice she has occasion to mention "in the summer I grew white with flame" (l. 70) and "it was hottest summer" (l. 215). "King Arthur's Tomb" begins "Hot August noon" (l. 1). Sir Galahad's Christmas mystery occurs on "the longest night in all the year, / Near on the day when the Lord Christ was born" (ll. 1-2). And the action of "The Chapel at Lyoness" climaxes on Whitsunday, the seventh Sunday after Easter. Further the poems are laden with imagery correspondent to their season: "The Defence of Guenevere" reverberates with heat imagery, beginning with her "cheek of flame" (l. 7) continuing through "a spout of blood on the hot land" (l. 214) and climaxing with her "cheek grew crimson" (l. 292). This heat imagery corresponds not only to the summer but also to the passion of Guenevere's love, as do the brilliant colors of blazing blues, greens, crimsons and golds. From the tomb at the center of the action, literally and figuratively, death resonates outward in "King Arthur's Tomb." The autumnal mood is reflected in the surroundings, the pale grey backgrounds that are omnipresent in the poem. The imagery is appropriate not only to the autumn setting but also to the tragedy of Lancelot's and Guenevere's love, whereby they must "die" to each other. In "Sir Galahad: A Christmas Mystery" accumulated detail produces an almost physical impression of cold and weariness, appropriate for the winter poem in which Sir Galahad ironically laments his separation from passionate love. In "The Chapel at Lyoness" images of dawn, baptism, spring, and spiritual renewal (Whitsunday traditionally represents the descent of the Holy Spirit) contribute not only to the poem's seasonal setting but also to the romantic theme of Ozana's healing from a spiritual wound and Galahad's concept of spiritual rebirth, recognized explicitly as growing out of love. As the four poems progress seasonally from summer through fall and winter to spring, then, the Arthurian cycle progresses from comedy through tragedy and irony and back to romance.

Morris' Arthurian poems were written not only from sources in Malory but particularly for students of Malory: that is, they require a knowledge of Malory for their full comprehension. As all readers of Malory know, the dissolution of Arthur's round table society had two causes: the tragic relationship of Lancelot and Guenevere (individual vs. social good) and the tragedy of the knights' inability to achieve the Grail quest (idealism vs. realism). More importantly, all readers of Malory know that "while Queene Guenevere lived she was a true lover and therefore she had a good end" [Sir Thomas Malory, *Morte D'Arthur*, Book XVIII]. It is this relationship between the two themes that Morris plays upon in his Arthurian poems. His cycle shows Arthur's court not only "when the full glory of the summer day has passed and there remains the last gleams of sunset beauty" but also when the glory is being reborn in transcendent spiritual value. His cycle presents the comedy of the birth of love in spring, the romance of that love's maturity in summer, the tragedy of love's failure in fall, the irony of love's absence in winter, and the comedy of love's rebirth in spring. Furthermore, by stressing the progress of Lancelot, representative of both themes and of both passionate and spiritual love, throughout the four poems, he shows that spiritual love grows out of the earlier love, which by dying had been saved.

The season of "The Defence of Guenevere" is implicitly summer, but first and last the poem looks back to the spring of the Queen's love for Lancelot and forward to her "good end." It is this that makes the question of Guenevere's guilt a moot point: her guilt is relative to the point of time in the cycle. She herself changes her refrain

from "whatever *may have happened* through *those* years" (l. 47) to "whatever *happened* on through all *those* years" (l. 143), only to conclude "Whatever *may have happened these* long years" (l. 284, italics mine). The change is comparable to her own change in position, as she first remembers "the kiss / Wherewith we kissed in meeting that spring day" (ll. 133-34), continues through the summer when she "grew white with flame" (l. 70), and looks forward symbolically to "Christ's dear tears" (l. 286). It is well to remember, too, that Guenevere chose "heaven's color, the blue" (l. 38), which proves to be not "hell," as the angel says, but a kind of purgatory.

Several critics have commented on Morris' making Gauwaine Guenevere's chief accuser rather than keeping Mordred in that role as Malory had done. There are several reasons for this important change. First of all, Morris' Guenevere, for all her passionate pleading and posturing, is a highly dignified and regal person; she would be above defending herself to Mordred as she is above defending herself to Mellyagraunce:

> so must I defend
> the honor of the Lady Guenevere?
> Not so, fair lords, even if the world should end
> This very day, and you were judges here
> Instead of God. (ll. 181-85)

More importantly, having Gauwaine as accuser gives Guenevere the chance to allude to his mother Morgause's death for adultery:

> Do I not see how God's dear pity creeps
> All through your frame, and trembles in your
>   mouth?
> Remember in what grave your mother sleeps,
> Buried in some place far down in the south,
> Men are forgetting as I speak to you;
> By her head sever'd in that awful drouth
> Of pity that drew Agravaine's fell blow. . . . (ll. 151-57)

Both of these references by Guenevere imply the difference between God's final judgment and the judgment of man. Furthermore, the references would recall to Malory readers the treacherous manner in which Agravaine and his brothers had slain their widowed mother and her lover, the renowned Lamorak, and the treacherous manner in which Mellyagraunce had trapped Guenevere and Lancelot. In both cases, Guenevere condemns Gauwaine by association as she aligns her cause with the side of God:

> You, Gauwaine, held his word without a flaw.
> (l. 171)
>   Yet Mellyagraunce was shent
> For Mellyagraunce had fought against the Lord;
> Therefore, my lords, take heed lest you be blent
> With all this wickedness. (ll. 220-24)

Most important of all for Morris' purposes, having Gauwaine as accuser gives Guenevere the chance to refer to

> the mad fit
> That caught up Gauwaine—all, all verily. (ll. 280-81)

In context, she is referring to Gauwaine's vehement accusations against herself and Lancelot, but the phrasing could not but call to a Malory reader's mind Gauwaine's other mad fits: those in which he slew a lady, in which he insisted on participating in the Grail quest although warned by Arthur of his unworthiness, and in which he insisted on avenging the accidental deaths of his brothers Gareth and Gaheris at the hands of Lancelot. All of these mad fits were instrumental in destroying Arthur's round table. Gauwaine's actions, in Morris' poem, are further paralleled with Guenevere's own madness:

> and I knew verily,
> A little thing just then had made me mad. (ll. 117-18)

Thus, in the very first poem, Morris refers to the two tragedies that caused the dissolution of the round table, and implies that growing out of these tragedies will be the transcendent spiritual value which will save that society:

> I love God now a little, if this cord
> Were broken, once and for all, what striving could
> Make me love anything in earth or heaven? (ll. 90-92)

The idea is carried further in "King Arthur's Tomb":

> If even I go to hell, I cannot choose
> But love you, Christ, yea, though I cannot keep
> From loving Lancelot: O Christ! must I lose
> my own heart's love? (ll. 173-76)

Guenevere is praying, and, as she does in her earlier "Defence," she uses the argument of her own beauty:

> dost thou reck
> That I am beautiful, Lord, even as you
> And your dear Mother? Why did I forget
> You were so beautiful, and good, and true,
> That you loved me so, Guenevere? (ll. 168-172)

Here, however, her beauty is not the beauty of Nature. In "The Defence of Guenevere," the unity of Guenevere with the earth, spring, the sun, and the sea is one of the primary themes. In "King Arthur's Tomb," that unity is ultimately with all the works of God. Guenevere, in the later poem, is able to move from "I kiss, kiss, kiss Christ's feet" to "Ah! now I weep" (ll. 181-82). As a result of that unexplained weeping, she loses her madness (l. 194), and, far more importantly, she is able to call on Christ to "help me to save his Lancelot's soul!" (l. 207). She helps to save his soul from lying "curl'd Body and face and limbs in agony" (ll. 384-85) by refusing him the kiss he begs "for God's love" (l. 204). Lancelot speaks truer than he is aware when he says:

> I pray you, love,
> . . . slay me really, then we shall be heal'd
> Perchance, in the aftertime by God above. (ll. 365-67)

Guenevere does in fact "slay" Lancelot, as she herself realizes:

> Now I have slain him, Lord, let me go too, I pray.
> *Lancelot falls.*

> Alas, alas! I know not what to do
> If I run fast it is perchance that I
> May fall and stun myself, much better so,
> Never, never again! Not even when I die. (ll. 388-92)

"King Arthur's Tomb" presents the death of the God of vegetation in autumn, with the ritualistic promise of rebirth in spring implicit. As the passionate rhetoric of Guenevere's final words makes clear, it is not her love for Lancelot that has died. The whole poem is replete with her continued passion for her former lover. The paradox is that she, for God's dear love, denies him the kiss he begs for God's dear love. Her love for Lancelot is translated (or begins to be translated) into spiritual terms.

Morris, again departing from his source in Malory, has Lancelot meet Guenevere at Glastonbury rather than at Almesbury. The reason is obvious. Glastonbury is the site of Arthur's tomb, the thematic center of the poem. However, Morris retains the spiritual associations of Almesbury as well. Guenevere, who in the poem has not yet joined a convent, is described as follows: "all her robes were black, / With a long white veil only" (ll. 129-30). The description obviously points toward her ultimate conversion and cloistering.

Similarly, Guenevere refers to past events in Camelot and her references are well chosen. The tournament she recalls is one in which Tristram and Lancelot, for love of Iseult and Guenevere, are champions:

> 'Tristram for Iseult!' 'Iseult!' and 'Guenevere!'
> The ladies names bite verily like steel. (ll. 359-60)

But her description also shows the weaknesses inherent in the romantic love of Tristram and Iseult, Lancelot and Guenevere (according to Malory, the only pairs of true lovers in Camelot); she refers also to

> scowling Gauwaine, like the night in day,
> And handsome Gareth, with his great white hand
> Curl'd round the helm-crest, ere he join'd the fray;
> And merry Dinadan with sharp dark face
> All true knights love to see. (ll. 330-34)

Gauwaine and Gareth, of course, recall the "Defence," and one is reminded that it was while rescuing Guenevere from the fire that Lancelot had accidentally killed Gareth, thereby causing the division that would eventually divide the whole society. Merry Dinadan, too, was slain in the Grail quest, and his thematic role in Morris' poems will become even clearer in the next poem, "Sir Galahad: A Christmas Mystery." The point here is that the tournament, representing the height of the romance of the round table, already contains the seeds of that society's destruction. Morris makes the point explicit when Guenevere refers also to Palomydes:

> helmet off,
> he fought, his face brush'd by his hair,
> Red heavy swinging hair, he fear'd a scroff
> So overmuch, though what true knight would dare
> To mock that face, fretted with useless care,

And bitter useless striving after love? (ll. 337-42)

Palomydes, Malory's valiant knight who throughout his career loved Iseult hopelessly and futilely, gains significance in the next poem, "Sir Galahad: A Christmas Mystery." In this poem, a questioning Galahad compares his situation unfavorably not only with that of Lancelot but also with that of Palomydes:

> Is he not able still to hold his breath
> With thoughts of Iseult? doth he not grow pale
>   with weary striving, to seem best of all
> To her, "as she is best," he saith? to fail
>   is nothing to him, he can never fall.
>
> For unto such a man love-sorrow is
>   so dear a thing unto his constant heart
> That even if he never win one kiss,
>   or touch from Iseult, it will never part.
>
> And he will never know her to be worse
>   Than in his happiest dreams he thinks she is;
> Good knight, and faithful, you have 'scaped the
>   curse
>   In wonderful-wise; you have great store of
>   bliss. (ll. 28-40)

The comparison is significant because the association of Lancelot and Palomydes implies the "spiritual" or Platonic aspect of the Lancelot-Guenevere relationship. The poem is set in winter because Galahad feels that he must give up the ennobling effects of love as well as its physical aspects, both the spirit and the flesh. The Christmas vision tries to warn him, telling him that Lancelot

> is just what you know, O Galahad,
>   This love is happy even as you say (ll. 105-06)

and that Palomydes

> wears away, my servant, too. (l. 121)

The vision also tells Galahad that Lancelot "old and shrivll'd . . . shall win my love" (l. 113), but more importantly the vision reminds him to

> Meantime, take note whose sword first made
>   him knight
> And who has loved him alway. (ll. 102-3)

The spirituality of Lancelot is further hinted when Galahad refers to him as "Father Lancelot." Galahad's reference is literal: Lancelot is his father; but the phrasing is also an implicit reference to Lancelot's later becoming a holy man.

"Sir Galahad: A Christmas Mystery," then, suggests that Lancelot is inherently spiritual. Galahad, however, fails to recognize this spirituality, and before he can find "Hard by, Sir Lancelot . . . in some short space upon that ship," he must first not only meet the sister of Percival, Percival, and Bors, but he must also be armed by the ladies of the vision. Quite significantly, the first of those ladies, who puts on his hauberk, is Margaret of Antioch, to whom Lancelot had compared Guenevere in "King Arthur's Tomb" (l. 78). Armed with the Biblical armor of righteousness, Galahad's first question is of Lancelot: "Tell me what news of Lancelot you have" (l. 183). The answer

comes from Sir Bors, who in Malory had been granted a glimpse of the Grail for his unselfish devotion to Lancelot's cause instead of his own:

> from the court nought good;
> Poor merry Dinadan, that with jape and scoff
>   Kept us all merry, in a little wood
> Was found all hack'd and dead: Sir Lionel
>   And Gauwaine have come back from the
>   great quest
> Just merely shamed; and Lauvaine, who loved
>   well
>   your father Lancelot, and at the king's behest
> Went out to seek him, but was almost slain,
>   Perhaps is dead now; everywhere
> The knights come foil'd from the great quest, in
>   vain;
>   In vain they struggle for the vision fair. (ll.
>   191-200)

And so the poem ends. Once again Morris has made reference to the causes of the destruction of Arthur's court, and the winter of Galahad's despair closes on that note of destruction; Gauwaine is shamed, Lauvaine cannot find Lancelot, and Dinadan, at whom Lancelot and Guenevere laughed in the summer of their love, is dead, slain treacherously by Mordred and Agravaine.

The narrative continues directly in the next and last of Morris' Arthurian poems, "The Chapel in Lyoness." The poem begins with Ozana's mystically rhythmic chant:

> All day long and every day
> From Christmas-Eve to Whit-Sunday
> Within that Chapel-aisle I lay,
>   And no man came a-near. (ll. 1-4)

Since "Sir Galahad: A Christmas Mystery" had occurred "near on the day the Lord Christ was born," the chapel represents a direct continuation of the narrative. Moreover, Ozana is presented suffering from a spiritual wound:

> Naked to the waist was I,
> And deep within my breast did lie,
> Though no man any blood could spy,
>   The truncheon of a spear.
>
> Many a time I tried to shout;
> But as in dream of battle-rout,
> My frozen speech would not well out;
>   I could not even weep. (ll. 5-8, 17-20)

The absence of blood makes clear that the wound is not merely a physical one; the inability to weep shows that it is a spiritual one.

Ozana was a more or less typical knight of Arthur's round table, and perhaps Morris chose him to represent the society for that reason. He is, however, connected with Lancelot and Guenevere in what is, perhaps, a tenuous way. He was one of the knights who accompanied Guenevere on her disastrous Maying expedition, which indicates that Ozana was one of the chosen knights of Guenevere. In Morris' poem, Galahad also associates Ozana with Lancelot:

> All my singing moved him not;
> As I sung my heart grew hot,
> With the thought of Lancelot. (ll. 37-39)

The association is central to Morris' poem, for it explains Ozana's two epitaphic songs:

> "Ozana of the hardy heart,
>   Knight of the Table Round
> Pray for his soul, lords of your part;
>   A *true* knight he was found"
> Ah! me, I cannot fathom it.
>
> "Ozana of the hardy heart,
>   Knight of the Table Round,
> Pray for his soul, lords, on your part;
>   A *good* knight he was found."
> Now I begin to fathom it. (ll. 29-33, 76-80, italics
>   mine)

Between the two songs, Galahad has picked a "faint, wild rose," laid the dew-laden flower across Ozana's mouth— "the sparkling drops seem'd good for drouth" (l. 51)—and given him the kiss of salvation. These acts of spiritual salvation, a form of the extreme unction, in fact, have changed Ozana from a "true" knight to a "good" knight and allowed him to "begin to fathom it." This is the change that Morris, taking his hint from Malory, has shown in Lancelot and Guenevere: while they lived they were true lovers, and therefore they had a good end. "The Chapel at Lyoness" even presents that good end in terms of the earlier passionate love:

> Ozana, shall I pray for thee?
>   Her cheek is laid to thine;
> No long time hence, also I see
>   Thy wasted fingers twine
> Within the tresses of her hair
>   That shineth gloriously,
> Thinly outspread in the clear air
>   Against the jasper sea. (ll. 85-92)

Here the man is Ozana and the woman is Percival's sister, but the vision concludes the cycle of Morris' Arthurian poems by showing the transcendent spiritual value that arose from the destruction of Arthur's court. In his cycle, Morris has shown that romantic love, born in spring, achieves its victory in summer; then, romantic love in an autumnal setting finds that reverence for the laws of the soul is necessary for mature love; finally, the one pure in heart achieves the consummation of holy love, showing how all loves unite finally in the love of Christ. (pp. 114-22)

> *Audrey Shaw Bledsoe, "The Seasons of Came-*
> *lot: William Morris' Arthurian Poems," in*
> South Atlantic Bulletin, *Vol. XLII, No. 4, No-*
> *vember, 1977, pp. 114-22.*

James Douglas Merriman

[*In the following excerpt, Merriman examines Sir Walter Scott's* The Bridal of Triermain, *Scott's one attempt to deal at length with the Arthurian legend. Merriman suggests that, since Scott accepted the poetic truth of the Arthurian legend and refused to alter or rearrange its major elements in his poem, the work "may be justly described as the first example of the distinctly modern reflowering of the legend."*]

[Sir Walter Scott's] acquaintance with chivalric romance was wide; his affection for it, a dominant motif in his imaginative life. And for the man who edited *Sir Tristrem* and for long contemplated doing the same for Malory, romance meant above all else the undying thrills of Arthurian romance:

> . . . on the ancient minstrel strain
> Time lays his palsied hand in vain;
> And . . . our hearts at doughty deeds,
> By warriors wrought in steely weeds,
> Still throb for fear and pity's sake;
> As when the Champion of the Lake
> Enters Morgana's fated house,
> Or in the Chapel Perilous
> Despising spells and demons' force,
> Holds converse with the unburied corse;
> Or when, Dame Ganore's grace to move,
> (Alas, that lawless was their love!)
> He sought proud Tarquin in his den,
> And freed full sixty knights; or when,
> A sinful man, and unconfess'd,
> He took the Sangreal's holy quest,
> And, slumbering, saw the vision high,
> He might not view with waking eye.

That Scott himself as late as 1807-1808 when these lines were written still intended to fulfill [the prediction that more would be written about Arthur] seems clear:

> The mightiest chiefs of British song
> Scorn'd not such legends to prolong:
>
>   . . . . .
>
> Warm'd by such names, well may we then,
> Though dwindled sons of little men,
> Essay to break a feeble lance
> In the fair fields of old romance.

Yet despite all his enthusiasm and all his knowledge, the quest was not for Scott. The subject lay outside his own creative range, and in the end, the lance that he did finally break in the lists of Arthurian romance was among his feeblest.

Of Scott's one attempt to deal at length with Arthurian materials, *The Bridal of Triermain* (1813), few of his admirers would be inclined to say that it is either very characteristic or very impressive as a poem. Even its genesis and the peculiar circumstances surrounding its publication suggest that Scott's own attitude toward the poem was one of uncertainty or uneasily mixed purposes. Begun originally with no intention beyond furnishing a fragmentary "imitation" of his own style printed under the name "Caleb Quotem," the poem seems to have strangely seized Scott's fancy. But even when he completed it as a serious work, he held on to the deception of publishing it as a professed imitation by an unnamed author who was suspected, as Scott intended, to be his friend William Erskine. Just what the ultimate motives were for this "systematic mystification" is not altogether certain; Scott's later explanation that it was a trap for the reviewers is probably honest as far as he knew his own mind, but certain elements in the deception suggest a more complex motive.

Even more obscure are the reasons for the peculiarly elaborated structure of the work as a whole. The poem begins with a lengthy Introduction in which a modern minstrel named Arthur woos his purse- and class-proud mistress Lucy by singing a romance "Of errant knight and damozelle; / Of the dread knot a wizard tied, / In punishment of maiden's pride" [I, viii]. Within the romance of the medieval Sir Roland de Vaux's quest which the lovesick minstrel sings, there is yet another romance, "a mystic tale, by bard and sage, / . . . handed down from Merlin's age" (I, ix), told by one Lyulph, which traces the antecedent history of Gyneth, the sleeping beauty whom Sir Roland finally rouses from the five hundred years' sleep to which her fatal pride had brought her.

The poem thus involves three lines of action. Of these the first, the framing device in which the narrator Arthur woos and ultimately wins the proud Lucy in spite of social and economic obstacles, seems on the surface to be a quite arbitrary addition to the romance of Roland and Gyneth. The various introductory and concluding passages in which the Arthur-Lucy story is developed are, it is true, in keeping with the general motif of the marriage quest, but it is equally true that they serve no necessary function of development or clarification of either that motif or of the poem as a whole. Even the pious Lockhart was constrained to describe them as "unfortunate" [in his *The Life of Sir Walter Scott,* 1937]. Nevertheless, if they have no function in the public poem, they may have had an important place in the poet's private fantasy world, and their presence hints at an explanation for Scott's curious impulses toward concealment manifested in both the publication of the poem and in the poem itself.

What the secret was is suggested by the fact that the scenery and the style of life portrayed in the framing story are clearly those of Gilsland, the small watering place where Scott himself had wooed and won Charlotte Charpentier in 1797. Following this clue, Dame Una Pope-Hennessy [in her *Sir Walter Scott,* 1948] has noted that "we may read a lyrical rendering" of Scott's courtship in the Introductions. Such a reading, however, scarcely accounts for the description of the young minstrel's love as "Lucy of the lofty eye, / Noble in birth, in fortunes high, / She for whom lords and barons sigh" (Introduction to Canto I, iii). There is nothing to suggest that Charlotte was haughty, and whatever other valuable qualities she may have had, she was if anything somewhat below her young husband in both rank and fortune. To find the real original of Lucy, we must look to Scott's earlier love, Williamina Belsches, a young lady whom Grierson describes as "certainly his most passionate . . . love" [*Sir Walter Scott, Barto: A New Life Supplementary to, and Corrective of, Lockhart's Biography,* 1938]. Williamina, unfortunately, had belonged "by birth and expectations . . . to a higher level of society" than her suitor, and she ended by rejecting a bitterly disappointed Scott in whose breast the pain of injured merit still rankled years afterwards. In real life there was nothing to be done about the "social wants that sin against the strength of youth," but in the world of fantasy the spirit could have its victory. Thus in the Introductions, Scott, reversing the unpleasant facts, handily combined the longed-for Williamina with the successful and lyric courtship at Gilsland of the obtained Charlotte. The actual winning of the proud fair, passed over in silence in the Introductions, was expressed in symbolic terms at yet

another remove from the hateful jars of reality; it is in the story of Sir Roland that the hero manages by overcoming dozens of supernatural obstacles to make clear his real worth and thus to liberate the lady from her spell of pride to live happily ever after with the poor but noble baron.

The process of redressing the disappointments of life by romantic fantasy was abiding in Scott. Usually it takes the relatively innocent form that we find in the story of Sir Roland, a form in which the frail, bookish, game-legged Edinburgh advocate was able to see himself as a noble and martial young man who wins fame, wealth, and love in a series of freely invented adventures. But that was not enough this time—the psychic damage of Williamina's rejection required stronger medicine, and thus the Introductions, wholly redundant and diffusive from an artistic standpoint, were added to satisfy the subconscious longing. But with this, the guilty wish came too near the surface. Hence the elaborate and prolonged efforts at concealment, at transferring—quite ambiguously to be sure—the authorship by means of an almost obsessively labored hoax to Erskine. And hence, perhaps, even the confusing structure and the strangely split moral burden of the poem. The overt moral of Roland's quest is unexceptionable: success attends valiant self-control; but there is another darker moral buried in the third layer of the poem, Lyulph's Tale: pride brings on a living death. It is as if the dangerous latent content had found a structural means to conceal itself—even from the poem's author. Such an interpretation is not labored for the cheap purpose of laying bare the pathetic self-deception of one of the most greathearted gentlemen our literature has known. Were that all to be derived from the inquiry, the mystery of the unsatisfactory structure of *The Bridal of Triermain* might well have been left unexplained. But the role of personal fantasy in the explanation of Scott's failure to write a great Arthurian poem is too large to be ignored.

What remains of the poem after the otiose Introductions are cleared away is a more or less typically Scottian romance into which an Arthurian episode of almost equal length has been inserted. Sir Roland de Vaux, Baron of Triermain, dreams in his sleep of a maiden so lovely that he decides she must be his bride; in order to find out if she is real, he sends to Lyulph, a "sage of power / . . . sprung from druid sires" (I, vi), who informs him that the damsel is indeed real and still to be won "though there have glided since her birth, / Five hundred years and one" (I, ix), a marvel which he explains in the lengthy intercalated "Lyulph's Tale." Learning that Gyneth, the maiden of his dreams, lies in spellbound sleep in a mysterious disappearing castle in the Vale of St. John, Roland goes there and after difficulties finally manages to enter the castle where he bravely strides unharmed through a hall of tigers, resists the riches offered by four maidens, and afterwards the advances of four oriental "slaves to love" (III, xxxi). Leaving them in order to go "where the feelings of the heart / With the warm pulse in concord move; / . . . where Virtue sanctions love" (III, xxxii), he next endures a dark, poisonous passageway, and finally the offer of royal power proffered by French, German, and Spanish maids. At his assertion that he prefers to be "A free-born Knight of England free, / Than sit on Despot's throne" (III, xxxvi), a fourth maiden—of England—declares that the spell has been broken by Roland, who has thus surmounted Fear and the "snares . . . / Spread by Pleasure, Wealth, and Pride" (III, xxxvi). Roland rushes on, finds and wakens the lovely Gyneth as lightning flashes, thunder rolls, and the castle falls asunder.

While there is nothing specifically Arthurian in this freely invented story, the range of Scott's vocabulary of stock medieval story motifs is a signal illustration of how long and how deeply he had drunk at the well of old romance. The central formula of the quest for the dreamed-of maiden is derived from Chaucer's *Tale of Sir Thopas,* as the motto on the title page of the poem as well as its irregularly rhymed octosyllabics and trimeters suggest. For such other standard motifs as the spellbound maiden and the disappearing castle that falls to the ground when a spell is broken, it is pointless to search for specific inspiration, although for the allegorized temptations that Roland overcomes, Spenser may be confidently offered as the source.

How Gyneth came to be in the situation from which Roland rescues her is the subject of "Lyulph's Tale," the only properly Arthurian part of *The Bridal of Triermain.* Long, long ago, King Arthur, having left Guenever at home and ridden out in search of adventure, entered a castle of maidens and there easily fell into dalliance with Guendolen, a child of a human mother and a pagan Genie. When the time finally came for Arthur's departure, Guendolen shed a tear and "pressed / The foldings of her silken vest! / At her reproachful sign and look, / The hint the monarch's conscience took" (II, vi-vii), and so he swore that if Guendolen's child should be a son, it would be his heir, and if a girl, then

> To chuse that maid a fitting spouse,
> A summer day in lists shall strive
> My knights,—the bravest knights alive,—
> And he, the best and bravest tried,
> Shall Arthur's daughter claim for bride. (II, vii)

In the fifteen years that followed, Arthur overcame the Saxons in twelve battles, killed the giant Rython, and defeated Lucius of Rome. Then one Pentecost day as Arthur sits feasting with his knights there comes a maid on a white palfrey. It is Gyneth, his daughter by Guendolen, and she claims the performance of his vow. In the competition that ensues, all the knights join save Tristrem, Lancelot, and Caradoc,

> And still these lovers' fame survives
> For faith so constant shown,—
> There were two who loved their neighbours' wives,
> And one who loved his own. (II, xviii)

Observing the heat of the conflict that follows, Arthur begs Gyneth to stop the fight before any of his knights are killed, but she proudly refuses, and he, bound by his oath, allows the fight to continue until "seemed in this dismal hour, that Fate / Would Camlan's ruin antedate, / And spare dark Mordred's crime" (II, xxv). Just at this moment, however, a young kinsman of Merlin's is mortally wounded, and the magician, arriving in a storm, stops the fight and lays on Gyneth for her pride a chilling curse: she

shall sleep in lone penance in the Vale of St. John until a knight "for feat of arms as far renowned / As Warrior of the Table Round" (II, xxvi) shall wake her. Who that knight will be some five hundred years later has already been seen.

In this episode, as in that of Roland de Vaux, Scott has again freely combined stock elements from medieval romance. The castle full of maidens with a princess who is got with child by a visiting knight he might have had from the story of either Lancelot or Percival; the coming to court of the child of such a liaison may easily have been derived from the story of Galahad. But it is not sources that are of real interest here. What is of the last moment is the approach that Scott has taken toward his material. Abandoning the method of arbitrary recasting of the central story that Spenser and Dryden had followed, Scott was content to sketch in the major outlines of the old legend unchanged, and to attach loosely to that story a new and original episode. It was, of course, the approach that many of the medieval romancers had followed, and by which the central legend of Arthur had been swelled to an immense body of stories. But more importantly, it was an approach born out of the new Romantic temper, a temper that fully and reverently accepted Arthurian romance as true—true poetically—and therefore not subject to arbitrary alteration and rearrangement. In this respect *The Bridal of Triermain* may be justly described as the first example of the distinctly modern reflowering of the legend.

This is not, of course, to say that it is fully satisfactory either as a treatment of the Arthurian story or even as a poem of any sort. Its structure, whatever subconscious satisfaction it may have afforded Scott, is defective, and its hero is an insipid projection of Scott's daydreams. Indeed, it is not too much to say that the whole poem is stultified by a pervasive immaturity, best suggested, perhaps, by the jejune "moral truth in fiction's veil" (Conclusion, ii) with which Roland de Vaux's adventure ends:

> . . . this was what remain'd of all
> The wealth of each enchanted hall,
>   The Garland and the Dame:—
> But where should warrior seek the meed,
> Due to high worth for daring deed,
>   Except from LOVE and FAME! (III, xxxix)

If such sentiments are innocuous, they are also vapid. Things are not quite that simple in either life or literature, and in fact such a view is likely to blunt the sense for finer distinctions in both ranges of experience.

Something of this coarsened perception seems to be involved, at any rate, in Scott's view of the central Arthurian story as it appears in *The Bridal of Triermain.* The standard fixtures of the legend, as we have seen, he leaves unaltered: the Arthur-Guenever-Lancelot triangle, Arthur's triumphs over Saxons, giants, and Rome, and the foreshadowed fatal battle at Camlan with Mordred. Similarly, the tradition of Arthur's court as a center of chivalry, a bulwark against anarchy and paganism, is carefully preserved:

> . . . all who suffered causeless wrong,
> From tyrant proud or faitor strong,
> Sought Arthur's presence to complain,

Nor there for aid implored in vain. (II, xi)

But Scott's reading of Arthur's character departs so widely from tradition that the final product is a great deal closer to an indiscreet Regency clubman than to the *flos regum* of romance. From the "wily monarch" who calculatingly "guess'd" that Guendolen's initial reserve showed "more ardent passions in the breast" (I, xxi) to the shamefaced lover who promises the injured maid to provide for his by-blow, Scott's Arthur cuts a poor figure, and the situation is little improved by the author's pedestrian reflection: "Where lives the man that has not tried, / How mirth can into folly glide, / And folly into sin!" (I, xxi). It is true, of course, that the younger Arthur of the old romances twice fell into amorous dalliance, but that was *before* his marriage with Guenevere. And there is nothing in the romances that could have justified an Arthur who "lies loitering in a lady's bower" while

> The Saxon stern, the pagan Dane
> Maraud on Britain's shores again.
>
> . . . . .
>
> Heroic plans in pleasure drown'd,
> He thinks not of the Table Round;
> In lawless love dissolved his life,
> He thinks not of his beauteous wife. (II, i-ii)

Nor does the discovery of this liaison disturb Guenever when she sees Gyneth's reception by Arthur; on the contrary, in what amounts to an ethic of sexual reciprocity, she gazes "unruffled at the scene, / Of human frailty construed mild, / Looked upon Lancelot, and smiled" (II, xv). Frere's Whistlecraft could scarcely have debased the conscience-searing tragedy of the lovers of the legend more ruinously.

This reduction of the "huge cloudy symbols" of romance to beings of such all-too-human stature suggests that it is perhaps just as well that Scott never attempted an independent retelling of the central story of Arthur's birth, triumphs, betrayal, and defeat. For although at first glance Scott, with all his antiquarian interests and his love for old romance, seems the ideal man to have presented that story anew to the world, the fact is that the legend was as far outside his creative range as its tragic spirit was beyond his sensibility. What did stir his creative impulses may be seen in one after another of Scott's chivalric romances: a poor but noble young man—a sort of Horatio Alger hero in plate armor—through a profusion of exciting deeds of derring-do manifests to all the world the ambition, valiance, strength, and honor that ultimately win for him fame, wealth, and love. It was, of course, Scott's beloved personal fantasy, but it was also a fantasy he shared with thousands upon thousands of readers. When to this formula Scott added his magical and lovingly detailed reconstruction of a glamorous past, he achieved the zenith of his own aims, and the delight of his audience—in whom the spirit of historical curiosity was steadily quickening under the influence of the Romantic revival—knew no bounds.

But the essential Arthur story was radically unsuitable for such development. In its somber world of strained and divided loyalties, of honor shattered on the paradoxes of existence, of high and noble aims grievously defeated, there was no place for facile wish-fulfillment to operate. Here ideals and bravery earned no automatic dividends, and here human love was not happy reward but melancholy pain. From such a story Scott's fantasying impulse doubtless drew back with a shivering awareness of its inability to survive in such dark waters. Nor was Arthurian romance congenial to Scott's other basic impulse—that of a sedulous reconstruction of the past. For the story of Arthur, as Scott must have realized, can be assigned to no actual past. Its King and his knights belong neither to the sixth century in which the annalists would put them, nor to the twelfth century from which they took their chivalric traits. They belong instead to a vaguely medieval world in which the physical facts that Scott loved to marshal matter little, and in which the emotional facts, which were beyond Scott's ability to deal with, count for everything.

Thus although long beguiled by the story, which he seems to have loved deeply and sincerely, Scott in the end produced only *The Bridal of Triermain* in which a hasty outline of the Arthurian legend is used as background for a newly invented and mythically irrelevant tale of adventure. It is significant of the coming attitude that Scott refrained from any wholesale recasting of the central story, and doubtless his example moved others to the same respect for the legend. But in terms of direct effect, outside of two hackwork dramatizations of the poem, *The Bridal of Triermain* seems to have had little influence on the subsequent development of the story in the nineteenth century. To that development Scott's contribution was made in other ways. He created not Arthurian poems, but rather an audience eager for them. He, more than any other man, made the world of medieval romance an integral part of the mental fabric of the nineteenth century, and, he, beyond all other exemplars, sent a generation of poets to

> . . . seek the moated castle's cell,
> Where long through talisman and spell,
> While tyrants rul'd, and damsels wept,
> Thy Genius, Chivalry, hath slept.

(pp. 150-58)

James Douglas Merriman, "Arthur Wakes in Avalon: Arthurian Literature of the Romantic Period," in his The Flower of Kings: A Study of the Arthurian Legend in England between 1485 and 1835, *The University Press of Kansas, 1973, pp. 137-77.*

THE ARTHURIAN LEGEND IN THE VISUAL ARTS

Debra N. Mancoff

[*In the following excerpt, Mancoff explores the close connections between literature, painting, and national identity as demonstrated in the treatment of the Arthurian legend during the Victorian period.*]

> There came a bark that, blowing forward, bore
> King Arthur, like a modern gentleman
> Of stateliest port; and all the people cried,
> Arthur is come again: he cannot die.
>   Alfred Tennyson, "The Epic," 1842

The idealistic spirit of the Victorian age found an eloquent incarnation in the figure of a medieval king. For the duration of Queen Victoria's reign King Arthur served as a potent symbol: for sovereignty, for national spirit, for gentlemanly virtue. The legendary king conceived by the Victorians, however, was neither the battle-worn chieftain of post-Roman conflicts nor the courtly king and leader of a renowned circle of champions. The Victorian Arthur was a fully contemporary man, medieval in dress and context but fully modern in ethos, intention, and sentiment. Arthur had been returned to the Victorians as Tennyson saw him, as "a modern gentleman/Of stateliest port."

To the Victorian imagination Arthur was not an historical man but a metaphor, a means to express the idealism and aspiration of the present in the ennobling raiment of a glorious past. The conceptual basis of the Victorian legend was the same as that behind the legend in medieval times, employing the legend as a didactic mirror, to express strong moral and social truths, gentled by a form and setting in the distant and undefined past. The lessons of the legend were regarded as the legacy of a mythic, golden age. Arthur existed in mythological times, not in history. In both use and in interpretation Victorian interest in the saga of King Arthur constituted a full-scale revival of the legend, the first since medieval times. In art it was nothing short of a renaissance.

Throughout its long history the Arthurian legend found its grandest expression in literature. It was first in the oral and then in the written tradition that Arthur and his story evolved. A gradual development transformed a shadowy war chieftain who struggled boldly against Saxon invaders into a monarch of incomparable status who presided over a sophisticated court. The high-medieval Arthur appeared in an aura of civility, virtue, and honor. Interest in the members of Arthur's court waxed and waned, but in Britain the warrior-turned-monarch maintained his firm position as a symbol for the culture.

From the twelfth century forward a tangential development occurred in the visual arts. Fully dependent upon the literature, medieval Arthurian imagery was narrative in form and existed in a sympathetic relationship with the literature through the latter's zenith in the late Middle Ages. During the Renaissance, when Arthurian reference served as propaganda for the Houses of Tudor and Stuart, imagery's supporting role was diminished. In the last decades of the seventeenth century and the first half of the eighteenth century, when interest in the legend lapsed into skepticism and burlesque, the literature declined, but the visual arts disappeared.

During the second half of the eighteenth century Britain's medieval heritage won new regard. The Gothic Revival turned attentive imagination to the relics of ancient national architecture and literature. A new audience began to school in the medieval tradition. Through this sensibility the decline of the legend in literature was slowly re-

versed; by the second decade of the nineteenth century Sir Thomas Malory's late-medieval epic *Le Morte Darthur* (1469-70), out of print for centuries, returned to circulation. The public, relearning the language of the legend, gained the intellectual and interpretative habits that would lead them to recraft the legend for themselves.

A full revival of the Arthurian tradition did not begin, however, until the first decade of the Victorian era. The Arthurian Revival was inextricably tied to the evolution of modern temper. The later years of the Gothic Revival had inspired new romances, peopled with figures possessed of modern sentiments in the novels of Sir Walter Scott. Chivalry had been reinterpreted for the modern age in the popular treatises of Kenelm Digby. It was not until these habits of thought converged with self-identity and nationalism that an audience, trained to project its own message into an ancient legend, could be found. This synthesis of thought occurred in the Victorian era when the public, at last fully fluent in the tradition, was ready to accept and understand a legend of its own. Only then did the contemporary audience find its own image in the poems of Alfred Tennyson, who wrote his society's Arthuriad, a project that endured for the length of his career. When the legend thus emerged as the sanctioned national epic in the Victorian era, it did so as a telling moral metaphor, speaking to a generation able to comprehend the ideals of present aspiration through allusion to the past.

It is significant that a major contribution of the Victorian era to the Arthurian tradition was a new interpretation of the legend in the visual arts. The interest in the legend early in the century had not significantly affected the arts. No new corpus of imagery accompanied the renewal of interest in ancient literature. The Arthurian Revival in the arts was, in every way, a Victorian phenomenon. It depended on the intellectual temper and the pervasiveness of the chivalric metaphor rather than familiarity with Arthurian story for its eloquence. Furthermore, the art of the Arthurian Revival marked an unprecedented achievement in the history of the tradition; the first works to address Arthurian subjects broke the customary narrative dependence on literary development and rose in an independent course. The Victorian interpretation of Arthurian subjects in art formulated a distinct set of visual and iconographic conventions. It was as representative of the currents of language in the visual arts as it was responsive to the inspiration of the canon of literature. Arthurian subjects were undertaken independent of text. Their communicative modes were derived from the practice of painting, rather than the narration of prose and poetry. For the first time in the history of the legend imagery developed as an entity distinct from the literature. During the Arthurian Revival the visual and verbal arts grew in parallel accord, defying the traditional dependency of image on text, and, in an unprecedented development, formative expressional ideas were manifest in art in advance of the literature.

To grasp the eloquence of this body of imagery it is necessary to set the works in their iconological context and to regard them as vessels for ideology throughout their stylistic and iconographical evolution. The study of these works demands the study of the conventions that shaped them, going out from the works to their sources—historical, philosophical, social, literary, and expressional—and returning to them to discover their original reception and, in result, return to them their original meaning.

The ability of the Victorian imagination to forge and extend the metaphor was born in the conventions of ideation developed during the Gothic Revival. What began as extrinsic factors of influence for the birth of the Revival became the intrinsic principles of Arthurian expression. The early, escapist fantasies of Gothic Revival literature led to the more scholarly, archaeological interest that, in turn, returned the legend first as fragment and then in Malory's canonical version to currency. The Gothic Revival created the audience for the Arthurian Revival, and the endeavors of resurrecting national literature gave that audience a fluency. Habits of the later Gothic Revival—popular medievalism, the revival of chivalry, and the creation of modern heroes in medieval guise—trained another generation in interpretation and in self-definition. The figures of the medieval world soon embodied a subtle familiarity, and their creeds were reinvented for the present. As a result the popular image of the chivalric hero came to resemble the modern man, and, conversely, the modern gentleman sought to emulate the ancient knight. The translation of the chivalric hero from a shadowy ancestor, known through arcane fragments of art and poetry, into a model for the modern British gentleman led directly to the interpretive mode at work in the Arthurian Revival.

In the decade before Victoria's accession chivalry reached a cult status. Young aristocrats enacted the conceits of earlier times in pageants, parties, and mock tournaments. At the same time, however, a strong link was forged between the ideals of the chivalric world and the quest for social improvement, seen in the ideological bases of treatises on chivalry and the formation of the Young England party. With the coronation of Victoria in 1837 came the promise of a new future. The conventions of thought of the immediate previous generations exerted a powerful influence on the present. The new idealistic intentions modified the vision of the past, and the Arthurian Revival, while drawing upon the interpretive methods and the widespread enthusiasms generated by the Gothic Revival, departed from the impulses that brought them into being. The Arthurian Revival must be seen in the context of the Gothic Revival, as a last and powerful surge of the forces that stimulated interest in medievalism, but at the same time, as a metamorphosis of that spirit that irrevocably changed its impetus and, through the Arthurian metaphor, led the revivalist spirit to its inevitable end.

When the Arthurian metaphor was instituted as an iconographic mode in the service of a governmental commission in painting, it was further subject to the conventions of art. The Arthurian subjects returned to the British artist's repertoire, after centuries of neglect, through a government commission. In 1848, upon the recommendation of Prince Albert, the painter William Dyce was contracted to design and execute a cycle of frescoes for the Queen's Robing Room in the new Palace at Westminster. The appropriate genre for the commission was history painting; it was from this that Dyce drew his mode of interpretation and his

---

> **During the Arthurian Revival the visual and verbal arts grew in parallel accord, defying the traditional dependency of image on text, and, in an unprecedented development, formative expressional ideas were manifest in art in advance of the literature.**
>
> —*Debra N. Mancoff*

---

conventions. Dyce used the Arthurian legend as a source for high-minded allegory. He regarded Arthur and his companions as personifications of timeless British virtues and he sought to use them in an allegorical framework. The Arthurian heroes presented by Dyce had only a shred of medievalism. In form, action, and message they were equivalent to the Neoclassical heroes that dominated the genre in the previous century.

Dyce took an ethical view of the legend as illustrative of national character. In his editorial voice and his moral stance he forecasted the approach Tennyson would take in the following decades in the *Idylls of the King*. For the duration of the Arthurian Revival in art Dyce remained the public voice of the legend. His works served as the prototypes for painters of the legend for the next two generations. He shared with Tennyson the position of premier interpreter of the legend. The court painter and the Poet Laureate gave the legend an official sanction. Not since the reign of Edward III had the Arthurian story been so closely and strongly tied to the government.

The fresco project in the Queen's Robing Room generated interest in Arthurian imagery in the 1850s. The publication of the first installment of the *Idylls of the King* at the end of the decade provided additional stimulus, and other artists undertook their own interpretation of the legend. The Pre-Raphaelites, already drawn to the poetry of Tennyson and the work of Dyce at Westminster, addressed the subject with energy and ingenuity. Soon two forms of the legend existed, the public and didactic saga of Dyce and the private and romantic vision of Dante Gabriel Rossetti and William Morris.

Arthurian expression came to full popularity in the 1860s and the 1870s. Every sector in the art world embraced the evocative iconography. Academic artists, including James Archer, Joseph Noël Paton, and Thomas Woolner, followed the examples set by Dyce, depicting monumental, classicizing figures engaged in noble actions, while adherents of Pre-Raphaelitism, most notably Rossetti, Edward Burne-Jones, and Arthur Hughes, preferred poignant vignettes of love. Literary sources were freely mixed. Artists drew from both Tennyson and Malory, as well as their own inventive visions, but it was painting rather than literature that influenced their interpretations. Eventually popular literature so widened the audience for Arthurian story that the expression in art inevitably changed. What began as an exclusive language in a monarchical commission expanded to address increasingly larger concerns in broader genre, from the world of Victorian art patronage through academic painting and works for private patrons to the general, literate public in illustrated books, in luxury and economy editions. This circumstance encapsulated the course of popularity of the legend in the medieval era; what began as a tradition attached to court patronage widened to the vernacular. Popular dissemination was the source of eventual demise.

During the last decades of the century Arthurian imagery began to betray the decline of Victorian aspiration. From its inception the art of the Revival was a mirror for national ideals, and with the increasing questioning and skepticism of the vague creeds of faith and aspiration by the last generation of Victorians came a darker vision of the legend. The image of the Fallen Hero supplanted that of the confident gentleman-knight. Subjects implying the failure of Arthur's order appear most significantly in the works of such artists as Joseph Noël Paton, William Holman Hunt, and John William Waterhouse and their obsession with the iconography of loss: the passing of Arthur and the Lady of Shalott. The heroic figure was replaced by an attenuated, androgynous form, seen in the languid knights of Burne-Jones and the erotic phantoms of Aubrey Beardsley. Implicit in the original choice of the legend was the cyclical narrative. The inherent structure of the legend dictates that Arthur's society must fail. In their optimism the early Victorians disregarded the warning of the legend, and their progeny were destined to act out the cycle. By the turn of the century Arthurian interest persisted only in book illustration, retreating into the former dependency on the literature. The debacle of World War I gave the death blow to Victorian idealism, and the Arthurian Revival, as conceived by its originators, faded into obscurity. Called into being as a self-conscious and self-defining allegory, the imagery of the Arthurian Revival charted the course of Victorian aspiration, flowering shortly after the coronation, developing through the reign, and waning at the end of the epoch.

Seen outside their Victorian context, the monuments of the Arthurian Revival in art are no more than romantic visions, illustrated narratives implying an absent text. Without the framework of original interpretive intention the metaphor remains mute. To release the message and to read the works as intended for their original audience it is necessary to explore the extrinsic factors that were significant to their conception, those habits of mind and communication that constituted the genesis of the metaphor and gave form to it, in art and in the course of the Revival itself. The development of Arthurian imagery was subject to specific demands that made the conveyance of the message possible. Tracing that development is an acknowledgment of the working of contemporary conventions, those of ideation, those of art, and those of interpretation. Furthermore, the tradition of the legend must not be diminished, for in choosing the tales of King Arthur to speak of themselves, the Victorian artists and writers made a conscious commitment to follow the legend through to its inevitable conclusion.

The Arthurian tradition has long tempered the fall of Ar-

thur's realm with a messianic assurance. In the concluding book of Malory's *Le Morte Darthur* is a promise of Arthur's return at the time of his nation's need. Malory tells that Arthur received a fatal blow in the last, fierce confrontation with Mordred, but also shares with the reader an epitaph attributed to Arthur's tomb: "Hic iacet Arthurus, Rex quondam Rexque futurus." The Victorians caused Arthur to fulfill his destiny as the "once and future king." In service to their idealism they summoned him out of Avalon and restored him to his former status, as the embodiment of the national spirit. Subject to the course of the legend, however, his return to oblivion was inevitable, but when Arthur resumed his slumbers, he was a changed being. Once a battle chieftain, a chivalric hero, and a courtly king, Arthur returned to Avalon as he appeared to his latest audience, a mirror of the rise and fall of aspiration in the Victorian era, a grand symbol of self-confidence and self-identity and, in the end, of true self-recognition. (pp. xvii-xxii)

> *Debra N. Mancoff, in an introduction to her* The Arthurian Revival in Victorian Art, *Garland Publishing, Inc., 1990, pp. xvii-xxii.*

FURTHER READING

Ashe, Geoffrey; Alcock, Leslie; Radford, C. A. Ralegh; Rahtz, Philip; and Racy, Jill. *The Quest for Arthur's Britain.* New York: Frederick A. Praeger, 1968, 282 p.
> Examines the development of the Arthurian legend and the historical foundations underlying it.

Chandler, Alice. "Sir Walter Scott and the Medieval Revival." *Nineteenth-Century Fiction* 19, No. 3 (December 1964): 315-32.
> Explores three influences on Sir Walter Scott's writing: "the scholarly, the Gothic, and the primitive."

———. *A Dream of Order: The Medieval Ideal in Nineteenth-Century English Literature.* London: Routledge & Kegan Paul, 1970, 278 p.
> An examination of the medieval revival as a reaction to changes in the social structure of Victorian England.

Gray, J. M. *Man and Myth in Victorian England: Tennyson's "The Coming of Arthur."* Lincoln, England: The Tennyson Society, 1969, 33 p.
> An interpretation of "The Coming of Arthur," the only poem in Tennyson's *The Idylls of the King* that was not based on the traditional Arthurian legend.

Gribble, Jennifer. *The Lady of Shalott in the Victorian Novel.* London: The Macmillan Press, 1983, 222 p.
> A comprehensive analysis of Victorian novelists' use of the Lady of Shalott from Arthurian legend as a recurring image in their fiction.

Houghton, Walter E. "Hero Worship." In his *The Victorian Frame of Mind: 1830-1870,* pp. 305-40. New Haven, Conn.: Yale University Press, 1957.
> Analyzes hero worship of such figures as King Arthur

as a sign of Victorian society's need for moral inspiration in a period of changing social values.

Johnson, E. D. H. "Shadow and Substance." In his *The Alien Vision of Victorian Poetry: Sources of the Poetic Imagination in Tennyson, Browning, and Arnold,* pp. 21-59. Princeton, N.J.: Princeton University Press, 1952.

> Suggests that dream, madness, vision, and quest motifs constitute "a neglected aspect of Tennyson's genius" in his *Idylls of the King.*

Priestly, F. E. L. "*Idylls of the King*—A Fresh View." In *Critical Essays on the Poetry of Tennyson,* edited by John Killham, pp. 239-55. London: Routledge & Kegan Paul, 1960.

> Maintains that "the *Idylls* are so far from being escape that they represent one of Tennyson's most earnest and important efforts to deal with major problems of his time."

Detective Fiction

INTRODUCTION

For discussion of related topics, see the Sherlock Holmes Centenary entry in *Twentieth-Century Literary Criticism,* Volume 26 and the Detective Fiction entry in *Twentieth-Century Literary Criticism,* Volume 38.

Crime and detection have been common elements in world literature throughout the ages, as exemplified by the biblical stories of Cain and Abel and Susanna and the Elders, as well as by such works as Sophocles' *Electra,* William Shakespeare's *Hamlet,* and Voltaire's *Zadig.* Most commentators agree, however, that while such early examples of crime literature contain both misdeeds and investigatory techniques, it was not until the mid-nineteenth century that the prototypical characteristics of the detective fiction genre appeared. In "The Murders in the Rue Morgue," first published in *Graham's* magazine in 1841, and several subsequent "tales of ratiocination," Edgar Allan Poe created the archetypal pattern for stories of detection: a mysterious crime is committed, a brilliant detective investigates and solves the puzzle with the aid of logical reasoning, and the perpetrator is revealed. The protagonist of Poe's stories, the perspicacious but eccentric C. Auguste Dupin, served as the model for numerous subsequent investigators.

Several political, social, and ideological forces unique to the nineteenth century are frequently cited by critics as reasons for the emergence of the detective fiction genre during this era. As societies grew more democratic and less subject to the authoritarian law-enforcement techniques of absolute rulers, criminals—who had often been viewed in the popular imagination as heroic in their defiance of governmental control—were increasingly seen as reprehensible in the eyes of a rising middle class with material goods to protect. At the same time, the police rose in popular esteem. Once maligned as agents of corrupt kings, members of the police force were now valued for the protection they provided, and the figure of the law enforcement officer became a fitting protagonist in literary works. In the intellectual realm, a profound respect for the reasoning process inherited from the eighteenth-century Enlightenment and a faith in the ability of science to solve social problems combined to create another hero, the scientist. Literature featuring a main character who combined the traits of both and focusing on the logical, scientific solution of a crime by a member of the police force or a well-informed amateur detective was therefore particularly suited to the interests of nineteenth-century readers.

While Poe's tales of ratiocination were relatively unknown in his own country during his lifetime, they strongly influenced the development of detective themes in the literature of France and England in the 1850s and 1860s. Although not exclusively concerned with detection, novels by Emile Gaboriau, Charles Dickens, and Wilkie Collins featured among other subjects the efforts of policemen to solve crimes in much the same manner as Poe's Dupin. The policeman-hero introduced by these writers inspired the growth of the French *roman policier* and the American police novel, branches of detective fiction that have flourished in the twentieth century. Other novelists of the time—Mary Elizabeth Braddon in England and Anna Katharine Green in America, for example—created the domestic detective novel in which crime investigation is combined with a realistic representation of the characters' everyday life, a form of detective fiction further developed in the twentieth century. By the 1890s, the short story form had eclipsed the novel in popularity and a number of short works appeared that were concerned exclusively with crime and detection. The Sherlock Holmes stories of Arthur Conan Doyle, which focus on the deductive talents of an eccentric amateur detective, are the best-known examples of these; their crystallization and popularization of the elements of Poe's short stories exerted considerable influence on the form and development of the twentieth-century detective story.

Commentary on the importance of nineteenth-century detective fiction concentrates on the cultural significance of the hero and the function of the genre in literary history. The detective of this era is seen as an "apostle of pure reason," who, by his defense of moral order, becomes a type of savior. At the same time, as Elliot L. Gilbert points out, his inevitable failures in an increasingly mechanized and godless society reflect late nineteenth-century awareness of the limitations of the reasoning process. Thus, the genre of detective fiction in the nineteenth century is often viewed as a transition between Romantic faith in the perfectibility of the world and Victorian disillusionment with its harsh realities.

REPRESENTATIVE WORKS

Aldrich, Thomas Bailey
   The Stillwater Tragedy (novel) 1880
Braddon, Mary Elizabeth
   Lady Audley's Secret (novel) 1862
   A Strange World (novel) 1875
   An Open Verdict (novel) 1878
   Just As I Am (novel) 1880
   Wyllard's Weird (novel) 1885
Bulwer-Lytton, Edward
   Pelham; or, The Adventures of a Gentleman (novel) 1828
   Eugene Aram (novel) 1832
   Night and Morning (novel) 1841
Collins, Wilkie
   The Woman in White (novel) 1860

The Moonstone (novel) 1868
The Law and the Lady (novel) 1875
Dickens, Charles
Bleak House (novel) 1853
The Mystery of Edwin Drood (novel) 1870
Doyle, Arthur Conan
A Study in Scarlet (novel) 1888
The Sign of Four (novel) 1890
The Adventures of Sherlock Holmes (short stories) 1892
The Memoirs of Sherlock Holmes (short stories) 1894
The Hound of the Baskervilles (novel) 1902
The Return of Sherlock Holmes (short stories) 1905
The Valley of Fear (novel) 1915
His Last Bow (short stories) 1917
The Case-Book of Sherlock Holmes (short stories) 1927
Farjeon, B. L.
119 Great Porter Square (novel) 1881
The Mystery of M. Felix (novel) 1890
Samuel Boyd of Catchpole Square (novel) 1899
Gaboriau, Emile
L'affaire Lerouge (novel) 1866
[*The Widow Lerouge,* 1873]
Le crime d'Orcival (novel) 1867
[*The Mystery of Orcival,* 1871]
Le dossier no. 113 (novel) 1867
[*File No. 113,* 1875]
Monsieur Lecoq (novel) 1869
[*Monsieur Lecoq,* 1880]
Le petit vieux des Batignolles (novella and short stories) 1876
[*The Little Old Man of the Batignolles; or, A Chapter from a Detective's Memoirs,* 1880]
Godwin, William
Things As They Are; or, The Adventures of Caleb Williams (novel) 1794; also published as *The Adventures of Caleb Williams; or, Things As They Are,* 1839
Green, Anna Katharine
The Leavenworth Case (novel) 1878
A Strange Disappearance (novel) 1879
The Mill Mystery (novel) 1886
Behind Closed Doors (novel) 1888
The Doctor, His Wife, and the Clock (novel) 1895
That Affair Next Door (novel) 1897
Lost Man's Lane (novel) 1898
The Golden Slipper (novel) 1915
Hoffmann, E. T. A.
Nachtstücke. 2 vols. (short stories) 1817
†*Die Serapions-Brüder.* 4 vols. (short stories) 1819-21
[*The Serapion Brethren.* 2 vols., 1886-92]
‡*Die letzen Erzählungen von E. T. A. Hoffman* (short stories) 1825
Hume, Fergus
The Mystery of a Hansom Cab (novel) 1886
Le Fanu, Joseph Sheridan
Ghost Stories and Tales of Mystery (short stories) 1851
Uncle Silas: A Tale of Bartram-Haugh (novel) 1864

Checkmate (novel) 1871
Morrison, Arthur
Martin Hewitt, Investigator (short stories) 1894
Chronicles of Martin Hewitt (short stories) 1895
The Adventures of Martin Hewitt (short stories) 1896
Poe, Edgar Allan
§*Tales by Edgar A. Poe* (short stories) 1845
‖*The Works of the Late Edgar Allan Poe.* 2 vols. (short stories) 1850
Shiel, M. P.
Prince Zaleski (short stories) 1895
Stevenson, Robert Louis
Strange Case of Dr. Jekyll and Mr. Hyde (novel) 1886
The Wrong Box [with Lloyd Osbourne] (novel) 1889
Sue, Eugène
Les mystères de Paris. 10 vols. (novel) 1842-43
[*The Mysteries of Paris,* 1896]
Vidocq, Eugène François
Mémoires. 4 vols. (memoirs) 1828-29
[*Memoirs of Vidocq, Principal Agent of the French Police until 1827,* 1828-29]
Wood, Mrs. Henry
East Lynne (novel) 1861
Zangwill, Israel
The Big Bow Mystery (novel) 1892

*This work contains the short story "Das öde Haus."

†This work contains the short story "Das Fräulein von Scuderi."

‡This work contains the short story "Die Marquise de la Pivardière."

§This work contains the short stories "The Murders in the Rue Morgue," "The Mystery of Marie Rogêt," "The Purloined Letter," and "The Gold-Bug."

‖This work contains the short story " 'Thou Art the Man'."

———

ORIGINS OF THE GENRE

Aaron Marc Stein

[*Stein was an American journalist and well-known writer of mystery novels. In the following excerpt, he traces the political, social, and intellectual influences on the origins and development of the detective story and explores some characteristics of the form.*]

Although it is generally agreed that the detective story had its beginnings with the tales of Edgar Allan Poe, it must be recognized that any work of art, if it is not to be "born to blush unseen and waste its sweetness on the desert air," needs more than a creator. It needs as well an audience to which it can speak, one that is prepared to receive it. In the long history of the arts there have been, it is true, occasional prophetic creations which by some miracle survived the indifference of their contemporaries to surface later into recognition, but it can be argued that even such works were not truly before their time. It was not that there was no contemporary audience prepared to listen, but rather that there was an audience not yet aware that it was so prepared.

In his own time Poe and his works were held in relatively low esteem in his native country. It has been suggested that his American contemporaries considered him to be overly preoccupied with death, therefore morbid and unhealthy. It has further been suggested that disapproval of Poe's private life may have also been a factor in the shaping of contemporary attitudes toward his work. Romantic preoccupation with the nonconformist antics of *la vie bohême* belongs to the end of the nineteenth century. The beginning of its fifth decade was too early for such titillations.

Be that as it may, the detective story, despite its American birth, had its earliest post-Poe development in France. This is not to say that the French of the mid-nineteenth century were less concerned with mental health than the Americans of that time, but that they probably defined it differently. It was a Frenchman, after all, who said *cogito ergo sum,* and it would be difficult to find a Frenchman, if not since the time of Pascal at least since the time of the Eighteenth-Century Enlightenment, who, whatever the evidence to the contrary, does not conceive of himself as a thinking man. To the sons of Voltaire and Diderot this new form of fiction in which a reasoned story line led to a neat and inevitable QED was irresistible.

The times in the English-speaking world were also ripe for it; it was only a short time before the word had crossed the channel and English authors avidly began to take up the detective story. From Britain it quickly made the return journey across the Atlantic to reroot itself lustily in the land of its birth.

Why then should this form of fiction have been so long in making its appearance? Why did it have to wait for Poe and the closing years of the first half of the nineteenth century? Tales of crime and its aftermath, and indeed of murder and its aftermath, are as old as the art of storytelling. One does not need to dig far into the works of the ancients to find examples of crime narratives which contain detective-story material.

Before exploring any of these it is well to establish some necessary distinctions. Any work of the imagination in which crime is a major factor may be placed in the broad category of crime fiction. That crime fiction ever since the beginnings of storytelling has constituted a large part of all forms of narrative literature is obvious.

Only recently, however, a matter of a century or less, has crime fiction, or at least some part of it, been institutionalized into a separate genre—that which is called mystery fiction. Although this is something of a misnomer, the term nevertheless has become firmly embedded in the language to cover all varieties of crime fiction which publishers for commercial reasons choose to present in a separate category and which critics, for possibly whimsical reasons, choose to regard as belonging to this separate category.

The border lines in this area have never been sharply defined. *An American Tragedy, The Great Gatsby, The Postman Always Rings Twice, Rebecca,* and *Lolita,* for example, were published not as mystery novels but simply as novels. *The Franchise Affair* and *A Kiss Before Dying,* on the other hand, were placed in the mystery category. Any argument that the distinction is based on considerations of literary merit is not supported by the evidence. Nobody could possibly contend that all, or even much, of what is published under the undepartmentalized label of the novel is of conspicuous literary merit. Among the works that have been published under the mystery label may be found a similar proportion of gold to dross.

Within the broad category of mystery fiction, furthermore, there is a more sharply defined subdivision called detective fiction, a distinct literary form originated by Poe. Detective fiction is a dramatization of a reasoning process concerned with assembling and interpreting data to arrive at the truth that underlies the events of a crime.

Since the detective story is a clearly definable form, it did come to be classified as a separate department of fiction writing. To a considerable extent, furthermore, it drew into its orbit other forms of crime fiction included in the broader category of the mystery, infusing them to a greater or lesser degree with elements of the reasoned search and in that way established the broader and vaguer catchall genre, the mystery story.

A brief examination of some ancient crime stories which contain detective-story material will clarify the distinction.

In the story of Cain and Abel, Genesis provides a passage of Q and A and even an example of that characteristic device of detective-story dialogue in which a suspect seeks to evade an incriminating response by countering question with question: "Am I my brother's keeper?" However, the account of Cain and Abel is not a story of detection. The Interrogator is omniscient. He questions Cain not in an effort to uncover the truth, but only to give the criminal an opportunity to mitigate his guilt by confessing to it. By definition, omniscience has no need for detection.

Sophocles in the *Electra* presents a passage of great detective-story writing. After a long absence Orestes returns to home and homicide. He has come incognito and if he is to hope to accomplish his bloody purpose, he must remain unrecognized. However, his sister, Electra, is on the home scene and she is potentially a valuable ally. He wants to make himself known to her and to her alone. We have, therefore, the recognition scene—a passage of dialogue in which brother and sister like a pair of strange dogs circle one another with equivocal questions until they make the breakthrough and arrive at the recognition.

This episode must be the envy of every detective-story writer, but it is only the one scene. The *Electra* as a whole is not a story of detection. It is not difficult to multiply such examples. Many centuries after Sophocles, though still much predating Poe, we have Shakespeare's *Hamlet,* a work that comes much closer to the form of detective fiction.

If we permit ourselves the barbarism of stripping *Hamlet*

of its manifold riches and baring it down to a crude outline of its plot, it can be recognized as a story of detection. It is not, however, a detective story; in modern publishing-house jargon it would be called a suspense story.

Many years ago I encountered *Hamlet* so stripped. It was an early German version—whether it was a tale known to Shakespeare and used as the outline of his tragedy, or just a crude paraphrase of the Shakespearean text is, I believe, not known. It is called *Bestrafte brudermord,* in English, *Fratricide Punished.* In the event that someone might be offended by the mauling of a masterpiece, let us say that we are discussing *Bestrafte brudermord,* a work nobody could call untouchable.

In the play the audience is expected to accept the ghost as genuine, to have no doubts of the ghost's veracity, and never to question Claudius's guilt. The suspense hangs not on learning who committed the murder, but on the uncertainty of the outcome of the struggle between Hamlet and Claudius. Who will emerge the winner? Who will be damaged along the way? Who will die?

If we undertake to determine what could be done to convert the plot into a detective story, we can in the process uncover part of the answer to the question we have posed: Why did the detective story have to wait for Edgar Allan Poe and almost the midpoint of the nineteenth century?

A detective-story writer, of course, cannot permit himself a ghost. He must build his proof entirely on hard, physically verifiable fact without any recourse to supernatural assistance. Assuming, however, that when *Bestrafte brudermord* was written ghosts were accepted as unassailable facts, let us permit the ghost.

There must, however, be a simple shift in what is assumed to be a ghost's supernatural knowledge if we are to start the tragedy off as a detective story. The play's assumption is that the ghost knows what happened to him just before he died, who caused his death, and how the murder was done. If we assume that a ghost's supernatural knowledge is not retroactive to even a moment before the spirit was separated from the body, then we can have the ghost tell Hamlet that he was asleep in his garden. He felt a trickle of liquid in his ear, a sensation which woke him. Someone had stolen up behind him while he slept. As the man bent over him, he could feel the man's hot breath on his skin. He tried to struggle, he tried to turn his head to see the man, but even in his moment of waking he was already under the effect of the poison. He couldn't move. He couldn't cry out. He couldn't turn his head to see his killer. He couldn't even raise his eyelids. The poison had paralyzed him.

That would be the whole of his information. He had been murdered. By whom he wouldn't know. It would then be Hamlet's job to determine that and to bring the killer to justice.

That's good enough for a beginning, but where can we go with it? An unsuspecting Hamlet takes the information to Uncle Claudius? The king, whom we must keep in character, would pretend to be shocked and concerned. He would tell Hamlet that this terrible thing touches him even

more deeply than it does Hamlet. The dead king was Hamlet's father, but he was Claudius's brother, and more than that, murder is a crime against the state. Regicide is the most serious crime against the state, and Claudius, now king, is the state.

"Justice is my responsibility. Rest assured, my boy. I shall leave no stone unturned. The murderer will be found. He will be brought to suitable punishment."

Claudius would then choose from the court some unfortunate he would just as soon have out of the way. The poor man would be taken into custody and put to the torture. His agony would wring from him a confession to the crime he had not committed, or failing that, it would continue until he died under it. There isn't much story there.

It is, however, not necessary to do it that way. Hamlet is no fool. Even on his way to see the king he would be thinking about the most likely suspects. It would occur to him that Claudius was the man who had profited most from the untimely death. He would recognize that the official approach wouldn't do, that he would have to go it alone.

So then we are back with the suspense story. There is, however, something to be learned from a quick look at Hamlet's methods of detection. He makes no search for a witness who may have seen Claudius on his way to the scene of the crime, or making his getaway afterward. He makes no attempt to discover the source of the poison. He doesn't question the friendly neighborhood alchemist. He doesn't so much as take a look at the strange old crone down at the end of the lane to whom people have been going for philtres and potions.

He follows the accepted methods of detection of his time. Circumstances, of course, make it impossible for him to put the king to the torture; he cannot haul his royal person off the throne and stretch him on the rack. The hand that holds the scepter cannot be fitted to the thumbscrews, but he does employ the one method of torture available to him—mental torture—and through it he attempts to torment Claudius into a confession, or at least into a damaging admission.

Here then lies part of the reason why the detective story did not make its appearance until the nineteenth century had been almost half-run. As long as the officially practiced, universally accepted means of crime detection was torture, the detective story was impossible.

A modern novelist could attempt a detective story set in some earlier century. A good man is suspected of a crime. The king's agents are searching for him. If they find him, he will be put to the torture. If no confession is wrung from him, the torture will continue until the good man has died under it. His friends spirit him away and keep him in hiding while they do the detection that leads them to the true criminal. By turning the culprit over to the king's agents, they clear their friend. Such a story would be the equivalent of one of those modern detective stories in which the evidence piled up against an innocent man has satisfied the police; he is saved only through the efforts of an amateur sleuth or a private eye who sets the police straight by uncovering the truth.

It is to be doubted that such a story could be done without attributing to characters of an earlier day modes of thought that might not have been possible for them. If we go all the way, however, and assume that such a story could have been written in that earlier day, there is a strong likelihood that it would have been suppressed. A society that looked askance at Beaumarchais' *Figaro* because it called into satiric question the morality of the ruling class, might well have reacted violently to a work that called into doubt the basis of its system of justice.

By Edgar Allan Poe's time there had filtered down into the popular consciousness some of the philosophic thinking of the Eighteenth-Century Enlightenment and with it the political thinking of the American and French Revolutions. Torture had fallen into disrepute, not only because it was cruel; but also because men of the Age of Reason had come to recognize that it wasn't good enough. Torture guaranteed only that punishment would follow crime; it offered no guarantee that it would fall on the right man.

The nineteenth century was a time of optimists. It was thought that if torture had not already disappeared from human societies, it was at least in the process of disappearing. In the twentieth century, one would like to believe that its disappearance has been accomplished, but there is too much evidence to the contrary.

Modern times, however, have brought an important difference: the universal public acceptance of torture is gone. When torture is practiced today it is either concealed and denied, or it is covered by apology. Nobody is advocating it as a good thing. At most it is presented as a disagreeable necessity. We are told that law and order demand it and that our own safety depends on it.

There was also another change crucial to the conception of the detective story. The nineteenth century saw the first organized police forces that were to be responsible only to the law. They displaced the agents of the king who had been responsible only to the royal will. The British bobby and the American cop appeared as ordinary citizens who were doing a job for the protection of the people. It could be believed that they were working in our interest and not for the advantage of someone in power who had hired them to molest us and tyrannize over us.

Earlier crime literature—if it did not deal with crime in high places, the violent deeds of gods and heroes and kings, if it did not in the words of Shakespeare's Richard II "sit upon the ground and tell sad stories of the deaths of kings"—was most likely to be on the side of the criminal. He emerged as the free man, the man who dared to stand up to tyrannical authority. He was Robin Hood. He was the hero of the picaresque novel.

At the level of less serious crime he was the beloved rogue or the merry clown. Plautus and Terence filled Roman comedy with scheming slaves who victimized their brutal owners with clever little dodges. Boccaccio built laughs on the witty confidence games worked by servants on their powerful and dull-witted masters. Although the small triumphs of the underdog and the entertaining antics of the turning worm persisted in literature through the nineteenth century, and still engage the talents of fiction writ-

ers to the undiminished delight of their audiences, the centuries-old automatic alignment with the lawbreaker was shaken where it was not destroyed.

Prior to the eighteenth-century emergence of free societies, crime could essentially be defined as any act that threatened the authority or prerogatives of the ruler. It was the commission of an act by a person whose station in life did not grant him the right to that act. In the face of the *droit du seigneur,* rape was not defined entirely by the act itself. Its criminality was at least to some extent determined by who committed the act. In societies where one class exercised an absolute and arbitrary power over life and death, murder could be regarded as the usurpation by someone of the lower orders of the ruling power's right to kill. The highwayman was a robber. The robber baron was a baron. Undertaken by the man up in the castle, kidnapping was high finance.

In any society where police authority is seen to be the protector of the powerful in their privileges, the sympathy of most men would tend to lie with the criminal. No man could be sure that one day he might not fall afoul of the royal whim.

It was only with the emergence of free societies that there developed in the consciousness of most men the concept of a delinquent class, a concept of clear separation between ourselves, the law-abiding, and the criminals. In such societies with the replacement of the agents of the king by an organized detective police force that operated under a body of law instead of under royal command, popular attitudes toward the police power changed. The bobby or the cop was seen to be on our side. He became an acceptable hero.

This new attitude became dominant, but it never completely displaced the old. It was a factor in making the detective story with its basically pro-establishment orientation possible, but in parallel development the anti-establishment, criminal-as-a-free-man, beloved-rogue story persisted.

Without these changes in political and social climate the detective story could never have evolved, but there was yet another event that more than any other was central to the invention and development of the form. It was a change in intellectual attitudes. Out of the Age of Reason there had come into the general consciousness a new hero, the man of science.

Out of his efforts there was to be created a better world, a world from which crime, want, inequity, and injustice would disappear. Consider, for example, that most optimistic of nineteenth-century philosophies that predicted the ultimate withering away of even the supreme criminal, government itself. It was, of course, the emergence of the man of science as the new hero that brought about science fiction.

The detective story developed as a form of science fiction. In its classic form, it is still a fictional celebration of scientific method, of the process of inductive reasoning. Nineteenth-century man was not blinded by his optimism. He recognized that in the brave new world the men of science and the men of reason were to create, some substitute for torture would be needed if crime was to be detected and controlled.

The new hero was to be the man who did the job. Proceeding by scientific method, he would examine the available data with the eye of a trained observer. The fact that in the work of the detective the data would be called evidence was a difference only of language. From the available data he would form a hypothesis. In accordance with Occam's razor it would be the simplest hypothesis that could contain the known facts. Guided by his hypothesis, he would search for additional data, new evidence. He would keep his hypothesis fluid, reshaping it as necessary to contain new evidence as it emerged. By this process he would accumulate all the evidence and would reason from it the final proof, the one and only hypothesis capable of containing all the evidence.

The nineteenth-century conception of science was far broader than the laboratory-oriented view of it commonly held in our time. The natural sciences were looked upon only as parts of the whole; philosophy, ethics, and law, for example, were also to be transformed by the application of scientific method. Vestiges of this attitude are still to be found in our university curricula. Courses are still given, for instance, in political science.

Central to this attitude was total reliance on observable fact and logical processes. The Eighteenth-Century Enlightenment had transformed men's minds, and men now were in the process of transforming their world. The detective-story hero, therefore, emerged as this nineteenth-century man, the devotee of fact, the child of reason. Of just such stuff Sherlock Holmes was made.

However, if the detective story was to have the tension it required, this genius of detection had to be opposed by a worthy adversary, a genius of crime who would provide a proper challenge through his skill at concealing the data, or masking them, or scrambling them into deceptive patterns. Holmes needed his Moriarty.

The detective story, accordingly, developed into a double contest. There was the battle of wits waged between the detective and the criminal, and there was also the contest of wits played between the author and his readers. The reader was drawn into competition with the detective in observation of the data and in reasoning from them.

Insofar as it was a game, it was necessary that it have rules, and the detective story developed as a highly structured, formal art. Robert Frost remarked of free verse that it was like playing tennis without a net; not necessarily a bad game, only a different one. A detective story that does not observe the rules, however, is like playing tennis with neither a net nor a court. It would degenerate into an aimless batting about of balls.

The rules are simple. All the data must be presented to the reader. When he is confronted with the solution, he must be left with the conviction that if he had not failed to take notice of a piece of evidence when it was given to him, or if he had reasoned properly from the available data, he would have achieved the solution on his own. If the sur-

prise of the solution depends on information not offered to the reader, then the author has violated the form. If misleading data are offered and are not counterbalanced by the presentation of other data that would identify the earlier evidence as irrelevant, then again the author is violating the form.

As the form developed, it inevitably departed more and more widely from the actualities of crime and detection. The genius detective, whether a police officer, a private operator, or a brilliant amateur, has seldom existed in the flesh. In the actual world the great scientific mind did not often apply itself to a career of crime detection. A young person of suitable potential, confronted with the choice between a university scholarship to study mathematics or physics and the opportunity to enroll in a police academy where he could earn while he learned, invariably would choose the university.

Why? Because the academic career is more prestigious? The acclaim that would come to a detective able to operate at the level of a Sherlock Holmes, a Nero Wolfe, a Hercule Poirot, or a Lord Peter Wimsey would be great enough to satisfy even the most immortality-hungry individual. Out of consideration for personal safety? Consider the scientific researchers who have pursued dangerous experiments, pressing forward in magnificent disregard of dangers to their health or even to their lives. It would be difficult to conceive of a moment of hazard that could exceed the one when Enrico Fermi gave the signal for the movement of the control rods that initiated the first chain reaction. The young who combine a lust to meet danger with a capacity for science aspire not to be detectives, but to be astronauts.

The choice of a career in one of the scientific disciplines over a career as a detective is made because the scientist is guaranteed a continuing challenge. The detective can expect to go through his whole career and rarely, if ever, be confronted with a case that will fully test his powers. He has little hope of ever confronting a worthy antagonist.

Criminals in the actual world are stupid people. Those who seem clever are merely the skilled practitioners of their specialties. Hotel thieves are glib. Pickpockets are manually dexterous. Confidence men are persuasive. None of these is a great brain. If one considers violent crime, one is likely to arrive at a picture of inverse proportion. The greater the level of violence, the lower the level of intelligence.

Of all criminals, the greatest dullards are likely to be the murderers. In cases where a murderer appears to be a person of any considerable mental capacity, during the commission of murder he is likely to be at least temporarily stupified by the emotional impact of his act. He will be in no condition to play intricate games of move and countermove with a genius of detection.

Any writer of detective stories must at some time have been haunted by the thought that out there in the real world there must be perfect crimes, murders that have never been solved because it was impossible to recognize them as murders; deaths that have successfully been staged to present the unassailable appearance of suicide or accident. If there are any such, they have been successful,

Two episodes from the life of the French detective Eugene Vidocq.

not because they presented evidence that could not be unscrambled, but because they presented no evidence at all.

A New York City Police Department detective defined the difference. "The detective of fiction," he said, "depends on clues. The police officer depends on informants."

Most actual murder cases that are solved solve themselves. In the event that a difficult one is handled successfully, it is probably because somebody talked. If the murder is not a family affair or the result of obvious hostilities in the victim's immediate circle, and if there is nobody to talk, the case will probably remain unsolved. The difference between a detective-story case and a baffling actual case is the difference between the difficult but complete jigsaw puzzle and the puzzle that can never be done because too many of the pieces are missing.

It must be conceded that there have been examples of successful police work in cases which at first sight did not solve themselves. At the simplest level a persistent mugger who kills and robs and leaves the scene unobserved might eventually be brought to justice if he works one area regularly, and if the police department can spare the manpower to play the patient game of keeping the area under surveillance until the mugger is caught in the act.

Valuable as such police work unquestionably is, it does not make a detective story. It is a story of patience, of dogged pursuit, and to a great extent, a story of luck. It cannot be converted into a celebration of the process of inductive reasoning.

For an illustration of the difference we can consider an actual murder case in which detectives, both professional and amateur, did attempt to operate at the detective-story level.

Some years ago in Manhattan's fashionable upper East Side the Wylie-Hoffert murders electrified the affluent and eminently respectable neighborhood. Three young women

shared an apartment. One of the three came home late in the afternoon to find in one of the bedrooms the murdered and mutilated bodies of her two fellow tenants.

The police, surveying the scene, arrived at the hypothesis that the killings were the work of a sex maniac. The nature of the mutilations inflicted on the two young women so indicated.

The police made all the available moves. They questioned the neighbors. Nobody had seen anything; nobody had heard anything. They inspected the apartment building and learned that inadequate security left the service entrance unprotected for considerable periods of time. They questioned the young women's office associates. They took a hard look at all the young men the two victims had been dating, investigating most assiduously those gentlemen whose hair lengths or life-styles were not in accordance with what police officers of that day considered suitable. They brought in for questioning all known sexual deviates they could locate. But on all sides they came up empty-handed. There were simply no clues.

While they were so engaged, across the river in Brooklyn a woman reported to the police that a youth had attempted to molest her sexually on a public street in the full daylight of mid-morning. The police scoured the neighborhood and picked up a young man, physically ill-favored, mentally deficient, unemployed, and aimlessly on the loose.

When they arranged for the complaining woman to view the youth, she identified him as her molester. The method used by the police to set up the viewing for identification was later called into serious question, but at that point the matter stood with the accused identified by the complainant.

Since in Manhattan the New York County police were looking at sexual deviates and the Kings County police in

Brooklyn had in custody a man accused of odd sexual behavior, a Manhattan detective crossed the East River to look at the accused.

Among the objects found in the young man's pockets at the time of his arrest was a snapshot of a pretty, well-dressed, well-groomed young woman. In the opinion of the Manhattan detective the photograph looked very much like the late Miss Wylie. He questioned the young man about it and all he could elicit was a statement that it was a photograph of his girl friend. The youth refused to divulge her name or her whereabouts.

Since the Manhattan crime was by far the more serious, the young man was turned over to the Manhattan police for questioning. He was soon charged with the murders and assigned a court-appointed attorney. The attorney examined the photograph. To his eye it was anything but an overwhelmingly convincing likeness of the murdered Miss Wylie.

He questioned his client about it, but he was unable to draw from the young man anything more than the story he had already given to the police. Not satisfied, the lawyer began to do some detective work. He learned that at the time of his client's arrest, the young man had only recently arrived in Brooklyn from a small town on the New Jersey shore.

The attorney then visited the town, and since he was a sound man, assiduous on behalf of his client and the proper administration of justice, and since the town was small, he succeeded in finding the young woman of the photograph. She identified it as a snapshot of herself, but was unable to explain how it could have come into the possession of the murder suspect.

He was not, and had never been, her boyfriend. She had never known him, had never seen him, and had never so much as heard of him. She had not liked the photograph. In her opinion, it did not do her justice. The last time she had seen it had been when she had thrown it away in the trash.

The lawyer also succeeded in locating a group of young men who had known the accused before he had left for Brooklyn. They knew the photograph. The young man had shown it to them and had boasted that it was a picture of his girl friend. They had never believed him. He was homely, he was not bright, and he spent most of his time scavenging in the garbage of the town dump. In the opinion of his peers it was hardly credible that he could have any girl friend, much less one who was clean, well-dressed, and well-groomed.

The attorney returned to New York. When he confronted his client with the information he had picked up in the youth's hometown, the young man broke down and admitted that the snapshot was just something he had salvaged from the dump. All the other fellows had girls. All the other fellows could boast of their conquests. He alone was different. He never had had a girl. With the picture he had only been trying to establish himself as one of the boys.

The lawyer took this information to the District Attor-

ney's office. The prosecutor agreed that the one item of evidence, the photograph, had been eliminated. It was his contention, however, that under questioning the accused had made damaging admissions. Although the youth's attorney was convinced that his dull-witted client could be manipulated into saying almost anything, it made no difference. The murder charge against the youth was not dropped.

While the unfortunate young man was in custody awaiting trial, an unsolicited informant appeared. He was a drug addict, who came in completely on his own to tell the police of another addict who had boasted to him of having done the Wylie-Hoffert murders. The police arrested this new suspect and, on questioning him, they learned that he knew details of the crime scene that had never been published; details that only the killer could have known.

The Wylie-Hoffert case had solved itself, and the poor lad who had never had a girl friend was returned to Brooklyn to stand trial on the lesser charge still pending against him there.

Any reader of the works of Erle Stanley Gardner will recognize that the court-appointed attorney in this case attempted to operate as both Perry Mason and Paul Drake. The Paul Drake part of the job he did and did well. The Perry Mason part—taking the information into court, blowing the case wide open, and confounding the prosecution by producing the true killer—he was unable to do.

It was, however, through no lack of will or lack of ability that he could not do it. It was because the evidence was not available. Furthermore, when it did become available, it was not through the efforts of anyone connected with the investigation or through the exercise of anyone's investigatory skills.

The detective story, therefore, developing as a celebration of scientific method through the dramatization of the process of inductive reasoning, created worlds of its own, worlds only tenuously connected to the world as we experience it. Before it may be condemned on these grounds, however, it is well to remember that in the total history of the arts, as men have practiced them through the millennia of historical record, and through earlier periods that are recorded for us only by their artifacts, naturalism, *verismo,* and slice-of-life representation speak for only one band of the great and various spectrum.

If one accepts the dictum that art, if it is to have any relation to truth, must be aleatory, operating as life appears to operate, pulled along by blind chance from chaos to chaos, then obviously the detective story does not qualify. But by this measure, virtually everything else man has called art will fall with the detective story, eliminated because it is contrived, an artifice, untrue.

If, therefore, we may except the aleatory, we must recognize that even the most naturalistic works are made with contrivance and artifice. If we accept that a work of art creates its reality through the cosmic organization of whatever piece of the chaos of actuality the artist has chosen to organize, we must recognize that the simple act of selection, as it lifts out of the surrounding chaos and isolates for representation one chosen piece, is a contrivance and an artifice.

The relationship of actuality to artistic realities can most easily be examined in the visual arts. On superficial acquaintance with painting and sculpture some people are inclined to assume that anything that diverges at all from the most literal naturalistic representation so diverges from a lack of skill on the part of the artist. On a slightly more sophisticated level there might be some recognition of the limitations of tools and of materials. Whether the artist alone is faulted, or whether he is permitted to share the fault with his tools and his materials, the judgment remains that for a work to fall at all short of literal naturalistic representation does constitute a fault. It is reasoned that if he had been good enough at his job, he would have created a likeness.

Exploration of the visual arts, however, quickly begins to chip away at this judgment. Works that make little or no concession to naturalistic literalness in representation frequently display such consummate skill and competence in other aspects of the art that it is difficult to believe that the artist could not have accomplished anything he chose to do. If he has produced no likeness, it would have to be concluded that doing a likeness had been no part of his purpose.

More direct evidence of the artist's intent is often available. Consider Byzantine mosaics where, with a dazzle of light and color, the artists delineated in rigidly schematized, highly formal style the characters of Old and New Testament stories and the figures of saints, of kings, and of queens. There are such mosaics where, along with the sternly schematized eminences, the artists chose to put in some ordinary people as observers of the scene. These little nobodies are represented with a high degree of naturalism. They have the look of portraits done from life.

Since the artists demonstrated their ability at handling this greater degree of naturalism, why did they deny it to the major characters in the stories they depicted?

It was done by intention. They were creating a deliberate distinction. There was the world of appearance and the ordinary people who inhabited that world, but there was also this other world the artists had created, the world of the divine personages. That kings and queens were included in this world of the divine was no anomaly. It was widely accepted that royal personages ruled by divine right.

Similarly, at Wells Cathedral in Somerset the great Gothic sculptures of the Holy Company are highly schematized. Where the South transept joins the crossing, however, there are carved capitals that show a woman drawing a thorn out of her foot and boys stealing apples—little naturalistic scenes of genre portraiture. Here again it is the deliberate establishment of a distinction between the world as it appears to be and a world as it doesn't appear to be, the contrast between the earthly and the divine.

There is no need to multiply examples. Artists select whatever aspect or segment of the actual world they choose to explore and celebrate. Through the process of isolation and development they convert what they have chosen into

a world of their own invention. Through this world a successful work of art has something to say about actuality and reality.

The choice made by the detective-story writers was the exploration and celebration of the process of inductive reasoning. For this purpose the detective, no matter how naturalistically he is characterized, is necessarily transferred to a world as it is not.

His world, so far as the progress of his own operations is concerned, has to be free of chance and accident. If there are to be lucky breaks, they will break only for his antagonist because the detective represents an abstraction, namely scientific method, just as the characters in the old mystery plays represent abstractions—Patience, for example, or Greed or Chastity or Folly.

As the puzzle-detective story developed, it took on more and more of the character of abstract art. By the end of the first quarter of this century it was moving toward the extremes of abstraction, but in that respect it was no more than moving in step with other arts of the time. Pablo Picasso and Georges Braque with the fragmentations of their analytical cubism were creating a world of their own for the exploration and celebration of the geometry of forms. Composers were well into the mathematical constructions of the twelve-tone row.

Among the arts involved in this move toward abstraction the detective story, however, was the only one that was truly a popular art. A painter could keep going with a few patrons. Composers fared less well but there were some funds for the subsidization of performances. The detective-story writers on the other hand, were producing entertainments, and entertainments were expected to be self-supporting.

The reading public that followed the detective story into this, its most formal and abstract phase, was enthusiastic and faithful, but its numbers were decreasing. As an example of this type of story, there is the Agatha Christie novel that appeared under three different titles but is perhaps most widely known as *And Then There Were None*. As an antidote to its abstraction it whipped up an atmosphere of unremitting menace and suspense, but at the cost of its validity as a detective story.

The game it played with its readers was essentially a fraud in that it engaged its audience in the detective-story contest to detect the killer and at its conclusion it failed to detect him, but instead aborting the puzzle by offering a confession in place of a reasoned solution.

In such stories the form was approaching the place where it would be almost totally cerebral, with characters recognizable only as symbols moved about in a game of wits: bloodless people, carrying bloodless corpses through the maze of a formal garden.

The detective story never quite reached that ultimate, since in that direction lay no wider public. It took instead the direction of a return toward a higher degree of naturalism. It emerged from those isolated country houses designed not so much for habitation as for the satisfaction of an Aristotelian unity of place. It fleshed out the characters who had been thinning down to symbols that were free of all vice but murder.

Despite these changes, however, it has remained at the heart of the matter what it had been, still a formal work in celebration of scientific method. Even though the detective might now be required to soak up in all the likely and unlikely parts of his anatomy a multitude of blows, even though his survival may have come to a large extent to depend on his ability to slug and shoot, he is still in there assembling the data and reasoning from it. That his cerebration may be taking place under a rain of bullets makes it no less a dramatization of the logical process.

Such changes reflected in the detective story, as similar changes did in other forms of the novel, a popular readiness to take a less limited view of the nature of man, to recognize him as possessed of not only mind and heart, but also of muscle, bone, blood, and the full assortment of glands and organs.

In the detective story, however, further changes appeared and are still appearing. Although that first post-Poe development did take place in France, it was writers in English who took the form to its full flowering. However much French writers may have been enamored of the logical story line, since they were working out of a culture that subscribed to the Code Napoleon, they were somewhat hampered in the processes of plot development. At the heart of the classic detective story lies that admirable eccentricity of Anglo-Saxon justice, the presumption of innocence. If you are to have readers who will take the side of the detective, you must either have detectives who are devoted to the presumption of innocence, or detectives who are working counter to the established system of justice.

Lawyers will object that in practice the presumption of innocence does not come into play as any part of the process of detection. It is instead an obligation on jurors when in their hearing of the evidence and in their deliberations on the proffered evidence, they must assess its validity.

In the detective story the presumption of innocence appears as a quality of the detective's mind. It is a corollary of his devotion to fact, to all facts. Georges Simenon's Inspector Maigret, even though he does operate under the Code Napoleon, is in this fashion so much dedicated to the presumption of innocence that again and again he contrives to hold his investigations away from the public prosecutor and the magistrates until he has assembled all the facts and has fitted them into an inescapable pattern of proof.

All through the period when the development toward extreme abstraction was taking place, there were other writers who took a tougher and more cynical view of the processes of crime and detection. They found justice in free societies not so much changed from the old ways when it was an instrument for the protection of the powerful. Their work appeared among the dime novels and the penny dreadfuls and in the pulp magazines. Although these outlets did run heavily to hack work, but perhaps no more heavily than did the hardcover product that was accepted as respectable, there was much good writing done

at this level, and it was here, possibly, that the twentieth-century crime story first developed social and moral sensitivity.

It was here that the so-called hard-boiled school took its shape, and from here it emerged into what was considered respectable publishing, coming as an alternative to the extremes of abstraction. It has been the strongest American contribution to the form, and it has had worldwide influence and popularity.

Dashiell Hammett's Continental Op can serve as an example. He is a dirty fighter engaged in a dirty game. He operates as he does because in a totally corrupt society there is no other way to operate, and the dirty game is the only game in town. His only loyalty is loyalty to his job and he is aware that in doing it he is also corrupted, but he never pretends that he stands apart from the corruption in which he lives.

Ever since the time of the turning away from the extremes of abstraction, the two styles—the classic whodunit and the more free-wheeling hard-boiled story—have coexisted, and have enjoyed a symbiotic relationship. The celebrations of the process of inductive reasoning have never disappeared. They have gained force and credibility insofar as they have been influenced by the hard-boiled school. On the other hand, the private eyes and the vigilante-minded individualists are also in some part men of reason.

The faith and the optimism out of which the detective story was born are, however, no longer as strong as they had been. The governments of free men that were to be created out of the Age of Reason are now found to be flawed. Faith in the perfectibility of man through intellectual processes has been shaken. Questions arise about the police and other government investigatory agencies. Are they, as we had thought, dedicated to our service, or have they become latterday equivalents of the agents of the king, engaged to molest us and tyrannize over us?

These doubts and these questions, earlier manifested in the pulps, are increasingly reflected in the detective story today. We have the private eye or the embattled citizen. He does the job because the police are ineffective, or because through corruption they have moved over to the side of the criminals. We have had the rogue cop, but we are also having the one honest cop who battles single-handedly against a rogue system. The spy story has moved from recounting the activities of incorruptible gentlemen in pursuit of international careers of derring-do to explorations of double-dealing where trust is folly and there is no wisdom that is not suspicion.

We also now have the city-street vigilante. He sees himself as detective, prosecutor, jury, judge, and executioner because he is convinced that the whole system has broken down and that there will be no justice but that which he metes out with his own hand. Where now is the presumption of innocence?

Whether we like these developments or not, they must be recognized for what they are: reflections of the malaise of our own time, just as the beginnings of the detective-story form were reflections of the faith in reason of the nineteenth-century inheritors of the thought of the Enlightenment. (pp. 29-59)

> *Aaron Marc Stein, "The Mystery Story in Cultural Perspective," in* The Mystery Story, *edited by John Ball, University Extension, University of California, 1976, pp. 29-60.*

Richard Alewyn

[In the following excerpt, Alewyn disputes the widely held belief that detective fiction is a product of the Enlightenment, arguing rather that it derives from nineteenth-century German Romanticism and the Gothic novel.]

A body is discovered. The circumstances permit no other diagnosis than murder. But who did it? That is the question that occupies and frightens everyone but that is not answered until the end of the story has been reached. The question becomes more urgent after a second murder has been committed, and a third. The search becomes feverish. Clues are found, pursued, and lost again. Hypotheses are constructed and refuted. But slowly some proven facts are sifted out. Their correct interpretation and correlation provide the answer to the mute question posed by the corpse, the reconstruction of the course of events, and the detection of the criminal.

What I have presented to you is a model in which you will recognize a literary phenomenon familiar to everyone: the detective novel. Reading a detective novel is one of the things people are willing to do but are not willing to talk about, at least not in good society and especially not among academics. Its material is indelicate, its style not always the most refined, its popularity knows no limits— reasons enough to disqualify it morally, esthetically, and socially, even if not to lessen its fascination. A couple of figures may provide evidence: in the United States alone, about 500 detective novels appear each year in book form, not counting the thousands of detective stories that are disseminated in magazines, radio, and television. One author sold in a single year four million volumes, while the total sales of another author's detective novels exceed 100 million copies. The pestilence began in America and England, but has spread over the whole world. And not only as opium for the people. We could name respectable representatives of politics and business, of literature and theology, who have confessed to this addiction. One can consider this disturbing, amusing, or perplexing; but one cannot ignore it.

What makes this phenomenon remarkable is not only its distribution, but also the fact that it is a modern invention. According to general opinion, the detective novel is not much more than a century old. The American Edgar Allan Poe is considered to be the discoverer of its formula, and his "Murders in the Rue Morgue" (1841) is taken as the classic example of the genre. But it did not begin its triumphal procession until fifty years later, under the leadership of Sherlock Holmes, the master detective created by Conan Doyle in London. Since then, however, the fruitfulness of this genre has never dried up, in spite of the frequent prophecies of its death.

How is it possible that so successful a fashion was not discovered earlier? Only if no need corresponded to it earlier. And, conversely, the current attractiveness of the detective novel can only be explained by its satisfying widespread needs. Whoever could succeed in figuring out what a detective novel really is would therefore not only have answered a question of literary history, he would perhaps also have acquired information about the masses of its readers and thus about the psychological condition of man in our time. Tell me what you read and I will tell you who you are.

What is a detective novel? This question has seldom been posed impartially. Though so many have thought, written, and spoken about it, most of them can be easily divided into two camps: its opponents and its defenders. It is not our intention to become embroiled in this debate, not because the question of a thing's value is unimportant, but because it cannot be answered as long as that thing is not recognized and understood. And the debate up to now has been so rich in misrecognitions and misunderstandings that inspecting its arguments provides the most unavoidable and most profitable starting point.

Everyone is familiar with the psychological argument. The objection is made against the detective novel that it deals with crimes of violence and numbs its readers to them or stimulates them to imitate them by showing them in a romantic light and removing the natural inhibitions against them. Hence, the detective novel is a school of crime. Against this, the response is that real criminals read no detective novels; they have no need to. Conversely, the readers of detective novels have no need to become criminals, since their reading permits them to rid themselves of their dormant criminal instincts innocently and harmlessly. Thus, the reader of the detective novel is subjected to the same catharsis as the viewer of Greek tragedy.

Both arguments have some plausibility and could certainly be corroborated. But we mention them only because they speak of an object which has often been mistaken for our own, which in practice probably intersects often enough with ours but is not identical with it, namely, the crime novel. In appearance, the difference is merely technical: the crime novel tells the story of a crime, the detective novel that of the solution of a crime. But this difference has far-reaching consequences. In the crime novel, the criminal is presented to the reader before the crime is, and the circumstances of the crime before its result. In the detective novel, on the other hand, the sequence is reversed. When the reader learns the identity of the criminal, the novel is necessarily at an end; he is informed of the result of the crime earlier than its circumstances; and he does not witness these circumstances, but instead learns of them by subsequent reconstruction. If the crime novel recommends itself by permitting the reader to empathize with the murderer and to experience the crime with him in his own mind, the detective novel denies its reader such sensational effects. Hence, the latter reader has neither a contagion to fear nor a cure to hope for, and if he is not spared excitement, it is of a different nature.

But, we hear the opponents say, even if the criminal remains anonymous until the end, that still does not alter the

Portrait of Sherlock Holmes by Frederic Dorr Steele.

regrettable fact that the detective novel always has to do with a murder. In response, its defenders can do little more than confess their embarrassment. They can neither deny the fact nor explain it convincingly. But they can point out that it is just as inevitable that the murderer be tracked down and bagged at the end. Hence, the detective novel teaches that crime does not pay, and thereby becomes a school of morality and justice. But this argument would be more convincing if the murderers were not represented so often as being more sympathetic than their victims and if their pursuers, the police and detectives, were always justified in considering themselves the champions of goodness.

But most of the apologists have gone even further: according to them, the detective novel is not only a school of justice but also an expression of democratic civic consciousness. They have started out from the correct observation that the detective novel has developed most fruitfully in England, the United States, and France, countries with liberal traditions, while it has never really succeeded in taking root in Germany or in Southern and Eastern Europe, and they have found it significant that the detective novel has been suppressed under totalitarian regimes. What is more plausible, they suppose, than to understand the detective novel as a democratic institution? They have also provided an explanation: in autocratically ruled countries, they suggest, the public is in the opposition and hence automatically stands on the side of the person who breaks the law. Here, therefore, only the crime novel, in which the criminal is glorified, could flourish. The detective novel, on the other hand, in which the reader's sympa-

thies are involved in the hunt for the criminal, his feelings satisfied and his convictions confirmed at the end by the restoration of the order of law, could only be conceived on the soil of democracy.

Every sentence in this argument has an error of fact or a mistake in logic. But let us try to keep listening. The apologists have pointed to an innovation in criminal procedure, allegedly not much older than the detective novel, namely, the introduction of circumstantial proof. Before the nineteenth century, we hear, nobody had bothered about circumstantial evidence. When no eyewitnesses could be found, the courts had been satisfied with torturing the defendant until he confessed. It is only since he, too, has enjoyed the protection of the laws himself that the public prosecutor has been obliged to prove the defendant's guilt to the court by a consistent chain of circumstantial evidence. But what else is the detective novel than such a circumstantial proof? Are not here, too, the circumstances of the crime consistently reconstructed, and thereby the criminal convicted, on the basis of clues? Hence, isn't the detective novel practically a textbook of liberal legal procedures, and could it have arisen before these arose?

Before we express our doubts about this argument, too, let us listen a bit longer. The apologists have pointed finally to certain public institutions created by the nineteenth century. They have claimed that there can only be detective novels once there are detectives, who have only existed since the creation in England in 1829 of a nonuniformed police force, from which Scotland Yard arose in 1842, and since the simultaneous organization in France of the Sûreté Nationale for investigating crimes. The spirit which produced these public institutions is, according to these writers, the same as the one that animates the detective novel.

But is all that, in fact, correct? We do not wish to ask now whether the claims concerning legal and cultural history (which have been taken over even by such clever and informed authors as Dorothy Sayers and Ernst Bloch) hold water. We need only pose a single question, one which can be answered by anyone who has read even only a couple of detective novels: is it then correct that in the detective novel it is an agency of the government which tracks down the murderer? Certainly, the police are usually at the scene of the crime en masse and get to work with commendable zeal. But do they accomplish anything other than finding a few tracks that quickly come to nothing or than throwing their nets around the wrong man? Would the criminal ever be found if a generally quite unauthorized person did not get involved, one who takes up the investigation to amuse himself or as a favor, without being appointed to do so by his office and often against the resistance of the police?

Doubtless, connoisseurs of detective literature will know that there are also successful detectives in the official police and will think, for example, of Georges Simenon's amiable Inspector Maigret or F. W. Croft's valiant Inspector French. But they will also concede that these are exceptions. (Estimates vary between ten and twenty percent.) Opposed to them stands the long series of amateur detectives that begins with E. A. Poe's Dupin and Conan Doyle's Sherlock Holmes and is gloriously continued by Chesterton's Father Brown, Agatha Christie's Hercule Poirot, Dorothy Sayers's Lord Peter Wimsey, Margery Allingham's Albert Campion, by Ellery Queen, by Raymond Chandler's Philip Marlowe, Rex Stout's Nero Wolfe, Erle Stanley Gardner's Perry Mason, and many others.

If a strange custom is observed so conscientiously, it is certainly more than a mere whim, and identifying it more than mere pedantry. There can be no doubt about its meaning. To be sure, the police and the detectives usually—if not always—cooperate cordially; but neither is the one side free from fits of jealousy nor the other from feelings of superiority, and both sentiments are not unjustified. Furthermore, the police are usually—by no means always—honestly and zealously on the job, but they are, even at their best, nothing more than capable routinists and ordinarily blind, narrow-minded, and unimaginative. And although the police have at their disposal an unlimited apparatus of persons and resources, they seldom avoid a dead end or a false clue. It is really impossible to derive from this a high opinion of the effectiveness of the agencies of the constitutional state.

But where the professionals make fools of themselves, the amateur shines. If anything at all is supposed to be glorified here, then it is certainly not the criminal, and not the state and police either, but instead the individual; and if we are looking for a political and sociological position for the detective or the detective novel, then it would make more sense to think of the liberalistic spirit of self-help which has been so impressively developed in the Anglo-Saxon countries and which has often enough not been especially pious towards the state.

But detectives are not only individuals; they are also outsiders. What lives they lead! They have no wife, they have no children, they have no profession, they live in messy rooms, they lead an irregular life, they turn the night into day, they smoke opium or raise orchids; indeed, they have unconcealed artistic inclinations, they quote Dante or play the violin. These detectives have the souls neither of civil servants nor even of citizens; these detectives are eccentrics and bohemians. This fact, too, has been often acknowledged, and not without astonishment; but it has never been explained. What does it mean when detective novels attribute with such striking unanimity precisely to these outsiders the success they withhold from the police? Certainly, not a vote of confidence for public institutions nor an acknowledgment of a social conformism. Instead, the suspicion obtrudes itself that precisely these aberrations from the social and psychological norm explain the success of the detective.

This leads us to examine a further attempt to explain the origin of the detective novel in terms of the spirit of the nineteenth century. It has been said that this century brought the exact sciences to victory. As a child of the Enlightenment, it banished the darkness that until then had lain upon all areas of life and thought. It determined to explain reality by methodically collecting and logically ordering facts. But, it has been asked, what is the detective

novel if not a model of this procedure? What else happens here than that a secret is elucidated by exact observation and controlled combination? And could that have been conceivable in the autocratic or totalitarian social orders in which thinking was prohibited?

Again, we do not wish to take up the terrible simplification at the basis of this theory, but only to examine the detective novel itself. In this case, to be sure, we will not have it so easy. There is no doubt that what is involved here is a process of the discovery of truth. At the beginning is a riddle, at the end comes the solution; the theme is nothing other than the search for this solution, and a large part of the tension is derived from this. Empiricism and logic, the methods of scientific thought, are also the methods with which the detective operates. He must combine many scattered and hidden traces with one another in such a way that a consistent correlation results. But does the object of these investigations have anything to do with our reality, and are their methods used in the same way as they are in the exact sciences?

I wish only briefly to point out that the world of the detective novel is constructed differently from that of our everyday experience. One of the recognized rules, for example, is that the criminal is one of the characters known to the reader from the beginning. It is considered impermissible to make an unknown character passing by chance the murderer. There are various reasons for this, but one is that it would otherwise be impossible for the reader to participate in the investigation. Hence, a circle of characters which is limited from the beginning is required. Frequently, this limitation is further marked by physical barriers. A weekend party at an isolated country house, a snowbound express train, a luxury yacht on a Mediterranean cruise, or a hermetically sealed house are therefore favored locations. These are artifical situations: they are possible in reality, but not especially frequent.

But the circumstances of the murder are just as carefully prepared. So that it can later be consistently reconstructed through mere combination, it must not only have been consistently planned but also brought off according to plan. Details of the sort that constantly require us in everyday life to change our plans and to postpone appointments—an unexpected call or visit, a downpour, or an occupied telephone booth—are not foreseen in the murderer's plan. The detective novel takes place in a world without chance, a world which is certainly possible, but is not the ordinary one.

But in other respects as well, what happens in the detective novel has little in common with everyday life. To begin with, a crime is already something that scarcely ever occurs in the experience of normal people; again, among all crimes, murder is fortunately the rarest. But not only does the detective novel insist upon murder with a curious pedantry: it makes its object precisely to dream up cases of such a complexity as rarely or never appear even in the experience of the police. And the reason for this is not only, as has been supposed, that the classic methods of murder, poison and the dagger, have become so clichéd that every new author is compelled to surpass his predecessors by more exotic inventions. The unusual murder stood already at the cradle of the detective novel. E. A. Poe's first murderer was very far from being everyday; it was an orangutan, and not by chance. Poe had his detective confess (and many have agreed) that the more exotic the method of a murder, the easier its solution. Hence, if it is true that the detective finds out the truth about a reality, this reality is not the usual one and is certainly not the one that obeys the laws of the natural sciences.

But what about the methods with which the detective operates? Certainly, he draws his conclusions from observations; it is not the obvious and most palpable facts that interest him, however, but rather extremely inconspicuous and insignificant things: a nail that has been broken off, a little bit of cigar ash, a clock that stopped or that did not stop—things that say nothing to an ordinary person, that have absolutely no significance in ordinary life, but that for the detective become the signs of a secret writing whose deciphering solves the riddle. But this art of reading clues and interpreting signs is denied to the ordinary person; indeed, in ordinary life it has no utility.

"Nothing deceives more than a naked fact," Sherlock Holmes is fond of saying and his successors are fond of repeating. But normal people (and to these belong especially the representatives of the police) inevitably let themselves get led astray by such "naked facts," palpable and evidently obvious facts of a case. And here we must mention an institution we have previously omitted, one which, though it has seldom been recognized, belongs, like the amateur detective, to the basic requirements of the detective novel: the motif of the false clue. Inevitably, all the circumstances point unanimously at the beginning to one person, who, in reality, is entirely innocent. And this error can be repeated until all the main characters of the novel have come into the gravest suspicion one after the other, with a single exception: the one who, in reality, is the criminal. It is a generally practiced rule that the most suspected person is innocent and the least suspected the criminal; naturally, the validity of this rule is not annulled, but only confirmed, when the author for once reverses the procedure in consideration of the clever reader and permits the really guilty party to seem so suspicious that he seems unsuspicious.

Misleading the reader in this way is designed to startle him and thereby to increase his pleasure. But it also betrays a doubt about the nature of the world and the aptitude of the organs of our experience, and it contains above all a scathing judgment of the reliability of circumstantial proof. So far from spreading trust in reason and science, it serves rather to undermine it. Just as little as the usual in the detective novel is the real, so little is the probable in it the true. Its world is not constructed according to the realistic and rationalistic model of positivism. Therefore, we shall have to seek its home elsewhere.

Before we inquire into this, we wish to recall once more the institutions which we bumped into while examining the popular theories about the spirit and origin of the detective novel and which we had to add to our first model. This model was: an enigmatic murder and its solution. The first addition was: this solution is the work, not of the police, but of an amateur who is an outsider socially and

an eccentric psychologically. The second addition was: the apparently guilty person is, in reality, innocent, the apparently most innocent person is, in reality, the guilty one. These are seemingly technical formalities, but the conscientiousness and unanimity with which they are observed betrays an unconscious need, which requires explanation.

And now, after so much dry theory, I am happy to tell, or rather to retell, a story. It takes place in Paris at the time of Louis XIV. The city has been alarmed for some time by a series of murders, all performed according to the same pattern. The victims are always isolated pedestrians who are supplied with expensive gifts and are on their way late at night to an amorous tryst. They are found in the morning, stabbed to death with the same weapon and robbed of their jewels. Police protection is increased and a special court is established, which succeeds in spreading a fear that causes even the most innocent to begin to tremble but not in getting hold of the murderer or even in preventing the continuation of his crimes. It is only when the respected goldsmith Cardillac is discovered murdered that the criminal is thought to have been found: Olivier Bresson, Cardillac's apprentice and lodger and the fiancé of his daughter Madelon, is arrested.

All the evidence speaks against him. He was found in Cardillac's room with the corpse, as was, with him, the weapon with which not only Cardillac but also all the earlier victims had been killed. He can supply no plausible explanation of the circumstances. He claims that his master left the house at midnight and ordered him to follow him at a distance of fifteen steps. From this distance he had seen Cardillac attacked by an unknown man. The murderer had vanished in the darkness, while he himself had dragged the dying man into his house and had also brought the murder weapon with him.

These statements are entirely implausible, as is demonstrated at length. For one thing, Olivier cannot explain what might have caused Cardillac to go out so late. Second, it appears to be impossible both that he could have left the house unnoticed at that hour and that Olivier could have brought him back unnoticed. Other people who live in the house attest (and this is checked and confirmed) that neither the lock nor the hinges of the house door can be moved without creating a loud noise which can be heard as far as the fourth floor. But on the third floor, two witnesses had spent the whole night without sleep. They clearly heard Cardillac bolt the door from inside at nine o'clock in the evening, as was his custom, and then nothing more until after midnight, when they heard, above the ceiling of their room, first heavy steps, then a muffled fall, and then a loud groan. The situation—well known to the theory and practice of the detective novel as the "locked room murder"—permits no other conclusion than that the murder was performed in the house. No other suspect comes into question but Olivier.

But then the earlier murders as well, which were performed with the same weapon under similar circumstances, must be laid to his account, and this suspicion becomes a certainty when, with the arrest of Olivier, the murders immediately cease. Neither the police nor the public doubt Olivier's guilt, especially as he was the fiancé of the daughter and sole heir of Cardillac and consequently would not have lacked an obvious motive.

Here we have the apparently consistent circumstantial proof which nevertheless goes completely astray. Olivier is not the murderer, but the unwilling and unhappy accessory who—as so often in detective novels—is compelled to silence by his regard for someone close to him. The real murderer is none other than Cardillac, who, as someone known as an honest craftsman and, moreover, as the apparently last victim in a long series of murders, is the apparently least suspicious character. A neurotic compulsion (whose origin, by the way, is explained according to psychoanalytic method) drove him to use murderous methods to take possession again of the jewels he had manufactured. A secret passage permitted him to leave the house without being noticed. During the last of these sorties he had been stabbed with his own dagger in self-defense by an officer he had attacked, and had been brought back into the house by Olivier, who had secretly followed him.

It is not through the work of the police that all this is brought to light. On the contrary, their methods practically prevented the solution. The terror they spread sealed the lips of Cardillac's murderer. The solution is rather the work of an outsider, Mlle de Scuderi, a little old lady who is as clever as she is plucky and who is a poet. She solves the crime, not, to be sure, like her later colleagues in the detective novel, by actively taking the investigation in hand, yet still not by accident, but by means of capabilities which the representatives of the court and the police entirely lack and which make her a poet, too: warmheartedness, wisdom, and an infallible emotional certainty. These capabilities encourage the unwilling murderer of Cardillac to entrust himself to her. It is to these capabilities (and to an earlier personal connection) that she already owed a confession that Olivier, to spare his beloved, had denied the police.

Next to some subordinate motifs, we find all together in this story the three elements that constitute the detective novel: first, the murder, or the series of murders, at the beginning and its solution at the end; second, the innocent suspect and the unsuspected criminal; and third, the detection, not by the police, but by an outsider, an old maid and a poet; and then fourth, the extraordinarily frequent, though not obligatory, element of the locked room. The story is entitled "Das Fräulein von Scuderi" ("Mlle de Scuderi"). Its author is the German romantic E. T. A. Hoffmann. It appeared in 1818, almost a quarter-century before E. A. Poe's "Murders in the Rue Morgue," with which, according to previous opinion, the history of the detective novel begins.

I do not intend to claim by this that Poe knew Hoffmann's story and was influenced by it. Determining this priority would have only an academic interest, and the history of the detective novel would not have to be rewritten if it were simply a matter of a lucky bull's eye. But the case is quite different. To be sure, this is the only time that all the essential characteristics of the detective novel are found together in a single story by E. T. A. Hoffmann (in Poe, by the way, this happens nowhere), but individually they

can be found easily everywhere in his works. In "Marquise de la Pivardière," retold from Pitaval, only the detective is missing. More importantly, the vast majority of his stories are constructed on the same pattern: a mystery and its solution. At the beginning one learns of an enigmatic event, or one encounters an unknown man with strange habits or an obscure past, or one is introduced into a whole circle of persons, a household or a clan or a court society, above whom a mystery hovers, or one enters a castle in a gloomy landscape or stands in front of an uninhabited house in a lively city, where there is something uncanny. The riddle awakens the reader's drive to investigate, when not that of one of the characters in the story, and this drive to investigate gives rise to discoveries that often yield new riddles but that confirm both the reader and the characters in the story in their sense of a subterranean connection. For a long time, all speculations or investigations lead to nothing or lead astray; but at the end, as is usually the case in the detective novel, everything obscure is clarified in a coherent report.

In this regard, E. T. A. Hoffmann is not alone. Mysteries and their solution provide the theme and the scheme of the romantic novel in Germany. All the novels of Tieck, Novalis, Brentano, and Eichendorff begin with riddles and questions and end with solutions and answers. If the characters in romantic novels are so willing to wander, this is also because a restlessness drives them on or a yearning draws them, but they are always also in search of something they once possessed but lost, their home, their father and mother, or a beloved. And during this search, it befalls them to encounter everywhere clues that say nothing to others but in which they recognize signs and messages, and these clues entwine themselves more and more closely into contexts in which everything that seemed isolated is connected and everything that seemed accidental attains a deeper significance, until at the end everything that had been lost is found again and all the riddles are solved. For romanticism, mystery is the condition of the world and all external appearance is merely the hieroglyph of a concealed meaning.

It is this romantic mystery that takes on the shadow of the uncanny in E. T. A. Hoffmann. But in his *Nachtstücke* (*Night Pieces*), the uncanny is always the sense of a crime concealed in the past or in the future. Hoffmann, like Poe after him, is one of the virtuosi of terror, and he is not the first who discovered and exploited this stimulus. Tieck had preceded him in Germany, and both Hoffmann and Tieck drew from a murky current which at the end of the eighteenth century had arisen in England and flooded all of Europe and had fertilized romanticism: the "Gothic" horror story.

The horror story is the abstinence neurosis of the aging Enlightenment. To a race starved by rationalism and bored with bourgeois security, it offered the forbidden fruits of mystery and of fear. If one strips away its nerve-shattering packaging—old castles in desolate mountains, around which at night the storm howls and the moon sheds an uncertain light—there remains a core similar to the simplest model of the detective novel; many inexplicable and uncanny phenomena turn out to be clues to secret connections, and these again reveal themselves slowly to be the consequences or omens of terrible crimes, whose roots are buried deep in the past and which are completely solved at the end when the criminal is unmasked and brought to justice.

These novels are often entitled *Mysteries:* between 1794 and 1850 over seventy novels appeared in England carrying this word in their title. Detective novels are still called mystery stories in English. The detective stories of E. T. A. Hoffmann and E. A. Poe are nothing but lateral shoots from this common root.

Now the detective novel is distinguished from the horror story by its locale. It does not carry its reader off into the dark Middle Ages. To be sure, it still occasionally makes itself at home in remote country houses and sleepy provincial towns, but it is happy to take residence in the modern metropolises and takes pleasure in turning precisely their well-known streets and buildings into the scene of extremely unusual occurrences and thereby making them strange in an uncanny manner. But this procedure, too, has its prehistory. In the middle of the nineteenth century, the Gothic mysteries had already receded when Eugène Sue's *The Mysteries of Paris* (1842-1843) unleashed a new wave of mystery novels in all of Europe, from whose fascination Balzac and Dickens, too, could not free themselves. In these novels, the apparently so prosaic and secure everyday life of the modern metropolis turned out to be nothing but a thin and brittle cover, undermined by a labyrinth of criminal conspiracies. Without being able to compete with the gloomy, colossal paintings of these metropolitan mysteries, E. T. A. Hoffmann had nevertheless here, too, already provided the model.

Romanticism had been just as dissatisfied with the trivial surface of the world and of life as the detective novel would be. Everywhere, in nature and in the soul, it tracked down hidden powers and secret meanings. It looked not only outside reality, but also *within* it, not on its surface, but into its depths. "Everything external is something internal transformed into the condition of mystery," says Novalis, and he means that for the favored gaze every phenomenon is a riddle whose key lies hidden in its depths. The whole world is a secret writing, and this applies to society no less than to nature.

It was E. T. A. Hoffmann who, thirty years before Eugène Sue and eighty years before Conan Doyle, developed this notion by turning not only lonely castles and cloisters but also the streets and squares, houses and places of entertainment of Paris and Berlin, Dresden, and Frankfurt, familiar to every native, into the scene of strange, mysterious, and criminal events, and lodging the unusual and the improbable in the middle of the everyday. In his story "Das öde Haus" ("The Deserted House"), in which behind the inconspicuous facade of a well-known and exactly specifiable house in Berlin, on the street Unter den Linden, gloomy secrets are revealed, he expresses the conviction "that the real phenomena in life often take on a much more marvelous form than everything the most active fantasy tries to invent." It sounds like an echo of this when Conan Doyle and his disciples repeat or vary countless times the saying, "Life is more fantastic than fantasy."

And conversely, E. T. A. Hoffmann would not have hesitated to sign Conan Doyle's creed: "Nothing deceives more than a naked fact." Romanticism saw reality as the detective novel does: an everyday and peaceful and deceptive surface, with abysses of mystery and danger underneath.

But in both cases, not everybody is capable of recognizing and disclosing these dark depths. Rather, two kinds of men correspond to these two levels of reality. The first are the prosaic and profane ones who have made themselves at home in everyday reality and resist every insight that could shake their confidence in the rational order of the world and in the reliability of common sense, and who consequently are blind to the unusual and not up to dealing with the improbable. Romanticism calls them Philistines. But then there are the others, a small minority, who are pretty useless for practical life because they are strangers to it, eccentrics and outsiders, but to whom, according to E. T. A. Hoffmann, "the power to recognize the wonders of our life is given like a special sense." Romanticism calls them artists.

These are the men who—again according to E. T. A. Hoffmann—"in every ordinary phenomenon, be it person, act, or event, immediately perceive the eccentric element to which we find nothing comparable in our ordinary life and which we therefore call marvelous, who notice, for example, what thousands of passers-by overlook, that there is something odd about a certain house in Unter den Linden." To such a person it can also happen that he "often follows for days on end unknown persons who have something wondrous in their gait, clothing, tone, or look, that he brings together things from the antipodes and imagines from them connections no one thinks of." Could one give a better description of the talent and activity of the detective?

The romantics populated their novels with people of this sort. They are called "artists," less because they practice some art than because their eccentric character and their extravagant life style exclude them from the society of ordinary men and make them useless for everyday life. Without family and without profession, without residence and without possessions, they are at war with society and state. Citizens and civil servants they consider a nuisance or ridiculous. But these émigrés or exiles are the ones who know how to read the clues and to interpret the signs which remain invisible or incomprehensible to normal men. For they are prepared for the reality of the unusual and immune against the deception of the probable. To this type of person belongs Mlle de Scuderi. To it belong also Poe's Dupin and Conan Doyle's Sherlock Holmes and all the other outsiders among the detectives.

In this way, the literary source and the spiritual home of the detective novel are secured. It is a child of rationalism only insofar as all romanticism has rationalism as its father. In this way, too, the question of its essence can be posed anew, and the question of the source of the fascination it exerts. So far from confirming everyday reality, the rational order, and bourgeois security, it serves instead to jeopardize them. Perhaps, in the course of such an investigation, the answer to the question which has often been put but never satisfactorily answered suggests itself—the question which is the scandal of all the opponents and the embarrassment of all the friends of the detective novel: Why in the world is the detective novel not satisfied with a more gratifying theme than a murder? (pp. 62-77)

> *Richard Alewyn, "The Origin of the Detective Novel," translated by Glenn W. Most, in* The Poetics of Murder: Detective Fiction and Literary Theory, *edited by Glenn W. Most and William W. Stowe, Harcourt Brace Jovanovich, 1983, pp. 62-78.*

Robert A. W. Lowndes

[Lowndes is an American science fiction and mystery writer. In the following excerpt, he ennumerates Poe's contributions to the development of detective fiction.]

Just how far back in time the mystery tale goes is a moot question, and the question of how far back goes the tale wherein a mystery is solved by the use of reason, rather than magic or divination, is also open. The Book of Daniel contains two episodes which make very respectable detective stories: "Bel and the Dragon" and "Susanna." However, these two stories, as far as we know, were not written as fiction or understood by their readers to be fiction. We must come far forward in time from those days, to the nineteenth century to be exact, to find the beginnings of what we now consider the detective story, wherein a fictional character solves a fictional mystery through the use of inductive and deductive reasoning—ratiocination, as this operation was called in the early nineteenth century. Such a story might indeed include thrilling events and action, but in no way does the solution of the mystery depend upon action. The detective may need to take steps in order to achieve justice, but the physical action derives from the solution to the mystery, at which the detective has arrived either by a combination of inspecting the premises and listening to or reading reports, or on the basis of reports alone, without ever having stirred from his chair.

The date to remember is April 1841 (in those days magazines were not dated ahead), and the publication to honor is *Graham's Magazine,* published in Philadelphia. It was here that readers saw "The Murders in the Rue Morgue," by an author who was already well known to followers of magazines: Edgar Allan Poe. This was the first of three tales of ratiocination devolving about a character named C. Auguste Dupin, whom Ellery Queen justly honors as "the world's first fictional detective in a modern sense." A little more than a year and a half later, the second Dupin tale, "The Mystery of Marie Rogêt," appeared as a three-part serial in *The Ladies' Companion,* November and December 1842 and February 1843. (Remember that one-month hiatus; it will become important later.) The final story, "The Purloined Letter," appeared in *The Gift,* late in 1844. An examination of these three tales will indicate the range of Poe's inventions in the detective story.

The first thousand or so words of "The Murders in the Rue Morgue" are devoted to an introductory essay on analysis. Some sort of introductory material preceding

Daguerreotype of Edgar Allan Poe.

what can properly be called the start of a story was common apparatus for 19th century authors; but most of Poe's stories (as opposed to pieces which are sometimes included among the "tales" but are little more than essays or whimsies) either start at once or begin after no more than a paragraph or two of introduction. This preliminary essay, then, is unusual for Poe. Whether he employed it for his own benefit (feeling his way, as it were, in a new type of story), whether he felt that the reader needed this introduction in order to comprehend or sympathize with what the author was doing, or whether it represents a combination of the two previous suggestions, is something I'll gladly leave to the experts. Having read it with care, I can assure you that today's reader does not need it at all. There is nothing in it that is not accomplished better in the course of the story, once the story starts. The introduction ends with this brief paragraph: "The narrative which follows will appear to the reader somewhat in the light of a commentary upon the propositions just advanced."

Now the story begins, with the introduction of Monsieur C. Auguste Dupin. "This young gentleman was of an excellent, indeed of an illustrious family, but, by a variety of untoward events, had been reduced to such poverty that the energy of his character succumbed beneath it, and he ceased to bestir himself in the world, or to care for the retrieval of his fortunes." Our narrator meets Dupin in an obscure library where both are in search of the same "very rare and very remarkable" volume. They find they are kindred souls in a sufficient number of ways so that they decide to share quarters, so long as our narrator stays in Paris. ". . . and as my worldly circumstances were somewhat less embarrassed than his own, I was permitted to be at the expense of renting, and furnishing in a style which suited the rather fantastic gloom of our common temper, a time-eaten and grotesque mansion, long deserted through superstitions into which we did not inquire, and tottering to its fall in a retired and desolate portion of the Faubourg St. Germain."

We see at once that the world's first private detective is an unusual person of unusual tastes and temperament; with Poe, it could hardly be otherwise. "Had the routine of our life at this place been known to the world, we should have been regarded as madmen—although, perhaps, as madmen of a harmless nature." My own feeling is that this represents more of the author's characteristic gestures—his routine manner of describing an intelligent and educated gentleman with whom he hoped to capture the readers' attention—than carefully thought-out harmony between story and character. The pair leave their quarters only at night, while "At the first dawn of the morning we closed all the massy shutters of our old building; lighted a couple of tapers which, strongly perfumed, threw out only the ghastliest and feeblest of rays. By the aid of these we then busied our souls in dreams—reading, writing, or conversing, until warned by the clock of the advent of the true Darkness. Then we sallied forth into the streets, . . . seeking, amid the wild lights and shadows of the populous city, that infinity of mental excitement which quiet observation can afford." Apparently this was before eyestrain was invented.

Nonetheless, despite the fact that the original portrait of Dupin is overdone (and later must be modified so that he can accomplish what he must accomplish), this very opening had tremendous influence upon subsequent authors of detective fiction. Sherlock Holmes, Father Brown, Hercule Poirot, Philo Vance, Sir Henry Merrivale, and Nero Wolfe—to list but a few—are all, to one degree or another, bizarre characters. And Dr. Doyle found that he had to modify a great deal of the description of Holmes' limitations as well as some of his habits (as presented in *A Study in Scarlet*) in order to fit him into later stories.

Poe goes on for slightly more than 800 words about the weird living style of the narrator and Dupin, then launches an episode wherein Dupin demonstrates his skill in induction and deduction, startling the narrator with a comment which would seem to indicate that Dupin could read his thoughts. Sherlock Holmes, you will remember, startled Dr. Watson at their first meeting, and Watson later compares Holmes to Dupin. Whereupon: "Sherlock Holmes rose and lit his pipe. 'No doubt you think that you are complimenting me in comparing me to Dupin,' he observed. 'Now, in my opinion, Dupin was a very inferior fellow. That trick of his of breaking in on his friends' thoughts after a quarter of an hour's silence is really very

showy and superficial. He had some analytical genius, no doubt; but he was by no means such a phenomenon as Poe seemed to imagine.' " (*A Study in Scarlet,* Chapter II.)

But as Michael Harrison notes in his essay on Dupin ("Dupin: The Reality Behind the Fiction," in *The Exploits of the Chevalier Dupin,* Mycroft & Moran, 1968), Doyle is really drawing a red herring across the reader's path, hoping thus to distract him from the size of the debt he actually owes to Poe and, in this first Holmes story, to "The Murders in the Rue Morgue" in particular. As Harrison indicates, Doyle was just beginning at that time, and was worried about being dismissed as a mere imitator of Poe; had he started writing about Sherlock Holmes after he was well established, he might have been more generous. (Later in *A Study in Scarlet,* Holmes tells Watson that his is a unique profession: the world's first consulting detective. For after all, Dupin was a fictional character.)

It is not until after the thought-reading episode that we get to the crime: Dupin and the narrator see an account "Extraordinary Murders" in the evening paper. However, the material preceding this point and dealing with the first meeting between the narrator and Dupin is not superfluous, however awkward some of the attempts to make Dupin himself seem extraordinary. The two friends follow the newspaper accounts for a time, then when the arrest of a particular person is announced, Dupin asks the narrator's opinions. He replies: "I could merely agree with all Paris in considering them an insoluble mystery. I saw no means by which it would be possible to trace the murderer."

We shall see later on in the story that the narrator, while not adept at ratiocination to anything like the extent of Dupin, is nonetheless able to observe and to ask intelligent questions. The difference between Dupin and the narrator in these tales is nowhere near the difference between Holmes and Watson. Of course our detective must be ahead of his Boswell (otherwise the story might as well be written from the viewpoint of the detective himself); but the difference between Dupin and the narrator in Poe's tales, and between Holmes and Watson, is particularly interesting. Poe was writing for readers who were on the whole far better educated and addicted to thought than the general public for which Doyle wrote. The magazines to which Poe contributed were read by the "gentle" class, and only incidentally here and there by members of the general populace. But in late 19th-century England, the popular magazines, though priced for the most part beyond the means of the lower classes (the so-called penny dreadfuls were for them), had a much broader circulation. It was not only Doyle's need to show but also the reader's need to see how extraordinary Holmes was that required Watson to be rather lazy-minded and decidedly slow on the uptake—outside of his profession, that is.

The beautiful thing about Holmes' line "You know my methods, Watson" is that Watson really did know Holmes' methods, but he didn't know he knew them. He employed them constantly as a doctor, but it never occurred to him to use them outside the practice of medicine.

Whether consciously or not, Doyle used a technique

which was perfectly appropriate for his general readership. He makes Watson a little denser than the reasonably well informed and alert reader, so that while the reader is perhaps rarely able to beat the great detective to the solution of the mystery, at least he's better than Watson. In respect to acumen, later authors have made their narrators pretty much either the Watson or the colleague-of-Dupin sort: Agatha Christie's Captain Hastings, whom she dropped after awhile for good reason, is more stupid than Watson (although he improves a bit after his marriage), and Archie Goodwin, while not up to Nero Wolfe's level, is at least as intelligent as the companion of Dupin.

Both Sherlock Holmes and Hercule Poirot said that their Boswells inspired genius, and we must suspect that one reason these sleuths are so fond of their companions is that the two masters appear so brilliant by comparison; in his heart each of the detectives realizes that he isn't as wonderful as his "friend and colleague" thinks he is. On the other hand, while Nero Wolfe has a certain fondness for Goodwin, he keeps Archie around because Archie is alert, intelligent and useful, more like the Poe than the Doyle type of narrator.

After the newspaper accounts of "The Murders in the Rue Morgue" comes a discussion of the police and their limitations.

> The Parisian police, so much extolled for *acumen,* are cunning, but no more. There is no method in their proceedings, beyond the method of the moment. . . . The results attained by them are not unfrequently surprising, but, for the most part, are brought about by simple diligence and activity. When these qualities are unavailing, their schemes fail.

There is in these tales a certain amount of competition and rivalry between Dupin and G———, the Prefect of Police, but neither is really contemptuous of the other. Dupin respects the police on their level of competence, and acknowledges readily that they can do better than he on *most* crimes; for most crimes are very ordinary affairs, perpetrated by people with little imagination, and thus readily susceptible to diligence and cunning. But when the police are up against the extraordinary crime, the criminal with both intelligence and imagination, their methods are often inadequate. Poe does not lean heavily on exalting Dupin by presenting G——— and the police as imbeciles.

Sherlock Holmes, on the other hand, is usually at loggerheads with Scotland Yard, and rarely has a good word for Lestrade and the others. They, quite humanly, resent Holmes' airs (in addition to his very presence which is itself something of an insult to them); but they cannot always withhold a grudging respect for him, and eventually Scotland Yard men will mourn his apparent death.

Agatha Christie plays it both ways. Poirot already has the respect of the police on both sides of the Channel before the time of the first case that Captain Hastings records (*The Mysterious Affair at Styles*), but at times he has difficulty with a particular police detective (like Giraud in *Murder on the Links*) who considers him a conceited has-been. Miss Marple never has trouble with the police: to criticize them would be out of character for her. Willard

Huntington Wright (S.S. Van Dine) wrote *The Benson Murder Case* as a burlesque, so the police are utter idiots. Philo Vance is a close friend of District Attorney Markham, and after one brief misunderstanding wins the respect of Sergeant Heath. As Wright began to find that he enjoyed writing murder mysteries he became less satirical, but I don't recall that the police ever go beyond the simplest level of competence in the series. Nero Wolfe and Archie Goodwin are in an endless feud with police authorities, who are constantly trying to get Wolfe's license revoked. Sir Henry Merrivale is a clown as well as a genius, but in general John Dickson Carr/Carter Dickson leans more toward Poe's rather than Doyle's method of handling the police. Father Brown, as a priest, renders unto Caesar that which is Caesar's.

But all the outstanding detectives of fiction who appear in a series of novels follow Poe in one respect: the murder or mystery is almost always an extraordinary one, not susceptible to the usual routine of diligence and cunning which at its best results in the solution of most crimes. Admittedly I have just presented a judgment disguised as a definition: I define outstanding fictional detectives as those who appear in cases of extraordinary crimes, requiring the methods of a Dupin, a Holmes, a Poirot or a Father Brown. My definition excludes crime stories where the only extraordinary element is the amount of violence, stupidity and sordidness that can be strung out before a simple and uninteresting "mystery" is solved. (Blood and horror are not barred *ipso facto:* "The Murders in the Rue Morgue" is as gruesome as any of the mindless gangster epics.)

To return to "The Murders," Dupin draws different conclusions than did the police from the facts available, one such conclusion being that there is something to be observed at the scene of the crime which the police did not notice. We do not know yet whether something right under their eyes escaped them, or whether they failed to look for something which hardly anyone would have noticed. These are two different possibilities, and Poe and his followers employed them both singly and in combination.

Another important element we find here is that it becomes necessary for the detective to observe at firsthand. (As we shall see, Dupin will solve a later case without stirring from his chair.) In the short story form we often find detectives who arrive at their solutions by sheer ratiocination, such as Miss Marple in *The Tuesday Club Murders* and a number of stories collected in other volumes; but in her novel-length cases she is required to move around a bit. Sherlock Holmes, for all his pipe-smoking and armchair deductions, is highly active in chasing down clues. Poirot scorns legwork that a police detective can do just as well, gets others to do most of the sniffing, and relies upon his gray cells—after, of course, getting everyone involved to talk at length about all sorts of matters seemingly unrelated to the crime. Father Brown goes around to a certain extent but is more of a Dupin than a Holmes. Nero Wolfe tries to give us the impression that he never leaves his brownstone, but it is astonishing how frequently he actually does go out; nonetheless his is the "gray cells" method, with Archie and subordinate private detectives such as Saul Panzer gathering the needed information preparatory to the climactic session in Wolfe's office.

When Dupin personally investigates the scene of the murders in the Rue Morgue, he discovers what he was looking for: a method of entering the murder room which was not considered possible. He knows now what he seeks as well as the type of person he seeks, and arranges for the person to come to him rather than going out to look for the party. There is a private confrontation and a confession, and Dupin's report to the police results in the release of the man who had been arrested and charged with the crime.

What was unique about "The Murders in the Rue Morgue"? Let us recapitulate some of the many elements in it that would be carried forward, or at least onward, by Poe's successors.

> 1. C. Auguste Dupin is a private citizen, neither presently nor formerly a policeman, nor associated with the police in their work.
>
> 2. Dupin is an eccentric, with a genius for induction and deduction as applied to human behavior.
>
> 3. Dupin has not made a special study of crime and criminal methods beyond the extent to which an ordinary well-read person of his time would have done so.
>
> 4. We see Dupin through the eyes of a close friend and associate, whose capabilities are above average, but lesser than Dupin's.
>
> 5. Dupin is attracted by the extraordinary features of the crime in the Rue Morgue; ordinary crimes do not interest him.
>
> 6. The case is a locked-room mystery.
>
> 7. Several important clues are presented squarely to the reader in the initial accounts of the crime that Dupin and the narrator read in the papers. The number of clues is not important; what is important is that the reader is given a fair chance to see an essential part of the truth before the detective reveals it.
>
> 8. But even if the reader follows these clues to a logical conclusion, the crime still appears to be impossible.
>
> 9. Dupin has apparently reached a tentative conclusion from reading the newspaper accounts. However, if this conclusion is correct, the police have overlooked something that is there to be seen.
>
> 10. Dupin arranges to examine the scene of the crime with the consent of the police. Relations between him and the Prefect show mutual respect and reasonable amity.
>
> 11. Dupin considers police methods adequate for most crimes, which are committed by people with very little imagination. He is interested only in the unusual cases, for which routine methods are inadequate. He acknowledges that the police can do better in the routine cases than can he.
>
> 12. Dupin is spurred to solve the riddle of the Rue Morgue by the fact that a person of whose innocence he is certain has been arrested and charged with the murders.
>
> 13. Dupin satisfies himself by an examination of the scene of the crime that his hypothesis is correct. The reader is shown the evidence, and, if astute, now knows essentially as much as Dupin does.
>
> 14. Dupin does not at once present his findings to the police, but sets a trap for the person he seeks.
>
> 15. Dupin does not turn this party over to the police after he has heard the entire story, a good deal of which he has deduced.
>
> 16. Dupin presents the police with just enough data to insure the release of the wrongly arrested gentleman.
>
> 17. Even if the astute reader has solved the puzzle in essence before Dupin reveals the whole truth, there are aspects of the final summation which are likely to surprise, and the summing-up is therefore rewarding to read. (My opinion is that in a well-done puzzle detective story, even the most alert and ingenious reader never figures out the whole truth as revealed at the end.)
>
> 18. There are no subplots in the story.
>
> 19. Dupin and the narrator neither run into danger nor are threatened with violence.
>
> 20. "The Murders in the Rue Morgue" is a short story. A writer before Poe's time would probably have made the same material into a long novel, filling it out with extraneous matter. Poe's story, however, contains nothing inessential except the introduction, which was necessary in this pioneering instance.

Had Poe never written another Dupin story, "The Murders in the Rue Morgue" would still be a monument for everyone today who loves the puzzle type of mystery tale, wherein the puzzle is solved by reason rather than physical violence, and the reader is given the clues he needs to solve the puzzle himself if he is astute enough. But in fact Poe did write more than one Dupin story; so let us look at what he did in the second story, "The Mystery of Marie Rogêt."

This, I am told, is the least popular of the three tales, although I should think that the person who enjoys true crime stories as I enjoy mystery-puzzle fiction would find it the best of the three. A young girl named Mary Cecilia Rogers had been murdered in the vicinity of New York. At the time Poe wrote his second Dupin tale, the crime had not been solved. So, fascinated by his own theories of ratiocination, Poe set out again to do something which (to my knowledge) had never been done in fiction before. He essayed to solve not a crime that had taken place in the dim past but a still-unsolved mystery of the present—one which might even be solved between the time his story was being printed and the time it came to the reader's attention. Poe was risking disaster for his theories.

For what Poe did was to take the Mary Rogers case and transpose each separate element of it, using nothing more than newspaper accounts. As the brief introduction to the tale states in part:

> The 'Mystery of Marie Rogêt' was composed at a distance from the scene of the atrocity, and with no other means of investigation than the newspapers afforded. Thus much escaped the writer of which he could have availed himself had he been on the spot and visited the localities.

Mary Rogers became Marie Rogêt, the essential facts of the real murder were duplicated in detail and the inessential facts were paralleled. Poe both draws the reader's attention to what he is really doing and disguises his objective in the brief introduction, where he speaks of coincidences which may seem almost supernatural but which actually are quite natural in the light of what he terms the "Calculus of Probabilities." And, he says, a prime recent example of such coincidence is the case of Mary Cecilia Rogers; for, *mirabile dictu,* a nearly exact parallel took place in Paris, "about two years after the atrocity in the Rue Morgue." And its solution was one of the most brilliant exploits of the narrator's friend, C. Auguste Dupin.

The crime is not extraordinary, but rather common and sordid. Why then does Dupin bother with the Marie Rogêt case?

> The first intelligence of the murder was brought us by G—, in person. . . . He had been piqued by the failure of all his endeavors to ferret out the assassins. His reputation—so he said with a peculiarly Parisian air—was at stake. Even his honor was concerned. The eyes of the public were upon him; and there was really no sacrifice which he would not be willing to make for the development of the mystery. . . .

Dupin gets his information from the police, from newspaper accounts, and from editorials in the papers. He makes no investigation of the scene of the crime, and he proposes his solution from the armchair. At the end of Dupin's solution appears the following paragraph, placed in square brackets.

> For reasons which we shall not specify, but which to many readers will appear obvious, we have taken the liberty of here omitting, from the MSS. placed in our hands, such portion as details the *following up* of the apparently slight clew obtained by Dupin. We feel it advisable only to state, in brief, that the result desired was brought to pass; and that the Prefect fulfilled punctually, although with reluctance, the terms of his compact with the Chevalier. . . .—*Eds.*

The "Eds." is generally taken as referring to the editors of *The Ladies' Companion,* in which "Marie Rogêt" was originally published; I cannot but wonder, though, whether the paragraph did not appear in Poe's own original manuscript. Since the Mary Rogers case was still open, surely Poe would have realized that, assuming his solution correct, revelation of the details whereby the essential clues should be followed up might serve to insure the culprit's escape.

An interesting feature of "Marie Rogêt" is that Poe therein punctures common notions about the behavior of corpses under water; this element too has been widely followed by subsequent authors. Of course, the question whether Dupin's certainties as to the facts are actually any less fallacious or superstitious than the opinions he is puncturing remains moot. New superstitions drive out old ones, and the notion that what drives out an old superstition cannot possibly be superstition itself is among the greatest of superstitions.

Poe, as noted above, took a considerable risk in publishing this story; for not only did he lack the advantage of examining the locale himself, but he was in danger of being misled by the sort of sloppy reporting that one frequently finds in the papers at any time in the history of journalism. Nevertheless, we are assured in a footnote to the story as it appears in book form that "the confessions of *two* persons (one of them the Madame Deluc of the narrative) made, at different periods, long subsequent to the publication, confirmed, in full, not only the general conclusion, but absolutely *all* the chief hypothetical details by which that conclusion was attained."

On the basis of this note, most readers of "Marie Rogêt" have accepted Poe's claim that he solved the actual murder of Mary Cecilia Rogers. But new light has recently been shed on this subject by John Walsh in his book *Poe the Detective* (Rutgers University Press, 1968). A former newspaperman, Mr. Walsh searched through the files of newspapers published in New York and New Jersey in 1841/42—i.e., Poe's own source material—and familiarized himself with the area of New York City where Mary Rogers lived and worked. Contemporary maps and woodcuts of the Hoboken-Weehawken area gave further assistance, so that it was possible for him to come up with nearly as much material as Poe had, as well as some that Poe did not have. Walsh then made a close examination of Poe's story in the light of known or probable events in the author's life during 1841-42, and compared the original magazine version of the story's final sections with the version later reprinted in hard covers, with numerous footnotes added. His conclusion is that Poe's claim to have solved the case in his story amounts not to a triumph of ratiocination but of flummery. The footnotes added to the hardcover reprint, plus a few ingenious alterations (both additions and deletions) in the text of the reprint, have given a misleading impression for well over a century.

At least that is Mr. Walsh's thesis, and the late Prof. Thomas Ollive Mabbott, who wrote the Introduction to *Poe the Detective,* found it convincing; as I do myself, mainly for the following reasons. (1) The issue of *The Ladies' Companion* which carried part three of the story was not January 1843 but February 1843. The first two installments appeared in the issues of November and December 1842, and there was a January 1843 issue; why then was Poe's final installment held up a month? Walsh's researches indicate that fresh material in the Mary Rogers case which threatened to refute Poe's solution came to light just around the time the final installment of "Marie Rogêt" was due to be printed. The most likely theory seems to be that publication was held up so that Poe could do a quick revision incorporating the newly discovered material. (2) Although Poe's original manuscript cannot be found, two slightly different texts exist. In his book Walsh prints the text we are familiar with, plus the alterations (the additions and deletions), so that we can see where the two versions differ, and correlate the variant texts with the footnotes which made Poe's claim so convincing to both readers and scholars up to the present time. (3) Walsh confirms my suspicion that Poe himself wrote the bracketed paragraph quoted above, which is signed *"Eds."* in the hardcover text. (Which raises the question, which never before occurred to me, Watson that I am: might not Poe have written *all* the footnotes?)

But regardless of whether or not it solved the actual murder of Mary Rogers, "The Mystery of Marie Rogêt" gives us some more firsts for Poe.

> 21. Dupin is the first fictional private detective to appear in a series of stories.
>
> 22. The police come to Dupin, imploring his help.
>
> 23. Dupin solves the mystery upon data brought to him, without leaving his quarters, thereby becoming the first armchair detective.
>
> 24. Dupin questions no one other than the Prefect, and solves the case solely on official data and newspaper accounts.
>
> 25. In this second appearance, Dupin is no longer presented as a bizarre character but only as a slightly eccentric fellow.
>
> 26. Dupin presents the police with data enabling them to apprehend the culprit, but takes no part himself in following up his deductions.
>
> 27. In the course of discussing the case, Dupin undertakes to explode popular notions on matters often connected with crime.

"The Purloined Letter," last of the Dupin series, is easily the best in a number of ways, but not in all ways. It is the best written, judged by the modern taste. "The Murders in the Rue Morgue" could not help but arouse suspicion that it was merely an invention to illustrate Poe's theory of analysis rather than an episode in the career of C. Auguste Dupin. An equal suspicion of ulterior motives lies behind "The Mystery of Marie Rogêt": Poe is so full of enthusiasms and messages, so quick with fables which "prove" his contentions! But "The Purloined Letter" has no such flaws; it starts at once, in Dupin's quarters, one autumn evening.

By a most interesting coincidence, the narrator and Dupin have just been discussing the two previous cases when Monsieur G—, the Prefect of Police, enters. What is more, he enters at the end of the very first paragraph. The game is afoot, as a spiritual son of Dupin will say.

In several pages of animated dialogue, we learn that the Prefect's problem is a stolen letter for which all search thus far has been futile but which must be recovered. Dupin says he can only suggest that the Prefect and his

men search once again, even more thoroughly, the premises where the letter must be hidden.

> "I have no better advice to give you," said Dupin. "You have, of course, an accurate description of the letter?"
>
> "Oh, yes!"—And here the Prefect, producing a memorandum-book, proceeded to read aloud a minute account of the internal, and especially of the external, appearance of the missing document. Soon after finishing the perusal of this description, he took his departure, more entirely depressed in spirits than I had ever known the good gentleman before.

It is generally contended that the reader has no fair chance to solve the mystery of the letter's hiding-place; and so far as the precise spot is concerned, I would agree. But it seems to me that the reader is given a fair enough opportunity to grasp the principle of concealment that is the point of the story.

A month passes, then the Prefect drops around to Dupin's quarters again, and admits that he is completely stumped. He again searched the premises of the man who stole the letter, as Dupin suggested, but to no avail. (There is no doubt who the culprit is, nor is there anything to be gained by arresting the man, for a royal scandal will ensue if the existence of the letter becomes known.)

Dupin asks if there is a reward for the return of the letter, and the prefect replies:

> " . . . I wouldn't mind giving my individual check for fifty thousand francs to anyone who could obtain me the letter. The fact is, it is becoming of more and more importance every day; and the reward has been lately doubled. If it were trebled, however, I could do no more than I have done."

After a little badinage, wherein the Prefect repeats that he would *really* give fifty thousand francs to anyone who could aid him in the matter, Dupin gets up, produces his checkbook, and replies: "In that case, . . . you may as well fill me up a check for the amount mentioned. When you have signed it, I will hand you the letter."

After the Prefect has signed the check, Dupin,

> unlocking an *escritoire*, took thence a letter and gave it to the Prefect. This functionary grasped it in a perfect agony of joy, opened it with a trembling hand, cast a rapid glance at its contents, and then, scrambling and struggling to the door, rushed at length unceremoniously from the room and from the house, without having uttered a syllable since Dupin had requested him to fill up the check.

And herewith G— exits from the series, for he does not return to learn how Dupin obtained the letter or where it had been hidden. Several pages of question and answer between the narrator and Dupin fill us in.

From this dialogue we learn something of Dupin's past, of the days prior to those misfortunes that left him in the rather sorry condition in which the narrator first met him

Auguste Dupin and his confidant listen to evidence from the prefect of police in an illustration for Poe's "The Mystery of Marie Roget."

in "The Murders in the Rue Morgue." Dupin's narration shows him taking action for once, and rather dangerous action; however, he had deduced in advance how to look for the letter, and that, of course, is the answer to the riddle. Although it has become astonishingly easy to locate the letter, recovering it is another matter, and Dupin resorts to assistance to create a diversion just long enough so that he can substitute a facsimile for the letter.

Although Dupin's explanation covers more pages than were taken to come to the delivery of the letter to the Prefect, Poe continues to hold the reader's interest. The pace slows a little, as it must when an illustrated lecture is being given; but the slow-down is more than compensated for by the suspense and the revelation of Dupin's character. Although it is actually somewhat longer than it appears to be, "The Purloined Letter" remains a remarkably swift-moving short story. From it we may add the following features to our list.

> 28. New facets of Dupin's character are revealed.

> 29. An element of humor (the practical joke on the Prefect) is worked in without appearing strained.

> 30. Dupin has a personal score to settle with the culprit.

> 31. The essential problem is not how to reveal but how to help officially conceal the existence of a crime.

> 32. Since the health of the state is involved, "The Purloined Letter" is a cloak-and-dagger story of intrigue in addition to being a genuine puzzle mystery.

My list of elements that subsequent authors derived directly or indirectly from Poe's Dupin stories comes to 32. It is a sizeable list, and I know of no subsequent author who has added half so much again to the list. Even if some of the elements can be traced back to writers predating Poe, he was the first to put them all together in a shorter total of words than you will find in any of the best novels that came after him. (pp. 1-18)

> *Robert A. W. Lowndes, "The Contributions of Edgar Allan Poe,"* in The Mystery Writer's Art, *edited by Francis M. Nevins, Jr., Bowling Green University Popular Press, 1971, pp. 1-18.*

HISTORY OF NINETEENTH-CENTURY
DETECTIVE FICTION

Julian Symons

[*Symons has been highly praised for his contributions to the genres of biography and detective fiction. His popular biographies of Charles Dickens, Thomas Carlyle, and his brother A. J. A. Symons are considered excellent introductions to those writers. Symons is better known, however, for such crime novels as* The Immaterial Murder Case *(1945),* The Thirtyfirst of February *(1950), and* The Progress of a Crime *(1960). In the following excerpt, he outlines the early history of detective fiction.*]

Historians are divided between those who say that there could be no detective stories until organized police and detective forces existed, and those who find examples of rational deduction in sources as various as the Bible and Voltaire, and suggest that these were early problems in detection. For the first group the detective story begins with Edgar Allan Poe, for the second its roots are in the beginnings of recorded history. Into the mud of this tiresome controversy I propose to dip no more than one long paragraphic toe.

The decisive point is that we should be talking about crime literature, while those who search for fragments of detection in the Bible and Herodotus are looking only for puzzles. The puzzle is vital to the detective story but is not a detective story in itself, and its place in crime literature generally is comparatively small. If we consider what Sayers calls the first four detective stories, we find that they involve the use of natural cunning rather than detective skill. In the tale of Susanna and the Elders, Daniel traps the Elders by an adroit question, but he has no means of knowing that Susanna is innocent and they are guilty, and in the story of the priests of Bel the reason for supposing them to be lying is theological, the fact that Bel is a heathen idol. The tale of King Rhampsinitus' attempts to catch the thief who stole from his treasure house is no more than a battle of wits with the rogue coming off best, and although the affair of Hercules and Cacus contains a deception about footprints, it bears no other relation to detection. The histories and fairy tales of which these are fragments are quite different in nature from crime literature. The trick or puzzle element is present in several of the Arabian Nights stories, often as an example of natural cunning used to escape a trap, on the level of the cock caught by a fox in Chaucer's 'The Nun's Priest's Tale' (mentioned by one historian) who persuades the fox to open his mouth and then flies away. The most interesting of these exercises is in Voltaire's *Zadig* (1747). Without seeing the Queen's bitch or the King's horse, both of which have disappeared, Zadig is able to say that the bitch recently had puppies, limps in the left foreleg and has long ears, and that the horse is five feet high, with very small hooves and a tail three and a half feet long. He adds that the horse is shod with silver of eleven deniers proof, with bosses on its bits of twenty-three-carat gold. When he insists that he has never seen the animals, Zadig is sentenced to be flogged. His explanation, made after the animals are found, is a piece of true deduction. In the case of the bitch,

hanging dugs and earmarks traced in the sand, with one paw more deeply impressed than the others, provided the clues. The horse had brushed off some leaves in an arcade at a height of five feet, and its tail had wiped away dust at a distance of three and a half feet. Marks left on stones showed the details about the bit and shoes. This brilliant fragment was borrowed by Voltaire from a romance by the Chevalier de Mailly published thirty years earlier, and at a further distance from the *Arabian Nights,* of which Zadig is an ironical imitation. Voltaire's prime concern is not to show the power of reason, but its inadequacy in dealing with all the unreasonable people in the world. This ingenious piece of analytical deduction is a flirt of the imagination in a book that does not bear the slightest resemblance to a crime story.

If we leave aside such puzzles and riddles, there is a great deal of fiction concerned with crime which goes back at least to the eighteenth century, including Fielding's *Jonathan Wild* and the tales of mystery and terror written by Mrs Radcliffe, Maturin and 'Monk' Lewis. But Fielding's book belongs to the tradition of the picaresque novel about the adventures of a rogue rather than to the genre of crime story, and although the Gothic novel bears a relationship to the detective story in the sense that it often poses a mystery to be solved, the solution is never in itself of much interest. The Gothic novelists wanted to arouse in their readers feelings of terror and delight at the horrific plight of the central character, and they used mysterious events to enhance these feelings. The solution of a puzzle was not for them the main object of a book. The characteristic note of crime literature is first struck in *Caleb Williams* by William Godwin (1756-1836), which appeared in 1794.

'Psychological novel, detective, adventure or pursuit novel, and political novel—these are the labels most often attached to *Caleb Williams,*' says Professor McCracken, introducing a modern edition of the book. The novel points up the weakness of any attempt to fit crime stories too closely into separate compartments. *Caleb Williams* is about a murder, its detection, and the unrelenting pursuit by the murderer of the person who has discovered his guilt. It was also for Godwin a means of expounding his Anarchist beliefs, and because of this is not usually considered as coming within the crime story's critical canon. Yet one has only to consider the account he gives of the book's conception to see how close he was in spirit to the modern crime story. He invented the last volume first, he says, as a volume of flight and pursuit with 'the fugitive in perpetual apprehension of being overwhelmed with the worst calamities, and the pursuer, by his ingenuity and resources, keeping his victim in a state of the most fearful alarm'. But how was he to account for this pursuit, why did it happen? He devised, as the material of the second volume, 'a secret murder, to the investigation of which the innocent victim should be impelled by an unconquerable spirit of curiosity'. And then, to make the implacable pursuit plausible, the first volume must show 'the pursuer . . . invested with every advantage of fortune, with a resolution that nothing could defeat or baffle, and with extraordinary resources of intellect'. This manner of working back from effect to cause, from solution to problem, is at the heart of crime literature, and no writer before Godwin had attempted it with his conscious deliberation.

Hazlitt thought that nobody who began *Caleb Williams* could fail to finish it, and that nobody who read it could possibly forget it, yet a summary of the plot may be useful. Falkland, a generous and charming country squire, is accused of stabbing to death his atrocious neighbour, Tyrrell. He is tried and acquitted. A tenant of Tyrrell's, named Hawkins, is then arrested, together with his son, and they are both tried and hanged. One principal piece of evidence against them is a knife found in their lodgings, the broken blade of which precisely fits the piece left in the wound. Caleb Williams is the narrator of the story—or most of the story, for Godwin introduces another narrator in a way that slightly anticipates *The Moonstone.* Caleb is a poor boy who enters Falkland's service as secretary at a time when the murder lies in the past. He suspects that his master had something to do with the crime, and pursues his investigation with the unquenchable curiosity of the amateur detective. After Caleb has discovered the truth, that Falkland killed Tyrrell and then planted clues against Hawkins, he is dismissed, put in prison on a charge of theft (Falkland has secreted jewellery among his belongings), and then pursued and persecuted by Falkland and his agent, Gines. The pursuit is relentless, frustrating Caleb's attempts at escape by disguising himself as an Irish beggar, a lower-class farmer and a Jew. In the end Caleb brings Falkland to trial and the squire, now a dying man, admits his guilt and praises his accuser.

Caleb Williams is a remarkable rather than a great novel. The second and third volumes are absorbingly interesting but the first, in which the nobility of Falkland's nature is contrasted with the brutishness of Tyrrell's, is heavy going for a modern reader. And Godwin's object in writing the book was political. In 1793 his *Enquiry Concerning the Principles of Political Justice* had appeared, and this outline of an ideal Anarchism, the book by which he is now remembered, at once made him famous. In it Godwin attacked practically all the institutions of the state, including the legal system, opposing to them the vision of a world in which 'there will be no war, no crimes, no administration of justice, as it is called, and no government'. In the bright dawn of the French Revolution this vision found many sympathizers, and Godwin became for a time the intellectual leader of the English Radical movement, as Tom Paine was its leader in action. *Political Justice* was an account of things as they might be, an expression of faith in the perfectibility of man. The original title of *Caleb Williams* was *Things As They Are,* and it is meant to show the corruption inherent in any legal system through which one man has power over another. Falkland is a good and generous man, and in Godwin's eyes his villainy springs from his trust in social institutions, which betray him until he commits and then has to conceal the ultimate crime of murder. Caleb's sufferings, in prison and throughout his wanderings, are forced on him directly by Falkland but indirectly through the authoritarian power exerted by evil institutions over the virtuous individual. And the climactic scene of Falkland's exposure is later seen by Caleb as his own terrible mistake. In desperation at the sufferings inflicted on him he too has invoked the force of law, where

he should have attempted 'the just experiment' by confronting Falkland privately: 'I despaired, while it was yet time to have made the just experiment; but my despair was criminal, was treason against the sovereignty of truth.'

The particular importance of *Caleb Williams* is that it denies all the assertions to be made later through the detective story. In the detective story the rule of law is justified as an absolute good, in Godwin's book it is seen as wholly evil. The important strand in modern crime fiction which looks for corruption in officialdom and bureaucracy, and often suggests a close alliance between police and gangsters, was expressed here by the crime story's most significant ancestor. Godwin's attitude often gives extraordinary power to his assertion of the heroic nature of the outlaw. At times he might be speaking with the voice of Brecht, as in the credo of Raymond, leader of a gang of thieves joined by Caleb: 'We, who are thieves without a licence, are at open war with another sort of men, who are thieves according to law.' And the proto-typical figure of the law-breaker turned thief-taker appears here for the first time in the person of Falkland's agent, Gines, who has been expelled from Raymond's band for his brutality, but becomes perfectly acceptable to society as an upholder of the law. There are some passages of biting sarcasm about the code of honour adhered to by such a figure as Gines.

It is a mark of Godwin's perceptiveness that he should have created such a character more than thirty years before the publication of the *Mémoires* of Eugène François Vidocq (1775-1857), the criminal who became in 1811 the first chief of the Sûreté, and later started the first modern detective agency, Le Bureau des Renseignements. We do not know much about Vidocq's criminal activities apart from what is said in his own highly coloured and ghosted autobiography. According to this he began by stealing 2,000 francs from his mother while in his early teens, joined the army and fought fifteen duels in six months, and then at the age of twenty-two received an eight-year prison sentence. He decided to become a police informer 'for the interest of honest men' and wrote to 'Papa' Henry, a divisional chief at the Paris prefecture, to offer his services. Dates and details are confused in the *Mémoires,* but there is no reason to doubt the substantial truth of Vidocq's story. He says that he spent twenty-one months as a police spy in prison, and during this time he proved his loyalty to the police. His 'escape' was arranged, and he was appointed Chef de la Sûreté with a staff originally of four men, a number eventually increased to twenty-eight.

Almost all of his agents were ex-convicts and there were persistent rumours that some of them, and perhaps Vidocq himself, engineered robberies that they later solved, instigated to do so by the arrangement through which they were paid no salary but received a fee and expenses for every arrest. These essentially probable offences were never proved, but in 1827 Vidocq's resignation was forced by his superior in the second Division, the Chevalier Duplessis. He was replaced by one of his most dubious ex-criminal agents, Coco Lacour, and although he returned to power in March 1832, he was never really trusted. In November he resigned again after a case in which one of his agents was accused of acting as *agent provocateur* in a case involving the arrest of several thieves. After this the authorities pursued him intermittently, and eventually succeeded in wrecking his Bureau. He lived on for more than twenty years after its destruction, writing, or at least producing, books, doing some private detective work, even still acting occasionally as a police agent.

The influence of Vidocq on writers of crime fiction in his own lifetime, and on detective story writers after his death, was immense. It did not rest on his skill in analytical detection, for he had none. He started a card index system at the Sûreté, and his *Mémoires* mention at one point taking impressions of footmarks, but it cannot be said that he was in any way a forerunner of later police methods, his perceptiveness being confined to such general observations as that many criminals are bow-legged. Vidocq's importance rested in his nature as the archetypal ambiguous figure of the criminal who is also a hero. The interpenetration of police with criminals, and the doubt about whether a particular character is hero or villain, is an essential feature of the crime story, and Vidocq embodied it in his own person. A typical passage in the *Mémoires,* relating to his own early days as a police spy, runs:

> I frequented every house and street of ill fame, sometimes under one disguise and sometimes under another, assuming, indeed, all those rapid changes of dress and manner which indicated a person desirous of concealing himself from the observation of the police, till the rogues and thieves whom I daily met there firmly believed me to be one of themselves.

The capacity for physical disguise is of course a mark of ambiguity, and there is no doubt that Vidocq was very successful in disguising himself. His ability to do so fascinated several contemporary writers, including Balzac and Bulwer-Lytton. Balzac heard from Vidocq's own mouth, and Lytton read in the autobiography, stories about the false wrinkles, pigtail, snowy ruffles and three-cornered hat that helped him to become a 'very respectable gentleman' when necessary, of the time when he had his hair and beard dyed black, stained his face with walnut liquor, and garnished his upper lip with coffee grounds plastered on with gum arabic, and of the mock blisters and fetter marks made on his feet and legs when he impersonated a criminal named Germain. When, in old age, he paid a visit to London, *The Times* gave his height as five feet ten inches 'when perfectly erect' (he was in fact five feet six inches tall), and added that 'by some strange process connected with his physical formation he has the faculty of contracting his height several inches, and in this diminished state to walk about, jump, etc.' The climactic emotional moment at which the man who has seemed to be bad is revealed as good and the true villain is exposed, comes often in the *Mémoires,* when Vidocq abandons disguise and proclaims 'I am Vidocq', and of almost equal symbolic importance are such occasions as those when Vidocq in disguise is set to search for and destroy himself. Vidocq started a tradition of disguise in the French detective force which persisted at least until the end of the century.

It was the criminal rather than the maintainer of law who fascinated Vidocq's contemporaries, and whom in some cases they admired. Balzac was a friend of Vidocq's and based upon him the character of Vautrin, who appears in *Le Père Goriot* and other books. Vautrin, alias Jacques Collin, is, like Vidocq, a master of disguise, and like him also is a figure both genial and sinister. He gives up criminal activities and enters the police. Balzac's interest, however, was not in painting a portrait of Vidocq but in using him to create a major character whose philosophy transcends the conventions of legality. 'In every million men there are ten who put themselves above everything, even the law, and I am one of them,' Vautrin says, and on the occasion of his arrest he is allowed a splendidly forceful declaration: 'Have you never seen a convict before? A convict such as I am is a man less cowardly than the rest, who protests against the hypocrisy of the social contract, as says Rousseau, whose disciple I am proud to call myself.' As A. E. Murch has pointed out, Balzac sometimes gave a hero's role to the criminal, but never made a hero out of a detective. His conception of the ethical relationship between crime, order and society is nearer to Godwin than to Wilkie Collins.

The most famous work of Eugène Sue (1804-57), *Les Mystères de Paris,* is a sensational novel owing a great deal to the Vidocq tradition, and indeed directly to the *Mémoires,* as well as something at a further distance to the horrors of Mrs Radcliffe. An impossibly virtuous aristocratic hero living in the Paris slums becomes mixed up in the activities of a gang of thieves and murderers. The adventures are often absurd, and although there is a great deal of information about criminal habits, the 'mysteries' hardly exist in a modern sense. There are several passages of deductive reasoning in the works of Alexandre Dumas Père (1802-70), including one by d'Artagnan in *Le Vicomte de Bragelonne* which closely resembles Zadig's reasoning about the horse and the bitch. Dumas was also the first writer to point out that an impression may be left on the second sheet of a pad of paper when the first has been torn off. But for the most part Dumas recounts ingenious tricks, like those featuring in the eighteenth-century picaresque novel, which are no more than deceptions practised on gulls.

In one or two of James Fenimore Cooper's romances there are similar incidents which anticipate the deductive methods of the detective story, the best known of them relating to the tracking exploits of the scout Hawkeye, as he points out the difference between one moccasin and another, but essentially these are repeating in a different time and country the feats of Zadig.

In England Edward Bulwer-Lytton (1803-73), later Lord Lytton, also stressed the romantic qualities of the criminal. Murch picks out for particular discussion his second novel, *Pelham* (1828), pointing out that Lord Pelham is confronted by a characteristic detective problem when his friend Sir Reginald Glanville is to be committed for trial on a charge of murder unless Pelham can 'by the day after to-morrow, ascertain any facts to elucidate this mysterious crime and point the inquiries of justice to another quarter'. This subsidiary plot, however, is far from being at the heart of the book, as murder is the central fact of *Caleb Williams,* but is rather evidence of Lytton's absorption in the world of the criminal as opposed to the world of authority. In Lytton's four genuine crime novels the hero is also a criminal. The best of them, *Night and Morning* (1841), points up frequently the distinction between Gawtrey, who commits crimes but is shown as essentially a good man led astray, and Lord Lilburne who breaks no laws but ruins the lives of others in pursuit of his own pleasure. *Eugene Aram* (1832) was based upon an actual case in which the scholarly and virtuous Aram was convicted and executed for a murder committed fourteen years earlier. But although these books of Lytton's have a genuine connection with modern crime stories, one should not overstate the case. The books sprang from the conception of the criminal as a romantic outsider, a man condemned to the life he led by the cruelty of an unjust society and a corrupt or ignorant judiciary, that was prevalent during the first half of the nineteenth century. Lytton's early Radicalism and his unhappy marriage led him to create characters who were outcasts from the respectable world, and to show them as sympathetic, but the point for him (in the case of Eugene Aram, that a single act can be 'at war with a whole life—blasting for ever the happiness') can hardly be the point for us.

The idea that detective fiction could not be written until organized detective forces existed is logically persuasive but not literally true, for the first detective stories were written by Edgar Allan Poe (1809-49), before a Detective Office had been established at Scotland Yard, and at a time when few American cities had any kind of police system. . . . [It] is a tribute to Poe's inventive genius that his stories had so little to do with actual police operations. He had read Vidocq, and it is right to say that if the *Mémoires* had never been published Poe would not have created his amateur detective, but one should immediately add that Poe owed to Vidocq only the inspiration that set light to his imagination. Almost every later variation of plot in the detective story can be found in the five short stories he wrote which, with a little stretching here and there, can be said to fit within the limits of the form. He is the undisputed father of the detective story, although he would have been disconcerted by many of his children and grandchildren.

It should be recognized also that Poe did not think of himself as writing detective stories (the word 'detective' was unknown at the time the first of them, 'The Murders in the Rue Morgue', appeared), or regard these particular stories as of much importance. Poe's roots as a prose artist lay, like those of Lytton and others at the time, in the romantic tale of terror. As Edmund Wilson has said, he was, far from being alien to the spirit of his age, one of its most typical figures, 'a thorough romantic, clearly akin to his European contemporaries', and it was probably fortunate for him as an artist that he spent his adult life in the tame literary enclosure of the United States. His work looks longingly towards Europe, but it was the irritant influence of the philistines surrounding him that helped to mature the pearl in this oyster. When T. S. Eliot calls Poe provincial, and Henry James says that 'to take him with more than a certain degree of seriousness is to lack seriousness oneself', they undoubtedly have in mind the endless endeavour he made to sound the artistic note of a civilization from which he was separated by the Atlantic. In prose, as

in verse and science, he longed always to produce something new, and his curiosity was endless. To quote Eliot again:

> The forms which his lively curiosity takes are those in which a pre-adolescent mentality delights: wonders of nature and of mechanics and of the supernatural, cryptograms and cyphers, puzzles and labyrinths, mechanical chess-players and wild flights of speculation. The variety and ardour of his curiosity delight and dazzle: yet in the end the eccentricity and lack of coherence of his interests tire.

Eliot's remarks are often taken as being in dispraise of Poe, but they should be regarded rather as outlining the limitations of his genius. The ingenuity and freshness of his mind were extraordinary, and throughout his writing life he was searching for new forms in which to express the ideas that crowded in on him, and in the horror stories to blend these with the neuroses by which he was increasingly obsessed. In these stories Poe was always driving towards perverse sexual themes with which he could not deal directly because of the limitations imposed by his society. The result can often be grotesque, as in 'Berenice', where the narrator is driven by some unspecified guilt not only to murder his epileptic cousin, but after she has been buried alive during a fit, to fulfil his obsession with her teeth by digging the living body out of the grave and extracting the thirty-two teeth with 'some instruments of dental surgery'. What he called the 'tales of ratiocination', like those involving his interest in cryptography, and his discovery that the Lamentations of Jeremiah were written in acrostic verse, are the obverse of this horrific romanticism. If we ask, as some writers have done, why he did not exploit the ratiocinative vein further, the answer is simply that it did not interest him enough—or, to put it another way, that his obsessions eventually became so overwhelmingly important that they did not permit the production of purely rational work.

What he did may be summarized briefly. 'The Murders in the Rue Morgue', which appeared in 1841, was the first of those hundreds of locked-room mysteries that propose the puzzle of a dead body found in a room which seems to be effectively sealed. Sometimes the problem in such stories concerns the murder method (how was X stabbed, shot, poisoned, when nobody could have entered the room and there is no trace of a weapon or the poison?), and sometimes the means of entry or exit. One common form of solution is that in which the murder was committed before the door was locked or after it had been re-opened, another depends upon some mechanical device like a murder weapon which will operate at a particular time, and another still is related to some possible means of entry which is not apparent. In Poe's story the investigator, Dupin, deduces that the murderer must have come in through the apparently securely nailed windows, and finds that the nail of one window is broken, so that it only appears to be holding the window, which is also retained by a concealed spring. The police, thinking that the nail was completely driven through the window, did not trouble to look for the spring. By various other deductions Dupin comes to the correct conclusion that the murders were committed by an orang-utan which must have escaped from its owner.

'The Mystery of Marie Rogêt' was written and published in magazine form during the following year. It follows closely the murder of a girl named Mary Cecilia Rogers in New York. She was killed in July 1841, and the case remained a mystery at the time Poe wrote of it, changing the scene from New York to Paris and putting forward a solution through the comments of Dupin. The innovation here is that the story is told through newspaper cuttings which, although attributed to French papers, are similar to those in the New York press. The cuttings are interspersed with the comments and conclusions of Dupin, who relies for his evidence wholly upon this sometimes contradictory press information, so that this story is the first piece of 'armchair detection', the precursor of all those tales in which the detective solves a crime simply by analysis of and deduction from the material with which he is presented.

The third of the Dupin stories, 'The Purloined Letter', first appeared in the American annual *The Gift*, and was dated 1845 but published in September 1844. The story was the prototype of detective novels and short stories based on the idea that the most apparently unlikely solution is the correct one, with the ingenious addition in Poe's story that what seems most unlikely is really perfectly obvious. A document 'of the last importance' has been 'purloined from the royal apartments'. The identity of the person who took it is known, but he is a Minister, too important to be arrested without proof. The police search without success, every night for three months, the hotel in which the Minister lives. They probe cushions with needles, remove table tops, look for cavities in bed legs, examine the rungs of every chair and the moss between bricks, measure the thickness of book covers to see if the bindings have been tampered with. At the end of all this Dupin pays a visit to the hotel and sees the letter at once. It is in full view, placed in 'a trumpery filigree card-rack of pasteboard', soiled and crumpled and torn nearly in two across the middle. It has been put into a place so obvious that the police have ignored it. Dupin goes to see the Minister again, and takes the letter when a diversion is created in the street with a musket by a man in his pay.

These three tales are directly associated with the detective story as we know it, but 'The Gold-Bug' and ' "Thou Art the Man" ' are so evidently the forerunners of much in later fiction that they should not be ignored. 'The Gold-Bug' is a puzzle story, the interest of which is linked to the mystery of the apparently sane Legrand's insistence that the Scarabaeus he has discovered is 'a bug of real gold'. We know from the beginning that Legrand will somehow be able to justify this statement, and he does so by deciphering a code on a scrap of paper left by the pirate Captain Kidd. Looked at in one way, the story is no more than a fictional exemplification of the principles laid down by Poe in his entertaining essay on cryptography, although the protagonist and the marshy island on which the bug is found have his characteristic imaginative strangeness, but many later writers are in debt to it. The directions for finding the pirates' treasure in *Treasure Island* and the Sherlock Holmes code story 'The Dancing Men' (in which

the cipher is a simple one, like that of 'The Gold-Bug', based on the predominance of the letter 'e') are among the first of the many stories and passages in books that would not have been written but for the example of Poe. ' "Thou Art the Man" ' blends Poe's interest in detection with the obsession about the narrow barrier between life and death shown in such a story as 'Facts in the Case of M. Valdemar', in which the body of a man who has been in a coma for seven months is roused to speech by mesmerism before disintegrating into 'a nearly liquid mess of loathsome—of detestable putrescence'. ' "Thou Art the Man" ' is a murder mystery. The wealthy Barnabas Rattleborough has disappeared, and several clues indicating that he has been murdered are found by his friend Charley Goodfellow, all of them leading to the conclusion that Rattleborough has been murdered by his dissipated nephew, Pennifeather. They include a bloodstained waistcoat and knife, both belonging to the nephew, and a bullet found in Rattleborough's dead horse, 'exactly adapted to the bore of Mr Pennifeather's rifle' and containing 'a flaw or seam' which 'corresponds precisely with an accidental ridge or elevation in a pair of moulds acknowledged by the accused himself to be his own property'. At a party given by Goodfellow to celebrate the arrival of a case of Château-Margaux, however, the case proves to contain not wine but the 'bruised, bloody and nearly putrid' corpse of Rattleborough, who sits up, looks at Goodfellow, and says clearly, 'Thou art the man.' A confession follows, with the revelation that all the false clues have been planted by Goodfellow, and the further revelation by the narrator that he had found the body, obtained the jack-in-the-box effect by thrusting whalebone down the corpse's throat and then doubling it up in the case, and used his ventriloquial ability to produce the few words of accusation. The originality of this improbable story from the detective point of view rests in the laying of false clues, in the fact that this is the first use of elementary ballistics, and in the commission of the crime by the most unlikely person. (Although actually the tone is one of such insistent levity about the absolute straightforwardness of 'old Charley Goodfellow', and indeed of anybody named Charles, that Poe clearly did not intend to deceive his readers.)

Here, then, is the announcement of the themes which later writers were to use, expand, elaborate: but Poe's originality does not end with the provision of material for plots used by writers who may well not have read his stories. He invented also the first detective of fiction, the Chevalier C. Auguste Dupin, and established the convention by which the brilliant intelligence of the detective is made to shine more brightly through the comparative obtuseness of his friend who tells the story. For nearly a century this was to be a fixed pattern for most detective stories. The friend might be exceptionally thick-headed like Dr Watson, Poirot's companion Captain Hastings, or Philo Vance's District Attorney, John F.-X. Markham, he might be a more or less neutral receiver of the detective's bright ideas like Ellery Queen's father the Inspector, or Thorndyke's friend Jervis, he might even be allowed his share of natural shrewdness like Hanaud's urbane dilettante, Mr Ricardo, but he had to be there as a recorder. At least that is one's first impression, although like all categorical statements this one has its exceptions. But still, the Dupin pattern of the omniscient amateur detective and his clumsy coadjutor was the one that nine out of ten writers were to follow.

Poe made Dupin in his own image, or rather in the image of what he desired to be. He was 'of an excellent—indeed of an illustrious family', partly because Poe detested the levelling idea of democracy, and partly as compensation for his own upbringing in the care of an unsympathetic foster father. He was poor, but like a romantic hero (and unlike Poe) regarded this very little, managing 'by means of a rigorous economy, to produce the necessaries of life, without troubling himself about its superfluities'. He believed, as Poe did, in the supreme importance of the intellect, yet a strain of wild romantic feeling led him to close the shutters of the apartment in which he lived at dawn, and to go out into the streets only when 'warned by the clock of the advent of the true Darkness'. Like Sherlock Holmes later on (and Conan Doyle fully acknowledged his debt), Dupin is able to interpret the thoughts of his companion by the way in which he reacts to exterior events like being pushed aside by a fruiterer carrying a basket on his head. He solves the problems presented to him by pure analytic deduction. Aristocratic, arrogant and apparently omniscient, Dupin is what Poe often wished he could have been himself, an emotionless reasoning machine.

A reasoning machine would not be interested in the motives and psychology of people, but only in making correct deductions about their actions. It should be repeated that Poe himself did not regard these stories very seriously. 'These tales of ratiocination owe most of their popularity to being something in a new key,' he wrote to a correspondent in 1846. 'I do not mean to say that they are not ingenious—but people think them more ingenious than they are—on account of their method and air of method.' The stories were exercises in analysis on matters that caught the interest of his brilliant mind, and he was right in mentioning their *air* of method, for all of the Dupin stories reveal under examination mistakes that are damaging to them as pieces of rational deduction.

The most notable, and least-known, of these are the criticisms made by Laura Riding of 'The Murders in the Rue Morgue'. They concern the way in which the ape got in and out of the window fastened by a secret spring undiscovered by the police. As she points out, this is in itself a most unlikely arrangement—why should such a mechanism be fitted in a fourth-storey room of an old shabby house? In relation to the window, one cannot do better than quote Miss Riding:

> The ape reached the window from the lightning-rod which was five and a half feet away, by a shutter three and a half feet broad which could shut like a door to cover the whole window and was now lying flat against the wall. He grasped the 'trellis-work' on the upper part of the shutter and swung himself into the room, landing unobserved directly on the head of the bed. [The head of the bed partly obstructed the window. *J.S.*] This is impossible. Poe at one point suggests that it was a double-sashed window: he speaks of the 'lower sash'. But he does not say, whether only the lower sash moved, or both sashes, or whether the two sashes were really one single piece. If only the lower sash moved, then the ape, grasping the shutter and kicking himself backwards (frontways is impossible) into the room, would have been obstructed by the upper half of the window from landing directly on the head of the bed, which was pressed close against the window. If only the lower half moved, then it was only the lower half that was open. If, however, the upper sash moved too, the ape, on climbing out and shutting the window behind him, as he is said to have done, could not have fastened this upper sash by the secret 'catch' . . . The window would have remained open.

I have never seen any answer made to this detailed criticism by writers about the detective story, who seem to be unaware of it. Poe made corrections in later versions of the story. He increased the length of the broken nail in the window frame, and reduced the distance between house and shutter, but the changes do not dispose of the criticism.

'The Mystery of Marie Rogêt' takes its flavour from the fact that it followed so closely an actual murder case. 'I have handled my design in a manner altogether novel in literature,' Poe wrote on 4 June 1842. 'I believe not only that I have demonstrated the fallacy of the general idea—that the girl was the victim of a gang of ruffians—but have indicated the assassin in a manner which will give renewed impetus to investigators.' Three years after the story's appearance he claimed in a footnote that 'the confessions of two persons . . . confirmed, in full, not only the general conclusion, but absolutely all the chief hypothetical details by which that conclusion was attained'. With one or two exceptions critics have taken this statement as being correct, and have said that Poe 'solved' the mystery. In fact he cheated by changing the newspaper stories when he needed to do so, and the case remained unsolved, with the balance of probability being that Mary Rogers died accidentally following an abortion. A year before his death Poe, who had said in the story that 'it was at once evident that murder had been committed', admitted this in a letter: 'The "naval officer" who committed the murder (rather the accidental death arising from an attempt at abortion) confessed it . . . but, for the sake of relatives, I must not speak further.' The naval officer existed, although we have only Poe's word for his confession: but the point really is that the story was based upon the idea that Mary Rogers had been murdered, and if she died accidentally the logic of the argument is destroyed.

Poe thought 'The Purloined Letter' to be 'perhaps the best of my tales of ratiocination', and he is probably right. The flaw here, noted by several writers, is not seriously damaging to the story. It lies in the fact that Dupin could have seen only the front or the back of the letter, and therefore could not possibly have observed at the same time the 'large black seal' (on the back) and the address 'in a diminutive female hand' (on the front).

Does such detailed criticism weigh too hard on Poe? It does, in the sense that almost any 'tale of ratiocination' would wilt if subjected to similar examination. Yet the criticism is important, because the prime merit claimed by

Poe for his puzzle stories was that they were model exercises in reasoning. If the reasoning is faulty the merit of the stories is reduced. For Poe these stories were above all an expression of his desire to oppose the forces in himself that were, as he said of Dupin, 'enamoured of the night for her own sake'. Against them is posed that longing for the morbid and perverse expressed in stories about a burden of unnamable personal guilt, like 'William Wilson', in which the central character feels himself responsible for 'unspeakable misery and unpardonable crime' and commits moral suicide when he stabs his black-masked double. In the pursuit of some completely original form by this figure of unmistakable genius, the detective and puzzle stories played a small part. Poe's paternity of the detective story is not in dispute, but his fatherhood was unintended. He thought his mistress was Art, but really she was Sensation. (pp. 27-41)

> *Julian Symons, "The Two Strands: Godwin, Vidocq, Poe," in his* Bloody Murder: From the Detective Story to the Crime Novel, a History, *revised edition, Viking, 1985, pp. 27-41.*

A. E. Murch

[In the following excerpt, Murch details the growth of English and American detective fiction from the 1860s to the 1890s.]

In the period that followed the publication of *The Moonstone* and *The Mystery of Edwin Drood,* detective fiction continued to be written in England, without reaching any notable heights until the final decade of the nineteenth century. Much of it, and perhaps the best known, was the work of women writers. . . . The authors to be reviewed [in this essay] were men who influenced the growth of the *genre* by introducing fresh ideas, or devising ways to interest readers of a different type. Some of them, better known for their work in other types of fiction, experimented with the detective novel in response to the increasing demand, or even as a light-hearted change from their usual choice of subject. Others chose to specialize in the *genre,* and it was during this quarter of a century that there appeared, for the first time, the 'detective-story-writer' who wrote nothing else.

Joseph Sheridan Le Fanu (1814-1873), the Irish author and journalist, was celebrated in his own country for humorous tales, ballads and lyrical poems, historical romances and stories of the supernatural. In England, his fame rests chiefly upon his ghost stories and one or two novels of crime and detection. *The House by the Churchyard* (1863), a ghoulish tale of supernatural horror, was followed by *Uncle Silas: a Tale of Bartram Haugh* (1864), equally sensational, but with the important difference that it deals with criminals, not ghosts, and introduces a certain amount of detective interest. The cunning schemes of Uncle Silas and his son to murder the heroine are at last found out and frustrated, and past crimes are eventually brought to light, but there is no central character acting as a detective, and no special emphasis is placed on deductive reasoning. *Uncle Silas* can hardly be considered a detective novel, but the introduction of analogous features

is significant and indicates a new trend in Le Fanu's work, a change that reached completion in his next novel, *Checkmate,* which appeared as a serial in *Cassell's Magazine* between September, 1870, and March, 1871, being issued in volume form in 1871.

In essence, *Checkmate* is constructed purely as a detective novel, and it contains one or two features not previously used. The investigations are followed step by step to their surprising *dénouement,* and despite the years that have elapsed since the first crime the murderer's guilt is proved beyond doubt. At the outset, *Checkmate* frankly acknowledges the truism that 'murders interest people so much' and proceeds to gratify this interest, surrounding the crimes with intriguing mysteries to intensify curiosity and suspense.

In the first volume the chief character is certainly the criminal, Walter Longcluse, adept in disguise and in contriving alibis, committing one murder after another while still retaining an honoured place in society. The first man to suspect Longcluse is Paul Davies, an 'ex-detective of the police office, recently dismissed from the Force for overzealous behaviour.' Le Fanu presents Davies as cunning and unscrupulous, clever enough to collect proofs of Longcluse's latest crime when the police fail to find a single clue. Davies blackmails Longcluse and is paid to leave the country, but before doing so he places the information he has gathered in the hands of David Arden, whose brother was murdered years earlier by a certain 'Yelland Mace' who eluded pursuit and vanished without trace.

Struck by certain similarities between Longcluse and the long-lost 'Yelland Mace,' Arden decides to investigate. In some respects he resembles his forerunner, Pelham, being a gentleman of wealth and title who undertakes a detective enquiry for strong personal reasons, an amateur, prepared to devote his own time and resources to unravelling a mystery. But Arden has a far more difficult and protracted task than Lytton's hero, and becomes more captivated by the thrill of the chase. He sets about it in a businesslike way, sending his 'confidential man' to undertake the tedious preliminary enquiries, and carefully studying his circumstantial reports, which are embodied in the text. Arden's Christopher Blount is by no means as skilled as Doctor Thorndyke's Polton, or Lord Peter Wimsey's Bunter, but he does place in his master's hand the thread that eventually leads him to the centre of the maze, and thereafter David Arden, fired with detective zeal, conducts the investigation personally. He shows no particular aptitude, makes no brilliant deductions, depending less upon inductive reasoning than on 'unaccountable suspicions,' good luck and an orderly habit of mind, but he finds out the truth and is solely responsible for the arrest of Longcluse at the end of the novel.

An innovation in *Checkmate* is that the criminal's features have been changed by a surgical operation, so that Arden comes up against an apparent deadlock that almost defeats him. In 1871, when the fingerprint system of identification was still unheard-of, there were serious difficulties to overcome before it could be proved that Walter Longcluse, the city magnate, was in reality the Yelland Mace of twenty years earlier, but Le Fanu handled the matter quite convincingly. Arden at last found the obscure surgeon who performed the operation. Plaster casts of the patient's face, before and after surgery, had been preserved with careful notes of the position and effect of every incision, each alteration in cartilage or bone structure, even information that certain teeth had been removed and artificial ones arranged at a different angle, so that identification from dental records, used occasionally in later fiction, finds some origin in *Checkmate.*

The plot is not solely concerned with David Arden's investigations, and introduces numerous melodramatic side-issues, but nevertheless the detective theme is certainly the main interest, an important new development. In spite of archaic phrases and various out-moded relics from the Tale of Terror, which made it in these respects old-fashioned even when first published, the detective part of the book is surprisingly in advance of its period. Le Fanu was well abreast of contemporary experiments in photography in his references to a 'silhouette made by machinery,' and ahead of his day in his introduction of plastic surgery, almost half a century before the general public became familiar with the idea. Thus *Checkmate,* though not a great novel, is of some importance as a landmark, and must be included in that small group of English detective stories which were written in the third quarter of the nineteenth century and influenced later fiction of this kind.

Checkmate suffered seriously, as a detective story, by being planned as a three-volume novel, the required length being filled up with various digressions. Until novels of that length had fallen out of favour, writers who perceived the dramatic possibilities of a detective theme had considerable difficulty in finding material to fill this conventional structure. Major Arthur Griffiths, one of H.M. Inspectors of Prisons, who must have possessed extensive first-hand knowledge of criminals and of how they had been brought to justice, was nevertheless unequal to the task of spinning out a detective mystery to fill three volumes, though his many novels of this type were well received by contemporary readers. *Fast and Loose* (1885), a typical example of his work, deals with a bank robbery for which an innocent man has been convicted. A baronet, with a flair for detection and the leisure to indulge it, sets himself to find out the real thief, for love of the prisoner's daughter, and by the end of the first volume his investigations are so well in hand that their conclusion is obviously imminent. The second volume and most of the third are devoted to various shady characters who have little or no connection with the main plot, until the baronet's detective activities are resumed and completed in the final chapters.

In contrast to *Fast and Loose* in this respect, we may notice G. Manville's *The Dark House,* published in the same year. The story itself has no special significance, but it broke away from the three-volume convention and presented a detective novel in one volume. Though detective novels in single volume form had been appearing in America ever since 1878, the English reading public was not quite ready for this innovation, and current reviews of *The Dark House* referred disparagingly to its lack of length, but it is interesting that the attempt was made in this country [England] in 1885, a year or two before Conan Doyle wrote his first single-volume detective novel, *A Study in Scarlet,* in which Sherlock Holmes made his *début.*

One other English novel that appeared in 1885, *A Hard Knot,* by Charles Gibbon, deserves mention because of its well-contrived plot and the character of its excellent police detective, Hadden, a competent officer and a kindhearted man whom the reader frequently sees in his home-surroundings, in addition to following his investigations into the mysterious murder of Jean Gorbal. Hadden is clearly akin to Charles Dickens's Detective-Inspector Bucket, and Gibbon, like Dickens, was a frequent visitor at Scotland Yard, where he had personal friends among the Detective police.

Meanwhile, in America, that section of the general public which enjoyed reading 'novelettes' and cheap magazines found its tastes in detective fiction catered for by a new series of single-volume novels. These tales, which form a subdivision of that vast section of American popular fiction known as 'The Dime Novel,' stemmed to some extent from native sources. Fenimore Cooper was as popular in his own country as in Europe, and his many imitators introduced not only the redskins and white settlers familiar to Cooper's readers, but also, as time went on, the new antagonists that faced a fresh generation of Indians, 'western' heroes such as Buffalo Bill and Kit Carson, who could out-ride and out-wit their Indian foes or even surpass them at woodcraft.

Such stories were extremely popular until social changes came about in the last quarter of the nineteenth century. When settlers had turned the rolling prairies into cattle ranches, and the Red Indians, confined in reservations, were to a large extent shorn of their earlier, mainly fictional, glamour, stories of warring cowboys and Indians began to lose their appeal. Publishers of cheap fiction sought some new device, a fresh setting for tales of action and excitement. Just as the trails of the covered wagons were replaced by railroads, and the scattered stockaded settlements by rapidly growing towns, so the redskins were superseded by mail-robbers, bandits and cattle rustlers, and the cowboys by detectives, of whom the best known, in this country as well as in America, was Nick Carter.

The Adventures of Nick Carter are, for the most part, hybrid productions, the settings being purely American and the detective themes often derived from French sources. The man who invented 'Nick Carter,' John R. Coryell, was at one time under contract to write a million words a year, and did so! With such a tremendous output it is not surprising that he borrowed extensively from various suitable sources, from Ponson du Terrail and especially from Gaboriau, whose detective novels were widely read in America, where Chistern, a New York importer of foreign books, published translations almost as soon as the originals appeared in France.

Nick Carter first appeared in a serial called *The Old Detective's Pupil,* which Coryell wrote for the *New York Weekly* in 1884. The tale appealed so strongly to readers that the circulation of the *Weekly* improved remarkably, and as soon as this 'case' reached its successful climax further stories followed, Nick Carter, private investigator, becoming the hero of a series that continued for half a century, all of them nominally written by 'Nicholas Carter,' but actually the work of several authors who adhered closely to the approved pattern, the hero retaining almost unaltered the characteristics given to him by Coryell.

In the first story, Nick Carter was introduced as a young lad whose father had just been killed, and he set himself the task of discovering the murderers as a filial duty. He employed much the same methods as Père Tabaret and Monsieur Lecoq, describing his suspects in detail after a brief examination of the scene of the crime, finding a single (but very informative) hair, and identifiable shreds of material under the victim's fingernails, exactly as the Frenchmen had done in *L'affaire Lerouge*. Lecoq was a master of disguise, employing it so habitually that only two or three of his colleagues at the *Sûreté* had ever seen his face as it really was, but Nick Carter carried the art to quite incredible lengths, and was able to masquerade convincingly as any character in the story, even as a woman. Rocambole, surpassing Lecoq in this respect, could assume a new identity at a moment's notice, but Nick Carter, and his assistants also, were clever enough to disguise themselves in the open street, without an instant's pause in the pursuit of their quarry. In some respects, Nick Carter resembles Rocambole even more closely than he does Lecoq. Both are incredibly clever linguists, for example. They have superhuman powers of mind and body, and perform similar feats of detection, yet they are both prone to find themselves trapped by the criminals they are hunting (which Lecoq never did), and have to be rescued from frightful peril by their faithful assistants.

The early Nick Carter stories, though without literary value, were nevertheless produced by men with experience and some skill in writing. Later examples, particularly those which were published in the twentieth century, sank to a much lower level. All of them, however, followed the original pattern fairly closely, opening in the middle of some sensational scene and building up from one excitement to another, with a little detective argument now and again: Their similarity was quite intentional, and was openly acknowledged on the back cover of the uniform, paper-backed volumes, where the following announcement appeared:

> Nick Carter stands for an interesting detective story. The fact that the books in this line are so uniformly good is entirely due to the work of a specialist. The man who wrote these stories produced no other type of fiction. His mind was concentrated upon the creation of new plots and situations, in which his hero emerged triumphantly from all sorts of trouble, and landed the criminal just where he should be—behind bars. If your dealer cannot supply you with exactly the book you want, you are almost sure to find in his stock another title by the same author which you have not read.

In other words, *The Adventures of Nick Carter* were written in conformity with a stock pattern for an uncritical public, and had two features, in particular, that never varied. 'The hero emerged triumphantly from all sorts of trouble,' danger to his person being implied, and 'the crim-

inal must be landed just where he should be, behind bars.' There is no character study, and no trace of that romantic indulgence towards rogues which was such a strongly marked feature of English and French novels earlier in the century. Not until the twentieth century did an equivalent attitude find expression in American fiction. In the Nick Carter stories, the criminal is simply a 'bad man,' and prison is the right place for him. The pattern shows an unvarying sequence of crime, flight, pursuit and capture, with physical endurance more important than detective acumen. (pp. 133-40)

While the early Nick Carter stories were reaching this country from America, English translations of Gaboriau's novels had become very popular in Australia, where Fergus Hume, a struggling young barrister with literary aspirations, learned from a Melbourne bookseller that these were his best selling lines. After studying Gaboriau's works carefully, Hume produced his first attempt at a detective story, *The Mystery of a Hansom Cab* (1887). The book met with some local success, and the copyright was then sold to a group of London speculators, who formed themselves into 'The Hansom Cab Publishing Company' and re-issued the novel in this country, where it met with a phenomenal reception, some 400,000 copies being sold. Wealthy Australian settlers were much in the news at that

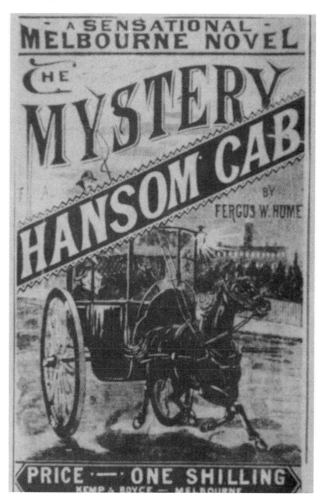

Cover for Fergus Hume's The Mystery of a Hansom Cab.

time, which gave the story a topical interest, and Melbourne's dockland slums provided a background that was new in detective fiction, although the tale itself was not strikingly original, nor was the mystery by any means baffling. Its success brought Fergus Hume to England, where he produced more than a hundred detective stories which enjoyed a certain prestige, being written by the author of *The Mystery of a Hansom Cab,* but which showed no great skill in invention or plot construction, and are of little interest today.

It was in the same year, 1887, that Sherlock Holmes made his first appearance, but this great figure did not immediately capture the imagination of the reading public, and meanwhile the current popularity of detective stories inspired other authors whose work deserves mention. B. L. Farjeon (1838-1903), in *Great Porter Square* (1884), gave English fiction a new type of detective hero, a keen young newspaperman who made his own investigations into a mysterious murder in the hope of securing a 'scoop.' He is the 'special crime-reporter' of the *Evening Moon,* and most of the story is told in the form of extracts from his 'despatches' to that paper. Farjeon's *The Mystery of M. Felix* (1890) has a police officer as its hero and a well-devised plot, but perhaps his best work is *Samuel Boyd of Catchpole Square* (1899). It contains several police officials, including Inspector Robson and a persistent French *agent,* Joseph Pitou, but Farjeon again places most of the detective enquiries in the hands of a reporter, Dick Remington, who is helped by a very intelligent little girl. The character-drawing shows considerable skill, and the story is made more interesting by an unusual psychological approach. Remington finds strong reasons for suspecting various people, in turn, but each time his further investigations reveal so much to their credit that he comes to doubt his first conclusions.

One might well have expected that Robert Louis Stevenson (1850-1894), who was so keenly aware of the trends of his day in popular fiction, and whose best work so often skirts the very fringe of the detective story, would have produced an outstanding novel of this type. An interesting comment in *The Wrecker* (which he wrote in collaboration with his stepson, Lloyd Osbourne) reveals that he gave serious consideration to the subject, but finally rejected it because of the artistic limitations from which such fiction inevitably suffers.

> We had long been at once attracted and repelled by that very modern form of the police novel or mystery story, [. . .] attracted by its peculiar interest when done and the peculiar difficulties that attend its execution; repelled by that appearance of insincerity and shallowness of tone, which seems its inevitable drawback. For the mind of the reader, always bent to pick up clues, receives no impression of reality or life, [. . .] and the book remains enthralling, but insignificant, like a game of chess, not a work of human art.

In *The Wrecker,* which appeared in 1892 but may have been written some years earlier, the authors set out to write a 'police novel,' but their attempts to give it 'life' and 'reality' made it a tale of adventure, rather than a detective story. In detective fiction, the background is usually familiar to the reader, and the clues are such that he can at least hope to interpret them from his own general knowledge. *The Wrecker,* however, is a tale of the Marquesas Islands and the blue Pacific; of sabotage and salvage, piracy, murder and opium smuggling; money-making schemes involving bankruptcies and fraudulent insurance claims. The landsman-reader knows so little about the world of sailing ships that he can scarcely follow, much less anticipate, the conclusions of the men who investigate the various plots and counterplots. He cannot, for instance, determine for himself whether *The Flying Scud* was really wrecked or deliberately beached. He has no idea of the normal stores of a brig, or what articles a skipper invariably takes with him if he has to abandon ship. The reader, therefore, is not equipped to deduce the solution of the mystery, as he hopes to do when entertaining himself with such fiction, and *The Wrecker* fails, as a detective story, not because it lacks a well worked out detective theme, but because its setting, its clues and arguments, are too remote from the general knowledge of the average reader.

Stevenson and Lloyd Osbourne had already published a detective novel written in a rollicking, humorous vein. *The Wrong Box* (1888), its original title being *A Game of Bluff.* In it, two penurious nephews take the utmost care of their aged uncle because, if he lives a little longer, he will inherit a fortune that they hope to acquire in due course. After a railway accident they find a body which they believe to be that of their uncle, and determine that no one shall suspect his death. (Actually, the old gentleman is unhurt, but has seized the opportunity of escaping from his irritating nephews). The unfortunate victim is never identified, but his body, concealed first in a water-butt and then in a locked piano, is sent from place to place, by train, delivery van or carrier's cart, in complete defiance of all probability, as well as of the normal canons of decency and decorum, until at last the cart is stolen, together with its incriminating load, and never heard of again.

This 'piece of judicious levity,' as the authors term it in their preface, is clearly a parody of contemporary detective stories, and, as such, is informative concerning the currently accepted view of this type of fiction, in particular that it was of French origin. All through *The Wrong Box* one character or another makes some facetious reference to 'French police fiction' or to its authors, in particular to Fortuné du Boisgobey. One young man in the story, 'inspired by the muse who presides over the police romance, a lady, presumably, of French extraction,' is himself the author of a detective novel called *Who Put Back the Clock?,* in which the investigator bore the would-be apposite name of Robert Skill.

> To readers of a critical turn, Robert appeared scarce upon a level with his surname, but it is a difficulty of the police romance that the reader is always a man of such vastly greater ingenuity than the writer.

Just at the time when *The Wrong Box* was published, detective fiction was at a critical juncture in its history. There was a good deal of truth in the view expressed by Stevenson and Lloyd Osbourne that it was 'enthralling but insignificant,' and after a long period of popularity it had reached the dangerous point when it was beginning to be laughed at, parodied and made to seem ridiculous. An American writer, T. B. Aldrich, much read in this country as well as in his own, had dealt detective fiction a shrewd blow in *The Stillwater Tragedy* (1880). It begins by following, quite seriously, the customary train of events. The crime is committed and discovered; the detective, Mr. Taggett, appears on the scene, carries out his investigations with meticulous thoroughness, and in due course reveals his discoveries and deductions. Unfortunately, they are all wrong! There is more than a hint of burlesque in such clues as Mr. Taggett's discovery of a half-burned match at the scene of the crime, and a box of similar matches in the room of his suspect. He counts them carefully, decides there is one missing and concludes it must be the one he has found, quite overlooking the fact that the matches have been in regular use since the 'fatal night,' if only to light the bedroom candles mentioned in the text.

Another American author, Ambrose Bierce (1842-1914?) in a volume of short stories, *Can Such Things Be?* (1893) wrote an even more broadly humorous example with the title 'My Favourite Murder' told by the dead man's nephew, who concludes his account with the 'surprise ending':—"Altogether, I cannot help thinking that, in point of atrocity, my murder of Uncle William has seldom been excelled."

Developments along such lines as these, with the central figure shown as a bungler or the subject treated humorously, would inevitably have brought the popularity of detective fiction to an end. Indeed, the vogue for the sensational 'police romance in the French manner,' fell sharply out of favour at this time. That the downward trend was halted, and that detective fiction entered, instead, on a new era of popularity, was almost entirely due to the work of Conan Doyle, who infused the *genre* with new vigour and gave it greater prestige than it had ever enjoyed. One particular feature of his stories had a far-reaching and immediate effect. In spite of the example of Poe and of Gaboriau, no English writer before Conan Doyle had created a detective-hero who appeared in a series of different tales. When *The Adventures of Sherlock Holmes* delighted English readers in the 1890's, they set a fashion for well-planned, well written short stories, with the same central figure displaying his detective skill in each of them.

Several writers quickly followed Conan Doyle's lead in this respect. The most prolific was "Dick Donovan," (Joyce Emmerson Muddock, 1843-1934), who from 1888 onwards related an almost interminable number of his own investigations in short stories that appeared in popular magazines, many of them in the *Strand,* which for some years published a 'Dick Donovan adventure' in almost every issue. Most of his comparatively simple mysteries concern the activities of sinister secret societies, or crimes committed unknowingly by people under the influence of drugs or of 'mesmerism.' Some long novels written in the third person, such as *The Man from Manchester* (1890), give his energies wider scope, but whatever their length the tales are generally trivial and unconvincing. "Dick Donovan" seldom displays any genuine aptitude

for detection, and his reports of his own successes inevitably make him appear insufferably conceited.

In striking contrast is the work of Arthur Morrison (1863-1945) a distinguished journalist who was for a time on the staff of the *National Observer.* Side by side with his realistic, penetrating studies of crime and social conditions in London's East End, *Tales of Mean Streets* (1894) and *A Child of the Jago* (1896), he wrote a number of short detective stories around the activities of Martin Hewitt, a gentlemanly hero, once a solicitor's clerk, who displayed such skill in collecting evidence for his employer's clients that he started in business on his own account as a private consultant. His methods, and the cases he investigates, are less spectacular than those of Holmes, and he 'has no system beyond a judicious use of ordinary faculties,' but the stories related by his journalistic friend, Brett, show Martin Hewitt to be more akin to Sherlock Holmes than were any other detectives of the period. A circumstance that may have stressed this similarity in the eyes of contemporary readers is that the Martin Hewitt stories, which first appeared in the *Strand Magazine* between March and December, 1894, were illustrated by Sidney Paget, the artist who had already illustrated Conan Doyle's *The Adventures of Sherlock Holmes,* published in the same magazine a year or so earlier. Arthur Morrison's stories were quickly re-issued in volume form, *Martin Hewitt, Investigator* in 1894, *The Chronicles of Martin Hewitt* in 1895, and *The Adventures of Martin Hewitt* in 1896.

There remains, in nineteenth century fiction, one other outstanding figure, the most remote and erudite detective of all, the high-born Russian exile, Prince Zaleski. He was created in the book of that name by Matthew Phipps Shiel, who had been studying surgery at Bart's Hospital and has related how he became 'sickened of knifing and gave it up, and lying idle one day, gazing at the sky, was given the idea to write my *Prince Zaleski.*' The volume, published in 1895, presents three of Zaleski's investigations, or, rather, his flights of inductive reasoning, for in only one of them does he leave his couch. The atmosphere of the tales, their background of exotic grandeur fallen into disuse and decay, is much more in tune with the Tale of Terror of a hundred years earlier than with the practical work-a-day world of Sherlock Holmes or Martin Hewitt. Prince Zaleski is more of a recluse than Dupin (and of still more exalted birth) more out of touch with normal living, more preoccupied with strange learning gleaned from distant ages and long-dead civilisations.

Shiel has acknowledged his debt to Edgar Allan Poe. [He] . . . was probably also influenced by Eugène Sue, for the similarities between Sue's Prince Rodolphe, or his Prince of Hansfield, and Shiel's Prince Zaleski seem too striking to be due entirely to chance. But many of Zaleski's eccentricities may well be due to a desire on Shiel's part to make him as different as possible from Sherlock Holmes, who was in the first flush of his popularity when *Prince Zaleski* was written. Except that they shared an addiction to drugs, the contrast between the two men could scarcely be greater than it is. Holmes loves the busy streets of London; Zaleski buries himself in a solitary retreat. Holmes is a 'scientist' whose knowledge is applied to practical purposes; Zaleski's studies are so vague and abstruse as to be almost beyond human understanding. The detection of crime is Holmes' most absorbing interest; Zaleski considers any such problem as an unwelcome interruption, and turns his mind to it only as a favour to his one personal friend, the anonymous narrator. Every detail of Holmes' face and figure is familiar to the reader; Prince Zaleski's appearance is nowhere described, and thus he remains a remote, unreal personality, who mingles prophecies with his detective deductions, for he possessed 'the unparalleled power not merely of disentangling in retrospect, but of unravelling in prospect, able to relate coming events with unimaginable minuteness of precision.' A further point of difference is that whereas Conan Doyle, and almost every other writer of detective fiction, uses plain, realistic language, Shiel's prose is ornate and polysyllabic, designed to conjure up an atmosphere of strange, unreal beauty, rather than to tell a straight-forward tale.

The stories themselves are equally remote from reality. In the first, 'The Race of Orven,' Zaleski's knowledge of the symptoms of hereditary insanity may be accurate, his interpretation of psychological reactions may be convincing, but his grasp of practical matters is not invariably sound. It is, for example, inconceivable that the police who searched the earl's mansion would have missed a series of holes cut through floors and ceilings, or the bloodstains caused by the accident to the maid. Such discrepancies would hardly have been overlooked by readers who had learned from the Sherlock Holmes stories to expect a precise and feasible interpretation of the evidence.

Another feature which is at variance with the normal pattern of detective fiction is the haughty, class-conscious snobbery which, though possibly natural to a Russian prince like Zaleski, is completely out of place in a story of this type. Even if, in view of Zaleski's royal blood, we are prepared to overlook his contemptuous reference to 'the yokels, jabbering uncouthly together,' or his savage scorn of the hard-working ill-used maid—'that poor specimen of humanity, a peering, hysterical caricature of a woman, we cannot accept his smooth generalisation that 'Earls' sons do not, in fact, go about murdering people,' for Lord Randolph is an unscrupulous, dangerous and brutal criminal. When a villain of this calibre figures in a detective story, the reader expects him to be brought to justice, and does not find satisfying an ending which merely hints at this event.

The second story, 'The Stone of the Edmundsbury Monks,' is more in the tradition of detective fiction, and concerns the mystery of a missing baronet. From a scrutiny of his diary, Zaleski discovers the reason for his disappearance and predicts his death at a specified time and place. In the third story, 'S.S.,' the mystery is more horrifying, and the urgency so intense that, for the first time, Zaleski leaves his retreat and returns to the outside world. Only by the most intense mental concentration does he fathom the secrets of the Society of Sparta and bring to an end their schemes for mass murder, without, however, taking any steps to inform against those responsible. It is, apparently, a sufficient triumph for Zaleski that the Society will plan no further crimes.

There is no one quite like Zaleski. He is the quintessence of the inductive, analytical reasoner, a student with an immense store of learning, created for readers capable of grasping clues derived from a Latin quotation, a couple of words in Greek, or some inconsistency in a sketch of mythological figures. He is the detective for the intelligentsia, the greatest possible contrast to Nick Carter, who is the detective of the uneducated. Each of them could appeal only to a limited section of the reading public, and neither could compare in popularity with their illustrious contemporary, Sherlock Holmes, who attracted readers of all classes of society and every educational level.

Several factors encouraged the remarkable growth of English detective fiction during the closing decades of the nineteenth century. The great scientific discoveries made at this time, particularly in the fields of chemistry, bacteriology and medicine (many of them concerned with preserving life and health or improving living conditions, and therefore of special interest to the general public) aroused lively admiration for men who were clever at finding things out, whatever their sphere of activity. The materialism of the period also had its effect, public opinion ranging itself increasingly strongly on the side of those whose function was to protect society from the depredations of criminals. A further point is that the changing economic conditions of the later nineteenth century created a vast, hardworked, often poorly-paid section of the community, city dwellers for the most part, who looked to the Free Libraries then springing up in all large towns, or to the many cheap magazines of the day, to provide entertainment for their brief leisure, an escape from the narrow realities of their daily life, an escape which the detective story most readily supplied.

A further explanation for the rapid growth of the detective story during the 1890's lies in 'the cult of the individual' which manifested itself everywhere in English fiction at that time. Detective fiction is a medium that lends itself particularly well to expressing this 'individualism,' and it was precisely at this period that English writers began to place special emphasis upon the personality of their detective heroes, all of them amateurs, not members of an organisation, and therefore free to act as individuals. It was the figure of Prince Zaleski, Martin Hewitt, Sherlock Holmes, or even Dick Donovan, that monopolised the reader's interest, the plot of each story being devised to give one more instance of the hero's amazing powers of detection.

The individuality of the author himself acquired a new significance. Earlier in the nineteenth century, English writers of popular fiction were prone to conceal their names from their readers, and the title page of a novel might simply state, for example, *'A Secret of the Sea,* by the author of *In the Dead of Night,'* or *'Done in the Dark,* by the author of *Recommended to Mercy.'* Even a writer as well-known as Miss M. E. Braddon observed the same convention, and the numerous romances that followed her first success were all described as being 'by the author of *Lady Audley's Secret.'* By the 1890's, however, this near-anonymity had become outmoded, and the writer's name, with very few exceptions, not only appeared on his work but also served to identify the specific type of story of which he was the inventor and sole producer. A 'Fergus Hume story,' an 'Arthur Morrison story,' or a 'Conan Doyle story,' implied a tale of a particular pattern already familiar to the reader, and though Conan Doyle occasionally produced fiction of a different type, the general public expected 'a Conan Doyle story' to be a tale about Sherlock Holmes.

At this period, perhaps to a greater degree than ever before, readers of popular fiction tended to limit their reading to whatever types of story best satisfied their individual preferences. For many people, then and later, their enjoyment of fiction depends largely upon the extent to which they can identify themselves mentally with the leading character, and this they may do more readily with a detective hero, particularly an amateur detective, than with almost any other type of hero, because the qualities on which his success is shown to depend, his powers of observation, deduction and intelligence, are precisely those which most people believe they themselves possess. Once the individuality of the detective had become the central point of interest, the individuality of the reader could find a special satisfaction by sharing in spirit his problems and his ultimate triumph.

Striking changes came about in detective fiction during the period reviewed in this [essay]. At the beginning of the 1870's, when Sheridan Le Fanu's *Checkmate* appeared, few English novels gave an important place to a detective theme, and those that did made the investigator one of the normal characters in the story, who undertook the enquiry for personal reasons, on a single occasion only. In the 1890's, detective fiction was being produced in great quantity, and though some excellent novels of this type were written, for example Israel Zangwill's *The Big Bow Mystery* (1891), one of the best of the 'crime in a sealed room' problems, the great majority of detective stories were short. The chief, often the only, interest was the theme of detection; the detective himself, in that capacity, was the dominating figure in a series of 'cases,' and a recognisable pattern had been evolved which was followed almost without variation for the ensuing quarter of a century. (pp. 141-51)

> *A. E. Murch, "From Sheridan Le Fanu to Matthew Phipps Shiel," in her* The Development of the Detective Novel, *1958. Reprint by Greenwood Press, 1968, pp. 133-51.*

Julian Symons

[*In the following excerpt, Symons examines Victorian social forces that contributed to the development of English detective fiction and traces the evolution of the detective hero in several works by Charles Dickens, Wilkie Collins, and Emile Gaboriau.*]

(i) The 'Unknown Public'

Poe was the founding father whose genius suggested the themes to be followed by other writers: but the pattern of the detective story as it formed in the eighteen-fifties and -sixties was closely related to the rise in Britain and America of a middle class with increasing leisure, the spread of reading, and the development of detective forces in several countries. Given these social factors, detective stories must inevitably have been written. The form they took was derived from Poe, but a look at their development in Britain shows how well the detective story was suited to the emotional needs of the growing middle class.

In 1858 Wilkie Collins wrote an essay on 'The Unknown Public', which was, he said, 'in a literary sense, hardly beginning, as yet, to read', and suggested that 'the future of English fiction may rest with this Unknown Public which is now waiting to be taught the difference between a good book and a bad'. The Unknown Public had been born with the Industrial Revolution, which brought with it a certain amount of education, strongly opposed by many who felt that to teach farm workers and domestic servants to read was no service either to them or to the country in which they lived. In the Sunday schools set up at the end of the eighteenth century only works tending to the improvement of religious education were read, but the creation of a semi-literate class of skilled workers, small shopkeepers, clerks and domestics had results not intended by Hannah More, who wanted everybody to be able to read religious books, or by the Utilitarians, who thought that 'the diffusion of useful knowledge' must be conducive to 'the future welfare of mankind'.

In the early part of the nineteenth century the high price of novels limited their circulation (the price was often a guinea and a half for a new work, and the sale usually not much more than 1,000 copies) and kept them out of the hands of the new readers, but as always demand created supply. A sub-literature sprang up to satisfy the needs of those who would in any case have found Scott, the best-selling novelist of the time, beyond their scope. It took the form of broadsheets and pamphlets, some of them political, but more concerned with crime. James Catnach published broadsheets and ballads about murders and executions, many of which sold up to a million copies, and other publishers and printers issued what were called 'blue books', abridgements or imitations of Gothic novels in thirty-six or, less often, seventy-two pages, which sold at sixpence. In 1841 Edward Lloyd, later the founder of *Lloyd's Weekly Newspaper,* put out books in weekly parts sold at a penny, which were called 'penny dreadfuls'. The dreadful thing about them was supposed to be their subject matter, although the stories were no more than amalgams of excitement and romance, often belying the promise of such titles as *Vice and its Victim: or, Phoebe, the Peasants' Daughter.* Some stories had a more directly violent or sexual content. G. W. M. Reynolds, who founded first of all *Reynolds' Miscellany* and later, like Lloyd, his own newspaper, wrote a series of enormously long 'Mysteries' which were issued in penny numbers with titles like *Mysteries of the Inquisition* and *Mysteries of the Court of London.* They were no more mysterious than Sue's work on which they were based, but Reynolds's early serials in particular are much concerned with torture and violence, up to the point of what Victorians considered permissible in open publication. In an obituary notice of Reynolds, who died in 1879, the *Bookseller* called him 'the most popular writer of his time'.

By the eighteen-fifties penny dreadfuls were being aimed more particularly at a juvenile market. Their readership changed largely because of the spread of subscription and public libraries, which in its turn reflected the rise of the new class created by the pressures of an increasingly industrial and urban civilization. Circulating libraries had existed in England for a long time, but they were given wide popularity by Charles Edward Mudie, who offered a yearly subscription for one guinea instead of his competitors' two, and arranged for an efficient delivery service in town and country. He found that the greatest demand was for novels, and although of course many of his country subscribers were the clergymen and gentry who had formerly bought books, in towns they were often the families of the highly respectable tradesmen and small businessmen who were anxious to move away from their origins and to assert their recently won privileges. All of these subscribers were able to feel assured that no work of a morally doubtful kind would be offered to them by Mudie, who was a Dissenter and had no hesitation in refusing to stock any book of which he disapproved.

So Mudie's, and other subscription libraries, helped to diffuse reading matter, if not always useful knowledge. They were supplemented by the free—that is, rate-supported—libraries which, after a good deal of opposition in the House of Commons on such grounds as that if the working classes read more they would damage agricultural interests by drinking less, were approved in 1850. Between Parliamentary approval and local readiness to establish libraries at the expense of ratepayers there was a considerable gap, and as late as 1887 only two parishes in London had rate-supported libraries. Their opponents felt that they were a sure road to ruin, and in the early eighteen-nineties a correspondent of the *Evening Standard* wrote of a young man in Brighton who spent all his time at the Public Library 'perusing light literature' and did no work. Another visitor to Brighton library said that 'no greater curse existed than these libraries', and he 'had rather see a young man hanging about a public-house than spending his time in these places'. The free libraries were not used by the gentry. A breakdown of borrowers by occupation at Manchester in the eighteen-fifties showed that 'artisans and mechanics' were by far the largest group of borrowers. Many of them wanted useful or improving books, but the demand for fiction was immediate and grew by what it fed on. As early as the mid fifties about half of the books lent or read at Sheffield Public Library were novels, and as the decades passed it was accepted that the purpose of libraries was to provide entertainment as well as education. Circulating and free libraries presented a threat to ordinary publishing which was countered by the issue of novels in monthly parts, and by the publication of still cheaper editions. The immense success of *Pickwick Papers* in monthly parts was the signal for much popular fiction to appear first in this form, sometimes simultaneously with publication in the new magazines that appeared at the end of the fifties. The first issue of the *Cornhill,* which included an instalment of Trollope's *Framley Parsonage* and Thackeray's *Roundabout Papers,* sold 120,000 copies. Cheap editions flourished too, encouraged greatly by the spread of rail travel and the length of the journeys. Every station of any size had its bookstall, and 'railway novels',

most of them yellowbacks with a picture on the front and advertisements at the back, were immensely successful. They sold at a shilling or one and sixpence, which may not seem cheap in comparison with modern paperbacks, but was within the price range of those who travelled by rail and ignored the free library.

This, then, was what Collins called the Unknown Public: a new generation of readers possessing literacy and some leisure, and with a vague but pressing need to read for amusement books which would in some degree confirm the permanence of their own newly won position in society. There were plenty of books in the Railway Library or the free libraries that were written from a social attitude with which they agreed, but not many that expressed the concern they felt about the importance of law and order, their interest in the prevention and punishment of crime.

(ii) The development of the police and detectives

There is a common impression that the Victorian age in Britain was one of settled calm, but that is not the way the early part of it looked to those who lived through it. It was not merely that the existing social order seemed threatened by the Chartist movement, but that the country was in fact a lawless place. Certain areas of London, as of New York and other big cities, were practically immune from visits by the police, and the detection of crime was in the hands of the Bow Street Runners, who were in effect private detectives operating partly for private reward, and widely thought to be susceptible to bribery. Even when a professional paid police force came into existence after the Metropolitan Police Act of 1829, the Bow Street Runners survived for another ten years. They were replaced in 1842 by the Detective Department, which consisted of two inspectors and six sergeants. The first head of the Department had distinguished himself two years before its foundation by what was then an unusual piece of detective work, when he noticed that apparent marks of forcible entry into a house had been faked, and that what appeared to be an 'outside' crime was really an 'inside' one.

It is impossible to understand the romantic aura which spread around detective departments and bureaus without realizing the thankfulness felt by the middle class at their existence. As they grew, the strand in crime writing represented by Godwin, Lytton and Balzac, in which the criminal was often considered romantic and the policeman stupid or corrupt, almost disappeared, although it could still be found in the penny dreadful. The detective, as the protector of established society, gradually replaced the criminal as hero.

In this capacity he was celebrated by Charles Dickens (1812-70), whose articles about various members of the Detective Department in *Household Words* were often expressed in terms of hero-worship. Dickens's ambivalent fascination with crime extended to the psychology of the criminal and the conditions of prison life. In several novels and short stories the idea of murder and its attendant guilt is examined, fretted over, viewed with distaste and even horror, yet considered as an act to which an evil character may be magnetically drawn. The psychological insight in the depiction of a figure like Bradley Headstone in *Our*

Mutual Friend sprang no doubt from Dickens's deepening awareness of his own criminal instincts. Our responses to the crimes of violence committed or attempted in the novels, from those of Bill Sikes and Jonas Chuzzlewit onwards, are all marked by our sense of the writer's own involvement.

Dickens's interest in prison conditions and his attempts to ameliorate their harshness were perfectly genuine, although his preference for the Silent System (by which all communication between prisoners was forbidden and infringements severely punished) over the Separate System (by which prisoners occupied individual cells and were masked or veiled when leaving them for religious instruction or any other purpose) may seem to us a liking for one form of barbarism over another. He viewed prisoners with the wrath and fear of one who senses a potential threat to his own social position, and echoed Carlyle in stressing the virtues of purposeless punishment: 'It is a satisfaction to me to see [a] determined thief, swindler, or vagrant, sweating profusely at the treadmill or the crank, and extremely galled to know that he is doing nothing all the time but undergoing *punishment.*'

It was natural that a man holding such views should extol the police, with whom he went out on expeditions, not only in London but also in Liverpool and New York. The articles that Dickens wrote, and others that he sponsored in his magazine *Household Words,* played a considerable part in forming the public view of detectives and changing the hostile or critical working-class attitude to the police. This hostility was based on two grounds: first that the police might be used as the state's arm to suppress reform movements, and second that they were inefficient. When a policeman was stabbed to death while helping to disperse a crowd at a political meeting in the eighteen-thirties the jury brought in a verdict of justifiable homicide. The efficiency in the early days of this collection of out-of-work tradesmen and unskilled labourers may be judged from the fact that in the first eight years of the Metropolitan Police Force's existence 5,000 men were dismissed and another 6,000 resigned. But by Dickens's time these growing pains were almost over, and he praised the imperturbability of the men in blue, although his greatest admiration was reserved for detectives. They were, he found, men of good deportment and unusual intelligence, never lounging or slinking about, showing signs of 'strong mental excitement', and (a common although unreliable test of honesty) 'they all can, and they all do, look full at whomsoever they speak to'. Dickens's particular hero was Inspector Field. When he entered a thieves' den 'every thief here comes before him, like a schoolboy before his schoolmaster'. His eye was keen and roving, he saw everything, he appeared to know everybody and to have access everywhere in criminal society. In the keenness and sagacity of Field (or Wield, as he appeared in other articles), and in his tricks of behaviour like 'the corpulent forefinger which is constantly in juxtaposition with his eyes or nose', we can see the outline of the professional detective of fiction, the bloodhound counterpart to Poe's aristocratic amateur. It is fitting that Dickens should have created the first English fictional police officer, natural that he should have been made in Field's image.

(iii) The pattern forms

'Inspector Bucket of the Detective', as he calls himself, was not precisely the first detective, even in Dickens. Before Bucket there was the insurance company investigator Nadgett in *Martin Chuzzlewit,* who carries cards saying that he follows all sorts of occupations from coal merchant to commission agent. Nadgett runs Jonas Chuzzlewit to earth, although he has to call on the police to make the arrest. Nadgett is a minor character, however, Bucket a major one. He makes his appearance about a third of the way through *Bleak House* (1853), in a manner appropriately unobtrusive, and indeed almost magical. Snagsby the stationer is talking to the lawyer Mr Tulkinghorn, when he is aware of a third person in the room, 'who was not there when he himself came in, and has not since entered by the door or by either of the windows. There is a press in the room, but its hinges have not creaked, nor has a step been audible upon the floor.'

Bucket has several physical resemblances to Field, including his use of a fat forefinger to make points. Like Field he is on familiar terms with lawbreakers, has an encyclopedic knowledge of their habits, and is greatly respected by them. He is able to disguise himself when necessary, an attribute no doubt derived from Vidocq. He is not at home among the upper classes, as is shown by his invariably addressing Sir Leicester Dedlock as 'Sir Leicester Dedlock, Baronet', but his plodding assurance is untouched by Sir Leicester's supercilious attitude. He is sympathetic to the poor, and capable of genially offering to fit a second pair of handcuffs on to an arrested man's wrists in case the first pair is uncomfortable. Bucket engages in no spectacular feats of detection, but is shown as a shrewd and sympathetic man. In a general way he serves as a model for many later professional detectives.

Dickens's unfinished last novel, *The Mystery of Edwin Drood,* is sometimes classed as a mystery or detective story. It was left unfinished at a peculiarly tantalizing point, when Drood has disappeared and the movements of the sinister John Jasper are being watched by several people, among them the obviously disguised Datchery. Had the book been finished these puzzles would of course have been resolved, and fascinating though they are in themselves they do not mean that the novel was intended to be, or would have appeared when completed as, a mystery story. An immense amount of ingenuity has been expended in solving these fortuitous puzzles, and the clues left by Dickens (who did not, one should perhaps stress, intend them as clues) and his illustrators can be interpreted in several ways. On the balance of probabilities Mr J. Cuming Walters is reasonable in suggesting that Datchery was Helena Landless in disguise, and that Jasper had killed Edwin, or at least believed that he had killed him, although I would have a small saving bet on the possibility suggested by Mr Michael Innes that Datchery may have been somebody who had not previously entered the story, but was closely connected with one of the leading characters. But these are mysteries related to Dickens's intentions, and probably the completed book would have been a mysterious thriller rather than a detective story, resembling *The Woman in White* rather than *The Moonstone.*

It is by these two books that Dickens's close friend Wilkie Collins (1824-89) is remembered today. Collins is generally regarded, as he was in his own lifetime, as a writer whose merits lie purely in the field of melodrama. 'Mr Collins is in the habit of prefixing prefaces to his stories which might almost lead one to think he looks on himself as an artist,' said the *Pall Mall Gazette* contemptuously in reviewing *The Moonstone*. 'A conjurer at a county fair has as much right to prate about his art . . . Is this, then, what fiction has come to? We scarcely see how anything could be meaner.' Yet, as T. S. Eliot has pointed out, in Collins's time 'the best novels *were* thrilling', and neither Collins nor his readers thought of him as writing down to them. In the preface to his second novel, *Basil*, Collins stated a creed from which he never wavered when he said that 'the business of fiction is to exhibit human life' and that it was permissible to depict 'misery and crime' if they were turned to 'a plainly and purely moral purpose'. The intentions of Collins were no less serious than those of Dickens. Both of them pursued, and indeed captured, the Unknown Public, and although Collins was not a genius like his friend, he was a melodramatic writer of the highest class, and perhaps the most skilful plot-constructor of the century.

His first novel which shows any detective element is *Hide and Seek* (1854), in which, as one critic has said, he borrowed Fenimore Cooper's Leatherstocking, had him scalped by Indians and set him down in London. The element of detection in the story, which relates to the unravelling of the history of an orphan and her mother, is real but slight. Some of the stories in the two collections *After Dark* (1856) and *The Queen of Hearts* (1859) also have a small claim to consideration. 'A Stolen Letter' in the first collection follows Poe's device in 'The Purloined Letter' so closely that it can almost be called a crib, and in the second 'Anne Rodway' is a murder story with an unusually convincing low-life background, and 'The Biter Bit' a comic detective story about a lawyer's clerk who has been accepted as a recruit for the 'Detective Police' and makes an appalling mess of his first and only case. Collins was particularly good at depicting bumptiously self-important characters, and this is one of the few successful comic detective short stories.

The Woman in White (1860) is the liveliest of Collins's crime stories, and the one most full of memorable characters. Upon the basis of an eighteenth-century French case, in which a woman was drugged and imprisoned so that she should be presumed dead and her estate pass to her brother, was built the idea of the substitution of one person for another, effected with the aid of a private asylum. In the interesting article about the book's construction Collins wrote a couple of years before his death, he discussed in detail the development from this original germ, the invention of the Italian Fosco because the crime was too ingenious for an English villain, the obesity which Fosco was given after the story had been begun because this was 'in opposition to the recognized type of villain' (in Victorian days fat men were jolly though sometimes unctuous, for us to be overweight is in itself sinister), the various false starts, and the ingenious shifts of viewpoint by which interest is maintained. But analysis of this kind does not fully account for the quality of the book. Marion Halcombe, almost the only moustached heroine in English fiction, and Fosco come through more clearly than any other Collins characters, and they do so because something about Marion's indomitable determination and about Fosco's charm struck a chord of romantic feeling in their author. This mild, genial little man, whose feet were so tiny that they were too small for women's shoes, had an obsession with physical deformity that is often ludicrous or disagreeable, but is urbanely comic in the picture of Fosco's monstrous fatness. The feeling was accompanied by a penchant for dominating ladies, seen at its most pleasant in Marion. Beyond this, the book has a high-spirited inventiveness that was uncommon even in Victorian fiction. The turns of the plot are always ingenious and often unexpected, and it is not surprising that Collins chose as a summary of his career on his tombstone: 'Author of *The Woman in White* and other works of fiction'.

From the beginning the book was a great success. In England Dickens's *All the Year Round* and in America *Harper's Magazine* began to carry it on the same date, 29 November 1859. On publication day the London crowds queued outside the magazine offices for it. Cloaks, bonnets and perfumes, waltzes and quadrilles, were called by its

A drawing by Frederick Walker for Wilkie Collins's The Woman in White.

name. Gladstone cancelled a theatre engagement to go on reading it, and Prince Albert sent a copy to Baron Stockmar. The book established Collins, in the minds of some readers, as a rival to Dickens. It is possible that some feeling of this kind was in Dickens's own mind, for although he published the book as a serial, he animadverted on it with unusual sharpness in a letter saying that 'the construction is wearisome beyond endurance, and there is a vein of obstinate conceit in it that makes enemies of readers'. In spite of a cool critical reception, the first edition of 1,500 copies (in the expensive three-volume form, it should be remembered) was quickly sold.

Judged purely as a novel of event and character, *The Moonstone* (1868) is not as good a book as *The Woman in White*. There are no characters in it equal to Fosco or Marion, and although Drusilla Clack, the spinster with her religious tracts, is a distinct comic figure, many readers have felt that they have had enough of her after a few pages. If we look at the originality of the conception, however, and at the skill shown in ordering the plot, *The Moonstone* is a masterly performance, a feat all the more memorable because shortly after beginning the book Collins was distressed by the illness and death of his mother, and during much of the later writing he was tortured by rheumatic gout so intense that several young men employed to take down from his dictation found his cries of pain unendurable and had to leave. Nothing of this comes through in a narrative told with an assurance, and a skill in varying style and tempo, equal to anything in Victorian literature.

But of course *The Moonstone* is not now judged primarily by these lights, but as the first detective novel written in English. Originality of this kind is something that doesn't last. As Sayers has said in writing about the book, 'when we have grown familiar with its successors and imitators the original classic no longer appears to us to have anything original about it'. This is not, however, quite true of *The Moonstone*. Collins's mind was so ingenious, and his skill in maintaining the deception about the jewel so great, that a reader who has been brought up on modern detective stories and then comes to the book is not likely to feel that this period piece was no doubt very good in its day, but rather that he is reading one of the few crime stories which combine great ingenuity in devising a puzzle with the ability to tell an absorbingly interesting story. The solution to the puzzle is perfectly fair, although its laudanum inspiration may now seem a little unsophisticated, and, as Sayers has said, the foundation for everything that happens later is laid in the first few chapters. The shifting of suspicion from one character to another is done with great adroitness, and the theft of an immensely valuable diamond, with its implied contrast between the mysterious East and the humdrum reality of Victorian life, gives full play to Collins's subdued romanticism. And, as a corrective to this, bringing what Collins sometimes called 'a breath of the Actual', there is Sergeant Cuff.

Cuff was founded upon Inspector Jonathan Whicher of the Detective Department, who appears in his days as a sergeant as 'Witchem' in a *Household Words* article. Whicher's career at the time Collins wrote had been a che-

quered one. In 1860 he had arrested Constance Kent on a charge of murdering her small brother Francis, and had suffered a blot on his reputation at her acquittal which was not quite wiped away when she confessed five years later. In 1861 he had been responsible in another murder case for the arrest of a man who was undoubtedly innocent. It is likely that the skills of Whicher, who was known before these calamities as 'the Prince of Detectives' were, like those of Field, much exaggerated, but Collins may have had in mind his rehabilitation. He used several details from the Constance Kent case and some of Cuff's deductions resemble those of Whicher, although there was no physical resemblance. Whicher was short, thick-set, pockmarked. Collins's portrait of Cuff, as described by the house-steward Gabriel Betteredge, shows what a splendid eye he had for externals:

> A fly from the railway drove up as I reached the lodge: and out got a grizzled elderly man so lean that he looked as if he had not got an ounce of flesh on his bones in any part of him. He was dressed all in decent black, with a white cravat round his neck. His face was as sharp as a hatchet, and the skin of it was as yellow and dry and withered as an autumn leaf. His eyes, of a steely light grey, had a very disconcerting trick, when they encountered your eyes, of looking as if they expected something more from you than you were aware of yourself. His walk was soft; his voice was melancholy; his long lanky fingers were hooked like claws. He might have been a parson, or an undertaker—or anything else you like, except what he really was.

Cuff is, like many later detectives, a master of the apparently irrelevant remark, the unexpected observation. Faced with a problem and asked what is to be done, he trims his nails with a penknife and suggests a turn in the garden and a look at the roses; asked who has stolen the moonstone he says blandly that nobody has stolen it. The fascination of such remarks is that their meaning just eludes us. We feel that we should be able to grasp it by making the proper deductions.

The first, the longest and the best of modern English detective novels': that was Eliot's description of *The Moonstone,* but its designation as 'the first' should certainly be corrected. . . . [There] is no doubt that the first detective novel, preceding Collins and Gaboriau, was *The Notting Hill Mystery.* This was published in book form in 1865, three years before *The Moonstone,* but first appeared in the magazine *Once a Week,* where publication began in November 1862 and continued well into the following year. Its primacy is thus unquestionable.

Its author, Charles Felix, remains mysterious. He wrote at least three other books, none of them a mystery, and although the name sounds like a pseudonym, research has not revealed another identity. *The Notting Hill Mystery* was no doubt an attempt to repeat the success of *The Woman in White,* with a sinister Baron playing the Fosco role, and although Felix had few of Collins's gifts as a story-teller, his book is in several ways an original work. It includes a map, a practice which was not to become common for a good many years, as well as facsimiles of a marriage certificate and of a fragment torn from a letter. The plot is in some ways strikingly modern in tone. The story is told in letters and reports sent to his employers by Ralph Henderson, investigator for a life assurance company. Their suspicions have been aroused after the death of Madame R by the fact that her husband, the Baron R, has taken out not one but five policies on her life, each in the sum of £5,000. Antimony is suspected as the cause of her death, but the Baron is able to prove that he never himself gave her food or drink. Henderson discovers that the 'Baron' is really a German named Carl Schwartz, and his conclusion is that Schwartz employed mesmeric powers to poison his wife through the sympathetic feeling existing between two sisters, so that poison given to one killed the other. The idea, preposterous to us, seemed less ridiculous to Victorians. The book ends with Henderson asking his employers what, if anything, can be done about a murder committed in this way. The level of the writing is far above Victorian hackwork, although equally far below that of Collins. But the essential point is that the book is a true detective novel, and the first of its kind.

This bow to the ghost of Charles Felix should not reduce appreciation of Collins. The combination of his particular gifts is rare. Perhaps if Somerset Maugham had written a detective story, instead of a spy story, and if he had been at the top of his form, the result might have been something like *The Moonstone*. Collins himself, in the two decades left to him, never wrote anything approaching in merit his two finest books, although historians of the detective story have surprisingly neglected *The Law and the Lady* (1875). The plot here owes something to the Scottish trial of Madeleine Smith, with its 'Not Proven' verdict. Eustace Macallan, like Madeleine, is tried for poisoning by arsenic and set free by a similar unsatisfactory verdict, and the story is concerned with the efforts of his second wife, Valeria, one of Collins's determined heroines, to prove him innocent. There is a genuine puzzle to be solved, and some parts of the book are excellent, particularly the long account of Eustace's trial. The quality of the writing, however, is very uneven, and the book is marred by one of his more unsuccessful grotesques, the self-styled poet Miserimus Dexter, a sort of legless Quilp.

Collins admired and kept upon his shelves the crime stories of Émile Gaboriau (1833-73), and *The Moonstone* may have been influenced by the French writer's first three crime stories, *L'affaire Lerouge* (1863), *Le crime d'Orcival* and *Le dossier no. 113* (1867)—dates given are those of the original serial publications in which Collins may have seen them, although *L'affaire Lerouge* first appeared in book form in 1866. Gaboriau was a hack writer of historical and sensational serials whose work was transformed by his discovery of the possibilities of the detective story. Gaboriau, like Dickens and Collins, was fascinated by police work and knew a great deal not only about the operations of the Sûreté, but about the functions of the interrogating judge and the local policeman. A passage in his finest work, the posthumously published long short story, *Le petit vieux de Batignolles,* shows that he was aware of the difficulty involved in making his hero a policeman. The narrator, an amateur detective on his first case, accompanies a professional named Méchinet into the Prefecture:

This was the first time in my life that I crossed the threshold of the Prefecture of Police, against which I had hitherto been quite as prejudiced as any other Parisian. Those who study social questions may well ask how it happens that the French police are so generally hated and despised. Even the ordinary street policeman is the object of aversion; and the detective is loathed as intensely as if he were some monstrous horror, in lieu of generally being a most useful servant of society.

It was, then, a daring stroke to create a policeman hero, and Gaboriau sugared the pill by providing an amateur detective who often keeps him company. In *L'affaire Lerouge,* Gévrol, Chief of the Sûreté, is quickly replaced as the chief investigator by an elderly retired pawnbroker named Père Tabaret, known as 'Tir-au-clair'. It is Tabaret who makes the brilliant deductions by which the crime is solved, explaining them as he goes along to a young policeman named Lecoq, first introduced as a minor character, 'an old offender reconciled with the law'. But although Père Tabaret does not disappear completely—at the end of *Monsieur Lecoq* (1869) he points out to the professional detective the clues he has missed—he moves into the background and Lecoq becomes the central figure, with Gévrol as his butt, and sometimes with a companion of inferior intelligence as his assistant. Gaboriau makes it clear that his hero was nothing like the hated detective of reality. 'The most obtuse shopkeeper is sure that he can scent a detective at twenty paces; a big man with moustaches, and a shining felt hat, dressed in a black, threadbare surtout, carefully buttoned up on account of the absence of linen. Such is the type.' Lecoq is nothing like that. His face is so mobile that he is able to 'mould his features according to his will, as the sculptor moulds clay for modelling'. He is a master of disguise, and on one occasion bitterly reproaches an agent for the inadequacy of his attempt to change his appearance. Unlike Cuff, Bucket or Dupin, he has a distinct eye on the main chance. When as a young detective he writes a report which by implication criticizes the inefficiency of Gévrol and does not sign his name to it, Gaboriau explains that the reason is not modesty but calculation, because 'by hiding oneself on well-chosen occasions, one gains greater notoriety when one emerges from the shadow'.

Lecoq is self-seeking and vain, but he is also honest—it is explained in a later story that the original mention of him as 'an old offender' was the result of a misunderstanding. He has reason to be vain, for his deductive feats are notable. He is the first detective of fiction to make a plaster cast of footprints, improvising for the purpose some old boxes, an earthen dish, plaster which he knocks off a wall, and water. He is the first also to observe that a striking clock may be used to tell the time a crime was committed, when he pushes the long hand of a clock round to half past three and it strikes eleven. He realizes in *Le crime d'Orcival* that the criminal has deliberately planted the material clues, so that 'I had only, to reach the truth, to take the contrary of that which appearance had indicated'. Since five glasses were on the table the number of people present was 'more or less than five, but they were not five', and since the remains of supper lay on the table, they neither ate nor drank. He is able to tell his assistant that a man they are following is 'of middle age and tall, wore a shaggy brown overcoat, and was probably married as he had a wedding ring on the little finger of his right hand'. The points are explained: his 'heavy and dragging step' shown in convenient snow marked middle age, his height was marked by a block of granite on which he had leaned, the ring appeared through the imprint of his hand in snow, the colour of his coat was indicated by a few flakes of brown wool torn off by a wood splinter. Dupin might at this point have sat back and solved the case, but Lecoq is not an armchair detective. 'We hold the clue; we will follow it to the end. Onward, then,' he cries.

Gaboriau's highly sensational themes often contrast oddly with the sobriety of his detection. The murder has usually been committed to prevent the revelation of a scandal, and passages of detection are interspersed with long explanatory flashbacks about family history. Sometimes the villain turns out to be an aristocrat. In *Monsieur Lecoq* the detective in disguise pursues the murderer on an immense tour of Paris. He conducts a search of a grand mansion but goes away baffled, unable to believe that the nobleman who receives him with weary courtesy is the man he wants. Much of this is tiresome today, but there are compensations other than the passages of detection in the accurate and interesting accounts of aspects of the French legal system and the battles of wits in the dialogues between examining magistrate and accused, from which Simenon probably learned something. And in *Monsieur Lecoq* the detective plays a fascinating game of cat and mouse with the prisoner, which ends with his realization that somehow he has been betrayed, and that the mouse knows exactly what the cat is doing. This is the best of the novels: but *Le petit vieux de Batignolles* is undoubtedly his finest piece of work, a story full of tricks and turns, in which the murderer overreaches himself in thinking that the police are certain to discover that his victim is left-handed. They fail to do so, and arrest the right man on a completely false basis of argument. Gaboriau lacked humour, and skill in characterization, but it is going much too far to talk as one critic has done of his tawdry puppetry, dull and irrelevant digressions, and dreary and artificial verbiage. He remains an interesting and still underrated writer, whose crime stories are rooted in sound knowledge of police procedure and marked by a keen analytical intelligence.

Collins and Gaboriau: after Poe, they set the pattern in which detectives were made. Poe created the aristocratic amateur who was to endure, and upon the whole to be supreme, until the Second World War. Collins and Gaboriau gave us the honest professional, often disdained by the amateur, who, as Auden says in relation to Freeman Wills Crofts's Inspector French, 'detects for the sake of the innocent members of society' and succeeds because he has 'the help of all the innocent people in the world who are doing their duty'. After Collins and Gaboriau the professional detective, whether uniformed or in plain clothes, no longer appears in fiction as the corrupt oppressor, but as the protector of the innocent. The detective's changed character in fiction reflected a change in the nature of society, and his standing as a watchdog against evil was only

seriously questioned after sixty years, in the work of Dashiell Hammett and Raymond Chandler. (pp. 42-56)

Julian Symons, "Dickens, Collins, Gaboriau: The Pattern Forms," in his Bloody Murder: From the Detective Story to the Crime Novel, a History, *revised edition, Viking, 1985, pp. 42-56.*

A. E. Murch

[*In the following excerpt, Murch investigates how women novelists contributed to the development of detective fiction in England and America during the latter half of the nineteenth century.*]

When the outcry against 'Sensation Novels' was at its height in the 1850's and 1860's, contemporary critics were considerably disturbed because many of them were written by women. In spite of the notable precedent set by Mrs. Radcliffe at the end of the eighteenth century and the popularity of her Tales of Terror, mid nineteenth century publishers seemed to feel there was something peculiarly indelicate about tales of crime or criminals being written by a woman, and were reluctant to print them, though stories of social or domestic life were readily accepted.

Elizabeth Cleghorn Gaskell (1810-1865) was among the first contributors to Charles Dickens's *Household Words,* which published *Cranford* between December, 1851, and May, 1853. Her next work, a comparatively short tale, appeared in the Christmas number of *Household Words* for 1853, with the title *The Squire's Story,* and deserves special notice for its discreetly-handled detective interest. The wealthy stranger who has settled in a small country town regularly leaves home for a few days 'to collect his rents,' but the reader is given clues suggesting that he is really a notorious highwayman, and his riches are derived from armed robbery. During one of his expeditions he commits murder, and though there seems nothing to connect him with the crime, suspicion is aroused by indicative trifles, evidence is gathered exactly as in a detective story, until he betrays guilty knowledge of details not reported in the newspapers and is arrested. It is a neat little tale of crime and detection, though presented as a social commentary, thus escaping the stigma of 'sensationalism.'

Most of the melodramatic novels written by women during the latter half of the nineteenth century were of little value in themselves . . . , except that they maintained the popularity of a background against which certain types of detective themes could show to advantage. In brief, they prepared the way for what may be called 'the domestic detective story,' in which the reader becomes acquainted with the normal daily life of the characters before the *motif* of a mysterious crime is introduced.

A few such novels did more than prepare the way. They travelled some distance in that direction, and enlivened the domesticity or social intrigues of their plot with a sensational crime, leading to investigations along detective lines, if not to the creation of a detective.

Of the hundreds of short stories and some forty novels written by Mrs. Henry Wood (1814-1887), scarcely more than one is instantly called to mind whenever her name is mentioned—*East Lynne.* It appeared as a serial in *Colborn's New Monthly Magazine* between 1860 and 1861, but its appearance in volume form was delayed by publishers' prejudice against 'sensation novels,' and it was rejected three times. Yet, when it was at last accepted and published by Richard Bentley, it was received with such enthusiasm that more than a million copies were sold during the author's lifetime.

Within the extensive framework of this romance is a well-constructed murder mystery. The problem is difficult, for years have elapsed since the crime, and an innocent man was, at the time, convicted on circumstantial evidence. New information is gradually discovered, an alias penetrated and an alibi proved false. Material witnesses must be traced before the case can be re-opened and the truth established. More interest is focussed upon the drama of these developments than upon the process of detection which brings them about, yet that process is clearly and logically followed through to a successful conclusion, and an orderly array of evidence is placed before the court at the trial which forms the culmination of this detective theme.

A point which links Mrs. Henry Wood with many later writers of detective fiction is her appreciation of what constitutes evidence, her accurate knowledge of the law. Her son commented on this detail in his biography:—

> The science and mystery of the Law had always possessed great charm and attraction for her. She followed out the points of any intricate case that might be going on with clearness and insight—in trials of mystery and complication quickly forming her opinion, which seldom proved wrong.

When *East Lynne* was published, the *Saturday Review* noticed this feature of the novel with considerable surprise:—

> What is more remarkable is that the legal proceedings taken when the murderer is finally discovered are all, or almost all, right. There is a trial with its preliminary proceedings, a real summing up, and a lively cross-examination. Mrs. Wood has an accuracy and method of legal knowledge which would do credit to many famous male novelists.

Perhaps the most important of the many favourable reviews of *East Lynne* was that which appeared in the *Times* on January 25th, 1862. Very few current works of fiction were similarly honoured, and the novel at once became known throughout the English speaking world. A French translation quickly followed, and versions in other European languages were soon available. America gave the story an even more enthusiastic reception than it received in this country [England], both as a novel and as a play. Though none of Mrs. Wood's later works equalled *East Lynne* in popularity or in detective interest, one or two of her *Johnny Ludlow* stories gave some place to crime mysteries, and in *The Story of Charles Strange,* published posthumously in 1888, she wove together no fewer than five

distinct problems and dealt skilfully with their ultimate solution.

The success of *East Lynne* had an immediate effect on the status of women fiction-writers, and also influenced 'sensation novelists' in general, especially in respect of plot construction. Many could, and did, imitate Mrs. Wood's descriptions of family affairs in aristocratic circles, with details of great estates, devoted servants, eccentric relatives and brilliant social events. Nor was it difficult to introduce a mysterious crime, with enough complications to fill three or even four volumes. But it required abilities of another calibre to create and develop a convincing detective theme, and most writers were content to reveal the explanation of the mystery through the confession of the guilty person, who forthwith committed suicide. It is patent that in such a plot there is little or no room for a detective, and the great majority of these novels are outside our present scope, but one or two women writers of the period approached the *genre* sufficiently closely to merit consideration in this connection.

In the same year which saw the publication of *East Lynne,* there appeared another extremely popular novel of somewhat similar type, *Lady Audley's Secret* (1861). It was the first successful work of a young writer, Mary Elizabeth Braddon (1837-1915), who was to become even more prolific than Mrs. Henry Wood, for she published her eightieth (and last) full length romance, *The Green Curtain,* in 1911, when she was seventy-four. It was to Wilkie Collins's *The Woman in White* that Miss Braddon owed her inspiration for *Lady Audley's Secret,* a melodramatic tale of bigamy, blackmail, murder and attempted murder. It contains nothing comparable to the detective theme in Collins's novel, but it deserves mention here because in it Miss Braddon devised an original method of presenting the story. Lady Audley enjoys an honourable social position and the complete trust of her elderly doting husband, but almost from the opening pages the reader is made aware of her real character. He suspects her of past crimes, watches her plan and carry out new ones, and his mounting suspense arises out of his uncertainty as to whether her schemes will succeed, and how, if at all, her guilt can be proved. Eventually she meets retribution through the efforts of a former victim, whose success is due to coincidence and good luck, rather than to any detective skill.

As one romance after another flowed from Miss Braddon's pen, she placed more emphasis upon the steps whereby the guilt of her villains is discovered. Her plots are conventional in the sense that evil-doers are all brought to justice, while the virtuous invariably triumph in the final chapters. The central mystery always concerns a secret crime—blackmail, fraud, or murder—and various characters do their best to solve whatever part of the problem affects them personally, but Miss Braddon never makes it the function of one particular figure to view the puzzle as a whole, or to collect and co-relate evidence in the manner of a detective.

Miss Braddon was a solicitor's daughter, and, like Mrs. Henry Wood, had a good working knowledge of English law. Perhaps her greatest influence upon detective fiction lies in the use she made of that knowledge, for she showed remarkable ingenuity in devising highly original ways of breaking the law, making the technique of crime so interesting that she was savagely attacked by contemporary critics as the most dangerous of the sensation novelists, and accused of encouraging criminals. But her appreciative public held a different opinion, and her novels were so popular that for almost three decades she was described in current periodicals as 'The Queen of the Circulating Libraries.'

Several of her later books give more place to the detection of crimes than to their sensational or technical aspects. In *A Strange World* (1875) the hero falls under suspicion in the first volume, and the reader is entertained by the conflicting attempts at detection by the hero and concealment by the villain until the final chapters of the third. *An Open Verdict* (1878) shows the heroine suspected of having caused her father's death. Her innocence is at last established, though the detective work that clears her of suspicion is overshadowed by her plans for punishing those who doubted her. The balance swings in the other direction in *Just As I Am* (1880), the love story of Morton Blake and Dulcie being less important to the plot than the mysterious crime and the detection of the murderer.

In *Wyllard's Weird* (1885) there are two love affairs and two strange crimes. Evidence has to be discovered in Paris, and Miss Braddon unravels the sensational clues in a manner very reminiscent of Gaboriau or Fortuné du Boisgobey. In so doing, she may have had in mind a wish to please her wide circle of French readers, for she was proud of the success of French translations of her novels, and was in close touch with literary circles in Paris. *Like and Unlike* (1887) tells of a bloodless murder that nearly succeeds in baffling detection, and the young nobleman who so carefully plans 'the perfect crime' is finally proved guilty. Almost without exception Miss Braddon's later novels deal with ingenious crimes and the circumstances that lead to the punishment of the criminal, and though she did not produce a detective hero, she certainly made some contribution to the detective fiction of the 1870's and 1880's.

Only one or two other women writers in England at this period followed Miss Braddon's lead in this respect, but there are points of special interest in *The Land of the Leal* (1878), by Miss Helen Mathers (1853-1920). The volume contains two comparatively short and unconnected tales (an innovation in itself) and in the first of them, 'As He Comes up the Stair,' Miss Mathers used a technique which does not seem to have been employed before that time. The story is told retrospectively, from the condemned cell, by a woman wrongly convicted of murdering her husband and his gipsy sweetheart. The husband has, in fact, been poisoned by the gipsy, and the wife shows considerable detective skill in discovering the truth, but falls under suspicion herself. Miss Mathers shows remarkable perception in depicting the thought-processes of the unfortunate woman, and for this alone the story deserves notice. The trial is related in detail, rather inadvisably in view of Miss Mathers' inaccurate impressions of judicial procedure. The same handicap mars the second tale, 'Stephen Hatton,' in which a man is convicted on circumstantial evi-

dence and executed, after which his supposed victim is found alive. Contemporary reviewers, who were beginning to expect writers of such fiction to have accurate legal knowledge, pointed out with some care just how far Miss Mathers was in error in her presentation of these matters.

Miss E. S. Drewry, in *The Death Ring* (1881) created a clever private detective, and this work could be considered an exciting detective novel if only the writer had not revealed, far too early in the story, details which would have been better concealed until the end. But Miss Drewry not only chose a title that disclosed the means, and indicated the identity of the murderer in the opening chapters, she went so far as to quote in her Preface an extract from the *Standard* describing an ancient ring lately discovered in Paris, which would inflict a poisoned scratch, causing death. It is by no means unusual for detective stories to be based upon such items found in newspapers, but by giving the explanation before the puzzle Miss Drewry sacrificed the element of mystery and deprived her readers of what could have been an entertaining problem.

A far clearer conception of how a detective novel should be constructed is shown in the work of an American writer, Anna Katharine Green (1846-1935), who exercised a considerable influence upon detective fiction in her own country and in England. She was the daughter of a distinguished defence lawyer of Brooklyn, and almost her first attempt at fiction, *The Leavenworth Case* (1878), achieved a remarkable success. She was the first woman to write a full-length detective story, and she described *The Leavenworth Case* in that way on the title page. Early in 1879 the book was re-issued in London, and her later novels were published more or less simultaneously on both sides of the Atlantic. While ostensibly obeying the contemporary convention that a full length novel should consist of several volumes, she made each 'volume' short enough to allow the whole story to be contained within one pair of covers. Almost without exception, the novels we have considered earlier were first issued in serial form, but *The Leavenworth Case* made its first appearance in the form of a complete detective novel in one volume.

In some respects Miss Green's novels resemble those of Mrs. Henry Wood and Miss Braddon in their introduction of such melodramatic features as guilty secrets behind a façade of wealth and luxury, unjust suspicions, dramatic revelations and noble reconciliations, but Miss Green uses them merely to provide a background and create the mystery. The paramount interest is clearly the theme of detection, and all her stories of this type are constructed upon a fairly uniform plan. A sensational puzzle is placed before the reader at the earliest possible moment; one enigma leads on to others even more baffling; false trails and temporary setbacks delay the investigations, but in the final chapters the detective triumphantly unmasks the criminal, generally someone quite unsuspected until that moment. Dickens had made a special explanatory chapter the culmination of the detective them in *Bleak House;* Collins had done much the same in *The Woman in White* and *The Moonstone;* Le Fanu had gone much further in *Checkmate,* but in none of these does the detective theme monopolize the reader's attention so completely as in Miss

Green's novels, and in her work we can discern for the first time, in its entirety, the pattern that became characteristic of most English detective novels written during the following fifty years.

Anna Katharine Green certainly knew the detective stories of her fellow-countryman, Edgar Allan Poe, and one of her shorter tales, 'The Mayor's Wife,' contains a cryptogram worked out in the same way as the one in 'The Gold Bug.' In *The Leavenworth Case,* the murderer needed to dispose quickly of two incriminating items, a letter and a key, and he reasoned in precisely the same way as the Minister D—in 'The Purloined Letter':—

> Hide them? I would not try to. Instead of that I would put them in plain sight, trusting to that very fact for their being overlooked. Making the letter into lighters, I carried them into the spare room and placed them in a vase. The key I placed within the ornamental metal-work of the gas-bracket.

Like Poe, Miss Green generally constructed her mysteries around a sensational murder, and worked out the explanation step by step, in logical sequence. Dupin (and also Lecoq) had figured in a series of different tales, and Miss Green followed this example, making her Mr. Gryce the central figure in several novels. But she did not give him an admiring friend to chronicle his exploits, nor did she begin her tale by relating anecdotes to illustrate his detective powers, as Poe did for Dupin, and as Conan Doyle did in later years for Sherlock Holmes. In this respect, and in making her detective a police officer, Miss Green was more akin to Gaboriau, whose tales of M. Lecoq had been well known in America for some ten years before she began to write in similar vein. His influence is also reflected in other aspects of her work, particularly in her concentration on intricately woven plots and in making her secondary characters 'types,' rather than individuals. In one or two points she improved upon Gaboriau's technique, for she kept her plots well within the bounds of probability, and contrived to reduce to a minimum the tiresome, but almost inevitable, passages relating the past histories of those concerned in the crime.

The Leavenworth Case opens dramatically when news of Mr. Leavenworth's murder is brought to his lawyer, Everett Raymond, who relates the story. The plot is unfolded skilfully with steadily increasing tension, and the atmosphere of the novel is so modern that little touches which reveal its period are encountered almost with a sense of shock. For example, the fact that Mr. Leavenworth had installed gas lighting in one or two of his private rooms is considered an ostentatious extravagance, the rest of the house being lighted 'in the ordinary way, with paraffin candles.' The police and the coroner cannot understand why a business man should employ a private secretary, for 'such an office in this country is not a common one.'

Mr. Ebenezer Gryce, 'one of our city detectives,' is introduced very early in the story, and at once assumes the leading rôle, by virtue of his personality as well as his official position. He is a quiet, competent, middle-aged man, quite unlike Dupin or Lecoq, and far more akin to Charles Dickens's Detective-Inspector Bucket. Miss Green's com-

ment on Mr. Gryce's first appearance shows clearly that a popular conception of a fictional detective already existed in the minds of American readers, and, like so many detective-heroes, Mr. Gryce was to be as different as possible from that conception.

> He was not the thin, wiry individual with a shrewd eye that seems to plunge into the core of your being, and pounce at once upon its hidden secret, that you are doubtless expecting to see. Mr. Gryce was a portly, comfortable personage with an eye that never pounced. . . .

His reputation precedes him, and Mary Leavenworth at their first meeting greets him thus:—

> Sir, I hear that you have great talents: that you can ferret out the real criminal from a score of doubtful characters, and that nothing can escape the penetration of your eye.

Mr. Gryce is sagacious, patient and imperturbable, with a mild, gentle manner that wins him the confidence of women in particular. He is hard-working rather than brilliant, and when at a loss he likes to arrange dramatic surprises for his suspects which usually prove informative. He is a pleasant, likeable human being, convincing as a detective and not lacking in strength or dignity. He believes, however, that his profession carries a social stigma, and discusses his difficulties in this respect with the young lawyer whose assistance he hopes to gain, commenting frankly that neither he nor any of his colleagues can ever hope to 'pass for a gentleman.'

In this regard, Mr. Gryce is certainly not a descendant of Poe's detective, the Chevalier C. Auguste Dupin, who was on visiting terms with the illustrious Minister D—, nor of Detective-Inspector Bucket or Sergeant Cuff, men of modest social status as private individuals, but fully capable, in their official capacity, of talking on equal terms with people of the highest rank. The memoirs of that most famous of all American detectives, Allan Pinkerton, do not convey the impression that in the democratic United States, during the 1870's, competent police officers suffered under such handicaps as Mr. Gryce describes. It may be that in exclusive Brooklyn, Miss Green's home, social distinctions were more rigidly observed, but it seems far more probable that, having little or no personal knowledge of the police of her own country, she was simply reflecting an impression she had gained from Gaboriau, possibly also from Balzac and from Dumas, about the position of the police in France.

However, just as Dumas' M. Jackal was assisted by Salvator, Mr. Gryce solves his difficulty by enlisting the help of the gentlemanly Mr. Raymond, while the less dignified detective work falls to the lot of Gryce's subordinate, 'Mr. Q.', a young man who rushes energetically here and there, following clues and collecting information for his chief, stopping on occasion to methods which are questionable, as, for instance, when he clambers over roofs to peer into windows, or searches rooms which he has no legal right to enter. With Mr. Raymond's co-operation in exalted spheres and the help of Mr. Q. in more menial researches, Mr. Gryce manages the case efficiently. He can talk as familiarly of firearms as of the 'science of probabilities'; has a good technical knowledge of such matters as the various grades of writing paper, and the distinctive ash that each type would form if burned; and knows business routine as well as he understands human nature.

In *The Leavenworth Case,* Anna Katharine Green not only made her detective the leading figure and formulated a plan of construction that later became conventional. She also introduced characters and incidents that were new in her day, though they have since become familiar in novels of this type: the rich old man, killed when on the point of signing a new will; the body in the library; the dignified butler with his well-trained staff; detailed medical evidence as to the cause and estimated time of death; the coroner's inquest and the testimony of expert witnesses; the authority on ballistics who can identify the gun that fired the shot. Miss Green even included a sketchmap of the scene of the crime and a reproduction of the torn-off fragment of a letter, not unlike the one that later occupied Sherlock Holmes's attention in 'The Reigate Squires.' It is rather remarkable to find such an assemblage of characteristic features in the first novel of this young American writer of detective fiction.

There followed a long sequence of novels from her pen, among the best of them being *A Strange Disappearance* (1879), *The Mill Mystery* (1886) and *Behind Closed Doors* (1887). *The Doctor, his Wife, and the Clock* (1893), though originally published as a slim volume, is little more than a short story in which Mr. Gryce personally relates one of his earliest cases, scarcely a successful one. A mysterious murder has been caused through an error made by a blind doctor, and though Gryce's enquiries lead him to suspect the truth, he fails to prevent or even to foresee the tragic *dénouement.*

That Affair Next Door (1897) is a long novel in which Mr. Gryce figures with some prominence, his detective work being at first handicapped and later assisted by a woman amateur detective, Miss Amelia Butterworth, who probes the mystery from motives of curiosity. It is possible that, before creating this character, Miss Green may have read a small book published in London in 1861, *The Experiences of a Lady Detective,* the author hiding behind the coy pseudonym of 'Anonyma.' The heroine of these slight tales was a Mrs. Paschall who darted busily here and there to solve various fairly simple problems, and was distinguished by her regard for 'ladylike conduct' and her personal appearance, rather than by any detective skill.

Miss Green created a far more entertaining and perspicacious amateur detective in Amelia Butterworth, a spinster of good family, uncertain age and enquiring mind who narrates the story of *That Affair Next Door.* When the body of an unknown girl is discovered in the house next to her own, she determines to learn for herself all the circumstances behind the mystery. She soon finds herself in disagreement with Mr. Gryce, the officer in charge of the police investigation, but their initial antipathy develops into mutual respect, and she helps him by pointing out clues he would not have noticed himself—the dead woman's 'indoor shoes that had recently been acquainted with the pavement,' and her hat which, though soiled and crushed, was nevertheless being worn for the first time,

since it had only once been pierced by a hatpin. Miss Butterworth, through her social contacts, obtains information to which Mr. Gryce has no access, and though they are often at cross purposes they each contribute materially to the eventual solution of the problem.

In a later novel, *Lost Man's Lane* (1898), Mr. Gryce seeks Miss Butterworth's help to fathom the mystery surrounding the disappearance, one after the other, of several visitors to a small country town. The suspense is fostered by such Radcliffiana as a gloomy mansion with vast, neglected rooms and hidden trapdoors; sinister bloodstains on the floor of a locked apartment; a secret midnight burial; even a 'phantom coach,' later accounted for rationally. But the chief interest lies in the detective work carried out with intelligence and courage by Amelia Butterworth, who shows herself a worthy forerunner of those shrewd observers Miss Marple, Miss Climpson and Hildegarde Withers, of half a century later.

There have been very few convincing women detectives in fiction, and Amelia Butterworth, notwithstanding her occasional prim fussiness, is a pleasing member of that small group, and one of the earliest.

Almost at the end of her long life, Miss Green created in *The Golden Slipper* (1915) another, far less competent, woman detective, Violet Strange, whose successes were largely due to her remarkably sagacious bloodhound. The tale follows much the same plan of construction as Miss Green's earlier novels, but the volume is of minor interest, except as showing that a manner of presentation and a style of writing that were new in 1879 had become old-fashioned, almost antiquated, by 1915, so greatly had detective fiction changed between those dates, particularly in England.

These changes began to make themselves felt far earlier, and were sweeping in their effect. It was not only that the 'domestic' background for fiction of this type, so much used between the 1860's and 1880's, had fallen almost completely out of favour by the closing decade of the nineteenth century, and did not become popular again until the second quarter of the twentieth. The full-length detective novel itself suffered a similar, though less prolonged, eclipse, for the magazine reading multitudes of the 1890's preferred short stories. Even Sherlock Holmes failed to surmount this intangible barrier when he was first introduced in the novels *A Study in Scarlet* (1887) and *The Sign of Four* (1889), but when he became the hero of a series of short detective stories in the *Strand Magazine* in 1891, he was at once received with tremendous acclaim.

The great and growing demand was for short stories presenting a sequence of individual 'cases,' all dealt with by the same 'specialist-consultant' on detective problems. An immediate result of this trend was that the detective himself became the real centre of interest. The 'cases' varied, but the familiar, dominant figure remained the same, greeted by the reader as an old friend whom he greatly admired. The popular detective hero of the period was not only a brilliant analytical reasoner, but could also draw upon an almost inexhaustible fund of specialised technical knowledge about such matters as the varieties of tobacco ash, the principles of ballistics or the workings of machinery. Above all, he tended to become more and more of a 'scientist,' seeking evidence in a test-tube or under the lens of a microscope. Such a hero could be convincingly portrayed only by a writer who possessed scientific knowledge, and at that time the path to a scientific education, particularly in medicine, was still closed to women.

At the turn of the century and for some years later, many of the notable writers of detective fiction in English were men with long years of specialised training and experience in science, often in medicine. Doctor Arthur Conan Doyle created Sherlock Holmes while waiting for patients to arrive at his surgery. Richard Austin Freeman was a surgeon with a distinguished professional career, before he began writing of Doctor John Thorndyke, the specialist in medical jurisprudence. Such men were familiar with the facilities of a laboratory, and could often describe scientific experiments—chemical analysis of material clues, for example, or tests to identify poisons—with an accuracy born of knowledge. Women at that time could not, and it is therefore hardly surprising that the advent of the 'scientific' detective brought to an end the period during which this type of fiction was first influenced by women writers.

The writers considered in this [essay], who were eagerly read by thousands of their contemporaries, influenced the development of the detective novel, rather than the shorter detective story, and though their effect was interrupted in the 1890's for almost two decades, yet it made itself felt later. The success of the detective investigations related in their novels depended upon a shrewd application of common sense to a puzzling problem, an urge to satisfy curiosity, and a quick eye for such informative details as sudden changes in household routine, an unusual choice of items on an invalid's breakfast tray, or the talk of a frightened child. Their skill lay in assessing the implications of an odd circumstance or an unexpected human reaction, and thus they played some part in foreshadowing the nonscientific, 'intuitional' or 'psychological' detectives of the twentieth century, such as Chesterton's Father Brown, who appeared when the popularity of the purely scientific detective had begun to wane.

It is noticeable that there is no Frenchwoman among the authors considered here, though during the same period there were in France many outstanding women writers of other types of fiction. Was this because of national differences in temperament, in education, in social or cultural background? A different assessment of the purpose and scope of fiction? There must be reasons to account for this discrepancy, and they may be the same reasons which explain why, though detective fiction was appreciably gaining popularity in England and America before the end of the nineteenth century, in France it was not recognised as an acceptable literary *genre* until the second quarter of the twentieth. . . . (pp. 152-66)

> *A. E. Murch, "Women Writers of Detective Fiction in the Nineteenth Century," in her* The Development of the Detective Novel, *1958. Reprint by Greenwood Press, 1968, pp. 152-66.*

LeRoy Lad Panek

[*Panek is an American critic and educator who specializes in the field of sensational fiction. In the following excerpt, he investigates the origins and influence of Arthur Conan Doyle's Sherlock Holmes stories.*]

When people read the Sherlock Holmes stories in the 1890s, they lived in a world radically different from that pictured by Collins, the sensation writers, or Gaboriau. In the old world, crime writers had to blush and apologize for introducing detectives, the crimes in fiction usually involved the rich and powerful, and the main concern of everyone involved was how to cover things up. Although a few atavistic twinges of these things remain in the Sherlock Holmes stories, Doyle wrote of a new world. In Doyle, people accept the fact that whenever a crime occurs, the police will be involved, and in the stories both the powerful and the humble seek out Holmes and Watson to air their problems before them. In Doyle, too, we get away from crime among the aristocrats. Holmes takes a high hand with the nabobs and robber barons who come to him and, in general, concentrates on the problems of the modest middle-class. Finally, Doyle, through his fictional narrator, takes it as a given that the public has a right to know about crime, criminals, policemen, and detectives.

These changes in detective fiction occurred because the world changed drastically between the 1860s and the 1890s. All sorts of technological innovations, such as electric lights and telephones, began to make life easier in Britain, and life also became more egalitarian and open. Part of this came about because of the reforms of the late Victorian era. Not only did mechanical innovations like the linotype revolutionize printing at the end of the nineteenth century, but labor laws and the Education Act of 1870 also broadened the reading public. Whereas in the 1860s, popular fiction and "best sellers" hardly existed, in the 1880s and 1890s they reshaped the world of publishing and the reading habits of millions. Add to this the facts that in the late 1880s Jack the Ripper was painting Whitechapel red and the Fenians were planting bombs even at Scotland Yard, and it is easy to see why the public asked not, why do we need snooping policemen, but, why aren't the police doing anything? Late in the 1880s, the public was ready for a new variety detective story and the editors were ready to publish anything which caught the public's fancy. It was, therefore, lucky that few people in Southsea chose to avail themselves of the medical services of young Arthur Conan Doyle (1859-1930).

Doyle always wanted to be a writer. Even during his medical apprenticeship, he began to write stories for the burgeoning Victorian periodical market. These started with "The Mystery of Sasassa Valley" (1879) in *Chambers,* and included pieces in *Cornhill Magazine* and *Boys' Own Paper.* By the time he opened his medical practice in Southsea, Doyle had written a novel, *The Firm of Girdlestone,* which publishers persisted in sending back to him. Then, in 1886, Doyle wrote a skimpy novel, or a hefty short story, entitled *A Study in Scarlet.* Because *A Study in Scarlet* introduced Sherlock Holmes, people endlessly asked the writer about its conception. In *The Westminster Gazette* of 13 December 1900, he emphasized plot:

At the time I first thought of a detective. . . .
I had been reading detective stories, and it
struck me what nonsense they were, to put it
mildly, because for getting to the solution of the
mystery, the authors always depended on some
coincidence. This struck me as not a fair way of
playing the game, because the detective ought
really to depend for his successes on something
in his own mind and not on merely adventitious
circumstances which do not, by any means, always occur in real life.

Twenty-four years later, in his autobiography, *Memories
and Adventures,* Doyle emphasized character as the motive for *A Study in Scarlet:*

Gaboriau had rather attracted me by the neat
dove-tailing of his plots, and Poe's masterful detective, M. Dupin, had from my boyhood been
one of my heroes. But could I bring an addition
of my own? I thought of my old teacher, Joe
Bell, of his eagle face, of his curious ways, of his
eerie trick of spotting details. . . . It was all
very well to say that a man is clever, but the
reader wants to see examples as Bell gave us
every day in the wards. The idea amused me.
What should I call the fellow? . . . First it was
Sherringford Holmes then it was Sherlock
Holmes. He could not tell his own exploits, so
he must have a commonplace comrade as a
foil. . . . A drab, quiet name for this unostenta-
tious man. Watson would do. So I had my puppets and wrote my *Study in Scarlet.*

Whether Doyle got his idea for *A Study in Scarlet* as a reaction to storytelling or from his detective character, he
wrote the book and began the soul-destroying job of sending it around to publishers. A handful sent it back to him
until Mrs. G. T. Bettany recommended the manuscript to
her husband. He recommended it to Ward, Lock & Company, which demurred at publishing the novel as a separate edition because of its brevity, but included it in the
1887 edition of the omnibus *Beeton's Christmas Annual.*
Not many people noticed *Beeton's Christmas Annual,* and
Doyle himself turned to writing historical novels, first
Micah Clarke (1889) and then *The White Company*
(1891). Meanwhile Stoddart, the American editor of *Lippincott's Magazine* (published in England by Ward, Lock),
contracted with Doyle for another Sherlock Holmes
novel. While working away at *The White Company,* the
author dashed off *The Sign of the Four* (1890). Appearing
in *Lippincott's, The Sign of the Four,* like its predecessor,
was not remarkable for its success.

Although Doyle held out great hopes for himself as a historical novelist, he continued to tinker with Sherlock
Holmes and the detective story. Since his slim novels still
ran counter to the accepted three-volume format, Doyle
decided to change his vehicle. Early in 1891, he says

It struck me that a single character running
through . . . [a] series, if it engaged the attention of the reader, would bind that reader to that
particular magazine. . . . Clearly the compromise [to the serial novel] was a character which
carried through, and yet installments which
were each complete in themselves. . . . I believe
I was the first to realize this.

Of course, Poe realized this a long time before Doyle did,
and so did Dickens. At this point, at any rate, Doyle decided to write short stories with Holmes as the hero. He
wrote six Holmes stories, beginning with "A Scandal in
Bohemia" (July 1891). His agent, A. P. Watt, sent them
to Greenhough Smith, the editor of *The Strand Magazine.*
Several things were in Doyle's favor here. First of all, in
the 1890s the short story was a relatively new form in Britain. Second, Doyle hit the beginning of the rage for the
popular illustrated magazine. *The Strand* was an aggressive magazine, fashioned to capture readers by including
some kind of illustration on every page. Finally, Doyle
was fortunate that Smith chose Sidney Paget to illustrate
his stories. All of these things combined with Doyle's fusion and fission of detective story elements and made the
first Holmes stories immensely successful. Naturally, *The
Strand* knew they had a winner. As the first stories began
to appear, Smith wrote to Doyle for more Holmes stories.
Thinking [of] himself as a historical novelist, Doyle at first
declined but then asked *The Strand* for fifty pounds a
story, a price he considered exorbitant. Smith, however,
agreed and Doyle contracted to write six more stories, beginning with "The Blue Carbuncle" (January 1892), a
Christmas piece. Originally, Doyle thought of killing
Holmes off in the twelfth story: "I think," he wrote to his
mother, "of slaying Holmes in the last and winding him
up for good and all. He takes my mind from better
things." This shocked his mother. "You won't! You can't!
You mustn't!" she wrote to him, and she sent him a story
idea which she cribbed from *The Woman in White* and
which Doyle converted into "Copper Beeches" (June
1892).

The Strand ran the first twelve Sherlock Holmes stories
from July 1891 to June 1892, and then George Newnes,
the founder of the magazine, published them as *The Adventures of Sherlock Holmes* (1892). In February 1892, as
the first series of Holmes stories was running out, *The
Strand* began begging Doyle for more. He "offered to do
a dozen more for a thousand pounds," but hoped this figure would put them off. It did not, and after Doyle took
a short break, "Silver Blaze" appeared in December 1892.
At the end of these twelve stories, Doyle reduced Holmes
and Moriarity to strawberry jam on the rocks of the Reic-
henbach Falls in "The Final Problem" (December 1893),
so he could devote himself to other things. Newnes published the second twelve stories as *The Memoirs of Sherlock Holmes* (1894), but that did not help *The Strand.* The
magazine wanted more Holmes tales, or lacking that,
more detective stories. When their Holmes stories ran out,
therefore, they put in this notice:

There will be a temporary interval in the Sherlock Holmes stories. A new series will continue
in an early number. Meanwhile, powerful detective stories will be contributed by other eminent
writers.

Doyle's first twenty-four Sherlock Holmes stories created
such a demand they turned people into detective story
writers overnight, and started the continuing development
of the detective story. Doyle, however, wanted nothing to
do with it.

From 1894 until 1901, Doyle ignored Holmes and Watson. He fed *The Strand* stories about Brigadier Gerard, his continuing character from the Napoleonic wars; worked on plays and historical novels; travelled to America; and volunteered for service in the Boer War. Out of the last experience, he wrote *The Great War* (1900), and *The War in South Africa: Its Causes and Conduct* (1902), which led to his knighthood in 1902. In 1901, because he picked up some provocative material about Dartmoor, he revived Holmes for his third detective novel, *The Hound of the Baskervilles* (August 1901 to April 1902). This got him back on the Holmes track, and, beginning with "The Adventure of the Empty House" (September 1903), thirteen new stories came out in *The Strand,* collected in *The Return of Sherlock Holmes* (1905). After the detective returned to life, Doyle wrote an occasional Holmes story for *The Strand* until the beginning of the Great War. During the war, he wrote *The Valley of Fear* (September 1914 to May 1915), based on shop talk with the American detective William J. Burns, and he also wrote "His Last Bow: The War Service of Sherlock Holmes" (September 1917). Between 1921 and 1927, he wrote twelve more stories for *The Strand* which became *The Case Book of Sherlock Holmes* (1927). There were no more stories about Holmes. Publishers wanted them, the public wanted them, but Doyle did not. He spent his last years thinking and writing about spiritualism, one of his life-long passions.

Just as the Sherlock Holmes stories mark the real beginning of the detective story as a continuing popular literary form, they also present real difficulties. First of all, Doyle wrote the Holmes tales over a period of forty years, from 1887 to 1927. During this span, human technology and social organization changed mightily. None of this affects the Holmes stories. Doyle is purposefully anachronistic and the stories written in the 1920s are set in the 1890s. For Holmes, the Russian revolution, the Great War (with one story excepted), manned flight, and myriad other changes in the culture never happened. Along with the world's transformation, the detective story changed too. Doyle began writing when Gaboriau was in vogue, and he continued to write Holmes stories well after Christie created Poirot, Sayers invented Wimsey, and American writers introduced the hard-boiled detective story. Further, even at his best, Doyle wrote very casually. After the first spurt of tales, he had to be bribed to continue writing detective stories. Doyle was, in fact, always sloppy about details—when he wrote "A Scandal in Bohemia," for example, he forgot he had named Holmes' landlady Mrs. Hudson—and cavalierly added and subtracted traits from Holmes as he progressed with the stories. Doyle's sloppiness, to be sure, has provided a lot of entertainment for Baker Street Irregulars and other Holmes fans, but it certainly stands in the way of a careful assessment of the Sherlock Holmes canon and the importance of Doyle's contribution to the development of the detective story.

The Sherlock Holmes stories start from Poe. Doyle freely and frequently acknowledged this and noted in one statement that he was not alone in his borrowings: "If every man who received a cheque for a story which owed its springs to Poe were to pay a tithe to a monument for the master, he would have a pyramid as big as that of Cheops." This being the case, Doyle would have had to finance a couple of courses of dressed stone near the base. As many people have recognized, the Holmes stories owed much of their popularity to the fact that they were short stories. This Doyle owed to Poe. But, he streamlines Poe's short stories. His essential Victorianism made him embarrassed about metaphysics, and his desire to be popular caused him to remove the abstruse. These things led him to eliminate Poe's lectures as well as his gropings for the great beyond and, as a consequence, Doyle brought the detective story closer to pure narrative than Poe's Dupin stories. Doyle also borrowed Poe's point of view. In the years between Poe and Doyle, with the exception of Collins, most detective writers used conventional third or first person points of view. Doyle, of course, realized the uses for plot and characterization of the detective's assistant as the narrator: the writer can use the narrator's ignorance to hide important facts and through him can praise the detective and keep him civilly reticent at the same time. Ever since Doyle introduced his narrator, this sort of figure in a detective story has been called a Watson, but, of course, Doyle borrowed the technique from Poe. Like this one, many motifs in the Holmes stories depend on Poe: the police versus the amateur, the detective's conceit, and so on. When Holmes interrupts Watson's thoughts, as he does in "The Cardboard Box" (January 1893) and "The Dancing Men" (December 1903), Doyle makes him acknowledge Dupin as the source of this dramatic but irritating bit of mental showmanship. Building Holmes on Poe's model, in fact, got Doyle tangled up in his own Victorianism. In Poe, we find a good bit of material on the Bi-Part Soul and the essential duality of genius, if not human nature. Dupin and Legrand both have spells, vital to the solution of the problems in the tales, where their eyes go blank and they go drifting off into other worlds and other seas. When Doyle introduced Holmes in *A Study in Scarlet,* he tried to come to grips with Holmes' genius in a chapter entitled "The Science of Deduction." Before mentioning that Holmes has written an article proving the observant person can reach conclusions "as infallible as so many propositions of Euclid" (thereby bringing in the coupling of math and deduction, itself derived from Poe), Doyle states that Holmes goes off into Dupin-like trances:

> . . . . for days on end he would lie upon the sofa in the sitting-room, hardly uttering a word or moving a muscle from morning to night. On occasions I have noticed such a dreamy, vacant expression in his eyes that I might have suspected him of being addicted to the use of some narcotic, had not the temperance and cleanliness of his whole life forbidden such a notion.

Doyle, however, immediately regretted this connection of Holmes with the inexplicable, ineffable, transcendent realm. He drew back from Poe's concept of genius, and in the second novel, *The Sign of the Four,* Doyle associated Holmes with the Decadents and made him a cocaine addict. Thereafter, Holmes' lassitude associates him with the Victorian theme of work, as well as with the Lotus Eaters, and moves away from the inexplicable realms hinted at by Poe's romanticism. Too late, Doyle realized the cocaine was a tactical error and he had to cure Holmes of his drug addiction by the time of the second set of stories.

If Doyle could not handle Poe's themes, he certainly could and did handle Poe's plot details. All of the cipher stories—"The Musgrave Ritual" (May 1893), "The Gloria Scott" (April 1893), and "The Dancing Men"—depend on "The Gold Bug." The treasure hunt business in "The Musgrave Ritual" likewise comes from Poe's tale. Holmes' device of inserting an ad in the newspaper and capturing the criminal who answers it (used in *A Study in Scarlet,* "Black Peter" [March 1904], "Abbey Grange" [September 1904], and elsewhere) goes directly back to Dupin's practice at the end of "The Murders in the Rue Morgue." More than anything else, Poe's signal importance for Doyle's detective stories is the fact that when he turned from the novel to the short story, he went immediately to "The Purloined Letter" for the plot of "A Scandal in Bohemia." Without Poe, Doyle might have given us Holmes in love as a contrast and sequel to Watson in love in *The Sign of the Four.* This, of course, is something we do not have to worry about. Doyle had absorbed enough Poe to be able to put the guts into his detective stories.

While Holmes grudgingly admits Dupin "had some analytical genius," in the next full paragraph of *A Study in Scarlet* he insists "Lecoq was a miserable bungler." He well may have been, but Doyle certainly cribbed enough from Gaboriau to give him higher marks. By Cooper out of Gaboriau, Doyle derived much of Holmes' tracking ability, and tracking constitutes a great deal of Doyle's detective stories. In the Holmes stories, Doyle pays little attention to modern criminology. Instead, almost all of the Holmes stories center on Holmes following the spoor or complaining the trail has been ruined by the impress of flat feet. We can track this motif from *A Study in Scarlet* through to the last stories. In one case, Holmes even uses plaster of Paris to preserve footprints. He imported all of this pretty directly from Gaboriau. Along these same lines, in *The Sign of the Four,* "The Missing Three Quarter" (August 1904), and "Shoscombe Old Place" (April 1927), Holmes borrows dogs to help him in his detective work. For Doyle, this was only the logical extension of the stories' multitudinous comparisons of Holmes to dogs, from hounds to fox hounds to retrievers. Doyle certainly found the detective-dog connection in Gaboriau, but it works in a somewhat different manner in the Holmes tales. The French, after all, are not a doggy nation; the British are. Gaboriau's comparisons of Lecoq to a bloodhound are, therefore, only intellectual. Doyle's comparisons bring with them the full panoply of the "view halloa," the association of British squirearchy and sport. And these things Doyle never found in Gaboriau. He did, however, find the development of the notion of the detective as the mathematically accurate crime-solving machine. In the early works, Doyle makes Holmes an instrument for detection. Holmes, Doyle says, knows nothing of literature, philosophy, or astronomy, and little of politics. He fills his cranial attic only with those things which help him solve crimes. In the early stories, Doyle applies machine images to Holmes, and many pieces begin with Holmes' complaint that Watson should describe his cases as exercises in reason rather than sensational adventures. Most of this came from Gaboriau, and Doyle, to his credit, got it out of his system pretty quickly. In the later stories, Holmes freely quotes literature from Shakespeare to Carlyle, and

in his retirement he settles down not only to bee-keeping but also to the study of philosophy. By the time of the "Naval Treaty" (October, November 1893), Holmes can say "What a lovely thing a rose is!" Doyle wrote Holmes out of the world of machines and toward the world of human beings. An analogous process goes on with Holmes' use of disguise, again something which Doyle borrowed from Gaboriau. In the early stories, Holmes, like Lecoq, plays a number of costumed roles. By the time of "The Reigate Squires" (June 1893), Holmes has dispensed with the wig and grease paint and become a method actor.

With all of these elements, Doyle goes beyond Gaboriau because he adapts the ideas to his culture and his sense of the fitness of things makes an interesting narrative. He does, however, borrow a couple of specific incidents from the Frenchman. The idea of the dirty prisoner in "The Man with the Twisted Lip" (December 1891) comes directly from *Monsieur Lecoq,* and Holmes' observation about wine glasses in "Abbey Grange" depends on an incident in *The Mystery of Orcival.* These things, like the character points, stimulated Doyle's imagination and helped him make his detective and his detective stories. He completely misjudged, however, the aesthetic suitability of Gaboriau's narrative structure. As late as 1924, Doyle spoke about the "neat dove-tailing" of Gaboriau's plots. Breaking apart a detective plot to insert a sentimental narrative did not prove to be a fit way to create a detective novel. Following Gaboriau's narrative pattern went a long way toward ruining *A Study in Scarlet, The Sign of the Four,* and *The Valley of Fear,* in all of which he uses the inserted story to provide a yawning anti-climax. Doyle also used the inserted narrative in a number of short stories, like "The Gloria Scott" and "The Crooked Man" (July 1893). In the short stories, Doyle condensed the historical material to make it appropriate to the narrative form, and over a time reduced his reliance on Gaboriauesque insertions. It was fortunate, then, that Doyle discovered the short story form, for Gaboriau disabled him as a detective novelist. Tangentially related to Gaboriau, and directly connected to Doyle's success and the success of detective stories in general, is the fact that Doyle limited the subject matter of his stories. . . . Gaboriau chose as one of his topics the murky and potentially frightening world of finance. Doyle, however, opted not to frighten his readers in this manner. In "The Reigate Squires," he makes Watson tell his readers they will find "no politics or finance" in the stories. Thus, although Holmes does handle a few spy cases ("The Naval Treaty," "The Bruce-Partington Plans" [December 1908], and "His Last Bow"), Doyle directs his detective stories away from disturbing or controversial public topics which might alienate readers. When he wishes to frighten his readers, he does so in the same ways English writers used from the days of Horace Walpole.

Doyle drew a good bit of his subject matter not from Gaboriau or Poe, but from Collins and the sensation novelists. Some of this shows up in his use of the Indian material in *The Sign of the Four* and "The Crooked Man." His dependence on sensation novel material, however, comes through more clearly in his use of the larger than life, gothic master criminal, as well as his frequent returns to the theme of inheritance. Holmes confronts powerfully evil men, of course, in "The Final Problem" and "The Empty House," but Professor Moriarty and Colonel Moran owe a bit more to Gaboriau than they do to the English tradition of villainy. This is not the case with "The Speckled Band" (February 1892) or "Copper Beeches." Grimesby Roylott in the former story owes much to the villain of the sensation novel, and in fact this story of a locked-room murder harkens back to *Uncle Silas*. Even more clearly, Jethro Runcastle in "Copper Beeches" is Doyle's remake of Count Fosco from *The Woman in White:* both are fat, jovial, threatening, and very bad. The later Holmes story, "The Disappearance of Lady Frances Carfax" (December 1911), reproduces the essentials of Collins' first sensation novel, with the substitution of persons, the larger than life villain, and the law's inability to prevent the crime. Going from these particular motifs of the sensation novel, we find underneath many of the short stories Doyle introduces the sensation novel assumption that thrilling fiction can be made from the thesis that women cannot handle their own affairs, and especially cannot deal with any sort of inheritance. Thus, "The Speckled Band," "Copper Beeches," "A Case of Identity" (September 1891), and "The Solitary Cyclist" (January 1904), all build on a helpless woman receiving an inheritance which the wolves and jackals of the world will snap up unless true and chivalrous men stop them.

Up to this point, all of Doyle's sources are natural and obvious, given the history of the detective story. In the 1880s, anyone could have combined Poe, Gaboriau, and the sensation novelists to form the next step in the evolution of the detective story. Not everyone, however, could have added Joseph Bell (1837-1911) to the formula. Dr. Joseph Bell, a consulting surgeon to the Royal Infirmary and Royal Hospital for Sick Children, was one of Doyle's teachers when he attended medical school in Edinburgh. Shortly after he finished the first set of short stories about Holmes, Doyle wrote to Bell, acknowledging his debt to him:

> It is most certainly to you that I owe Sherlock Holmes. . . . I do not think that his analytical work is in the least an exaggeration of some effects which I [have] seen you produce in the out-patient wards.

Holmes' background in Joe Bell provides a fair amount of what is unique in him. To some extent, Doyle based Holmes' appearance on the lean-faced, hawk-nosed Bell, but this is difficult to argue since Doyle does not detail Holmes' appearance and his illustrator, Paget, established the popular notion of Holmes' looks using his brother as a model. More significant than this, Doyle drew Holmes' deduction demonstrations from Bell. Almost all of the Holmes stories begin, not with a crime, but with a curtain raiser in which Holmes demonstrates his powers of observation and analytical skill. Watson's shoes, hat, watch, and fingers all provide material for seemingly outlandish and magical assertions which Holmes proceeds to explain as simply routine results of methodical looking and thinking. This kind of "You have been in Afghanistan, I perceive," is the sort of thing Joe Bell used to do in the

wards—telling patients about themselves and their ailments before they had a chance to announce where it hurt. Doyle's readers, as shown in countless parodies, clearly thought this analytical skill provided much of what was fascinating and valuable about Holmes.

Almost as important for Holmes' character as the deduction demonstrations is the fact that Doyle modelled Holmes on a physician. In his first draft of *A Study in Scarlet,* Doyle jotted down that Holmes was to be "a consulting detective." Even though Doyle threw out some of his original ideas for his protagonist, he kept the notion of Holmes as a consulting detective. This came from Bell, who was a medical consultant, as well as from Doyle's own work as a physician. Thus, in the stories and novels when Lestrade, Gregson, and assorted other Scotland Yarders run up against a case they cannot diagnose or cure, they call in Holmes, just as the perplexed general practitioner summons a consultant when he finds an ailment beyond his skill and power. Although in the later stories Doyle eases out of this concept, making Holmes simply a private detective and in the 1920s giving him a rudimentary agency, the concept of the consultant operated in the early ones. Indeed, it may have given Doyle the idea for Holmes' Baker Street rooms. Baker Street is only a stethoscope's throw away from Harley Street. The background as a physician, moreover, contributed several other things to Doyle's fashioning of his detective. On occasion, he metaphorically describes Holmes as a physician (in "Charles Augustus Milverton" [April 1904] and "Abbey Grange"), he introduces us to Holmes at St. Bartholomew's hospital, and in "The Beryl Coronet" (May 1892) he even gives the character something of a bedside manner. Holmes' constant references to historical criminal cases in the early stories smacks more of a physician reading *The Lancet* than a policeman reading *The Police Gazette.* Finally, in the last series of stories, Doyle virtually turns Holmes into a physician. Holmes diagnoses a case of leprosy in "The Blanched Soldier" (November 1926), traces peculiar behavior to monkey-gland shots in "The Creeping Man" (March 1923), and straightens out a case of poisoning and sibling rivalry in "The Sussex Vampire" (January 1924).

But Doyle derived more for Holmes from his recollections of Joe Bell than the logical diagnoses and other qualities of a physician. Bell was also a teacher and so in many ways is Holmes. We tend to forget, in these days of "that's right, but" and "that's certainly an interesting idea," that simpler times viewed humiliation and abuse as valuable ways of motivating students. Part of what Doyle put into Holmes, as a result of either using his old professor, or professors in general, is some marked pedagogical characteristics. Holmes teaches and has plenty of scholars. Doyle specifically tells us that detective Stanley Hopkins in "Black Peter" has "the respect of a pupil" for Holmes and his methods. Watson in "Abbey Grange" listens to Holmes "like an interested student who observes the demonstration of his professor," and even Lestrade in "The Norwood Builder" (November 1903) has an air of "a child asking questions of its teacher." During the course of the stories, Doyle creates for Holmes passages which can only be described as lectures—thus the cryptography material in "The Dancing Men" and the walk-through geometry lesson in "The Musgrave Ritual." In this same category come the various tests Holmes administers to Watson. Watson squeaks out a gentleman's C in the quiz about the hat in "The Blue Carbuncle," but here the importance of the test resides not in the experience itself but in that Holmes feels impelled to point out Watson's errors and to show him how to do the thing correctly. Holmes' professorial qualities show through in his little monographs, like the famous one on tobacco ash or the one about human ears mentioned in "The Cardboard Box." They also appear in his running argument with Watson about the nature of Watson's narratives. Holmes, again and again, wants the narratives to be didactic, stressing the intellectual side rather than the less dignified sensational elements incidental to crime and detection. Doyle wisely makes Watson decline to do this, but as a compensation and as intellectual veneer, he places considerable stress on the professorial qualities of Holmes. This may be, in fact, one of the secrets of the character. What we view as endearing grumpiness and delightful perversity in our teachers (usually in retrospect), becomes in unemployed geniuses like Dupin or upstart policemen like Lecoq a royal pain.

The Holmes stories also have some definite and persistent connections with the entrenched ideas about detectives and policemen as a class. As I noted at the beginning of this chapter, people, all sorts of people, willingly take their problems, trivial ones as well as big ones, to Holmes. This is a far cry from Walter's refusal to consult the police in *The Woman in White.* We find, in fact, a reversal of the detective's position shown in Gaboriau. In *L'affaire Lerouge,* Papa Tabaret fears his friends will not shake his hand if they discover his detective activity, but in "Scandal in Bohemia" Holmes has enough self-assurance to refuse the proffered hand of the King of Bohemia. Part of this new attitude toward detectives occurs because toward the end of the century Scotland Yard and the reorganized C.I.D. established their legitimacy and competence. Part of it, too, came from the fact that Doyle was a physician. People are more helpless, honest, and willing when they visit a physician, particularly a high-powered consultant, than they are when they visit a lawyer. Here Doyle's own experience differed from that of the lawyer-writers of the last generation. Nevertheless, throughout the stories, Doyle constantly brings up the issue of the detective's discretion. Doyle's mention of royalty in two of the first three short stories serves partly to demonstrate that Holmes has been discreet for the crowned heads of Europe. He carries this theme through "The Missing Three Quarter", and in his efforts to demonstrate Holmes' sensitivity, he goes a long way toward destroying the story. The discretion theme in Doyle carries over a century's worth of fear that the police will not respect individual privacy. With the theme of discretion, of course, Doyle has to have it two ways: he is, after all, telling about the detective's locked lips at the same time he details his cases for the public. Doyle throws a sop in the direction of professional propriety by having Holmes protest against the publication of his cases, by Watson's conscious limitation to old cases in which the participants are all dead, and by telling us, in some stories, the real names have been changed. In the majority of the cases, especially those like "The Second

Stain" (December 1904) and "The Noble Bachelor" (April 1892) involving important persons, Doyle appeals to the public's voyeuristic tastes. He realized, as did other late Victorian writers and publishers, the number of people who like to read gossip was far larger than the number who become the subject of gossip. This attitude reflects a major cultural shift and it, in turn, has its effect upon the tone of Doyle's detective stories. In *Caleb Williams,* detection is the stuff of tragedy. For some of Doyle's early stories, too, detection specifically touches on something akin to traditional tragedy: "The Boscombe Valley Mystery" (October 1891) and "The Five Orange Pips" (November 1891) pointedly use the term "tragic" and bring in judgment from weightier realms than mere human justice. As the Holmes stories progress, however, Doyle uses "tragedy" in its loose sense, meaning anything shockingly depressing, and he concentrates instead on writing detective stories which will appeal to and gratify his readers.

Doyle inherited another police theme from all of the detective writers before him: the boob policeman. In his early works, official policemen display all sorts of truculent ignorance and wrong-headedness. They never see the truth and frequently want to arrest the wrong person. Gregson and Lestrade are, in the traditions of the detective story, the ignoramuses installed for Holmes to dally with as he finds the real facts. Doyle, over the years, changed this. Look at what happens to Lestrade. In *A Study in Scarlet,* he is stupid and, to use Doyle's word for him, ferret-like. Friston's illustration in *Beeton's Christmas Annual* shows him as a nasty little piece of work. By the time of "The Second Stain" (1904), however, Doyle describes him as having "bulldog features", and Paget's illustrations change accordingly. Between these two stories, too, Lestrade becomes more civil and humble, and Doyle introduces other policemen, like Stanley Hopkins, whom Holmes considers almost bright. By the time of "Wisteria Lodge" (September and October 1908), we find policemen like Inspector Baynes who arrives at the correct solution at the same time the Great Detective does. To some extent, then, Doyle worked himself out of the rut of the convention of stupid policemen—probably because there were manifest examples this was wrong. He proceeded from fantasy to occasional glimpses of reality.

With another traditional detective theme, Doyle worked the other way, towards fantasy instead of away from it. The genius detective, from Poe onward, is supposed to be infallible. Contrary to popular notions of the character, Holmes fails pretty often in the early cases. He fails with Irene Adler, he fails in "The Five Orange Pips," he fails in "The Engineer's Thumb" (March 1892), in "Copper Beeches," and in a few other stories. Holmes assures Mrs. St. Clair her husband is dead in "The Man with the Twisted Lip," he tells Grant Munro his wife is being blackmailed in "Yellow Face" (February 1893), and so on. Hardly the great detective. Doyle even has Holmes talk to Watson about his errors in the introductions to several stories. Of course, Doyle is again having it both ways, and we forget about Holmes' incompetence when we read the stories, but the evidence is there nonetheless—in the early tales. Probably because of his need to create Moriarty to dispose of Holmes in 1893, and then because of the emergence of thriller writers like John Buchan, as well as the advent of World War I, Doyle moved gradually toward stories dealing with master criminals. As a response to this, and as a response to the efficiency latent and manifest in the early stories, Doyle made Holmes much more infallible in the later tales.

In the main, Doyle displays little interest in police work. Yet he wrote the Holmes stories at a time when modern, scientific criminology was aborning. This fascinated other writers and provided details for the lesser detective writers of the 1890s and early twentieth century, but it did not greatly inspire Doyle. At best, he gives Holmes only a wash of scientific criminology. In the first series of stories, Holmes frequently alludes to parallel historical cases, but, with the exception of Palmer and Pritchard mentioned in "The Speckled Band," Doyle made most of them up. As I have said before, Holmes' practice smacks a bit more of reading medical literature than it does of police work. While Doyle eases up on these historical citations in the stories collected in *The Memoirs,* he does seed chemistry throughout the whole canon. We see Holmes fiddling with beakers and retorts in a number of stories. Holmes' chemistry, however, has only an occasional connection to criminology. Mostly he precipitates this or that without concern for its detective application. In "The Adventure of the Empty House," in fact, Holmes spends some of the missing years studying coal tar dyes, suggesting he is more interested in making a million by inventing a new color than in devising criminological tests. This lackadasical attitude toward chemistry extends to the toxicology and medicine in the Holmes stories. Doyle did not care (nor, in justice, did his readers) whether the snake in "The Speckled Band" or the poison in "The Dying Detective" (December 1913) really existed. In spite of his professional training, Doyle was willing to introduce "brain fever" whenever he wanted a character out of the way, as in "The Cardboard Box" and "The Naval Treaty." If he was casual about things he should have known about, Doyle was downright unconcerned about actual advances in scientific criminology. Holmes may mention Bertillon, but, aside from "The Norwood Builder," fingerprints do not figure in the stories. Rather than reading up on crime and criminals, Doyle developed details for his detection from his own imagination, or from perfunctory reading of popular magazines like *The Strand,* where he got the idea about the disguised horseshoes he used in "The Priory School" (February 1904).

All of this casualness with his detective stories presents a reversal of Doyle's usual practice in his historical fiction. In books like *The White Company,* he attempted to make his background information as accurate as possible. This, however, he coupled with the most puerile of story lines. But in spite of their unfitness for adult consumption, Doyle's composition of historical novels does have a real impact on the Holmes stories. One of the reasons for Doyle's affection for Gaboriau lay in the fact that the Frenchman demonstrated the stuff of the historical novel could be levered into the detective story. With the exception of *The Hound of the Baskervilles,* Doyle included in the Holmes novels stories which carry us to past events in exotic places—granting, of course, that Utah and Pennsyl-

vania are exotic. In the short stories, too, Doyle frequently hooks on an excursion into the past after Holmes has nabbed the criminal. One of the detective story's pulls on Doyle was as a medium for telling more than one story, usually the criminal's and the detective's. If we already have two, why not add a third story, a historical one? Not only, then, did Doyle find in the detective story an excuse for including small historical romances, he also found in his own historical novels a framework for characterizing the detective. The author, like his Victorian contemporaries, was caught up in the glamorization of chivalry, chivalry modulated by contemporary attitudes toward sexuality as well as by imperialism. Much of this comes out in *The White Company,* in which Doyle depicts his own hearty and healthy view of the Middle Ages. Fundamental to this historical romance, Doyle creates the ideal of the chivalric hero who is "fearless to the strong, humble to the weak, [and who dispenses] chivalry to all women . . . Help to the helpless, whosoever shall ask for it." This concept forms the character basis of the Holmes stories. We can see it, specifically, in "Charles Augustus Milverton":

> The high object of our mission, the consciousness that it was unselfish and chivalrous, the villainous character of our opponent, all added to the sporting interest of the adventure. . . . I knew that the opening of safes was a particular hobby with him [Holmes], and I understood the joy which it gave him to be confronted with this green and gold monster, the dragon which held in its maw the reputations of many fair ladies.

Doyle certainly heaps on the metaphors of knighthood in this passage, and, indeed, interpreting the stories in light of chivalry adds another necessary level to their meaning. In the first series of stories, four women bring their problems to Holmes because they have no one else to turn to. Only one of *The Adventures of Sherlock Holmes,* "The Engineer's Thumb," involves a healthy, intelligent, and active man. That is the "chivalry toward all women" and "help to the helpless." The knight's quality of being "fearless to the strong" shows up in Holmes' anti-aristocratic bias in stories from "Scandal in Bohemia" to "Mazarin Stone" (October 1921). In the first story, we can almost say Holmes accepts Irene Adler's photograph because he cannot get her scarf or her sleeve.

The chivalry Doyle transplanted from *The White Company* to his detective stories links up directly to the element in the Holmes stories coming from the Victorian schoolboy story and its reincarnation in the popular novels of Stevenson and Haggard. *A Study in Scarlet* resembles in many ways Stevenson's *Treasure Island* (1883) and H. Rider Haggard's *King Solomon's Mines* (1886). All of these novels aim what begins as a schoolboy story at a slightly older and more mature audience. The schoolboy story originated in periodicals, like *Boys' Own Paper,* and developed in novels like Hughes' *Tom Brown's Schooldays* (1857). These outlets dispensed exciting fiction for boys, but, specifically opposed to the Penny Dreadful of the early 1800s, fiction which inculcated morality into its pubescent readers. The schoolboy story was, in effect, the tool of imperialistic values. To appeal to schoolboys, however, this class of fiction adopted character patterns familiar to boys. Thus we endlessly find the teacher and his students along with the head boy and his fags. Doyle began his career as a writer doing pieces for *Boys' Own Paper*, and we have seen his exploitation of the teacher-student side of the Holmes-Watson relationship. The teacher-student pattern, in fact, is one Doyle could not escape, and he included it in the Sir Nigel stories as well as in the Professor Challenger pieces. In the Holmes stories, too, Doyle introduces a bit of fagging with Holmes acting as the superior older boy and Watson playing the awestruck, eager fag. Further, the manly virtues of the schoolboy story join with Doyle's sense of chivalry to produce Holmes' protection of the weak, his adherence to conscience and principle versus external law, and his independence when faced with the rich and powerful. Finally, Doyle's contemporaries rather quickly picked up the Holmes stories as means of instructing boys. That Baden-Powell suggested Boy Scout group leaders have their boys read Sherlock Holmes stories not only indicates the Victorian ratification of their ways of dealing with the material world, but testifies to their moral fitness for the Empire's leaders.

With the Holmes stories, however, Doyle purposely leaned far heavier on the *dulce* of adventure than on the *utile* of imperial morality or scientific method. The detective stories and novels may start with a gloss of the intellectual, but Doyle invariably ends with adventure. In part, Doyle wrote the Holmes tales out of protest against torpid contemporary fiction. When, in "The Boscombe Valley Mystery," Watson picks up a "yellow-backed novel," he quickly becomes bored with it and drops it in favor of thinking about the business at hand. The substance of the Holmes stories is not intellectual, but emotional. Doyle, of course, knew this and went as far as incorporating Holmes' complaint "you slur over work of the utmost finesse and delicacy in order to dwell upon sensational details which may excite but cannot possibly instruct the reader." For word counters, we can see the bias of the Holmes stories in the fact that *The Strand* labelled thirty-five of the stories as "adventures." And, even in the earliest stories, words like "strange," "unusual," "fantastic," and "singular" by far outnumber terms like "reason" and "deduce." Throughout, the hunt, the chase, the capture, and the shock of action mean more than the mental questions of detection. In "The Solitary Cyclist," in fact, Doyle comes right out and says the stories depend on "the ingenuity and dramatic quality of the solution."

When he discusses Holmes' mental powers, Doyle betrays amazing casualness even in the early stories. As with stalactites and stalagmites, he confuses the meanings of the terms induction and deduction. When Holmes or Mycroft tells us about a person or material object, they do not, strictly speaking, deduce anything (i.e. reason from general to specific). If anything, they use inductive reasoning and go from specific to general. To be sure, Doyle discovered the word "deduce" does not open up the possibility of confusion which turning inductive reasoning into a verb does: Holmes can hardly say "I induce you have been ill." At any rate, by the time of "The Six Napoleons" (May 1904), he does admit the detective uses "a connected chain of inductive reasoning." Although in the early stories

Doyle makes a great deal out of Holmes as a thinking machine and puts particular stress on the detective's employment of strict methodology, most of the stories show not that Holmes reasons better, but that he observes better than anyone else. In one story, in fact, he specifically says observing is his trade. Thus, the solutions to many of the fictions begin with Holmes seeing things others have missed because he is a "scientific searcher." Coupled with these facts, Doyle put new emphasis on one of the traditional metaphors for the detective's activity. When Doyle started out as a detective writer, he picked up on the standard detectival metaphor of the clue; he originally was going to entitle *A Study in Scarlet* as *A Tangled Skein* to take advantage of the thread background tied up with the word "clue." He did, in fact, keep the phrase "a tangled skein" in the finished novel. However, he switched quickly to talking about his detective forging links into a chain, rather than exclusively using metaphors of magic thread. On the one hand, the chain metaphor serves to enhance the air of reasoning about Holmes: forging links becomes akin to building syllogisms. On the other hand, it moves Doyle away from the concept of the detective simply following a preordained path to justice. As far as its total effect on character goes, however, all of Doyle's talk about calculating reason is just that, talk. Simple observation plays a part in Holmes' success in the stories, and so do intuition and imagination. Doyle eventually came to admit this in *The Case Book of Sherlock Holmes* where, in one story, Holmes says Watson "has given an exaggerated view of my scientific methods," and in another admits a "mixture of imagination and reality . . . is the basis of my art."

Doyle's stories succeed, in part, because he glued a scientific veneer to his detective and clamped a thin layer of reason to his sensational plots. Sherlock Holmes came from Doyle's combination and modification of preexisting literary motifs. He succeeded because of Doyle's addition of his own flourishes and arabesques: Doyle transformed the somewhat wooden character of the detective when he made Holmes. One way Doyle followed toward making Holmes interesting was to keep him in reserve. The stories suggest Holmes is a complex and fascinating man, but they do not say much about him. Doyle effected this by using Watson as the narrator, but he also designed the action of the stories to keep the focus away from Holmes. Usually the client's story as told to Holmes and Watson takes up more space than the detective action does. In the stories, we learn nothing of Holmes' life. We do not know he has a brother until the twenty-second story, and we never hear anything about his father. The stories mention only the scantiest details of the hero's appearance, and Doyle, by omission or commission, left the physical delineation of Holmes to Paget, his illustrator. The few details we remember about Holmes are his habits, the shag tobacco, and the Persian slipper. These stick in our minds because others have harped on them, not because Doyle repeats them. On the whole, the author keeps Holmes under wraps to heighten the wonder of the surprise at the end of the story. Holmes, nevertheless, is a creature of immense attraction. Part of this comes from the character's name. If Doyle had a genius for nothing else, he had a positive genius for creating names. Grimesby Roylott in "The

Speckled Band" can only be a villain, just as Hilton Cubitt in "The Dancing Men" can only be a solid English squire. Changing his detective's name from "Sherringford Holmes" in the first draft of *A Study in Scarlet* to Sherlock Holmes in the finished version was one of the smartest things Doyle ever did. We can see the power of the name in that it was the first thing parodists latched onto: burlesque creations from Sherlock Abodes to Sheerluck Omes testify to the power of the name.

Not everyone would be comfortable living with such an original and half-flamboyant name. To match the name, Doyle picked up on the genius-generated eccentricities he found in Poe's Dupin. As Watson knows, Holmes has little peculiarities, from scraping on the violin to pocking V.R. in the plaster with his revolver. He is magnificently moody and close-mouthed. Here, Doyle particularizes from hints in Poe. He also fleshes out in a practical way the genius' mind. Dupin may be intelligent, but we discover in the stories that Holmes knows everything and can do anything. The steady accretion of Holmes' knowledge and abilities depends, of course, on Doyle's writing off the top of his head. It does demonstrate genius, but it appeals only to the most naive part of our imaginations. On a slightly more sophisticated level, Holmes attracts readers because of the dualism Doyle consciously manufactured for his character. From Poe's romantic and metaphysical concept of the Bi-Part Soul with which Doyle flirted in *A Study in Scarlet,* he built into Holmes a more secular and popular split personality. Holmes is a rational drug addict, a sloppy precision, and a lazy athlete. He does not jog, do executive exercises, practice boxing or singlestick, and uses his revolver only to the depredation of Mrs. Hudson's plaster. Yet he is accomplished at all these things: he is an expert boxer, marksman, and so on. Here he embodies almost everyone's fantasy of being accomplished without effort, and the very fact that Holmes is an expert without working at it and is able to snap out of lassitude into action also contributes to our estimation of his genius. In their practical application, these elements of Holmes' character lead to other areas of his attraction. One of Holmes' problems as a genius is boredom. He constantly complains about the sorry state of criminality which cannot produce a problem worthy of his attention. Boredom, of course, is the epidemic problem of modern life. To counter this, Doyle graciously provides things for his detective to do, and once Holmes grabs hold of a trivial problem it quickly becomes absorbing and, in stories like "The Red Headed League," important. Here Doyle gives us a practical demonstration of Carlyle. Coupled with this, he makes Holmes laugh. Especially in the early stories, Holmes laughs often to express his joy, not only in the foibles of others but also in the exhilaration of the hunt and chase. That Holmes can manipulate events to become jokes in "Silver Blaze" and "The Naval Treaty" shows Doyle's beginning awareness of new opportunities for the detective story.

Although he wrote fifty-six short stories and four novels about Sherlock Holmes, Doyle did not invent many detective plots. Scraped down to their essentials, Doyle's detective plots fall into a small number of categories: the returned avenger, the unusual occupation, the circumstantial delay, the stolen inheritance, the secret society, the duel, the hunt, and one or two others. These he simply repeated in new guises and combined together to write new stories. We have already seen where most of the plots come from, and as plots they are hardly remarkable or vital or interesting. Doyle does, nevertheless, tell stories in a workmanlike fashion, and he also happened upon some narrative devices which look forward to the detective story of the twentieth century. The first of these, we can find codified in the opening sentences of "The Three Garridebs" (January 1925) when Watson says "It may have been a comedy, or it may have been a tragedy." Although this comes in 1925, Doyle from quite early in his career wrote many Holmes stories as mixtures of non-serious and serious material. "The Red Headed League," for instance, begins with the patently comic adventures of Jabez Wilson, but then shifts tone to end with the thrilling action in the bank vault. This is not an isolated example; many stories mix comedy with serious action. Unlike the majority of detective writers before him Doyle came to realize, by accident or choice, the detective story can profit from a combination of non-serious, comic, and playful with the serious, tragic, and human implications of crime. By striking a balance between these two attitudes, the detective story can be both seriously moral and pleasingly entertaining. This combination is one of the things which enables the genre to be popular, and it forms the basis for one branch of twentieth-century detective fiction. The other modern narrative element of the detective story Doyle flirted with is the so-called "fair play" technique. The Holmes stories never become the kind of reader-writer game envisioned by S.S. VanDine and other twentieth-century writers. Doyle does not give readers all the facts, but, as he says in "The Crooked Man," retains "some factors in the problem which are never imparted to the reader." He, rather, builds stories so "the facts slowly evolve before your eyes and the mystery clears gradually away as each discovery furnishes a step which leads to the complete truth." That is what he says in "The Engineer's Thumb," and the stories bear out the statement. In some of the stories, however, he includes the sort of visual evidence which becomes a standard part of the "fair play" story. Doyle does occasionally give us architectural drawings, fragments of letters, and, of course, the code of the dancing men. He found this sort of thing in Gaboriau, and included it for the same reason—as a superficial advertisement for the realism of the stories. Although Doyle never intended to invite his readers to an intellectual wrestling match, he appreciated that curiosity played a large part in attracting the audience to the detective story. He began to learn that inviting readers to make the wrong guesses heightened the surprise at the end of the story. When he wrote "Silver Blaze," in fact, he bet his wife a shilling that she could not name the murderer. In response to this idea, Doyle made Holmes acknowledge in the later stories that the facts of the case can generate several alternate explanations: in "The Norwood Builder" Holmes says he can supply a half-dozen solutions which fit the facts of the case. Over the long haul, Doyle did not exploit this line of development. Most of the Holmes' adventures are single-option stories, principally formed to produce wonder at the detective's achievement. Indeed, the short story cannot really develop into the multiple-suspect, multiple-option detective story because it is too short. Doyle, however, thought about this a long time before it became a standard part of the detective novel.

Doyle thought about a lot of things connected with the detective story. He received the form from Poe, Gaboriau, and the sensation writers, and he passed it on to the short story writers of the 1890s and the novelists of the 1920s. It has been one hundred years, now, since Doyle wrote *A Study in Scarlet,* and over fifty since "Shoscombe Old Place," the last Holmes story. It has become increasingly difficult, however, to tell the dancer from the dance. Sherlock Holmes has become William Gillette, Eille Norwood, John Barrymore, Clive Brook, Raymond Massey, Basil Rathbone, and a number of other twenty-feet tall faces on the cinema screen. The stories have been plagiarized, parodied, burlesqued, updated, and rewritten so many times the originals have disappeared, smothered by their progeny. For the whole culture, too often Holmes has become a deerstalker hat and a calabash pipe saying "Elementary, my dear Watson." The Holmes stories have become public domain in more ways than one. Yet Doyle did little that was entirely new. The detective story existed before him and would have continued had Watson never met young Stamford, or had Jefferson Hope never loved Lucy Ferrier. Further, in some ways it would have been the same kind of detective story Doyle wrote: some sort of fusion of Poe, Collins, and Gaboriau was inevitable. But it would not have been the same in the most significant ways. Never could the detective story have inspired the kind of popularity achieved by Holmes without Doyle. Never would the detective story have fused adventure, intellect, and sentiment without Doyle. Never would it have developed precisely the same combination of humanity and flamboyance Doyle caught in Holmes. Never would it have become more than the sum of its parts. (pp. 76-95)

> LeRoy Lad Panek, "Doyle," in his An Introduction to the Detective Story, *Bowling Green State University Popular Press,* 1987, pp. 76-95.

SIGNIFICANCE OF NINETEENTH-CENTURY DETECTIVE FICTION

Elliot L. Gilbert

[*In the following excerpt, Gilbert examines the significance of the fictional detective in the nineteenth century as a symbol of both faith in and disillusionment with the powers of human reason.*]

Recently, interest in detective fiction has been running high among book collectors. At the famous London auction house of Sotheby's, hard-to-obtain copies of mystery novels and short story anthologies have, according to the *Times Literary Supplement,* been bringing up to a hundred pounds each; and in the same number of *TLS* appears a review of *Victorian Detective Fiction,* a catalogue of the "small, choice collection" of nineteenth-century detective stories made by Dorothy Glover and Graham Greene.

Thus, bibliographically speaking, the detective is booming these days. There is no sign, however, that he is also being "rediscovered" as a significant literary figure or even as a sociological phenomenon. Indeed, the anonymous reviewer of the Glover-Greene catalogue makes this point directly. "We find no hint," he writes, "either in Graham Greene's preface or John Carter's introduction, that these early detective stories are worth *reading,* or even—not that we should expect it in such company—that they throw an interesting sociological light on, etc. . . . " Yet it would surely be strange if the detective, so ubiquitous in our literature since his first appearance there in the middle of the nineteenth century, should have nothing at all to tell us about our civilization. One question, for example, inevitably suggests itself: if there is no meaningful connection between the detective as a literary figure and the century which gave him birth, why were there no detective stories—that is, no stories whose main subject is the professional detection of crime—before the nineteenth century?

Howard Haycraft, in his book *Murder for Pleasure,* suggests, in answer to this question, that "there could be no detective stories until there were detectives," and he further points out that "professional detectives did not appear in history until the nineteenth century." But why then were there no detectives before the nineteenth century? Haycraft's answer to this is to associate the sudden appearance of professional detectives in this period with the rapid development of democracy, and in particular with the growing acceptance of the rule of reason which democracy implies. " 'Detectives,' " Haycraft writes: " 'cannot flourish until the public has an idea [of] what constitutes proof.' . . . And of all the democratic heritages, none has been more stubbornly defended . . . than the right of a fair trial safeguarded by known, just, and logical rules." Thus, the critic sees the detective as a function of all that is most rational and progressive in nineteenth-century society.

It is, of course, extremely satisfying to view the detective—that apostle of pure reason—as the product and even the symbol of a reasonable age. But if reason had its triumphs in the nineteenth century, it also had its failures, and the detective was a product of these as well. To be sure, reason had discovered the laws which made men masters of the physical universe. But, as if to testify to the intransigence of chaos, these same laws also gave rise to the dark, satanic mills and sprawling slums that blighted industrial Europe and America during this period. Man's shaping mind, which had set out to build Jerusalem in England's green and pleasant land, had built Tom-all-Alone's instead. And from the dark and terrible slums of Tom-all-Alone's there sprang a new kind of crime—impersonal, anonymous—that required for the first time great hordes of impersonal, anonymous policemen for its detection, policemen who, simply by undertaking to solve these crimes, became themselves unwilling dwellers in the slums that reason had built. If, then, the detective was a metaphor for the nineteenth century's faith in man's problem-solving abilities, he was just as importantly a symbol of growing nineteenth-century disillusionment with reason as a meaningful response to the human condition.

Nothing, for example, could more perfectly epitomize both the possibilities and the limitations of human reason than the life history of Edgar Allan Poe, author of the first detective story. The details of Poe's biography are too familiar to require elaboration here: a painful childhood and adolescence, increasing loss of control, and, by 1840, complete collapse and delirium; and then, suddenly, the possibility of regeneration, one last chance—so to speak—for the mind to master the dark.

Poe was offered the editorship of *Graham's Magazine* on the condition that he give up his "irregular" behavior, and for a time his efforts in this way were successful. Through the sheer force of a fine intellect kept under precise control, he shaped the world to his own design, making of *Graham's* the first mass circulation magazine in America and at the same time writing the tales of ratiocination which were to be the basis of all future detective fiction. It is surely no coincidence that Poe wrote these stories during the months when he was struggling successfully against an impending dissolution no less terrible than M. Valdemar's. As Joseph Wood Krutch has put it, "Poe invented the detective story that he might not go mad."

It was, then, the ape of insanity in man that the writer was after, the murderous ape of the Rue Morgue which, in one ingenious disguise or another, had prowled unchallenged through dozens of the earlier nightmare tales. And now at last the ape had met its match in the author's super-intellectual alter ego, Auguste Dupin. The mind had triumphed. But was the victory final? Unhappily for Poe, the period of perfect lucidity which produced the detective stories was all too brief. Soon the writer had slipped back into the old ways and into the old stories. He produced no more tales of ratiocination, for the detective had been given his chance and had been found wanting. The descent was a precipitate one back into the familiar maelstrom of "waking dread" from which not even Auguste Dupin could rescue him.

Poe's disillusionment with reason as the key to man's salvation was, of course, merely the accident of his private life. The fact, however, that during this same period other writers, in the deliberateness of their art, chose to express this same disillusionment, and chose to do so in stories about detectives, is more suggestive. Charles Dickens, for one, in creating in *Bleak House,* the first detective in an English novel, deliberately refrained from portraying, through this character, the complete triumph of reason. Indeed, the police force in *Bleak House,* like the Court of Chancery and the great mills and factories in the book, is shown by Dickens to be just one more potentially disastrous product of man's intellect. The courts, created to dispense justice, are instead the great centers of injustice; the factories, dedicated to the elimination of human discomfort, only make men more uncomfortable; the police force, designed to drive out crime with the pure strength of reason, merely corrupts reason with the terrible vitality of crime.

For it is clear from *Bleak House* that just as a jailer becomes a prisoner of the men he guards, so Inspector Bucket is as much the *creature* of crime as he is its nemesis. The machinery of detection must wait, in the first place, upon

the commission of the crime. Thus, crime is passionate, self-starting, independent, while detection is initially powerless, nearly always fighting its battles on the enemy's ground, and in the end often obliged to become a part of what it seeks to destroy. Bucket, for example, succeeds in avenging the inhumanity of murder only by coldly perverting the human obligations of friendship and sympathy.

In this respect, Dickens' detective is very much like Hugo's Javert in *Les miserables,* another mechanical man, fated, in his pursuit of the sewer-dwellers, to plunge into the sewers himself. Nor did the nineteenth century exhaust this metaphor of the detective as a slave rather than a master of darkness. In his recent play, *Victims of Duty,* Eugene Ionesco has a detective sum up his life with these words: "My duty, you know, my dear sir, is simply to apply the system." And when one of the other characters protests, saying, "You're not just a civil servant, you're a *thinking being* (emphasis mine)," the detective dismisses the suggestion. "I am only a soldier, monsieur," he says.

This preoccupation of the nineteenth and twentieth centuries with detectives as thinking beings whose intellects cannot cope with the disorder of the world may in part account for the period's great interest in two other literary figures—Hamlet and Oedipus. Both these characters are, as has frequently been noticed, detectives of a sort; that is, they are both obliged to solve murder mysteries, and at first glance they both seem ideally suited for the job.

Hamlet, just home from the university, is called upon to restore order to his dissolute country by bringing the murderer of his father to justice. But though the prince, a man of considerable intellect, is aware of the importance of his mission, and though he recognizes that if no action is taken to root out the corruption in Denmark the whole court may well be destroyed, he nevertheless cannot manage to put off the final massacre. *Why* he could not do so has fascinated generations of playgoers and readers, and each generation has sought its own answer to the question. Significantly, the answer which the early nineteenth century (and in particular Coleridge) found was that Hamlet's undoing was precisely that instrument which was supposed to save him—his mind. In the end, according to this explanation, reason was no match for the rottenness in Denmark.

As Hamlet was an obsession in the first years of the nineteenth century, so Oedipus, through the imagination of Freud, began to be an obsession in the last. Like Hamlet, Oedipus is also well-suited to the role of detective. He has gained his throne by solving the riddle of the Sphinx, and he is therefore highly qualified to investigate the murder of Laius. But once again the mind is no match for the horror; indeed, by a grim irony, it is the very act of investigation, the very application of reason, which brings on the tragedy. In the same way, Oedipus' success in answering the riddle of the Sphinx does not really lift the curse from Thebes as it appears to do, it simply shifts the curse to another quarter, just as the nineteenth-century's application of the new physical laws to its problems only succeeded—nightmare-like—in creating new and more serious problems.

The man who, more than anyone else, gave Oedipus to the nineteenth and twentieth centuries—Sigmund Freud—was himself, as Stanley Edgar Hyman has noted in *The Tangled Bank,* a "great detective." Hyman remarks that a number of exchanges of dialogue between doctor and patient in Freud's case histories read like passages from Sherlock Holmes stories, nor is this surprising when we recall that Conan Doyle based the character of Holmes on Dr. Joseph Bell, a teacher of his at medical school. Conversely, the detective Porfiry in Dostoevsky's *Crime and Punishment* is, in his sensitive investigation of Raskolnikov, as much a psychoanalyst as he is a policeman, there being, however, an important distinction between him and a real-life doctor. For where the psychoanalyst-detective in the novel manages to rescue his prisoner-patient from the darkness—though not, to everyone's taste, convincingly—the real-life psychoanalyst was not always so successful. Sometimes, Freud would encounter a patient whose hysterical lameness, for example, would vanish after deep probing into the victim's unconscious. But often the same patient would return only a few months later, this time with hysterical paralysis of some other limb or perhaps with symptoms of hysterical blindness. The Sphinx had not been killed after all; her destructive energies had only been displaced a little and would never finally be overcome.

Even in his own life, Freud was helpless to forestall the famous prophecy of the oracle which had come both to Oedipus and to Laius; that is, he could not himself avoid growing from Oedipus into Laius, from son into father, from heir presumptive into king. Nor, when the time came, could he keep himself from violently dismissing most of his disciples—his professional sons—just as if, for all his knowledge and understanding, there still rang in his ears the dread and not-to-be-ignored warning: "If you have a son, he will kill you."

Of course, in spite of Bucket and Javert, in spite of Hamlet and Oedipus and Freud, detectives were not universally ineffectual in nineteenth-century literature and experience. In popular mystery fiction, for example, they were almost invariably triumphant spokesmen for human reason. Indeed, during the century and a quarter that have passed since Poe created the detective story, the genre has spawned literally thousands of detective-geniuses from whom nothing can be hidden and who always succeed in restoring order to a murderous world. But even as the mystery story industry has been grinding out these optimistic tales for readers who would certainly not devour them so eagerly if they were not aware of the stubborn persistence of evil in the real world, that real world has been encroaching on the fictional one. Among the more recent popular literary detectives, for instance, such figures as Raymond Chandler's Philip Marlowe and Dashiell Hammett's Sam Spade begin, realistically, to blur the distinctions between detective and criminal. Then there is a character like Mickey Spillane's Mike Hammer, who neither in actions nor in values differs in the least from the people he pursues.

It may be objected, of course, that Mike Hammer was never intended to be an apostle of reason and that there-fore his surrender to the violence he is supposed to eliminate is not meaningful. But even about Sherlock Holmes, that very type of the perfect intellect triumphing over a chaotic universe, it is possible to raise disquieting questions. All of those successful cases which permit us to flatter ourselves that man's mind is indeed in control of the world—do they not, according to Watson, constitute only a portion of the mysteries which Holmes investigated? Do we not hear with alarming frequency of cases which trailed off inconclusively or, even more astonishing, of cases which in the end left Holmes baffled? And with the introduction of the sinister Professor Moriarty and his complex network of world crime, do not even Holmes' greatest successes—successes with lost jewels and curious cyphers and ingenious bank robbers—come to seem rather pallid and, in the long run, insignificant?

The story called "His Last Bow" makes this point most incisively. Time and again in the early days, Holmes, by the simple expedient of discovering the hiding place of the top-secret plans or of revealing the activities of international spies, had single-handedly kept Europe from going to war. Now, however, it is August, 1914, and though the great man has come out of retirement to do battle once more with the forces of darkness, and though his mind seems as quick as ever, this time the darkness is not to be denied. To be sure, Holmes foils the German agent, but World War I, the ultimate symbol of irrationality, cannot so easily be put off. It has a vitality too terrible even for the great detective, who withdraws once more to the Sussex Downs and to his bees, never again to appear in the world.

Can it be that in the end even Sherlock Holmes, whose creator—Conan Doyle—was himself to move from the realm of reason to the world of the occult, had come to doubt the efficacy of intellect, had come to see that if the detective was a metaphor for the nineteenth century's faith in ratiocination, he was also symbolic of the age's profound disillusionment with human reason? We have the evidence of his own words in one of the late stories. At the end of "The Adventure of the Cardboard Box," Holmes asks solemnly,

> What is the meaning of it, Watson? What object is served by this circle of misery, violence and fear? It must tend to some end, or else our universe is ruled by chance, which is unthinkable. But what end? *There* is the great standing perennial problem to which human reason is as far from an answer as ever.

(pp. 256-62)

Elliot L. Gilbert, "The Detective as Metaphor in the Nineteenth Century," in Journal of Popular Culture, *Vol. 1, No. 3, Winter, 1967, pp. 256-62.*

Steven Earl Forry

[In the following excerpt, Forry links the emergence of detective fiction in the nineteenth century to such economic and social forces as the rise of industrialization

and the loss of spiritual belief and analyzes the literary function of the detective during this era.]

In chapter XI of *Pickwick Papers* Samuel Pickwick discovers "a small broken stone, partially buried in the ground" on which are carved what he interprets as runic inscriptions. Pickwick pays ten shillings for the stone and carries it to his hotel room for a closer examination. When he arrives, Dickens describes the scene:

> The stone was uneven and broken, and the letters were straggling and irregular, but the following fragment of an inscription was clearly to be deciphered:
>
> +
>
> BILST
>
> UM
>
> PSHI
>
> S.M.
>
> ARK
>
> Mr. Pickwick's eyes sparkled with delight as he sat and gloated over the treasure he had discovered . . . In a country known to abound in remains of the early ages . . . he . . . had discovered a strange and curious inscription of unquestionable antiquity, which had wholly escaped the observation of the many learned men who had preceded him.

The "unquestionable antiquity" of the stone is effectively quashed, however, when Mr. Blotton—who earlier in the novel cast dubious eyes on Pickwick's Tittlebation Theory—deciphers the message as the orthographically imperfect inscription of a village yokel: "BILL STUMPS, HIS MARK."

Although Pickwick receives the brunt of our laughter, the gist of Dickens' argument lies deeper than comedy. In the text, interpolated between the discovery of the stone and its deciphering, lies a tale entitled "A Mad Man's Manuscript." The evening of the discovery of the supposed runic inscriptions, Pickwick turns to the "somniferous influence" of "A Mad Man's Manuscript" to ease, what Dickens calls, his "disagreeable state of mind." Throughout the novel these nocturnal "pockets of darkness" reflect the states of mind of Samuel Pickwick in that they release internal pressures that cannot be accommodated in the Pickwickian world of sunlight and salutation. Juxtaposed as it is between Pickwick and Blotton, the manuscript not only captures Pickwick at his most radical distortion of reality—at his most "insane"—but also signifies, in Blotton, the necessity of empirical order in a world rapidly becoming more complex, more indecipherable.

This bifurcated focus—on the desire for and the loss of oracular insight, and the necessity of forming a cogent response to an increasingly relativistic universe—occupies a key position in the formation of artistic tastes out of which nineteenth-century literature emerged. For when we enter the Victorian world we are entering a fallen or falling world—what Silas Wegg accurately terms the "falling off" of civilization. As described by Henry Adams, mid-century England was "in its last stage of decomposition." By 1850 the dynamos of Michael Faraday had long replaced the "subterraneous music" that Words-

worth's Michael encountered in the hills of Grasmere; and, like the Renaissance Madonna extolled in "The Dynamo and the Virgin," the "youthful Poets" of Wordsworth's "Pastoral Poem" had at long last been supplanted. The world that emerged was a world striving to regenerate itself, yet caught in its own seeming paralysis. As J. Hillis Miller comments, in his aptly titled *The Disappearance of God,* "the nineteenth and twentieth centuries seem to many writers a time when God is no more present and not yet again present, and can only be experienced negatively, as a terrifying absence. In this time of the no longer and not yet, man is 'Wandering between two worlds, one dead, / The other powerless to be born.'" Somewhere order had to be injected into what Carlyle envisioned as the "ever-living, ever-working, Chaos of Being"; somewhere had to be found a challenger for the amorphous "Hyrcanian tiger, the Behemoth of Chaos," which stalks *Past and Present.*

Into this pandemonium stepped the detective, a descendant of Daniel in a world descending to Beelzebub. In this [essay] I propose that the emergence and fruition of detective fiction can be correlated as a direct response to the influences of a rapidly industrializing nation coupled with the loss or questioning of God in the nineteenth century. In this sense, the calling forth and development of the detective reflects a reaction to the lack of stability inherent in an increasingly mechanized—or "Wemmickized"—society. In his ability to introduce into society order and moral strength, the detective conquered a world that demanded the tempering of imagination with the dross of disillusion. In this context the sudden rise of detective fiction at the beginning of the last century may be conceived of as a Romantic invention which survived and, by its very nature, thrived on adversity. What began as an incipient rejoinder to "stormtost seas, French Revolutions, Chartisms, [and] Manchester Insurrections," of *Past and Present* burgeoned into a full-fledged rebuttal of that self-same chaos. Thus the growth of detective fiction marks the stages of transition in England from Romantic to Victorian in that it charted the disintegration of pastoral ideals into urban actualities: as the hills of Grasmere lost their poets, the Bow Street Runners inherited the streets of London.

It is not coincidental, therefore, that Mary Shelley published *Frankenstein* at the beginning of that century. By no small incongruity the first words spoken by the first "hideous progeny" of the nineteenth century are "Pardon this intrusion." That violence and destruction should so politely announce themselves betokens an irony which can only be appreciated in hindsight; yet, clearly, the perfect metaphor for an age of revolution and invention is Frankenstein's creature. As the quintessential ordering principle and interface between two worlds, the secular and the sacred, the detective represents the perfect medium by which Frankensteinian chaos may be turned into rational order.

In her incisive *The Development of the Detective Novel,* Alma Murch defines the detective story as ". . . a tale in which the primary interest lies in the methodical discovery, *by rational means,* of the exact circumstance of a mysterious event or series of events." Murch distinguishes between the detective and the crime story (such as the Newgate Calendar and the Newgate Novel), in that the crime story does not recognize the activities of the criminal as reprehensible and, in fact, regards the criminal as a source of amusement or admiration. Thus, rather than the controlling force of the action, in the crime story the police figure acts as a mere backdrop for the more exciting actions of the criminal.

Murch sharply delineates the difference between the detective and the mystery story in that the latter involves the supernatural. This point cannot be over-emphasized: in detective fiction the detective alone discovers "by rational means" the cause or causes of the enigma. Moreover, since this rationality substitutes as a kind of providence, with the loss of God in the nineteenth century, the detective introduced into the world a human element that could combat chaos, perceive meaning, and reaffirm order. For, as Thackeray so poignantly stated in a reference to *Vanity Fair,* by 1850 society had truly become "a set of people living without God in the world."

Hence, although for King Belshazzar Daniel interprets MENE TEKEL PERES, by the nineteenth century only Inspector Bucket can interpret Allegory for the society of *Bleak House;* only William Legrand, in Poe's "The Gold Bug," can properly decipher the cryptogram left by Captain Kidd on Sullivan's Island; and only Sherlock Holmes, in "The Adventure of the Dancing Men," has the power to decipher the hieroglyphs written by Abe Slaney to Elsie Cubitt. In the last two stories both men use similar procedures to arrive at similar solutions because in the modern society the act of semiotic interpretation belongs not to the sacred but to the profane. In the final case, Holmes becomes so proficient in the art of decoding that he writes his own hieroglyph which leads to the arrest of Slaney in the murder of Mr. Cubitt.

By the time of the Industrial Revolution Daniel's visions have become referential misprisions. Once doubt has been introduced concerning the sacrosanct, ancient remedies dissolve into nostrums—"Morrison's Pills"—for modern ailments. " 'Do you believe in ghosts, Max?' " queries the assistant of Max Carrados in "The Ghost of Massingham Mansions." " 'Only as ghosts,' replied Carrados with decision." Carrados then disproves the belief that ghosts inhabit the mansions. To a similar question posed in "The Sussex Vampire," Sherlock Holmes responds definitively: " 'Are we to give serious attention to such things? This Agency stands flat-footed upon the ground, and there it must remain. The world is big enough for us. No ghosts need apply.' "

Writers such as Poe, Dickens, Wilkie Collins, Arthur Conan Doyle and even Bulwer-Lytton developed the detective into a superior man, a superman, who stepped forth to command a world of heretofore hidden facts. In the introductory pages of "The Murders in the Rue Morgue," which I include in this study of British fiction because of Poe's enormous influence on detective fiction in general, the narrator defines the character of the detective. His comments prove to be the detective's manifesto:

> As the strong man exults in his physical ability . . . so glories the analyst in that moral activity which disentangles. . . . He is fond of enigmas, of conundrums, of hieroglyphics; exhibiting in his solutions of each, a degree of acumen which appears to the ordinary apprehension praeternatural. His results, brought about by the very soul and essence of method, have, in truth, the whole air of intuition.

In the opening pages of "Rue Morgue" Auguste Dupin evinces these characteristics when he reconstructs his companion's private ruminations simply by attending to his friend's physical movements as they stroll through Paris:

> "I will explain," he said, "and that you may comprehend all clearly, we will first retrace the course of your meditations, from the moment which I spoke to you until that of the *rencontre* with the fruiterer in question. The larger links of the chain run thus—Chantilly, Orion, Dr. Nichol, Epicurus, Stereotomy, the street stones, the fruiterer."

In "The Adventure of the Cardboard Box" Conan Doyle reflects his indebtedness to Poe's story when Holmes alludes to Dupin's penetrating insights in "Rue Morgue" and then proceeds to exhibit the same power by deducing Watson's unstated reflections on the American Civil War. In another story ("The Adventure of the Yellow Face") he deduces Watson's past health by the present state of his slippers. And in a third story ("The Adventure of the Stockbroker's Clerk"), Holmes reconstructs not only a man's physiognomy, but also his social habits and economic class by analyzing a pipe. Finally, from the mere trace of chalk on Watson's hand, Sherlock Holmes reconstructs how Watson passed an entire evening as well as how he plans on investing his money:

> Here are the missing links of the very simple chain: 1. You had chalk last night. 2. You put chalk there when you play billiards to steady between your left finger and thumb when you returned from the club the cue. 3. You never play billiards except with Thurston. 4. You told me four weeks ago that Thurston had an option on some South African property which would expire in a month, and which he desired you to share with him. 5. Your cheque-book is locked in my drawer, and you have not asked for the key. 6. You do not propose to invest your money in this manner.

In *The Moonstone* only Sergeant Cuff is perspicacious enough to notice a smear on Rachel Verinder's newly varnished door. He concludes that since the varnish dries in twelve hours, and since it was applied at 3 p.m., it was still wet at midnight. Therefore the theft of the gem must have occurred between midnight and 3 a.m. As the thief was the only person moving through the house between those hours, his nightdress must have been stained with varnish. From this dab of paint, his deductions set in motion the process that leads to the apprehension of Godfry Ablewhite. As Cuff observes elsewhere:

> I made a private inquiry last week . . . At one end of the inquiry was a murder, and at the other

end there was a spot of ink on a tablecloth that nobody could account for. In all my experience along the dirtiest ways of this dirty little world, I have never met with such a thing as a trifle yet.

In the early twentieth century these traits converge in the hero of Ernest Bramah's novels, Max Carrados. Although he is inhibited by blindness, his handicap seems to have crystalized and heightened his intuitive and rational senses. As Bramah comments:

> You will notice that [Carrados] is blind—quite blind; but so far from that crippling his interests in life or his energies, it has merely impelled him to develop those senses which in most of us lie half dormant and practically unused.

Returning now to *Bleak House,* I wish to conclude my discussion of detection by concentrating on the method by which the detective's interpretation of reality supplies meaning to his society. Inspector Bucket infuses his world with a symbolic mode by which to live when he elucidates the meaning of Allegory, the protean fresco in the ceiling of Tulkinghorn's study. Just as Legrand and Holmes interpret their ciphers, so Bucket interprets his conundrum, Allegory. It is noteworthy that the fresco no longer serves as a natural conflux of societal beliefs—no longer serves its "allegorical" purpose; rather it has been reduced to a meaningless, albeit imposing, plaster decoration. In translating Allegory, therefore, Bucket can lead us to not only the murderer of Tulkinghorn, but also to the body of Lady Dedlock.

At our first encounter with Allegory "it" points out the door. At our second, "it" points out the window. By chapter XLVIII, Allegory has become vivified enough to be called "he":

> He is pointing at a table . . . He is pointing at an empty chair, and at a stain upon the ground before it. . . . These objects lie directly within his range. An excited imagination might suppose that there was something in them so terrific, as to drive the rest of the composition, not only the attendant biglegged boys . . . [but] the very body and soul of Allegory, and all the brains it has—stark mad.

At this stage Allegory has not only a body but a soul and brains as well. More is involved here than Dickens' penchant for animism. As Allegory gains life—illustrated by the changing pronouns—his role as justice crystallizes into action. Indeed one could say that Allegory rather than Hortense is responsible for the vengeance wreaked on Tulkinghorn. After all, every object in the room lies "directly within his range" of fire. Allegory is the sole witness, and the "person" from whom Bucket obtains the final clues for solving the murder. As we read: "A few hours afterwards, he and the Roman will be alone together, comparing forefingers."

Bucket's forefinger "never rests." It is called his "admonitory finger" and "his familiar demon." When he queries Sir Leicester with his suspicions of Lady Dedlock, Dickens refers to "the cruel finger that [probes] the life-blood of [Sir Leicester's] heart." The finger lures Mrs. Snagsby, crooks with sagacity, and hooks when it understands. It

also gives Bucket the scent of the traverse of Lady Dedlock, and acts as a moral cudgel when interrogating Hortense: Bucket "shakes the finger at her . . . making no demonstration, except with the finger." At the heart of his interrogation "Mr. Bucket bends forward in some excitement . . . and inaugurates what he is going to say with one ghostly beat of his forefinger in the air. . . . " Bucket also inherits Allegory's extended and admonitory hand, literally becoming the long arm of the law: " 'Do you see this hand,' he queries, 'and do you think that I don't know the right time to stretch it out, and put it on the arm that fired the shot?' "

Now that Bucket emerges, society takes on an homologous form; a communal telepathy establishes itself between the community and the Inspector. In chapters LVII through LIX, which describe the search for Lady Dedlock, "everybody seemed to know" Bucket.

A sense of community redemption establishes itself in these closing chapters. Still, one feels that the efforts of Bucket represent a last-ditch attempt on the part of Dickens to forestall a sense of universal entropy. As Mr. Jarndyce says, "The universe . . . makes rather an indifferent parent." The mysteries of the universe are catalogued and hope should reign. Yet one cannot ignore the fact that Lady Dedlock dies because Bucket could not track her down. In the world of mortals, sheer human intelligence can only accomplish so much; although of superior intellect and intuition, the detective is still a human being. As Sergeant Cuff tells Franklin Blake: "It's only in books that the officers of the detective force are superior to the weakness of making a mistake."

As the next century approaches, even the partial and temporary unity achieved at the conclusion of *Bleak House* vanishes. "Life knows us not and we do not know life" Conrad was to write not forty-five years after the publication of *Bleak House.* Few images representing the futile impotence of mankind are stronger than the image Conrad invokes to describe the mutilated body of Señor Hirsch hanging from the rafters of a building gutted by fire. Here Conrad describes Hirsch as ". . . an opaque long blotch in the semi-transparent obscurity of the room between the two tall parallelograms of the windows full of stars." The image symbolizes more than man's inhumanity to man. It represents a metaphor for man's place in the cosmos: beaten and savaged, he hangs silhouetted in the unfeeling geometry of the world, shaded by the benign image of stars that twinkle (one imagines) to distant children who look to the stars and make fantastic wishes. The juxtaposition is unbearable, yet the incongruity is unavoidable.

As if referring to this image of Sr. Hirsch, Edmund Wilson writes [in his *Axel's Castle: A Study in the Imaginative Literature of 1870-1930*]:

> It was the effect of the theory of Evolution to reduce man from the heroic stature to which the Romantics had tried to exalt him, to the semblance of a helpless animal, again very small in the universe and at the mercy of the forces about him. Humanity was the accidental product of

heredity and environment, and capable of being explained in terms of these.

Perhaps Wilson overstates the tenor of the first half of his argument; however, he argues persuasively when he emphasizes the psychological ramifications of a world "ordered" by chance and environment. For, as I have stated, in a world directed by providence, pattern occurs as part of an inherent design. Remove providence and one removes the organizing system. The results are as terrifying as multifarious.

In this world of the no longer and the not yet, the detective attempted to ferret out new directions while reasserting the power of individuals over their circumstances. In his attempt to insert pattern into the non-providential, the detective mediated between thundering industrialism and subterraneous music, and between the almighty dynamo and the enfeebled Virgin. His emergence could not have taken place in any preceding century. Perhaps one should be solaced that he did not arrive too late. (pp. 92-104)

> *Steven Earl Forry, "The Detective as Hero," in* Perspectives on Nineteenth-Century Heroism: Essays from the 1981 Conference of the Southeastern Nineteenth-Century Studies Association, *edited by Sara M. Putzell and David C. Leonard, Studia Humanitatis, 1982, pp. 92-104.*

Brigid Brophy

[*Brophy is an Anglo-Irish novelist, dramatist, and critic. Influenced by Sigmund Freud and Bernard Shaw, she has created social satires of middle-class morality and hypocrisy strongly marked by elements of farce and wordplay. As a literary critic, Brophy is known for her provocative and acerbic remarks, particularly the iconoclasm of* Fifty Works of English and American Literature We Could Do Without *(1967), in which she and coauthors Michael Levey and Charles Osborne attack such works as* Hamlet, Wuthering Heights, *and* Moby-Dick. *In the following essay, Brophy analyzes the mythic qualities of detective fiction, focusing on Poe's "Murders in the Rue Morgue" as a prototype of the genre.*]

The question mark [in the title of this essay, 'Detective Fiction: A Modern Myth of Violence?'] is casting doubt on the violence, not the modernity or the myth—both of which are, indeed, exactly to the point.

Admittedly it is only in a longish historical view that one can call something modern which is a hundred and twenty-two years old. But in that longish view, a hundred and twenty-two is just about the age of modernity itself—of our present, industrialised phase of civilisation. From what went before we are cut off socially by the industrial and intellectually by the French Revolution. People before that demarcation are unaccountable creatures in fancy dress; after it, they are ourselves, modern man, in—if they are men in the sexual sense as well—trousers. There are sound reasons why detective fiction and modernity are roughly coeval. Of its nature, the detective story could not have been invented in the (to us) age of fancy dress. The detective quintessentially wears trousers.

In a longer view still, the contrast with 'modern' is 'ancient'—A.D. is opposed to B.C.; and in this view the detective story has a fairly precise claim to be one of the few equivalents the modern world can put forward to the myths of the ancient. We incline to toss off the word 'myth' inexactly: we call Marilyn Monroe a myth (when we really mean a goddess—a myth being, by etymology, a story and not simply a personality, however touching); novels should be myths, according to some of their theorists (who seem to mean, if anything, that novels should make manifest material from the unconscious). The detective story itself is not a myth in the very strictest sense of an anonymous, undated fiction passing itself off as truth. But it does share one characteristic of myths: it runs to type. In the ancient world, which set so much less store than we do by novelty and originality, many poems or plays, by several authors, might repeat the story of a single myth; and, quite over and above that, the single mythical story itself was often a good deal less singular than it seemed. Very many—perhaps most—of the Greek myths can be divided into groups, the myths in each group being in fact variations on a single skeleton narrative. The countless stories we generically call 'the detective story' resemble a group of myths, inasmuch as there is really only one skeleton detective story, on which detective writers invent variations consciously (which probably separates them from the anonymous and no doubt multiple authors of myths) and more or less ingeniously.

In the ancient world itself, Ovid pointed out by implication that myths tend to run to type when he compiled his *Metamorphoses.* The entire collection has a single underlying story: some*one* is transformed into some*thing.* Within this, there are sub-groups, according to why the transformation takes place—as a reward, to save a virgin from a fate worse than metamorphosis, and so forth; and every now and then one of the myths makes a conspicuous, though wholly superficial, bid for independence by tying itself to, and claiming to account for, the genesis of a particular species of bush or the invention of a particular musical instrument. In the same way, a single skeleton lies inside several of the stories of the Greek heroes. A hero was often tied very conspicuously to local patriotism, being claimed for the royal dynasty or as the founding-father of one of those Greek city-states which were so notoriously unwilling to surrender their sovereign independence.

The granular individualism of Greek politics is reflected in the unwillingness of Greek mythology to amalgamate its heroes into a single national hero. Had mythology cared to do it, the job would not have been hard, because the heroes, for all their seeming individualism, are remarkably unoriginal. Quantities of them conform to a type of *the* hero. He is usually of royal or divine parentage, and at his birth someone prophesies for him a future so disturbing to his father or, which may be the same thing, the ruler that it is decided to kill him in infancy. But by one mechanism or another he escapes death—and also the city of his birth. He is brought up by strangers in a foreign land. Sometimes his fosterparents disclose his true identity to him when he comes of age (or when they are about to die); sometimes he has to wait until he is identified by someone in his native city when he returns there. Return there, whether by chance or in order to claim his inheritance, he always does; and he always finds the city in urgent need of a hero. Some innocent party, perhaps the king's daughter, perhaps the whole population, is under threat from some monstrous tyranny. The hero arrives just in time to destroy the dragon—or whatever form the monster takes—by a display of heroic courage or magic or both. He may perform other, incidental wonders and shew forth the signs of his true identity; he is acclaimed as a saviour; if he is the king's son he is publicly acknowledged, and if he is not he usually becomes the king's son-in-law. Eventually, whether by inheritance, marriage or being co-opted by the grateful population, he becomes king.

This story was capable not only of local variation but of crossing a major frontier and adapting itself to the mœurs of a different civilisation. The Greek custom of exposing unwanted children, which gave the baby hero in Greek versions of the myth so many opportunities to be saved by a tender-hearted nurse or fortuitously found by a humane shepherd, was not practised in Palestine, where (although the shepherds remain, rather gratuitously, in the story) King Herod has to resort to the wholesale slaughter of the innocents. That, it may be, is a rather clumsy and extravagant variation, but in other items of the myth transplantation brings a gain in gravity and in the rarity of the hero's standing. In Greek mythology, with its multiplicity of lecherous gods, the hero who is the son of a god and a mortal woman was bound to be rather common. Shifted into the sphere of influence of the jealously monotheistic and on other occasions sexless Jewish god, the hero's claim became much more impressive—so much so, indeed, that it was blasphemous; and that enabled it to fit neatly in, from the point of view of the mechanics of the plot, with the important and emotionally very significant change the Christian myth makes in the ending of the story.

For a modern audience, the Greek hero is in danger of losing our sympathy. In the contest between the hero (or his Christian successor, St George) and the dragon, we are apt to take sides with the dragon. The danger became plain indeed when an ancient, though not Greek, hero was music-dramatised by Wagner. Siegfried (one of the heroes, incidentally, who is always seeking the truth about his parentage) behaves like the nastiest sort of boy bully when he wantonly wakens, provokes and kills Fafner. Wagner does, just, make us swallow the situation—he seduces us by the beauty of the horn calls with which Siegfried summons the sleeping dragon; but Wagner the impresario was evidently not quite confident that Wagner the artist had succeeded, since he took monstrously extravagant—and therefore inartistic—pains to build up the poor dragon by stage-carpentry into something that should pass for an opponent of Siegfried's own calibre.

From the danger of creating a sadistic hero the Christian myth escaped by the nearest masochistic emergency exit. The new version of the myth was calculated to appeal to a modern audience and in fact, in making its tremendously wide appeal, it transformed the ancient world into the modern. In the Christian version, the population does not recognise the distinguishing marks which identify the hero

as the royally and divinely descended person of whom so much has been prophesied; instead, it denies him and makes his claim to be his father's son the occasion for accusing him of blasphemy. He is executed and triumphs only after death, when he enters into his inheritance of a kingdom that is not of this world. In this world his part is that of innocent victim, offering himself in place of the people—who in this version are not innocent but guilty of sins which culminate in their denial of the hero.

This convenient exit proved in the end ill advised. It had the effect of amalgamating the hero's father with the tyrant who threatens the people, creating a monster-god capable of accepting his son's self-sacrifice in lieu of the sinful population, at the same time as requiring the population to do endless penance for their sins or else forgo the benefits the son has bought for them. The masochistic trap-door had led to a god whose sadistic tyranny was redoubled because it was also sanctimonious. This issue was not, however, foreseen when the new version of the myth appeared. It quickly made enough emotional headway in the Greco-Roman world for its adherents to acquire some political power; and since of all the sects in that world (with the exception of the Jews, who did not, however, proselytise), the Christian was the only one to be absolutely non-tolerating of all the others, the Christians quickly used their political power to shut down the whole of pagan mythology by force of law.

The monster god who then clamped his tyranny over Christendom naturally monopolised Christendom's faculty for inventing and launching myths. That faculty was constrained to flow almost exclusively into the lives of the saints (which often followed a minor heroic pattern) and into the acts of magic performed by their relics, acts which shewed an even greater tendency than the feats of the heroes to reduplicate a type. The myth-making capacity revived a little before it was overtaken and virtually extinguished by a written culture, but many of Christendom's myths are Christian-tinted. The tint is not always so blatant as it is in witchcraft, whose mythology is simply the Christian one written, bravely but unimaginatively, back to front, but it is usually perceptible. A light and charming Christian varnish washes the whole concept of chivalry, whose ladies do not escape a certain conflation with the madonna and whose knights and troubadours are not wholly distinct from crusaders, while King Arthur suffers the quests of his knights errant to be merged with a quest for the Holy Grail. Perhaps the first figure to revive anything of the heroic pattern in a wholly secular tone is Robin Hood, who seldom enters a church except to rescue the sweetheart of one of his merry men when she is being sacrificed as an innocent victim to a monstrous man she does not love.

Compared with the Greek or even the medieval world, ours is short of myths. That does not, of course, mean that our imaginative life has been impoverished. On the contrary. But it is now carried on chiefly through stories which bear a date, an authorship and the open announcement that they are fictions. Great changes have taken place in our attitude to both authorship and fiction—ultimately as the result, no doubt, of the change from an oral to a written culture. Long after Greek culture became literate it remained predominantly, in the very nature of its traditions and conventions, oral—indeed, it remained specifically rhetorical. It did so, probably, because it could. The city-state had a small enough population for the whole electorate to be addressed by an orator, and the Greek world had a small enough geography for a rider or even a hiker to get from one sovereign city to another in a day. Nothing made change pressing; whereas in modern Europe, with its bigger territories and populations, the printing press, which is what eventually enabled culture to entrust itself almost wholly to written media, was one of the few inventions which really have been mothered by urgent necessity. The necessity had already existed, but no one had come forward with an answer to it, in the Roman Empire, whose great areas and population were too unwieldy to be steered with any precision by the rhetorical conventions of Roman law courts and which quickly dropped even the pretence of being governed by the rhetorical conventions of the Roman Senate.

So long as culture remains genuinely oral, it is inevitable that poems and stories will be altered as they are passed on. To that extent, a work of literature in an oral culture really does have no—that is, no single—author; and where the conventions of oral culture persist, they will go on behaving as though there were no authors even when books are in fact circulating with the authors' names on them. Because the stories that are anonymously handed down by an oral tradition count traditionally as history, which provokes pride in the whole community instead of in a single author, fiction was slow to acquire an intellectual standing in the ancient world. History books were in fact written by named historians and fictions by named authors of fiction, and yet neither classical language makes provision in its vocabulary for succinctly drawing the distinction between fiction and non-fiction. The Latin from which we derive 'fiction' also, and significantly, gives us 'feign'. Inventing an original story was not properly distinguished from inventing falsehoods, a circumstance in which authors of fiction might well be less anxious than they are today to own to their work. Rather than see his fiction confused with a falsehood, an author might be glad, even though this involved the loss of his own name from public view, to see his work pass under the anonymous authority of history or the hallowed, semi-mythical and thus almost anonymous authorship of Homer.

In modern Europe, printing led first to licences to print and from there to (under English law, early in the eighteenth century) the first stages of establishing copyright. An author was enabled first to fix his text and thus make sure he *was* the sole author of it, and presently to draw from it not only any kudos but also any royalties it might earn, though it was and remains rare for either to amount to very much. The old prestige of history lingered so forcefully that authors of fiction were for a long time (and in some quarters are still) less esteemed than redactors of facts. Prose fictions, which never acquired a distinctive descriptive name in the ancient world, had to wait a long time before acquiring one in the modern. Fictions long and short had been written and recognised for many years before the ambiguous name 'history' and the morally am-

biguous name 'romance' ('romancing' is scarcely better than 'feigning') were driven out, in some languages at least, by 'novel' and 'novella'—words which positively announce that the story is, precisely, new: that is, original to its author.

This claim to originality is not only a boast: it is an obligation. The novelist nowadays is obliged to warrant his publisher by contract that the work *is* his own. This does not mean he must be artistically original: artistic originality is acknowledged to be a virtue, but examples of it are seldom praised or even recognized until some time after they appear. It is only in a letter-of-the-law sense that a novel must be novel. Yet there are departments of fiction in which even this rule is, in a special way, tacitly abrogated. This is not a question of a literary form, which prescribes, exactly, form and not content: no one will accuse me of plagiarism if I publish a series of poems of fourteen lines each, but neither does the sonnet sequence lay down what the poems be about. Again, a literary genre does not say so much what the subject should be as what the treatment should not: not too searching, if it's light comedy; not too subtle, if it's farce. Even the pulp-reading which is often said to be turned out to a formula relies less on a positive than on a negative formula—a set of boundaries which the author cannot cross without losing some of his market. There is a kind of fiction distinct, though at the edges only vaguely, from all of these. It is popular in that it makes small intellectual or imaginative demands on its readers, though its readers in some cases are, unlike pulp-readers, capable of responding to such demands when they are made by a different sort of book; but it is not necessarily popular in the sense of having large sales. Or, rather, it is rare for any one novel in the category to have a very big sale, but the category as a whole may sell enormously, relying not so much on numerous as on deeply addicted readers, who seem to need to consume one novel a week in their chosen category, much as (the comparison is not idle) Christians need to consume one communion wafer a week in their chosen denomination.

It is these fictions which are our latterday myths. Although they carry an author's name (or, very often, pseudonym), they shew the mythological tendency to repeat a standard pattern with variations conspicuous but superficial, and their heroes come close to the mythological type of *the* hero. For the equivalent to one metamorphosed Greek, Narcissus, we have to look to the theatre (and the theatre as depicted by the cinema), where a *vedette,* wearing spangled tights and singing either 'On with the Motley' or 'There's no business like show business', personifies show business holding up a mirror to show business. The vedette has a female version, but apart from her we have few heroines. We have no counterpart to the maiden saved from rape; we can represent her only by her opposite, the tart with the heart of gold, who is closely related to the female vedette and probably goes back mythologically to St Mary Magdalene—who herself may well be, like another passage from the New Testament, a plagiarism from the Greek theatre of Menander. Heroes, however, we have profusely: the spy (Ulysses?); the mad scientist (Prometheus, undoubtedly—via Mary Shelley's 'modern Prometheus'); the gangster—who shades into the outlaw (Robin

Hood, Dick Turpin, Ned Kelly); and, above all, the heroes of two vast and very distinct groups, the western and the detective story.

The hero of the western borrows from the outlaw tradition and at the same time exemplifies a modern tradition of chivalry. Like both Dick Turpin and the knight errant, he is so far inseparable from his horse that it is tempting to trace him to an ultimate mythological prototype in the centaur. It is the hero of the detective story who sticks most closely to the centre of the track beaten by the Greek hero, though he has abbreviated it at both ends. The detective story does not finish with the detective becoming king—though he *is* acclaimed by a grateful population. He is a democratic hero, a superman perhaps, but not by divine right, and his apotheosis consists of his becoming famous. (Like all democratic heroes, he has bashfully to deprecate his fame.) At the beginning of the story, the circumstances of the hero's birth are omitted; but echoes of the prophecy about the hero may remain inasmuch as the detective is forerun by his celebrity, and the conspiracy against him, which in the Greek myth happens in the hero's babyhood, may be displaced to later in the story when the criminal may feel himself threatened (as the ruler was by the hero's birth) and make an unsuccessful attempt on the detective's life. In essence the detective story opens about a third of the way through the heroic story, at the point where the hero comes back to the city. For the detective it is not a matter of coming *back* (though it may be of coming *again*—to another case in his career). The detective comes by chance or because he has been 'called in'—he borrows his professional status chiefly from the consultant ranks of the medical profession. He is accompanied, like the Greek hero in the Greek theatre (or in the theatre of Racine), by a confidant (who borrows a touch also from the chivalrous tradition—he is the detective's squire, his Sancho Panza). In the theatre, the confidant's job is to elicit from the hero in conversation what is going on in the hero's mind and so make the heroic thoughts accessible to the audience. In the detective story he does the same job more selectively: he must elicit some of the detective's thoughts, but not those whose premature revelation to the reader would cut the story too short. The confidant is a device whereby the narrative can keep close to the detective without wholly entering his consciousness. The confidant is also there, of course, as a foil: where the confidant warns that a certain action is dangerous, the detective fearlessly insists on doing it; where the confidant is baffled, the detective astutely sees the sense of the clue. Unlike the Greek hero, the detective cannot shew forth signs which identify him as the long-lost royal son or the prophesied messiah, but he invariably shews forth distinguishing marks—idiosyncrasies of speech, dress and habits which raise him to a heroic level above the other characters in the book. Then, like the Greek hero, he proceeds to perform miracles.

In the detective's case, the miracles are very pointedly not done by magic. They rely on nothing but common sense, which, however, the detective uses to an uncommon, heroic degree. The cause in which he uses it remains the same as that in which the Greek hero uses his magic powers and talismans—the deliverance of the population from a

threat. The Greek hero comes to the city and finds the whole people grieving under menace from a monster: the detective comes to a closed community (a family, a house party, a country inn cut off by snow, a school, a campus) where a murder has been committed and the whole surviving community is under suspicion. The writer deliberately makes use of the closed community in order to limit the number of suspects and thereby increase the pressure of suspicion bearing down on each. It may even be that the police are already investigating the crime and about to accuse an innocent person—perhaps even the pretty girl in the story, who plays the same rôle as the King's daughter who is about to be sacrificed to the monster. In this stricken community the detective appears as the saviour. He does not go so far as the Christian hero who takes the guilt on himself. More rationally, he uses rational methods to discover the real murderer—often arranging in the penultimate scene a reconstruction of the crime which brings the murderer's guilt home in the sight of all: and thus he takes the only exhaustively convincing way available of lifting the suspicion of guilt from the community as a whole.

Like the heroic myth, this pattern is—and must be—varied. It can even establish an equivalent to local patriotism: brand loyalty. Sometimes the publisher tries to set this up for his series of books by various hands, but it is more successful, and more mythological in spirit, when it is done by the author, who makes his detective the centre of a cycle—the case of the this, the case of the that—much as King Arthur and Robin Hood are the centres of their cycles. One of the variable factors, the eccentricities and idiosyncrasies of the detective, may therefore be repeated from novel to novel; the other, the details and method of the crime, must be fresh for each novel or short story. Provided I can think up fresh variations at these two points (or have already invented a detective of my own in an earlier novel), I may offer my publisher tomorrow a novel written precisely to the outline sketched above; so far has that outline become public—anonymous—property that I can in good conscience warrant him, and he will unblinkingly accept, that it is all my own work. Yet it is in fact the plot of thousands of detective novels. Indeed, with one modification (the elaborateness of the scene where the crime is reconstructed—a scene the detective tradition has, as a matter of fact, borrowed from *Hamlet*), it is exactly the plot of the first detective story ever written.

That was published in 1841, written by an American and set in France. Edgar Allan Poe's decision to set 'The Murders in the Rue Morgue', as well as his two later detective stories, in France is usually explained by Poe's great interest in and knowledge of French culture. Strictly speaking, however, those only *enabled* him to set his fictions there; they do not in themselves provide a positive impulsion, for which I think we ought to look in a combination of history and psychology. Briefly, I think that Poe set his detective stories in France because the French Revolution had been set in France.

Moreover, I think it was the French Revolution which was the positive impulsion towards the particular invention of the detective story by Poe and its general adoption as a myth pattern. Here again, there is a distinction between what positively impelled and what merely enabled detective fiction to come into being. Obviously, just as novelists could not set their stories in the neighbourhood of fictitious gasometers until real gasometers had been invented, fictitious detectives had to wait until real detectives and detection had been invented—which happened in England and in France (where the organisation of an effective police force was a direct result of the Revolution) about 1800. But we are entitled to seek also a positive factor which turned the real-life invention into a much repeated fictitious myth. No such factor seems to exist in gasometers. Evidently the detective, as fictionalised by Poe at that particular moment in history, contained a peculiar myth-creating potential.

Sherlock Holmes, who is still probably the most famous detective hero and the one who commands the greatest brand loyalty, speaks on one occasion of 'my scientific methods'; and they are indeed scientific, but in a restricted sense. They hardly touch on experimental science. Indeed, it was probably in order to borrow some of the kudos of experimental science, which did not rightfully belong to it, that detective fiction evolved its elaborate reconstruction scene, which is at once an experiment in the technique of the murder and, like the play scene in *Hamlet,* an experiment on the criminal's guilty psychology. Again, Sherlock Holmes's methods touch, but only lightly, on technology. His amateur laboratory is sketched in very cursorily indeed: 'the scientific charts upon the wall, the acid-charred bench of chemicals' are enough—the enumeration of his tools goes straight on to 'the violin-case leaning in the corner' (which, in the philistine world Holmes inhabits, counts as one of his eccentricities). Only once in the twelve stories in his *Case-book* do we actually come upon Holmes 'bending for a long time over a low-power microscope'. In fact Holmes himself gives a narrower and more accurate description of his method when he calls it 'my familiar method of logical analysis'. And 'analysis' is the word Poe chooses to epitomise the method of the prototypical detective Dupin in the prototypical case in the Rue Morgue.

In other words, although the detective may call in 'laboratory aids', they are as a rule amateur ones of the sort you might have found in the home of a dilettante, philosopher or man of letters in the eighteenth century—Goethe, say, or Voltaire himself, who expressed his ideal as *'passer d'une expérience de physique à un opéra ou à une comédie'.* Nineteenth-century figure though he is, the detective preserves the fashion of the eighteenth-century Enlightenment in carrying elegantly a veneer at least of both arts and sciences. Dupin is something of a classical scholar; Holmes has his violin as well as his microscope. As for the methods which the detective's scientific smattering helps out, they are less those of science at large than of scientific scholarship, the methods of the historian, the art historian, the textual critic. They consist of pure deductive logic. They are remarkable and specialised only in the rigour and thoroughness of the mind which applies them, a mind which considers no detail beneath and no reputation above scrutiny, and which refuses to accept preconceptions and conventions about what a thing *must* be but insists on enquiring for itself what it *is*.

Here, too, the detective preserves the eighteenth-century spirit. His habit of looking at content instead of nimbus is the essence of Candide's near-naïf vision. Candide is still surprised enough by everything to take nothing for granted. On the battlefield where others have been trained to see honour and glory, Candide sees the actual content of the ground—*'des cervelles . . . répandues sur la terre à côté de bras et de jambes coupés'.* It is by a narrowing of Candide's vision to a particular problem that, in the too-familiar-to-be-remarked-by-anyone-else figure of the postman, the detective sees the one person who could have entered and left the scene virtually invisibly. And in fact Voltaire himself did, in another of his *naïf* heroes, Zadig, anticipate the detective's methods—an instance mentioned in histories of detective fiction but, quite rightly, disallowed because Zadig's deductions do not help solve a crime. (In fact they get him unjustly accused of one.) The crime had, so to speak, not yet been committed.

In the widest and most social sense Voltaire might have maintained that his own deductive acumen *was* deployed towards exposing a crime, since it was used to the end he expressed as *'écrasons l'infâme'.* His was only the nimblest hammer in the labour of demolition carried out by the eighteenth-century Enlightenment as a whole. The weapons of *naïf* vision, ridicule, irony, scholarship, textual criticism and logic were used to bring down the whole numinous superstructure, social and theological, of Christendom. Deep buried under the rubble was the guilt European man had consciously entertained ever since he accepted exclusively the Christian hero who died for him. Having refuted the supernatural, the Enlightenment pinned its curiosity and hopes to the natural, by which, since its concept of Nature was barely biological and not at all psychological, it meant chiefly the material—hence all those dilettante hours at the amateur laboratory bench. However, natural philosophy was not yet wholly separated from philosophy, and the philosophers were able to slip between the physicist and his lens the notion that the Nature under inspection must be not merely natural but naturally benevolent. Man having shed his supernatural soul (together with the myth of his Fall), the benevolence of Nature logically extended to human nature, too. The tyranny of Christian superstition exploded, man was pronounced not guilty of original sin and found to be inherently good—though in practice corrupted by unnatural tyrannies. Unfortunately, at the end of the century which had pulled off this enormous intellectual feat, its findings were tested in an experiment. The monarchy which had tyrannised France by virtue of feudal numinous awe was removed, and French citizens were set free to—as Pope had urged at the beginning of the century—'follow Nature': whereupon they proclaimed the noblest slogan ever coined by a body politic and, setting up the guillotine, began severing one another's heads from their bodies in a way that would have horrified the ex-tyrant had they not earlier done the same to him. And, having leapt out of the frying-pan into the fire, they proved unable to call up any fire engine except Napoleon, in whose wars cannon- and musket-fire eventually killed far greater quantities of them than tyrant and Terror combined.

It is impossible to exaggerate the scar left in our cultural consciousness to this day by the French Revolution. The generation immediately after it became all but emotionally and intellectually prostrate in its efforts to sew together the lips of the trauma. The real-life heroes of this period are the first of the anti-heroes, tormented and *maudit;* they are exemplified in Kierkegaard, Newman, Poe himself and Poe's disciple Baudelaire. Reason, it seemed, had led to man's proving himself not benevolent but monstrous by nature. And yet reason had not been wrong: it was impossible to go back with genuine belief to the numinous world: or, supposing one could force oneself to do so, that, as Kierkegaard experienced, was merely to succumb on irrational instead of rational grounds to the conviction of man's guilt. Half of Poe's violently dichotomised imagination was given to creating nightmares in which doom descends in punishment of a guilt whose source is not understood; and the other half was given to constructing stories—those about Dupin's detection, and also Poe's cryptogram and puzzle stories—in which a mystery proves understandable and soluble in strictly rational terms. And in the detective stories, the only ones which laid down the pattern of a myth, it is guilt which is rationally understood and traced to its source.

Having created his detective-hero-deliverer, Poe even tried to make him deliver Poe and solve the mystery of Poe's own dichotomy between imagination and reason. The narrative of 'The Murders in the Rue Morgue' is preceded by a discourse on the analytical faculty, in the course of which Poe elaborates Coleridge's antithesis between fancy and imagination in such a way (a way that might have had the approval of Coleridge himself, another of the tormented romantic-rationalists of the period) as to bring imagination and rationality into analogy and almost identification with one another: 'It will be found, in fact, that the ingenious are always fanciful, and the *truly* imaginative never otherwise than analytic.'

Reason, when liberated in the French Revolution, seemed to have laid human nature under the imputation of blood guilt. What Poe invented in the first detective story was a hero who delivers the community—the inhabitants of the 'quartier St Roch'—from just that imputation, and does it not by supernatural means, which would involve a reaction to the *ancien régime* no longer possible, but by a *better* application of reason. One of the strictest rules of the detective-story convention is that the supernatural may be (in the words of Dorothy Sayers, quoted by Howard Haycraft in his history of the detective story) 'evoked only to be dispelled'. The rule was obeyed by Sherlock Holmes ('This Agency stands flatfooted upon the ground . . . No ghosts need apply'—this despite his creator's belief in spiritualism) and had been laid down by Dupin in the prototype: 'It is not too much to say that neither of us believe in praeternatural events. Madame and Mademoiselle L'Espanaye were not destroyed by spirits.'

Disdaining the supernatural, the detective disdains also any last attenuated rag of feudal superstition: the last wisp of the heroic tradition whereby the triumphant hero be-

comes a king or even a god was disdainfully shrugged away when Holmes refused a knighthood. Nevertheless, the detective *is* (witness his disdain) an aristocrat—but a natural one, just as he is merely rational but more incisively so than common people. On a small scale he represents the fantasy which, of all fantasies, post-Revolutionary society wished *could* be true: he offers a way of returning to the aristocratic principle without violating reason. His superiority does not rest on breeding, which is wholly irrational, or on talent, which people may disagree about and which cannot be rationally proved, but on a process of reasoning which, when he explains it, can be followed and concurred in by everyone—including, by implication, a jury, that microcosm of a democratic society. The detective's superiority cannot be rationally refuted, and therefore he is justified, as the aristocrat by blood was not, in exhibiting his eccentricities and his essentially aristocratic disregard of the bourgeois reaction to them. In two cardinal instances, Holmes and Dupin, one of the main eccentricities is keeping irregular hours—the aristocratic mark of the man who does not have to go out to work next morning. Ordinary, blunt-witted rationality—indeed, flat-footed rationality—is represented in the detective myth by the men who do have to go out to work, who investigate the crime by routine methods as part of the routine of their job and not because the problem (or an old friend or a pretty woman) has appealed to them: the flat-foots, the police.

In life, the police came first and were aped by the private detective: but it is significant that in fiction the detective was a private eye from the start. Later detective fictions may deviate from this pattern in fact but not in spirit. The fictitious detective is sometimes a policeman, but he is almost invariably an unorthodox one, whose methods disturb his orthodox colleagues or superiors (this happens to the young Maigret) or bring him into rivalry with another department—which the French judicial system in particular makes plausible. Even English detective writers can postulate a rivalry between Scotland Yard and the local force; Simenon positively pits the Police Judiciare against the Palais de Justice. The middle-aged Maigret has a permanent rival in the judge Coméliau, who *'s'était toujours méfié du commissaire et de ses méthodes'*. The rational-democratic essence of the detective hero is brought out in the fact that between Maigret and Coméliau there is a social contrast: Maigret is plebeian born, but an aristocrat of reason; Coméliau is by breeding an aristocrat but limited to *'le point de vue de son milieu'*. By going beyond police routine and evolving his own unorthodox methods, Maigret becomes, as it were, a private detective who, needing to earn a living, happens to be employed by the police. He sticks to the myth pattern in which both the aboriginal Dupin and the central Holmes are private detectives (Holmes already using the word 'Agency' for his partnership with his slow-witted confidant). Holmes is the aristocratic consultant who receives fees, the police the routine artisans who are paid wages. Dupin actually mentions the famous real-life French policeman Vidocq—as 'a good guesser, and a persevering man', who, being 'without educated thought . . . erred continually'.

In fact, the competition between the detective hero and the

police is indispensable to the myth, because it is the police, with their propensity to err continually, who are the threat to the population of the story. The pattern is already firm set in 'The Murders in the Rue Morgue', where the police arrest an innocent man. The lax reasoning of the police in detective fiction is the inheritor of the lax reasoning whereby the Revolutionary juries condemned innocent men; the detective is the hero who rescues the innocent—not, like the aristocratic Scarlet Pimpernel or Napoleon himself, who founded a new aristocracy as well as a new tyranny, by a plunge into reaction and irrationality, but by superior rationality.

To recognise the detective as primarily a deliverer is in itself to refute—or at least greatly shift the emphases of—the theory most usually advanced as a psychological account of the detective story's popularity. There is, of course, another but this time quite superficial theory, namely that it is popular simply as a puzzle: but that is easily disposed of, since it does not explain why the puzzle grew into a literary myth. Poe's purely puzzle stories laid down no myth pattern and have few imitators. It seems that the actual content of the detective puzzle, unlike, say, the significance of the words which answer the clues in a crossword puzzle, is a material and indispensable element. This is in fact assumed by the usual psychological theory—which also assumes, however, that the important part of the content is violent death: the death of the victim and then the death of the murderer in expiation. According to this theory, the detective story is an opportunity for reader and writer to commit at least one murder in their imaginations; the writer is said to have a *nostalgie de la boue,* and both reader and writer are said to have a 'blood-lust' which can be 'sublimated by reading and writing fiction murders'. The words are those of 'Nicholas Blake', a detective-story writer who contributed an introduction to the Howard Haycraft book (*Murder for Pleasure*) I have already cited. The book was published in 1942, and the introduction by 'Nicholas Blake' goes on to suggest that, had the Germans sublimated their blood-lust through detective fiction they 'would certainly have less zest for murdering real Poles'. This 'certainty' is supported by two arguments: that the Nazis banned imported detective fiction; and that in any case detective stories were not popular in Germany. These facts (if the second *is* a fact—after all it was in the German language that *Emil and the Detectives* had carried the detective myth to the very nursery) cannot have been very telling even at the time. (The Nazis banned a good range of cultural imports, not all of which offer an opportunity for sublimating murder.) Now that we have seen some of the post-1942 behaviour of the countries, America, England and France, where the detective story undoubtedly is popular, they do not seem a very solid support for so large a hypothesis.

The view that the reader commits murder in his imagination is not always stated explicitly, yet it seems to be implied by a very commonly drawn contrast. 'Nicholas Blake' himself, in the same introduction, draws it when he asks 'From what dark incentive, by what devious and secret psychological passages have detection writers—timid and law-abiding persons for the most part, who faint at the sight of blood and tremble when the eye of a policeman

is turned upon them—first set out upon the sinister paths of crime fiction?' A hundred other cliché-writers have said the same thing in not very different words. It all goes back, I rather think, to some journalistic commonplace of the 'thirties, which still turns up in the English press on Sundays, to the effect that detective stories are the favourite reading of bishops. What with these (presumably) Anglican bishops, the fictitious detective Father Brown and the detective-fiction writer Father Ronald Knox, it must have seemed in England in the first three decades of this century that detective aptitude was conferred by the laying on of hands.

As a matter of fact, to see so prompt a contrast between murder and the priesthood is an example of our un-Candide-like vision, our habit of heeding people's professions about their professions rather than the content of their professions. Were we to see the priest as a man whose daily routine is to feed first himself and then others with the body and blood of a person who was tortured to death, we might think it less surprising if the priest's imagination *were* blood-boltered. Yet if the detective myth really is analogous to the heroic one, then in fact the priests must be acquitted of blood-thirst at least in their spare-time reading. The detective myth appertains to a different priestly function.

The place of the detective story in our society does distantly imply a general confession of blood guilt—but of guilt which is there before, and quite independently of, the story. Reading the story does not bring the guilt into existence: rather, it is the existence of the guilt which impels the repeated writing and reading of the story in its many variations. The detective myth, which did not exist before it, is a repeated admission that the French Revolution took place. It admits a wish to kill as inherent in human nature, inasmuch as it repeatedly builds a fictitious situation in which all the human beings involved need to be cleared of the suspicion of guilt: we might all be murderers. (Before the French Revolution it was possible to disbelieve that proposition.) But the detective story does not pile yet more guilt onto its readers by seducing them into imaginatively participating and concurring in a murder. On the contrary: its form is carefully calculated to make participation impossible. By the very terms of the puzzle, the reader cannot follow the act of murder through the consciousness of the murderer.

Some recent detective stories do slip in a passage seen through the eyes of the murderer, but he has to remain anonymous to the reader—a device which in itself tends to set him beyond the reader's power to identify himself with the characters; and the device is usually employed to arouse fear in the reader of the person who is least identifiable with oneself, the stranger, the prowler who may jump out at you; indeed, if anything, the device identifies the reader with a potential victim rather than the murderer. The reader cannot be in a position wholly to identify himself with the murderer in a detective story until the story is over. Only when the puzzle is solved does the reader come into possession of the facts—the murderer's name and the technique of the crime—which enable him to put himself in the position of the criminal during the act; and by then the act is finished and done with. If the reader can follow the murderer's consciousness at the time, then the story is by definition not a detective story but a thriller or psychological thriller like *Crime and Punishment.*

In the detective story proper, murder is less an act than stage machinery. It sets the scene and starts the story moving. (Further murders may re-set the scene and give the story a fresh impetus.) More often than not the murder happens off-stage, frequently before the story opens. Neither the act of murder nor the hunting down of the murderer (which in societies which still practise capital punishment may imply a further murder, committed in vengeance for the original one) occupies the centre of the narrative stage, because it is not on those that the suspense in the story rests. The suspense is generated by the race between the detective's powers and the doom of unjust suspicion which is descending on the population. Blood there has, admittedly, to be; admittedly, without the pre-existing blood guilt there would have been no story; and usually a murderer has to be indicted because that is the only way to provide the rest of the cast with an acquittal wholly satisfying to reason. But the psychological purpose of the story is summed up in that acquittal. The detective myth exists not to provoke or endorse guilt but to dissipate it. The solution pronounces the general absolution.

Usually that can be done only at the cost of excepting one person and accusing him of murder, but it would be wrong to think the myth exacts his blood and makes the reader an imaginative participator in the act of vengeance. The murderer is required as a piece of machinery without which the solution would not be plausible. The narrative is often a touch shame-faced about its need to employ him—more shame-faced, in fact, than it is about requiring a victim to be murdered to start the story off in the first place. If that often happens off-stage at or before the start, the murderer, once detected, is positively rushed off-stage at the end. His death on the scaffold, so far from being gloried in, is scarcely hinted at. In this the author may be following the sound commercial practice of not offending the susceptibilities of any class of readers, even if it is probably a minority, when there is no need to; and commercial practice certainly makes it clear that the pattern of the story does *not* need an emphatic and blood-thirsty revenge against the murderer. Or the writer may be acting on his own convictions, many detective writers being no more in favour of capital punishment than of murder. (And in one notable instance at least, when a detective writer conspicuously played the detective in real life, it was with the same essential purpose as the fictitious detective, namely to establish innocence. Conan Doyle worked strenuously to clear the wrongly convicted Oscar Slater—just as Voltaire earlier gave his deductive and literary brilliance to clearing Callas and Sirven.) With no matter what motive, the detective writer regularly makes not the most but the least of the criminal's punishment. If he plausibly can, he often takes the comparatively humane way out by suggesting that the murderer will be found insane or by allowing him to commit suicide.

Even the rule that someone must be guilty is not absolutely essential to the myth pattern. All that really matters to

it is innocence. This is clear from the first detective story, which laid the pattern down. It is highly significant that, in that story, there are murders but (although Poe may have intended an allegory about the bestial aspect of human nature and certainly perpetrated a slander against orang-outang nature) what the solution shows is that there is no murderer. (pp. 121-42)

> *Brigid Brophy, "Detective Fiction: A Modern Myth of Violence?" in her* Don't Never Forget: Collected Views and Reviews, *1966. Reprint by Holt, Rinehart and Winston, 1967, pp. 121-42.*

FURTHER READING

Anthologies

Bleiler, Everett F., ed. *A Treasury of Victorian Detective Stories.* New York: Charles Scribner's Sons, 1979, 406 p.
> Collection of nineteenth-century detective fiction that includes works by Charles Dickens, Mary Elizabeth Braddon, Emile Gaboriau, Mrs. Henry Wood, Wilkie Collins, Arthur Conan Doyle, and Anna Katharine Green.

Greene, Hugh, ed. *The Rivals of Sherlock Holmes: Early Detective Stories.* New York: Pantheon Books, 1970, 351 p.
> Reprints short detective fiction by contemporaries of Arthur Conan Doyle. In an introduction, the editor offers biographical and critical commentary about the authors included.

Wright, Willard Huntington, ed. *The Great Detective Stories: A Chronological Anthology.* New York: Charles Scribner's Sons, 1945, 483 p.
> Selection of short detective fiction chosen by the editor to "show the evolution of the modern detective story." The collection includes works by Edgar Allan Poe, Wilkie Collins, Anna Katharine Green, and Arthur Conan Doyle, as well as an introduction to the genre by Wright.

Secondary Sources

Aisenberg, Nadya. *A Common Spring: Crime Novel and Classic.* Bowling Green, Ohio: Bowling Green University Popular Press, 1979, 271 p.
> Suggests that the crime novel is linked thematically and structurally to such archetypal literary forms as the myth and fairy tale, and that it serves a similar function—confirming and reinforcing the moral order in which its readers believe. Included in Aisenberg's study are a chronological survey of nineteenth-century detective fiction and a chapter devoted to Dickens and the crime novel.

Altick, Richard D. "Literature with a Sanguinary Cast." In his *Victorian Studies in Scarlet,* pp. 67-85. New York: W. W. Norton & Co., 1970.
> Examination of the subject of murder in the "penny dreadful," the Newgate novel, the works of Dickens and Collins, and other examples of Victorian popular literature.

Barzun, Jacques. "From *Phèdre* to Sherlock Holmes." In his *The Energies of Art: Studies of Authors Classic and Modern,* pp. 303-23. New York: Harper & Brothers, 1956.

Outlines the history of detective fiction and suggests that the strict conventions of the genre limited its possibilities for development.

Barzun, Jacques, and Taylor, Wendell Hartig. *A Catalog of Crime.* Second edition. New York: Harper & Row, 1971, 831 p.

Annotated bibliography of nearly thirty-five thousand novels, short stories, anthologies, magazines, and dramas of detection, crime, mystery, and espionage, as well as secondary literature on the subject.

Bedell, Jeanne F. "Melodrama and Manners: Changing Attitudes toward Class Distinctions in English Detective Fiction, 1868-1939." *CLUES: A Journal of Detection* 1, No. 1 (Spring 1980): 15-24.

Analysis of nineteenth- and twentieth-century English detective literature that contends: "the virtual exclusion of working-class and radical characters from serious consideration in detective fiction not only reflects bourgeois dominance during its formative period but also reveals its kinship to two dramatic forms, melodrama and comedy of manners, and that the fusion of these two forms in detective fiction accounts for the rigid limitations of the genre."

Binyon, T. J. *'Murder Will Out': The Detective in Fiction.* Oxford: Oxford University Press, 1989, 166 p.

History of the detective character in literature from Edgar Allan Poe's Dupin to the modern policeman.

Bloom, Clive. "Reading and Death: Considering Detective Fiction in the Nineteenth Century." In his *The 'Occult' Experience and the New Criticism: Daemonism, Sexuality and the Hidden in Literature,* pp. 80-9. Sussex, England: Harvester Press, 1986.

Examination of nineteenth-century detective literature that attempts to "consider the formal properties of detective fiction and the complex interrelations between detective fiction, reading and death, between murder and creation."

———— et al., eds. *Nineteenth-Century Suspense: From Poe to Conan Doyle.* New York: Macmillan, 1988, 139 p.

Includes essays on the works of Edgar Allan Poe, Wilkie Collins, and Arthur Conan Doyle in a collection of criticism of suspense, mystery, and horror fiction of the period.

Christopher, J. R. "Poe and the Tradition of the Detective Story." In *The Mystery Writer's Art,* edited by Francis M. Nevins, Jr., pp. 19-36. Bowling Green, Ohio: Bowling Green University Popular Press, 1970.

Exploration of Edgar Allan Poe's contributions to detective fiction through an analysis of seven of his short stories.

Craig, Patricia, and Cadogan, Mary. *The Lady Investigates: Women Detectives and Spies in Fiction.* New York: St. Martin's Press, 1981, 252 p.

Examines the origins and development of the female detective character in English and American fiction from Victorian times to the present.

Cruse, Amy. "Crime Fiction." In her *After the Victorians,* pp. 138-48. London: George Allen & Unwin, 1938.

Surveys the crime literature of the late nineteenth century.

Dorff, Susan L. "The French Connection." *The Armchair Detective* 22, No. 4 (Fall 1989): 374-80.

Provides a history of the French *roman policier* from its beginnings in the *Mémoires* (1828-29) of François Eugène Vidocq to modern examples of the genre.

Haines, Helen E. "The Lure of Crime." In her *What's in a Novel,* pp. 218-38. New York: Columbia University Press, 1942.

Brief survey of detective fiction that begins with William Godwin's *Caleb Williams* (1794) and continues into the twentieth century.

Haining, Peter. *Mystery! An Illustrated History of Crime and Detective Fiction.* New York: Stein and Day, 1977, 176 p.

Chronicles the history of detective literature to World War II.

Hardy, Thomas John. "The Romance of Crime." In his *Books on the Shelf,* pp. 219-35. 1934. Reprint. Freeport, N.Y.: Books for Libraries Press, 1970.

History of detective fiction that emphasizes nineteenth-century British contributions to the development of the genre.

Haycraft, Howard. *Murder for Pleasure: The Life and Times of the Detective Story.* New York: D. Appleton-Century Co., 1941, 409 p.

Highly regarded chronicle of detective fiction that outlines "the main progress of the detective story" to the mid-twentieth century.

Hirsch, Gordon. "*Frankenstein,* Detective Fiction, and *Jekyll and Hyde.*" In *Dr Jekyll and Mr Hyde after One Hundred Years,* edited by William Veeder and Gordon Hirsch, pp. 223-46. Chicago: The University of Chicago Press, 1988.

Analysis of *Dr Jekyll and Mr Hyde* that "explores the book's strong connection with its most important gothic predecessor, Mary Shelley's *Frankenstein,* as well as its relation to the emergent nineteenth-century genre of detective fiction, to which it belongs, but which it also deconstructs."

Hubin, Allen J. *The Bibliography of Crime Fiction: 1749-1975.* San Diego: University Extension, University of California/Publisher's Inc., 1979, 697 p.

Comprehensive listing of detective novels, plays, and short stories published in English.

Hutter, Albert D. "Dreams, Transformations, and Literature: The Implications of Detective Fiction." *Victorian Studies* 19, No. 2 (December 1975): 181-209.

Finds that detective fiction echoes the process of dreaming "by taking as both its form and its subject a conflict between mystery and unifying solution." Hutter focuses on an examination of Wilkie Collins's *The Moonstone* as representative of the genre.

Johnson, Timothy W., and Johnson, Julia, eds. *Crime Fiction Criticism: An Annotated Bibliography.* New York: Garland Publishing, 1981, 423 p.

Annotated bibliography of secondary sources.

Kalikoff, Beth. *Murder and Moral Decay in Victorian Popu-*

lar Literature. Ann Arbor, Mich.: U.M.I. Research Press, 1986, 193 p.

Analyzes "the discussion and enactment of murder in street literature, newspapers, middle-class journals, melodrama, and fiction" during the Victorian era in order to "understand the direction of Victorian beliefs and fears." In the course of her study, Kalikoff examines a number of nineteenth-century works of detective fiction including Mary Elizabeth Braddon's *Lady Audley's Secret* (1862), Charles Dickens's *Bleak House* (1853), and Arthur Conan Doyle's *A Study in Scarlet* (1888).

Knight, Stephen. *Form and Ideology in Crime Fiction.* Bloomington: Indiana University Press, 1980, 202 p.

Examines the social and cultural values inherent in selected works of crime fiction. Knight includes chapters on the works of Edgar Allan Poe, Poe's precursors, and Arthur Conan Doyle.

Matthews, Brander. "Poe and the Detective-Story." In his *Inquiries and Opinions,* pp. 111-36. New York: Charles Scribner's Sons, 1907.

Glowing account of Poe's contributions to the development of detective fiction.

Melvin, David Skene, and Melvin, Ann Skene. *Crime, Detective, Espionage, Mystery, and Thriller Fiction & Film: A Comprehensive Bibliography of Critical Writing through 1979.* Westport, Conn.: Greenwood Press, 1980, 367 p.

Annotated bibliography of literature and film criticism that includes nineteenth-century detective fiction.

Ousby, Ian. *Bloodhounds of Heaven: The Detective in English Fiction from Godwin to Doyle.* Cambridge: Harvard University Press, 1976, 194 p.

History of detective fiction in England.

Peterson, Audrey. *Victorian Masters of Mystery: From Wilkie Collins to Conan Doyle.* New York: Frederick Ungar Publishing Co., 1984, 235 p.

Charts the development of nineteenth-century English detective fiction through an examination of selected works by Wilkie Collins, Charles Dickens, and Joseph Sheridan Le Fanu, among others.

Porter, Dennis. "Crime Literature." In his *The Pursuit of Crime: Art and Ideology in Detective Fiction,* pp. 11-23. New Haven, Conn.: Yale University Press, 1981.

Exploration of forms of crime in eighteenth- and nineteenth-century works of detective fiction.

Queen, Ellery. *The Detective Short Story: A Bibliography.* Boston: Little, Brown and Co., 1942, 145 p.

Bibliography of short detective fiction providing first publication information, physical descriptions of books, and brief annotations.

————. *Queen's Quorum: A History of the Detective-Crime Short Story as Revealed in the 106 Most Important Books Published in this Field since 1845.* Boston: Little Brown and Co., 1951, 132 p.

Provides a critical overview of the genre.

Rollason, Christopher. "The Detective Myth in Edgar Allan Poe's Dupin Trilogy." In *American Crime Fiction: Studies in the Genre,* edited by Brian Docherty, pp. 4-22. Houndsmills, England: Macmillan Press, 1988.

Examines the character of Dupin in "The Murders in the Rue Morgue" (1841), "The Mystery of Marie Rogêt" (1842-43), and "The Purloined Letter" (1844).

Rosenheim, Shawn. " 'The King of "Secret Readers" ': Edgar Poe, Cryptography, and the Origins of the Detective Story." *ELH* 56, No. 2 (Summer 1989): 375-400.

Theorizes that the plot and narrative form of the detective story emerged from Poe's interest in cryptography.

Routley, Erik. *The Puritan Pleasures of the Detective Story: A Personal Monograph.* London: Victor Gollancz, 1972, 253 p.

Appreciation of the genre. Routley includes four chapters on the Sherlock Holmes stories.

Sayers, Dorothy L. Introduction to *The Omnibus of Crime,* edited by Dorothy L. Sayers, pp. 9-46. New York: Payson and Clarke Ltd., 1929.

Discusses the early development of detective fiction, focusing on the seminal works of Edgar Allan Poe and Arthur Conan Doyle.

Stewart, R. F. *. . . And Always a Detective: Chapters on the History of Detective Fiction.* Newton Abbot, England: David & Charles, 1980, 351 p.

Critical history of the genre.

Symons, Julian. *The Detective Story in Britain.* Bibliographical Series, edited by Bonamy Dobrée. London: Longmans, Green & Co., 1962, 48 p.

Outlines English developments in detective fiction through the mid-twentieth century.

Thomson, H. Douglas. *Masters of Mystery: A Study of the Detective Story.* 1931. Reprint. Richard West, 1978, 288 p.

Provides an overview of detective fiction.

Wells, Carolyn. *The Technique of the Mystery Story.* The Writer's Library, edited by J. Berg Esenwein. Springfield, Mass.: The Home Correspondence School, 1913, 336 p.

First full-length discussion of the elements of narration, plot, and characterization in detective fiction. Wells devotes several chapters to the works of Edgar Allan Poe, Emile Gaboriau, and Arthur Conan Doyle.

Williams, H. L. "The Germ of the Detective Novel." *The Book Buyer* XXI, No. 4 (November 1900): 268-74.

Account of the genesis of the detective novel in France that also traces late nineteenth-century developments in the genre in England and America.

Williams, Valentine. "The Detective in Fiction." *The Fortnightly Review* 134 (September 1930): 381-92.

Examination of the detective fiction of Edgar Allan Poe, Emile Gaboriau, and Arthur Conan Doyle.

Woeller, Waltraud, and Cassiday, Bruce. *The Literature of Crime and Detection: An Illustrated History from Antiquity to the Present.* Translated by Ruth Michaelis-Jena and Willy Merson. New York: Ungar, 1988, 215 p.

History of detective fiction that includes discussion of the often overlooked German contributions to the genre.

European Romanticism

INTRODUCTION

The movement known as European Romanticism arose in the late eighteenth century and dominated European literature throughout much of the nineteenth century. Attempts to define Romanticism have been complicated by the difficulty of unifying the distinct manifestations of the movement throughout Europe, as well as the problem of accounting for the various time periods in which it arose in different countries. However, critics are moving toward a recognition of Romanticism's homogeneity; they have agreed that the movement arose as a reaction against the aesthetic tenets of Neoclassicism, which emphasized formal regularity and emotional restraint, and that the European Romantics were unified in stressing the importance of the imagination and the validity of individual expression in artistic creation. The Romantic temperament is distinguished by a yearning for the inaccessible, which arises from an idealization of all that is beyond reach and expresses the artist's desire to transcend the limits of human existence. The futility of this aspiration often destines the Romantic hero to a sense of dejection apparent in his introspective and self-conscious nature, which often leads to passivity or even paralysis in situations that require action.

The unbridled subjectivity of the Sturm und Drang movement, led by Johann Wolfgang von Goethe and Johann von Schiller, and the transcendental philosophy of Immanuel Kant prepared for the advent of Romanticism in Germany in the late eighteenth century. Kant, Schiller, and Goethe independently advanced theories of symbolic, dialectical poetry that were later codified by Friedrich and August Wilhelm Schlegel, who became the most influential advocates of Romanticism in Germany. This first generation of Romantics produced the philosophical theory underlying the movement, and, in the nineteenth century, writers such as E. T. A. Hoffmann, Ludwig Tieck, and Johann Gottfried Herder fulfilled in their writing the precepts established by the Schlegel circle. Although Romanticism was slowed in France by the firmly entrenched Neoclassical tradition, by 1830 Madame de Staël's call for new literary styles in response to the cultural changes of the French Revolution was answered by Victor Hugo. He was the first French writer to reject the dramatic unities as stringently practiced by Jean Racine and Molière, and his break with the past was followed by the poets Alfred de Musset, Alphonse de Lamartine, and Chateaubriand. Italian Romanticism arose during the period following the collapse of Napoleon's empire in 1814; some critics find the roots of Romanticism in eighteenth-century Italian culture and deny the importance of outside influence. Critics similarly see Spanish culture as historically consistent with the tenets of Romanticism so that the literature of the 1830s was in effect a reaffirmation of national tradition.

The Romantic artists attempted to reconcile the intellect with emotion, reason with imagination, the outer world with the inner life, and the past with the present. Critics maintain that, despite the impossibility of such syntheses, the Romantic movement produced a large number of lasting works of great brilliance and power. In addition, most agree that European Romanticism has had an immeasurable impact on art and literature, as seen in such movements as Symbolism, Naturalism, Impressionism, and Expressionism; as Jacques Barzun has noted: "Romanticism does not die out in 1850 but branches out under different names like a delta."

DEFINITIONS

Arthur O. Lovejoy

[*Lovejoy was a German-born American philosopher, educator, and critic. In the following lecture, originally delivered in December of 1923, subsequently published in* PMLA *in 1924, and later reprinted in his* Essays in the History of Ideas, *he argues that the term Romanticism has been used to describe a number of disparate phenomena and should therefore be abandoned.*]

We approach a centenary not, perhaps, wholly undeserving of notice on the part of this learned company. It was apparently in 1824 that those respected citizens of La-Ferté-sous-Jouarre, MM. Dupuis and Cotonet, began an enterprise which was to cause them, as is recorded, "twelve years of suffering," and to end in disillusionment—the enterprise of discovering what Romanticism is, by collecting definitions and characterizations of it given by eminent authorities. I conjecture, therefore, that one of the purposes of the Committee in inviting me to speak on this subject was perhaps to promote a Dupuis and Cotonet Centennial Exhibition, in which the later varieties of definitions of Romanticism, the fruit of a hundred years' industry on the part of literary critics and professors of modern literature, might be at least in part displayed. Certainly there is no lack of material; the contemporary collector of such articles, while paying tribute to the assiduity and the sufferings of those worthy pioneers of a century ago, will chiefly feel an envious sense of the relative simplicity of their task. He will find, also, that the apparent incongruity of the senses in which the term is employed has fairly kept pace with their increase in number; and that the singular potency which the subject has from the first possessed to excite controversy and breed divisions has in no degree diminished with the lapse of years.

For if some Dupuis of to-day were to gather, first, merely a few of the more recent accounts of the origin and age of Romanticism, he would learn from M. Lassere and many others that Rousseau was the father of it; from Mr. Russell and Mr. Santayana that the honor of paternity might plausibly be claimed by Immanuel Kant; from M. Seillière that its grandparents were Fénelon and Madame Guyon; from Professor Babbitt that its earliest well-identified forebear was Francis Bacon; from Mr. Gosse that it originated in the bosom of the Reverend Joseph Warton; from the late Professor Ker that it had "its beginnings in the seventeenth-century" or a little earlier, in such books as "the *Arcadia* or the *Grand Cyrus*"; from Mr. J. E. G. de Montmorency that it "was born in the eleventh century, and sprang from that sense of aspiration which runs through the Anglo-French, or rather, the Anglo-Norman Renaissance"; from Professor Grierson that St. Paul's "irruption into Greek religious thought and Greek prose" was an essential example of "a romantic movement," though the "first great romantic" was Plato; and from Mr. Charles Whibley that the Odyssey is romantic in its "very texture and essence," but that, with its rival, Romanticism was "born in the Garden of Eden" and that "the Serpent was the first romantic." The inquirer would, at the same time, find that many of these originators of Romanticism—including both the first and last mentioned, whom, indeed, some contemporaries are unable to distinguish—figure on other lists as initiators or representatives of tendencies of precisely the contrary sort.

These differing versions of the age and lineage of Romanticism are matched by a corresponding diversity in the descriptions offered by those of our time who have given special care to the observation of it. For Professor Ker Romanticism was "the fairy way of writing," and for Mr. Gosse it is inconsistent with "keeping to the facts"; but for Mr. F. Y. Eccles (following M. Pellissier) "the romantic system of ideas" is the direct source of "the realistic error," of the tendency to conceive of psychology as "the dry notation of purely physiological phenomena" and consequently to reduce the novel and the drama to the description of "the automation-like gestures of *la bête humaine.*" To Professor Ker, again, "romantic" implies "reminiscence": "the romantic schools have always depended more or less on the past." Similarly Mr. Geoffrey Scott finds "its most typical form" to be "the cult of the extinct." But Professor Schelling tells us that "the classic temper studies the past, the romantic temper neglects it; . . . it leads us forward and creates new precedents"; while for some of the French "Romantic" critics of the 1820s and 1830s, the slogan of the movement was *il faut être de son temps.* Mr. Paul Elmer More defines Romanticism as "the illusion of beholding the infinite within the stream of nature itself, instead of apart from that stream"—in short, as an apotheosis of the cosmic flux; but a special student of German Romanticism [Marie Joachimi] cites as typical Romantic utterances Friedrich Schlegel's "alles Sichtbare hat nur die Wahrheit einer Allegorie," and Goethe's "alles Vergängliche ist nur ein Gleichnis"; and for a recent German author [Julius Bab] the deepest thing in Romanticism is "eine Religion die dieses Leben hasst . . . Romantik will die gerade Verbindung des Menschlichen mit dem Überirdischen."

Among those for whom the word implies, *inter alia,* a social and political ideology and temper, one writer, typical of many, tells us that "Romanticism spells anarchy in every domain . . . a systematic hostility to everyone invested with any particle of social authority—husband or *pater-familias,* policeman or magistrate, priest or Cabinet minister"; but Professor Goetz Briefs finds "the climax of political and economic thought within the Romantic movement" in the doctrine of Adam Müller, which sought to vindicate the sanctity of established social authority embodied in the family and the state; "by an inescapable logic the Romanticist ideology was drawn into the camp of reaction." From M. Seillière's most celebrated work it appears that the Romantic mind tends to be affected with an inferiority-complex, "une impression d'incomplètude, de solitude morale, et presque d'angoisse"; from other passages of the same writer we learn that Romanticism is the "imperialistic" mood, whether in individuals or nations—a too confident assertion of the will-to-power, arising from "the mystic feeling that one's activities have the advantages of a celestial alliance." The function of the human mind which is to be regarded as peculiarly "romantic" is for some "the heart as opposed to the head," for others, "the Imagination, as contrasted with Reason and the Sense of Fact"—which I take to be ways of expressing a by no means synonymous pair of psychological antitheses. Typical manifestations of the spiritual essence of Romanticism have been variously conceived to be a passion for moonlight, for red waistcoats, for Gothic churches, for futurist paintings; for talking hero-worship, for losing oneself in an ecstatic contemplation of nature.

The offspring with which Romanticism is credited are as strangely assorted as its attributes and its ancestors. It is by different historians—sometimes by the same historians—supposed to have begotten the French Revolution and the Oxford Movement; the Return to Rome and the Return to the State of Nature; the philosophy of Hegel, the philosophy of Schopenhauer, and the philosophy of Nietzsche—than which few other three philosophies more nearly exhaust the rich possibilities of philosophic disagreement; the revival of neo-Platonic mysticism in a Coleridge or an Alcott, the Emersonian transcendentalism, and scientific materialism; Wordsworth and Wilde; Newman and Huxley; the Waverley novels, the *Comédie Humaine,* and *Les Rougon-Macquart.* M. Seillière and Professor Babbitt have been especially active in tracing the progeny of Romanticism in the past century; the extraordinary number and still more extraordinary diversity of the descendants of it discovered by their researches are known to all here, and it therefore suffices to refer to their works for further examples.

All this is a mere hint, a suggestion by means of random samples, of the richness of the collection which might be brought together for our Centennial Exposition. The result is a confusion of terms, and of ideas, beside which that of a hundred years ago—mind-shaking though it was to the honest inquirers of La-Ferté-sous-Jouarre—seems pure lucidity. The word "romantic" has come to mean so many things that, by itself, it means nothing. It has ceased to perform the function of a verbal sign. When a man is asked, as I have had the honor of being asked, to discuss

Romanticism, it is impossible to know what ideas or tendencies he is to talk about, when they are supposed to have flourished, or in whom they are supposed to be chiefly exemplified. Perhaps there are some who think the rich ambiguity of the word not regrettable. In 1824, as Victor Hugo then testified, there were those who preferred to leave *à ce mot de romantique un certain vague fantastique et indéfinissable qui en redouble l'horreur,* and it may be that the taste is not extinct. But for one of the philosopher's trade, at least, the situation is embarrassing and exasperating; for philosophers, in spite of a popular belief to the contrary, are persons who suffer from a morbid solicitude to know what they are talking about. (pp. 228-32)

What, then, can be done to clear up, or to diminish, this confusion of terminology and of thought which has for a century been the scandal of literary history and criticism, and is still, as it would not be difficult to show, copiously productive of historical errors and of dangerously undiscriminating diagnoses of the moral and aesthetic maladies of our age? The one really radical remedy—namely, that we should all cease talking about Romanticism—is, I fear, certain not to be adopted. It would probably be equally futile to attempt to prevail upon scholars and critics to restrict their use of the term to a single and reasonably well-defined sense. Such a proposal would only be the starting-point of a new controversy. Men, and especially philologists, will doubtless go on using words as they like, however much annoyance they cause philosophers by this unchartered freedom. There are, however, two possible historical inquiries which, if carried out more thoroughly and carefully than has yet been done, would, I think, do much to rectify the present muddle, and would at the same time promote a clearer understanding of the general movement of ideas, the logical and psychological relations between the chief episodes and transitions, in modern thought and taste.

One of these measures would be somewhat analogous to the procedure of contemporary psychopathologists in the treatment of certain types of disorder. It has, we are told, been found that some mental disturbances can be cured or alleviated by making the patient explicitly aware of the genesis of his troublesome "complex," i.e., by enabling him to reconstruct those processes of association of ideas through which it was formed. Similarly in the present case, I think, it would be useful to trace the associative processes through which the word "romantic" has attained its present amazing diversity, and consequent uncertainty, of connotation and denotation; in other words, to carry out an adequate semasiological study of the term. For one of the few things certain about Romanticism is that the name of it offers one of the most complicated, fascinating, and instructive of all problems in semantics. It is, in short, a part of the task of the historian of ideas, when he applies himself to the study of the thing or things called Romanticism, to render it, if possible, psychologically intelligible how such manifold and discrepant phenomena have all come to receive one name. Such an analysis would, I am convinced, show us a large mass of purely verbal confusions operative as actual factors in the movement of thought in the past century and a quarter; and it would, by making these confusions explicit, make it easier to avoid them.

But this inquiry would in practice, for the most part, be inseparable from a second, which is the remedy that I wish, on this occasion, especially to recommend. The first step in this second mode of treatment of the disorder is that we should learn to use the word "Romanticism" in the plural. This, of course, is already the practice of the more cautious and observant literary historians, in so far as they recognize that the "Romanticism" of one country may have little in common with that of another, and at all events ought to be defined in distinctive terms. But the discrimination of the Romanticisms which I have in mind is not solely or chiefly a division upon lines of nationality or language. What is needed is that any study of the subject should begin with a recognition of a *prima-facie* plurality of Romanticisms, of possibly quite distinct thought-complexes, a number of which may appear in one country. There is no hope of clear thinking on the part of the student of modern literature, if—as, alas! has been repeatedly done by eminent writers—he vaguely hypostatizes the term, and starts with the presumption that "Romanticism" is the heaven-appointed designation of some single real entity, or type of entities, to be found in nature. He must set out from the simple and obvious fact that there are various historic episodes or movements to which different historians of our own or other periods have, for one reason or another, given the name. There is a movement which began in Germany in the seventeen-nineties—the only one which has an indisputable title to be called Romanticism, since it invented the term for its own use. There is another movement which began pretty definitely in England in the seventeen-forties. There is a movement which began in France in 1801. There is another movement which began in France in the second decade of the century, is linked with the German movement, and took over the German name. There is the rich and incongruous collection of ideas to be found in Rousseau. There are numerous other things called Romanticism by various writers whom I cited at the outset. The fact that the same name has been given by different scholars to all of these episodes is no evidence, and scarcely even establishes a presumption, that they are identical in essentials. There may be some common denominator of them all; but if so, it has never yet been clearly exhibited, and its presence is not to be assumed *a priori.* In any case, each of these so-called Romanticisms was a highly complex and usually an exceedingly unstable intellectual compound; each, in other words, was made up of various unit-ideas linked together, for the most part, not by any indissoluble bonds of logical necessity, but by alogical associative processes, greatly facilitated and partly caused, in the case of the Romanticisms which grew up after the appellation "Romantic" was invented, by the congenital and acquired ambiguities of the word. And when certain of these Romanticisms have in truth significant elements in common, they are not necessarily the same elements in any two cases. Romanticism A may have one characteristic presupposition or impulse, X, which it shares with Romanticism B, another characteristic, Y, which it shares with Romanticism C, to which X is wholly foreign. In the case, moreover, of those movements or schools to which the label was applied in their own time, the contents under the label sometimes changed radically and rapidly. At the end of a decade or two you had the same men and the same party appellation, but profoundly different ideas. As everyone knows, this is precisely what happened in the case of what is called French Romanticism. It may or may not be true that, as M. A. Viatte has sought to show [in *Le Catholicisme chez les Romantiques,* 1922], at the beginning of this process of transformation some subtle leaven was already at work which made the final outcome inevitable; the fact remains that in most of its practically significant sympathies and affiliations of a literary, ethical, political, and religious sort, the French "Romanticism" of the eighteen-thirties was the antithesis of that of the beginning of the century.

But the essential of the second remedy is that each of these Romanticisms—after they are first thus roughly discriminated with respect to their representatives or their dates—should be resolved, by a more thorough and discerning analysis than is yet customary, into its elements—into the several ideas and aesthetic susceptibilities of which it is composed. Only after these fundamental thought-factors or emotive strains in it are clearly discriminated and fairly exhaustively enumerated, shall we be in a position to judge of the degree of its affinity with other complexes to which the same name has been applied, to see precisely what tacit preconceptions or controlling motives or explicit contentions were common to any two or more of them, and wherein they manifested distinct and divergent tendencies.

Of the needfulness of such analytic comparison and discrimination of the Romanticisms let me attempt three illustrations.

1. In an interesting lecture before the British Academy a few years since, Mr. Edmund Gosse described Joseph Warton's youthful poem, *The Enthusiast,* written in 1740, as the first clear manifestation of "the great romantic movement, such as it has enlarged and dwindled down to our day. . . . Here for the first time we find unwaveringly emphasized and repeated what was entirely new in literature, the essence of romantic hysteria. *The Enthusiast* is the earliest expression of complete revolt against the classical attitude which had been sovereign in all European literature for nearly a century. So completely is this expressed by Joseph Warton that it is extremely difficult to realize that he could not have come under the fascination of Rousseau, . . . who was not to write anything characteristic until ten years later." Let us, then, compare the ideas distinctive of this poem with the conception of *romantische Poesie* formulated by Friedrich Schlegel and his fellow-Romanticists in Germany after 1796. The two have plainly certain common elements. Both are forms of revolt against the neo-classical aesthetics; both are partly inspired by an ardent admiration for Shakespeare; both proclaim the creative artist's independence of "rules." It might at first appear, therefore, that these two Romanticisms, in spite of natural differences of phraseology, are identical in essence—are separate outcroppings of the same vein of metal, precious or base, according to your taste.

But a more careful scrutiny shows a contrast between them not less important—indeed, as it seems to me, more important—than their resemblance. The general theme of Joseph Warton's poem (of which, it will be remembered, the sub-title is "The Lover of Nature") is one which had been a commonplace for many centuries: the superiority of "nature" to "art." It is a theme which goes back to Rabelais's contrast of Physis and Antiphysie. It had been the inspiration of some of the most famous passages of Montaigne. It had been attacked by Shakespeare. Pope's *Essay on Man* had been full of it. The "natural" in contrast with the artificial meant, first of all, that which is not man-made; and within man's life, it was supposed to consist in those expressions of human nature which are most spontaneous, unpremeditated, untouched by reflection or design, and free from the bondage of social convention. "Ce n'est pas raison," cried Montaigne, "que l'art gagne le point d'honneur sur notre grande et puissante mère Nature. Nous avons tant rechargé la beauté et richesse de ses ouvrages par nos inventions, que nous l'avons tout à fait étouffée." There follows the *locus classicus* of primitivism in modern literature, the famous passage on the superiority of wild fruits and savage men over those that have been "bastardized" by art.

Warton, then, presents this ancient theme in various aspects. He prefers to all the beauties of the gardens of Versailles

> Some pine-topt precipice
> Abrupt and shaggy.

He rhetorically inquires:

> Can Kent design like Nature?

He laments

> That luxury and pomp . . .
> Should proudly banish Nature's simple charms.

He inquires why "mistaken man" should deem it nobler

> To dwell in palaces and high-roof'd halls
> Than in God's forests, architect supreme?

All this, if I may be permitted the expression, was old stuff. The principal thing that was original and significant in the poem was that Warton boldly applied the doctrine of the superiority of "nature" over conscious art to the theory of poetry:

> What are the lays of artful Addison,
> Coldly correct, to Shakespeare's warblings wild?

That Nature herself was wild, untamed, was notorious, almost tautological; and it was Shakespeare's supposed "wildness," his non-conformity to the conventional rules, the spontaneous freedom of his imagination and his expression, that proved him Nature's true pupil.

Now this aesthetic inference had not, during the neo-classical period, ordinarily been drawn from the current assumption of the superiority of nature to art. The principle of "following nature" had in aesthetics usually been taken in another, or in more than one other, of the several dozen senses of the sacred word. Yet in other provinces of thought an analogous inference had long since and repeatedly been suggested. From the first the fashion of conceiving of "nature" (in the sense in which it was antithetic to "art") as norm had made for antinomianism, in some degree or other—for a depreciation of restraint, for the ideal of "letting yourself go." There seems to be an idea current that an antinomian temper was, at some time in the eighteenth century, introduced into aesthetic theory and artistic practise by some Romanticist, and that it thence speedily spread to moral feeling and social conduct. The historic sequence is precisely the opposite. It was Montaigne again—not usually classified as a Romanticist—who wrote:

> J'ai pris bien simplement et crûment ce précepte ancien: 'que nous ne saurions faillir à suivre Nature' . . . Je n'ai pas corrigé, comme Socrate, par la force de la raison, mes complexions naturelles, je n'ai aucunement troublé, par art, mon inclination; je me laisse aller comme je suis venu; je ne combats rien.

It was Pope who asked:

> Can that offend great Nature's God
> Which Nature's self inspires?

and who spoke of

> Wild Nature's vigor working at the root

as the source of the passions in which all the original and vital energies of men are contained.

Aside from a certain heightening of the emotional tone, then, the chief novelty of Warton's poem lay in its suggesting the application of these ideas to a field from which they had usually been curiously and inconsistently excluded, in its introduction of antinomianism, of a rather mild sort, into the conception of poetic excellence. But this extension was obviously implicit from the outset in the logic of that protean "naturalism" which had been the most characteristic and potent force in modern thought since the late Renaissance; it was bound to be made by somebody sooner or later. Nor was Warton's the first aesthetic application of the principle; it had already been applied to an art in the theory and practice of which eighteenth-century Englishmen were keenly interested—the art of landscape design. The first great revolt against the neo-classical aesthetics was not in literature at all, but in gardening; the second, I think, was in architectural taste; and all three were inspired by the same ideas. Since, the "artful Addison" had observed [in the *Spectator,* No. 144], "artificial works receive a greater advantage from their resemblance of such as are natural," and since Nature is distinguished by her "rough, careless strokes," the layer-out of gardens should aim at "an artificial rudeness much more charming than that neatness and elegancy usually met with." This horticultural Romanticism had been preached likewise by Sir William Temple, Pope, Horace Walpole, Batty Langley, and others, and ostensibly exemplified in the work of Kent, Brown, and Bridgman. Warton in the poem in question describes Kent as at least doing his best to imitate in his gardens the wildness of Nature:

> He, by rules unfettered, boldly scorns
> Formality and method; round and square
> Disdaining, plans irregularly great.

It was no far cry from this to the rejection of the rules in the drama, to a revulsion against the strait-laced regularity and symmetry of the heroic couplet, to a general turning from convention, formality, method, artifice, in all the arts.

There had, however, from the first been a curious duality of meaning in the antithesis of "nature" and "art"—one of the most pregnant of the long succession of confusions of ideas which make up much of the history of human thought. While the "natural" was, on the one hand, conceived as the wild and spontaneous and "irregular," it was also conceived as the simple, the naïve, the unsophisticated. No two words were more fixedly associated in the mind of the sixteenth, seventeenth, and early eighteenth centuries than "Nature" and "simple." Consequently the idea of preferring nature to custom and to art usually carried with it the suggestion of a program of simplification, of reform by elimination; in other words, it implied primitivism. The "natural" was a thing you reached by going back and by leaving out. And this association of ideas—already obvious in Montaigne, in Pope, and scores of other extollers of "Nature"—is still conspicuous in Warton's poem. It was the "bards of old" who were "fair Nature's friends." The poet envies

> The first of men, ere yet confined
> In smoky cities.

He yearns to dwell in some

> Isles of innocence from mortal view
> Deeply retired beneath a plantane's shade,
> Where Happiness and Quiet sit enthroned,
> With simple Indian swains.

For one term of the comparison, then, I limit myself, for brevity's sake, to this poem to which Mr. Gosse has assigned so important a place in literary history. There were, of course, even in the writings of the elder Warton, and still more in other phenomena frequently called "Romantic," between the 1740's and the 1790's, further elements which cannot be considered here. There is observable, for example, in what it has become the fashion to classify as the early phases of English Romanticism, the emergence of what may be called gothicism, and the curious fact of its partial and temporary fusion with naturalism. It is one of the interesting problems of the analytic history of ideas to see just how and why naturalism and gothicism became allied in the eighteenth century in England, though little, if at all, in France. But for the present purpose it suffices to take *The Enthusiast* as typical, in one especially important way, of a great deal of the so-called Romanticism before the seventeen-nineties—a Romanticism, namely, which, whatever further characteristics it may have had, was based upon naturalism (in the sense of the word which I have indicated) and was associated with primitivism of some mode or degree.

2. For in this fundamental point this earlier "Romanticism" differed essentially from that of the German aesthetic theorists and poets who chose the term "Romantic poetry" as the most suitable designation for their own literary ideals and program. The latter "Romanticism" is in its very essence a denial of the older naturalistic presuppo-

sitions, which Warton's poem had manifested in a special and somewhat novel way. The German movement, as I have elsewhere shown, received its immediate and decisive impetus from Schiller's essay *On Naïve and Sentimental Poetry;* and what it derived from that confused work was the conviction that "harmony with nature," in any sense which implied an opposition to "culture," to "art," to reflection and self-conscious effort, was neither possible nor desirable for the modern man or the modern artist. The *Frühromantiker* learned from Schiller, and partly from Herder, the idea of an art which should look back no more to the primitive than to the classical—the notions of which, incidentally, Schiller had curiously fused—for its models and ideals; which should be the appropriate expression, not of a *natürliche* but of a *künstliche Bildung;* which, so far from desiring simplification, so far from aiming at the sort of harmony in art and life which is to be attained by the method of leaving out, should seek first fullness of content, should have for its program the adequate expression of the entire range of human experience and the entire reach of the human imagination. For man, the artificial, Friedrich Schlegel observed, *is* "natural." "Die Abstraktion ist ein künstlicher Zustand. Dies ist kein Grund gegen sie, denn es ist dem Menschen gewiss natürlich, sich dann und wann auch in künstliche Zustände zu versetzen." And again: "Eine nur im Gegensatz der Kunst und Bildung natürliche Denkart soll es gar nicht geben." To be unsophisticated, to revert to the mental state of "simple Indian swains," was the least of the ambitions of a German Romantic—though, since the unsophisticated is one type of human character, his art was not, at least in theory, indifferent even to that. The Shakespeare whom he admired was no gifted child of nature addicted to "warblings wild." Shakespeare, said A. W. Schlegel, is not "eine blindes wildlaufendes Genie"; he had "a system in his artistic practise and an astonishingly profound and deeply meditated one." The same critic seems to be consciously attacking either Joseph Warton's or Gray's famous lines about Shakespeare when he writes: "Those poets whom it is customary to represent as carefree nurslings of nature, without art and without schooling, if they produce works of genuine excellence, give evidence of exceptional cultivation *(Kultur)* of their mental powers, of practised art, of ripely pondered and just designs." The greatness of Shakespeare, in the eyes of *these* Romantics, lay in his *Universalität,* his sophisticated insight into human nature and the many-sidedness of his portrayal of character; it was this, as Friedrich Schlegel said, that made him "wie der Mittelpunkt der romantischen Kunst." It may be added that another trait of the Romanticism found by Mr. Gosse in Joseph Warton, namely, the feeling that didactic poetry is not poetic, was also repudiated by early German Romanticism: "How," asked F. Schlegel again, "can it be said that ethics *(die Moral)* belongs merely to philosophy, when the greatest part of poetry relates to the art of living and to the knowledge of human nature?"

The difference, then, I suggest, is more significant, more pregnant, than the likeness between these two Romanticisms. Between the assertion of the superiority of "nature" over conscious "art" and that of the superiority of conscious art over mere "nature"; between a way of thinking of which primitivism is of the essence and one of which the idea of perpetual self-transcendence is of the essence; between a fundamental preference for simplicity—even though a "wild" simplicity—and a fundamental preference for diversity and complexity; between the sort of ingenuous naïveté characteristic of *The Enthusiast* and the sophisticated subtlety of the conception of romantic irony: between these the antithesis is one of the most radical that modern thought and taste have to show. I don't deny anyone's right to call both these things Romanticism, if he likes; but I cannot but observe that the fashion of giving both the same name has led to a good deal of unconscious falsification of the history of ideas. The elements of the one Romanticism tend to be read into the other; the nature and profundity of the oppositions between them tend to be overlooked; and the relative importance of the different changes of preconceptions in modern thought, and of susceptibilities in modern taste, tends to be wrongly estimated. I shall not attempt to cite here what seem to me examples of such historical errors; but the sum of them is, I think, far from negligible.

Between the "Romanticism" which is but a special and belated manifestation of the naturalism that had flourished since the Renaissance (and before it) and the "Romanticism" which began at the end of the eighteenth century in Germany (as well as that which appeared a little later in France) there is another difference not less significant. This is due to the identification of the meaning of "Romantic" in the later movement with "Christian"—and mainly with the medieval implications of that term. This was not the central idea in the original notion of "Romantic poetry" as conceived by Friedrich Schlegel. Primarily, as I have elsewhere tried to show, the adjective meant for him and the entire school "das eigentümlich Moderne" in contrast with "das eigentümlich Antike." But it early occurred to him that the principal historic cause of the supposed radical differentiation of modern from classical art could lie only in the influence of Christianity. He wrote in 1796, before his own conversion to what he had already defined as the "Romantic," *i.e.,* modern, point of view:

> So lächerlich und geschmacklos sich dieses Trachten nach dem Reich Gottes in der christlichen Poesie offenbaren möchte; so wird es dem Geschichtsforscher doch eine sehr merkwürdige Erscheinung, wenn er gewahr wird, dass eben dieses Streben, das absolut Vollkommene und Unendliche zu realisiren, eine unter dem unaufhörlichen Wechsel der Zeiten und bei der grössten Verschiedenheit der Völker bleibende Eigenschaft dessen ist, was man mit dem besten Rechte modern nennen darf.

When, after reading Schiller's essay, Schlegel himself became a devotee of those aesthetic ideals which he had previously denounced, he wrote (1797):

> Nachdem die vollendete natürliche Bildung der Alten entschieden gesunken, und ohne Rettung ausgeartet war, ward durch den Verlust der endlichen Realität und die Zerrüttung vollendeter Form ein Streben nach unendlicher Realität veranlasst, welches bald allgemeiner Ton des Zeitalters wurde.

"Romantic" art thus came to mean—for one thing—an art inspired by or expressive of some idea or some ethical temper supposed to be essential in Christianity. "Ursprung und Charakter der ganzen neuern Poesie lässt sich so leicht aus dem Christentume ableiten, dass man die romantische eben so gut die christliche nennen könnte," said Richter in 1804, repeating what had by that time become a commonplace. But the nature of the essentially Christian, and therefore essentially Romantic, spirit was variously conceived. Upon one characteristic of it there was, indeed, rather general agreement among the German Romanticists: the habit of mind introduced by Christianity was distinguished by a certain insatiability; it aimed at infinite objectives and was incapable of lasting satisfaction with any goods actually reached. It became a favorite platitude to say that the Greeks and Romans set themselves limited ends to attain, were able to attain them, and were thus capable of self-satisfaction and finality; and that modern or "romantic" art differed from this most fundamentally, by reason of its Christian origin, in being, as Schiller had said, a *Kunst des Unendlichen.* "Absolute Abstraktion, Vernichtung des Jetzigen, Apotheose der Zukunft, dieser eigentlich bessern Welt!; dies ist der Kern des Geheisses des Christentums," declared Novalis. In its application to artistic practice this "apotheosis of the future" meant the ideal of endless progress, of "eine progressive Universal-poesie" in the words of Fr. Schlegel's familiar definition; it implied the demand that art shall always go on bringing new provinces of life within its domain and achieving ever fresh and original effects. But anything which was, or was supposed to be, especially characteristic of the Christian *Weltanschauung* tended to become a part of the current connotation of "Romantic," and also a part of the actual ideals of the school. Preoccupation with supersensible realities and a feeling of the illusoriness of ordinary existence was thus often held to be a distinctive trait of Romantic art, on the ground that Christianity is an otherworldly religion: "in der christlichen Ansicht," said A. W. Schlegel, "die Anschauung des Unendlichen hat das Endliche vernichtet; das Leben ist zur Schattenwelt und zur Nacht geworden." Another recognized characteristic of Christianity, and therefore of the "Romantic," was ethical dualism, a conviction that there are in man's constitution two natures ceaselessly at war. The Greek ideal, in the elder Schlegel's words, was "volkommene Eintracht und Ebenmass aller Kräfte, natürliche Harmonie. Die Neueren hingegen sind zum Bewusstsein der inneren Entzweiung gekommen, welche ein solches Ideal unmöglich macht." Directly related to this, it was perceived, was the "inwardness" of Christianity, its preoccupation with "the heart" as distinguished from the outward act, its tendency to introspection; and hence, as Mme de Stael and others observed, "modern" or "Romantic" art has discovered, and has for its peculiar province, the inexhaustible realm of the inner life of man:

> Les anciens avaient, pour ainsi dire, une âme corporelle, dont tous les mouvements étaient forts, directs, et conséquents; il n'en est pas de même du coeur humain développé par le christianisme: les modernes ont puisé dans le repentir chrétien l'habitude de se replier continuellement sur eux-mêmes. Mais, pour manifester cette existence tout intérieure, il faut qu'une grande variété dans les faits présente sous toutes les formes les nuances infinies de ce qui se passe dans l'âme.

It is one of the many paradoxes of the history of the word, and of the controversies centering about it, that several eminent literary historians and critics of our time have conceived the moral essence of Romanticism as consisting in a kind of "this-worldliness" and a negation of what one of them has termed "the Christian and classical dualism." Its most deplorable and dangerous error, in the judgment of these critics, is its deficient realization of the "civil war in the cave" of man's soul, its belief in the "natural goodness" of man. They thus define "Romanticism" in terms precisely opposite to those in which it was often defined by the writers who first called their own ideals "Romantic"; and this fashion, I cannot but think, has done a good deal to obscure the palpable and important historical fact that the one "Romanticism" which (as I have said) has an indisputable title to the name was conceived by those writers as a rediscovery and revival, for better or worse, of characteristically Christian modes of thought and feeling, of a mystical and otherworldly type of religion, and a sense of the inner moral struggle as the distinctive fact in human experience—such as had been for a century alien to the dominant tendencies in 'polite' literature. The new movement was, almost from the first, a revolt against what was conceived to be paganism in religion and ethics as definitely as against classicism in art. The earliest important formulation of its implications for religious philosophy was Schleiermacher's famous *Reden* (1799) addressed "to the cultivated contemners of religion," a work profoundly—sometimes, indeed, morbidly—dualistic in its ethical temper. Christianity, declares Schleiermacher, is *durch und durch polemisch;* it knows no truce in the warfare of the spiritual with the natural man, it finds no end in the task of inner self-discipline. And the *Reden,* it must be remembered, were (in the words of a German literary historian) "greeted by the votaries of Romanticism as a gospel."

Now it is not untrue to describe the ethical tendency of the "Romanticism" which had its roots in naturalism—that is, in the assumption of the sole excellence of what in man is native, primitive, "wild," attainable without other struggle than that required for emancipation from social conventions and artificialities—as anti-dualistic and essentially non-moral. This aspect of it can be seen even in the poem of the "blameless Warton," when he describes the life of the state of nature for which he yearns. But as a consequence of the prevalent neglect to discriminate the Romanticisms, the very movement which was the beginning of a deliberate and vigorous insurrection against the naturalistic assumptions that had been potent, and usually dominant, in modern thought for more than three centuries, is actually treated as if it were a continuation of that tendency. Thesis and antithesis have, partly through accidents of language and partly through a lack of careful observation on the part of historians of literature, been called by the same name, and consequently have frequently been assumed to be the same thing. An ideal of ceaseless striving towards goals too vast or too exacting ever to be wholly attained has been confused with a nostalgia for the untroubled, because unaspiring, indolent, and unselfconscious life of the man of nature. Thus one of the widest and deepest-reaching lines of cleavage in modern thought has been more or less effectually concealed by a word.

3. This cleavage between naturalistic and anti-naturalistic "Romanticism" crosses national lines; and it manifestly cuts, so to say, directly through the person of one great writer commonly classed among the initiators of the Romantic movement in France. The author of the *Essai sur les révolutions* and of the earlier-written parts of *Atala* may perhaps properly be called a Romantic; the author of the later-written parts of the latter work and of the *Génie du Christianisme* may perhaps properly be called a Romantic; but it is obvious that the word has, in most important respects, not merely different but antithetic senses in these two applications of it to the same person. Chateaubriand before 1799 represented in some sort the culmination of the naturalistic and primitivistic Romanticism of which Mr. Gosse sees the beginning in Joseph Warton; he had not only felt intensely but had even gratified the yearning to live "with simple Indian swains." That the Chateaubriand of 1801 represents just as clearly a revolt against this entire tendency is sufficiently evident from the repudiation of primitivism in the first preface to *Atala*:

> Je ne suis point, comme M. Rousseau, un enthousiaste des sauvages; . . . je ne crois point que la *pure nature* soit la plus belle chose du monde. Je l'ai toujours trouvée fort laide partout où j'ai eu occasion de la voir . . . Avec ce mot de nature on a tout perdu.

Thus the magic word upon which the whole scheme of ideas of the earlier writing had depended is now plainly characterized as the fruitful source of error and confusion that it was. And in his views about the drama the Chateaubriand of 1801 was opposed *both* to the movement represented by *The Enthusiast* and to the German Romanticism of his own time. Shakespeare was (though mainly, as we have seen, for differing reasons) the idol of both; but Chateaubriand in his *Essai sur la littérature anglaise* writes of Shakespeare in the vein, and partly in the words, of Voltaire and Pope. In point of natural genius, he grants, the English dramatist was without a peer in his own age, and perhaps in any age: "je ne sais si jamais homme a jeté des regards plus profonds sur la nature humaine." But Shakespeare knew almost nothing of the requirements of the drama as an art:

> Il faut se persuader d'abord qu' écrire est un art; que cet art a nécessairement ses genres, et que chaque genre a ses règles. Et qu'on ne dise pas que les genres et les règles sont arbitraires; ils sont nés de la nature même; l'art a seulement séparé ce que la nature a confondu . . . On peut dire que Racine, dans toute l'excellence de son art, est plus naturel que Shakespeare.

Chateaubriand here, to be sure, still finds the standard of art in "nature"; but it is "nature" in the sense of the neo-classical critics, a sense in which it is not opposed, but equivalent, to an art that rigorously conforms to fixed rules. And the "great literary paradox of the partisans of Shakespeare," he observes, is that their arguments imply that "there are *no* rules of the drama," which is equivalent to asserting "that an art is not an art." Voltaire rightly felt

that "by banishing all rules and returning to *pure nature,* nothing was easier than to equal the *chefs-d'oeuvre* of the English stage"; and he was well advised in recanting his earlier too enthusiastic utterances about Shakespeare, since he saw that "en relevant les beautés des barbares, il avait séduit des hommes qui, comme lui, ne sauraient séparer l'alliage de l'or." Chateaubriand regrets that "the *Cato* of Addison is no longer played" and that consequently "on ne se délasse au théâtre anglais des monstruosités de Shakespeare que par les horreurs d'Otway." "Comment," he exclaims, "ne pas gémir de voir une nation éclairée, et qui compte parmi ses critiques les Pope et les Addison, de la voir s'extasier sur le portrait de l'apothicaire dans *Roméo et Juliette.* C'est le burlesque le plus hideux et le plus dégoûtant." The entire passage might almost have been written with Warton's poem in mind, so completely and methodically does this later "Romanticist" controvert the aesthetic principles and deride the enthusiasm of the English "Romanticist" of 1740. It is worth noting, also, that Chateaubriand at this time thinks almost as ill of Gothic architecture as of Shakespeare and of *la pure nature:*

> Une beauté dans Shakespeare n'excuse pas ses innombrables défauts: un monument gothique peut plaire par son obscurité et la difformité même de ses proportions, mais personne ne songe á bâtir un palais sur son modèle.

We have, then, observed and compared—very far from exhaustively, of course, yet in some of their most fundamental and determinative ideas—three "Romanticisms." In the first and second we have found certain common elements, but still more significant oppositions; in the second and third we have found certain other common elements, but likewise significant oppositions. But between the first and third the common elements are very scanty; such as there are, it could, I think, be shown, are not the same as those subsisting between either the first and second or the second and third; and in their ethical preconceptions and implications and the crucial articles of their literary creeds, the opposition between them is almost absolute.

All three of these historic episodes, it is true, are far more complex than I have time to show. I am attempting only to illustrate the nature of a certain procedure in the study of what is called Romanticism, to suggest its importance, and to present one or two specific results of the use of it. A complete analysis would qualify, without invalidating, these results, in several ways. It would (for one thing) bring out certain important connections between the revolt against the neo-classical aesthetics (common to two of the episodes mentioned) and other aspects of eighteenth-century thought. It would, again, exhibit fully certain *internal* oppositions in at least two of the Romanticisms considered. For example, in German Romanticism between 1797 and 1800 there grew up, and mainly from a single root, *both* an "apotheosis of the future" and a tendency to retrospection—a retrospection directed, not, indeed, towards classical antiquity or towards the primitive, but towards the medieval. A belief in progress and a spirit of reaction were, paradoxically, joint offspring of the same idea, and were nurtured for a time in the same minds. But it is just these internal incongruities which make it most of all evident, as it seems to me, that any attempt at a *general* appraisal even of a single chronologically determinate Romanticism—still more, of "Romanticism" as a whole—is a fatuity. When a Romanticism has been analyzed into the distinct "strains" or ideas which compose it, the true philosophic affinities and the eventual practical influence in life and art of these several strains will usually be found to be exceedingly diverse and often conflicting. It will, no doubt, remain abstractly possible to raise the question whether the preponderant effect, moral or aesthetic, of one or another large movement which has been called by the name was good or bad. But that ambitious inquiry cannot even be legitimately begun until a prior task of analysis and detailed comparison—of the sort that I have attempted here to indicate—has been accomplished. And when this has been done, I doubt whether the larger question will seem to have much importance or meaning. What will then appear historically significant and philosophically instructive will be the way in which *each* of these distinguishable strains has worked itself out, what its elective affinities for other ideas, and its historic consequences, have shown themselves to be. The categories which it has become customary to use in distinguishing and classifying "movements" in literature or philosophy and in describing the nature of the significant transitions which have taken place in taste and in opinion, are far too rough, crude, undiscriminating—and none of them so hopelessly so as the category "Romantic." It is not any large *complexes* of ideas, such as that term has almost always been employed to designate, but rather certain simpler, diversely combinable, intellectual and emotional components of such complexes, that are the true elemental and dynamic factors in the history of thought and of art; and it is with the genesis, the vicissitudes, the manifold and often dramatic interactions of these, that it is the task of the historian of ideas in literature to become acquainted. (pp. 234-53)

> *Arthur O. Lovejoy, "On the Discrimination of Romanticisms," in his* Essays in the History of Ideas, *1948. Reprint by George Braziller, Inc., 1955, pp. 228-53.*

Lilian R. Furst

[*Furst is an Austrian-born American professor and critic who has written many works on European Romanticism. She once explained that "the concepts elaborated by the romantics on the role of the artist, on the creative process, on the function of art, on freedom to experiment—all these are still of central relevance to our thinking and our experience today." In the following essay, she surveys the archetypal, historical, and aesthetic aspects of European Romanticism.*]

It was Arthur O. Lovejoy who first suggested, in a well-known article published in 1924 [in *Publications of the Modern Language Association* XXXIX; reprinted in *Essays in the History of Ideas,* 1948] ('On the Discrimination of Romanticisms'), 'that we should learn to use the word "Romanticism" in the plural'. To discriminate between romanticisms would, he argued, 'clear up, or . . . diminish, this confusion of terminology and of thought which

has for a century been the scandal of literary history and criticism'. Almost a century before Lovejoy, Musset had already satirised that confusion in the serio-comical deliberations of Monsieur Dupuis and Monsieur Cotonet. Each month, with the arrival of the Parisian journals in their rural retreat at La-Ferté-sous-Jouarre, these innocent devotees of culture became more and more bewildered by that prominent and obviously fashionable term 'romantic'. Did it, they wonder, mean this?—or that?—or that? running through a whole gamut of possibilities, each sufficiently close to contemporary controversies to remain credible, yet sufficiently ludicrous to expose the absurdity of the entire discussion. Dupuis and Cotonet never find that absolute, final answer, for which they grope with such tenacity for years on end. Their fundamental error, like that of so many of their successors, lies in their pursuit of *the* single, ultimate definition that will provide the key to the understanding of Romanticism and that will, moreover, be valid for ever. It is this common, but mistaken assumption that was first seriously called into question by Lovejoy's article: that is its main importance. In its recognition of the plurality of romanticisms, it marks a vital turning-point in the history of the critical evaluation of European Romanticism.

Lovejoy's distinctions are, admittedly, quite conservative. In spite of his contention that 'the discrimination of the romanticisms which I have in mind is not solely or chiefly a division upon lines of nationality or language', he first differentiates between 'a movement which began in Germany in the seventeen-nineties' and 'another movement which began pretty definitely in England in the seventeen-forties', and a third 'which began in France in 1801'. Later on he does elaborate on the divergence in character between the German Romanticism of the 1790s and the English Romanticism of the 1740s. However, Lovejoy's examples, illuminating though they are in themselves, are all drawn from the eighteenth and early nineteenth centuries, i.e. from the time of the Romantic movements in literature and the arts. But the term is so frequently used of other periods too that it continues to engender that uncertainty that Lovejoy deplored and sought to remedy. In order to achieve his purpose of diminishing 'this confusion of terminology', we must, I believe, make broader and bolder discriminations than he did. If we are to grapple with the appearance of 'romantic' in relation to phenomena both long before and long after the accepted bounds of the historical movement, as we patently have to, we need some divisions that transcend outer historical limitations. My modest proposal is that we identify three separate, though closely interconnected, spheres of reference: the archetypal, the historical, and the aesthetic. These represent the major contour lines of European Romanticism.

The archetypal denotes the 'forever recurring emotional condition', as Henry H. H. Remak has so aptly called it [in "West European Romanticism: Definition and Scope," in *Comparative Literature: Method and Perspective,* edited by Horst Frenz and Newton P. Stallknecht, 1961]. Remak, like many other critics, categorically excludes consideration of this strand from his article on 'West European Romanticism' because his focus is on the literary movement of the later eighteenth and of the nineteenth century. But no attempt to chart the contours of Romanticism can ignore its existence. As a constant modal temper, it has for one of its cardinal features a quintessential independence of time and place. To acknowledge this at the outset immediately helps to dispel and obviate certain of the difficulties attendant on the usage of 'romantic'. For instance, it removes the grounds for Lovejoy's surprise that H. C. J. Grierson [in "Classical and Romantic," in *The Background of English Literature,* 1925] should have referred to Plato as 'the first great romantic'; that astonishment reflects Lovejoy's too exclusive linking of the notion 'romantic' to a specific period. The actual appropriateness of the term to Plato or to any other writer or thinker of the Classical Age is open to question. What must be recognised, however, is the validity of 'romantic' as an archetypal concept. Once this is done, it may be applied at any period and in any setting to any individual bearing its marks, irrespective of connections to the literary movement known as Romanticism.

There is no more cogent phrase to characterise the archetypal romantic than that with which Virgil in the *Aeneid* (Book VI, line 314) described the dead awaiting passage across the Styx in Charon's ferry, stretching out their hands 'ripae ulterioris amore' ('with love for the yonder bank'). The romantic by temperament is always intuitively drawn by a yearning for the yonder bank. The contrast with the realist's sober, sensible contentment with the blessings of this bank is well brought out in Goethe's ballad *Adler und Taube* (Eagle and Dove). A young eagle with a broken wing lands in a grove of myrtle-trees, a pleasant spot with shade, warmth, a stream, soft moss, and golden sand. But to the eagle, to be earth-bound is tantamount to death; he longs to soar on high, and derives little comfort from the well-meant advice of the dove who chances on him as he frets at his limitations. After enumerating the advantages of life in the myrtle-grove, the dove concludes:

> O Freund, das wahre Glück
> Ist die Genügsamkeit,
> Und die Genügsamkeit
> Hat überall genug.

> (Oh friend, true happiness
> Lies in contentedness,
> And contentedness
> Is everywhere content.)

To which the eagle can only reply:

> O Weise, sprach der Adler, und tief ernst
> Versinkt er tiefer in sich selbst,
> O Weisheit! Du redst wie eine Taube!

> (How wise, said the eagle, and deep in thought
> He sinks deeper into himself,
> Oh wisdom! you speak like a dove!)

This little fable has implications far beyond its immediate relevance to Goethe's autobiographical self-portrayal as an eagle straining to escape the confines of Frankfurt's bourgeois society. It summarises, in a brilliant miniature, the polarity between the archetypal realist and the archetypal romantic: the dove with his sagacious, pragmatic enjoyment of the here and now, as against the eagle with his

longing for a way of life less comfortable perhaps than his present state, but incomparably more exciting.

Such yearning for the inaccessible is the hallmark of the romantic temperament. It springs largely from the idealisation of all that is beyond reach; the very fact of its inaccessibility indeed greatly heightens its potential attractiveness. Frequently, though not invariably, the yearning is associated with motifs familiar from the old tales of romance; it may be a love object, or glory in combat, or the thrill of adventure, or some dream of life either in the past (or future), or in a remote part of the world, that is invested with the attributes of perfection.

The romantic's intrinsic urge to transcend the confines of his existence may unleash dynamic energies. Of this the prototype is Goethe's Faust, whose ethos of perpetual striving is a variation of the romantic's innate yearning. Conversely, the romantic's vague longings may prove destructive. Witness the case of Emma Bovary who resembles the eagle in her spurning of the one man with any genuine affection for her: her pathetic husband, Charles. Though her tastes may have been perverted by the spiritual diet of her adolescence, by the sentimental 'keepsakes' she cherishes, by her reading of *Paul et Virginie* and the novels of Scott, her appetite for these fantasies so remote from her rural, middle-class background, is in itself an indication of her inherent temperament. Emma is indefatigable in her pursuit of her mirage: 'Elle se promettait continuellement, pour son prochain voyage, une félicité profonde' ('She kept on promising herself immense happiness on her next expedition'); only at length, when she 'retrouvait dans l'adultère toutes les platitudes du mariage' ('came in adultery upon all the platitudes of marriage'), does she ask herself: 'D'où venait donc cette insuffisance de la vie, cette pourriture instantanée des choses où elle s'appuyait?' ('What was the source of this shortfall of life, this immediate rotting of all the things to which she turned?'). She does eventually pose that crucial question, but she cannot answer it. Significantly, Flaubert follows that question-mark with suspension points ('. . .') as if to invite an answer from the reader who must first and foremost point to Emma's constitutional disposition: that of the romantic entranced by a vision and impelled by the urge to seek it out. In its striking delineation of the archetypally romantic personality lies one of the greatnesses of *Madame Bovary*.

Once the existence of such an archetypal romanticism without allegiance to period or locale is posited, certain problems of literary classification are more readily overcome. For example, it is with equal reluctance that one includes Hölderlin among the *Romantiker* or excludes him. His poetry shows distinct romantic traits, notably in his aspiration towards the ideal. But this should be recognised for what it is: an expression of archetypal romanticism, rather than an affiliation to any one school. The same holds true of poets more remote temporally from the nineteenth-century Romantic movement, such as Tasso, or Yeats with his Celtic ideology. It could indeed be argued that no major poet is without some degree of this kind of romanticism. The so-called Hellenism of several nineteenth-century poets, which has puzzled many critics, could also be regarded as a manifestation of this archetypal phenomenon. And it is an exploitation of our latent yearning for romance that leads to the marketing of perfumes, lingerie and holiday places under that magically evocative adjective, 'romantic'. There is obviously a streak in human nature that is strongly drawn to a primordial romanticism of this sort.

The correlation of this archetypal romanticism with the historical romanticism of the late eighteenth and early nineteenth centuries is like that between the endemic and the epidemic. The comparison with the demographic outbreak of a disease is not intended as a value judgement, but merely as a quantitative measure. The archetypal romanticism that had always existed as a sporadic human trait became the dominant mode at the turn of the eighteenth century. It was—to a greater or lesser degree, according to local circumstances—systematised into a number of artistic movements. It grew and spread in both extent and complexity, but it still remains an entity whose contours can be traced. At this point, Lovejoy seems to be overstating his insistence on confusion when he maintains that:

> When a man is asked, as I have had the honor of being asked, to discuss Romanticism, it is impossible to know what ideas or tendencies he is to talk about, when they are supposed to have flourished, or in whom they are supposed to be chiefly exemplified.

Let us take Lovejoy's strictures one by one. First, 'when they were supposed to have flourished': whatever other controversies surround historical romanticism, there is a wide measure of agreement on its timing; the European Romantic movement was at its zenith in the closing decade of the eighteenth century and the first thirty or so years of the nineteenth century. The exact dates vary from country to country, depending on the retarding or impelling effect of local conditions. Remak cites the 1790s to 1830s for Germany, 1800 to 1843 for France, 1780 to the 1830s for England, 1830-1845 for Spain, and 1816 to the 1850s for Italy. The position is perhaps not quite so simple, as I shall go on to suggest later, but by and large these are generally accepted time-spans for historical romanticism.

The second of Lovejoy's objections concerns the identity of the Romantics: 'in whom they are supposed to have been chiefly exemplified'. In this area, the approach has undergone considerable refinement in recent years, above all in the refutation of the earlier simplistic categories that had been the product of positivistic scholarship which often sought to label poets like chemicals in a laboratory. C. H. Herford's divisions, for instance, in *The Age of Wordsworth* now seem facile:

> English poetry in the age of Wordsworth had three characteristic haunts. It throve in seclusion among the mountain glens of England, in society among her historic Borderlands, and in exile beyond the Alps. Stowey and Grasmere, Tweedside and Ettrick, Venice and Rome, were the scene of potential activities as alien as the places, and yet all embodying some element of the Romantic revival.

The first, the Wordsworth group, was said to comprise Wordsworth, Coleridge, Bowles, Crabbe, Bloomfield, Clare and Elliot; the second, the Scott group, consisted of Scott, Campbell, Moore, Southey, Leyden, Hogg, Cunningham, Motherwell, Rogers, Keble, J. Montgomery, Heber, Milman and Mrs Hemans; while the third, the Shelley group, was made up of Byron, Shelley, Keats, Landor, Tennant, Frere, Horace Smith, Wells, Wade, Darley and Procter. The sheer incongruity of this assortment of major and miniscule poets illustrates the artificiality of such a method. Later classifications into the 'Lake School' and the 'Satanic School' are hardly more helpful. All of them, remarkably, omit any reference to Blake. Such synthetic arrangements have been superseded by the appreciation of each poet's individual voice; but there can be no reasonable doubt as to the identification of the English Romantics.

In France the contours have usually been drawn by generation. In the volume devoted to Romanticism in the standard history of French literature [*Le Romantisme*, 1957], Pierre Moreau singles out first 'La Génération de René' which includes, alongside Chateaubriand, Mme de Staël, Ballanche, Joubert, Constant, and Joseph de Maistre. Then comes the period of the *Cénacle:* Hugo, Vigny, Lamartine, Nodier, Lamennais, Barante, and Augustin Thierry; and finally, 'Le Romantisme de 1830', composed of many of the writers associated with the *Cénacle* with the addition of Musset and, somewhat later, George Sand and Nerval. Again, the overlapping from one to the other underlines the unreliability of such generational slicing. Division of the French Romantics according to their political alignment or religious beliefs into Liberals, Royalists, Catholics, etc. is even less satisfactory because of the rapid shifts of opinion. Here, too, the old static compartmentalisation is giving way to a greater flexibility that grows from an awareness of the dynamic developmental flow of literature.

Only in Germany does the traditional split into two major groups have any real validity. There was certainly a continuity, both personal and ideological, between the *Frühromantik* (the Early Romantics) and the *Hochromantik* (the High Romantics), but the differences are great enough to warrant a distinction. In many fundamental respects the interests of the two generations were at variance. The *Frühromantiker,* with their marked predilection for the metaphysical, focused their attention mainly on the transcendental and on the mediation of their mystical perception of the infinite. The *Hochromantiker,* by contrast, less speculative and more practical, concentrated on the creation of the *Märchen* (wondrous tales) and *Lieder* (songs) for which German Romanticism is best known. Moreover, while the *Frühromantiker* were cosmopolitan in outlook, the *Hochromantiker* inclined increasingly to a fervent patriotic nationalism. Nevertheless, in none of these literatures, nor in those of Spain, Italy and other European countries, should Lovejoy have encountered any serious dilemmas in identifying the Romantics in the historical sense.

His third heading, 'what ideas or tendencies', is indeed a thornier matter, but even here a consensus of opinion has been reached. The definitive statement of the cardinal unitary features of European Romanticism, given by René Wellek in his essay, 'The Concept of Romanticism in Literary History' [in *Concepts of Criticism,* 1963], has been widely endorsed:

> If we examine the characteristics of the actual literature which called itself or was called 'romantic' all over the continent, we find throughout Europe the same conception of poetry and of the workings and nature of the poetic imagination, the same conception of nature and its relation to man, and basically the same poetic style, with a use of imagery, symbolism, and myth which is clearly distinct from that of eighteenth-century neoclassicism.

To these basic tenets a variety of features may be added, and some modifications made. Morse Peckham, for instance, in his attempt [in "Toward a Theory of Romanticism," in *PMLA* LXVI (1951)] to lessen the conflict he perceived between Lovejoy's plea for discrimination and Wellek's synthesising tendencies, suggested the following amendment:

> What then is Romanticism? Whether philosophic, theologic, or aesthetic, it is the revolution in the European mind against thinking in terms of static mechanism and the redirection of the mind to thinking in terms of dynamic organicism. Its values are change, imperfection, growth, diversity, the creative imagination, the unconscious.

To prove much the same point, Henry H. H. Remak has evolved his own method, a schematic catalogue of the prime qualities of European Romanticism with an assessment of their relative force in Germany, France, England, Italy and Spain. These are the characteristics he lists as yard-sticks: imaginativeness, cult of strong emotions, restlessness and boundlessness, individualism, subjectivism, introversion, cult of originality, interest in nature, greater emphasis on religion, mysticism, *Weltschmerz,* liberalism, cosmopolitanism, nationalism, interest in folklore and primitivism, medievalism, anti-neoclassicism, interest in Nordic mythology, supremacy of lyrical moods and forms, historical drama and novel, reawakening of national epic, greater flexibility of form, irony, vagueness, symbolism, rhetoric, exoticism, and realism in local colour. Needless to say, not all these traits of Romanticism are present in each national movement. Remak's tables are studded with such qualifying phrases as 'but', 'less strong', 'within limits', 'relatively', 'not primary', 'notable exceptions' and so on. These indicate the perceptible fluctuations in the strength of the various features in different countries, as well as some dissimilarity in the forms they assumed, determined as they were by local circumstances and native traditions. But such national differences can only be established on the basis of an acknowledgement of the fundamental common elements of historical Romanticism. This is, to invert Coleridge's terms, unity in multeïty. The recognition of its homogeneity as a movement throughout Europe is perhaps the most important advance in the comparative approach to Romanticism since Lovejoy's day. The doubts that he harboured in 1924

as to 'what ideas and tendencies' were meant, have to a large extent been dispelled in the past fifty years.

Not entirely, however. The demarcation of historical Romanticism still poses some problems, foremost among them that raised originally by Lovejoy himself in his discrimination between the two major strands of Romanticism. He summarised the contrast as follows:

> Between the assertion of the superiority of 'nature' over conscious 'art' and that of the superiority of conscious art over mere 'nature'; between a way of thinking of which primitivism is of the essence and one of which the idea of perpetual self-transcendence is of the essence; between a fundamental preference for simplicity— even though a 'wild' simplicity—and a fundamental preference for diversity and complexity.

As an example of the first type of Romanticism Lovejoy cites Joseph Warton's *The Enthusiast,* written in 1740; for the second he refers to the theories of the *Frühromantik* in the 1790s. The objections to Lovejoy's arguement are fairly obvious: the fifty-year interval separating his two examples, during which the nascent Romanticism of the 1740s underwent further evolution, not to say, a mutation; the unfortunate imbalance inherent in the comparison of a rather second-rate poem with a complicated aesthetic theory; and the fact that Warton's *Enthusiast* belongs, ideologically as well as temporally, to Pre-romanticism, which differs in several vital respects from the Romantic movement that it foreshadows. Nonetheless, in spite of these reservations, Lovejoy's thesis is of great importance. Two currents do clearly run side by side in historical Romanticism: the naturalistic whose prime emphasis was on naturalness, primitivism and simplicity; and the transcendental which stressed the superiority of conscious art, and showed a preference for diversity and complexity, to use Lovejoy's apt terms. To the former belong not only Pre-romanticism, and notably the *Sturm und Drang* (Storm and Stress) of the 1770s, but also a number of the English poets: Wordsworth, Clare, Crabbe, possibly Keats. The outstanding expression of the naturalistic strain during the period of historical Romanticism comes, however, in the French Romantic movement. The *romantisme* of the early years of the nineteenth century plainly bears the marks associated with the first type of Romanticism. Its preference for naturalness, primitivism and simplicity are best understood as part of the revolt against all that Neoclassicism had represented: artificiality, over-refinement, and arabesques of convention. The impact of Rousseau's writings with their advocacy of a return to nature in the widest sense reinforced its rebellious tendencies. As a result, French *romantisme* has more in common with the *Sturm und Drang* than with the *Frühromantik.* On the other hand, a striking affinity of ideals, aims and idiom links the *Frühromantik* to the French poets of the later half of the nineteenth century from Nerval and Baudelaire onwards through the French Symbolists. They, together with Coleridge, Blake and Shelley, pertain to the second, the transcendental direction of Romanticism. There are good grounds for maintaining, as Albert Béguin [in *L'Ame romantique et le rêve,* 1939] and some of his successors have done, that it was only with this later wave of poets that the second type of Romanticism came to play a vital part in France. Be that as it may, Lovejoy's thesis of two Romanticisms cuts across the comfortable periodisation that sites historical Romanticism neatly between 1790 and 1830. In order to include the earlier manifestations of naturalistic Romanticism as well as the later expressions of transcendentalism, the dates would have to be extended to, at least, 1740-1895.

While the contours of archetypal romanticism follow a stable course along steady lines, those of historical Romanticism are of a conspicuous, though by no means unchartable sinuosity. But this sinuosity in the contours of historical Romanticism leads to some blurring of the silhouette at this point. For if the *terminus a quo* of historical Romanticism is none too easy to determine with any assurance, the *terminus ad quem* is even more perplexing. The very diversity that is universally conceded to be one of the salient features of historical Romanticism has fostered a beguiling and hazardous elasticity in the use of the term.

'Romantic' recurs in literary and artistic criticism with stubborn persistence and generally with little or no attempt at a designation of its precise meaning. . . . [Two] major recent collections of poems, *Sphere* by A. R. Ammons, and *High Windows* by Philip Larkin, were enthusiastically hailed as 'romantic', and in another recent review-article the word was applied [by Harold Bloom] with equal liberality to T. S. Eliot, Hart Crane, Allen Tate, Whitman and Wallace Stevens. This is not a matter of careless misuse, yet there is a disturbing vagueness in such usage. The implication would seem to be that these poets were writing within a tradition represented by their predecessors in the historical Romantic movement. These examples offer in fact a significant pointer to what has become a common assumption: the existence of a third dimension to the term 'romantic', distinct from the archetypal or the historical connotations, namely as a broad aesthetic concept. As such it has long become part of the critical vocabulary of our day. In meaning it is patently indebted to the archetypal and the historical alike, from which it derives its main thrust, though it lacks the relative explicitness of either. That is at one and the same time its strength and its weakness; its breadth of reference increases its usefulness, though its want of specificity detracts from its force. Its convenience as a portmanteau term all too easily exposes it to over-use and abuse.

How then are the contours of this third sense of 'romantic' to be traced? One possibility is to envisage them as an outer perimeter to historical Romanticism. The development from the historical to the aesthetic is then considered as a process of expansion into ever widening circles. Jacques Barzun chose the image of a river when he wrote [in *Classic, Romantic, and Modern,* 1961]: 'romanticism does not die out in 1850 but branches out under different names like a delta'. Another of his favourite images, that of the family, is particularly illuminating in this context if the transition from the historical to the aesthetic sense of 'romantic' is likened to the growth of the nuclear into the extended family. In essentials the features of the far-flung family echo and repeat those of the original nucleus,

but with varying degrees of intensity. Thus as a general aesthetic term 'romantic' continues to signify the primacy of the individual consciousness, an emphasis on emotion rather than reason, the espousal of irrationalism rather than rationalism, the reliance on vision rather than the orientation to reality, the trust in subjective reactions rather than objective standards, obedience to the dictates of an inner, rather than an outer imperative of order. Perhaps the most appropriate succinct definition of this aesthetic connotation of 'romantic' is that which Rémy de Gourmont coined for Symbolism: 'une littérature très individualiste, très idéaliste, au sens strictement philosophique du mot, et dont la variété et la liberté mêmes doivent correspondre à des visions personnelles du monde' ('a literature that is highly individualistic, highly idealistic in the philosophical sense of the word, and whose very variations and freedoms reflect, of necessity, personal visions of the world').

Although Rémy de Gourmont intended to characterise only Symbolism, his phrases have a significance beyond his original purpose. The contour lines are freely drawn here, with a generous sweep. For in its aesthetic sense, 'romantic' surpasses the limits of any specific movement or movements to denote one of the basic directions of art. Ultimately it betokens that imaginative transfiguration that is the opposite of the mimetic imitation called 'realistic'. Those are the two contrary poles. If the realist leads us through the honest gates of horn, as Harry Levin has taught us [in *The Gates of Horn: A Study of Five French Realists,* 1963], the romantic takes us through the extravagant gates of ivory, the portals of dreams, illusions and fantasies—of horror as well as of beauty. When 'romantic' in the aesthetic sense is interpreted in this way as a basic tendency, it obviously has some relation to the archetypal meaning. But whereas the archetypal manifestations of romanticism are not subject to temporal or spatial demarcations, those of aesthetic romanticism do, in practice, follow on the historical movement, from which they derive. The artistic modes of aesthetic romanticism devolve from the matrix of historical romanticism; they reflect the momentous changes in manner and style that resulted from the enthronement of the subjective imagination as the prime source of perception and creativity. Thus it is the literary and artistic schools of the late nineteenth and early twentieth centuries that are the best examples of the romantic in this third connotation.

Symbolism is clearly romantic, and indeed in a dual sense, sited as it is in that area where the contours of the historical and the aesthetic run closest to each other. Its direct descent from historical romanticism is evident in the Symbolists' striking affinity to the German *Frühromantiker*. The two groups share many basic ideals and techniques: the underlying belief in transcendental idealism and in the metaphysical nature of art; the conception of the artist as a visionary prophet and mediator of the infinite; the quasi-religious and magical aura surrounding creativity; the paramount role of the symbolic image as the vehicle for the expression of the inexpressible; the tendency to modify traditional forms in an experimental search for new means more fitted to the presentation of the ineffable vision. So intimately is Symbolism connected to historical Romanti-

An 1810 drawing of Friedrich Schlegel by Philipp Veit.

painting is essentially visionary, imaginative and personal, and must therefore stand in the lineage of Romanticism.

This holds true of Surrealism too, though it departs in some respects from the Romantic paradigm, particularly in its rejection of mysticism and in its attachment to this earth. But its main tenets point to its origins in the Romantic tradition: the primacy of the free-wheeling imagination, released from any restraints of logic; the conviction that the true essence of being can best be revealed through art; the leading role of the irrationally inspired mind in a poetic state open to Orphic insights; the flexibility of artistic forms; the belief in the actuality of a 'féerie intérieure' ('an inner realm of the wondrous'), as André Breton called it [in *Qu'est-ce que le surréalisme?*, 1934]. These are the characteristics that justify the use of the term 'romantic' in its third, aesthetic sense, in relation to Surrealism.

Expressionism offers yet another variant. Like Surrealism, it has certain deviant distinguishing features, such as its concern for the typical rather than the individual, the shrill stridency of its tone, and that tendency to inflation that was to lead towards the grotesque. However, in its opposition to naturalistic mimeticism as well as to automatism; in its emphasis on inner vision, on the creative powers and on the imagination; in its intense subjectivity; in the importance it attached to the almost autonomous image; in its championship of the supremacy of the artist as creator, as the passionate centre of a dynamic vortex; in its frequent mingling of the arts: in all these attributes Expressionism appears as yet another recrudescence of the romantic in its wider, aesthetic signification.

There is no need to multiply these examples any further, or to list instances of the occurrence of 'romantic' in recent literary and artistic criticism. The word and the idea obviously continue to flourish long after the demise of the Romantic movements of the late eighteenth and early nineteenth centuries. Its repeated usage can be understood only if its existence as a broad aesthetic concept is accepted in addition to its specifically historical—and archetypal—sense.

To use the term 'Romanticism' in the plural, as Lovejoy urged, and to discriminate between its varied manifestations: between the timbre of the national historical movements, between their successive waves, and between its differing connotations outside its historical boundaries—such discriminations are the starting-point for a truer understanding of European Romanticism. But this understanding does not lead to fixities and definities; rather, it is conducive of an appreciation of the character, potentialities, and also the problems inherent in Romanticism. Its kernel lies in change, growth and development, for Romanticism is essentially dynamic and organicist. As van Tieghem suspected, it is Protean, and it may well be comparable—as he thought—to a serpent in its dangerous windings, but it is not cloud-like. Its contours can be charted, even though the map will never attain a diagrammatic neatness. And at those very points where the contours crowd together most closely, where the lines converge in the densest configuration, Romanticism can be

cism that it is tempting to regard it as a final, grandiose wave of that sprawling movement, just as the *Sturm und Drang* may be considered a preliminary flood of the tide. Through its filiation to historical Romanticism on the one hand, and on the other, its prefiguration of subsequent poetic modes, Symbolism stands at a crucial point of transition. Its aesthetics represent a heavy contour line on the map of modern literature.

While Symbolism is at the convergence of the contour lines, Impressionism is already in the outer, the aesthetic perimeter. The Impressionists have—quite wrongly—been taken for realists because they painted directly from nature. Yet their purpose was far from the faithful reproduction of reality. The subject as such was of minor importance to them, a pretext more than a topic. What mattered was the perception of the subject; to borrow Zola's famous phrase [from *Le roman experimental*, 1923], it was 'un coin de la nature vu à travers un tempérament' ('a corner of nature seen through a temperament'), through a certain individual pair of eyes. For this reason the Impressionists would happily paint the same scenes over and over again, the same apparently mundane hay-stacks, the same water-lilies, the same cathedral front. The repetition of the same held a particular fascination for them insofar as the object would appear different at different times of day or year, under different illumination. And it was the recording of this subjective view that was their paramount aim. Their seen in its richest—and often perplexing—abundance. (pp. 1-15)

Lilian R. Furst, "The Contours of European Romanticism," in her The Contours of European Romanticism, *University of Nebraska Press, 1979, pp. 1-16.*

Furst on the difficulty of defining Romanticism:

It lies in the nature of Romanticism that any study of it should lead to an awareness of its inherent problems rather than to the sort of absolute conclusions that would allow us to close the book on Romanticism once and for all. Its extraordinary wealth of poetic works, its wide spread both geographically and historically, its great range of interests and techniques undoubtedly encourage a continuing pre-occupation with the Romantic movement. But the fundamental reason for its endless fascination resides in its very essence: in abandoning the certainties of Rationalism, Romanticism threw the doors wide open to searching of every kind, in aesthetics, in metaphysics, in religion, in politics and social sciences as well as in literary expression. It is a movement that begs questions, questions that are often without answer.

Lilian R. Furst, in her Romanticism, *Methuen, 1969.*

René Wellek

[*Wellek's* A History of Modern Criticism: 1750-1950 *(1955-65) is a major, comprehensive study of the literary critics of the last three centuries. Wellek's critical method, as demonstrated in his* History *and outlined in his* Theory of Literature *(1949; with Austin Warren), describes, analyzes, and evaluates a work solely in terms of the problems it poses for itself and how the writer solves them. For Wellek, biographical, historical, and psychological information is incidental. Although many of Wellek's critical methods are reflected in the work of the New Critics, he was not a member of that group and rejected their more formalistic tendencies. In the following excerpt, he examines the similarities among various European Romantic writers, concluding that the concept of a unified Romanticism is valid.*]

If we examine the characteristics of the actual literature which called itself or was called "romantic" all over the continent, we find throughout Europe the same conceptions of poetry and of the workings and nature of poetic imagination, the same conception of nature and its relation to man, and basically the same poetic style, with a use of imagery, symbolism, and myth which is clearly distinct from that of eighteenth-century neoclassicism. This conclusion might be strengthened or modified by attention to other frequently discussed elements: subjectivism, mediævalism, folklore, etc. But the following three criteria should be particularly convincing, since each is central for one aspect of the practice of literature: imagination for the view of poetry, nature for the view of the world, and symbol and myth for poetic style.

German literature is the clearest case; in both so-called romantic schools we find a view of poetry as knowledge of the deepest reality, of nature as a living whole, and of poetry as primarily myth and symbolism. This would hardly need to be argued with anyone who had read only Novalis. But it is impossible to accept the common German view that romanticism is the creation of the Schlegels, Tieck, Novalis, and Wackenroder. If one looks at the history of German literature between the date of Klopstock's *Messiah* (1748) and the death of Goethe (1832), one can hardly deny the unity and coherence of the whole movement which, in European terms, would have to be called "romantic." Some German scholars, such as H. A. Korff, recognize this and speak of "Goethezeit" or "deutsche Bewegung," terms which, however, obscure the international character of the changes.

One must, of course, grant distinctions between the different stages of the development. There was the "storm and stress" movement in the seventies which exactly parallels what today is elsewhere called "pre-romanticism." It was more radical and violent than anything corresponding in England or France, but it must be recognized as substantially the same movement, if we realize that the most important single influence was that of Rousseau and understand the extraordinary extent to which the ideas of Herder were prepared by the English and Scottish critics of the eighteenth century. The usual German terminology, "die Klassiker," is grossly misleading, since the authors grouped together as the German "classics" form two quite distinct groups; Lessing and Wieland belong to neoclassicism, while Herder was an extremely irrationalistic pre-romanticist, as were the early Goethe and Schiller. Only these last two authors went through a phase of "classicism," and that for the most part only in their theories. It is hard to find anything classical in Schiller's practice. The nostalgic hymn, "Die Götter Griechenlands," is rather a typical romantic dream. Goethe, while under the impression of his trip to Italy, for a time expounded a classical creed, especially in his writings on the plastic arts; and he wrote some works which must be considered in any history of neoclassicism: *Iphigenie* (1787), *Römische Elegien, Achilleis, Hermann und Dorothea, Die natürliche Tochter* (1804), possibly *Helena.* Still, however successfully their classical spirit could be defended, Goethe's greatest works are the subjective lyrics, *Faust,* the very influential *Meister,* and of course, *Werther.* It seems a strange preconception of many Germans to judge their greatest writer only according to one stage in his development and in accordance with his quite derivative and conventional taste in the fine arts. All the artistic power of Goethe is in the lyrics, in *Faust,* and in the novels, where there is scarcely any trace of classicism. If we examine Goethe's views of nature, it is obvious that he was an enemy of the Newtonian cosmology, the eighteenth-century world machine, and that he not only defended poetically a dynamic, organic view of nature, but also attempted to buttress it by scientific experiments and speculations (the *Theory of Colors,* the *Metamorphosis of Plants*) and by the use of concepts such as teleology, polarity, and so forth. Goethe's views are not identical with those of Schelling, but they are not easy to distinguish from them, and Schelling was the father of German *Naturphilosophie.* Goethe was also a symbolist and mythologist both in theory and practice. He interpreted language as a system of symbols and images. All philosophizing about nature was to him only anthropomorphism. Goethe was apparently the first to draw clearly the distinction between symbol and allegory. He attempted to create new myths, such as the Mothers in the second part of *Faust,* and tried to define poetically the relation of "Gott und Welt." One could use as a commentary to these poems the neo-Platonic cosmology Goethe claimed was his own at the age of twenty-one. Goethe's one abstractly philosophical paper [the so-called "Philosophische Studie," 1784-85] clearly formulates what even in 1812 he declared to have been "der Grund seiner ganzen Existenz," i.e. to see God in nature and nature in God. Thus, Goethe perfectly fits into the European romantic movement which he, as much as any single writer, helped to create.

There was, one must admit, a pronounced stage of Hellenism in the German movement; its roots are in Winckelmann, an ardent student of Shaftesbury, and this Hellenic enthusiasm early became extremely fervid in Germany. Its main documents are Schiller's "Die Götter Griechenlands," Hölderlin's *Hyperion* and *Archipelagus,* some of the writings of Wilhelm von Humboldt, Goethe's *Winckelmann und sein Jahrhundert,* and the early writings of Friedrich Schlegel. Still, one need not speak of a "Tyranny of Greece over Germany." There was, after all, a comparable Hellenic enthusiasm in France and England. It seems a mistake to underrate these parallel developments because they did not find such embodiment as in Germany's Goethe. French neo-Hellenism has at least one great poet, André Chénier. One cannot ignore the Hellenic enthusiasms and interests of even Chateaubriand and Lamartine, or the "Dionysiac" conception of Greek mythology charmingly expressed by Maurice de Guérin. We must not forget the Greek revival in painting and sculpture: Canova, Thorwaldsen, Ingres, Flaxman, none of whom were Germans.

In England, the role of romantic Hellenism has been studied only recently; it was widespread in the eighteenth century and finds poetic expression of great power in Byron, Shelley, and Keats. The whole of neo-Hellenism, German, English, and French, is not necessarily contradictory of romanticism. Homer was interpreted as a primitive poet. Leopardi, arguing against romanticism, appealed to a pastoral, romanticized, primitive Greece. Surprisingly early the "Orphic," orgiastic side of Greek civilization was recognized: by Friedrich Schlegel, by Schelling, by Maurice de Guérin. The conception of antiquity emerging from Keats' *Hyperion* is far removed from any eighteenth-century neo-classicism.

If this view that a large part of Hellenism is romantic is justified, it will be possible to minimize the excessive stress the Germans have traditionally put on the supposed conflict between their "classicism" and "romanticism." This conflict was in part purely personal, as a detailed history of the relations between Goethe and Schiller and the Schlegels shows, and in part it expressed a return of the so-called romantics to the ideals of the *Sturm und Drang* which Goethe and Schiller had attempted, somewhat too strenuously, to repudiate. Still, there is a fundamental

unity in the whole of German literature from roughly the middle of the eighteenth century to the death of Goethe. It is an attempt to create a new art different from that of the French seventeenth century; it is an attempt at a new philosophy which is neither orthodox Christianity nor the Enlightenment of the eighteenth century. This new view emphasizes the totality of man's forces, not reason alone, nor sentiment alone, but rather intuition, "intellectual intuition," imagination. It is a revival of neo-Platonism, a pantheism (whatever its concessions to orthodoxy), a monism which arrived at an identification of God and the world, soul and body, subject and object. The propounders of these ideas were always conscious of the precariousness and difficulty of these views, which frequently appeared to them only as distant ideals; hence the "unending desire" of the German romantics, the stress on evolution, on art as a groping towards the ideal. Exoticism of many kinds is part of the reaction against the eighteenth century and its self-complacency; the suppressed forces of the soul seek their analogies and models in pre-history, in the Orient, in the Middle Ages, and finally in India, as well as in the unconscious and in dreams.

The German romantic writers are the contemporaries of the flowering of German music: of Beethoven, Schubert, Schumann, Weber, and others, many of whom used German poetry of the age as texts for their songs or, like Beethoven, as inspiration for their symphonies. The fact of this collaboration is significant but hardly sufficient to make it the distinguishing characteristic of all romanticism. Such an emphasis obscures the international character of the movement, since the collaboration with music was practically non-existent in England and fairly late and slight in France. It points to the undeniable fact that romanticism in Germany was far more pervasive than in the other countries and that it affected all human endeavors—philosophy, politics, philology, history, science, and all the other arts—there much more thoroughly than elsewhere. But in this respect also the difference between Germany and the other countries is only relative. There was a romantic philosophy, philology, history, politics, and even science, not to speak of painting and music, in other countries, especially in France (Delacroix, Berlioz, Michelet, Cousin). The apparent isolation of Germany is exaggerated by German writers who see in romanticism a purely German style, and by antiromantics and recently by anti-Hitler propagandists who want to prove that all the ills of the last two centuries came from Germany. The only view which takes account of all factors holds that romanticism is a general movement in European thought and art and that it has native roots in every major country. Cultural revolutions of such profound significance are not accomplished by mere importations.

Romanticism was more completely victorious in Germany than elsewhere for very obvious historical reasons. The German Enlightenment was weak and of short duration. The Industrial Revolution was late in coming. There was no leading rationalistic bourgeoisie. Both the derivative, unoriginal Enlightenment and the peculiarly rigid religious orthodoxies seemed unsatisfactory. Thus social and intellectual causes opened the way for a literature which was created mostly by unattached intellectuals, tutors, army surgeons, salt-mine officials, court clerks, and the like, who revolted against both feudalism and middle-class ideals. German romanticism, more so than English and French, was the movement of an intelligentsia which had loosened its class ties and hence was particularly apt to create a literature remote from ordinary reality and social concerns. Still, the aestheticism and lack of social "engagement" of writers such as Goethe has been very much exaggerated. One hears too much about the "Olympian" Goethe. It is not realized that the quotation "ein garstig Lied, pfui, ein politisch Lied!" is the dramatic pronouncement of a student in "Auerbachs Keller."

While it would be absurd to deny the special features of the German romantic age (we may pause to reflect that every age has its special features), almost all its views and techniques can be paralleled elsewhere. It is no denial of originality to see that the great German writers drew freely on foreign sources (Rousseau, English preromanticism) or on sources in the remote past, both foreign and native, which had been available to the other European nations: neo-Platonism, Giordano Bruno, Böhme, a reinterpreted Spinoza, Leibniz. The Germans, in turn, influenced other countries; but their influence, for obvious chronological reasons, comes too late to make them the only source of the turn towards the ideas and poetic myths usually called romantic. In England, Böhme was important for Blake, Schelling and August Wilhelm Schlegel for Coleridge, Bürger and Goethe for Scott (though hardly centrally so), Goethe and Jean Paul for Carlyle. But the German influence on Wordsworth, Shelley, Keats, and even Byron is negligible. In France, German influences came much later; A. W. Schlegel . . . was very important for the introduction of the new critical terminology. German interests are strong in Nodier, in Gérard de Nerval, and in Quinet, who studied Herder and Creuzer. Some argument can be made for the importance of the German song *(Lied)* for the French romantic lyric; but certainly the central figures, Chateaubriand, Lamartine, Vigny, Hugo, Balzac, Sainte-Beuve have few German affinities, and similarities must be explained by identical antecedents in England and an analogous literary and cultural situation.

As for France, our view is blurred by the official insistence on beginning the romantic movement with the triumph of *Hernani* (1830), a minor event in a later perspective, which obscures the fact that, outside of the drama or rather the Parisian official stage, a profound change had come over French literature many years before. This has been widely recognized in France, even though the centenary of romanticism was celebrated in 1927. The very first historian of romanticism in France, F. R. de Toreinx, says that romanticism was born in 1801, that Chateaubriand was its father, Madame de Staël its godmother (he is silent about the mother). In 1824 *La Muse Française* noticed the decisive role of Rousseau and Bernardin de St. Pierre; Alfred Michiels, in his *Histoire des idées littéraires en France* (1842), was of the opinion that the whole of romanticism can be found in Sébastien Mercier. Some have tried to find the ancestors of romanticism even further back in the past; Faguet interpreted French poetry around 1630 with reference to Lamartine, and Brunetière claimed to see the germs of melodrama in *Phèdre*. But more sober views have

prevailed. The romantic elements in French eighteenth-century literature have been investigated quite systematically and, on the whole, convincingly; there is today some very fine work by Pierre Trahard and André Monglond on the history of sentimentalism, usually traced back at least as far as Prévost. Daniel Mornet has studied the reawakening of the feeling for nature and Gilbert Chinard has devoted much attention to French exoticism and primitivism. Auguste Viatte has shown [in *Les Sources occultes du romantisme,* 2 vols., 1928], most impressively, the large undercurrent of illuminism and theosophy in eighteenth-century France. Saint-Martin assumes a large role not only for France (De Maistre, Ballanche), but also for Germany (Hamann, Baader, even Goethe, Novalis). Rousseau, of course, has never ceased to attract attention; he has even been made the wellspring of all romanticism, by friends like J.-J. Texte or by enemies who try to reduce romanticism to Rousseauism. But Rousseau is unduly overrated if he is made the originator of attitudes which he helped popularize but did not invent. Still, all these scattered French studies show isolated anticipations of romantic attitudes, ideas, sentiments, rather than a real romantic literature in eighteenth-century France. That such a literature existed has best been demonstrated by Kurt Wais, who has shown [in *Das antiphilosophische Weltbild des französischen Sturm und Drang (1760-89),* 1934] that there was a whole group of French writers who attacked the *philosophes* and the neoclassical tradition, stressed primitivism, thought that there is cultural decay rather than progress, attacked science, felt well inclined toward religion and even toward superstition and the marvelous. Many of the authors quoted are very minor and even minimal; Ramond de Carbonnières' *Les dernières aventures du jeune d'Olban* (1781) is only a mediocre imitation of *Werther.* But Wais has established that there was a widespread "irrationalism" in writers like Mercier, Chassaignon, Loaisel de Tréogate, and others, which can be compared with the German *Sturm und Drang.*

This French preromantic movement received a temporary setback through the Revolution, which fostered classicism and rationalism, and by the Empire, which also had its official classicism. But among the *émigrés* romanticism flourished. Madame de Staël was the propagandist of the German romantics. Chateaubriand cannot be made out a classicist, whatever his interests in classical antiquity and his reservations against Shakespeare or against many of his contemporaries. *Le Génie du Christianisme* (1802) is a romantic poetics. If we apply our tests, it is obvious that Chateaubriand expounds an organic, symbolic order of nature, that he is a mythologist and symbolist *par excellence.* But Madame de Staël and Chateaubriand were by no means alone in their time; even Chénier conceived the idea of a new mythic poetry, especially in the fragment *Hermès.* In Sénancour's *Obermann* (1804) we find the romantic view of nature in full bloom. "La nature sentie n'est que dans les rapports humains, et l'éloquence des choses n'est rien que l'éloquence de l'homme. La terre féconde, les cieux immenses, les eaux passagères ne sont qu'une expression des rapports que nos cœurs produisent et contiennent." Obermann constantly finds in external things analogies which give us the feeling of a universal order. Even flowers, a sound, a smell, a gleam of light become the "materials which an external idea arranges like figures of an invisible thing." The states of mind described by Sénancour are extraordinarily similar to Wordsworth's, but unlike Wordsworth (not to speak of Novalis' "magic" idealism) Sénancour experiences them almost as a curse. He complains bitterly that fate has condemned him to have only [in the words of Albert Béguin, *L'Âme romantique et le rêve,* 1946] a "dream of his existence." His art is rather that of passive rêverie.

In Charles Nodier also we find the whole repertory of romantic themes and ideas. Nodier was a quite technical entomologist who mythologized the world of insects. He sees in nature an alphabet which needs deciphering. In the world of insects and infusoria he finds a grotesque parallel to the forms of human art, and in the universe a process of *"syngénésie,"* a fantastic evolution toward a human Utopia. Nodier knew Swedenborg and Saint-Martin, and used the work of an Italian physiologist, Malpighi. He wrote romantic fairy tales *(La Fée aux Miettes)* and fantasies such as *Lydie ou la Résurrection* (1839), which has obvious affinities with Novalis' *Hymnen an die Nacht.*

Lamartine's *Harmonies poétiques et religieuses* (1830) ties completely into our scheme; one could hardly find a more precise expression of the romantic view of nature as a language, as a concert of harmonies. The whole universe is conceived of as a system of symbols, correspondences, emblems, which at the same time is alive and pulsates rhythmically. The task of the poet is not only to read this alphabet, but to vibrate with it, to sense and reproduce its rhythm. *La Chute d'un Ange* (1838) has a mythological conception of the epic similar to Ballanche; there is the scale of being, there is the concept of the transformation of each atom and element into thought and sentiment.

Vigny is different. He does not accept the romantic concept of nature, but embraces a dualism of man and nature, a pessimistic titanism which is a continuous protest against the order of nature. Nature is dead, silent, and even hostile to man. But this sharp ethical dualism of man versus nature is, in Vigny, combined with a totally romantic symbolism: "The men of greatest genius are those who made the justest comparisons. They are the branches to which we can cling in the void which surrounds us. . . . Each man is nothing but an image of an idea of the general mind." Many of Vigny's poems are organized around such symbols as *Le Cor, La Neige, La Bouteille à la mer.* Vigny's preoccupation with myth is obvious; he planned a most ambitious series which was to include a Last Judgment and "Satan Sauvé." Only *Eloa,* a "mystery," and *Le Déluge* were carried out.

Victor Hugo, later in his life, became the most ambitious mythologist, symbolist, prophet of a new religion, of all the romantics. His fame has declined in the twentieth century, but recently several attempts have been made to rescue these late works—parts of the *Légende des Siècles, La Fin de Satan, Dieu.* These attempts emanate not only from academic scholars, but also from surrealist poets. They stress the mythic, eerie, grand, and sometimes absurd late Hugo. He fits into our scheme beautifully, whatever we may think of the quality of the poetry. Historians of ideas "have marvelled at the unperturbed serenity of a synthesis which does not flinch before self-contradiction, which, at once pantheist and deist, shows God disseminated in the universe and yet transcendent and personal; which draws from all sources, from the modern Platonists and Pythagoreans . . . Swedenborg, Ballanche, from the contemporary Illuminati, from Cabbalists, but persists in wresting originality out of a many-sided indebtedness." Hugo expounds a panpsychism of nature; a conviction of omnisentience (e.g. *Le Sacre de la Femme*), of the "victory of unity over diversity, of All over the ephemeral, the victory of universal and palpitating life over all that limits, curtails, frustrates, and denies." In *Le Satyre* the satyr is haled before the gods and asked to sing in order to amuse the contemptuous Olympians. "Le satyre chanta la terre monstrueuse." His stature increases in singing, he becomes an incarnation of nature and life. The faun declares himself in the concluding line: "Place à tout! Je suis Pan, Jupiter, à genoux!" In *La Fin de Satan,* Satan is pardoned and dies in a surprising conclusion, God saying: "Satan est mort! renais, o Lucifer céleste!" Evil is reabsorbed because Satan actually loved God, was himself a part of the providential scheme. In *Dieu,* Hugo passes in review the different philosophies he rejects or ridicules: atheism, scepticism, dualism, Greek polytheism, the Hebrew Jehovah. A spiritual pantheism is expounded by an angel: "Tous les êtres sont Dieu; tous les flots sont la mer." The poem concludes in a hymn to God, who is conceived as a bewildering series of contradictions, a dazzling light which is, at the same time, darkness. "Rien n'existe que Lui; le flamboiement profond." In Hugo, then, all the romantic convictions and themes are summarized: organic, evolving nature, the view of poetry as prophecy, the view that symbol and myth are the instruments of poetry. In Hugo the reconciliation of opposites, the stress on the grotesque and evil ultimately absorbed in the harmony of the universe, is particularly clear and was clear even in his early aesthetic theories, as in the preface to *Cromwell.* His prophetic fervor, intensity, and grandiose gestures may have become pretentious and absurd to generations who have lost this view of poetry. But Hugo marshalled all the possible arguments for the romantic view of nature, for man's continuity with nature, the great scale of nature, and the final perfection of man.

Balzac is not usually considered a romantic and he may not be one in many aspects of his stupendous work. But E. R. Curtius [in *Balzac,* 1923] has rightly stressed an aspect which must have struck every reader of the *Human Comedy*—Balzac's interest in magic and the occult. A study of Balzac's religious views reveals that he declared himself a Swedenborgian many times. In *Louis Lambert,* which contains much that is autobiography, there is an exposition of a system which must be substantially Balzac's and exuberant praise of Swedenborg as the "Buddha of the North." *Seraphita* also is full of Swedenborgianism, a theosophical and pantheistic philosophy of immanence, which Balzac must have considered compatible with Catholicism and his specific endorsement of political Catholicism. Whatever Balzac's exact religious views, he certainly held this organic view of nature which he calls *magisme.* He was deeply impressed by contemporary biology, especially by Geoffrey Saint-Hilaire and his view that there is only *one* animal. He was absorbed and taken in by all forms of magnetism, mesmerism, and phrenology, all of which uphold the "unity of nature." Like the romantics, Balzac had a theory of intuition, to which he applies the queer term, *spécialité,* distinguishing it from instinct and abstraction. He was also an ardent mythologist, giving a symbolic interpretation to all rites, cults, myths, mysteries of religion, and creations of art. "Today hieroglyphics are not any more impressed in Egyptian marble, but in mythologies which are unified worlds." Balzac said of *La Peau de Chagrin,* "tout y est mythe et figure." He himself constantly gave symbolic interpretations; e.g. *La Vieille fille* contains a strange symbolic use of *Orlando Furioso.* Though wide stretches of Balzac's work may not show it, he was inspired by a peculiar type of romantic metaphysics, physics, or energetics, with its supposed laws of compensations, polarities, fluids, etc.

Among the authors less well known today many fit in with our criteria. Pierre-Simon Ballanche had a mystical, Pythagorean conception of nature and the harmony of the spheres (the seven numbers produce an endless concert); an apocalypse is presented in which matter will be spiritualized by a new magnetism and the animals disappear as their life, by assimilation, becomes the life of man. Ballanche was not only a mythologist and fantastic philosopher of nature but also a symbolist who, long before Mallarmé, conceived the unity of the senses.

Edgar Quinet is related to Ballanche and, of course, to the Germans. To him, religion was the business of the poet; the poet destroys the fixed symbols of dogma in order to renew them. Quinet believed also in some future universal epic which will "reconcile all legends by fusing them into one."

Maurice de Guérin also fits into our scheme. He shows the major points of agreement: the views of the substantial unity of nature, the continuity in the chain of creation, the primacy of the intuitive faculty in man, which is especially active in poets, whose role is to decipher the "flottant appareil de symboles qu'on appelle l'univers." His sense of identity with nature is finely expressed in his journal. "Se laisser pénétrer à la nature . . . s'identifier au printemps . . . aspirer en soi toute la vie . . . se sentir à la fois fleur, verdure, oiseau, chant, fraîcheur, élasticité, volupté, sérénité." Guérin wants to "sentir presque physiquement que l'on vit de Dieu et en Dieu." He aspired to create neopagan myths, like *Le Centaure,* and to spiritualize nature, as in the *Méditation sur la mort de Marie;* he had the romantic thirst to ascend to the origins of mankind and of himself as a child, to find the "point de départ de la vie universelle."

Gérard de Nerval is the most mystical, "supernatural," of the French romantics, the nearest to the most fantastic Germans whom he knew and loved. The symbolists have recognized him as their precursor. *Aurélia,* especially, is a series of visions and dreams which attempt to change the whole life of the author himself into a myth. Nerval, exactly like Keats, believed in the literal truth of anything imagination has invented. The whole of Nerval's work is a world of dream symbols and myths. He is full of Swedenborgianism and other occult beliefs; nature is emblematic through and through. He speaks of "a vast conspiracy of

all animate beings to reestablish the world in its first harmony": "How can I have existed so long, I said to myself, outside Nature without identifying myself with her? Everything lives, everything acts, everything corresponds; the magnetic rays emanating from myself or others traverse unimpeded the infinite chain of created things; it is a transparent network which covers the world, and its fine threads communicate from one to another to the planets and the stars. I am now a captive on the earth, but I converse with choiring stars, who share my joys and sorrows!"

I have already suggested some of the sources of French romanticism—Swedenborg, Saint-Martin, the Germans. But we must realize that in all phases of French thought there was a considerable parallel activity. In history Michelet propounded a "historical symbolism." The numerous neo-Catholic French thinkers shared many of the main romantic tenets and motifs. There is "striking similarity between the doctrines of Hegel and Bonald." Joseph de Maistre, in his youth at least, was steeped in the mythical, Masonic, and Illuminati ideas of the time, and they left strong traces on his mature thought. A letter to Bonald states that "the physical world is nothing but an image or, if you prefer, the formula, a repetition of the spiritual world." Matter does not exist independently of mind. Catholicism does not totally reject polytheism; it rather explains and corrects the Graeco-Roman mythology. "The name of God, no doubt, is exclusive and incommunicable; still, there are many gods in heaven and earth. There are intelligences, better natures, deified men. The gods of Christianity are the saints."

Illustration by Delacroix for Part I of Goethe's Faust.

The whole eclectic movement, fed as it is in part from German sources, especially Schelling, fits into our scheme, and much in the French science of the time, particularly biology, helps to re-create the whole mental "climate" in which French romanticism flourished. (pp. 160-78)

Much space would be required to examine all the other European literatures adequately from this point of view. Italy has sometimes been considered an exception; it has even been denied that it had any "real" romanticism. But, while one may grant the strong survivals of neoclassicism, the peculiarly vehement political orientation, and the absence of some themes of the Northern romantic literatures, Italy cannot be considered to deviate from the pattern. Leopardi certainly is in profound agreement with his great contemporaries across the Alps, even though his literary theories have many neoclassical traits. For his romantic concept of nature the early poem *L'infinito* (1819) is evidence. His speculations on the great poetic harmony, the "effetto poetico" of the totality of nature, and his nostalgia for early Greece link him with the Germans. Foscolo and Manzoni, both as critics and as artists, are part and parcel of the European romantic movement. Gioberti expounded an aesthetics similar to Schelling's.

Allison Peers has argued that Spanish romanticism was of very short duration and disintegrated very soon after its triumph in 1838. This may be true of romanticism as a "school," but hardly of romantic Spanish literature of the nineteenth century. Espronceda, especially, seems to fit our pattern very closely.

In the Scandinavian countries, German romanticism, especially Schelling, was most influential. Among the Swedes a whole group of critics viewed the work of art as a symbol of the universe. *Naturphilosophie* was widely accepted, and mythologizing was at the very center of the whole Nordic revival.

The Slavic romantic movements present special features and special problems. The Russians drew heavily on the Germans, especially on Schelling and Hegel. Lermontov fits into our pattern as does, of course, Vladimir Odoevsky, whose stories of artists, such as "Johann Sebastian Bach," are full of the theory of correspondences, the view of art as a mediator between man and nature. Pushkin, to a certain extent, is an exception; his clear form seems neoclassical and recent Russian literary scholarship excludes him from the romantic movement. But this is hardly warranted if one considers not only the usually quoted affinities with Byron, but recognizes also Pushkin's nature symbolism, which has been studied, possibly oversubtly, by Gershenzon, or if one considers his myth of the destructive statue, in the *Stone Guest,* the *Bronze Horseman,* and the *Tale of the Golden Cockerel.*

Polish romantic literature is the most romantic of all minor literatures: Mickiewicz and Slowacki share fully the romantic view of nature, the romantic concept of the imagination, the use of symbol and mythology, and express them even extravagantly. So do such Polish romantic thinkers as Hoene-Wroński. The Czech romantic movement has at least one great poet, Karel Hynek Mácha, who shares the concept of nature, of imagination, and of symbol with his German and Polish contemporaries. One important argument for the coherence and unity of the European romantic movement emerges from an investigation of the minor literatures—the "predictability" of their general character. If we had never heard anything about the Czech romantic movement, it would still be possible, within limits, to assert the presence and absence of certain themes, views, and techniques.

My conclusion concerning the unity of the romantic movement may be distressingly orthodox and even conventional. But it seems necessary to reassert it, especially in view of Lovejoy's famous attack. "On the Discrimination of Romanticisms" proves, it seems to me, only that Joseph Warton was an early naturalistic preromanticist, that Friedrich Schlegel was a highly sophisticated, self-conscious intellectual, and that Chateaubriand held many classicist views on literary criticism and on Shakespeare. The fact that Chateaubriand was conservative and Hugo ended in liberalism does not disrupt the continuity of French romanticism as a literary movement. On the whole, political criteria seem grossly overrated as a basis for judging a man's basic view of the world and artistic allegiance.

I do not, of course, deny differences between the various romantic movements, differences of emphasis and distribution of elements, differences in the pace of development, in the individualities of the great writers. I am perfectly aware that the three groups of ideas I have selected have their historical ancestry before the Enlightenment and in undercurrents during the eighteenth century. The view of an organic nature descends from neo-Platonism through Giordano Bruno, Böhme, the Cambridge Platonists, and some passages in Shaftesbury. The view of imagination as creative and of poetry as prophecy has a similar ancestry. A symbolist, and even mythic, conception of poetry is frequent in history, e.g. in the baroque age with its emblematic art, its view of nature as hieroglyphics which man and especially the poet is destined to read. In a sense, romanticism is the revival of something old, but it is a revival with a difference; these ideas were translated into terms acceptable to men who had undergone the experience of the Enlightenment. It may be difficult to distinguish clearly between a romantic and a baroque symbol, the romantic and the Böhmean view of nature and imagination. But for our problem we need only know that there is a difference between the symbol in Pope and in Shelley. This can be described; the change from the type of imagery and symbolism used by Pope to that used by Shelley is an empirical fact of history. It seems difficult to deny that we are confronted with substantially the same fact in noting the difference between Lessing and Novalis or Voltaire and Victor Hugo.

Lovejoy has argued that the "new ideas of the period were in large part heterogeneous, logically independent and sometimes essentially antithetic to one another in their implications." If we look back on our argument it will be obvious that this view must be mistaken. There is, on the contrary, a profound coherence and mutual implication between the romantic views of nature, imagination, and symbol. Without such a view of nature we could not believe in the significance of symbol and myth. Without symbol and myth the poet would lack the tools for the insight into reality which he claimed, and without such an epistemology, which believes in the creativity of the human mind, there would not be a living nature and a true symbolism. We may not accept this view of the world for ourselves—few of us can accept it literally today—but we should grant that it is coherent and integrated and, as I hope to have shown, all-pervasive in Europe.

We can then go on speaking of romanticism as one European movement, whose slow rise through the eighteenth century we can describe and examine and even call, if we want to, preromanticism. Clearly there are periods of the dominance of a system of ideas and poetic practices; and clearly they have their anticipations and their survivals. To give up these problems because of the difficulties of terminology seems to me tantamount to giving up the central task of literary history. If literary history is not to be content to remain the usual odd mixture of biography, bibliography, anthology, and disconnected emotive criticism, it has to study the total process of literature. This can be done only by tracing the sequence of periods, the rise, dominance, and disintegration of conventions and norms. The term "romanticism" posits all these questions, and that, to my mind, is its best defense. (pp. 193-98)

René Wellek, "The Concept of Romanticism in Literary History," in Concepts of Criticism, *Yale University Press, 1963, pp. 128-98.*

Romanticism, so often ill defined, is in the final analysis, and here is its real definition, if one considers only its militant aspect, nothing other than liberalism in literature.

—Victor Hugo, in his preface to Hernani, *1830.*

Morse Peckham

[Peckham is an American educator and critic who explained that virtually all his writing "developed from an effort to develop a theory of romanticism." In the following excerpt, Peckham attempts to reconcile the theories of Lovejoy and Wellek in a definition of Romanticism determined by the unity of countries and genres.]

Can we hope for a theory of Romanticism? The answer, I believe, is, yes. But before proceeding further, I must make quite clear what it is that I propose to discuss.

First, although the word "Romanticism" refers to any number of things, it has two primary referents: (1) a general and permanent characteristic of mind, art, and personality, found in all periods and in all cultures; (2) a specific historical movement in art and ideas which occurred in Europe and America in the late eighteenth and early nine-

teenth centuries. I am concerned only with the second of these two meanings. There may be a connection between the two, but I doubt it, and at any rate whatever I have to say refers only to historical Romanticism.

Second, in this historical sense "Romanticism" as a revolution in art and ideas is often considered to be only an expression of a general redirection of European life which included also a political revolution, an industrial revolution, and perhaps several others. There may be a connection between the revolution in ideas and the arts and the more or less contemporary revolutions in other fields of human activities, but for the time being, at any rate, I think it is wise to dissociate the Romanticism of ideas and art from these other revolutions. Just as one of our greatest difficulties so far has arisen from assuming an identity between general and historical Romanticism, so much of our difficulty in considering the nature of historical Romanticism has come from assuming its identity with all of the other more or less contemporary revolutions. Let us first isolate the historical Romanticism of ideas and arts before we beg any questions about the nature of history. For example, I think it is at present wiser to consider Romanticism as one of the means then available for hindering or helping the early nineteenth-century movement for political reform than it is to assume that Romanticism and the desire for political reform and its partial achievement are the same thing.

With these two distinctions in mind, I repeat, Can we hope for a theory of the historical Romanticism of ideas and art? Such a theory must be able to submit successfully to two tests. First, it must show that Wordsworth and Byron, Goethe and Chateaubriand, were all part of a general European literary movement which had its correspondences in the music, the painting, the architecture, the philosophy, the theology, and the science of the eighteenth and early nineteenth centuries. Second, it must be able to get us inside individual works of literature, art, and thought: that is, to tell us not merely that the works are there, to enable us not merely to classify them, but to deliver up to us a key to individual works so that we can penetrate to the principles of their intellectual and aesthetic being. Can we hope for such a theory? *Dare* we hope for such a theory? To this question I answer, "Yes, we can." I feel that we have it almost within our grasp—that one or two steps more and we shall have mastered this highly perplexing literary problem.

Certainly there is no generally accepted theory of Romanticism at the present time. Twenty years ago, and for more than twenty years before that, the problem of Romanticism was debated passionately, not least because of the redoubtable but utterly misdirected attacks of Babbitt and More. In his *Romanticism and the Modern Ego* (1943), Jacques Barzun has made a good collection of some of the definitions that have been more or less widely used in the past fifty years: a return to the Middle Ages, a love of the exotic, the revolt from reason, a vindication of the individual, a liberation of the unconscious, a reaction against scientific method, a revival of pantheism, a revival of idealism, a revival of Catholicism, a rejection of artistic conventions, a return to emotionalism, a return to nature—and so on. The utmost confusion reigns in the whole field. In the past fifteen or twenty years, most scholars have done one of two things. Either they have given up hope for any sense to come out of this tangle and have stoutly denied that there was such a movement, or, less pessimistically, they have continued to use one or more concepts or ideas—theories which they feel to be unsatisfactory yet which they continue to employ because there is nothing better. Most students are convinced that something happened to literature between the death of Pope and the death of Coleridge, but not very many are willing, when you question them sharply, to tell you exactly what happened. The situation is all the more discouraging in that it is generally conceded that Romanticism is a central problem in literary history, and that if we have failed to solve that problem, we can scarcely hope to solve any general problems in literary history.

Too many scholars, then, will try either to avoid the term entirely, or failing that strategy—and it always fails—will isolate some idea or literary effect and will say, "This is Romanticism." Or such a scholar will use the term with the full knowledge that the reader will recognize the difficulties involved and will charitably permit him to beg the question. He will very rarely begin with a theory of Romanticism and seek to place a particular poem or author in relation to that theory or seek to use the theory in unlocking a baffling and complex work, or even a simple one for that matter. He will fit his ideas into whatever notion of Romanticism he may have, usually without specifying what it might be, but very rarely, at least in public and in print, will he use a considered theory of Romanticism as a starting point for his investigations. It is a discouraging situation, but my purpose is to suggest that it is not so discouraging as it appears.

In the last few years there have been signs that some scholars at least are moving toward a common concept of Romanticism. In 1943, Jacques Barzun spoke [in *Romanticism and the Modern Ego*, 1943] of Romanticism as a biological revolution; and in 1949, he defined [in "Romanticism: Definition of a Period," *Magazine of Art* XLII (1949)] it as part of "the great revolution which drew the intellect of Europe . . . from the expectation and desire of fixity into desire and expectation of change." Stallknecht, in his fascinating book on Wordsworth, *Strange Seas of Thought* (1945), spoke of how Romanticism established the sentiment of being in England and then, reversing his statement, suggested that the sentiment of being established Romanticism. In his admirable introduction to his edition of *Sartor Resartus* (1937), C. Frederick Harrold—whose death has deprived us of one of the most valuable of contemporary students of Victorian literature—wrote of Carlyle's ideas about organicism and dynamism. And in his and Templeman's excellent anthology of Victorian prose (1938), there is an appendix "illustrative of nineteenth-century conceptions of growth, development, evolution." But the most recent attempt to tackle the problem, the best yet, though I think not entirely satisfactory, has been René Wellek's two-part article "The Concept of Romanticism," published in 1949 in the first two issues of *Comparative Literature* [later reprinted in *Concepts of Criticism*, 1963]. There he offered three

criteria of Romanticism: imagination for the view of poetry, an organic concept of nature for the view of the world, and symbol and myth for poetic style.

Wellek does establish to my mind three things in his article: first, that there *was* a European intellectual and artistic movement with certain intellectual and artistic characteristics, a movement properly known as Romanticism; second, that the participators in that movement were quite conscious of their historic and revolutionary significance; and third, that the chief reason for the current skepticism in America about a theory of Romanticism was the publication in 1924 of Arthur O. Lovejoy's famous article, "On the Discrimination of Romanticisms" [in *PMLA;* later reprinted in *Essays in the History of Ideas,* 1948]. In this article Lovejoy pointed out that the term is used in a fearful variety of ways, and that no common concept can include them all. Indeed, the growth of skepticism about any solid conclusions on Romanticism does seem to begin—or at least start to become very powerful and eventually dominant—with the publication of that article. Wellek decries what he calls Lovejoy's excessive nominalism and skepticism, and refuses to be satisfied with it. He also puts in the same category of nominalism and skepticism Lovejoy's 1941 article, "The Meaning of Romanticism for the Historian of Ideas." Here Lovejoy offered three criteria of Romanticism, or rather the three basic ideas of Romanticism, "heterogeneous, logically independent, and sometimes essentially antithetic to one another in their implications." These ideas are organicism, dynamism, and diversitarianism. Now in discussing Lovejoy's 1941 paper, Wellek has made, I think, an error. He seems to have confused the nature of the two articles, because, apparently, he has forgotten about the last three chapters of *The Great Chain of Being* (1936).

Lovejoy's great book is a landmark of scholarship, and also for scholarship. It is a book on which some of the most useful scholarship of our times has been based, and it is as useful to the teacher who uses it with intelligence as it is to the scholar. Twenty-five years from now, scholars of literature will look back on the publication of *The Great Chain of Being* as a turning point in the development of literary scholarship; for it has been of astonishing value in opening up to our understanding in quite unexpected ways the literature of the sixteenth, seventeenth, and eighteenth centuries. But, so far as I know, almost no use has been made of the last three chapters, especially of the last two, in explaining Romanticism and Romantic works. It is a curious situation; for these chapters contain the foundations for a theory of Romanticism which will do everything that such a theory must be able to do—place works and authors in relation to each other and illuminate individual works of art as they ought to be illuminated.

By ignoring (at least in his two papers) *The Great Chain of Being,* Wellek concluded that the same kind of skepticism was present in both Lovejoy's 1924 and 1941 articles. Actually *The Great Chain of Being* is an answer to Lovejoy's 1924 article. Without emphasizing the fact, Lovejoy *did* in 1933 and 1934, when he delivered the lectures on which the book is based, what in 1924 he said could not be done. To be brief, in 1936 he stated simply that literary

Romanticism was the manifestation of a change in the way of thinking of European man, that since Plato European man had been thinking according to one system of thought—based on the attempted reconciliation of two profoundly different ideas about the nature of reality, both stemming from Plato—and that in the late eighteenth and early nineteenth centuries occidental thought took an entirely different direction, as did occidental art. Furthermore, he says that the change in the way the mind works was the most profound change in the history of occidental thinking, and by implication it involved a similar profound change in the methods and objects of European art.

What I wish to do here is, first, to explain what these new ideas of the late eighteenth century involved, to reconcile Wellek and Lovejoy, and Lovejoy with himself, and to show the relevance of certain other ideas about Romanticism I have mentioned; and second, to make one addition to the theories of Lovejoy and Wellek, an addition which I hope goes far toward clearing up an essential problem which Lovejoy scarcely faced and with which Wellek is unable to come to terms.

It is scarcely necessary to outline what *The Great Chain of Being* implied. Yet I should like to reduce the concepts involved to what I think to be their essentials. Briefly, the shift in European thought was a shift from conceiving the cosmos as a static mechanism to conceiving it as a dynamic organism: static—in that all the possibilities of reality were realized from the beginning of things or were implicit from the beginning, and that these possibilities were arranged in a complete series, a hierarchy from God down to nothingness—including the literary possibilities from epic to Horatian ode, or lyric; a mechanism—in that the universe is a perfectly running machine, a watch usually. (A machine is the most common metaphor of this metaphysic.) Almost as important as these concepts was that of uniformitarianism, implicit both in staticism and in mechanism, whenever these two are separated, as frequently happens. That is, everything that change produces was to be conceived as a part to fit into the already perfectly running machine; for all things conformed to ideal patterns in the mind of God or in the nonmaterial ground of phenomena.

If, in short, you conceive of the universe as a perfectly ordered machine, you will assume that any imperfections you may notice are really things you do not understand. You will think of everything in the universe as fitting perfectly into that machine. You will think that immutable laws govern the formation of every new part of that machine to ensure that it fits the machine's requirements. And, although with delightful inconsistency—as Pope made his *Essay on Man* the basis of his satires—you will judge the success of any individual thing according to its ability to fit into the workings of the machine, your inconsistency will be concealed, for a time, by the influence of either original sin, if you are an orthodox Christian, or the corruptions of civilization, if you are a deist or a sentimentalist—not that there is much difference. Your values will be perfection, changelessness, uniformity, rationalism.

Now this mighty, static metaphysic, which had governed perilously the thoughts of men since the time of Plato, collapsed of its own internal inconsistencies in the late eighteenth century—or collapsed for some people. For most people it still remains the unrealized base for most of their values—intellectual, moral, social, aesthetic, and religious. But to the finer minds of the eighteenth and nineteenth centuries it was no longer tenable. There are a number of reasons why this should have been so. The principal cause was that all its implications had been worked out; they stood forth in all their naked inconsistency. It became impossible to accept a theodicy based upon it. More and more, thinkers began searching for a new system of explaining the nature of reality and the duties of men.

I shall omit the development of the new idea. The grand outlines have been magnificently sketched by Lovejoy, and the details are steadily being filled in. Rather, I shall present the new idea in its most radical form. Let us begin with the new metaphor. The new metaphor is not a machine; it is an organism. It is a tree, for example; and a tree is a good example, for a study of nineteenth-century literature reveals the continual recurrence of that image. Hence the new thought is organicism. Now the first quality of an organism is that it is not something made, it is something *being* made or growing. We have a philosophy of becoming, not a philosophy of being. Furthermore, the relation of its component parts is not that of the parts of a machine which have been made separately, i.e., separate entities in the mind of the deity, but the relation of leaves to stem to trunk to root to earth. Entities are an organic part of that which produced them. The existence of each part is made possible only by the existence of every other part. Relationships, not entities, are the object of contemplation and study.

Moreover, an organism has the quality of life. It does not develop additively; it grows organically. The universe is alive. It is not something made, a perfect machine; it grows. Therefore change becomes a positive value, not a negative value; change is not man's punishment, it is his opportunity. Anything that continues to grow, or change qualitatively, is not perfect, can, perhaps, never be perfect. Perfection ceases to be a positive value. Imperfection becomes a positive value. Since the universe is changing and growing, there is consequently a positive and radical intrusion of novelty into the world. That is, with the intrusion of each novelty, the fundamental character of the universe itself changes. We have a universe of emergents. If all these things be true, it therefore follows that there are no pre-existent patterns. Every work of art, for instance, creates a new pattern; each one has its own aesthetic law. It may have resemblances even in principle to previous works of art, but fundamentally it is unique. Hence come two derivative ideas. First, diversitarianism, not uniformitarianism, becomes the principle of both creation and criticism. The Romantics, for example, have been accused of confusing the genres of poetry. Why shouldn't they? The whole metaphysical foundation of the genres had been abandoned, or for some authors had simply disappeared. The second derivative is the idea of creative originality. True, the idea of originality had existed before, but in a different sense. Now the artist is original because he is the instrument whereby a genuine novelty, an emergent, is introduced into the world, not because he has come with the aid of genius a little closer to previously existent pattern, natural and divine.

In its radical form, dynamic organicism results in the idea that the history of the universe is the history of God creating himself. Evil is at last accounted for, since the history of the universe—God being imperfect to begin with—is the history of God, whether transcendent or immanent, ridding himself, by the evolutionary process, of evil. Of course, from both the old and the new philosophy, God could be omitted. Either can become a materialism.

In a metaphysical nutshell, the older philosophy grounded itself on the principle that nothing can come from nothing. The newer philosophy grounded itself on the principle that something *can* come from nothing, that an excess can come from a deficiency, that nothing succeeds like excess.

I have presented these ideas in a radical form to make them as clear as I can and to bring out in the strongest possible colors the contrast between the old and new methods of thought. Now I should like to apply them to Lovejoy and Wellek. Lovejoy stated that the three new ideas of Romantic thought and art were organicism, dynamism, and diversitarianism. He says that they are three separate and inconsistent ideas. I agree that they often appear separately, but I am convinced that they are all related to and derived from a basic or root metaphor, the organic metaphor of the structure of the universe. Strictly speaking, organicism includes dynamism, for an organism must grow or change qualitatively, but I prefer to use the term "dynamic organicism" in order to emphasize the importance of imperfection and change. Diversitarianism, of course, is in these terms a positive value; for the diversity of things and their uniqueness are proof of the constant intrusion of novelty in the past, the present, and the future.

Turning to Wellek and his three criteria, I have already included one, organicism; the other two are imagination and symbolism. Wellek means the creative imagination, and a little thought will show that the idea of the creative imagination is derived from dynamic organicism. If the universe is constantly in the process of creating itself, the mind of man, his imaginative power, is radically creative. The artist is that man with the power of bringing new artistic concepts into reality, just as the philosopher brings new ideas into reality. And the greatest man is the philosopher-poet, who, supremely gifted, simultaneously does both. Furthermore, the artist is the man who creates a symbol of truth. He can think metaphorically, and if the world is an organic structure only a statement with the organic complexity of the work of art can create an adequate symbol of it. And is this not the method of symbolism? In allegory, a symbolic unit preserves its meaning when taken from its context. The Cave of Error *is* the Cave of Error. There is a direct one-to-one relationship between any unit in the world of phenomena and any unit in the world of ideas. But in symbolism, a symbolic unit has power only because of its relationships to everything else in the work of art. Ahab has symbolical value because of the whale, and the whale because of Ahab. In symbolism the interrelationships of the symbolic units involved are equated with the interrelationships of a group of concepts. Let a series of 1, 2, 3, 4, etc., stand for a series of ideas in

the mind, and a similar series of a, b, c, d, etc., stand for a series of things in the real world or in the world of the concretizing imagination. Now in allegory, if "a" is a symbolic unit, it stands for "1," "b" for "2," and so on. Thus the Dragon in the *Faerie Queene,* Canto i of Book I, stands for Error, whether the Red Cross Knight is there or not, and the Knight, on one level of interpretation, stands for Holiness, whether the Dragon is there or not. But in symbolism, "a" or "b" or "c" has no direct relation to "1" or "2" or "3". Rather, the interrelationships among the first three have symbolic reference to the interrelationships among the second group of three. Moby-Dick has symbolic power only because Ahab is hunting him; in fact, he has symbolic power only because almost everything else in the book has symbolic power as well.

The now current though probably not widely accepted critical principle that a symbolic system is capable of an indefinite number of equally valid interpretations is itself a Romantic idea, in the sense that the work of art has no fixed or static meaning but changes with the observer in a relationship between the two which is both dialectical, or dynamic, and organic.

Thus we may conclude that Wellek's three criteria—organicism, imagination, and symbolism—are all derivable from the basic metaphor or concept of dynamic organicism.

There is yet another profoundly important idea which I have not so far mentioned, the idea of the unconscious mind, which appears in Wordsworth, in Coleridge, in Carlyle, and indeed all through the nineteenth and twentieth centuries. In 1830, in his magnificent essay "Characteristics," Carlyle says that the two big ideas of the century are dynamism and the unconscious mind. The idea of the unconscious mind goes back to Hartley, to Kant, to Leibniz, and is implicit in Locke. Indeed, it goes back to any poet who seriously talks about a muse. But it appears in full force only with the appearance of dynamic organicism. Best known to the English Romantics in the mechanistic associationism of Hartley, it became a central part of their thought when they made the mind radically creative. Heretofore the divine had communicated with man either directly through revelation or indirectly through the evidence of his perfect universe. But with God creating himself, with an imperfect but growing universe, with the constant intrusion of novelty into the world, how can there be any apprehension of truth? If reason is inadequate—because it is fixed and because historically it has failed—the truth can only be apprehended intuitively, imaginatively, spontaneously, with the whole personality, from the deep sources of the fountains that are within. The unconscious is really a postulate to the creative imagination, and as such continues today without the divine sanction as part of present-day critical theory. It is that part of the mind through which novelty enters into the personality and hence into the world in the form of art and ideas. We today conceive of the unconscious spatially as inside and beneath; the earlier Romantics conceived of it as outside and above. We descend into the imagination; they rose into it. The last method, of course, is the method of Transcendentalism.

Furthermore, . . . not only was the unconscious taken over from Locke and Kant and Hartley and converted into something radically creative, it also became an integral part of dynamic organicism because a number of the early Romantics proved it, as it were, empirically, by their own personal experience. It became to them proof of the validity of the new way of thinking. Hence also Romantic subjectivism, the artist watching his powers develop and novelty emerging from his unconscious mind.

What then is Romanticism? Whether philosophic, theologic, or aesthetic, it is the revolution in the European mind against thinking in terms of static mechanism and the redirection of the mind to thinking in terms of dynamic organicism. Its values are change, imperfection, growth, diversity, the creative imagination, the unconscious.

Perhaps the result of my remarks so far is to make a much larger group of determined skeptics on the subject of Romanticism. The proof of the Martini is in the drinking, and in the rest of what I have to say I hope to show not only that a group of literary works can be related in terms of the ideas I have given but also that particular literary works can be genuinely illuminated by these ideas, can be given richer content, can be more readily understood. And in addition I wish also to advance one more concept, the only one indeed to which I lay any claim of originality, for what I have already said is only an attempt to reconcile various ideas about Romanticism which seemed to be fairly close together and to develop them into some consistent whole, on the basis of Lovejoy's statement that the coming of Romanticism marked a great turn in the direction of European thought. For instance, Barzun's "desire and expectation of change" is an important part of my proposal; Stallknecht's "sentiment of being," i.e., of a living universe, is right at the heart of it; Harrold's ideas of growth are equally central. Nevertheless, the theory is still incomplete.

Dynamic organicism, manifested in literature in its fully developed form, with all its main derivative ideas, I have called "Radical Romanticism." To this term I should now like to add "Positive Romanticism," as a term useful in describing men and ideas and works of art in which dynamic organicism appears, whether it be incomplete or fully developed. But by itself "Positive Romanticism" for the purposes of understanding the Romantic movement is not only frequently useless; it is often worse than useless. It is often harmful. If some of my readers have been muttering, "What about Byron?" they are quite right in doing so. Positive Romanticism cannot explain Byron; Positive Romanticism is not enough. To it must be added the term "Negative Romanticism," and to that I now turn.

It may at first seem that I am here denying my basic aim of reducing the multiplicity of theories of Romanticism to a single theory, but this is not really so. Negative Romanticism is a necessary complement to Positive Romanticism, not a parallel or alternative to it, with which it must be reconciled. Briefly, Negative Romanticism is the expression of the attitudes, the feelings, and the ideas of a man who has left static mechanism but has not yet arrived at a reintegration of his thought and art in terms of dynamic organicism. I am here, of course, using a method of analysis which is now so common that one inhales it with the dust of our libraries, the method of analyzing the works of a man in terms of his personal development. Before we study any artist, we begin by establishing his canon and chronology. We *begin,* that is, by *assuming* that there is a development in his art. I hope I am not being merely tedious in pointing out that this method is in itself a particular application of one of the main ideas derived from dynamic organicism, or Positive Romanticism—the idea of evolution in the nineteenth-century sense. (pp. 3-16)

And now to define Negative Romanticism. I have, of course, taken the term from Carlyle's Everlasting No. As various individuals, according to their natures, and their emotional and intellectual depths, went through the transition from affirming the meaning of the cosmos in terms of static mechanism to affirming it in terms of dynamic organicism, they went through a period of doubt, of despair, of religious and social isolation, of the separation of reason and creative power. It was a period during which they saw neither beauty nor goodness in the universe, nor any significance, nor any rationality, nor indeed any order at all, not even an evil order. This is Negative Romanticism, the preliminary to Positive Romanticism, the period of *Sturm und Drang.* As the nineteenth century rolled on, the transition became much easier, for the new ideas were much more widely available. But for the early Romantics the new ideas had to be learned through personal and painful experience. The typical symbols of Negative Romanticism are individuals who are filled with guilt, despair, and cosmic and social alienation. They are often presented, for instance, as having committed some horrible and unmentionable and unmentioned crime in the past. They are often outcasts from men and God, and they are almost always wanderers over the face of the earth. They are Harolds, they are Manfreds, they are Cains. They are heroes of such poems as *Alastor.* But when they begin to get a little more insight into their position, as they are forced to develop historical consciousness, as they begin to seek the sources for their negation and guilt and alienation, they become Don Juans. That is, in *Don Juan* Byron sought objectivity by means of satire, and set out to trace in his poem the development of those attitudes that had resulted in himself. As I said earlier, Positive Romanticism cannot explain Byron, but Negative Romanticism can. Byron spent his life in the situation of Wordsworth after the rejection of Godwin and before his move to Racedown and Nether Stowey, of the Mariner alone on the wide, wide sea, of Teufelsdröckh subject to the Everlasting No and wandering through the Centre of Indifference.

It is the lack of this concept that involves Wellek's second article and much of Barzun's book, for all their admirable insights, in certain difficulties, in such a foredoomed attempt to find in figures who express Negative Romanticism and figures who express Positive Romanticism a common and unifying element. Theirs is the same difficulty as that with which Auden gets involved in *The Enchafèd Flood.* It is true that both Positive and Negative Romanticism often cause isolation of the personality, but, as Coleridge of these three men alone realized, Negative Romanticism causes isolation and despair because it offers no cosmic explanations, while Positive Romanticism offers cosmic explanations which are not shared by the society of which one is a part. To Arnold, "Not a having and a resting, but a growing and a becoming, is the character of perfection as culture conceives it." His ideas isolated him from Barbarians, Philistines, and Populace; they were impressed but they did not follow; for they could not comprehend, so far were his fundamental attitudes separated from theirs. Picasso has in his painting expressed profoundly the results of the freedom that Romanticism has given to the creative imagination, but he is detested by most people who have seen his Cubist or post-Cubist paintings—as well as by a great many who have not. He is at home in the universe, but not in his society.

My proposal is now complete. This theory does, I firmly believe, what such a theory must do. It gets us inside of various works of art, and it shows the relevance of one work of art to another. Consider Beethoven's Fifth Symphony. It builds to a triumphant close. Unlike the symphonies of Haydn and most of those of Mozart, its last movement, not its first or second, is the most important and the most fully developed, for it is an affirmation which is the result of a tremendous struggle. Between the third and fourth movements is a bridge passage which repeats the rhythm and the harmonies of the opening theme, and the whole work is developed from germinal themes, ideas from which are derived the themes of subsequent movements. It is a symphony developmental and organic in construction. It is the record of a process, of an experience. It is a symbol of the cosmos conceived of as dynamic organism.

The same insights can be extended to painting, to impressionism, for example, with its evocation and record of a particular moment; or to modern architecture, especially to the work of Wright, with his lifelong search for an "organic architecture" of houses that are part of their sites, with living rooms and gardens which interpenetrate. But I cannot here offer a full history of the development of modern culture. Rather, I wish to make one final suggestion, to issue a warning to anyone who may be taken with these ideas enough to try to employ them.

Although Negative and then Positive Romanticism developed by reaction out of the static-mechanistic-uniformitarian complex, with its cosmic Toryism, its sentimentalism, and its Deism, they were also superimposed upon it. At any point in nineteenth- or twentieth-century culture it is possible to take a cross section and find all three actively at work. The past 150 years or so must be conceived as a dramatic struggle, sometimes directly between Positive Romanticism and static, mechanistic thought, sometimes three-cornered. It is a struggle between minds and within minds. It is seen today in the profound disparity between what is sometimes called high art and popular art; it is expressed in the typical modern cultural phenomena of the avant-garde, which is as modern as Wordsworth and Coleridge. It appeared in the struggle over the "packing" of the Supreme Court and in the wearisome but still vital quarrels about progressive education. It appears in the antagonism between our relativistic critics and our absolutistic critics. It appears in the theological struggle between the theology of such a man as Charles

Raven and the proponents of the "theology of crisis." A very pure Positive Romanticism is at the heart of Ruth Benedict's *Patterns of Culture;* her ideal of a good society is organic, dynamic, and diversitarian. In short, the history of ideas and the arts in the nineteenth and twentieth centuries is the history of the dramatic struggle among three opposing forces: static mechanism, Negative Romanticism, and Positive Romanticism. In this drama, to me the hero is dynamic and diversitarian organicism, and I think Goethe and Beethoven and Coleridge and the other founders of the still vital Romantic tradition—a tradition often repudiated by those who are at the very heart of it, and understandably—have still much to say to us, are not mere intellectual and aesthetic curiosities. Nevertheless, I am aware that to many scholars and thinkers, Positive Romanticism is the villain, responsible for all the ills of our century. The drama may indeed turn out to be a tragedy, but if it does, it is because static mechanism persists in staying alive.

Of course, the fact that my attitude towards the continuing and future usefulness of Positive Romanticism may not after all be justified is not essential to my argument, or even germane to it. I ask only that my readers take under serious consideration, and test in their studies, in their reading, and in their classrooms the theories about Romanticism which I have outlined. I trust that many of

---

George Santayana praises Romanticism:

The great merit of the romantic attitude in poetry, and of the transcendental method in philosophy, is that they put us back at the beginning of our experience. They disintegrate convention, which is often cumbrous and confused, and restore us to ourselves, to immediate perception and primordial will. That, as it would seem, is the true and inevitable starting-point. Had we not been born, had we not peeped into this world, each out of his personal eggshell, this world might indeed have existed without us, as a thousand undiscoverable worlds may now exist; but for us it would not have existed. This obvious truth would not need to be insisted on but for two reasons: one that conventional knowledge, such as our notions of science and morality afford, is often top-heavy; it asserts and imposes on us much more than our experience warrants,—our experience, which is our only approach to reality. The other reason is the reverse or counterpart of this; for conventional knowledge often ignores and seems to suppress parts of experience no less actual and important for us than those parts on which the conventional knowledge itself is reared. The public world is too narrow for the soul, as well as too mythical and fabulous. Hence the double critical labour and reawakening which romantic reflection is good for,—to cut off the dead branches and feed the starving shoots. This philosophy, as Kant said, is a cathartic: it is purgative and liberating; it is intended to make us start afresh and start right.

George Santayana, "Romanticism," in his
Little Essays, *edited by Santayana and*
Logan Pearsall Smith, Scribners, 1934.

them will find these ideas useful, even though they with-hold final assent. (pp. 21-6)

Morse Peckham, "Toward a Theory of Ro-manticism," in his The Triumph of Romanti-cism, *University of South Carolina Press, 1970, pp. 3-26.*

Morse Peckham

[*In the following excerpt, Peckham updates his theory of Negative Romanticism presented in his earlier essay excerpted above.*]

If order is perceived as structured into the empirical world—natural and social—value (i.e., what is variously referred to as "meaning" or "purpose") and identity are also thus seen. Consequently, the perception of order is felt to be interchangeable with the perception of value, and the perception of both is accompanied by the emergence of identity, perceived in terms of a socially structured role. Nevertheless, because of the disparity between an orienta-tion and the data it is called upon to organize, the individ-ual, if he is to adapt successfully to his environment, *must* perceive a disparity between the order affirmed by orienta-tion and his actual experience of randomness. In the West-ern tradition there have been two primary pseudo-explanations for this disparity. The first is the myth of par-adise and the Fall. That it is an emotionally and pragmati-cally satisfactory resolution is evidenced by its continuing vitality. An environment such that the orientation corre-sponds exactly with the experienced world would be para-dise, a place of pure order, pure value, and never-threatened identity, that is, salvation. From this point of view the reason for the Fall is of no importance. The possi-bilities for explaining it are infinite. The important ele-ment is the contrast between the prelapsarian state and the postlapsarian, between perfect orientation and the world as we experience it. The Platonic solution, at least after the Neo-Platonists had their way with it, exhibits the same pattern, nonhistorically. A real world of pure order and value is set against the experienced, shadowy, imitated world, of disorder and little or no value. Thus the myth of the Fall and the Neoplatonic epistemological myth can be perfectly synthesized by containing time in eternity. The Middle Ages were founded on a world hypothesis ac-cording to which the world of space and time is disordered and of only partial and occasional value, in which even perceived order can be used as a temptation by Satan, the spirit that denies value; the moral task is to maintain as much order and value as possible until death, or the last judgment, when the individual would either re-enter para-dise, a world of total order, value, and salvation, or identi-ty, or be forever plunged into its opposite. Since such a scheme embraced orientation and perception, order and disorder, good and evil, in an all-embracing orientation, it exhibited remarkable stability, and continues to do so.

However, the Renaissance brought out a different atti-tude; in the older scheme the source of the order was reve-lation and the means of its transmission was the Church, through its redemptive power. The progressive organiza-tion and accumulation of knowledge in medieval science and philosophy led to a situation in which some individu-als began to believe that it was possible to arrive at the vi-sion of order outside of the Church, and even outside of religion. The human mind, it was decided by a few, could achieve the truth of revelation without the instrumentality of ecclesiastical transmission and sanction. A revival of Neo-Platonism was the consequence, or rather the separa-tion of Neo-Platonism from its Judeo-Christian twin. Re-cent investigations have shown the Neo-Platonic back-ground of both Galileo and Newton; and Descartes's deci-sion to think through the world, since order was thought of as discovered and not ascribed, and value and identity as given, led, with the aid of Galileo and Newton, to a wholly new orientation. The sensational results have been admirably described and the roots investigated in the re-markable contributions to the history of science made in the past ten years, and for the literary scholar in Marjorie Nicolson's *Mountain Gloom and Mountain Glory: The De-velopment of the Aesthetics of the Infinite* and particularly in Ernest Tuveson's *The Imagination as a Means of Grace: Locke and the Aesthetics of Romanticism*. The new orien-tation was that this is not a fallen world, nor a shadowy world, but that order and value are structured into the perceived world, and that identity is given with the exis-tence of each biological human entity. Society is a natural emergent, not the result of divine fiat. The disparity be-tween the orientation and the experience lies in the fact of our ignorance—a notion easily demonstrated—not in the fact that we are faced with a corrupt world. Man is natu-rally part of that order; the moral task is to restore his originally perfect adaptation by exploiting his civilization and knowledge. Since the natural order grants perfect ad-aptation, what has been lost through ignorance can be re-gained through knowledge. Or—and here was the rub—since man is the product of nature, he is not in fact mal-adapted at the present time. His task is to adapt himself morally and emotionally to the order in which we now find ourselves. In either case observable order assures that value is structured into the universe. However, in the long run neither perspective offers any means to make moral discriminations. Down one can be seen Soame Jenyns, down the other, Robespierre. Rigorously interpreted, whatever moral decision you make, you cannot be wrong; you can only be ignorant. If you wish to persuade people that they are in a perfect world, you are quite justified in your choice of means, since by definition the ends, which will be arrived at by a natural process, have order and value structured in them; and De Sade's frustration emerges: it is impossible to perform an unnatural act. Re-cent studies in Enlightenment pessimism have shown that as the eighteenth century wore on, more and more En-lightenment figures became aware of the difficulty. An im-portant consequence for students of literature was the steady development in intensity and quantity of sentimen-talism. Its original source was the necessity to discharge the tension consequent upon the affirmation that the world is radiant with order and value which any mind free from superstition, tyranny, and priestcraft could arrive at for itself, and the inconsistent perception that it is not. An aesthetic stimulus came to be valued for its power to dis-charge that tension in tears and enthusiasm. Further, the more the basic instability became apparent, the more ne-cessity there was to fall back upon an emotional affirma-tion of order, value, and identity as qualities structured into the real world. From this point of view Ossian was a typical late Enlightenment phenomenon. The enthusiastic poet and the man of feeling dominated the scene. As Professor Tuveson has so well demonstrated, Nature, through the exercise of the imagination, redeemed man. If you wish, as many do, to use the term "Romanticism" to refer to this Enlightenment and enthusiasm and sentimentalism and natural redemption, I have no objection. One long tradition has always called it Romanticism. But nothing could be more different from what I am talking about when I use that word. When the crash came, when a tiny minority of Enlightenment personalities, themselves a cultural minority, saw through Enlightenment pretensions and saw that it is impossible to maintain them, and when the Enlightenment was put to the test in the French Revolution and its superficiality revealed, a major cultural break occurred.

The logical possibilities of identifying Nature with order and value had been exhausted. If it is not true that order and value once were in this world and no longer are, or that they are outside the world, if it is not true that order and value are in the world, where are they? They do not exist at all, cries in anguish the Negative Romantic. But it is impossible for people at a high level of culture and civilization to endure for long such total disorientation. In such a situation was (and still is) any individual who enters the Negative Romantic stage, unless he can turn back to a pre-Enlightenment orientation or successfully repress his doubts about the Enlightenment construct. If he can do neither, he turns the world inside out.

Long ago George Herbert Mead said that Romanticism is marked by the separation of the role from the self. With the collapse of the Enlightenment there also collapses the natural social structure, and with it the possibility of playing a role. Hence the social alienation which accompanies the cosmic isolation, or loss of relatedness to the perceived world. The first step at reconstituting value, then, is to strip bare the self, or, more accurately, to invent the self, to conceptualize the sense of identity. To survive, one asserts pure identity as the basic datum. As two recent studies have pointed out, Schelling and Wordsworth attempted to assert the self as real and the world as a symbol of value [David Ferry, *The Limits of Mortality*, 1960, and E. D. Hirsch, Jr., *Wordsworth and Schelling*, 1960]. Wordsworth eventually regressed, for such a position is a compromise. To be sure, there is all the difference between perceiving the world as evidence of divine order and perceiving it as a symbol of divine value, and finding order in the act of perception itself, but the latter, or symbolic, perception is extremely unstable, since it really asserts the existence of two sources of value and order, the self and the world. Rather, the more stable solution is to perceive the world as symbol of the self, and order and value as projected upon the world by the self. I think Professor Tuveson is in error, therefore, when he thinks of eighteenth-century Enlightenment and enthusiastic "early Romanticism" as the predecessor of "high Romanticism" (*my* Romanticism), which is its fulfillment. Rather, *my* Romantics used the same words, but sang them to a different tune. Imagination is a means of grace, to be sure, but Nature does not redeem man. Rather, man, through the exercise of the imagination, redeems Nature. Value enters the world through the self, which is not supported by any perceptible social or cosmic order, and the self projects upon the world an order which serves to symbolize that self-generated value. To be sure, for a time, and for some, the self was seen as the portal of the divine, a mythological symbolization for the sense of value. This was the transcendental stage of Romanticism; but side by side, and eventually superseding it, was a nonmetaphysical realization that the only conceivable source of value was the necessity for the individual self to create it in order to maintain itself. In short, the self does not emerge through the perception of order and value in the world; rather, order and value emerge from the perception of the self. Nature is not the source of value, but the occasion for projecting it.

Man therefore redeems the world; and since in the poet the imagination is predominant, the poet is the primary source of value—in traditional language, redemption. The Romantic poet thus takes upon himself the role of Christ; he becomes Christ, and he is himself his own redeemer and the model for the redemption of mankind. Eventually this task of the artist is extended to every human being. Further, if man is to redeem the world, it is only this world which can be redeemed. After yielding up moral questions in despair, because they are ultimately unsolvable by the Enlightenment orientation, Wordsworth grasped both horns of his dilemma. Nature is the source of both disturbance and equilibrium, of disorientation and orientation. To see what a gulf has here been crossed it is sufficient to call to mind that, to the Enlightenment, Nature was the source of orientation only. Hence the frequent marriages of heaven and hell in the Romantic tradition. Kubla Khan's garden includes both. Here or nowhere we find our home. Since it is this world which must be redeemed, the first task of the Romantic is to face fully the horror, the brutality, and the evil which before had been either thought away or dismissed or regarded as either temporary or ultimately unreal. The flower of value must be plucked not on the sunny mountaintop, but in the very abyss. The worship of *sorrow* is divine. The world must be redeemed, in its absurdity and ugliness, as well as in its order and beauty. Hence Romanticism leads directly to the realism of Dickens and Balzac and so down to the present. It is the Romantic's tradition that is really tough-minded. To him nothing is so beautiful as fact, nor does anything offer such sweet bones to gnaw on as the empirical world itself, the only world we can know, for the self can only be symbolized, not known. And hence the profoundest way to symbolize it is to recognize and assert its existence in another; and this emphatic assertion is the basis of Romantic social morality.

From this fundamental percept of the self as the source of order flows Romanticism's essentially antimetaphysical character. With and without the aid of Kant, an orientation is now seen not as a discovery but as a projection. Thus a metaphysical theory is thought of as an instrument, not as a reality, not as something in Nature, but as something imposed upon it. On the one hand it is conceived as an instrument for symbolizing the self or value; on the other it is thought of as an epistemological instrument. Further consequences flow from this. If an orientation is only instrumentally, not constitutively, valid, it is useful only temporarily. But then value, identity, and order can be experienced only temporarily, in moments of illumination, spots of time. Further, the Romantic knows from history, his own and man's, that the great human temptation is to regard an orientation as final and that succumbing leads to disaster, for Christianity and the Enlightenment had ultimately collapsed. Consequently his moral task is to break down an orientation once it has been fully realized. His only means is self-disorientation. Hence the judgment often made that the Romantic values emotional disturbance for its own sake. Not at all; he values it as a means to break down an orientation which, as a human being, he is tempted to preserve but, as a Romantic human being, he knows by definition is inadequate. As Browning implied, the only failure is success. Hence throughout the nineteenth century the use of drugs, alcohol, sex, and Asiatic theologies as means of deliberately dislocating the senses so that new worlds may emerge. Only with the breakthrough into modern art did the Romantic artist and thinker learn how to break down an orientation without partially disintegrating his personality.

From this perspective it is possible to develop a more adequate explanation of the presence of dynamic organicism in the Romantic tradition than the one I proposed several years ago. To begin with, it is now apparent—and perhaps was then, though not to me—that organicism is a product of the Enlightenment, that the increasing dependence on the natural world was bound to lead to conceiving the cosmos on the model of an organism rather than of a machine, and did. Further, the values of diversity, change, growth, and uniqueness, derived from organicism, are mainly late Enlightenment values, though, to be sure, relatively rare. From this point of view Herder, for example, appears as an Enlightenment figure, not a Romantic one. The organic episode in the development of Romanticism occurred partly because it was in the culture and could be used to symbolize the subjective experience of the Romantic personality, the emergence of the self, partly because it was a novelty to many Romantics, who did not realize its Enlightenment origins. Nevertheless, to the Romantic it is always an instrument, while to nineteenth-century Enlightenment thinking it is constitutive. Although it was the most important metaphysical episode in the history of Romanticism, it was abandoned, as all Romantic world hypotheses are abandoned, for by definition they are inadequate; and this process continues until Romanticism learns that it can do entirely without constitutive metaphysics and can use any metaphysic or world hypothesis as a supreme fiction.

To conclude with a phrase from Wallace Stevens is, I think, appropriate, for I still believe what I said years ago and what is now, in fact, becoming almost a platitude, that modern art is the triumph of Romanticism, that modern culture, in its vital areas, is a Romantic culture, and that nothing has yet replaced it. Since the logic of Romanticism is that contradictions must be included in a single orientation, but without pseudo-reconciliations, Romanticism is a remarkably stable and fruitful orientation. For the past 175 years the Romantic has been the tough-

minded man, determined to create value and project order to make feasible the pure assertion of identity, determined to assert identity in order to engage with reality simply because it is there and because there is nothing else, and knowing eventually that his orientations are adaptive instruments and that no orientation is or can be final. The Romantic artist does not escape from reality; he escapes into it. We may expect that the present revival of interest in nineteenth-century Romanticism among younger scholars and artists will continue, for, as a consequence of the current widespread breakdown of the Enlightenment tradition, Romanticism is at last beginning to receive an adequate response. (pp. 28-35)

> *Morse Peckham, "Toward a Theory of Romanticism: II. Reconsiderations," in his* The Triumph of Romanticism, *University of South Carolina Press, 1970, pp. 27-35.*

ORIGINS OF THE MOVEMENT

Lilian R. Furst

[In the following excerpt, Furst examines the developments in eighteenth-century literature that prepared for the Romantic movement.]

The roots of the Romantic movement lie in the eighteenth century in a series of interlocking trends of cumulative effect: the decline of the Neo-classical system led to the questionings of the Enlightenment, which in turn was conducive to the infiltration of the new notions current in the latter half of the century. Although the appellation 'pre-Romantic' is generally reserved for certain writers and thinkers who were direct forerunners of the Romantics in ideas or style (e.g. Rousseau, Young, Macpherson, Bernardin de Saint-Pierre), in a wider sense the term is appropriate to the entire line of development in the eighteenth century, in so far as it paved the way for the crystallization of the Romantic movement. A major reorientation of critical standards and methods was an essential pre-condition for the blossoming of Romanticism, and this took place in the course of the eighteenth century. Thus the Romantic movement, though it effected a literary revolution at its decisive break-through, was in itself in fact the product of a protracted process of evolution. The direction and form of this evolution points to the nature of the Romantic revolution.

• • • • •

The period that equated 'romantic' with 'chimerical' and 'ridiculous' was that of Neo-classicism, which was at its height in the seventeenth century, notably in France. Since the revival of Classical standards in the Renaissance, the main concern had been the establishment, elaboration and spread of a view of literature inherited from Greek and Roman antiquity. The chief sources of aesthetic ideas were, for over two centuries, Aristotle, Horace, Quintilian and Longinus. The major topic of discussion was the revival and imitation of the Ancients, who enjoyed unlimited authority and inspired a strong craving to conform to their patterns. This is most evident in France, where the Neo-classical attitude was codified by critics as powerful as Boileau and where the strict observance of the three unities was considered of paramount importance. Moreover, the passage of time brought an increasing emphasis on a merely repetitive formalism, a hollow clinging to the outer practices of Neo-classicism without any deeper understanding of its aims such as had inspired the great poets of the seventeenth century. This dogmatism was buttressed in France by the dominance of an absolute monarchy allied to the Catholic Church so that the literary as well as the political and religious regime was close to totalitarianism. In the England of parliamentary rule and easy-going Protestantism there was never the same degree of conformity; the approach to both political organization and literary taste was far more flexible, not to say unsystematic, partly no doubt as a result of Shakespeare's disregard of the Neo-classical canons. It is, nevertheless, worth recalling that the early eighteenth century could and did dismiss *Hamlet* on the grounds of its 'incorrectness'.

The authoritarianism of the Neo-classical period stemmed from an unqualified belief in the powers of the mind, the intellect, in short, reason. Descartes in his famous 'Cogito ergo sum' deduced the very existence of man from his powers of thought; in Germany the philosopher Christian Wolff conceived God as 'reiner Verstand' ('pure reason') and the world as a mechanism that functioned logically according to set laws, while in England Pope maintained, in the *Essay on Man* 'that REASON alone countervails all the other faculties'. The scientific discoveries of the age, specially those of Newton, helped to foster the conviction that all things were knowable, and what is more, knowable by means of rational understanding. This total commitment to, indeed trust in, reason was what Isaiah Berlin had very aptly called the backbone of European thought for generations—the backbone which the Romantics were to crack.

In the arts, as in politics, ethics and morals, the Neo-classicists hoped to do what Newton had achieved in physics: to discern universal truths and establish standards of lasting validity. Hence they sought to formulate once and for all the basic 'laws' of aesthetics, the rules of writing which, properly observed, would guarantee a correct (and therefore necessarily good) composition, just as a recipe, carefully followed, will produce a fine dish. The artist, like the scientist, was expected to operate by calculation, judgement and reason, for, to borrow La Bruyère's revealing comparison, the making of a book was considered a task like the making of a clock. Art was thus conceived as a reasonable and reasoned imitation of reality, the artist as a skilful manipulator, and the ultimate aim of the whole exercise as an intellectual statement of moral precepts, in which pleasure was no more than a means to an end. This view is well illustrated by Gottsched's instructions for 'the making of a good tragedy' from his *Kritische Dichtkunst (Ars Poetica)* of 1730:

> Der Poet wählet sich einen moralischen Lehr-
> satz, den er seinen Zuschauern auf eine sinnliche

Art einprägen will. Dazu ersinnt er sich eine allgemeine Fabel, daraus die Wahrheit seines Satzes erhellet. Hiernächst sucht er in der Historie solche berühmte Leute, denen etwas Ähnliches begegnet ist, und von diesen entlehnet er die Namen vor die Personen seiner Fabel, um derselben also ein Ansehen zu geben. Er erdenket sodann alle Umstände dazu, um die Hauptfabel recht wahrscheinlich zu machen, und das werden die Zwischenfabeln oder Episodia genannt. Dieses teilt er denn in fünf Stücke ein, die ungefähr gleich gross sind, und ordnet sie so, dass natürlicherweise das letztere aus dem vorhergehenden fliesset, bekümmert sich aber weiter nicht, ob alles in der Historie so vorgegangen oder ob alle Nebenpersonen wirklich so und nicht anders geheissen.

(Let the poet first choose a moral precept which he wants to impress on his audience by means of the senses. Then he invents a general story to illustrate the truth of his precept. Next he looks in history for famous people to whom something similar has happened, and from them he borrows names for the characters in his story in order to give it a semblance of reality. After this he thinks up all the attendant circumstances necessary to make the main story really probable, and these are called the sub-plots or episodes. He then divides his material into five pieces, all of approximately equal length, and arranges them so that each section follows from the preceding one, but he does not bother further whether everything corresponds to the historical happenings, nor whether the subsidiary characters bore these or other names.)

That this conception of art and of the artist's role was in the long run untenable is self-evident, whatever arguments may be advanced in its defence. The weaknesses of Neo-classical aesthetics are only too numerous: its view of art was extreme in its weighting towards the rational, simplified to the point of standardization and so rigid as to induce sterility, or at least a repetition of a fixed pattern. It had also many contradictions concealed in its system, as Wellek has pointed out in his lucid and fair assessment of the Neo-classical position in the first chapter of his *History of Modern Criticism,* and as these contradictions were opened up, there was a growing unease with the doctrine as a whole. Its fabric began to dissolve as men became increasingly conscious of the vast areas which it had chosen to ignore completely. This in fact was its most damning defect, that it took virtually no account of the *irrational* aspects of the creative process: what we call rather vaguely 'inspiration', the inner impetus of the artist, and the instinctive response on the part of the reader. In keeping with this omission, the imagination was relegated to a very minor role because it was considered a mere caprice, incapable of producing a judicious poem. Its function was almost exclusively decorative: the addition of 'wit' to truths already known. Thus Gray, when asked by an aspiring poet how to turn a flat piece of prose into a poem, advised him to 'twirl it a little into an apophthegm, stick a flower in it, gild it with a costly expression'. Far from being the mainspring of poetry, the imagination was no more than a storehouse of images in some remote attic of the brain.

The imitative, rationalistic view of art offered no real scope for the individual imagination: this was the cardinal source of its inadequacy and the eventual cause of its decline in the eighteenth century.

Pre-Romanticism is inspired by a real revulsion from all that Neo-classicism was thought to stand for: dull rules, superficial elegance, formality, orderliness, finite views, artificiality, convention, didacticism, courtly civilization, the preservation of the *status quo*.

—Lilian R. Furst

The dissolution of the Neo-classical system meant more than the replacement of one set of aesthetics by another. Neo-classicism had not only been the dominant attitude for a considerable period, and had enjoyed a veneration reflected from its Classical antecedents. It had also offered men a coherent, stable view of the world, derived from the certainty of a well-established order in the universe, thereby giving to literature too a sure frame of reference. With the abandonment of the old system, its sense of security was lost in life as in art. This is a break of such far-reaching consequences that its effects, even today, can hardly be overestimated. Our relativism, our ambivalence, our hesitations of judgement, our unwillingness (or inability?) to settle on any firm standards—all these are, in the last resort, developments from that crucial jettisoning of the Neo-classical definites and the tentative questionings of the Enlightenment. The objective order was slowly and surely displaced by a principle of subjective reference.

• • • • •

The dawn of the Enlightenment was like the opening of shutters that had been tightly clamped down. The image of increasing light is very appropriately suggested in its name in the three major European languages: Enlightenment, *Lumières* and *Aufklärung,* of which the latter two also imply the idea of light and clarity (*'lumière'* and *'klar'*). This is apposite in that the essence of the Enlightenment is a quest for new light on issues that had become stereotyped. What had hitherto been accepted (for instance, the absolute validity of the three unities in drama) was now questioned as the basic Neo-classical assumptions were re-examined in an attempt to separate the chaff from the grain. This process of critical assessment was a slow one, and it was still founded on a respect for reason. There was neither blatant defiance of the Neo-classical canons nor a wholesale introduction of startlingly new ideas; the shift of emphasis was reasoned and reasoning and the mood was one of cautious compromise. The change of tone is, however, unmistakable: from the old dogmatism to a far greater flexibility that was ready to admit into aesthetic discussion certain notions (e.g. genius, beauty, phantasy) beyond the domain of reason.

During the Enlightenment these factors came to be recognized as an integral part of the work of art.

The pace and extent of the advance during the Enlightenment was directly related to the strength of the Neo-classical conventions. Thus it was slowest in France, the land of Descartes, where the long-established traditions were so deeply entrenched as to persist far into the eighteenth century. As late as 1799 La Harpe, in his *Cours de littérature ancienne et moderne* still presented a codified summary of the old outlook with its characteristic insistence on the eternal principles, the rules of literature. Voltaire too, in spite of his political radicalism, was a conservative in literary matters, looking back with a nostalgic admiration to the age of Racine. Though opposed to excessive rationalism and summary judgements according to immutable criteria, Voltaire did stress the need for good taste, moderation, decorum, what was called *bienséance* in art. His concessions are grudging: in admitting 'enthusiasm' into his *Dictionnaire philosophique,* he demands that it must always be 'reasonable', i.e. held in check by an intellectual control. When he wrote to a friend in 1753: 'Je n'estime la poésie qu'autant qu'elle est l'ornement de la raison' ('I value poetry only in so far as it is an ornament of reason'), he revealed the order of priorities in his mind, and there can be no doubt that reason headed the list. It was by no means as simple for Diderot, who put forward many progressive ideas in the prefaces to *Le Fils naturel* (1757) and *Le Père de famille* (1758). In place of the lofty type of tragedy hitherto customary and upheld by Voltaire, Diderot here advocated 'domestic' tragedy, in which realistic devices could be used to intensify the emotional effect. Moreover, Diderot extolled the power of genius over the authority of the rules, useful though these could be in an age of decadence. On the whole he considered rationalization to be detrimental to poetry, and in *Le Rêve de d'Alembert* (*The Dream of d'Alembert,* 1769) he seems to be hinting at a theory of imagination as a perception of hidden analogies. Had he developed or even only sustained these notions, Diderot would have been in the forefront of the Enlightenment. Indeed *Le Neveu de Rameau* (1762) presents the Enlightenment's own profoundest self-criticism in its confrontation between the eighteenth century's right-minded conformist sage and the free-flowing demonic inventiveness of the social parasite, the marginal man, who foreshadows both the Romantic hero and the modern anti-hero. As he grew older, however, partly under the government's threats to radical writers, Diderot became increasingly circumspect and prudent. His final position is baffling: he appears unable to choose between two worlds, fascinated by Shakespeare, yet faithful to the native creed. Diderot's ambiguous attitude is in many ways symptomatic of eighteenth-century France, of a period of transition that no longer wholeheartedly espoused the ideals of the previous century without, however, going so far as to abandon them. It is no coincidence that the term *Lumières* has relatively little currency in France. The timidity of its Enlightenment, its comparative backwardness in emancipating itself from the Neo-classical system were to prove important factors in shaping the character of the French Romantic movement.

The Enlightenment was a time of complex countercurrents in English literature too. While it is tempting to emphasize the many departures from outworn theories and practices, it is well to remember that this was also the age of Johnson. His massive personality looms large, and if not reactionary, he was stoutly conservative in his basically rationalistic views, representing a position not unlike that of Voltaire in France. Reason in fact continued to enjoy considerable prestige, specially in the attenuated guise of reasonableness, which was tantamount to sound common sense. Herein lies perhaps a typically English example of compromise: whereas in France the rules were arbitrarily imposed as a *conditio sine qua non* of art, in England they were considered the outcome of good sense and sound reason rather than absolute authority. Consequently they became for the French a tyrannical yoke, which could only be cast off eventually by outright rebellion, while in England they were continuously tempered and modified to fit changing conceptions of what was reasonable practice. Even Pope conceded in his *Essay on Criticism* (1711) that

> Those RULES of old discovered, not devis'd,
> Are nature still, but nature methodiz'd.

Dryden went much further when he advocated that rules should be stretched or broken in preference to sacrificing any great beauty. This is a most important opinion because it shows the emergence of a new approach in literary criticism: the evaluation of a work of art by positive aesthetic standards, i.e. the appreciation of its beauties, rather than by the negative, pedantic yardstick of counting its infringements of the rules. This new attitude, in turn, discouraged too strict a formalism, and there were numerous protests against making poetry 'a mere mechanical art' as well as against over-much moralizing didacticism. The Neo-classical tenets were thus questioned sooner and more radically in England than in France, and they were more readily refashioned because they had never achieved the same intransigent power as in the France of the seventeenth century. The English could and did look back to their pre-Restoration heritage, to Shakespeare and the Elizabethans, who provided models quite different from the Classical tradition. There was, therefore, a far greater freedom, range and variety in Augustan writing than in the comparable period in France. Elegance, moderation and correctness were indeed highly prized; but at the same time there is also evidence of a certain agility in both thought and expression that is the very epitome of the Enlightenment. The England of the mid-eighteenth century was clearly open to new ideas.

This is even more true of Germany, partly because it had at this point nothing in its history comparable to Shakespeare and the Elizabethans in England or the French 'golden age' of Corneille, Racine, Molière, etc. At the start of the Enlightenment Germany was very much the poor relation in Europe, a fragmentary patchwork of small states without a unifying cultural centre, economically backward, impoverished, still suffering from the backwash of the Thirty Years' War. In many respects the state of affairs in Germany in the first half of the eighteenth century is the antithesis to that in France: on one side of the Rhine a proud awareness of a brilliant past, leading naturally to a reluctance to depart from the practices that had produced so glorious a harvest; whereas on the opposite bank,

Drawing of Friedrich Hölderlin by Franz K. Hiemer, 1792.

little sense of achievement in the past, and consequently a far greater willingness to experiment with new ideas and techniques. For in the long run it was, paradoxically, the initial backwardness of Germany that was to make her the leader of the Romantic movement in Europe, where France, with her powerful Classical tradition, lagged behind. The failure of Gottsched's attempt to introduce the Neo-classical system into Germany proved fortunate; firstly because it meant that there was no burden of accepted practice to hinder progress, and secondly because Gottsched's extreme views provoked the opposition of Bodmer and Breitinger. Not that these two Swiss critics were particularly revolutionary in their ideas; their *Kritische Dichtkunst (Ars Poetica)* of 1739 is still redolent of Neo-classical attitudes, but there is a distinct advance in the recognition that poetry springs not from the intellect but from the spirit and the imagination. Bodmer even had some inkling of the creative powers of the imagination, which he called more potent than 'alle Zauberer der Welt' ('all the magicians in the world'). By an interesting coincidence that phrase dates from the same year, 1741, when Hume maintained in his essay *Of the Standard of Taste* that 'to check the sallies of the imagination, and to reduce every expression to geometrical truth and exactness, would be the most contrary to the laws of criticism.' The questioning note of critical reassessment is as plain in Hume as in Bodmer and Breitinger.

Nowhere is this more evident than in the criticism of Lessing, who appears the very incarnation of the Enlightenment. Drawing on his profound knowledge of the Classics, Lessing was able to analyse their actual practices and to compare them with modern usage. The best example of this method is in section XLVI of the *Hamburgische Dramaturgie,* where he demonstrates the sensible, even profitable application of the unities in Classical drama as against the dogmatic adherence of the French to rules that became senseless with the abolition of the Chorus. The Neo-classical tenets are here not merely questioned, but made to seem absurd and hypocritical. And Lessing's criticism is so convincing because he is eminently reasonable in the logical sequence of his thought and the close-knit structure of his style. These are not the wild shots of an angry opponent, but the devastatingly thorough attack of the moderate man, very sure in his aim. Nor was Lessing just a destructive critic; each of his onslaughts has its complement of constructive suggestions. For instance, the section on the observance of the unities points to the significance of the 'irregular' English drama, adding the comment: 'Möchten meinetwegen Voltaires und Maffeis *Mérope* acht Tage dauren und an sieben Orten in Griechenland spielen! Möchten sie aber nur die Schönheiten haben, die mich diese Pedantereien vergessen machen' ('For all I care, Voltaire's and Maffei's *Mérope* could go on for eight days and be set in seven different places in Greece! But would that they were of a beauty to make me forget these pedantic considerations'). This implies the same vital change in critical standards as Dryden's identical preference of great beauty over the rules.

With its questionings the Enlightenment achieved emancipation from the authoritarianism of the Neo-classical creed. The advances were perhaps still only modest, but the trend is clear enough: away from the neat, finite, regular schemes of the old system towards a growing appreciation of the irregular beauties of the irrational imagination.

• • • • •

While the old was disintegrating under the questionings of the Enlightenment, the new was already appearing in the works of those writers of the mid- and later eighteenth century now known as 'Pre-Romantics'. This is an awkward portmanteau term, used as vaguely as 'romantic' itself, and, of course, meaningful only in relation to the major movement which it pre-figured in various ways. As a critical term it is useful to denote the many innovations in attitudes, ideas and techniques introduced at this time as part of the tentative search for something to replace the Neo-classical system of aesthetics and style of writing. In its positive beginnings Pre-Romanticism is complementary to the Enlightenment which was primarily directed towards a critical assessment of past, received notions. At some points the two trends interlock, as in the enthusiasm for Shakespeare and in the growing importance attached to the imagination of the genius. But whereas the Enlightenment represents a critique of the old, Pre-Romanticism is inspired by a real revulsion from all that Neo-classicism was thought to stand for: dull rules, superficial elegance, formality, orderliness, finite views, artificiality, convention, didacticism, courtly civilization, the preservation of the *status quo.* Not that the Pre-Romantics had any coherent programme to replace the old system—that in itself would have savoured too much of a rational approach. Hence the essentially haphazard, sporadic character of Pre-Romanticism which is made up of a number of individual starts rather than a concerted effort. Nevertheless certain common factors can be discerned in disparate works of the years 1740-80 which reveal the dominant concerns of this period. In every field the emphasis was on the natural in contrast to the rational, the spontaneous in place of the calculated, freedom instead of regimentation. This freedom led to the bewildering variety in the manifestations of Pre-Romanticism, but the basic trend is everywhere evident: in the new modes of feeling and their more direct expression, in the choice of new pastures and also in the new aesthetics. (pp. 15-27)

• • • • •

Since the dissolution of the old Neo-classical system a new theory of poetry had gradually been evolving. Dryden's and Lessing's plea for the appreciation of beauties, Diderot's 'realism', Lessing's championship of Shakespeare as an original genius all marked significant new starts. The keywords 'genius', 'originality' and 'creation', as well as 'spontaneous' and 'natural' were in fact already current during the Pre-Romantic period, as Logan Pearsall Smith has established in his analysis of 'Four Romantic Words', in which he lists a series of critical dissertations published between 1751 and 1774 by such writers as Joseph and Thomas Warton, Richard Hurd, William Duff, Edmund Burke, William Sharpe on topics like the genius of Pope, originality in authors, original genius, the genius of Shakespeare, etc. Among these dull tracts ('the dusty Saharas and Dead Seas of literature' in Smith's words), one alone was of lasting interest: Young's *Conjectures on Original Composition* (1759). Not that Young's ideas were intrinsically novel; many attempts have indeed been made to prove the extent of his indebtedness to his predecessors. The *Conjectures* are none the less important because they summarize and crystallize the new lines of thought, stating them more cogently and more vividly than ever before. Young draws clear distinctions between imitation and originality, learning and genius, the rules and free creation, the ancients and the moderns:

> An original may be said to be of a vegetable nature, it rises spontaneously from the vital root of genius; it grows, it is not made; imitations are often a sort of manufacture wrought up by those mechanics, art and labour, out of pre-existent materials not their own.

Young here even uses the image of organic growth subsequently favoured by Goethe and Coleridge. In his advocacy of an adventurous approach, his insistence on the divine inspiration of the genius, his emphasis on originality and spontaneity, and also in his vivid phraseology, Young was foreshadowing the poetic theory of the Romantics. The *Conjectures* are not a further amendment of the Neo-classical code in the manner of the Enlightenment; they are a replacement of the old with a new, in many ways antithetical set of notions.

The *Conjectures* had less immediate resonance in England

than abroad, particularly in Germany, where the first translation in 1760 received prompt and wide attention. Young's aesthetic programme seemed tailor-made for the *Sturm und Drang (Storm and Stress)* movement of the early 1770s. These youthful writers—Goethe (1749-1832), Schiller (1759-1805), Herder (1744-1803), Klinger (1752-1831), Lenz (1751-92), Bürger (1747-97)—were in rebellion against any organized creed, literary, social, political or religious. In their dynamic urge to break out of the bonds of the past, they rejected every facet of the *status quo.* All that mattered, in life as in art, was the original, creative genius of the individual who must be free to express his personal experience spontaneously. No wonder that the *Storm and Stress* is alternatively known as the 'Age of Genius'.

Thus once again in the spread of the new aesthetics, as in the sentimental novel, in the expression of melancholy and in the discovery of primitive poetry, the vital impetus during the Pre-Romantic period came from England, although many of these innovations had a greater and more rapid effect across the Channel than in their country of origin. The liberal English tradition of freedom to air one's views from any soapbox has always been conducive to a wealth of new ideas. On the other hand, this very freedom, together with a fine native literature, produced less need for radical reform than in Germany, where men were avid for a new start after a long stretch of relative sterility. The violence of the *Storm and Stress* and the extremism of the German Romantic movements reflect the desire to 'catch up' and indeed outdo others. In France there was a little of both these attitudes: immense pride in and loyalty to the indigenous Classical writers, mingled with a growing longing for something new and a curiosity about 'foreign' notions. In this way the pre-history of the Romantic movement not only elucidates the meaning of Romanticism as a whole, but already determines the character of individual Romantic groups. (pp. 36-8)

> *Lilian R. Furst, "The Pre-history of the Romantic Movement," in her* Romanticism, *second revised edition, Methuen & Co. Ltd., 1976, pp. 15-38.*

ROMANTIC THEORY

Ernst Behler

[*Behler is a German educator and critic. In the following excerpt, he surveys the concept of German Romantic irony, focusing on the sources of Friedrich Schlegel's ideas.*]

[Irony] is a phenomenon intimately related to the Romantic movement in all of its phases and in all its various national manifestations. More than in any other period of Western literature the ironic attitude appears as the distinctive hallmark of the Romantic generation, deeply affected as they were by the antagonism of heart with intel-

lect, of spontaneity with reflection, of passion with calculation, and enthusiasm with scepticism. It is in this epoch that we encounter individuals who, out of their "dédoublement", engage in infinite reflection—that is, in an infinite mental spiral in which the individual ego hovers between naive experiences and critical reflection on its experiences while viewing its own passions with disillusioned detachment. Irony and masquerade become the devices for this intellectual attitude which often cloaks a vulnerable personality plagued by melancholy, loneliness, and profound suffering.

A theory of irony—in the sense of a critical formulation of what irony really constitutes—was however almost exclusively the preoccupation of the German representatives of this movement. This theme was indeed closely bound to philosophical developments in Germany at that time, especially to the philosophy of transcendental idealism. Theoretical reflections on the nature of irony in fact determine the evolution of Germany's Romantic movement and provide instructive indications of the mood and the changing mentality of this generation. Critical statements on irony also tell us something about the profound alterations in the romantic view of the world and the role of the poet in it.

The first and most important phase in the development of a critical theory of irony is the era of the periodical *Athenaeum* (1798-1800) and that of the early Romantic school before the turn of the century when Friedrich Schlegel proudly claimed to have placed irony "on the agenda". This early concept of irony clearly reflects the lofty mentality and playful subjectivity of the young Schlegel, his progressive republicanism, emancipatory liberalism, and optimistic messianism with its futuristic belief in infinite perfectibility. Irony is presented here as the "lofty urbanity of the Socratic muse", the "freest of all licences", as "artistic reflection and beauteous self-mirroring", and as a mood which rises infinitely above all finiteness. Irony is a mode of "poetic reflection" which can "raise this reflection to higher and higher powers and can multiply it, as it were, in an endless array of mirrors".

Only a few years later this confidence had disappeared and been replaced by a profound scepticism against irony as a legitimate principle in poetic creation. This is noticeable, for instance, in the famous debate on irony and humor which became an essential aspect of the German preoccupation with irony. Inaugurated by Jean Paul in his *Vorschule der Asthetik* of 1804 and continued by E. T. A. Hoffmann in the tale *Die Prinzessin Brambilla* of 1820, this debate lasted until well into our own century. In its early version the controversy was noticeably flavored by Germany's awakening nationalism preceding the wars of liberation. The central issue was whether irony rightfully deserved the pivotal position in literary theory that Schlegel had accorded it or whether humor should preempt it. More specifically irony was faulted with being too intellectual, sophistically Erasmic, deceiving, haughty, dandyish, and coldly Western, whereas humor was seen as genuine, open, honest, and heartfelt or "herzaufquellend" (as Thomas Mann later put it) and native to that region in the German soul termed *Gemüt*.

Yet in spite of these reservations and Hegel's vitriolic attacks against the "infinitely absolute negativity" of irony, new critical theories of the phenomenon continued to emerge during the Romantic period—theories, however, which tended to turn from the initial optimism of joyous freedom toward sadness, melancholy, and despair. This trend is especially noticeable in the school of Swabian Romanticism, in authors such as Justinus Kerner, Eduard Mörike, and Ludwig Uhland; in Gotthilf Heinrich Schubert's *Ansichten von der Nachtseite der Naturwissenschaft* of 1808 and *Die Symbolik des Traumes* of 1814, and most profoundly presented in its metaphysical aspect by Karl Wilhelm Friedrich Solger in his *Vorlesungen über Ästhetik* (1819) and the dialogue *Erwin* (1815). Basically, this melancholic note of irony devolves from the contradictory experience of infinite longing in the face of the finitude of life. Immeasurable sadness permeates every form of life, since the absolute can only appear in limited, finite, and transitory form. Pain is the basic timbre of nature, transitoriness the mark of art, and the death-wish the desire of him who encounters such experiences. At best, we can only mask and in irony disguise this "Weltschmerz" through feigned laughter and gaiety. Marx and Engels explained this attitude simply as a reflection of what they called the predominant "German misery". Yet these pessimistic feelings about the world were by no means limited to the Romantic generation in Germany, but extended to Romantics in other European nations as well. Here they were often fused with predilections for sickness, decadence, and decay. They were enhanced, especially in the French and Byronic forms of Romanticism, by feelings of damnation, world-weariness, despair, and ennui.

In Germany, however, the development of melancholic irony is almost inseparably linked with the emergence of the theory of tragic irony and the recognition that in literature irony is not restricted to the realm of the comic, but is essential to tragedy as well. Irony becomes manifest in tragedy when the protagonist, misjudging reality, makes in his hubris self-assured statements which affect the discerning audience ironically. The most impressive embodiment of this type of irony was to be seen in Attic drama, especially in Sophocles' *Oedipus Rex* when the protagonist, in order to satisfy the oracle, makes every effort to identify the king's murderer, only to discover that it was he himself. Tragic irony was also to be found in modern drama, especially in Shakespeare, and in Schiller's *Wallenstein* when the protagonist, shortly before his murder, says: "I think I'll take a long sleep." The interpretation of such double-edged speech as ironic has since become commonplace for us. It was however, not at all usual when Adam Müller, in his *Vorlesungen über die dramatische Kunst* of 1806, first introduced the topic of tragic irony. As a matter of fact, August Wilhelm Schlegel protested vigorously against this critical innovation in his *Vorlesungen über dramatische Kunst und Literatur* of 1808. Solger, however, reaffirmed the conception of tragic irony in 1819 in his review of August Wilhelm Schlegel's lectures. Yet the concept was not firmly established in literary criticism until Connop Thirlwall, influenced by German sources, published his article "On the Irony of Sophocles" in the *Philological Museum* of 1833.

These stages in the development of the theory evince a considerable pessimism in the understanding of the concept of irony which had been first so optimistically introduced by Friedrich Schlegel. Over the years Schlegel himself had modified his view of irony, so that when in his last lectures of 1829 he broached the subject again, he said: "Genuine irony is the irony of love. It arises from the feeling of finiteness and of one's own limitations and the apparent contradiction of these feelings with the concept of infinity inherent in all genuine love." A further step in this direction was taken with the concepts of "God's irony" (Gottes Ironie), "world historical irony" (welthistorische Ironie), and "general irony of the world" (allgemeine Ironie der Welt). These new formulations all bear a close affinity with the theme of God's death and are predicated upon the absurdity of our world. The first to anticipate this topic was Benjamin Constant, who already in 1790 had toyed with the idea "that God, i.e., the author of us and our surroundings, died before having finished his work . . . that everything now finds itself made for a goal which no longer exists, and that we especially feel destined for something of which we ourselves have not the slightest idea". But Constant advanced this speculation in a letter which was not published until the beginning of the present century and thus could hardly have occasioned the rise of this nuance in the development of Romantic theory. It was Hegel who first coined the term "general irony of the world", and Kierkegaard drew our attention to it. Hegel used this phrase in his *Vorlesungen über die Geschichte der Philosophie* regarding the dialectical evolution of world history which proceeds through contradictions and must necessarily destroy forms of life so that other newer and higher forms can emerge. More specifically Hegel sensed irony in the dialectical point of view whereby existing historical accomplishments appear as both firmly established and yet at the same time subject to a necessary destruction. He was of course convinced that this whole process was governed by reason and that the world spirit moved on, despite all destruction, "exalted and glorified". Yet what if at this point we were to introduce Benjamin Constant's speculation about "la mort de Dieu"? It was Heinrich Heine who asked this question in his *Reisebilder* as early as 1826 and went on to develop the concepts of "irony of the world" and "God's irony", predicated precisely upon the lack of any reason and discernable plan in the course and eventual fate of our world.

With such ideas we are but a step removed from Nietzsche and the twentieth century. These are, in summary, the main stages in the history of the theory of irony in German Romanticism, a theory which now will deserve closer scrutiny and elaboration.

When Friedrich Schlegel decided to term the mood which permeates certain of the works of Cervantes, Ariosto, Pindar, Goethe, and Sterne "ironic" and wrote in 1797 that "there are ancient and modern poems which breathe throughout, in their entirety and in every detail, the divine breath of irony", he effected a fundamental change in the concept of irony in Western literary theory. The authors he mentioned certainly would have been astonished to hear him interpret their literary creations as displaying irony—to say nothing of Shakespeare and other older models of ironic style. The only reason why we today do not find anything remarkable in Schlegel's statement is that his usage of the term took root and became established. Until then and far into the eighteenth century the word irony retained its strict and consistent connotation of an established form of speech or literary communication which could be reduced to the simple formula: "a figure of speech by which one indicates the opposite of what one says." This quotation was taken from the renowned French *Encyclopédie* of 1765 and contains the essence of the definitions of irony as found in numerous handbooks of the various European literatures as they had developed from the older manuals of rhetoric concerning the art of public speaking and persuasion. If in this schematized structure of classical rhetoric we were to seek the topic of irony, we would find it first in the column of the tropes— that is, among indirect modes of speech (including metaphor, allegory, metalepsis, irony, hyperbaton); and second under the rubric of figures of speech—that is, of unusual verbal constructions (including question, anticipation, hesitation, consultation, apostrophe, illustration, feigned regret, and intimation). But the most basic characteristic of all forms of classical irony is always that the intention of the speaker is opposed to what he actually says and that we understand the contrary of what he expresses in his speech ("For Brutus is an honourable man"). We should perhaps add to this definition of classical irony that according to ancient opinion, in order to distinguish irony from mere lying, the entire tenor of speaking including intonation, emphasis, and gesture was supposed to reveal the real meaning to the initiated.

As opposed to this limited use of the term irony in particular instances and under definite conditions, Schlegel's new understanding of irony extended first of all to the entirety of a work of literature and even assumed a metaphysical meaning in the sense of a general world view. This is what Benedetto Croce had in mind when he referred to the "transition from the usual concept of irony to a metaphysical understanding" at Schlegel's time and when he illustrated this metaphysical understanding with "God's eye, looking on movement in creation, and loving every thing equally, good and evil, the greatest and the smallest in man, even the grain of sand, because He has created all this and finds movement in everything, eternal dialectic, rhythm, and harmony". In his reference to the entirety of a work of literature, Schlegel's new understanding of irony bears a strong resemblance to his other innovations in literary criticism. He himself described this novel tendency as a departure from a search for "beautiful instances and single images", so dominant in eighteenth century criticism, to attempt instead the empathic comprehension of a whole work of the imagination and the formulation of this sentiment in words.

Modern critics credit Schlegel for this innovation and refer to his usage of the word irony as a "coinage of a term". But given the original domain of the word, calling Schlegel's neologism a change of term or reformulation of a concept would perhaps be more appropriate. Hegel called Schlegel the "father of irony" and the "most prominent ironic personality", epithets which were certainly not intended as compliments. Adam Müller characterized

Schlegel's new understanding of irony as the reestablishment of an originally Greek concept and praised his literary theory generally for having accomplished an "aesthetic" or "critical revolution", meaning by this a total departure from neoclassicism and as such a general critical upheaval.

As Adam Müller's remark indicated, Schlegel's redefinition of irony bears a startling resemblance to his critical operation in general which may be considered a reconstitution for the modern world of basic Greek concepts. This was his way of reaching what he considered the "ultimate goal of all literature", that is, the "harmony of the classical and the romantic" and of fulfilling his motto "to live classically and to realize in practice the ancient world within oneself". This was also Schlegel's device to rid himself of the dominant French, Roman, and Aristotelian impact upon Western criticism in exchange for a closer bond with the Greeks and especially with the Platonic tradition. In neoclassicism and in previous periods of criticism the Greeks had maintained their influence upon history of aesthetics chiefly through the Romans as well as through various adaptations of Aristotle's *Poetics*. Following Winckelmann and the tradition of Goethean humanism, Schlegel attempted to terminate this form of classicism by establishing a close connection with the aesthetics of the Greeks and by referring directly to Plato and the Platonic tradition. As is evident in the presentation of almost every aspect of his early theory, Schlegel scrupulously avoided presenting the tenets of his doctrine as original ideas in that he painstakingly tried to derive all of it from classical Greek sources. To be sure, all these concepts gain their characteristic profiles only through a particular process of "re-functioning" or reformulation according to the views of idealistic philosophy, especially those of Kant and Fichte.

As to the new understanding of the concept of irony, Schlegel's model was obviously the Platonic Socrates. He appreciated to a certain extent "rhetorical irony which, if sparingly used, has an excellent effect, especially in polemics". But his real intention was to replace this glossy and formal device of neo-classicism by the human and metaphysical irony of Socrates and he said: "Compared to the lofty urbanity of the Socratic muse, rhetorical irony is like the pomp of the most brilliant oration compared to the noble style of an ancient high tragedy." The classical rhetoricians knew of course that irony was originally a Greek phenomenon and that their ironic devices had been modeled after the Socratic manner of argumentation. Cicero termed irony "that form of dissimulation which the Greeks named $\epsilon\iota\rho\omega\nu\epsilon\iota\alpha$" and considered Socrates the prototype of this witty and refined art of conversation. After having discussed irony as a trope and a figure of speech in his *Institutio oratoria*, Quintilian mentions a third and more comprehensive form of irony which transcends the scope of mere rhetoric and was represented by Socrates:

> Nay, a man's whole life may be colored with irony, as was the case with Socrates, who was called an ironist because he assumed the role of an ignorant man lost in wonder at the wisdom of others.

Aristotle in his *Nicomachian Ethics* had already exemplified the noble attitude of ironic dissimulation with Socrates, who did not deviate from the truth for his own advantage but only from a dislike for bombast and to spare others the feeling of inferiority. This view of irony which had been replaced by rhetorical devices was reaffirmed by Schlegel toward the end of the eighteenth century.

Schlegel was clearly aware that the original manifestation of irony according to his etymologies was in philosophy and that, as he put it: "Philosophy is the true homeland of irony, which we might like to define as logical beauty." We are touching here upon the metaphysical aspect of irony as illustrated earlier in the quote from Croce concerning God's eye contemplating his creation. Schlegel was of the opinion that poetry and literature can rise to this height of philosophy if they are not merely "based on ironical instances, as rhetoric". He illustrated in Goethe's novel *Wilhelm Meister* how this was to be achieved and in a fragment of 1797 drew the first parallel between irony in philosophy (Socrates) and irony in literature (Goethe): "Meister = ironic poetry as Socrates = ironic philosophy, because it is the poetry of poetry," that is, it is self-conscious and self-reflective poetry. Later, in his famous review of Goethe's novel, he described the "irony hovering above the entire work" with phrases clearly reminiscent of Socrates. He refers to the "air of dignity and self-possession, smiling at itself " and the "utmost prosaic in the middle of the poetic mood" as particular characteristics of the novel and adds:

> One should not let oneself be fooled when the poet himself treats persons and events in an easy and lofty mood, when he mentions his hero almost never without irony, and when he seems to smile down from the heights of his spirit upon his masterwork, as if this were not for him the most holy seriousness.

Shlegel's "revolution" in the history of the notion of irony can thus be characterized as follows. The modern author's attempt to communicate with his reader seemed to parallel Socrates' situation as a philosopher vis à vis his disciples. Since the classical age, the problem of literary communication had become increasingly complex. Shaftesbury had indicated how ridiculous it would have been for a contemporary author to refer to the inspiration of his Muse as the ancients had done. Confronted with this obstacle, the modern writer assumed more of a Socratic attitude toward his readers. He understated his talents, parodied old patterns, pretended to draw on lost manuscripts, commented upon himself and his creation, and included the reader in his creative task by establishing a contrast between expectation and actual narration. Socratic irony thereby helped overcome a fundamental dilemma and enabled him to convey a message which otherwise could hardly have been communicated. In a word, Socratic irony became the force by which he could—in Schlegel's terms—"infinitely rise above himself ".

Yet this summary of Schlegel's adaptation of Socratic irony falls short in two essential aspects, namely, the roguish, hoaxing, and teasing character of Socratic irony and the rhythm of reflection inherent in Platonic dialectics. The first aspect has become a famous theme of European

literature certainly familiar to Schlegel and indeed integrated into his final definition of Socratic irony. This view of Socratic irony refers back to Alcibiades' eulogy on Socrates in Plato's *Symposium* when he compares Socrates with the Sileni, those carved figures with exterior satyrlike and grotesque images which contain within them figures of gods, pure gold, and other valuables. This is clearly a reference to the contrast between the philosopher's outer appearance and his covert intellectual quality which can be interpreted as a form of ironic dissimulation or, in Nietzsche's term, a "mask". Toward his fellow man, Socrates assumes the mask of one who tends to fall in love with goodlooking young men and who is to all appearances universally ignorant. But once beneath the surface we discover that he disdains the attractions of physical beauty just like those of wealth and popular esteem and that he possesses an unparalleled degree of self-control. Using the Greek term $\epsilon\iota\rho\omega\nu\epsilon\iota\alpha$ for this type of dissimulation, Alcibiades explains to his drinking companions: "He spends his whole life pretending and playing with people, and I doubt whether anyone has ever seen the treasures which are revealed when he grows serious and exposes what he keeps inside." In the *Physiognomy* ascribed to Aristotle the influence of Alcibiades is detectable in the image of the ironist as possessing older age and having wrinkles around the eyes reflecting a critical power of judgment. In his *History of Animals* Aristotle even considers eyebrows rising upwards toward the temples as marks of the mocker ($\mu\omega\chi os$) and ironist ($\epsilon\iota\rho\omega\nu$). Schlegel obviously had all these manifold elements of the literary tradition in view when in 1797 he gave his portrait of Socratic irony:

> Socratic irony is the only entirely involuntary and yet completely deliberate dissimulation. It is equally impossible to feign it or to divulge it. For him who does not possess it, it will remain a riddle even after the frankest avowal. It is intended to deceive none but those who consider it to be deceptive, who either enjoy its delightful roguery of mocking at everybody or else become angry when they suspect that they too are meant. In it, everything should be both playful and serious, both frank and obvious and yet deeply dissimulated. It originates in the union of savoir vivre and scientific spirit, in the conjunction of a perfectly instinctive and a perfectly conscious philosophy. It contains and arouses a feeling of the insoluble conflict between the absolute and the relative, the simultaneous impossibility and necessity of a complete account of reality. It is the freest of all licences, for through it one transcends oneself; and still the most legitimate, for it is absolutely obligatory.

This image of Socrates is also clearly discernible in the conclusion of aphorism 42 of the *Lyceum* of 1797, where with regard to literary works displaying irony Schlegel says:

> Internally (they are permeated by) the mood that surveys everything and rises infinitely above all limitations, even above the poet's own art, virtue, and genius; externally, in their execution, (they have) the histrionic style of an ordinary good Italian buffo.

The decisive shift in the understanding of irony from the usual rhetorical concept to the philosophical notion probably did not occur abruptly and may very well have been prepared by a progressive change in consciousness from the eighteenth to the nineteenth centuries. Norman Knox, who has studied this process mainly as it occurs in English literature, comes to the conclusion that the new concept of irony did not arise from the head of an Aristotle and did not find expression in a critical scheme, but rather evolved from the every day criticism prevalent during the latter decades of the eighteenth century. The German concept of irony, however, took its own course at that time and differentiated itself in particular from the concept of irony in the English-speaking world. Whereas many critics, especially in England, still mean "double-edged speech" when they speak of irony, German authors since the beginning of the nineteenth century view irony rather as a metaphysical attitude which, to quote Goethe, "rises above objects, above happiness and unhappiness, good and evil, death and life and gains thereby possession of a truly poetic world". And in its espousal of this metaphysical attitude the German mind was certainly influenced by Greek sources, especially by Socrates, who had been so forcefully thrust into modern German intellectual history by Hamann.

This debt to Greek sources is evidenced by a brief glance at some authors who shortly after the turn of the century mention irony and who were not necessarily influenced by Schlegel's reformulation of the concept. In 1803 Herder published a short allegorical dialogue, *Kritik und Satyre,* in which criticism is the aunt of her niece satire. When satire attempts to embrace criticism as her relative, she is rejected as a low and presumptuous companion. Satire admits that in her youth she had been a frivolous and merry girl, roving about in ancient comedy and the satyr play with mockery and jest, but then, through the instruction of the foreigner El Gusto, had learned the art of refined persiflage and urbane raillery (obviously representing rhetorical irony). She also became an expert in parody—technique, however, which incorporates the danger of depicting its objects in extreme ugliness, as Swift's works demonstrate. At this point in the dialogue, Sophron (sober reason), the father of satire, appears to inform her of her original given name, namely "irony", but "in the noble meaning of the Greeks". This name and meaning, once forgotten, have now been rediscovered. Criticism is now ready to accept her niece as a legitimate relative who in turn promises from now on to become important "in conversation, in the dialogue, the sermon, the tale, but most of all in the novel which combines all of these." After the revelation of her real name, all authors lacking recognition as representatives of irony can be retroactively rehabilitated. Irony singles out as her favorites Socrates and Lucian, Horace and Galiani, Cervantes, Addison, Swift, Voltaire, and Sterne and she does not forget her Jean Paul, whose own genius is fused with that of Swift, Fielding, and Sterne. Criticism rejoices in her niece's change of name, removing her former symbol, the whip, and now bestowing bow and arrows as designating irony. Father Sophron does not give a material present to his daughter but advises her always to perceive the general in the particular and to refer back from the general to the particular. Whoever

creates without this talent—obviously representing symbolic creation—is no poet, and whoever judges without it is no critic. Now irony is released with criticism's admonition: "The world is in need of you; inform me soon about your accomplishments."

Goethe also provides a good illustration of the change in the concept of irony since he uses the term in both senses—that of rhetorical dissimulation and that of a metaphysical view of the world. This latter aspect comes to the fore when Goethe emphasizes in Goldsmith's *Vicar of Wakefield* the author's "lofty spirit" manifesting itself throughout as irony and making this work "both wise and charming". In another instance he praises the Spanish romances because of their "high-minded view of life" which he again considers as irony. For Goethe, this irony has "something roguish along with the grand, and the most common does not become trivial". Later, in his remarks on the sketches for Casti's fables, *Die redenden Tiere* of 1817, he emphasizes the "gay and dispassionate irony" in these sketches, "softening the bitterness of the jest which stresses the animalistic in man and providing a tasteful additional enjoyment for the witty reader".

Even Jean Paul, a true advocate of humor, testifies to the Greek and Platonic inspirations for the new concept irony when in his *Vorschule der Ästhetik* of 1804, he distinguishes, in analogy to world-humor, a world-irony manifest in Plato's philosophy and says:

> Plato's irony (and at times Galiani's) could be called world-irony, on an analogy with world humor: it hovers singing and sporting not only above errors (as world-humor not only above follies), but above all knowing, free like a flame, consuming and rejoicing, volatile and yet rushing only toward heaven.

The Socratic-Platonic inspiration for Schlegel's concept of irony is still manifest when after a long interval he again dealt with this topic in the lectures *Über die Philosophie der Sprache* delivered shortly before his death in Dresden in 1829. On several occasions Schlegel tried to distinguish the "true" from "false" irony and insisted "that this word in its modern usage had sunk several stages below its original meaning" and often signified little more than "common ridicule", or an irresponsible, "acid and bitter irony", soaring above everything and devolving from a "general negation". That irony, however, "which is characteristically germane to the speeches and argumentations of Socrates and is found especially in the Platonic writings", has for Schlegel the nature of being intimately interwoven "with the highest enthusiasm for the divine in higher truth and is almost completely identical with it". This irony arises "from the feeling of one's own incapacity to grasp in words and to render in language the abundance of that divine, as our spirit truthfully perceives it".

Within this context, Schlegel makes an important observation with regard to the technique of Socratic irony. He links it intimately to the Platonic version of dialectics and dialectical movement, that is, with the pursuit of truth through question and answer in the medium of speech alone. Schlegel says:

In this original Socratic sense . . . irony simply means nothing but this astonishment of the thinking mind about itself which often dissolves into a gentle smile; and again this smiling of the mind which nonetheless hides beneath a cheerful surface and incorporates a deeply hidden sense, another higher meaning, and quite often the most sublime seriousness. In this thoroughly dramatic development and presentation of thought in Plato's works, the dialogue form is so predominant that even if we eliminated the titles and names of persons, all addresses and responses, and the entire dialogue format as well, and stressed only the inner thread of thoughts in their cohesion and progression—the whole would still remain a dialogue in which each answer calls forth a new question and which in the alternating flow of speech and counter-speech, or rather of thought and counter-thought, moves forth in lively fashion.

When Schlegel delivered these lectures he was far removed from the intellectual world of the *Athenaeum* and most eager to point out the Platonic basis of his thought which indeed can be traced back to the beginnings of his critical career. Yet when reading and contemplating his presentation of irony as an "alternating flow of speech and counter-speech, or rather of thought and counter-thought", one can hardly escape the impression that Schlegel deliberately ignored one philosopher whom in earlier years he had called "the greatest metaphysical thinker now alive", and who for many years exerted the most profound influence on him, namely Fichte.

How closely Schlegel actually associated Fichte with his interpretation of Platonic dialectics can easily be detected in an earlier text, namely, Schlegel's anthology of *Lessings Gedanken und Meinungen* of 1804. In the dedicatory preface to this anthology Schlegel attempted to characterize Lessing's style of thought and prose, the best illustration of which was an analogy to the manner of thinking in Plato's dialogues. With direct reference to Plato's thought process he said:

> A denial of some current prejudice or whatever else can effectively surmount innate lethargy constitutes the beginning; thereupon the thread of thought moves imperceptibly forward in constant interconnection until the surprised spectator, after that thread abruptly breaks off or dissolves in itself, suddenly finds himself confronted with a goal he had not at all expected: before him an unlimited wide view, but upon looking back at the path he has traversed and the spiral of conversation clearly before him, he realizes that this was only a fragment of an infinite cycle.

This dedicatory preface, however, is addressed to Fichte, and Schlegel refers to him as "honorable friend", trying thus to include Fichte among the representatives of this thought process. One year earlier in his periodical *Europa* he had stated more pointedly that Fichte had "shaken consciousness to its innermost creative depths" by "organizing into an art free thought about oneself." Schlegel compared Fichte's manner of thinking to that science

"which Plato called dialectics and Jakob Böhme theosophy, namely, the science of that which alone is truly real."

It was Hegel who emphatically maintained that the dialectical rhythm animating Friedrich Schlegel's understanding of irony was actually an offspring of Fichte's philosophy. Indeed, Schlegel's model of an infinite thinking and counterthinking was certainly inspired by Fichte, who is commonly credited with being the initiator of the age of reflection. Fichte's attempt to attain self-understanding through pure contemplation of self or through thinking about thinking made philosophizing a technique of pure reflecting upon the self. As Hegel put it, Fichte brought "the knowledge of knowledge to consciousness" and conceived of philosophy as "a consciousness of consciousness in which I am conscious of what my consciousness is doing." The intellect, as Fichte understood it, "looks at itself" in philosophizing and thereby comprehends all that which it contains. This was for Fichte the true nature of the intellect which was no longer one unified entity, but rather a duality, one aspect of which was its actual being, the other a reflection upon its being. Philosophy had become the philosophy of philosophy.

In his *Grundlage der gesamten Wissenschaftslehre* of 1794 Fichte was the first to attempt to unfold "before the eyes of the reader or listener" the entire content of consciousness in a transcendental history of consciousness. In its desire to be entirely by itself and with itself, that is to be completely free, the ego constantly encounters barriers and finds itself in otherness and alienation. After having overcome one barrier, the ego is confronted with yet another, and so the transcendental thought process moves on toward absolute self-consciousness and self-determination. Hegel described this mode of philosophizing as "a continuous alternation of negation and affirmation, an identity with itself which immediately succumbs to negation, but then is immediately reconstituted".

This alternation of affirmation and negation, of emerging from and returning to the self, of expansion and contraction, is the basic model of Fichte's philosophical reflection which became the stimulus for Schlegel's theory of "poetic reflection" and "transcendental poetry". These are but different names for the attitude usually called irony and defined as the "form of the paradox", a "clear consciousness of eternal agility", as a "soaring" on the "wings of poetic reflection", and as a reflection which we can "raise to higher and higher powers and multiply it, as it were, in an endless array of mirrors." This reception of Fichte can be traced back as far as 1795-1796 and happened in close cooperation or "symphilosophizing", as they called it, between Friedrich Schlegel and Novalis. It is mainly in this context of a transformation of Fichte's philosophical reflection to new and more artistic modes of consciousness that Novalis is relevant for the theory of irony in German Romanticism.

Of course, this adaptation of Fichte's reflection did not take place without decisive modifications. Fichte's attempt to deduce the categories of reason in their entirety and to propel this process to absolute self-consciousness was disdained as the mere "letter" of his philosophy or, as Novalis put it, a "monstrous spiral of reflection". Only the basic model of Fichte's reflection was accepted as his "spirit", that is, the ceaseless rhythm of affirmation and negation, of exuberant emergence from oneself and self-critical retreat into oneself, of enthusiasm and scepticism, reformulated by Schlegel as a "constant alternation of self-creation and self-destruction". Schlegel and Novalis also believed that Fichte had too arbitrarily restricted the process of self-understanding to logic and philosophy. They demanded greater freedom for this type of reflection and wanted to exercise it in other domains as well such as art (and especially poetry), religion, and so forth. A further decisive step in this artistic transformation of Fichte's reflection was a readiness on the part of Schlegel and Novalis to engage in the unlimited process of thinking and to recognize reflection as infinite. Fichte had been careful to limit the infinite process inherent in his thought in order to avoid what Hegel called "schlechte Unendlichkeit", the undesirable infinity. For Schlegel and Novalis, however, such thought had by nature no limit.

Thus toward the end of the eighteenth century there originated with Schlegel and Novalis that which Walter Benjamin has designated as "infinite reflection" (unendliche Reflexion)—a thought process in which thinking incessantly reflects upon itself and in the infinity of ever new series strives toward ever higher modes of self-recognition. In a different context I have tried to demonstrate that Schlegel and Novalis had a vision of reflection as art which toward the end of the nineteenth century was taken up by Nietzsche, whom Thomas Mann has called a "lyricist of knowledge". This revival of the art of reflection was again accompanied by considerable modifications. Yet the link between Nietzsche and the two Romantics lies in the conviction that artistic representation of such thinking will impose unity or at least coherence upon it—a representation, however, which would never be fully achieved, but must remain fragmentary. This is what the two friends understood by "Fichtesizing" (Fichtisieren) and what Novalis had in mind when he said that the "inventor himself might not be the most skillful and ingenious artist on his instrument". He felt that there would be "people who will fichtesize much better than Fichte himself", especially if one began to practice "fichtesizing in an artistic fashion". Then "marvelous works of art" could result.

One way of "fichtesizing in artistic fashion" was pursued by Friedrich Schlegel with his theory of irony. Schlegel's early writings of 1795-1798 on Greek literature already reflect this process. They are dominated by that axiom of transcendental idealism postulating a strong antagonism of nature and human freedom which marks the early phase of idealistic thought as represented by Kant, Schiller, and finally Fichte. Schlegel depicted the entire course of Greek literature as a dramatic exemplification of this process. Out of the long night of barbaric darkness the world of the Homeric epic arises ushering in the dawn of Hellenic poetry in which, however, nature still impinges heavily upon freedom. With the rise of the lyric age, accompanied by an awakening republicanism, the poetic ego gains freedom and self-determination. Finally the birth of tragedy in Athens forms the climax of this development and unites epic with lyric poetry, action with chorus, and nature with freedom. This origin of the highest form of art

coincided with the moment in political life when all citizens were equal, free, and united. As to the development of irony in this process, the epic age is of no relevance because of its complete lack of any image of infinity and the accompanying Dionysian experience of bliss and horror. The character of the Homeric man was for Schlegel "quiet circumspection, not divine intoxication". The intuition of the absolute and the infinite, however, is the "step into an entirely different world" and marks the lyric, but especially the dramatic age. Now a "Bacchic enthusiasm" replaces the former naiveté and discharges itself in "solemn joyfulness", in "orgiastic dances" and in "blissful rapture". In Nietzsche's terms, the Apollonian world of Homer is replaced by a Dionysian experience. In these early studies Schlegel held the opinion that this effervescent poetic enthusiasm can turn against itself. "The most intense passion", he said, "is eager to wound itself, if only to act and to discharge its excessive power." He presented irony as a destructive reaction against the primordial Dionysian ecstasy and said:

> This self-infliction is not ineptitude, but deliberate impetuousness, overflowing vitality, and often has a positive, stimulating effect, since illusion can never be fully destroyed. Intense agility must act, even destroy; if it does not find an external object, it reacts against a beloved one, against itself, its own creation. This agility then injures in order to provoke, not to destroy.

Examples of such counter-actions were to be found in lyric poetry, "when the social mind of the poet looks at himself and he seems to contemplate himself in the mirror of his inner being with happy astonishment and noble enjoyment." As this quote indicates, Schlegel, by applying the Fichtean model, interpreted the awakening of Greek lyric poetry as a return of the poetic mind to itself. Whereas during the epic age, the poetic mind had emerged from within itself and had almost lost itself in the external world, now historical conditions and particular circumstances motivated the poetic mind "to return into itself, to restrain and lovingly to contemplate itself", and to make the creator simultaneously the subject of his own creation. The most prominent classical expression of this counter-action, however, was seen in the appearance of the chorus in Greek tragedy and ancient comedy. More specifically, Schlegel refers to the dramatic technique of parabasis ($\pi\alpha\rho\alpha\beta\alpha\sigma\iota\zeta$) in ancient comedy, i.e., addresses of the poet to the audience through the medium of the chorus which were generally unconnected with the action and displayed, as Schlegel saw it, utmost capriciousness, frivolity, and a disruption of the play. In a fragment of 1797 he says laconically: "Irony is a permanent parabasis", whereby he understands this emergence of the author from his work certainly in the broadest sense, relating it to phenomena of both ancient and modern literature in all of its genres.

In Schlegel's aphorisms of the *Lyceum* (1797) and the *Athenaeum* (1798-1800), the original, enthusiastic stimulus of the poet appears as "self-creation" (Selbstschöpfung), whereas the counteracting scepticism toward one's own productive drive is labeled "self-destruction" (Selbstvernichtung). A similar and recurrent formulation of the same phenomenon is the phrase "developed to the point of irony", by which Schlegel understood the highest artistic perfection—a perfection, however, which precisely because of its utmost achievement necessarily leads to self-criticism, and thus shifts to its contrary. As is evident from these observations, Schlegel found two antagonistic forces in the author's creative drive, namely the creative strivings of poetic enthusiasm for expression which are counteracted by the scepticism of irony. More specifically, the function of irony does not reside so much in the destruction of creative production, but rather in a hovering, mediating position between enthusiasm and scepticism. Schlegel defined irony as a shifting between two poles, as "alternation between self-creation and self-destruction", and termed the result of this ironical alternation "self-restraint" (Selbstbeschränkung), i.e., the disciplined mastering of the creative drive. This idea is expressed in the following aphorism: "It is just as fatal for a thinker to have a system as not to have one. He will therefore have to decide to combine both."

Although this oscillation between self-creation and self-destruction, enthusiasm and scepticism, forms the essential meaning of Schlegel's concept of irony, upon closer examination we see that there are still other nuances of irony delineated in the *Athenaeum*. In the third volume of the periodical (1800) a symbolic concept of irony emerges, deviating from the "beautiful self-mirroring" of the author also referred to as "poetic reflection". According to the *Gespräch über die Poesie* (also in the third volume of the *Athenaeum*), in irony "things which individually excite, move, occupy and delight our senses, our hearts, understanding, and imagination appear to us to be only a sign, a means for viewing the whole." This viewing of the whole is illustrated through the works of Cervantes and Shakespeare, exhibiting for Schlegel "this artistically arranged confusion, this charming symmetry of contradictions, this wonderfully perennial alternation of enthusiasm and irony." More specifically, he refers to this idea of the whole in the following aphorism, also from the third volume of the *Athenaeum:* "Irony is clear consciousness of the eternal agility, the infinitely abundant chaos." For Wilhelm Dilthey this concept of irony manifests the "aesthetic and moral mood of pantheism"; it relates to "that which Goethe called resignation and which Schleiermacher's *Speeches on Religion* referred to as melancholy." This new attitude clearly reflects the second phase of idealistic philosophy, namely the philosophy of identity, in which the grim antagonism between freedom and nature, firmly maintained by Kant and Fichte, had given way to an amiable cooperation between nature and human freedom. Now, to use Schelling's language, nature appeared as visible spirit and spirit as visible nature, and the former antagonism was replaced by an identity of the real and the ideal. Correspondingly, Schlegel saw man no longer confronted with nature, but as part of a greater whole or an "infinitely abundant chaos". And this awareness expressed itself in a type of irony that already foreshadowed the melancholic irony of the following romantic generation. (pp. 43-62)

One main aspect connected with the origin of Romantic irony appears to be a basic change in man's relationship to the world—a change relating to his perception and manner of speaking about the world. Rhetorical irony in its classical fashion was basically dissimulation, yet as this word already emphasizes by its negative formulation, the underlying assumption was that there is truth objectively discernible and recognizable by every intelligent person. In Romantic irony this point of reference in the sense of an objectifiable truth has vanished, and what has been substituted is the infinite self-mirroring of the individual in the mirrors of his ego and the world. Similarly, up to the pre-Kantian era, reality was considered a pregiven entity which the subject was able to understand and interpret more or less successfully. Romantic irony represents an entirely different correlation of man and world, namely, a net of subject-object relationships based on infinitely many perspectives which oppose, contradict, and support one another. Later representatives of the ironic mode bring about a dramatic evolution in the sense of an increasing pessimism sometimes bordering on the feeling of absurdity. The question arises as to what reasons there are—societal, political, psychological, ideological—which made this new attitude possible.

As to the aesthetic implications of Romantic irony, we realize that generally speaking pre-romantic art attempted to mirror reality, whereas during the Romantic period the author became increasingly aware that he was projecting something basically different. One way to resolve the difficulties implied in this awareness was for the author to admit openly the fictional character of his work and by relativizing it, release his creation into its own and authentic sphere of reality. Here we leave the existential terrain of irony—characterized by the "recognition of the fact that the world in its essence is paradoxical and that an ambivalent attitude alone can grasp its contradictory totality"—and are entering, to use post-Wittgensteinian terms, that sphere of reality which is immanent in language alone and where irony merges entirely with the text. Irony becomes a "principle of structure" as it has been developed by critics such as Cleanth Brooks [in *The Well-Wrought Urn: Studies in the Structure of Poetry*, 1947] in the sense of ambiguity ("the art of saying something without really saying it"), by I. A. Richards [in *Principles of Literary Criticism*, 1960] as the integration of a multiplicity of heterogeneous impulses into the structure of an all-inclusive work, and by William Empson as the "pressures of a context".

From our theme of the theory of Romantic irony, it is quite easy to realize how Thirlwall's dramatic and tragic irony, still entirely based on action, could also be perceived solely from the context of the text. Yet with this, we are only at the surface of this dimension of Romantic irony. In order to understand the implications of the romantic theory for contemporary structuralist and linguistic thought more fully, one would have to re-read Schlegel's observations about symbolic form in authors such as Fichte, Lessing, and Plato, his remarks on thought and counter-thought, speech and counter-speech in Socrates, about Plato's dialectics as a search for truth in the medium of language alone, as well as Solger's presentation of irony as the dialectic of the absolute and the relative, the infinite and the finite. (pp. 80-1)

Ernst Behler, "The Theory of Irony in German Romanticism," in Romantic Irony, *edited by Frederick Garber, Akadémiai Kiadó, 1988, pp. 43-81.*

An excerpt from Friedrich Schlegel's *Athenäum Fragments*

We cannot see God, but we can see the divine everywhere, most immediately and truly, however, at the core of an understanding human being, in the depths of a living human work. You can feel and think nature and the universe directly, but not the divinity. Only the human being among human beings can create and think in a divine way, and live with religion. No one can be a direct mediator unto himself for his own spirit, because the mediator must be simply object, whose centre the contemplator posits outside himself. One chooses and posits one's mediator, but one can only choose and posit him who has already posited himself as such. A mediator is he who perceives the divine in himself, and who self-destructively surrenders his self in order to proclaim and communicate this divine perception, and to present it to all mankind in ethos and action, in words and works. If this urge does not follow, then what was perceived was not divine or not personal. To mediate and to receive meditation is mankind's whole higher life, and every artist is a mediator for all others.

Quoted in European Romanticism: Self-Definition, *edited by Lilian R. Furst, Methuen, 1980.*

Lilian R. Furst

[*In the following excerpt, Furst distinguishes between traditional irony, in which the characters are the focus, and romantic irony, in which the reader is the focus.*]

The greatest challenge in grappling with romantic irony is to try to get away from Schlegel's cryptic terminology so as to evolve not so much a portable definition as a robust understanding of the phenomenon in its bewildering ramifications. Such an endeavour must take as its point of departure not the postulates of German Romantic theory but the actuality of romantic irony as it becomes manifest in the works of some of its outstanding exponents. By delineating the differences between their irony and that of traditional ironists, the relationship between the two modes can be brought out, and with it the specific character of romantic irony.

Fundamental distinctions can be drawn between traditional, classical irony and romantic, modern irony. Traditional irony is an irony of discrimination that springs from the security of knowledge held with assurance. Buttressed by faith in the existence of truths and absolute standards, it is an expression of moral judgement as well as of social values. Among the possible alternatives facing him, the traditional ironist is able to distinguish sharply between what he considers 'true' and what he regards as 'false'. His confidence in his knowledge is rooted in the solidity of the ethical framework and in the widespread acceptance of

norms held to be sound. His world possesses the coherence of firm contours, and he himself maintains a steady perspective on it; in saying the opposite to what he means, he knows what he means, and what he wants to attain. From the vantage-point of his detachment, and with a slightly supercilious sense of his moral and intellectual superiority over the masses, the traditional ironist uses irony as a means of sceptical evaluation and as a weapon for clarification, seeking to elicit and establish the truth by an argumentation *per contrarium*. His irony is generally local and concrete, focused on contraries that can be resolved. Such stable irony is akin to satire in so far as it is a means to an end, though the ironist always harbours a deeper scepticism about the human condition than the satirist, together with an awareness that its innate ambivalence may in part defy resolution. His mask must, however, remain fairly transparent and his irony finite if they are to achieve the purpose for which they are designed. For the mask and the rhetoric of irony are the visible manifestations of a vision of the universe, from which they must not be divorced. Irony is never merely a figure of speech; all irony, whether traditional or romantic, originates in a vision of the universe, though that vision is quite different in the two modes. Beneath his ambiguities and equivocations, the traditional ironist aspires to an affirmation of certainty.

Socratic irony is a good example of traditional irony at its most subtle. Often regarded as a dialectical tool and a method of inductive polemics, it far exceeds these circumscribed limits in its reach. Whether Socratic irony is deemed [in the words of George G. Sedgewick in *Of Irony, Especially in Drama*, 1948] 'a war upon Appearance waged by a man who knows Reality', or whether its essence lies 'in Socrates' commitment to the process of intellectual self-enquiry combined with a skepticism concerning the ultimate conclusions it might yield' [Stuart M. Sperry, "Toward a Definition of Romantic Irony in English Literature," in *Romantic and Modern*, edited by George Bornstein, 1977] is largely immaterial. What matters is the staunch commitment to the worth of the process and, beyond that, to the validity of the vision inspiring it. The pretence of ignorance and the mocking assertions of the contrary to what Socrates believed are intended as provocations to uncover falsehoods. In this sense Socrates' systematic irony represents an oblique profession of faith in the efficacy of rational enquiry as well as in the authenticity of the standards upheld. The teasing method of ironical rhetoric peculiar to Socrates springs not from a doubting state of mind but from strongly held convictions, from the urge to attain truth and, what is more, to lead others towards that truth.

The unceasing questions of romantic irony, by contrast, are less a pursuit of enlightenment than an assent to, indeed an affirmation of continuing doubt. For romantic irony is an irony of uncertainty, bent primarily on the perplexities of searching. Alert to the plurality of all meaning and the relativity of every position, the romantic ironist probes an open-ended series of contradictions which bound into a chaos of contingencies instead of coming to rest in a state of resolution or comprehension. In the context of a changing, disjointed world of shifting values, his quest is for transcendental certainty, even while he may question its existence. His irony is therefore pervasive and infinite, absorbing everything in its exponential progression. It is not a perspective on a situation, but a presence within each situation. So its effect is one of kinetic, relativistic perspectivism. Irony is not used to differentiate the true from the false because for the romantic ironist all options may be true, or false; nor can he manipulatively say the opposite to what he means because he cannot be sure of any meaning. Thus whereas the traditional ironist, who accepts authority and has a hold on knowledge, exposes the disparity between appearance and reality, the romantic ironist, who suspects that each successive reality may be as illusory as the previous one, subjects appearance and reality alike to an unrelenting ontological scrutiny. And the greater the gaps in the knowledge held, the more radical the doubts, and the larger and deeper the spaces occupied by irony. In short, far from *using* irony, as the traditional ironist does, the romantic ironist *is* ironic. His irony is the instrument for registering the obdurate paradoxicality of a universe in eternal flux.

The divergence between traditional and romantic irony is thus as much a matter of ontology and epistemology as of literary technique. The form that the discourse takes devolves from the underlying philosophic vision. But it is in the discourse itself that the difference between the two modes becomes fully apparent.

In narration this can most cogently be expressed in terms of the narrative stance. The dynamics of the tripartite relationship between the narrator, the narrative, and the reader are distinctively at variance in the two kinds of irony. Traditional irony resides in the space between the narrative and the reader who is able to reconstruct the intended covert meaning with the aid of clues deliberately planted by the knowing narrator who acts as an invisible guide because he wants his irony to be understood. The narrator's stance is impersonal and detached; he functions as an extraneous observer, purposefully uncovering subversive implications which are brought to the reader's attention through indirect but unmistakable signals. The presentation of Casaubon's feelings in *Middlemarch,* cited in the first chapter, is a fine instance of such irony. The narrator, while maintaining his aesthetic distance, is in collusion with the reader, behind the protagonists' backs, so to speak. The irony is transparent in that the words carry meanings other than those on the surface, and it is finite in application and stable in that there is no further demolition of the reconstructed meaning.

Romantic irony, on the other hand, is situated primarily in the space between the narrator and his narrative. The discreet, assured chronicler of traditional irony is replaced in romantic irony by a self-conscious, searching narrator who openly stands beside his story, arranging it, intruding into it to reflect on his tale and on himself as a writer. He portrays himself in the act of writing alongside his story as an integral part of his narrative, operating not from behind the scenes, but groping his way across the stage in the presence of his protagonists and his readers. So the romantic ironist assumes a prominence in the text that is the antithesis of the reticent role of the traditional ironist. The distance between the mask and the persona of the narrator is significantly foreshortened to the point where the mask takes possession of the persona. The sense of a dissembling that is meant to be seen through has vanished, and so has the consistent texture of traditional irony. With the romantic ironist the mask merges with the persona in a displacement likely to generate disorientation. The narrator abdicates his controlling, directing function, or at least appears or pretends to do so, becoming in effect a narrative gamesman who delights in sporting with his creation, exploiting it as a medium for displaying the fireworks of his creativity. While traditional irony is *between* the lines, romantic irony is *in* the lines.

One immediate result of this shift of emphasis is a drastic reduction in the status of the story. While the created, finished product and the effects it achieves attract most interest in such works as *Pride and Prejudice, Middlemarch,* and *Effi Briest,* it is the actual business of story-telling that demands greatest attention in *Tristram Shandy, Don Juan,* or *Jacques le fataliste.* The romantic ironist has forgone that supremacy over the world and over his story that enables the traditional ironist to order, to explain, and to resolve. The romantic ironist's self-conscious embroilment in the strategies of narration is at the expense of his narrative. An important mutation occurs here in the art of narration. Not only is linear plot replaced by associative arabesque; in fact, classical aesthetic theory, which held that writers should adapt their style to their tale, is inverted when manner takes precedent over matter. The insistence on the essentially fictional, illusory nature of art furthers this transference. The prominence and space given to the narrated situation declines in proportion to that devoted to the narrative situation. In the *Flegeljahre* and in *Don Juan* the two are roughly equal, but in *Jacques le fataliste* and certainly in *Tristram Shandy* it is on the tactics of narration rather than on the stories narrated that the spotlight falls. With the romantic ironist narration usurps the centre of the stage, dislodging the story from its customary privileged place. Classical narrative expectations are overturned when narration asserts its autonomy in this way. Literature as product yields to literature as process.

This shift of focus has far-reaching consequences for the reader. The traditional ironist looks outwards to his narrative and also to his listeners; through a network of oblique but comprehensible signals he maintains a tacit rapport with the reader to whom the ironic countermeaning is to be communicated. The stance of the romantic ironist, on the contrary, is introverted; his gaze is directed inwards onto the work he is creating and onto himself as its creator. The reader, even when he is specifically addressed, is no more than an audience of the creative spectacle at best, and at worst merely an eavesdropper. For although the romantic ironist assumes an audible and visible role in his intrusive running commentary on his narration, he has a tenuous connection to the reader despite his vociferous presence because of his overriding interest in himself and in the problems of writing. This entails another fundamental alteration in the entire narrative set-up. The contract between narrator and reader loses its reliability as the basis for communication. Once perspective is converted into perspectivism, the reader is deprived of his sense of assurance *vis-à-vis* the narrative. The signals that he catches from the mercurial narrator may be loud and manifold, but they are inevitably conflicting and confusing since the narrator himself has no firm position or clear insight. So in romantic irony [in the words of David Simpson in *Irony and Authority in Romantic Poetry,* 1979] 'the meaning is not simply "reversed" in any determinate and identifiable sense; it is unsettled'. It is 'unsettled' through the reciprocal suspicion of narrator and reader. On the one hand, the unreliable narrator implies that it is the reader who is unreliable; on the other, the reader comes to query the narrator's competence and to doubt his knowledge. The resultant irony is wholly different in nature to that engendered by a mutually trusting narrator and reader whose shared intelligence is contrasted with the ignorance of the protagonists. In place of the reader's participation in knowledge, as is the case in traditional irony, in romantic irony he is, by devious manoeuvres, made to realise the unattainability of truth and the prevalence of paradox. It is the reader who becomes the disconcerted victim of irony, whereas in traditional irony he is a party to the whisperings and snickerings at the expense of the protagonists, the duped objects on whom he preys in concert with the narrator.

Because of these divergences in narrative disposition and in the underlying vision of the universe, the discourse of romantic irony is a palpable departure from that of traditional irony. The ironic discourse of such contemporary writers as Barthelme, Kafka, Beckett, Borges, or Nabokov has been characterised [by Robert Scholes in *Semiotics and Interpretation,* 1982] as one 'that invites its own ironies upon itself, through the deliberate introduction into both story and discourse of gaps, contradictions, and absurdities'. It contrasts with that of, say, Balzac, Austen, or George Eliot, where irony 'was controllable only at the price of introducing a highly coercive and manipulative discourse'. The phrase 'only at the price of', together with the adjective 'coercive', contains a value judgement that is hardly warranted. However, the essential distinction between the two modes of discourse is legitimate and important. Almost equally important is the fact that the specification of twentieth century irony is apposite to romantic irony without need of modification or qualification. The close similarity between the discourse engendered by the irony known as 'romantic' and that intrinsic to many modernist texts is the surface stylistic manifestation of the kinship between them. Like its modern descendant, romantic irony emanates from an open sense of self which is projected into images of hovering identity and which finds its aesthetic format in the eschewal of enclosure. The literary structures of romantic as of modern irony are nurtured by the perception of art as a self-generating dynamic process. The consciousness of its own mainsprings is incorporated into the composition and determines its intrinsic form.

The transformation wrought in fiction by romantic irony has a wider significance that extends far beyond the disposition and tactics of narration into the approach to representation in the arts in general. A bold postulate has recently been put forward in the field of art history which has a direct relevance in this context. In *Absorption and Theatricality,* Michael Fried documents and analyses 'a major shift in the relationship between painting and be-

holder' in mid-eighteenth century French painting. He chooses the terms 'absorption' and 'theatricality' to indicate two disjunctive positions. By 'absorption' he means the representation of a group of figures hermetically engrossed in whatever they are doing and hence perfectly oblivious to anything extraneous, including the beholder's presence. This corresponds in effect to the situation in traditionally ironic narrative. 'Theatricality', by contrast, denotes the primacy of dramatic and expressive considerations and 'the accomplishment of an ontologically prior relationship, at once literal and fictive, *between painting and beholder*' (italics are Fried's). The thrust for theatricality entailed 'the fracturing of perspectival unity, which makes it virtually impossible for the beholder to grasp the scene as a single instantaneously apprehensible whole'. The parallelism in presupposition and in impact to romantic irony in narration is quite striking, as is the timing of this shift during the 'pivotal period':

> starting around the middle of the eighteenth century in France, the beholder's presence before the painting came increasingly to be perceived by critics and theorists as something that had to be accomplished or at least powerfully affirmed by the painting itself; and more generally that the existence of the beholder, which is to say the primordial convention that paintings are made to be beheld, emerged as problematic for painting as never before.

Such a perception is animated by the same self-consciousness of art as an illusory theatrical play with its own possibilities and with its audience as romantic irony. What is more, it produced in painting a paradox closely akin to that implicit in narration:

> the recognition that paintings are made to be beheld and therefore presuppose the existence of a beholder led to the demand for the actualization of his presence: a painting, it was insisted, had to attract the beholder, to stop him in front of itself, and to hold him there in a perfect trance of involvement. At the same time, taking Diderot's writings as the definitive formulation of a conception of painting that up to a point was widely shared, it was only by negating the beholder's presence that this could be achieved: only by establishing the fiction of his absence or nonexistence could his actual placement before and enthrallment by the painting be secured. This paradox directs attention to the problematic character not only of the painting-beholder relationship but of something still more fundamental—the *object*-beholder (one is tempted to say object-'subject') relationship which the painting-beholder relationship epitomizes. (italics are Fried's)

The outcome of romantic irony in narrative is equally contradictory. To all appearances the reader is actively invited, indeed cajoled and coerced, into energetic participation in the making as well as in the reading of the narrative. But in reality his efforts are neutralised by the teasing mistrust of which he is the victim; the multiple invocations to the reader are no more than a disarming strategy. He remains an outsider to the transactions between the narrator and his narrative on which the text pivots. He has ultimately a lesser stake in the dynamics of romantic irony than in traditional irony where the confiding narrator, though sparing of explicit appeals, counts on him for comprehension. Thus traditional irony may be said to depend on the reader's relationship to the text, while romantic irony hinges on the narrator's orientation towards his own construct. (pp. 227-34)

The metamorphosis in the conceptualisation of irony in the late eighteenth and early nineteenth century marks the crucial turning-point where the qualitative transformation is voiced and asserted. But in literary practice the lines of demarcation between traditional and romantic irony are too fluid to be subordinated to any rigorous paradigm. It is perhaps a fitting hallmark of irony that it should be so resistant to schematisation.

In the light of this theory of romantic irony, some commonly held beliefs about it can be dispelled as fictions.

First, the thesis that it is [in the words of Ingrid Strohschneider-Kohrs in *Die romantische Ironie in Theorie und Gestaltung,* 1977] 'ein historisches Phänomen' ('a historical phenomenon'). Through the name attached to it by Hettner it has come to be associated with a specific period of literary history. Not without some justification either, since it was the leading theoretician of German Romanticism, Friedrich Schlegel, who identified the phenomenon, recognised its importance, and delineated its characteristics. It was, moreover, at a particular phase in history, roughly contemporaneous with its cognitive formulation, that this kind of irony became widespread and prominent in fiction. Yet it is a curious reflection of its jumbled time-schema that the opening volumes of *Tristram Shandy* appeared within five years of Dr Johnson's *Dictionary.* Despite some such inconsistencies in its upsurge, romantic irony does have a historical constituent, but it would be erroneous to insist on its historicity, and quite wrong to envisage it along purely historical lines.

Many critics have indeed made passing reference to the tendency of romantic irony to surpass its conventional historical boundaries. Strohschneider-Kohrs cautiously concedes: 'das von der Romantik konzipierte Prinzip der künstlerischen Ironie und die mit dieser Konzeption hervorgehobene Möglichkeit der Kunst trägt eine gewisse Antizipation von Problemen der modernen Kunst in sich' ('the principle of artistic irony as conceived by the Romantics and the potential for art brought out in this conception includes a certain anticipation of problems of modern art'). Muecke [in *The Compass of Irony,* 1969] resorts to a slightly evasive witticism: 'To study Romantic Irony is to discover how modern Romanticism could be, or, if you like, how Romantic Modernism is'. Muecke's cardinal example of romantic irony in the modern period is Thomas Mann's *Doktor Faustus* (1947). One could just as well cite James Joyce's *Ulysses* (1922), André Gide's *Les Fauxmonnayeurs* (1926; *The Coiners*), Samuel Beckett's *Molloy* (1951), Italo Svevo's *La Coscienza di Zeno* (1920; *Confessions of Zeno*), Saul Bellow's *Herzog* (1964), almost any of the fictions of Jorge Luis Borges, Max Frisch's *Mein Name sei Gantebein* (1964; *A Wilderness of Mirrors*) or *Der Mann erscheint im Holozän* (1979; *Man in the Holocene*), Delmore Schwartz's story, 'In Dreams Begin Re-

sponsibilities' (1948), or such very recent works as Stanislaw Lem's *Doskonale próżnia* (1974; *A Perfect Vacuum*), E. L. Doctorow's *Loon Lake* (1980), Gilbert Sorrentino's *Mulligan Stew* (1979), Juan Benet's *Una meditácion* (1970; *A Meditation*), or Italo Calvino's *Se una notte d'inverno un viaggiatore* (1979; *If on a Winter's Night a Traveler*). This is a random sample of twentieth-century fictions that draw heavily on practices central to romantic irony. The continuing relevance, indeed the crucial importance, of this kind of irony to modern fiction is cogent evidence of its transcendence of the limits of historicity.

Equally telling is its existence before the cultural segment called Romanticism. Friedrich Schlegel and the Romantics were themselves fully aware of the historical antecedents on which they based their perception of irony. It is no coincidence that *Don Quixote* held pride of place among their reading. Tieck published a new German translation of Cervantes' novel in 1799-1801, and even if [according to Anthony Close in *The Romantic Approach to "Don Quixote"*] the Romantics did misread certain aspects of *Don Quixote,* they were the first to appraise adequately the teasing ambivalences it insinuates into the narrator-reader relationship. *Don Quixote* was indisputably the foremost model to the Romantics of uses of irony other than those habitual among the Augustans. They also idolised Shakespeare, not only for the spontaneous originality of his genius, but specially for that imaginative perspectivism that enabled him to transport himself into every situation and every character with a mobility that never ceased to astonish them. It is for this quality that Shakespeare is granted an irony that is romantic in its stance, though Schlegel still asserted: 'Cervantes ist doch romantischer als Shakespeare' ('Cervantes is even more romantic than Shakespeare'). The sporadic occurrence of an irony akin to romantic irony before the Romantic period and its frequent recurrence thereafter vitiates the argument that it is predominantly a historical phenomenon. It must be accorded archetypal as well as historical status. It encompasses a typological approach to the manipulation of fictional illusion together with an open-ended querying epistemology and an ontology that embraces an order of disorder quite distinct from orderliness. Such an approach becomes preeminent at an identifiable historical period, but it is by no means confined to that period. To disregard the archetypal dimension of romantic irony is to forfeit an element of momentous significance for an understanding of the art of narration and, above all, for the devices and structures of modern fiction.

Any enquiry into the historicity of romantic irony must needs beg another question: if romantic irony is not to be associated solely with the Romantic period, how appropriate is its name? To put it more bluntly, should it be deemed a misnomer? It is well to recall at this juncture that this name was not in fact accepted usage among the originators of the concept, but was popularised only later by mid-nineteenth century scholars. The Romantics themselves, with an intuitive sense of its wider implications, chose to refer to it as 'artistic' irony. They would, however, emphatically have affirmed the integral function of such irony within the metaphysical and aesthetic edifice they built. Irony was the essential dynamic force in a progressive process in which the work of art was to be deconstructed and re-constructed into a closer approximation of the ideal. Irony is thus one of the major instruments of Romantic idealism [in the words of Ingrid Strohschneider-Kohrs]: 'sie erscheint als eines ihrer "Mittel", ist erkennbar als ein inneres agens, eine der Bedingungen romantisch-poetischer Möglichkeit' ('it appears as one of its "means", it is recognisable as an inner activating force, one of the conditions for the romantic-poetic endeavour'). What is more, a number of other cardinal tenets of Romanticism, such as the supremacy of the subjective vision, the belief in the transcendental nature of art and in the artist's divine creative powers, and the consequent explosion of self-consciousness have a direct bearing on the crystallisation of the new concept of irony. So it is a facet of the philosophical, aesthetic, and literary reorientation that is at the core of the Romantic movement. It is no coincidence that an innovative perception of irony and new uses of irony in fiction came into the forefront at that time. In this sense, therefore, there is a certain aptness in the name 'romantic' irony. Yet it has also proved an unfortunate misnomer in so far as it has fostered too exclusive an identification of this type of irony with a limiting period concept. The irony normally described as romantic irony represents an aesthetic category independent of the Romantic movement. Its name has, regrettably, contributed to the underestimation of the phenomenon it denotes by triggering an automatic association that has resulted in a failure to appreciate to the full its importance beyond the Romantic period.

Partly because of the misleading implications of its name, romantic irony has acquired the reputation of being a peculiar caprice of a few esoteric writers at the turn of the eighteenth into the nineteenth century, resistant to common comprehension and of slight relevance anyway. Such a view of romantic irony is a grave misconception. There is admittedly no denying the intricacy of the concept nor the often rebarbative formulation of ideas by its sponsors from Friedrich Schlegel to Kierkegaard. But these objections do not impugn the worth of the ideas in themselves, although they make them less accessible. What is ultimately at issue in romantic irony is nothing other than the authority of the invented fictional world both unto itself and in relation to the world of our experience. The authenticity of the self-contained illusion remains intact in traditional irony, whereas it is incessantly undermined and questioned in romantic irony. A progressive deconstruction of illusion takes place: first it is broken within the fiction by the impulse to self-representation in mirror images and in those labyrinthine arabesques so favoured by Romantic and modern narrators. The illusion becomes controversial at a second level through the continual arousal of the reader's awareness of the text's standing as fiction. This has a strangely contradictory impact: for the pretence of realism is heightened when the contingencies of the known world appear to be faithfully noted as they beset the narrative; but at the same time the sense of artifice is strongly reinforced through the reader's realisation of the games that are being played. Taken far enough, as in *Tristram Shandy,* such games can finally draw the entire text into an ironic state of relativity. In the transition from traditional irony to romantic irony, irony within the frame-

work of the fiction is transmuted into an irony of the fiction which may then be potentiated into an irony of fictional irony—and of the fictionality of existence. It is a process that starts with ambiguity, edges from ambivalence to paradox, and ends in an alienating derangement of the text and of the world. So romantic irony, far from being the remote preserve of a small coterie of specialists roaming the byways of the late eighteenth and early nineteenth century, must be of urgent concern to all who travel the highways of fiction and of life. (pp. 235-39)

> *Lilian R. Furst, "In Search of a Theory," in her* Fictions of Romantic Irony, *Cambridge, Mass.: Harvard University Press, 1984, pp. 225-39.*

D. L. Fanger

[*Fanger is an American educator and critic who has written extensively on nineteenth-century Russian literature. In the following essay, he examines the development of the concept of historicism in Romantic cultural theory.*]

A manifesto, in the modern sense, is a published document that aspires to be an event. Aiming in some sense at marking a fresh start, it implies a rejection of older attitudes. It may range in decorum from stateliness to exhibitionism, in method from scholarship to bare assertion; but its unvarying hallmark is a self-conscious air of innovation. The major critical texts of continental romanticism, by this standard, can be called manifestoes, but some of them, clearly, are manifestoes *manqués*—Sismondi's, for example. The student of incipient romanticism must be prepared to qualify every generalization and almost every term generously and variously. The development which a dozen texts trace is not uniform or disciplined; the romanticism to be deduced from them is not consistent or single. Degrees of innovation are not always easy to assess; it is sometimes an offhand remark, sometimes a sheer weight of emphasis, which justifies the title.

A case in point is La Harpe, who is (with qualifications) a convenient point of departure. Had he made good his promises in the preface to *Le Lycée,* he would belong at least to the fringe of Madame de Staël's group. That he defaulted on them is a measure of his inability to break through the limitations of his neoclassical taste—and it is this taste and this prejudice, expressed or residual, which Madame de Staël, Chateaubriand, the Schlegels, Sismondi, Manzoni, Stendhal, Hugo, and Heine were united in rejecting. La Harpe's failure was a failure to indulge a historical sense whose value he conceded in principle; this was a not uncommon eighteenth-century phenomenon. The historical interpretation of literature compels a respect for more diversity than the codes—applied under the aspect of eternity—could admit. It meant discovering traditions which would then demand comparison with *the* tradition; and this would mean diminution of *the* tradition; even a verdict of *prima inter pares* would be a comedown, and comparison once embarked on could by no means guarantee a verdict of primacy.

La Harpe's intended innovation consists, he says, in offering to the public "une histoire raisonnée de tous les arts de l'esprit et de l'imagination, depuis Homère jusqu'à nos jours, qui n'exclut que les sciences exactes et les sciences physiques." Furthermore, "la philosophie de la critique" will involve "l'examen des rapports généraux du théâtre avec les mœurs des nations." If this statement of intentions seems to anticipate Madame de Staël's in *De la littérature,* a series of demurrers punctuates the actual performance, so that the period "depuis Homère jusqu'à nos jours" becomes, in his opening lecture, "les cinq siècles qui ont marqué dans l'histoire de l'esprit humain." If La Harpe was the father of historical criticism in France, as Faguet maintained, his role in its birth was the usual father's role; the fruitful conception of "la littérature considérée dans ses rapports avec les institutions sociales" was Madame de Staël's, in her book by that name.

The catholicity of Madame de Staël's interest was announced early; she too, including in the term literature all but the physical sciences, strove to trace "l'histoire des progrès de la pensée depuis Homère jusqu'à nos jours." This meant, however, not five remarkable centuries, but a conscientious effort "pour suivre les progrès, et pour observer le caractère dominant des écrivains de chaque pays et de chaque siècle." She did not carry out her task fully, but not for the reasons that made La Harpe default. In the first place, Madame de Staël simply lacked the knowledge. Her chapters on classical literature, on much of English literature, and on the Middle Ages generally, betray her lack of firsthand familiarity. In the second place, her temperament barred her from a thoroughness which she would probably—and wistfully—have called Germanic. Thibaudet has noted that her book "reste soutenu par le mouvement d'une conversation," and this might be said in lesser degree of the work on Germany as well. The real

Portrait of Madame de Staël by Elisabeth Vigée-Lebrun.

point about *De la littérature* is not that it failed to be fully what it promised to be (for these promises were plural), but that it succeeded enough to justify its character as manifesto. Madame de Staël at least remained faithful to her method.

The historicism of that method took several lines. It was governed throughout by her theory of perfectibility, which saw a constant development of Western civilization from its beginnings and which, relating literature to social institutions, climate, and geography, found literature in some sense subject to a parallel development. In any case, her very attention to these external factors made it clear that (as against La Harpe's claim that literature always imitates nature, and that nature is always and everywhere the same) each literary work occurs at a unique juncture, and that the critic must consequently have a variable scale on which to measure it. Though she was reluctant to say so outright, the implication is plain that one *goût*—itself the product of particular conditions—is inadequate to the critic's job. One might even claim that *De la littérature* was a pioneer effort in the field of comparative literature. "Vous ne pouvez juger qu'en comparant," she wrote, and brought into the field of comparison much that the neoclassicists had ignored.

Another line her criticism took amounted to an adumbration of the *Zeitgeist.* There is, she found, a general spirit of modern literature—a concomitant of the modern sensibility which chivalry and Christianity produced. This point, pursued to obsession by Chateaubriand, was further particularized by Madame de Staël in terms of geography and climate (and, of course, of her own temperament). Thus she states that, "à l'époque où nous vivons, la mélancolie est la véritable inspiration du talent: qui ne se sent pas atteint par ce sentiment, ne peut prétendre à une grande gloire comme écrivain; c'est à ce prix qu'elle est achetée." Place this alongside the observation that "la mélancolie . . . semble appartenir presque exclusivement aux climats du Nord," and the twofold revolutionary impact becomes clear. In the first place, a new content is urged for contemporary literature which would set it off sharply from a classical tradition unable to supply models for it. In the second place, not only is a literature like the English allowed a legitimacy for the first time, but it is advanced as worthy of emulation. As Lanson notes [Gustave Lanson, *Histoire de la littérature française,* 1912], Madame de Staël spoke of the English and the Germans "comme personne encore n'avait parlé chez nous." She did so, further, with special attention to social institutions and to the politics that support these institutions. Shakespeare's tragedies and histories are explained not by genius or race alone, but by the fact that they were written at the conclusion of a period of civil war, when violence and violent contrasts were still in the air. English national history, she suggests, produced more abundant tragedy than the French—for the freer English writers to embellish into literature.

The novelty of this applied method cannot be overstressed. Despite its dependence on her unsteady mixture of thought and emotion, on her dogma of perfectibility, on her penchant for slenderly based speculation and often on her downright ignorance, it dignified a whole series of questions by raising them seriously, and paved the way for the *débat romantique* which broke out in earnest during the following decades.

"Ma folie est de voir Jésus-Christ partout, comme madame de Staël la *perfectibilité*." So wrote Chateaubriand apropos of his *Génie du Christianisme*, but the statement is badly misleading. Its largest truth is to indicate the subordination of both books to an a priori thesis. But, even here, Madame de Staël left herself a greater freedom for independent judgment by pointedly exempting imaginative literature from her thesis of *le progrès*. Within her limits, she set out to make distinctions; within his very general distinctions, Chateaubriand was busy remaking beauties. A measure of his failure to see essential differences is his fondness for comparing texts in terms of such irrelevancies as the marriage relationship (Ulysses and Penelope versus Adam and Eve), or, for that matter, his failure to distinguish Catholicism from the Christianity he purports to discuss.

Since the essence of the historical method is that faculty for particularization which Madame de Staël proclaimed and tried to practice, Chateaubriand's contribution to literary historicism would seem to be small indeed. Seeing the modern period as distinct from the ancient, after all, was hardly a discovery. And yet, seeing modern cultures as *qualitatively* distinct from the ancient was new. Madame de Staël had hinted at this in *De la littérature;* but, perhaps because her enthusiasm did not extend to Catholicism, she could not be so thorough in exploring the difference. Perhaps also her dynamic conception of "les progrès de l'espèce humaine" unfitted her for that trait which Thibaudet calls the core of Chateaubriand: "le sens d'une durée, la familiarité avec une durée." The Christian dualism, the intuition of the infinite, the sense of "une certaine vérité cachée," the dichotomy between reason and passions, the ubiquitous presence of grace—in short, the whole intellectual apparatus of Catholicism—is marshalled by Chateaubriand not so much to describe the modern sensibility as to demonstrate it. And from this exaggerated awareness, based as it is on a historical truth, can come such a reasoned perception as that of the superiority of Racine's *Phèdre*, which offers "une gradation des sentiments, une science de la tristesse, des angoisses et des transports de l'âme, que les anciens n'ont jamais connues." Chateaubriand, in sum, put the *querelle* on a new basis by using a historical touchstone; he found, by his lights, that ancient and modern poets offered different superiorities, and in that sense he resolved the *querelle*—for himself, at least.

Beyond this, though he has a neat chapter summarizing the national characters of Europe, and though he criticizes the German epic for lacking *vraisemblance des mœurs*, Chateaubriand inclines more to the contemplation of timeless generalities than to a search for historic junctures—for him there is only one. In Isaiah Berlin's figure, he is a hedgehog of romantic criticism—*the* great hedgehog, in fact. But from the very amplitude of his vision came more than one insight for the foxes who came after to develop.

Echoes of Chateaubriand are in fact not far to seek in August Wilhelm Schlegel's *Vorlesungen über dramatische Kunst und Literatur*, delivered in Vienna in the spring of 1808. In his first lecture, speaking of what distinguishes romantic (modern) from classical (Greek) literature, Schlegel remarks:

> Man can never altogether turn aside his thoughts from infinity, and some obscure recollections will always remind him of the home he has lost . . . . Religion is the root of human existence. Were it possible for man to renounce all religion, including that which is unconscious, independent of the will, he would become a mere surface without any internal substance. When this centre is disturbed, the whole system of the mental faculties takes a new shape. And this is what has actually taken place in modern Europe through the introduction of Christianity.

And, echoing both Chateaubriand and Madame de Staël, he sees the modern temper marked by a penchant for melancholy—a trait alike of the Christian outlook and of the character of northern peoples.

Schlegel was, of course, an independent scholar, and the depth of his scholarship alone sets his work apart from the works mentioned so far. And yet, if we consider Madame de Staël a pioneer of the historical method, we must recognize Schlegel as a more thoroughgoing complement to her, equipped with knowledge as she was not and, because he was educated outside the French tradition, free to go further than she into that genuine relativism which the historical interpretation of literature requires. The great degree to which he used that freedom is what gives this course of lectures its character—especially for a French audience—as manifesto.

Schlegel states all this forcefully at the outset, requiring of the true critic "universality of mind" and flexibility "to adapt himself to the peculiarities of other ages and nations—to feel them, as it were, from their proper central point, and . . . to recognize and duly appreciate whatever is beautiful and grand under the external accessories which were necessary to its embodying, even though occasionally they may seem to disguise and distort it." Applied in practice, Schlegel's theory subverted the whole neoclassic monolith. Specifically, probably his greatest contribution to historical criticism was a discriminating scrutiny of the classical theater. He explained Greek tragedy as dependent far more on the nature of the Greek stage and religion and mores than on any assumed discovery of universal laws of poetic creation. Greek comedy emerged as a sort of mirror image of tragedy, reversing its modes as it reversed the earnestness of the tragic poet. His method vindicated by its illumination of the Greek works, he transferred it to the Romans and found that their poetry, far from being a parallel expression of the genius of Roman society and civilization, was derivative. For the first time a qualitative distinction was thus made between a genuine classical form—the Greek tragedy—and a spurious (because grafted-on) form, the *Trauerspiel* of the Romans. This, with its burden of scholarly application to the works of Shakespeare and his continental peers, is the heart of Schlegel's contribution to the historical interpretation of literature: the notion not only of a general *Zeitgeist,* but of a *Volksgeist,* and the perception that a literature which is not in consonance with these is, in the deepest sense, not true to itself, or indeed to any clearly understood tradition.

Madame de Staël in *De la littérature* had felt her conclusions and labored through a speculative-critical-historical essay to give them a basis; Chateaubriand had put on rose-colored spectacles and then catalogued in splendid prose the infinitude of rose-colored objects he saw around him; Schlegel had essayed new territory in considering the drama as a genre and then, through careful attention to its various historical settings, proceeded to discover how variety of setting gave to the drama its various forms and manners. J. C. L. Simonde de Sismondi, with the easy cosmopolitanism of the Swiss, feeling personally the impact of Madame de Staël's ideas and the friction of Schlegel's, proposed for himself a somewhat different aim in writing *De la littérature du Midi de l' Europe.* Subordinating both theory and criticism to historical exposition, he aimed "seulement de rassembler et de présenter aux gens de goût ce qu'il leur convient de savoir sur les littératures étrangères."

Despite bows to La Harpe and Marmontel, the whole ponderous weight of his argument opposes them precisely as Madame de Staël's book had done after a similar obeisance. In pursuing his intention "de faire juger le lecteur pour lui-même," he was working for a democracy of literary taste to replace an established oligarchy. In distinguishing between "règles conventionnelles de chaque littérature" and "règles fondamentales," he was adumbrating Manzoni's, Stendhal's, and Hugo's proclamation of a single fundamental unity. In relating literature to politics and to a national character, he was developing De Bonald's and Madame de Staël's ideas—and correcting some of the latter. In all of this lies the character of the book as manifesto, and it is only the mummification of these arguments in historical exposition that makes it a manifesto *manqué.*

There is a prophetic passage in Sismondi's work where, having called the epic the noblest of poetic genres, he nevertheless goes on to deduce from history a special claim for the lyric, in words which prefigure the great role of the lyric in nineteenth-century romantic poetry: "Le genre lyrique est le premier qui soit cultivé dans chaque langue au renouvellement de toute littérature; c'est le seul où le poète s'abandonne sans but à ses impressions . . . Le poète lyrique . . . chante parce qu'il est ému, parce qu'il est inspiré." One is tempted to revise these words a little to see in them the Madame de Staël of *De l'Allemagne:* "Elle s'abandonne avec un but à ses impressions; elle écrit parce qu'elle est émue, parce qu'elle est inspirée." One object at least of her book was clear enough to the minister of police, who banned it in 1810, observing, "Il m'a paru que l'air de ce pays-ci ne vous convenait point, et nous n'en sommes pas encore réduits à chercher des modèles dans les peuples que vous admirez."

The method of *De l'Allemagne* is somewhat different from that of *De la littérature.* That had been a speculative essay; this was a work of reportage. The same capacity for re-

marking particular differences informs it: Saxony is distinguished from Weimar, Vienna from Berlin. The same attempt is made to relate literature to society. But here her material forces a change of terms, for Madame de Staël finds the influence of solitude on German writers greater than that of society. This means, in the first place, that Germany forms its writers not through institutions but through *les mœurs,* which are deeply and *non-institutionally* national. There is not even *le monde,* in the sense of a class repository of sophistication, to set the tone of German writing. "Un auteur allemand," in all the naive freedom of his solitude, "forme son public." In the absence of mediating laws, literature's relation is directly with an intangible but recognizable entity, *la nation.* A second result of her discussion of German solitude is a recognition that the character of German philosophy, quite as much as that of the literature, is traceable to it. National character produces both, by the same process, from the same source. Hence the impossibility of maintaining the distinction she had made in her earlier work between *poésie* and *philosophie*—the distinction on which had rested her theory of perfectibility. *De l'Allemagne* thus is less encumbered by preconceptions; and the historical interpretation of literature becomes a task chiefly of discriminating genuine manifestations of the genius of a nation from the spurious ones.

The Germans, needless to say, come off far better on this score than the French. The tyranny of society in France cramps the writer's ability to express his own individuality; fear of ridicule limits him to conventions which may develop his acuteness but isolate him from nature—his own, and his country's. So strictly is this limitation maintained that its exceptions are not French at all! "J.-J. Rousseau, Bernardin de Saint-Pierre, Châteaubriand, etc., dans quelques-uns de leurs ouvrages, sont tous, même à leur insçu, de l'école germanique, c'est-à-dire qu'ils ne puisent leur talent que dans le fond de leur âme." In drawing such essentially hortatory comparisons, Madame de Staël shows the usefulness of her historical approach to literature; towards the end of the book this is stated openly, in a paragraph which could stand independently as her manifesto in small:

> Les nations doivent se servir de guide les unes aux autres et toutes auroient tort de se priver des lumières qu'elles peuvent mutuellement se prêter. Il y a quelque chose de très-singulier dans la différence d'un peuple à un autre: le climat, l'aspect de la nature, la langue, le gouvernement, enfin surtout les événements de l'histoire, puissance plus extraordinaire encore que toutes les autres, contribuent à ces diversités, et nul homme, quelque supérieur qu'il soit, ne peut deviner ce qui se développe naturellement dans l'esprit de celui qui vit sur un autre sol et respire un autre air: on se trouvera donc bien en tout pays d'accueillir les pensées étrangères; car, dans ce genre, l'hospitalité fait la fortune de celui qui reçoit.

After *De l'Allemagne* come the abolitionists among the romantic manifesto writers: Manzoni with his *Lettre à M. Chauvet,* and Stendhal with *Racine et Shakespeare.* Neither is concerned primarily with practical criticism; both are frankly polemical. Manzoni's book is a cogent and concentrated attack on the theory of the two unities (for he accepts unity of action as inherent in an achieved drama, defining it simply as "la représentation d'une suite d'événements liés entre eux"). His method is unexceptionable—to consider with strict logic the neoclassical claim that the rules facilitate imitation of nature. Having disposed of the rules, he proposes history—by which he seems to mean historically verified events—as a guide to dramatists, who should be allowed to heighten effects but not to sacrifice *la vraisemblance* (as, in fact, he claims the rules do). Since his argument is almost entirely confined to theory, a real historicism enters only by way of allusion; at one point he criticizes the application of rules to masterpieces "hors de toute comparaison dans le système suivant lequel ils ont été conçus." And, towards the end, he sees contemporary progress in historical study as an ally in a way that suggests Schlegel and Sismondi as possible examples.

From the *Lettre à M. Chauvet* it appears that Manzoni would abolish the neoclassical rules in order to write a better neoclassical drama, with a truer imitation of nature (for he does in fact call himself "un bon et loyal partisan du classique," and he objects as such to Shakespeare's mixing of genres). Stendhal, his fellow abolitionist, has quite a different end in view. His clearing action is to make way for a new, romantic drama, and *Racine et Shakespeare* is aimed as much at specifying its type as at removing the obstacles to it. In using "romantic" to mean "responsive to the *Zeitgeist*," he seeks to free the word from its geographical, historical, and religious connotations; and, for all its flippancy, his famous definition of *le romanticisme* and *le classicisme* does actually refine the idea of the *Zeitgeist* by making the generation a measure for changes of taste. If, ultimately, Stendhal's vigorously polemic manifesto lacks any unity beyond what his temperament inevitably gives it, its direction is still clear. The new literature he hails is realistic; this would seem to be the point of his praise for Werner's nuanced treatment of Luther, as well as for his advocacy of prose tragedy. He makes an important application of historical criticism in observing that, in modern times, the majority of readers replaces royal patrons as an instrument of conformity. Some implications of this formed the subject of Sainte-Beuve's "De la littérature industrielle" fourteen years later. Otherwise, while the pamphlet is full of interesting *aperçus,* it is also full of statements which are never developed to the point of persuasiveness, and which perhaps never could be. One intriguing speculation concludes a discussion of the best idiom to employ in the drama: "Peut-être faut-il être *romantique* dans les idées: le siècle le veut ainsi; mais soyons *classiques* dans les expressions et les tours: ce sont des choses de convention, c'est-à-dire à peu près immuables ou du moins fort lentement changeables." One would expect the term romantic, as Stendhal conceives it, to cover automatically "des choses de convention" so long as they were not anachronistic; but there is more clarity in the prose of this pamphlet than in its ideas.

From the standpoint of historicism, Hugo's *Préface de Cromwell* is largely a derivative essay in the vein of speculative history which his predecessors had worked. Cultures are seen as infant, adolescent, and mature, much as Madame de Staël saw them. Roman culture is seen with August Wilhelm Schlegel as separate and inferior to the Greek. The modern era, defined by "une religion spiritualiste" and marked by "un sentiment [inconnu des anciens] qui est plus que la gravité et moins que la tristesse, la mélancolie," begins with the Middle Ages. This last comes straight from Chateaubriand, but the development is new; the classic muse recognized only one type of the beautiful, and limited its imitation of nature to that type. But "la muse moderne verra les choses d'un coup d'œil plus haut et plus large. Elle sentira que tout dans la création n'est pas humainement beau, que le laid y existe à côté du beau, le difforme près du gracieux, le grotesque au revers du sublime, le mal avec le bien, l'ombre avec la lumière." Hugo's insistence on the legitimacy of the ugly and the grotesque in art—as one half, in fact, of the union which produced "le génie moderne"—is a tremendously important forward step, and one which even the most strident of his predecessors, Stendhal, balked at taking. The union of the grotesque and the sublime being a criterion of modernity, it follows that Dante, Milton, and Shakespeare should be hailed as the three giants of modern literature. It follows also that tragicomedy, the mixing of genres, should be welcomed as the embodiment of that union. And it follows, finally, that, with the discarding of the classical outlook, the classical insistence on two unnecessary unities should also be discarded. "Toute action a sa durée propre comme son lieu particulier." Ergo, recognizing a historical imperative, the call: "Mettons le marteau dans les théories, les poétiques et les systèmes . . . Le poète, insistons sur ce point, ne doit donc prendre conseil que de la nature, de la vérité, et de l'inspiration qui est aussi une vérité et une nature."

De Bonald had observed the part that literature played in preparing the French Revolution; Madame de Staël, sharing that awareness, had hoped to guide literature in preparing the new, postrevolutionary society. In the historical imperative she saw a need to break the hegemony of neoclassical aesthetics—at least to the point of sympathetically studying foreign political and literary experiences. French literary greatness was not to be disparaged; the question was rather of continuing to justify it in the new era by new modes. To us this seems an unexceptionable notion. But to the neoclassicists its premise was unthinkable. The models of antiquity seemed to them as bright and as serviceable as ever—and it followed that no national literature that disregarded them could be worth the notice of the heirs of Greece and Rome. "Il n'y a pas longtemps encore," Manzoni could write with truth in 1820, "que juger avec impartialité lés génies étrangers attirait le reproche de manquer de patriotisme."

Under these circumstances, the methods and the failings of all the romantic manifesto writers become understandable. For they were all, willy-nilly, abolitionists of the antihistorical dogmas. They were all, in this sense at least, the voice of the young man in Stendhal's epigraph to Part II of *Racine et Shakespeare.* To those whose recommendation for French literature was "Continuons," they all—even Chateaubriand, in his way—replied, "Examinons."

And their examination led them inevitably to geographical as well as to historical comparisons. Their subject was *la littérature comparée*. The causal relation is implied in Sainte-Beuve's remarks on the history of literature in France: "Ce ne fut qu'au sortir de la Révolution qu'un genre de curiosité purement intellectuelle, le besoin de savoir ce qui se pensait et s'écrivait au dehors, vient s'emparer de quelques esprits studieux." *Besoin* here must be accorded its full force. Their need, that is, determined their subjects; but another kind of necessity contributed to the character of their works. The very fact that they were pioneers meant that they lacked any body of wholly reliable scholarship on which to build, and so explains their tendency to indulge in expositions so lengthy that questions of analysis and even of principle might get lost beneath them. If historicism was necessary, exposition had to precede it. The writer forms his public, Madame de Staël noted of the Germans (anticipating Wordsworth's similar declaration of five years later), implying that the German public was willing to be formed, as the French was not. For such a willingness open minds were needed, and a knowledge of foreign literatures was—as it still is—one way of opening them.

At this point political questions once again impinge on literary ones. Originally, it had been the revolutionary situation that touched off the debate and defined its terms. In the early 1800s, the Consulate, issue of the revolution, continued to point up the tie of literature with politics in the most practical way. We have seen how Napoleon's minister of justice had reacted to *De l'Allemagne*. Edmond Eggli has summarized the dilemma of the literary critics over the same book:

> L'ouvrage de Mme de Staël mit la presse française dans un cruel embarras. Sur la littérature et la philosophie allemandes peu de critiques étaient assez documentés pour discuter avec compétence ses jugements. Quant aux tendances générales du livre, elles suggéraient des appréciations difficilement conciliables, suivant qu'on les considérait du point de vue politique ou du point de vue littéraire. Et même, du point de vue politique, la perspective se modifiait complètement selon qu'on envisageait en France la situation nationale ou la question dynastique. Louer le livre *de l'Allemagne,* en mai 1814, c'était répudier les actes du gouvernement napoléonien et faire acte de loyalisme légitimiste: mais c'était renoncer à l'hégémonie européenne de l'esthétique française: c'était accepter, après Leipzig et l'invasion, une humiliation non moins sensible de la littérature nationale. Blâmer Mme de Staël, c'était affirmer l'idéal esthétique du classicisme français, c'était repousser l'invasion littéraire du Nord: mais c'était approuver Napoléon, qui avait reproché au livre *de l'Allemagne* de n'être pas français.

In the dilemma as here posed, the accuracy of Madame Staël's reportage was assumed! Only under Heine's rebuttal, when the book was subjected to a sharper discrimination, did it appear against its full political implications. "L'ensemble de cet ouvrage," Heine wrote in his own *De l'Allemagne,* "montrera que cette école [romantique] était toute différente de celle qu'on a désignée en France sous

ce titre, et que son but était tout-à-fait distinct du but des romantiques français." The exposition all goes to demonstrate that the Middle Ages themselves are not the same for Germany as for France, nor is Christianity. The rediscovery of the Catholic Middle Ages in Germany, Heine argued, represented a reactionary nationalism which went much deeper than mere literature:

> Les Français sont sortis depuis longtemps du moyen-âge, ils le contemplent avec calme, et peuvent apprécier ses beautés avec une impartialité philosophique ou artistique. Nous autres Allemands, y sommes encore enfoncés, dans ce moyenâge: nous combattons encore ses caducs représentans; nous ne pouvons donc l'admirer avec une grande complaisance. Il nous faut au contraire nous échauffer d'une haine partiale pour que notre force destructrice ne soit point paralysée.

Though *De la littérature* had noted the effects of literature upon society, most of the subsequent manifestoes considered here had used society almost exclusively to explain literature—because, among other reasons, their writers were interested in literature more than in politics. That is to say, up until Heine the theory of literary-political rapport had been a one-edged sword, good only in the paper fight against neoclassicism. Now Heine gave it another edge, and turned it into a weapon in the *Kulturkampf.*

By 1839 the situation, in France at least, had changed. Sainte-Beuve, writing "De la littérature industrielle," observed that "la chose littéraire . . . semble de plus en plus compromise"—not for any restriction of genius by rules, or for any lack of talent, or for political reasons. "Mais voilà qu'en littérature, comme en politique, à mesure que les causes extérieures de perturbation ont cessé, les symptômes intérieurs et de désorganisation profonde se sont mieux laissé voir." In the discussion that followed, Sainte-Beuve limited himself to the discussion of literature, for what he saw was a new stage in the politics of literature, based on the economics of literature. Here was, in effect, a sketch for a sociology of literary taste a century before Schücking. Madame de Staël had wondered a generation earlier: "Comment la littérature peut-elle se former dans un pays où l'on publie près de trois mille volumes par an? . . . Le vrai talent a peine à se reconnaître au milieu de cette foule innombrable de livres." When Sainte-Beuve wrote, "le démon de la propriété littéraire" was much more clearly visible: literature was becoming industrialized; authorship was becoming a means of livelihood and notoriety, abetted by collusion in the popular press. *La marche de l'esprit humain* was becoming *le marché de l'esprit humain.*

With Sainte-Beuve's essay, the historical method had caught up—had been forced to catch up—with contemporaneity. The notion that an author was in some sense a creature of his times was by now accepted—but the nature of his times was a matter calling for new and deeper study. The critic had seen this; so had the novelist. Seeking to anatomize his society, Balzac noted:

> La société française allait être l'historien, je ne devais être que le secrétaire. En dressant l'inventaire des vices et des vertus, en rassem-

blant les principaux faits des passions, en peignant les caractères, en choisissant les événements principaux de la société, en comparant des types par la réunion des traits de plusieurs caractères homogènes, peut-être pouvais-je arriver à écrire l'histoire oubliée par tant d'historiens, celle des mœurs.

No longer merely an inspiration, the *Zeitgeist* had become itself a subject for literary treatment, and by a literary form for which no one could claim models in antiquity. With Balzac, the growing historical consciousness which is traceable in the earlier manifestoes is finally assimilated into literature and, to reverse Thomas Mann's formula, *Kritrik wird Kunst.* (pp. 153-66)

> *D. L. Fanger, "Romanticism and Comparative Literature," in* Comparative Literature, *Vol. XIV, No. 2, Spring, 1962, pp. 153-66.*

THEMES AND TECHNIQUES

Henry H. H. Remak

[*Remak is a German educator and critic who has written extensively on French and German literature. In the following essay, he rejects the common assumption that Romantic literature is characterized by dichotomies and examines the Romantic artists' attempts to establish synthesis and balance.*]

This will be an arch-romantic essay: it attempts the impossible. Romanticism has often, with tossed-off facileness, been declared undefinable. Its built-in dichotomies have provided such a field day for students of romanticism that they have increasingly tended to throw the idea of a synthesis out of the ballpark. But scholarship cannot accept such taboos. If it did, it would deny its own raison d'être. To shirk the responsibility would be even more of a strikeout today, when rampant relativism has become the dominant fashion of literary theorizing. No individual, no society, can endure without some visible coherence. Analysis must lead to synthesis. There is today a pervasive underlying bias among Western intelligentsia and the corresponding segment in scholarship against intellectual ordering and especially literary syntheses. It is suspected that those arguing for the past and potential viability of synthesis are relics or prophets of ages of tutelage in claiming that all is ultimately for the best in this world.

We may freely admit that there is a particular American need for synthesis, for without it this immigrant continent could not function as a nation. But the general—by no means universal—success of this society in achieving a working balance of pluralism and coherence out of stupendous diversity perhaps gives Americans a relevant cultural experience in addressing related questions to very different contexts such as romanticism. Romanticism offers an iron test of our unfashionably positive premise: for no cultural current more explosive and yet more enduring has

hit European civilization in modern times. Individual and collective divergence and uniqueness has been one of its hallmarks. If such a centrifugal force can also generate centripetal counteraction, then maybe we are not in as bad a shape ourselves as the prevailing intellectual mode suggests. For in essence we face the same quandary as romanticism, though aggravated by the tremendous surge of technology. On the one hand, today cost-effectiveness demands, for competitive survival, galloping collectivization and impersonal mergers (read: nation building in and through romanticism). On the other hand, the cataclysmic violence of World War II (read: the French Revolution, the Napoleonic wars) has been followed by a period of liberal aspirations and confident assertions of individualism (stifled but not strangled by reactionary pressures in the romantic period). As in the romantic era, our society has a difficult time reconciling the proliferation of individual options (which correspond to Enlightenment as well as romantic values, though with different emphases), with the equally existential need for security—liberty with order. Both eras are the immediate heirs of enlightened rationalism (the eighteenth century; the on the whole remarkably peaceful progress, proletarization notwithstanding, of Western mankind between 1815 and 1914); both were shattered by brutal upheavals after which arose the effort, with varying success, to preserve both individual liberties and social responsibilities, to maintain a difficult equilibrium in the social contract that demands, as the price of tolerance, individual and collective discipline. In the field of artistic expression, in the arts, music, and literature, there was then, and is now, a particular urgency and, in general, disposition to defend and nurture the nonconformist imaginative wellsprings without which neither the arts nor the intellect and religion can flourish. The quest for synthesis of romanticism is not *only* of historic interest.

Our approach cannot be immune to the limitations of cohesive inquiry. Any synthesis has to be reductionist. This one, geared principally to nonspecialized readers, will be even more so. What it tries to offer is not only evidence for romantic attempts at synthesis but also illustrations of the process and problems of identifying them. It will limit itself, in essence, to Western European romanticism in space and to the romantic era in time (approximately the 1790s to the 1840s), cognizant that the most effective romantic syntheses may well be located in the postromantic culture: in the literature of Baudelaire and the symbolists (Rimbaud, Verlaine, Mallarmé, Ibsen, and Strindberg), in sculpture (Rodin), painting (Renoir, impressionism), philosophy (Schopenhauer, Nietzsche), psychology (Freud), and music (Wagner, Richard Strauss, Debussy). Even more painful, given the all-embracing ambitions of romanticism, will be the short shrift made of nonliterary areas running parallel to historical romanticism and deeply imbued with it: philosophy (Fichte, Schelling, Hegel), painting and illustrations (Blake, Fuseli, Friedrich, Delacroix, Géricault), and music (Beethoven, Weber, Schubert, Mendelssohn, Chopin, Schumann, Berlioz). The immense secondary literature will only be sampled, as will be the larger synthesis extant when one looks at European romanticism as a whole; that is, what may be lopsided in a particular national romanticism or genre is balanced by a differently oriented romanticism of another culture. This symbiotic arch most certainly amounts to a romantic synthesis *in European terms.* But for the purpose of this essay we will mainly concern ourselves with the synthesis proposed, explicitly or implicitly, by single romantic authors chiefly indigenous to Germany, England, France, Italy, and Spain. Our intention is: (1) to delineate the term *synthesis;* (2) to make a prima facie case for synthesis as an organic element in Western European romanticism; and (3) to give some illustrations of the quest for synthesis in specific works of West European romantics.

All the nonchemical definitions of *synthesis* given by Webster correspond to our use of the term: "the combining of often diverse conceptions into a coherent whole" fits our purpose particularly well. Translated into theoretical-methodological and philosophic terms, Webster reads: "the dialectic combination of thesis and antithesis into a higher stage of truth." This definition denotes more than a compromise, complementariness, compensation, reconciliation: it describes an ascent. But it does not postulate an impossible "seamlessness," a perfect unity, an infinite fusion, an ultimate truth, nor necessarily a wholly conscious process. That distinguishes—if in practice only by degrees, but by significant degrees—romanticism from classicism: romanticism is process-oriented, it is more likely to claim synthesis for one particular generation in a particular cultural environment. "Dynamism" is an essential part of the most satisfying definitions given of it. No vital synthesis can be permanent. It remains primarily functional for a certain stage of culture. It can be admired and even emulated by posterior cultures, but it cannot be substituted *telle quelle* for a synthesis at a different place at a different time. Romantic flux is not, however, directionless. It is a merging flux, a rhythm: centrifugal—centripetal. The constituents of the "coherent whole" are "diverse conceptions."

The case for romantic antitheses is also very strong. It would be folly to underestimate the striking differences between and within the various romanticisms as well as the existential contradictions uncovered by romanticism. Examples: Tony Tanner concludes a wide-ranging, truly "cultural" essay ["Notes for a Comparison Between American and European Romanticism," in *Diverging Parallels,* edited by A. N. J. Hollander, 1971] by saying that human integration into one's natural habitat is much more thorough in European than in American romanticism, whose environment was menacingly expansive. Heine finds there is not only no sense to the existential calvary of man but God himself is having fun with our misery ("Zum Lazarus" ["About Lazarus"] in *Das Buch Lazarus* [*Book Lazarus*]). Heaven gives no answer to the question: what is the meaning of man? (Heine, "Fragen" ["Questions"] in *Die Nordsee* [*The North Sea*]). The only dignified answer to the contempt shown for man by all natural and supernatural forces is indifference to them (Leopardi, "A se stesso" ["To Himself"]).

Furthermore, there is always an element of gamesmanship in the jockeying of terms such as *antithesis* and *synthesis.* The difference between dialectics and reality is never clear-cut. How much reality is there in the intellectually beguiling paradigm of Friedrich Schlegel, which elevates

irony to the common denominator of a romantic literature whose claim to revolutionary universality supersedes that of politics? And how can Schlegel's cult of the fragment and of the arabesque contribute to such a synthesis? How much reality is there even in a much more elaborate scheme such as Novalis's, which sees in the king the promise and guarantee of ultimate equality of human rights through a process of assimilation of the ordinary citizen to regal quality? And who can decide whether Nietzsche represents the ultimate synthesis or the ultimate antithesis?

The tensions within romanticism can, for a beginning and very simply, be divided between external and internal drives: the active versus the passive, Prometheus versus Orpheus, expansion versus aesthetic-musical propensities, Dionysus versus Apollo, passion and vitality versus contemplative reflection and self-analysis, the prophetic-communal versus the egocentric-narcissistic, the absolute versus the relative, the whole versus the fragment, monism versus dualism. But without tension there is no coherence, without antithesis no synthesis. Separation cannot be the ultimate aim of man. Unlike classicism, the Parnassians, symbolism, or dada, romanticism is, by nature, expansive. Isolation for it can only be a stage of self-assessment, of making sure that the uniqueness of "self" is not lost. And we are speaking of a *quest* for synthesis, which is not synonymous with the *achievement* of synthesis.

Syntheses may be diachronic as well as synchronic. Corresponding to syntheses composed of phenomena occurring more or less simultaneously in different cultures constituting European civilization is a potential synthesis of the two or more roughly sequential phases of romanticism within the larger movement. Historicism provides, especially in Germany, "a much larger perspective within which romanticism as such appears as only one phase in a larger evolution of thought."

Seen from the consecutive angle, the differences in historical evolution not only between the five countries but also within one national entity and within one and the same person are striking. The most complex of all constituents is, in all likelihood, the political element. The principal supranational events influencing political attitudes and shifts in European romanticism are the early phases of the French Revolution, the later phases of the French Revolution, and the restoration. The variables are local, regional, and national factors of history, social structure, economics, religion (for example, parentage between religious and political orthodoxy, on the one hand, and between applied Christianity and socialism, on the other), education, philosophy, family, friends, genes, health, aging, or early death. The individual evolution seems to be toward conservatism, but the political coloration of the two romantic generations—the one coming to the fore in the 1790s and the other one asserting itself twenty to thirty years later—is bewildering. Very tentatively and with weighty reservations, one makes out a drift from more theoretical, aesthetic, idealistic, transcendental, mystic positions (Herder [Böhme], Schiller, Novalis, Friedrich Schlegel, Fichte, Schleiermacher, Schelling, Blake, Coleridge, Chateaubriand, Alfieri) to worldlier applications of romanticism whether conservative or liberal. Second, one finds in all countries a shift, in the same writer, from earlier, more liberal attitudes (usually corresponding to the more pluralistic initial stages of the French Revolution) to steadily more conservative positions reflecting the impact, immediate or delayed, of the Terror: Chateaubriand, Madame de Staël, Schiller, Fichte, Klopstock, Wieland, Herder, Gentz, Görres, Novalis, Friedrich Schlegel, Schelling, Hegel, Coleridge, Wordsworth, Southey, Manzoni. Some positions are, however, equivocal: Klopstock, Herder, Kant, Blake, Monti. There are also shifts, in later stages of romanticism, from conservative to (more) liberal; Hugh and Lamartine are cases in point.

Writers and poets reacting to Napoleon are in an especially difficult quandary. To the extent he is the executor of the egalitarian, if not the libertarian, and modernizing thrust of the French Revolution, he is attractive to liberals such as Heine and Stendhal; to the extent he enhances the glory of France and suffered exile on a remote island from France's archenemy, he appeals even to French liberals (Hugo) and German patriots (Rückert, Platen). His charisma, genius, and "superman" stance entice corresponding affinities among the romantics (Hugo, Manzoni, Byron, Heine), but his authoritarian suppression of internal liberties and his insatiable conquest of foreign lands, draining them as well as his own, evokes the very opposite reactions (Arndt, Kleist, Körner, Scott). The repressive restoration eras in Austria and Germany (1815-48) and in France (1815-30), followed by the materialistic, comfortably musty reign of the "roi bourgeois," Louis-Philippe, revived Napoleonic sympathies. As a result of the many variables and glossing over the many nuances, one finds, third, and contrary to the common assumption that romanticism is politically conservative, nay reactionary, an approximate equilibrium of politically conservative and liberal romantics. On the more conservative side: Klopstock, Wieland, Fichte, Görres, Gentz, Hegel, Schelling, Brentano (all in their later stages), Schiller, Goethe (both considered romantics outside of Germany), Novalis, Kleist, Adam Müller, Friedrich Schlegel, Arnim, Fouqué, Arndt, Körner, Eichendorff (Germany); Coleridge, Southey, Wordsworth (in their later years), and Carlyle (England); Chateaubriand, Joseph de Maistre, De Bonald, Vigny (France); the later Manzoni and the elusive Monti (Italy). On the more liberal side: in addition to the German writers mentioned above (who turned from earlier liberalism toward more conservatism due to the course of the French Revolution), there are Jean Paul, Hölderlin (who, to be sure, was mentally *hors de concours* from about 1802 to 1806 on) and, in the next generation, Heine and Uhland; in England, Burns, Blake (a very complex case), Byron, Hazlitt, Hunt, Shelley (plus the early Coleridge, Southey, and Wordsworth); in France, Madame de Staël (a conservative liberal), the later Hugo, Lamartine, George Sand, Stendhal, Lamennais, and the communal socialist Christianity of Saint-Simon, Leroux, Fourier, and Proud'hon; in Italy, the earlier Manzoni, Monti (?), Berchet, Foscolo, Gioberti, Mazzini, Pellico, and Stendhal, never mind his French nationality (nor must the tremendous impact of Verdi's liberal romanticism be forgotten). (Lermontov and Pushkin would fit into the liberal romantic category in Russia.) Spain was caught in searing inter-

nal and external political struggles (peninsular war, civil wars). It had to fight against foreign military and cultural domination (France) and absolutism at home. Spanish romanticism is essentially liberal (Espronceda, Larra, Duque de Rivas, Martínez de la Rosa), but with a conservative turn in later romanticism (Zorrilla). Portuguese romanticism, arising in a country with a great past but strong dependence on the Spanish neighbor and Great Britain, poor as well as economically backward, is epitomized by the charismatic and liberal Joao Batista Almeida Garrett (poet, dramatist, folklorist), who had close ties to French romanticism.

This is a preliminary sorting that at this point hardly justifies any hypothesis of sequential synthesis; at most one can speak of compensatory shifts. The terms *liberal* and *conservative* are slippery in some respects. Open-mindedness toward the French Revolution in its incipient stages certainly showed a liberal attitude, but could a real liberal continue to support it after the events of September 1792? Are conservatives in England, for example, less concerned with fundamental human rights than liberals? Are not the motivations of populism, so characteristic of romanticism—running the gamut from arch-conservative to ultraliberal—so heterogeneous as to preclude a substantive synthesis? (A better case for a more genuine synthesis of conservative and liberal romanticism can be made on behalf of present-day environmentalism.)

More promising are diachronic syntheses combining premedievalism, medievalism, classicism, Renaissance, and Enlightenment with romanticism. The carry-over of the past into the present is a fact of life in all cultures at all times, but it tends to be covered up by the dialectics of historical scholarship, which is inclined to enshrine the particular moment in time on which the scholar in question has chosen to focus his attention. Romanticism has a very personal hold on many scholars (myself not excepted), addicted to it in the belief that it represents one of the most revolutionary turnabouts ever in Western civilization and of determinative (if not exclusive) influence on the Western Hemisphere in the last century and a half. Hence there are ideological and psychological obstacles to sequential syntheses felt as diluting the case for the more largely synchronic concept of a coherent romantic movement. Our answer to this dilemma is that diachronic syntheses do not exclude synchronic syntheses and vice versa: both are legitimate but different approaches to a comprehensive and complex phenomenon.

Counteracting the "save romanticism" instinct is an experience rediscovered and nurtured by romanticism itself: memory. For cultures it means the reintegration of distant collective memories into present consciousness; hence the unprecedented flowering of the historical genres in the romantic era in all Western cultures except the American one: the historical drama (Hugo, Kleist, Shelley's *The Cenci,* Musset's *Lorenzaccio,* Martínez de la Rosa's *La conjuración de Venezia* [The Conspiracy of Venice]), the historical novel and novella (Hugo, Kleist, Scott, Alexis, Vigny's *Cinq-Mars,* Manzoni, Stendhal), ballads, and more. For individuals, the rediscovery of memory means the reintegration of infancy and adolescence into maturity. Wordsworth's delicate observation is applicable to the cultural as well as the individual level: "but that the soul, remembering how she felt, but what she felt remembering not, retains an obscure sense of possible sublimity." The child, the naïve (in the sense of Schiller's *Über naive und sentimentalische Dichtung* [On Naive and Sentimental Poetry, 1795-96]), is more immediately and intuitively in tune with the divine at dusk, with the rhythmical wholeness of day and night, the everlasting union of heaven and sea, than the "solemn thought" of the adult father ("It is a beauteous evening"). "The child is father of the man"—only apparently paradoxical—is a prerequisite for a fulfilled life on the individual level. An adult is viable only so long as he maintains his childlike capacity for internal movement, for emotional quickness, for instinctive response to "natural piety" evoked by a wonder of nature: "My heart leaps up when I behold a rainbow in the sky: so was it when my life began, so is it now I am a man, so be it when I shall grow old, or let me die."

Novalis's language is more ecstatic than Wordsworth's, but it extols childhood and childlikeness in the same universalist terms as the English romantic. Heinrich von Ofterdingen sees two roads to truth: the first one is the path of practical experience, but he perceives it as "wearisome and without visible goal, with countless twists and turns"; whereas the other, "hardly more than a single leap," is "the way of intuition," an uninhibited "childlike simplicity" that "hits upon the right path through the labyrinth of our mundane affairs more certainly than a shrewdness misled and hemmed in by concern for private advantage and blinded by the inexhaustible sum of new contingencies and complications." The strength of childlike intuition is that it is closer to the "infinite source" that gives the child unearned superiority "in the highest and holiest matters." The nostalgia of old people for tales of childhood exemplifies the overarching continuity of life—like Wordsworth's rainbow—whether in man or in nature: the old man sitting in his garden is among his children, "and I look upon myself as an old tree from whose roots this youthful throng has sprouted." Henry's father, practical as he is, nevertheless spends his happiest hours among his flowers; that explains, says Heinrich, his openness toward children "since flowers are the images of children." "Clouds are perhaps the manifestation of a second, higher childhood, of paradise regained, and hence let their showers fall so beneficently on this other childhood": flowers.

Vertical synthesis joins horizontal synthesis to produce an organic personal and social whole. Romanticism had a particular affinity for distant memories, for the earliest, deepest roots in the subconscious complementing the synchronic and conscious experience of collective adulthood (see, for example, Rousseau's social contract). It delved sympathetically into prehistoric and early historic, pre-Christian and non-Christian times and spaces, into the origin of peoples, of poetry, into *Urmythen*, into the struggle between "alien" Christianity and indigenous paganism (Oehlenschläger's *Hakon Jarl* [Earl Hakon] and his "Guldhornene" [Golden Horns]; Fouqué's Nordic dramas). But in so doing romanticism had to pick up potent seminal leads engendered by Enlightenment's Nordic and Celtic Renaissance: the scholarship and literary activities

of Vico, Mallet, Herder, Percy, MacPherson (see the several pages of excerpts from Ossian in Goethe's arch-romantic *Werther*, 1774), Gray, Collins, Klopstock, Bodmer, and Wieland. In its search for the Mediterranean Renaissance, for the non-Christian, nonclassicistic, nonformalist, nontraditional Dionysian forces of occidental antiquity, romanticism secured, it is true, its identity vis-à-vis reigning classicism and found it confirmed in the unbroken *élan vital* of such *locales romantiques par excellence* as Italy (Heinse, Madame de Staël, Shelley, Byron, Eichendorff, Stendhal, Musset, Quinet), Corsica (Mérimée), Greece (Byron), and Spain (Byron, Hugo, Mérimée). Its Hellenism, however, could not but be affected by classicism of long standing (principally in France and Italy, but also in Spain and England) or, as in Germany, the immediately preceding and simultaneous impact of classicism (Schiller, Goethe, Hölderlin, the Humboldt brothers, even Lessing and Wieland), the chief representatives of which (Wieland, Schiller, Goethe, and Hölderlin) struck and still strike non-Germans as "romantics."

What work is hailed in 1798 by the arch-prophet and chief theoretician of literary romanticism, Friedrich Schlegel, because it comes closer to the holistic ideal of romanticism than any other prose text? Goethe's *Wilhelm Meisters Lehrjahre* (*Wilhelm Meister's Apprenticeship Years*, 1795-96), an apex of German classicism to be sure, but according to Schlegel with an admixture of romantic elements: "natural poetry [*Naturpoesie*] which suffuses the whole romantic magic and music." Admittedly, says Schlegel, the internal and the external, feeling or reflection and social activity, seem to be dichotomous from the beginning of the work on, and even "with the most beautiful and most intimate concordance and oneness the ultimate nexus of thoughts and emotions may be felt as lacking." Just *because* of that it is, asserts Schlegel, a "living oneness" (*lebendige Einheit*), a "harmony of dissonances."

The evidence for synthesis marshaled by Schlegel in one of the exemplary reviews of modern times is encompassing: means and goal; striving, will, and feeling; nature and the formation of self (*Bildung*); the external and the internal; the theater as the merger of art and society; living and art ("The art of all arts is the art of living" [*Lebenskunst*]), art and science; religion becoming art—and the whole overarched by serenity and irony. After the moral failure of the political revolution in France, Schlegel believes in art as the revolutionary synthesis, in literature, whether in verse or in prose and including criticism, as the marriage of language and music, reality and beauty. Protagonist and work unite in their drive toward the whole. Schlegel romanticizes classical architecture by comparing the uncle and the abbé in Goethe's novel to mighty pilasters, with Lothario as the cupola striving heavenwards. He describes the work as the wedding of the "allegorical" (symbolic?) and universal with the specific, a complete poetics of the world à la Shakespeare to which creator and critic, empathy and reflection, self and cosmos, the subjective and the objective, make their fused contribution. To put it epigrammatically: classicism objectifies the subjective, romanticism subjectivizes the objective. Both are syntheses with different departures but related goals.

How typical this link between German classicism and romanticism is—and in view of the impact of German romanticism on European literature, of romanticism as a European phenomenon—is confirmed by August Wilhelm von Schlegel's *Vorlesungen über dramatische Kunst und Literatur* (*Lectures on Dramatic Art and Literature,* 1809-11). Here romantic "poetry"—taken in the same universal, nongeneric sense as by his brother—blends everything that is opposed: nature and art, poetry and prose, seriousness and jest, memory and foreboding, spirituality and sensuality, the terrestrial and the divine, life and death. Poetry, to A. W. Schlegel, is the manifestation of the secret pull, hidden beneath ordered creation in its very womb, toward chaos, forever struggling for new and wonderful births.

In other European countries, romanticism and classicism have close bonds not because they are, as in Germany, largely simultaneous phenomena of the highest caliber in a culture with relatively weak previous classicistic patterns. On the contrary, romanticism is, especially in France and Italy, an alien upstart trying to assert itself against a long and profoundly acculturated classical and classicistic tradition strong enough to be part of the romantics themselves. In Italy, above all, almost all romantics are also classicists: Alfieri, Foscolo, Pellico, Monti, Leopardi, Manzoni. In France, classicistic influences are unmistakable in the styles of Chateaubriand, Madame de Staël, George Sand, Lamartine, Vigny, Musset, and Stendhal. Even in Spain, with the forceful *siglo de oro* in its recent past and a strong indigenous folkloristic tradition, classicistic influences nevertheless persisted in Larra, Martínez de la Rosa, and the Duque de Rivas. The political situation strongly affects the survival of classicism and the problems of romanticism in France, Italy, and Spain; it is therefore far too early to speak of a synthesis of classicism and romanticism in these countries, not only because of pronounced national variations and sharply profiled polemical antitheses put forward by both camps but also because of the intermingling of romanticism and classicism, of expansion and contraction, in one and the same author.

There is, however, copious evidence for a much greater balance in the romantic movement between the rationalism championed by the Enlightenment and the cult of emotions and imagination typical of romanticism. Research in the last four decades has effected a rapprochement between the two consecutive and simultaneous waves by enlarging the notion of Enlightenment to cover the liberation of emotions as well as of reason and, conversely, emphasizing the distinctly rationalistic, intellectual, and scientific qualities of romantics (such as Novalis). A similar assertion can be made about the emergence of realism from romanticism.

Even more incontrovertible proof exists of the very conscious attempt to integrate medieval times into romanticism, which revived and reshaped the memory for the Middle Ages, whose "darkness" was precisely what fascinated romanticism. There, too, a synthetic memory operates, combining the extrovert, daring-do for damsels-in-distress swordsmanship of the embattled hero ("The Eve of St. Agnes," *Ivanhoe*), the great deeds against terrible odds of chivalry, feudal loyalty, the crusades, tournaments, of unbroken faith and passionate determination, with the religious internalism of a still unified Christianity (see, for example, Novalis's *Die Christenheit oder Europa* [*Christendom or Europe,* 1799]) in a fusion of reason and faith that the surge of Protestanism or of pragmatism, materialism, and science had subsequently—so the hypothesis goes—unbalanced. Romanticism's nostalgia for the normative-collective binding found by a leap back into the Middle Ages compensated for the equally romantic assertion of individual uniqueness, for its modernist cult of subjectivity; together the normative and the unique constitute the essence of literary scholarship: history and criticism. D. W. Robertson, Jr., contrasts a "dominant medieval convention, the tendency to think in terms of symmetrical patterns," with a corresponding modern convention "to think in terms of opposites"; but this does not lead, he thinks, to a perpetuation of antitheses but to vital interaction resulting in synthesis. He sees the romantic critic, to be sure, as one who stands "in dynamic opposition to the conventions of his society" but whose task is precisely to "synthesize, resolve the tensions thus produced in his art." Hoffmeister [in *Deutsche und europäische Romantik,* 1978] interprets Novalis's *Christendom or Europe* as aiming at a new political and religious synthesis for which the romanticized Middle Ages serve as a poetic metaphor rather than a specific solution.

A romantic amalgamation of medieval introversion, unbroken vigor, and modernism is sought and found in the (especially Italian) Renaissance: Heinse's *Ardinghello und die glückseligen Inseln* (*Ardinghello and the Blissful Isles,* 1787), Wackenroder and Tieck's *Herzensergiessungen eines kunstliebenden Klosterbruders* (*Outpourings of the Heart of an Art-loving Friar,* 1797), Lamb's and Hazlitt's essays, Vigny's *La maréchale d'Ancre* (*The Wife of the Marshal d'Ancre,* 1831, late Italo-French Renaissance), Musset's *Lorenzaccio* (1833), Stendhal's Italian chronicles and novellas as well as his merger of contemporary and Renaissance motifs in *La chartreuse de Parme* (*The Charterhouse of Parma,* 1839), and Tieck's *Vittoria Accorombona* (1840).

With their general orientation toward the past, it is no great surprise that the strongest literary influences on romanticism are attributable not to contemporary writers (above all, Byron, Scott, E.T.A. Hoffmann, Hugo, Dumas Père, authors who often preferred historic subjects themselves) but to more remote poets such as Dante, Shakespeare, Cervantes, Calderón, and Milton, themselves "historic." Compared to its predecessor (the Enlightenment), romanticism, though in some of its aspects excessively historistic, made up in historical perspective not only for its immediate antecedent but also for its immediate successor, realism, both more centered on subjects of direct contemporary relevance. In this sense romanticism had better equilibrium than they did.

Romanticism's total absorption with the various levels of the past can perhaps be subsumed under the heading of the search for comprehensive authenticity. Premedieval and medieval times cultivated the imagination, the yearning for togetherness, or exquisite formalism in literature and art, but lacked opportunities for self-expression of nonprivileged individuals. The Renaissance furnished romanticism with unbridled forcefulness but little ethics and few norms. Classicism excelled in moral, social, and formal norms but repressed passion and in the end, no matter how understanding, punished noncompliance and spontaneity; the experiences it described were too remote from the personal encounters, internal and external, of the author. The Enlightenment, by drawing on the middle classes and lower-level aristocracy (see, for example, the *Marriage of Figaro*), makes the artistic experience more authentic by anchoring it in personal living, and it has good balance between the normative and the individualized, but it curtailed imagination, defused faith, and diluted the tragic. Romanticism caps the movement toward authenticity by resting its literary art on the reality of the "I," but it had to look for vitalistic individual and collective compensations in the past.

In a recent paradigmatic essay ["Societal Models as Substitute Reality in Literature," *Poetics Today* (1984)], Virgil Nemoianu has convincingly argued that preromantic "changes—exoticism, historic nostalgia, subjectivity" developed by the eighteenth century were combined by romanticism in a "unifying principle": expansion in time, space, variety, and depth. The pre- and pararomantic "additions" to eighteenth-century rationalism (we could perhaps go a step further than Nemoianu and call them modifications) are now integrated from "the previous model into a new wholeness. The result is a tremendous grasp for totality in Blake, Novalis, Hölderlin, Schelling, Coleridge, and Wordsworth. . . . The ultimate purpose of the core romantics (Blake, Coleridge, Novalis, young Schelling, Wordsworth, F. Schlegel, and Shelley) was to regenerate human potential itself by identifying the self with nature and/or divinity." But Nemoianu, agreeing here implicitly with Morse Peckham's pioneering flux-and-process oriented works on romanticism, recognizes that this model is too explosive to be stable (contrary, we might add, to the endurance of classicism or Enlightenment rationalism even when displaced as dominant patterns). "Hence the change in later romanticism," he argues, to "the taming of the hero" from a macroimage to a smaller, more tangible but still relatively comprehensive scale such as national history and revival or social rebellion, a domestication of the cosmic scope of a Blake and a Novalis, an infusion into absolute romanticism of poetic realism or Biedermeier. In England, Lamb, Hazlitt, and Hunt civilize the threatening audacities of high romanticism by essayistic, entertaining, sparkling, intellectual, personal stylishness, by humor and charm. The hero is detached from himself by his own or the narrator's ironical stance: Büchner's Leonce, Byron's Don Juan, Musset's Fantasio, Pushkin's Eugene Onegin. Enlightenment and classicism patrimonies continue to moderate romanticism. Scott, Hugo, Manzoni, and Alexis secularize romanticism by healthy doses of social realism.

Nemoianu agrees with the classic analogy of M. H. Abrams between biblical Eden-Fall-Redemption and its "high" romantic secularization as innocence-alienation-regeneration. Tracing the antithesis confronting romanticism to man's "primal fracture" between his mind and outer nature, to his loss of the original harmony of impulse and action, to the split between necessity (natural human instincts) and reason (choice between right and wrong) resulting from man's self-consciousness, Abrams, relying here particularly on Schelling, concludes his section entitled "Unity Lost and Unity Regained" [in *Natural Supernaturalism*, 1973]: "Romantic philosophy is thus primarily a metaphysics of integration, of which the key principle is that of the 'reconciliation,' or synthesis, of whatever is divided, opposed, and conflicting."

Friedrich Schlegel, in his famous definition of romanticism in the *Athenäum-Fragmente* No. 116 (*Atheneum Fragment*, 1798), spells out the process and extent of this synthesis without including the metaphysical dimension:

> Romantic poetry is progressive universal poetry. Its destination is not merely the reunification of all separated genres and the contact of poetry with philosophy and rhetoric. It wants and ought to mix or fuse poetry with prose, genius with criticism, poetry as art with poetry as nature, render poetry alive and sociable, life and society poetic, poeticize wit, fill and saturate the forms of art with sterling cultured substance of every kind, and animate it with the vibrations of humor.

Schlegel's intimate friend Novalis may be considered the creative executor of this definition. It is no easy task to separate and crystallize his syntheses, not because they are elusive, complex, or obscure (they are not), but because they *are* his work.

History is a great synthesizer for Novalis. He sees the link between past, present, and future as an apotheosis for continuity. This applies, as we have noted, to the course from childhood to adulthood of man in general as well as man in particular. History is both backward- and forward-looking: it is pieced "together out of hope and memories." "Youth reads history only out of curiosity, like an entertaining fairy-tale; those of riper years find in it a heavenly, comforting, and edifying friend who through wise discourse prepares them gently for a higher, more comprehensive career and by means of vivid imagery makes them familiar with the unknown world." History and poetry are fused in the Bible. But there is also the history of the earth, with its childhood and adulthood and old age: caves and caverns as the testimonies and preservers of early civilization, as the refuge of animals and man, play an important role in *Heinrich von Ofterdingen,* and miners appear as astrologers in reverse, interpreting not the future (sky) but the past (earth).

To these sequential syntheses correspond spatial syntheses. The practical northern father of Heinrich nevertheless loves the arts, "had the makings of a great sculptor," and marries a poetic southern woman. While businesslike himself, he allows his wife to guide his son's upbringing. The result of their union, Heinrich, is poetically inclined. But he does justice to his father and, while he argues with the merchants, respects their point of view. They have been to Swabia, Italy, and France, and Heinrich enjoys their storytelling ability. Compare this differentiated, complementary family harmony with the fatherless and, for all intents and purposes, motherless Werther and René. Heinrich's journey from Eisenach to Augsburg is also a spiritual journey from the fiercely industrious north to the enjoyment-of-life-oriented south, whose "nearness to the Latins is revealed in their free and easy behavior and in their appealing conversation." The actual goal of Heinrich's voyage is to find the right balance of the metaphysical and the physical, a synthesis that is also supported by the marriage of Occident and Orient, the latter personified by Zulima and her child. Christinaity itself is a merger of south and north, East and West, pre-Christian and Christian elements, of imagery that has not lost, far from it, its sensual, nay, sexual flavor, particularly in Novalis's *Hymnen an die Nacht* (*Hymns to the Night*): "I journey across; all pangs will be some day the stings of ecstasy. A brief time yet, and free above, I shall lie drunken in the lap of love. Unending life swells grandly in me; I gaze from on high below upon thee. . . . O breathe me, Beloved, with might above so I sleep into death and come to love. I feel now Death's youth-giving flood, to balm and aether is changed my blood. For I live by day full of faith and desire, in the nights I die in holy fire."

The material and the immaterial, the external and the internal components of existence are equally cherished in the second, not completed part of *Heinrich von Ofterdingen:* after "Expectation" ("Die Erwartung") comes "Fulfillment" ("Die Erfüllung"). The mortal and the immortal, fear and promise, are engendered and reflected by cloud formations running from "the terrors of hell" descending from "gloomy and grave and terrible overcloudings," "destructive bolts" and "crashing thunderclaps," "echoes of a primitive inhuman nature," to bright and cool clouds that "pick us up and take us with them" in their "foretelling of an unknown, ineffiable splendor." This "higher nature" corresponds to the victory of "heavenly consciousness in us" (*Gewissen*). Ethics and aesthetics have fused, "meager ethical receptivity and lack of charm in freedom" have been overcome.

Ethics versus aesthetics; that is the core of poetry. To Heinrich, "consciousness, this power which generates the universe and meaning, this germ of all personality, appears . . . like the spirit of the world poem [*der Geist des Weltgedichts*], like the accident of the eternal, romantic confluence of the endlessly changeable totality of life." Poetry is the great synthesizer via the magical power of language, the restorer of the original unity of prophet and poet, the harmonizer of language, ideas, music, nature, love, youth, old age, heaven, and earth: poetry is magic realism. But to be effective, chaos as the subject matter of the poet must only "shimmer through the regular veil of orderliness": "Not the material but the execution is the purpose of art." Poets must learn from composers and painters and vice versa. Intellect, reason, distance, craftsmanship, and competence are essential to the effectiveness of poetry: "The poet is pure steel, as sensitive as a fragile glass thread and as hard as unyielding flint." The comprehensiveness and (at least theoretical) equilibrium and solidity of Novalis's synthesis is precisely due to this mining engineer's integration of mind, science, and skill into his romantic *Weltbild,* balancing inspiration, faith, heart. As Heinrich's merchant father was a sculptor, so Zulima plays the lute and Mathilda will teach Heinrich to play the guitar. Only demanding and trained competence can ensure the quality of the fusion of fairy tale, legend, poetry, philosophy, didactic purpose, and utopian dimensions in Novalis's magic realism and promote the credibility of romantic synaesthesia of the arts.

Music and religion, Orpheus and Jesus, antiquity and Christianity—all are to be fused. Consciousness—which encompasses the harmony between mastery and freedom, science and religion, crafts and creativity, man and God— is embodied in every genuine work of art. Freedom of creating is synonymous with mastery ("Freiheit ist Meisterschaft"). "The master exercises unfettered power in a purposeful, definite, and deliberate manner. . . . Every act of the master is . . . a proclamation of the lofty, simple, uncomplicated world—God's world. . . . Consciousness . . . is the vicar of God on earth." "Fable" is virtue under a "smiling disguise." "There is a startling similarity between a genuine song and a noble deed. . . . Like virtue, fable too is the godhead immediately operative among men." The artist restores grace to man who has fallen from it.

Novalis expressed this conviction in his own poetry:

Ludwig Tieck.

> All things must into all others flow,
> Each through the other thrive and grow,
> And each in all others [be] represented.

> Alles muss ineinander greifen,
> Eins durch das andere gedeihn und reifen,

Jedes in allen dar sich stellt.

Never has the inevitability of this process of union been more perfectly described in thought and in form than in the untranslatable poem Novalis addressed to Adolph Selmniz ("An Adolph Selmniz") between 1794 and 1797:

> What fits, must round off,
> What understands, find the other,
> What is good, combine,
> What loves, be together,
> What hinders, must recede,
> What's crooked, straighten out,
> What's distant, get together,
> What germinates, must grow.

> Was passt, das muss sich rûnden,
> Was sich versteht, sich finden,
> Was gut ist, sich verbinden,
> Was liebt, zusammen sein.
> Was hindert, muss entweichen,
> Was krumm ist, muss sich gleichen,
> Was fern ist, sich erreichen,
> Was keimt, das muss gedeihn.

Novalis died before his twenty-ninth birthday, yet in his systematic quest for synthesis hardly one major component of the universe has been omitted: tradition and revolution, the male and the female principles, eros and agape, day and night, reality and dream, time and space, time and infinity (life—death—God), death as the gateway to life via Christ, the world and ourselves (as Thoreau puts it in "The Village" in *Walden:* "Not till we have lost the world, do we begin to find ourselves and realize where we are"), science and poetry, science and religion (their synthesis: theology), object and subject fused under the auspices of the self through the unifying power of the imagination.

The romantic struggle for cohesiveness, far from being dismissible by fin-de-siècle twentieth-century skepticism as of purely historic interest, prefigures our modernist and postmodernist quandary: the relative pushing back the absolute, the specific strangling the universal, complexity overwhelming unity. But it kept a sense of the whole: "The universe breaks down into an infinite number of worlds, each in turn contained by larger ones. In the end, all minds are *one* mind. *One* mind like *one* world gradually leads to all worlds, but everything has its own time and its own manner." This is not dated monism; this is synthesis though under new auspices—that of the self.

Of the new caveats that can be adduced against the validity of Novalis's vision, the most obvious and justified one is that it has always been much easier to create syntheses on paper than to live them. Professional thinking dominating the late twentieth century would also say that reality *is*—and is *only*—words, language, codes, conventions: that there is no objective reality behind signs, that the medium *is* the message, that philosophy (logical positivism, Wittgenstein) is simply reflecting what is (and what is not) in twentieth-century primary literary texts from Kafka and Proust via Mann and Joyce to Sartre and Beckett, and that the roots of this pluralism are to be found in romanticism prior to the twentieth-century relativity theories now prevailing in most intellectual domains. True enough, as far as it goes, though even in the twentieth century [in the

words of Richard Ellman and Robert O'Clair in *Modern Poems: Introduction to Poetry,* 1976] "for T. S. Eliot the fragmentariness of the world was intolerable, and he was determined to mend it . . . but Pound preferred to accept and exploit this disjunctiveness." Many romantics stayed with what Morse Peckham has called "negative romanticism," but far more remarkable is the perseverance of those who aspired to "positive romanticism," and none of these is more affirmative of the adequacy of words to reality than Novalis.

Another criticism of Novalis seems more justifiable: his synthesis of internal and external, near perfect as it is in *theory,* is not matched by its *literary* implementation through society-oriented activities in his creative works: the discrepancy between talking, talking about doing, and realistic doing is admittedly a problematic landmark of the German Bildungsroman though more excusable for romanticism than for realism. It must also be conceded that his syntheses are less viable in the second half of the twentieth century, when science and technology, social services, effective representation of just about all special interests of any consequence, anticipations of comfort, and happiness as a birthright have mushroomed to such an extent that mental and verbal reconciliation of all these elements has become more elusive than practical compromise, which carries no expectations of intellectual integrity. But that is not the whole story. Even romanticism, the immediate heir of the long-contained breakthrough of the Enlightenment, had a big problem on its hands. Our own task today has become still more difficult. Why? Less, perhaps, because we have to face complexities undreamed of by romanticism. Graver yet may be the circumstance that we have lost the *desire* for synthesis. Synthesis cannot come about without determination for synthesis, and that determination has largely disappeared from academia and even nonacademic intelligentsia: it is unchic. To propel it the romantics had a subjective as well as objective drive, and among the best in that direction (Blake, Wordsworth, Coleridge, Shelley, Keats, Scott, Hugo, Manzoni, Goethe, Schiller, Hölderlin, Novalis, Kleist, August Wilhelm and Friedrich Schlegel, E.T.A. Hoffmann, Eichendorff, Emerson, Thoreau) that propelling force was joy, love, humor, ecstasy, intensity, and vitality even in despair.

What is the result of our reflections? There is no use in minimizing the antitheses and differentiations in romanticism. But neither is it justified to ignore the remarkable attempts at synthesis. If our illustrations seem somewhat top-heavy in the direction of German and English romanticism, it is not that French, Italian, and Spanish romanticism are less interested in the equilibrium of coherence and apparent incoherence but—aside from our severe limitations of space—that English and in particular German romantics were readier to articulate this search for synthesis conceptually, whereas their Mediterranean siblings were more inclined to practice rather than to preach. All things told, I see no reason to abandon the tentative keystone theory I proposed eighteen years ago: "Romanticism is the attempt to heal the break in the universe, it is the painful awareness of dualism coupled with the urge to resolve it in organic monism, it is the confrontation with chaos followed by the will to reintegrate it into the order of the cosmos, it is the desire to reconcile a pair of opposites, to have synthesis follow antithesis." (pp. 331-48)

> *Henry H. H. Remak, "New Harmony: The Quest for Synthesis in West European Romanticism," in* European Romanticism: Literary Cross-Currents, Modes, and Models, *edited by Gerhart Hoffmeister, Wayne State University Press, 1990, pp. 331-51.*

Henry H. H. Remak

[*In the following essay, Remak explains how the exotic provided Romantic artists with "diversely combinable geographic and cultural backgrounds that served as outlets for Romantic frustrations, nostalgias."*]

> Why do those cliffs of shadowy tint appear
> More sweet than all the landscape smiling near?—
> 'Tis distance lends enchantment to the view
> And robes the mountain in its azure hue.
>
>   Thomas Campbell, "The Pleasures of Hope"
>   (1799)

> On commence à comprendre de nos jours que la localité
> exacte est un des premiers éléments de la réalité.
>
>   Victor Hugo, *Préface de Cromwell* (1827)

What are the stringencies and latitudes inherent in the term "exoticism"? What use did Romantics make of exoticism? What conceptual and functional links exist between a few selected aspects of exoticism in West European Romanticism?

First, the term. We must try to differentiate, difficult as it is, and more deliberately than previous scholarship however distinguished (Chinard, Jourda, Van Tieghem), between exoticism and xenophilia. The record discloses that "exotic" means both less than "foreign" and more than "exotic" normally does. Less than "foreign" because it denotes a foreign culture with which there has been little or no authentic contact and which presents features extraordinarily different from the vantage point of a particular majority culture of Western Europe. More than the usual connotation of "exotic" because it goes beyond the customary reference to southern, far eastern, or far western location, beyond a predilection for tropical or subtropical climates, beyond a floral and faunal, aesthetic, sensual as well as philosophical nostalgia of inhabitants of colder, drabber climates, working hard to stay warm, for sun and lushness and relaxation ensconced in a traditional, binding, serenely fatalistic order, thus combining—or so it would appear—the best of two possible worlds.

The etymology of the word foreshadows a wider as well as a more specific interpretation of the term. Greek "exotikos," Latin "exoticus," from the Greek adjective and adverb "exo," mean "outside," "beyond" both spatially and temporally. The concept denotes a phenomenon outside and beyond our normal cultural experience, not only one spatially remote, or culturally remote even if spatially fairly close, but potentially also one lying back so far in time that even if it has been part of our own culture its remoteness in time (not necessarily in years) creates the same effect as the contemporary remoteness in space or in culture. Of the connotations given in Webster, "strikingly or excitingly different" and "strikingly unusual in color and design" indicate the wider ramifications of the term which seem more congruent with the expansive nature of Romanticism than a more conservative or conventional definition. It would be nice to have a secure and inflexible delimitation of "exotic" once and for all, but the intricate cultural patterns existing in fact call for more relative, flexible and authentic distinctions. We must not only break down larger units and test differentiated components as to their exotic potential but must also ask: "exotic" to whom, to what other cultures?

Cultures that share essential analogies are not exotic to each other even when transgressing national borders. It is arguable that cultures significantly different from each other after continuous contact over time may still be exotic to each other because the contacts have not resulted in penetrating adjustments on either side (Britain and India in their reciprocal relationships might be a case in point), but they would not be exotic to each other in the historical context of Romanticism if the element of newness, of discovery, were absent or considerably reduced.

Exoticism—not the term but the phenomenon—, whatever the obvious first connotation ("very remote, non-Western"), represented to the Romantics a far more extended and differentiated interest embracing also Northern and Northeastern cultures, contemporary, regional, non-majority subcultures or alien elements (Jews, Gypsies) in Western Europe, and past cultures (including sometimes their own). The emphasis is on the strikingly different and the non-familiar, granting, however, that these two concepts are not necessarily synonymous.

Some examples. In providing them one must be careful not to superimpose automatically the notion of "country" or "nation"—political concepts sometimes much posterior to Romanticism—on a geographical or cultural area whose profile may then have been more strongly determined (and still may be today, e.g. Belgium) by other elements: ethnic, linguistic, religious, or otherwise cultural. Being aware of this danger is not, however, a guarantee that I have entirely neutralized it in my own illustrations.

Thus Sweden was not, at the time of Romanticism, an exotic country for Norwegians, Danes, Finns, Baltic peoples of German origin, or for the Pomeranians in Northern Germany, though Bavarians would undoubtedly have taken her for such. Rome was not necessarily experienced as an exotic city by the Germans whose *Italiensehnsucht* had taken many, especially the cultured among them, to her, in body or in spirit, for at least six hundred years before Romanticism. Whatever the depth, culturally speaking, of the Channel between England and France during Romanticism and even today, France could not be regarded in her totality as an exotic country by English Romantics, considering the constant connections between the two nations. Spain, on the other hand, much more separate from the rest of Europe than France or Italy for many reasons including rugged geographical obstacles (the Pyrenees), her greater aridity, her Arab/African impregnation, her rigid brand of Catholicism, her more somber character, could well be—and was—felt to be exotic by the Romantics even in the immediately neighboring country of France.

Cultural divisions of great significance ran and run through countries. Calabria, Sicily, and Sardinia were surely viewed as exotic not only by Germans and Austrians and French who would not have thought of Lombardy, Tuscany, or Rome in that manner, but these three regions might have appeared "exotic" to Northern Italians as well, as did Corsica to the French in the days of Romanticism (Mérimée, *Colomba*). Scotland at the time of Romanticism was an exotic region not only to the French and Germans but also to many English, Brittany to most Frenchmen outside the peninsula's boundaries, the Basques to most Spainiards. Norway was, for most Europeans during the Romantic period, an unknown, mysterious, nebulously grandiose region enshrouding paganism survivals; the Provence (but not Paris) was exotic to many non-French and Northern French as well, and Germany as a cultural area was surely exotic to most French intellectuals—not to speak of the others—when Madame de Staël wrote *De l'Allemagne,* though the converse is much less true. Athens, while much farther away from Berlin than Warsaw, would have qualified as far less exotic to Berlin Romantics than Poland (see, e.g., Heine's *Über Polen,* 1822).

The term "exotic" is, to be sure, not infinitely stretchable, or it will lose its usefulness, but it must correspond more closely to its functional potential.

A second functional phenomenon of Romantic exoticism is the interchangeability of exotic locales, of exotic predilections, of exotic moods among a number of West European writers. The extent of this analogy exchange surprised me, for I had supposed that what distinguished Romanticism from Enlightenment was precisely the selective empathy with very unique, very specific, very diverse national or regional cultures instead of the universalism of culture promoted by the Enlightenment. To some extent this interchangeability results from the survival and, indeed, prevalence of stylized landscapes and *Sittenbilder* inherited from the Enlightenment. A second cause may lie in the personalized, subjective origin of Romantic exoticism. Exoticism is not only the discovery of a peculiarly profiled foreign civilization, it is a state of mind. This state or rather fermentation of mind will not terminate with the exploration of a particular culture: it will look for additional satisfaction of these expectations in somewhat analogous but not identical cultures elsewhere, or take off in search of a different set of cultural elements in order to satisfy psychic and/or physical *Wanderlust.*

The restlessness of Romantics, while not universal, is proverbial. Chateaubriand roamed over North America, England, the entire Mediterranean, and Central Europe. Madame de Staël, when not confined to Coppet by Napoleon, wandered compulsively all over Europe from Italy to Russia. Hugo, Lamartine, Musset, Mérimée, Stendhal, Nerval, Dumas père, Gautier traveled extensively abroad, a feature hardly in the mainstream of French cultural tradition. The traditional *Wanderlust* of the Germans took on

a psychic syndrome in Kleist, the early Hölderlin, Chamisso, E.T.A. Hoffmann, and Brentano, though it has to be conceded that the travels of German Romantics were more bookbound than actual. Wordsworth and Coleridge settled down soon after their early continental safaris, but Byron has become the epitome of the peripatetic poet, and Mary Shelley tells us that "but for our fears on account of our child, I believe we should have wandered over the world, both being passionately fond of traveling." To the personal *Wanderlust* corresponds the restlessness of the Romantic personae: René, Childe Harold, Manfred, Don Juan, the Ancient Mariner, Peter Schlemihl, Eichendorff's Taugenichts, Scott's Richard the Lion-Hearted, many figures of E.T.A. Hoffmann, etc. The causes of this search for experience in foreign lands are complex and not easily disentangled. Roughly speaking, there is a positive and a negative escapism involved. Byron delineates the positive one in *Childe Harold* (1816):

> Where rose the mountains, there to him were
>   friends;
> Where roll'd the ocean, thereon was his home;
> Where a blue sky, and glowing clime, extends,
> He had the passion and the power to roam;
> The desert, forest, cavern, breaker's foam,
> Were unto him companionship; they spake
> A mutual language, clearer than the tome
> of his land's tongue . . .

Shelley, too, in the preface to his *Revolt of Islam* (1817), has found magnificent words for the inclusion of this facet of the explorative urge of man in the total creative process of the poet. Negative, fatalistically serene escapism also appears in *Childe Harold:*

> "Self-exiled Harold wanders forth again,
> With nought of hope left, but with less of gloom;
> The very knowledge that he lived in vain, . . .
> Had made Despair a smilingness assume, which
>   though 'twere wild, . . .
> Did yet inspire a cheer, which he forbore to
>   check."

The complex fusion of positive and negative features in this Faustian nostalgia reflect the aspirations and frustrations of the Romantic; they provide a network of unexpected cross-references within Romantic exoticism.

Some illustrations. There are analogies between René's visits, in Chateaubriand's story, to the ruins of Rome and Athens, his return to the paternal mansion, and the narrator's approach to the House of Usher in Poe's story. In going to Italy and Greece, René visits "the peoples who are no longer there," monuments "of strong and productive memory, where palaces are buried in the dust and the mausolea of kings are hidden under the brambles. O strength of nature, feebleness of man! A blade of grass often pierces the hardest marble of these tombs which all these dead, so powerful, will never raise. Sometimes a tall column stood alone in the desert . . . I meditated on these monuments . . . at all hours of the day." Let it be noted that Chateaubriand had not yet been either to Italy or to Greece when he wrote this.

Compare this to René's subsequent return to the castle that used to be ruled by the 'family king', so to speak—his father—, his return to *his* childhood home in Brittany rather than civilization's childhood home in Greece. Some details are similar. More importantly, the mood is the same: deserted courtyards, closed or half-broken windows, thistles growing at the foot of the walls, the front entrance stone steps on which he visualizes his father standing, surrounded by faithful servants, the gillyflower growing among disjointed and tottering stones. The pathos of general history and the pathos of individual history are made of the same fabric. So is, with some hyperbolic reinforcement and several touches of southern subtropical putrefaction added, the narrator's approach to the "melancholy House of Usher," whose owner had been a boyhood friend, "through a singularly dreary tract of country." With "a sense of insufferable gloom," he sees "bleak walls," "vacant, eye-like windows" (twice), a "building. . of an excessive antiquity," "minute fungi (that) overspread the whole exterior," "the crumbling condition of the individual stones." Even the episode of the brusque servant in *René* suddenly opening the doors and that of the "valet of stealthy step" taking the narrator to the chamber of Roderick Usher bear some resemblance.

We cannot dwell here on the equally important differences, but do want to bring out two fundamental analogies in Romantic concept and mood: 1) mankind (René in Italy and Greece) and individual man (René, Poe's narrator) "can't go home again": general and personal history coincide, and 2) the close connection between the spatial and temporal factors in Romantic exoticism to which we shall return later.

Another illustration, this time the partial—only partial, to be sure—interchangeability of the Caledonian motif with other geographic and cultural units. This is noteworthy in itself since Scotland has a highly profiled history, complexion, and mood. Certain analogies between Scotland and Brittany are evident: a wholly or partly Celtic, rather inaccessible region bounded by the sea on all but one side, a pious, Christianized area transferring to the new religion a serious and somber nature-boundness while clinging to traditions and memories preceding the Christian era. The paternal château and its environment in *René*, "located in the middle of forests, near a lake, in a remote province," with rain-soaked hills in the neighborhood, the storms, the mournful story of René's sister—all this carries a strong Ossianic flavor. Byron's and Shelley's initial exposure to the Highlands was a conditioning or at least symptomatic factor for their subsequent love for Swiss mountains and lakes. In the "Dedicatory Epistle" of *Ivanhoe,* Scott himself connects the phenomenon of Scottish social and political structure in the recent past with a more current kind of exotic primitivism: "It was not above sixty or seventy years . . . since the whole north of Scotland was under a state of government nearly as simple and patriarchal as those of our good allies the Mohawks and Iroquois." Scott also tells us in the same location that his well received portrayals of Scottish antiquity had led him to do the same for England—which proved equally successful.

Madame de Staël's discovery of Germany was not her only iron in the fire: *Corinne ou l'Italie* (1806) contains, besides much melodrama, substantive cultural and psy-

chological insights into Italy and even brings about the unlikely fusion of Scotland and Italy in the person of the heroine. The four great interpreters of German literature and thought in France during the Romantic period, Charles Nodier, Gérard de Nerval, Edgar Quinet, and Jean-Jacques Ampère had multi-pronged foreign competences: Nodier added Scotland, Switzerland, and Spain, Nerval the Orient, Quinet Italy and Greece, and Ampère Scandinavia, Egypt, and America to their German expertise. Interchangeability of interest in one Mediterranean country with another one is not so surprising: in Byron's work the diversity of his attention to Spain, Portugal, Italy, Albania, and Greece is held together not only by shared scenic, climatic, and cultural characteristics but by his overriding involvement in their struggle for liberty. Shelley's concern with Italy and Greece comes from the same roots. Likewise, the role of America, Hungary, and Poland in Romantic exoticism is closely linked to their fight for independence. A certain similarity in the Romantic treatment of two, to put it mildly, much less advantaged kinds of underdog, the Jews and the Gypsies, indicate analogies between these exotic outsiders-without-a-country despite their fundamental differences: compare, e.g., the scenes between the Templar and the Jewess Rebecca in *Ivanhoe* with the confrontations of Claude Frollo and the alleged Gypsie Esmeralda in Hugo's *Notre-Dame-de-Paris.*

The transferability of one exotic ambiance to another one is particularly striking when the passages in question are quite specific and flavorful:

> The natives were wilder than the place. Our near neighbours . . . were more like savages than any people I ever before lived among. Many a night they passed on the beach, singing, or rather howling; the women dancing about among the waves that broke at their feet; the men leaning against the rocks and joining in their loud wild chorus. We could get no provisions nearer than . . . , at a distance of three miles and a half off, with the torrent of the . . . between; and even there the supply was very deficient.

What part of the world is the author describing? Micronesia? Melanesia? Polynesia? Africa? South America? Not at all: it is Mary Shelley talking about the environment of their house in the Bay of Spezia between Genoa and Leghorn. She herself comments: "Had we been wrecked on an island of the South Seas, we could scarcely have felt ourselves farther from civilization and comfort."

The extreme in the interchangeability of exotic regions was probably reached by De Quincey, whose opium gave him, it seems, tremendous range: "Under the connecting feeling of tropical heat and vertical sun-lights, I brought together all creatures, birds, beasts, reptiles, all trees and plants, usages and appearances, that are found in all tropical regions, and assembled them together in China or Indostan. From kindred feelings, I soon brought Egypt and all her gods under the same law." In breathtaking succession, he takes us from monkeys, parakeets, and cockatoos to pagodas where he is both worshipped and sacrificed, from ibises and crocodiles to mummies and sphinxes; like the Ancient Mariner, he is taken uncomfortably close to "all unutterable slimy things," to "ugly birds" and snakes, and compelled to live for centuries with the "cursed crocodile." Coleridge's range is only slightly less impressive: his two preferred locations in the tropics were the West Indies (at one time he had thoughts of emigrating to the island of St. Nevis), and the sources of the Nile. To be fair to the northern regions, he also lavished his affection on Greenland, Lapland, and Spitzbergen. Balzac ironizes this merry-go-round fashion of exotic locales by advising a client:

> Je pourrais vous dire d'étudier la couleur locale de la Laponie, et vous nous construiriez un admirable Spitzberg avec des glaces bien naturelles, une aurore boréale que vous n'auriez pas vue, et les rennes, les arê tes de poisson, l'huile de baleine, l'horizon de neige, les ours blancs et les lichens . . . Bah! ce ne serait plus cela! . . . Quand vous nous apporteriez votre microcosme tout imprimé, la girouette littéraire aurait tourné vers les forêts vierges du Brésil.

Earlier, Byron had advised Thomas Moore to heed exotic opportunism: "Stick to the East;—the oracle, Staël, told me it was the only poetical policy."

There are, to be sure, also obstacles in the way of exotic or semi-exotic interrelationships. Scott tells us that English readers will find it much easier to believe stories about remote Scotland than tales about their own country some years back:

> If he be of the ordinary class of readers, he has either never seen those remote districts (of Scotland) at all, or he has wandered through those desolate regions in the course of a summer tour, eating bad dinners, sleeping on truckle beds, stalking from desolation to desolation, and fully prepared to believe the strangest things that could be told him of people wild and extravagant enough to be attached to scenery so extraordinary. But the same worthy person, when placed in his own snug parlour, and surrounded by all the comforts of an Englishman's fireside, is not half as much disposed to believe that his own ancestors led a very different life from himself.

This perceptive remark—relevant, by the way, to the *Rezeptionsästhetik* currently much debated—leads us to greater awareness of another, strategic aspect of exoticism in literature. It might be assumed that the farther removed the exotic locale from the reader in space and time, the less its credibility. But the contrary may be truer: the reader is more inclined to give credence to unusual locales, events, and personae if they are sufficiently removed from his era and habitat than to extraordinary even though 'true' events reported about his own region or time. This consideration may have led Romantic writers to move stories to an exotic locale to make them more credible. The Italian setting of Kleist's *Die Marquise von O . . .* and of his *Bettelweib von Locarno,* the Chilean background of his *Erdbeben in Chili* are probably, in large part, the result of the poet's decision that the credibility of stories reporting happenings so extraordinary as to strain the reader's faith in their veracity or plausibility is enhanced when moved to a foreign, unfamiliar or less familiar locale. The suitor of the Marquise von O . . . is Russian, but there is nothing specifically Russian about him. Kleist likely made him into an 'exotic', unpredictable Russian rather than an Austrian or German (which he could have managed easily) to gain credibility for the extremes of the hero's behavior: the raping of an unconscious woman, on the one hand, and the demonstration of nobility, gentlemanliness, and loyalty toward the same woman, a behavior so odd that the orderly German reader might not tolerate it or even believe it on the part of his own nationality, whereas a Russian . . .

The mountains and the sea, as the ultimate in height and stability and the ultimate in depth and flux, respond to the "beyondness" of exoticism. It is perhaps the concurrence of these poles of existence in the shape of islands and peninsulas that is at the heart of Romantic predilection for such sites as much as, or more than, the elements of remoteness, isolation, and pristineness. Emphasis on one of these two phenomena at the expense of the other one (on the sea, perhaps, for Coleridge and Heine and Shelley, on the mountains, perhaps, for Byron), or the use of "ice" imagery compatible with both may tell us something more fundamental about the writer than preference for Italy over Spain, for Scotland over Germany. Snakes of the most exotic colors hold great fascination for Coleridge and E.T.A. Hoffmann (not forgetting Goethe's deeply romantic *Märchen*). The mythology, the timelessness revolving around this reptile, not only its geographical habitat and its zoölogical characteristics, have surely something to do with this lure. Caves and mines combine mystery, riches, and timeless stability, and are in that sense exotic. Novalis describes the metals discovered by Heinrich von Ofterdingen in the mine, as well as the miners' conversation and songs, in terms of exotic mystery. Heinrich also discovers in the cavern inhabited by the hermit, written in what seems at first a mysterious language but turns out to be Provençal, a manuscript which like a kaleidoscope reflects his past and present, actual and potential experiences.

This episode, combining spatial and temporal exoticism (the Provence in the twelfth century), reminds us of the temporal dimensions of the term "exo." Indeed, much of the impact of exoticism lies in the fusion of space and time. Ossianism, Romantic Hellenism, the Gothic revival, medievalism in general (often accompanied by the use of archaic diction) and in particular as reflected, e.g., in the cult of the Rhine country and castles of Nuremberg: all these images require for full effect a temporal scope. In some cases the temporal element is decisive. The English landscape: pretty, charming, garden-like, harmonious, civilized, and English mores, rather subdued, do not lend themselves to an image of exoticism were it not for the pomp and circumstance, the color and the glory of the English past. The time lag often permits a more sympathetic attitude toward past happenings, it romanticizes unpleasant features of historical circumstances such as, e.g., the Moorish domination of Spain. The Orient would be exotic even today, but the antiquity of its culture intensifies its exotic attraction (see, e.g., Heine's poem, "Der Dichter Firdusi"). Novalis' demand in *Heinrich von Ofterdingen* that the historians should be poets was implemented soon afterwards by Michelet. Novalis himself is a prime example for the other imperative: that the poet should also be a historian.

Not all such fusions of space and time have cheerful consequences. René's nostalgia for the recapture of his and his sister's Edenic childhood in the Celtic ambiance of Brittany is defeated by the impossibility of going back in time. De Quincey is not only compelled to live with "the cursed crocodile" but, on top of it, "for centuries."

One may tentatively conclude that however much the Romantics championed the unique coloring of national, ethnic, or cultural identities, Romantic exoticism arose from and served primary purposes other than the accurate in-depth discovery of specific cultures. Rather, it furnished diversely combinable geographic and cultural backgrounds that served as outlets for Romantic frustrations, nostalgias, for different options. In recognition of the manifold conceptual, functional, and strategic links between and among exotic targets, several of which seem, to varying extent, interchangeable, Romantic exoticism requires both a wider and a more differentiated definition and interpretation. Some of the richest effects of Romantic exoticism result from the combination of spatial and temporal, geographical and historical, with psychologic elements, and from the dynamics of symbols. (pp. 53-62)

Henry H. H. Remak, "Exoticism in Romanticism," in Comparative Literature Studies, *Vol. XV, No. 1, March, 1978, pp. 53-65.*

A drawing of E.T.A. Hoffmann in 1821 by Wilhelm Hensel.

Henri Peyre

[*Peyre is a French-born critic who has lived and taught in the United States for most of his career. One of the foremost critics of French literature, he has written extensively on modern French literature and is a staunch defender of traditional literary forms that examine the meaning of life in modern society and the role of individual destiny in an indifferent universe. Peyre disagrees with critical trends that attempt to subsume literary analysis under the doctrines of restrictive theories, such as those of structuralism. Regarding his critical stance, Peyre has written that "there is no single approach that is infallible or systematically to be preferred when dealing with literature. Pluralism seems to me to be a far more fruitful attitude." In the following excerpt, he examines the tragic mood that characterizes nineteenth-century French literature, explaining that although it was "dramatic and immoderate in expression, ridiculous at times in its excesses, it also included genuine grief."*]

Alfred de Musset, the most tragically "damned" of all the French romantic poets and the one who, more than Nerval and even Baudelaire, stubbornly persisted in bringing down malediction upon his own head, has left us some dramatic or rather melodramatic pages dealing with the malady which, according to him, afflicted his entire generation of followers of romanticism. Unquestionably, the moral of his *Confession d'un enfant du siècle* (1836) is unskilfully presented. The author himself admitted to Franz Liszt that these types of works "are not nearly authentic enough to be memoirs, nor are they make-believe enough to be novels." But the grandiloquent introduction, evoking those children conceived between two battles during the wars of the Empire, who were suddenly in great trouble due to the fall of the master who had for a long time been crowned with glory, and who were even more deceived by the mediocrity of the Restoration, affirmed peremptorily:

> All that afflicts the present century results from two causes: the nation which has suffered through the period of '93 and of 1814 bears the scars of two mortal wounds.

> All that existed before exists no longer; all that will come into being one day is not yet in existence. There is no need to look further for the cause of our afflictions.

Rarely had there been such an abrupt break in history, or at least it had hardly ever seemed so abrupt to contemporaries. It was all very well for future historians, supported by statistics and able to see events in their proper perspective half a century later, to show that a great deal of continuity persisted if one looked beyond superficial upheavals, and that already widespread reforms in the allocation of property and economic progress had been accomplished in France before 1789 or in Russia before 1917. The psychological shock experienced after political revolution leaves, nonetheless, a mark on sensibilities. Posterity has acknowledged that the "mal du siècle", which the romantics gloried in or complained about, retained the importance of a great myth; and it is likely that, in the future, at the beginning of every new century, men will feel that they are afflicted by the same malady and will display their restlessness as their privilege and as a sign of being special, just as at the end of every century (from 1970 onwards, the twentieth century has begun to use these terms lavishly), men will think that their times are characterized by decay and will analyse with secret pride their own decline. Actually, like so many other aspects of romanticism, the one characterized by wailing, cursing existence, making a show of anguish, and continually wishing, quite sincerely moreover, for death—the prelude perhaps to a desired revival—did not disappear from Europe, and especially not from France, once the so-called romantic period was over. The generation of Flaubert, Leconte de Lisle, Jean Lahor, then that of Laforgue, Elémir Bourges, Suarès, of Gissing and A. E. Housman in England, still later that of Roger Martin du Gard, Mauriac, Ribemont-Dessaignes, and Pierre-Jean Jouve, and finally in our times, those pessimists contemptuous of their age and fostering little hope in man, men like Montherlant, Green, Céline, and Cioran, are no less imbued with disillusioned romanticism, inspired by pride or melancholy pity, depending on the individual case.

It is obvious that this "mal du siècle", felt most acutely by Aloysius Bertrand, Nerval, Musset, Maurice de Guérin, Gautier, and Mme Ackermann (all born between 1807 and 1812), was nothing radically new or unique. . . . [The] obsession of suicide, discussed at length by Saint-Preux and Milord Edouard in Rousseau's novel, had troubled a great many suffering souls and weak-willed people in France between 1760 and 1789. The theme of death had become predominant at that time in the poetry of several nations of Europe, but it was treated more skilfully and with more stirring and colorful rhetoric by Young and Gray, and then by Novalis and Foscolo, in languages other than French. The role played by fashion in literature and art is considerable, even if our minds, craving for rational explanations, revolt at attributing too much to chance or the contagion of a rather ineffectual mimesis. There are feelings that our parents had undoubtedly experienced before us (pantheistic impulses inspired by landscapes, delight in solitude, contemplation of a moonlit night, a desire for death or revolt against it), feelings that it had not been fashionable to express; or else they did not have the necessary vocabulary, the gift of inventing images, or the lack of modesty needed to display one's inner self. The literary, musical, or pictorial expression of a feeling makes us suddenly aware of its intensity. Finding it thus magnificently expressed or boldly orchestrated in the art of our period, we feel this mood more intensely, we analyze it in our letters or our private diary, and we, in our turn, help to spread it.

• • • • •

The historian may pursue his inquiry into the more general causes which helped to infect a great number of "preromantic" souls during 1775-1785, and later the romantics, during 1815-1830, with the contagion of this collective fashionable malady, which sometimes reached epidemic proportions, or which prepared the way for it. But it is very difficult to specify the effect of these causes in each individual case. One of the causes most often alleged by

the victims of this malady of the century, for it is convenient and ennobling to use this as an excuse, is the loss of religious faith by them and those around them. As a matter of fact, there were very few people after 1789 who considered themselves "delighted atheists" or felt an unbridled joy in attacking Christianity head on after having received an ecclesiastical education like Boulanger, Mably, Morellet, or Toussaint. The weakening of the power of traditional religion inevitably made many social institutions totter and shook the framework of daily life. Those who craved most for a firm faith found it easy to transfer their need to believe in something to an anticlerical or revolutionary doctrine. Those whose religious faith was based on emotional needs or who, according to the words of Ninon de Lenclos, had never had enough of it to want to change it, were perhaps more at a loss. But it would be useless to try to explain a great variety of temperaments by a single category of causes. These romantics who reached their thirties around 1800—Sénancour, Constant, Chateaubriand, and Napoleon—and whose melancholy is best revealed to us through their writings and letters, were not really religious people. The clever remark made by the émigré Chateaubriand, on the death of his mother, "I wept and I believed," is perhaps a sincere statement by this man who was sincere about many things successively (or even simultaneously), but his religion was above all a source of literary inspiration, and it did not form an integral part of the lives of even his characters such as Atala, Amélie, the Bianca of *Le Dernier Abencérage,* or Eudora, but only served to stimulate conflicts which we do not take very seriously. Benjamin Constant, throughout his life, through all the troubles he endured as lover of several women at the same time, through his debauchery and his betrayals, dreamed of writing a work in which he would show, without having any more faith than Bourget, Barrès, or Maurras would have later on, that it was necessary to believe, and he would support his arguments by erudition. He finally wrote this work in five volumes in the autumn of his troubled life and published the five volumes between 1824 and 1830. It did not reveal at any point the kind of heartbreak that breaking away from their religious faith caused Jouffroy or even Renan. In any event, the "mal du siècle" certainly did not affect only unbelievers suffering from the loss of their intellectual or emotional comfort: Shelley, Keats, Leopardi, and the Goethe of *Werther* did not regret for a minute the fact that they no longer believed or that they had never believed. On the other hand, neither Lamartine, at the time when his faith was still intact, nor Lamennais, saying over and over again that "his soul had been born with a gaping wound," nor even Kierkegaard owed the sadness that they expressed and felt to a lessening of their religious beliefs. The Danish philosopher, torn at the same time by anguish and irony, noted at the age of thirty-five, in 1847, in his *Journal:* "From my earliest youth on, an arrow of grief has been stuck in my heart. As long as it stays there, I am ironical. If it is pulled out, I will die."

The feeling of political and social insecurity has undoubtedly affected more those men who, with the downfall of the monarchy, the imprisonment of the king, civil war in many French towns, and the abruptly revealed class hatreds, had witnessed the collapse of the relative order in which they had grown up. The sight of the massacres perpetrated by the enraged crowd in August and September 1792, the news of the "noyades" in the Loire at Nantes, mass executions at Lyons, the atrocities of the civil war in the Vendée could not help but upset well-balanced people who, only a few decades before, had admired Voltaire's hymns to tolerance and had stigmatized the persecutions attributed to "Intolerance." Strangely enough, however, contemporary writers reveal little trace of indignant condemnation of these massacres, just as the writers of 1670 or 1685 did not criticize the havoc wrought in the Palatinate or the repeal of the Edict of Nantes, nor did the non-Jewish Germans of 1933-1943 protest against the Nazi crimes. Benjamin Constant survived these political upheavals by remaining more preoccupied with his love affairs than with the misfortunes of the country. He lashed out against the spirit of acquisition and usurpation in firm and strong language, but he had few qualms about abandoning first one regime and then another in 1814-1815 and, after Waterloo, in noting cynically as he rushed for the spoils: "Time is pressing if I want to be in at the death." Sénancour preferred to live in seclusion and remain uninvolved, and he undoubtedly showed the most nobility of all these semi-sick souls. Chateaubriand showed very little remorse for having fought along with the princes against his own country; his attitude towards Napoleon varied considerably from being fascinated by the genius of the First Consul, to being envious of him and wishing to have the same glory as the warrior and politician, and to being vexed as a nobleman by the off-hand manner in which the upstart Corsican treated certain aristocrats. But several others were excited about the overthrow of the old order, and Talleyrand was among the very first of them, even though he deeply regretted the end of "the pleasant life." The insecurity of the times helped especially to increase their desire for power and their ambition. In 1800 and again in 1830, love of money, position, and power were found side by side with the spiritual vacuum felt by certain people and complaints about the ennui of life and the weakening of wills, and this has been brought out very well in *La Comédie humaine.*

For quite some time, social classes had no longer been separated by the watertight bulkheads which have been too often ascribed to French society under the monarchy. Saint-Simon had already expressed several complaints about the rise of the newly rich and the conferring of titles on commoners. People from the provinces and foreigners (Law, Abbé Galiani, Casanova, Cagliostro) met with little opposition when they ventured to beguile the Courts of the Regency, of Louis XV, and of Louis XVI. But the less ambitious individual was still fairly closely tied to his family, his social and political group, and the district of Paris in which he lived; or else he found without too much difficulty a new social life, a literary circle with which he could identify himself. With the breakdown of social life brought about by the Revolution and the political rather than literary or philosophical nature of the clubs which soon multiplied rapidly in Paris, many writers felt estranged from their class, cut off from their provincial or family ties. The feeling of moral solitude that the romantic poets and moralists were to express so often, has rarely been experienced as intensely as by Sénancour, Chateaubriand in his *René*

and his *Mémoires,* and that romantic Bonaparte, a man of letters who soon became a man of action. At the age of seventeen, on May 3, 1786, the young officer wrote: "Always alone as I am in the midst of men, I retire within myself to dream alone and to indulge in the vividness of my melancholy." He avidly read Ossian and *La Nouvelle Héloise.* From Egypt, where he was victorious and fawned upon, he confided to his brother Joseph, in 1799: "I need solitude. I am tired of greatness and bored by glory. At the age of twenty-nine, I have nothing more to look forward to." The thought of suicide had obsessed him since his adolescence, just as, according to Goethe, such an idea must have crossed the mind of every man worthy of the name, at least once in his life. In May 1786, when he was still unknown, he had exclaimed: "What is to be done in this world? Since I must die, is it not as well to kill myself?" Indeed, he was as familiar with *Werther* as with Ossian, and he liked it just as much.

• • • • •

Romantic suicide or the literary theme of suicide (for the dramatic element was inextricably blended with what might have been sincere in the confessions written by men who were already old and were reliving their turbulent adolescence) was actually omnipresent in literature, from Preromanticism to Flaubert, Maxime du Camp, and Baudelaire. It would be a worthy subject of a monograph which ought not to be uniquely sociological or medical. A specialist in mental illnesses and psychiatrist of the nineteenth century, Brière de Boismont, studied this phenomenon as early as 1865 in his book *Du Suicide et de la folie suicide;* and E. Caro, a moralist with considerable insight, wrote an essay of about a hundred pages about this book, which he included in his *Nouvelles Etudes morales sur le temps présent* (Hachette, 1869). Goethe, in recollections in which poetry and truth are intertwined, has brought out the intense feeling of the futility of everything—studies, future careers, joys of nature—which had overpowered him when he was an adolescent and knew deep down within him that he was destined for great fortunes which, however, were too slow in coming for his liking. The monotony and absurdity of existence overwhelmed him. He thought admiringly of the Emperor Othon, who had stabbed himself to death. He himself placed the point of a dagger against his chest, but shrank from the deed and preferred to rid himself of the temptation of suicide by writing *Werther.* The novel, inspired by the actual suicide of a young man in love, by the name of Jerusalem, led, it is said, a few readers too quickly affected by literature to kill themselves, while Goethe marched on to conquer serenity.

Threats or promises to commit suicide, made to himself or various confidants, abounded in Benjamin Constant's *Journal intime.* At the very time when he was reading *Adolphe* to his friends and was finally going to publish, in 1816, this short novel on which his reputation is based today, he was courting without success Juliette Récamier and, frustrated and jealous, he solemnly wrote (as he had previously done during many other lover's intrigues): "Made up my mind to die . . . I will not reverse my decision to die" (September 5, 1815 or October 9, 1815):

"Spent the night writing to Mme de Krudener that I want to kill myself." He was at the time almost a quinquagenarian, but he took pleasure in feeling and acting inconsistently and in believing that he was eccentric and an enigma to himself. Many romantics, after this keen analyst of passions who could not live without them, gazed at themselves in like manner in a mirror, astonished and naively proud of their duality. He confided in his *Journal,* with the self-conceit of one of Molière's aristocratic fops (April 11, 1804): "I have excellent qualities of pride, generosity, and devotion." He added however this strange statement that a seventeenth century Frenchman would never have made: "But I am not a completely real person." And his novel of transparent cruelty, like that of Laclos, seemed to have frightened him to the point where he wrote a fictitious letter to the publisher assigning to it a moral aim and he made every effort elsewhere to generalize this particular case which had been more or less his own (the inability to love along with an invincible need to love) and to present it, long before Musset, as a malady of the new century:

> I wanted to describe in *Adolphe* one of the chief moral maladies of our century: that stress, that uncertainty, that lack of strength, that constant analysis which makes mental reservations about all sentiments and thereby spoils them from the beginning.

Chapter 14 of the third part of *Mémoires d'outre-tombe,* entitled "Temptation", evokes once again the romantic childhood of Chateaubriand, his intense fear of his strange father, the joy he felt in scouring the countryside in autumn, "the season of storms," his reveries about some woman being at hand, a Sylph, the fallen Eve or Phryne, and his anguished questions about the significance of life. He alternated between self-contempt and the pride of knowing that he was so exceptional that no one would ever appreciate him. He related that finally one day he loaded an old shotgun and placed its muzzle in his mouth. By chance it did not fire. He added in a more modest tone than that of other similar reflections recalling the *qualis artifex pereo* of Nero: "If I had killed myself, all that I have been would have been buried with me. . . . I would have increased the number of nameless unfortunate people; people would not have followed the trail of my sorrows like a wounded man can be tracked by the trail of blood he leaves behind."

There is undoubtedly some affectation in the awe-inspiring attitude of melancholy which Chateaubriand took pleasure in adopting, as he listened to the secrets whispered to him by the sea or the forest. But it is too easy to accuse the enchanter of insincerity. In his work, as in that of so many other writers who were in his line of descendants, from Barrès to Malraux, Drieu, and Camus, there was a blend of sincerity and love of verbal ostentation which made the writer exaggerate the expression of an impression. Several avowals found in the *Mémoires* confessed this ambiguity which always affected his personality, and, he maintained, that of superior men since the advent of Christianity. Already, in the last pages of *René,* when his sister confessed to the hero "her guilty passion" and when true sorrow took the place of his vague, languishing sadness, which until then had been without cause

the traveller to the country of the Natchez remarked: "What is odd is that from the moment I was really unhappy, I no longer wanted to die." Instead of killing himself, he traveled across the ocean to the New World. A similar duality filled him with pride for having been the first in France to have analyzed the "mal du siècle" with complacency and communicated it to his successors; then, irritated by them or jealous of the French admirers of Byron who made these vague yearnings and this obsession of death commonplace, he maintained that he wanted to stigmatize "this new type of vice and present the fatal consequences of love exaggerated by solitude." Chactas nonetheless consoled the querulous René by assuring him that "a great soul must contain more grief than one less great" and that suffering from a malady mainly imaginary and without a precise cause brings a pleasure unknown to the majority of men.

Certainly none of these sentiments, which caused deep distress to Chateaubriand or the young men of 1820 to whom he communicated the contagion of his moral malady, were very new; it is as difficult to invent new sentiments as new sensation. Even before the advent of Christianity, the ancients had bewailed the instability of all things, the passing of time (*eheu! fugaces labuntur anni*) and the slow and sure death of all the affections of the heart. Pascal, whom the author of *Le Génie du christianisme* greatly admired, had denounced, after Montaigne, the need for new obstacles, or goals that are no longer desired once they are attained, a need on the basis of which Chateaubriand modulated so many of his best orchestrated sentences: a difference of religious or civilization, a suspicion of incest were not enough for him; even women, fascinated by him although they detected his self-centeredness (or perhaps captivated by that very element), readily succumbed to him. His own wife, neglected, waited and suffered, almost uncomplainingly. He discerned in advance the vanity of everything that he pursued, but he did not go to the point of making the Pascalian wager which would make him reject these fleeting or illusory pleasures for an immortality in which he just could not really believe. The feeling of the eternal haunted him, as it later haunted Lamartine and Musset: human destiny is to leave us with this gloomy fact that our existence—our pleasures as well as our afflictions—is short-lived, and therefore spoiled in advance by the presentiment of their end; human beings are incurably incomplete and dream of a plenitude which they declare impossible to achieve or of a joy which they know, deep down within them, cannot be lasting without becoming insipid. Jean-Pierre Richard and other recent critics of Chateaubriand have stressed how constant the obsession of death was in his work. The word "death" was the *leitmotiv* of his *Mémoires,* just as it was later in the *Anti-Mémoires* of Malraux. Death for him, however, was not, as it was for Hugo, the gateway to a true life ("Do not say die; say be born"—Sixth book of *Contemplations*) or a vision of paradisal felicity like that of Dante at the end of his long tour. In one of his magnificent sentences, he has evoked the gracious end our life can have:

> On our death, the earth opens its bowels to us and throws over our remains a covering of plants and flowers, while it transforms us secretly into

its own substance, in order to reproduce us in some graceful form.

At other times, he has evoked in a more gloomy manner, forestalling Gautier, Hugo, and Baudelaire, worms feeding on the carcass in the tomb, the body of Talleyrand eaten away by gangrene, or Rancé, that Ninon, who "devoured by time, was only left with a few intertwined bones, such as one sees in Roman crypts."

The symptoms of this moral malady, so often condemned by moralists but analyzed with complacency by the very people who suffered from it and thus intensified their suffering, are well-known; however, each case was a specific one and the depth of anguish felt varied depending on the temperament of the individual. The accusation of charlatanism made against them by men, during the romantic period itself (almost unanimously by critics and by doctrinaire and bourgeois politicians), and later during the antiromantic reaction of 1900-1925, was most unjust. To be sure, Balzac and Hugo were also extremely ambitious men and they were plagued by financial troubles and worry about their reputation. The notes they exchanged were often typical of men of letters, heedful of the most likely strategy to advance their success or attentive to the minute questions of language, versification, and technique that writers raise, just as painters and musicians exchange views on their own professional dodges. But the grimace of sorrow frozen on their face, doubts about the significance and goal of life which beset them, formed nevertheless a new psychological phenomenon in Western Europe. Almost all creative geniuses who have followed them have inherited this malady.

An acute state of nerves was undoubtedly at the root of this greater capacity for suffering. From Virgil to Pascal, Racine, and Marivaux, there had always been vulnerable, susceptible, and sensitive souls; but never had so many sick souls or excessively touchy people been affected this way before. Rétif, Laclos, and Sade, who had placed this cultivation of feelings in the forefront of literature, nonetheless lived long lives, perhaps because they were stimulated by the obstacles and dangers which they had faced: poverty at times, revolution and political upheavals, imprisonment. They had rarely been prostrated by a dismal sluggishness or apathy. The chasm that separated the ideal that they dreamed about and dull reality had not made them despair. They had not transfigured the woman of their dreams into an inaccessible goddess, as Stendhal, Nerval or, in other countries, Novalis or Shelley did later. According to the famous little statement—supposedly by Thucydides—that Stendhal presents in *Lucien Leuwen,* the romantics "will spread their nets too high." Even in art their ideal seemed inaccessible to them as it was so far above them, and the deficiencies of linguistic or pictorial resources in relation to their dream led them to despair. La Fontaine or Voltaire had not bewailed thus the inadequacy of expression with respect to the conception of ideas. It was after enthusiasm was considered as the surest sign of genius in art that the men of the new century felt threatened by these repercussions of enthusiasm which undermine creativeness.

There were many individual cases of the dire consequences of the "mal du siècle" in several European countries. Goethe did not succumb to it, and Schiller died young; but there were several others in Germany who were most distressed by the impossibility of fulfilling their dream and became neurasthenic or mad or resorted to suicide. Soon after he was thirty, Hoelderlin's mind became unhinged, and, in a few brilliant flashes of lucidity, he uttered cries of revolt like the following: "Like a man buried alive, my spirit revolts against the darkness in which it is fettered." Heinrich von Kleist committed suicide with Henriette Vogel, after having once again shrunk from consummating his love. Caroline de Gunderode killed herself at the age of twenty-six, for love of a professor (Creuzer); Charlotte Stieglitz did the same, in order to inspire her husband to genius; Lentz failed in his suicide attempt, but became mad. Novalis died before reaching the age of thirty, after the most chimerical, and in the opinion of the wise, the most foolish of impossible loves for a young girl. Jean Paul wrote to a friend: "Man reaches out toward the infinite; all our desires are only fragments of a great boundless desire." Friedrich Schlegel, however learned he might have been, was no more sensible in matters concerning his love life; at least, he deceived himself with complete awareness of what he was doing and a little of what Baudelaire later called "love of lying" in one of his strangest poems. "I first pretended a passion which I soon came to feel," he confided in his singular and gauche novel, *Lucinde,* which toyed often with the idea of suicide. Wackenroder died at the age of twenty-five, not quite right in his mind. Much later, not long after Nerval's suicide in a Parisian alley, the musician Schumann died in an insane asylum (1856), after having failed in an attempt to drown himself in the Rhine to put an end to his anguish.

Among the English romantics there were fewer unhappy souls who considered suicide as an alternative to their over-ardent dreams: the painter Haydon, the poet and dramatist Beddoes (in 1849). But De Quincey and Coleridge sought salvation in opium; Charles Lamb, who lived in close proximity to madness (his sister who was mad had murdered their mother), succeeded in taking his mind off it by humor. Many others, from the second half of the eighteenth century onwards, had lapsed into neurasthenia. Cries of despair echoed in the verses of Byron and Shelley and sometimes even in those of Keats, who was to die of tuberculosis at the age of twenty-five. It is a well-known fact that, in France, Hugo dreaded intensely becoming insane as one of his brothers, Eugène, had done, on the very day of the marriage of the poet, and as his daughter did later. Balzac was also afraid of the same thing. Antoni Deschamps, who was more gifted than his brother Emile, lived at Dr. Blanche's place in order to receive treatment for his mental crises, and tried to find deliverance through poetry and the translation of Dante. Musset went through crises which made him seem half mad to George Sand and later to his brother Paul de Musset. The minor romantics in France, with the exception of Nerval, were more easily engulfed in the abyss within them than the more richly talented poets who found in their more successful creativeness a distraction from their malady; their psychology was nevertheless peculiar and it is through them that we have an inkling of how deeply romantic moods distressed Frenchmen steeped in literature around 1825-1850 and even later: Charles Lassailly, author of the peculiar work *Roueries de Trialph,* who in 1843, at the age of thirty-seven, killed himself; Charles Dovalle, who died in a foolish duel in 1829, at the age of twenty-two, after having believed that he was dogged by a dismal fate; Alphonse Rabbe, author of *Album d'un Pessimiste,* committed suicide in 1829, and Victor Hugo evoked him in a long poem of *Chants du crépuscule* (XVII):

> Oh Rabbe, my friend,
> Rigorous historian asleep in the tomb

the eloquence and the passion of the Provençal who was secretly fed up with living. Esquiros, another Southerner, lived longer, wretched, exiled under the Second Empire for his political views, unbalanced, without any will. In 1942, Desnos, who was already marked down by the German police, who were responsible for his death in a concentration camp in 1945, asked the question which will undoubtedly remain unanswered: "What Baudelaire scholar will be able to enlighten us about the relationship between the author of *Les Fleurs du mal* and Esquiros? . . . [Can it be] that his tone, muffled in the verses of Pétrus Borel or Esquiros, had preceded him and was awaiting him to be finally articulated by him alone, in a loud and clear voice?" (pp. 71-82)

• • • • •

The facility which Lamartine has called "the grace of genius" and which at times seems more to be something that prevents talent from rising to the level of genius, had not been bestowed on the "minor romantics" as we call them today, or on [Astolphe de] Custine, who had more of a bent for personal writings or travel narratives than fiction-writing. It had, however, been meted out, and too liberally, to George Sand, who was fourteen years younger than him. Her ancestors had had just as stormy and as irregular an existence as had those of Custine, during those times which we would like to picture as more stable and wiser than our own. Disgracefully treated by a brutal husband, she sought other consolations. But she expected too much from sensual satisfactions and, in the first version of *Lélia,* she did not conceal this incapacity for fully experiencing sensual love which she arrogated to herself: "My heart remains detached even in the most intimate situations," Lélia confessed to Sténio, whom she loved in a motherly fashion and who loved her madly and ended up by drowning himself out of unrequited love for her. The former convict Tremor later strangled Lélia to punish her. The strange priest Magnus fascinated her but he passed judgment on her. "I could not be anyone's equal in love. My frigidity made me inferior to the most despicable women; the exaltation of my thoughts made me superior to the most passionate men." She was the counterpart of the heroes of Byron of the opposite sex, attracted by other women more than by male lovers to whom she would have liked to be able to yield but whom she ended up looking after like a motherly nurse. No work depicted more unwisely and more faithfully the exacerbations of the "mal du siècle" than this novel of 1833. The author toned it down later and produced a less revealing version of it in 1839. It is well known that she transferred her intellectual passion to socialist reformers, wrote innocuous but charming pastoral novels, a strange epical and mystical novel, *Spiridion* (1838), which was perhaps her masterpiece, and she confessed one day to Juliette Adam: "If I had to begin my life over again, I would be chaste." But she did not regret having suffered pangs of this "mal du siècle" which had been the prerogative of her generation. In 1865, she confessed to Flaubert, who showed her affectionate respect: "Grief is not unhealthy; it prevents us from becoming insensitive." The following year, responding to those who made fun of the earlier victims of the "mal du siècle" of 1830, she replied boldly and proudly:

> Perhaps our malady was better than the reaction that followed it, that craving for money, pleasures without ideals, and unbridled ambitions, which does not seem to characterize very nobly the "moral well-being of our century."

An excerpt from Alfred de Musset's *Confessions of a Child of the Century*

. . . [Two] poets, whose genius was second only to that of Napoleon, consecrated their lives to the work of collecting the elements of anguish and of grief scattered over the universe. Goethe, the patriarch of a new literature, after painting in his *Werther* the passion which leads to suicide, traced in his *Faust* the most sombre human character which has ever represented evil and unhappiness. His writings began to pass from Germany into France. From his studio, surrounded by pictures and statues, rich, happy, and at ease, he watched with a paternal smile his gloomy creations marching in dismal procession across the frontiers of France. Byron replied to him in a cry of grief which made Greece tremble, and hung Manfred over the abyss, as if oblivion were the solution of the hideous enigma with which he enveloped him.

Pardon, great poets! who are now but ashes and who sleep in peace! Pardon, ye demigods, for I am only a child who suffers. . . . Oh, God! I who speak to you, who am only a feeble child, have perhaps known sorrows that you have never suffered, and yet I believe and hope, and still bless God.

When English and German ideas had passed thus over our heads there ensued disgust and mournful silence, followed by a terrible convulsion. For to formulate general ideas is to change saltpetre into powder, and the Homeric brain of the great Goethe had sucked up, as an alembic, all the juice of the forbidden fruit. Those who did not read him, did not believe it, knew nothing of it. Poor creatures! The explosion carried them away like grains of dust into the abyss of universal doubt.

It was a denial of all heavenly and earthly facts that might be termed disenchantment, or if you will, despair; as if humanity in lethargy had been pronounced dead by those who felt its pulse. Like a soldier who is asked: "In what do you believe?" and who replies: "In myself," so the youth of France, hearing that question, replied: "In nothing."

Alfred de Musset, in his Confessions of a Child of the Century, *translated by Henri de Bornier, Current Literature, 1910.*

Along with all that the anguish of these first generations of romantics contained that was dramatic and immoderate in expression, ridiculous at times in its excesses, it also included genuine grief, impatience with limits imposed on the ambitions and dreams of man, dissatisfaction with the present and a desire to change it after having analyzed its defects. Without these romantics who were discontented with themselves and who ruthlessly analyzed their aboulia or their passion that was never completely satisfied, mankind would be poorer and duller. Lamartine, George Sand, Delacroix, Quinet, Michelet, Hugo and many others were, after all, men of action and reformers of their art and often of the society around them. Like the young eagles in a sentence of *Fantasio* which Taine liked to quote, they shot out of their nest with the indignation of the young generation which hopes to change life. They failed only partially in their endeavor. (pp. 85-7)

> *Henri Peyre, " 'Mal du Siècle' and Romantic Pessimism," in his* What is Romanticism? *translated by Roda Roberts, The University of Alabama Press, 1977, pp. 71-87.*

Victor Brombert

[*Brombert is a German educator and critic who has written extensively on nineteenth-century French literature. In the following essay, he discusses Romantic fascination with prison as an opportunity for rebirth; he explains that, for the Romantics, inventiveness arises from the repressed freedom which rejuvenates the dramatic potential of the soul.*]

Prison haunts our civilization. Object of fear, it is also a subject of poetic reverie. The prison wish does exist. The image of immurement is essentially ambivalent in the Western tradition. Prison walls confine the "culprit," victimize the innocent, affirm the power of society. But they also, it would seem, protect poetic meditation and religious fervor. The prisoner's cell and the monastic cell look strangely alike.

Poets in particular, as Albert Béguin remarked, are taken with the prison image. Is this because they have been frequent inmates of jails, ever since jails have existed? Béguin [in *Création et Destinée,* 1973] suggests a deeper reason: the poet sings of freedom. Between his vocation and the prisoner's fate there appears to be "a natural and substantial bond, a significant affinity." For the freedom in question is of the mind; it can be attained only through withdrawal into the self. It is the turbulence of life that the poet—a "spiritual anarchist"—comes to view as exile or captivity.

Romanticism, especially in France, has endowed the prison symbol with unusual prestige. This is not to deny that grim jails—real and metaphoric—served to bring out themes of terror and oppression; that images of labyrinths, undergrounds, traps, buried secrets, crushing covers, and asphyxiating encirclements provided the symbolic décor for a tragic awareness. The motif of the gloomy prison became insistent toward the end of the 18th century, in large part for political and ideological reasons. The symbolic value attributed to the Bastille and other state prisons viewed as tyrannical constructs, the nightmarish architectural perspectives in the famous "Prigioni" etchings of Piranesi, the cruel fantasies of the Marquis de Sade conceived in prison and projected into further enclosed spaces, the setting of Gothic novels in dungeons, vaults, and oubliettes—all this can tell us a great deal about the structures of the Romantic imagination, and the favored dialectical tensions between oppression and the dream of freedom, between fate and revolt, between the awareness of the finite and the longing for infinity.

The link between enclosure and inner freedom is at the heart of the Romantic sensibility. The title of Stendhal's novel, *La Chartreuse de Parme,* has puzzled many a reader, not merely because Parma is without a charterhouse, but because not even a fictional charterhouse appears in the novel's field of vision. It is clear, however, that the charterhouse in question is really none other than the Farnese Tower—in other words, the prison-fortress. The title thus proposes the central metaphor, as well as the parable of a fear translated into a blessing. The link between enclosure and spirituality is unmistakable. Paul Jacob, one of the strangest figures of the period, noted in his preface to Saintine's *Picciola*—the story of a disbeliever who regains his faith while in jail—that the prisoner in his dungeon and the monk in his cell are "eternal sources of reverie and meditation."

Fictional metaphors and social problems overlap. The monastic model is explicitly brought to bear on utopian penology. Prison reform, very much debated since the end of the 18th century, became a burning issue under the Restoration. The controversy, which was to reach fever pitch under the July Monarchy, centered on the question of the cellular prison régime. Was the cell a redemptive punishment? Tocqueville and Beaumont travelled to the United States to observe and compare the model penitentiaries in Philadelphia and Auburn. Which was preferable, the cenobitic or the anchoritic system? One thing was clear: the monastic model seemed the pattern for the future. In 1838, Léon Faucher (*De la Réforme des prisons*) came to the conclusion that the original inspiration for prison punishment (hence the word "penitentiary"!) was monastic existence, "voluntary penitence." In 1847, the International Penitentiary Congress pronounced itself in favor of solitary confinement. Isolation in the cell was to be redemptive, regenerative. Salvation and rehabilitation were increasingly viewed as dependent on the privacy of the cell. *Punitur ne pecatur:* a prison historian [Jacques Leauté, in *Les Prisons,* 1968] somewhat ironically recalls this formula, after reminding his readers that it was the French Revolution, destroyer of the Bastille, which elevated prison to the dignity of rational punishment.

The monastic prison image is reflected in the popular imagination. Prison inmates themselves seem aware of the metaphor. A recent survey by the politically activist GIP (Groupe d'Information sur les Prisons) quotes a prisoner in the "model" prison of Fleury Mérogis: "No complaints about the cells. They're not very big, but they're clean. They're a little like a monk's cell" (*ça fait un peu cellule de moine*). The underlying shuttle or reversibility of images is profoundly revealed in a book that has left its imprint on generations of readers. Dantès, the hero-prisoner of *Le Comte de Monte-Cristo,* is fated to be reborn and liberated in the cell occupied by the monastic figure of Father Faria. The prisoner-monk and the monk-prisoner: the two images converge in Alexandre Dumas' novel.

The place of enclosure and suffering is also conceived of as the protected and protective space, the locus of reverie and freedom. Our tradition is rich in tales that transmute sequestration into a symbol of security. *Securum carcer facit.* The motto is devoloped in lines that go back to the 17th century:

> Celui qui le premier m'osta la liberté
> Me mit en sureté:
> De sa grace je suis hors de prise et de crainte.
>
> (He who first took away my freedom
> Put me in safety:
> Thanks to him, I am beyond reach and fear.)

But, even earlier, folklore, legends, fairy tales, the tradition of romance, provide variations on the theme of protective custody. The motif occurs repeatedly in Renaissance epics. The magician Atlantes builds an enchanted castle to lock up his favorite hero Rogero, the better to shield him from danger. Merlin renders similar service in the Arthurian legend. Psychoanalysis has since confirmed the yearning for the enclosed space, the latent fear of the threatening outside. Agoraphobia is a recognizable symptom. Constriction is not necessarily a feared condition. Bertram D. Lewin, in *The Psychoanalysis of Elation,* suggests that the idea of the closed space corresponds not to an anxiety phantasm but to a phantasm of safety.

But with the safety dream goes the dream of freedom through transcendence. The spirit wills itself stronger than prison bars.

> Stone Walls do not a Prison make,
> Nor Iron bars a Cage . . .

writes the poet Richard Lovelace, who sings of the victory of the prisoner's mind over suffering:

> Tryumph in your Bonds and Paines,
> And daunce to th' Musick of your Chaines.

It is in the same spirit that Byron conjures up the figure of the poet-prisoner Tasso to extol the tragic liberation through confinement. The "wings" of the mind make it possible to soar beyond oppressive walls:

> For I have battled with mine agony,
> And made me wings wherewith to overfly
> The narrow surface of my dungeon wall.

Heine's famous epigram is apposite: "The love of freedom is a prison flower" (*Die Freiheitsliebe ist eine Kerkerblume*). In this perspective, the characteristic Romantic figure of the convict—the *forçat*—acquires a special meaning. Larger even than the figure of revolt (Balzac's convict Vautrin) looms the figure of salvation (Hugo's convict Jean Valjean). For, in its mythic dimension, the carceral imagery implies the presence of a threshhold, the possibility of a passage, an initiation—a passage from the inside to the beyond, from isolation to communion, from punish-

ment and suffering to redemption, from sadness to that profound and mysterious joy which poets such as Hugo associate with the eternal secret of human bondage.

The prison fear and the prison dream have been powerful literary themes. But never, it would seem, have they so persistently pressed themselves on the writer's imagination as during the 19th century. History and politics are no doubt largely responsible. The arbitrary arrests (*lettres de cachet*) and the state prisons of the Ancien Régime, the symbolism of the Bastille and of its epic fall, the revolutionary jails, the political detentions throughout Metternich's Europe, the shadow of the Spielberg, where Silvio Pellico and other victims languished, the police repressions of popular uprisings—all conspired to dramatize and poetize the prison image. This pervasive prison concern explains in part why the 19th-century sensibility was incapable of separating moral indignation from poetic vision. The ambivalence was to be vividly illustrated, toward the end of the century, in the fictional biography of the revolutionary socialist Louis Auguste Blanqui. Gustave Geffroy's *L'Enfermé* (*The Captive*) is a documentary novel on the strange destiny of this political activist whose prison vocation made him live out his own fiction. For Blanqui, the *enfermé,* viewed himself as determined by literary models: the Mont-Saint-Michel fortress, where he and other inmates became fascinated with the prison fate of Silvio Pellico, is repeatedly referred to as the "French Spielberg"; his "cup of bitterness" makes of him, in his own eyes, a "Job" and a victim of "Dante's hell"; the spiritual "freedom" discovered in jail becomes so precious to him that, having returned to "free life," he reconstructs his own cell. "Prison followed the man, reconstituted itself around him by his own volition, no matter where he was."

The Romantic imagination exploits the dramatic potential of sequestration and exile. But the importance of the carceral themes is clearly prefigured in the literature of the 18th century. The nightmarish locales of the Gothic novel indicate a yearning for the irrationality of depths and labyrinthine constriction. Their oneiric structures are graphically confirmed in Piranesi's imaginary prisons, his *carceri d'invenzione.* These dizzying descents to the underground, these crushing stone constructs, appear again in many a Romantic text. But it is not fortuitous if the taste for Piranesi and for Sade's rape scenes (always in situations of confinement) corresponds historically to the growing dream of political freedom and individual dignity. The 18th century is known to be the age of "reason"; but it is also—especially as the century comes to a close—an age that delighted in horror, and was fascinated by all the manifestations of coercion. The obsession with walls, crypts, forced religious vocations, inquisitional procedures, parallels the beginnings of a revolt against arbitrariness.

Imaginary plight and real plight reflect each other. Events were to confirm the latent sense of anguish. Many families, at this turning point of history, underwent the harrowing experience of imprisonment. It was in prison that André Chénier composed some of his most powerful poems. The new century added further distress. For the young Hugo, as for the young Vigny, the word "prison" was to retain

Alfred de Vigny.

a grim resonance. The fall of Napoleon plunged Europe into a renewed fear of political detentions. If the image of the Bastille, after 1815, continued to function as a symbol, this is because it had come to mean more than itself. This Bastille metaphor was clearly understood as a meaningful anachronism: the prisons of post-Napoleonic, reactionary Europe were being denounced obliquely. Michelet, for whom the Bastille myth was a lasting inspiration, diagnosed the anachronism. He knew full well that, from the Spielberg to Siberia, Europe was covered with prisons more terrible than the destroyed Bastille. Casanova, who had been detained in the infamous Piombi of Venice, knew it too: "I have seen at the Spielberg, in Moravia, prisons far more gruesome. . . . " It is against this political background that one must assess the prestige of Casanova, Cellini, Sade, Baron von der Trenck, Latude, Linguet, Pellico, Andryane, as well as many other prison heroes past and present.

Certain favorite themes might also explain the intense interest of Romantic writers in the prison image: tragic beauty of solitude, glorification of the individual and concern for the problem of identity, existential anguish (Freud was later to insist on the relation between *Angst* and *angustiae*), spatio-temporal motifs (*arrested* prison

time viewed as an utopian atemporality), exaltation of the rebellious outlaw who indicts society as a prison and himself becomes the hero of a double drama of fall and redemption, pride in any punishment under the dual aegis of Prometheus-Lucifer.

The *topoi,* or commonplaces, of prison literature can also be listed: the sordid cell and the hospitable cell, the cruelty of jailors (but also the presence of the "good" jailor), glimpses of the landscape and of the sky, the contrast between the ugliness of the "inside" and the supposed splendor of the surrounding scenery, prisons within the prison (the image of the iron mask), the insanity of the captive, the inscriptions in the stone, the symbolism of the wall as an invitation to transcendence. If even the most atrocious jail can be transformed into a mediating space where consciousness learns to love despair and takes full possession of itself, it is no doubt because—as Gaston Bachelard put it [in *La Poétique de l'espace,* 1957]—man is a "great dreamer of locks." Even man's consolatory prison activities, as repeatedly presented in Romantic literature, betray the urge to exploit creatively the possibilities of concentration and expansion. On the one hand, mental prowess and experimentation (geometric progressions formulated without help of paper, imaginary chess games); on the other hand, an outward reach, love at a distance (often for the jailor's daughter), conversations with the beloved (in fairy tales the beloved may be changed into a bird!), a movement of the mind toward the *outside* which makes the prisoner reinvent communication. For the "other" remains a presence. Hence the obsession with writing, secret alphabets, tappings on the walls, underground communications.

Two opposing and simultaneous movements can here be followed: the one toward an inner center (a search for identity, knowledge, the operations of memory); the other toward a transcending outside which corresponds to the joys of the imagination and the *ecstasy* of spiritual escape. Intimacy with the elusive self is the aim of the first movement, the quest within. Essentially unheroic, the movement toward the internal cell of meditation corresponds to a nocturnal lyricism, to a quest for authenticity which, at its extreme point, tolerates no histrionics, leaves no room for any pose. Novalis speaks of the mysterious road that leads to this interior region. The most diverse texts, in our literary tradition, confirm this association of the prisoner's descent into the self with the quest for a personal truth, the quest for an original identity. Robinson Crusoe is an exemplary figure: on his prison-island, he is quick to create further limits within limits; he builds a fortification, he erects walls, not merely to ward off danger, but to *surround himself,* to confine himself—and thus to *define* himself. Rousseau, on another island, dreams of living for the rest of his life as a happy prisoner. In one of the basic texts for an understanding of Romanticism—the fifth "Promenade" in the *Rêveries* (where the Bastille image occurs in association with the very notion of reverie)—Rousseau describes his happy stay on the island of Saint Pierre, and expresses the desire to see the island refuge become for him a "prison perpetuelle." The key words (*circonscrite, enfermé, asile, confiné*) all suggest an interiorization of the prison image which corresponds to the sense of almost God-like self-sufficiency (this state in which *"on se suffit à soi-même comme Dieu"*), and points to the central metaphor of Rousseauistic solipsism: *" . . . ce séjour isolé où je m'étais enlacé de moi-même . . ."* (this isolated abode where I did entwine with myself . . .).

But as Albert Béguin observed [in *L'Ame romantique et le rêve,* 1939]—precisely in talking about Novalis—the inward movement implies a glance toward what lies beyond, an ascent, an expansion. Neither the island nor the narrowest of cells represents an obstacle, in metaphoric terms, to the dynamics of escape. A wall asks to be scaled. The eye seeks the chink, measures the distance. The mind is carried through space. Nothing appears more constant than the notion of freedom associated with the cell—freedom, as it were, from the imperatives of time and space. Poets repeatedly sing of this *utopia* and of this *atemporality.*

> There were no stars, no earth, no time

writes Byron in the admirable ninth stanza of *The Prisoner of Chillon,* entirely based on a series of negative constructions. To which Tristan Corbière, in a poem ironically entitled *Libertà—A la Cellule IV bis* (*prison royale de Gênes*), seems to provide an echo:

> *Plus de jours, plus de nuits. . . .*

What is involved is an affirmation of tragic elation and dauntlessness. In Schiller's *Die Raüber,* not exactly the setting of a happy imprisonment, it is in the darkest dungeon that the dream of freedom penetrates "like lightning in the night" (. . . *wie ein Blitz in der Nacht*).

It is of course perfectly logical that the dynamics of escape (and escapism) should affirm themselves most powerfully within the context of captivity. Balzac evokes the *art* of convicts who know how to conceive and execute masterful schemes. Escape becomes a challenge to human ingeniousness. Nineteenth-century readers were likely to appreciate Benvenuto Cellini's defiant advice to his jailors ("*guardatemi bene*"—"lock me up well"), for he promised that he would do all he could to escape. (Pope Paul III, exvirtuoso of prison escape, had spoken of Cellini's feat admiringly as a *"maravigliosa cosa."*) The 19th century rediscovers Cellini. And Romantic literature is crowded with its own virtuoso jail-breakers: in the works of Stendhal, Alexandre Dumas, and above all Victor Hugo, who describes with relish the "muscle science" of convicts and the "incredible art" of rising perpendicularly. Hugo . . . does not merely praise the unusual skill in fabricating escape instruments of precision ("There are Benvenuto Cellinis in the penitentiary"); he sees in any man fired by the frightful thirst for liberty an "inspired" dreamer struggling toward the "sublime."

The darkest dream of freedom, in the Gothic novel particularly, carries an otherworldly intentionality. Clare, in *The Monk,* evokes with rapture the "glorious sunbeams." But this spiritualized yearning for escape also appears in works far removed from the Gothic, or even Romantic, tradition. Jack London, in a prison novel entitled *Star Rover,* partly a documented denunciation of torture and human degradation in California penitentiaries, invents a prisoner-hero who, through a process of mental concentration and self-hypnosis, attains a temporal and spiritual freedom that allows him, at will, to "leave" not only his cell, but his era and the limits of this world. The levitationascent leads to a walk "among the stars." The confrontation with anguish and nothingness in a prison setting, the tête-à-tête with ultimate fear, are of course recurrent motifs fully exploited in the Existentialist tradition. Leonid Andreyev, in *The Seven Who Were Hanged,* pungently conveys the sense of absurdity as the prisoner, awaiting execution, views the most ordinary objects and gestures with a feeling of terror and incongruity. Yet even Andreyev's protagonist, from within the cellular limits symbolizing the limits of his existence, experiences the "divine spectacle" of walls that vanish, of time and space that are destroyed, leaving him with the impression that he is in the presence of a "supreme being."

The link between visible loss and secret victory underlies the prison theme. It is not unrelated to the Christian notion of lost paradise and *felix culpa.* Robinson Crusoe, very much in favor with the Romantics, is once again exemplary, as he declares never to have been happier than in his "forsaken solitary condition," and gives thanks to God for having there opened his eyes and provided cause "to praise Him for dungeons and prisons." Simone Weil, in our time, has given the Christian paradox its deeper resonance, stressing [in *La Pesanteur et la grâce,* 1948] the dialectics of *absence* and *presence* ("One must therefore love that which does not exist") and suggesting that the relation of man to God is dependent on a barrier. The knocking against the wall becomes a metaphysical symbol. "Every separation is a bond." This religious thematization of the prison image confirms its metaphysical power. *The Imitation of Christ* teaches indeed that he who will cherish his cell will find peace. Western literature provides countless illustrations of the salvational virtue of the prison cell. Mary Stuart, in Schiller's play, comes to consider her prison as fitting for the visit of the celestial messenger who will show her the way to eternal freedom. Dimitri, in *The Brothers Karamazov,* declares that one cannot exist in prison without God. He discovers that a "new man" has risen up in him as he confronts the peeling walls that enclose him.

A wide range of mediating and stereotyped images links the dream-prisoner to what lies beyond the symbolic walls: windows, hills, clouds, birds—even water. The image of the bird seems favored, perhaps because it lends itself to a fundamental ambiguity. For the bird, in its free flight, brings to mind the cage from which it might have escaped, the cage that awaits it, the cage that it perhaps regrets. If indeed the quest for spiritual freedom and the redemptive thrust carry toward an elsewhere, a reverse impulse tends toward the still center, toward another form of release, a deliverance from the causal world of phenomena. It is at this still center, this still point of the turning world, that the hidden secret, the ineffable treasure, the perception of the *numen,* are to be found. Enclosure becomes the warrant of perfect fulfillment. It allows the constricted spirit to leave behind what Villiers de L'Isle-Adam calls the *"geôle du monde,"* the worldly jail, and to escape from the world of Becoming.

The dream of the happy prison defies the worldly jail. How else is one to interpret King Lear's elation, toward the end of the play, at the thought of imprisonment together with Cordelia? "Come, let's away to prison"—he seems almost impatient to be locked up. How is one to explain this impatience and hint of joy? Is it battle fatigue (he has indeed incurred the worst!); is it mental derangement; is it despair? All is lost, to be sure—but Cordelia has been found. In twelve intensely suggestive lines, Shakespeare indicates the reason for this unexpected delight. For father and daughter, so Lear hopes, prison will be an enchanted cage. Indeed like "birds i'the cage" they will be able to sing their poem of love, forgiveness and innocence:

> So we'll live,
> And pray, and sing, and tell old tales, and laugh
> At gilded butterflies.

In this cage they will feel freed from life's snares and servitudes; they will—so the old king dreams—be endowed with superior vision and glimpse the mystery of things "as if [they] were God's spies."

The idea that prison can be the locus of spiritual freedom and revelation is not merely a dream of mad, sinned-against kings. A similar notion determines Benvenuto Cellini, in his *Vita,* to write a chapter in praise of incarceration (*In Lode di detta prigione*) and to insist—he the fiery adventurer-artist—on the spiritual initiation he underwent in jail.

> *Chi vuol saper quant'è il valor de dio,*
> *e quant' un uomo a quel ben si assomiglia,*
> *convien che stie'n prigione, al parer mio.*

Similar effusions inspire the famous *Le Mie Prigioni* by Silvio Pellico, the Milanese liberal who experienced years of "hard prison" (*carcere duro*) in Metternich's political prison, the Spielberg. There were those who loudly deplored his Christian lyricism, discovered in jail, as a weakness. But the unusual success of Pellico's book (in France alone there were five translations during the first year after publication in 1833) suggests that its tone and message had immense appeal. Pellico insists on the rediscovered light; he copies with deep emotion the edifying graffiti on his prison walls (*Benedico la prigone*); he glorifies suffering. A century and a half later, his name is still revered by another famous political prisoner, Solzhenitsyn. The author of *The Gulag Archipelago* indeed sums up the prison theme: "It has been known for many centuries that prison causes the profound rebirth of a human being. The examples are innumerable—such as that of Silvio Pellico." And Solzhenitsyn adds, as his own testament to the future: " . . . I turn back to the years of my imprisonment and say, sometimes to the astonishment of those about me: '*Bless you, prison!*' "

The rebirth in question implies the redemptive powers of imagination. Repressed freedom and poetic inventiveness are intimately related. This would explain the specific prestige of the sequestered artist. Tasso in jail continues to be a subject of inspiration for other poets. The enclosed space is also the locus of artistic creativity.

We return to the figure of the writer. If indeed poets experience an affinity for the world of walls, bars, and locks, it is because it reflects the image of their own condition. Leopardi, in the imaginary dialogue between Tasso and his own *genio familiare* exalts sequestration because it rejuvenates the soul (*ringiovanisce l'animo*) and galvanizes the imagination—the *virtu di favellare*. Gérard de Nerval imagines the jailor as eternally jealous of the prisoner's dreams. Tristan Corbière is more explicit still; in his poem on liberty-in-jail, he proclaims the lyric joy of the prisoner-poet singing about the inspiration of (and to) his happy cage:

> —*Moi: jamais je n'ai chanté*
> *Que pour toi, dans ta cage,*
> *Cage de la gaité.*

The joyous confinement is here clearly associated with the creative act. It is also viewed as a sanctuary.

> *Prison, sûre conquête*
> *Où le poète est roi!*

Metaphor implies reversibility and the negation of literal meaning. The abhorred prison becomes a holy place. "A prison is a sacred asylum," affirms one of the characters in Pétrus Borel's *Madame Putiphar*. And Byron, whose *Prisoner of Chillon* explains in the final stanza that "These heavy walls to [him] have grown/ A hermitage," writes even more directly in the *Sonnet on Chillon* (referring to "the eternal spirit of the chainless mind"):

> Chillon! thy prison is a holy place,
> And thy sad floor an altar. . . .

But the figurative sense is also convertible. Poetry *becomes* prison, just as the mind (more specifically the skull) becomes the substitute for the abstract notion of closed space. Hugo provides rich examples of this interiorization of enclosure. The *noir cerveau* of Piranesi in the poem *Les Mages* prepares for the metaphor of the brain-jail (*crâne-cachot*) where the spider suspends its web. What the brain of the poet holds locked up preciously is nothing less than the infinite dimension of poetry and the secret of the world. "Un poète est un monde enfermé dans un homme" (A poet is a world locked up in a human being).

This internalized prison space is not merely the trope for the writer; it is the metaphor of the textual space. What is involved is the question of spatial form, and specifically the challenge of formal contraction as well as the fecund struggle with the limits of language. It is surely not a coincidence that Wordsworth, in his defense of the sonnet form, strings together a series of monastic and cellular images:

> Nuns fret not at their convent's narrow room;
> And hermits are contented with their cells . . .

and that Baudelaire, also celebrating the sonnet, develops the notion that constricting forms give a deeper sense of infinity.

But beyond strictly formal problems, beyond the *circumscription of space* (as Edgar Allan Poe put it), there is the emblem of the writer's vocation. Enclosure conjures up the image of the writer-at-work: Balzac's *mansarde féconde,* the "fertile garret"; Vigny and the ivory tower; Stendhal and the *prison de soie,* the "silken prison"; Flaubert and his study with its shutters closed, the Croisset cell where he gets drunk "on ink" (". . . I live like a monk"); Huysmans and the decadent retreat, the *thébaïde raffinée;* Kafka and the life-prison converted into a pleasure castle; a *Lustschloss;* Sartre for whom writing *is* sequestration ("I envied the famous prisoners . . . "). The list is far from complete.

The textual space and the prison space of salvation ultimately merge. Proust, for whom the shuttle operation between reading and writing required the intimacy of the secluded room (the darkened room offering the *spectacle total de l'été*), proposes an image that might well serve as epigraph for this study. This image strikingly telescopes a metaphor of enclosure and a metaphor of survival: the invalid's room transformed into a diluvial ark. "I understood then that Noah never saw the world so clearly as from inside the ark, though it was closed and there was darkness on the earth." (pp. 3-17)

> *Victor Brombert, in an introduction to his* The Romantic Prison: The French Tradition, *Princeton University Press, 1978, pp. 3-17.*

ROMANTICISM IN GERMANY

George Brandes

[*Brandes, a Danish literary critic and biographer, was the leader of "Det moderne gennbruch" ("the modern breaking-through"), the intellectual movement that helped to bring an end to Scandinavian cultural isolation. Writing during the latter part of the nineteenth and the early part of the twentieth century, he departed from the influence of G. W. F. Hegel and developed a critical approach based on the psychological criticism of Charles Augustin Sainte-Beuve and the sociological criticism of Hippolyte Taine. Brandes believed that literature reflects the spirit and problems of its time and must be understood within its social and aesthetic context. His major critical work,* Hovedstrømninger i det 19de aarhundredes litteratur *(1871;* Main Currents in Nineteenth Century Literature, *1872-90), traces the development of European literature in terms of writers' reactions to eighteenth-century thought. In the following excerpt, Brandes examines the origins of Romanticism in Germany.*]

Any one who makes acquaintance with the Germany of today, either by travelling in the country or by reading about it, and then compares it with the Germany of the beginning of the century, is astounded by the contrast. What a distance between then and now! Who would believe that this Realistic Germany had ever been a Romantic Germany!

Public utterances, private conversation, the very physiognomy of the towns, bear in our days a distinct stamp of realism. Walk along any street in Berlin, and you meet men in uniform, officers and privates, erect, decorated.

The literature in the windows of the bookshops has for the most part a practical tendency. Even the furniture and ornaments are influenced by the new spirit. One cannot imagine anything more prosaic and warlike than the shop of a Berlin dealer in fancy articles. On the clocks, where of old a knight in armour knelt and kissed his lady's finger-tips, Uhlans and Cuirassiers now stand in full uniform. Conical bullets hang as trinkets from watch-chains, and piled muskets form candelabra. The metal in fashion is iron. The word in fashion is also iron. The present occupation of this nation of philosophers and poets is assuredly not poetry-writing and philosophising. Even highly cultured Germans know little about philosophy now-a-days—not one German student in twenty has read a word of Hegel; interest in poetry, as such, is practically dead; political and social questions rouse a hundred times more attention than problems of culture or psychical conundrums.

And this is the people which once was lost in Romantic reveries and speculations, and saw its prototype in Hamlet! Hamlet and Bismarck! Bismarck and Romanticism! Unquestionably the great German statesman succeeded in carrying all Germany with him chiefly because he offered to his country in his own person the very qualities of which it had so long felt the want. Through him politics have been substituted for æsthetics. Germany has been united; the military monarchy has swallowed up the small States, and with them all their feudal idylls; Prussia has become the Piedmont of Germany, and has impressed its orderly and practical spirit upon the new empire; and simultaneously with this, natural science has supplanted or metamorphosed philosophy, and the idea of nationality has superseded or modified the "humanity" ideal. The War of Liberation of 1813 was pre-eminently a result of enthusiasm; the victories of 1870 were pre-eminently a result of the most careful calculation.

The idea which is the guiding star of the new Germany is the idea of organising itself as a whole. It pervades both life and literature. The expression "In Reih' und Glied"— In Ordered Ranks—(the title of a novel by Spielhagen) might be the universal watchword. The national aim is to gather together that which has been scattered, to diffuse the culture which has been the possession of too few, to found a great state, a great society; and it is required of the individual that he shall sacrifice his individuality for the sake of adding to the power of the whole, of the mass. The power of the mass! This idea may be traced in all the most remarkable phenomena of the age. Belief in it underlies the calculations of Bismarck, the agitation of Lassalle, the tactics of Moltke, and the music of Wagner. A desire to educate the people and unite them in a common aim is the mainspring of the literary activity of the prose authors of the period. A common feature of all the works which most clearly reflect the times is that they keep to the subject, to the matter in hand. The influence of the great idea, "the power of the mass," makes itself felt here too. In the new literature the relation of the individual to the State, the sacrifice of personal volition and originality entailed by the yoking of the Ego to the State chariot, presents itself in marked contrast to the Romanticist workshop of the talented individual with all his peculiarities, and the

Romanticist indifference to everything historical and political. Romantic literature was always pre-eminently drawing-room literature, the ideal of Romanticism being intellectual society and æsthetic tea-parties (*vide* the conversation in Tieck's *Fantasus*).

How different everything was in those old days! In both life and literature the detached Ego, in its homeless independence, is omnipresent. The guiding star here is, indeed, nought else but the free, unhistorical Ego. The country is divided into a multitude of small States, ruled by three hundred sovereigns and fifteen hundred semi-sovereigns. In these States the so-called "enlightened" despotism of the eighteenth century prevails, with its narrow, petrified social conditions and relations. The nobleman is lord and master of his serfs, the father, lord and master of his family—everywhere stern justice, but no equity. There are in reality no great tasks for the individual, hence there is no room for genius. The theatre is the only place where those who are not of princely birth can gain any experience of all the manifold phases of human life, hence the stage mania of literature. Lacking any social field in which to work, all activity necessarily takes the form either of war with reality or flight from it. Flight is prepared for by the influence of the rediscovered antique and of Winckelmann's writings; war, by the influence of the sentimentally melancholy English writers (Young, Sterne) and of Rousseau, reverenced as the apostle of nature, who, as Schiller expressed it, "would fain out of Christians make men."

Our first proceeding must be to trace the rising of this star, the genesis of this free, Romantic Ego, to whom, be it remembered, all the greatest intellects of Germany stood sponsor.

It was Lessing who laid the foundations of the intellectual life of modern Germany. Clear of thought, strong of will, indefatigably active, he was a reformer in every matter in which he interested himself. With perfect consciousness of what he was doing, he enlightened and educated the German mind. He was the embodiment of manly independence and vigorous, tireless militancy. His personal ideal, as it is revealed in his life and writings, was proud independence in combination with a wise love of his fellow-men, which overcame all differences of creed. Hence, solitary as he stood in his own day, his Ego became a source of light. He was the "Prometheus of German prose." His great achievement was that of freeing German culture for all time from the swaddling bands of theology, as Luther had freed it from those of Catholicism. His life and his criticism were action, and to him the essence of poetry too was action. All his characters are instinct with dramatic passion. In opposition to the theological doctrine of punishment and reward, he maintained that to do right for the sake of doing right is the highest morality. And for him the history of the world became the history of the education of the human race. To a certain extent the word "education" is employed by him merely as a concession to his readers, who, he knew, could not conceive of any development without a divine educator; but, all the same, the idea of natural development is not an idea with which he was familiar. To him, history is the record of "enlightenment." The Ego to him is not nature, but pure mind.

In reality, all that was best in Lessing was entirely unsympathetic to the new group of Romanticists; they had less in common with him than with any other of the great German authors, Schiller not excepted. Nevertheless, it was natural enough that they should refuse to acknowledge any connection between Lessing and those of his disciples (men such as Nicolai, Engel, Garve, and Schütz), who were, from the "enlightenment" standpoint, their bitter enemies and ruthless persecutors. This was done by Friedrich Schlegel in an essay in which, while praising the power and the width of Lessing's grasp, he lays chief stress upon everything in him that is irregular, boldly revolutionary, unsystematic, and paradoxical, dwells on his bellicose wit, and draws attention to everything that can be construed into cynicism. The Romanticists could not possibly claim a champion of reason, pure and simple, as their forerunner, hence they attempted to characterise the nutritive element in Lessing's works as mere seasoning, as the salt which preserves from corruption.

They owed far more to Herder. They evidence their descent from him both by their continuation of the *Sturm und Drang* period and by their capacity of understanding and reproducing the poetry of all countries. In Herder the new century germinated, as in Lessing the old had come to its close. Herder sets genesis and growth above thought and action. To him the true man is not only a thinking and moral being, but a portion of nature. He loves and sets most store by the original; he prefers intuition to reason, and would overcome narrow-mindedness, not by reason, but by originality. The man of intuitions is to him the most human. His own genius was the genius of receptivity. He expanded his Ego until it comprehended every kind of originality, but it was by virtue of feeling that he comprehended, that he absorbed into his soul a wealth of life, human and national.

From Herder the Romanticists derive that which is most valuable in their literary criticism—the universal receptivity which finds expression in the impulse to translate and explain; from him they derive the first stimulus to a scientific study of both European and Asiatic languages; from him comes their love for what is national in both their own and foreign literature, their love of Spanish romance and of Shakespeare's plays. Herder grasped things in their entirety as did Goethe after him. His profound comprehension of national peculiarities becomes in Goethe the genius's intuition of the typical in nature, and is exalted by Schelling under the name of "intellectual intuition." The objection of the Romanticists to the idea of aim or purpose may be traced back to Herder. His theory of history excluded the idea of purpose: what happens has a cause and is subject to laws, but cannot be explained by anything which has not yet happened, *i.e.* by a purpose. The Romanticists transferred this theory into the personal, the psychical domain. To them purposelessness is another name for Romantic genius; the man of genius lives without a definite purpose; purposelessness is idleness, and idleness is the mark and privilege of the elect. In this caricature of a philosophy there is not much resemblance to Herder's. But he is the originator of a new conception of genius, of the belief, namely, that genius is intuitive, that it consists in a certain power of perceiving and apprehending without any resort to abstract ideas. It is this conception which, with the Romanticists, becomes scorn of experimental methods in science, and approbation of extraordinary vagaries in art.

Goethe was the fulfilment of all that Herder had promised. To him man was not merely theoretically the last link in nature's chain; the men in his works were themselves natures; and in his scientific research he discerned with the eye of genius the universal laws of evolution. His own Ego was a microcosm, and produced the effect of such on the most discerning of his younger contemporaries. "Goethe and life are one," says Rahel. So profound was his insight into nature, so entirely was he a living protest against every supernatural belief, that he did what in him lay to deprive genius of its character of apparent incomprehensibility and contrariety to reason, by explaining (in his autobiography, *Wahrheit und Dichtung*) his own genius, the most profound and universal of the age, as a natural product developed by circumstances—thereby creating the type of literary criticism to which the Romanticists were strongly opposed.

From Goethe the young generation derived their theory of the rights and the importance of the great, free personality. He had always lived his own life, and had always lived it fully and freely. Without making any attack whatever on the existing conditions of society, he had remoulded, according to his own requirements, the social relations in which he found himself placed. He becomes the soul of the youthful and joyous court of Weimar, with the audacity of youth and genius drawing every one with him into a whirl of gaiety—fêtes, picnics, skating expeditions, masquerades—animated by a wild joy in nature, which is now "lightened," now "darkened" by love affairs of a more or less dubious character. Jean Paul writes to a friend that he can only describe the morals of Weimar to him by word of mouth. When we hear that even skating was a scandal to the worthy Philistines of that town, we are not surprised by old Wieland's ill-natured remark, that the circle in question appeared to him to be aiming at "brutalising animal nature." Thus it was that the sweet, refined coquette, Frau von Stein, became Goethe's muse for ten whole years, the original of Leonore and Iphigenia; and later he created a still greater scandal by taking into his house Christiane Vulpius (the young girl whose presence had become a necessity to him, and who, in spite of her faults, never embittered his life by making any demands upon him), and living with her for eighteen years before obtaining the sanction of the Church to their union.

Goethe's as well as Schiller's youthful works had been inspired by what the Germans call the "Freigeisterei" of passion, its demand for freedom, its instinct of revolt. Both breathe one and the same spirit, the spirit of defiance. Goethe's *Die Geschwister* treats of the passion of brother for sister. The conclusion of *Stella,* in its original form, is a justification of bigamy; and Jean Paul, too, in his *Siebenkäs,* treats of bigamy as a thing perfectly permissible in the case of a genius to whom the first tie has become burdensome. *Götz* represents the tragic fate of the man of genius who rises in revolt against a lukewarm and corrupt age. Schiller's *Die Räuber,* with its device *In Ty-*

rannos, and its motto from Hippocrates, "That which medicine cannot cure iron cures, and that which iron cannot cure fire cures," is a declaration of war against society. Karl Moor is the noble-hearted idealist, who in "the castrated century" is inevitably doomed to perish as a criminal. Schiller's robbers are not highwaymen, but revolutionaries. They do not plunder, but punish. They have separated themselves from society to revenge themselves upon it for the wrongs it has done them. Schiller's defiance is still more personally expressed in those poems of his first period which were written under the influence of his relations with Frau von Kalb, poems re-written and entirely altered in the later editions. In the one which ultimately received the title *Der Kampf,* but which was originally called *Freigeisterei der Leidenschaft,* he writes:—

> Woher dies Zittern, dies unnennbare Entsetzen,
> Wenn mich dein liebevoller Arm umschlang?
> Weil Dich ein Eid, den auch nur Wallungen verletzen,
> In fremde Fesseln zwang?
>
> Weil ein Gebrauch, den die Gesetze heilig prägen,
> Des Zufalls schwere Missethat geweiht?
> Nein—unerschrocken trotz ich einem Bund entgegen,
> Den die erröthende Natur bereut.
>
> O zittre nicht—Du hast als Sünderin geschworen,
> Ein Meineid ist der Reue fromme Pflicht,
> Das Herz war mein, das Du vor dem Altar verloren,
> Mit Menschenfreuden spielt der Himmel nicht.

Comical as this naïve sophistry sounds, and unreliable as is the assurance that Heaven will not permit itself now and again to play with human happiness, the spirit of the verses is unmistakable; and, as Hettner aptly observes, Don Carlos uses almost the same words: "The rights of my love are older than the ceremonies at the altar."

The model for Schiller's young Queen Elizabeth was Charlotte von Kalb. This lady, the passion of the poet's youth, had been unwillingly forced into matrimony by her parents. She and Schiller met in 1784, and in 1788 they were still meditating a permanent union of their destinies. Soon after Schiller left her, she became Jean Paul's mistress. (Caroline Schlegel jestingly calls her Jeannette Pauline.) Jean Paul characterises her thus: "She has two great possessions: great eyes (I never saw their like) and a great soul." He himself confesses that it is she whom he has described in one of his principal works as the Titaness, Linda. In *Titan* (118 Zykel) we are told of Linda that she must be tenderly treated, not only on account of her delicacy, but also in the matter of her aversion to matrimony, which is extreme. She cannot even accompany a friend to the altar, which she calls the scaffold of woman's liberty, the funeral pyre of the noblest, freest love. To take, she says, the best possible view of it, the heroic epic of love is there transformed into the pastoral of marriage. Her sensible friend vainly insists that her aversion to marriage can have no other ground than her hatred of priests; that wedlock only signifies everlasting love, and all true love regards itself as everlasting; that there are as many unhappy free-love connections as marriages, if not more, &c.

Frau von Kalb herself writes to Jean Paul:

> Why all this talk about seduction? Spare the poor creatures, I beg of you, and alarm their hearts and consciences no more. Nature is petrified enough already. I shall never change my opinion on this subject; I do not understand this virtue, and cannot call any one blessed for its sake. Religion here upon earth is nothing else than the development and maintenance of the powers and capacities with which our natures have been endowed. Man should not submit to compulsion, but neither should he acquiesce in wrongful renunciation. Let the bold, powerful, mature human nature, which knows and uses its strength, have its way. But in our generation human nature is weak and contemptible. Our laws are the outcome of wretchedness and dire necessity, seldom of wisdom. Love needs no laws.

A vigorous mind speaks to us in this letter. The leap from this to the idea of *Lucinde* is not a long one, but the fall to the very vulgar elaboration of *Lucinde* is great. We do not, however, rightly understand these outbursts until we understand the social conditions which produced them, and realise that they are not isolated and accidental tirades, but are conditioned by the position in which the majority of poetic natures stood to society at that time.

Weimar was then the headquarters and gathering-place of Germany's classical authors. It is not difficult to understand how they came to gather in this little capital of a little dukedom. Of Germany's two great monarchs, Joseph the Second was too much occupied with his efforts at reform, too eager for the spread of "enlightenment," to have any attention to spare for German poetry; and the Voltairean Frederick of Prussia was too French in his tastes and intellectual tendencies to take any interest in German poets. It was at the small courts that they were welcomed. Schiller lived at Mannheim, Jean Paul at Gotha, Goethe at Weimar. Poetry had had no stronghold in Germany for many a long year, but now Weimar became one. Thither Goethe summoned Herder; Wieland had been there since 1772. Schiller received an appointment in the adjacent Jena. Weimar was, then, the place where passion, as poetical, compared with the prosaic conventions of society, was worshipped most recklessly and with least prejudice, in practice as well as theory. "Ah! here we have women!" cries Jean Paul when he comes to Weimar. "Everything is revolutionarily daring here; that a woman is married signifies nothing." Wieland "revives himself" by taking his former mistress, Sophie von la Roche, into his house, and Schiller invites Frau von Kalb to accompany him to Paris.

We thus understand how it was that Jean Paul, when in Weimar, and under the influence of Frau von Kalb's personality, exclaimed: "This much is certain; the heart of the world is beating with a more spiritual and greater revolution than the political, and one quite as destructive."

What revolution? The emancipation of feeling from the conventions of society; the heart's audacious assumption of its right to regard its own code of laws as the new moral code, to re-cast morals in the interests of morality, and occasionally in the interests of inclination. The Weimar circle had no desire, no thought for anything beyond this, had neither practical nor social reforms in view. It is a genuinely German trait that outwardly they made deep obeisance to the laws which they privately evaded. In conversation, Goethe, in his riper years, invariably maintained that the existing conventions regulating the relations of the sexes were absolutely necessary in the interests of civilisation; and in their books authors gave expression to revolutionary sentiments which were more or less their own, only to recant at the end of the book. The hero either confesses his error, or commits suicide, or is punished for his defiance of society, or renounces society altogether (Karl Moor, Werther, Tasso, Linda). It is exactly the proceeding of the heretical authors of the Middle Ages, who concluded their books with a notice that everything in them must of course be interpreted in harmony with the doctrines and decrees of Holy Mother Church.

Into this Weimar circle of gifted women Madame de Staël, "the whirlwind in petticoats," as she has been called, is introduced when she comes to Germany. In the midst of them she produces the effect of some strange wild bird. What a contrast between her aims and their predilections! With them everything is personal, with her by this time everything is social. She has appeared before the public; she is striking doughty blows in the cause of social reform. For such deeds even the most advanced of these German women of the "enlightenment" period are of much too mild a strain. Her aim is to revolutionise life politically, theirs to make it poetical. The idea of flinging the gauntlet to a Napoleon would never have entered the mind of any one of them. What a use to make of a lady's glove, a pledge of love! It is not the rights of humanity, but the rights of the heart which they understand; their strife is not against the wrongs of life but against its prose. The relation of the gifted individual to society does not here, as in France, take the form of a conflict between the said individual's rebellious assertion of his liberty and the traditional compulsion of society, but of a conflict between the poetry of the desires of the individual and the prose of political and social conventions. Hence the perpetual glorification in Romantic literature of capacity and strength of desire, of wish; a subject to which Friedrich Schlegel in particular perpetually recurs. It is in reality the one outwardly directed power that men possess—impotence itself conceived as a power.

We find the same admiration of *wish* in Kierkegaard's *Enten-Eller* (*Either-Or*). "The reason why *Aladdin* is so refreshing is that we feel the childlike audacity of genius in its wildly fantastic wishes. How many are there in our day who dare really wish?" &c. The childlike, for ever the childlike! But who can wonder that *wish*, the mother of religions, the outward expression of inaction, became the catchword of the Romanticists? *Wish* is poetry; society as it exists, prose. It is only when we judge them from this standpoint that we rightly understand even the most serene, most chastened works of Germany's greatest poets. Goethe's *Tasso*, with its conflict between the statesman and the poet (*i.e.* between reality and poetry), its delineation of the contrast between these two who complete each other, and are only unlike "because nature did not make one man of them," is, in spite of its crystalline limpidity of style and its keynote of resignation, a product of the self-same long fermentation which provides the Romantic School with all its fermentative matter. The theme of *Wilhelm Meister* is in reality the same. It, too, represents the gradual, slow reconciliation and fusion of the dreamed of ideal and the earthly reality. But only the greatest minds rose to this height; the main body of writers of considerable, but less lucid intellect never got beyond the inward discord. The more poetry became conscious of itself as a power, the more the poet realised his dignity, and literature became a little world in itself with its own special technical interests, the more distinctly did the conflict with reality assume the subordinate form of a conflict with philistinism (see, for instance, Eichendorff's *Krieg den Philistern*). Poetry no longer champions the eternal rights of liberty against the tyranny of outward circumstances; it champions itself as poetry against the prose of life. This is the Teutonic, the German-Scandinavian, that is to say, the narrow literary conception of the service that poetry is capable of rendering to the cause of liberty.

"We must remember," says Kierkegaard,

> that Tieck and the entire Romantic School entered, or believed they entered, into relations with a period in which men were, so to speak, petrified, in final, unalterable social conditions. Everything was perfected and completed, in a sort of divine Chinese perfection, which left no reasonable longing unsatisfied, no reasonable wish unfulfilled. The glorious principles and maxims of 'use and wont' were the objects of a pious worship; everything, including the absolute itself, was absolute; men refrained from polygamy; they wore peaked hats; nothing was without its significance. Each man felt, with the precise degree of dignity that corresponded to his position, what he effected, the exact importance to himself and to the whole, of his unwearied endeavour. There was no frivolous indifference to punctuality in those days; all ungodliness of that kind tried to insinuate itself in vain. Everything pursued its tranquil, ordered course; even the suitor went soberly about his business; he knew that he was going on a lawful errand, was taking a most serious step. Everything went by clockwork. Men waxed enthusiastic over the beauties of nature on Midsummer Day; were overwhelmed by the thought of their sins on the great fast-days; fell in love when they were twenty, went to bed at ten o'clock. They married and devoted themselves to domestic and civic duties; they brought up families; in the prime of their manhood notice was taken in high places of their honourable and successful efforts; they lived on terms of intimacy with the pastor, under whose eye they did the many generous deeds which they knew he would recount in a voice trembling with emotion when the day came for him to preach their funeral sermon. They were friends in the genuine sense of the word, *ein wirklicher Freund, wie man wirklicher Kanzleirat war.*

I fail to see anything typical in this description. Except

that we wear round hats instead of peaked ones, every word of it might apply to the present day; there is nothing especially indicative of one period more than another. No; the distinctive feature of the period in question is the gifted writer's, the Romanticist's, conception of philistinism. In my criticism of Johan Ludvig Heiberg's first Romantic attempts, I wrote: "They (the Romanticists) looked upon it from the philosophical point of view as finality, from the intellectual, as narrow-mindedness; not, like us, from the moral point of view, as contemptibility. With it they contrasted their own infinite longing. . . . They confronted its prose with their own youthful poetry; we confront its contemptibility with our virile will." As a general rule, then, they, with their thoughts and longings, fled society and reality, though now and again, as already indicated, they attempted, if not precisely to realise their ideas in life, at least to sketch a possible solution of the problem how to transform reality in its entirety into poetry.

Not that they show a spark of the indignation or the initiative which we find in the French Romantic author (George Sand, for instance); they merely amuse themselves with elaborating revolutionary, or at least startling fancies.

That which Goethe had attained to, namely, the power of moulding his surroundings to suit his own personal requirements, was to the young generation the point of departure. In this particular they from their youth saw the world from Goethe's point of view; they made the measure of freedom which he had won for himself and the conditions which had been necessary for the full development of his gifts and powers, the average, or more correctly the minimum, requirement of every man with talent, no matter how little. They transformed the requirements of his nature into a universal rule, ignored the self-denial he had laboriously practised and the sacrifices he had made, and not only proclaimed the unconditional rights of passion, but, with tiresome levity and pedantic lewdness, preached the emancipation of the senses. And another influence, very different from that of Goethe's powerful self-assertion, also made itself felt, namely, the influence of Berlin. To Goethe's free, unrestrained humanity there was added in Berlin an ample alloy of the scoffing, anti-Christian spirit which had emanated from the court of Frederick the Great, and the licence which had prevailed at that of his successor.

But both Goethe and Schiller paved the way for Romanticism not only positively, by their proclamation of the rights of passion, but also negatively, by the conscious attitude of opposition to their own age which they assumed in their later years. In another form, the Romanticist's aversion to reality is already to be found in them. I adduce two famous instances of the astonishing lack of interest shown by Goethe, the greatest creative mind of the day, in political realities; they prove at the same time how keen was his interest in science. Writing of the campaign against France during the French Revolution, a campaign in which he took part, he mentions that he spent most of his time in observing "various phenomena of colour and of personal courage." And after the battle of Jena Knebel writes: "Goethe has been busy with optics the whole time.

We study osteology under his guidance, the times being well adapted to such study, as all the fields are covered with preparations." The bodies of his fallen countrymen did not inspire the poet with odes; he dissected them and studied their bones.

Such instances as these give us some impression of the attitude of aloofness which Goethe as a poet maintained towards the events of his day. But we must not overlook the fine side of his refusal to write patriotic war-songs during the struggle with Napoleon. "Would it be like me to sit in my room and write war-songs? In the night bivouacs, when we could hear the horses of the enemy's outposts neighing, then I might possibly have done it. But it was not my life, that, and not my affair; it was Theodor Körner's. Therefore his war-songs become him well. I have not a warlike nature nor warlike tastes, and war-songs would have been a mask very unbecoming to me. I have never been artificial in my poetry." Goethe, like his disciple Heiberg, was in this case led to refrain by the strong feeling that he only cared to write of what he had himself experienced; but he also tells us that he regarded themes of a historical nature as "the most dangerous and most thankless."

His ideal, and that of the whole period, is humanity pure and simple—a man's private life is everything. The tremendous conflicts of the eighteenth century and the "enlightenment" period are all, in consonance with the human idealism of the day, contained in the life story, the development story, of the individual. But the cult of humanity does not only imply lack of interest in history, but also a general lack of interest in the subject for its own sake. In one of his letters to Goethe, Schiller writes that two things are to be demanded of the poet and of the artist—in the first place, that he shall rise above reality, and in the second, that he shall keep within the bounds of the material, the natural. He explains his meaning thus: The artist who lives amidst unpropitious, formless surroundings, and consequently ignores these surroundings in his art, runs the risk of altogether losing touch with the tangible, of becoming abstract, or, if his mind is not of a robust type, fantastic; if, on the other hand, he keeps to the world of reality, he is apt to be too real, and, if he has little imagination, to copy slavishly and vulgarly. These words indicate, as it were, the watershed which divides the German literature of this period. On the one side we have the unnational art-poetry of Goethe and Schiller, with its continuation in the fantasies of the Romanticists, and on the other side the merely sensational or entertaining literature of the hour (Unterhaltungslitteratur), which is based on reality, but a philistine reality, the literature of which Lafontaine's sentimental bourgeois romances, and the popular, prosaic family dramas of Schröder, Iffland, and Kotzebue, are the best known examples. It was a misfortune for German literature that such a division came about. But, although the rupture of the better literature with reality first showed itself in a startling form in the writings of the Romanticists, we must not forget that the process had begun long before. Kotzebue had been the antipodes of Schiller and Goethe before he stood in that position to the Romanticists. (pp. 17-32)

There had, most undoubtedly, been a time when Goethe and Schiller themselves were realists. To both, in their first stage of restless ferment, reality had been a necessity. Both had given free play to nature and feeling in their early productions, Goethe in *Götz* and *Werther,* Schiller in *Die Raüber.* But after *Götz* had set the fashion of romances of chivalry and highway robbery, *Werther* of suicide, both in real life and in fiction, and *Die Raüber* of such productions as *Abällino, der grosse Bandit,* the great writers, finding the reading world unable to discriminate between originals and imitations, withdrew from the arena. Their interest in the subject was lost in their interest in the form. The study of the antique led them to lay ever-increasing weight upon artistic perfection. It was not their lot to find a public which understood them, much less a people that could present them with subjects, make demands of them—give them orders, so to speak. The German people were still too undeveloped. When Goethe, at Weimar, was doing what he could to help Schiller, he found that the latter, on account of his wild life at Mannheim, his notoriety as a political refugee, and especially his pennilessness, was regarded as a writer of most unfortunate antecedents. During the epigram war (Xenienkampf) of 1797, both Goethe and Schiller were uniformly treated as poets of doubtful talent. One of the pamphlets against them is dedicated to "die zwei Sudelköche in Weimar und Jena" (the bunglers of Weimar and Jena). It was Napoleon's recognition of Goethe, his wish to see and converse with him, his exclamation: "Voilà un homme!" which greatly helped to establish Goethe's reputation in Germany. A Prussian staff-officer, who was quartered about this time in the poet's house, had never heard his name. His publisher complained bitterly of the small demand for the collected edition of his works; there was a much better sale for those of his brother-in-law, Vulpius (author of *Rinaldo Rinaldini*). *Tasso* and *Iphigenia* could not compete with works of such European fame as Kotzebue's *Menschenhass und Reue;* Goethe himself tells us that they were only performed in Weimar once every three or four years. Clearly enough it was the stupidity of the public which turned the great poets from the popular path to glory; but it is equally clear that the new classicism, which they so greatly favoured, was an ever-increasing cause of their unpopularity. Only two of Goethe's works were distinct successes, *Werther* and *Hermann und Dorothea.*

What were the proceedings of the two great poets after they turned their backs upon their surroundings? Goethe made the story of his own strenuous intellectual development the subject of plastic poetic treatment. But finding it impossible, so long as he absorbed himself in modern humanity, to attain to the beautiful simplicity of the old Greeks, he began to purge his works of the personal; he composed symbolical poems and allegories, wrote *Die Natürliche Tochter,* in which the characters simply bear the names of their callings, King, Ecclesiastic, &c.; and the neo-classic studies, *Achilleis, Pandora, Palœophron und Neoterpe, Epimenides,* and the *Second Part of Faust.* He began to employ Greek mythology much as it had been employed in French classical literature, namely, as a universally understood metaphorical language. He no longer, as in the *First Part of Faust,* treated the individual as a type, but produced types which were supposed to be individuals. His own *Iphigenia* was now too modern for him. Ever more marked became that addiction to allegory which led Thorvaldsen too away from life in his art. In his art criticism Goethe persistently maintained that it is not truth to nature, but truth to art which is all-important; he preferred ideal mannerism (such as is to be found in his own drawings preserved in his house in Frankfort) to ungainly but vigorous naturalism. As theatrical director he acted on these same principles; grandeur and dignity were everything to him. He upheld the conventional tragic style of Calderon and Alfieri, Racine and Voltaire. His actors were trained, in the manner of the ancients, to stand like living statues; they were forbidden to turn profile or back to the audience, or to speak up the stage; in some plays, in defiance of the customs of modern mimic art, they wore masks. In spite of public opposition, he put A. W. Schlegel's *Ion* on the stage—a professedly original play, in reality an unnatural adaptation from Euripides, suggested by *Iphigenia*. Nay, he actually insisted, merely for the sake of exercising the actors in reciting verse, on producing Friedrich Schlegel's *Alarkos,* an utterly worthless piece, which might have been written by a talentless schoolboy, and was certain to be laughed off the stage. To such an extent as this did he gradually sacrifice everything to external artistic form.

It is easy, then, to see how Goethe's one-sidedness prepared the way for that of the Romanticists; it is not so easy to show that the same was the case with Schiller. Schiller's dramas seem like prophecies of actual events. The French Revolution ferments in *Die Räuber* (the play which procured for "Monsieur Gille" the title of honorary citizen of the French Republic), and, as Gottschall observes, "the eighteenth Brumaire is anticipated in *Fiesko,* the eloquence of the Girondists in *Posa,* the Cæsarian soldier-spirit in *Wallenstein,* and the Wars of Liberation in *Die Jungfrau von Orleans* and *Wilhelm Tell.*" But in reality it is only in his first dramas that Schiller allows himself to be influenced, without second thought or ulterior purpose, by his theme. In all the later plays the competent critic at once feels how largely the choice of subject has been influenced by considerations of form. Henrik Ibsen once drew my attention to this in speaking of *Die Jungfrau von Orleans;* he maintained that there is no "experience" in that play, that it is not the result of powerful personal impressions, but is a composition. And Hettner has shown this to be the relation of the author to his work in all the later plays. From the year 1798 onwards, Schiller's admiration for Greek tragedy led him to be always on the search for subjects in which the Greek idea of destiny prevailed. *Der Ring des Polykrates, Der Taucher,* and *Wallenstein* are dominated by the idea of Nemesis. *Maria Stuart* is modelled upon the *Œdipus Rex* of Sophocles, and this particular historical episode is chosen with the object of having a theme in which the tragic end, the appointed doom, is foreknown, so that the drama merely gradually develops that which is inevitable from the beginning. The subject of the *Jungfrau von Orleans,* in appearance so romantic, is chosen because Schiller desired to deal with an episode in which, after the antique manner, a direct divine message reached the human soul—in which there is a direct material interposition of the divinity, and yet the human

being who is the organ of the divinity can be ruined, in genuine Greek fashion, by her human weakness.

It was only in keeping with his general unrealistic tendency that Schiller, though he was not in the least musical, should extol the opera at the expense of the drama, and maintain the antique chorus to be far more awe-inspiring than modern tragic dialogue. In *Die Braut von Messina* he himself produced a "destiny" tragedy, which to all intents and purposes is a study in the manner of Sophocles. Not even in *Wilhelm Tell* is his point of view a modern one; on the contrary, it is in every particular purely Hellenic. The subject is not conceived dramatically, but epically. The individual is marked by no special characteristic. It is merely an accident that raises Tell above the mass and makes him the leader of the movement. He is, as Goethe says, a "sort of Demos." Hence it is not the conflict between two great, irreconcilable historical ideas that is presented in this play; the men of Rütli have no sentimental attachment to liberty; it is neither the idea of liberty nor the idea of country that produces the insurrection. Private ideas and private interests, encroachments on family rights and rights of property, here provide the mainspring of action, or rather of event, which in the other dramas is provided by personal or dynastic ambition. It is explicitly signified to us that the peasants do not aim at acquiring new liberties, but at maintaining old inherited customs. On this point I may refer the reader to Lasalle, who develops the same view with his usual ingenuity in the interesting preface to his drama, *Franz von Sickingen.*

Thus, then, we see that even when Schiller, the most political and historical of the German poets, appears to be most interested in history and politics, he is dealing only to a limited extent with reality; and therefore it may be almost considered proved, that distaste for historical and present reality—in other words, subjectivism and idealism—were the characteristics of the whole literature of that day.

But the spirit of Herder, Goethe, and Schiller is only one of the motive powers of Romanticism. The other is the philosophy of Fichte. It was the Fichtean doctrine of the Ego which gave to the Romantic individuality its character and force. The axioms: All that is, is for us; What is for us can only be through us; Everything that is, both natural and supernatural, exists through the *activity of the Ego,* received an entirely new interpretation when transferred from the domain of metaphysics to that of psychology. All reality is contained in the Ego itself, hence the absolute Ego demands that the non-Ego which it posits shall be in harmony with it, and is itself simply the infinite striving to pass beyond its own limits. It was this conclusion of the *Wissenschaftslehre* (Doctrine of Knowledge) which fired the young generation. By the absolute Ego they understood, as Fichte himself in reality did, though in a very different manner, not a divine being, but the thinking human being. And this new and intoxicating idea of the absolute freedom and power and self-sufficiency of the Ego, which, with the arbitrariness of an autocratic monarch, obliges the whole world to shrink into nothing before itself, is enthusiastically proclaimed by an absurdly arbitrary, ironical, and fantastic set of young geniuses, half-geniuses, and quarter-geniuses. The *Sturm und Drang* period, when the liberty men gloried in was the liberty of eighteenth-century "enlightenment," reappeared in a more refined and idealistic form; and the liberty now gloried in was nineteenth-century lawlessness.

Fichte's doctrine of a world-positing, world-creating Ego was at variance with "sound human reason." This was one of its chief recommendations in the eyes of the Romanticists. The *Wissenschaftslehre* was scientific paradox, but to them paradox was the fine flower of thought. Moreover, the fundamental idea of the doctrine was as radical as it was paradoxical. It had been evolved under the impression of the attempt made by the French Revolution to transform the whole traditional social system into a rational system (Vernunftstaat). The autocracy of the Ego was Fichte's conception of the order of the world, and therefore in this doctrine of the Ego the Romanticists believed that they possessed the lever with which they could lift the old world from its hinges.

The Romantic worship of imagination had already begun with Fichte. He explained the world as the result of an unconscious, yet to a thinker comprehensible, act of the free, yet at the same time limited, Ego. This act, he maintains, emanates from the creative imagination. By means of it the world which we apprehend with the senses first becomes to us a real world. The whole activity of the human mind, then, according to Fichte, springs from the creative imagination; it is the instinct which he regards as the central force of the active Ego. The analogy with the imaginative power which is so mighty in art is evident. But what Fichte himself failed to perceive is, that imagination is by no means a creative, but only a transforming, remodelling

Oil painting of Jean Paul Richter by Friedrich Meier, 1810.

power, since what it acts upon is only the form of the things conceived of, not their substance.

Fichte says that he "does not require 'things,' and does not make use of them, because they prevent his self-dependence, his independence of all that is outside of himself." This saying is closely allied to Friedrich Schlegel's observation, "that a really philosophic human being should be able to tune himself at will in the philosophical or philological, the critical or poetical, the historical or rhetorical, the ancient or modern key, as one tunes an instrument, and this at any time and to any pitch."

According to the Romantic doctrine, the artistic omnipotence of the Ego and the arbitrariness of the poet can submit to no law. In this idea lies the germ of the notorious Romantic irony in art, the treating of everything as both jest and earnest, the eternal self-parody, the disturbing play with illusions alternately summoned up and banished, which destroys all directness of effect in many of the favourite works of the Romanticists.

The Romanticist's theory of art and life thus owes its existence to a mingling of poetry with philosophy, a coupling of the poet's dreams with the student's theories; it is a production of purely intellectual powers, not of any relation between these powers and real life. Hence the excessively intellectual character of Romanticism. Hence all the self-duplication, all the raising to higher powers, in this poetry about poetry and this philosophising on philosophy. Hence its living and moving in a higher world, a different nature. This too is the explanation of all the symbolism and allegory in these half-poetical, half-philosophical works. A literature came into being which partook of the character of a religion, and ultimately joined issue with religion, and which owed its existence rather to a life of emotion than a life of intellectual productiveness. Hence we understand how, as A. W. Schlegel himself says, "it was often rather the ethereal melody of the feelings that was lightly suggested than the feelings themselves that were expressed in all their strength and fulness." It was not the thing itself that the author wished to communicate to the reader, but a suggestion of the thing. It is not in bright sunlight, but in twilight or mysterious quivering moonlight, on a far horizon or in dreams, that we behold the figures of Romanticism. Hence too the Romantic dilution or diminution of the terms expressing what is perceived by the senses (Blitzeln, Aeugeln, Hinschatten), and also that interchange of the terms for the impressions of the different senses, which makes the imagery confusedly vague. In *Zerbino* Tieck writes of flowers:

> "Die Farbe klingt; die Form ertönt, jedwede
> Hat nach der Form und Farbe Zung' und Rede.
>
> . . . . .
>
> Sich Farbe, Duft, Gesang Geschwister nennen."

The essential element in this literature is no longer the passion of the *Sturm und Drang* period, but the free play of fancy, an activity of the imagination which is neither restrained by the laws of reason nor by the relation of feeling to reality. The higher, poetic sequences of ideas now introduced declare war against the laws of thought, ridicule them as philistine. Their place is taken by caprices, conceits, and vagaries. Fancy determines to dispense with reality, but despised reality has its revenge in the unsubstantiality or anæmia of fancy; fancy defies reason, but in this defiance there is an awkward contradiction; it is conscious and premeditated—reason is to be expelled by reason. Seldom has any poetic school worked under such a weight of perpetual consciousness of its own character as did this. Conscious intention is the mark of its productions.

The intellectual inheritance to which the Romanticists succeeded was overpoweringly great. The School came into existence when literature stood at its zenith in Germany. This explains the early maturity of its members; their way was made ready for them. They assimilated in their youth an enormous amount of literary knowledge and of artistic technique, and thus started with an intellectual capital such as no other young generation in Germany had ever possessed. They clothed their first thoughts in the language of Goethe, Schiller, and Shakespeare, and, beginning thus, proceeded to create what Goethe called "the period of forced talents." For the study of real human character and the execution of definite artistic ideas they substituted the high-handedness of turbulent fancy. Common to all the very dissimilar endeavours and productions of the Romanticists—to Wackenroder's *Klosterbruder,* with its spiritual enthusiasm for art and ideal beauty, to *Lucinde,* with its sensual worship of the flesh, to Tieck's melancholy romances and tales, in which capricious fate makes sport of man, and to Tieck's dramas and Hoffmann's stories, in which all form is lost and its place supplied by the caprices and arabesques of whimsical fancy—common to them all, is that law-defying self-assertion or assertion of the absolutism of the individual, which is a result of war with narrowing prose, of the urgent demand for poetry and freedom.

The absolute independence of the Ego isolates. Nevertheless these men soon founded a school, and after its speedy disintegration several interesting groups were formed. This is to be ascribed to their determination to make common cause in procuring the victory, insuring the universal dominion, of the philosophy of life which had been evolved by the great minds of Germany. They desired to introduce this philosophy of the geniuses into life itself, to give it expression in criticism, in poetry, in art theories, in religious exhortation, in the solution of social, and even of political problems; and their first step towards this was violent literary warfare. They were impelled partly by the necessity felt by great and strong natures to impart one will and one mind to a whole band of fellow-combatants, and partly by the inclination of men of talent, whose talent is attacked and contested, to confront the overwhelming numbers of their opponents with a small but superior force. In the case of the best men, the formation of a school or a party was the result of exactly that lack of state organisation which was the first condition of their isolating independence. The consciousness of belonging to a people without unity as a nation, and without collective strength, begot the endeavour to imbue the leading spirits of the aristocracy of intellect with a new rallying principle. (pp. 34-43)

> *George Brandes, "The Pioneers of Romanticism," in his* Main Currents in Nineteenth Century Literature: The Romantic School in German, Vol. II, *translated by Diana White and Mary Morison, The Macmillan Company, 1902, pp. 17-43.*

An excerpt from Friedrich Schlegel's *Athenäum Fragments*

Romantic poetry is a progressive universal poetry. It is destined not merely to reunite the separate genres of poetry and to link poetry to philosophy and rhetoric. It would and should also mingle and fuse poetry and prose, genius and criticism, artistic poetry and natural poetry, make poetry lively and sociable, and life and society poetic, poetise wit, fill and saturate the forms of art with worthy cultural matter of every kind, and animate them with a flow of humour. It embraces all that is poetic, from the greatest art system that enfolds further systems, down to the sigh, the kiss uttered in artless song by the child creating its own poetry. It can so identify with what is being represented that one might well think its sole aim was to characterise poetic individuals of every sort; but there is as yet no form designed fully to express the author's mind: so that some artists, who want only to write a novel, have come to portray themselves. Romantic poetry alone can, like the epic, become a mirror to the whole surrounding world, an image of its age. At the same time, free of all real and ideal interests, it can also float on wings of poetic reflection midway between the work and the artist, constantly reinforcing this reflection and multiplying it as in an unending series of mirrors. It has the potential for the highest, most manifold evolution by expanding not only outward but also inward, for each thing destined to be a whole entity is organised uniformly in all its parts, so that the prospect is opened up of a boundlessly developing classicism. Among the arts Romantic poetry is what wit is to philosophy, and what sociability, friendship and love are to life. Other types of poetry are complete and can now be wholly analysed. Romantic poetry is still in the process of becoming; this indeed is its very essence, that it is eternally evolving, never completed. It cannot be exhausted by any theory, and only a divinatory criticism could dare to try to characterise its ideal. It alone is infinite, just as it alone is free, recognising as its prime law that the poet's caprice brooks no law. Romantic poetry is the only type of poetry that is more than merely a type of poetry; it is in fact the very art of poetry itself: for in a certain sense all poetry is or should be romantic.

> *Quoted in* European Romanticism: Self-Definition, *edited by Lilian R. Furst, Methuen, 1980.*

L. A. Willoughby

[In the following essay, Willoughby discusses early German Romantic poetry.]

If to the Classicists the ideal of poetry was plastic, statuesque, to the Romanticists it was musical. Where Goethe had aimed at transforming the word into perception, Tieck 'thought in sound, and made music with words and thoughts'. Hence to the Romanticists, as it had been to Herder, language was the expression of life, the symbol of the living things themselves. For Novalis or Hölderlin the word itself possessed a magic property. To Goethe language was never quite adequate for thought, it necessarily suffered from the metaphorical force inherent in words, and was but an imperfect reflection of the idea. To the Classicists language appealed primarily to the eye—for the Romanticists to the ear.

So, too, it is possible to make a distinction between Classicism and Romanticism in their use of rhythm. While to Klopstock rhythm was a means of expression, and in his search for the perfect welding of matter and form he invented free rhythm, to the Classicists Goethe and Schiller it was a device for investing poetry with a distinctive garb, which should separate it from reality. Hence in their use of classical metres, especially in the elegy, they returned to the stricter scheme of the Ancients and, in true classical style, even sacrificed the natural accent to metrical need. Similarly the iambic verse of Goethe and Schiller has a tendency towards stricter form in its preference for self-contained lines and the avoidance of enjambment, for a fixed caesura; compared with which the verse of Kleist or Werner returns to the freedom of musical rhythm of which the most characteristic example are the polymeters of Jean Paul, or the later rhythmic prose of Hölderlin. It would seem strange at first sight that the Romanticists should have introduced again the trammels of rhyme, were it not for the mystic meaning with which they invested it. Rhyme became for them a symbol of love, of the longing for an echo in answer, of the mating and blending of the feminine and masculine. It is true that neither Goethe nor Schiller had any feeling of enmity towards rhyme such as moved Klopstock to consider it as 'romanesque trifling'. But they used it structurally rather than musically, as a means of rounding off a line or building up a strophe. It was only when the Romanticists had opened his eyes to its musical properties that Goethe became reconciled to its 'lovely consonance' as in *Faust II,* and especially in *Der Westöstliche Divan.* And as the Romanticists found a mystic meaning in rhyme, so too the multiple combinations of rhyme forms which they introduced from Romance sources—the sonnet, the terza rima, the canzone, the gloss, rondeau, ritornelle, sestina, and triolet, appealed to them for the same reason. The sonnet because, although in itself perfect, it might not be repeated like the strophe; the terza rima because it was hallowed by Dante's use, and by its mystic unity in trinity; the canzone because its labyrinth of rhymes suggested the way to an inner and hidden depth; the gloss because the elaboration of the thought was congenial to their sense of movement; the others because in them all the end returns again to the beginning and thus, in the figure of a circle, presents a symbol of the infinite in the finite, of Romantic eternity. In its continuous striving for movement, Romanticism combined ancient and modern and even Eastern rhythms, iambs, trochees, alexandrines, 'Knittelverse', free rhythms, in constant musical variations.

Just as the form of the Romantic lyric is characterized by the lack of repose, so also is its content: like the poetry of the *Volkslied* it consists of numerous 'leaps and digressions and lack of transition', it aims at producing the impression of depth rather than of clearness, and often loses itself in mysticism. It has all the movement of musical

composition rather than the plastic serenity of the Classicists, and whereas the theme in a poem of Goethe's or Schiller's is circumscribed and complete in itself, that of Tieck or Eichendorff is fragmentary, or ends with a discord. The Classical poem calls up a picture for the eye, the Romantic sings a melody for the ear; Classicism reproduced nature in its typical aspects, in those timeless constant forms which Goethe called 'Ur-Phänomene'; Romanticism was first struck by the changing picturesque phenomena of nature, and then sought to penetrate into the spirit which produced them. 'Nach innen geht der geheimnisvolle Weg' Novalis taught. Hence it was that Goethe, even in the days when most in sympathy with Romanticism, essayed in vain to compose a great epic of cosmogony and made over the plan to Schelling. The Classicists delight in the architectural beauty of the landscape, Goethe loved especially a garden, the work and sphere of man; to Schiller, again, a fine landscape was but a symbol of the moral harmony of the human soul. The gardens of Eichendorff are formless and wild, and overgrown. Romantic is the forest with its mysterious darkness, or the mountain because of its elemental mass, or the endless distance, because it awakened longing or remembrance. If Goethe had a predilection for the plastic arts, and for engravings with their sober black and white, the Romanticists favoured painting and high colours. It pleased Goethe to conceive of colours as specific entities in themselves, which could be classified as modifications of the primary white or black. To the Romanticists, on the other hand, Newton's theory of light as a synthesis of colours was in accordance with their mystic transfiguration of all bodies into pure spirit. And the Romanticists carried the blending of the arts a step further when, in anticipation of our musical critics, they identified colour and sound: 'No colour', said Jean Paul, 'is as musical as a sound'. A. W. Schlegel was not alone in identifying certain vowels with definite colours: *a* was for red, *o* for purple, *u* for black. Even a latecomer like Heine could speak of 'ein Meer von blauen Gedanken'. E. T. A. Hoffmann was only going a step further when he maintained the agreement of all the impressions from the senses: 'of sound, colour, and even odours'. It was a truly Romantic attempt to reach the ultimate reality underlying all perceptions, although the Romanticists always returned to music as the most divine of the arts, and that most in tune with the infinite.

Most of these characteristics appear in all the Romantic poets, but especially in the pioneer, Ludwig Tieck. His poems are essentially the reflection of moods, 'Stimmungen', such as the famous *Waldeinsamkeit* or the *Mondbeglänzte Zaubernacht.* There is little in his poetry of the erotic element, and his love songs have no force or passion. And, in anticipation of some modern Expressionists, Tieck uses language essentially for its musical properties and not for its meaning, or as he expressed it, 'why should it be just the contents which constitute a poem?' He thought he found confirmation of these views in the minnesingers, to whom Wackenroder had drawn his attention, and whom he was the first to make widely known by his *Minnelieder aus dem schwäbischen Zeitalter* (1803). His theory necessarily influenced his form, and the value of Tieck's lyric poetry lies entirely in the pictorial colouring and musical feeling. He revels in soft, rich colours, reds and golds and forest green, and his favourite lights are those of morning or evening, or, better still, the silver gleam of the moon. Musical effects play an even more important part: alliteration and assonance abound, and sounds have a definite meaning assigned to them. A good example is afforded by the romance *Die Zeichen im Walde,* in which scores of assonances in 'u' are used to arouse a spirit of melancholy and mourning. *Die verkehrte Welt* even contains a symphony in words divided into movements: *andante, piano, crescendo, fortissimo,* in which the words and phrases keep pace with the time and expression; an experiment which foreshadows the similar attempts of Brentano in *Gustav Wasa* and of E. T. A. Hoffmann in the *Kreisleriana.*

The lyric sentiment was present in some degree in every member of the school, and since according to Wilhelm Schlegel technique was merely a question of practice, all of them, Friedrich, Schleiermacher, Fichte, Schelling, Dorothea, Caroline, indulged their lyric bent in stanzas of the most intricate character. As a receptacle for this poetry was founded, in 1801, the *Musenalmanach für d. J. 1802 von A. W. Schlegel und L. Tieck* which was intended to take the place of Schiller's defunct *Almanach.* The undertaking was not a success, chiefly owing to quarrels of the editors and contributors, and the *Almanach* ceased to appear after the first year. As a kind of continuation we may regard the *Dichtergarten* of Novalis's brother, Karl von Hardenberg, which already forms a transition to the younger school of Heidelberg.

Apart from Tieck, Wackenroder and Novalis, none of these authors possessed real poetic talent. Friedrich Schlegel wrote a series of nature poems difficult of comprehension and fanciful in tone: the *Romanze vom Licht,* the cycle *Abendröte.* His best lyric work lies, however, in the patriotic poems *Gelübde* and *Freiheit,* inspired by the reaction from a trip to France and the national uprising against Napoleon. Through his Rhine songs he became the creator of the typically Romantic attitude to the German river, even before Brentano and Arnim, and Cologne became to him as a second home. A. W. Schlegel had begun as a follower of Bürger and Schiller. From the former he learned appreciation for form in poetry; the latter inspired his early ballads *Pygmalion* and *Prometheus* in which the influence of *Die Götter Griechenlands* is plainly visible. He took an especial delight in practising the most complicated romance metres, but his main achievement was the introduction of the sonnet, which he brought to a high degree of perfection. Typical are the *Gemäldesonette,* composed in concert with Caroline and published in the *Athenæum.* Each of these sonnets is inspired by a famous picture in the Dresden art gallery and attempts to reproduce in verse the impression made by the painting, not descriptively, but by transmuting painting into language and transferring it from space into time. Schlegel thus became the founder of a new genre in which art and poetry, painters and poets were the theme. Even beyond the confines of Germany the sonnet became a vehicle for literary and artistic characterization, as it is often with Sainte-Beuve in France or Swinburne and Rossetti in England.

There is more poetry, however, in a sonnet cycle which commemorated his step-daughter, Auguste Böhmer, whose death aroused the greatest grief among the little circle in Jena. The *Totenopfer* have the additional interest of instigating a new poetic genre, the *Kindertotenlieder* in which the younger generation of Romanticists, Eichendorff, Rückert, and Paul Heyse attained much excellence. It awakened an echo in France with the *Contemplations* of Victor Hugo over the loss of his daughter.

Even Goethe, though hostile at first, was induced by the example of Schlegel to try his hand at the sonnet. But it was not for Goethe, as it was for the Romanticists, a symbol of the infinite, and he emphasized rather its plastic completeness: 'in der Beschränkung zeigt sich erst der Meister.' The intercourse with Zacharias Werner, himself a consummate master of the sonnet, provided a further incentive. But it was for Goethe never more than a literary pastime, and even the cycle dedicated to Minna Herzlieb has so little individuality and passion that Bettina von Arnim could plausibly have claimed it as written in her honour. Most of the Romanticists wrote sonnets with distinction, but the great master was Graf von Platen, whose sonnets attain a classic finish and beauty.

Wackenroder wrote few lyrics, and these are so insignificant as to be omitted from most editions of his works. Of the importance of Novalis and his *Hymnen an die Nacht* for the whole trend of German Romanticism mention has already been made. He and Hölderlin were the most genuinely lyrical of this early group, and both wrote out of the fulness of a passionate heart. Neither owed anything to the formal intricacies of Tieck or the Schlegels; Novalis drew his inspiration from the Protestant German hymn, and his songs are filled with even deeper religious mysticism. It is only rarely, as in the songs interspersed in *Heinrich von Ofterdingen,* that his poetry attains to lightheartedness. Hölderlin, though dependent on the Greeks for both form and matter, has none of their serene joy of life. Dionysos rather than Apollo was his ideal, and it is this that makes him into a Romantic and not a Classic poet. It has been well said of him that 'he romanticized the Greeks', for he saw in them not types of complete humanity as did Goethe, but rather examples of a naïve people yet in touch with holy nature. His love for Greece was born of romantic 'Sehnsucht', of longing for escape from the political and social unrest of his time, into an imaginary Utopian existence which he found in an idealized Greece, just as Novalis had discovered it in an imaginary Middle Ages.

Friedrich Hölderlin (1770-1843) began as a disciple of Klopstock and Schiller, and it is characteristic that one of his early poems long passed as the former's. His first rhymed poems, the *Hymnen an die Ideale der Menschheit* (as the critic Dilthey aptly entitles them), are echoes of Schiller's philosophical poetry. They treat of similar abstract themes dear to eighteenth-century rationalism: freedom, immortality, humanity, beauty, friendship, and with all their pomp and rhetoric they are among the purest poetry the great age of German humanitarianism produced. The decisive change came with Hölderlin's love for Frau Gontard, the wife of his Frankfurt employer, whom he has immortalized as Diotima. She inspired the elegiac novel

Hyperion, 'die Frucht unserer seelenvollen Tage', and with it the beautiful *Schicksalslied.* She was to him 'die letzte Griechin', an ideal personality in which nature and humanity were in perfect equipoise; and like the hero of his novel, Hölderlin found in her 'fate, gods, and love'. His devotion attained its supreme expression in the elegy *Menons Klage um Diotima,* a love-plaint with which only Goethe's *Marienbader Elegie* can compare for depth of feeling and lofty resignation.

The Frankfurt poems *Der Wanderer* and *Der Äther* are both typical of his new conception of nature. It is no longer, as it was for Schiller, an idyllic abstract state of mind, but a real living concrete thing, which he found symbolized in his own beautiful Swabian countryside. Nature to Hölderlin was not only a sensuous, living experience, but already he had learned to revere in her the mysterious, mystical forces of the cosmos. And these forces were sympathetic, even friendly to man and made for a world of order of which already the Stoics had preached. Romantic, too, and due perhaps to Schelling's 'Weltseele', is his conception of the all-pervading, all-nourishing 'father Aether', not indeed in any physical sense, but as a symbol both of the infinite and the circumscribed, forming with the earth and with light a 'holy trinity'. Thus the gods of Greece to whom Hölderlin sang his hymns were no longer the deified, idealized men of Winckelmann or Goethe, but elemental forces. Perhaps for this reason they found but little favour with Goethe, who thought them 'mehr naturhistorisch als poetisch'; and for the same reason they stamp Hölderlin as a Romantic poet, inasmuch as his chief concern is nature rather than man.

Some of the finest poetry Hölderlin ever wrote is contained in the *Odes,* the form of which was particularly suited to his dithyrambic genius. His favourite metres, the Alcaic or Asclepiadic strophe, he uses with a mastery and ease free from any virtuosity or pedantry, which make them the most suitable medium for the dignity and sublimity of these perfect poems, so full of tenderness and grace. They ascend in a series of from one to seven or more strophes, culminating in the famous *Dichterberuf* and *Gesang der Deutschen.* The former expresses Hölderlin's conviction of the poet's sacred office: he is the seer and prophet of the human race. The latter is a magnificent paean to his fatherland which he praises as the 'heart of the nations and the soul of the world'. Thus from the quest of the Greek ideal Hölderlin brought back, not perfect man in a timeless world like the Classicists, but the sense of a national community, such as Friedrich Schlegel had proclaimed. Hölderlin transferred to his own age the conception he had formed of Greek culture as the perfect relationship of nature and man, of gods and heroes, and he looked forward to the time when this dream would be realized in his German fatherland. And this thought is the chief inspiration of the great cycle of *Elegien* which receive their note of sadness from his unhappy love. They are at the same time a theodicy, a vindication of this life for the sake of its divine nature; for it needs evil to elevate man to good.

Archipelagos, the ode which is Hölderlin's most inspired and yet most actual vision of Greece, is at the same time a prophetic announcement that a similar ideal awaits the German, will he but open his eyes and ears to love. For it is the poet's holy mission to awaken men's hearts to the new religion which, like that of the Greeks, was to be founded on a common tradition and belief, and on a love of art and nature in all their manifestations. Hence in these later elegies the insistence on popular festivals like the vintage, as expressed in *Die Herbstfeier,* or the symbolic fusion of Christ and Dionysos, both 'des Höchsten Sohn', in *Brod und Wein.* This synthesis of East and West was accentuated in the later hymns in free rhythms, and the ecstatic trait which had always attracted him so strongly in Greek poetry, and which he had expressed so forcibly in his translation of Sophocles, now led him to the original home of Dionysos, to Asia and India. *Die Wanderung* is a symbolic account of how the Germans once mixed with the Caucasians to form an ideal people. Even the Rhine (in *Der Rhein*) originally turned Asia-wards until fate headed it to the north. In *Patmos* Hölderlin dreams of the new invisible church of Revelation, set up by the apostle of love in memory of the God of love. Yet this approximation to Christianity in no sense implies a negation of his pantheistic nature religion, but rather the conviction that the religion of Christ and that of the Greeks are one. To Hölderlin love is the need which man feels for communion with nature, his sense of unity with the soul of the universe which comes upon him in moments of inspiration. It awakens in the poet's soul splendid visions of harmony in which spirit and senses are in equipoise. The poet's aim is to educate mankind, and in particular his beloved Germans, to this ideal state which once the Greeks possessed. That this dream is capable of realization is shown by the great personalities which arise from time to time to bear witness to the soul's harmony. It is a state to which all may attain and which for Hölderlin was near at hand.

It is obvious that with his deep conception of life Hölderlin's poetry could never be popular. During his lifetime much of it remained unpublished, or it passed unnoticed scattered in various journals, and it was not until 1826 that a collected edition of his *Gedichte* was made by his countrymen Schwab and Uhland. But it was late in the nineteenth century before any real interest in his poetry was aroused, and it is only within the last few years that he has met with full recognition. His thought and his language are both difficult; to the great multitude he must ever remain a sealed book. To the intellectual élite, on the other hand, he appeals with ever-increasing force, and Thomas Mann has made the significant prophecy that German civilization of the future will be a synthesis of the harmonious national community for which Hölderlin yearned and the communistic Utopia imagined by Karl Marx. Hölderlin is perhaps the best example in German literature of the 'vates sacer', of the god-inspired poet filled with a poetic frenzy. For it was given to Hölderlin to see deeper into the heart of things than most mortals, and it was as though the gods, in fear and jealousy lest he should reveal their inmost secrets, clothed his mind with madness. (pp. 36-45)

L. A. Willoughby, "The Early Romantic Lyric," in his The Romantic Movement in Germany, *1930. Reprint by Russell & Russell, 1966, pp. 36-45.*

Marshall Brown

[*Brown is an American educator and critic. In the following excerpt, he examines the manifestation of Friedrich Schlegel's dualistic world vision in German Romantic novels.*]

To say that literature wishes to succeed where life cannot is to say that there is, in later romantic poetry, a definite will to form: an aspiration to create a surrogate image in words for the unification that is impossible in experience. Deemphasizing the all-inclusive "progressive universal poetry" of the earlier Schlegel, the poets searched for a controlled means adequate to the task of expressing the erratic eccentricities of life. And the remarkable thing is that such forms were found, indeed many such forms. I have analyzed elsewhere, at greater length than I can do here, three of these solutions: the marble image and chiseled imagery of Brentano's *Godwi,* which subsume the polarities of life into a firm ethical postulate; Humboldt's willed ideal of classical form, in which the self can put its own provisional status at a distance without self-betrayal; Eichendorff's supple rhetorical mastery, which allows the constantly varying flow of time itself to be given a firm shape. These are some of the noteworthy individual attempts to give, in art, a centered and coherent expression to man's incoherent experience. But beyond such individual solutions a group effort was also made to arrive at a common solution available to all. A new, quintessentially romantic form evolved, bicentral in nature. By encompassing both poles within it, literature for the romantics became truly central. This new form was the generic expression of the later romantic world view.

Schlegel's notebooks contain the most helpful comments on the nature of bicentral literary form. In order to interpret these comments correctly, however, we must make a detour for a few paragraphs to see how thoroughly the notebooks are permeated with Böhmist imagery. Beginning as early as 1799 frequent references to two centers or to two poles reflect the effort to evaluate and exploit Böhme's conceptions in many different ways. Thus Schlegel says that harmony and allegory are two centers of poetry, that Locke and Descartes are two poles of philosophy, that Sophocles and Spinoza are two poles of morals, that politics and mysticism are two poles of morals, that art and nature are the centers of morality. In addition, some fragments describe a particular quality as the "other center," even though they do not clearly identify a first center. One fragment from 1799 is particularly interesting in attempting to relate Böhmist bicentrality to the metaphor of central forces associated with Fichte (and also Schelling): "*Mysticism* and *magic* each a center of religion, centripetal and centrifugal principle." In another fragment Schlegel experiments with a whole series of concepts, always grouping them in pairs: "*Law* and *love* probably are the poles of immortality; both united in the classical; or law and mystery, force and generality."

Although many fragments speak only of a single center, which was the customary symbol of an individual organism, Schlegel seems to have fully accepted the Böhmist bicentral or elliptical explanation of the structure of the whole universe and to have tried with considerable regu-

larity to clarify and apply it. . . . [The] best evidence that Schlegel considered the bicentral explanation to be the normal and most adequate one is negative; it consists of some fragments asserting that various phenomena have only one center. In the Kantian corpus only one work is central, only nature is central, there can be only one mediator at a time. Such things would be unworthy of remark unless it were in some way limited or unusual to have only one center; the normal condition is to have a divided or double center. In this connection a somewhat later fragment (probably from 1802) is particularly revealing, a fragment whose strong tone probably reflects exasperation rather than absolute conviction: "The *center of the earth* is SINGLE, that much is clear." That much may or may not be clear. What is clear, when this fragment is taken in conjunction with the rest of what is known about Schlegel, is that the center of the *universe* was in his eyes not single but double.

A recognition of this pervasive theme in the notebooks makes possible the interpretation of another group of fragments. These are the fragments that speak of a central center. Examples of this type are "The ideal is the center of the center," and "The encyclopedia is a textbook of universality, centrum centrorum." Syntactically, this is the type of expression familiar from the Bible—as in "the holy of holies"—and in Hebrew it is merely the common form of the superlative, there being no synthetic form corresponding to our "holiest." But to Schlegel these expressions certainly meant more than just "the absolute center." Schlegel's statement that "religion is the central center, that is clear," suggests the image of a bicentral universe with some other principle such as material causality as the "terrestrial" center of attraction and religion as the second and higher center (metaphorically the sun) around which the lower center revolves. It suggests, in other words, a bipolar universe, a double center. The abbreviation actually used by Schlegel in his notebook—"Rel ist CtCt, das ist klar"—in fact gives a visual image of the Böhmist notion that the divine center divides itself, emanates an earthly center, and in this very process verifies and recognizes its superiority and spirituality. Repetition, as incipient self-consciousness, confers status.

Two are one and one is two—that is the structural principle governing Schlegel's speculations in these years: "There is no dualism without primacy—for all dualism results from the procession of the infinite out of itself and the positing of something finite." Or, as Novalis wrote in a late fragment which already anticipates much later speculation, "The true dividual is also the true individual." The absolute enters this world through duplication, and the double, or "CtCt," is the finite form that represents the infinite center. This self-division of the finite world (the temporal inner distance from self to self) is associated in particular with language: in the center is the "reciprocity" of "dialogue." Language, as Baader says, divides thing from image (it "speaks asunder"), and yet this very action of fission carries within it a re-collection of the higher, original, "central action" of Creation, when the Word was made flesh. Thus, the form that best manifests the ubiquitous bicentrality of the universe will be a language of repetition.

The perfected language of repetition is poetry. A number of Schlegel's fragments exalting poetry presuppose the belief that reduplication is the finite garb that makes visible the transcendent unity of the infinite. Thus, when Schlegel calls poetry "absolutely central in every respect," he must be understood to mean that it is the highest, repeated, central center. The common formulas π^2 (Schlegel's shorthand notation) and "Poesie der Poesie" are the graphic and syntactic representations of a poetry that has reached the level of self-reflection (as are also the formulas "der romantische Roman" and "Ironie der Ironie"). The value of true poetry resides in its reflected quality, that is to say, in its eminent centrality: "The ancients can only be understood through CtCt poetry. All prose about the most high is incomprehensible."

Repetition is a principle of representation. Hence the Böhmist orientation affects the form of romantic poetry as well as its ethos. Only reduplicated forms can be truly central and can render "the most high," and only such reduplicated forms as suggest a temporal and ontological ordering of original and derived, hidden and revealed. In verse such duplications are inherent: "The caesura is a turning point in the verse, an inner dualism." An inner dualism is, of course, not an absolute opposition; the two halves of the verse are two foci of meaning subordinate to a single primary (and presumably allegorical or structural) meaning: "The repetition of the sound in rhyme [is] only a reduction to the language of nature." And more generally, "There lies an *infinite duality* in the sonnet—always anew. For that very reason the sonnet is appropriate for mystical thoughts, for prayer."

The main divided, mystical form of romantic literature, however, is not verse, but the novel. (It should be remembered, however, that Schlegel used the word *Roman* for any work that fulfilled his postulates for romantic literature. The characteristics I am about to enumerate are not limited to the novel but are widespread in all the "epic" forms, including stories and tales, verse narratives, and pageant dramas such as *Faust.*) It is the romantic novel that provides the adequate structural correlative to the bicentral world view and its most highly developed expression. A few fragments before speaking of the caesura as the inner dualism of verse, Schlegel had already spoken of the dualism of novels: "That the *novel* desires two centers indicates that every novel wants to be an absolute book, indicates its mystical character. This gives it a mythological character, it becomes a *person.*" The fragment preceding this one names Schlegel's model, which is *Don Quixote,* rather than a novel of the romantic period, but his description of the bicentrality of *Don Quixote* could be applied without alteration to several of the most important romantic novels: "The chief character in the second part of *Don Quixote* is the first part. It is, throughout, the work's reflection on itself." *Don Quixote* has, and any novel desires, two centers and two levels of meaning. First comes the level of action: part one of *Don Quixote* consists of the violent adventures that befall Don Quixote and, with more serious consequences, the characters associated with the inserted novellas. Then follows the level of reflection, the second part of the novel, consisting largely of prepared charades reflecting and playing on the adventures of the

first part. In this second part are unfolded the significance, depth, and, as Schlegel calls it, personality of the actions. Similar relations hold between the two parts of *Godwi,* between the two *Wilhelm Meister* novels, and (I believe) between Hegel's two major treatises as well: the *Phenomenology of Mind* was Hegel's *Bildungsroman,* while the later *Science of Logic,* more deliberate in its pacing, reflects on the *Phenomenology* so as to ground its dialectic and ultimately to serve as an introduction to it. Thus, the romantic novel leads from action to significance or—as Loeben phrases it in a nearly identical formulation—to the unification of action with significance: "The coincidence of the visible and the invisible center in the novel, in one point, can be considered as its highest moment, as its solution, its close, and indeed no novel in which a man is given as the ideal center of the poetry can close with any other resolution."

Duality of form, then, is characteristic of romantic literature in general and of the romantic novel in particular. An account of the formal presuppositions of German romanticism leads naturally to a study of romantic narrative. A full-scale phenomenology of the romantic novel would require another whole volume, of course, and I do not propose to attempt that here. But I would like at least to comment on some of the salient peculiarities of the romantic novel that are related to the bicentral conception of experience, for it is here that the language of time finds its fullest realization.

Chronic dualism. My title phrase comes from E. T. A. Hoffmann's well-known "capriccio," "Prinzessin Brambilla." It names the disease from which the double hero of this bizarre narrative is suffering. In a brilliant reading Jean Starobinski has presented the story [in "Ironie et mélancholie (II): La 'Princesse Brambilla' de E. T. A. Hoffmann," *Critique* 22 (1966)] as an allegory of the human psyche, whose chronic Fichtean schizophrenia is cured by the comic theater. Paul de Man has responded [in "The Rhetoric of Temporality," in *Interpretation: Theory and Practice,* edited by Charles S. Singleton, 1969] that the story remains ironic to the end, with no saving reconciliation of opposites. But both agree in seeing duality exclusively in negative terms. In so doing they overlook the double meaning of the crucial phrase. For in this story, as throughout later romanticism, the Cartesian division into opposing worlds of mind and matter is replaced not (as Fichte still desired) by a unitary first principle, but by temporalized bicentrality. The disease of chronic *dualism* is in fact cured, but the cure is none other than *chronic* dualism. To the end the hero leads a double life, as the actor Giulio Fava and as the mythical prince among princes, Cornelio Chiapperi (whose guiding spirit, "the old, fabulous Prince Bastianello of Pisa," is still present in the final tableau). He does not overcome his split personality, but he learns to conduct his life on two planes at once: ideal and real, in the imagination and in the senses, in allegory (utopian myth) and in ironic, demystified self-awareness. Earlier in the story Hoffmann has already described the tempered and temporal dualism that characterizes human life: "Everyone who is gifted with any imagination [*Fantasie*] suffers, as can be read in some book fraught with worldly wisdom, from an insanity which steadily rises and falls, like ebb and flow. The time of the latter, when the waves crash ever louder and stronger, is the fall of night, as the morning hours just after awakening, with a cup of coffee, count as the highest point of the ebb." Outsiders see as the irreconcilable poles of madness and sanity what insiders recognize as the mutually supplementary times of fantasy and earnest sobriety. Hoffmann's tone here is only semi-serious, but one worldly-wise book he may have had in mind is his own *Serapionsbrüder,* whose title character is a raving lunatic at night but nearly sane in the morning. Chronic dualism is thus the sign under which all of Hoffmann's fiction stands, and indeed, it seems to me, all the major fiction of the later romantics.

This is not a story. There are many different manifestations of this chronic dualism, though in all its forms it may be said that the narrative exists on two different temporal levels. The most flamboyant type is Hoffmann's novel *Kater Murr,* where sections of the cat's memoirs are interlarded with fragments from the apparently unrelated biography of the musician Kreisler. Much more common are framing effects: the inclusion within the narrative of a fairy tale that recapitulates and idealizes the action or (a favorite device of Brentano's) the magical translation of a human tale into the animal realm and back again. In Kleist's tales a different, but still related dualism, is to be found. With only one set of events, careful management of the diction (combined, in some cases, with a framing effect achieved by inversion of the narrative sequence) creates a dual perspective on them, as fluctuating contingency and as driving fate. In the fiction of the 1790s chronic dualism does occur, but in characteristically indeterminate, "eccentric" forms. Thus, both the completed portion of *Heinrich von Ofterdingen* and Goethe's *Unterhaltungen deutscher Ausgewanderten* conclude with fairy tales (rather than encapsulating the tales in a finished narrative) and consequently open outward. And Hölderlin's *Hyperion* superimposes a gradually developing narrator on a gradually maturing hero, but without reaching any definite conclusion. Other dualisms pervade every level of romantic fiction. Organizationally, for instance, we find the diptych structures of works like Brentano's "Kasperl und Annerl" and Eichendorff's "Eine Meerfahrt," thematically the widespread use of *Doppelgänger* figures, and stylistically the formulaic prose that makes the fiction sound like the repetition of long-familiar patterns. Yet all these various dualisms are marked as romantic and bicentral by the fact that they never involve mere repetition or mere opposition, but always indicate variation and hierarchy. Indeed, even the most mechanical and stylized dualism, Hoffmann's ubiquitous trick of repeating the initial word of a quotation before and after naming the speaker, is often used to give a witty effect of variation or even reversal of meaning: " 'Doubt,' responded the charlatan with a polite, almost respectful greeting, 'doubt not . . . ' " In *Kater Murr* the hierarchy is guaranteed by the sequence of events, for the cat's "opinions" belong to a later period than the portion of Kreisler's biography being reported. Other works distinguish in different ways between their two components, but the result always conforms to the bicentral ideology, with a human world unfolding through time and imperfectly reflecting a timeless ideal. Classically, in the works of Cervantes and Fielding, inserted stories are related to

the principal narrative by analogy or negative analogy, but in the romantic novel the relationship is more complex, as Novalis suggests: "The state of nature is a *strange image* of the eternal realm. The world of the fairy tale is the world *exactly opposite* to the world of truth (history)—and precisely for that reason so *thoroughly similar* to it—as *chaos* is to the *accomplished creation.* " The ideal and the real, fiction and truth, are different yet somehow related, for man lives in both worlds. Hence the ideal second world of romantic fictions never appears cut off from the first world, as the Man of the Hill is from Tom Jones, or the Latin tale of the nosy Slawkenbergius from Tristram Shandy's noseless environment. A characteristic reflection of the relationship of real frame to ideal insertion is the topos "this is not a story," which sometimes introduces an inserted narrative. It is not a story because it is a part of life itself, seen from a higher perspective. "Do not take my story for a fairy tale," says Bertha at the beginning of Tieck's "Der blonde Eckbert," and this is a sign not only that the story is true, but also that it unlocks the mysteries of Eckbert's soul. "Do not take the affair for a poem," says St. Boniface at the beginning of the scene "Wüste" in Tieck's *Genoveva,* and yet his narrative monologue in ottava rima stands out as a particularly poetic section of the verse drama. But it is more than a mere poem, for it is the bridge passage between the two parts of the drama and completes the transition from the neo-Shakespearian history play of the opening to the Christian mystery of the conclusion. It is not a poem because it lies above, rather than outside, the prose world of everyday experience.

Poems in prose. Like the speech of Time in *The Winter's Tale,* Boniface's monologue comes at a dead point in the play. Seven blank years pass while the action is stopped. Boniface does report a few events from the interval, but mostly of a supernatural rather than a historical character, and the steady rhythm of the stanzas joins with an irregular alternation of tenses to create a general atmosphere of timelessness. Such timelessness characterizes lyric interruptions of the flow of events in general. Thus earlier in the same play, in the scene "Garten. Mondschein," Golo and Genoveva sing a beautiful lyric describing a moment of natural stasis. The song has an unearthly, seductive effect, against which Genoveva warns Golo: "Desist, Golo, from words of flattery which captivate my ear at dead of night like a fable and poem from a distant time; moonbeams invite poetry and invention, which is distant from truth as from the sober light of day." And indeed, after a second song and a sonnet the lyric interview is finally interrupted by a trumpet call announcing news from the battle front. Poetry is the night side of history, as imagination is of reason.

Of romantic bicentral forms the most widely used combines history and poetry: it is the prose narrative with inserted lyrics. The poems are of many types: folk songs evoking an ancient national culture, or songs (like Mignon's) that are the relics of an idealized lost childhood, prophecies, the effusions of madness such as Peregrina's songs in Mörike's *Maler Nolten,* magical incantation, or the dialogue of fairy tale creatures (particularly in Brentano). The poems can also be improvisations or recent compositions that express otherwise ineffable sensations;

indeed, at times, as in Klingsohr's tale in *Heinrich von Ofterdingen* or as in parts of *Godwi,* the narrative or the dialogue simply breaks into verse under the pressure of heightened emotions. Whatever the format, the poems give access to a timeless world that is the ground of our mortal existence.

The interplay of the realms of prose and poetry is a special phenomenon of German romanticism. Even Hoffmann, who was much less given to poetry than Tieck, Brentano, Arnim, or Eichendorff, has Murr interrupt his narrative to deliver a verdict on the subject: "Verses in a book written in prose should perform the same as bacon in wurst, to wit, strewn hither and yon in little bits, they afford the whole mixture more radiance of richness, more sweet grace of taste." Despite the playful simile, the judgment is well considered. We know from an incident in "Nußknacker und Mäusekönig" that wurst without bacon is contemptible, and poems likewise provide an indispensable higher plane (a radiance and grace, in Murr's words) without which novels are mere entertainment. At the same time Murr pinpoints the weakness of some early examples of the type, such as Moritz's *Anton Reiser* and the first version of *Franz Sternbald,* when he adds that biographical novels should not be simply a framework and an excuse for publishing a mass of inferior verse. The decorum of romantic novels differs sharply in this respect from that of the fiction that precedes and follows. In the later nineteenth century even novelists who were active poets (the French "romantics," Eliot, Melville, Keller, Fontane, and so forth) seldom or never insert poems into their prose works. And both before and after the romantic period the rare inserted poems are liable to be felt as disturbing intrusions and to be associated with danger or evil; thus in chapter 4, "L'Enigme," of Voltaire's *Zadig* the hero almost loses his head for having written a poem; in Musset's "Fils du Titien" the hero turns to verse only to confess his lack of talent; in Dickens's *Our Mutual Friend* the balladeer Simon Wegg is the villain. When Hardy then revived the *genre mêlé* at the end of the century, it was already an archaic form appropriate to the primitive and repressed passions of his characters.

Pastoral and gothic. The historical distribution of the *genre mêlé* is worth pondering. Its popularity is invariably associated with romance forms, but of two widely divergent types. An outgrowth of the *razos,* or lives, of the Provençal poets, the prose narrative with inserted poems was a late medieval invention best known from Dante's *Vita Nuova;* it reached its first flowering in the line of Renaissance pastorals, which began with Boccaccio's *Ameto* and ran through Sannazaro, Montemayor, and Sidney. Pastoral society brings man into immediate contact with nature, and the profusion of verses studding the narrative bespeaks the easy intercourse of prose and poetry, low and high, natural and artificial, primitive and sophisticated. It is "the nature of this clime to stir up Poeticall fancies," as one of Sidney's characters says:

> All the people of this countrie from high to lowe,
> is given to those sportes of the witte, so as you
> would wonder to heare how soone even children
> will beginne to versifie. Once, ordinary it is
> among the meanest sorte, to make Songes and

> Dialogues in meeter, either love whetting their
> braine, or long peace having begun it, example
> and emulation amending it. Not so much, but
> the clowne *Dametas* will stumble sometimes
> upon some Songs that might become a better
> brayne: but no sorte of people so excellent in that
> kinde as the pastors; for their living standing but
> upon the looking to their beastes, they have ease,
> the Nurse of Poetrie.

The other romance tradition employing the *genre mêlé* is the English gothic. Here, in Radcliffe and Lewis, as later in some of Poe's stories, poetry is felt to be an interruption of the prose and hence a sign of mental alienation. This can take various forms: the simple foolishness of "poetical paroxysm," in chapter 5 of Lewis's *The Monk;* revelation of a hidden secret, as in Poe's "Assignation"; or, most often, as in "The Fall of the House of Usher," subjection to a ruling passion: "They must have been, and were, . . . the result of that intense mental collectedness and concentration to which I have previously alluded as observable only in particular moments of the highest artificial excitement. . . . In the under or mystic current of its meaning, I fancied that I perceived, for the first time, a full consciousness on the part of Usher of the tottering of his lofty reason upon her throne." The novels of Scott and Cooper are more complex in their inspiration, but they likewise employ poems most often to mark the distance between the supernatural and the natural realms: the "wild and irregular spirit" of Waverly (*Waverley,* chapter 5), the ravings of Madge Wildfire, the magical simplemindedness of David Gamut.

The *genre mêlé* of German romanticism combines the two romance traditions. A fusion of the frenzied, "impetuous time" of the gothic with the static, reflective time of pastoral has long been recognized as characteristic of romanticism. And the German romantic version of the *genre mêlé* formalizes this duality of mood. Although many significant variations occur in the distribution of modes, in general it may be said that gothic elements of plot, imagery, and atmosphere are assigned to the prose, and the unchanging, circumscribed pastoral world of love and nature is evoked in the poems. The poems and the prose present alternative kinds of interest, whereas in both Renaissance pastoral and English gothic the poems are in harmony with the prose. (In *Don Quixote,* the other important formal model, the poems are confined to pastoral interludes, which are represented as an alternative folly to the violent, impetuous folly of chivalry.) The prose is the focus of human action, and the poetic pastoral is the ideal focus, the higher or central center of the novels: "Aesthetics has a center and it is just that of—humanity, beauty, art; golden age is the center of this center." The ideal poem is a still point of reference in an unquiet world, the tonic on which the plot sings a descant, the centerpiece within the arabesque. Such a relationship Eichendorff found in two earlier German works, Grimmelschausen's *Simplicissimus* and Müller's *Genoveva,* and described in a passage that distills many essential formal elements of the romantic novel: "A deeply religious and specifically Catholic feeling threads its way through this wide world, indeed the beautiful song of the hermit, 'Komm Trost der Nacht, o Nachtigall!' just like Golo's song in Genoveva, could be regarded as the root chord [*Grundaccord*] that sounds through the whole, until finally Simplicissimus rescues himself as a hermit on a desert island out of the shipwreck of the world, as from out of a dream in which he has lost time and virtue."

Discontinuity, repetition, and variation. Eichendorff's imitation of the hermit's song, "Komm Trost der Welt, du stille Nacht," resounds during a magical moonlit interlude of the story "Eine Meerfahrt," between a demonic chase and a dark, ghostly battle scene. The song reverses many of Grimmelshausen's emphases: his echoing bird songs are excluded, and silent night appears as a protective envelope rather than a threatening blankness. Outlines are blurred, figures merge, and chronologies overlap as shade comes drowsily to shade to drown the wakeful anguish of the soul. If time (as Baader said) is a suspension of eternity, then the protected world of Eichendorff's hermit is a suspension of time in a world of inspirited things rather than living beings: " 'Quiet there!' he cried; 'what drives you to break the night with this coarse noise? The wild sea only mutters in the distance at the foot of the rocks, and the blind elements had all kept peace here for thirty years in a beautiful concord of nature, and the first Christians whom I see bring war, revolt, death.' "

Although the contrast between propulsive narration and lyrical pause is not often so schematic as here, it nevertheless is fundamental in German romantic fiction. The interaction of the two worlds is explored in countless modulations: the song may be a sudden revelation or a distraction, an analogue or a pointed irrelevance; the ideal it evokes may be true or fallacious, it may continue or vary motifs from the prose context or suggest an alien world. But whatever the specific circumstances, the very regularity of rhythm and rhyme constitutes an interruption (on occasions a failed interruption) of the linear impetus of time. As a temporality without forward movement, rhythm and rhyme of themselves constitute the ground or "tonic chord" of human time.

The essence of the lyric mode, of the pastoral "central center" of time, is repetition. Something happens, yet nothing changes, for the ideal is unvarying. Not all poems in German romantic fiction are equally central (nor are all plots equally propulsive), but the lyrical high points are marked by a well-developed art of repetition. Thus, the hermit's song in "Eine Meerfahrt" repeats elements both externally (from its literary model) and also internally (through its refrain as well as through thematic duplications). "Der Abend" is actually sung twice in "Aus dem Leben eines Taugenichts," and its repetition breaks through all realistic hindrances and unleashes the comic opera "emigration to Arcadia," which concludes the story. Within this framework of repetition, variation offers the possibility for flexibility and also the threat of decomposition. Undoubtedly, the best-known instance is the thrice-varied song "Waldeinsamkeit" in Tieck's story "Der blonde Eckbert." With each version Bertha's forest solitude preempts a new aspect of time—first eternity, next mutability, and lastly repetition—until it has become an all-encompassing demonic space from which consciousness can find no escape.

The fictional space. Over an all but unbounded landscape the wandering hero of a romantic novel traces his figure. His character is his fate; nothing external seriously impedes his progress or shapes his destiny. Even the romantic madman, such as Nathanael in Hoffmann's "Sandmann," is possessed only by his own demon, "the wild beast in the breast," as Eichendorff repeatedly called it, and not by an external power. Yet within this world of unconfined subjectivity lies a fixed point of reference, a circumscribed world of timeless stability. Man lives in both worlds, and neither may safely take exclusive possession of his imagination. His accomplishment is measured, not by absolutes, but by the distance maintained between the freedom of prose and the order of verse. Two suns shine on the romantic hero and the romantic novel, a fire within and a light without, and the life of the fiction lies in the difference between these two illuminations.

Difference is the key word, and not opposition or ambivalence. It is true that Novalis, in a late fragment, speaks of the "battle of poetry and unpoetry" as one of the "unities of the novel." But this is a battle in which there are no losers; indeed, it is rather a contest in which both sides are strengthened through competition, "an arch-poetic game": "Throughout Shakespeare's historical plays there is a battle of poetry with unpoetry. The common appears witty and relaxed—when the great appears stiff and sad, etc. Lower life is pitted throughout against higher—often tragically, often parodically, often for the sake of contrast. . . . Just the opposite of true history and yet history as it ought to be." Opposition is true friendship—not because opposites are united, but precisely because they are different enough to open a space for creativity: "The art of *estranging* in a *pleasing* way, of making an object strange and yet familiar and attractive, that is the romantic poetic."

The last prophetic word may be left to the earlier Novalis. It is not a final judgment or even a clear one, for these are not Novalis's virtues. But in its enthusiastically evocative way, it is a programme for the bicentral novel of the romantics and for that true life situated in the differential space of fiction:

> It would be a fine question, whether the lyrical poem is actually a *poem,* plus-poetry, or whether prose is minus-poetry? As the novel has been taken for prose, so has the lyric poem been taken for poetry—both in error. The highest, truest prose is the lyric poem.

> So-called prose arose from the limitation of absolute extremes—It is only there ad interim and plays a subaltern, temporary role. A time is coming where it will no longer be. For out of limitation has grown interpenetration. A true life has arisen, and poetry and prose are thereby most intimately united and put in alternation.

(pp. 199-214)

Marshall Brown, "Romantic Temporality," in his The Shape of German Romanticism, *Cornell University Press, 1979, pp. 181-214.*

ROMANTICISM IN FRANCE

George Brandes

[*In the following excerpt, Brandes discusses the development of Romanticism in France and delineates its major characteristics, especially as manifested in Victor Hugo's drama* Hernani.]

The literature produced in France between the years 1824 and 1828 is important and admirable. After the upheavals of the Revolution, the wars of the Empire, and the lassitude of the reign of Louis XVIII., there arose a young generation that applied itself with eager enthusiasm to those highest intellectual pursuits which had so long been neglected. During the Revolution and the wars of Napoleon the youths of France had had other vocations than the reformation of literature and art. The best energies of the nation had been diverted into the channels of politics, mili-

---

An excerpt from Jean Paul Richter's "On the Novel"

The most indispensable element in the novel is the romantic, into whatever form it may be hammered or cast. Up to now, however, the stylicists have demanded from a novel not the romantic spirit but its exorcism; the novel was supposed to repress and expel what little romanticism still glimmers in reality. The stylistic novel, an unversified didactic poem, became a thick almanac for theologians, philosophers, and housewives. The spirit became an agreeable dressing for the body. . . .

Certainly poetry teaches and should teach, and the novel should do so as well, but only as a blossoming flower which through its opening and closing and even through its fragrance announces the weather and the times of day. Its tender stem will never be cut, carpentered, and confined to the wooden teacher's desk or preacher's pulpit; the wooden frame and the person standing therein do not replace the living breath of spring. And what does it mean to give lessons? Simply to give signs. But the whole world and all time are full of signs already. Yet these letters are not read; we need a dictionary and a grammar of the signs. Poetry teaches us to read, while the mere teacher belongs among the ciphers rather than among the deciphering chancery-clerks.

A man who expresses a judgment about the world gives us his world, a miniature fragment of world instead of the living extended one, a sum without the reckoning. Poetry is indispensable, because it renders to the spirit only the spiritually reborn world and does not impose any casual conclusion. In the poet humanity alone speaks to humanity alone, not this man to that man.

Quoted in German Aesthetic and Literary Criticism: The Romantic Ironists and Goethe, *edited by Kathleen M. Wheeler, Cambridge University Press, 1984.*

---

tary enterprise, and civil administration. Now a great volume of intellectual force which had long been confined was suddenly set free.

The period of the restored Bourbon kings and the Monarchy of July may be defined as that of the decisive appearance of the bourgeoisie on the historical stage. With the fall of Napoleon the industrial period of history begins. Confining our attention to France, we observe that the new division of the national property which had been made during the Revolution, and which it had been Napoleon's economic mission to vindicate to the rest of Europe, now began to produce its natural consequences. All restrictions had been removed from industry and commerce; monopolies and privileges had been abolished; the confiscated lands of the Church and estates of the nobility, broken up and sold to the highest bidder, were now in the hands of at least twenty times as many owners as before. The result was that capital, free, floating capital, now began to be the moving power of society and consequently the object of the desires of the individual. After the Revolution of July the power of wealth gradually supersedes the power of birth and takes the power of royalty into its service. The rich man is received into the ranks of the nobility, acquires the privileges of a peer, and, by utilising the constitution, manages to draw ever-increasing profit from the monarchical form of government. Thus the pursuit of money, the struggle for money, the employment of money in great commercial and industrial enterprises, becomes the leading social feature of the period; and this prosaic engrossment, which contrasts so strongly with the revolutionary and martial enthusiasm of the foregoing period, helps, as background, to give the literature of the day its romantic, idealistic stamp. One only of its eminent authors, one of the greatest, Balzac, did not feel himself repelled by the period, but made the newborn power of capital, the new ruler of souls, money, the hero of his great epic; the other artists of the day, though it was often the prospect of material gain which inspired their labours, kept in their enthusiasms and their works at as great a distance as possible from the new reality.

The decade 1825-35, the most remarkable and most fertile period from the literary point of view, was from the political, colourless and inglorious. Its focus is the Revolution of July, but this Revolution is a solitary blood-spot amidst all the grey. (pp. 1-2)

It is against this grey background, this foil of Legitimist cowls and Louis-Philippe umbrellas—in this society where the new-born power of capital, strong as Hercules, has, even in its cradle, strangled all the external romance of life—on this stage upon the grey walls of which an invisible finger has written in grey letters the word *Juste-milieu*—that a fiery, glowing, noisy literature, a literature enamoured of scarlet and of passion, suddenly makes its appearance. All the conditions were present in combination which were certain to impel young, restless minds towards romantic enthusiasm, towards ardent contempt for public opinion, towards worship of unbridled passion and unrestrained genius. Hatred of the bourgeoisie (as in Germany a generation earlier hatred of the Philistines) becomes the watchword of the day. But whereas the word

"Philistine" conjures up a picture of the chimney-corner and the pipe, the word "bourgeois" at once suggests the omnipotence of economic interests. Its essential antipathy to utilitarianism and plutocracy turned the intellectual current of the day, in the case of the men of talent already before the public, and still more strongly in the case of the budding geniuses, in the direction of antagonism to everything existing and accepted, at the same time mightily increasing the force of the current. The religion of art, and enthusiasm for liberty in art, suddenly took possession of all hearts. Art was the highest, art was light, art was fire, art was all in all; its beauty and audacity alone imparted value to life.

The young generation had heard in their childhood of the great events of the Revolution, had known the Empire, and were the sons of heroes or of victims. Their mothers had conceived them between two battles, and the thunder of cannon had ushered them into the world. To the young poets and artists of the day there were only two kinds of human beings, the flaming and the grey. On the one side there was the art which meant blood, scarlet, movement, audacity; on the other, a strictly regular, timid, bourgeois, colourless art. Everything in the life of their day seemed to them unpoetic, utilitarian, devoid of genius, grey; they desired to show their contempt for such a day, their admiration of genius, and their hatred of the bourgeois spirit. For now, since the middle-class had become the influential one, this spirit had become a power.

Seen from the point of view of our own day, the young men of those days appear to have been younger than youth generally is—younger, fresher, more richly gifted, more ardent and hot-blooded. And we see the youth of France, who in the days of the Revolution had by their devotion changed the political and social conditions of the country, and in the days of the Empire had risked their lives on every battlefield in France, Italy, Germany, Russia, and Egypt, now devoting themselves with the same ardour to the culture of literature and the arts. Here, too, there were revolutions to be made, victories to win, and countries to conquer. During the Revolution they had worshipped liberty, under Napoleon martial glory; now they worshipped art.

For the first time in France the word art came to be regularly applied to literature. In the eighteenth century literature had aimed at transforming itself into philosophy, and much was then included under this denomination to which we no longer apply the word; now it aimed at the name and dignity of art.

The explanation of the change is, that the analytical and reasoning tendency which distinguishes both the imaginative and reflective works of the classical period, had in the new century slowly made way for interest in the actually existing, in what is perceivable by the senses. And the deeper-lying reason of this new preference was that men now placed nature, original, unconscious, rustic, uncultivated nature, above all the culture of civilisation. Why? Because a historically minded age had succeeded to a rationalising one. A man no longer coveted the title of philosopher, for it was now considered a greater distinction to be original than to be a self-conscious thinker. The poet-

ical literature of the eighteenth, nay, even that of the seventeenth century was despised, because it was purely intellectual; because, bloodless and elegant, it seemed to have been produced by attention to conventions and rules, not to have been born and to have grown. For whereas the eighteenth century had held thinking and acting to be the highest forms of activity, the children of the new age regarded origination, natural genesis, as the highest. It was a German idea, Herder's and Goethe's, by which men's minds were unconsciously occupied, and which produced in them an aversion for rules and academic principles. For how could art as unconscious, natural production be subjected to arbitrary external rules!

An intellectual movement had begun which recalled the Renaissance. It was as if the air which men breathed intoxicated them. In the long period during which France had been at an intellectual standstill her great neighbours, Germany and England, had hastened past her, had got a long start in the work of emancipation from old, hampering traditions. She felt this, felt it as a humiliation, and the feeling gave a sharp impulse to the new art enthusiasm. And now the works of foreign authors, both the new and the hitherto unknown older books, made their way into the country and revolutionised the minds of the young; every one read translations of Sir Walter Scott's novels, of Byron's *Corsair* and *Lara,* and devoured Goethe's *Werther* and Hoffmann's fantastic tales. All at once the votaries of the different arts felt that they were brothers. Musicians studied the literature both of their own country and of other nations; poets (such as Hugo, Gautier, Mérimée, Borel) drew and painted. Poems were read in painters' and sculptors' studios; Delacroix's and Devéria's pupils hummed Hugo's ballads as they stood at their easels. Certain of the great foreign authors, such as Scott and Byron, influenced poets (Hugo, Lamartine, Musset), musicians (Berlioz, Halévy, Félicien David), and painters (Delacroix, Delaroche, Scheffer). Artists attempt to overstep the limits of their own in order to embrace a kindred art. Berlioz writes Childe Harold and Faust symphonies, Félicien David a Desert symphony; music becomes descriptive. First Delacroix and then Ary Scheffer choose subjects from Dante, Shakespeare, and Byron; the art of the painter at times becomes illustration of poetry. But it was the art of painting which was most powerful in influencing the sister arts, especially poetry, and that distinctly for good. The lover no longer, as in the days of Racine, prayed his mistress "to crown his flame." The public demanded naturalness of the author, and refused to accept representations of impossibilities.

In 1824 Delacroix exhibits his *Massacre of Scios,* a picture with a Grecian subject and a reminiscence of Byron, in 1831 *The Bishop of Liège,* which illustrates Scott's *Quentin Durward,* in May 1831 *Liberty at the Barricades.* In February 1829, Auber's opera, *La Muette de Portici,* makes a great sensation; Meyerbeer's *Robert le Diable* follows in 1831. In February 1830 Victor Hugo's *Hernani* is played for the first time at the Théâtre Français; in 1831 Dumas' *Antony* is a grand success. The authors Dumas and Hugo, Delacroix the painter, the sculptor David d'Angers, the musical composers Berlioz and Auber, the critics Sainte-Beuve and Gautier, Frédéric Lemaître and Marie Dorval the scenic artists, and, corresponding to them, the two great dæmonic musical virtuosi Chopin and Liszt—all these make their appearance simultaneously. One and all proclaim the gospel of nature and of passion, and around them assemble groups of young men who apprehend and cultivate literature and art in a spirit akin to theirs.

These men did not always realise that in the eyes of posterity they would constitute a natural group. Some of the greatest of them felt as if they stood alone, and believed that the spirit and tendency of their work was different from that of their contemporaries', nay, actually antagonistic to it. Nor were they entirely wrong, for there are very essential points of difference between them. Yet common excellences, common prejudices, common aims, and common faults unite them and make of them a whole. And it happened much more frequently than is generally the case, that those whom reflection inclines us to class together actually did feel themselves drawn to each other; many of the best among them early joined hands and formed a league.

Seeking the connecting links we find, as it were, a chain which binds the group together.

When, after the lapse of many years, we dryly say or write the words, "they formed a school," we seldom take the trouble to conjure up any adequately vivid impression of what the formation of a school of literature and art signifies. There is a mysterious magic about the process. Some one remarkable man, after a long unconscious or half-conscious struggle, finally with full consciousness, frees himself from prejudices and attains to clearness of vision; then, everything being ready, the lightning of genius illuminates what he beholds. Such a man gives utterance (as did Hugo in a prose preface of some score of pages) to some thoughts which have never been thought or expressed in the same manner before. They may be only half true, they may be vague, but they have this remarkable quality that, in spite of more or less indefiniteness, they affront all traditional prejudices and wound the vanity of the day where it is most vulnerable, whilst they ring in the ears of the young generation like a call, like a new, audacious watchword.

What happens? Scarcely are these words spoken than there comes with the speed and precision of an echo a thousand-tongued answer from the wounded vanities and injured interests, an answer like the furious baying of a hundred packs of hounds. And what more? First one man, then another, then a third, comes to the spokesman of the new tendency, each with his own standpoint, each with his revolt, his ambition, his need, his hope, his resolve. They show him that the words he has spoken are incarnated in them. Some communicate directly with him, some with each other in his spirit and his name. Men who but lately were as unknown to each other as they still are to the public, who have been spiritually languishing, each in his separate seclusion, now meet and marvel to find that they understand each other, that they speak the same language, a language unknown to the rest of their contemporaries. They are young, yet all are already in possession of what to them constitutes life; the one has his dearly-bought joys, the other his bracing sufferings; and from these life-

elements each has extracted his own portion of enthusiasm. Their meeting is electric; they exchange ideas with youthful haste, impart to each other their various sympathies and antipathies, enthusiasms and detestations; and all these wellsprings of feeling flow together like the streams that form a river.

But the most beautiful feature in this crystallisation of artistic spirits into a school is the reverence, the awe which, in spite of the unanimity of their opinions, and in spite of their good comradeship, each feels for the other. Outsiders are apt to confuse this with what is satirically called "mutual admiration." But nothing is in reality more unlike the interested homage paid in periods of decadence than the naïve admiration of each other's talents exhibited by the men who are unconsciously forming a school. Their hearts are too young, too pure, not to admire in real earnest. One young productive mind regards the other as something marvellous, which holds surprises in store. To the one the workshop of the other's mind is like a sealed book; he cannot guess what will next appear from it, has no idea what pleasures his comrade has in store for him. They honour in one another something which they value higher than the personality, than the usually as yet undeveloped character, namely, the talent by virtue of which they are all related to the deity they worship—art.

Seldom, however, in the world's history has the mutual admiration accompanying an artistic awakening been carried to such a pitch as it was by the generation of 1830. It became positive idolatry. All the literary productions of the period show that the youth of the day were intoxicated with the feeling of friendship and brotherhood. Hugo's poems to Lamartine, Louis Boulanger, Sainte-Beuve, and David d'Angers; Gautier's to Hugo, Jehan du Seigneur, and Petrus Borel; De Musset's to Lamartine, Sainte-Beuve, and Nodier; and, very specially, Sainte-Beuve's to all the standard-bearers of the school; Madame de Girardin's articles; Balzac's dedications; George Sand's *Lettres d'un Voyageur*—all these testify to a sincere, ardent admiration, which entirely precluded the proverbial jealousy of authors.

They did not only praise one another, they communicated ideas to each other and helped each other. Now it is an inspiring influence, now an artistic criticism, now some actual service rendered, which knits the bond of friendship between two authors of this period. Émile Deschamps inspires Victor Hugo to borrow themes from the old Spanish Romancero; Gautier writes the beautiful tulip sonnet in Balzac's *Un grand Homme de Province à Paris,* and helps him to dramatise certain of his plots; Sainte-Beuve reads George Sand's manuscripts and aids her with his criticism; George Sand and De Musset influence one another powerfully at a certain stage of their career; Madame de Girardin, Méry, Sandeau, and Gautier collaborate in a novel written in letters; Mérimée is the bond of union between the realists Beyle and Vitet and the romanticists.

The short period during which all meet and combine is the blossoming time of literature. Before many years pass Nodier is in his grave, Hugo is living in exile in Jersey, Alexandre Dumas is turning literature into a trade, Sainte-Beuve and Gautier are to be found in Princess Mathilde's circle, Mérimée is presiding over the Empress Eugénie's courts of love, De Musset sits solitary over his absinthe, and George Sand has retired to Nohant.

One and all in their riper years made new connections, connections which aided their development; but their boldest and freshest, if not always their most refined and beautiful work was done at the time when they were holding their first meetings in Charles Nodier's quarters at the Arsenal, or in the apartments in the Rue Notre-Dame-des-Champs where Hugo and his pretty young wife kept house on their 2000 francs a year, or in Petrus Borel's garret, where the host's Hernani cloak decorated the wall in company with a sketch by Devéria and a copy of a Giorgione, and where, owing to lack of chairs, at least half of the company had to stand.

These young Romanticists felt like brothers, like fellow-conspirators; they felt that they were the sharers in a sweet and invigorating secret; and this gave to the works of the school a flavour, an aroma like that of the noble wines of a year when the vintage has been more than ordinarily good. Ah! that bouquet of 1830! There is no other in the century that can be compared with it.

In all the arts a break with tradition was aimed at and demanded. The inward fire was to glow through and dissolve the old musical forms, to devour lines and contours and transform painting into colour symphonies, to rejuvenate literature. In all the arts colour, passion, and style were aimed at and demanded—colour with such urgency that the most gifted painter of the period, Delacroix, neglected drawing for it; passion with such ardour that both lyric poetry and the drama were in danger of degenerating into hysteric foolishness; style with such artistic enthusiasm that some of the younger men, such as those two opposite poles, Mérimée and Gautier, neglected the human groundwork of their art and became devotees of style pure and simple.

The original, the unconscious, the popular was sought after and demanded. "We have been rhetoricians," men cried; "we have never understood the simple and the illogical—the savage, the people, the child, woman, the poet!"

Hitherto the people had only served as a background in literature—in Victor Hugo's dramas the passionate plebeian, the avenger and requiter, appeared on the scene as the hero. Hitherto the savage had talked like a Frenchman of the eighteenth century (Montesquieu, Voltaire)—Mérimée in *Colomba* and *Carmen* depicted savage emotions in all their wildness and freshness. Racine's child (in *Athalie*) had spoken like a miniature edition of a grown-up man—Nodier with a childlike heart put simple, innocent words into his children's mouths. In the French literature of an earlier period, woman had generally acted with full consciousness, arriving at conclusions like a man; see the works of Corneille, Racine, and Voltaire. Corneille paid homage to virtue, Crébillon the younger to frivolity and vice, but both the virtue and the vice were conscious and acquired. George Sand, on the contrary, depicted the innate nobility and natural goodness of a noble woman's heart. Madame de Staël in her *Corinne* had represented the gifted woman as a being of great and commanding tal-

ent—George Sand, in *Lélia*, represented her as a great sibyl. In olden days the poet had been a courtier, like Racine and Molière, or a man of the world, like Voltaire and Beaumarchais, or simply an ordinary decent citizen, like Lafontaine. Now he became the neglected step-child of society, the high-priest of humanity, often poor and despised, but with the starry brow and the tongue of fire. Hugo hymned him as the shepherd of the people, Alfred de Vigny represented him in *Stello* and *Chatterton* as the sublime child who prefers dying of hunger to degrading his muse by common work, and dies blessing his fellowmen, who acknowledge his worth when it is too late. (pp. 8-16)

At first Romanticism was, in its essence, merely a spirited defence of localisation in literature. The Romanticists admired and glorified the Middle Ages, which the culture of the eighteenth century had anathematised, and the poets of the sixteenth century—Ronsard, Du Bellay, &c.—who had been supplanted by the classic authors of the age of Louis XIV. They attacked pseudo-classicism, the tiresome and monotonous Frenchifying and modernising of all ages and nationalities. They took as their watchword "local colouring." By local colouring they meant all the characteristics of foreign nations, of far-off days, of unfamiliar climes, to which as yet justice had not been done in French literature. They felt that their predecessors had been led astray by the premise that every human being was simply a human being, and, moreover, more or less of a Frenchman. In reality, there was not such a thing as universal humanity; there were separate races, peoples, tribes, and clans. Still less was the Frenchman the typical human being. It was imperative, if they were to understand and represent human life, that they should free themselves from themselves. This idea gave the impulse to the art and criticism of nineteenth-century France.

Authors now made it their endeavour to train their readers to see things from this new point of view. They no longer wrote to please the public—and it is this fact which gives value to the books of the period. Therefore a critic who, like myself, is engaged in tracing the main currents of literature, must dwell upon many a seldom read and still more rarely bought Romantic work, and do little more than mention such a talented dramatist as Scribe, who for a whole generation dominated the stage in every country in Europe.

For if an author does not penetrate to the essential in the human soul, to its deepest depth; if he has not dared, or has not been able to write his book regardless of consequences; if he has not ventured to represent his ideas in statuesque nakedness, has not imaged human nature as it showed itself to him, improving nothing and modifying nothing, but has taken counsel with his public, been guided by its prejudices, its ignorance, its untruthfulness, its vulgar or sentimental taste—he may have been, probably has been, highly distinguished by his contemporaries, he may have won laurels and wealth by his talents; for me he does not exist, to what I call literature his work is valueless. All the offspring of the author's *mariage de convenance* with that doubtful character, public opinion, all those literary children which their author begets, giving a side-thought to the taste and morality of his public, are defunct a generation later. There was no real life and heat in them, nothing but timorous regard for a public which is now dead; they were nothing but the supply of a demand which has long ceased to exist. But every work in which an independent writer has, without any side-thought, uttered what he felt and described what he saw, is, and will continue to be, no matter how few editions of it may be printed, a valuable document.

There is only a seeming contradiction between this condemnation of the literary work produced to please the public, and the doctrine of the sound natural influence of society on the author. It is certain that the author cannot separate himself from his age. But the current of the age is not an undivided current; there is an upper and an under one. To let one's self drive with or be driven by the upper one is weakness, and ends in destruction. In other words, every age has its dominant and favourite ideas and forms, which are simply the results of the life of former ages, that were arrived at long ago and have slowly petrified; but besides these it owns another whole class of quite different ideas, which have not yet taken shape, but are in the air, and are apprehended by the greatest men of the age as the results which must now be arrived at. These last are the ideas which form the unifying element of the new endeavour.

In 1827 an English theatrical company visited Paris, and for the first time Frenchmen saw Shakespeare's masterpieces, *King Lear, Macbeth, Othello,* and *Hamlet,* admirably played. It was under the influence of these performances that Victor Hugo wrote that preface to *Cromwell* which is regarded as the programme of the new literature.

The literary war of liberation began with an assault upon French classical tragedy, the weakest and most exposed point in literary tradition. Hugo knew very little about the attacks upon its authority which had been made in other countries; and to those who have read the utterances delivered on the same subject many years previously by Lessing, Wilhelm Schlegel, and the English Romantic writers, his manifesto offers little that is new. But it was, of course, an important step to carry the war into France itself. The vigorous arguments expended in proving the unnatural-

ness of compressing the action of every drama into twenty-four hours and a single pillared hall, seem to the reader of to-day almost as uninteresting as the absurdities attacked; but he must remember that Boileau's authority was then still supreme, still unshaken in France.

Of interest as regards Hugo's own development are the passages in which he expounds his private theory of poetry; although he is so much of the poet and so little of the thinker that his arguments are, as a rule, sadly inconclusive.

What he attacks is the idealistic, pseudo-classic tendency of tragedy. This he does, oddly enough, in the name of Christianity, and by means of a great historical survey, made on as false a system as any of those of his contemporary, Cousin, of whom it reminds us. He distinguishes three great periods—the primitive, when poetry is lyric; the period of ancient civilisation, when it is epic; and the age of Christianity, which is the period of the drama. The peculiar characteristic of the poetry of the Christian, which he treats as synonymous with the modern, period is that it (having learned from religion that man consists of two elements, an animal and a spiritual, body and soul) makes place in the same work for the two elements which in literature have hitherto excluded each other, the sublime and the grotesque. It is no longer imperative that tragedy should be solemn throughout; it may venture to develop into drama.

If we pay less heed to what Hugo says than to what he really intends to say, we find that the sum and substance of this tolerably foolish argument is a naturalistic protest against pure beauty as the proper or highest subject of art. His idea is: We will renounce convention; we will not feel ourselves in duty bound to exclude everything from serious poetry which directly reminds us of the material world. We see this from the examples he gives. The judge is to be allowed to say: "Sentenced to death. And now let us dine." Queen Elizabeth is to be allowed to swear and speak Latin; Cromwell to say: "I have the Parliament in my bag and the King in my pocket." Cæsar in his triumphal car may be afraid of its upsetting. And Hugo calls Napoleon's exclamation: "There is only one step from the sublime to the ridiculous," the cry of anguish which is the summary of both drama and life.

Exaggerated as Hugo's language may be, his meaning is plain. What he asserts is the æsthetic value of the ugly. He maintains that the beautiful only comprehends form as absolute symmetry, form in its simplest relations and most intimate harmony with our being, whereas the ugly is a detail in a much greater, harmonious whole which we are unable fully to discern. He declares that the ugly has a thousand types, whereas the beautiful is poor, and has but one; which last theory we may be excused for calling one of the most absurd ever advanced by a poet. It was parodied by his opponents in the axiom: *Le Laid c'est le Beau* ("Foul is fair," as the witches sing in *Macbeth*), and combated with the objections which the Romanticists themselves offered in the Seventies to extreme realism.

Was not this French Romanticism, then, after all simply a thinly-veiled naturalism? What did Victor Hugo de-

A painting by Albert Bernard depicting the uproar during the first performance of Hugo's Hernani.

mand in the name of the young generation but nature—faithful reproduction, local and historical colour? Is not George Sand Rousseau's daughter? the preacher of a gospel of nature? And Beyle and Mérimée, are they not half-brutal, half-refined worshippers of nature? Is not Balzac nowadays actually honoured as the founder of a naturalistic school?

The answer is simple. Hugo's watchword was, undoubtedly, nature and truth, but it was at the same time, and first and foremost, contrast, picturesque contrast, antithesis founded upon the medieval belief in the confliction between body and soul; that is, a dualistic Romanticism. "The salamander heightens the charm of the water-nymph, the gnome lends beauty to the sylph," he says. He desired truth to nature, but he believed it was to be arrived at by making nature's extremes meet, by placing opposites in juxtaposition—Beauty and the Beast, Esmeralda and Quasimodo, the courtesan's past and the purest love in Marion Delorme, bloodthirstiness and maternal tenderness in Lucrèce Borgia.

In his early youth nature was to Victor Hugo a great Ariel-Caliban, the product of a superhuman ideality and an unnatural bestiality, the result obtained by the combination of two supernatural ingredients. But this conception of nature, which corresponded exactly with that of Germanic Romanticism, at times made way in Hugo's case for the magnificent pantheism which found typical expression in that profound and beautiful poem, "Le Satyre," in *La Légende des Siècles.*

The combination of love of nature with predilection for the unnatural, is to be traced far on into the new literature. All its authors chant the praises of nature. But what they detest and shun under the name of the prosaic and the commonplace is very often the simple nature that lies nearest them. Romantic nature alone is dear to them. George Sand escapes from the world of dreary, hard realities into that of beautiful dreams, Théophile Gautier into the world of art. George Sand in *Lélia,* Balzac in *Père Goriot,* make the ideal or the omnipotent galley-slave the judge of society; Balzac actually writes fantastic legends in Hoffmann's style. And they are even more inclined to shun the plain and simple in their language than in their characters. They soon evolved a pompous diction, which far outrivalled that of the classic periods. These were the golden days of the glowing, dazzling adjective. Picturesque, enthusiastic words, with which the narrative was inlaid as with so many transparent jewels, opened up endless vistas. In so far, therefore, it may be said that both the style and the predilections of these young authors were purely romantic. But only in so far.

In Victor Hugo, the founder of the school, the dual love of the natural and the unnatural was the result of a personal peculiarity. His eye naturally sought and found contrasts; his mind had an innate tendency towards antithesis. In *Inez de Castro,* the melodrama of his earliest youth, and later in *Marie Tudor,* we have the throne on one side of the stage, the scaffold on the other, the monarch and the executioner face to face. About the time when the preface to *Cromwell* was written, Hugo was, his wife tells us, in the habit of walking on the Boulevard Montparnasse.

"There, just opposite the Cemetery, tight-rope dancers and jugglers had erected their booths. This contrast of shows and funerals confirmed him in his idea of a drama in which extremes meet; and it was there that the third act of *Marion Delorme* occurred to him, the act in which the tragic, fruitless attempt of the Marquis de Nangis to save his brother from the scaffold forms the counterpart to the antics of the jester." In the preface to *Cromwell,* when he is asserting the necessity of representing an action in the place where it actually happened, he writes: "Could the poet dare to have Rizzio murdered anywhere but in Mary Stuart's chamber? . . . or to behead Charles I. or Louis XVI. anywhere but on these sorrowful spots within sight of Whitehall and the Tuileries, which seem as if they had been chosen in order that the scaffold might contrast with the palace?" In spite of all his asseverations this poet does not really see natural environments with an understanding eye. He does not see them act as formative influences upon the human soul; he employs them as great symbols of the tremendous reverses of fate; he arranges them like the stage scenery of a melodrama.

If we look deeper, what reveals itself to us in this? A characteristic which is to a certain extent distinctive of many of the French Romanticists, and which may be most briefly expressed thus: French Romanticism, in spite of all the elements it has in common with general European Romanticism, is in many ways a classic phenomenon, a product of classic French rhetoric.

Words undergo strange vicissitudes in this world of ours. When the word *romantic* was introduced into Germany it signified almost the same as Romanesque; it meant Romanesque flourishes and conceits, sonnets and canzonets; the Romanticists were enthusiastic admirers of the Roman Catholic Church and of the great Romanesque poet Calderon, whose works they discovered and translated and lauded. When, a century later, Romanticism reached France, the same word meant exactly the opposite thing—it meant the German-English tendency as opposed to the Greco-Latin Romanesque tendency; it meant Teutonic. The simple explanation of this is, that whatever is strange and foreign produces a romantic impression. The art and literature of a people of a homogeneous civilisation and culture, like the ancient Greeks, are classic; but when one civilised, cultured nation discovers another civilisation and culture which seem to it strange and wonderful, it is at once impressed by it as romantic, is affected by it as by a landscape seen through coloured glass. The Romanticists of France despised their own national excellences, the perspicuity and rational transparency of their own literature, and extolled Shakespeare and Goethe because these poets did not, like Racine and, to a certain extent, Corneille, break up human life into its separate elements, did not represent isolated emotions and passions which offered dramatic contrasts, but, without any rhetorical recurrence to the fundamental elements, flung real human life on the stage in all its complex cohesion. The Frenchmen determined to follow this great example.

But what was the result? Under their treatment, in the hands of Lamartine, Alfred de Vigny, George Sand, Sainte-Beuve, real life was dissolved and disintegrated anew. In the hands of Victor Hugo and Alexandre Dumas its extremes formed symmetrical contrasts, exactly as in classic tragedy. Order, moderation, aristocratic refinement, a transparent, severely simple style distinguished Nodier, Beyle, and Mérimée, exactly as they had done the classic authors of the eighteenth century. The light, free, airy fancy which intermingles all the most varied imaginations of the poetic mind, which unites near and far, to-day and hoary antiquity, the real and the impossible, in one and the same work, which combines the divine and the human, popular legend and profound allegory, making of them one great symbolic whole—this real romantic gift was not theirs. They never saw the dance of the elves, nor heard the thin, clear tones of their music floating across the meadows. Although Celts by birth, these men were Latins; they felt and wrote as Latins; and the word Latin is equivalent to classic. If we understand by Romanticism what is generally understood, that is, an overwhelming of the style by the subject-matter, contents uncontrolled by any laws of form, such as we have in the writings of Jean Paul and Tieck, and even in Shakespeare and Goethe (*A Midsummer Night's Dream* and the second part of *Faust*), then all the French Romanticists are classic writers— Mérimée, George Sand, Gautier, and even Victor Hugo himself. Hugo's romantic drama is as disintegrative, regular in construction, perspicuous, and eloquent as a tragedy of Corneille.

At the mention of this name my thoughts turn involuntarily and naturally from the characteristics common to the periods to the common characteristics of race. In Hugo, Corneille's apparent antagonist, Corneille lives again.

There are many veins in the French character. There is a vein of scepticism, jest, sarcasm—the line Montaigne, La Fontaine, Molière, Mathurin Régnier, Pierre Bayle, &c.; there is the true, thoroughbred Gallic vein—Rabelais, Diderot, Balzac; and amongst the rest there is the heroic vein, the vein of enthusiasm. It is this last which pulsates so strongly in Corneille; and in Victor Hugo the blood begins to course in it again. If we compare Hugo in his stateliness with other poets, we shall find that there is probably not one in the whole world whom he resembles so much as he does old Corneille. There is something Spanish about the French eloquence of both, and Spain had certainly made its impression on them both; in Corneille's case a literary impression, in Hugo's a personal, received in his childhood. The drama to which Corneille owes his fame is the *Cid,* in which a Spanish theme is treated in a Spanish spirit, in imitation of Spanish models. The drama which makes Hugo famous is *Hernani,* Spanish in its subject, and permeated by the spirit of Calderon's code of honour. But in both these dramas it is heroism pure and simple which is inculcated and exhibited. They are schools for heroes. It is not human nature in its manysidedness, but heroic human nature which Corneille represents; in Victor Hugo this same heroic human nature is merely symmetrically complemented by wildly passionate human nature.

Let us glance at this *Hernani,* round which the great conflict between the party of the future and the party of the past raged. The story of the first performance has often been told. Adherents of the old school listened at the doors during the rehearsals, and picked up single lines, which they caricatured; and a parody of the play was acted before the play itself. The author had a hard struggle with the censor; he had to fight for his play almost line by line. There was a long correspondence on the subject of the one line: "C'était d'un imprudent, seigneur roi de Castille, et d'un lâche." And the actors and actresses regarded the work with equal disfavour; only one of the company applied himself with goodwill to the study of his part. Hugo was determined to dispense with the paid claque, but he arranged to have three hundred places at his disposal for the first three nights. The most faithful of his followers, young men who, according to their own confession, spent their nights in writing "Vive Victor Hugo!" all over the arcade of the Rue de Rivoli, with no other aim than to annoy the respectable citizen, now enlisted a corps of young painters, architects, poets, sculptors, musicians, and printers, to whom Hugo gave the watchword *Hierro,* and who were prepared to present an iron front to the foe. The moment the curtain rose the storm burst, and every time the play was performed there was such an uproar in the theatre that it was with the greatest difficulty it could be acted to the end. A hundred evenings in succession was *Hernani* hissed, and a hundred evenings in succession was it received with storms of applause by young enthusiasts, who for their master's sake did not weary of listening to the same speeches evening after evening and defending them line by line against the hate, rage, envy, and superior power of his opponents. The fact may seem unimportant, yet it is worthy of observation, that France is the only country in which such *esprit de corps,* without the existence of any tangible *corps,* such unselfish devotion to the cause and honour of another, has ever been witnessed.

The enemy took boxes and left them unoccupied, in order that the newspapers might report an empty house; they turned their backs to the stage; they made disgusted grimaces, as if the play were more than they could stand; they affected to be absorbed in the newspapers; they slammed the box doors, or laughed loud and scornfully, or hooted and hissed and whistled; so that a resolute defence was absolutely necessary.

There is not an emotion in *Hernani* which is not strained to its extremest pitch. The hero is a noble-minded man of genius, the genius and noble-mindedness being of the type which exists in the imagination of a young man of twenty. His genius impels him to lead the life of a brigand chieftain, and out of pure high-mindedness and contempt for ordinary prudence he does the most foolish things— betrays himself, lets his mortal enemy escape, gives himself up again and again. As chieftain he exercises unbounded power over other men, but it seems to be his courage alone which gives him this, for all his actions are as unreasoning as a child's. Nevertheless there is life and reality in the play.

This noble and disinterested highwayman, who lives at war with society and is the leader of a band of faithful enthusiasts, reminds us of the poet himself, the literary outlaw, who filled pit and gallery with a band of young men quite as remarkable in appearance and attire as his brigand troop. Madame Hugo describes the contingent of spectators who appeared on the first evening in answer to her husband's invitation as "a troop of wild, extraordinary creatures, with beards and long hair, dressed in every fashion except that of the day—in woollen jerseys and Spanish cloaks, Robespierre waistcoats and Henry III. caps—displaying themselves in broad daylight at the doors of the theatre with the clothing of all ages and countries on their backs." Their frantic devotion to Hugo was as great as that of Hernani's band of robbers for its captain. They knew that Hugo had received an anonymous letter in which he was threatened with assassination "if he did not withdraw his filthy play," and, improbable as it was that the threat would be literally fulfilled, two of them accompanied him to and from the theatre every evening, though he and they lived in the farthest apart quarters of Paris.

Amongst Hugo's papers of this date there is a quaint note from the painter Charlet, which expresses the feelings of these youths.

> Four of my Janissaries offer me their strong arms. I send them to prostrate themselves at your feet, begging for four places for this evening, if it is not too late. I answer for my men; they are fellows who would gladly cut off heads for the sake of the wigs. I encourage them in this noble spirit, and do not let them go without my fatherly blessing. They kneel. I stretch out my hands and say: God protect you, young men! The cause is a good one; do your duty! They rise and I add: Now, my children, take good care of Victor Hugo. God is good, but He has so much to do that our friend must in the first instance rely upon us. Go, and do not put him you serve to shame.—Yours with life and soul,
>
> CHARLET.

Supported by such devoted enthusiasts as these in its struggle with fanatic opposition, romantic art stormed the enemy's first redoubt and won its first important victory.

What these young men heard from the stage was the expression of their own defiance and thirst for independence, of their courage and devotion, their ideal and erotic longings, only pitched in a still higher key; and their hearts melted within them.

The time was February 1830, five months before the Revolution of July. The dullest materialism made life colourless. France was as regularly ordered as the avenues of the gardens of Versailles; it was ruled by old men, who patronised only such young ones as had written Latin verse to perfection at school, and had since qualified themselves for office by absolute correctness of behaviour. There they sat, these correct, faultlessly-attired youths, with their neckcloths and stiff standing collars. Contrast with them the youths in the pit, one with locks reaching to his waist and a scarlet satin doublet, another with a Rubens hat and bare hands. These latter hated the powerful Philistine bourgeoisie as Hernani hated the tyranny of Charles V. They gloried in their position; they, too, were freebooters, poor, proud—one a cherisher of Republican dreams, most of them worshippers of art. There they stood, many of them geniuses—Balzac, Berlioz, Théophile Gautier, Gérard de Nerval, Petrus Borel, Préault—taking the measure of their opponents of the same generation. They felt that

they themselves were at least not place-seekers, not tuft-hunters, beggars, and parasites like those others; they were the men who a few months later made the Revolution of July, and who in the course of a few years gave France a literature and art of the first rank. (pp. 17-28)

> *George Brandes, in his* Main Currents in Nineteenth Century Literature: The Romantic School in France, Vol. V, *translated by Diana White and Mary Morison, William Heinemann, 1904, 391 p.*

Furst on French and German Romanticism:

In spite of the sound and fury attendant on its birth, French Romanticism was in effect more modest in scope and objective than German Romanticism. This is the paradox inherent in the emergence of the two Romantic movements: that it was the seemingly quieter one that proved in the long run more deeply revolutionary than its rumbustious cousin. The overshadowing presence of Goethe, the forestalling impact of the Storm and Stress, and the closure of political expression drove the German Romantics onwards to adumbrate an aesthetic far ahead of their time. Just as the forces of retardation predominated in France, so a forward thrusting momentum emanated from the unique set of pressures operative in Germany. This is at the root of the time-lag, as well as of the differences in character, separating the emergence of the Romantic movements in the two countries. And it was this also that led to those later diagonal relationships in the nineteenth century, making French Romanticism the counterpart to the Storm and Stress, and French Symbolism that of the *Frühromantik*.

> *Lilian R. Furst, in her* Counterparts: The Dynamics of Franco-German Literary Relationships 1770-1895, *Wayne State University Press, 1977.*

Lloyd Bishop

[*Bishop is an American educator and critic whose expertise is French literature. In the following excerpt, he delineates the characteristics of the French Romantic hero.*]

The French romantic hero, especially in fiction, is introspective, and is the first to marvel at his strange uniqueness. This introspection usually makes of him a man of moods more often than a man of action. His self-consciousness seems more marked than that found in heroes of other romantic literatures. As Walter L. Reed says, in his *Meditations on the Hero:* "The heroes of French Romanticism are more prone to self-consciousness themselves, more passive than active. As with Constant's Adolphe and Musset's *enfant de notre siècle,* they exhibit the disease of the age rather than provide its remedy." In *Either/Or* Kierkegaard has noticed the peculiar self-consciousness of modern heroes:

> In ancient tragedy the action itself has an epic moment in it; it is as much event as action. The reason for this naturally lies in the fact that the

ancient world did not have subjectivity fully self-conscious and reflective. Even if the individual moved freely, he still rested in the substantial categories of state, family, and destiny. This substantial category is exactly the fatalistic element in Greek tragedy, and its exact peculiarity. The hero's destruction is, therefore, not only a result of his own deeds, but is also a suffering, whereas in modern tragedy the hero's destruction is not really suffering, but is action. In modern times, therefore, situation and character are really predominant. The tragic hero, conscious of himself as a subject, is fully reflective, and this reflection has not only reflected him out of every immediate relation to state, race, and destiny, but has often reflected him out of his own preceding life.

Kierkegaard's statement about ancient heroes moving within the "substantial categories of state, family and destiny" is echoed by Lukács' view of ancient society as "bounded" and well integrated whereas modern society is unbounded and its literary heroes all lonely wanderers and questors. No god plots the modern hero's path or walks ahead of him. As David H. Miles comments [in "Portrait of the Marxist as a Young Hegelian: Lukács' *Theory of the Novel,*" in *PMLA* 94 (1979)], Lukács believes that "the farther we travel from the unselfconsciousness of the Greeks, the more we suffer from the burden of consciousness itself, and the novel hero becomes emblematic of this suffering." And Kierkegaard's observation about the modern tragic hero's self-consciousness reflecting him out of every immediate relation to state, race and destiny is echoed in Erich Heller's analysis of the modern artist's "journey to the interior" or toward self-absorbed contemplation resulting in "the disinherited mind." The romantic hero does not enjoy the ancient hero's sense of belonging with regard to his "home" or his world. Homelessness, or rootlessness, is his basic situation; his wanderlust it not so much a retreat *from* but a futile search *for* a true home.

The romantic hero, then, is a solitary hero, the very antithesis of the ideal man of seventeenth-century classicism: the eminently sociable *honnête homme.* Sartre, we recall, has noted that self-consciousness is basically a "nihilating" consciousness, it is the consciousness of *not being* anything else in one's phenomenal field. But the original romantic hero at least is not the emblem of a negative ontology. He is solitary because he is superior, he stands *above* ordinary mortals, a fact that is usually symbolized in spatial terms, by his penchant for high places, the mountain top especially. The hero's superiority lies in his keen sensibility, his enlarged capacity for feeling, and in his total sincerity rather than in the traditional virtues. He considers himself beyond what others call good and evil. As [Walter L.] Reed says [in *Meditations on the Hero,* 1974]: "The definition of the hero as one who 'represents . . . a socially approved norm' . . . does not apply at all to the romantic hero." He does not inspire "epic awe" but rather a mixture of fascination and repulsion; he is the victim of other men's incomprehension and jealousy. He makes others feel uneasy. If one compares him to Aristotle's idea of the tragic hero, he exhibits two or three essential differences. Aristotle's hero is above average but recognizabley human. Romantic heroes tend to see themselves as a superior breed. The mis-

fortune of Aristotle's hero is brought on in part by his *hamartia* or tragic flaw and is accompanied by some measure of tragic guilt; the misfortune of the romantic hero, on the other hand, is usually attributed to the fault of other men or to a flawed universe. The epic hero's tragic flaw is usually related to *hubris,* but the inordinate and overweening pride of the romantic hero is simply the result of a total (and often embarrassing) sincerity that does not allow of false modesty. If *hubris* is invoked, as at the end of [Chateaubriand's] *René,* it is rather unconvincing, that is, it does not come off as a dominant theme.

The romantic hero, says [George Ross] Ridge [in *The Hero in French Romantic Literature,* 1959], is also a seeker, a man of fate, a pathological hero, a poet-prophet and a rebel. As a seeker, he is usually in search of one of three things: new and exotic sensations or emotions; new values; and finally what he calls *un bien inconnu,* a spiritual dimension or ground of being that underlies—or lies beyond—the quotidian. René was in search of all three. The romantic *hantise de l'absolu* is usually a tacit form of metaphysical anguish and is the forerunner of our own century's *hantise de l'absurde.*

As seeker, the romantic hero can be considered as continuing in some measure the medieval romance tradition: [in the words of Raney Stanford, "The Romantic Hero and that Fatal Self-Hood," *The Centennial Review* 12 (1968)] "The romantic knight is mostly anguished and roams in an apparently purposeless universe in search of an object which usually seems increasingly vague even to him." But the knight-errant usually finds that object whereas the romantic hero, like most modern heroes, is doomed to a never-ending quest. If the knight-errant was uneasy about worldly and otherworldly values, he found consolation in his own values (e.g., valor) and in his undying love for his lady. This is also true, on the whole, of romantic heroes, who often find further consolation, or at least good company, in Nature.

Like the hero of classical tragedy, the romantic hero is a fatal hero, but unlike the former, he is profoundly conscious of himself in this role. While the classical hero is not aware of the catastrophe that fate and a tragic flaw will bring upon him until the anagnorisis at the end of the play, the romantic hero [in the words of Ridge in *The Hero in French Romantic Literature*] "watches himself struggle in the mesh of fate" from beginning to end. He is doomed to misfortune and tragedy because life cannot fulfil his extraordinary and insatiable desires, live up to his superior values, or satisfy his "romantic" imagination. His fate is tied, then, to his exceptional nature and to the fact that his genius is envied by both men and gods who conspire to hurt him and seal his doom. Of all this he is tragically aware from the very beginning of his story; there will be no dramatic or Sophoclean irony in the romantic drama. If others do not actively conspire to harm him, they are bound to misunderstand and ostracize him. He becomes an outcast, a pariah. Harm inevitably comes also to those close to him, those who love him or follow him into exile. His embrace, like Manfred's, is fatal; his *voeux,* like René's, are *malédictions.*

The romantic hero usually begins his career with a short

and uncomfortable stay in ordinary society, which strikes him immediately as artificial, hypocritical and vain. Society, he feels, is more interested in symbols of status than in true worth. If he is not cast out from society for being different, he has three options: retreat (e.g., René's self-imposed exile into the wilderness), open rebellion (e.g., Dumas's Antony) or concealed rebellion in the interests of both self-realization and self-preservation (e.g., Julien Sorel).

As everyone knows, the romantic hero, like his famous progenitor, Werther, is a melancholy hero. His reaction to ordinary life is either disgust, ennui or both. His estimate of his fellow man is low. His prospects for the future seem dim. The ensuing *taedium vitae* leads almost always to the famous "romantic" or Wertherian death wish, which represents for people like René, Lamartine and Nerval not only a rejection of this life but a mystic quest for another, "truer" life. For others, like Obermann, Nodier's Charles Munster (in *Le Peintre de Salzburg*, 1803, a pallid imitation of *Werther*) and Vigny's Moses, death is not the entrance into some Platonic or religious paradise but simply a surcease from turmoil. For still others (e.g., Antony and René of *Les Natchez*) a truly "romantic" (here, in the sense of extreme) passion is so beyond the ordinary that only death can consummate it.

Actually, there are at least four different forms of romantic melancholy, and I should like to urge at once that the following terms not be used interchangeably since they represent four rather distinct states of mind: (1) *le mal de René;* (2) *le vague des passions;* (3) *le mal du siècle;* (4) *Weltschmerz.*

(1) *Le mal de René.* First, let's go to the source:

> La solitude absolue, le spectacle de la nature, me plongèrent bientôt dans un état presque impossible à décrire. Sans parents, sans amis, pour ainsi dire seul sur la terre, n'ayant point encore aimé, j'étais accablé d'une surabondance de vie. Quelquefois je rougissais subitement, et je sentais couler dans mon coeur comme des ruisseaux d'une lave ardente; quelquefois je poussais des cris involontaires, et la nuit était également troublée de mes songes et de mes veilles. Il me manquait quelque chose pour remplir l'abîme de mon existence. . . .
>
> Toutefois cet état de calme et de trouble, d'indigence et de richesse, n'était pas sans quelques charmes.

This is not pure melancholy but ambivalence; there is an important admixture of expectancy and even exuberance. What we really have here is adolescent anguish concerning one's identity and one's future. Our young hero seeks a precise object for his burning passions (or, more precisely, his libidinal impulses) and for his unspent energy. He needs a role to play in life, and even more urgently right now, a woman to love. He wants to realize his great potential. Will his life—will *he*—be worthy of his gifts? Will life satisfy these intense (but basically normal) longings? "Does what I love really exist?" he wonders. This state of mind is not only one of intense anxiety but of guarded, cautious *hope*. There is no feeling yet that these aspirations

are impossible of attainment. There is no ennui here, no *taedium vitae,* no lassitude.

(2) *Le vague des passions.* Again, let us go back to the source, which is not the above passage but the *Génie du christianisme* proper.

> Il reste à parler d'un état de l'âme qui, ce nous semble, n'a pas encore été bien observé: c'est celui qui précède le développment des passions, lorsque toutes les facultés jeunes, actives, entières, mais renfermées, ne se sont exercées que sur elles-mêmes, sans but et sans objet. Plus les peuples avancent en civilisation, plus cet état du vague des passions augmente; car il arrive alors une chose fort triste: le grand nombre d'exemples qu'on a sous les yeux, la multitude de livres qui traitent de l'homme et de ses sentiments, rendent habile sans expérience. On est détrompé sans avoir joui; il reste encore des désirs, et l'on n'a plus d'illusions. L'imagination est riche, abondante et merveilleuse, l'existence pauvre, sèche et désenchantée. On habite, avec un coeur plein, un monde vide, et sans avoir usé de rien, on est désabusé de tout.

Here the victim is a bit older. He is not much more experienced in life but has read and reflected more. His books (in *René* his travels) have shown him most of life's typical experiences and sentiments; he becomes jaded and blasé through vicarious satiety; he concludes that there is no reasonable hope for happiness. "Spleen" sets in and he becomes bitter ("L'amertume que cet état de l'âme répand sur la vie est incroyable.") This surely is a new note. The *mal de René* passage speaks of *richness* and of a *surabondance de vie;* this one speaks of *une existence pauvre* and of a *monde vide.* The first passage is one of both anxious and eager expectancy; the second of disillusionment. The world, it is now concluded, will not live up to one's rich, romantic imagination. (In the interests of his general argument Chateaubriand adds that this feeling is encouraged by the *contemptus mundi of Christianity.)*

René will experience this phase too, but *later*. The time lapse is rapid (among other things, the romantic hero is precocious), but there *is* a time lapse and there is a *new* state of mind. The indications of time lapse between the two states are fleeting and vague and have gone unnoticed.

> Cette vie qui m'avait *d'abord* enchanté [!], ne *tarda pas* à me devenir insupportable.
>
> Je luttais *quelque temps* contre mon mal . . . *Enfin,* ne pouvant trouver de remède à cette étrange blessure de mon coeur. . . .

Finding no remedy, he passes into another state, more morbid than "normal".

(3) *Le mal du siècle.* As this term suggests, or ought to, we are dealing with a more precise form of melancholy. It is linked with history and not just adolescent psychology (which is still present, however). It derives in part from that legacy of skepticism concerning all traditional values bequeathed by the Enlightenment and in part from the confusion of values brought on by political instability, social anarchy and the acceleration of history ("Les événements couraient plus vite que ma plume," writes Chateau-

briand in his memoirs). During the very brief period between 1789 and 1815 France experienced absolute monarchy, revolution, a Directorate, a Consulate, an Empire and a restored but constitutionalized or "characterized" monarchy criticized by the *ultras* as being too liberal—from extreme absolutism to extreme revolution to extreme reaction. Political and religious opinions were so diverse that France was becoming, nay, had already become a centrifugal civilization. By 1820 young men did not know where to turn for faith, hope or ideals. The glorious Emperor was gone and was already the victim of revisionism. The Restoration offered its youth no lofty goals and produced no inspiring leaders.

Henri Peyre [in *What is Romanticism?*, 1977] thinks that the *mal du siècle* was radically new only by virtue of its ruthless self-analysis and in purely quantitative terms: the fact that it reached epidemic proportions. But it was radically new in qualitative terms as well. It was not just an expression of the insecurities of adolescence, it was a new sensitivity to History. Before the Revolution, the Terror, the Empire and the Fall, artists did not react so violently to contemporary history. From the reign of Louis XIV to the early years of Louis XVI the political régime and the social order seemed stable if imperfect. But the Terror, to take just the greatest trauma, not only weakened belief in divine Providence, it destroyed the Enlightenment's law of irreversible secular progress. When writers after 1815 spoke of the "void," they were not simply speaking of a vague discontent but of a vacuum that was specifically political, religious and social. The fact of Terror showed many that History was being written not by God, as Ballanche and Lamennais still endeavored to believe, but by the shaky hands of men. The guillotine, says Manuel de Dieguez [in *Chateaubriand ou le poète face à l'histoire,* 1963], seemed to function solely by men's will and not by God's long-range plans for humanity.

The best description of the *mal du siècle* is not in *René,* where it is tactfully and tactically kept hidden (there are, for instance, no specific references to the Revolution or to emigration, only hints, "displacements") but in Quinet's *Histoire de mes idées* and Musset's *Confession d'un enfant du siècle.* Quinet himself makes a distinction between the *mal* of his generation and the earlier generation's *vague des passions.*

> Je ne voyais autour de moi ni un guide auquel je pusse me fier, ni même un compagnon dans la route où je tremblais et brûlais à la fois de m'engager. J'avais le presentiment qu'il s'agissait d'un renouvellement presque entier des choses de l'esprit . . . Quoique cette souffrance allât souvent jusqu'au désespoir, il n'y avait là pourtant rien qui ressemblât au spleen, à l'ennui de la vie, à tout ce que l'on a appelé le vague des passions, vers la fin du dernier siècle. C'était, il me semble, à bien des égards, le contraire de la lassitude et de la satiété. C'était plutôt une aveugle impatience de vivre, une attente fiévreuse, une ambition prématurée d'avenir, une soif effrénée de l'âme après le désert de l'Empire. Tout cela joint à un désir consumant de produire, ce créer, de cela joint à un désir consumant de produire, ce créer, de faire quelque

chose, au milieu d'un monde vide encore. Ceux que j'ai interrogés plus tard sur ces années m'ont dit avoir éprouvé quelque chose de pareil. Chacun se croyait seul comme moi: chacun pensait, rêvait comme dans une île déserte.

The important differences are two in number: although *le mal du siècle* can and usually does include the late-adolescent "impatience de vivre" of *le mal de René* and the *vague des passions,* it contains none (or *need* not contain any) of the latter's lassitude, spleen or ennui, and more importantly, it is explicitly informed by a sense of history: a healthy if anxious ambition (Balzac called it *impatience d'avenir*) is struggling among "the ruins of the Empire." The young man's whole life is ahead of him, but where is it leading? The old régimes are dead; a new order is certainly in the making, but as yet it has taken no definite shape nor even a specific direction. One is adrift in History without a guide. There is no consecrated authority. One feels utterly alone. Quinet sums it up well: "un désir consumant de produire, de créer, de faire quelque chose, au milieu d'un monde vide encore."

Quinet takes up this image of the void in another significant passage:

> Les grandes invasions de 1814 et de 1815 avaient laissé un fond d'impressions, d'images, à travers lesquelles j'entrevoyais toutes choses. L'écroulement d'un monde avait été ma première éducation. De quelque côté que je voulusse tourner mes yeux, je trouvais à l'horizon un grand vide; je sentais ce vide dans la poésie, dans l'histoire, dans la philosophie, dans toute chose; j'en souffrais parce que j'étais incapable de le combler, et je ne savais pas que d'autres esprits souffraient de même mal.

Quinet adds that at the root of his *mal* was not just his tender age nor his peculiar psychological makeup but the precise historical situation of France. The similarity between Quinet's *mal* and René's is the mixture of energy, expectation and hope with a very deep anxiety about an uncertain future. The major difference is the historization, or what Pierre Barbéris [in *Balzac et le mal du siècle,* 1974] calls "the politization of the *mal du siècle*"—a difference that separates, according to Barbéris, pre-romanticism from romanticism proper. I should like to modify Barbéris's formula by proposing that the *mal du siècle* is a historization of the *vague des passions* that is, it involves, by definition, not only one's self-assessment but also, and even more, an assessment of History.

Alfred de Musset's assessment of History is more pointedly negative and his particular *mal* is more poignantly disillusioned. "Toute la maladie du siècle présent vient de deux causes: le peuple qui a passé par '93 et par 1814 porte au coeur deux blessures. Tout ce qui était n'était plus; tout ce qui sera n'est pas encore. Ne cherchez pas ailleurs le secret de nos maux." The romantic sense of alienation is here a *historical* awareness. Seventeen ninety-three was the year the Revolution aborted or at least turned sour; it was the year the Revolution failed to keep its promises: Freedom became Tyranny; Fraternity turned into Terror; Equality existed but it was now obvious that some were more equal than others. Eighteen fourteen was the end of another dream; an era of excitement and glory was followed by an era of ennui, of reaction and revisionism; a mercantile-industrial society was founding a new order and a new moral code built upon Money.

(4) *Weltschmerz.* This has been defined [by Peter L. Thorslev, in *The Byronic Hero,* 1962] in terms of two contradictory drives within the romantic hero: "one toward egoistic and skeptical self-assertion, a passionate holding fast to the feeling of self as a separate and individual identity; the other an equally passionate longing for commitment to absolutes outside the self." I would define it rather as a nihilistic denial of absolutes, a premonition of the Absurd. It is more than personal sorrow, and it is more than metaphysical anguish; it is cosmic despair. The hero has come to a philosophical conclusion: This world is essentially evil and the "other world" is either unknowable, unattainable or non-existent.

René Jasinski [in *Histoire de la littérature française,* 1947] has distinguished three generations of the *mal du siècle*: that of René, that of Musset, and that of Gautier, Flaubert and Baudelaire. A more useful distinction, however, is the one I am trying to make here, a distinction between four or five distinct "maladies." The first can be characterized, briefly, as *impatience et inquiétude du désir* (René); the second heavily stresses the *inquiétude* (René again, but later); the third is *impatience et inquiétude d'avenir* (Quinet); the fourth heavily stresses the *inquiétude* (Musset); the fifth is *avenir bloqué* (Flaubert).

The trouble with "generations" is (1) they tend to overlap and (2) they are not monopolized by a single malady. Vigny, while more contemporary to Musset and Quinet than to Chateaubriand, harks back to the latter's aristocratic, "passéiste" melancholy, that of a nobleman ostracized by a revolution. Senancour, while more contemporary to Chateaubriand, exhibits a *Weltschmerz* more typical of later generations, of Flaubert's—and ours.

It is tempting, but it would be impractical to assemble here all the definitions and descriptions of romantic melancholy from all the many histories of romanticism in order to show that these four terms have been taken by and large as synonymous. For the moment, let two examples suffice:

> It is significant that the *mal de René* is synonymous with the *mal du siècle,* for no other hero epitomized the romantic type so well as René. [Ridge, *The Hero in French Romantic Literature,* 1959]

> [In *René,* Chateaubriand] presented the first authentic portrayal of that new state of spiritual frustration and moral isolation which is called *le mal du siècle.* Yearning for a vague but indefinite ideal impossible of attainment, obsessed by haunting dreams of a bliss that can neither be found nor formulated, the victim of this malady suffers from langour and paralysis of the will, broods self-indulgently on his melancholy and anguish of soul, and, fleeing from the bitter realities of life which he is unable to face, sinks into thoughts of death and suicide. [Ramon Guthrie and George E. Diller, *French Literature and Thought since the Revolution,* 1942]

One problem here is that several different states of mind are presented as equivalent or as existing simultaneously. In the case of René, this is simply not true. . . . In the case of other romantic heroes, only one or two states may be applicable. Another problem is that the *mal du siècle* is being divorced from History and thus deprived of its main ingredient.

Another recurrent feature I have found in the romantic hero is that although very young he is "old before his time." The *puer senex* topos, as has been shown by Ernst Robert Curtius [in *European Literature and the Latin Middle Ages,* 1953], is as old as Latin antiquity. Says Curtius: "All early and high periods of a culture extol the young and at the same time honor age. But only late periods develop a human ideal in which the polarity youth-age works toward a balance." Thus Virgil praises the virile mind that is found in Iulus' youthful body:

> Ante annos animumque gerens curamque virelem.
> (Having manhood's spirit and forethought before man's years)

And Ovid will extol such a combination of youth and maturity as a heaven-sent gift granted to emperors and demigods. Similarly, the ancient Armenian poets frequently used the following formula to laud their young hero:

> Other children grow by years,
> But David grew by days.

The topos becomes a cliché of hagiographic literature and survives into the Latin Middle Ages and beyond. Curtius has traced it, in both sacred and secular texts the world over, up to (i.e., as late as) the seventeenth and eighteenth centuries. He believes that the topos is explained less by delight in antithesis or oxymoron than as the expression of a human ideal and that its persistence over such a long period of time and over such a large area of the world is evidence of the presence of an archetypal image, an expression of the collective unconscious.

What is significant for our purposes is the radical change the topos undergoes in romantic literature. The romantic hero describes himself as a *puer senex* ("jeune et pourtant vieux"; "un vieillard né d'hier," etc.), but the stress is on the negative implications: "J'ai le malheur de ne pouvoir être jeune," says Obermann. It is cynical old age that we find in our young romantic hero. This old-young romantic is disillusioned with life before fully tasting it; he is jaded and blasé either because he passes through the normal range of human experiences with lightning speed or because his hypersensitivity or heightened imaginativeness rejects in advance the homely pleasures of terrestrial life. He is "old" too because his future is blocked by his fate.

So, rather than a sense of classical "balance" that the topos seems to work toward in late periods of a culture, we have a sense of imbalance, of a world out of joint. The negative connotations will become exacerbated in the decadent hero of the end of the century who finds himself in a culture that is not just late but overripe and decaying. The topos will continue in even more radicalized form with some of the anti-heroes of twentieth century literature. What we may have here is nothing less than a change in Western man's collective unconscious, in any case a radical change in sensibility.

The romantic hero is an enigmatic hero. He has the mysterious birth and orphanhood of many ancient heroes, whom he resembles in a surprisingly large number of ways. Otto Rank, in *The Myth of the Birth of a Hero,* notes that the normal relations of the ancient hero toward his father and mother regularly appear impaired, the hero being, or feeling himself to be, an orphan, a foundling or a step child. The romantic hero has the same feeling; in fact he usually *is* an orphan. Rank sees in the orphan motive a manifestation of an Oedipal hostility toward the Father that makes of the youthful hero a rebel: "The hero himself, as shown by his detachment from his parents, begins his career in opposition to the older generation; he is at once a rebel, a renovator, and a revolutionary. However, every revolutionary is originally a disobedient son, a rebel against the father." (The incest motive, intimately connected with the Oedipal situation, is also frequently found among romantic heroes, but, through displacement perhaps, usually involves a sister rather than a mother.) For the romantic hero, the Father is presented either directly or—through displacement again—indirectly in the form of established authority, organized society or traditional morality. There is also, I am convinced, a metaphysical dimension, the feeling of being abandoned by God (the heavenly Father). This is clear for instance in Vigny's Jesus (*Le Mont des Oliviers*).

The many obstacles that are put in the way of the hero's birth and childhood lend themselves, according to Rank, to both a positive and a negative interpretation. The positive interpretation underscores the youthful hero's triumph over adversity. But it is the negative interpretation that is especially germane to the romantic hero's situation: "Another interpretation may be admitted, according to which the youthful hero, foreseeing his destiny to taste more than his share of the bitterness of life, deplores in pessimistic mood the inimical act which has called him to earth. He accuses his parents, as it were, for having exposed him to the struggle of life, for having allowed him to be born." Rank, by the way, traces the comparison of birth to a shipwreck from Lucretius to Schiller's *Robbers.*

The romantic hero, like Tristan, is born in sorrow, and, like most traditional heroes, is early exposed to envy, bitter jealousy and calumny. In this connection Rank has uncovered what he thinks to be the paranoid structure of the hero-myths: they are equivalent in many essential features to the delusional ideas of certain psychotics, especially delusions of persecution and grandeur. The paranoid is apt to claim that the people whose name he bears are not his real parents, but that he is actually the son of a princely personage. Julien Sorel, we recall, was apt to do the same. Furthermore, the egotistical and passive nature of the typical paranoid is found in many romantic heroes.

I am not urging here a psychoanalytical interpretation of the romantic hero's unconscious motives but am merely suggesting a few leads to those who might want to explore this potentially fruitful topic. I am more interested in our hero's conscious motives and feelings, his sensibility, his

own appraisal of his relation to society, to history and to the future.

The romantic hero does not know whence he comes nor, except for his premonition of disaster, whither he goes. He is an enigmatic, inscrutable "force qui va." His heroic otherness is underscored not only by his mysterious origin and catastrophic end but also by the remote settings to which he is attached or into which he is exiled: the American wilderness for René, the moors and crags of Yorkshire for Heathcliff, the forbidding sea for Melville's Ahab, the uninhabited mountains for Lermontov's Pechorin, Byron's Manfred, Hugo's Hernani. Even Vigny's Christ "knows the rocks better than the smooth paths." When the romantic hero tells his own story in the first person, it is often framed by an authorial, editorial or other narrative point of view underlining the "hermeneutic distance" between the enigmatic hero and his audience. In *Werther* for instance the "Editor" warns the reader that it is difficult to discover the true and innermost motives of men "who are not of the common run."

Although a man of noble impulses, the romantic hero's intense individualism and hypersensitivity often result in morbid or pathological tendencies. His acute awareness of being persecuted or misunderstood borders at times on paranoia; his melancholy often degenerates into involutional melancholia, masochism, or even mere petulance; his egocentrism verges dangerously at times on egomania, narcissism and solipsism. His frequent willingness to be caught in the enemy's trap is another symptom of masochism, while his frequent association of love and death is a sure sign of sadism.

According to Mario Praz, the romantic movement produced a new and perverse sensibility in which pleasure and pain, love and hate, tenderness and cruelty are intimately linked. Praz claims the romantics to be the first in the history of art to see beauty in the grotesque and to delight in the revolting. *The Romantic Agony,* despite the author's protestations to the contrary, tends to reduce romanticism to this perverse sensibility—a savage reduction indeed. But it is undeniable that there is in the romantic hero, alongside his good qualities, a penchant for the perverse.

Unlike ancient and medieval heroes with their highly unified personality, the modern hero tends to be a divided, quasi-schizoid self. As Goethe's Faust laments:

> Two souls abide, alas, within my breast,
> And each one seeks for riddance from the other.
> The one clings with a dogged love and lust
> With clutching parts unto this present world,
> The other surges fiercely from the dust
> Unto sublime ancestral fields.

The dialectical tensions in which the romantic hero is involved do not produce a satisfactory synthesis but at best a tenuous equilibrium which breaks down eventually and leads either to the hero's self-destruction or to a paralysis of the will or heroic resolve. (pp. 2-18)

Lloyd Bishop, "Portrait of a Hero," in his The Romantic Hero and His Heirs in French Literature, *Peter Lang, 1984, pp. 1-28.*

An excerpt from Alphonse de Lamartine's *On the Fortunes of Poetry*

Poetry will be reason set to song, that is its destiny for long to come; it will be philosophical, religious, political, social, like the periods that mankind will go through; above all, it will be intimate, personal, meditative and serious, no longer a play of wit, a melodious caprice of flighty, superficial thought, but the deep, true and sincere echo of the mind's loftiest ideas and the soul's most mysterious impressions. It will be man himself, and no longer his image, man in all his truth. The prefigurations of this transformation of poetry have been apparent for more than a century; they are increasing in our times. Poetry has more and more rid itself of its artificial form, it has almost no other form than its own. As the world has become more spiritual, so too poetry. It no longer wants puppets or contrivances; for the first thing that the reader does is to push aside the puppets and contrivances and to seek only poetry in the poetic work, to seek also the poet's soul within his poetry.

But will it be dead because it is truer, more sincere, more genuine than ever before? Of course not; it will have more life, more intensity, more effectiveness than ever before!

Quoted in European Romanticism: Self-Definition, *edited by Lilian R. Furst, Methuen, 1980.*

John Porter Houston

[*Houston was an American educator and critic who specialized in French literature. In the following excerpt, he discusses Gothic melodrama as an influence on Romanticism and studies the exoticism, violence, and sensuality that characterize French Romanticism.*]

The first definition made in France of the adjective *romantique* was an iconological one. Letourneur, the translator of Shakespeare, tried to explain it by evoking English gardens, the Alps, and the paintings of Salvator Rosa, the latter being a curious sort of link between baroque and early romantic taste. The relatively new adjective *pittoresque* was associated with the *romantique* from the very beginning, and it will be useful to recall some of the late eighteenth century's favorite poetical images. Autumnal landscapes, such as we have seen in the verse of Delille, were popular, as well as suggestions of sunset and night. More interesting perhaps, for our purposes, is the fondness for funeral objects: tombs, cenotaphs, mausoleums, urns, and weeping willows. Monasteries, hermitages and their inhabitants belong also to this strain of taste, for monks and nuns were coming, even in Catholic France, to be conceived of as being totally absorbed in thoughts of death—if not of something worse. Ruins, obvious symbols of death and decay, complete the picture, and melancholy is the dominant mood. The sources for these scenes would seem evidently to be English literature—Young's *Night Thoughts* come to mind—but it is easier to observe this phenomenon than to assign precise origins to it.

Well before Hugo and Sainte-Beuve made their first decla-rations about poetic style in the late 1820's, the French were already beginning to speak of a *genre romantique* which they identified by certain kinds of subject matter, that, while not necessarily new, were not found in the pure stream of neoclassicism. Hugo's first poems in the *genre romantique* will provide a good example. They were published in the fourth and fifth books of *Odes* and retain some of the manner of the more conventional odes while being quite distinct:

> Soeur du hibou funèbre et de l'orfraie avide,
> Mêlant le houx lugubre au nénuphar livide,
> Les filles de Satan t'invoquent sans remords;
> Fuis l'abri qui me cache et l'air que je respire;
> De ton ongle hideux ne touche pas ma lyre,
> De peur de réveiller des morts!
>
> ("La Chauve-souris")

The poet is addressing a bat. He does not appear really to have much to say to the creature, but obviously takes some pleasure in imagining its sinister habits and attributes:

> Sors-tu de quelque tour qu'habite le vertige,
> Nain bizarre et cruel, qui sur les monts voltige,
> Prête aux feux du marais leur errante rougeur,
> Rit dans l'air, des grands pins courbe en criant
>   les cimes,
> Et chaque soir, rôdant sur le bord des abîmes,
> Jette aux vautours du gouffre un pâle voyageur?

It becomes clear that these descriptive details do not support a theme, nor do they have any pattern of development or contrast among themselves. They are there, each for its own sake, to create a certain mood just like the subject matter of a painting. The bat, the owl, the tower, the dwarf, the vultures, the abyss, and the pale face will recur in the work of Hugo and other poets, creating a tone of malaise and fear for which no explanation is given. They are part of the iconography of French romanticism whose function and character can bear some comparison with that of the contemporary plastic arts.

Until recently, romantic painting as a whole has not received the critical attention and public interest accorded to other periods in the history of art. European painting on the eve of modernism has certain characteristics which have made it uncongenial to eyes disciplined by Cézanne, cubism, and the other forms of abstraction current in our century. To begin with, its subject matter seems far more obtrusive than that of earlier periods of art; in romantic painting the subject is determined through its strangeness to draw attention to itself to a degree we do not feel in the more conventionalized work of the renaissance and baroque. The most obvious example that comes to mind is Delacroix, whose subjects seem to vie for our attention with his technical brilliance. In the "Exposition universelle de 1855," Baudelaire even went so far as to say of him, "Another very great, very profound quality of M. Delacroix's talent, one which makes him the favorite painter of poets, is the fact that he is essentially literary." Other romantic artists remain peculiarly associated in our minds with the novelty of their subjects: Goya and his grotesque or sinister figures, Géricault and his madmen, Caspar David Friedrich and his disturbing landscapes, Fuseli and his nightmares. The scornful critic will claim that romantic painting is literary, unpainterly. And conversely much of French romantic poetry can be called pictorial. Like Hugo's "Chauve-souris" it tends to evoke objects for their own sake; it indulges in complacent descriptiveness.

The curious fact is that perhaps at no other period or place have painters and poets shared so similar an iconology as in romantic France. The high periods of painting have often occurred in times and places whose literary activity was mediocre. In the nineteenth century, however, Parisian poets and artists frequented one another, exchanged ideas, and on occasion tried their hand at another art form. Hugo's drawings are well known. The supreme example, of course, of the double artist is to be found in contemporary England: William Blake attempted a union of the arts which others were incapable of. Book illustration, whether practices with Blake's imagination or more pedestrianly, is a typical nineteenth-century art form, showing the seriousness with which artists treated the verbal image.

The iconography which dominates French romantic verse and European romantic painting is characterized by violence, exoticism, and the sinister. Nightmares, wild animals, ominous birds, threatening landscapes, executions, sensual scenes in Mediterranean lands, and presages of death are favorite motifs. It would be an idle quibble to ascribe the frequency of such images to the *Geist,* dear to Germanic thought, or to an elaborate concatenation of influences. To explain the presence of such material in French verse, however, we should recall two minor literary genres of the early nineteenth century which, because of their popular, even vulgar character, have not perhaps received due recognition for their impact on romantic sensibility. These are the Gothic novel and the commercial theater.

The Gothic novel must have been one of the wonders of the age when the first translations of Anne Radcliffe and Monk Lewis appeared in France. The tradition of literary decorum and urbanity had already been nicked and chipped by certain writers of the revolutionary period, but the wild imagination of the English Gothic novelists is completely irreconcilable with the whole French neoclassical concept of letters. Nor does the palpable sensationalism of the *roman noir* seem to have disgusted serious, elevated writers: Hugo's "Chauve-souris" quoted earlier has an epigraph taken from Mathurin's *Bertram.* To evaluate the novelty and surprise of the Gothic novel, let us summarize certain lurid aspects of *The Monk,* which is perhaps the most utterly Gothic of its genre: the action takes place in a strange country (Spain) where lust and superstition seem to motivate everything; among the characters are monks and nuns torn between God and Satan; the solution to most problems in the novel is violent death, and, finally, the setting is a dangerous labyrinth of chambers, staircases, hidden courtyards, and subterranean vaults. Monk Lewis had created what amounted to a new vision of evil.

The other minor genres which had a surprisingly large influence on French literary sensibility were theatrical ones: the *mélodrame,* the *féerie,* and similar forms of what has been called the *théâtre du merveilleux.* The role of these sub-literary plays in forming taste often tends to be ob-

scured; literary historians like to make far too much of the originality of Hugo's *drame romantique* in order to establish facile antitheses between it and "classical" plays. The truth is less clear cut. In the early nineteenth century, Parisian theater life was divided between the Comédie française, which specialized in verse plays along traditional lines, and the great theaters on the boulevard du Temple, the Gaîté, the Ambigu, and the Porte-Saint-Martin, which welcomed "irregular" plays and novelties of any sort. Guilbert de Pixerécourt was their greatest author, and his success was international. The dominant genre was the *mélodrame,* a sensational play with incidental music. The source of the plot was sometimes a *roman noir,* and, in any case, the two genres are intimately related by their subject matter. The titles of a few of Pixerécourt's plays will adequately suggest their similarity to Gothic fiction: *Les Maures d'Espagne, Coelina ou l'enfant de mystère, L'Ange tutélaire ou le démon femelle, La Tête de Mort.* We might add *Marguerite d'Anjou* to show how Hugo had been anticipated in historical subjects. The melodrama, like the Gothic novel, represents an important development in sensibility: both are concerned with evil but see it, not in the traditional theological context, but in a purely secular fashion. The consequences are far-reaching. Violence and bloodshed no longer belong to a larger scheme of things; they are sensational in the most literal meaning of the adjective: sheer unreasoned emotion is their product. Satan, too, is secularized: the villain emerges as the active agent in these dark matters. The villain is the incarnation of absolute evil, like the devil in Christian thought, but he is all the more sinister for acting gratuitously. The melodrama ceased to believe in the old Christian view of the world and did not yet have any psychological theories to account for evil.

The French romantics' conception of life is often melodramatic in just the way we have been describing. Sinister images like Hugo's arsenal of bats, owls, and demons obtrude for no evident reason. Teratology, the study of monstrosities and abnormalities, is essential. Certain words begin to occur incessantly in French verse and critical writings after 1820: *frénétique, fantastique, grotesque, macabre. Ange* and *démon* lose their traditional meanings and become terms which the characters in Hugo's plays constantly apply to one another. The old paradox about the "realism" of French romanticism can be readily explained by the tremendously varied ways which Hugo and his contemporaries found to express unpleasant feelings. We must have recourse to the idea of an iconology, an iconology of evil, in order to account for the shape and detail of much of the poetry of the 1820's and 1830's.

We have seen Hugo, in "La Chauve-souris," handling a quite unexpected subject in a somewhat overripe neoclassical style. The subject is unexpected because of the traditional character of most of his odes, but it should not surprise us if we recall that his first prose works, *Han d'Islande* and *Bug-Jargal,* are examples of the *frénétique* manner. From Lamartine's pastiches of Chateaubriand to the reading of *Salammbô* which resulted in Mallarmé's "Hérodiade," nineteenth-century French literary history is filled with examples of prose, always freer, anticipating and nourishing verse. Hugo never had a neoclassical prose style parallel to the manner of his odes; from the start he was committed to the fantastic-realist genre. In verse, however, the *Ballades* and *Orientales* constitute his first lengthy use of the *genre romantique,* and their subject matter will help us elucidate the character of much romantic writing.

The title *Orientales* does not seem really to fit the collection, at least if we take the term—a neologism—to mean poems treating the Near East. At the same time, however, the mood of the book is sustained; we do not feel any discrepancy between the poems about the Greeks and Turks and those about Napoleon or Spain. The reasons for this are complex and involve the whole function of exoticism for the French romantics as well as Hugo's conception of Napoleon. To begin with, the Ottoman Empire is, for Hugo, like Spain, like the Rhineland later, like Italy for some other poets, not a concrete place in historical reality but a fantasy world where actions of a lurid nature can take place. And what are these actions? They are violent or erotic outbursts; they are selfish and libidinous; in short, they are the actions appropriate to a demonic world. Hugo's Turks are not only non-Christian; their love of destruction identifies them as villains or secularized demons. Their harems are a dark paradise.

Spain, though clearly less sinister, has something of the same meaning in Hugo's symbolism. In poems like "La Légende de la nonne," in the *Ballades,* or in the plays *Hernani* and *Ruy Blas,* Spain is a country where lives are under the sway of a somber destiny. For fate is the term Hugo found to summarize his visions of the demonic. It is the key notion of his plays as well as of *Notre-Dame de Paris,* where *ananké* is inscribed on the cathedral. The Middle Ages belong also to the dark realms: the picturesque medieval vignettes of earlier writers undergo a change in high French romanticism. Finally, the figure of Napoleon remained for Hugo, throughout his career, charged with ambivalent grandeur. "Tu domines notre âge; ange ou démon, qu'importe?" he says in the fortieth *Orientale,* and this ambiguous attitude persists in "L'Expiation" and *Les Misérables.*

The unity of *Les Orientales,* and, I suggest, the unity of French romantic poetry lie in the pervasiveness of demonic symbols and themes. These can have varying degrees of intensity. In the *Ballades,* Hugo's first collection marked by a sinister strain, the devils and hobgoblins are presented as quaint, picturesque folklore. The closing of "Les Deux Archers" is characteristic; the poem has told of two archers who have desecrated a sanctuary and have been destroyed by Satan:

> Si quelque enseignement se cache en cette his-
>   toire,
> Qu'importe! il ne faut pas la juger, mais la croire.
> La croire! Qu'ai-je dit? ces temps sont loin de
>   nous!
> Ce n'est plus qu'à demi qu'on se livre aux croy-
>   ances.
> Nul, dans notre âge aveugle et vain de ses sci-
>   ences,
> Ne sait plier les deux genoux!

The ambivalence and uneasiness of the conclusion are

quite typical of Hugo's work before the exile: he was fascinated by the demonic and could not justify this obsession to himself. Other romantic writers tried ironic approaches to the demonic. The Byronic verse tale, which Musset put into fashion with his *Contes d'Espagne et d'Italie,* is an attempt to handle lurid material—any romantic tale taking place in Spain or Italy is bound to have eroticism and violent death in it—with a superficial glaze of sophistication. Other treatments too are possible, and we shall now consider the contributions made to the demonic iconology by Sainte-Beuve, Gautier, Petrus Borel, and Philothée O'Neddy.

The importance of Sainte-Beuve's poetry has often been mentioned but seldom with much explanation. His influence on Gautier, on Baudelaire, and perhaps even on Verlaine is certain, but this influence was of a very special sort. Much of Sainte-Beuve's verse, especially in his first and most famous collection, *La Vie, Poésies et Pensées de Joseph Delorme,* is conventional elegy, whose neoclassical style is only occasionally relieved by oddities of syntax and vocabulary. A contemporary cartoonist had great fun with the following lines, although the curious image is nothing but Racinian metonymy:

> Pour trois ans seulement, oh! que je puisse avoir
> Sur ma table un lait pur, dans mon lit un oeil
>   noir . . .
>
>   ("Voeu")

In a few poems, however, Sainte-Beuve, spurred perhaps by a sense of rivalry with Hugo, succeeded in creating a very distinctive tone of his own, which, while he never exploited it fully, was to suggest further possibilities to Gautier and Baudelaire. The feeling which Sainte-Beuve was trying to express is somewhat different from traditional elegiac sentiment: it is not so much a sense of loss as one of spleen and emptiness, and in certain poems Sainte-Beuve worked out a quite new and personal set of "objective correlatives" to render it. Images of city life, of the dingy, sordid quarters on the fringes of Paris translate his feeling of universal disgust. Here, for example, is the conclusion of "Les Rayons jaunes," a poem in which the speaker has thought of various deaths:

> —Ainsi va ma pensée, et la nuit est venue;
> Je descends, et bientôt dans la foule inconnue
> J'ai noyé mon chagrin:
> Plus d'un bras me coudoie; on entre à la guingu-
>   ette,
> On sort du cabaret; l'invalide en goguette
> Chevrote un gai refrain.
>
> Ce ne sont que chansons, clameurs, rixes
>   d'ivrogne,
> Ou qu'amours en plein air, et baisers sans ver-
>   gogne,
> Et publiques faveurs;
> Je rentre: sur ma route on se presse, on se rue;
> Toute la nuit j'entends se traîner dans ma rue
> Et hurler les buveurs.

After an unctuous poetic meditation on tapers burning yellow in church and yellow winding sheets, these images of proletarian conviviality (expressed in harsh rhythms and cacophonic juxtapositions of sounds) add a grotesque complement to the speaker's melancholy: his sorrow is complacent, solitary, and spiritual, while the popular crowd is bestially good humored. Each reflects unpleasantly on the other, and the city which brings them together seems to soil both.

A poem of Sainte-Beuve's which Baudelaire particularly admired was "La Veillée" written for the birth of Hugo's son François-Victor.

After a conventional description of the parents' watching over the newborn child, he continues:

> —Moi, pendant ce temps-là, je veille aussi, je veille,
> Non près des rideaux bleus de l'enfance vermeille,
> Prés du lit nuptial arrosé de parfum,
> Mais près d'un froid grabat, sur le corps d'un défunt.
> C'est un voisin, vieillard goutteux, mort de la pierre . . .

The Hugolian diction of the first lines yields quite abruptly to a very low level of style exemplified by the mention of kidney stones. This fondness for ugly commonplace material has often been ascribed to Sainte-Beuve's acquaintance with the English lake poets, but no one familiar with Wordsworth is likely to take this hypothesis too seriously. The seventeenth-century satirist Régnier, whose influence in the romantic period we shall come back to, has been proposed as a more likely model. In any case, Sainte-Beuve was clearly determined to exploit subjects which were not only low but also somewhat repulsive in their realistic immediacy. "Moi, j'aime entre deux beaux yeux un sourire un peu louche . . . ," he exclaims in what is also probably an imitation of a baroque model.

As a final example of Sainte-Beuve's imagination, we can isolate in the following "sonnet imitated from Wordsworth" the distinctive note which is his own:

> Je ne suis pas de ceux pour qui les causeries,
> Au coin du feu, l'hiver, ont de grandes douceurs;
> Car j'ai pour tous voisins d'intrépides chasseurs,
> Rêvant de chiens dressés, de meutes aguerries,
>
> Et des fermiers causant jachères et prairies,
> Et le juge de paix avec ses vieilles soeurs,
> Deux revêches beautés parlant de ravisseurs,
> Portraits comme on en voit sur les tapisseries.
>
> Oh! combien je préfère à ce caquet si vain,
> Tout le soir, du silence,—un silence sans fin;
> Etre assis sans penser, sans désir, sans mémoire;
> Et, seul, sur mes chenets, m'éclairant aux tisons,
> Ecouter le vent battre, et gémir les cloisons,
> Et le fagot flamber, et chanter ma bouilloire!

The sonnet of Wordsworth's in question is the first of the series "Personal Talk," which is by no means an encomium of utter silence; a conversation with the poet's sister takes place, in which he compares the delights of reading to the monotony of gossip. As for the details of idle chatter:

> These all wear out of me, like Forms, with chalk
> Painted on rich men's floors, for one feast-night.

We can see how little Sainte-Beuve's imitation really has to do with Wordsworth's sonnet. In the latter the poet's solitude is rich and productive; the scene is intimate rather than bleak. The winter night and pounding wind are Sainte-Beuve's inventions. In his poem the speaker lives in the midst of a distasteful society of brutes and sex-crazed old maids; he longs for insentience—for one infers that memory and desire are his greatest torments. Monotonous, lulling sensation provides an escape from himself, an hypnotic release from inner and outer realities. Though the conclusion of Wordsworth's poem also evokes the sensations of the hearth, Sainte-Beuve makes the final images far more intense by their contrast with the quatrains.

If, through Sainte-Beuve, Wordsworth had any influence on French verse, I think we must conclude that it was in the revival of the sonnet. Sainte-Beuve knew Ronsard's work, but the example of a contemporary English poet exploiting this form may have been decisive. The abundance of sonnets in *Joseph Delorme* inspired three younger poets, Gautier, Nerval, and Musset, but the suitability of the sonnet for intimate reflective poetry was not generally realized until later in the century. Baudelaire points the way, and many of the next generation of poets—Verlaine, Mallarmé, Rimbaud, Corbière, Hérédia—worked with variations on the traditional sonnet forms.

Although the poems of *Joseph Delorme* cannot, in any strict sense, be called demonic or even sinister, they did contribute to French verse a new mood and iconolgoy, which were to merge with darker themes. The feeling of ennui, weariness with the self, and moral indifference, was to obtrude more and more in younger poets, while the imagery of ugly, commonplace urban objects and scenes became an invaluable means of conveying alienation and malaise. There is also in Sainte-Beuve an important strain of decadent religiosity, concerned more with incense and guilt than with redemption or good works. If Sainte-Beuve is only a quite minor poet, still in those few pieces in which he strove after a new manner of verse there occur passages that anticipate French poetry for many decades.

Théophile Gautier's poetry has had, in our century, the curious fate of being seriously mentioned more often in English-speaking countries than in France: the imitations of *Emaux et Camées* that Pound and Eliot made around 1920 have assured him of that even slight renown which he does not enjoy in his own country. And yet his greater contemporaries considered him a poet of some importance. *Les Fleurs du mal* are dedicated to Gautier, and his death elicited superb poems by both Hugo and Mallarmé. As a prose writer, he was one of the most brilliant stylists of his day and greatly expanded the literary vocabulary. His novel *Mademoiselle de Maupin,* a mock confession-novel, is the most elegant blend of parody and seriousness in French romantic prose. In short, the neglect into which Gautier has fallen seems to me more the result of academic obtuseness than of any failing of his splendid if minor gifts. Gautier's poetic production was not immense, yet still, as in the case of many lesser writers, we must discount much of it if we are to get to the truly seminal part of his work. Our concern here is with Gautier's poems of the 1830's. The better known *Emaux et Camées* (1852)—

which Baudelaire evidently cared less for—belong to another area of verbal experiment than the high romantic.

Gautier was part of the second generation of romantic poets, along with Musset and Nerval, men of the 1830's rather than of the Restoration. Their careers followed a somewhat different pattern from those of Lamartine, Sainte-Beuve, Hugo, and Vigny: from the very beginning the *genre romantique* constituted the whole scope of contemporary poetry for them. No hesitation between a traditional, neoclassical style and a modernist one occurred in their first published works; Hugo, Sainte-Beuve, and Byron had, in certain poems, set a definitive example to follow. However, the younger poets were not mere imitators. A number of circumstances imposed on them a rather new conception of the role of poetry and of the poet in society, which is not without some relation to their style and subject matter. To begin with, official honors played little part in their careers: the contemporary public tended to ignore them, at least as poets, and they were among the first writers to evolve that ironic attitude toward society which characterizes much of nineteenth-century French literature. Skepticism seemed the only possible way for them to look at politics, democracy, and nationalism. Gautier and Nerval belonged, furthermore, to the original Bohemia, an independent colony of artists, poets, actors, journalists, and others whose callings were repugnant to bourgeois values. The character of the French public was such as to inspire in these poets a radically modernist attitude to-

A portrait of Chateaubriand by Girodet-Trioson (1809).

ward literature, and this is what Gautier elaborated in his writings on *l'art pour l'art.*

Art for art's sake is a commonly misinterpreted slogan. Even people associated with it, such as Baudelaire, loathed the expression. To try to determine what complex of ideas it represented for Gautier, we must reflect somewhat on polemics over poetry at the time when Gautier began to write. The major young poet of the day was Victor Hugo, and in the prefaces to *Les Orientales* and *Les Feuilles d'automne* he had spoken of "pure poetry" and "a pure work of art." These expressions seem to indicate both exotic subjects and poems which have no reference to public events, for Hugo makes some matter over the propriety of publishing non-political verse in the wake of a revolution. The whole discussion over *l'art pour l'art,* which Gautier fed with his prefaces to *Albertus* and *Mademoiselle de Maupin,* seems to center around Hugo, local color, and the freedom of the imagination. It is directed against the neoclassical conception of the poet as a composer of odes on public questions. As an affirmation of the autonomy of art, the theory of *l'art pour l'art* is an essential hypothesis of modern esthetics, but it acquired several corollaries in the course of the nineteenth century which are of less value. Opposition to both industrialism and movements of social reform came to color what at first had been merely a reaction to neoclassicism. Finally, immoralism was associated with *l'art pour l'art.* What the phrase most generally and essentially meant, however, can be summed up as follows: the artist and public have no mutual obligations. In theory at least, the way was prepared for the unprecedented and interlocking series of poetic experiments which form the history of French verse from the 1830's to the end of the century.

In accordance with the theory of *l'art pour l'art,* Gautier's poems display right from the beginning a descriptive richness and intimacy of tone judiciously derived from Hugo and Sainte-Beuve. Symbols of death and urban imagery abound:

> . . . la ville aux cent bruits
> Où de brouillards noyés les jours semblent des
>   nuits,
> Où parmi les toits bleus s'enchevêtre et se cogne
> Un soleil terne et mort comme l'oeil d'un
>   ivrogne . . .
>
> ("Paris")

Something of Gautier's originality can be felt in these lines: despite the inversion of *de brouillards,* a device which Gautier normally avoids, the language is free of self-consciously poetic usage. The bleakness of the city, which Sainte-Beuve had less concretely depicted, is reinforced by the imagery of an infernal sky, heavy and dark. The avoidance of banality and the pursuit of the pictorial were Gautier's guiding principles in style.

Although many fine passages occur in all of Gautier's verse, we need not dwell on his second volume, *Albertus:* this is a Byronic verse tale about witches and *sabbats,* which must be seen as a parody, for as seriously and complacently as the French romantics took demonology, their self-irony could also be immense. Demonic imagery is handled quite gravely, however, in *La Comédie de la mort*

(1837), in many ways Gautier's most interesting collection and certainly the one which most profoundly influenced Baudelaire. The title poem is intentionally Dantesque: a romantic visit to the underworld forms its subject and "La Comédie de la mort" is almost a summa of the imagery of spleen and death which the 1830's cultivated. The poem begins at the end of autumn; the sky is prison-like:

> C'était le jour des Morts: une froide bruine
> Au bord du ciel rayé, comme une trame fine,
> Tendait ses filets gris;
>
> Un vent de nord sifflait; quelques feuilles rouil-
> lées
> Quittaient en frissonnant les cimes dépouillées
> Des ormes rabougris . . .

There follows a long meditation on the dead in their coffins, which Baudelaire was to make use of in "La Servante au grand coeur. . . . " Night falls and the crows, owls, vampires, and other creatures of the sinister, romantic bestiary emerge. The poet hears a dialogue between a dead girl and the worm whose "marriage" to her is about to be consummated: necrophilia is a favorite demonic mode of sexuality. The speaker then returns home to a room furnished with a coffin-like bed, a picture of the dying Christ, and a skull. Raphael appears in order to announce the end of the human race. "Death in life" is the subject of the following section and a guide presents herself to lead the poet down the *funèbre spirale:*

> Pour guide nous avons une vierge au teint pâle
> Qui jamais ne reçut le baiser d'or du hâle
> Des lèvres du soleil.
> Sa joue est sans couleur et sa bouche bleuâtre,
> Le bouton de sa gorge est blanc comme l'albâtre
> Au lieu d'être vermeil.

The figure of the pale woman with black hair occurs regularly in romantic literature and painting. Virginity, frigidity, or sterility are among her attributes, and sexual barrenness can carry numerous symbolic meanings as it later does in Mallarmé's "Hérodiade." Here the guide represents not simply death but the poet's muse, statue-like, *sinistre et charmante.* The Dantesque pattern of the journey is continued, and the poet meets successively Faust, Don Juan, and Napoleon, three personages who fired the romantic imagination through their defiance of deity and mortal bounds. The description of Don Juan is a fine example of the grotesque:

> Tout ce luxe, ce fard sur cette face creuse,
> Formaient une alliance étrange et monstrueuse.
> C'étaient plus triste à voir
> Et plus laid qu'un cercueil chez des filles de joie,
> Qu'un squelette paré d'une robe de soie,
> Qu'une vieille au miroir.
> . . . . . .
> Dis, que fais-tu donc là, vieillard, dans les ténè-
> bres,
> Par une de ces nuits où les essaims funèbres
> S'envolent des tombeaux?
> Que vas-tu donc chercher si loin, si tard, à
> l'heure
> Où l'Ange de minuit au beffroi chante et pleure,
> Sans page et sans flambeaux?

Don Juan, Faust, and Napoleon admit defeat in their search for love, knowledge, and power, and the poet returns from the underworld overwhelmed by the idea of death. He makes a last attempt to throw off this obsession, but in place of the healthy Hellenic muse he has invoked there appears, in a new guise, the infernal guide:

> Chantons Io, Péan! . . . Mais quelle est cette
> femme
> Si pâle sous son voile? Ah! c'est toi, vieille in-
> fâme!
> Je vois ton crâne ras;
> Je vois tes grands yeux creux, prostituée im-
> monde,
> Courtisane éternelle environnant le monde
> Avec tes maigres bras!

The association of death and eroticism is reaffirmed, and the poem closes on a note of inexorability.

Most of Gautier's poems are more interesting for their details than for their overall structure. "La Comédie de la mort" is characteristic in this respect: a certain colloquial note—evident in our citations—lends itself to discursiveness and rambling. Indeed, the relation between Gautier and Baudelaire becomes clearer when we compare the concision of the younger poet to Gautier's wordiness: often, as in the opening of "La Comédie de la mort," many scattered phrases in Gautier will be drawn together by Baudelaire and forced into a tighter, more dramatic form. But in mood and phrasing Gautier frequently anticipated effects which we commonly ascribe to Baudelaire. The complex of feelings connected with spleen, horror of movement, ebbing life, and nostalgia for the cloister is eloquently expressed in such a poem as "Thébaïde":

> Donc, reçois dans tes bras, ô douce Somnolence,
> Vierge aux pâles couleurs, blanche soeur de la
> Mort,
> Un pauvre naufragé des tempêtes du sort!
> Exauce un malheureux qui te prie et t'implore,
> Egrène sur son front le pavot inodore,
> Abrite-le d'un pan de ton grand manteau noir,
> Et du doigt clos ses yeux qui ne veulent plus voir.
> Vous, esprits du désert, cependant qu'il som-
> meille,
> Faites taire les vents et bouchez son oreille,
> Pour qu'il n'entende pas le retentissement
> Du siècle qui s'écroule, et ce bourdonnement
> Qu'en s'en allant au but où son destin la mène
> Sur le chemin du temps fait la famille humaine!

The ancient Christian adoration of immobility as the perfect state, which Pascal so movingly represents, is summed up in lines which convey a dread of historical process, seen not as progress but as decay.

Gautier is so seldom credited with having any thoughts or deep feelings that it may come as a surprise to realize that, in a completely secularized and rather esthetic way, he saw his own age as the end of a great classical-Christian historic cycle, in which a spiritual night was drawing over the West. Predictably, he conceived of human history only as the history of the *beaux arts,* but he had sufficient taste to recognize the relatively impoverished and derivative character of painting, sculpture, and architecture in his day. "Melancholia," suggested by the Dürer engraving, is a meditation on Northern Renaissance painting and Trecento frescoes: it attempts to order the stages of our civilization's decay and concludes that the nineteenth century will remain unredeemed by its art. (Perhaps for the first time in French poetry, a religious vocabulary is here transferred to esthetic matters.) The most thorough statement of Gautier's feelings about history, however, is "Ténèbres," a poem in which thoughts on individual spleen and contemporary decay are cast in terza rima, a form particularly associated with Gautier:

> Taisez-vous, ô mon coeur! taisez-vous, ô mon âme!
> Et n'allez plus chercher de querelles au sort;
> Le néant vous appelle et l'oubli vous réclame.
>
> Mon coeur, ne battez plus, puisque vous êtes mort;
> Mon âme, repliez le reste de vos ailes,
> Car vous avez tenté votre suprême effort.

A theme which Baudelaire and Gautier share, and which is connected with the mood called spleen, is the voluntary imitation of death: through spite at life and apprehension of the future, the soul tries to anticipate its inevitable destruction, the thought of which is tinged with overtones of consolation.

The same imagery of futile movement which Baudelaire was to employ in "Le Voyage" occurs as the poet begins to résumé his experience of life:

> Hélas! le poète est pareil à l'amant,
> Car ils ont tous les deux leur maîtresse idéale,
> Quelque rêve chéri caressé chastement:
>
> Eldorado lointain, pierre philosophale
> Qu'ils poursuivent toujours sans l'atteindre jamais;
> Un astre impérieux, une étoile fatale.
>
> L'étoile fuit toujours, ils lui courent après;
> Et le matin venu, la lueur poursuivie,
> Quand ils la vont saisir, s'éteint dans un marais.

The plaint of the despairing artist, so frequently echoed by later poets, seems to have been an invention of Gautier's. The antinomy of aspiration and achievement is expanded on:

> Il est beau qu'un plongeur, comme dans les ballades,
> Descende au gouffre amer chercher la coupe d'or,
> Et perce triomphant les vitreuses arcades.
>
> Il est beau d'arriver où tendait son essor,
> De trouver sa beauté, d'aborder à son monde,
> Et, quand on a fouillé, d'exhumer un trésor;
>
> De faire, du plus creux de son âme profonde,
> Rayonner son idée ou bien sa passion,
> D'être l'oiseau qui chante et la foudre qui gronde;
>
> D'unir heureusement le rêve à l'action . . .

"Certes, je sortirai, quant à moi, satisfait / D'un monde où l'action n'est pas la soeur du rêve . . . " wrote Baudelaire, taking up Gautier's antithesis, which is another variation on the opposing realms characteristic of nineteenth-century thought: being and becoming, the ideal and the real, appearance and reality, and so forth. The feeling of disparity or *décalage* is typical of the romantics, and Gautier attributes it to the late and fallen character of his epoch; "Ténèbres" concludes with the world waiting for a redemption that will never come:

> Le Christ, d'un ton railleur, tord l'éponge de fiel
> Sur les lèvres en feu du monde à l'agonie,
> Et Dieu, dans son Delta, rit d'un rire cruel.
>
> Quand notre passion sera-t-elle finie?
> Le sang coule avec l'eau de notre flanc ouvert;
> La sueur rouge teint notre face jaunie.
>
> Assez comme cela! nous avons trop souffert;
> De nos lèvres, Seigneur, détournez ce calice,
> Car pour nous racheter votre Fils s'est offert.
>
> Christ n'y peut rien: il faut que le sort s'accomplisse;
> Pour sauver ce vieux monde il faut un Dieu nouveau,
> Et le prêtre demande un autre sacrifice.
>
> Voici bien mille ans que l'on saigne l'Agneau;
> Il est mort à la fin, et sa gorge épuisée
> N'a plus assez de sang pour teindre le couteau.
>
> Le Dieu ne viendra pas. L'Eglise est renversée.

This vision of the cycle of Christian history drawing to its sinister close is an important aspect of romantic historical theory with its Hegelian penchant for sharply defined ages. But Gautier does not place it in the context of prophetic poetry as Nerval, Hugo, and Yeats were to do; for him the imminence of a new cycle is unthinkable. Gautier had not evolved a framework of poetic thought in which he could thoroughly exploit his feeling about history, for his intellect was perhaps too timid to lead him into the abstruse metaphysical concepts cherished by his friend Nerval. But the intuition of a demonic God—a central theme in French romanticism . . .—was perfectly consonant with his temperament. His mocking Christ and sardonic God anticipate many later and greater visions of an evil deity. (pp. 43-60)

To conclude our examination of demonic iconology . . . we shall consider the verse of two of Gautier's friends of the 1830's. Both are lesser poets and were probably not influential, but their work represents the extremes of early romantic sombreness and linguistic perversity. Philothée O'Neddy and Petrus Borel—to use their chosen names—were among the great literary eccentrics of their day. Often their verse is conventional, but occasionally their reputation for bizarreness is fully justified. O'Neddy was the less peculiar of the two; here is his version of the metamorphosis of woman into skeleton:

> Je rêvais, l'autre nuit, qu'aux splendeurs des orages,
> Sur le parquet mouvant d'un salon de nuages,
> De terreur et d'amour puissamment tourmenté,
>
> Avec une lascive et svelte Bohémienne,
> Dans une valse aérienne,
> Ivre et fou j'étais emporté.
>   · · · · ·

Oh! pitié!—je me meurs.—Pitié! ma blanche fée!
Disais-je d'une voix électrique, étouffée.
Regarde.—Tout mon corps palpite incandes-
    cent.—
Viens, viens, montons plus haut, montons dans
    une étoile.
—Et là, que ta beauté s'abandonne sans voile
A ma fougue d'adolescent!

Un fou rire la prit . . . rire désharmonique,
Digne de s'éployer au banquet satanique.
J'eus le frisson, mes dents jetèrent des strideurs.
Puis, soudain, plus de fée à lubrique toilette!
Plus rien dans mes bras qu'un squelette
M'étalant toutes ses hideurs!

                        ("Succube")

The living room of clouds with its shifting floor is a strik-ing way of rendering acrophobic dreams, and the lumi-nous storm (*splendeurs* suggests brightness) anticipates the odd and novel adjective "electric," as well as "incan-descent," freakily placed in an adverbial position. Linguis-tic oddity at any cost was O'Neddy's great concern: the colloquial *fou rire* mingles with neologisms like *strideurs* and *désharmonique*, while the expression *sans voile* is pure neoclassicism. The abundance of k-sounds in the last stan-za quoted violates the traditional canons of euphony, in order apparently to suggest the clatter of bones. What we have in "Succube" is a good example of Bohemian taste, which values insubordination above all. To some degree, the *espirit de bohème* penetrated nearly all of French ro-manticism, but it is more covert in major figures. O'Neddy's poem can be taken as a common denominator of the romantic impetus to find the *new* at any cost.

Petrus Borel was a stranger figure than O'Neddy: "one of the stars in the somber romantic sky," to quote Baude-laire's words. In the preface to his *Rapsodies* Borel wrote, "Je suis républicain comme l'entendrait un loup-cervier; mon républicanisme, c'est de la lycanthropie." The Were-wolf, as Borel called himself, seems to have been a deeply disturbed person, incapable of subsisting even in the *bo-hème* of journalists and lesser poets. Baudelaire regretted the incompleteness and botched character of his talent while maintaining that Borel was essential to romanti-cism. His linguistic imagination was certainly at times im-pressive:

Autour de moi voyez la foule sourcilleuse
S'ameuter, du néant son haut coeur est marri.—
Dites de ce vieux chêne où va le tronc pourri?—
Poudre grossir la glèbe.—Et vous, souche or-
    gueilleuse!
Un ogre appelé Dieu vous garde un autre sort!
Moins de prétentions, allons, race servile,
Peut-être avant longtemps, votre tête de mort
Servira de jouet aux enfants par la ville! . . .
Peu vous importe, au fait, votre vil ossement;
Qu'on le traîne au bourbier, qu'on le frappe et
    l'écorne . . .
Il renaîtra tout neuf, quand sonnera la corne
Du jugement!

                        ("Rêveries")

The archaisms of the first lines are not gratuitous but iron-ically characterize the crowd as high minded. The blunt dialogue heightens the angry undertone, as does the

strange use of *poudre*. Borel is either omitting subject and verb (*il va, poudre . . .*) or else construes it as an infini-tive ("to crumble or rot") by analogy with a series of un-usual and defective verbs, and treats it as a verb of motion like *aller grossir la terre*. *Glèbe*, a poetic term suggesting fertility, is again ironic: death is meaningless, and proof of God's malevolence. And, finally, the advent of the Last Judgment demonstrates the senseless incoherence of God and His scheme of things: sloughing off one's body only to get it back again is offered as a sardonic consolation.

Borel did not write much verse; after the volume of *Rapso-dies* there remains only the Prologue to the novel *Madame Putiphar*. This piece is an allegory about three apocalyptic horsemen who war in the poet's heart. The world and the cloister are the first two, but his favorite is death:

Le dernier combattant, le cavalier sonore,
Le spectre froid, le gnôme aux filets de pêcheur,
C'est lui que je caresse et qu'en secret j'honore,
Niveleur éternel, implacable faucheur,
C'est la mort, le néant! . . . D'une voix souter-
    raine
Il m'appelle sans cesse:—Enfant, descends chez
    moi,
Enfant, plonge en mon sein, car la douleur est
    reine
De la terre maudite, et l'opprobre en est roi!
Viens, redescends chez moi, viens, replonge en
    la fange,
Chrysalide, éphémère, ombre, velléité!
Viens plus tôt que plus tard, sans oubli je ven-
    dange
Un par un les raisins du cep Humanité.
Avant que le pilon pesant de la souffrance
T'ait trituré le coeur, souffle sur ton flambeau;
Notre-Dame de Liesse et de la Délivrance,
C'est la mort! Chanaan promis, c'est le tombeau!

These lines are cast in an odd verse form: they are ar-ranged as if in verse-paragraphs, but the rime pattern is stanzaic. The poet seems to be striving for a combination of sustained discourse and lyrical effect. The especially in-teresting thing about this passage is its cosmology: the un-derground is seen both as man's origin and end. "*Redes-cends*," "*replonge*," cries the horseman, who offers the lib-eration of original insentience—a theme we have already encountered in Gautier. The colorfulness of the language is also worth noting: "Notre-Dame de Liesse et de la Dé-livrance" introduces an unctuous note of religiosity, while "cep Humanité" is a super-concise construction usually associated with the late work of Hugo.

In the Prologue to *Madame Putiphar*, as elsewhere in Borel, as in the work of Gautier, or in Hugo's volumes be-fore the exile, the abundance of imagery connected with death, the demonic supernatural, or the absence of God cannot be said to correspond to a stable, coherent pattern of thought. It would be vain to construct a "philosophy" from this verse. As yet, death and the devil are merely ob-sessive preoccupations. In this sense, we may speak of them as belonging to a French romantic iconology: they create favorite moods rather than symbolize ways of thinking. In the course of the nineteenth century, howev-er, as the strain of poetry darkens and diversifies, several figures stand out for the breadth of their poetic vision and its coherence. After 1840, the poetry of Vigny, Baudelaire, Nerval, and Hugo absorbs and orders the fragments of romantic thought and sensibility. (pp. 66-9)

> *John Porter Houston, "Toward a Romantic Iconology," in his* The Demonic Imagination: Style and Theme in French Romantic Poetry, *Louisiana State University Press, 1969, pp. 43-69.*

ROMANTICISM IN ITALY

Kenneth McKenzie

[*In the following essay, McKenzie discusses the growth of Italian Romanticism as a response to the reactionary government and personal misfortune that followed the fall of Napoleon.*]

Italy, for obvious reasons, always kept closer than other countries to ancient classical literature. There the classic spirit was native, for the Italians were always conscious of being the heirs of the ancient Roman Empire; there Humanism and the Renaissance arose; there the counter-Reformation resisted the Protestant spirit of the northern countries; there Arcadian academies and pseudo-classicism flourished. But the Romantic attitude was present in many Italian writers from the Middle Ages on. Petrarch was romantic in his introspective melancholy, Ariosto was romantic in his love of picturesque adventure; yet both are classic in the perfection of their style as well as in their knowledge of antiquity. Thus the two tendencies existed side by side, frequently in the same man, although in theory Italy remained classicist until the end of the eighteenth century. The pre-romantic literature of France, England, and Germany was modified in Italy by the prevalent classical tradition, but it found there a fertile soil. As a literary movement, Romanticism in Italy is best considered as represented by a group of writers in the period which followed the collapse of Napoleon's empire.

By creating the Regno d'Italia in 1805, Napoleon had intended to make northern Italy a dependency of France; but in spite of himself he gave the Italians an object lesson which showed the possibility of national unity. When his empire came to an end in 1814, the former rulers returned to their possessions. The problem then was not only to achieve unity, but to end foreign domination. The nucleus from which grew the Italian nation was the small kingdom of Piedmont; but this fact was not recognized in the early years of the nineteenth century, and the movement toward unity and independence centered in Milan. There a reaction against the classicism which had flourished during the Napoleonic period was fused with the revolutionary political movement. Romanticism had its political aspect in other countries, but nowhere to the same degree as in Italy. It follows that Italian romanticism was practical, altruistic, and patriotic. With these circumstances in mind,

some critics have denied that the term *romantic* can properly be applied to this period of Italian literature.

The explosion of the spirit of revolt, as Farinelli expresses it, began in northern Europe; but the spiritual movement which arose in all nations is not to be judged by doctrinaire criticism. It is absurd, he says, to identify romanticism with Germanism, and classicism with Latinity. It is true that the Italian romanticists, like the French, believed that literary art has its practical use, while the Germans emphasized its inactive side; but this does not mean that either aspect is more authentic than the other. In fact, cosmopolitanism is one feature of the Romantic movement. It became Italian in the sense that it undertook to liberate classicism from conventional academic restrictions, not to abolish it. The distinction between *classic* (or *classicist*) on the one hand and *romantic* on the other hand was never very clear in Italian literature, in spite of critical discussions. But the elements of development from ancient to medieval and modern were present in Italy as well as in France, where also the classic spirit was still powerful; whereas in Germany, England, and Spain literature had long shown traits which afterwards were called romantic, and classicism was foreign to the national character.

Some critics find the foundation of romanticism in eighteenth-century Italy, believing that the importance of foreign influences on Italian writers was on the whole superficial. De Sanctis in his *Storia della Letteratura Italiana* declares that the romantic school in Italy, while connected with German traditions and French methods, in essence remained Italian in its purposes and its forms. Certain it is that eighteenth-century Italy experienced an intellectual awakening which perpetuated itself in the following century. Gravina and Vico, with their interpretations of history, anticipated Herder, Hegel, and other Germans. Muratori published documents and studies which revived interest in the national history. Goldoni turned comedy from imitation of conventional models to realistic representation of the life of the people. Parini had in his satire a moral and educational motive; while he himself was satisfied with moderate social progress, he prefigured the Revolution. Alfieri was always an aristocrat and a classicist, yet no one contributed more than he to spreading the germs of revolt. All these men seem to have exercised less influence on literature than their importance as authors would lead us to expect; but in stimulating a spirit of independence their influence was immense. Thus the awakening of the Italian spirit, conditioned by the classic tradition, while it was helped, was not caused, by foreign influences.

The leading Italian poets during the Napoleonic period were Vincenzo Monti and Ugo Foscolo. Monti was influenced by all types of literature, but attachment to antiquity formed the unity of his art. Foscolo began his career with the ultra-romantic *Ultime lettere di Jacopo Ortis* (1796–1802), in which he lamented both his personal misfortunes and the unhappy condition of Italy. This combination of motives gives the key to Italian romanticism. In his *Sepolcri* he was still interested in the condition of his country, but in his later poem *Le Grazie* he reverted to Greek mythology. After the romanticists had condemned the use of classical mythology, Monti wrote a "sermon" in defence of it. Monti and Foscolo, both classicists at heart, belong to the period of pre-romanticism.

The restoration of the former rulers in Italy after the fall of Napoleon disappointed the patriots who had hoped for a united country. Since the restored governments were reactionary, the promoters of a romantic revolt were under suspicion and were opposed by the classicists, who generally supported the existing political system. Thus romanticism inevitably came to be one aspect of the political Risorgimento. In purely literary matters the romanticists were not particularly unconventional. However, they studied the modern literature of their own and other countries, condemned imitation of the ancients, and aimed to put literature at the service of national education, an ideal scarcely known in previous ages. The two greatest Italian writers of the first half of the nineteenth century—Manzoni, who became the acknowledged leader of the romantic movement in so far as it was literary and educational, and Leopardi, who was at heart more romantic than Manzoni—kept aloof from the political polemics of the day; but their works nevertheless made an important contribution to the regeneration of the country.

It is usual to take as the beginning of the definite romantic movement in Italy the publication in 1816 of Mme de Staël's article exhorting the Italians to rouse themselves from their complacency and learn what was going on in other countries. But already in the previous year Manzoni had published his *Inni Sacri,* which De Sanctis has called "the first voices of the nineteenth century"; and in August, 1815, enormous enthusiasm had been aroused by the performance in Milan of Silvio Pelico's *Francesca da Rimini.* This tragedy, based on the best-known passage in Dante, is classical or at least Alfierian in form, with only four speaking characters and with observation of the rule of the unities; but its plot is medieval and national, and it is filled with romantic passion. It speedily became known all over Italy, although not printed until 1818. The passage that attracted particular attention was the monologue in which Paolo laments having fought in foreign wars when he should have reserved his sword for Italy; this speech was an anachronism in a play of the thirteenth century, but it seemed extraordinarily timely in the nineteenth, when in everyone's mind were the Italians in Napoleon's army who had laid down their lives in Germany and Russia. Pellico later wrote tragedies which in many ways departed from the classic rules, but none met the same success as *Francesca da Rimini.*

In 1816, under the patronage of the Austrian authorities in Milan, a periodical, *Biblioteca Italiana,* was established, which continued publication for many years. It soon became the organ of the classicists, since the Austrians used it for propaganda against the liberal movement. In the beginning, however, it was impartial and objective in its attitude, and not averse to introducing German ideas in northern Italy. The first number contained the famous article written by Mme de Staël especially for the *Biblioteca* and translated into Italian with the title "Sulla maniera e sulla utilità delle traduzioni." Her work was already well known; in 1807 she had published *Corinne ou l'Italie,* a story containing descriptions of Italian scenes. An Italian translation of *De l'Allemagne* appeared in 1814. The main point of the article in the *Biblioteca* was that Italians would do well to study foreign literature, in translation if necessary, not to imitate it but to broaden their outlook. Mme de Staël's article alarmed the classicists, who feared the corruption of their fixed ideals, and it angered nationalistically minded critics who chose to believe that she was belittling Italian genius. A furious debate arose; Mme de Staël was violently attacked and valiantly defended. In the same year (1816) there appeared a work which is spoken of as a manifesto of Romantic doctrines comparable to the "Préface de Cromwell" in France. This was the *Lettera semiseria de Grisostomo* by Giovanni Berchet. The author pretended to advise his son to write according to the dictates of his heart and the spirit of his country, abandoning the academic rules and standards of the prevailing classicism; as an example, he accompanied the letter with a translation of two ballads from the German of Bürger. Berchet knew English and German literature better than most of his Italian contemporaries, and the *Lettera semiseria,* as well as the patriotic ballads which he afterwards wrote in exile, contributed to the development of a national spirit by suggesting that Italians could do for their own country what other races were doing for theirs. As a matter of fact, a knowledge of foreign literatures was no new thing to the Milan of 1816, for that had begun half a century before. Thus both native and foreign elements combined to form the outlook of the intellectuals who were in revolt against the classicist restrictions on literary production and at the same time against the political impotence of Italy.

The houses of two Milanese aristocrats, Luigi Porro Lambertenghi and Federico Confalonieri, not themselves literary men, were centers where many forward-looking Italians and foreign visitors gathered to discuss questions of the day. So much dissatisfaction was felt with the growing conservatism of the *Biblioteca Italiana* that the project arose of establishing a journal to give voice to the ideas of the liberal group. After several abortive attempts, the semi-weekly *Conciliatore* was started in September, 1818. Silvio Pellico, Porro's secretary, had charge of seeing the journal through the press, and was the most regular contributor. His task was far from easy, for at the last moment the censor frequently required him to cut or rewrite articles, or to substitute new material. The various contributors differed among themselves in many matters, but were a unit in their devotion to the romantic movement in literature and in their determination to change the political situation. Although the romantic tendency of the articles published was confined to literary questions and perforce avoided politics, the connection between the two orders of ideas was clear to the Austrian authorities. Pellico was several times warned to be more careful, and finally in October, 1819, the attitude of the police became so threatening that it was decided to cease publication. The diffusion of the journal was slight; but its influence, both literary and political, was considerable. Finally, several of the *Conciliatore* group were arrested and condemned for high treason; others escaped from Italy and lived for years in exile. Pellico's *Le mie Prigioni,* written in 1832 after his release from prison, became one of the most famous books of the century. Patriotism continued to express itself in the theory and practice of romanticism until in 1859 Italy began in fact to free herself from foreign domination. During all this period, literature was employed in the service of the fatherland. But at the same time we may consider the ideas expressed in the *Conciliatore* from a purely literary point of view.

In the prospectus which Pietro Borsieri wrote for the first number the words *romantico, romanticismo* do not occur, but they appear in many of the later numbers. An article by the eminent economist Gian Domenico Romagnosi begins:

> Are you romantic?—No.—Are you classicist?—No.—What then?—I am *ilichiastico,* to say it in Greek; that is, adapted to the present age . . . Every age must find principles which obey only the laws of taste, reason and morality . . . We are always the children of the age and the place in which we live . . . To maintain among us the exclusive dominion of the classics is to wish a dead Italian poetry and a dead Italian language.

A long article by Ermes Visconti, entitled "Idee elementari sulla poesia romantica," begins as follows:

> If the discussion for and against romanticism were in style only here in Milan, it would perhaps be well to let the style pass. But beyond the Alps the new literary system is discussed and will continue to be discussed, because it opposes many old errors and offers opportunity for many useful observations. True it is that its usefulness is diminished by the disagreement of various German writers as to the phrase *poesia romantica.* This phrase was invented to Germany to distinguish the proper characteristics of the art of modern poets from the qualities belonging exclusively to the ancient classics, so as to give due praise to the originality of the former in contrast to the pedantic partisans of those who merely copy antiquity.

In a "Dialogue on the dramatic unities of time and place," Visconti anticipates many of the arguments used later by Manzoni and Hugo; this was written and published in January, 1819—before the publication of Manzoni's tragedies or of his celebrated letter on the unities. The discussion of romantic principles also appears in private letters of the time. Thus in 1819 Pellico wrote to his brother:

> From the way in which you speak of Romanticism you seem to think of it as a party into which I have been dragged. You are wrong. The word was not well chosen; but the doctrine is held by everyone who has clear-sighted intelligence. You know how Monti and Foscolo appreciated Shakespeare and Schiller before the word Romantic was used. Now perhaps they would call themselves Classicists. Time will clear away these uncertainties.

The connection of the literary movement with the political situation comes out clearly in a letter from Pellico to Porro: "At Turin, as in our cities in Lombardy, to say 'liberal' one says 'romantic'; no distinction is made. And 'classic' has become the synonym of reactionary, of spy."

From the period of which we have been speaking until after Rome had become the capital of united Italy, there lived in Milan a greater literary genius than any of the *Conciliatore* group, who sympathized with their purpose without sharing their activities. This was Alessandro Manzoni (1785-1873). In 1818 Manzoni began the historical studies on which were based his two tragedies, *Il Conte di Carmagnola* (1820) and *Adelchi* (1822), dealing with Italian history of the fifteenth and the eighth centuries respectively. These tragedies, like Alfieri's, are in blank verse, but, unlike them, employ many characters and do not observe the unities of time and place. They were adversely criticized in France by a certain Chauvet, whose name is now remembered only on account of the reply which Manzoni made to his criticism: this "Lettre à M.C. . . . sur l'unité de temps et de lieu dans la tragédie," together with Claude Fauriel's translation of the tragedies, was published in Paris in 1823. Victor Hugo can hardly have failed to see this publication; in any case, many of Manzoni's ideas reappear in the "Préface de Cromwell" (1827). It is true that some of these ideas were already more or less current both in France and in Italy; but it should be noted that Manzoni's thoroughly romantic tragedies antedate the French romantic drama. However, they did not lead to a development of a new dramatic form in Italy. On the other hand, Manzoni's great historical novel, *I Promessi Sposi* (1827), was followed by a host of imitations in the second quarter of the century, many of which are still read with interest. Later, fiction turned to realism but toward the close of the century in the novels of Fogazzaro it reverted to the moralizing romanticism of Manzoni.

If Berchet's *Lettera semiseria* may be called the militant manifesto of the Italian romanticists in their "Sturm und Drang" period—namely, from 1815 to the breaking up of the *Conciliatore* group by imprisonment and exile—a letter which Manzoni addressed in 1823 to Cesare d'Azeglio is to be regarded as the serene, carefully pondered statement of the principles of the school as understood and practised by the greatest Romantic writer of Italy. Manzoni's central idea was that literature should be useful; in his famous phrase, "che la poesia, e la letteratura in genere, debba proporsi l'utile per iscopo, il vero per soggetto, e l'interessante per mezzo." This principle was to him more important than any consideration of school; when asked if romanticism would last, he replied that the name was already being forgotten, but that the influence of the movement would continue. The negative doctrines of the school were easy to define: to abandon imitation of the classics (they should be studied, as Mme de Staël had said of modern foreign literature, but not copied); to reject ancient mythology, which seemed to Manzoni idolatrous and contrary to Christianity; to base rules for writing not on arbitrary decisions, but on the human mind. The positive side of romantic doctrine was less easy to specify, and the romantic writers had been criticized for not agreeing among themselves. The basis of romanticism is individuality; yet all should agree, and according to Manzoni in general they do agree, in believing that literature must be useful, and must have as its source historical and moral truth. Just what is meant by "il vero" is, to be sure, open to discussion; but by excluding the false, the useless, the harmful, romanticism defines the truth. In Italy, Manzoni concludes, with an eye to the German models that were sometimes proposed, romanticism does not consist of a confused crowd of ghosts and witches, of search for the extravagant, of negation of common sense—such a romanticism Italians have good reason to reject and forget. In regard to the linguistic problem which had been debated with heat ever since the time of Dante, Manzoni rejected the arbitrary rules which tended to impede growth and make Italian a dead language: he based his style on the best contemporary usage, particularly that of Tuscany.

It should be evident from what precedes that the Italians were not ignorant of the methods of romantic writers in other countries, and that in adopting the principle of liberalism in art they restricted it with rules based on the conditions which confronted them in their own country at the moment. Manzoni did not advance the need for political revolution as a guiding principle in the literary movement; but nevertheless he aided the revolution, both by his insistence on strength of character and morality and by his picture, in *I Promessi Sposi,* of the abject condition of Lombardy under the Spanish dominion in the seventeenth century—a picture which drew attention, perhaps more pointedly than he intended, to the evils of the Austrian rule in his own day. The combined efforts of the romantic-minded Italians, whether or not they formally espoused romanticism, finally made the political Risorgimento a reality. In this process the purely literary contribution of the generation of 1815 must not be overlooked, even though the contributions of the less gifted members of the group now have in many cases little intrinsic interest. This generation did in fact produce significant literary works: noble lyric poetry, keen critical discussions, important tragedies, and splendid historical fiction.

To sum up: In the eighteenth century Germany brought to a focus a movement which had long existed in different parts of Europe; the movement spread to Italy and France, where classicism was strongly entrenched, and there, as well as in England and Spain, it assumed forms peculiar to each country. It ran its course as a definite school, but its influence pervades all modern literature. The need for a renewal of vitality was characteristic of all countries, both those which were normally and fundamentally classic and those which were already romantic in a general sense. It is evident, then, that even though romanticism as a school originated in Germany, one of its important elements is its cosmopolitan and general European character. Manzoni's masterpiece is one of the great novels of world literature. The sublime poems of Leopardi, classical in their perfection of form, are filled with the spirit of romanticism; his "noia" is as significant in modern literature as the "sorrows" of Werther and the "ennui" of René. The critic Carducci observes that Manzoni was attracted more by the art of Goethe and Schiller than by that of men like Novalis, Tieck, and the Schlegels, and reduced to a clear expression of reality the nebulous spirit of German romanticism; while Leopardi romanticized the purity of the Greek attitude toward life and renewed the classic expression of the conflict of modern thought. Both these writers, by representing two different pyschological states that were common to all Europe, became more universal than their immediate Italian predecessors. Both kept aloof

from political agitation, yet their writings were transformed into battlecries and Italy responded with the will to fight; with astonishment Europe saw this nation, which had been called the land of the dead, rise to throw off the shackles of foreign domination and affirm its independence. In 1902 the popular dramatist Rovetta produced a play dealing with the revolt against the Austrians in northern Italy in 1854; and the title of this play is appropriately *Romanticismo.* (pp. 27-35)

Kenneth McKenzie, "Romanticism in Italy," in PMLA, *Vol. LV, No. 1, March, 1940, pp. 27-35.*

ROMANTICISM IN SPAIN

F. Courtney Tarr

[In the following essay, Tarr discusses the historically Romantic literature of Spain and examines how Spanish culture served as a theme and inspiration for Romantic writers in Germany, England, and France.]

During the romantic era Spain enjoyed for perhaps the first time in her history a genuine European vogue. The theorizers of romanticism in Germany, England, and France—especially Germany—discovered in Spanish literature, as they imperfectly knew it—chiefly the *Don Quixote,* the ballads, and the theatre of Calderón— ammunition for their critical and anticlassical campaign, while the creative writers of these countries found in the land and its people, their history, legends and letters, a new and rich store of themes and settings, made as if to order in response to the demand of the moment for the picturesque and the passionate, the chivalresque and the medieval. But having little interest in Spain for herself nor (Mérimée excepted) any real knowledge of her language, history, or culture, they recreated a conventional, literary Spain according to their own needs, desires and imaginations, that "romantic" Spain best typified perhaps in the *Carmen* of Mérimée and of Bizet, a conception which has persisted in the popular mind down to the present and against which Spaniards and Hispanophiles—then and now—have reacted more or less violently and in vain. (And, may I add, not with complete justification, for creative artists are hardly to be censured for not being exact historians or archeologists.)

Furthermore, even the romantic caricature of Spain, to say nothing of the more sober and sounder vision of a few critics and travelers, brings out for the first time, to any considerable extent, those peculiar traits of Spanish culture and the Spanish temper which have increasingly come to be regarded (even among Spanish critics) as essentially romantic, or perhaps, with greater accuracy, as essentially unclassic: the co-existence and clash of extremes, the persistence of medieval and national themes and attitudes, the intense individualism and resistance to rules, schools, and all forms of purely human authority, the preponderance of the popular and the spontaneously creative over the aristocratic and the critical.

Nevertheless, the great creations of the Spanish spirit, both artistic and vital—in the interplay of these two forces lies the key to the creative genius of Spain—lack, because of their very vitality, one fundamental aspect of romanticism. The Spanish spirit and Spanish letters are individualistic, but not subjective; extrovert, not introvert. (Save in the best of Larra and Espronceda, in a few minor writers in the romantic period itself, and especially, sixty to seventy years later, in some outstanding authors of the "generation of 1898," the one really romantic generation in Spanish literature.) The epic and the dramatic, especially the dramatic, predominate over the lyric, and form, or rather expression, over sentiment and feeling. It is not around the latter, but around action, even mental action— the *ingenio* so characteristic of the race—that Spanish letters revolve. The "tragic sense of life" is ever present, as Unamuno reminds us, but rarely in the form of *Weltschmerz* or *mal du siècle.* The original Spanish Don Juan is completely extrovert, as is the rebellious Cid of the ballads. The romantic exaltation of Don Quixote as the rebellious dreamer, started in Germany and England and carried to its zenith by Unamuno as late as 1905 (in his *Vida de D. Quijote y Sancho*), is a one-sided distortion, and has served to obscure, until quite recently, the essential genius of his creator.

It is not without significance, then, that in their recreations of Spain, the romantics in Germany, England, and France should emphasize and exaggerate the external rather than the internal. For this is precisely what occurs, although in different tones and modes, in the writers of the Romantic period in Spain itself.

Literary romanticism comes late to Spain, later even than to Italy. In February of 1828 Mariano José de Larra, then not quite nineteen years of age, published as his first article of dramatic criticism a scathing denunciation of Ducange's *Trente ans ou la vie d'un joueur,* one of the translated melodramas which, along with sentimental and spectacle plays (also in translation) had formed, despite the fulminations of the critics, an increasingly large part of the repertory of the Madrid stage ever since the turn of the century. In this juvenile outburst Larra upbraids the French for having abandoned, and extols the Spaniard Moratín and his followers for continuing to uphold, those external rules of literary and dramatic art and propriety for the violation of which the Frenchman Boileau had condemned the great Spanish dramatists of the seventeenth century. And, taking Ducange's play as a horrible example, Larra ridicules romanticism as a silly, ephemeral, and degenerate French fad.

Hostile and naïve, not to say ignorant, as this article is in its conception of romanticism, it is nevertheless representative of the critical attitude prevailing at the time in Spain. It reveals the strong patriotic pride in the achievement of the Spanish neoclassicists and the equally strong anti-French feeling inherited from the eighteenth century and intensified by the War of Independence as vital forces in the critical opposition to romanticism. It also reveals how little the latter, either in precept or in practice, was

understood or even known in Spain as late as 1828. The faint breath of a native pre-romanticism (melancholy, a feeling for nature, and a passion for liberty) discernible in the poets of the eighteenth century had been stifled by the declamatory ode on contemporary social and patriotic themes introduced by Quintana and furthered by the War of Independence. The political upheavals—foreign invasion, civil strife, anarchy, and bloody repression—which had racked the country since 1808 had arrested, if not destroyed, that notable revival of learning and letters which had taken place in the last decades of the eighteenth century. Intellectual intercourse with the rest of Europe was largely cut off. As later during the romantic period (which coincides roughly with the first Carlist war (1833-39) and subsequent strife until the "pacification" of 1843-45) politics was the primary preoccupation with intellectuals and writers. The debate over the neoclassic esthetic in its relation to Spanish literature, which since 1737 had raged intermittently for nearly a century, was largely stilled. Almost single-handed the great Hispanist Böhl von Faber, inspired by Herder, Grimm, and the Schlegels, strove to focus attention on the ancient folk poetry and to exalt the drama of the seventeenth century as superior to the revered "rules." Although translations of English, German, and French pre-romantics (Young, "Ossian," Goethe, Rousseau, Chateaubriand, and Lamartine) are seen and heard in the last years of the eighteenth and early decades of the nineteenth century, they had no great popularity (save possibly *Atala*) and certainly little immediate influence. Only sporadic references to romanticism as such are found prior to 1818; and the first serious critical discussions, moderate and conciliatory, like those of the Italian *Conciliatore,* by which they were indeed influenced, are those of the Italian Monteggia and the Catalán López Soler, published in the short-lived *El Europeo* (1823–24) of Barcelona. Yet the public had applauded for decades the type of play denounced by the youthful Larra and his contemporaries and predecessors, and had devoured the romantic novels of Chateaubriand and the pseudo-historical and sentimental fiction of Mme de Genlis, Mme Cottin, the Vicomte d'Arlincourt, and Miss Roche (to say nothing of the thrillers of Mrs. Radcliffe). And from 1825 on, the novels of Walter Scott, and Cooper, too, whose vogue in the rest of Europe was echoed in Spain, were almost immediately accepted by the critics and men of letters who were still indifferent or hostile to romanticism in general. As a consequence, romanticism made its initial appearance in Spain in its newest and least romantic form—the first of the many paradoxes to be encountered in our survey—in the historical novel in the manner of Walter Scott, initiated in 1830 by López Soler and continued almost immediately by other writers—among them Larra and Espronceda—with the deliberate purpose of enriching the national literature by adapting this new and widely acclaimed form to Spanish soil and the Spanish spirit, so congenial to historical and legendary themes and settings. But (again the paradox) the pseudo-archaeological novel proved alien to the Spanish temper, precisely because of its antiquarianism, and dragged out a feeble existence in the thirties and forties. The vivid, living recreation of the national past took place, not in the novel, at least not until the historical novels of Pérez Galdós, but in the theatre and in narrative poetry. And here the opposition to romanticism had first to be overcome, at least in part.

As seen in Larra's review, there were deeper reasons for this opposition than a pardonable ignorance due to isolation and an understandable scorn for the vulgar taste in fiction and in the theatre. The belated and limited, yet sound and solid, renaissance of culture in eighteenth-century Spain was in its literary aspects almost exclusively the work of two generations (symbolized by the Moratíns, father and son) of writers and scholars imbued with the patriotic desire to reform and restore Spanish letters on the basis of the neoclassic precepts, to the failure to observe which they attributed the shortcomings of the national literature, particularly the theatre, of the seventeenth century and its subsequent decadence. And it was under the direct example and even guidance of these men (Jovellanos, Moratín the younger, Quintana, Lista, etc.) that the literary generations of the first half of the nineteenth century grew up. Thus not only did neoclassicism flower late in Spain, but the prestige of its exponents, even more than of its precepts, was at its peak in the first three decades of the nineteenth century. This prestige was political as well as literary. The eighteenth-century *reformadores* had met with great opposition—not so much, again, on doctrinal as on patriotic grounds—which took the form of a vigorous defense of the national drama and continuous satire of French culture and customs and of its supporters. But during and after the War of Independence the *reformadores* and their followers, with few exceptions, took the lead, not only in resisting the invader, but also in the liberal and constitutional movements of 1810–14 and 1820–23. Imprisonment, exile, and even death was the portion of many of them in the reactions of 1814–20 and 1823–33. No wonder, then, that they and their disciples should oppose romanticism, as they imperfectly knew it, identified as it was, in their eyes, with the figure of Chateaubriand, the arch-enemy of liberal Spain. For them romanticism represented reaction, political and literary, the very opposite of their own principles of progress and reform. Not until the political and literary revolution of 1830 in France, in which some of them were participants, did their attitude change. And then only in part. Thus it was that the patriotic impulse, which had animated both the eighteenth-century neoclassicists and their opponents, although to opposite ends, worked before 1830 against the introduction of romanticism, just as after that date it was to further its conditional acceptance and its adaptation to national soil and literary traditions. First, and, on the whole unsuccessfully, in the novel, next in the drama, and finally in lyric, or rather narrative poetry.

In these latter genres the first important essays in romanticism take place outside of Spain, in Paris, after the revolution of 1830 and among the liberal and neoclassicist exiles gathered there. The most outstanding figure, literary and political, among them, Martínez de la Rosa, composed—on the heels of his preceptist *Poética* (1827) and his pseudo-Sophoclean *Edipo* (1828)—a historical drama in French, *Aben-Humeya, ou la révolte de Maures sous Philippe II,* played at the Porte-St. Martin in June of 1830. (This, by the way, is by no means the only instance of literary composition in French, or in English, by the Spanish *emigrados.*) In the same year Martínez de la Rosa published, also in Paris, his *Conjuración de Venecia,* the first Spanish historical drama with external romantic, or melodramatic, trimmings. This was not played in Madrid until 1834, after the death of Ferdinand VII in 1833 had given rise to the Carlist revolt, the return of the *emigrados* to aid the cause of Isabel II, and the elevation of Martínez de la Rosa to head the government. Yet by the year 1837 the romantic drama was firmly established, as a part, although not the dominant one, of the theatrical repertory. But only when purged of some of its "excesses" and garbed in native dress, as initiated by *El Trovador* (1836) and *Los amantes de Teruel* (1837), of two young and relatively unknown poets, García Gutiérrez and Hartzenbusch, respectively. The romantic drama in Spain, after 1837, perhaps its year of greatest vitality, represents a cross between the French *drame romantique* and the Spanish *comedia* of the seventeenth century, but stressing the elements present in the latter: themes from national history and legend, freedom from the "rules," exuberance of rhetoric and varied versification—Lope and Calderón brought "up to date"!

In lyric poetry the course of events was slower, but much the same. The long narrative poem (*El Moro Expósito*), published in 1834 in Paris by the former liberal exile and neoclassicist Duque de Rivas, had little direct influence until followed in 1840 by the author's *Romances históricos,* much more definitely modelled on the old ballads (*romances*). This turn was the one finally to triumph: one more distinctly historical and legendary in subject-matter, more directly Spanish and Catholic in spirit, more superficial and declamatory in expression. It was initiated by Zorrilla in his *Poesías* (1837–39) and sealed by the same poet's *Cantos del Trovador* (1841). The years 1840–41 also saw the appearance of numerous other volumes of the *leyenda* and ballad type. In the meantime, however, the outstanding poet was the ex-revolutionary Espronceda, in whose meagre yet magnificent verses (not published in collected form until 1840) is to be found the almost perfect fusion of Spanish forms and themes with those of foreign inspiration (Byron, Hugo, Béranger). Espronceda died in 1842 and the field was left to the bard Zorrilla and lesser poets. For two decades and more the rhetorical reverberations of the national ballad, of Quintana, and of Victor Hugo—the variegated fountain heads of inspiration for the period—dominate the scene, to drown out the timid and tardy but genuinely romantic voices, the exquisitely simple and poignant verses, of Bécquer and Rosalía de Castro.

Doctrinaire romanticism gained little or no headway in Spain. *El Artista,* the organ of the small group sworn to advance the cause, a *jeunesse dorée* of young intellectuals and artists, had only a year (1835–36) of precarious existence, and the ill-advised attempt of the same group to convert the death and funeral of Larra into a public glorification of suicide met with crushing disapproval. In February of 1837, just nine years after his first review, Mariano José de Larra shot himself, in utter despair (despite his unparalleled success as a critic and satirist) at his country's desperate plight and his own (to him) hopeless situation, a self-created victim of political persecution and of unrequited love. This genuine Wertherian gesture and the scandal of his funeral mark the turning point in the history of Spanish romanticism: the disappearance of the most profoundly romantic temperament of his times and the theatrical emergence, reciting verses at his very grave, of the youthful Zorrilla, whose poetry, both dramatic and narrative, is to strike the dominant note in the romanticism of the forties and beyond: the historical, the legendary, and the rhetorical.

Thus romanticism in Spain presents, in its main lines, like the land itself and the genius and culture of the race, a veritable panorama of paradox. To judge from the popularity of Spanish themes and settings among the romantics of Germany, England, and France, to judge from the apparently romantic qualties inherent in the great enterprises and creations of the Spanish spirit, it would seem that literary romanticism should flourish there as in few countries. Yet the contrary is rather the case. Until the eighteen sixties and after, the German romantics were at best mere names in the Peninsula. Of the English romantics only Byron and, especially, Scott had any influence, and this was by no means decisive. The ideas of the *Conciliatore* were echoed almost immediately and, although almost immediately forgotten, were unconsciously fulfilled in Spain perhaps more completely than in Italy. Indeed, the history of romanticism in Spain has more direct analogies, in the decisive interplay of literary and political factors, with the situation in Italy than even with that in France, although it is French romanticism alone that exercises any important literary influence. Yet even French romanticism made a late entry, was combated or, at best, comprehended but imperfectly, and had in the theatre only a brief moment, in the late thirties, of qualified success. Only in the forties and beyond are Hugo and Lamartine—never Vigny or Musset—definitely incorporated into the stream of Spanish poetry.

The co-existence of the past and the present so peculiar to Spain, the struggle between the weight of the past and the pressure of the present—the tragic dilemma lying at the core of modern Spanish history—is reflected throughout modern Spanish letters and nowhere more clearly than in the nature and course of romanticism in Spain.

—*F. Courtney Tarr*

At first opposed by intellectuals and men of letters in the name of patriotism, literary and political, romanticism of the French variety was, after the revolution of 1830, accepted (with reservations) and practiced (with modifications) by the very same group and for the same patriotic motives. But only because it had been seen—and after it had been made—to conform to the national temper and tradition. The dyed-in-the-wool romantic dramas of Hugo

and Dumas and their Spanish counterparts—notably the *Don Alvaro o la fuersa del sino* (1835) of the Duque de Rivas—awakened more opposition than applause. Earlier attempts to acclimate a new genre, the historical novel, were on the whole disappointing, if not frankly unsuccessful. Romantic lyric poetry gained no great foothold until after the revival of the *romance* or ballad. Thus romanticism, which was in its first Spanish phases largely an international, not to say cosmopolitan, manifestation—witness the activities of the *emigrados* in France and England—came, once it was established in Spain (in modified form, of course) and once the European vogue of Spanish themes and letters had been tardily appreciated—and speedily exaggerated—quickly to be regarded and practiced as a peculiarly national heritage, the direct descendant of the ballads and of the *comedia* of the Golden Age. Indeed, as early as 1837 Victor Hugo is accused (by Mesonero Romanos in his satiric sketch *El romanticismo y los románticos*) of having propagated, not the pure romanticism he absorbed in Spain as a boy, but a deliberately false and adulterated version!

But this Spanish brand of romanticism, incarnate in the figure of Zorrilla, is at best external and rhetorical. Divorced from contact with newer literary currents and with the realities of the times, it reflects only the husks, rarely the spirit, of the past. Its chief vehicle is, naturally enough, dramatic and narrative verse. Of true lyricism there is little. Characteristic romantic themes and attitudes—for instance, the feeling for nature—are few and limited. Significant works of thought and criticism are conspicuously absent. The outstanding prose *genre* is the *artículo* (later *cuadro*) *de costumbres* (humorous and satirical sketches of manners and customs), an eighteenth-century form in origin—it goes back, of course, to Addison and Steele—and romantic only in its preoccupation, in the *cuadro* stage, with picturesque and popular scenes and types. Only in the later *artículos* of Larra, those in which he distills his own satiric despair, identifying, like the true romantic he is, his own and his country's plight, is the *artículo* romantic, romantic in feeling, but not in form or theme.

The genuine romantic personalities either disappear early (Larra, Espronceda) or are obscure or belated figures (Bécquer, Rosalía de Castro). Yet their product, small as it is, is not without distinction. Spanish literature of the romantic period can boast no Byron, Shelley, Wordsworth, or Keats, no Goethe, Schiller, or Heine, no Leopardi, not even a Hugo or a Vigny, yet it does have, in Espronceda and Bécquer, two poets of genuine accent and expression, and in Larra a profoundly romantic personality, as well as a prose artist of the first rank.

Taken as a whole, Spanish letters of the romantic period form the first considerable body of literature of respectable stature since the golden days of Lope and Cervantes. But in Spain as elsewhere, literary productivity is not wholly, nor even predominantly, in the romantic mode. Introduced by a generation steeped in the liberal and neoclassical traditions, romantic drama and poetry were continued by a younger group brought up in the same ideals and who consequently alternated their romantic compositions with the literary types and practices of the preceding era. Although these latter actually predominate from the quantitative standpoint, the period still deserves the label "romantic" (or "pseudo-romantic") because the major literary achievements were in that mode. The romantic period in Spain, then, represents no complete rejection, save for a brief moment and then only in a few extreme cases, of neoclassical principles and personages, but rather a compromise with them, the very compromise, although in reverse order, between national tradition and universal standards advocated since the end of the eighteenth century. In literature, as in politics, there came to reign, after a short flurry of revolt even less fundamental in literature than in politics, a sort of *justo medio (juste milieu)*. The two literary traditions, the age of Cervantes and Lope and that of Jovellanos and Moratín, were both respected, but with emphasis increasingly on the former.

Although some aspects of romanticism (notably literary patriotism and the reaction against the "rules") go far back into the eighteenth century, it does not enter Spain as a conscious literary force until 1830. Yet by 1840 many of its externals have been assimilated and continue to flourish, in increasingly modified form, in the poetry and the theatre of the entire second half of the nineteenth century. But in the group known as the "generation of '98" (in whom the Silver Age of Spanish literature, begun in the novel by Galdós and his contemporaries, is carried to fruition in poetry, drama, and the essay as well) are to be found some of the most genuinely romantic personalities and attitudes in Spanish letters. Their romanticism is vital and functional, not formal or rhetorical. It lies at the root of their attitude toward life and of letters, and is manifest in that blend of personal and national introspection, that fusion of the intellectual and the passionate, of the creative and the critical, which constitutes the peculiar hall-mark of their genius as individuals and as a generation. And, inspired both by contemporary European currents and fundamental national realities, they, especially the most profoundly romantic among them—Unamuno, Baroja, Azorín—deliberately repudiate the literary romanticism of the nineteenth century with its stress on the verbal, the external and the superficially historical, excepting only Larra (in whom they saw a forerunner), Rosalía de Castro, and, with reservations, Espronceda and Bécquer.

Fundamental, then, to the understanding of romanticism in Spain, as elsewhere, is the distinction between the external and the internal between "romantic" and "romanticist." Fundamental too, from the historical rather than the esthetic angle, is the chronological differential, the "time lag" of roughly fifty years or more which, save for occasional moments and individuals, has characterized, from the eighteenth century on, Spanish history and culture with respect to those of England and France. Corollary to this is the patriotic preoccupation which, in one form or other, in one direction or other, permeates the warp and woof of modern Spanish intellectual activity. The co-existence of the past and the present so peculiar to Spain, the struggle between the weight of the past and the pressure of the present—the tragic dilemma lying at the core of modern Spanish history—is reflected throughout modern Spanish letters and nowhere more clearly than in the nature and course of romanticism in Spain. (pp. 35-46)

F. Courtney Tarr, "Romanticism in Spain," in PMLA, *Vol. LV, No. 1, March, 1940, pp. 35-46.*

IMPACT AND LEGACY

Jacques Barzun

[*Barzun is a French-born American critic whose wide range of learning has produced distinguished works in several fields, including history, culture, musicology, literary criticism, and biography. Barzun's writing style has been praised as elegant and unpretentious. In the following excerpt, he surveys the impact of Romanticism, examining the reactions to what he sees as its weaknesses: overexpressiveness, overdramatization, and carelessness.*]

Throughout the *eighteenth* century, all over Europe, signs appeared of new interests and new feelings about neglected elements in life and art. This is sometimes called eighteenth-century romanticism or pre-romanticism. It covers the period from Dyer and Thomson to Cowper, from Klopstock and Wieland to late Lessing and early Goethe, from Marivaux to Marmontel and Chénier—a fairly spontaneous rise of novelty everywhere, in spite of crosscurrents of influence. But this movement is not as yet romanticism. There is in it too great an intermingling of the old with the new, and the all-important new forms, which are the mark of decisive cultural change, are still lacking.

Departure in form appears at widely spaced intervals in the several countries of Europe, and first in Germany—partly because her eighteenth-century literature was largely of French importation, partly because her rich tradition of German folklore was never stamped out by a centralized absolutism. Under Lessing's vigorous and brilliant attacks, second-hand and second-rate classicism fell away and the new forms appeared as early as the 1770s with Bürger's *Lenore,* Goethe's *Götz von Berlichingen,* and Schiller's *Robbers.*

In England, the shock that broke the dominant tradition seems to have been the French Revolution. We can date romanticism from Burns and Blake. Then Scott and Wordsworth sharpen the break in the decade 1789 to 1799, all four deeply moved by the meaning of the events across the Channel. But understandably enough, those same events in France itself had the effect of delaying the outburst of new ideas. Dictatorship, at first revolutionary, then Napoleonic, stifled expression and directed energies to political ends. The most gifted French poet alive in 1789, Chénier, went to the guillotine in 1794. Three years later, the young Viscount René de Chateaubriand was in exile in England, where he published his *Essay on Revolutions,* a mixture of rationalism and the historical spirit, of Rousseau and traditional monarchism. It was not until 1800 that he returned to his native land and saw his fame assured with the *Genius of Christianity,* in which, as someone has said, Pascal triumphs and becomes a poet.

But there were further delays. The Napoleonic censorship suppressed original thought, and the encouragement that Mme. de Stael meant to give to the new ideas by her book on Germany was cut off by the police in 1810. It was not in fact until ten years later that the young genius of Lamartine made itself heard. Between 1820 and 1830, then, is the incubating time of French romanticism, which burst forth in full-blown vigor towards the end of the decade with Hugo's Preface to *Cromwell,* Stendhal's *Racine et Shakespeare,* Delacroix's *Death of Sardanapalus,* and Berlioz's *Fantastic Symphony.*

In Spain, Italy, Poland, and Russia, the establishment of romanticism paralleled in time its coming of age in France. Italy—or rather Milan—was perhaps in advance of Paris, and Spain and Russia a trifle lagging, unless we except the ripe genius of Goya, which reached its high point during the Spanish war of liberation from Napoleon. Everywhere, the new developments were the outcome of deeply rooted national traditions, combined with a common recovery from the eighteenth-century blight on poetry. Russia and Poland offer particularly good examples, their romantic revivals being in fact their first great and original literary epoch since the Renaissance. It is now called, as a result, the "classic period" of their literary history. With Pushkin, Gogol, and Lermontov in Russia, Mickiewicz, Slowacki, and Krasinski in Poland, these two countries not only made lasting contributions to European literature, but explored and gave form to their own past and present, their own reality and ideals, with a fullness and power that nothing in their previous pseudo-classical and pseudo-French tradition could have led one to expect. Here as elsewhere, the quick reception of influences, as shown in, say, Pushkin's Byronism, is a sign, not of imitation but of pre-established sympathy between minds independently tending towards the same goals.

Romanticism as a European phenomenon, then, comes of age between 1780 and 1830, and remains undisputed master of the field until about 1850. This period constitutes what I find it convenient to regard as the first phase. By the latter date, 1850, some of the greatest names in romanticism belong to the dead: Burke, Burns, Byron, Shelley, Blake, Keats, Scott, Wordsworth, Coleridge, Hazlitt, Lamb, Pushkin, Lermontov, Espronceda, Goya, Büchner, Beddoes, Chateaubriand; Leopardi, Beethoven, Chopin, Mendelssohn, Schubert, Schumann, Bellini; Bonington, Géricault, Balzac, Stendhal, Gérard de Nerval, Goethe, Schiller, Hegel, Schelling, Schleiermacher, Hoffmann, Kleist, Hölderlin, Novalis, Wackenroder, and the brothers Schlegel.

This list reveals that in seventy years, two semigenerations—an older and a younger group—have made their contribution and left the stage; yet in the short working time of twenty to twenty-five years allotted to each group, all the forms, ideas, perceptions, tendencies, genres, and critical principles have been put forward which the rest of the nineteenth century is to make use of in its further development. What I am suggesting is that the first phase of romanticism is one of extraordinary, un-

remitting, "unspecialized" production in all fields. The next three phases, which we are about to examine, are efforts at specialization, selection, refinement, and intensification. Romanticism sounds all the themes of the century in its first movement. The next three movements develop one theme each. These next three movements are: Realism, Symbolism—which may also be called Impressionism—and Naturalism. The divisions in time are roughly: 1850 to 1885 for Realism, and 1875 to 1905 for the other two movements.

Each of these takes the form of a strong reaction against its predecessor, with the exception of Naturalism, which reacts against its own contemporary, Symbolism. This strong reaction is accompanied, of course, by theories which tell us that the preceding movement has failed, but which generally point at the same time to some part of that movement as containing the germs of a solution to the new problems of the particular art. Thus, for instance, the realistic Russian novelists admire and vindicate parts of Gogol, but separate them from what they are pleased to call his romanticism, as if the artist had not been himself in both aspects of his genius.

In the nature of things, the movements that follow the "failure of romanticism" are, like any specialization, easier to grasp and define. They are more consistent and concentrated; they have more the air of a school about them. But when closely examined they show such clear marks of stemming from the main trunk that no doubt can arise about the thesis here presented: romanticism does not die out in 1850 but branches out under different names like a delta.

This has sometimes been remarked, but usually in piecemeal fashion. The relation of the Pre-Raphaelites to Blake, and of the Impressionists to Turner and Delacroix, is perhaps the most visible, and hence the most often noted, but it is not necessarily the closest. In some cases, as with Zola and Flaubert, the debt to Hugo and Balzac has been admitted by the artists themselves. This is also true of the debt owed by the Russian Five to Glinka, Weber, and Berlioz. That owed by Debussy and the whole French school to Berlioz has also been demonstrated. Often, where the kinship between a romantic and a post-romantic may seem tenuous, the appearance can generally be accounted for by a quantitative difference: there is much more Impressionism in an Impressionist than in Delacroix, because Impressionism is all there is in an Impressionist. What is plain in the later man is but one aspect of the work of the earlier.

I need not add that opinions are free to vary as to which of any two phases is preferable—the first, encyclopedic, or one of the later, selective. With this question of taste we are not concerned. Modern feeling, for understandable reasons, works against a just appreciation of romanticist performance. Even so, to choose among artists otherwise than in the light of one's own enjoyable perceptions is foolishness, and to want styles immutable is but to quarrel with history: there is neither the need nor the possibility of a new full-scale renaissance or romanticism every twenty years, and after an epoch of revolutionary triumphs, artists can only refine.

If there were any doubt about this, the doubt would be removed by the tendency, noticeable in many romanticists, to end their career with a conscious effort at refinement and simplification. Tieck and Pushkin, Berlioz and Goethe, are good examples, for whom there is no need to invoke the misleading cliché of "reformed romantic" as if there were something of the repentant criminal in a change of manner. It is very likely that if a certain type of artist lived for two hundred years while his contemporaries lasted the usual span, he would follow without constraint or imitation the curve of their successive changes of style. This is not artistic determinism. It suggests not a cause but a condition of art, namely that its problems and techniques follow an inner logic, at the same time as they respond to that outside pressure of the times which the greatest artists have seldom wished to resist.

With these generalities in mind, we are in a position to do for Realism what I have tried to do for Romanticism: to see as far as possible through the eyes of its representative figures. Since Realism began with the assumption that romanticism had failed, what is meant by this failure? Obviously romanticism had failed to please the younger generation. But had it failed absolutely? It seems a paradox to speak of failure and yet go back to haggle over works and men as critics and artists have been doing for a century. If the first phase of romanticism ended in bankruptcy, why the waste of time over the wreckage? Undoubtedly what is meant is failure*s*, in the plural.

For unquestionably romanticism failed at many things. It failed to establish a universal order, permanent peace, and a common language of art and philosophy. As E. M. Forster has said, history is a series of messes. From these, temporary and local achievements stand out like isolated peaks. This is in fact what romanticism asserts about the world, and the paradox would be to have its clearest perception belied by its own results. In classicism, the peak is the establishment of fixed order for a small class by the exclusion of real but disturbing facts. In romanticism the peaks are individual achievements, serviceable to others not by enforced imitation but by free choice. Consequently romanticism is rich in successes, and proportionately rich in failures. Who tries for much stands to gain or lose much. No concealment in mediocrity is possible, even if desire for concealment were present.

As heralds of defeat one thinks first of those disheartened German romantics who turned joylessly to Catholicism, neo-medievalism, and political nationalism, because a more inclusive and more perfect order did not win the support of their fellow nationals. Next, one looks at the so-called Victorian Compromise, which followed the Reform Bill of 1832 and the rise of industrialism. There one sees political order achieved by a class who voluntarily accepted the strictest code of morality as a substitute for force and a guarantee against revolution. That purpose was fulfilled by subtracting from the romanticist program a certain freedom of individual behavior and certain expressions of the feelings. At this cost intellectual freedom alone was saved out of the larger romanticist scheme.

On the Continent, where between 1830 and 1848 a similar attempt was made by a part of the bourgeoisie, one thinks

of the series of uprisings and revolutions which precluded compromise while seeking a short cut to the good life, that is to say, the concrete goods romanticism had desired: individual liberty within the social organism; the satisfaction of man's needs under the spur of imagination; and the pursuit of the intellectual, national, and religious life without superstition or intolerance. By 1850 all these legitimate aims were disappointed, whether they had been expressed as liberalism, as cultural nationalism, or as Utopian socialism.

The rebound from this disappointment was Realism. The very word wants to convey that what romanticism desired was not possible and that the romanticists' methods would not work. Realism is the fox in the fable who said the grapes were sour. This likeness does not prejudge the case against Realism, though to this day no one can affirm that the romantic aims are not achievable by the romantic means. Realism, meanwhile, was sure that they were not, and hence turned to two familiar devices—force and materialism. It developed *Realpolitik,* which means the abandonment of principle—on principle—and the adoption of cynicism in its place. The signs and successes of this new method were seen in the unification of Italy under Cavour, that of Germany under Bismarck, and the emergence of the second French Empire under Napoleon III.

In thought, materialism played the same role that force played in politics. In the highly symptomatic work of Karl Marx, the two are united. Force replaces either the concerted good will of the earlier socialists or the individualist-mutualist schemes of a Fourier or Proudhon. In German philosophy, the materialistic school flourished in the fifties with Moleschott, Ludwig Büchner—the brother of the dead romantic poet—and Feuerbach, whose writings influenced another symptomatic character of the period—Richard Wagner.

Behind all these manifestations of force and matter was the august authority of physical science, particularly chemistry and the new physics, which had just established the theories of the conservation of matter and the mechanical equivalent of heat. Here, too, unification was going on, and a new world system was being built which seemed a bridge reaching back to Newton over the dead body of romantic, vitalist biology. For this was also the time when the work of Spencer and Darwin once again delivered biology over to materialism. So ripe was the occasion that within five years after the appearance of the *Origin of Species,* the belief began to spread that science was synonymous with *Darwinismus.* The return to eighteenth-century mechanism was complete, and it looked as if romanticism had never been, except for the fact that Realism discovered and gave fame to a neglected romantic philosopher—not a materialist, but a stoic who had proclaimed the inescapable badness of things—Arthur Schopenhauer.

What had in fact occurred? A *reduction* of romantic perceptions and methods to a single term: Realism meant force *without* principle, matter *without* mind, mechanism *without* life. And what was the motive of this simplification? The quicker or surer achievement of some of the romantic aims: nationhood, social order, intellectual unity, the improvement of the human lot. Marx's socialism proceeds from all the motives of his so-called Utopian pre-decessors, but scorns morality and persuasion while presenting itself to the public as science. Finally, what method served this realistic reduction? It was the method of appeal to a common denominator. Liberals, conservatives, and radicals were united by their common desire for tangible, territorial nationhood; scientific hypotheses were tested by their suitability to mechanical representation or analogy—it was the heyday of the luminiferous ether; while force, which is by its nature the great leveler, was applied as the universal solvent of social contradictions and complexities.

This notion of a common denominator ruthlessly adhered to is of course essential to science, though it may make a difference to science itself which denominator is chosen. But Realism had as yet no inkling of this. It equated science with the common denominator of matter, which is why the post-romantic period seems in all ways so scientific. It felt it had at last reached solid ground, not only in the study of nature but in that of history, philology, law, economics, and anthropology. It prided itself on correcting the errors and "extravagances" of the romanticists—though as one candid scholar pointed out, if the romanticists had not been, there would have been nothing to correct.

This pattern appears with identical effect in the domain of art. The Realist schools that sprang up in the fifties and sixties were inspired by the desire to correct and amend romanticism. Here again, what were the characteristic romantic failures? Some have already been mentioned—overexpressiveness; unsuccessful attempts at new forms; an exuberance of animal spirits, translated, as in Elizabethan England, into an exuberance of language; a too zestful appetite for dramatic contrast, intensity, and distortion. To these may be added a certain roughness and carelessness of treatment, side by side with the most finished and minute detail—Gothic or Shakespearean characteristics, which are frequent in the works of men conscious of their strength and indifferent to proving it.

Repelled and irritated by all this, the realists applied as their new criterion of the "really real" the denominator of common experience. Flaubert supplies the classic example of Realism so defined and made into a method. *Madame Bovary* is the bible of Realism as *Faust* is the bible of romanticism. We have often enough been told how hard Flaubert worked and we know from successive drafts of his novel what he was working toward. He strove for truth through the exclusion of subjective detail, by which—if the reader will recall our earlier definition—I do not mean fanciful detail, but simply individual and possibly uncommon perception. In the various stages of a description of rain falling on Rouen and the surrounding hills, for example, Flaubert flattens out every image, removes every salient word, docks every "original" idea, until what is left is what anybody might have said about the scene—though nobody, of course, but Flaubert could have said it. Scene and prose are objectified by being made completely intersubjective.

Now a noteworthy fact about the master of Realism is that he began as a romanticist. He himself recorded the trans-formation. "How did you spend your youth?" he inquires of a friend in 1858. "Mine was very beautiful *inwardly*. I had enthusiasms which I now seek for in vain; friends, alas, who are dead or changed. A great confidence in myself, splendid leaps of the soul, something impetuous in my whole personality. I dreamed of love, glory, beauty. My heart was as wide as the world, and I breathed all the winds of heaven. And then gradually, I have grown callous, tarnished. I accuse nobody but myself. I gave myself over to absurd emotional gymnastics. I took pleasure in fighting my senses and torturing my heart. I repelled the human intoxications which were offered me. Furious with myself, I uprooted the man in me with both hands, two hands full of pride and strength. I wished to make of that tree with verdant foliage a bare column in order to place on its summit, as on an altar, I know not what divine flame. . . . That is why I find myself at thirty-six so empty and at times so weary. Is not this story of mine a little like your own?"

The secret of Realism lies in this change, in these "emotional gymnastics." It was not only Flaubert's story but that of all his self-aware contemporaries who at the sight of the material conditions of their time determined to replace the "tree with verdant foliage" by a bare column. Flaubert, as we shall see, underwent another spiritual change and ended as a symbolist, but his importance for us here is that he first crucified romanticism in himself, knowing that had he not done so, his romanticism would have been secondhand, anachronistic, inadequate; just as it was in Emma Bovary, who, as we all know, read Scott in her adolescence and dramatized herself as a heroine throughout life. When Flaubert reached the point of saying, "*I* am Emma Bovary," the Realistic *coup d'état* had become history.

Because Flaubert had to blind himself to the realism in Scott and to pick and choose among the elements of Balzac does not mean that he was ungrateful or unjust as a critic. It means only that specialization had set in. A different order of genius was being used upon selected materials. "Flaubert," as John Peale Bishop aptly said, "already represents a deterioration of the romantic will in which both Stendhal and Byron, with the prodigious example of Napoleon before them, could not but believe."

For fifty years or more after Flaubert, the novel was to be the plausible and minute recital of commonplace events. More than that, because the setting and routine of life were being made increasingly drab by industry, the contents of the novel became more and more dreary and dull, until that moment in George Gissing's *New Grub Street* when the wretched Biffen loses the manuscript of the most realistic of all novels—so like life that its dullness will make it impossible to read.

That the great realistic novels of the mid-century are anything but dull hardly disproves the validity of Realism as a method. For though by it the real is defined as the commonplace and tends towards the sordid, it yet covers and cultivates so wide a field that to see it systematically exploited is in itself a pleasure. The romanticists—Scott, Balzac, Hugo, Stendhal, George Sand, Gogol—had shown in famous chapters what could be done with the commonplace and even the sordid. And the new, total Realism did not always achieve the naked form that Flaubert sought for. In Dickens, in Thackeray, in George Eliot, and even in Trollope—partly because they were born during the heyday of romanticism, and partly because of the Victorian moral tone—realism often appears side by side with an agreeable make-believe which I have termed second-hand romanticism. I mean such things as the story of Amelia and Dobbin in *Vanity Fair* or the change of plot forced on Dickens in *Our Mutual Friend.* (pp. 96-106)

It remains to explain what symbolism means, since it is clear that all art whatever uses symbols. The specialization that deserves the new name consists either in new combinations of symbols—be they words or shapes—or in the unexpected transfer of a symbol from its usual meaning and context to a new one. The "scarlet cry" is the familiar poetic example, one of many in romantic verse. Blake's poems are almost wholly made up of such transferred and reshuffled verbal symbols, his difficult Prophetic Books, like their illustrations, being nothing but a systematic use of the device. We readily see its usefulness for reacting against Realism. By limiting itself to words and images that are universally current, Realism rapidly wears out its symbols. It keeps the context eternally the same, for fear of falling into an individual variation of the true. Artists tired of realism have no choice but to revivify symbols by putting them to unaccustomed uses in unaccustomed places.

Or rather, artists have a choice between this attempt to refresh the conventions and a return to an older set. And to put this alternative in its proper relation to all the post-romantic efforts, I must here digress. The marginal doctrine I have in mind is nineteenth-century neo-classicism. Being a purely individual, though recurrent tendency, it has no distinct place in the chronology. But some of the men who followed a neo-classic course are important enough to mention briefly. Puvis de Chavannes, who decorated the walls of the Boston Public Library and many public buildings in France, fairly represents the quality of the neo-classical mood. Its keynote is calm, austerity, determined anti-Realism as well as anti-romanticism.

It is in fact anti-present-day-ism. Though it takes the arts seriously, it regards them as the decoration rather than the expression of life; hence, like its parent classicism, it believes in rules independent of time and space. Thus did the poet Leconte de Lisle polish many beautiful verses about subjects antique and oriental; and thus in the second half of their careers did Brahms and César Franck seek to restore purity and "form" to music. They generally meant by this aloofness or piety combined with academicism. Matthew Arnold himself was tempted by an imaginary Greek ideal and produced the tragedy of *Merope* under its inspiration; but it was a vision that had obviously paled since the day when Sophocles saw life steadily and whole.

None of these five fully succeeded in welding their derivative subject matter to their would-be classical form. Theirs was a reaction against Realism which may be truly called reactionary, and it is this which lends a characteristic flavor to their work. What could be more refreshing than to see the contemplative Grecians who in Puvis's work represent chemistry and physics, industry and trade; or to think that in the middle of the toilsome nineteenth century he should paint "The Fisherman's Family" as a collection of pink and placid athletes, grouped about a smack that has never been to sea? Clearly, these are the fishermen of a golden age when the day's catch jumps ashore into the net. Neo-classicism is a sometimes moving expression of that distant hope, but in the century of romanticism the gap was still too great. Classicism had as yet no social role to play.

Having made this brief circuit, we can return to the third genuine and powerful phase of romanticism: symbolism. With the Pre-Raphaelites, as we saw, it took the guise of the "new simplicity" in order to work at the revivification of pictorial and poetic symbols. What we now call "arty" is the exaggeration of these tendencies, which Gilbert and Sullivan satirized in *Patience,* this play, incidentally being directed not at Oscar Wilde, as is usually said, but at the Pre-Raphaelites who were Wilde's forerunners. For symbolism did not stop with the relatively mild "strangeness" of Rossetti and his friends, still under the realistic afterglow. Symbolism developed in the direction of increasing subjectivism in word, image, and sound, and finally presented such a united front against the older Realists as to deserve the name of neo-romanticism.

Flaubert shows the gradualness of the transition very clearly. *Madame Bovary* is Realism: *Salammbô* is realism laid in a foreign setting, with the result that the commonplace for Carthage is nevertheless strange and wonderful for Europeans. This historical novel is, as it were, a way of playing truant from the Realist school without incurring the charge of romanticism. For the next step, Flaubert pulls out his old manuscript on the *Temptation of St. Anthony* and, by pruning it, shapes a work without plot, without visible bearing upon common life, occasionally without literal intelligibility, a veritable symbolist "prose poem." In it, as already in *Salammbô,* we find a sensuous pleasure in words, a sought-after musicality, which are contrary to Realistic tenets. In *St. Anthony,* there is added a multiple allegory that relates the work to symbolism. In a parallel manner, Wagner, the great idol of the Symbolist poets, straddles both movements. He appealed to the Symbolists by virtue of the allegorical, legendary, and atmospheric elements of his operas, while he taught them and their elders the meaning of the music "realistically" through its close association with concrete objects.

The musical impressionists, who came later and of whom Debussy is the best-rounded example, made the break with Realism complete. They not only chose their texts from the Symbolist poets themselves, beginning with Rossetti, but they were symbolists (or impressionists) in their disregard of the rhetoric of melody and chord, which they broke up and rejoined in new contexts. Here as elsewhere, the sign of the passage from realism to symbolism is the deliberate abandonment of established syntax.

The poetical creed of a Verlaine, the obscurities of a Rimbaud, the involution of images in Mallarmé, the impalpable atmosphere of Whistler's nocturnes, are but the working out of the premise that Realism is a very narrow and short-lived convention, which fails to give permanent unity to experience. Symbolism attempts the reunion of the two halves of experience—the inner or subjective part with the outer and communicable part—as against the divorce, productive of sentimentality and materialism, which Realism dictates. As we shall see later, and as indeed we all know from reading Proust, Joyce, and Gertrude Stein, the work of remaking language for the sake of a new synthetic experience is by no means over.

A comparable course of action explains the development of the school of painting known as Impressionism. By refining more and more on the perceptions of the human eye, by making use of the scientific truth that white light is made up of colors, and that complementary colors heighten each other's intensity when set close together, the Impressionists followed a worthy "realistic" bent which soon landed them clean outside the photographic reality. The effects achieved by their divided palette and the pointillism that gives such a wonderful brightness and shimmer to their canvases were so exactly studied and managed that the original beholders thought the painters were mad or making fun of the public. The retort was that realism was itself an arbitrary selection from among visible objects, and that the impressionist goal was to convey a new truth by means of a new set of symbols—dots and dashes of bright paint. Outline may have disappeared in the process, just as fixed views of natural objects had proved illusory under changing lights, "but"—prophesied the Impressionists—"you will soon see Nature as we do"; an outcome which Oscar Wilde was to erect into the principle that Nature imitates art.

Looking back on these three groups—the commonplace realists, the faithful impressionists, and the evocative symbolists—we are permitted to draw an important conclusion about the evolution of style. Strictly speaking, every school of art pretends to capture reality and every successful school does it. The classicist dwells on the reality of the abstract and the general; the romanticist on the concrete particular, both mental and physical; the Realist with a capital *R*, on the commonplace and physical; the Impressionist, on the individual impression of the physical; the Symbolist on the need to extend the range of his impressions and to make them vivid once more by defying realism and convention. Each doctrine takes in more or less; each doctrine at the beginning of its trial has validity; each doctrine, when repetition and imitation have set in, disintegrates from lack of meaning and conviction—and falls a prey to its successor.

This leaves us with one more wave of the romanticist impulse to discuss, namely, Naturalism. It is the fourth phase, but not in order of time, since its manifestations coincided with those of Symbolism and Impressionism. There occurred a split, in other words, in the generation that protested against dogmatic Realism. One group—generally the poets—preferred to exploit the subjective domain of idea, dream, word-music, and legend. These are the symbolist poets from Rossetti down to Rimbaud, Mallarmé, and Maeterlinck. The other group, chiefly novelists, were unwilling to forget the collective reality of late nineteenth-century Europe—its cities, factories and slums, its wars, social problems, and scientific beliefs. In

this group Zola, the Goncourt brothers, Strindberg, Dostoevski, Huysmans, Sudermann, and Verhaeren belong. Some men, finally, divided their allegiance—the Goncourts, to begin with, who are the true precursors of modernism in taste as in style; and such men as Ibsen, Verlaine, Hauptmann, William Morris, John Davidson, and George Moore. I do not pretend to give a survey of the period or even to fit these names with finality, but to suggest tendencies.

In music, naturalism was made a conscious program by some members of the French school, principally Alfred Bruneau, and interpretation has extended the meaning of the word to apply to such composers as Moussorgsky, Chabrier, Charpentier, and most of all to Richard Strauss. In painting it may not be too farfetched to class Cézanne and the Post-Impressionists with the naturalists, as men who said in effect, "Objects exist—and not merely light—but Realism is too narrow. We shall restore the solidity of objects, but we shall paint either the commonplace or the uncommon, as we please; and in a manner suited to our temperaments, whatever the photograph-minded public may think." The Post-Impressionists also brought to light the genius of the romanticist Daumier, whom his contemporaries—excepting Balzac and Delacroix—had dismissed as a mere political cartoonist.

An interesting difference between the literary naturalists and the post-impressionists is that whereas the latter took their stand squarely on the artistic requirements of the situation in painting, the former pretended to treat of life according to scientific methods. At least the French naturalists, led by Zola, believed for a time in the possibility of making their novels "experimental researches" into the nature of reality. The device of accumulating genuine case histories from the newspapers—a practice which Dickens and Charles Reade had already followed; the "working up" and insertion of technical dissertations into the body of the novel—which Balzac and George Eliot were wont to do; and more importantly, the selection of subjects that involved the study of social plague spots—these things constituted the naturalistic stock-in-trade. The contradiction between the claim to scientific dispassionateness and the reforming zeal is only on the surface. Zola would have answered that his work was *applied* science. But in applying it, it was evident that the individual was re-entering the scene he had left under Realist theory, and Zola ultimately admitted that naturalism was a corner of life seen through a temperament.

When this admission was made, the outlook of science itself had begun to change. The hypothesis of materialism was undergoing a thorough riddling at the hands of critics such as William James, Nietzsche, Samuel Butler, Bergson. These men did not attack science or its method, but only its temporary ally, mechanistic materialism. It was becoming ever clearer that science did not copy reality in full but selected from it and created symbols—verbal or mathematical—to fit the relevant facts. The language of science was as arbitrary and manmade as that of art: It was both Symbolist and Naturalistic.

The result of casting loose from narrow Realism was a kind of scientific neo-romanticism: in biology and evolutionary theory, the work of De Vries and Bateson was creating a non-mechanical science of genetics. In psychology, James and Freud were displacing Spencer and overturning mid-century dogmas. In morals and art criticism, Nietzsche had revised all the "Realistic" values and discredited the authority of Darwin, Marx, and Wagner. In physics, Max Planck and Einstein had revised Newtonianism and raised more questions than Newton or the nineteenth century could answer. For by this time we have reached the twentieth, the first world war is on the verge of breaking out, and the cultural work of western man is about to suffer another of its periodic eclipses. (pp. 109-14)

> *Jacques Barzun, "The Four Phases of Romanticism," in his* Classic, Romantic and Modern, *revised edition, Little, Brown and Company, 1961, pp. 96-114.*

Henri Peyre

[*In the following excerpt, Peyre examines the impact of Romanticism on late nineteenth-century French writers and the survival of its influence in the twentieth century.*]

Ernest Seillière, one of the most "romantic" prophets of the past in our century, and one of the most stubborn adversaries of European romanticism, had given the name "imperialism" to what he considered most to be dreaded in romantic sensibility. We would not like to be guilty of another sort of imperialism by trying to connect with romanticism all that followed this tremendous agitation of the nineteenth century. There were many Frenchmen who repudiated romanticism's aesthetics, its search for very obvious effects, its cultivation of excess and horror, its immodesty at times, and its tolerance of a plebeian sentimentalism. Furthermore, no literary or artistic period ever consents to being only the imitation or banal continuation of one which has preceded it, the grandeur of which overwhelms it; and no writer, however little ability he may have, willingly resigns himself to being a mere follower. The very exacerbation of individualism, which was one of the romantic traits, drove the successors of Byron, Schiller, Hugo, and Delacroix to become themselves as much as possible.

We are concerned here with another aspect of romanticism. We maintain that romanticism can no more be limited by very clearly defined dates than it can be restricted to any definition. One cannot, without artifice, hold up the date of 1843, or consider Victor Hugo's failure in the theater or Ponsard's short-lived success as a reason for entitling a chapter of our textbooks "the end or the death of romanticism." Sainte-Beuve, in one of his moments of anti-romantic bitterness which clouded his clearsightedness, made a mistake about this. Other critics, misled by their conservative and moralistic prejudices, have also rung the knell of a movement which had always seemed dangerous to them. But neither Balzac, nor Vigny, nor Delacroix, nor above all Hugo had ceased to be of consequence in the period 1843–1850. Gautier, Nerval, Pétrus Borel had continued to write. And it was these masters, born around 1800 or 1810, that the young generation, which was preparing a new literary period, ecstatically ad-

mired. They did not care about *La Preface de Cromwell* or the old quarrel about unities and noble or proletarian words. But René, Obermann, Raphaël of *La Peau de chagrin,* Lucien of *Illusions perdues,* and Musset's Octave were their elder brothers and their heroes.

It is almost inevitable that a rising literary generation should try at first to assert itself by opposing those who immediately precede it and by indicating forcefully its differences in point of view, ideals, and method. For sons to act differently towards their fathers, for gifted disciples to act otherwise towards their masters, would be to confess that their presence in the world was quasi-useless and that everything had been said and accomplished before them and for them. So they join forces to emphasize the deficiencies of their elders and repudiate the doctrines (romantic, impressionist, symbolist, cubist, existentialist, structuralist) that their predecessors have professed and sometimes used. That is all the more natural as any generation which is thus going to assert itself sees immediately before it not the giants who had triumphed in their time and imposed their successful innovations, but their followers, daunted by the greatness of their elders: those who had exploited already conquered territory, applied the new tricks of the trade, and often exaggerated the mannerisms or peculiarities of those who had been the true literary conquerors.

In France in particular, where journalists, critics, and professors find it convenient to group writers by "schools," a second generation of romantics, born around 1810, who have been mentioned above, had, about 1835-1840, caused some stir by its peculiar behavior and by some of its literary lucubrations. They have been called by different names: "groupe de la rue du Doyenné," "Jeunes-France" (after an amusing book of Théophile Gautier), "the generation of art for art's sake" (to the extent that the aggressive preface of *Mademoiselle de Maupin* was their manifesto). They have not been studied very much in painting or literature, and that is a pity: for they were often more unhappy than true rebels and they suffered from their bohemianism, their relative lack of success (nobody had any idea then about the apotheosis which would one day transfigure Nerval into a sacred monster!), the isolation to which the literary and almost official success of Hugo, Balzac, Vigny, and Delacroix was going to relegate them. It was against these minor romantics, considered as humbugs or incurable failures, that a part of literature between 1850 and 1870 reacted—the part which was taking shape mainly in Paris and preferred to look beyond these "minor romantics," as they are called today, to the great men who had preceded them and were more powerful and prolific. Chateaubriand, Hugo, Balzac, Delacroix continued to inspire respect in the men of letters of the Second Empire, and even in their envious contemporary, Sainte-Beuve.

But it was provincials, both important and insignificant, who had moved to Paris, who left their mark on French literature, particularly in the nineteenth century, young men who were champing at the bit in the Grenoble of Stendhal and Berlioz, the Touraine of Balzac, the Normandy of Flaubert, the South of Daudet and Zola. Fromentin experienced in his Charente a youthful and melancholy love and dreamed of painting in a Parisian studio; Leconte de Lisle, in his distant island and later at Rennes, balked even more at the dull middle-class; Renan and then Taine remained, even in Paris, the hardworking natives of their province and gathered knowledge and reflections to later force their way into the academies and change the insipid philosophy of their predecessors. All of them, intoxicated by what they read, even more Byronian at the start of their career than the men of 1820 or 1830 had ever been, borrowing from Byron a few themes and a type of conventional hero, experienced romanticism through their sensibility and the dreams of their senses or their mind.

In spite of all that unites a generation at its beginnings—shared disdain, hatreds, and admiration—each of those who are a part of it remains an individual. As soon as he feels he has found himself in his first books or pictures, he accentuates the features which distinguish him from his contemporaries, whose passions and ambitions he had shared when they were together at school, at cafés, or in the same studio. Each of the writers who asserted their authority in France during the Second Empire, and each of the painters of the Salon des Refusés (exhibition of rejected works), almost all of whom drew inspiration from Delacroix without imitating him, deserve a study of their connections with romanticism and the romantics, and of what was romantic in them: this last point of course presupposes an agreement on the main elements of a definition.

There was one failing of the romanticists that almost all their successors noticed and vowed they would avoid: a cheap display of emotion. It is very difficult to decide at what moment the expression of personal sensibility becomes a slightly puerile sentimentality, and finally a display of one's sufferings, of one's intimate life, of the pity inspired in us by others, and of the self-pity that the term "maudlin sentimentalism" evokes. Even the greatest writers have not been able to avoid it; these include the first great English romantics, for example, Wordsworth in "The Idiot Boy" or "The Afflictions of Margaret," or the moving story in verse of his encounters with Simon Lee, an old hunter, or with an old beggar of Cumberland. Shelley, in some of his slightly over-facile songs, also lays himself open to the reproaches of those who criticize a certain mawkishness in art. The aesthetes that professors of literature quickly become, lovers of refined art and of a certain irony which cures the self-pity of every lyricist or elegist, severely criticize this "keepsake" literature appealing to young British girls. This is perhaps a necessary stage in the formation of taste and one which it would be foolish to be ashamed about later. From Tennyson's *Enoch Arden,* Poe's "Ulalume," or Verlaine's musical expression of tears shed over a town and his own heart, the lover of poetry then comes to more restrained works. He guesses fairly rapidly that, as Verlaine himself remarked maliciously about E. A. Poe, the immodest poet or the devout painter who manages to move him is the one who is smart and wily. Traditionally, in the last hundred years or more, we have rejected, as the most discomfiting and outdated aspect of romanticism, the excessively languid poems, embarrassing to our sense of modesty, of Longfellow, Heine, Lamartine, and Musset, the emotion of Hugo about his

children and, of course, patriotic poems. We reserve our tears for the sentimental songs sung at cafés or played on the barrel-organ. This involves curious problems of the psychology of taste, or perhaps of psychoanalysis, which literary critics have preferred not to tackle so far. They prefer to make fun of the poor taste displayed by Goethe in admiring Béranger or even by Taine writing with deference to that old song-writer in June 1853; or they treat as the tall stories of a dandy or the mistaken ideas of a young man the very embarrassing praise that Baudelaire bestowed on that detestable woman poet Marceline Desbordes-Valmore, on Hégésippe Moreau, and on Pierre Dupont in 1861. And yet at that time he was forty years old.

The same Baudelaire attacked elsewhere the display of personal emotion by Musset. It may even be, as he insinuated in a letter to his mother in which he boasted about being extremely good at lying, that he had been repulsed by the sentimentality and social pity of *Les Misérables* even as he was praising the work in public and in writing. Leconte de Lisle and Rimbaud likewise rejected Musset as just good enough for high school adolescents, and were barely lukewarm in their attitude towards Lamartine's elegies. Furthermore, they thus distorted the image of Musset, a poet even more damned than those whom Verlaine called "les poètes maudits" (more than Mallarmé certainly, and Corbière), and a virtuoso artist who, in his better moments, demanded much from himself. There continued in fact to be a great deal of sentimentality in the works of the Parnassians and Verlaine, Samain, and Laforgue, as well as in Gide, who was always ready to weep over what he read, and Proust, who was moved by *François le Champi* and by *Mill on the Floss.* But this sentimentality is expressed slightly differently. The immodest naivety of the romantics lost popularity. In about the middle of the twentieth century, immodesty is transferred from the heart to the body and endeavors to be more brutal, or more wholesome.

It was not only against the tendency towards sentimentality, but also against what was at times slipshod, vague, and limp in construction and expression (among poets and novelists) in romantic literature, that the following generation protested—the generation that is sometimes called Parnassian, giving too much honor to a poetic collection that was on the whole very modest. A great deal, if not all, has been said about the cult of impassivity on the part of some of these poets, about their substitution of history, archaeology, and a review of defunct religions and past centuries for the expression of the wretched and egotistic self of the romantics. The determination of Flaubert, who had been extremely sentimental and hyperbolic at the start of his career, to compose an objective, well-ordered novel, almost the antithesis of the novel of Balzac, is well known. There is no doubt that there was unfairness in some of his peremptory judgments, in his *Correspondance,* or in Leconte de Lisle's prefaces. In actual fact, in the best works of Balzac, Hugo, and Vigny, there had been organization, structure, and deliberate adaptation of means to the goal aimed for. It was against the failings and excesses of its elders that the new generation, very naturally, stormed, as it was anxious to mark the difference between them and to take their place. Nothing would have been worse for the Parnassians than to have been contented with imitating Hugo; for Flaubert, Fromentin, the Goncourts, and Zola than to have done over again works like Balzac's or George Sand's. It was not by their aesthetics, but by their sensibility, that the writers of 1845-1875 were still romantics, and by the dreams of their imagination dissatisfied with the present and their country. They too were rebels. The development of society, between 1830 and 1860, having brought about a reinforcement of the state and the growth of technology, made their revolt only more hopeless. They did not fall into line later, as Hugo, Mérimée, and Sainte-Beuve had done when they had become peers of France or senators of the Empire, or like Lamartine, when he was minister for a while. None of the novelists of the period 1850–1880 were even admitted to the Académie. The Parnassian poets were only admitted into it later, and the painters were poorly treated in the official art exhibitions for an even longer period. (pp. 149-54)

There had undoubtedly been adolescents tormented by dire anxiety, eager to experience life but refusing the conditions that their social sphere imposed on them, inclined to ruthless self-analysis, long before those whom we call the preromantics. But if Virgil, Botticelli, El Greco, Shakespeare, Racine, or Montesquieu had suffered from being in conflict with the world, they had not revealed it. Rousseau and his contemporaries greatly enlarged the domain of psychology and analytical literature by authorizing what one of the enemies of romanticism, Ernest Seillière, called *Le Mal romantique* (*The Romantic Malady*) in the title of one of his works. There have been very few men who have not been affected by it, among those whose correspondence and intimate works have given us information about their youthful crisis. One could mention in this context the Goncourt brothers, Huysmans, Mallarmé, Claudel, Gide, Suarès, Alain Fournier, Mauriac, Lyautey (who, according to the letters he wrote as a young officer, was bored to death in his garrison), and many more contemporary men.

Of course, this youthful period of revolt and despair can only be a passing crisis. Those who have gone through it later become angry with themselves for having uttered adolescent complaints and having felt a disgust for life before having lived or acted. Sometimes, they turn in shame and anger against those romantic poets in whom they had felt they could see themselves. They punish themselves for having been taken in by them. This was what happened with Zola and to some extent with Valéry after his "Nuit de Gênes," when he resolved not to feel any more pity for women and himself. At the same time, they repudiate in romantic aesthetics what seemed to encourage facility, doleful complaints, flabbiness of style, and a lack of rigor in thinking. They hold up to ridicule love elegies, idealizations of the angelic woman, and protestations of sincerity. Mallarmé and Valéry made fun of that poetry based on the theme of love, written by men (Lamartine, Musset, or Hugo) who were fully aware of carnal realities. And Mauriac himself, in spite of the fact that he was inspired by Maurice de Guérin, Baudelaire, and Barrès, sometimes spoke harshly about the romanticism which he had fostered in himself.

But what writers might have said for a century for or against their romantic predecessors counts for less in our opinion than the traits of their sensibility and their temperament by which romanticism is recognized: literary, moral, and metaphysical revolt; solitude and despair; lack of moderation, a passion for the great and tremendous; a need to embrace nature and the world in their fierce "imperialism"; finally, an implicit or instinctive pantheism. In the generation which was born around 1840 and grew up during the Second Empire, Cézanne (born in 1839), Monet or Redon (born in 1840), Rodin (1840), and in literature, Villiers de L'Isle-Adam (born in 1838), Mallarmé and Charles Cros (1842), Verlaine (1844), Corbière (1845), Lautréamont (1846) could be chosen as examples. Daudet (in books like *Le Petit Chose* or *Sappho*) and Zola, both born in 1840, were the most typical of them all. A few lines on Zola will have to suffice here. The letters he wrote, when he was young, to his three friends from Aix—Valabrègue, Cézanne, and especially Baille—give us a clear picture of him.

Brunetière, who bluntly opposed him but who was basically fascinated by him, said very rightly somewhere: "Flaubert, whom I would call the last of the romantics if Zola had not existed." Seillière, who was a supporter too of tradition and morals, entitled the first chapter of his book on Zola: "The stigmata of the romantic temperament." By that he meant faith in the natural goodness of man, the will for power, and even nervous instability, which in Zola's case was undoubtedly real. Zola had confided his constant anguish about his work to Dr. Toulouse, who had observed and studied him as a nevropath: "Oh! what a poor hurt soul I am!" The first of Zola's novels which are of consequence, *La Confession de Claude* (1866), is indeed the still maladroit work of a hyper-romantic, eager, notwithstanding, to react against the romantic clichés. *La Faute de l'abbé Mouret* (1875), the work of his maturity, was undoubtedly the most luxuriant and exuberant of the romantic novels of the entire century. Nature was even more ardently alive in it than in *Les Misérables* or *Les Travailleurs de la mer*. Meadows, flowers, birds—everything was stamped with a diffuse sensuality and sang a hymn celebrating the love of the priest and the wild and tender young girl, a new Daphnis and Chloe as they have been called, but much less soft-spoken than the characters of Longus' pastoral novel.

> The vine plants trailed like great insects; the thin corn-stalks, the wilted plants were like batallions armed with long spears; the trees were dishevelled by running, they stretched out their limbs, like wrestlers preparing for a fight; the fallen leaves and the dust of the roads were marching forward.

And in another part of this work, he described the pagan ecstasy which took possession of the sense of sight, the sense of smell, of all the senses of the young priest captivated by this sweet-smelling Garden of Eden in which the sense of sin disappeared:

> A warm joy of light filtered into a floating gold dust, a certainty of perpetual greenery, an attraction of continuous perfume.

Like so many others at that time, the adolescent Zola had begun by being intoxicated by Hugo and Musset. He knew entire poems of Hugo by heart and, he reported in those curious articles written for a Russian newspaper and later published in France under the title *Documents littéraires* (1881), his friends and himself, returning home in the evenings, recited Hugo and synchronized their steps "to the rhythm of his verses which were as sonorous as trumpet blasts." In the same work, he evoked his escapades with his two friends in the countryside of Aix. One wet morning, one of them had brought along a volume of Musset, a poet about whom one took good care not to breathe a word in high school. The rain was falling in torrents. The wind was making the branches creak. But "in the ditch . . . , in the little room of the village inn, Musset was with us and was enough to make us happy." They thus reread "Rolla" and "Les Nuits" more than twenty times, in the midst of nature. Michelet, at the end of his career, when he wrote *La Femme, L'Amour, L'Oiseau,* impressed him just as much, as he also impressed Van Gogh and many others at that time, by sentimental and sensual exaltation and the confused yet deferential cult of woman, which had been diffused in these works by the historian who became a naturalist and was more than ever a romantic. From his first works which were filled with declamatory sincerity, Zola showed himself to be what he always remained: a romantic, dissatisfied with the present, worshiping the purity which he attributed to woman, strangely chaste and puritanical, drunk with that despair which, from the time of *René* onwards, he declared in his essay on Chateaubriand, "has blown for a while over all the summits of the mind."

Perspicacious as he was (he proved to be one of the best critics of his century on Stendhal, Balzac, Hugo, and Manet), he soon realized that he had too much creative energy, too great a passion for certain aspects of the truth which had not struck his predecessors, to remain a mere follower of romanticism. *La Débâcle, Nana* particularly, and even *La Terre* with its poetry of ugliness were great romantic novels. Sandoz, in *L'Oeuvre,* uttered wild pantheistic cries to the world. But Zola understood that one had to destroy in order to replace and that the most fruitful message of romanticism urged him to imitate, not the aesthetics or the work of the romantics, but the daring they had shown in renovating everything. So he included romanticism in his "hatreds." Naturalism, of which he was the theoretician, was a product of romanticism, and he recognized this. Its role was then to move away from romanticism and fight against it, if it was to take its place. A fig for the mess of the poorer romanticism! An end to the total condemnation of their age begun by the romantics! They had been too enamored of the past and the idealization of reality. In a strange statement (in an article on Gautier, reprinted in *Documents littéraires*), he even accused romanticism of having been "a leprosy which has corrupted our national genius. . . . A school of rhetors, battling for form, without trying to base its conquest on the scientific evolution of the century." He was surprisingly hard on Baudelaire himself. In his *Roman expérimental* (1880), he proposed as a goal: "Reality being accepted and then dealt with in poetry." Again elsewhere, without suspecting how romantic he was in the statements that he

made as leader of his literary school (*Le Naturalisme au théâtre,* 1881), he exclaimed:

> Poetry is everywhere, in everything, even more in the present and reality than in the past and abstraction. Every act, at every hour, has its poetic and splendid aspect.

And in his correspondence, he found a more poetic and striking formula to specify his aim as a novelist:

> A leap to the stars from the springboard of precise observation. Truth rises to the level of symbolism in one rapid leap.

It would be almost too easy to indicate the points of similarity between the "damned poets" such as Verlaine, Corbière, or Rimbaud, and the romantics who had been the first to express their revolt against the world, their yearning for a more or less reinvented love, and their frantic attempt to broaden man's horizons and change life. The "damned poets" too could have cried: "I revolt against death," and cursed western civilization for what was bourgeois and pettily commercial in it. On the other hand, from the point of view of aesthetics, they were not satisfied with the techniques or efforts of the romantics. The romantics had opened the way for them. It was now up to them to be more daring than their predecessors, to make poetic language more familiar and popular, and to dislocate the verse by adding meters which were opposed to the alexandrine or the octosyllable. Verlaine, an artist who was very conscious of his means and a virtuoso metrist, succeeded marvellously in doing this. Rimbaud had been impressed by the poems of Hugo the visionary, and even more by *L'Homme qui rit* from which he borrowed his allusion to "comprachicos," and certainly by *Les Travailleurs de la mer.* But it was in the youthful poems of Mallarmé that all the feelings of tenderness, ideal purity, and melancholy of the romantic poets and their heir Baudelaire were expressed with the greatest emotion and charm. The earlier volumes of his *Correspondance* show him to be one of the most moving and subtly ironical letter-writers of his century. Like Zola, it was in his youthful letters that this man revealed himself most. Alas! after he was forty, too often he only wrote letters to editors, notes to colleagues, and advice to disciples. Once past that age, few men can still lay bare their hearts.

It is well known that Mallarmé, with his exquisite politeness but also undoubtedly in all sincerity, had a very high opinion of Zola and exchanged several letters with him. "As for me, admiring as I do a designed and colored poster . . . , as much as a ceiling or an apotheosis, I do not know one point of view in art which is inferior to another," he wrote to Zola on November 6, 1874, after having attended one of his plays which the public had not liked. He felt that Zola was a poet in his own way and sought the ideal. However, at the same time, Zola, who was less observant or less lucid, only considered Mallarmé as a Parnassian who was so enamored of pure art that he became a bit cracked because of it. Mallarmé's letters about the young German girl with whom he fell in love and whom he finally married after many tears shed on both sides were full of sentimental effusions (very natural at the age of twenty), of tenderness nicely tinged with irony and moral idealism. She gave herself to him and this only made her seem purer in his eyes. Would she understand his poetic dreams? His friend and confidant Cazalis (Jean Lahor) asked him this question. Like all lovers who have a bent for teaching, he replied that he would bring her up to his level:

> She is as intelligent as a woman can be without being a monster. It is I who will make her an artist. Moreover, to whom does the pleasant task of teaching fall? To the husband. . . . After two years spent with me, Marie will be my reflection. (Letter of September or October 1862.)

Both of them were very poor when he was in a position, as he expressed it very nicely, to "legalize the throbbings of their two hearts." But at least, said Mallarmé, who was as scornful of the bourgeois as his romantic predecessors or Flaubert, his children "would not have the blood of merchants in their veins." For he could not bear to "feel running through his hair a hand which had served customers and had rattled coins on a counter." How could he "drink infinity" in the eyes of a tradesman's daughter? For shame! He already had a love of unhappiness and knew that he was predestined for it, just like the hero of Byron. But the sentimental tone of his letters brings to mind Lamartine. To the young conscience-stricken governess, frightened by the future and already by the "what will people say" around her, the only consolation he offered was Victor Hugo's advice: "you who suffer because you are in love, love even more."

He declared to his friends, who were, like him, just beginning their poetic careers and were just as obscure and poor at that time: "Happiness in this world is ignoble" (June 3, 1863). One of his first poems, "Les Fenêtres," published in the *Parnasse contemporain* of 1866, expressed a great dislike, similar to that professed by Leconte de Lisle, for "the hard-hearted man / Wallowing in happiness" and avid for wealth. And that was not a literary complaint made during one particular moment of spleen, for there were many such moments in the days of the young devotee of "the bitter ideal." Villiers had declared, in the same year, 1866, that Mallarmé and himself were both equally indifferent to happiness and would remain so. Such was the destiny of these heroes of a rejuvenated romanticism. Their dream was too idealistic and had to devote itself to preserving its purity. Twenty years later, in 1886, in a magnificent and revealing "divagation" on Hamlet, a character who, he confessed, exercised over him "a fascination akin to anguish," Mallarmé stated solemnly: "For, rest assured, that is the question: the conflict between man's dream and man's fate as decreed by a higher Fate." Delacroix, Musset, Baudelaire had already suspected this in their insistent meditation upon the Shakespearean character.

There is obviously no question of reducing Mallarmé completely to the young melancholic man revealed in his confidential letters to his friends, and to this elegiac romanticism. At the same time, in his letters of July 1866 to Théodore Aubanel, this anguished man in exile at Tournon released the most glorious bulletins of victory that any poet has ever written:

> I have laid the foundations of a magnificent work . . . I have died and come to life again with the key to the precious stones of my last spiritual casket . . . I have found the key to myself . . . a center where I remain like a sacred spider on the main threads which have already emerged from my mind . . .

The expressions he used (cult of beauty, for example) still recalled the Parnassians. Moreover, Mallarmé was sincere in his long-lasting admiration for Banville and even more for Gautier. Claudel reported how, at one of Mallarmé's Tuesday receptions, the poet had cast a withering glance at him and rebuked him when the young man had dared to make a blunt statement against Victor Hugo. Later, he broke away from a certain Parnassian aesthetics which had become static and had been spoilt by clumsy followers, whose virtuosity was only formal. We know that he criticized them in his famous reply to Jules Huret's inquiry in 1891; and in those few lines, and in another even more striking declaration to Léo d'Orfer, he assigned to poetry the goal of expressing "the mysterious meaning of existence." But if he reproached the descendants of the Parnassian school for lacking tremendously in mystery, he proposed a definition of symbolic art very similar to those which various romantics, including Vigny, had presented in a more clumsy fashion. The mood that the object evokes or that poetry "draws from the subject by a long deciphering process" counts for much more than the skill in making a few gems sparkle. (pp. 171-77)

Few critical doctrines are more casual, and more misleading, than those which attribute to a certain epoch a spirit or an essence of the epoch, a unique *Zeitgeist,* which makes it easy to label it forever. Everything must conform to this allegedly dominant current, which is also considered the tide of the future, and must move in the direction of history. Dissident doctrines or nonconformist talents that do not move in the direction which is proclaimed inevitable are, metamorphically at least, excluded or suppressed, as they could be in politics by a dictator or a single party. Zola had believed that his Naturalist novel alone followed thus the direction of history, between 1865 and 1880. He became rapidly undeceived, both by disciples who disowned him and by the continuing existence around *Les Rougon-Macquart* of other types of novels, of imaginative poetry and painting, and of an idealistic philosophy. What we consider here as romantic in the symbolists is of course only one of the many elements of their credo and their personality. Moreover, many other quests and creations coexisted at that time with symbolism.

But the romantic current continued to overflow into the last twenty years of the century. From time to time, it broke out with a temperament that was excessively fond of self-expression (Barrè professing his cult of the ego for a while, Loti with his monotonous laments, Mme de Noailles with a heart filled with wonder, who enchanted Proust) or of passionate vitality. Nietzscheism, which was then spreading in France, exacerbated even more this revival of egotism, and it was believed that German thinkers or Stirner, the prophet of the unique, provided a philosophical justification for this arrogant solipsism. In the case of Verhaeren, Loti, Mme de Noailles, or Barrès, it was not merely a question of a youthful outburst; they were just as romantic at the end of their lives as at the beginning. Barrès created a great stir with his conversion to nationalism and came to praise above all the French and Lorraine tradition. But, until the end of his life, he was obsessed by the romantics, in whom he recognized his elder brothers. He romanticized Pascal. His last project was to recount, with some addition of imaginative fantasy, the relations, which might have been amorous, and which he considered very romantic, of Descartes and Princess Elisabeth. In an article in *L'Echo de Paris* (September 28, 1912) on "Les Maitres romantiques," he confessed:

> I love and admire always the great romantic works. I consider them useful as a description of the suffering endured by elite beings, trying to reach the bank through storms and raging waves . . . I would like to write a history of the romantics.

To be sure, personalities whom we have been able to call "classiques" (in painting, Seurat or Signac) or who considered themselves as such after having sown their wild oats (Moréas) coexisted perfectly with the hyper-romantics (also called expressionists) between 1885 and 1910. Cubism, in which may be seen a return to the priority of form over color, to David and Ingres rather than Delacroix, and its quasi-scientific quests through still-life coincided very exactly with Fauvism about 1905-1910. Fauvism, however, was an outburst of exuberance, a return to the sentiments of tragedy and anguish, a will of aggressive coloring, of which Géricault and Delacroix were the most authentic distant ancestors. Vlaminck (whose little book, *Tournant dangereux,* published by Stock in 1929, is one of the most explosive and naive works ever written by a painter), and Delaunay, and more than anybody else the great tormented romantic Soutine, all of them in love with brute sensation and intensity, were the most genuine romantics in art in the first half of the twentieth century.

In the literature of the twentieth century, there are so many authors with a romantic sensibility that one is forced to choose, almost arbitrarily, two or three of them as examples. Proust had been inspired by the poets of the first half of the century and by Baudelaire. On the other hand, he seemed to have taken little interest in the efforts of Mallarmé, the minor reviews of symbolism which Valéry loved, the first works of Apollinaire and Claudel. For his aesthetics of enchantment, dream, and assiduously cherished memory, for his love of long, involved sentences with their rich train of adjectives, for the Balzacian sense of mystery in his characters, he deserves to be styled "romantic." He was also romantic by his faith in art reinterpreting and immortalizing life, and his cult of the artist as the true hero. In a note in his *Pastiches et mélanges* ("Journées de lecture"), he even added that "the classicists have no better commentators than the romanticists. As a matter of fact, only the romanticists know how to read classical works, for they read them as they were written, romantically." Gide took some time to get rid of what he knew was disturbed and maudlin in him; after having given free rein to this plaintive romanticism in *André Walter,* and to a more exalted and pagan romanticism in *Les Nourritures terrestres,* without ceasing to cultivate his ego

and to pursue his quest of sincerity, he had preferred to bring to light another facet of himself, that of irony. Suarès, who was his friend for a while, impetuous and proud, draped in his haughty solitude, fond of brilliant prose, preferred all his life to cherish his loneliness as a social misfit and a despiser of the modern world. He was one of the most nobly Byronic Frenchmen. Bernanos, so different from him, but just as lost in his century, against which he vituperated with verbosity and outbursts of anger, did not attain the so-called classical serenity either. Malraux, from his earliest works which were very like those of Chateaubriand and Barrès, then through his heroes who, too, were proudly aloof and obsessed by their fight against fate, and by his often sumptuous prose, is certainly the great romantic of the middle of the twentieth century; he is also romantic by his meditations on art and the artist who is the rival of reality and emulator of God. Perhaps, in the opinion of posterity, the best aspects of Camus, once that part of his work which has ideological pretensions has been excluded, will be found in the bitterness of *La Chute* and in the romantic resonance of his first essays and travel accounts in *Les Noces* and *L'Été.* Aragon's novels, his poetry of war and love, the Moorish décor of the love poems in *Le Fou d'Elsa* (1963), everything in him indicates an impenitent romantic, who is by no means embarrassed to recall at times the indiscreet opulence of Hugo, at other times the tones and display of sentiments of Alfred de Musset.

The excesses, aggressiveness, and transports of a certain romanticism, proliferated further by the audacity of the Naturalists, were found again in the most obdurate of the romantics of this period, Céline. More than any of his predecessors, Céline proclaimed his need to revolt coupled with a feeling that the only outlet for modern man is to fume and curse. The restraints of society and administration blocked all the openings around him. As early as October 4, 1933, in an article "Hommage à Zola" in *Marianne,* Céline saw on all sides around modern man a quasi-mystical passion for death.

> The current unanimous sadism arises above all from a desire for nothingness which is deeply embedded in man and especially in the mass of men, a sort of amorous, almost irresistible and unanimous impatience for death. With coyness, of course, and a thousand denials, but the tropism is there, and it is all the more powerful as it is perfectly hidden and silent.

The omnipresence of death (in the work of Céline as well as in that of Julien Green, Malraux, Camus, and Bonnefoy) is indeed one of the obsessions which, after the great slaughter of 1914-1918, recalls the obsession of death which afflicted the romantics after the Napoleonic wars. But the rebound to hope in the future had been more rapid one hundred and fifty years ago. Finally, Élie Faure, one of the first men in France to have understood and helped Céline (who was not at all grateful to him for this), one of the most perspicacious art critics of his time and, in his best moments, a profound and passionate essayist, was not afraid to reveal his personal sentiments in his work and to express himself with vehemence and often with turgidity. In the fourth volume of his *Histoire de l'art,* he made the affirmation which pervaded his entire thinking: "France would not be France without French romanticism." In France, even rationalism, while trying to impose the reign of reason, becomes romantic.

> From David up to and including cubism, all of French painting, or almost all of it, has been romantic, even in those of its internal movements which were born with the avowed purpose of opposing romanticism . . . Zola is the most romantic, not only of the disparagers, but also of the champions of romanticism.

Whatever might have been said about it, it is very seldom by its classical qualities of lucidity, order, moderation, and respect for venerable traditions that French art and literature have exercised such a powerful influence over Germany, England, and America. Dreiser who admired Balzac and Zola, Faulkner who rewrote a *Comédie humaine* in the South of the United States, Henry Miller who was intoxicated by Rimbaud, Giono, and Céline, twenty disciples or translators of Apollinaire, so many admirers of surrealism who reinterpreted this movement, the first enthusiasts of Claudel, all these men have sought in the France of today the country par excellence of a romanticism which has never been stamped out and is always renascent.

It is in poetry just as much as in painting, however, that a romantic sensibility is manifested most fully, and for the observer that the critic becomes in these matters, the advantage lies in the fact that he has at his disposal many more confidences and written testimonies than in the case of painters, who are less inclined to explain themselves clearly, or in the case of sculptors or musicians. Here again, a few references relating to poets as diverse as Apollinaire, Breton, and Claudel will have to suffice for illustration.

Few poems are as personal as those of Apollinaire. He himself remarked that each of his poems commemorated an event in his life. His personality, which was moreover engaging and which had won him so many warm friendships among artists and poets, was exposed in his poems, at times smiling in its melancholy and weeping over a dead love ("Love died in your arms") with accents which brought back to mind Musset or Heine, at other times tragically anguished, as in his long autobiographical poem *Zone,* written after the break with Marie Laurencin:

> The anguish of love chokes you
> As if you were never to be loved any more . . .
> I have lived like a mad man and I have wasted
>   my time . . .

Also, like so many romantics, he combined his intimate memories and his impulses of evasion with fragments of popular songs ("Rosemonde," "Marie") and visions of chimerical palaces. Nobody since Baudelaire had expressed sadness in more poignant verse. But he was peculiarly hard on Baudelaire in the few notes which he wrote about him, and he was even more distant from the symbolists. He had more affinity with Verlaine and Musset than any other Frenchman. He was romantic in his exalted conception of the poet as the supreme creator, the one who creates or recreates for us a world which, without him,

would remain uninteresting or incomprehensible to us. "To contrive a new universe" was one of his definitions of the function of the poet as seer and architect of a more harmonious world than the one in which we struggle. To one of the women whom he courted and loved, Madeleine Pagès, when she showed herself incapable of understanding a poet as a lover, he wrote the following very solemn lines: "Poets are creators. So nothing is born on earth, nothing is presented to the eyes of women, if it has not first been imagined by a poet."

He was well aware of the fact that every true romantic, once adopted by posterity if not by his contemporaries, became a classic. And he never spoke ill of the so-called classical values, and certainly not of the poets of the seventeenth century called "baroque" (Théophile or Maynard), whom the romantics had rediscovered. In his aesthetics, he always fought for "the most energetic art" of a period, the one which has the best chances of survival.

If, from Rousseau to Rimbaud, the great romantic outburst had been a revolt against the world and a tremendous impetus to transform it by transforming man, none of the revolts since that time equals in verbal violence and in bitterness that of the surrealists. They dreamed of nothing less than a total remodeling of man. Their revolt was social, like that of the romanticists who had come into contact with Saint-Simonism and Fourierism, had been eager to change religion with Lamennais, and had understood that one had to "cure the universal human malady" not only by theories but by political action. It was moral to an even greater degree, in its effort to transform the relations between the sexes, as George Sand and Michelet had no doubt dreamed of doing, and this on the strength of passion loudly asserting its rights. In the text entitled "La Confession dédaigneuse" (*Les Pas Perdus,* 1924), Breton had asserted this, when he was still very young, invoking his favorite moralists, Vauvenargues and Sade:

> The moral question preoccupies me. . . . Morals are the great conciliator. To attack them is to still pay homage to them. It is in them that I have found my main subjects of exaltation.

He had proclaimed very emphatically the unique influence of Rimbaud, more profound in the moral sphere than in the poetic domain, in his *Position politique du surréalisme.* Even before he became an acknowledged admirer of Fourier, he had wished to establish morals on desire, distinguished from animal lust. The sexual revolution which the young people of several countries prided themselves on in 1970 could justly have claimed him as their most direct precursor.

Like the romantic revolt, which had constantly come up against the limits assigned to the human condition and had been fond of the image of man as a bat, colliding incessantly with the walls and roof of his prison, the revolt of Breton and his friends was metaphysical. Against the "ridiculous conditions of all existence," according to another sentence of *Les Pas perdus,* Breton wanted to retrieve all the psychic forces which lie, untapped, in us. He had recourse to the coincidences of objective chance, to automatism (much less, in fact, to automatic writing than he had seemed to announce in a few statements which had aroused a great deal of interest), and particularly to the unconscious and dreams. Here again, Breton turned, not to the symbolists (about whom he spoke unkindly, preferring the naturalist novelists to the "symbolists who, during the same period, endeavoured to stun the public with their more or less rhythmical lucubrations" [*Les Vases communicants*]), but to Nerval, Hugo, and a few German romanticists for a few features which he tackled with a more fierce persistency. With the impeccable virtuosity in reasoning which characterizes French revolutionaries in all spheres, he proposed to exalt the method of analogical thought at the expense of the use of logic. He cast out the word *"car"* as the most baneful of the language. Elsewhere, *"Signe ascendant"* (1947), he expressed the desire to destroy forever the little word *"donc"* "with all the vanity and morose enjoyment that it involves." He went as far as to suppose, and soon to affirm, the existence of a connection between real automatism and forms of poetry, between personal automatism and universal automatism, borrowing from Friedrich Engels his enigmatic expression "objective chance" to describe it.

The task that he proposed for his combative energy was a Herculean one. Fighting against and going beyond reason, man, transformed and craving for liberty (as the German and French romantics had already described him), could only avoid sinking into despair by struggling against the skeptics and rational logicians, against corrupt society and against God. He had to have recourse to powers which were perhaps magical and at least mythical, and to believe (as Balzac had done) that miracles themselves are within our reach. Man, carrying out the vertiginous descent into himself that Novalis and Nerval had asked, had to draw from there the force required to rise much higher. "Every artist must resume on his own the pursuit of the golden fleece," this new argonaut declared in his *Prolégomènes*. . . . Here again, the symbolic names of Prometheus and Icarus, heroes of the romantics, were those which were recalled by the exhortations of Breton, who wished to attain, and help others attain, a state of grace. He said himself in a very important article, "Le Merveilleux contre le mystère" (1936), included in *La Clé des champs* (Sagittaire, 1953), what a high regard he had for romanticism, from which dates—and not from Baudelaire or from symbolism—"the will for the total emancipation of man." A glimmer of this had shone in "the gigantic façades of Hugo," in "Musset's admirable song of February 3, 1834" (undoubtedly "A saint Blaise, à la Zudecca . . ."), in Nerval, and lastly in Lautréamont. Again, elsewhere, he expressed his admiration for *Bug-Jargal, Han d'Islande,* and for the poems of Hugo's twilight years. How romantic still was the famous passage that concluded *Nadja,* which, along with *Arcane 17,* was the most romantic work of the twentieth century: "Beauty will be convulsive or it will not be."

The most constant preoccupation of Breton and of those who, for a while at least, were his disciples—Eluard, Desnos, Péret, and Char—was even more romantic, and without any fear of ridicule: the preoccupation of restoring total, deified love to its true place, by far the foremost position, both in literature and in life. As early as 1924, in *Poisson soluble,* Breton exclaimed: "We will reduce art to its simplest expression, which is love." In 1929, repeated: "There is no solution outside of love," and he would agree to receive into the surrealist clique only those who could answer to his own satisfaction the question: "What sort of hope do you place in love?" Much later still, at the age of fifty-six, in his *Entretiens,* Breton showed that he had not wavered on this central point of his credo: "All subjects of exaltation peculiar to surrealism converge . . . toward love. The highest human ambition lies in elective love." It was not a question principally of eroticism and, in spite of the admiration proclaimed for the divine Marquis, there was even less a question of anything sadistic, but entirely of sentiment and deferential declarations to woman, which were generally chaste, even in the quasi-Petrarchan enumeration of the charms of the partner (*Union libre*). Sentences like the following from *Arcane 17* could have been written by Chateaubriand pursuing the sylph of his dreams, by Lamartine to Elvire, by Hugo to Juliette:

> Before knowing you, I had encountered unhappiness and despair. Before knowing you? Nonsense! These words have no sense. You know very well that when I saw you for the first time, I recognized you without the slightest hesitation.

The love that the poet celebrates in prose and verse, that "crazy love," idealizes woman as a fairy Mélusine, a woman-child or even a woman-serpent, an intermediary between man and nature. She unites existence and essence in herself, declared Breton. She brings him faith. She alone can inspire and guide him in his struggle against the menacing war and the governments which threaten to reduce half of humanity to slavery.

She is always the same, even though those to whom the adoration of the male is directed are continually changing. This is not quite the same as Musset's not very gallant cry, "What does the flask matter provided one gets intoxicated!" or Goethe's epigram comparing women to plates of crockery or silver on which men place their golden apples. Rather, it is faith in the future, in the infinite possibilities that this future offers us, faith that love creates and renews. Old age and death are conquered:

> Men despair stupidly of love. They live a slave to the idea that love is always behind them, never before them. . . . And yet, for each one, the promise of this hour to come contains the whole secret of life, capable of revealing itself one day, accidentally, in another being.
>
> (*L'Amour fou*)
> (pp. 179-86)

This outline of what we call the survival, and often the exacerbation, of romanticism since 1840 has been centered on the one modern literature we feel we know, the French. But it would not be difficult for scholars of other literatures of this century to show that the vitality of romanticism has been even more evident in Germany, where one has rightly been able to deplore in Hitlerism a destructive explosion of the irrational and an outbreak of Faustian elements, enamored of the colossal and of nihilism, which Germany has often paradoxically associated with its genius for meticulous organization and obedience to the administrative hierarchies. The America of the mid-twentieth century, after having witnessed a few attempts, begun by sober-minded academics, to establish a neo-humanism favoring moderation, order, and moral and aesthetic restraints, proclaims itself incurably romantic through its Black, Jewish, Southern, and other kinds of writers, swearing only by the sexual, social, political, moral, or supramoral revolution. As one of its novelists and critics, Leslie Fiedler, has admitted, at the end of long discussions on the rules with which the novel should comply, the American writer, no matter how hard he tries to be "classical" with conviction, always ends up by becoming romantic. Never before had the youth of the country, which was considered to be dedicated to the qualities of efficiency and hard work, fed so much on utopias (some of which had been revived from Fourier's and Cabet's times) as after 1965. England had witnessed, after the First World War, especially with the most uncompromising anti-romantic, T. S. Eliot, a systematic attempt to extol the cult of traditional and intellectual values. The attempt soon proved abortive. Twenty years after his death in 1930, D. H. Lawrence became the idol of readers, even of academics and—supreme ratification—of film directors. Stephen Spender did not manage to avoid in his poetry the romantic clichés of former times; he was a better essayist than poet, and he campaigned on behalf of a more accurate appreciation of romanticism in *The Destructive Element, a Study of Modern Writers and Beliefs* and especially in his sympathetic presentation of the English romantics in an article published in *The English Review* (XIV, March 1947). Francis Scarfe, a scholar of French literature, a poet and a discriminating commentator of poetry, was one of the first to protest, as early as 1942, against the excessive sophistication of English poetry of the period between the two World Wars, in his work *Auden and After: the liberation of Poetry, 1930-1941*. The experience of life after he had lost his father in the First World War, his brief encounters with surrealism and communism, the shock of the Civil War in Spain had opened his eyes. He wanted to testify for the younger generation which was attracted by the expression of ardent emotions in literature. Several of these young men of 1945-1960 had assembled in groups with the slogan of *La Nouvelle Apocalypse* (1939) or *Le Cavalier blanc* (1941). Their motto was total freedom in art and the individual pursuit by each artist of his creative originality [in the words of Stefan Schimanski and Henry Treece]:

> The Romantic artist is in the vanguard of human sensibility; he leaves the world richer than he had found it. . . . Romanticism is the spirit which springs into life; it is the spark of the Creator, which, one day, will flash like lightning from tired eyes and perceive the paradise that God has tried to create.

The most sonorous and the best virtuoso among the neo-romantic poets, who, on the other side of the English Channel, had undoubtedly rallied to surrealism, is the Welshman Dylan Thomas. His poetry—rich in sounds, in images, in leaps over the links of coherent language, and obsessed by death—and his intense life, which had been foolishly wasted (he died in 1953 at the age of thirty-nine), consist of the purest romanticism of Byron or Beddoes relived a century and a half later.

In all these countries, the romanticism of the twentieth century constitutes, like the romanticism of the previous hundred and fifty years, a claiming of spontaneity in art, of creative liberty against the forces which, more and more, want to reduce man to a mere cog in the machinery of compartmentalized civilization. The greatness of this romanticism lies in having taught us that harmony does not necessarily exist between the order of things (or perhaps their fundamental disorder) and the consciousness of man, eager for clarity and for well-ordered security in his thoughts. Camus saw in this irremediable discord the great source of the sentiment of the absurd which should drive modern man first to revolt, then to the creation of a different universe, that of art. There is sometimes a certain affectation in this revolt and some intoxication of words in this return to emotion, to the irrational, to the forces of instinct, which can only be savagely destructive. But in all this, there is also a legitimate protest against traditional humanism, which, until the irruption of these romantics, enjoyed its intellectual complaisance too indolently and imagined itself free from anguish in its firm belief that the reign of rational progress had begun. By repressing or avoiding this romanticism, too many artists risk growing poorer or condemning themselves to a dull barrenness. One of the most genuine poets of this century, Pierre Reverdy, whose style is severe, and who, more than anyone else, has avoided any declamation and flamboyant histrionism, has rightly stated in his *Gant de crin:*

> It is difficult for the artist to live without romanticism. If he does not introduce it in his works, he introduces it into his life; if he does not introduce it into his life, he preserves it in his dreams. . . . When one has got rid of romanticism, one has generally lapsed into a distressing dullness.

(pp. 192-94)

Henri Peyre, "The Survival and Vitality of Romanticism," in his What Is Romanticism? *translated by Roda Roberts, The University of Alabama Press, 1977, pp. 149-94.*

FURTHER READING

Atkins, Stuart Pratt. *The Testament of Werther in Poetry and Drama.* Cambridge: Harvard University Press, 1949, 322 p.
Examines the influence of Goethe's novel on German, English, and French Romantic literature.

Behler, Ernst. "Techniques of Irony in Light of the Romantic Theory." *Rice University Studies* 57, No. 4 (Fall 1971): 1-17.
Traces the roots of Romantic irony.

Blackall, Eric. *The Novels of the German Romantics.* Ithaca, N.Y.: Cornell University Press, 1983, 315 p.
Examines the work of the major German novelists and their relationship to the German Romantic theorists.

Eichner, Hans. "The Rise of Modern Science and the Genesis of Romanticism." *PMLA* 97, No. 1 (January 1982): 8-30.

Examines the connections between the increasingly mechanistic view of the world during the eighteenth century and the Romantic belief in an organic, evolving universe.

Fass, Barbara. *La Belle Dame Sans Merci & The Aesthetics of Romanticism.* Detroit: Wayne State University Press, 1974, 311 p.

A comprehensive study of the Romantic artists' fascination with humans in love with supernatural beings. Fass interprets this as an expression of the artists' perception of the dichotomy between art and life.

Furst, Lilian R. *Counterparts: The Dynamics of Franco-German Literary Relationships 1770-1895.* Detroit: Wayne State University Press, 1977, 210 p.

An examination of the different cultural backgrounds that caused a "time lag" between French and German Romanticism.

Garber, Frederick, ed. *Romantic Irony.* Budapest: Akadémiai Kiadó, 1988, 395 p.

A complete examination of Romantic irony, including articles on German, French, Scandinavian, Eastern European, and Portuguese forms.

Gautier, Théophile. *A History of Romanticism.* 1909. Reprint. New York: Howard Fertig, 1988, 114 p.

Contains Gautier's personal reminiscences of the Romantic age, including his impression of the first performance of Victor Hugo's *Hernani.*

Hoffmeister, Gerhart. "Goethe's *Faust* and the *Theatrum Mundi*-Tradition in European Romanticism." *Journal of European Studies* 13, Nos. 1-2 (1983): 42-55.

Discusses how *Faust* stimulated the Romantic artists to address theatrum mundi, "the idea that human life is like a play . . . in which each player is given his allotted role."

———, ed. *European Romanticism: Literary Cross-Currents, Modes, and Models.* Detroit: Wayne State University Press, 1990, 369 p.

A collection of essays addressing such topics as the Napoleonic image in literature, the *femme fatale*, exoticism, irony, and the grotesque.

Immerwahr, Raymond. "The Subjectivity or Objectivity of Friedrich Schlegel's Poetic Irony." *The Germanic Review* XXVI, No. 3 (October 1951): 173-91.

Claims that Schlegel's irony is characterized by both subjectivity and objectivity and that the critical controversy over Schlegel's definition of irony is "in large measure one of semantics."

Lacoue-Labarthe, Philippe and Nancy, Jean-Luc. *The Literary Absolute: The Theory of Literature in German Romanticism.* Translated by Philip Barnard and Cheryl Lester. New York: State University of New York Press, 1988, 167 p.

Examines the complexity of the Schlegels' formulation of Romanticism, which the authors contend is not encompassed by current use of the term.

Man, Paul de. "Intentional Structure of the Romantic Image." In his *The Rhetoric of Romanticism,* pp. 1-18. New York: Columbia University Press, 1984.

Examines the Romantic artists' use of poetic imagery with the understanding that "an abundant imagery coinciding with an equally abundant quantity of natural ob-

jects, the theme of imagination linked closely to the theme of nature, such is the fundamental ambiguity that characterizes the poetics of Romanticism."

Nemoianu, Virgil. *The Taming of Romanticism: European Literature and the Age of Biedermeier.* Cambridge: Harvard University Press, 1984, 302 p.

Examines the influence of late German Romanticism throughout Europe, including an examination of Eastern European literature.

Peckham, Morse. *The Triumph of Romanticism.* Columbia: University of South Carolina Press, 1970, 462 p.

A collection of essays originally published between 1950 and 1969 examining the theory, applications, and consequences of Romanticism.

Praz, Mario. *The Romantic Agony.* Translated by Angus Davidson. New York: Meridan Books, 1956, 502 p.

Examines such Romantic themes as suffering female beauty, ecstasy and horror, and the union of the beautiful and the sad.

Remak, Henry H. H. "West European Romanticism: Definition and Scope." In *Comparative Literature: Method and Scope,* edited by Newton P. Stallknecht and Horst Frenz, pp. 223-59. Carbondale: Southern Illinois University Press, 1961.

Surveys the definitions of Romanticism and provides an evaluation of the movement in different countries to explore its various manifestations.

———. "A Key to West European Romanticism?" *Colloquia Germanica* I, No. 2 (1968): 37-46.

An extension of Remak's earlier work (cited above) in which he suggests that "instead of a keystone theory, we may have to admit the alternative of variable clusters of Romantic norms."

Robertson, J. G. *Studies in the Genesis of Romantic Theory in the Eighteenth Century.* Cambridge: Cambridge University Press, 1923, 298 p.

An examination of the Italian influence on the formulation of French and German theories of Romanticism.

Rosenblum, Nancy L. "Romantic Militarism." *Journal of the History of Ideas* XLIII, No. 2 (April-June 1982): 249-68.

Studies the Romantic artists' vision of war as an occasion for self-development and self-expression.

Schenk, H. G. *The Mind of the European Romantics: An Essay in Cultural History.* London: Constable, 1966, 303 p.

Examines Romanticism as a revolt against eighteenth-century rationalism and as a revival of Christianity.

Shroder, Maurice Z. *Icarus: The Image of the Artist in French Romanticism.* Cambridge: Harvard University Press, 1961, 287 p.

Studies the French Romantics' use of the Icarus myth to symbolize the ambition and failure of the artist.

Tarr, F. Courtney. "Romanticism in Spain and Spanish Romanticism: A Critical Survey." *Bulletin of Spanish Studies* XVI (1939): 3-37.

Argues that because Spanish literature was always Romantic, the movement in Spain was actually a reaffirmation of traditional aesthetics.

Thorlby, Anthony, ed. *The Romantic Movement.* London: Longmans, 1966, 176 p.

A collection of essays addressing the definitions of Romanticism and examining its manifestation in science, philosophy, political thought, art, and music.

Ward, Patricia A. "Encoding in the Texts of Literary Movements: Late European Romanticism." _Comparative Literature Studies_ XVIII, No. 3 (September 1981): 296-305.
    Discusses the relation between literature and culture, focusing on how the work of the late Romantic artists reflects or embodies the ideas of the early Romantic theorists.

Weintraub, Wiktor. "The Problem of Improvisation in Romantic Literature." _Comparative Literature_ XVI, No. 2 (Spring 1964): 119-37.
    Examines the Italian tradition of improvisation, in which the poet would create verse in the presence of the audience, as a theme of Romantic literature.

Wellek, René. "Romanticism Re-examined." In _Romanticism Reconsidered,_ edited by Northrop Frye, pp. 107-34. New York: Columbia University Press, 1963.
    Rearticulates his opposition to theories of Romanticism that focus on specific time periods rather than common characteristics and surveys the recent work done in the field of defining Romanticism.

————. "German and English Romanticism: A Confrontation." In his _Confrontations: Studies in the Intellectual and Literary Relations Between Germany, England and the United States During the Nineteenth Century,_ pp. 3-34. Princeton: Princeton University Press, 1965.
    A comparison of English and German Romanticism that emphasizes the distinctive characteristics of German Romanticism.

Naturalism

INTRODUCTION

Naturalism, a literary movement which espoused the application of scientific principles to fictional works, emerged in late nineteenth-century France. A combination of factors, including an increasing interest in scientific experimentation, widespread economic disparity, and political repression, gave rise to a group of writers committed to the eradication of social ills through objective observation and faithful description of human experience. Adherents to Naturalism therefore viewed all of life as their province: they pledged to defy conventional restrictions on subject matter through the frank treatment of sex and the graphic portrayal of brutality, corruption, and decay. Applying to literature theories of determinism, derived primarily from the works of Charles Darwin, Naturalistic writers in Europe and America portrayed characters as helpless victims, subject to hereditary and environmental forces beyond their control and comprehension.

Emile Zola, the founder of literary Naturalism, outlined his views in his collection of essays *Le roman expérimental* (1880; *The Experimental Novel*). In the title essay Zola acknowledged his debt to physiologist Claude Bernard, who, in his 1865 work *Introduction à l'étude de la médecine expérimentale* (*Introduction to the Study of Experimental Medicine*), had advocated the application of the experimental methods to medicine, a discipline that had previously been viewed as an art rather than a science. Zola asserted that Bernard's scientific principles could be applied to the novel as well, arguing that "if the experimental method leads to the knowledge of physical life, it should also lead to the knowledge of the passionate and intellectual life." Zola's theories were also influenced by the writings of H. A. Taine. In his *Histoire de la littérature anglaise* (1863-64; *History of English Literature*), Taine described the three factors—race, surroundings, and epoch—which produce the elementary moral state in all people. Adapting Taine's doctrines, Zola formulated his definition of Naturalism as the study of heredity and environment. The works of Honoré de Balzac were also influential in the development of Zola's approach to literature. In the spirit of Balzac's forty-seven-volume *Comédie Humaine,* Zola wrote a twenty-novel masterwork chronicling the history of the Rougon-Macquart family. This cycle, intended to demonstrate Zola's view of the immutable laws of heredity, includes *L'assommoir,* a novel examining the effects of alcoholism and squalid living conditions that Oscar Cargill has described as "the one perfectly plausible exposition of the philosophy of Naturalism."

Due to the firmly entrenched Victorian morality, which insisted upon individual responsibility, Naturalism failed to develop into a substantial movement in England, though Thomas Hardy and George Moore successfully incorporated some of Zola's theories into the British novel of the period. Hardy's *Return of the Native, Tess of the d'Urbervilles,* and *Jude the Obscure* illustrate his doctrine of pessimistic determinism, while Moore's novels *Confessions of a Young Man* and *Esther Waters* adhere to the Naturalist principle of verisimilitude. Naturalism gained prominence among writers in the United States at the turn of the century. The American Naturalists formed a more clearly identifiable group than had their British counterparts, and their works had a tremendous impact on future generations of American writers. Although novelists such as Stephen Crane, Frank Norris, and Theodore Dreiser were influenced by Darwinism, and concurred with the European Naturalists in the importance of applying scientific principles to literature, their works reflected a set of circumstances uniquely American. In the early twentieth century, as Dreiser has stated, "America was just entering upon the most lurid phase of that vast, splendid, most lawless and most savage period in which the great financiers were plotting and conniving at the enslavement of the people and belaboring each other." The American Naturalists, many of whom began as journalists, approached fiction as they did newspaper reporting: as detached, objective observers; but, as Malcolm Cowley has stated, "Try as they would, they could not remain merely observers. They had to revolt against the moral standards of their time." Although many of their works suggest the pessimistic notion that people are governed by forces outside of their control, the American Naturalists, as Cargill has averred, "are by no means *convinced* Naturalists—they betray themselves by pet schemes for human betterment, schemes in which no genuine and thorough-going pessimist has any legitimate interest." In the name of such virtues as strength and candor, these novelists vehemently condemned intolerance and hypocrisy.

Writing with the intention of shocking their readers' genteel sensibilities, the Naturalists effectively sparked furious debate, and their works were often heavily censored. Amidst the controversy, the Naturalists developed a relatively small but impassioned following. The movement as defined by the tenets of Zola flourished only for a brief time, though it profoundly and permanently altered conventional notions about the accurate representation of reality and experience in literature. James T. Farrell, an American Naturalist writing in the mid-twentieth century, has asserted that Naturalism "has had more force and more impact, and has been able to nourish and give more energy to successive generations than any other tradition."

REPRESENTATIVE WORKS

Chekhov, Anton
  Chayka: Komediya v chetyryokh deystviyakh
    (drama) 1896
    [*The Sea-Gull*, 1912]
Crane, Stephen
  Maggie: A Girl of the Streets (A Story of New York)
    (novel) 1893
  *The Red Badge of Courage: An Episode of the
    American Civil War* (novel) 1895
Dreiser, Theodore
  Sister Carrie (novel) 1900
  An American Tragedy (novel) 1925
Hardy, Thomas
  Return of the Native (novel) 1878
  Tess of the d'Urbervilles (novel) 1891
  Jude the Obscure (novel) 1895
Hauptmann, Gerhart
  Vor Sonnenaufgang (drama) 1889
    [*Before Dawn*, 1909]
  Die Weber: Schauspiel aus den vierziger Jahren
    (drama) 1892
    [*The Weavers*, 1899]
Ibsen, Henrik
  Gjengangere (drama) 1881
    [*Ghosts*, 1888]
Maupassant, Guy de
  Bel-Ami (novel) 1885
    [*Bel-Ami; A Novel*, 1891]
  Pierre et Jean (novel) 1888
    [*Pierre et Jean; The Two Brothers*, 1889]
Moore, George
  Confessions of a Young Man (novel) 1888
  Esther Waters (novel) 1894
Norris, Frank
  McTeague: A Story of San Francisco (novel) 1899
  The Octopus: A Story of California (novel) 1901
  The Pit: A Story of Chicago (novel) 1903
Strindberg, August
  Fröken Julie (drama) 1889
    [*Countess Julia*, 1912; also published as *Miss Julie*,
    1918]
Zola, Emile
  Thérèse Raquin (novel) 1867
    [*The Devil's Compact*, 1892]
  *Les Rougon-Macquart (novels) 1871-93
  Le roman expérimental (essays) 1880
    [*The Experimental Novel*, 1880]

*This twenty-novel series includes *L'assommoir*, 1877 [*Gervaise*,
1879]; *Nana*, 1880 [*Nana*, 1880]; *Germinal*, 1885 [*Germinal*, 1885];
and *La terre*, 1886 [*The Soil*, 1886; also published as *Earth*, 1954].

DEFINITIONS AND THEORIES

Emile Zola

[*In the following essay, Zola defines the term Natural-*
ism, outlines the purpose of the movement, and discusses
its manifestation both in novels and on the stage in
nineteenth-century France.]

In the first place, is it necessary to explain what I understand by "naturalism"? I have been found fault with on
account of this word; some pretend to this day not to understand what I mean by it. It is easy to cut jokes about
this subject. However, I will explain it again, as one cannot
be too clear in criticism.

My great crime, it would seem, has been to have invented
and given to the public a new word in order to designate
a literary school as old as the world. In the first place, I
cannot claim the invention of this word, which has been
in use in several foreign literatures; I have at the most only
applied it to the actual evolution in our own literature.
Further, naturalism, they assure us, dates from the first
written works. Who has ever said to the contrary? This
simply proves that it comes from the heart of humanity.
All the critics, they add, from Aristotle to Boileau, have
promulgated this principle, that a work must be based on
truth. All this delights me and furnishes me with new arguments. The naturalistic school, by the mouth even of
those who deride and attack it, is thus built on an inde-
structible foundation. It is not one man's caprice, the mad
folly of a group of writers; it is born in the eternal depth
of things, it started from the necessity which each writer
found of taking nature for his basis. Very well, so far we
are agreed. Let us start from this point.

Well, they say to me, why all this noise? why do you pose
as an innovator and revealer of new doctrines? It is here
the misunderstanding commences. I am simply an observer, who states facts. The empiricists alone put forth invented formulas. The savants are content to advance step by
step, relying on the experimental method. One thing is certain, I have no new religion in my pocket. I reveal nothing,
for the simple reason that I do not believe in revelation;
I invent nothing, because I think it more useful to obey the
impulses of humanity, the continuous evolutions which
carry us along. My rôle as critic consists in studying from
whence we come and our present state. When I venture
to foretell where we are going it is purely speculation on
my part, a purely logical conclusion. By what has been,
and by what is, I think I am able to say what will be. That
is my whole endeavor. It is ridiculous to assign me any
other rôle; to place me on a rock, as pope and prophet; to
represent me as the head of a school and on familiar terms
with God.

But as to this new word, this terrible word of naturalism?
I should have pleased my critics better had I used the
words of Aristotle. He spoke of the true in art, and that
ought to be sufficient for me. Since I accept the eternal
basis of things and do not seek to create the world a second
time, I no longer have need of a new term. Truly, are they
mocking me? Does not the eternal basis of things take
upon itself divers forms, according to the times and the degree of civilization? Is it possible that for six thousand
years each race has not interpreted and named, according
to its own fashion, the things coming from a common
source? Homer is a naturalistic poet—I admit that at once;
but our romanticists are not naturalists after his style; be-

tween the two literary epochs there is an abyss. This is to judge from an absolute point of view, to efface all history at one stroke; it is to huddle all things together and keep no account of the constant evolution of the human mind. One thing is certain, that any piece of work will always be only a corner of nature as seen through a certain temperament. Only we cannot be content with this truth and go no further. As we approach the history of literature, we must necessarily come upon strange elements, upon manners, events, and intellectual movements which modify, arrest, or precipitate literatures. My personal opinion is that naturalism dates from the first line ever written by man. From that day truth was laid down as the necessary foundation of all art. If we look upon humanity as an army marching through the ages, bent upon the conquest of the true, in spite of every form of wretchedness and infirmity, we must place writers and savants in the van. It is from this point of view that we should write the history of a universal literature, and not from that of an absolute ideal or a common æsthetical measure, which is perfectly ridiculous. But it must be understood that I cannot go as far back as that, nor undertake so colossal a work; I cannot examine the marches and counter-marches of the writers of all nations, and set down through what darkness and what lights they passed. I must set myself a limit, therefore I go no further back than the last century, where we find that marvelous expansion of intelligence, that wonderful movement from whence came our society of to-day. And it is just there that I discover a triumphant affirmation of naturalism, it is there that I meet with the word. The long thread is lost in the darkness of the ages; it answers my purpose to take it in hand at the eighteenth century and follow it to our day. Putting aside Aristotle and Boileau, a particular word was necessary to designate an evolution which evidently starts from the first days of the world, but which finally arrives at a decisive development in the midst of circumstances especially favorable to it.

Let us start, then, at the eighteenth century. We have at that period a superb outburst. One fact dominates all, the creation of a method. Until then the savants had worked as the poets did, from individual fantasy, by strokes of genius. A few discovered truths, but they were scattered truths; no tie held them together, and mixed with them were the grossest errors. They wished to create science at one bound the way you write a poem; they joined it on to nature by quack formulas, by metaphysical considerations which would astound us to-day. All at once a little circumstance revolutionized this sterile field in which nothing grew. One day a savant proposed, before concluding, to experiment. He abandoned supposed truths, he returned to first causes, to the study of bodies, the observation of facts. Like a schoolboy he consented to become humble, to learn to spell nature before reading it fluently. It was a revolution: science detached itself from empiricism, its method consisted in marching from the known to the unknown. They started from an observed fact, they advanced from observation to observation, hesitating to conclude before being in possession of the necessary elements. In one word, instead of setting out with synthesis, they commenced with analysis; they no longer tried to draw the truth from nature by means of divination or revelation; they studied it long and patiently, passing from the simple

to the complex, until they were acquainted with its mechanism. The tool was found; such a way of working was to consolidate and extend all the sciences.

Indeed, the benefit was soon apparent. The natural sciences were established, thanks to the minute and thorough exactitude of observation; in anatomy alone an entirely new world was opened up; each day it revealed a little more of the secret of life. Other sciences were created— chemistry and natural philosophy. To-day they are still young, but they are growing, and they are bringing truth to light in a manner harassing from its rapidity. I cannot examine each science thus. It is sufficient to name in addition cosmography and geology, two sciences which have dealt so terrible a blow to religious fables. The outburst was general, and it continues.

But everything holds together in civilization. When one side of the human mind is set working other parts are affected, and ere long you have a complete evolution. The sciences, which until then had borrowed their share of imagination from letters, were the first to cut free from fantastic dreams and return to nature; next letters were seen in their turn to follow the sciences, and to adopt also the experimental method. The great philosophical movement of the eighteenth century was a vast inquiry, often hesitating, it is true, but which ended by bringing into question again all human problems and offering new solutions of them. In history, in criticism, the study of facts and surroundings replaces the old scholastic rules. In the purely literary works nature intervenes and reigns with Rousseau and his school; the trees, the waters, the mountains, the great forests, obtain recognition and take once more their place in the mechanism of the world; man is no longer an intellectual abstraction; nature determines and completes him. Diderot remains beyond question the grand figure of the century; he foresees all the truths, he is in advance of his time, waging a continual war against the worm-eaten edifice of conventions and rules. Magnificent outburst of an epoch, colossal labor from which our society has come forth, new era from which will date the centuries into which humanity is entering, with nature for a basis, method for a tool!

This is the evolution which I have called naturalism, and I contend that you can use no better word. Naturalism, that is, a return to nature; it is this operation which the savants performed on the day when they decided to set out from the study of bodies and phenomena, to build on experiment, and to proceed by analysis. Naturalism in letters is equally the return to nature and to man, direct observation, exact anatomy, the acceptance and depicting of what is. The task was the same for the writer as for the savant. One and the other replaced abstractions by realities, empirical formulas by rigorous analysis. Thus, no more abstract characters in books, no more lying inventions, no more of the absolute; but real characters, the true history of each one, the story of daily life. It was a question of commencing all over again; of knowing man down to the sources of his being before coming to such conclusions as the idealists reached, who invented types of character out of the whole cloth; and writers had only to start the edifice at the foundation, bringing together the greatest number of human data arranged in their logical order. This is naturalism; starting in the first thinking brain, if you wish; but whose greatest evolution, the definite evolution, without doubt took place in the last century.

So great an evolution in the human mind could not take place without bringing on a social overthrow. The French Revolution was this overthrow, this tempest which was to wipe out the old world, to give place to the new. We are the beginning of this new world, we are the direct children of naturalism in all things, in politics as in philosophy, in science as in literature and in art. I extend the bounds of this word naturalism because in reality it includes the entire century, the movement of contemporaneous intelligence, the force which is sweeping us onward, and which is working toward the molding of future centuries. The history of these last one hundred and fifty years proves it, and one of the most typical phenomena is the momentary rebound of the minds which succeeded to Rousseau and Chateaubriand; that singular outburst of romanticism on the very threshold of a scientific age. I will stop here for an instant, for there are some very important observations to make on this subject.

It is rarely the case that a revolution breaks out calmly and sensibly. Brains become deranged, imaginations become frightened, gloomy, and peopled with phantoms. After the rude shocks of the last century, and under the tender and restless influence of Rousseau, we find poets adopting a melancholy and fatal style. They know not where they are going. They throw themselves into bitterness, into contemplation, into the most extraordinary dreams. However, they also have been breathed upon by the spirit of the Revolution. They also are rebels. They bring about a rebellion of color, of passion, of fantasy; they talk of breaking outright with rules, and they renew the language by a burst of lyrical poetry, sparkling and superb. Moreover, truth has touched them, they exact local coloring, they believe in resurrecting the dead ages. This is romanticism. It is a violent reaction against classical literature, it is the first revolutionary use which the writers make of the reconquered literary liberty. They smash windows, they become intoxicated; maddened with their cries they rush into every extreme from the mere necessity of protesting. The movement is so irresistible that it carries everything with it, not only the flamboyant literature, but painting, sculpture, music, even; they all become romantic; romanticism triumphs and stamps itself everywhere. For one moment, in view of so powerful and so general a manifestation, one could almost believe that this literary and artistic formula had come to remain for a long time. The classical style had lasted at least two centuries; why should not the romantic style, which had taken its place, remain an equal length of time? And people were surprised when, at the end of a quarter of a century, they found romanticism in its last agony, slowly dying a beautiful death. Then truth came forth into the light. The romantic movement was without question but a skirmish. Poets, novelists of great talents, a whole generation full of magnificent enthusiasm had been able to start a wrong scent. But the century did not belong to these overexcited dreamers, to these children of the dawn, blinded by the light of the rising sun. They represented nothing definite; they were but the ad-

vance guard, charged with clearing away the *débris,* and insuring the future conquest by their excesses. The century belongs to the naturalists, to the direct sons of Diderot, whose solid battalions followed, and who will finally found a true state. The ends of the chain came together once more; naturalism triumphed with Balzac. After the violent catastrophes of its infancy, the century at last took the broad path marked out for it. This romantic crisis was bound to be produced, because it corresponded to the social catastrophe of the French Revolution in the same manner that I willingly compare triumphant naturalism to our actual republic, which bids fair to be founded by science and reason.

This is where we stand to-day. Romanticism, which corresponded to nothing durable, which was simply the restless regret of the old world and the bugle call to battle, gave away before naturalism, which rose up stronger and more powerful, leading the century of which it is in reality the breath. Is it necessary to exhibit it everywhere? It arises from the earth on which we walk; it grows every hour, penetrates and animates all things. It is the strength of our productions, the pivot upon which our society turns. It is found in the sciences, which continued on their tranquil way during the folly of romanticism; it is found in all the manifestations of human intelligence, disengaging itself more and more from the influences of romanticism which once for a moment seemed to have submerged it. It renews the arts, sculpture, and, above all, painting; it extends the field of criticism and history; it makes itself felt in the novel; and it is by means of the novel, by means of Balzac and Stendhal, that it lifts itself above romanticism, thus visibly relinking the chain with the eighteenth century. The novel is its domain, its field of battle and of victory. It seems to have chosen the novel in order to demonstrate the power of its method, the glory of the truth, the inexhaustible novelty of human data. To-day it takes possession of the stage, it has commenced to transform the theater, which is the last fortress of conventionality. When it shall triumph there its evolution will be complete; the classical formulas will find themselves definitely and solidly replaced by the naturalistic formula, which should by right be the formula of the new social condition.

It seemed to me necessary to insist upon and to explain at length the meaning of this word naturalism, as a great many pretend not to understand me. But I will drop the question now; I simply wish to study the naturalistic movement on the stage. But I must at the same time speak of the contemporaneous novel, for a point of comparison is indispensable to me. We will see where the novel stands and where the stage stands. The conclusion will thus be easier to reach.

I have often talked with foreign writers, and I have found the same astonishment expressed by them all. They are better able than we are to judge of the drift of our literature, for they see us from a distance, and they are outside and away from our daily quarrels. They express great astonishment that there are two distinct literatures with us, cut adrift from each other completely: the novel and the stage. No parallel exists among our neighbors. In France it seems that for half a century literature has been divided in two; the novel has passed to one side, the stage remains on the other; and between is dug a deeper and deeper ditch. Let us examine this situation for a moment; it is very curious and very instructive. Our current criticism—I speak of newspaper critics, whose hard task is to judge from day to day new pieces—our criticism lays down the principle that there is nothing in common between a novel and a dramatic work, neither the frame nor the development; it even goes so far as to say that there are two distinct styles, the theatrical style and the novelist's style, and a subject which could be put in a book could not be placed upon the stage. Why not say at once, as strangers do, that we have two literatures? It is but too true; such criticism has but stated a fact. It only remains to be seen if it does not aid in the detestable task of transforming this fact into a law by saying that this is so, because it cannot be otherwise. Our continual tendency is to draw up rules and codify everything. The worst of it is that, after we have bound ourselves hand and foot with rules and conventions, we have to use superhuman efforts to break the fetters.

In fact, we have two literatures entirely dissimilar in all things. Once a novelist wishes to write for the stage they mistrust him; they shrug their shoulders. Did not Balzac strand himself? It is true that M. Octave Feuillet has succeeded. I am going to take up this question at the beginning in order to solve it logically. But first let us study the contemporaneous novel.

Victor Hugo wrote poems, even when he descended to prose; Alexander Dumas, *père,* was but a prolific story-teller; George Sand gave us the dreams of her imagination in an easy and happy flow of language. I will not go back to those writers who belong to that superb outburst of romanticism, and who have left us no direct descendants. I mean to say that their influence is felt to-day only by our rebound from it, and in a manner of which I will speak later. The sources of our contemporaneous novel are found in Balzac and in Stendhal. We must look for them and consult them there. Both escaped from the craze of romanticism: Balzac because he could not help himself; and Stendhal from his superiority as a man. While the whole world was proclaiming the triumphs of the lyrics, while Victor Hugo was noisily crowned king of literature, both died almost in obscurity, in the midst of the neglect and disdain of the public. But they left behind them in their works the naturalistic formula of the century; and the future was to show their descendants pressing to their tombs, while the romantic school was dying from bloodlessness, and survived only in one illustrious old man, respect for whom prevented the telling of the truth. This is but a rapid review. There is no need of explaining the new formula which Balzac and Stendhal introduced. They made the inquiry with the novel that the savants made with science. They no longer imagined nor told pretty stories. Their task was to take man and dissect him, to analyze him in his flesh and in his brain. Stendhal remained above all else a psychologist. Balzac studied more particularly the temperaments, reconstructed the surroundings, gathered together human data, and assumed the title of doctor of social sciences. Compare "Père Goriot" or "Cousine Bette" to preceding novels, to those of the seven-

teenth century as to those of the eighteenth, and you will better understand what the naturalistic evolution accomplished. The name "romance" alone has been kept, which is wrong, for it has lost all significance.

I must now choose among the descendants of Balzac and Stendhal. First, there is M. Gustave Flaubert, and it is he who will complete the actual formula. We shall see in him the reaction from the romantic influence of which I have spoken to you. One of Balzac's most bitter disappointments was that he did not possess Victor Hugo's brilliant form. He was accused of writing badly, and that made him very unhappy. He sometimes tried to compete with the ringing lyrics, as for instance when he wrote "La Femme de Trente Ans," and "Le Lis dans la Vallée"; but in this he did not succeed; this great writer never wrote better prose than when he kept his own strong and fluent style. In passing to M. Gustave Flaubert the naturalistic formula was given into the hands of a perfect artist. It was solidified, and became hard and shining as marble. M. Gustave Flaubert had grown up in the midst of romanticism. All his leanings were toward the movement of 1830. When he published "Mme. Bovary" it was as a defiance to the realism of that time, which prided itself on writing badly. He intended to prove that you could talk of the little provincial *bourgeoisie* with the same ampleness and power which Homer has employed in speaking of the Greek heroes. But happily the work had another result. Whether M. Gustave Flaubert intended it or not, he had brought to naturalism the only strength which was lacking to it, that of that perfect and imperishable style which keeps works alive. From that time the formula was firmly established. There was nothing for the newcomers to do but to walk in this broad path of truth aided by art. The novelists went on and continued M. Balzac's inquiry, advancing more and more in the analysis of man as affected by the action of his surroundings; only they were at the same time artists, they had the originality and the science of form, they seemed to have raised truth from the dead by the intense life of their style.

At the same time as M. Gustave Flaubert, MM. Edmond and Jules de Goncourt were laboring also for this brilliancy of form. They did not come from the romantic school. They possessed no Latin, no classical aids; they invented their own language; they jotted down, with an incredible intensity, their feelings as artists weary of their art. In "Germinie Lacertéaux" they were the first to study the people of Paris, painting the faubourgs, the desolate landscapes of the suburbs, daring to tell everything in a refined language which gave beings and things their proper life. They had a great influence over the groups of naturalistic novelists. If we found our solidity, our exact method, in M. Gustave Flaubert, we must add that we were very much stirred by this new language of the MM. Goncourt: as penetrating as a symphony, giving that nervous shiver of our age to all objects, going further than the written phrase, and adding to the words of the dictionary a color, a sound, and a subtle perfume. I do not judge, I but state my facts. My only end is to establish the source of the contemporaneous novel, and to explain what it is and why it is.

These, then, are the sources clearly indicated. First, Balzac and Stendhal, a physiologist and a psychologist, weaned from the rhetoric of romanticism, which was nothing but an uprising of word-lovers. Then, between us and these two ancestors, we find M. Gustave Flaubert on one side, and MM. Edmond and Jules de Goncourt on the other, giving us the science of style, fixing the formula in new modes of expression. In these names you have the naturalistic novel. I will not speak of its actual representatives. It will suffice to indicate the distinctive characteristics of this novel.

I have said that the naturalistic novel is simply an inquiry into nature, beings, and things. It no longer interests itself in the ingenuity of a well-invented story, developed according to certain rules. Imagination has no longer place, plot matters little to the novelist, who bothers himself with neither development, mystery, nor *dénouement;* I mean that he does not intervene to take away from or add to reality; he does not construct a framework out of the whole cloth, according to the needs of a preconceived idea. You start from the point that nature is sufficient, that you must accept it as it is, without modification or pruning; it is grand enough, beautiful enough to supply its own beginning, its middle, and its end. Instead of imagining an adventure, of complicating it, of arranging stage effects, which scene by scene will lead to a final conclusion, you simply take the life study of a person or a group of persons, whose actions you faithfully depict. The work becomes a report, nothing more; it has but the merit of exact observation, of more or less profound penetration and analysis, of the logical connection of facts. Sometimes, even, it is not an entire life, with a commencement and an ending, of which you tell; it is only a scrap of an existence, a few years in the life of a man or a woman, a single page in a human history, which has attracted the novelist in the same way that the special study of a mineral can attract a chemist. The novel is no longer confined to one special sphere; it has invaded and taken possession of all spheres. Like science, it is the master of the world. It touches on all subjects: writes history; treats of physiology and psychology; rises to the highest flights of poetry; studies the most diverse subjects—politics, social economy, religion, and manners. Entire nature is its domain. It adopts the form which pleases it, taking the tone which seems best, feeling no longer bounded by any limit. In this we are far distant from the novel that our fathers were acquainted with. It was a purely imaginative work, whose sole end was to charm and distract its readers. In ancient rhetorics the novel is placed at the bottom, between the fables and light poetry. Serious men disdained novels, abandoned them to women, as a frivolous and compromising recreation. This opinion is still held in the country and certain academical centers. The truth is that the masterpieces of modern fiction say more on the subject of man and nature than do the graver works of philosophy, history, and criticism. In them lies the modern tool.

I pass to another characteristic of the naturalistic novel. It is impersonal; I mean to say by that that the novelist is but a recorder who is forbidden to judge and to conclude. The strict rôle of a savant is to expose the facts, to go to the end of analysis without venturing into synthesis; the facts are thus: experiment tried in such and such conditions gives such and such results; and he stops there, for if he wishes to go beyond the phenomena he will enter into hypothesis; we shall have probabilities, not science. Well! the novelist should equally keep to known facts, to the scrupulous study of nature, if he does not wish to stray among lying conclusions. He himself disappears, he keeps his emotion well in hand, he simply shows what he has seen. Here is the truth; shiver or laugh before it, draw from it whatever lesson you please, the only task of the author has been to put before you true data. There is, besides, for this moral impersonality of the work a reason in art. The passionate or tender intervention of the writer weakens a novel, because it ruins the clearness of its lines, and introduces a strange element into the facts which destroys their scientific value. One cannot well imagine a chemist becoming incensed with azote, because this body is injurious to life, or sympathizing with oxygen for the contrary reason. In the same way, a novelist who feels the need of becoming indignant with vice, or applauding virtue, not only spoils the data he produces, for his intervention is as trying as it is useless, but the work loses its strength; it is no longer a marble page, hewn from the block of reality; it is matter worked up, kneaded by the emotions of the author, and such emotions are always subject to prejudices and errors. A true work will be eternal, while an impressionable work can at best tickle only the sentiment of a certain age.

Thus the naturalistic novelist never interferes, any more than the savant. This moral impersonality of a work is all-important, for it raises the question of morality in a novel. They reproach us for being immoral, because we put rogues and honest men in our books, and are as impartial to one as to the other. This is the whole quarrel. Rogues are permissible, but they must be punished in the wind-up, or at least we must crush them under our anger and contempt. As to the honest men, they deserve here and there a few words of praise and encouragement. Our impassability, our tranquillity in our analysis in the face of the good and bad, is altogether wrong. And they end by saying that we lie when we are most true. What! nothing but rogues, not one attractive character? This is where the theory of attractive characters comes in. There must be attractive characters in order to give a kindly touch to nature. They not only demand that we should have a preference for virtue, but they exact that we should embellish virtue and make it lovable. Thus, in a character, we ought to make a selection, take the good sentiments and pass the wicked by in silence; indeed, we would be more commendable still if we invented a person out of the whole cloth; if we would mold one on the conventional form demanded by propriety and good manners. For this purpose there are ready-made types which writers introduce into a story without any trouble. These are attractive characters, ideal conceptions of men and women, destined to compensate for the sorry impression of true characters taken from nature. As you can see, our only mistake in all this is that we accept only nature, and that we are not willing to correct what is by what should be. Absolute honesty no more exists than perfect healthfulness. There is a tinge of the human beast in all of us, as there is a tinge of illness. These young girls so pure, these young men so loyal, represented to us in certain novels, do not belong to earth; to make them mortal everything must be told. We tell everything, we do not make a choice, neither do we idealize; and this is why they accuse us of taking pleasure in obscenity. To sum up, the question of morality in novels reduces itself to two opinions: the idealists pretend that it is necessary to lie to be moral; the naturalists affirm that there is no morality outside of the truth. Moreover, nothing is so dangerous as a romantic novel; such a work, in painting the world under false colors, confuses the imagination, throws us in the midst of hair-breadth escapes; and I do not speak of the hypocrisies of fashionable society, the abominations which are hidden under a bed of flowers. With us these perils disappear. We teach the bitter science of life, we give the high lesson of reality. Here is what exists; endeavor to repair it. We are but savants, analyzers, anatomists; and our works have the certainty, the solidity, and the practical applications of scientific works. I know of no school more moral or more austere.

Such to-day is the naturalistic novel. It has triumphed; all the novelists accept it, even those who attempted at first to crush it in the egg. It is the same old story; they deride, and then they praise and finally imitate it. Success is sufficient to turn the source of the current. Besides, now that the impetus has been given, we shall see the movement spreading more and more. A new literary century is beginning for us.

I pass now to our contemporaneous stage. We have just seen to what place the novel has risen; we must now endeavor to define the present position of dramatic literature. But before entering upon it I will rapidly recall to the reader's mind the great evolutions of the stage in France.

In the beginning we find unformed pieces, dialogues for two characters, or for three at the most, which were given in the public square. Then halls were built, tragedy and comedy were born, under the influence of the classical renaissance. Great geniuses consecrated this movement— Corneille, Molière, Racine. They were the product of the age in which they lived. The tragedy and comedy of that time, with their unalterable rules, their etiquette of the court, their grand and noble air, their philosophical dissertations and oratorical eloquence are the exact reproduction of contemporaneous society. And this identity, this close affinity of the dramatic formula and the social surroundings, is so strong that for two centuries the formula remains almost the same. It only loses its stiffness, it merely bends in the eighteenth century with Voltaire and Beaumarchais. The ancient society is then profoundly disturbed; the excitement which agitates it even touches the stage. There is a need for greater action, there is a sullen revolt against the rules, a vague return to nature. Even at this period Diderot and Mercier laid down squarely the basis of the naturalistic theater; unfortunately, neither one nor the other produced a masterpiece, and this is necessary to establish a new formula. Besides, the classical style was so solidly planted in the soil of the ancient monarchy that it was not carried away entirely by the tempest of the Revolution. It persisted for some time longer, weakened, degenerated, gliding into insipidity and imbecility. Then the romantic insurrection, which had been hatching for years, burst forth. The romantic drama killed the expiring

tragedy; Victor Hugo gave it its death-blow, and reaped the benefits of a victory for which many others had labored. It is worth noticing that through the necessities of the struggle the romantic drama became the antithesis of the tragedy; it opposed passion to duty, action to words, coloring to psychological analysis, the Middle Ages to antiquity. It was this sparkling contrast which assured its triumph. Tragedy must disappear, its knell had sounded; for it was no longer the product of social surroundings; and the drama brought in its train the liberty that was necessary in order boldly to clear away the *débris*. But it seems to-day as though that should have been the limit of its rôle. It was but a superb affirmation of the nothingness of rules, of the necessity of life. Notwithstanding all this uproar, it remained the rebellious child of tragedy; in a similar fashion it lied; it costumed facts and characters with an exaggeration which makes us smile nowadays; in a similar fashion it had its rules and its effects—effects much more irritating, as they were falser. In fact, there was but one more rhetoric on the stage. The romantic drama, however, was not to have as long a reign as tragedy. After performing its revolutionary task it died out, suddenly exhausted, leaving the place clear for reconstruction. Thus the history is the same on the stage as in the novel. As a result of this inevitable crisis in romanticism, the traditions of naturalism reappear, the ideas of Diderot and Mercier come more and more to the surface. It is the new social state, born of the Revolution, which fixes little by little a new dramatic formula in spite of many fruitless attempts and of advancing and retreating footsteps. This work was inevitable. It produced itself and it will be produced again by the force of things, and it will never stop until the evolution shall be complete. The naturalistic formula will be to our century what the classical formula has been to past centuries.

Now we have arrived at our own period. Here I find a considerable activity, an extraordinary outlay of talent. It is an immense workroom in which each one works with feverish energy. All is confusion as yet, there is a great deal of lost labor, very few blows strike out direct and strong; still the spectacle is none the less marvelous. One thing is certain, that each laborer is working toward the definite triumph of naturalism, even those who appear to fight against it. They are, in spite of everything, borne along by the current of the time; they go of necessity where it goes. As none in the theater has been of large enough caliber to establish the formula at a stroke by the sheer force of his genius, it would almost seem as if they had divided the task, each one giving in turn, and with reference to a definite point, the necessary shove onward. Let us now see who are the best known workers among them.

In the first place, there is M. Victorien Sardou. He is the actual representative of the comedy with a plot. The true heir of M. Scribe, he has renovated the old tricks and pushed scenic art to the point of prestidigitation. This kind of play is a continuous and ever more strongly emphasized reaction against the old-time classical stage. The moment that facts are opposed to words, that action is placed above character, the sure tendency is to a complicated plot, to marionettes led by a thread, to sudden changes, to unexpected *dénouements*. The reign of Scribe was a notable event in dramatic literature. He exaggerated this new principle of action, making it the principle thing, and he also displayed great ability in producing extraordinary effects, inventing a code of laws and recipes all his own. This was inevitable; reactions are always extreme. What has been for a long time called the fashionable stage had then no other source than an exaggerated principle of action at the expense of the delineation of character and the analysis of emotion. The truth escaped them in their effort to grasp it. They broke one set of rules to invent others, which were falser and more ridiculous. The well-written play—I mean by that the play written on a symmetrical and even pattern—has become a curious and amusing plaything, which diverts the whole of Europe. From this dates the popularity of our *repertoire* with foreigners. Today it has undergone a slight change; M. Victorien Sardou thinks less of the cabinetwork, but though he has enlarged the frame and laid more stress on legerdemain, he still remains the great representative in the theater of action, of amorous action, this quality dominating and overpowering everything else. His great quality is movement; he has no life, he has only movement, which carries away the characters, and which often throws an illusive glamour over them; you could almost believe them to be living, breathing beings; but they are in reality only well-staged puppets, coming and going like pieces of perfect mechanism. Ingenuity, dexterity, just a suspicion of actuality, a great knowledge of the stage, a particular talent for episode, the smallest details prodigally and vividly brought forward—such are M. Sardou's principal qualities. But his observation is superficial; the human data which he produces have dragged about everywhere and are only patched up skillfully; the world into which he leads us is a pasteboard world, peopled by puppets. In each one of his works you feel the solid earth giving way beneath your feet; there is always some far-fetched plot, a false emotion carried to the last extremity, which serves as a pivot for the whole play, or else an extraordinary complication of facts, which a magical word is supposed to unravel at the end. Real life is entirely different. Even in accepting the necessary exaggerations of a farce, one looks for and wants more breadth and more simplicity in the means. These plays are never anything more than vaudevilles unnecessarily exaggerated, whose comic strength partakes altogether of caricature. I mean by that that the laughter evoked is not spontaneous, but is called forth by the grimaces of the actors. It is useless to cite examples. Everyone has seen the village which M. Victorien Sardou depicts in "Les Bourgeois de Pont-Arcy"; the character of his observation is here clearly revealed—silhouettes hardly rejuvenated, the stale jokes of the day, which are in everyone's mouth. Compared with Balzac, for instance, of how low an order are these plays. "Rabagas," for instance, the satire in which is excellent, is spoiled by a very inferior amorous intrigue. "La Famille Benoiton" in which certain caricatures are very amusing, has also its faults—the famous letters, these letters which are to be found throughout M. Sardou's writings, and which are as necessary to him as the jugglery and the presto-change to the conjurer. He has had immense success, a fact easy of explanation, and I am very glad he has. Remark one thing, that, though he very often runs counter to the truth, he has nevertheless been of great service to naturalism. He is one of the workmen of whom

I spoke a short time ago, who are of their period, who work according to their strength for a formula which they have not the genius to carry out in its entirety. His personal rôle is exactness in the stage setting, the most perfect material representation possible of everyday existence. If he falsifies in filling out the frames, at least he has the frames themselves, and that is already something gained. To me his reason for being is that above all things. He has come in his hour, he has given the public a taste for life and tableaux hewn from reality.

I now turn to M. Alexander Dumas, *fils.* Truly, he has done better work still. He is one of the most skillful workmen in the naturalistic workroom. Little remains for him but to find the complete formula, and then let him realize it. To him we owe the physiological studies on the stage; he alone, up to the present time, has been brave enough to show us the sex in the young girl, the beast in the man. "La Visite de Noces," and certain scenes in the "Demi-Monde" and the "Fils Naturel," possess analysis which is absolutely remarkable and rigorously truthful. Here are human data which are new and excellent; and that is certainly very rare in our modern *repertoire.* You see I do not make any bones about praising M. Dumas, *fils.* But I admire him with reference to a group of ideas which later will cause me to appear very severe upon him. According to my way of thinking, he has had a crisis in his life, he has developed a philosophic vein, he manifests a deplorable desire for legislation, preaching, and conversion. He has made himself God's substitute on this earth, and as a result the strangest freaks of imagination spoil his faculties of observation. He no longer makes use of human observation save to reach superhuman results and astonishing situations, dressed out in full-blown fantasy. Look at "La Femme de Claude," "L'Étrangère," and other pieces still. This is not all: cleverness has spoiled M. Dumas. A man of genius is not clever, and a man of genius is necessary to establish the naturalistic formula in a masterly fashion. M. Dumas has imbued all his characters with his wit; the men, the women, even the children in his plays make witty remarks, these famous witticisms which so often give a play success. Nothing can be falser or more fatiguing; it destroys all the truth of the dialogue. Again, M. Dumas, who before everything is a thorough playwriter, never hesitates between reality and a scenic exigency; he sacrifices the reality. His theory is that truth is of little consequence provided he can be logical. A play becomes with him a problem to be solved; he starts out from a given point, he must reach another point without tiring his public; and the victory is gained if you have been agile enough to jump over the breakneck places, and have forced the public to follow you in spite of itself. The spectators may protest later, cry out against the want of the reality, fight against it; but nevertheless they have belonged to the author during the evening. All M. Dumas' plays are written on this theory. He wins a triumph in spite of paradox, unreality, the most useless and *risque* thesis, through the mere strength of his wrists. He who has been touched by the breath of naturalism, who has written such clearly defined scenes, never recoils, however, before a fiction when he needs it for the sake of argument or simply as a matter of construction. It is the most pitiable mixture of imperfect reality and whimsical invention. None of his plays escape this double current. Do you remember in the "Fils Natu-rel" the incredible story of *Clara Vignot,* and in "L'Étrangère," the extraordinary story of *La Vierge du Mal?* I cite at haphazard. It would seem as though M. Dumas never made use of truth but as a springboard with which to jump into emptiness. He never leads us into a world that we know; the surroundings are always false and painful; the characters lose all their natural accent, and no longer seem to belong to the earth. It is no longer life, with its breadth, its shades, and its good nature; it is a debate, an argument, something cold, dry, and rasping in which there is no air. The philosopher has killed the observer—such is my conclusion, and the dramatic writer has fin-ished the philosopher. It is to be deeply regretted.

Now I come to Émile Augier. He is the real master of our French stage. His was the most constant, the most sincere, and the most regular effort. It must be remembered how fiercely he was attacked by the romanticists; they called him the poet of good sense, they ridiculed certain of his verses, though they did not dare to ridicule verses of a sim-ilar character in Molière. The truth was that M. Augier worried the romanticists, for they feared in him a powerful adversary, a writer who took up anew the old French tra-ditions, ignoring the insurrection of 1830. The new formu-la grew greater with him; exact observation, real life, true pictures of our society in correct and quiet language, were introduced. M. Émile Augier's first works, dramas and comedies in verse, had the great merit of appearing at our classical theater; they had the same simplicity of plot as the best classical plays, as in "Philiberte," for example, where the story of an ugly girl who became charming, and whom all the world courted, was sufficient to fill three acts, without the slightest complication; their main point was the elucidating of character, and they possessed also a spirit of genial good nature and the strong, quiet move-ment that would naturally arise among people who drew apart and then came together again as their emotions im-pelled them. My conviction is that the naturalistic formula will be but the development of this classical formula, en-larged and adapted to our surroundings. Later M. Émile Augier made his own personality more strongly felt. He could not help employing the naturalistic formula when he began to write in prose, and depicted our contempora-neous society more freely. I mention more particularly "Les Lionnes Pauvres," "Le Mariage d'Olympe," "Maître Guerin," "Le Gendre de M. Poirier," and those two come-dies which created the most talk, "Les Effrontés," and "Le Fils de Giboyer." These are very remarkable works, which all, more or less, in some scenes, realize the new theater, the stage of our time. The bold, unrepentant effrontery, for instance, with which *Guerin,* the notary, dies, so novel and true in its effect; the excellent picture of the newly en-riched *bourgeois* in the "Gendre de M. Poirer"; both of these are admirable studies of human nature; *Giboyer,* again, is a curious creation, quite true to life, living in the midst of a society depicted with a great deal of excellent sarcasm. M. Augier's strength, and what makes him really superior to M. Dumas, *fils,* is his more human quality. This human side places him on solid ground; we have no fear that he will take those wild leaps into space; he re-mains well balanced, not so brilliant, perhaps, but much more sure. What is there to prevent M. Augier from being

the genius waited for, the genius destined to make the nat-uralistic formula a fixture? Why, I ask, does he only re-main the wisest and the strongest of the workmen of the present hour? In my opinion it is because he has not known how to disengage himself from conventions, from stereotyped ideas, from made-up characters. His stage is constantly belittled by figures *"executés de chic,"* as they say in the studio. Thus it is rarely that you do not find, in his comedies, the pure young girl who is very rich and who does not wish to marry, because she scorns to be married for her money. His young men are equally heroes of honor and loyalty, sobbing when they learn that their fathers made their money unscrupulously. In a word, the interest-ing character predominates; I mean the ideal type of good and beautiful sentiments always cast in the same mold, that mere symbol, that hieratic personification outside of all true observation. This commandant *Guerin,* this model of military men, whose uniform aids in the *dénouement; Giboyer's* son, that archangel of delicacy, born of a man of ill repute, and *Giboyer* himself, so tender in his baseness; *Henri,* the son of *Charrier* in "Les Effrontés," who goes bond for his father when he has dabbled in an equivocal affair, and who finally induces the latter to reimburse the men whom he has wronged—all these are very beautiful, very touching; only as human data very unlikely. Nature is not so unmixed, neither in the good nor in the evil. You cannot accept these interesting characters except as a con-trast and a consolation. This is not all; M. Augier often modifies a character by a stroke of his wand. His reason is easily seen; he wants a *dénouement,* and he changes a character after an effective scene. For instance, the climax in the "Gendre de M. Poirier." Really it is very accommo-dating; you do not make a light man out of a dark one so easily. Considered from the point of genuine observation these brusque changes are to be deplored; a temperament is the same to the end, or at least is only changed by slowly working causes, apparent only to a very minute analysis. M. Augier's best characters, those which will remain lon-gest, because they are the most complete and logical, to my thinking, are *Guerin* the notary, and *Pommeau* in "Les Lionnes Pauvres." The climax in both plays is very good. Reading "Les Lionnes Pauvres" over I bethought me of *Mme. Marneffe,* married to an honest man. Compare *Seraphine* to *Mme. Marneffe,* place M. Émile Augier and Balzac face to face for one instant, and you will under-stand why, notwithstanding his good qualities, M. Émile Augier has not firmly established the new formula on the stage. His hand was not bold enough to rid himself of the conventionalities which encumber the stage. His plays are too much of a mixture; not one of them stands out with the decisive originality of genius. He softens his lines too much; still he will remain in our dramatic literature as a pioneer, who possessed great and strong intelligence.

I would like to have spoken of M. Eugène Labiche, whose comic vein is very refreshing; of M. Meilhac and M. Halé-vy, these sharp observers of Parisian life; of M. Goudinet, who by his witty scenes, depicted without any action, has given the last blow to the downfall of the formula of Scribe.

But it must be sufficient for me to explain myself by means of the three dramatic authors whose work I have just analyzed and who are really the most celebrated. Their talent and their different gifts I greatly admire. Only I must say, once more, I judge them from the point of view of a group of ideas and the place which their works will hold in the literary movement of the century.

Now that all the elements are known I have in my hands all the data which I need for argument and conclusion. On one side, we have seen what the naturalistic novel is at the present time; on the other, we have just ascertained what the first dramatic authors have made of our stage. It remains but to establish a parallel.

No one contests the point that all the different forms of literary expression hold together and advance at the same time. When they have been stirred up, when the ball is once set rolling, there is a general push toward the same goal. The romantic insurrection is a striking example of this unity of movement under a definite influence. I have shown that the force of the current of the age is toward naturalism. To-day this force is making itself felt more and more; it is rushing on us, and everything must obey it. The novel and the stage are carried away by it. Only it has happened that the evolution has been much more rapid in the novel; it triumphs there while it is just beginning to put in an appearance on the stage. This was bound to be. The theater has always been the stronghold of convention for a multiplicity of reasons, which I will explain later. I simply wish, then, to come down to this: The naturalistic formula, however complete and defined in the novel, is very far from being so on the stage, and I conclude from that that it will be completed, that it will assume sooner or later there its scientific rigor, or else the stage will become flat, and more and more inferior.

Some people are very much irritated with me; they cry out: "But what do you ask? what evolution do you want? Is the evolution not an accomplished fact? Have not M. Émile Augier, M. Dumas, *fils,* and M. Victorien Sardou pushed the study and the painting of our society to the farthest possible lengths? Let us stop where we are. We have already too much of the realities of this world." In the first place, it is very naïve in these people to wish to stop; nothing is stable in a society, everything is borne along by a continuous movement. Things go in spite of everything where they ought to go. I contend that the evolution, far from being an accomplished fact on the stage, is hardly commenced. Up to the present time we have taken only the first steps. We must wait until certain ideas have wedged their way in, and until the public becomes accustomed to them, and until the force of things abolishes the obstacles one by one. I have tried, in rapidly glancing over MM. Victorien Sardou, Dumas, *fils,* and Émile Augier, to tell for what reasons I look upon them as simply laborers who are clearing the paths of *débris,* and not as creators, not as geniuses who are building a monument. Then after them I am waiting for something else.

This something else which arouses so much indignation and draws forth so many pleasantries is, however, very simple. We have only to read Balzac, M. Gustave Flaubert, and MM. de Goncourt again—in a word, the naturalistic novelists—to discover what it is. I am waiting for them, in the first place, to put a man of flesh and bones on the stage, taken from reality, scientifically analyzed, without one lie. I am waiting for them to rid us of fictitious characters, of conventional symbols of virtue and vice, which possess no value as human data. I am waiting for the surroundings to determine the characters, and for characters to act according to the logic of facts, combined with the logic of their own temperament. I am waiting until there is no more jugglery of any kind, no more strokes of a magical wand, changing in one minute persons and things. I am waiting for the time to come when they will tell us no more incredible stories, when they will no longer spoil the effects of just observations by romantic incidents, the result being to destroy even the good parts of a play. I am waiting for them to abandon the cut and dried rules, the worked-out formulas, the tears and cheap laughs. I am waiting until a dramatic work free from declamations, big words, and grand sentiments has the high morality of truth, teaches the terrible lesson that belongs to all sincere inquiry. I am waiting, finally, until the evolution accomplished in the novel takes place on the stage; until they return to the source of science and modern arts, to the study of nature, to the anatomy of man, to the painting of life, in an exact reproduction, more original and powerful than anyone has so far dared to place upon the boards.

This is what I am waiting for. They shrug their shoulders and reply to me that I shall wait forever. Their decisive argument is that you must not expect these things on the stage. The stage is not the novel. It has given us what it could give us. That ends it; we must be satisfied.

Now we are at the pith of the quarrel. I am trying to uproot the very conditions of existence on the stage. What I ask is impossible, which amounts to saying that fictions are necessary on the stage; a play must have some romantic corners, it must turn in equilibrium round certain situations, which must unravel themselves at the proper time. They take up the business side; first, any analysis is wearisome; the public demands facts, always facts; then there is the perspective of the stage; an act must be played in three hours, no matter what its length is; then the characters are endowed with a particular value, which necessitates setting up fictions. I will not put forth all the arguments. I arrive at the intervention of the public, which is really considerable; the public wishes this, the public will not have that; it will not tolerate too much truth; it exacts four attractive puppets to one real character taken from life. In a word, the stage is the domain of conventionality; everything is conventional, from the decorations to the footlights which illuminate the actors, even down to the characters, who are led by a string. Truth can only enter by little doses adroitly distributed. They even go so far as to swear that the theater will cease to exist the day that it ceases to be an amusing lie, destined to console the spectators in the evening for the sad realities of the day.

I know all these reasonings, and I shall try to respond to them presently, when I reach my conclusion. It is evident that each kind of literature has its own conditions of existence. A novel, which one reads alone in his room, with his feet on his andirons, is not a play which is acted before two thousand spectators. The novelist has time and space before him; all sorts of liberties are permitted him; he can use one hundred pages, if it pleases him, to analyze at his leisure a certain character; he can describe his surroundings as much as he pleases; he can cut his story short, can retrace his steps, changing places twenty times—in one word, he is absolute master of his matter. The dramatic author, on the contrary, is inclosed in a rigid frame; he must heed all sorts of necessities. He moves only in the midst of obstacles. Then, above all, there is the question of the isolated reader and the spectators taken *en masse;* the solitary reader tolerates everything, goes where he is led, even when he is disgusted; while the spectators, taken *en masse,* are seized with prudishness, with frights, with sensibilities of which the author must take notice under pain of a certain fall. All this is true, and it is precisely for this reason that the stage is the last citadel of conventionality, as I stated further back. If the naturalistic movement had not encountered on the boards a difficult ground, filled with obstacles, it would already have taken root there with the intensity and with the success which have attended the novel. The stage, under its conditions of existence, must be the last, the most laborious, and the most bitterly disputed conquest of the spirit of truth.

I will remark here that the evolution of each century is of necessity incarnated in a particular form of literature. Thus the seventeenth century evidently incarnated itself in the dramatic formula. Our theater threw forth then an incomparable glitter, to the detriment of lyrical poetry and the novel. The reason was that the stage then exactly responded to the spirit of the period. It abstracted man from nature, studied him with the philosophical tool of the time; it has the swing of a pompous rhetoric, the polite manners of a society which had reached perfect maturity. It is the fruit of the ground; its formula is written from that point where the then civilization flowed with the greatest ease and perfection. Compare our epoch to that, and you will understand the decisive reasons which made Balzac a great novelist instead of a great dramatist. The spirit of the nineteenth century, with its return to nature, with its need of exact inquiry, quitted the stage, where too much conventionality hampered it, in order to stamp itself indelibly on the novel, whose field is limitless. And thus it is that scientifically the novel has become the form, *par excellence,* of our age, the first path in which naturalism was to triumph. To-day it is the novelists who are the literary princes of the period; they possess the language, they hold the method, they walk in the front rank, side by side with science. If the seventeenth century was the century of the stage, the nineteenth will belong to the novel.

Let us admit for one moment that criticism has some show of reason when it asserts that naturalism is impossible on the stage. Here is what they assert. Conventionality is inevitable on the stage; there must always be lying there. We are condemned to a continuance of M. Sardou's juggling; to the theories and witticisms of M. Dumas, *fils;* to the sentimental characters of M. Émile Augier. We shall produce nothing finer than the genius of these authors; we must accept them as the glory of our time on the stage. They are what they are because the theater wishes them to be such. If they have not advanced further to the front, if they have not obeyed more implicitly the grand current

of truth which is carrying us onward, it is the theater which forbids them. That is a wall which shuts the way, even to the strongest. Very well! But then it is the theater which you condemn; it is to the stage that you have given the mortal blow. You crush it under the novel, you assign it an inferior place, you make it despicable and useless in the eyes of future generations. What do you wish us to do with the stage, we other seekers after truth, anatomists, analysts, searchers of life, compilers of human data, if you prove to us that there we cannot make use of our tools and our methods? Really! The theater lives only on conventionalities; it must lie; it refuses our experimental literature! Oh, well, then, the century will put the stage to one side, it will abandon it to the hands of the public amusers, while it will perform elsewhere its great and glorious work. You yourselves pronounce the verdict and kill the stage. It is very evident that the naturalistic evolution will extend itself more and more, as it possesses the intelligence of the age. While the novelists are digging always further forward, producing newer and more exact data, the stage will flounder deeper every day in the midst of its romantic fictions, its worn-out plots, and its skillfulness of handicraft. The situation will be the more sad because the public will certainly acquire a taste for reality in reading novels. The movement is making itself forcibly felt even now. There will come a time when the public will shrug its shoulders and demand an innovation. Either the theater will be naturalistic or it will not be at all; such is the formal conclusion.

And even now, to-day, is not this becoming the situation? All of the new literary generation turn their backs on the theater. Question the young men of twenty-five years—I speak of those who possess a real literary temperament; they will show great contempt for the theater; they will speak of its successful authors with such faint approval that you will become indignant. They look upon the stage as being of an inferior rank. That comes solely from the fact that it does not offer them the soil of which they have need; they find neither enough liberty nor enough truth there. They all veer toward the novel. Should the stage be conquered by a stroke of genius to-morrow you would see what an outpouring would take place. When I wrote elsewhere that the boards were empty I merely meant they had not yet produced a Balzac. You could not, in good faith, compare M. Sardou, Dumas, or Augier to Balzac; all the dramatic authors, put one on top of the other, do not equal him in stature. The boards will remain empty, from this point of view, so long as a master hand has not, by embodying the formula in a work of undying genius, drawn after him to-morrow's generations.

I have perfect faith in the future of our stage. I will not admit that the critics are right in saying that naturalism is impossible on the stage, and I am going to explain under what conditions the movement will without question be brought about.

It is not true that the stage must remain stationary; it is not true that its actual conventionalities are the fundamental conditions of its existence.

Everything marches, I repeat; everything marches forward. The authors of to-day will be overridden; they cannot have the presumption to settle dramatic literature forever. What they have lisped forth others will cry from the house top; but the stage will not be shaken to its foundations on that account; it will enter, on the contrary, on a wider, straighter path. People have always denied the march forward; they have denied to the newcomers the power and the right to accomplish what has not been performed by their elders. The social and literary evolutions have an irresistible force; they traverse with a slight bound the enormous obstacles which were reputed impassable. The theater may well be what it is to-day; to-morrow it will be what it should be. And when the event takes place all the world will think it perfectly natural.

At this point I enter into mere probabilities, and I no longer pretend to the same scientific rigor. So long as I have reasoned on facts I have demonstrated the truth of my position. At present I am content to foretell. The evolution will take place, that is certain. But will it pass to the left? will it pass to the right? I do not know. One can reason, and that is all.

In the first place, it is certain that the conditions existing on the stage will always be different. The novel, thanks to its freedom, will remain perhaps the tool, *par excellence,* of the century, while the stage will but follow it and complete the action. The wonderful power of the stage must not be forgotten, and its immediate effect on the spectators. There is no better instrument for propagating anything. If the novel, then, is read by the fireside, in several instances, with a patience tolerating the longest details, the naturalistic drama should proclaim before all else that it has no connection with this isolated reader, but with a crowd who cry out for clearness and conciseness. I do not see that the naturalistic formula is antagonistic to this conciseness and this clearness. It is simply a question of changing the composition and the body of the work. The novel analyzes at great length and with a minuteness of detail which overlooks nothing; the stage can analyze as briefly as it wishes by actions and words. A word, a cry, in Balzac's works is often sufficient to present the entire character. This cry belongs essentially to the stage. As to the acts, they are consistent with analysis in action, which is the most striking form of action one can make. When we have gotten rid of the child's play of a plot, the infantile game of tying up complicated threads in order to have the pleasure of untying them again; when a play shall be nothing more than a real and logical story—we shall then enter into perfect analysis; we shall analyze necessarily the double influence of characters over facts, of facts over characters. This is what has led me to say so often that the naturalistic formula carries us back to the source of our national stage, the classical formula. We find this continuous analysis of character, which I consider so necessary, in Corneille's tragedies and Molière's comedies; plot takes a secondary place, the work is a long dissertation in dialogue on man. Only instead of an abstract man I would make a natural man, put him in his proper surroundings, and analyze all the physical and social causes which make him what he is. In a word, the classical formula is to me a good one, on condition that the scientific method is employed in the study of actual society, in the same way that the chemist studies minerals and their properties.

Emile Zola, the founder and principal theorist of Naturalism.

As to the long descriptions of the novelist, they cannot be put upon the stage; that is evident. The naturalistic novelists describe a great deal, not for the pleasure of describing, as some reproach them with doing, but because it is part of their formula to be circumstantial, and to complete the character by means of his surroundings. Man is no longer an intellectual abstraction for them, as he was looked upon in the seventeenth century; he is a thinking beast, who forms part of nature, and who is subject to the multiplicity of influences of the soil on which he grows and where he lives. This is why a climate, a country, a horizon, a room, are often of decisive importance. The novelist no longer separates his character from the air which he breathes; he does not describe him in order to exercise his rhetorical powers, as the didactic poets did, as Delille does, for example; he simply notes the material conditions in which he finds his characters at each hour, and in which the facts are produced, in order to be absolutely thorough in order that his inquiry may belong to the world's great whole and reproduce the reality in its entirety. But it is not necessary to carry descriptions to the stage; they are found there naturally. Are not the stage settings a continual description, which can be made much more exact and startling than the descriptions in a novel? It is only painted pasteboard, some say; that may be so, but in a novel it is less than painted pasteboard—it is but blackened paper, notwithstanding which the illusion is produced. After the scenery, so surprisingly true, that we have recently seen in our theaters, no one can deny the possibility of producing on the stage the reality of surroundings. It now remains for dramatic authors to utilize this reality, they furnishing the characters and the facts, the scene painters, under their directions, furnishing the descriptions, as exact as shall be necessary. It but remains for a dramatic author to make use of his surroundings as the novelists do, since the latter know how to introduce them and make them real.

I will add that the theater, being a material reproduction of life, external surroundings have always been a necessity there. In the seventeenth century, however, as nature was not taken into consideration, as man was looked upon only as a purely intellectual being, the scenery was vague—a peristyle of a temple, any kind of a room, or a public place. To-day the naturalistic movement has brought about a more and more perfect exactness in the stage settings. This was produced little by little, almost inevitably. I even find here a proof of the secret work that naturalism has accomplished in the stage since the commencement of the century. I have not time to study any more deeply this question of decorations and accessories; I must content myself by stating that description is not only possible on the stage, but it is, moreover, a necessity which is imposed as an essential condition of existence.

There is no necessity for me to expatiate on the change of place. For a long time the unity of place has not been observed. The dramatic authors do not hesitate to cover an entire existence, to take the spectators to both ends of the world. Here conventionality remains mistress, as it is also in the novel. It is the same as to the question of time. It is necessary to cheat. A play which calls for fifteen days, for example, must be acted in the three hours which we set apart for reading a novel or seeing it played at the theater. We are not the creative force which governs the world; our power of creation is of a second-hand sort; we only analyze, sum up in a nearly always groping fashion, happy and proclaimed as geniuses when we can disengage one ray of the truth.

I now come to the language. They pretend to say that there is a special style for the stage. They want it to be a style altogether different from the ordinary style of speaking, more sonorous, more nervous, written in a higher key, cut in facets, no doubt to make the chandelier jets sparkle. In our time, for example, M. Dumas, *fils,* has the reputation of being a great dramatic author. His "mots" are famous. They go off like sky rockets, falling again in showers to the applause of the spectators. Besides, all his characters speak the same language, the language of witty Paris, cutting in its paradoxes, having a good hit always in view, and sharp and hard. I do not deny the sparkle of this language—not a very solid sparkle, it is true—but I deny its truth. Nothing is so fatiguing as these continual sneering sentences. I would rather see more elasticity, greater naturalness. They are at one and the same time too well and not well enough written. The true style-setters of the epoch are the novelists; to find the infallible, living, original style you must turn to M. Gustave Flaubert and to MM. de Goncourt. When you compare M. Dumas' style to that of these great prose writers you find it is no longer correct—it has no color, no movement. What I want to

hear on the stage is the language as it is spoken every day; if we cannot produce on the stage a conversation with its repetitions, its length, and its useless words, at least the movement and the tone of the conversation could be kept; the particular turn of mind of each talker, the reality, in a word, reproduced to the necessary extent. MM. Goncourt have made a curious attempt at this in "Henriette Maréchal," that play which no one would listen to, and which no one knows anything about. The Grecian actors spoke through a brass tube; under Louis XIV. the comedians sang their rôles in a chanting tone to give them more pomp; to-day we are content to say that there is a particular language belonging to the stage, more sonorous and explosive. You can see by this that we are progressing. One day they will perceive that the best style on the stage is that which best sets forth the spoken conversation, which puts the proper word in the right place, giving it its just value. The naturalistic novelists have already written excellent models of dialogue, reduced to strictly useful words.

There now remains but the question of sentimental characters. I do not disguise the fact that it is of prime importance. The public remain cold and irresponsive when their passion for an ideal character, for some combination of loyalty and honor, is not satisfied. A play which presents to them but living characters taken from real life looks black and austere to them, when it does not exasperate them. It is on this point that the battle of naturalism rages most fiercely. We must learn to be patient. At the present moment a secret change is taking place in the public feeling; people are coming little by little, urged onward by the spirit of the century, to admit the bold reproduction of real life, and are even beginning to acquire a taste for it. When they can no longer stand certain falsehoods we shall very nearly have gained our point. Already the novelists' work is preparing the soil in accustoming them to the idea. An hour will strike when it will be sufficient for a master to reveal himself on the stage to find a public ready to become enthusiastic in favor of the truth. It will be a question of tact and strength. They will see then that the highest and most useful lessons will be taught by depicting what is, and not by oft-dinned generalities, nor by airs of bravado, which are chanted merely to tickle our ears.

The two formulas are before us: the naturalistic formula, which makes the stage a study and a picture of real life; and the conventional formula, which makes it purely an amusement for the mind, an intellectual speculation, an art of adjustment and symmetry regulated after a certain code. In fact, it all depends upon the idea one has of literature, and of dramatic literature in particular. If we admit that literature is but an inquiry about men and things entered into by original minds, we are naturalists; if we pretend that literature is a framework superimposed upon the truth, that a writer must make use of observation merely in order to exhibit his power of invention and arrangement, we are idealists, and proclaim the necessity of conventionality. I have just been very much struck by an example. They have just revived, at the Comédie Française, "Le Fils Naturel" of M. Dumas, *fils*. A critic immediately jumps into enthusiasm. Here is what he says: "*Mon Dieu!* but that is well put together! How polished, dove-tailed, and compact! Is not this machinery pretty? And this one, it comes just in time to work itself into this other trick, which sets all the machinery in motion." Then he becomes exhausted, he cannot find words eulogistic enough in which to speak of the pleasure he experiences in this piece of mechanism. Would you not think he was speaking of a plaything, of a puzzle, with which he amused himself by upsetting and then putting all the pieces in order again? As for me, "Le Fils Naturel" does not affect me in the least. And why is that? Am I a greater fool than the critic? I do not think so. Only I have no taste for clockwork, and I have a great deal for truth. Yes, truly, it is a pretty piece of mechanism. But I would rather it had been a picture of life. I yearn for life with its shiver, its breath, and its strength; I long for life as it is.

We shall yet have life on the stage as we already have it in the novel. This pretended logic of actual plays, this equality and symmetry obtained by processes of reasoning, which come from ancient metaphysics, will fall before the natural logic of facts and beings such as reality presents to us. Instead of a stage of fabrication we shall have a stage of observation. How will the evolution be brought about? Tomorrow will tell us. I have tried to foresee, but I leave to genius the realization. I have already given my conclusion: Our stage will be naturalistic, or it will cease to exist.

Now that I have tried to gather my ideas together, may I hope that they will no longer put words into my mouth which I have never spoken? Will they still continue to see, in my critical opinions, I know not what ridiculous inflations of vanity or odious retaliations? I am but the most earnest soldier of truth. If I am mistaken, my judgments are there in print; and fifty years from now I shall be judged, in my turn; I may perhaps be accused of injustice, blindness, and useless violence. I accept the verdict of the future. (pp. 109-57)

Emile Zola, "Naturalism on the Stage," in his The Experimental Novel and Other Essays, *translated by Belle M. Sherman, 1894. Reprint by Haskell House, 1964, pp. 109-57.*

An excerpt from Zola's essay, "The Experimental Novel" (1880)

Now, science enters into the domain of us novelists, who are to-day the analyzers of man, in his individual and social relations. We are continuing, by our observations and experiments, the work of the physiologist, who has continued that of the physicist and the chemist. We are making use, in a certain way, of scientific psychology to complete scientific physiology; and to finish the series we have only to bring into our studies of nature and man the decisive tool of the experimental method. In one word, we should operate on the characters, the passions, on the human and social data, in the same way that the chemist and the physicist operate on inanimate beings, and as the physiologist operates on living beings. Determinism dominates everything. It is scientific investigation, it is experimental reasoning, which combats one by one the hypotheses of the idealists, and which replaces purely imaginary novels by novels of observation and experiment.

George Wilbur Meyer

[In the following essay, Meyer delineates Zola's theory of Naturalism as outlined in The Experimental Novel *(1880), and explains some common misconceptions about Naturalism.]*

Probably no significant movement in modern literature has been more consistently misunderstood than the Naturalistic novel. Ever since Émile Zola defined the Naturalistic or "Experimental" novel in 1880, students of the subject have mistaken its purpose and its philosophy. So radical and frequent were the misinterpretations of Naturalism in his own day that Zola, in a moment of exasperation, felt obliged to voice this rather strong complaint: "What always puzzles me is the manner in which my words are read. For more than ten years I have been repeating the same things, and I must really express myself very badly, for the readers are very rare who will read 'white' when I write 'white.' Ninety-nine people out of a hundred persist in reading 'black'. . . . For example, do they not say foolish enough things about this poor naturalism? If I were to gather together all that has been published on this question, I should raise a monument to human imbecility."

Zola no doubt would choose kinder words to describe the performance of modern critics of Naturalism. Unlike Zola's contemporaries, the critics of today, instead of regarding the Naturalistic novel as a vulgar exercise in slang and obscenity, unworthy of their attention, accept its subject matter and make serious efforts to understand its philosophic and social implications. Yet, if Zola could return and scan the most recent commentaries, he would still have reason to complain that the critics persist in reading "black" when he wrote "white." My purpose is to show that the Naturalistic novel, as Émile Zola originally conceived of it, was based not upon a philosophy of pessimism, as is commonly supposed, but upon a philosophy of optimism; and that its fundamental purpose was not a mere objective description of life as a trap, dirty and mean, but the immediate betterment of human society.

To make certain that we are not tilting with straw men in this discussion, let me first establish the point that current definitions describe Naturalism as a philosophy of pessimistic determinism. Vernon Louis Parrington, in 1930, wrote that Naturalism was "pessimistic realism," and that the type of realism called Naturalism by Émile Zola "conceived of the individual as a pawn on the chessboard of society." In 1934, Harry Hartwick remarked that "At the foundation of Zola's method lay a belief in scientific determinism, which conceives of man as an unimportant experiment in the vast laboratory of Nature, a being shaped and conditioned by circumstances beyond his control." More recently, Oscar Cargill, in his *Intellectual America,* asserts that "*Naturalism,* of which Zola was the first comprehensive exponent, is pessimistic determinism—the conviction that we are hurried towards evil and ignominious ends whether we will or not, that degeneracy is the common history of man."

According to this definition, the Naturalistic novel cannot have a social and reformatory purpose. If man is impotent and quite incapable of controlling, or even of modifying, the powerful forces which shape his character and hurry him down the path to inevitable degeneracy and sordid death, obviously a novel devoted to portraying this impotence cannot logically express any desire of its author to improve or reform society. On the contrary, a novel written by a pessimistic determinist can have no purpose other than the author's masochistic urge to show a man like himself defeated by the world and—like a beetle on a pin—made the squirming, pathetic victim of a brutal, cosmic jest. The tragedy of such a novel, if it can be called a tragedy, will lie, as Parrington suggests, in the "pity and irony with which we contemplate man and his fate in the world."

But such confusion has resulted from the assumption that Naturalism is pessimistic determinism, and from the further assumption that the Naturalistic novel cannot have a social purpose, that this definition is automatically suspect. Critics have had difficulty reconciling the notion that all Naturalists are pessimistic determinists with the acknowledged fact that almost all Naturalistic novelists have attempted to reform society. The curious and somewhat embarrassing conclusions to which this discrepancy leads are nowhere better illustrated than in the hundred and twenty-odd pages which Oscar Cargill devotes to his study of Naturalism. Attempting to stick to the definition of Naturalism as pessimistic determinism, Professor Cargill is forced to admit that the best known naturalists, including Zola—the recognized founder of the movement—are not really Naturalists at all. Professor Cargill's remarks on Theodore Dreiser are particularly interesting in this connection. Having found that the Naturalism of Zola was impure because of its reformatory implications, Professor Cargill begins his analysis of Dreiser by announcing that he is the "very quintessence of Naturalism" because he "believes in nothing and works for nothing." Yet, when he has completed his examination of Dreiser's novels, Professor Cargill concludes that Dreiser plays favorites with his characters, that he wants society to remain Christian, and that he must therefore be condemned as a "double-standard" Naturalist, something which a genuine Naturalist should never be. Finally, Professor Cargill closes his discussion by asserting "that the leaders in the American Naturalistic school are by no means *convinced* Naturalists—they betray themselves," he says, "by pet schemes for human betterment, schemes in which no genuine and thorough-going pessimist has any legitimate interest." It seems reasonable to suggest at this point that if Émile Zola, Stephen Crane, Frank Norris, Theodore Dreiser—and we may as well include such writers as Dos Passos and John Steinbeck—that if they cannot be made to fit a definition of Naturalism, there is something wrong, not with the novelists, but with the definition. If these writers "betray themselves by pet schemes for human betterment . . . in which no genuine and thorough-going pessimist has any legitimate interest," it would seem that these writers—with the possible exception of Dreiser—are not pessimists,

and that the definition of Naturalism should be altered accordingly. A brief examination of *The Experimental Novel* will show even more clearly the need for a new definition by revealing that Émile Zola, for one, worked, not only in practice but in theory, from premises that were unmistakably optimistic, with the specific purpose of reforming society.

In the first two chapters of *The Experimental Novel,* the so-called Bible of Naturalism, Zola, relying constantly on the scientific authority of Claude Bernard, the author of the *Introduction to the Study of Experimental Medicine,* defines the experimental method, and explains how it may be used by the novelist. Quite simply, the method is based upon the principle, accepted by scientists, that no natural phenomenon, animate or inanimate, human or inhuman, exists without a cause. According to this principle of determinism, there is a chain of causation which, when it is divulged, will explain the position and the shape of a rock on the side of a hill. There is also a sequence of events and influences which, if it can be accurately described, will account for the character and the actions—no matter how abnormal they may seem to be—of the individual man in society. The immediate object of the experimental method is to lay bare the determining causes of phenomena—the causes, that is, without which the phenomena could not exist. In the hands of physicians the experimental method will be used to expose the determinism of diseases of the body. Once the determinism of such a disease has been disclosed, the disease may be brought under control and perhaps completely destroyed by the physicians. To illustrate this, Claude Bernard cited the example of scabies, better known as mange, or the itch. "Today," he wrote, "the cause of this disease is known and determined experimentally; the whole subject has become scientific, and empiricism has disappeared. A cure is surely and without exception effected when you place yourself in the conditions known by experiment to produce this end."

Zola devotes the entire third chapter of his essay to an account of what the novelist may accomplish by the experimental method. The particular subject which the experimental novelist should investigate Zola describes as the "reciprocal effect of society on the individual and the individual on society." In Zola's judgment, the experimental novelists, like the men in white coats in medical laboratories, can contribute much toward mankind's mastery of disease. "We are . . . experimental moralists," he exclaims, "showing by experiment in what way a passion acts in a certain social condition. The day in which we gain control of the mechanism of this passion we can treat it and reduce it, or at least make it as inoffensive as possible. And in this consists the practical utility and high morality of our naturalistic works. . . . " A few lines further on, Zola suggests that the possibilities of experimental fiction for the reform of society are virtually unlimited: " . . . when we are in possession of the different laws," he writes,

> it will only be necessary to work upon the individuals and the surroundings if we wish to find the best social condition. In this way we shall construct a practical sociology, and our work will be a help to political and economical sciences. I do not know . . . of a more noble work,

nor of a grander application. To be the master of good and evil, to regulate life, to regulate society, to solve in time all the problems of socialism, above all, to give justice a solid foundation by solving through experiment the questions of criminality—is not this being the most useful and the most moral workers in the human workshop?

Finally, in the concluding sentences of this chapter, Zola makes it clear that Naturalism is the very opposite of pessimistic determinism, and that the prime purpose of the Naturalistic novel is the betterment of society:

> we . . . content ourselves with searching out the determinism of social phenomena, and leaving to legislators and to men of affairs the care of controlling sooner or later these phenomena in such a way as to develop the good and reject the bad, from the point of view of their utility to man.
>
> In our rôle as experimental moralists we show the mechanism of the useful and the useless, we disengage the determinism of the human and social phenomena so that, in their turn, the legislators can one day dominate and control these phenomena. In a word, we are working with the whole country toward that great object, the conquest of nature and the increase of man's power a hundredfold.

So far as I have been able to discover, the erroneous belief that Zola and his Naturalistic descendants are pessimistic determinists arises from a confusion of determinism with fatalism, and from the resulting idea that whatever is is not right but inevitable. This confusion had arisen in Zola's day, and he attempted to expel it by declaring flatly that the two terms were not synonymous. "I reach thus," he says,

> the great reproach with which they think to crush the naturalistic novelists, by treating them as fatalists. How many times have they wished to prove to us that as soon as we did not accept free will, that as soon as man was no more to us than a living machine, acting under the influence of heredity and surroundings, we should fall into gross fatalism, we should debase humanity to the rank of a troop marching under the baton of destiny. It is necessary to define our terms: we are not fatalists, we are determinists, which is not at all the same thing. Claude Bernard explains the two terms very plainly: "We have given the name of determinism to the nearest or determining cause of phenomena. We never act upon the essence of phenomena in nature, but only on their determinism, and by this very fact, that we act upon it, determinism differs from fatalism, upon which we could not act at all."

The critics of Naturalism and pessimists like Theodore Dreiser contend that the sores and wounds of society in a world of determinism are inevitable, like the revolutions of the earth or the wetness of rain. But Zola recognizes a distinction between natural phenomena, for which God alone is responsible, and social phenomena, for which man is at least partly responsible. Zola insists that a social disease is inevitable only until its determinism has been disen-

gaged and understood by men. In *L'Assommoir,* for example, he shows us how Coupeau and Gervaise disintegrate under the influence of alcohol—a commodity certainly not forced upon them by an act of God. Zola provides a detailed description of the nature and the consequences of alcoholism so that we may understand its determinism and take steps to prevent the degeneracy to which it leads. Zola's own account of the moral to be taken from the book proves that he regarded *L'Assommoir* as a temperance tract, designed to show the need for comprehensive social legislation: "Educate the worker, take him out of the misery in which he lives, combat the crowding and the promiscuity of the workers' quarters where the air thickens and stinks; above all prevent drunkenness which decimates the people and kills mind and body. . . . " Accomplish these things, he urges, and this social evil will disappear.

The passages I have cited from *The Experimental Novel,* and the example of *L'Assommoir,* make it clear that according to Zola, a pessimistic Naturalist is a contradiction in terms. Zola would never accept Theodore Dreiser, for example, as a member of the fraternity of experimental novelists. He would regard Dreiser as a mere impostor who had borrowed the technical machinery of the Naturalists, the better to communicate his perverse and hopeless doctrines. The chief difference between Zola and Dreiser is the difference between one who acts to improve his condition, and one who accepts his condition and invites us to pity his submission. This is the difference between an authentic Naturalist and a pessimistic determinist. Zola might agree with Dreiser that the tragedy of Clyde Griffiths was inevitable, but he would object to Dreiser's implication at the end of *An American Tragedy* that a repetition of the disaster is inevitable. Zola would explain that if Dreiser had performed properly the true function of the Naturalistic novelist, he would have revealed the determinism of Clyde's downfall so clearly as to make unnecessary a recurrence of the circumstances which caused Clyde's destruction. He would argue that just as soon as Dreiser disclosed the determinism of the social disease from which Clyde suffered, it became the duty of rational men to alter or destroy the conditions necessary for its existence. If men permit the noxious conditions to remain unchanged, the disease will continue to prosper, but its continuation will not have been inevitable. But Dreiser maintains that the disease will continue to flourish because men are irrational, or at least too indifferent to alter existing conditions. Zola, however, would not agree. He insists that men can and will correct social evils, once their determinism has been divulged, just as medical science could and did control tuberculosis, once its determinism had been sufficiently disengaged. Zola, I think, has the better of the argument, for not even Dreiser can deny that great numbers of men, having been instructed in the determinism of tuberculosis, diphtheria, cholera, and typhoid, have been rational and energetic enough to profit from their information. However, the main point I wish to make about Dreiser is that he does not move further from authentic Naturalism when, as in *An American Tragedy,* he appears to sympathize with his characters and suggest that radical social reforms are imperative unless the tragedy is to recur again and again. By suggesting that such reforms be effected, even though he himself has no genuine hope that they ever will be, Dreiser, far from impairing further his claims to the title of Naturalist, actually comes closer to the original purpose of Naturalism—as Zola conceived of it—than he has ever done before.

By way of conclusion, I should like to add that the Naturalistic novel was merely a late nineteenth-century continuation in prose fiction of a movement that began in the eighteenth century, if not earlier, and took rather definite literary form in the poetry of William Wordsworth. Philosophically the movement is based on the old idea of progress and the perfectibilitarian principle that man has an infinite capacity for improving himself and his environment. The purpose of Naturalism, moreover, is primarily utilitarian—that of stimulating and strengthening man's ability to better his society. The movement takes its name from the belief of its exponents that human society, if it is to be successful, must rest upon a precise and comprehensive understanding of nature and its immutable laws. Zola adopted Naturalism because he believed in its high promise for the future of mankind, and because he wished to add dignity and significance to the French novel. In his hands, the novel had for its aesthetic object, not a futile pity for the impotence of man, but the revelation that vital knowledge can be made to spring from human suffering. As Zola understood it, knowledge of nature is the greatest force in nature. Without it man is indeed, in Parrington's phrase, a "pawn on the chessboard of society"; possessed of knowledge, the otherwise helpless individual becomes the master of nature and a morally responsible free agent. Finally, by insisting upon the responsibility of the novelist to keep abreast of the discoveries of scientists and men of learning in all fields, Zola performed a service of immense value to literature and humanity. When all writers have recognized this responsibility, and have persuaded their readers to follow their example, we shall, as Zola predicted sixty years ago, "enter upon a century in which man, grown more powerful, will make use of nature and will utilize its laws to produce upon the earth the greatest possible amount of justice and freedom." (pp. 563-70)

> *George Wilbur Meyer, "The Original Social Purpose of the Naturalistic Novel," in* The Sewanee Review, *Vol. L, No. 4, Autumn, 1942, pp. 563-70.*

Haskell M. Block

[*Block is an American educator and critic. In the following excerpt, he discusses the discrepancy between Naturalism as delineated in Zola's theoretical essays and as employed in the writer's novels. Block asserts that an accurate and useful definition of Naturalism can be determined only by an examination of both the novels and the essays.*]

Naturalism, like all generalizations which serve to order and classify literature, is a most difficult term to define with absolute precision. Its vagueness is inherent in the very attempt to impose a broad unifying concept on so seemingly free and diverse an activity as literary creation. The labels devised by both writers and readers to clarify the meaning of literature often give rise to as much confusion as clarification, but the widespread use of such terms and their enormous impact on both the making and the understanding of literature testify to their real importance. Like classicism, Romanticism, and realism, naturalism has served to emphasize common elements of individual works and to blur their differences, yet these common elements are not hypothetical but correspond to qualities actually present in the works themselves. The term "naturalism" as applied to the modern novel would not have lasted for almost a century if it did not in fact help define and illuminate some of the general characteristics of the modern novel as well as the salient attributes of specific novels. In the course of its usage, naturalism has been defined and redefined so many times that perhaps it would be more accurate to speak of "naturalisms" rather than naturalism, to indicate the multiplicity of meanings expressed in a single term. Most writers and readers, however, are less demanding in such matters than historians of ideas or of literature. Rather than discard the term because of its ambiguities, we should try to use it with with what precision it will allow, recognizing that such broad classifications can never adequately define the complexities of literary art.

Naturalism has been most commonly described as either a literary group or school, a literary movement or period, a way of looking at literature and life, a method for the creation of literary works, or a literary technique and style. These descriptions are not mutually exclusive, nor do they constitute a complete list. Some students of naturalism see it as an intensified and exaggerated mode of realism, thereby shifting but not resolving the problem of definition. Still others have insisted that naturalism, in expression if not in theory, is a mode of Romanticism. For most students of the modern novel, however, naturalism, with all its ambiguities, is distinct from both Romanticism and realism. When used to designate a group of writers, naturalism commonly refers to Emile Zola and his followers; Zola, however, insisted that he did not invent the term and denied that there was a naturalistic *cénacle,* or school. To speak of a naturalistic movement or period, extending perhaps from 1870 to 1900, is to simplify unduly the variety of conflicting and contradictory assumptions and norms that prevailed during the closing decades of the past century. In its historical context, naturalism was but one of many literary tendencies of the day. As an attitude, naturalism may be considered a constant element in human experience, free of dependence on any particular time and place, and asserting a view of both art and life that may be held not only by writers but by anyone. As a method, naturalism is generally regarded as an instrument and a procedure derived from the natural sciences and applied to literature. It is in this sense that Zola usually employs the term. Finally, as a literary technique or style, naturalism may be viewed as a distinct way of ordering the elements of an art form. In this sense, the term has been used by literary critics and historians to characterize individual novels and to group under a common classification novelists embodying the specific qualities ascribed to naturalistic art. On occasion, such groupings have led to the formulation of naturalism as a "period style" or as a literary current or tradition that is present in several literatures but is discontinuous in its manifestations. The usual definition of naturalism employed today is still that provided by Zola himself, for it was as a direct result of Zola's own efforts both as theorist and novelist that the concept of naturalism came to be generally adopted as a literary term.

Any approach to the critical study of the naturalistic novel must therefore begin with Zola. This is not to say that Zola's definition of naturalism will describe any and all naturalistic novels, whether by Zola himself or by novelists who responded to his program. Yet, if we are to view naturalism in a broad perspective, we must recognize Zola's enormous impact. Despite his insistence that naturalism was neither new nor limited to his own theory and expression, as a literary technique and style it is essentially Zola's invention; its widespread emulation and acceptance in Zola's time and in our own is a tribute not only to the power of his art but also to the force of his incessant propaganda on behalf of the new impulse.

The term "naturalism" had a long history before Zola made it into a battle cry. Generally, it had been used to indicate any materialistic, secular, or scientific attitude toward human experience. In the middle years of the nineteenth century in France, "naturalist" was a synonym for natural scientist, but it was also used to describe writers whose procedures resembled those of the scientist. Early in his career, well before he was recognized as a novelist, Zola praised the positivist critic Taine as "a naturalist philosopher who declares that the intellectual world is subject to laws in the same way as the material world." Taine had called special attention to the similarity of Balzac's methods in his novels and those of scientific naturalists. Zola repeatedly employed the term "naturalistic" in this sense in his journalistic articles as early as 1866, long before the appearance of his manifesto of naturalism, *Le Roman expérimental* (*The Experimental Novel*), in 1880. Indeed, both the term and the program which it embodies are clearly set forth by Zola in his preface to the second edition of his novel *Thérèse Raquin* (1868). The preface is a polemical reply to those who assailed the novel as "Putrid Literature"; it indicates unmistakably that Zola's essential convictions were formulated some years before he read Claude Bernard's account of the experimental method, on which *Le Roman expérimental* is based. In writing *Thérèse Raquin,* Zola insists, "my aim was above all a scientific one." Each chapter, he contends, is the study of "a curious physiological case." The novelist's cold and objective analysis of passion is viewed by Zola as exactly the same as "the analytical work which surgeons perform on cadavers." For Zola, the strength, boldness, and violence of his novel are all in keeping with its fidelity to experience. In the final lines of his preface he declares: "The group of naturalist writers to which I have the honor to belong has enough courage and energy to produce strong works, which will carry their own defense."

Sympathetic readers of *Thérèse Raquin,* such as Taine, admired the novel for its convincing analysis of physiological and psychological forces, but Taine urged Zola to cast a wider net in his subsequent novels and to take Balzac and Shakespeare as his models. Undoubtedly, Taine played an important part in helping Zola to plan the great design of the *Rougon-Macquart* series of novels as a mirror of a whole society. Clearly inspired by Balzac's gigantic conception of *La Comédie humaine,* Zola's *Rougon-Macquart* is grandiosely subtitled "A Natural and Social History of a Family during the Second Empire." Yet, for some time before the conception of this vast project, Zola had seen his approach to reality as somewhat different from that of Balzac—in his more acute awareness of the coercive force of heredity and environment. To the influence of milieu, derived chiefly from Balzac and Taine, Zola added the rigorous determinism of the laws of heredity as proclaimed by the biologists of the day. In the preface to *Thérèse Raquin,* he describes his central figures as "human beasts," totally devoid of free will, "dragged along each act of their life by the fatalities of their flesh." From the beginning of his theoretical formulations, the analogy between the novelist and the scientist and the insistence on a thoroughgoing biological and social determinism in human events are the foundations of Zola's naturalism.

Zola's collection of essays *Le Roman expérimental* is by far the best known statement of his doctrines. His most ambitious formulations occur in the title essay, a polemical document which is not as measured or as carefully qualified in its assertions as some of the other essays in the collection. Precisely because of its extreme and categorical claims, the essay entitled "The Experimental Novel" is one of Zola's weakest theoretical statements, yet its programmatic definition of naturalism is primarily responsible for the way the term has been understood by most readers since Zola's time. The experimental novel, he contends, is "the literature of our scientific age." The novelist must employ the same methods as the scientist if his novels are to constitute a truthful representation of life:

> In a word, we must operate on characters, passions, human and social events, as the chemist and physician operate on brute matter, as the physiologist operates on living beings. Determinism dominates everything. It is scientific investigation, it is experimental reasoning, which combats one by one the hypotheses of idealists, and which replaces the novels of pure imagination by novels of observation and experimentation.

Repeatedly in this essay, Zola insists that naturalism is neither a school nor an activity of a particular writer or group; it consists solely of "the application of the experimental method to the study of nature and man." The method is everything, and, as a method, Zola believes that naturalism will come to dominate all literature. It should be noted that Zola explicitly states that naturalism is not a form, a style, or a technique. These will follow from the method, which implies for Zola not only an attitude and a perspective but also a distinct mode of procedure in fictional composition.

In *Le Roman expérimental* Zola does not seem to regard naturalism as a literary movement, but in the polemical essays which he wrote soon afterward he fuses the notions of a method and a movement. In an essay entitled "Naturalism," included in the collection *Une Campagne (A Campaign,* 1882), he writes of naturalism as the third great movement of French literature, after classicism and

Romanticism. The first period of the nineteenth century, he asserts, was dominated by Romanticism; the second period will be that of naturalism. Here, naturalism is plainly defined as a historical movement as well as a literary method. Zola's introduction of a historical concept is unquestionably one of the principal sources of confusion in the definition of naturalism which has prevailed since his time. Proof of the persistence of this confusion in our own day may be found in almost any of the standard handbooks and dictionaries of literary terms.

As a result of Zola's five volumes of criticism proclaiming the ascendency of naturalism in the novel, the term came into vogue almost at once. Unquestionably, the growing success of Zola's novels, particularly after the publication of *L'Assommoir* in 1877, helped to attract attention to his theories. By the time he wrote *Le Roman expérimental,* he was an experienced and a successful novelist, and there is perhaps more than a little malice in Edmond de Goncourt's account of Zola's alleged declaration that naturalism was nothing more than a way of calling attention to his work and of promoting his literary career. As we have seen, the main elements of Zola's naturalistic theory were completely formulated a decade before 1878, the year in which he first came to know Claude Bernard's *Introduction to the Study of Experimental Medicine.* Despite the extreme character of Zola's theories in "The Experimental Novel," there can be no doubt of his solidity of conviction and seriousness of purpose.

Nevertheless, it has not been difficult for readers in either Zola's time or our own to point to contradictions in his theories. These contradictions are in fact expressions of tensions in his mind and art which are all but submerged in the manifesto in which he proclaims the experimental method. In an essay of 1881, restating a formula expressed fifteen years earlier, Zola defines a literary work as "a corner of nature seen through a temperament." In this recognition of the role of the artist's temperament in literary creation, he implicitly repudiates any reduction of art to photography or to a mechanical transcription of external reality. Even in "The Experimental Novel," he insists on the importance of genius and the modifying power of selection in the application of the experimental method. In subsequent essays, he goes further, declaring that the canon of value of a literary creation is not its accuracy of representation, but rather the grandeur of the spectacle of nature, the intensity of the writer's view of reality: "the powerful way he deforms it to make it fit into his mould, the imprint he leaves on all he touches, this is real creation, the true sign of genius." Clearly, if we look beyond "The Experimental Novel" to Zola's letters and his later critical essays, we shall find that his definition of naturalism is not as wooden and as mechanical as has frequently been contended.

A similar inconsistency can be seen in juxtaposing Zola's novels and his doctrines. His works reflect not only his scientific and sociological preoccupations but also his exuberant fantasy and his penchant for extraordinary incidents that issue in violent drama and colossal symbolic configurations. As his American follower Frank Norris points out, the citation of Zola as a realist is "a strange perversion." Basing his account of naturalism on Zola's novels rather than on the theories of "The Experimental Novel," Norris asserts [in *The Literary Criticism of Frank Norris,* 1964]:

> The naturalist takes no note of common people, common in so far as their interests, their lives, and the things that occur in them are common, are ordinary. Terrible things must happen to the characters of the naturalistic tale. They must be twisted from the ordinary, wrenched out from the quiet, uneventful round of every-day life, and flung into the throes of a vast and terrible drama that works itself out in unleashed passions, in blood, and in sudden death.

Zola himself was acutely aware of the large distance between the theories of "The Experimental Novel" and his boldly imaginative art. As he remarks in a letter of December 28, 1882: "It is certain that I am a poet and that my works are built like great musical symphonies. . . . I am steeped in romanticism up to my waist." The definition of naturalism which emerges from Zola's novels is at such variance with his programmatic doctrines that some readers have contended that his theories are altogether irrelevant to his novels. This, too, may be an extreme position. On the whole, Zola was a rather good critic with a keen awareness of the theoretical bases of his art. It is nonetheless evident that the problem of defining naturalism and of describing the salient characteristics of naturalistic novels has been rendered more difficult by the wide gap separating the doctrines of "The Experimental Novel" from the art of Zola's fiction.

The expansion of the subject matter of the novel in France was accomplished as much by Zola's predecessors, notably Balzac and Flaubert, as by Zola himself. Yet because of the fullness of detail with which Zola, in some of his novels, depicts scenes of depravity and vice, particularly among characters drawn from the lower classes, naturalism for many readers came to be associated with sordid and brutal events and "low" characters. In vain did Zola protest that naturalism as a method could be applied to any subject and to any plane of society. For most readers, naturalistic fiction was defined not only by its embodiment of deterministic laws of nature but also by its portrayal of harsh events and crude characters. Thus, in an essay entitled "The New Naturalism" in *The Fortnightly Review* in 1885, W. S. Lilly declares that "the results obtainable by his [Zola's] researches in the latrine and brothel are of precisely the same value as those which the vivisector derives from the torture trough." It is difficult for readers today to understand the almost pathological reactions of anger and disgust aroused by naturalistic novels at the end of the past century. In claiming all of life as their province, Zola and his followers merely intensified a development in the novel that was well under way before Zola's proclamation of his credo. The naturalists provided not so much a new subject matter as a new emphasis on areas of experience which had been ignored if not repudiated by most earlier novelists. For Zola himself, the enlargement of subject matter was simply a necessary part of the novelist's responsibility to the social and natural forces of his time. The novel as the naturalists conceived it is not a mode of casual amusement but an instrument for the discovery of truth.

In the essays which constitute *Le Roman expérimental,* as well as in his conversations with young writers and interviews with journalists, Zola describes at great length the process by which he felt the naturalistic novelist arrives at truth in art. In keeping with the analogy of the novelist and the scientist, the novel as a controlled experiment must be based on observation. The novelist's point of departure and the "solid terrain" of his characters and events are the observer's "facts as he has observed them." This observation must be thorough, impartial, and exact if the novel is to be a truthful representation of experience. For the naturalistic novelist, Zola insists, observation is the indispensable starting point of fictional creation.

The result of the method which Zola set forth for the composition of a naturalistic novel is to make the fictive almost completely dependent on the real. The fidelity to experience of the novel is based above all on the novelist's documentation of his characters and their milieu. Clearly, Zola views the process of documentation as crucial, not only in his own art but in that of any novelist who would adopt the naturalistic method. The process is most fully described in an essay entitled "Le Sens du Réel" ("The Sense of the Real"), included in *Le Roman expérimental.* In the naturalistic novel, Zola says, the romantic assertion of the imagination is suppressed: "All the efforts of the writer tend to conceal the imaginary beneath the real." He does not claim that the imagination is totally absent in the new novel, but rather that the sense of the real is achieved essentially through documentation, in a process which he describes in some detail:

> It would be a curious study to describe how our great contemporary novelists work. They base almost all of their works on notes, taken at great length. When they have studied with scrupulous care the terrain on which they are to move, when they have investigated all the sources and have in hand the many documents they need, only then do they decide to write. The plan of the work is given them by the documents themselves, for it happens that facts classify themselves logically, this one before that. A symmetry is established, the story composes itself out of all the collected observations, all the notes, one leading to another by the very enchainment of the life of the characters, and the conclusion is nothing more than a natural and inevitable consequence.

Thus, documentation furnishes the materials of art; the author need only attend to their disposition. Zola also admits, however, that the novelist's use of his materials is by no means as automatic as this preoccupation with factual investigation would suggest. At the very end of his essay, he recognizes that, in the work of a truly significant novelist, the sense of the real must be accompanied by the power of personal expression: "A great novelist, in our time, is one who has the sense of the real and who expresses nature with originality, by making it live with its own life." In insisting on the necessity for the novelist to create an autonomous and independent world, Zola moves beyond his earlier assertion of the total dependence of the fictive on the real.

Despite his recognition that documentation alone is insufficient to produce great art, Zola's elaborate account of his own processes of composition helps to explain why, for many of his readers, naturalistic fiction is defined as the depiction of sordid events based on painstaking documentation. It is precisely in this sense that Henry James, who knew Zola's work well and responded to it with grudging admiration, describes, in a letter of December 12, 1884, his preparations for the writing of a prison scene in *The Princess Casamassima:*

> I have been all the morning at Millbank prison (horrible place) collecting notes for a fiction scene. You see I am quite the Naturalist. Look out for the same—a year hence.

James could hardly be described as a naturalistic novelist, but it is important to note that naturalistic methods and values enter into the work of many novelists whose art is in most respects quite remote from that of Zola. Clearly, for James, documentation is only a phase of fictional creation, a way of making the novel a more convincing and lifelike work of art; but this may also be the case for more naturalistic novelists as well. The main difference in this respect might only be one of emphasis. Presumably, documentation is more vital to the naturalist and consequently more detailed so as to underscore the requisite sense of fact. A further and more important difference between naturalistic novels and others lies in the enchainment of material circumstances in the naturalistic novel, demonstrating the deterministic role of natural and environmental forces in the movement of events.

Like so many of Zola's premises, determinism in the naturalistic novel turns out to be more of a tendency than a dogma. As Zola's *L'Assommoir* clearly illustrates, accident may play a crucial role in the relentless movement toward catastrophe in the novel. The tensions of freedom and determinism in the naturalistic novel are analogous to the conflicting claims of the fictive and the real. These tensions seem to be particularly marked in American naturalistic novels, but they may also characterize the works of Zola and of his European followers as well. No naturalistic novelist seems to have written in absolute accord with the doctrines set forth by Zola in his manifesto. If we adopt Zola's definition, all naturalistic novelists, including Zola himself, are impure. Despite the contentions of some of Zola's doctrinaire followers, there are no "consistent naturalists" whose works are of high artistic value.

When we direct our attention to the study of particular novels composed, at least to some extent, under the impact of naturalistic theories, we are confronted with an immense range of individual differences, depending, as Zola himself admitted, on the temperament of the novelist and on the distinct combination of artistic elements in his work, elements on occasion totally unrelated to or even at variance with naturalism. Nevertheless, all naturalistic novelists share with Zola a recognition that some dependence on the literal and the actual is indispensable if the novel is to represent a cross section of life with the requisite degree of verisimilitude. It is therefore no surprise to find in the composition of representative naturalistic novels a considerable reliance on factual documentation, often based on the personal experience of the novelist but also on his use of oral and written sources. The importance of these sources, however, should not be overemphasized. Of primary significance in the making of a novel—or of any work of art—is not the mere existence of specific sources but their transformation into art. If this transformation does not take place in the act of composition, the work itself remains only a document, devoid of aesthetic value. The situation of the naturalistic novelist in his deliberate closeness to actuality may be extreme, yet the problem of the assimilation and transformation of life into art may ultimately prove to be no different for him than for other novelists.

The problem of defining naturalism cannot be resolved as long as we insist on a rigorous conformity to the theories set forth in "The Experimental Novel." A useful definition must be based on the novels themselves as well as on the novelist's theoretical assumptions. Indeed, the latter are important only insofar as they are actually embodied in works of art. (pp. 3-14)

> *Haskell M. Block, in an introduction to his* Naturalistic Triptych: The Fictive and the Real in Zola, Mann, and Dreiser, *Random House, 1970, pp. 3-15.*

H. A. Taine on the elementary moral state:

Three different sources contribute to produce [the] elementary moral state—RACE, SURROUNDINGS, and EPOCH. What we call the race are the innate and hereditary dispositions which man brings with him into the world, and which, as a rule, are united with the marked differences in the temperament and structure of the body. . . .

We must [also] consider the surroundings in which [a race] exists. For man is not alone in the world; nature surrounds him, and his fellow-men surround him; accidental and secondary tendencies overlay his primitive tendencies, and physical or social circumstances disturb or confirm the character committed to their charge. . . .

There is yet a third rank of causes; for, with the forces within and without, there is the work which they have already produced together, and this work itself contributes to produce that which follows. Beside the permanent impulse and the given surroundings, there is the acquired momentum. When the national character and surrounding circumstances operate, it is not upon a *tabula rasa*, but on a ground on which marks are already impressed. According as one takes the ground at one moment or another, the imprint is different; and this is the cause that the total effect is different.

> *H. A. Taine, in his* History of English Literature, *Vol. 1, translated by H. Van Laun, Edmonston and Douglas, 1873.*

CRITICAL DEBATES ON NATURALISM

Clarence R. Decker

[Decker was an American educator and critic. In the following essay, he surveys the reactions of nineteenth-century theorists to Naturalism.]

Victorian society, however emphatic its hostility to French Naturalism, was not unanimous in its disapproval. Indeed, many of the bitterest critics softened their reproaches as the century advanced. Robert Buchanan, for example, not only modified his earlier position in later years, but became a staunch defender of Zola. In 1877 he had aligned himself with the forces of virtue and goodness as embodied in the Society for the Suppression of Vice, the aim of which was to save the land from the blasphemers Rabelais, Boccaccio, Baudelaire, Swinburne, Rossetti, Meredith, Zola, Ibsen, Wagner, George Moore, and many others. Ten years later he published an appreciative brochure on Zola, in which he wrote:

> As one grows older, one wonders less at the proverbial philosophy of contemporary criticism. While the *Saturday Review* still exists, though toothless and moribund, a journalistic Dogberry proclaiming the watches of the literary night to a generation still unaware of sunrise and Mr. Spencer, there will always be a class of readers which takes its opinions on faith and eagerly echoes the anathemas pronounced by senile watchmen against "one deformed" and other disturbers of the peace. We smile at Dogberry, though it is sad to reflect that never once, from the beginning of his official career, has he done a sane or a generous thing, has he recognized a new thought or a rising reputation, has he ceased to regard all men of genius as malefactors, and all mediocrities as men of genius. [*A Look Around Literature*, 1887]

Zola, he continues, is among the great men of the age who are "run-in" by the old-fashioned literary watch. Buchanan is amused when lesser men repeat the old cry of immorality, as when they told Thackeray that he was "no gentleman" and Dickens that his *Tale of Two Cities* was mere rubbish, but he is amazed when a Stevenson accuses Zola of an "erotic madness":

> Zola is to literature what Schopenhauer is to philosophy—the preacher of a creed of utter despair. No living writer has a stronger and purer sense of the beauty of moral goodness; no living man finds so little goodness in the world to awaken his faith or enlarge his hope. But if Zola is "erotic," then a demonstrator of morbid anatomy is a sensualist, and a human physiologist is a person of unclean proclivities.

Just as ten years earlier Buchanan had arrayed himself against the Pre-Raphaelites and others who were defending the "modernistic" literature, so now he found himself opposed to another group of critics, many of them writers themselves, who condemned Naturalism not so much because of its alleged perversion of public morality as for its unsound philosophic and aesthetic assumptions.

Thus far in . . . studies in Victorian literary taste, I have been concerned largely, but not exclusively, with the critical journals, the censorship, the newspapers, the clergy, and the layman whose protests against the literature that brought "the mantling blush to the maiden cheek" were made largely on moral grounds. These protests reached their most vehement stage in the reaction against foreign authors and movements of the Naturalistic variety. But to complete the picture, it remains to trace the part played by the aesthetic and philosophic critics in crystallizing the shifting literary taste of the period. With them, as with the moralists, the challenge of foreign Naturalism provided a battleground of conflicting points of view. But they were less concerned with specific authors than with the implications and influences of their writings. I shall therefore round out and conclude these studies with a survey of the main ideas of the theorists.

Andrew Lang, who had attacked Zola in 1882 [in the *Fortnightly Review* XXXVII, April 1882], again took up the cudgels five years later [in the *Contemporary Review* LII, November 1887]. On this occasion he is perturbed primarily by the philosophy underlying Naturalism. Eschewing partisanship in the current controversy between Realism and Romance, he judges a work of art solely by the significance of its aim and the beauty of its expression. And on both these grounds he finds Naturalism wanting. Its manner is crude and its interpretation of life distorted. It sacrifices the good and the beautiful on the altar of the vulgar and unpleasant. Comprehensive and truthful observation of human society reveals men and women in all ranks of the social order who are kind, courteous, good-humoured and well-bred. In their exclusive emphasis upon the sordid, contemporary Realists, Lang argues, lack the breath and humour of Fielding, Scott, and Thackeray.

> Perhaps mean people are more easily drawn than generous people; at all events from the school of Realists we get too many mean people—even from a Realist who is as little a Realist as the king was a royalist—from M. Zola. These writers appear not to offer up Henry Fielding's prayer to the Muse, "Fill my pages with humour, till mankind learn the good nature to laugh only at the follies of others, and the humility to grieve at their own."

". . . if the battle," Lang concludes, "between the crocodile of Realism and the catawampus of Romance is to be fought out to the bitter end—why, in the Ragnarök, I am on the side of the catawampus."

John Addington Symonds, less troubled by the popular moral questions of the Realism-Romance controversy, probed into more of the fundamental issues than most of his contemporaries. Applying Darwin's evolutionary concepts to literary criticism, he attempts to liberate the mind from dogma through the instrumentality of science, to reconcile Hellenism, Christianity, and modern scientific thought, and to justify the democratic spirit in art.

> Delivered from scholastic traditions regarding style and the right subjects to be handled—delivery from pedantry and blind reactionary fervour—delivered from dependence upon aristocratic and ecclesiastical authority—sharing

the emancipation of the intellect by modern science and the enfranchisement of the individual by new political conceptions—the artist is brought immediately face to face with the wonderful world of men and things he has to interpret and to recreate. The whole of nature, seen for the first time with sane eyes, the whole of humanity, liberated for the first time from caste and class distinctions, invite his sympathy. [*Essays Speculative and Suggestive*, 1893]

Modern art, conditioned by new scientific concepts, inevitably forms the Realistic approach:

> Science has made one fact manifest, that the more we come to know instead of dreaming about things, the less can we tolerate having those things misrepresented in accordance with some whimsical or obsolescent fancy. Science has rendered our sense of veracity acute. Under its influence we tend to become positively shy of anything which seems untrue to fact, intolerant of a merely allegorical use of known things, to express visions however beautiful, or aspirations however honourable. . . . Art, obliged to obey the mental stress of the epoch, deprived of a widely-accepted body of sensuous religious thoughts, leans of necessity more to Realism than it did in the Athens of Pericles or in the Florence of Lorenzo de Medici. [*Fortnightly Review* XLVIII, September 1887]

But Symonds is not a Realist or Naturalist as these terms were commonly used. With the Naturalist, to be sure, he feels that truth, scientific and experimental, is the chief object of art and that no aspect of life is unworthy of examination. Nevertheless, chivalry, adventure, beauty, modesty, the chastity of saints, the strength of athletes, manhood, temperance, hope, love are quite as much the proper subject of art as ugliness and impudicity, the licentiousness of harlots, and the flaccid feebleness of debauchees. Realism, he insists, cannot separate itself from the Ideal, for the latter is an inherent part of experience.

The first duty of the artist—whether he be painter, sculptor, or writer—is veracity:

> The painter must depict each object with painstaking attention to its details. He must aim at delineating the caper and columbine as faithfully as Titian did, armour as accurately as Giorgione, pearls and brocade with the fidelity of John Van Eyck, hands with the subtlety of Leonardo da Vinci, faces with the earnest feeling after character displayed in Raphael's Leo or Velasquez' Philip. [*Essays Speculative and Suggestive*]

But this is only the first step. The artist soon discovers the impossibility of an absolute reproduction: his eye is not that of the camera. Actually, the artist reproduces himself. The object imitated becomes the object imagined by a personality. Twenty cameras under identical conditions will reproduce an object identically; twenty draftsmen will produce twenty different chiaroscuro drawings. Thus absolute Realism, no less than art for art's sake, is impossible. An artist cannot represent life without injecting himself into his work; neither can he depict a beautiful object completely dissociated from reality. His representation will convey thoughts and feelings of good and evil, nobility and baseness, from the point of view of his personality.

Thus the basis of all art is selection. Great art, whether Realistic or Idealistic, sees life truthfully only by avoiding the transitory, the exceptional, and the particular. The Greek sculptors, in their recognition of this principle, are our surest teachers. Idealism and Realism at their best are one, but no artist ever achieves this perfect harmony. Successive ages have emphasized a crude Realism or an unsubstantial Idealism, each striving to correct the other. It is this emphasis that seems to separate their aims into two opposing tendencies [as stated by Symonds]:

> Realism is the presentation of natural objects as the artist sees them, as he thinks they are. It is the attempt to imitate things as they strike the senses. . . . Idealism is the presentation of natural objects as the artist fain would see them, as he thinks they strive to be. It is the attempt to imitate things as the mind interprets them.

The art history of the nineteenth century has turned from an exaggerated Idealism to an equally exaggerated Realism:

> The one regarded man's incapacity to rival a machine with pride, and deemed his power of independent imagination sufficient for itself. The other, indignant at the miserable consequences of such arrogance, strives to reduce man's mind, so far as possible, to the condition of an imitative machine.

The genuine artist, whatever his aesthetic credo, in actual practice reconciles these conflicting points of view.

Zola, for example, in *La Bête humaine* selects and rearranges his material, violates the experimental method of science, and creates an illusion of reality rather than reproducing reality itself. Imagination and emotion profoundly color his best work. Indeed, his very enthusiasm for the ugly and the vulgar has all the ardor of the Romanticist glorifying the beautiful and the lovely.

> The ponderousness of his method, the tedium of his descriptions, and the indecencies in which he revels, do not justify his claim to stand outside the ranks of those who treat reality from an ideal point of view. Walt Whitman, one of the staunchest idealists who ever uttered prophecy, might be made to pass for a realist on the same grounds of heaviness, minuteness, and indecency. The fact is that Zola, like Whitman, approaches his art-work in the spirit of a poet. [*The Key of Blue*, 1896]

Symonds' sympathy with contemporary science, his acceptance of the rising democratic spirit, his compromise of Romanticism and Naturalism, and his insistence on the importance of the whole life of man, reveal him as one of the sanest critics of the period. His modernity was neither puerile nor unrooted; his traditionalism was neither sterile nor dogmatic.

Meredith and Stevenson might be described as "Romantic-Realists." Both revolted against sentimentality and improbability in the novel, and both stood out against the ap-

plication of science and the scientific method to art. One of Meredith's characters sums up his attitude toward sentimentality when she says, "Sentimental people . . . fiddle harmonics on the strings of sensualism, to the delight of a world gaping for marvels of musical execution rather than for music." Philosophy must fortify us; then we can write the truth, and that truth will be neither Romantic nor Realistic. In the Prelude to the *Egoist* he writes:

> . . . the realistic method of a conscientious transcription of all the visible, and a repetition of all the audible, is mainly accountable for our present brainfulness, and for that prolongation of the vasty and the noisy, out of which, as from an undrained fen, streams the malady of sameness, our modern malady. . . . We drove in a body to Science the other day for an antidote; which was as if tired pedestrians should mount the engine-box of headlong trains; and Science introduced us to our o'er-hoary ancestry—then in the Oriental posture: whereupon we set up a primeval chattering to rival the Amazon forest nigh nightfall, cured, we fancied. And before daybreak our disease was hanging on us again, with the extension of a tail. We had it fore and aft. We were the same, and animals into the bargain. That is all we got from Science.

Art is the remedy for this false approach to life. The "Comic Spirit" (a commonsense philosophy colored by a vivid sense of humour, or a feeling for the incongruities of life) combined with the method of art, the method of selection and clarification and beauty, will correct the pretentiousness, the inflation, the dullness, the vestiges of rawness and grossness to be found about us. "She is the ultimate civilizer, the polisher, a sweet cook. . . . She watches over sentimentalism with a birchrod."

Meredith's antipathy toward Naturalism, repeatedly expressed in his letters, is summed up in the opening chapter of *Diana*. With an adequate philosophy

> . . . the novelist's Art, now neither blushless infant nor executive man, [will] have attained its majority. We can then be veraciously historical, honestly transcriptive. Rose-pink and dirty drab will alike have passed away. Philosophy is the foe of both, and their silly cancelling contest, perpetually renewed in a shuffle of extremes, as it always is where a phantasm falseness reigns, will no longer baffle the contemplation of natural flesh, smother no longer the soul issuing out of our incessant strife. Philosophy bids us see that we are not so pretty as rose-pink, not so repulsive as dirty drab; and that instead of everlastingly shifting those barren aspects, the sign of ourselves is wholesome, bearable, fructifying, finally a delight. . . . Peruse your Realists—really your castigators for not having yet embraced Philosophy.

Philosophy, spiritual comprehension, alone provides "Reality's infinite sweetness."

Like Meredith, Stevenson held out against the Realistic domination of life and letters in the late nineteenth century. With the exception of a few essays in the realm of Realistic writing, writing which, unlike that of the French Realists, did not emphasize the sordid, Stevenson's literary efforts and theories were Romantic. "A Gossip on Romance," published in *Longman's Magazine* in 1882 sets forth his aesthetic credo. For him the novel is a means of escape from life. It is to the grown man what play is to the child. The more we identify ourselves with the characters and the progress of the story, the greater has been the author's triumph. Literature is not a transcript of life, but a mood, a mood which satisfies the imagination. The writer of a story must draw his materials from real life, but this is his method, not his objective. He has to arrange and select his subject matter so that the impression on the reader is that of a satisfying illusion. In the ideal novel "situation is animated with passion, passion clothed with situation. Neither exists for itself, but each inheres indissolubly with the other." The true character of Romance is to subordinate character, passion, and thought to incident in such a way that the situation will be brought strikingly and dramatically to the mind's eye. It is thus that the reader forgets the characters and loses himself in the excitement of fresh experience; thus that he

> . . . changes the atmosphere and tenor of his whole life. And when the game so chimes with his fancy that he can join in it with all his heart, when it pleases him with every turn, when he loves to recall it and dwells upon its recollection with entire delight, fiction is called romance.

In "A Note on Realism," first published in the *Magazine of Art* in 1883, Stevenson points out that the great change which has come over the novel since Scott is the admission of detail—a change due to the influence of the semi-romantic Balzac and his more or less wholly unromantic followers. For a while this detail expressed a more ample contemplation of the conditions of a man's life; "but it has recently (at least in France) fallen into a merely technical and decorative stage." The use of detail has become a mere "feux-de-joie" of literary trickery. Thus it is that a "man of the unquestionable force of M. Zola spends himself on technical successes. To afford a popular flavour and attract the mob, he adds a steady current of what I may be allowed to call the rancid." For Stevenson the essential problem lies not in the clash between Realism and Romanticism or Idealism. All representative art which lives is both Realistic and Ideal. The Realism to which he objects is simply the external Realism of the French Naturalists.

> The immediate danger of the realist is to sacrifice the beauty and significance of the whole to local dexterity, or, in the insane pursuit of completion, to immolate his reader under facts; but he comes, in the last resort, and as his energy declines, to discard all design, abjure all choice, and, with scientific thoroughness, steadily to communicate matter which is not worth learning. The danger of the idealist is, of course, to become merely dull and lose all grip of fact, particularity, or passion.

The nineteenth century, however, errs on the side of Realism, and Stevenson cautions the contemporary novelist "to begin no work that is not philosophical, passionate,

dignified, happily mirthful, or, at the last and least, romantic in design."

In "A Humble Remonstance," published in *Longman's Magazine* for December, 1884, Stevenson criticizes Henry James' theory that a novel is a transcript of life. Life is too complex to be reproduced between the covers of a book. It is

> . . . attended by the most various and surprising meteors; appealing at once to the eye, to the ear, to the mind—the seat of wonder, to the touch—so thrillingly delicate, and to the belly—so imperious when starved. It combines and employes in its manifestation the method and material, not of one art only, but of all the arts. Music is but an arbitrary trifling with a few of life's majestic chords; painting is but a shadow of its pageantry of light and colour; literature does but drily indicate that wealth of incident, of moral obligation, of virtue, vice, action, rapture, and agony with which it teems.

No art can possibly hope to give an exact transcript of life. But it can give a representation that is typically true. From life which is monstrous, infinite, illogical, abrupt, and poignant, comes art which is neat, finite, self-contained, rational, flowing, and emasculate.

Thus Art remakes life by selection and arrangement and the product is true if the artist has not falsified the relationships of man to man, and of man to nature. If he has falsified his interpretation, he has created an immoral work,

> . . . for any book is wrong that gives a misleading picture of the world and life. The trouble is that the weakling must be partial; the work of one proving dank and depressing; of another, cheap and vulgar; of a third, epileptically sensual; of a fourth, sourly ascetic. [*Fortnightly Review,* April 1895]

It is impossible, of course, in literature, as in conduct, to do absolutely right. But we can strive earnestly and patiently and honestly. Then it is likely we shall not fall far short of the true, the good, and the beautiful, whether our method be Classic, Romantic, or Realistic.

George Moore's observations on contemporary authors are less criticisms than pictorial interpretations of what the writers attempted to express. His article on Balzac in the *Fortnightly Review* [October 1889] will illustrate:

> . . . As a traveller in the unknown East, standing on the last ridge of the last hill, sees a city, and in awe contemplates the walls fabulous with terraces and gates, the domes and the towers clothed in all the light of the heavens, so does the imaginative reader view the vast sections into which the Human Comedy is so eloquently divided. . . . His [Balzac's] criticism of life seems to me as profound as Thackeray's is trivial and insignificant, and as beautifully sincere and virile as George Eliot's is canting and pedantic; and today it is more living than when he wrote, for he was enormously, incomprehensibly in advance of his time and able by intuitive knowl-

Illustration for Zola's L'assommoir *by Pierre-Auguste Renoir.*

edge of the inherent qualities of things to divine all latent possibilities.

Moore is an impressionist in his reaction to men and to life. Balzac to him is the greatest of all creative geniuses because of his profound perception into human passion and his understanding of the "racking inquietude of existence," because he lived in the midst of the Romantic movement yet never succumbed to it, and because he was a Realist yet never allowed himself to drift "among the mud-banks and shallow shores of Naturalism."

Rather than classify the novelists as Realist or Idealist, Romantic or Naturalist, Moore suggests that we differentiate them into the "thought-mind" and the "fact-mind." Zola's force comes from his fact-mind; Turgenev's from his thought-mind. It is to this latter type that Moore gives approval:

> . . . For it is thought, and thought only, that divides right from wrong; it is thought and thought only that elevates or degrades human deeds and desires; therefore turgid accounts of massacred negroes, and turgid accounts of fornicating peasants, are in like measure distasteful to the true artist. . . . What I wish to establish here is that it is a vain and fruitless task to nar-

rate any fact unless it has been tempered and purified in thought and stamped by thought with a specific value. [*Impressions and Opinions,* 1891]

Impersonality in art is one of the vainest of delusions. Art means personality. *Madame Bovary,* objective as it appears, is one of the most personal of books. Even Zola is no Realist. His novels synthesize life and rise from Realism to poetry and philosophy. They are based on personal observation and are subjective. Zola's critics have closed their eyes to the form of his works and have been deceived by the matter. They must be reminded that the mire is not more real than the clouds. Zola's use of factual material and detail gives the air of reality, but basically he is a Romanticist. He carries the use of minute detail to the limit. His method can go no farther. It is sterile.

Whatever Moore's affection for the Naturalists in his youth, it was a passing fancy. His later life and art show how closely he was drawn to the "Art for Art's sake" group. His emphasis on form, his aversion for the more outward detail, his love for the fine phrase and the selected word, his appreciation of the impressionist painters, his affection for Pater and for Stevenson, all show how foreign his mind really was to Naturalism. To be sure in the bitter attacks of the English against the Naturalists, he aligned himself definitely with the Naturalists. He was vehement in his denunciations of the censorship, and, in fact, of all charges of immorality brought against artists. But in this he was insisting only on the novelist's right to choose his own material, whether or not that material happened to fit in with the conventional thought and practice of the period. George Moore bridges the gap between the Realists of the eighties and the Æsthetes of the nineties. His emphasis on the necessity of actuality as a basis for art, his insistence on style, form, beauty, impressionism, and his belief that art was its own justification, link him with the Naturalists as well as with the Impressionists.

Oscar Wilde is the leader of the "art for art's sake" group just as Zola is the high priest of Naturalism. Meredith and Stevenson had revolted against the latter group on the grounds that their art was not true, that it failed to consider the whole of life. The Wilde group revolted against Naturalism on much the same grounds. In contrast with Zola's preoccupation with the ugly and low, with his neglect of style, with his insistence that art must be an exact copy of life, and with the seriousness with which he approaches the business of writing, is the fastidious, stylized, imaginatively clever and flippant writing of Wilde. The Preface to *Dorian Gray,* published originally in the *Fortnightly Review* for March, 1891, summarizes his creed:

> The artist is the creator of beautiful things. . . .

> Those who find ugly meanings in beautiful things are corrupt without being charming. This is a fault. . . .

> There is no such thing as a moral or an immoral book. Books are well written, or badly written. That is all.

> The nineteenth century dislike of Realism is the rage of Caliban seeing his own face in a glass.

> The nineteenth century dislike of Romanticism is the rage of Caliban not seeing his own face in a glass.

> The moral life of man forms part of the subject-matter of the artist, but the morality of art consists in the perfect use of an imperfect medium. . . .

> It is the spectator, and not life, that art really mirrors.

> Diversity of opinion about a work of art shows that the work is new, complex and vital. . . .

> All art is quite useless.

His antagonism toward Naturalism is set forth in his essay "The Decay of Lying," published in the *Nineteenth Century* for 1889:

> Art never expresses anything but itself. It has an independent life, just as Thought has, and develops purely on its own lines. It is not necessarily realistic in an age of realism, nor spiritual in an age of faith. . . .

Yet Wilde's theories were large enough to embrace many of the nineteenth-century Realists, as this passage from his review of Balzac indicates:

> Many years ago, in a number of *All the Year Round,* Charles Dickens complained that Balzac was very little read in England, and although since then the public has become more familiar with the great masterpieces of French fiction, still it may be doubted whether the *Comédie Humaine* is at all appreciated or understood by the general run of novel readers. It is really the greatest monument that literature has produced in our century, and M. Taine hardly exaggerates when he says that, after Shakespeare, Balzac is our most important magazine of documents on human nature. . . . The distinction between such a book as M. Zola's *L'Assommoir* and such a book as Balzac's *Illusions Perdues* is the distinction between unimaginative realism and imaginative reality. . . . He was, of course, accused of being immoral. Few writers who deal directly with life escape that charge. . . . The morals of the personages of the *Comédie Humaine* are simply the morals of the world around us. They are part of the artist's subject-matter; they are not part of his method. [*Pall Mall Gazette,* September 13, 1887]

Nor did Wilde neglect the Russians:

> Of the three great Russian novelists of our time Tourgenieff is by far the finest artist. . . . Count Tolstoi's method is much larger, and his field of vision more extended. . . . Dostoieffski differs widely from both his rivals. He is not so fine an artist as Tourgenieff, for he deals more with the facts than with the effects of life; nor has he Tolstoi's largeness of vision and epic dignity; but he has qualities that are distinctively and absolutely his own, such as a fierce intensity of passion and concentration of impulse, a power of dealing with the deepest mysteries of psychology and the most hidden springs of life, and a realism that is pitiless in its fidelity, and terrible because it is true. [*Pall Mall Gazette,* May 2, 1887]

But for Wilde, as for Meredith, Stevenson, and Symonds, essential reality is not to be found in the surface appearance of life. It is to be found in the interpretation of objective phenomena. And all interpretation is subjective. Wilde asks, What is truth? and replies: "In matters of religion, it is simply the opinion which has survived. In matters of science, it is the ultimate sensation. In matters of art, it is one's last mood." Such is the glorification of individuality and personality which Wilde constantly emphasizes. It is the antithesis of Flaubert's impersonalism, of the Goncourt's experimentalism, of Maupassant's objectivism, and of Zola's Naturalism. Only at one point does Wilde agree with the Naturalists; namely, that art and morality are distinct categories:

> Besides, I must admit that, either from temperament or taste, or from both, I am quite incapable of understanding how any work of art can be criticized from a moral standpoint. The sphere of art and the sphere of ethics are absolutely distinct and separate; and it is to the confusion between the two that we owe the appearance of Mrs. Grundy, that amusing old lady who repre-

sents the only original form of humour that the middle classes of this country have been able to produce. [*St. James Gazette,* June 25, 1890]

Despite Arthur Symons' early connection with the Realistic and Naturalistic movements, and despite his sympathy for their efforts to produce a higher art, the whole tone of his later criticism is impressionistic. He was profoundly influenced in many ways by the Naturalists, but by temperament he was more the artist than the scientist. Like Pater, he sought to convey the spirit of a work of art through a prose style that would express every nuance of meaning. To him art is more than nature.

> The art of Rodin competes with nature rather than with the art of other sculptors. Other sculptors turn life into sculpture, he turns sculpture into life. . . . But for the living representation of nature in movement, something more is needed than an exact copy. This is a certain deliberate exaggeration; not a correction, not a deviation, but a means of interpretation, the only means by which the softness and energy of nature can be rendered into clay. [*Studies in the Seven Arts,* 1907]

Like Huysmans, Symons in his youth turned to literature to find a representation of life; in his maturity he turned to literature, if not as an escape from life, at least as a means for making life bearable.

> Allowing ourselves, for the most part, to be but vaguely conscious of that great suspense in which we live, we find our escape from its sterile, annihilating reality in many dreams, in religion, passion, art; each a forgetfulness, each a symbol of creation; religion being the creation of a new heaven, passion the creation of a new earth and art, in its mingling of heaven and earth, the creation of heaven out of earth. Each is a kind of sublime selfishness, the saint, the lover, and the artist having each an incommunicable ecstacy which he esteems as his ultimate attainment, however, in his lower moments, he may serve God in action, or do the will of his mistress, or minister to men by showing them a little beauty. But it is, before all things, an escape; and the prophets who have redeemed the world, and the artists who have made the world beautiful, and the lovers who have quickened the pulses of the world, have really, whether they knew it or not, been fleeing from the certainty of one thought: that we have, all of us, only our one day; and from the dread of that other thought: that the day, however used, must after all be wasted. . . . Well, the doctrine of Mysticism, with which all this symbolical literature has to do, of which it is all so much the expression, presents us, not with a guide for conduct, not with a plan for our happiness, not with an explanation of any mystery, but with a theory of life which makes us familiar with mystery, and which seems to harmonize those instincts which make for religion, passion, and art, freeing us at once of a great bondage. [*The Symbolist Movement in Literature,* 1919]

The reputation of the Naturalists in Victorian society was attacked by the philosophical critics, who, unlike the mor-

alists, objected not so much on the grounds that Naturalism dealt with "the seamy side of life" as that it dealt with "the seamy side of life" in a way that was neither truthful nor beautiful. The aesthetic revolt represents an assault upon the major premises of Naturalistic dogma. It does not deny the importance of using the whole of human experience as fit material for fiction. But it does insist that experience must be clarified and interpreted, that the work of the artist can never be objectively scientific. It is this aspect of Victorian literary criticism that was partially responsible for the deflection of Naturalism into the numerous subjective Realisms of late nineteenth and early twentieth century fiction. (pp. 844-56)

> *Clarence R. Decker, "The Aesthetic Revolt Against Naturalism in Victorian Criticism," in* PMLA, *Vol. LIII Summer, 1938, pp. 844-56.*

A nineteenth-century English journalist's condemnation of Naturalism:

The only acquaintance which the writer of this article has with Zola's novels is from two pages of one of the most notorious of them placed open in the window of a well-known bookseller in the City of London. The matter was of such a leprous character that it would be impossible for any young man who had not learned the Divine secret of self-control to have read it without committing some form of outward sin within twenty-four hours after. In this case a boy, apparently about fourteen years old, was reading the book. The writer immediately went into the shop, and accosting the manager in a loud voice, demanded that he should 'step outside and see this boy reading this infernal book in your window.' The shop was full of customers, and the manager naturally looked thunder-struck. Half-an-hour afterwards, when the writer passed, the book was gone.

> *George J. Becker, ed.,* Documents of Modern Literary Realism, *Princeton University Press, 1963.*

Roger Sherman Loomis

[*Loomis was an American educator and critic specializing in medieval literature, particularly Arthurian legend. In the essay below, he illustrates and justifies the basic tenets of Naturalism in response to objections raised by the movement's critics.*]

Naturalism is a word with as many phases of meaning as pacifism or patriotism, and about it rages nearly as fierce a conflict. When Zola issued his well-known pronunciamento that Naturalistic art was Nature seen through a temperament, he stressed the word "Nature." Nature and Nature only must be the subject of art: to face Nature frankly and openly, to present her dulnesses and stupidities and shames with scrupulous impartiality must be the aim of the artist. Now modern English criticism has preferred to call such full-length and unflattering portraiture of Dame Nature, even the emphasis upon her wry neck, bow legs, and squint eyes, by the name of Realism. Accordingly, when the critic nowadays quotes Zola's definition of Naturalism, he stresses the word "temperament." Naturalistic art is Nature seen through a certain temperament, or through a certain formula created by that temperament. Naturalism, we are told, is not simply a reproduction of the homely and repulsive side of Nature's physiognomy, but an attempt to read in it a certain character.

With Zola's profession faithfully to portray Nature the critics have now no quarrel, but with his practice of giving a certain interpretation of her character they and a great body of readers beg leave, more or less politely, to differ. Realism, though not admitted to so high a seat as idealizing poetry and romance, has been received into the company of the immortals, and Howells and Bennett are permitted to sit down to dinner with self-respecting critics. But Naturalism, Zola's interpretation of Nature, the high priests of criticism hold up to mocking and execration. Flaubert, Ibsen, Hardy, Moore, Brieux, and Masters were all at first denounced in the reputable journals as devils from the pit: and they are still ostracized by good society as if a sulphurous vapor hung around them.

To the question, "What is this interpretation, this formula which brings down upon its enunciators the formidable wrath of the critics?" we are likely to receive several answers. The first genial and rubicund gentleman of letters whom we interrogate over a bottle of Burgundy is apt to reply simply: "These fellows are arrant pessimists. They do not assure us that 'God's in his heaven, all's right with the world.' They are notoriously addicted to depressing surroundings and unhappy endings. Literature should not upset one's ideas about anything, and should be either soothing, inspiring, or funny." Apparently, for all his assumed superiority the genial critic demands just about the same remoteness from the workaday world and the same comfortable ending as the tired business man, whom he professes to despise.

If we approach some gentleman who has perhaps felt a little more than our genial friend the brunt of pain and perplexity, we are likely to get a somewhat more illuminating answer. "Naturalism is Bestialism. Man is not a beast." To be sure, Zola has much to say of the Bête Humaine, and undoubtedly does stress in us the ape and tiger strains. But will anyone deny that the strains are there? Now and then a human being sprouts an atavistic tail or fell of hair. So, too, now and then, human beings commit atrocities at Louvain or East St. Louis. Let him that is without a streak of the beast in him cast the first stone at the Bête Humaine. After all, what most critics of this class object to is not the recognition of the animal, but the recognition of the animal as a serious problem. The emphasis on the beast in *L'Assommoir, Jude the Obscure,* and *Spoon River* shocks the conventional critic, who is accustomed to hear such things mentioned only over his after-dinner cigar: he feels it very deeply when he sees them in print where they can be read by ladies, and where apparently they are treated not as jests to roll under his tongue but as grit to break his teeth on. He is ready enough to recognize the beast, but only as a joke or a German. So long as it can be laughed away or blown to bits with high explosive, he is quite ready to appreciate it in his Boccaccio or his Bryce re-

ports. But when the naturalistic author shows him the beast everywhere about him, in the office, the church, and the home, and by no means to be got rid of by such simple methods as laughter or trinitrotoluol, and he realizes that only a reorganization of all his ideas in the light of what sociological, economic, and psychological experts tell him can make this abundant *élan vital* galvanize rather than blast our society, he kicks like a Missouri mule and refuses to recognize the Bête Humaine.

Perhaps, however, we have put our question to some more rational critic, and he replies that he confesses the beast in man, but that he also finds a demigod: Naturalism denies the demigod. True enough, if by the demigod is meant some infusion of a supernatural or mystical element into the beast. But if by the demigod be meant simply those qualities which men have ascribed to gods as their chief and worthiest title to worship—justice and love, beauty and reason—then, of course, the Naturalist does not deny the demigod, though like the Nazarene he often discovers him in the less reputable circles of society. Furthermore, he finds embryonic even in the beast all that is popularly considered peculiar to man—art, altruism, remorse, some of the simpler forms of reasoning and foresight. In the most primitive types of humanity he finds a religion claiming as much supernatural sanction as the Roman Church or Bahaism. When confronted, then, with the fact that even animals possess the supposedly divine traits, and that as divine revelation the totem pole and the Cross claim equal authority, the Naturalist comes to the conclusion that the supernatural is only a development of the natural, and that mystical experience, however valuable as a dynamic, is worthless as a directive. Only reason acting upon the facts supplied by experience can guide us to the truth.

Accordingly the Naturalist discards as obsolete three supernaturalistic concepts—Providence, absolute morality, and freedom of the will. In his novels and plays Providence is represented as a blind bungler, conventional morality is scouted and even flouted, and man is displayed as a puppet worked by the forces of Heredity and Environment. It is about these three phases of the Naturalistic interpretation of Nature that the battle of the critics still rages. What may be said in defense of these tenets of Naturalistic doctrine—a cosmic order without justice, a morality without sanction or stability, and a will, free within limits to choose what it likes best, but determined as to what it likes best?

The idea of a Providence in the affairs of men, working out a sort of poetical justice, has, to be sure, a certain basis in fact. No one can help observing that certain acts cause pain, directly to himself or indirectly through others. The relation is far from being uniform and inevitable, but despite the exceptions certain general causal relations are recognized. It is obvious that to overindulge in Welsh rarebit or to spoil a child with petting brings its own retribution with it. But Nemesis as an instrument of God's jealous vengeance upon the mortal who dares disobey his fiat seems a superfluous explanation of these facts. For it occurs to the Naturalist that a sane ethics calls only those deeds evil which generally bring suffering in their train: and if occasionally that suffering falls upon the evil-doer there is no occasion for seeking an explanation in some mysterious Nemesis. Surely never was an absurder piece of writing than Emerson's dithyramb on *Compensation*. To him it would be a cause for wonder and awful speculation that Providence had provided a dark brown taste in the mouth to balance the exhilaration of drunkenness, and had made fire burn to punish the child for putting its finger in the flame. The fundamental idea is worthy of the good old lady who thanked the dear Lord for providing such excellent harbors where the cities of New York and San Francisco were to spring up. Nemesis is a law, just as gravitation is a law; but like gravitation it is offset a billion times a minute by other laws: and inasmuch as it is therefore less successful than any human penal system in saddling the heaviest penalty on the worst offender, it scarcely deserves all the mystified veneration that has been lavished upon it.

Let us turn next to the Naturalist's morality. We have noted that whether an act is right or wrong depends upon whether joy or pain in the long run follows. This, in turn, depends upon the human and other sentient beings involved. These, in turn, will be affected by climate, heredity, education, and a thousand other things. Naturalistic morality differs, then, from orthodox morality in its relativity. The notion of an eternal code, confided by Infallible Wisdom to the visions of seers and the conscience of every individual, does not appeal to the Naturalistic thinker. If conscience be an infallible guide to right conduct, why did the conscience of 1700 encourage duelling, the conscience of ancient Sparta stealing, the conscience of the devout Mohammedan polygamy, and why was what we now regard as a loathsome sexual perversion practised unblushingly in Periclean Athens? The Naturalist has come to believe that conscience, an emotional assurance of the rightness of one's action, varies so uniformly with the social conventions about it that it can no more be relied on than a compass in the neighborhood of masses of iron. If the moral law is carved on tables of adamant for all times and all places, why is it that when the moral law interferes too severely with the right to life or happiness, we all by common consent make and approve exceptions thereto? We agree that the starving child cannot be blamed for stealing, the invalid must be kept alive by falsehoods, self-defense justifies killing, a noble purpose takes the taint from suicide. I know a clergyman, who had one of the greatest shocks of his life when I wrote him that I believed in comparative freedom of divorce, who yet not long after met with a case of domestic unhappiness, which not only led him to approve a divorce but actually to officiate at the remarriage of the divorced wife. The unpardonable sin, to use a manner of speaking, for the Naturalist is to let a taboo stand in the way of human happiness.

Naturalistic ethics, then, are hedonistic. The greatest happiness of the greatest number is the end and criterion of action. But the Naturalistic thinker does not believe that to obey each moment's passing whim brings the maximum of happiness either for the individual or for the group. He perceives that man is a highly complex organism, whose nature includes, besides the passions, a social instinct, an artistic instinct, and a reason. In the harmonizing of all these factors lies happiness. To give controlled expression to the passions and to sublimate them, to enjoy the pleasures of social intercourse and social approval, to do all things beautifully, and viewing all these things in their relation, to harmonize them by reason,—this is the art of living. Individuals here and there may attain degrees of happiness in spite of, even by the partial denial of one or another of these four elements. One may even kill the artistic impulse and yet live in moderate pleasure. But to deny the fundamental passions or the claims of society or of reason is to court destruction. On the other hand, to follow too eagerly the seductions of any one is to distort the growth of the organism, and evil results appear either in the later development of the individual or in the society which imitates him.

What does duty mean to the Naturalistic thinker? The root of the word supplies the key. Duty is simply the debt which the individual owes to society. If society gives him much,—wealth, power, education,—society has a right to demand much. If it gives him little, it should demand little. The product of the slum, the ten hour day, and the gin palace, owes nothing to society. Society's demand that he make himself an intelligent human being and refrain from burglary, rape, and murder is an impossible impertinence on the part of society; though society will doubtless continue to enforce the payment of loans which it never made. Duty, then, is simply a claim by society upon the individual.

Since, however, the individual craves happiness and the way to complete happiness does not lie in antagonism to society and wholesale infringement of social interests, it will always be expedient for him, no matter how little society has done for him, to work for social ends. On the whole, it pays to cash up when society sends in a bill.

What have the Naturalistic writers done for morality? We may admit at once that they have done more to throw down rotting conventions than to build up new moral and social laws. But the former service is not to be minimized. Zola built his ponderous engines of destruction up against the walls of clerical imposture and vice in many forms; Hardy battered at the undemocratic walls of Oxford colleges and laid bare the shallowness of revivalism; Wells in his Naturalistic period exploded the bladder of the patent medicine and the whole vast imposture of advertising; Galsworthy attacked a jingoistic patriotism, and enacted for us the farce-tragedy that is sometimes played under the title of "Justice"; and Masters in his *Spoon River Anthology* has pierced to the root of nearly every wrong and folly and sham that festers in the modern social body.

Greatest has been the service of the Naturalistic school to the cause of labor and the cause of women. There are Naturalists who have been indifferent or hostile to both, but they form a small minority. From Zola to Verhæren, from Arthur Morrison to Ernest Poole, the majority of Naturalists have insistently claimed for labor that right to the pursuit of happiness which is so tantalizingly offered in our revolutionary Declaration of Independence.

For women Naturalistic literature has done the enormous service of telling the truth and the whole truth about sex. Conventional literature gave glimpses of purple mountain peaks, encircled with clouds of gold; it told besides of a vast tract hidden by sulphurous vapors, where the unwary wanderer felt the earth's crust crumble beneath him, and sank into a seething cauldron. Conventional literature charted only the most obvious parts of this region: where the concealed dangers were perhaps greatest it gave no direction. It prescribed for women one entrance only, a gate called marriage, and gave many details of the route thither. But for all the tract that lay beyond or outside of it the details were meagre and sometimes false. Now all this region has been faithfully charted and published abroad. I venture to say the reading of half a dozen novels of the Naturalist school will exhibit more of the rationale of sex than any other body of literature ever written. Wifely subjection, the double standard of morals, prostitution, the seduction of working-girls, long sanctioned or condoned in much conventional literature, have received no quarter here. Among what school of writers are we to find one particular form of criminal folly so scarified as in *Ghosts, Damaged Goods,* and "Willard Fluke" of the *Spoon River Anthology*? Burke's famous generalization that no discoveries are to be made in morality breaks down before such a case. For while, doubtless, the ethical principle of which this is an application is as old as society, yet the perception of its application and the forcible presentation of the evil and its consequences, leading at last to recognition in our legislatures, is new and may be placed in large measure to the credit of the Naturalists.

Look at Tom Jones, the hero of what has been called by the conventionalists the greatest English novel. Tom is scarcely more than a slave of the moment's appetite. To be sure, he has too much sense of fair play ever to seduce women, but women have not the slightest difficulty in seducing him. The possibility that any of his adventures may have dire consequences is never faced, except when the sensational possibility of committing incest for a time horrifies him. This amiable gentleman, rather than soil his hands, resolves to sell himself to a lady in return for his keep. At last, he marries the chaste Sophia and rears a lusty brood. I should like to know what those who charge the Naturalistic novel with a predilection for feeble heroes and heroines have to say for this flabby protagonist of their greatest English novel. As a picture of random sex relations it betrays a facile optimism that no realist would be capable of.

Now by way of contrast let us look at a novel of the Naturalistic extreme,—*Sanine,* by Artzybasheff. The book is not a typical example of Naturalism, for the author derides the exercise of reason and humanitarian effort. But even though in these respects it falls short of the saner Naturalism characteristic of Zola, Ibsen, Hardy, and Masters, even though it glorifies sexual experiences as the greatest thing in the world, yet it is so far superior to *Tom Jones* as a criticism of life that it does not flinch from the tragic possibilities in such experience, and it makes a sharp differentiation between the putrescent koprophagy of the garrison town and the artistic expression of a healthy desire. While in my opinion the author does not sufficiently recognize that human nature has other summits than those reached in the culmination of the mightiest elemental passion, and does not realize the limitations which soci-

ety has a right to place upon mating, yet in his demand that passion be beautiful as a Greek statue is beautiful, and in his recognition of the woman, not as a plaything but as a personality, he admits the place of the artistic and social impulses and justifies his classification as a Naturalist. Neither *Sanine* nor *Tom Jones* gives us anything like an exhaustive study of sex, but *Sanine* penetrates beneath the crust of convention; *Tom Jones* does not: *Sanine* has an idealism of sex; *Tom Jones* has none.

The larger Naturalism, then, founded upon the view of happiness as the goal of life, of the all round development of the individual as the way, and of the golden mean as the guiding principle, has been gradually making over our morality, ridding it of the relics of primitive taboos, and establishing it upon the demands of human nature.

But the third fundamental principle of Naturalism, determinism, is a stumbling block to many. The conventionalist is sure to object.

> Granted that Naturalism has laid bare the ulcers and cancerous growths in the body of society, and has been as plainspoken as the Old Testament or Shakespeare about things that are never mentioned in polite society, it destroys all incentive to salve those sores because it denies the freedom of the human will. It so impresses on us the thorough corruption of society that we feel that it is condemned to an eternity of disease. We see these men, as one reverend critic phrases it, "concentrating attention on the shadiness and seaminess of life, exploiting sewers and cesspools, dabbling in beastliness and putrefaction, dragging to light the ghastly and gruesome, poring over the scurvy and unreportable side of things, bending in lingering analysis over every phase of mania and morbidity, going down into the swamps and marshes to watch the phosphorescence of decay and the jack-o'-lanterns that dance on rottenness"; and we conclude forsooth that if this is life, there is no hope for the world.

Naturalism may at once plead guilty to the doctrine of determinism: but it does not admit that the doctrine is inconsistent with optimism of the future or that it robs man of incentive to moral action. The argument that optimism can be justified only by belief in an outside power pumping virtue into humanity by slow degrees is not convincing to anyone who realizes what is meant by potential energy. It is not necessary to believe that if a pound of radium could emit electrical energy for thousands of years it must be connected with a celestial dynamo. Neither is it necessary to believe that the human race is incapable of improving itself, however unhappy its present condition. No man can tell the potential energies latent in the human race, energies that may express themselves through reason, social feeling, and the love of beauty to make the superman. Determinism is no foe to an optimism of the future. Professor Santayana puts the theory admirably:

> We are a part of the blind energy behind Nature, but by virtue of that energy we impose our purposes on that part of Nature which we constitute or control. We can turn from the stupefying contemplation of an alien universe to the building of our own house, knowing that, alien as it is,

that universe has chanced to blow its energy also into our will and to allow itself to be partially dominated by our intelligence. Our mere existence and the modicum of success we have attained in society, science and art, are the living proofs of this human power. The exercise of this power is the task appointed for us by the indomitable promptings of our own spirit, a task in which we need not labor without hope.

The conventionalist pursues his point. "This all sounds mighty fine. But experience shows that a belief in the freedom of the will and moral responsibility is all that keeps us from wallowing in a sensual sty." As the Rev. Dr. S. Law Wilson puts it,

> What, we ask, would be the effect of persuading the masses of mankind to believe that all the evil of which they are guilty is necessitated, and all the blame must be laid to the door of blood, or birth, or environment, or the tyranny of impulse? Indoctrinate the masses of our population with this pestiferous teaching, and there be some of us who shall not taste of death till we see the reign of moral anarchy and disintegration set in.

Now let us see what the real effect of acting upon the doctrine of free will is as contrasted with the effect of acting upon its denial. The theory of the freedom of the will, apart from its incompatibility with the generally accepted law of causation as implying an agent that, without being itself caused, initiates or causes action, involves the doctrine of complete responsibility. For if the will could have refrained just as well as not from the immoral act, no matter how powerful the pressure of heredity and environment, the man is absolutely responsible. His guilt has no extenuation. Punishment heavy and merciless is but his due. The only thing for society to do is impress upon him the enormity of his crime and urge him to repentance.

Now the old penal methods were in entire accord with this theory. Criminals were in prison to be punished. No treatment was too bad for them. The prison chaplain dilated on their essential wickedness, and told them that they had only themselves to thank for the plight in which they found themselves. If they would freely confess their guilt and accept the inspiration of religion, though society would not forgive them, God would. Now the results of such a logical application of the doctrine of moral responsibility to the criminal class are notorious. Everyone knows that the men who went to the penitentiary did not come out penitent, far less did they come out with any propensity to good. These men had learned what the doctrine of free will was in its application to them. Somehow there seems to have been a perverse conspiracy among criminals throughout the world to discredit the doctrine of free will and its corollary, moral responsibility.

What, however, are the results of determinism as applied to these same men? Mr. Osborne, whose work at Sing Sing we all know, has without knowing it acted upon this principle. He has brought into the prison pleasure and social life and a system of stimuli in the form of rewards. He has created a society where the criminal naturally did his duty to society because society had done something for him. He has taught the men trades and made openings for them in

Thomas Hardy.

the world, and as a result he has made citizens out of outlaws. Of his success there can be no question. What here the individual could not do for himself, environment did for him. It mattered little whether he thought his will free or not: it responded inevitably to the right stimuli. Little need have we to fear the spread of the determinist theory among the masses, if only we have intelligence enough to practice as well as to preach it.

The conventionalist once more objects. "But turn away from life to your own Naturalistic novels. Are they not shrieking in our ears that man is feeble and doomed to failure? Are not their heroes and heroines weaklings who fall unresisting under the bludgeonings of Fate?"

Now it may well be admitted that the Naturalists, in order to show where the rocks lie, have usually represented their human barks as breaking upon the reefs rather than gliding smoothly into harbor. But in doing so the Naturalists have done only what every tragic writer has done. If the Mayor of Casterbridge or Madame Bovary fell through a combination of defects of character with adverse circumstances, what else may we say of Hamlet and Lear? Are we to despise Tess of the D'Urbervilles because though she often showed great strength of character, at certain crises of her fate timidity prevailed over purpose? When the conventionalists begin to call the great tragedies decadent on the same grounds that they condemn the Naturalistic novels; when they scorn Desdemona because when her husband suspected her she did not call up the Pinkerton's detective agency of Cyprus and probe the matter to the bottom, and because on her deathbed she did not wrestle courageously, but murmured merely, "A guiltless death I die," then we may listen patiently when they apply these standards to works not in the classic tradition. Until then some of us are inclined to believe that these critics unconsciously act upon the principle that any stick is good enough to beat a dog with.

Dr. Johnson once said that if he had no duties and no reference to futurity he would spend his life in driving briskly in a post-chaise with a pretty woman. To such a declaration the appropriate Johnsonian reply is, "You lie, sir." If the Doctor would permit of any further explanation, we might go on to say: In the first place, Fate might refuse. Fate, in the form of the pretty woman, might politely decline the invitation. She might prefer other company to that of the hectoring oracle of the Mitre, the polysyllabic proser of the *Rambler* papers: she might object to being referred to as an unidea-ed girl. In the second place, if the woman found it agreeable, the Doctor himself would soon have found it disagreeable. It may be an impertinence to presume that we know the Doctor better than he knew himself, but Boswell has made the claim possible. Now the Doctor had certain hereditary traits that would never have been satisfied for long with sitting in a post-chaise beside a pretty woman. He had too active a brain, he was too much of a clubman, and, as a matter of fact, despite all his complaints of indolence, he had an instinct for work. Moreover, it is difficult to imagine that Samuel Johnson would have let the American Revolution go by without leaping from the post-chaise and scratching off *Taxation No Tyranny.* At the very least, he would have had to stop for a moment, stretch his limbs, and perhaps roll down a hill for the fun of it. Without disparaging the worthy Doctor's sincerity, one may say that, granted his pecuniary and other restrictions, he would have lived much the same life if he had had no theories of duty beyond what every social being holds, and no more reference to futurity than the desire that the rest of life contain as much happiness as he could put into it.

Moreover, one cannot help thinking that if Doctor Johnson had exerted his great influence, not as a conventionalist and Tory, but as a Naturalist and democrat, the whole course of events in Europe might have been changed. His posthumous power might have offset the Bourbonism of Burke; England might not have thrown her strength on the side of that Holy Alliance of Prussian, Austrian, and Russian despotisms; the contagion of a liberal England and France might have liberalized Europe; and the world might have been made safe for democracy a hundred years ago. But it was not to be.

There are people who see in Naturalism the origin of this war [World War I] and in the triumph of the Allies the vindication of Providence. Such a view is only possible through a misconception of the facts. The insane policies of German imperialism found ready support throughout the ranks of the German supernaturalists, and palliation in that inviolate citadel of supernaturalism, the Vatican. On the other hand, the bitterest and most courageous of the foes of German imperialism were a small group of atheistic socialists in Germany, whose creed was the creed of Naturalism. As for the victory of the Allies I can see nothing but a confirmation of the blunt statement erroneously attributed to Napoleon that God is always on the side of the heaviest battalions. The feeble succor afforded by St. Michael at Mons hardly leads one to rely much upon the heavenly powers for aid. The despairing prayers of millions went unheeded until material force came to the aid of spiritual yearnings. One who can believe in supernaturalism after this war possesses, indeed, a faith which serves as an evidence of things not seen. Let him have his angels of Mons and be happy. But the rest of us, in this time momentous and critical as scarcely any other time in the world's history, can hardly afford to base our hopes for the future on any efforts but our own, or afford to direct those efforts by any but Naturalistic principles: for these must bring happiness in their wake, or *ipso facto* cease to be the principles of Naturalism. (pp. 535-48)

> *Roger Sherman Loomis, "A Defense of Naturalism," in* Documents of Modern Literary Realism, *edited by George J. Becker, Princeton University Press, 1963, pp. 535-48.*

NATURALISM IN THEATER

John Gassner

[Gassner, a Hungarian-born American scholar, was a great promoter of American theater, particularly the work of Tennessee Williams and Arthur Miller. He edited numerous collections of modern drama and wrote two important dramatic surveys, Masters of Modern Drama *(1940) and* Theater in Our Times *(1954). In the following excerpt, Gassner assesses the impact of Naturalism on modern drama, finding it eclipsed by the more pervasive influence of realism.]*

Naturalism can be defined broadly or narrowly. [I have] employed this rather ambiguous term as though it were generally interchangeable with "realism." This has, indeed, been the case on the European continent, as Europeans will say "Naturalismus" or "naturalisme" when we would say "realism."

As an intensive term, however, naturalism signifies not only a strict, often extreme, mode of realism, but a rather narrow dogma introduced into dramatic theory by Emile Zola in 1873, in his familiar and perhaps overrated preface to *Thérèse Raquin,* the unsuccessful play that he had fashioned out of his own naturalistic novel. Zola formulated a creed that was consonant with nineteenth-century idolatry of mechanistic science as the key to all truth. He especially reflected the advances made in physiology by Claude Bernard (1813-1878), the founder of experimental medicine, with whose researches, as recorded in *An Introduction to the Study of Experimental Medicine* (1865), Zola was extremely impressed.

Zola's program for the theatre called upon writers to concentrate on data arrived at objectively, and to adopt the hypothesis that man is primarily an animal whose emotions can be submitted to the same laboratory tests as "sugar and vitriol," to use Taine's expression. The strictly naturalistic view was mechanistic, physiological, and deterministic. The individual was to be exhibited as the product, puppet, and victim of the inexorable forces of heredity, instinct, and environment, for man was to be regarded as a wholly natural object subject to natural processes. Since the naturalists could consistently consider moral issues only as manifestations of the "laws" of physiology and psychology, they were more inimical to Victorian moralism than were Ibsen and Shaw, who were strong believers in the moral will. Naturalists subordinated morality to the order of nature.

The strict application of these standards of naturalism to playwriting resulted in the presentation of environments and of more or less animal (that is, instinctive) behavior on the stage. Pictures of degradation, disease, and sexual license abounded in advanced theatrical circles after 1880. (As usual, there was a time lag in the theatre; naturalism had established itself in European fiction about two decades earlier.) Among plays reflecting the naturalist dogma are Gerhart Hauptmann's *Before Sunrise* (1889), *The Beaver Coat* (1893), and *Rose Bernd* (1903); Strindberg's *The Dance of Death* (1901); and Schnitzler's *Reigen* (1897), best known here by the title of the French motion picture made from it, *La Ronde.* Naturalism became a *cause célèbre,* and its progress was punctuated by conflicts with censorship.

Naturalists required of the actor the utmost authenticity in speech, appearance, and movement, even encouraging him to turn his back to the audience when the action called for it, thus giving the proscenium arch the character of a fourth wall. They also called for the utmost naturalness in playwriting, discouraging plot maneuvering even more than Ibsen did, and favoring the employment of dialect. They advocated dialect not for poetic effect, but for the sake of realism of the phonograph, supplementary to their ideal realism in scenery, which constituted a realism of the camera. Dialect in a play by Hauptmann or Galsworthy was, indeed, likely to be unlovely and jangling.

Zola's passion for naturalism in 1873 also made him a quixotic advocate of "naturalness." He seemed bent on liberating the drama from dramatic structure, although his *Thérèse Raquin,* a play of murder and revenge, was anything but uncontrived. He declared somewhat grandiosely, "The word *art* displeases me: it contains I do not know what ideas of necessary arrangements. . . . To make art, is it not to mistake something which is outside man and outside nature?" Zola was successful, perhaps, in helping to rid the stage of romantic "heroic drama" and its "paraphernalia of armor, secret doors, poisoned wines and the rest," which were to find a refuge ultimately in the Hollywood factories of historical romance. But Zola came up against the refractoriness of the dramatic medium, which requires that a story must be greatly condensed and arranged. And the natural opposition of the artist to a consistent naturalism was stated, or rather thundered, by

Nietzsche in *Twilight of the Idols* when he deplored the results of nonselection, "a mass of daubs, at best a piece of mosaic," and protested that "nature is no model. . . . This lying in the dust before trivial facts is unworthy of the thorough artist." Zola's call for thoroughly "unarranged" drama was heeded only to a limited extent. The realistic plays of Ibsen and Strindberg and Shaw were certainly not "unarranged," and Chekhov's only seemed so. The realists' use of the materials of social reality was interpretative, whereas Zola's "scientific" program for naturalism demanded absolute objectivity and clinical detachment.

Naturalism, however, did not cause any changes in dramatic form that were not implicit in realism as practiced by courageous playwrights. If the naturalistic theatre encouraged the use of dialect on the stage, so did the poetic-nationalistic Irish movement. In demanding that the drama consist of "slice of life" scenes, Zola and his followers also discouraged plottiness and theatrical contrivance; but so did realists, such as Ibsen and Shaw, who opposed drama of intrigue without embracing a Naturalist program. Of the preference for naturalness erected (and somewhat distorted) into an article of naturalistic faith by Zolaism, the kindest thing to be said is that it was, on the negative side, a renunciation of easy and banal means of winning public interest; and, on the positive side, that it expressed one of the oldest ideals of art—namely, the Horatian one of the art of concealing art. Perhaps Randall Jarrell has expressed it best in contemporary terms when, in writing of Robert Frost's poetic power, but mentioning also Thomas Hardy's, he referred to "the tremendous strength . . . of things merely put down and left to speak for themselves" [*Poetry and the Age,* 1955]. But, as in the case of all theories of art, the worse practice of the theory prevailed far more frequently than the better.

For my argument, then, the term "naturalism" has no particular meaning not already embodied in the term "realism." I would note only two historically important points: the first is that the naturalists led by Zola, most of whom had a flair for publicity, were particularly effective in championing dramatic realism and encouraging its extension. They supported the plays of Ibsen, Strindberg, and Tolstoy, and they were the first to rally to the support of Antoine's historic Théâtre Libre, although Antoine himself tried to disclaim exclusive adherence to naturalism. A second fact to bear in mind is that doctrinaire naturalists soon alienated the public with the grossness of their plays and the tawdriness of their stage productions. Naturalism was responsible to a considerable extent for the antirealistic reaction represented by Maeterlinck's "symbolist" plays and Rostand's flamboyantly romantic pieces before the nineteenth century came to a close. Deterministic views and fascination with raw animalism, however, received too much support from the social conflicts and wars of the twentieth century to permit them to wither away quietly. And it may also be argued that by minimizing the role of reason in human life, naturalism prepared the ground for the excesses of expressionists and surrealists. (pp. 66-70)

John Gassner, "The Modernization of Dramatic Art," in his Directions in Modern Theatre and Drama: An Expanded Edition of Form and Idea in Modern Theatre, *Holt, Rinehart and Winston, Inc., 1965, pp. 3-78.*

Martin Esslin

[*Esslin, a prominent and sometimes controversial critic of contemporary theater, is perhaps best known for coining the term "theater of the absurd." His* The Theatre of the Absurd *(1961) is a major study of the avant-garde drama of the 1950s and early 1960s, including the works of Samuel Beckett, Eugene Ionesco, and Jean Genet. In the following essay, he discusses the origins of Naturalism, specifically its manifestation in the theater, and he emphasizes the movement's influence on contemporary theater.*]

Nothing tastes staler than the revolutions of the day before yesterday; the bitter flavor of great expectations disappointed clings to them; they make us feel superior for having seen through their ridiculous pretensions and sorry for our fathers and grandfathers for having been taken in by them. That Naturalism in the novel and in the theatre still leaves such an aftertaste on our own palates is, in a way, a tribute to the intensity of emotion it aroused in its day and the length of time during which it acquired and held a dominant position. After all: it was in the 1870's that Zola shocked the world with his new concept of Naturalism; Ibsen's *Ghosts* was first published in 1881; Strindberg's *Father* in 1887, *Miss Julie* in 1888; Hauptmann's *Before Sunrise* had its first performance in 1889; Chekhov's *Seagull* in 1896. Yet the Expressionism of the 1920's, Brecht's epic theatre of the Thirties and Forties, the Theatre of the Absurd of the Fifties and Sixties were still essentially both continuations of and reactions *against* Naturalism (or at least against its latter-day exponents, who still dominate the more conservative sector of our theatre: Broadway, the London West End, and the Paris Boulevard, not to speak of Moscow). A movement which started out as a furious attack on the conventions of what was then regarded as the well-made play, as an iconoclastic, revolutionary onslaught against the establishment, has now turned into the embodiment of "squareness," conservatism, and the contemporary concept of the well-made play. In the West End of London early Shaw and Ibsen have become safe after-dinner entertainment for the suburban business community—the equivalents of Scribe, Sardou and Dumas *fils* in their own day—the very authors whom they had wanted to replace because they were safe and establishment-minded.

Such, however, is the dialectical law of historical development: each hour has its own necessity, its own imperative; and what is essential is precisely the insight and the courage needed to obey it. Once the hour is passed, the new molds have been created, lesser spirits will inevitably continue to use them; and that is how the revolutionary contents and forms of yesteryear turn into the clichés of today.

What matters, therefore, for any objective assessment of a movement like Naturalism, is to see it in its historical context; to understand the moral and artistic impulse behind it; and to pursue its manifestations into our own time:

we shall then find that the impulse behind the Naturalist movement is still very much alive, very relevant for our own time and well worth our study and understanding.

The mid-19th century was one of dismal stagnation in the European theatre. The achievements of the classical and romantic movement in Germany and of the romantic revolution in France had congealed into an empty routine; the theatre was discredited as a serious art form. Looking back on those days Strindberg reported that

> if one wanted to submit a play to the Royal Dramatic Theatre in the Sixties and Seventies the following conditions had to be met to get it performed: the play had to have five acts, each act had to run to about 24 sheets of writing paper, thus the whole play to 5 times 24 = 120 foolscap pages. Changes of scene within the acts were not liked and were considered a weakness. Each act had to have a beginning, a middle and an end. The curtain lines had to give rise to applause through oratorical figures; if the play was in unrhymed verse, the last two lines had to rhyme. In the play there had to be "turns" for the actors which were called "scenes"; the monologue was permissible and often constituted a highlight; a longish emotional outburst or invective, a revelation were almost compulsory; there also had to be narrative passages—a dream, an anecdote, an event . . . This dramaturgy had a certain justification and even a certain beauty; it stemmed in the last resort from Victor Hugo and had been a reaction against the obsolete abstractions of Racine and Corneille in the Thirties. But this art form degenerated like all others, when it had had its day, and the five-act form was used for all kinds of subjects, even for insignificant minor history or anecdote . . .

Strindberg here confirms the diagnosis which Zola made in his preface to *Thérèse Raquin* (dated July 25, 1873):

> Drama is dying of its extravagances, its lies and its platitudes. If comedy still keeps on its feet in the collapse of our stage, that is because it contains more of real life, because it is often true. I defy the last of the romantics to put on the stage a heroic drama; the old iron of the middle ages, the secret doors, the poisoned wines and all the rest would only make one shrug one's shoulders. Melodrama, this bourgeois offspring of romantic drama, is even more dead in the affection of the people; its false sentiment, its complications of stolen children and recovered documents, its impudent grandiloquence have brought it, at long last, into such disrepute that one holds one's ribs at any attempt to resuscitate it. The great works of the 1830's will remain as milestones of a struggle, as literary red-letter days, as superb efforts that brought down the classical trappings. But now that all this is overturned, the cloaks and the daggers have become unnecessary. The time has come to create works of truth. To replace the classical tradition by a romantic tradition would amount to a failure to make use of the freedom which our elders conquered for us. There must be no more schools, no more formulas, no more literary panjandrums of any kind; there is just

life itself, an immense field where everybody can explore and create at his heart's content.

No more schools, no more formulas, no more literary panjandrums of any kind! Here lies the impetus behind the Naturalist movement which is still active and immensely relevant. No wonder Zola's impassioned manifesto reads so well and seems fresh and tropical today. The romantic movement had overthrown the dominance of the rigid formula of French classical drama, but it had imposed its own narrow conception of subject matter, technique and objective on all serious theatre. Comedy, stemming from Molière and his realism of observation and language, had remained much freer from the blight of the schoolmen. Now the Naturalists called for a fresh start in *complete* freedom; art, as philosophy, was making the transition from a *closed* to a totally open system. The Naturalists were the first to formulate such a new, open view of aesthetics.

It had taken half a century for Auguste Comte's positivist philosophy to be taken up by the creative artists—Comte's *Système de philosophie positive* had appeared in 1824. It reached Zola via the works of a physiologist, Claude Bernard, notably his *Introduction à l'étude de la Médecine expérimentale* (1865), and a literary and social historian, Hippolyte Taine, whose epoch-making *Histoire de la littérature anglaise* had appeared in 1864. What Zola took from Claude Bernard is the basic concept of the *scientific method* of observation and experiment. Zola's essay *Le Roman Expérimental* (1890), the basic formulation of the Naturalists' creed, is little more than an anthology of quotations from Claude Bernard's book on experimental medicine. "All experimental reasoning must be founded on doubt, for the experimenter must have no preconceived ideas when confronting nature; he must always preserve his freedom of mind." Bernard had stressed that the scientific, experimental method implied a *determinist* view of nature; experimentation uncovers the chain of cause and effect behind seemingly arbitrary phenomena. But it was from Taine that Zola took his own specific determinism. In his history of English literature Taine sought to explain each writer through three main factors that determined his nature and his style: race, milieu, moment. This concept allowed the Naturalists to reintroduce the classical source of tragedy—preordained, inescapable *fate*—into drama in a new and highly respectable "scientific" guise. Man's fate was preordained through a combination of heredity, environment and history. It was this idea of heredity that stalked through *Ghosts, Before Sunrise* and *Miss Julie.*

Taine's determinism was oversimplified and scientifically untenable. (Modern genetics soon showed that the real workings of heredity were far more complex than Taine, or even Darwin, had imagined; that neither Oswald's syphilis nor the alcoholism which Hauptmann's Helene, in *Before Sunrise,* seemed destined to inherit would in fact have been transmitted from father to son, from father to daughter). But—and this must be stressed again and again in the face of a present-day tendency to scoff at the Naturalists precisely for being scientifically out-of-date—these mistakes in scientific detail are not of the essence of their

attitude. Their fundamental and essential belief has not become obsolete:

> Naturalism, in literature . . . is the return to nature and to man, direct observation, correct anatomy, the acceptance and the depiction of that which *is*. The task is the same for the scientist as for the writer. Both have to abandon abstractions for realities, ready-made formulas for rigorous analysis. Hence no more abstract characters in our works, no more history of everyone, the web and woof of daily life. It is a matter of a totally new start, of getting to know man from the very well-springs of his being, before reaching conclusions in the manner of the idealists who *invent* their types. Writers from now on are constrained to build from the foundation upward by presenting the largest possible number of human documents, put forward in their logical order . . . (Zola, *Le Naturalisme au théâtre*).

This spirit of free enquiry, totally unprejudiced, unburdened by preconceived ideas, liberated immense energies. That it consciously aimed beyond the immediate techniques and subject matters of the moment is clearly shown, for example, by the manifesto with which Otto Brahm, the great critic and director of German Naturalist drama, opened the Berlin *Freie Buehne* (Free Stage) on January 29, 1890:

> Once upon a time there was an art which avoided the present and sought poetry only in the darkness of the past, striving in a bashful flight from reality to reach those ideal distant shores where in eternal youth there blooms what has never happened anywhere. The art of our time embraces, with its tentacles, everything that lives: nature and society; that is why the closest and subtlest relations bind modern art and modern life together; and anyone who wants to grasp modern art must endeavor to penetrate modern life as well in its thousand merging contours, in its intertwined and antagonistic instincts. The motto of this new art, written down in golden characters by our leading spirits, is one word: truth; and truth, truth on every path of life, is what we are striving for. Not the objective truth, which escapes the struggling individual, but individual truth, freely arrived at from the deepest convictions, freely uttered: the truth of the independent spirit who has nothing to explain away or hide; and who therefore knows only one adversary, his arch-enemy and mortal foe: the lie in all its forms.

No other programme is to be recorded in these pages. We swear by no formula and would not dare to chain into the rigid compulsion of rules that which is in eternal flux—life and art. Our striving is for that which is in the act of becoming and our eyes are directed toward the things which are about to arise far more attentively than those elements of an eternal yesterday which have the presumption to tie down in conventions and rules, once and for all time, mankind's infinite potential. We bow in reverence before all the greatness that past epochs have preserved for us, but it is not from them that we draw our lodestone and norms of life; for it is not he who ties himself to the views of a dead world, but only he who freely feels the demand of the present hour, who will penetrate the spiritual power activating our age as a truly modern man . . . No barrier of theory, no sanctified model of the past must inhibit the infinity of development which constitutes the essence of our species . . . Friends of naturalism, we want to stride along with it for a fair stretch of the way, but we shall not be astonished if in the course of this journey, at a point we cannot as yet foresee, the road might suddenly turn, opening up surprising new vistas in art or life. For the infinite development of human culture is bound to no formula, not even the newest; and in this confidence, in this faith in infinite potentiality, we have erected a free stage for modern life.

These are noble words; they show the genuine freedom of the spirit, transcending all narrow dogmatism of literary movements or coteries, which inspired the best minds among the champions of Naturalism. Seldom in the history of literature has the call for *absolute truth* been voiced with such uncompromising conviction, such relentless courage. Chekhov wrote in 1887,

> Artistic literature is called so just because it depicts life as it really is. Its aim is truth—unconditional and honest . . . I agree with you that the "cream" is a fine thing, but a *littérateur* is not a confectioner, not a dealer in cosmetics, not an entertainer; he is a man bound, under compulsion, by the realization of his duty, and by his conscience; having put his hand to the plow he must not plead weakness; and no matter how painful it is to him, he is constrained to overcome his aversion, and soil his imagination with the sordidness of life. He is just like an ordinary reporter. What would you say if a newspaper reporter, because of his fastidiousness or from a wish to give pleasure to his readers, were to describe only honest mayors, high-minded ladies and virtuous railroad contractors? To a chemist nothing on earth is unclean. A writer must be as objective as a chemist; he must abandon the subjective line; he must know that dungheaps play a very respectable part in a landscape and that evil passions are as inherent in life as good ones . . . (Letter to M. V. Kiselev, January 14, 1887).

The decisive and truly revolutionary element in this attitude—this I believe must be stressed above all—was exactly this passionate proclamation of the *primacy of content over form,* the conviction that any subject matter could be treated, and that each subject matter would call for the form most adequate and suitable to express it. Artistic form thus came to be seen as the *organic expression* of its content.

> We are through with intrigue, with artificial plot, through with the play as a kind of chess game; the ability to perceive and to express, which is the secret of each true artist, is his natural style, his inner form, his inner turn of phrase. In these the great rhythm and the great dynamism of life are reduced to an individual

rhythm, an individual dynamism. There may be a tradition in this, but it has become flesh and blood! A tradition which, like those of eating and drinking, is carried by ever new hunger and thirst. Traditional, external dogmas cannot have a bearing on this process. Such useless and pointless external dogmas are: the dogma of plot, the dogma of the unities of space and time, the dogma of exposition in twenty to thirty lines at the opening of the first act, and others. (Gerhart Hauptmann, ca. 1910.)

Yet in their demand for truth, the primacy of subject matter over form, the Naturalists were never—as is nowadays often thoughtlessly assumed—naive enough to believe in the possibility of a truly objective representation of nature. In the above quotation Hauptmann insists on the artist's *individual* ability to perceive and to express as the starting point. And Zola himself coined the famous slogan: *"Il est certain qu'une oeuvre ne sera jamais qu'un coin de la nature vu à travers un tempérament"* (A work of art cannot but be a corner of nature seen through a temperament).

This recognition of the subjective nature of all perception marks the really decisive breach with any theory of art which believed in the possibility of embodying absolutes, *eternal verities,* in great enduring works. As such, the Naturalists were the first conscious *existentialists* in the realm of aesthetics. (The link from Kierkegaard to his fellow Scandinavian Ibsen is only too clear, although Ibsen was at pains to stress that he had "read little and understood less" of Kierkegaard. Mere awareness of the debate around Kierkegaard must have been enough to acquaint him with the essence of his ideas. While denying that Kierkegaard had been the model for Brand, Ibsen added: "But, of course, the depiction of a man whose sole aim in life is to realize his ideals will always bear a certain resemblance to Kierkegaard's life.") There is no contradiction between the ruthless pursuit of truth, observed, scientifically tested, *experimental* truth on the one hand; and the continual awareness of a subjective point of view on the part of the observer on the other. Indeed, the notion that the observer's subjectivity will always have to be reckoned with is the hallmark of a truly scientific attitude. Zola used the term *"document humain"* to show that any truthful description of human experience, however subjective, also has an objective value as a contribution to man's knowledge of himself. Hence Strindberg's violent denunciation of the tyranny of women over men could be seen as equally valid as Shaw's passionate advocacy of the rights of women. Each one of these dramatists was ruthlessly truthful, precisely *because* he gave the fullest possible expression to nature seen through *his* temperament.

From this acceptance of the individual's point of view there followed also the rejection of any ethical absolutes, the denial of the notion that it was art's purpose to propagate the accepted moral code. "The idealists," says Zola, "pretend that it is necessary to lie in order to be moral, the naturalists assert that one cannot be moral outside the truth. . . . " Truthfulness, accuracy of observation and the courage to confront the results of this observation thus became the only moral absolutes for the artist.

And this is the impulse which still inspires the literature

of today—as indeed it does all the other arts. It is the impulse that has led to abstract painting as much as to the Theatre of the Absurd. Once it is realized that the view of Naturalism as a mere attempt to create photographic reproductions of external reality is a very superficial one; and that, indeed, the essence of the Naturalists' endeavor was an existential, value-free, scientific and experimental exploration of reality in its widest possible sense (including the subjective reality of the artist's temperament through which he perceives external reality); and that this approach logically led to the rejection of all ready-made formal conventions and implied the acceptance of organic form dictated by the nature of the subject matter—all else follows.

Admittedly, the earliest Naturalists did not all have the ability or the desire to follow the theoretical implications of their views to their logical conclusions. Zola's own *Thérèse Raquin* had more in common with a well-made play à la Dumas *fils* than with later naturalist drama (while its basic melodramatic image, the paralyzed observer unable to communicate his knowledge of a crime to his visitors, comes directly from that arch-romantic novel by Dumas *père, The Count of Monte Cristo*); and Ibsen's great social dramas used the stage technique of Sardou, while Shaw openly proclaimed his determination to emply the convention of popular drama to put over modern ideas in a play like *You Never Can Tell.* But who, on the other hand, would doubt that Ibsen's later symbolic myths were the direct and logical development of his determination to explore his own inner, as well as objective external, reality, and that Strindberg's dream plays did not continue the impulse behind his naturalistic explorations of society and its hypocrisies.

As early as 1887 Georg Brandes had pointed out that Zola himself constantly invested the nature he was describing and exploring with symbolic, mythical significance, that in fact his naturalism took far more from Zola's own poetic temperament, his way of looking at the world, than from the mere transcription of external phenomena. Art, unlike experimental science, deals with a reality which includes the *emotional* reaction of the observer; even the most prosaic object, when seen in a human context, becomes a symbol: Hedda Gabler's pistols, Solness' church tower, Hedwig Ekdal's wild duck transform themselves into images of inner, psychological realities, become the embodiments of dreams and dark desires. It is often said that Naturalism soon lost its impact because its main practitioners turned to symbolism and new-romanticism. This is true only insofar as the dramatists concerned—Ibsen, Strindberg, Hauptmann—followed their initial impulse to its logical consequences. In Hauptmann's *Hannele,* the sick child's dream vision leads us straight from the ultra-naturalist environment of a workhouse into the poetic world of neo-romantic visions of the Savior surrounded by angels. Likewise Strindberg, in *The Ghost Sonata* or *To Damascus,* merely translated the psychological situation of the chief character of a play like *The Father* into a direct, concrete image of his nightmares and obsessions. Oscar Wilde's *Salomé* (1892) and Hugo von Hofmannsthal's *Elektra* (1903) are both clearly derived from Naturalism in their ruthless determination to delve into the

depths of human nature, yet at the same time they also bear the mark of aestheticism and neo-romanticism. Max Reinhardt, the greatest of the neo-romantic directors, had first excelled as the interpreter of the Naturalists, and can be regarded as one of the founders of the truly naturalist style of acting by his creation of the *Kammerspiele,* a chamber theatre specially designed for intimate dialogue and subtle psychological effects (1907). Quite analogously, Stanislavski also subsequently developed his style towards neo-romanticism and invited Gordon Craig to direct a highly stylized neo-romantic *Hamlet* (1912). "The theory of environment ends where the subconscious starts," Stanislavski declared—in other words, the naturalism of external reality merges into the dreamlike reality of man's inner life.

This, of course, is not to say that symbolism, neo-romanticism, or the expressionism which Strindberg's dream plays had inspired, are styles *identical* with Naturalism in its accepted sense. It is merely to draw attention to the fact that once the basic position of the Naturalists had been reached a *new phase* of art history had begun, a phase in which the same basic impulse carried all before it, so that—as Otto Brahm had predicted—new vistas quite naturally opened up at bends in the road, and the wayfarers travelling on it naturally entered a succession of new landscapes: Ibsen, who had consciously chosen the path of realism with *Pillars of Society* ("I believe I may say with certainty that we shall both be satisfied with this play of mine. It is modern in all respects and completely in tune with the times. . . . " (Letter to Frederik Hegel, Ibsen's publisher, July 29, 1877—six years after Zola's *Thérèse Raquin*) almost imperceptibly turned into a symbolist; Hauptmann into a neo-romantic; and Strindberg gradually evolved from a ruthless Naturalist (*Miss Julie* was subtitled 'A Naturalistic Tragedy') into the first Expressionist; and at the end of *The Cherry Orchard* even Chekhov, the most rigorous Naturalist, could not resist introducing that famous, mysterious symbolic sound like the breaking of a string.

This line of evolution was dictated not only by the logic behind the basic philosophical concept that had inspired the Naturalist movement, but also by the parallel logic of the development of the *organic form* which, of necessity, had to adapt itself to its subject matter. Zola, Becque, Ibsen still followed in varying degrees the formal pattern of the well-made, social melodrama of the Parisian Boulevard. Yet with the gradual implementation of the underlying theory, with its rejection of intrigue and artificial shape, dramatists came closer to fulfilling Jean Jullien's slogan that drama should become a *tranche de vie*—a slice of life. It was Hauptmann who perfected this new technique in plays like *The Weavers* and *Florian Geyer.* Each act of these massive dramas became a series of loosely connected snapshots, with characters emerging from the crowd and then sinking back into it, half-finished episodes out of which the total mosaic gradually coalesced. These plays could dispense with the old division of the cast into heroes and supporting actors. *The Weavers* has no hero; its principal character is the mass of Silesian weavers, just as the subject of the play is not the fate of one man, but that of a whole social class. This is the multi-focal technique of playwriting which was also used with such immense effect by Gorky in *The Lower Depths* (triumphantly produced by both Stanislavski and Reinhardt) and by Chekhov. (Elmer Rice's *Street Scene,* Saroyan's *The Time of Your Life* and O'Neill's *The Iceman Cometh* fall within the same category. O'Neill is, of course, also a notable example of the closeness of naturalistic and the expressionistic impulse; his development closely parallels that of Strindberg).

This multi-focal snapshot technique makes the playwright concentrate on a single static segment of *time.* Hauptmann tended to build his plays in this style from a sequence of such static pictures. But he was also aware that there might be subjects requiring a completely different approach. In a note dated August 9, 1912, he remarked: "The modern dramatist, being a biologist, may sometimes strive for a drama which, like a house, a work of architecture, stands still in one spot without moving from its position. Or he may have cause to comprehend life in a horizontal direction, having already grasped it in the vertical. He might prefer the *epic flow* of life to its *dramatic stasis.* The true biologist will not want to do without either of these two possibilities of form. . . . " Here Hauptmann already clearly anticipates Brecht's idea of an epic theatre, in which the loving depiction of minute detail gives way to the swift flow of action in a horizontal direction through time. That Brecht's concept of the theatre as a sociological laboratory also stems from the original impulse of the Naturalists' experimental concept hardly needs to be stressed. His demand for a theatre that would be able to deal with reality in an age of science very closely resembles Zola's original manifesto. Equally, Brecht's view that drama should be used to stimulate thinking in the audience has much in common with Hauptmann's view—noted down in 1912—that "drama as literature is not so much the ready-made result of thought as the *thinking process* itself. It is the living presentation of the socially-manifested content of consciousness. From this it follows that none of the truths it presents can lay claim to final, absolute, self-contained validity. Each is valid only insofar as it is conditioned by the inner drama." (I.e., the particular conception of a particular poet's consciousness of a particular event.)

Hauptmann saw the dramatist as a biologist; Zola took his basic concepts from the physiologist Claude Bernard. It is surely no coincidence that George Buechner (1813-1837), the greatest forerunner of naturalistic drama, who inspired both Hauptmann and Brecht, was a physiologist, that Brecht had started as a medical student and that both Chekhov and Schnitzler were practicing physicians. Arthur Schnitzler (1862-1931), another great dramatist (far too little known in the English-speaking world) who wrote both in a strictly naturalistic and in a neo-romantic style, also used drama as a means of exploration—of depth psychology. His series of dialogues, *Reigen* (1896), was the first attempt to put the sexual act on the stage and to illustrate, with bitter irony and sparkling wit, the extent to which the purely physiological side of sex is overshadowed by social ambition, snobbery and the struggle for domination. Sigmund Freud himself regarded Schnitzler as a kind of double of himself, a co-discoverer of the world of the sub-conscious. On the occasion of Schnitzler's sixtieth birthday he wrote to him:

> . . . again and again, in looking into your creations, I have thought to find, behind the make-believe of fiction, the same endeavors, interests and results, that I knew to have been my own. Your determinism as well as your skepticism—what people call pessimism—your being captivated by the truths of the unconscious, of the instinctive nature of man, your disruption of the safe assumptions of love and death, all this has always struck me with an uncanny familiarity . . . Thus I gained the impression that not by intuition—but, in fact, by subtle self-observation—you came to know all that which I have uncovered through painstaking work on other people. Yes, I believe, fundamentally you are a psychological depth explorer, as honestly unprejudiced as any . . . (Freud, Letter to Schnitzler, May 14, 1922).

Among the explorations which Schnitzler undertook was one of the earliest examples of a work of literature which consisted entirely of the thoughts and feelings of an individual—*monologue intérieur.* This was Naturalism pressed to its utmost consequence—nature as perceived in and through a single temperament, an attempt to encompass the totality of the existential process of a human being. Schnitzler's novella *Leutnant Gustl* (1901)—the thoughts of a young officer compelled to commit suicide by a ridiculous "affair of honor"—marks, among other things, a point of contact between the novel and the drama. (In his essay *Le naturalisme au théâtre* Zola had deplored the fact that "an increasingly deep gulf " had opened up between the novel and the drama). For the very fact of being couched in the form of a monologue—a soliloquy—turned the short story into a dramatic representation of reality: the reader was made to *witness* a sequence of events *as it happens* rather than being told about it as a past event. Here again the Naturalists' rejection of rigid categories and preordained forms had led to a creative merging of ancient distinctions. The internal monologue was to become one of the main forms of the vast literature of introspection which arose in the 20th century.

Leutnant Gustl was only one of the earliest examples of internal monologue; the very first came from France: Edouard Dujardin's short novel *Les Lauriers sont coupés* (1887), which James Joyce regarded as the model for his own use of internal monologue in *Ulysses* and *Finnegans Wake.* Here, then, is another direct link between the Naturalists and the avant-garde literature of introspection, dream and fantasy which culminated in Surrealism and the Theatre of the Absurd. Again, as in the case of the link between the Naturalists and neo-romantics, the connection is narrow, organic and initially so gradual as to amount to an imperceptible merging. Joyce started as an admirer of Ibsen, he learned Norwegian to read Ibsen in the original, his first works of fiction were meticulously observed slices of life; the step from the careful description of external reality to the plan to encompass not only the exterior but also the interior of the hero's life was logical and inevitable.

In the French novel, and in the wake of Dujardin, and certainly by the same inner logic, Proust's monumental at-tempt to capture the process of time through his hero's consciousness also led to an *internalization* of the concept of reality: the same scenes, the same people appear differ-ently to an eager young, and a disillusioned middle-aged, Marcel. And this, again, is a process entirely analogous to the subjective vision behind Strindberg's *To Damascus, A Dream Play* and *Ghost Sonata.* Antonin Artaud directed Strindberg's *Dream Play* in 1928. Arthur Adamov derived his inspiration for his first absurdist plays from Strindberg as well as from Artaud himself; and Samuel Beckett's dra-matic *oeuvre* forms part of a wider exploration of the inner world of the internal monologue closely related to the ideas and the example of James Joyce. Thus we can ob-serve the initial impulse behind the Naturalist revolution spreading, and still active, in the manifold manifestations of contemporary theatre.

However revolutionary the ideas of the early Naturalists may have been, they saw themselves as part of a tradition. Zola proclaimed that "Naturalism is Diderot, Rousseau, Balzac and twenty others." He even regarded Homer as a naturalist and consciously emulated Homeric passages. Taine, who admired English literature, derived many of the ideas which later inspired Zola from the English realis-tic social novel of the 18th and early 19th century. In Ger-many the dramatists of the *Sturm und Drang* period (Lenz, Zacharias Werner, Klinger) as well as the early Goethe and Schiller must clearly be regarded as forerun-ners of Naturalism; and so must Kleist and Buechner, Grabbe and Hebbel. In Russia, Gogol, Tolstoy, Dos-toyevsky and Ostrovsky exercised a powerful and decisive influence on Chekhov and Stanislavski, Gorky and Leonid Andreyev. In the English-speaking theatre, T. W. Robert-son's *Caste* (1867) must be regarded as a forerunner of the realism of Shaw and Granville-Barker.

The coming of the Naturalist revolution was inevitable. It was an expression of the *Zeitgeist*—the rapid industrial-ization of Europe and North America, the growth of sci-ence, the impact of Darwinism and positivism, and the consequent collapse of old certainties and established faiths. What the early pioneers and theoreticians of Natu-ralism achieved was no more than the systematization and clear, programmatic expression of the spirit of their age. Nevertheless, the effect was overwhelming—a feeling of excitement, of liberation. And it was this excitement which released the most valuable element in the Naturalist revolution: by opening up a vast new field of subject mat-ter, by removing age-old inhibitions and taboos, by de-stroying time-honored rules and recipes for writing dia-logue and structuring plot, Naturalism opened the flood-gates for a stream of new poetic possibilities in the theatre. Whatever their ideas, their social purpose, their political commitment may have been, the great Naturalists— Ibsen, Strindberg, Shaw, Hauptmann, Chekhov, Gorky, Schnitzler—must ultimately be judged as great poets, poets of a new kind: for they discovered the magic that lies behind the seemingly commonplace surface of ordinary life, the tragic greatness of simple people, the poetry of si-lences and reticences, the bitter ironies of unspoken thoughts: Mrs. Alving hearing the ghosts of the past in the next room; the old drunken doctor, Chebutykin, washing

his hands in the night of the fire in *Three Sisters;* the "Baron's" barely articulate account of his life in *The Lower Depths*—these are examples of a poetry *of* the stage, a poetry arising out of, and entirely in tune with, an indus-trialized, urbanized society and the image of man which it had created. To have bridged the gulf between literature and theatre, which had opened up so disastrously in the middle of the 19th century, to have restored the dignity of the theatre not only as an art but also as an instrument of serious thought and enquiry and to have created a new kind of poetry—these are the true achievements of the early Naturalists. The contemporary theatre, to a very large extent, still draws its impetus and energy from their ideas, their courage, their liberating influence. (pp. 67-76)

Martin Esslin, "Naturalism in Context," in The Drama Review, *Vol. 13, No. 2, Winter, 1968, pp. 67-76.*

Raymond Williams

[*Williams was an English educator, author, and critic whose literary theory is informed by his socialist ideology and his belief that a reader's perception of literature is directly related to cultural attitudes which are subject to change over the course of time. As a literary critic, Wil-liams is best known for* Modern Tragedy *(1958), which asserts that modern tragedy derives from the inadequa-cies of social systems rather than weaknesses of charac-ter, as in classical tragedy. In the following essay, he traces the reasons why Naturalism failed to have a sig-nificant impact on nineteenth-century English theater.*]

THREE SENSES OF NATURALISM

There are three relevant senses of 'naturalism', and of the associated 'naturalist' and 'naturalistic'. The first, and most popular, indicates a method of 'accurate' or 'lifelike' reproduction. The second, and historically earliest, indi-cates a philosophical position allied to science, natural his-tory and materialism. The third, and most significant in the history of drama, indicates a movement in which the method of accurate production and the specific philosoph-ical position are organically and usually consciously fused.

The first sense began in English around 1850, mainly in relation to painting and especially landscape painting. Thus [in the *Oxford English Dictionary*]: 'the mannerism of the Italians, and the naturalism of the Flemish painters' (1852); 'the Gothic naturalism advancing gradually from the Byzantine severity' (1853); 'the Naturalist-landscape school, a group of painters who threw overboard the tradi-tions of Turner' (1893). There was a common association of such a method with simplicity of attitude—'a natural-ism without afterthought' (1850)—and, through the asso-ciation with 'nature' and 'natural', of subject.

The second sense was already more generally established. It began in the late sixteenth century in a form of con-scious opposition, or at least distinction, between revealed (divine) and observed (human) knowledge, and was used in close association with accusations of atheism: 'atheists or men . . . who will admit of nothing but Morality, but Naturalismes, and humane reason' (1641); 'those blasphe-mous truth-opposing Heretikes, and Atheisticall naturalists' (1612). With growing confidence from the seventeenth through to the nineteenth centuries it acquired the more positive associations of a method and practice and body of knowledge, in natural history and the natural sciences. 'Naturalist' in this sense became neutral, but 'naturalism' was still a doctrine in which there was appeal to and reliance on natural laws, forces and explanations, as distinct from and eventually consciously opposed to 'supernaturalism', and also in which, in matters of morality, there was appeal to and reliance on human reason and a (secular) natural law.

The third sense, in specific application to a particular kind of novel or play, and thence to a literary movement, appeared in French in the late 1860s and is common in English from the 1880s. Its relations with the two earlier senses are complex. On the one hand its conscious linkage of literary method with scientific method and with the laws of natural history was sharp, distinct and at times aggressive. On the other hand, in very general tendencies in fiction and drama before this period, many steps in this linkage had been practically taken. The link between painting and science had been made by Constable [in his *Fourth Lecture at the Royal Institution,* 1836]:

> Painting is a science, and should be pursued as an inquiry into the laws of nature. Why, then, may not landscape painting be considered as a branch of natural philosophy, of which pictures are but the experiments?

This was indeed the landscape-painting which had attracted the apparently simple technical term 'naturalist'. More generally, since the early eighteenth century, in plays and novels, there had been a practical reliance on a secular human dimension, in action, description and interpretation. Bourgeois literature, with increasing confidence, was in a distinguishing sense, by comparison with earlier literature, secular and social; an explicitly or implicitly metaphysical dimension was steadily and in the end without argument excluded. This is particularly evident in the drama, most clearly in bourgeois tragedy (from Lillo, *The London Merchant,* 1731), with its consciously secular, contemporary, social and socially extended emphasis, but it had many seventeenth-century precedents in prose comedy and in isolated examples of what would later be called 'domestic drama'. Within this powerful general movement towards a predominantly secular and social literature, many elements of 'naturalism' became habitual, but the conscious description awaited one further emphasis, in which the key term is 'environment'. It is one thing to present character and action in exclusively secular and social terms. It is or can be quite another to see and to show character and action as determined or profoundly influenced by environment, either natural or social. The novelty of the naturalist emphasis was its demonstration of the *production* of character or action by a powerful natural or social environment. This is radically distinct from exemplifications of 'permanent' human characteristics in an accurately reproduced natural or social 'setting'. The intellectual basis for the new emphasis is then a sense of historical production, both in the social sense that character is determined or profoundly influenced by its social environment, with the later and more penetrating observation

that this social environment is itself historically produced, and in the wider sense of natural history, in the evolution of human nature itself within a natural world of which it is an interacting part. The theory of naturalism, in fiction and drama, is then a conscious presentation of human character and action *within* a natural and social environment. It is a specific culmination of a long tendency of bourgeois theory and practice. It only ceases to be bourgeois (and then, strictly, ceases to be naturalism) when, as in Marxist theory, action is seen not only within an environment but as itself, within certain limits and pressures, producing an environment.

Relations between the first and third senses of 'naturalism', in descriptions of works of art, are then inevitably complex. In popular and semi-professional usage naturalism means no more than accurate or lifelike reproduction of a character, an action or a scene. In a stricter historical use naturalism is an artistic method in which a particular environment is reproduced, of course as accurately and fully as possible, not because it is an observed feature but because it is a causal or symptomatic feature. Naturalism in the first sense is a general product of a bourgeois secular tendency, with its preference for a practical and recognisable everyday world. Naturalism in the third sense is the extension to art of the philosophical positions originally described as 'naturalism', in a conscious reliance on observed natural history and on human reason. Dramatic naturalism in the first sense can be plausibly related, but with complications that we shall notice, to developments in the means of production of physical theatrical effects. Dramatic naturalism in the third sense can never be so reduced, since it does not reproduce a physical feature or environment because it is technically available or interesting, but because such features and environments are integral parts of the dramatic action, indeed, in a true sense, are themselves actors and agencies.

It is a curiosity of dramatic history that naturalism, in the third sense, was relatively weak in England, by comparison with France, Scandinavia and Russia. Indeed, paradoxically, it was only after naturalism in the first sense had been modified that there were significant naturalist plays, in the third sense, in English. This is at first sight very surprising, since the intellectual movements which led to conscious naturalism were especially strong in England. The purest doctrine of the production of character by environment was that of Robert Owen, from as early as 1815. The most influential exponent of natural history as the production of human nature was, of course, Darwin. If anywhere, it might then seem, conscious naturalism would be developed it would be in England, and indeed the case can be positively argued in the development of English painting and the English novel. In the drama, however, the case is quite otherwise, and the specific reasons for this need careful examination.

PHYSICAL REPRODUCTION IN THE THEATRE

Limited to the first sense of naturalism, the history of 'lifelike' reproduction on the English stage has often been traced. It is worth looking at the main elements of this history, both for their own sake and for the light they throw on the limitations of any merely technical definition of naturalism.

'The modern stage affects reality infinitely beyond the proper objects of dramatic representations', complained an observer in 1827 [J. Boaden, in his *Memoirs of Mrs. Siddons*]. This was no sudden development. The indoor theatres, from the Restoration, had developed more and more complicated and effective types of painted scenery, but in the turn from the eighteenth to the nineteenth century there was a further decisive change. This can be summarised as the development of the 'set scene' from the system of scenic mobility which had dominated the eighteenth-century theatre. A crucial element in this was the steady reduction and eventual abolition of the apron-stage. This, together with the elaboration of backcloths and profiles as an alternative to moveable flats and wings, made the stage at once more integrated, more static and more enclosed. It was not until much later in the century, after prolonged controversy about the old kind of proscenium doors, that the fully enclosed picture-frame stage was established. The first was perhaps the Gaiety of 1869, but a description of the new Haymarket, in 1880 [by P. Fitzgerald, in his *The World Behind the Scenes*], makes the point:

> A rich and elaborate gold border, about two feet broad, after the pattern of a picture frame, is continued all round the proscenium, and carried even below the actor's feet. There can be no doubt the sense of illusion is increased, and for the reason just given; the actors seem cut off from the domain of prose; there is no borderland or platform in front; and, stranger still, the whole has the air of a picture projected on a surface.

The whole development thus achieved points forward, certainly, to major features of the naturalist drama: in particular its specific central feature of the stage as a room. It points forward also, interestingly, to film and television drama: 'a picture projected on a surface'. Yet the dramatic intentions within this development have an ambiguous relation to naturalism. Vestris and Mathews, at the Olympic between 1831 and 1838, were perhaps the first to develop the drawing-room stage, and a reviewer noted that the 'more perfect enclosure gives the appearance of a private chamber, infinitely better than the old contrivance of wings'. Moreover, in a further innovation, these rooms were fully furnished, including floors and 'walls'. But the plays performed in them, usually adapted French short comedies, were hardly concerned with the 'lifelike', and a sense of luxury rather than accuracy seems to have been the main staging motive. The wider development of technical means for more 'realistic' production is at an even greater distance from naturalism. Indeed, in all its early phases, technical innovation was primarily for spectacle. It is often asserted that naturalistic staging owed much to the introduction of gas-lighting, which was getting into theatres by 1820. Yet the main use of the new lighting was for new spectacular effects, such as sunrise dispersing early mist. Indeed one of its most powerful applications, burning lime in a gas-jet to produce limelight, became almost synonymous with a new kind of spectacle, and was extensively used in the development of melodrama. Per-

haps the most interesting, because intermediate, case is the development of technical staging for historical productions and in particular for the staging of Shakespeare. Elsewhere the new means of production made for increased spectacle; here, while spectacle remained as an intention, there was also an emphasis on 'correctness' of setting. This is evident as early as Planché's work for Kemble in the 1820s and is best known from Kean's 'antiquarian' productions in the 1850s. The interest in 'historical accuracy', and its intended priority over what Kean distinguished as 'theatrical effect', has something genuinely in common with elements of naturalism. What is intended is a *reconstructed* environment, and, as in the case of the historical novel, with its formative effects on the novel of social realism, this is a transitional phase towards the presentation of a specific physical environment as symptomatic or causal. Nevertheless, the very sense of historical reconstruction, looking backward, characteristically, to more splendidly clothed and furnished times, worked in the opposite direction, against the contemporary environment outside the theatre, which was to be a decisive influence in naturalism.

It was in the 1870s that the fully enclosed box-set began to be used to replace wings, flats and back-cloths, in close relation, of course, to the fully enclosed picture-frame

Theodore Dreiser, circa 1908.

stage. This provided a technical means for one of the central conventions of naturalism: the stage as an enclosed room. Yet even in this development, as in technical developments throughout the century, dramatic intentions remained variable. Spectacular illusion was as common as naturalistic illusion; or, to put it another way, even the motive for much naturalistic illusion was spectacular: the impressive reproduction of a 'real' environment, for its own sake rather than as an integral dramatic agency. This allows us to recall that in the theatre as in any other area of cultural technology, the doctrine of technological determinism—the creation of a form seen as determined by technical development; naturalism as the consequence of improvements in stage-carpentry—is false. And this in turn allows us to see the distinction, so decisive in the history of the drama, between naturalism as a technique among others, a particular staging effect among other varieties of spectacle, and naturalism as a dramatic form, in which the production or reproduction of a social environment, symptomatic or causal, is not just the setting for an action but is part of the action itself.

CHANGING SOCIAL RELATIONS IN DRAMA AND THEATRE

One dimension especially excluded by merely technical accounts of the development of naturalism is that of social relationships in the theatre. This is an especially significant exclusion in the case of English nineteenth-century theatre, where the changes in social relationships, in the course of the century, were radical.

We can distinguish three periods: that before 1830; from 1830 to 1860; and from 1860 to 1914. In the first period there was a completion of the long process, traceable from around 1700, in which the theatre moved back towards a more popular audience. This is not, in spite of some accounts, the entry of the 'mob' into the theatres. On the contrary it was the narrowing of the theatre audience which preceded this movement, from the 1620s to the 1690s and reaching a point of extreme class selectivity in the Restoration theatre, which was the novel phenomenon. In the course of the eighteenth century the audience broadened again, as well as increasing. In 1600 there had been some six successful theatres in London; in 1700, after the narrowing of the Restoration, there were only two. By 1750 there were again seven theatres in London, and a growing number of established theatres in the provinces. This process is usually summarised as the return of the middle class to the theatres. But social classes are not immortal, and the new eighteenth-century playgoers were in fact a new class: the greatly extended middle and lower-middle class of the developing cities: in a modern sense, a bourgeoisie. Until the end of the eighteenth century this was much more evident in London than elsewhere, for it was there that the explosive growth of a new kind of city had begun. By the beginning of the nineteenth century this urban bourgeoisie and petit-bourgeoisie had in effect taken over the London theatres, and a similarly 'popular' audience had become the mainstay of the multiplying provincial theatres. Many of the internal changes in theatre structure—the pit driving back the apron stage, the conversion of upper galleries to boxes—were directly related to this at once growing and changing audience. The Old

Price riots at Covent Garden in 1809 are only the most striking among many manifestations of these class tensions and changes. 'Polite society', as it called itself, was in effect first invaded, then driven from the pit to boxes, then driven out altogether. This made the tension between the monopoly patent theatres, established under Restoration conditions to restrict serious drama to minority audiences, and the so-called 'minor theatres', pushing up everywhere, using every device and exploiting every ambiguity of definition, very much more severe. In the period before 1830, 'minor theatres' such as the Lyceum, the Haymarket and the Adelphi were only nominally distinguishable from the old patent theatres, Covent Garden and Drury Lane, while south of the Thames, especially at Astley's and Surreyside, the 'transpontine theatre', more open, more popular and more spectacular in style, was serving new audiences.

The inevitable happened. A repeal of the monopoly legislation passed the House of Commons in that classic year of middle-class triumph, 1832, but was thrown out by the House of Lords. In 1843 the law was finally changed. Covent Garden, in 1847, became an opera house, with a more fashionable audience. Drury Lane became the centre of spectacles. The majority development of the English theatre went on in the middle-class theatres, which grew from seven in 1800 to nineteen in 1850. Astley's became the Royal, Surreyside the Olympic. In outlying districts new large theatres were opened, and from the 1840s the music-halls began their extraordinary development, both taking over variety from the minor theatres which had now moved up to drama and providing newly organised entertainment for the vastly growing population of the city. London had grown from just over a million to over two and a half millions in the first half of the century. The industrial cities now followed the same patterns. In this period, between 1830 and 1860, the theatre, like the press and publishing, became open, varied and in its own forms vigorous. It could have gone in any of a number of ways.

What actually happened in the third period, after 1860, is again characteristic of general developments in the culture. There was an even faster rate of growth, but new dividing lines appeared between the 'respectable' and the 'popular', and at the respectable end there was an integration of middle-class and fashionable audiences and tastes. This integration, decisive in so many areas, had marked effects in the theatre. The 'popular' audience was now, in the new terms of an urban industrial society, largely working-class and lower middle-class, but on the whole they were not in the theatres, except on special occasions; they were in the music-halls. In the theatres what was happening was the process usually described as making theatre 'respectable' again: a process which included putting carpets and seats into the old pit; serving more discreet refreshments; altering times to fit with other social engagements. In the Restoration theatre there had been early afternoon performances, for the Court and its circle. Through the eighteenth century the time was steadily moved towards the evening, when people could attend after business and work. Early nineteenth-century performances usually began at six and went on four or five hours: an entire night out at the theatre. From the 1860s the time was moved to eight o'clock, and the performance ended at about eleven: largely to allow for dinner and supper engagements on either side. Matinées came in, for a new kind of leisured audience. What we now think of as West End theatre was established.

This social change must be remembered within the impressive statistics of growth. The whole point of the newly respectable integration was that it offered to be self-recruiting; it was socially inclusive, at a given level of price, taste and behaviour, rather than categorically exclusive, as in an older kind of society. London grew from the two and a half millions of mid-century to six and a half millions by 1900. Internal transport, in railways, omnibuses, and eventually the underground both increased possible audiences and permitted the physical concentration of theatres. From the 1860s an extraordinary wave of building, rebuilding and refurnishing began. In 1850 there had been nineteen theatres; in 1900 there were sixty-one, as well as some forty music-halls. What we think of as the modern theatre and its audience—though it is not modern, since it pre-dates cinema, radio and television which were to cut it back again—had been more centrally and more solidly established than at any other time, before or since.

MELODRAMA

It is in relation to these connected social factors—changes in audiences and physical changes in the theatres—that we can begin to consider the development of dramatic forms. The first important problem, in a way just because it seems to be at the opposite pole from naturalism, is the case of melodrama which, at least in the first half of the nineteenth century, can be reasonably claimed to be the only significant formal innovation. Yet melodrama is an especially difficult 'form' to define.

Some elements of its development are clear. The original 'melodrama'—mime to music in France, dialogue intermissions with music in opera in Germany—was not widely imitated in England, and where it was, usually passed under other names, connected with other precedents. By the time that it was recognised as a form in England its connection with music was little more than incidental or indeed tactical (one of the effects of the restriction of 'legitimate' drama to the patent theatres was to encourage the minor theatres to describe plays as anything but plays; if the inclusion of a song or a mime would do the trick with the Licensing Office—the Lord Chamberlain—then managers and authors would try it). What really came through, under this title, was a new kind of sensational drama, with close connections with the popularity of the Gothic novel. Monk Lewis's *The Castle Spectre* (1797) is an early English example, among a flood of similar imports from Germany (especially Kotzebue) and France. If we correlate this development with the changes of audience already noted, we can see connections between the replacement of sentimental comedy by melodrama and the replacement of a relatively restricted and 'polite' audience by a more open and more vigorous 'popular' audience. Yet within this, and also overriding it, are more complex elements. In France the melodrama, in the sense of sensational drama, had become overtly political during the Revolu-

tion, especially in the 'Bastille' plays (Pixérécourt). These sensational plays of prison, tyranny and liberation became popular in adaptation in England, but their political element was excluded, in the period of danger before 1830, when censorship of a conscious political kind was extensive. The English 'prison' melodrama then became more purely sensational. A certain radicalism, nevertheless, was inseparable from all English popular culture between about 1820 and 1850; a close correlate was the new kind of Sunday paper, combining sensation, scandal and radical politics. Much of the subsequent development of English social drama, with obvious effects on the case of English naturalism, was affected by this linkage and by its many contradictions and ambiguities. On the one hand, within the restrictions imposed by the status of the minor theatres, there was a constant pressure on authors to avoid more traditional dramatic forms, and the internal habits of these theatres, trained to action and to spectacle rather than to sustained dialogue, increased this. While it is still a question of the simple sensational drama there are no difficult analytic problems. Indeed in one sense this was the heir of Renaissance drama, in most of its external elements, but with the supernatural losing its metaphysical dimension, and the exploring moral and social energy declined to stereotypes: a process most evident in the reduction of dramatic language to rhetoric and stereotype, carriers of the shell of the action, the living body dead inside it. Yet from the 1820s onwards there was a discernible attempt to put new content into this sensational form. This is the attempt at once recognised and exaggerated by the description 'radical melodrama'.

The significant case is that of Douglas Jerrold. He had made his name in 1829 with *Black-Ey'd Susan*: melodrama in the simple transitional sense: a plot of innocence in danger, of miraculous rescue, tied, characteristically, to a ballad (Gay's), and with some marginal consciousness of the poor man (the sailor) as exposed and victimised. It is significant that then, in 1832, Jerrold wrote two plays, *The Rent Day* and *The Factory Girl*, which were quite open attempts to dramatise a new social consciousness. *The Rent Day*, which has survived, is again transitional. Based on a picture by David Wilkie, which the opening tableau directly reproduces, it is a 'domestic drama' in which a farm-tenant suffers from an absentee landlord and a cheating steward: in this sense radical but assimilated to an older consciousness and an older kind of play. The absentee landlord, initially taken as the representative figure gambling away his rents, has returned in disguise to see what is happening; he exposes the dishonest steward. Thus the actual social tension, which was especially acute in the period when the play was written, is at once displaced—the agent substituting for the landlord as villain—and sensationalised, in that through the magic of disguised and providential authority a happy ending to what had in fact no ending is contrived. *The Factory Girl*, which we know only by report, has many features in common, but what happened to it is, in its way, a significant moment in nineteenth-century culture. This account is taken from the contemporary *Figaro in London*:

> Writers like Mr Jerrold deserve our gratitude as
> well as our admiration, for their aim is not mere-

ly to amuse, but to plead, through the medium of the stage, the cause of the poor and oppressed classes of society. Such is the author's object in *The Factory Girl,* in which he has drawn with lamentable truth the picture of a weaver's lot, which is to be the slave of the inhuman system of overworking in English factories, and too often a victim of the petty tyranny of those who are placed in authority over him . . . The story has interest and incident which would with the general good writing throughout the piece, and the quaint satirical humour of Harley's part, have carried off *The Factory Girl* triumphantly had it not been in some degree marred by the dénouement, in which letters were pulled out of bosoms, a labourer finds a brother in a rich merchant, and an extensive relationship is discovered among the principal characters. This comfortable arrangement for a happy ending naturally excited a smile which gave to the ill-natured a plea for sending forth their venomous breath in loud blackguard shouts of 'off' . . .

This can be read in more than one way: as confirming the tendency, as in *The Rent Day,* to solve the insoluble by the devices of the sensational drama; as evidencing an audience which was becoming critical of this; or, with the specification of the 'ill-natured', as an example of the cross-pressures of the period. The play was taken off after two nights and never printed. There may be many reasons, but the contrived ending is not likely to be one of them, since it was, indeed, standard practice. Jerrold himself was sure that it was the new theme of the victimised industrial worker which made the play unpopular.

It is now some six years since the writer of this paper essayed a drama, the purpose of which was an appeal to public sympathy in the cause of the Factory Children: the drama was very summarily condemned . . . The subject of the piece 'was low, distressing'. The truth is, it was not then *la mode* to affect an interest for the 'coarse and vulgar' details of human life, and the author suffered because he was two or three years before the fashion.

He refers to the subsequent success, in such subjects, of a 'lady writer', presumably Frances Trollope. The terms in which *The Factory Girl* was attacked may remind us of the arguments that raged around naturalism in the 1880s. Yet the history, again, is complex. There was nothing in the new naturalist or realist drama of the 1880s which, in terms of the vulgarity of low life or of the violence of events, was new to the English nineteenth-century theatre, and especially to the melodrama. There had been a long run of crime plays, from the stories of Maria Marten and Vidocq (both dramatised by Jerrold in the 1820s) through *The Factory Assassin* (Rayner, 1837), with a falsely accused mute, to the 'detective' plays beginning with Taylor's *The Ticket-of-Leave Man*—the appearance of the archetypical Hawkshaw—in 1863. Mayhew's *London Labour and London Poor* was dramatised, with the sub-title *Want and Vice*, at the Whitechapel Pavilion in 1860. Plays of city poverty and orphanage, including many adaptations of Dickens, were commonplace. In *Lost in London* (1867) a miner's wife was abducted by a wealthy London-

er, and there were scenes of contrast between Bleakmore Mine and a London champagne party. In Charles Reade's *It's Never Too Late To Mend* (1865) an actress dressed as a boy died on a meticulously staged treadmill (incidentally provoking a critic to get up in the theatre and shout 'Brutal realism'—one of the earliest examples of what was to become a standard phrase). Sexual or at least marital scandals were common after the success of *East Lynne* (1861) and *Lady Audley's Secret* (1862), the latter including a scene of the wife hitting her husband with an iron bar and pushing him down a well, though he reappears in the final scene. Moreover, to look at it another way, there was a certain radicalism in many of the most popular melodrama plots: wicked landlords seduced the daughters of tenants, foreclosed mortgages, turned mothers and children into the snow; wicked officers and other wealthy young men did their best to emulate them. It is possible, from these examples, to speak of the radical melodrama, with close connections to other elements of the new urban popular culture. What has then to be observed is a paradox: that elements of the social and moral consciousness which was to inform serious naturalism went mainly, in England, into the melodrama, which at the same time preserved, as the foundation of its conventions, providential notions of the righting of wrongs, the exposure of villainy, and the triumph or else the apotheosis of innocence. At the same time, as we shall see, the more naturalistic presentation of scenes, characters and actions moved in general away from themes based in a radical consciousness. The result was a muddle. Melodrama touched every nerve of nineteenth-century society, but usually only to play on the nerves and to resolve crisis in an external and providential dramatic world. Its methods became a byword for sensational exaggeration, against which the more blurred and muted tones of English domestic naturalism made their way with the false reputation of a more essential truth. But this is not simply an internal history of the forms. The changes already noted in the social character of the theatre, after 1860, including especially the split between a 'respectable' drama and 'popular' entertainment, prevented, on either hand, the emergence of any sustainable adequate form. Melodrama, which in its own way had got nearest to the crises of that dislocated, turbulent and cruel society, became, in the end, no more than sensational presentation and then, inevitably, a mode to be patronised or mocked.

DOMESTIC NATURALISM

It is orthodox to date the appearance of English naturalism from Robertson's *Caste* (1867), or perhaps the earlier *Society* (1865). But it is again a matter of definition. It is indeed a world away from melodrama. A preliminary definition might be comedy of manners with a consciously social topic. But then this does not begin with Robertson. Bulwer Lytton's *Money* (1840) is an obvious earlier example. Its plot involves the familiar scheming for an inheritance, and the readjustments of all the finer feelings after it is known where all the money has gone. In fact to come to *Money* after *The Plain Dealer* or *The Way of the World* is to feel a certain continuity, though its language and incident are firmly contemporary. Or take Jerrold's *Retired from Business* (1851), in which a greengrocer retires to the country and is persuaded by his wife, as a matter of prestige, to change his name from Pennyweight to Fitzpennyweight. The anxious snobbery of this (suburban) country society is mocked in the character of Creepmouse, who at any mention of the actual world can exclaim:

> Pumpkinfield is threatened with revolution. Retail marriage menaced at our firesides, and property barricaded with its own hearthstones.

To go from Bulwer Lytton or Jerrold to Robertson's *Society* is hardly to feel the breeze of innovation. The plot is a standard account of the *nouveaux riches* trying to buy their way into fashionable society, and making the conventional coarse errors. In minor ways it is a nineteenth-century world: one of the Chodds' schemes, to acquire influence, is to start a newspaper, or rather two newspapers: the *Morning* and the *Evening Earthquake*. In the end, after scheming and counter-scheming, Chodd Junior rejects 'blue blood' and would 'rather have it the natural colour'. But this does not prevent the play ending with the triumph of the impoverished barrister as Sir Sidney Daryl, Member of Parliament:

> Countrymen, &c, wave hats—band plays, &c.

Caste extends the social reference. An aristocratic officer courts the daughter of an unemployed and drunken workman; she is an actress. This outrages his mother, the Marquise. The girl, left with his child, becomes poor when he is reported killed in India and her father has spent the money left for her. But D'Alroy resurrects, the Marquise is reconciled, and the old workman, the only embarrassment, is pensioned off to drink himself to death in Jersey. Of course remarks are made about the silliness of 'caste' feeling when compared with the claims of true love, but to go from *Caste* or *Society* to the pushing world of mid-Victorian England, with its ready conversion of business fortunes into peerages, its movement of actresses into the old aristocracy, to say nothing of the general triumph of the new social integration of 'respectability', is to perceive a theatrical convention as impervious as anything in melodrama. It can then be said that the difference is the 'naturalness' of the dialogue, and it is true that the writing of *Society* and *Caste,* and for that matter of *Money* and *Retired from Business,* can be sharply contrasted with the exclamatory and incident-serving dialogue of, say, *Lady Audley's Secret.* In fact what is principally evident is a developed colloquialism at all but the critical points. Yet this again is not a novelty: *The Ticket-of-Leave Man,* slightly earlier, has more sustained colloquial speech, with less edge of caricature, within its 'melodramatic' plot. (Indeed it is an irony that the only words widely remembered from the play are the detective's, on emerging from disguise: 'Hawkshaw, the detective', which became a comic catchphrase. The speech of most of the play is the most sustained 'naturalism', in the popular sense, in the English nineteenth-century theatre.)

What then is new in Robertson? It is naturalism in the most technical sense: that of the 'lifelike' stage. There were, as we have seen, precedents for this, in Vestris and Mathews and in the 'archaeological' productions. But Robertson fixed the form, in the new theatres and the new staging of the 1860s. The changes in the social character

of the theatre helped him: single-play evenings, at the new later hours; longer runs. The technical means had only to be brought together, in an integrated production of an 'enclosed' play. It is in this exact sense that it is true to say that Robertson invented stage-management, and indeed invented the modern figure of the producer or director, impressing an overall atmosphere and effect. Styles of acting were modified to fit into this general effect, and the plays, in a real sense, are scripts for these productions, in a way that has since become very familiar. Robertson's detailed stage-directions are the most obvious evidence of this kind of integrated production, and the motive is undoubtedly, as in all technical definitions of naturalism, the 'appearance (illusion) of reality': 'the ivy to be real ivy, and the grass to be grass matting—not painted'. In local ways these effects of environment are intended to be symptomatic: 'holding out kettle at arm's length. Hawtree looks at it through eyeglass', in a familiar contrast of social habits. But the informing consciousness is always illustrative, and naturalism of this kind is properly described in terms of 'setting' or 'background'. The distinction that then matters can be explored by comparing this kind of reproduction of a known and recognisable environment with the superficially similar production of a symptomatic or causal environment in high naturalism: for example, the room and the garret beyond it in Ibsen's *The Wild Duck;* the trapped interior of Strindberg's *The Father;* or the social presence and social history of the orchard in Chekhov's *The Cherry Orchard.* It is not only, though it is also, a matter of dramatic reach and scale. It is a question of a way of perceiving physical and social environment, not as setting or background through which, by other conventions, of providence, goodwill, freedom from prejudice, the characters may find their own ways. In high naturalism the lives of the characters have soaked into their environment. Its detailed presentation, production, is thus an additional dramatic dimension, often a common dimension within which they are to an important extent defined. Moreover, the environment has soaked into the lives. The relations between men and things are at a deep level interactive, because what is there physically, as a space or a means for living, is a whole shaped and shaping social history. It is characteristic that the actions of high naturalism are often struggles against this environment, of attempted extrication from it, and more often than not these fail. The prenaturalist conventions of providential escape or of resolution through recognition fall away in the face of this sombre assessment of the weight of the world: not a world which is a background, nor an illustrative setting; but one which has entwined itself in the deepest layers of the personality. It is this practice which makes sense of Strindberg's argument [in his *On Modern Drama and Modern Theatre,* 1889]:

> Naturalism is not a dramatic method like that of Becque, a simple photography which includes everything, even the speck of dust on the lens of the camera. That is realism; a method lately exalted to art, a tiny art which cannot see the wood for the trees. That is the false naturalism, which believes that art consists simply of sketching a piece of nature in a natural manner: but it is not the true naturalism, which seeks out those points

in life where the great conflicts occur, which rejoices in seeing what cannot be seen every day.

There is room for confusion, here, between 'naturalism' and 'realism', especially since later distinctions, of a comparable kind, have usually reversed the terms. But the central point is evident, and the reference to 'conflict' clarifies it. This view of a shaping physical environment and a shaping social environment is the intellectual legacy of the new natural history and the new sociology of the nineteenth century. Whatever the variations of subsequent attitude, among individual dramatists, this absolute sense of real limits and pressures—in physical inheritance, in types of family and social relationship, in social institutions and beliefs—is common and preoccupying. To produce these limits and pressures, in actually staged environments, was the common aim of the varied and brilliant period of dramatic experiment which this sombre consciousness provoked. Even where, eventually, the struggles and conflicts became internal, as in early expressionism, they were still between the physical limits and pressures of a shaped and shaping natural and social world, and the determined sense of a self, a possible self, which could try to get beyond them, though it usually failed.

It is hardly necessary to say that, set beside high naturalism, what became known as naturalism in the English theatre, after Robertson, is of another and much smaller dimension. But to follow the argument through we must look at what happened after Robertson, in the confident theatres of late Victorian and then Edwardian society.

NATURALISM AND THE PROBLEM PLAY

The key to an interpretation of the development of English drama between Robertson and the end of the century is the social character of the West End theatre, newly established in this form in the same period. Its audience, as we have seen, was not 'aristocratic' or even 'fashionable'; it was an integrated middle-class audience, in what was now at once a metropolitan and an imperial capital. But then, as in other areas of the culture of the period, and especially in those closely dependent on institutions (from parliament and education to the theatre) the dominant tones were those of an assumed and admired class: 'Society'. This is a radically different situation from theatres with a direct court or aristocratic linkage, notably the Restoration theatre, in which actions, audience and writers were, however narrowly, socially integrated. In the late Victorian theatre, to put it crudely, a largely middle class audience was spellbound by an image of 'fashionable Society'; the theatres were among the principal agencies for its display. Dramatists such as Henry Arthur Jones, originally a commercial traveller with a nonconformist upbringing, or Pinero, a legal apprentice and then an actor, were not of this displayed class but, like other theatre people, serving it and, as agents of the image, making their way into it. It is striking evidence of the prepotence of the display form that Jones and Pinero did not, as might have been supposed, succeed in writing bourgeois drama but what it was agreed to call 'Society drama'. It was not that they did not briefly try. Jones's *Saints and Sinners* (1884) grafted the problems of nonconformist dullness and respectability on to the old melodrama plot of the innocent girl seduced by a villainous officer and, though rescued, dying of a lost reputation. Pinero, in a late play, *The Thunderbolt* (1908) moved away from London society to a provincial (brewing) middle-class family; the play was found to be drab. In what was now overwhelmingly a bourgeois commercial society, the displacement represented by 'Society drama' would be almost incredible, were it not for the special character of the institutional cultural integration. It is instructive to go from Jones's *Saints and Sinners* to Stanley Houghton's *Hindle Wakes* (1912), not only because Houghton has moved into a bourgeois manufacturing world, but because Fanny Hawthorn, formal successor to the long line of compromised innocents (she has gone to Blackpool with the son of a rich manufacturer) refuses her conventional fate: he is not man enough for her to marry, she has had a good time and now she will make her own way. It is a generation later, of course, but the more significant difference is that the play developed and was produced outside the special atmosphere of the London theatre, in Miss Horniman's Repertory at Manchester. In its refreshing note of self-confidence it illuminates, by contrast, the extraordinary cultural subordination of the earlier bourgeois dramatists.

There is nothing difficult in the diagnosis of 'Society drama' as a form. It is the intrigue play moved up-stage, with strong scenes for display. What is more interesting is the interaction of this form with what became known as the 'problem play', for this is a crucial question in the matter of naturalism. Jones and Pinero, in their drawing-room plays, to some extent muted and blurred—or to put it another way, simplified and naturalised—the detail of the intrigue play. At the same time they developed characteristic intrigues to the status of 'problems': notably the old plot of the lady with a 'past'. The problem, here, was one of moral judgement, and there was an obvious loosening from the rigidities of, say, *Lady Audley's Secret*. The best-known example is Pinero's *The Second Mrs Tanqueray*, in which the problem is directly discussed. Tanqueray's first wife, a virtuous woman who also, it is suggested, 'kept a thermometer in her stays and always registered ten degrees below zero' has insisted on a convent education for her daughter, before she dies. Tanqueray's second marriage is to a woman, Paula, whose 'past' is known to him: a succession of unmarried affairs. The problem of 'respectability' is then posed at two levels: the conventional prejudices of his circle against the second Mrs Tanqueray, including their fears about her influence on the daughter; second, the explosive situation in which the daughter falls in love with one of her stepmother's former men. Paula tells the truth and kills herself. The daughter wishes she had 'only been merciful'. It is a strongly emotional play, but it is the interaction of 'intrigue' and 'problem' that is significant, and that is significantly unresolved by the form. The sensational coincidence of the daughter falling in love with one of the stepmother's young men remains within the orbit of the intrigue drama, though one can easily see that, taken straight, it could lead directly to issues of relationship, including sexual rivalry and jealousy, which the major naturalist drama was exploring. It is not so taken, though the hint is there, and some of the ground has been laid for it, in the last scene of confrontation. On the other hand the generalised 'problem' is of a quite different kind. All the right questions are asked: do not men have 'pasts'; is not prejudice often hypocritical; even, are there not connections between respectability and frigidity? The points go to and fro, but of course that whole discussion is blown to pieces by the actual event, when the abstract question enters an intractable area of primary relationships. What happens is then a compromise, with neither the relationship nor the problem carried through.

Indeed the general character of the 'questioning' in the problem plays of Society drama is in the end strictly suggestive. The basic reason is that the conventions, alike of the structure of feeling and of the form, are restricted to the uneasy terms of the social integration. No sense of any life or any idea beyond the terms of this displayed society can be dramatically established; not even any strictly bourgeois viewpoint, since this is overlaid and compromised by the preoccupation with 'Society' (there is markedly less frankness about money, for example, than even earlier in the century). English naturalism, in this first phase, could then, inevitably, be no more than a technical matter.

Some breaks came. As in most other European situations, a new kind of drama needed a new kind of theatre audience. Virtually all the important new work in European drama of this period was done in breakaway independent theatres, based on a minority audience which separated itself at once from its own class and from the 'theatrical' integration. In England this minority was already large, in other fields, but in the theatre it was slow to organise: The Dramatic Students (1886), the Independent Theatre Society (1891), the Stage Society (1899). But it was through these organisations that different work came into the theatres: Shaw's *Widower's Houses* at the Independent Theatre in 1892; the *Plays Pleasant and Unpleasant;* and ultimately the Vedrenne-Barker régime at the Court Theatre between 1904 and 1907. By the last ten years before the war a different kind of English drama had an independent base, though the West End continued to be dominated by Society drama (Sutro, Hankin, early Maugham) and, even more, by musical comedy.

Was this then, even if late, the period of English naturalism, in the most serious sense? In a way, yes. The plays of Galsworthy (*Strife,* 1909 and *Justice,* 1910) have a new breadth of reference and concern, and are specifically naturalist both in the technical sense and in the sense of a conscious correlation between character and environment. Barker's plays (*The Voysey Inheritance,* 1905, and *Waste,* 1907) are highly developed naturalism, in the technical sense, though their themes belong more to the anti-romantic, exposure-of-respectability, strain than to any positive naturalism. It is a significant but limited achievement, and the main reason for this is that Shaw, who most consciously adopted the naturalist philosophical standpoint, and indeed whose expositions of it are more conscious and explicit than those of any of the major naturalist dramatists, chose, for tactical reasons connected with the predominant styles of the orthodox theatre, to work mainly with old forms and then to alter them internally. In some plays, *Widowers' Houses, Mrs Warren's Profession*

and the later *Heartbreak House,* the material is transformed; the last under the direct influence of a genuinely original naturalist form in Chekhov. But the main thrust of Shaw's drama is a sustained and brilliant polemic, in both plays and the significantly ancillary prefaces, within the terms of the established Society drama and the associated romantic intrigues, historical reconstructions and even the earlier melodrama and farce. It is unquestionably the most effective body of drama of the period, but it never attempted, in any sustained way, the specifically naturalist conjunction of philosophy and form, and it was supported in this by the reaction against naturalism which was already evident in the avant-garde theatre elsewhere. For of course high naturalism, as a form, itself broke down, under the tensions of its own central theme: the interaction of character and environment. To go more deeply into the experience of the self consciously trapped by environment the new subjective expressionism of Strindberg was already necessary. Also, to see environment actively—not as a passive determining force, but as a dynamic history and society—needed the new and more mobile conventions of social expressionism. Shaw has connections with the second of these tendencies, though significantly none with the first, and this must be seen as a reason for his actual development. But another reason is the prepotence of the theatrical forms then current within the special case of the English (London West End) theatre.

To trace the subsequent development of English naturalist drama is beyond the scope of this essay. We can only briefly note the extraordinary revival of naturalist drama in the theatre of the mid- and late-1950s, and its extensive and dominant transfer into television drama. We can also add that the persistence of a limited technical sense of naturalism has allowed many people, including especially directors and writers, to claim that they have abandoned, 'gone beyond', naturalism, when it is clear, on the one hand, that the great majority of plays now produced, in all media, are technically naturalist, and, on the other hand, that many 'non-naturalist' plays are evidently based on a naturalist philosophy: not only character and environment but the 'scientific' sense of natural history and especially physical inheritance. What remains to be emphasised is the special character of the social basis of theatre in England since the changes of the 1860s. It is significant that in centres other than London a different kind of drama has been evident. I have already given an example of the work at Manchester. Even more significant is the case of the Irish drama, which in spite of the very different preoccupations and influence of Yeats, produced in Synge's *Riders to the Sea* an especially pure naturalist tragedy, in his *Playboy of the Western World* a significantly localised naturalist comedy, and in O'Casey's early plays, for all their difficulties, work which belongs in the mainstream of European naturalist drama. A final example is of a negative kind: D. H. Lawrence, in his early writing years, worked consistently and sometimes successfully in a kind of naturalist drama, with a quite different social base and with a language significantly revitalised by contrast with the terms of the middle-class problem plays. *The Widowing of Mrs Holroyd,* in spite of limitations which he overcame when writing the same experience in the more flexible form of narrative, would also take its place in a European mainstream, and more work might have followed, but for the fact that, in the special conditions of the English theatre, he could not get his plays produced and so came to rely, as generations of English writers had done before him, on the more open medium of print.

CONCLUSION

The special conditions for the limitation and lateness of English naturalism are then reasonably clear. Some of these conditions indeed still exist in parts of the English theatre, though television has bypassed them. What remains for reflection is the very difficult question of the relations between naturalist method and what can still be distinguished, though the labels are often changed, as naturalist world-views and structures of feeling. The specific fusion of method and structure which we know historically as high naturalist drama has always to be seen in these terms, but it also, quite as much as the fashionable London theatre, had its specific historical conditions. The question about other forms of such a fusion, both actual and potential, remains central in the history of twentieth-century drama, and it is made very much harder to ask, let alone to answer, if, in loose ways, we go on describing naturalism as if it were only a set of techniques. English naturalism, in its very limitations, provides, in its real history, ample evidence against that. It also provides evidence for what is still the central inquiry: into the formation of forms and, which is another way of saying the same thing, into the relations between forms and social formations, crucial everywhere in art but in the drama always especially central and evident. (pp. 203-23)

> *Raymond Williams, "Social Environment and Theatrical Environment: The Case of English Naturalism," in* English Drama: Forms and Development, Essays in Honour of Muriel Clara Bradbrook, *edited by Marie Axton and Raymond Williams, Cambridge University Press, 1977, pp. 203-23.*

EUROPEAN NATURALISM

Oscar Cargill

[*An American educator, historian, and literary critic, Cargill edited critical editions of the works of such major American authors as Henry James, Walt Whitman, Frank Norris, and Thomas Wolfe. In the following excerpt, he examines the works and philosophies of the major nineteenth-century Naturalists in France and England, from the perspective of their impact on their American successors.*]

THE GENESIS OF DESPAIR

Although Naturalism, the first of the European schools of thought to make itself felt in America, has been described as one result of interpretation of the doctrines of Evolution, it must not be forgotten that there was a long prepa-

ration for it in France in the early part of the nineteenth century. One cannot ignore the fact that Auguste Comte's development of a science of society and his tremendous concern for the renovation of the family must have had an influence upon Émile Zola even if the latter did not read a book of Comte's, any more than one can forget the fact that Charles-Augustin Sainte-Beuve, thinking of his almost scientific examination of the minutiae of biography, described himself in the preface to his *Port-Royal* as "a kind of naturalist of souls (*un espèce de naturaliste des esprits*)." And Taine, too, might well be considered a naturalist in literary history, before Zola became *the* naturalist in literature. Indeed, the sottishness of the Angles and Saxons and Jutes, the influence of their environment upon them, as it appears in the irritating, but highly diverting, early pages of Taine's *History of English Literature,* must have been very suggestive to the novelist. Zola later corresponded with both Taine and Sainte-Beuve in an effort to find their origins. Naturalism, then, has a background in Positivism, a more comprehensive evolutionary science than Darwinism.

The truth is, Zola aroused so much hostility in France in his lifetime that his thought, his Naturalism, has never been properly studied, nor has it received the consideration due it there. The sum of French criticism upon Zola can very nearly be found in the none-too-profound observations that his Rougon-Macquart cycle owes something to Balzac's "Comédie Humaine," and that the writings of the physiologist Claude Bernard influenced him—though Bernard's influence appears to lie wholly in buttressing quotation in *The Experimental Novel.* Matthew Josephson, an American, has done more to set Zola fairly before the world than have all his countrymen. Havelock Ellis in *The New Spirit* and Henry James in his *Notes on Novelists* both broke lances for Zola, but the Frenchman's greatest servant, aside from Josephson, was his English publisher, translator, and biographer, Ernest Vizetelly, who went to jail in 1889 for printing his books.

Émile Zola, the son of an engineer who was part Greek and part Italian, was born in Paris, on April 2, 1840, but passed his boyhood and youth in Aix, in Southern France, which figures in his novels as the town of Plassans. His only heritage on his father's death was a lawsuit against this town for the latter's services in constructing a canal. A final settlement of this suit, after the litigation of years, gave Zola his education at the Collège Bourbon, in Aix, where he had for a schoolfellow the future Post-Impressionist painter, Paul Cézanne. At eighteen he went up to Paris to live in hunger in the Latin Quarter, possibly setting traps, like Maupassant, on the roof for sparrows, until eventually he was glad to take a position in the firm of Hachette and Company as clerk. While hitherto he had written poetry, he now turned to fiction, shifting his allegiance from Alfred de Musset to Honoré de Balzac. His early work in this field is relatively unimportant, even for an understanding of Zola himself. *Contes à Ninon,* a book of short stories, published in 1864, attracted some attention; in 1865 *Les Confessions de Claude,* a novel depicting life in Bohemia, was roundly and justly abused in the press; while *Thérèse Raquin,* given the public in 1867, shocked with its gruesomeness. More important, however, were the articles he contributed to various newspapers and to the *Figaro,* the staff of which he joined in 1866. His fervid, though mistaken, articles on the Impressionists who were then undergoing attack, his ironical review of Louis Napoleon's *History of Julius Caesar,* and his defense of the Goncourts' *Germinie Lacerteux* won him recognition as a fair and fearless controversialist who could hit with either hand. When he predicted, in 1867, that Manet would one day be in the Louvre, he was deemed insane by the conservative critics.

At twenty-eight, with six books behind him, Zola seems to have done his first serious thinking about his profession. He saw that his talent was not for carefully wrought, psychological portraits like *Madame Bovary* and *Germinie Lacerteux.* He could never be *précieux.* Yet though long rhythms, broad panoramas, and great masses affected him most powerfully, he would not, like Balzac, indulge in mere portraiture or try to paint the whole of contemporary society. Balzac, like life itself, seemed to him to need an interpreter. Taine had taught him that, above everything else, the novelist must have a philosophy. Convinced that this was his own great lack, Zola deliberately started reading in the Imperial Library with a view to finding a philosophy (not forming one!) which should fit his work. He seems, in the elaborate notes which he took up to the summer of 1869, to have been chiefly influenced by Doctor Prosper Lucas, a minor disciple of Darwin. Lucas' *Treatise on Natural Heredity* is hardly a scientific work, for while it asserts the existence of laws of transmission and the possibility that traits might lie dormant for a generation, it also maintains the possibility of "atavism," a complete return to an earlier ancestor, and the "crossing" of the characteristics of the mother and father, so that the son resembles the mother and the daughter the father, and like nonsense. Though Zola utilized later most of the scientific "facts" of this treatise, the greatest impression that it, and other similar volumes, made upon him was that one absolutely cannot escape his origins, but is completely the creature of heredity. Thus Naturalism, which we have defined as pessimistic determinism, was born.

In his Preface to *The Fortune of the Rougons,* printed in book form in 1871, Zola boldly announced his intention to study the history of a single family in a series of novels that should compass the events between Napoleon's seizure of the government in 1852 and his fall in 1870, an event which he needed artistically, "and which, as if by fate, I ever found at the end of the drama, without daring to hope that it would prove so near at hand . . . the terrible, but necessary, *dénouement* for my work." Although in his notes for his great cycle of twenty novels he had affirmed, *"If I accept an historical frame, it is solely to have a milieu which reacts . . . ,"* history has a larger significance in his books. A Republican, in spite of himself and his confrères, he believed that the Second Empire pandered to men's appetites, corrupted and seduced the people, and betrayed France for ambition. Such a conviction led him to begin his cycle with "the ambuscade of the *Coup d'État"* and to conclude it with "the treachery of Sedan." Thus, while each novel in his cycle deals with the individual lives of members of the Rougon-Macquart family, through these "dramas" is seen the greater tragedy of

the country. In *The Fortune of the Rougons* a bewildered peasantry swarm over the countryside, into Plassans and out again to their doom. In *His Excellency, Eugène Rougon* (1876) the stupid herd is shown contentedly grazing while one of the favorites of the Empire rises to fame at their cost. In *Nana* (1880), the study of a courtesan who is symbolic of all those who enervated the court of Louis Napoleon and also of the extreme degeneracy of the Rougon-Macquarts, this same herd, with bands playing and with frenzied shouts *"À Berlin! à Berlin! à Berlin,"* passes beneath the open window of the room in which her pustular body lies deserted, dead from small pox. And finally, in the "terrible *dénouement"* which he needed for his work, in *La Débâcle* (1892), Zola describes the marching and confused counter-marching of the French armies before they were bottled up in Sedan, that terrible defeat, and then the bloody fighting in Paris between the Communists and the Republicans—really but an episode, as he sees it, in the death of the nation when, like a great beast mortally stricken, it claws frantically at the wound in its own bowels. It is useless to insist that Zola's history is nothing; the shadow which moves behind the "dramas" of the Rougon-Macquart series is the greatest actor of all, the solid shadow of a nation tottering to destruction. One is never unaware of it; it illustrates destiny better than the puppets on the proscenium. There is no God or Fate in the matter; the French people are themselves decadent, responsible (but not in a moral sense) for their own disaster.

Yet despite all their faults, of which the chief is their waning strength, the French people are betrayed. Zola's Republicanism gets the better of his philosophy. Nowhere does this receive clearer illustration than in the initial volume, *The Fortune of the Rougons.* Miette and Silvère, lovers as well as young Republican revolutionaries, are led to death, while the scheming Pierre Rougon and his wife Félicité through the plots hatched in their yellow drawing room lay the basis for the family fortune. On them, Zola lavishes a hatred of the bourgeoisie, which, while it may have been derived from the author of *Madame Bovary,* is personal and bitter. In no other book of his does Republicanism seem so much a chimera for the destruction of youth and the profit of the selfish middle class as in this. *The Fortune of the Rougons* is not a great book—aside from Félicité (who is out of Balzac), its people are cardboard people—but it illuminates the whole series. Zola's bitterness towards Republicanism is the bitterness of disillusioned youth (he was only thirty), the bitterness of a Republican who has hoped for too much. He is never again, no, not even towards the Emperor and his consort, who are Pierre Rougon and Félicité all over, quite so apparent and personal as here. *The Fortune of the Rougons* aids us in seeing that cupidity, rather than blind force, as Zola would have us believe (but cannot believe himself), is responsible for the downfall of France.

It is remarkable in Zola's notes to discover that he did not wish to be "political, philosophical, or moral," but "purely naturalistic, purely physiological." In only one of his novels did he succeed in being "purely physiological." That is in *Le Ventre de Paris* (1873), an astonishing novel with its setting in Les Halles, the great public market of Paris. Here all men are classed as Thin or Fat, and the Fat

Stephen Crane in Athens, 1897.

live off the Thin, which, for the time being, Zola noisily insists is the law of life. In no other book of his is the *milieu* more important; yet the tale is not an ideal illustration of the influence of environment upon the human animal— it is too bizarre, Rabelaisian, fantastic. The observations are not those of a photographer, but those of a caricaturist. In this book, however, Zola exploited for the first time successfully the reportorial method of assembling all the minutiae of his background for a studied effect, a method which to many minds is Naturalism itself. Yet the one thing the Naturalists have in common is not this technique, as we shall see, but the philosophy of determinism.

L'Assommoir, which created a sensation when run serially in the *Bien Public* in 1876, is all things that *Le Ventre de Paris* is not. One of the half-dozen great novels of the nineteenth century, it is the most plausible exposition of the dogma that heredity and environment make completely a man or a woman. It tells how Gervaise Macquart, a country girl of easy disposition, is abandoned in Paris by her lover Lantier, how she later weds a roofer by the name of Coupeau, and how they prosper together, even running a little laundry with success, until Coupeau has a bad fall, during the convalescence from which he becomes lazy and takes to drink, gradually losing all ambition and eventually reducing his wife to his own lax habits. Lantier, the for-

mer lover, returns, and the two men become boon companions, sharing Gervaise and living off her until the shop is gone. Lantier again deserts Gervaise, Coupeau dies a lunatic from drink in an asylum, and Gervaise perishes of starvation beneath the stairs of the very apartment in which she had first known prosperity. One cannot resist the argument of the book: Gervaise's pliant nature led her into the very circumstances which destroyed her; even her willingness to work encourages her husband's laziness; the return of Lantier is prepared for in the softening of Coupeau; and debauchery and death are sequels as inevitable as the going down of the sun. *L'Assommoir* may be counted the one perfectly plausible exposition of the philosophy of Naturalism.

The book is written with great gusto, Zola employing the slang of the shops and gutters, a sludge of words, even in his descriptions. The result is that there is no good translation of *L'Assommoir* in English, and no just appreciation of the raciness of the style. Yet the French themselves were not prepared to admire the book on this score. A people of no conspicuous chastity, they rarely forgive an author who is not chaste in his style, and many a writer, like Jacques Anatole Thibault, who has had little else but style, has gained enormous success in France. Zola was the first Frenchman after Rabelais to employ the living speech and was denounced for his pains. The coarseness of his expression, from the moral point of view, led to inane and emasculated English translations, with the result that Zola in translation has been a license for slack writing by British and American Naturalists.

More offensive even than the style was the fact that Zola intended *L'Assommoir* as a picture of the French working class. A vulgar, vain, foolish, and sottish people is revealed, and with a malice which was at once resented. Zola's delight in his mockery is patent to all who read the book, and the easy life with husband and lover which he pressed upon Gervaise (who is meant to represent the lax morals of her class) roused no more indignation than her comic wedding to Coupeau earlier in the book, or her famous fight with Virginie, another laundress, before her marriage. To Frenchmen the loose woman is less offensive than the hussy. Paris and the provinces shook with indignation, and Zola was made.

Yet Vizetelly assures us that, following the siege of Paris, the workingman was as degraded as Zola represented him, while the novelist himself insists that the book is a tract:

> When *L'Assommoir* appeared in a newspaper, it was attacked with unexampled brutality, denounced, accused of every crime. Is it really necessary to explain here in a few lines my intentions as a writer? I have sought to picture the fatal downfall of a family of work people in the pestilential atmosphere of our faubourgs. After drunkenness and sloth come the loosening of family ties, filth engendered by promiscuity, progressive forgetfulness of all upright sentiments, and then, as a finish, shame and death. The book is simply a lesson in morality.

How, we may fairly ask, can the book be at once a moral tract and a piece of naturalistic reporting? The answer is, it cannot. In theory, Gervaise is responsible neither for her nature nor for what happens to her; and in fact, the novelist has made this altogether reasonable. If, then, she and her husband, and all those around her, are symbolical of the French working people, how is any tract going to save them? Right here we are at the crux of the whole matter: the truth is, Gervaise is representative of no one but herself; the story is convincing because she is an individual, possessed of certain characteristics which bring about her wholly plausible doom. Zola is revealed as a moralist eager to generalize from a particular case which for once his art has clearly set before us. Paradoxically, he is less of a Naturalist at heart than some of his followers, although *L'Assommoir* triumphantly illustrates the workings of determinism in the life of a single person, for the Naturalist would see the absurdity of reproaching the pliant woman for her forgetfulness of upright sentiments, just as he would realize the weakness of selecting such a character to demonstrate his philosophy.

The moralist and Puritan is even more visible in *Nana.* Bunyan's Mrs. Love-the-flesh, Mrs. Filth, and Madam Wanton are all rolled into this one daughter of Gervaise and Coupeau, whom, as Ernest Boyd points out, Zola produced to show the prostitute as she really is, stripped of the romantic glamour in which she had been enveloped by Dumas *fils,* Hugo, and Augier. The novelist knew nothing about the woman whom he sought to describe, and had to rely upon the reminiscences of his friends, who were not above deceiving him, and upon what information he could gather from the ladies of the high-class *demi-monde* of the Second Empire to whom he was given introductions. Edmond de Goncourt was probably responsible for Zola's meetings with the infamous La Païva from whose own narrative he drew some of the most startling episodes of the book, among them notably the suicide of young Georges and the imprisonment of his brother and rival, Philippe, who stole twelve thousand francs from the chest of his regiment to buy baubles for Nana. Yet one courtesan did not suffice Zola: through the saintly Ludovic Halévy, author of *L'Abbé Constantin* and connoisseur in the field of Zola's interest, he gained information about the tastes and habits of such creatures as Cora Pearl, Zulma Bouffar, Hortense Schneider, La Castiglione, and La Bellanger. Nana represents them all, and in consequence, is an allegorical, rather than a human, figure. While the novelist accomplished much by showing the depraved woman as an utterly selfish and calculating animal, he is not convincing on the score of Nana's charms. This is what Anatole France meant when he remarked that "Zola is never voluptuous enough when he paints human degradation." Here the method of the compiler was fatal. The appeal of this courtesan to men of taste and good breeding (even gentlemen of the Second Empire) is a stated fact rather than a seductive force in the book. Zola is too much repelled by an object which he should somehow make attractive to be convincing, and the novel is another polemic directed against the immorality of the last days of Louis Napoleon. Yet the book has elements of greatness: the scene at the race track is a memorable one, the police raid upon the low hotel where Nana took refuge is real enough, Count Muffat is palpably well drawn, and Satin, whose amorous fondness for her own sex distinguishes her, is

perhaps one of the novelist's most original figures. Nevertheless *Nana* is the novel one should cite as most fulfilling Zola's requirements in fiction: as little imagination as possible and no plot whatsoever. Driven by his strong moral nature to punish Nana, yet unwilling to make her punishment the result of her actions and the culminating episode in a plot, Zola has her stricken by small pox, an altogether loathsome thing, at the end of the tale. Robert Henryson, the Scotchman, punished Criseyde for infidelity in a like manner and improved not at all on Chaucer, but rather revealed the incensed moralist. A similar revelation lies at the end of *Nana.*

The effect of heredity or of environment may be studied in the case history of a single individual, as in *Nana,* or in the story of a whole society, as in *Germinal* (1885), Zola's next important novel. In the bulk of his books Zola is interested in biological determinism; in *Germinal* he is for once fairly absorbed by economic determinism. The book is a study of the revolt of the coal miners of Montsou, ground down by the operatives, brutalized by long hours, small pay, unsanitary and dangerous working and living conditions. They are led by Étienne Lantier, child of Gervaise and her lover, who is slowly won over to Communist doctrine which has filtered in from the North. Of course, the workers are defeated, but there are some magnificent scenes in the book where, when they are completely out of hand, they smash and burn and destroy as only an outraged mob can. The terrible abuse they visited upon the body of the dead bread-dealer, Maigrat, a filthy animal who had cheated and robbed them all and seduced their daughters, is not soon forgotten. *Germinal* ends, however, in the sheerest melodrama. When the mines are flooded in an effort to destroy them, Étienne is caught below ground with Catherine, his loved one, and with Chaval, his rival; the three wall themselves up against the water, Étienne destroys his rival, but cannot keep Catherine alive till help comes. Troops restore order, the miners return to the mines, and Étienne leaves the coal fields on foot as he had come. Although the workers have turned from him as a leader, he is aware that this first revolt of the miners is but the beginning of a strife which will continue until something more like justice is realized. It is spring and the fields around are germinating; beneath the ground sprout also the seeds of other revolts.

Étienne saw, too, that failure had come out of cross purposes, out of inadequate preparation, and out of jealous leadership:

> . . . Thus, this famous International which would have revived the world, had failed for lack of power, after having seen its formidable army divide and crumble with interior quarrels. Was Darwin then right, was the world only a battlefield where the strong devoured the weak, for the beauty and the continuity of the race? This question troubled him although he decided it as a man content with his own knowledge. But one idea scattered his doubts and enchanted him, that of taking up again his old explanation of the theory, the first time that he should speak. If it was necessary that one class should be devoured, was it not the common people, long-lived and still new, who would devour the bourgeoisie,

weakened by enjoyments? The new society would be of new blood. And in this expectation of an invasion of the barbarians regenerating the old decrepit nations, reappeared his absolute faith in the next revolution, the true one, that of the workers, the flames of which would set on fire the end of the century with that purple of the rising sun that he saw bleeding even to the heavens.

He still walked along, dreaming, striking with his cane of cornelian the pebbles on the road, and as he cast his eyes around him, he recognized parts of the country. Just there, at the Fourche-aux-Boeufs, he remembered that he had taken command of the band the morning of the sacking of the pits. To-day the brutish work, killing and badly paid, was recommencing. Under the ground, down there, at seven hundred mètres, he seemed to hear deadened blows, regular and continuous; these were the comrades that he had just seen go down, the black comrades, who were striking in their silent rage. Without doubt they were vanquished, they had left there their money and their dead; but Paris would not forget the fiery blows of Voreux, the blood of the empire too would flow from that unquenchable wound; and if the industrial crisis was drawing to its close, if the manufactories were opening again, one by one, the state of war was not any less declared for peace was not hereafter possible. The coal workers had counted their men, they had tried their strength, they had aided the workers of all France by their cry for justice. Thus did their defeat reassure no one, the bourgeoisie of Montsou, troubled in their victory by the ill sound of the strike of the morrow, were looking behind them to see whether their end was not inevitably there at the end of this great silence. They understood that the revolution would be born again without ceasing, perhaps tomorrow, with a general strike, the union of all workers having funds and so being able to hold on for months, eating their own bread. This time, still, it was only a shoulder blow given to a society in ruins, but they had heard in it the cracking under their own feet, and they felt rising up other shocks and still others, even to that which would destroy the old edifice, already shaken, and would engulf it as the Voreux, going down to the abyss.

Étienne's ideas for the moment seem to be Zola's: the novel is not a "scientific" study, but rather a proletarian manifesto, and its popularity in the coal fields about Mons is readily understood. Zola has affected to believe that his naturalism has something in common with Marxism, and the general decadence of the upper classes is to be offset by the inherent strength of the proletariat. Yet he has forgotten the proletariat of Paris whom he pictured in *L'Assommoir;* indeed, he has even forgotten the proletariat of the earlier pages of *Germinal* who were debauched and sodden and hopeless before Étienne inspired them. He has proved the fire there is in the Marxian doctrine, but he has not shown that the workers, either of Montsou or Paris, are of the splendid barbarian physical stuff to regenerate the world. The evidence he offers and the conclusion he draws conflict with each other.

After having discovered economic determinism in *Germinal,* Zola deliberately thrust it aside as a theme in his later books. In *La Terre* (1887) he had an unusual opportunity to employ it effectively and to his disadvantage refrained from doing so. Although this story is written around the miserable fortunes of the peasant Fouan's two sons and daughter, and has only an incidental connection with the Rougon-Macquart cycle through the presence of Jean Macquart, the novelist had a chance to draw a comparison between the sensible scientific program of the landed agriculturalist, Hourdequin, and the ignorant ways of the peasants who are ever dividing their land into smaller and smaller parcels, none of which can be cultivated advantageously. Instead, equal disaster overtakes both, and Hourdequin, anticipating the common catastrophe of small landowner and large, can only exclaim, "Let everything go to smash and all of us perish, and the whole soil be covered with weeds and brambles, since our race is decayed and the land exhausted!" Had Zola possessed strong convictions in economics, he should have made some distinction in the lots of peasant and large landowner. Had he been more of an artist, the exhaustion of the soil of France (very largely hypothecated, one thinks after a visit to Les Halles) might have been made to chime with the melancholy note of his whole great cycle, but it does not. Had he been a political doctrinaire and not a professional pessimist, he would not have repudiated equally, as he does, Hyacinthe with his " '89" and his humanitarian motto of "Liberty, Equality, and Fraternity," and Canon, the Communist, "with his schemes for the compulsory and scientific reorganization of society." Instead, all is ground into the earth in *La Terre:* both types of agricultural program and all schemes of social salvation as well. *La Terre* is proof that the author of *Germinal* was a man possessed by a mood and not by a conviction.

La Terre is the most dismal of all Zola's dark books, perhaps because it is the most animalistic. The reader's sympathies are soon attached to the girl Françoise Mouche in her heroic efforts to resist the brutal physical attacks of her sister's husband, Butteau, which she is successful in doing, even though the sister's aid is invoked against her, until she is married to Jean Macquart, when, with child, she is at last overcome—only to realize, during the attack, that she is in love with Butteau. Him she protects after a fatal quarrel in which she is thrown upon a scythe, closing her lips to her devoted husband as she lies for hours dying. Françoise's extraordinary realization of her love seems intended to convey the theme of the book—the bestial quality of all affection—symbolized by the notorious and over-discussed fecundating of a cow at the beginning of the book. Yet Françoise's defection—and it may fairly be called that—is beyond the credulity of the reader. All the people in the novel live like swine save she; she seems, up to the last thousand words, to be the exception necessary for the proof of the rule and for artistic contrast in the story; when, therefore, she is shown to be like the others, the reader has had a surfeit of proof. His mind rebels. Zola has ridden the theme too hard. A countryside as lascivious as that in *La Terre* (no other examples of repression are noted) simply has no counterpart in life, neither in Africa, New England, nor France. Perhaps through hyperbole the book accomplished something in leading to franker discussions of the sexual basis of affection, though a good many other books had to be written before this was in any degree accomplished.

While *La Terre* adds nothing to the Rougon-Macquart cycle, *La Débâcle,* completed five years later, brings the story of defeated France to the climax Zola wished for it. In this novel Jean Macquart, outsider in *La Terre,* is spectator to one of the greatest pageants ambition has unrolled. Yet the fact that he is the selected witness is of no consequence so far as his degenerate family is concerned, any more than that he was a minor actor in *La Terre.* His low station, however, gives the novelist an opportunity to comment on the folly of his superiors, responsible for the disaster at Sedan and the fighting in Paris. The American reader has little interest in the precise share of the Emperor, Marshal MacMahon, General Ducrot, General Douay, General de Wimpffen, and others in these fatal events, nor in the politics of the book, which together have made it the best selling novel of Zola's in France; indeed, they make the book difficult for him, yet he may enjoy as much as any Frenchman the spectacle of the whole French army as tragic hero, the subordination of individuals to the mass, the fidelity of drawing in all the war scenes—specifically the massacre of the civilian defenders of Bazeilles, the horrors of the inadequate factory-hospital of Delaherche in Sedan, and the vileness of the prison-concentration camp on the island in the Meuse. Yet he must not mistakenly assume, from the effect of these scenes on him, that *La Débâcle,* like so many recent war novels, is a pacifist tract. Through the educated Maurice, Corporal Macquart's friend, Zola spikes that assumption. To his sister, who cannot see why nations do not adjust their differences without shedding blood, Maurice replies that war is itself existence, the universal law. "Would not the end of war be the end of humanity?" While *La Débâcle* may be as effective anti-war propaganda as Barbusse's *Under Fire,* this was not the author's intention. That a degenerate race must expect pain and punishment in conflict with a "newer and more vigorous strain" is his whole theme. Had France not been debauched by the Empire, the tone of the story might have been quite different, for Zola was altogether capable of writing a romance on war.

Zola concluded the Rougon-Macquart cycle with one of his poorest novels, *Le Docteur Pascal,* in 1893, a book worthy of brief examination, however, since certain deductions may be made from it in regard to Zola. For narrative interest it has the aged Doctor Pascal's love for his niece Clotilde—a pretty piece of sentimentalism based, it is said, upon an illicit autumnal affair which the novelist himself had. To Pascal, however, is attached more than an amatory interest, for this elderly scientist has kept complete records of the whole Rougon-Macquart family and from these has formulated a science of heredity. The story develops into a contest between Pascal and Madame Félicité Rougon for the possession of these documents: he, to give them to the world; she, to destroy them for the sake of family pride. Clotilde shifts her allegiance from one to the other as the arguments of love and religion have force with her. In the end, however, the old lady triumphs and the documents are burned. Thus the novelist dodges the responsibility of summing up his "science" and his philoso-

phy, which is plainly the task he should have set himself in the book that was to be the capstone of the series. While fatigue may be pled in his behalf—he had been occupied by the cycle for twenty-three years, it is not a valid excuse, since the novelist possessed sufficient energy to complete six more books and plan a seventh, which he doubtless would have finished, had not accidental death intervened.

The reason why *Le Docteur Pascal* is no summary of the Rougon-Macquart cycle, no statement of the laws of heredity, no final exposition of a philosophy, is that such a summary, statement, or exposition was for Zola impossible. In *Le Roman Expérimental* he had recognized the need of the scientist for caution, especially in regard to his conclusions:

> One studies nature and man, one classifies his documents, one advances step by step in employing the experimental and analytic method, but one must beware of settling things.

Yet this pronouncement is not typical of Zola. The man who proclaimed that heredity has its laws like gravity and accepted the notion that "vice and virtue are products like vitriol and sugar" had none of the instinctive caution of a Renan who would accompany every phrase by a "perhaps." Indeed, all Zola's creative work prior to this was preparation for a grand generalization. The whole purpose in writing novels, he frequently averred, was that these investigations should lead to developing the best elements and to exterminating the worst in man. Why, then, did he not summarize the best and the worst in *Le Docteur Pascal,* save that he was no longer so sure about the "laws" as he once had been? Had his going up and down the earth, had his investigations of workingmen (*L'Assommoir*), of domestics (*Pot-Bouille*), of peasants (*La Terre*), of miners (*Germinal*), of railwaymen (*La Bête Humaine*), of shopkeepers (*Au Bonheur des Dames*), of financiers (*L'Argent*), of politicians (*Son Excellence, Eugène Rougon*), of artists (*L'Oeuvre*), of soldiers (*La Débâcle*), of priests (*La Faute de l'Abbé Mouret*), had his unrivaled experience and observation shaken his faith in absolute determinism?

The answer perhaps is suggested in those novels which were written after the cycle was done, the trilogy called "The Three Cities": *Lourdes, Rome, Paris* (1894-1898) and the series called "The Four Gospels": *Fécondité, Travail, Vérité,* and *Justice,* of which he completed only the first three (1899-1903). *Lourdes,* the most important book in the trilogy, tells how the young Abbé Pierre, a skeptic in love with the crippled Marie de Guersaint, goes with her up to Lourdes in the hope that she may be cured through the miracles wrought there by Our Lady and that his faith may perhaps be restored to him. Since he had suspected her invalidism to be the product of nerves, he does not regard her cure as a miracle and is not himself converted. Further, he loses Marie for ever because she has taken a vow that she will never marry if cured. Instead of railing at the trick fate has played upon him (as Hardy would have had him do), Pierre contents himself with the hope for a new religion which shall make larger concessions to natural life. We are at once reminded of Comte's nonmetaphysical, non-theological religion of humanity, his international association functioning under the aegis of science. Unable to make the anti-ethical, non-moral deductions implicit in Naturalism, Zola turned back to Comte for support. He shares Comte's respect for Catholicism ("the chief political masterpiece of human wisdom") without avowing it. Although it is common to assert that the trilogy is anti-clerical, it is so to a far less degree than one would have anticipated it to be—particularly when one reflects that Zola had thrown science and his own writing repeatedly against religion and that the Boulangist crisis was just passed.

In "The Four Gospels" series Zola at last generalizes about those elements which are best in human life and which are the positive virtues apparently in his new "natural" religion—fecundity, work, truth, and justice. Yet as virtues these are partially debatable even in a "natural" religion. For example, epicurean idleness has as much to commend it as work, and mere fruitfulness is under most conditions (one writes as a critic) a curse. Zola failed to summarize his thinking in *Le Docteur Pascal* and botched it in the novels which followed, for the system there produced has no consequential relationship to the Rougon-Macquart cycle. Though Naturalism owes something to Comte, there is a gulf between it and Comte's philosophy which Zola could not fill with seven books. It is doubtful, however, if Zola ever perceived this gulf, for he was, after all, not a thinker, but an ideologist, like Rousseau. This, perhaps, is why he has to be reckoned with in the modern world.

One cannot quit the man without paying tribute to his courage, so conspicuously manifested in the Dreyfus case. After the establishment of the Third Republic many German-Jews came to France, driven out of the Central European countries by anti-Semitism, and attracted by the bourgeois prosperity there. On these Jews Edouard Drumont opened fire in 1886 in a book entitled *La France Juive,* which made a point of the evil influence of Jewish financiers on the national life. Having aroused a good deal of race hatred with his book, Drumont continued his campaign in *La Libre Parole,* a newspaper which he founded for this purpose. He asserted that the anti-clerical policies of the government were of Jewish origin and that Jews in the French army were German spies. This probably suggested to a group really guilty of espionage the possibility of fixing their crime upon Captain Dreyfus, a General Staff officer of Alsatian-Jewish origins. Dreyfus was given a secret military trial, convicted, and sent to Devil's Island, the whole affair being played up by *La Libre Parole.* New evidence and confession led to a demand to reopen the case, which Zola phrased most strongly in an article headed "J'accuse." Zola had no other motive in entering the case than to see justice done. Indeed, his long hatred of the bourgeoisie, to which class the Jews generally belonged, might have silenced him had it not influenced him to take the other side in the matter. The result of his charges against the War Office officials was his own indictment and forced flight to England. Dreyfus, however, through the efforts of Zola and other French liberals was eventually vindicated. The Dreyfus case would be for Zola what Missolonghi was for Byron except that Zola throughout his career had shown a moral earnestness,

never perceived by the public, which not only functioned in this episode but is the motivating force in all his writing. The question we are left with is, whether a Naturalist can be a moralist or, at least, the kind of moralist that Zola was?

The detachment, the philosophical firmness lacking in Zola are found in Flaubert who, however, because of his intellectual and artistic superiority, had faults which are harder to condone than Zola's. Because only one of his books has had any influence in America, and because at best he is a very dubious Naturalist, he will receive but brief consideration here. Flaubert, son of a Normandy surgeon, planned novels as a child and turned to the writing of them after the death of his father made it possible for him to give up the legal studies which he detested. After seven years of unremitting labor, he permitted his masterpiece, *Madame Bovary,* to be published serially in the *Revue de Paris* in 1857. On this book, on *L'Éducation Sentimental,* and on the unfinished *Bouvard et Pécuchet* rests whatever claim he has to be considered as a Naturalist, for Flaubert in his other work was a Romantic of the character of a Delacroix. He recognized a conflict within himself, though as he phrased that conflict the forces are somewhat obscured. "There are two distinct men in me," he wrote, "one who is in love with bellowing, with lyricism, with great eagle flights, with all the sonorities of the phrase and with the summits of the idea; another who digs and delves into the true as deeply as he can, who loves to bring out the little fact as powerfully as the big, who would like to make you feel almost materially the things he reproduces." Had he stated instead that there was in him a gross sensualist, fond of color, music, Orientalism, over whom the artist with torture kept a semblance of control, he would have been more nearly correct. This sensualist was the author of *Salammbô,* of *Herodias,* of the *Temptation of St. Anthony,* and of *St. Julian the Hospitaler.* Just two elements have kept these books from being ranked where they belong—on a plane with the work of Pierre Louys. The first of these is style—the most meticulous prose in any language, and the second is emphasis. A fault has here preserved the artist's rank. So obsessed is Flaubert with detail in these stories that by overwhelming them with detail he has buried their grossness. One has only to compare the verbose *Herodias* with Anatole France's "The Procurator of Judea" (which, in a sense, it doubtless inspired) to understand how lacking in economy it is. Yet Flaubert's passion for archeological detail diverts attention from some of his palpable faults, for example the sadistic pleasure the author derived from the slaughter of humans in *Salammbô* and of animals in *St. Julian.* Who can deny that the death of Salammbô, when realization comes to her of the love of Matho, is the sheerest melodrama?

On the other hand, how few nineteenth century novels measure up to *Madame Bovary, L'Éducation,* or even the unfinished *Bouvard et Pécuchet* for style, minute observation, and cumulative effect! The unfamiliarity of most Americans forty years ago with the French language kept them from appreciating what is best in Flaubert with the result that only *Madame Bovary* of all his work has exerted any considerable influence here, and its influence has been chiefly thematic. The heroine, convent-reared, is through her reading a hopeless romantic, and when she becomes the wife of a provincial physician, without really loving him although he adores her, she is shortly bored with him and plays him false with one lover, then another, growing all the while more self-indulgent, until through extravagance she has involved him in financial ruin. When she has prepared for him inextricable difficulty and for herself exposure, when she has reached the perigee of her moral declension, she takes poison as a way out. The tragedy of Emma lies not wholly in the fact that her surroundings and acquaintance are bourgeois, but also in the further fact that her head was filled with romantic nonsense for which temperamentally she had an insatiable taste— that her end was predetermined. All this, however, is implicit rather than explicit in the book, for Flaubert, although he was firmly convinced of the evil in the constitution of things, was equally sure that the novelist should not fill the rôle of interlocutor. "In the ideal I have of art," he wrote George Sand, " . . . the artist ought not to appear in his work any more than God in nature." And he insists that one should make even "an effort of the soul" to get inside his characters and not draw them from himself. In this regard, it is important to remember that *Madame Bovary* was based on a real incident and that the function of the novelist was, as he described it, to enter "into skins which are antipathetic to me." For Flaubert hated every character in *Madame Bovary,* as he did the vast majority of his fellow men, for their mediocrity. It should be noted, however, that this was not class-hatred (as it is generally understood in America), for Flaubert says flatly, "I call bourgeois whoever thinks meanly." Yet with a contempt for his characters which amounted almost to obsession, Flaubert entered into them so perfectly that they all live—Emma, Charles, Homais, Rodolphe, and Bournisien. And so, too, do the scenes against which he sets them: the brief glimpses of the French countryside strike one as better, or at least more convincing, than the whole of *La Terre.* Yet out of all this Americans have got . . . , in the main, only the theme of the oppression of a spirit in uncongenial surroundings. Flaubert's conviction of the essential meanness in that spirit they have missed altogether.

Besides Zola and Flaubert, these several other novelists contributed to the rise of French Naturalism in an important way: Edmond and Jules de Goncourt, Alphonse Daudet, Guy de Maupassant, and Joris-Karl Huysmans. Of these writers, the Goncourts and Huysmans as Naturalists were practically unread in America before the 'twenties and certainly were not directly influential here; Daudet was popular in translation (even Theodore Roosevelt quoted from him!), but his two best known books in this country—*Le Petit Chose* in the schools and *Sappho* in the boudoirs—appear to have provoked absolutely no reflection; and Guy de Maupassant, sold in complete sets and spread broadcast in anthologies of the short story, was yet far less influential than Zola, who was read, in the main, surreptitiously.

The Goncourt brothers endure in French literature primarily because of their famous *Journal,* rich in anecdotes of the literary and artistic world of the second half of the

century (1851-1892), and an astonishing piece of self-dissection and revelation, deliberately planned as a work of art. Many years before Zola defined the experimental novel, the two brothers had approached the novel from the standpoint of science. Thus, in 1865, they observed, "The novel of to-day is made with documents narrated or copied from nature, just as history is made with written documents." Unfortunately, while the Goncourts gathered facts with great industry, they never evaluated properly their facts, so that anything approximating perfect synthesis is lacking in their novels. Describing themselves as "unhealthy impressionables," they had so great a flair for the abnormal that their books are all pathological. Although *Manette Salomon* (1867), with its picture of studio life, is probably the most authentic of their works, it is *Germinie Lacerteux* (1865), which, in a roundabout way, through George Moore, has exerted some slight influence in this country. This is the story of a serving girl, seduced and preyed upon by a rogue, who nevertheless satisfies her craving for love, a craving which drives her into utter degradation, since she is a nymphomaniac, when he deserts her. The authors describe their book as a clinical study of love, and indeed it is, since Germinie was drawn from a serving girl in the employ of their aunt who was unaware of the girl's dual life (as is the mistress to whom Germinie is devoted in the book) until after her death. Done with a pity lacking in their other works, *Germinie Lacerteux* had force enough to move George Moore to do something infinitely superior.

Besides their pathological Naturalism, the Goncourts are the originators of a flamboyant style, totally out of keeping with their professed "scientific" approach, yet well adapted to their morbid subject matter, to which they gave the name "impressionism." It is this style which Maupassant cursed as "the weird, complicated, overloaded, and Chinese vocabulary imposed upon us nowadays under the name of artistic writing." Impressionism came to America in the 'nineties, yet those who introduced it were probably completely unaware of any debt to the Goncourts.

Daudet, notebook-keeper, impressionist, follower of the Goncourts, brought to French Naturalism the gift of a warm nature which won him a popular success. The best elements in him are not easily copied (the pathos and humor of *Le Petit Chose* and the two collections of short stories, *Lettres de mon Moulin* and *Contes du Lundi*) or if copied, are more easily imitated from Dickens, hence his influence in America is, as has been remarked, undetectable. The "religious Naturalism" of Huysmans, an important departure from the work of Zola, decadent in character, probably owes its little appeal in America to its Catholic subject matter and its lack of constructive imagination.

To Guy de Maupassant, however, must be conceded the largest American reading public over the years of any French Naturalist: yet it has been an uncritical audience which has confined itself to the short story and merely noted the Norman's great economy of means, his faultless plotting, his studied objectivity, in a word, his *virtuosity,* rather than his meaning or significance. He meant to most of his readers what Hemingway means to most of his today. The anthologists apologized for his "melancholy tone," little realizing apparently how complete a material-ist and pessimist he was. "The mediocrity of the universe astonishes and disgusts me, the littleness of everything nauseates me, and the poverty of human beings crushes me," he declared. His conviction of the smallness of hu-mans made him content when he had found one salient trait in his character's soul: his people are all animated vices, and the fact that we cannot remember one of them explains adequately why his influence has been less than that of Zola and Flaubert. We remember an old woman who burned alive the Prussian soldiers billeted with her out of vengeance for her son's death ("La Mère Sauvage"), we remember a fiend possessed, but that is all we do re-member. We draw nothing new about life from such a story as this. Maupassant's failure where psychological penetration is needed, as in the novel *Fort comme la Mort,* is the failure of a man who was by temperament impatient with the world. There is more than melodrama in that ut-terance to a friend in November, 1891, when it was appar-ent that he would die insane: "I entered literary life like a meteor, I will leave it like a thunderbolt."

BRITISH PESSIMISM

It was important for the development of American Natu-ralism that this philosophy was but little strained through the coarse, yet choked, mesh of British intelligence before reaching this country. The Victorian Englishman had so many concessions to make to propriety that his mind more nearly resembled a valve than a sieve. Fortunately Ameri-can Naturalists were in the main directly influenced by the French. Nevertheless one Englishman and one Irishman materially modified French Naturalism in individual ways which have left their mark on American writing. Thomas Hardy and George Moore were converts to the philosophy of pessimistic determinism at a time when public disap-probation was a foregone conclusion for one who espoused unconventionality in anything, let alone thinking.

For many Americans Thomas Hardy stands for Natural-ism, one book of his, either *The Native* or *Tess,* being per-haps the only Naturalistic book they have ever read. Yet Thomas Hardy, though by temperament fatalistic, did not settle into the Naturalistic way of expression until comparatively late in his career. A native of Higher Bock-hampton, early apprenticed to an architect, and attracted to the writing of fiction only by the uncertainty of his pro-fession, Thomas Hardy lived outwardly the conventional-ly good, average, quiet British life, which, if it is artistic, must produce extravaganzas of action and event by way of compensation, for your superior Englishman is by he-redity an adventurer, ill at ease in contemplative rôles. And there is much that is primitive British in Thomas Hardy despite his Norman name, much that reminds us of Taine's comments on his forebears—an interest in drink, a fascination in sudden death, and a profound rev-erence for *weird* or fate. Hardy's first book, *Desperate Remedies* (1871), which his publisher called "a blood-curdling story," was written under the influence of the sensational Wilkie Collins, another average Englishman who did his swashbuckling in the imagination. A heavily overplotted story, with a murder, a suicide, a criminal im-personation, and an incredible tangle of relationships, *Des-*

perate Remedies is sadly typical of much that Hardy wrote. Mr. Joseph Warren Beach, devoted admirer and apologist for the novelist, has this to say about his work:

> The most remarkable thing about Mr. Hardy's novels, for anyone who takes them in sequence, is their extreme unevenness of quality. It is ev-erywhere agreed to rank the author of *Tess of the d'Urbervilles* as the most serious English novelist of his time. No one doubts that he has produced works of noble beauty, has made illuminating representation of life, has ranged his facts in the light of a significant philosophy. And yet this artist, this philosopher, this scientist in human nature, is the author of works that by their crudeness positively put his lovers to the blush.

Ten novels out of fifteen which Hardy published are in various ways wretched, and the high position assigned the author is maintained not only by the merits of five books but also by lack of serious challenge or rivalry. The solitar-iness of Hardy has been used as an argument for his apo-theosis, and indeed his persistence almost alone in an ad-verse time speaks for his courage, yet it cannot be denied there is a degree of luck for the man who did not believe in good fortune in the very fact of his lonely circumstance. Monadnock, rising solitary from the plain, looks more like a mountain than it would if it were set among the White Hills to the north of it.

If Thomas Hardy is placed against the French Naturalists, it will at once be seen that his work had no meaning and little artistic significance before *The Return of the Native* was published in 1878. To be sure, *A Pair of Blue Eyes* (1872) dangles the daughter of a country vicar on a line in a fashion which some are pleased to call "ironical," and *Far from the Madding Crowd* (1874) keeps three male puppets in motion about a country doll with a dexterity which is amazing, considering the shortness of the strings. The author, who is never to achieve the Flaubertian ideal of self-effacement in his writing, notes "many miserable incongruities" in these earlier tales, but when all is said and done, justly rewards competence and merit where he finds it in his characters. Thus Smith and Knight who are hardly worthy of Elfride lose her to Lord Luxellian, and Gabriel Oak by devoted service wins his Bathsheba in the end, though it must be admitted she is a somewhat soiled article. The animadversions of the novelist, his vague fum-blings for meaning, do not count against the argument of events in his tales.

With *The Return of the Native* (1878), however, all is dif-ferent. The situation of *Madame Bovary,* of a woman ill content with her surroundings, is here repeated, with this exception, that Eustacia Vye is tied to Egdon Heath through marriage, not to a dull fellow, but to an idealist, Clym Yeobright, who has returned from Paris to the Heath with the fixed purpose of passing his life there as a teacher to the natives. When she married him, she hoped to win him over to her views, but it is he who prevails. Eu-stacia, moreover, is a woman with a past—*à la* Wilkie Col-lins,—for before Clym's return she had experimented with love with Mr. Wildeve, the gentlemanly innkeeper, who, now coming to fortune, offers her a way of escape when she quarrels and separates from her husband. In the end, however, she cannot go through with it and jumps into the millrace to be followed by Wildeve and Clym. When their bodies are dragged out, only Clym lives, a broken spirit, to preach his resignation to the world. The subplot of Thomasin Yeobright's marriage to Diggory Venn, after she had been wronged by Wildeve, is of small consequence, for the fortunes of Eustacia and Clym are, by the novelist's ordering, all with which we are concerned. They are defeated, not so much by their cross purposes—Eustacia's desire to reach the bright world of Paris and Clym's to stay on the Heath—as by "some indistinct, colossal Prince of the World" who has framed their situation and rules their lot. The Heath for them is His prison yard, a symbol of His ever perverse Presence, filling even the devoted Clym with foreboding. Hardy, through the pathetic fallacy, has elevated the *milieu* of Flaubert into an actor, the villain of the piece. As art, this is suspect, but it is enormously effective, like tilting the camera in photographing the cinema-melodramas so that the floor rocks dizzily under the characters. The "untameable, Ishmaelitish thing" is opposed not to one, but to both of them, nay, is the "enemy of civilization" itself, and the novelist in pity sees the victims of Egdon Heath far fairer than they could ever have been in life—Clym's face only a Pheidias of the future may cut, while "Eustacia Vye was the raw material of a divinity . . . The new moon behind her head, an old helmet upon it, a diadem of accidental dewdrops round her brow, would have been adjuncts to strike the note of Artemis, Athena, or Hera respectively!" Of course, this is nonsense, but it is nonsense which forces exaggeration throughout the tale, so that men cannot even throw dice without some unusual stage effect, in this case, absurdity of absurdities, the light of glow-worms! The heightening of the narrative in all its parts leads to the greater plausibility of the tragedy of Shadwater Weir, yet set that scene beside a similar one in Hawthorne's *Blithedale Romance* and the terrific exaggeration of Hardy bursts with overwhelming force. Had Flaubert been blind to the faults of Charles and Emma, had he lifted them into gods, then piled the Pelion and Ossa of the countryside upon them, *Madame Bovary* would perfectly resemble *The Return of the Native*, but we should have exchanged a work of art for something less—a polemic on the injustice of God to man. Yet Hardy has convinced legions of the uncritical of the actual hostility of Nature, of its sentient malice, through the power of his prose, one of the most magnificent pieces of over-writing, of passionate argument, in British literature.

The writing of *The Native* so exhausted its author that he had not the strength to lift his next six books (whose stuff is not radically dissimilar to that of *The Native*) into significance, although some of the author's great passion is responsible for the convincing delineation of Henchard in *The Mayor of Casterbridge* (1886), who, breaking through a web of incredibility, stands erect among Hardy's finest characters. *The Woodlanders* (1887), curiously suggestive of Henry James, has some moving situations, but its snarled and improbable plot deprives it of effectiveness. It is with *Tess of the D'Urbervilles* (1891), the simplest of his novels, that Hardy, after the longest hiatus in his creative career, an interval of four years, recovers the full strength of the earlier book. Again passion sweeps the reader off his

feet, but in this case it is suppressed passion, felt under the deadly calm of what, for the author, are calculated statements of fact. Tess Durbeyfield, or D'Urberville, a beautiful girl, is ravished by Alec D'Urberville, an unprincipled gentleman of whom she had obtained employment in the hope of helping her wretchedly impoverished family. After her child dies, she is reëmployed in a great dairy where she meets Angel Clare, a young man of fine character, who in season declares his love for her. Tess has a fixed conviction of her unworthiness, but is persuaded by her mother to keep her past a secret from Angel Clare, which she does until circumstances convince her of the dire need of revelation. She does not discover, however, until the morning of her wedding day that the letter which she had prepared, telling all, and thrust under the door of Angel Clare's room had gone under the carpet, too, so that her fatal secret is still preserved. In the evening after the wedding she thinks she has a favorable opportunity when Angel Clare reveals an indiscretion of his own, and she confesses to her husband. Yet Clare is shocked, cannot overcome his repugnance for her, and leaves her for South America. Tess goes back to her family; together they suffer great misfortune; then literally to save the others from starvation, when she feels that Angel Clare will never return, Tess becomes the mistress of Alec. But Clare does come back, all contrition, to discover her living with Alec. In her desperation she kills her seducer, flees with her husband, but is taken at Stonehenge and hanged for the murder. When he sees her body swing at the end of its tether against the sky, Hardy's full passion bursts out: "Justice was done, and the President of the Immortals (in the Aeschylean phrase) had ended his sport with Tess."

Tess of the D'Urbervilles is a very deceptive book: blow on it anywhere as you would on iron and you will discover the hot passion of Hardy beneath—what was visibly dangerous in *The Return of the Native* has here been allowed to cool to blue and gray, but you take it only at great hazard. The flaw in Hardy's reasoning is that, the universe being what he makes it out to be, the raising of Tess to the stature of a figure set in opposition to it, a milkmaid deserving the pity of all mankind, is patently absurd. Hardy demands a Christian evaluation of the single life in a system which he represents as wholly without Christian ethics. His book would be a total failure if he did not depend upon readers with values that are ridiculous in the natural world of his vision. How many phrases in the novel serve only the purpose of arousing pity for Tess! Yet there is no deliberate chicanery in this; Thomas Hardy was a man who preferred a God who marked the sparrow's fall, and the fact that his suspicions have been aroused that the President of the Immortals is indifferent to such an accident stirs his deepest resentment; he is determined to charge Him with moral responsibility, which is another matter, since the devout may argue that the circumstances leading to the fall in reality are not the same as those of Mr. Hardy's contriving. It is a little difficult to hold God responsible for Mr. Hardy's plots—or for Victorian morality which determined Angel Clare's course of action following his wife's revelations. The French Naturalists more logically eliminated all metaphysical considerations: Zola was "satisfied to be a scientist"; he scoffed at Fate as "an old tool, absurd. . . . " Flaubert, a more genuine skeptic than Hardy, never allows Fate or God to appear as a cause in his books. The Victorian handicap under which Hardy labored in his scientific approach was such that he could not wash his thought of God, or of Fate, which he at times identifies with God. *Tess* is a tract thrown in the direction of a heavenly footstool which Mr. Hardy is not absolutely sure does not exist.

Tess of the D'Urbervilles was followed, in 1892, by a fantastic book called *The Well-Beloved,* in which the sex-instinct is symbolized in the passion of a sculptor, a worshipper of Aphrodite, for various feminine objects all of whom are for the moment the Well-Beloved. Despite the slight merit of the tale, it is the prototype of many similar things in America of even less worth. It would seem that there is an almost fatal stipulation that one kind of thinker, much preoccupied with the hostility of the universe and the remoteness of God, should write some time in his career a fevered book with the eternal pursuit of a nymph for its theme. The Freudians probably have an explanation for this.

Jude the Obscure, begun in *Harper's* in December, 1894, under the title *The Simpletons,* brought the career of the novelist to a close. So great was the outcry against this book that Hardy determined to write no more fiction. In this last novel Jude Fawley, who has aspired to study divinity at the university city of Christminster, is trapped by a coarse girl into marriage—a tie which makes it impossible, even when she has deserted him, for him to pay court to his cousin Sue Bridehead, whom he later meets and loves. Meanwhile, on his application at the university, he has been told to practice his trade of stone mason and not to aspire beyond his position. Seeing him drunk, without appreciating the causes, Sue becomes engaged to Jude's former teacher and inspirer, the aged Phillotson. During her engagement the two cousins are thrown much together, and Jude for the first time tells Sue of his marriage to Arabella, only to precipitate her wedding to Phillotson. Sue, however, cannot endure the schoolteacher, and the latter generously releases her from her bonds, whereupon she goes to live with Jude. Yet she will not be his mistress, and Jude lives with her in peculiar torment until the return of Arabella from Australia arouses Sue's fear that she will lose him, and so she yields herself to him. Sue is divorced by Phillotson; Arabella has an opportunity to make a good match if Jude will legally release her and take their child, who has been born without his knowledge. Jude agrees to both these stipulations, and he and Sue are now free to wed, yet the pair cannot bring themselves to the ceremony, because each has had such a bitter experience with legal wedlock. Thus they drift along in natural union, Jude finding it increasingly difficult to support Sue and the children born to them. Some vague comprehension of the burden these children are creeps into the queer little mind of Arabella's child, who, while Jude and Sue are away, takes his own life and the lives of the others. This grim tragedy powerfully affects Sue, the hitherto flippant skeptic, who now conceives it her religious duty to return to Phillotson.

The threshing scene from Hardy's Tess of the d'Urbervilles. *Illustration by Hubert Herkomer for the serialization of* Tess *in the* Graphic, *December 5, 1891.*

The schoolteacher welcomes her back and again is formally married to her. Jude, deserted, is once more game for Arabella, whose husband is dead. Drunk again, he marries her, but the will to live in him is gone. The novel closes with Jude's death after a painful illness.

Summing up, before she becomes converted, her bitter experiences with Jude, Sue declares, "There is something external to us which says, 'You shan't!' First it said, 'You shan't learn!' Then it said, 'You shan't labor!' Now it says, 'You shan't love!' " Jude, on his part, quotes from a chorus of *Agamemnon:* "Nothing can be done. Things are as they are, and will be brought to their destined issue." It is clear that the author has a firmer conviction than his characters that they are deliberately plotted against. We again ask the question, Who is it that has arranged this plot? The daily paper is filled with incomprehensible events, yet we can recall no such Lappet weave of relationships in the most sensational journalistic story as appears in *Jude.* While disaster is inherent in a marriage based wholly upon sexual attraction or in a marriage where one member is as strongly impelled towards the sexual act as the other is repelled by it, is it likely, in the first place, that Jude would exercise an appeal for women of such different temperaments as Arabella and Sue? Is it probable that Sue, book-wise and not unacquainted with men (having lived in London with an Oxford student before the story opens), would have ever become engaged, much less legally wed, to Phillotson, who, by way of what is called "irony," was originally Jude's inspirer? Is it possible that Jude and Sue in the course of the novel would each suffer such a neat reversal of attitude—the pious, hymn-singing Jude becoming a complete skeptic, while the frivolous Sue is little short of a religious fanatic at the end of the tale, submitting her quivering flesh to the torture of Phillotson's embraces like a martyr? Is not Phillotson's first release of Sue a little breath-taking? Argue that he was glad to see her go (this is not Hardy's explanation) and his magnanimity in receiving her back is difficult to explain. In the first event, he is too enlightened for his experience; in the second, too blind and selfish for his earlier enlightenment.

There is also a little too much poetic justice in the fact that Arabella, who led Jude into marrying her by a deliberately false claim that she was pregnant, bears him a child eight months after separating from him. Would the sexually irresistible Arabella normally steer a course among all other males straight back to another marriage with Jude? Were none of the characters in the book capable of learning anything? Perhaps Jude, Sue, and Phillotson were not, but surely Arabella was. *Jude the Obscure* is challengeable on so many scores in regard to verisimilitude, that, powerful though the total effect of the prose is, the thesis of the author is flatly not demonstrated for anyone with any intelligence. On the other hand, it is very gratifying to meet in Hardy characters who are not god-like in beauty (as were the principals in *The Native*) or bucolically "pure," like Tess. *Jude the Obscure* has the further great merit of discussing the impulsions of sex with a frankness no other British author achieved for two decades, yet with a dignity which (since it has not been said before) is one of the salient characteristics of Hardy's best work. Indeed, the chief merit of Thomas Hardy is that he compelled serious

reflection in the most evasive decade in British and American history—the last ten years of Victoria and at the end of the Gilded Age. A man who could do this, whatever his artistic faults, is worthy of lasting respect.

More influential upon the rise of Naturalism in America than Thomas Hardy's *Native, Tess,* or *Jude* were two books by George Moore, *Confessions of a Young Man* (1888) and *Esther Waters* (1894). "Zola was the beginning of me," Moore wrote very truthfully, but before he encountered Zola, Moore had stored up a good deal of experience which was later exploited in his books. Son of a member of Parliament with a claim to distant relationship to Sir Thomas More, he was born at Moore Hall, County Mayo, Ireland, in 1852. An extraordinarily introspective youth, according to his own account, he early fell in love with Shelley who sustained him through the monotony of his school days at Oscott. When home, his father's racing stable was the focal point of his interest, and there he picked up all the curious lore about horses and jockeys and betting which he later used so admirably. The death of his father and a small talent in painting gave him the excuse at twenty to go to Paris which was his residence for the next ten years.

George Moore gravitated in the French city into what was then the most creative group of artists in the world, Monet, Renoir, Degas, Pissarro, and Manet, the last named becoming an especial friend. In this company he quickly learned that he was no painter, and turned to decadent verse for expression, Gautier and Baudelaire furnishing him models. Two volumes of poetry of "the fleshly school," *Flowers of Passion* (1878) and *Pagan Poems* (1881), attest to the fact that Moore might have easily become a minor Swinburne. Before these books were published, however, he had read with astonishment an article by Zola on the novel and immediately had become a convert to that man's theories. He returned to London, probably with the intention of reforming the English novel as a critic, but his style was "so rotten with French idiom" that the better journals would not tolerate his essays, and he was forced into fiction.

Moore's first novels are unimportant. *A Modern Lover,* in 1883, is a story of three women who sacrifice themselves for a shallow youth; while *A Mummer's Wife* (1885) studies the effect of sensual appetite on two quite different characters, good-natured Dick Lennox and his more temperamental wife Kate. They are perhaps not beneath the aims of a man who described art as a "sublime excrement." *A Drama in Muslin* (1886) is a slight book, but the drawing is better and firmer. None of these novels attracted any attention in America nor, singularly, did they find many readers here after George Moore became better known.

In 1888 George Moore published *Confessions of a Young Man,* an account of his early youth and days in Paris, with much incidental criticism and explanation of Decadence and Naturalism. The visit of Oscar Wilde to America had awakened considerable interest in the former, and the *Confessions* were widely read by those who wanted to inform themselves on topics that his advent brought into popular discussion. Moreover, the hero of the *Confessions,*

"Edward Dayne," furnished young American aesthetes with a model for a sophisticate, sufficiently different to seem original. There are some bright quips in the book, like that on Hugo's poetry—"the structure of the verse was too much in the style of public buildings to please me," but the criticism is none too sound and the explanations are altogether too facile for the *Confessions* to serve as a manual. Nevertheless countless Americans learned all they know about Impressionism, Decadence, and Naturalism from this book, and some few were stimulated by it to inquire further into the subjects there scanned and to acquire a sounder knowledge of them.

The popularity of the *Confessions* in America prepared the way for a more serious consideration, at least by creative writers, of Moore's best novel, *Esther Waters,* issued in 1894, than was accorded the book in England. We had perhaps not the class prejudices to overcome which made the story unattractive to the average British reader. For Esther is a serving girl who, to the end of her tale, never even dreams of becoming a princess: she is seduced and has a child, but not by one of the gentry, rather by one of her own class, a servitor in the house in which she was then employed. Driven from Barfields because of her condition, she endures every hardship in order to rear her child (at the end of the book she has the pleasure of seeing him, a stalwart young man, in a soldier's uniform!), endures without bitterness or complaining, clinging to her purpose as she clings to her narrow religious faith, blindly, stubbornly, yet heroically. When at last she may make an advantageous marriage to a book clerk, the lover reappears, and it is to him, in recognition of the power of animal attraction, that she is wed. William Latch, her husband, is a bookie who cannot give up betting once he has acquired a bar, and the ultimate forfeiting of his license ruins him. After William's death Esther returns to the service of her first mistress following a painful interlude as a drudge in a cheap lodging house.

The merits of *Esther Waters* are great: it may bluntly be said that the author has more nearly achieved verisimilitude in this one book than has Hardy in all his novels. And curiously, this is one of the most English books ever written: where else is there a better study of the betting fraternity, of the whole serving class, of the British "pub" than here? In the decay of British genius it took an Irishman to do it, but that has in no way affected the authenticity or accuracy of the work. The characterization of Esther herself is the prime achievement of the novel, yet the minor people are sharply limned and live beyond the story's duration. Stack and Journeyman who have different systems for the horses, Mrs. Spires who "cares" for the unwanted children of serving girls until they conveniently expire, Sarah who steals her mistress' silver for a lover who deserts her, Fred Parsons who becomes a captain in the Salvation Army after Esther chooses William Latch in his stead—all these may be seen in any East End tavern. Without challenging credulity, Moore has given Esther an amazingly rich experience in order to reveal the great variety of ways in which the serving girl is victimized by those who employ her. As wet nurse, she is expected to allow her own child to die in order that the infant of higher birth may be properly suckled; she must, when receiving a mere

pittance as housemaid, resist the temptation to pick up the small coin which has been deliberately "planted" merely to test her; and her duty is to report the foolish attentions of a son to her mistress though it means the forfeiture of her job. Esther displays a fine fortitude in the most trying situations, yet all that her pluck does for her is to land her precisely where she was at the beginning of the story, back at Barfields as a servant. Moore succeeds in convincing us, however, that without her strength of character Esther would have been forced down and down into prostitution and early death. She is the exception which really does prove the rule, and the thesis that the odds are against human beings, like herself, creatures of the lower class, is as well illustrated here as in any novel. Yet determinism is a generally conceded fact at the instinct level of intelligence, and what, after all, Moore has illustrated best is the blind nobility of maternal sacrifice in Esther Waters. It is a flawless character study.

Moore followed *Esther Waters* with *Evelyn Innes* (1898) and *Sister Teresa* (1901), ordinarily considered among his better novels. They are, however, of less consequence to us, since they are really inferior to *Esther Waters* and since they exerted but a slight influence in America. They are more definitely "written" and indicate the passing of Moore as an important Naturalist writer. Moore discovered the "last temple of my soul" in Pater's *Marius the Epicurean* in the late 'eighties, and the magic style of that book completely captivated him. Even when he penned the *Confessions* he acknowledged that Zola had no style—one could find anything in him from Chateaubriand to the reporting in the *Figaro*. The late suddenness with which the importance of style burst upon Moore reminds us of Wilde's remark to the effect that Moore had to write for seven years before he knew there was such a thing as grammar and for another seven before he realized that a paragraph had structure. Yet from 1888 onward Moore was more occupied with form than with substance. Style, however, he never achieved and frequent revisions of his books have not eliminated their stylistic defects. *Esther Waters* is rather a neatly planned book, and there are vivid bits of writing in it (one remembers Parson's blonde moustache, receding chin, and "the red sealing-wax lips"), yet there remain in the novel innumerable head-and-tailless sentences, like the following:

> On week days he wore a short jacket, and every day a ring of discoloured hair, neither brown nor red, but the neutral tint that hair which does not turn grey acquires under his chin.

Moore, after all, was more definitely Decadent than Naturalistic in his tastes, and it is not surprising to find him who had loved Gautier, Baudelaire, and Mallarmé swinging to Pater. *Marius the Epicurean,* with its aesthetic Christianity and its fake classicism, is responsible for *The Brook Kerith* (1916) and *Heloïse and Abelard* (1921) which Moore chose to regard as his most finished work. These novels must have been an enormous labor for their author with his little equipment, for they are more than passably well written, but they are as meaningless as the later work of Huysmans to Moore's contemporaries or to posterity. The Irishman's best is in *Esther Waters.*

Thomas Hardy and George Moore are the chief English sources of influence upon American Naturalism. Discovery and appreciation of George Gissing and Samuel Butler came too late to have any pronounced effect in this country. Naturalism was an established trend and Decadence had full momentum before we made thumbed classics out of *The Private Papers of Henry Ryecroft* and *The Way of All Flesh* in cheap American editions (1927). Americans had nothing to learn from the adulterated Naturalism of Arnold Bennett, and in the work of Rudyard Kipling and Joseph Conrad it was the Primitivistic rather than the Naturalistic (though they are related . . .) that caught American attention. Although the British influence upon creative artists was thus confined, there must be conceded to it the tremendous importance of loosening up the popular mind in America for our own Naturalists. Moore and Hardy in the 'eighties and 'nineties won the first considerable American reading public that Naturalism had, and whoever blinks this fact does the British authors a great injustice. How fortunate it is that crusaders in thought recognize no international law and respect no national boundaries. (pp. 48-82)

> *Oscar Cargill, "The Naturalists," in his* Intellectual America: Ideas on the March, *The Macmillan Company, 1941, pp. 48-175.*

An excerpt from Emile Zola's *Germinal* (1885)

Then Étienne went mad. A red mist swam before his eyes and blood surged up to his head. The blood-lust was upon him, as imperious as a physical need, as a lump of phlegm in the throat that makes you cough. It rose up in him and his will-power was swept away before the onrush of his hereditary taint. He laid hold of a flake of shale in the wall, tugged it from side to side until it came away. Huge and heavy though it was he raised it in both hands, and with superhuman strength brought it down on Chaval's skull.

He did not even have time to jump back, but went down with his face smashed in and skull split open. His brains spattered the gallery roof and a red flood streamed like a steady flowing spring, making a pool which reflected the smoky flame of the lamp. Darker shadows seemed to invade the narrow enclosed space, and the black corpse on the ground looked like a heap of slack.

Etienne stood over him, staring with dilated eyes. So he had done it, he had killed a man! All his past struggles swam through his consciousness; the unavailing fight against the latent poison in his system, the slowly accumulated alcohol in his blood. And yet he was far from drunk now, unless it were with hunger. The drunkenness of his parents long ago had sufficed. Though his hair stood on end at the horror of this murder, though all his upbringing cried out in protest, his heart was beating faster with sheer joy, the animal joy of an appetite satisfied at last. And then there was pride, the pride of the stronger. He had a fleeting vision of that young soldier's throat slit by a knife—killed by a child. Now he had killed, too.

> *Emile Zola, in his* Germinal, *translated by L. W. Tancock, Penguin Books Ltd., 1954.*

William C. Frierson

[In the following excerpt, Frierson examines the themes and techniques in the works of the French Naturalists in terms of their effect on English literature.]

It is hard for us to imagine the post-Victorian development of English fiction along strictly English lines. Perhaps the tendency would have been toward regionalism. Perhaps it would have been toward romantic realism and realistic romance in line with the effort of Blackmore, Stevenson, Haggard, and Kipling. Perhaps the "matter-of-fact romance" would have continued. Perhaps with the approach of the critical spirit in the twentieth century the tendency would have been toward satire.

As it so happened, the translation into English of French naturalistic novels furnished the occasion for a revaluation of the English novel's aims. Change was slow in coming. As will later be shown, the years 1885-95 were years of fierce controversy. But critical standards were altered, and the great figures of 1900-1917 were all in one way or another subject to strong naturalistic influence—Gissing, George Moore, Henry James, Arnold Bennett, Galsworthy, Wells, Maugham, Joyce.

Indeed, the naturalistic conception of fiction as a cosmic commentary—an outgrowth of Flaubert's theories—has generally prevailed in twentieth-century fiction. Up to World War I, writers in England were progressively concerned with the material details of human enterprise, the influence of circumstances upon individuals and classes, the mixture of qualities which make personality, the problem of fulfillment. Their spirit of inquiry was not that of the Victorians, and the presentation was based upon a logical sequence of events which could not have been of English origin.

There can be no adequate understanding of post-1885 English fiction without a knowledge of French naturalism. A million copies of translated naturalistic works were circulated in Britain before 1890, according to Ernest Vizetelly, whose father was chief publisher of the translations. Even in India during the nineties the translations crowded English novels off the market. English authors began to learn from naturalism, each in his own particular way.

The English modifications of naturalism produced the modern English novel. We shall later be interested in noting the temperamental limitations of English authors and the extent to which naturalism proved palatable to English taste.

The Victorian realists sought to present with conventional reticence the *matter* of life but allowed themselves full liberty to alter its typical *manner*. On the other hand, the French naturalists sought to portray both the *matter* and the *manner* of life. They would give the results of an impersonal study of representative men and women of their own time. In extreme cases their presentations were actually similar to clinical monographs. French naturalism is distinctive for its social consciousness. Since the effort was to reveal life, and therefore to expose it, the attitude of the author was necessarily critical. Man was a creature of circumstance, thwarted and degraded by certain specific causes. The novelist, taking his cue from experimental science, would become an experimental moralist by checking against the facts of life an observed or documented case of typical human behavior. The theories of Zola as propounded in *Le roman expérimental* were based upon the application of experimental science to physiology as developed in the writings of Dr. Claude Bernard.

Obviously since truth-telling was the aim, the naturalistic novelist would be brutally frank. He would give detailed descriptions of seductions, and in describing married life he would not stop at the doorways to bedrooms. He would describe the lives of harlots and he would enter houses of prostitution. He would expose vice and "foul passions." Equally important was the fact that the naturalists were debunkers of the romantic view. It served their purpose, therefore, to show that dreams and pleasant illusions are at variance with the harsh facts of life. The naturalists took pains to imply that God is unresponsive to prayers and to good intentions, and that violations of the moral code generally go unpunished. They treated the spirit and flesh as elements of the same central substance; today we would call them monists.

Certain phrases often applied to naturalism are misleading. It is sometimes said that naturalism is "literary photography," "a cross section of life." Obviously the terms are ill applied, for they exclude selection as a principle of composition. They exclude the alteration and grouping of material as it passes through the mind of the author, and the naturalists did not forbid rearrangement.

In striving to be impersonal the naturalists made painful efforts to conceal their temperamental likes and aversions. Yet Flaubert, who most nearly approached impersonality in his writings, realized the limits of any attempt and merely advised that the author extend as far as possible the moral horizon of his judgments. In perspective we see the naturalists as a group with humanitarian sympathies and a conviction of the cruelty and irrationality of human life. We see them aspiring to form and proportion; we see them bent upon showing the logical sequence of events; we see them stressing, often overstressing, motivation. We see them, within the limitations of their temperaments, endeavoring not to distort life; and we see them, bound by the spirit of a school, presenting selected aspects of life which give us a special and exceptional view of it. We realize now that this group spirit was characterized by a sympathy with the varied phases of human fallibility and a feeling that conventional valuations are awry. Even advocates of the naturalists admit a certain justification in Bouvier's unsympathetic comment that the naturalists' "principles of artistic conscience" were "hatred of the bourgeois, dislike of industrial civilization and a normally regulated life, sympathy for outcasts, eccentrics, lawbreakers, and nomads" [*La bataille réaliste*, 1914].

In form we note that the naturalists strove to show the direct relation of cause and effect; that they attempted to expose the influence of circumstance—though Zola was also concerned with heredity; that they followed in the main Zola's precept in *Le roman expérimental*—to show "what a certain 'passion,' aroused under certain circumstances and in a certain environment, will result in as regards the individual and society."

Surveyed in its general nature, the work of the naturalists is distinctive for its exposure of the framework of society, for its clarification of the springs of action, particularly among the lower orders, for its exploration of the network of evils attendant on industrial civilization, and for its vital presentation of the masses in action. Walter Myers gives a convenient summary [in *The Later Realism,* 1927]:

> Naturalism disdains literary graces and purports to tell the truth about life as it has been revealed by science. In telling the truth naturalism professes to follow exactly the method of science, that is, collection of detailed evidence, induction from this evidence, and impersonal setting forth of the conclusions. Unlike native British realism, naturalism opposes the use of any typification or idealization which will not serve to demonstrate that all men are by nature akin to the beasts, particularly in matters of sex. Moreover naturalism asserts, as Eliot and Meredith never did, the supreme importance of heredity and environment; and it finds its best material in the most degraded classes and in the revolting aspects of life.

One should avoid too close a definition of naturalism. The naturalists differed widely in their practices, and scarcely any two French critics have agreed on who are the naturalists and what naturalism really is. Louis Cons, who has a closer knowledge of the French writers than Professor Myers, is wary of generalizations:

> Naturalism is a label we put for convenience' sake on certain writers who differ widely from one another but who have in common a certain attitude towards Life and (this last point is very important) towards the Public. If I were obliged at the point of a sword to define this attitude, I would say it consists in admitting to the field of the novel all manifestations of life and in expecting the reader to stand the shock, or that naturalism is a literary anticipation of *Behaviorism* in that it describes life as a chain of reflexes responding to stimuli. Thus Zola, whose novels tend towards clinical monographs as a limit, is the typical Naturalist. Flaubert, Goncourt, Maupassant are less consistent Naturalists, for they still at times see Nature as a setting, as a landscape in which Man moves, and not exclusively as the inflexible Scheme of Things in which man is engulfed. In Maupassant we still hear the rustling of wind and water. In Zola, we hear only the swish of the whip of Man's Slave-drivers, Hunger and Sex. [*Journal of English and Germanic Philology,* October 1928]

The divergences among the naturalists necessitate a somewhat careful treatment of the important figures in the movement. Each author extended the conception of the term "naturalism," and each author influenced English writers. It would be tedious . . . to pause for clarification of each separate influence. The exposition of the spirit and technique of individual naturalists made in this [essay] will doubtless be valuable for reference purposes. Furthermore an effort will here be made to call attention to qualities of kinship. Insofar as possible the term "naturalism" will be extended to cover divergences within the school.

We are not here concerned with the minor figures in the movement. Our concern is with the unifying tendencies among the masters. Naturalism as a literary label has become part of the international literary vocabulary, and the law of custom has bound inseparably the names of Flaubert, the Goncourts, Zola, and Maupassant. Let us first consider the ideas and purposes common to these writers.

Naturalism arose, on the one hand, from the psychological theories propounded by Taine and, on the other, from the influence of Balzac. These influences, of course, were dissimilar; that of Taine was direct, that of Balzac indirect. Taine expounded the great doctrine of "causes": "no matter if the facts be physical or moral, they all have their causes; there is a cause for ambition, for courage, for truth, as there is for muscular development, for digestion, for animal heat. Vice and virtue are products, like vitriol and sugar; and every complex phenomenon arises from other more simple phenomena on which it hangs. Let us then seek the simple phenomena for moral qualities, as we seek them for physical qualities" [*History of English Literature*, 1873].

Balzac's influence was to inculcate the taste for document-like precision when dealing with the facts of life. We find in his writings a careful insistence upon the details of material circumstance, a concern with heredity, and a preoccupation with habits of mind. Nevertheless, we cannot call Balzac a naturalist, because naturalism is essentially a study of a significant phase of life. Balzac's studies are exceptional, oblique, romantic. They testify to the endless variety of life, to the caprices of temperament, of obsession. Balzac is an expressionist who concerns himself with the naturalistic treatment of fevered and overbalanced minds. His stories are based upon conceptions rather than upon observation. Life furnished hints, starting points, settings. It was a tropical wilderness where he wandered, picking out strange multicolored flowers which he would arrange according to his own conceptions into a well-ordered garden. Sometimes nature's careless grouping would furnish him with an idea, but often he was too intent upon his own bizarre designs to seek guidance from nature.

Thus Balzac created the taste for reality in fiction without completely satisfying it. A closer approach to reality was made by Flaubert when he published in 1857 *Madame Bovary*.

Before *Madame Bovary* was written, no novelist had taken the theme of his story from a human event of a seriously significant nature, analyzed the motives which had been the directing forces, and rendered the result of his investigation without partiality or prejudice, changing it only in so far as to make it fit in with a rationalized scheme of human action and a technical plan of dramatic effectiveness.

Flaubert attempted an objective and passionless rendering of naturally arranged human phenomena. "The artist should be in his work, like God in Creation, invisible and all-powerful," he writes in a letter. "He should be felt ev-

erywhere and seen nowhere. And then art should be raised above personal affections and nervous susceptibilities. It is time to give it the precision of the physical sciences by means of a pitiless method." The new approach is associated in Flaubert's mind with a style of clarity and exactness. "I love before everything," he writes, "the nervous, substantial, clean phrase with swelling muscle, gleaming skin; I like masculine, not feminine phrases."

But Flaubert did more than establish a new procedure in the method of writing novels. He adopted a spirit of approach to his material which was not without its influence. He would show human weakness and incapacity "in a fashion to set one musing"; he would "inspire a pathetic contemplation, like that of the stars." Humanity was tainted, cursed by God, and hence irresponsible: "However well we may feed the animal man, however thickly we may gild his stable, even though we give him the softest and most luxurious litter, he will ever remain a beast. The only progress upon which one can count is to make the beast less of a cannibal. But as to raising the level of his ideas, or inspiring the masses with a broader conception of God, I doubt it, I doubt it." For humanity, therefore, he felt not love but compassion. "Tout comprendre est tout pardonner." "Christ's blood which stirs in us, nothing can extirpate that, nothing can drain its source; our business is not to dry it up, but to make channels for it." [*Correspondence*, 1893]

The persistent contemplation of human misery and the analysis and explanation of human action according to a mechanistic conception are the distinguishing features in the realistic writings of Flaubert and those of his associates and followers whom we gather loosely together under the title of "naturalists." "All human observers are sad and must be so," write the Goncourts. "They are but spectators of life, witnesses; they take part neither in what will deceive nor in what will intoxicate. Their normal condition is that of a melancholic serenity." And again, "The telescopic and microscopic researches of the present day, the exploration of the infinitely great and of the infinitely little, the science of the star and of the microscope, lead to the same infinite depth of sadness. They lead the human thought to something far sadder to man than death—to a conviction of that nothing which is his lot even while alive" [*Idées et sensations*, 1886].

"Ah, the poor wretches, the poor wretches," says Maupassant after visualizing in reverie the forms of relief from life taken by Paris' thousands of yearly suicides, "how well I have felt their anguish, how really I have felt myself dying their own death! I have been through every phase of their miserable lives. I have known all the sorrows, all the tortures that brought them there; for I have felt the deceitful infamy of life better than anyone has ever felt it before" [*Misti*, 1912].

"Que c'est triste, la vie!" are words uttered by a young painter standing beside the corpse of a woman who has killed herself.

> Comme il y a des êtres malheureux! Je sentais peser sur cette créature humaine l'éternel injustice de l'implacable nature. . . . Et je comprenais qu'elle crût à Dieu, celle-là, et qu'elle eût

espéré ailleurs la compensation de sa misère. Elle allait maintenant se decomposer et devenir plante à son tour. Elle fleurirait au soleil, serait broutée par les vaches, emportée en grain par les oiseaux, et chair des bêtes, elle redeviendrait de la chair humaine. Mais ce qu'on appele l'âme s'etait éteint au fond du puits noir.

Zola, for his part, had certainly no pleasant illusions about life. In moments of depression he was wont to think, with his own Dr. Pascal, that the only hope for humanity was regeneration through the injection of a serum! The exposure of human tares was his specialty, and no one, before or since, has found so many of them. Like the other naturalists, he had no pleasant illusions about an afterlife and considered death as "la déchéance au fond d'un cabanon, l'abominable décomposition de l'être."

Flaubert, the Goncourts, and Maupassant were humanitarians only artistically. They pitied and blamed not, but they were unconcerned with plans for human betterment. Zola, however, had faith in human progress, progress which was to be attained by pitiless truth and publicity. "If I were conducting a school of morals," he wrote in 1869, "I would hasten to put into the hands of my pupils *Madame Bovary* and *Germinie Lacerteux,* convinced, as I am, that truth alone can instruct and sustain generous souls." Enlightenment, therefore, exposure, and the further seeking of truth constituted a plan of action to which he adhered with something of religious faith. He might well have spoken the creed of Dr. Pascal: "I believe that the pursuit of truth by science is the divine ideal which a man should prescribe for himself. I believe that all is illusion and vanity which does not contribute to the treasure of those slowly acquired truths which will never be lost. I believe that the sum of these truths, augmented continually, will in the end give to mankind incalculable power and serenity, if not happiness. Yes, I believe in the final triumph of life."

In matters of technique there were many points upon which the naturalists agreed. Plots in the old sense were discountenanced and human action re-examined from what they chose to call a scientific point of view. If abnormal relations were considered, an attempt was made to generalize upon the abnormality—similar cases were investigated and the principles of conduct there determined were applied to a particular incident. Malice was largely eradicated from the characters; evil became a form of ignorance. Conflicts were portrayed in the lives of persons groping for happiness in blind and pathetic fashions. Simple, or at least uncultivated, types were generally chosen in order that universally recognized motives be attributed to them, and in order that the natural or physical aspects of life be shown as the controlling forces. Anything of a spiritual nature was but "a more finely-woven flesh." Startling or significant phases of life were selected for investigation, and the artist tried "not to belittle art for the sake of an isolated personality."

But differences are immediately in evidence. Flaubert chose to delineate character and its development through vivifying the mental processes of certain individuals. "What Flaubert strove to do in revealing scientifically the special quality of a certain human mind was to show the

thoughts and sensations which ran through it, and to stress by repetition and rhythm the more significant ones," writes Paul Bourget [in *Essais de psychologie contemporaine,* 1901]. "Authors of monologues do this, and the author of *Madame Bovary* follows their procedure. His characters are associations of ideas which walk." Each thought or idea reveals, therefore, a significant trait of the person who conceives it, and the poetic qualities of the human soul are revealed through the rhythm and form by which its preoccupations are presented.

As regards the presentation of incidents, Flaubert is not to be distinguished from the other naturalists by the fact that his method is "scenic," but by the fact that his work is more "scenic" than theirs. A rather evident feature is that the foreground rather than the background is made prominent. He portrays few landscapes and vistas; there are houses, streets, a chemistry shop, an inn, and, above all, people. Color, as in an impressionist's picture, is reflected. Speech, ideas, emotions, and customs—all have their interplay and effect. Figures are never isolated; there are no mere portraits; we are shown at close view a succession of scenes.

Sensitiveness and acuteness of vision account for the visual quality of Flaubert's work. "There is at present such a gulf fixed between myself and the rest of the world," he writes, "that I sometimes experience a feeling of astonishment when I hear even the most ordinary and casual things; there are certain gestures, certain intonations of voice which fill me with surprise, and there are certain silly things which nearly make me giddy." It was these

Frank Norris at the time he was writing his Epic of the Wheat, which included The Octopus *(1901) and* The Pit *(1903).*

startling and significant gestures and phrases which were to Flaubert the essence of pictorial art; they could stand for pages of careless description. "The unexpected is in everything," he told Maupassant. "The least object contains an unknown element or aspect. Find that" [Maupassant, Introduction to *Pierre et Jean,* 1925].

Perhaps the casual reader will note that the story of *Madame Bovary* is too interesting to be taken from life. Flaubert transformed his material by elevating certain characters and by eradicating the artistic crudities of his material to fit in with a rational scheme of human action and a technical plan of dramatic effectiveness. It was in this way that he attempted to give "truth rendered by beauty."

The method of the Goncourts is in striking contrast to that of Flaubert. As the researches of Olin H. Moore conclusively show, the Goncourts were unconcerned with consistent characterizations and with modifying human action so that it would seem reasonable. Believers in "l'illogique du vrai," they neglected unified effects. To quote Mr. Moore:

> The Goncourts, with their photographic method, often attempt to attribute to "A" as it were the *exact* finger-print of "X," the *exact* head of "Y," and the *exact* temperament of "Z." Their method would be less vulnerable if "A's" finger bore only an ordinary resemblance to that of "X." The difficulty is that the Goncourts, by renouncing the principle of selection in art, are prone to insist upon an *absolute resemblance*— their notes frequently being thrust into their novels without alteration. Thus their characters, though possessing features, living in surroundings, and speaking a language precisely such as have been observed in real life, and jotted down with infinite pains upon the author's pads, are far from being truly realistic. They are contrary to "nature," to "history," and to the medical science of which the Goncourts professed themselves disciples. Many a romantic character of the early nineteenth century novel, though improbable, was at least possible, while the characters of the Goncourts would seem, if our reasoning is just, to be in many cases impossible. [*PMLA,* XXXI]

In reading the novels of the Goncourts, one feels that their practice was to write more in accord with documentary evidence than did Flaubert, but with less artistic comeliness of design. Abnormal and exceptional elements abound in both the characters and the story. There is much of newspaper veracity in their accounts, but one feels that these accounts often reveal no more significant aspects of life than do the daily papers. Their characteristic procedure is to portray human beings of a low order of intelligence who are made unhappy by an assembly of unfortunate circumstances. The influence of environment and incidents is, by inference, overstressed; the human will is all but obliterated.

Furthermore, the novels of the Goncourts take the form of chronicles. In the main there is an avoidance of epic or dramatic treatment. Incidents are related rather than portrayed, and the gradual development or disintegration of character is indicated by the delineation in separate chapters of incidents which may be supposed to have produced certain effects.

One strong point of similarity between Flaubert and the Goncourts, however, is their hypersensitiveness. In *Idées et sensations* we find the state of mind mentioned:

> I perceive that literature and observation, instead of deadening my sensibility has extended and refined it, developed it and laid it bare. . . . By observing and noting relations one becomes, instead of hardened, a sort of creature without skin, who is wounded by the least impression, utterly defenseless and seeping blood.

In such states both Flaubert and the Goncourts sought for an unknown element or aspect of the least object, but their procedure was different. While Flaubert attempted an objective description of clarity and exactness, the Goncourts under the influence of a "forte fièvre hallucinatoire" sought to portray the scene or object in mind subjectively, in associating with the scene or object their own reactions to it. In order to record precisely their sensations they fashioned similes and metaphors of a certain originality, employing words outside of their usual connotations, and applying adjectives usually considered appropriate to one object as applicable to another.

Both Flaubert and the Goncourts seemed unconscious that they wrote to perpetuate their particular illusions of life—in the case of the Goncourts an illusion of life fostered by a rather dogmatic determinism; in that of Flaubert "une vision personelle du monde" in which the limitations and incapacity of humanity are the most evident features. It remained for Maupassant, Flaubert's pupil, to render his vision of life with humility. The "truth" which he portrays is consciously that which seems significant according to his particular temperament. Realism, he holds, should not be considered the portrayal of "reality" but that of personal visions of life. To decide which happenings are significant is the function of the artist. He elects and rearranges in accord with the dictates of his artistic temperament.

Maupassant was at great pains to refute the slander that the group of writers to which he belonged were bent upon giving a cross section of life. A photographic presentation of life would show it to be "brutal, made up of disconnected and unrelated segments, full of unexplainable, illogical, and contradictory catastrophes." Art, he says, consists in showing relations, in selection and regrouping with the aim of making visible a certain special truth which the artist feels to be significant and profound. Again he says:

> No one can claim to portray "reality." The truths that we see are the products of our conceptions, and therefore of our organs. Our eyes, our ears, our noses, our different tastes create as many truths as there are men on the face of the earth. And our spirits, receiving instruction from these differently constituted organs, analyze and pass judgment as if each of us belonged to another race. . . . Each of us creates his illusion of the world, and the great artists are those who impose upon humanity their own particular illusions. [Introduction to *Pierre et Jean*]

Maupassant's particular illusion of life did not differ materially from that of the other naturalists—pity for, and scorn of, humanity's helpless blundering, hatred of sham and hypocrisy, and a sad or bitter acceptance of the imperfectibility of humanity and of the relentless influence of circumstance. But his vision was not rigid or uniformly severe. A pervading Gallic animalism by some strange magic tints the pitiful with the pathetic in his writings; the immensity and organic unity of creation seemed ever in his thoughts, lending perspective to the affairs of mice and men. Maupassant's theory was that the adroit grouping of "petits faits" would show the profound and concealed significance of happenings. But he did not depend upon the grouping alone for interpretation. A deft phrase or sentence, sometimes keenly insinuating, sometimes grimly pathetic, sometimes of a sophistical nature, gives point to his accounts; often carries suggestions of universality. And the artist must be a close and careful student of life.

> He must show how the feelings are modified under the influence of environmental circumstance, how the sentiments and passions develop, how people love one another, how they hate one another, how struggles evolve in all the ranks of society, how within an individual the varied bourgeois interests fight for dominance—the interests of family and of money and of politics.

Aside from *Bel-Ami,* which stands as the perfect example of the "experimental novel," Maupassant's stories are his most naturalistic writings. In them he could give expression to disconnected, unrelated "truths." But when he tried to associate the varied phenomena of life, as is necessary in a novel, he often evaded the artistic principle of detachment which Flaubert taught him. I refer in particular to *Mont-Oriol, Notre cœur,* and *Fort comme la mort.* In these his personal sympathies are in evidence. He shows a fondness for the well-dressed and cultivated beau, and a leaning, rather conventionally French, toward the romance of intrigue. Even the sorrows and languors are romantic; the stark, naturalistic note of tragedy is lacking.

In two novels, however, he shows himself to be the detached and critical student of life. *Pierre et Jean* is a psychological portrayal. The author uses the magnifying glass upon a family situation. Social considerations are neglected and attention forced upon a soul tortured by the stain of illegitimacy upon his name and the dishonor reflected upon his father's household. Maupassant's other naturalistic novel, *Bel-Ami,* follows the procedure typical of Zola. A particular phase of society is exposed through the delineation of a life history. The author chooses for his central figure an ambitious and good-looking young journalist who is without delicate scruples. The journalist rises to a position of prominence through the influence of women, and the organic functioning of society is critically shown in a delineation of journalistic influence, political corruption, and feminine power.

We note that with the exception of *Bel-Ami*—which was written after Zola had attained a position of dominance in French fiction—the realistic work of Flaubert, the Goncourts, and Maupassant dealt largely with the nature of the human heart. Society was of importance in its relation to the individual. Zola looks through the other end of the telescope. Individuals are of importance in their relation to society.

As Henry James so ably points out, Zola's novels deal with Things in a gregarious form—classes, crowds, confusions, movements, industries. Zola gives us individual life reflected in generalized terms; he shows the effect of character and passion in the lump and by the ton; and his particular talent lies in making his characters swarm, and in giving them a great central Thing to swarm about—"some highly representative institution or industry of the France of his time, some seated Moloch of custom, of commerce, of faith, lending itself to portrayal through its abuses and excesses, its idol-face and great devouring mouth" [*Notes on Novelists,* 1914].

We may illustrate what is meant by "great central Thing" by specific reference. *Le ventre de Paris* deals with the process of feeding the huge city, with the great markets as the focal point of attraction; *Au bonheur des dames,* the spread of the mammoth department store showing "its ravage amid the smaller fry of the trade, of all the trades, picturing these latter gasping for breath in an air pumped clean by its mighty lungs"; *Germinal,* the coal miner and life in the underworld of the pits; *L'Assommoir,* drink among the lower orders and the depravity to which it may lead; *La Bête humaine,* the great railway; *L'Argent,* finance, banking, and the French stock market; *La Débâcle,* the Franco-Prussian War; *Faute de l'Abbé Mouret,* a critical study of ecclesiastical life; *Vérité,* the evils of clerical influence and popular prejudice; *Nana,* the demimonde; *La Curée,* the decline of the second empire.

When we consider that one of the central features of Zola's labors was to assimilate an unbelievable variety of the details of human enterprise, a natural curiosity leads us to the moral theory underlying his portentous documentation. The theory, when we discover it, shows how closely Zola is allied in spirit to the other naturalists, for Zola was perhaps more conscious than the others of the variety of human taints and the well-nigh irremediable depravity brought about by man's inhumanity. Havelock Ellis adequately phrases this aspect of Zola's conception:

> All are the victims of an evil social system, as Zola sees the world, the enslaved workers as well as the overfed masters; the only logical outcome is a clean sweep—the burning up of the chaff and the straw, the fresh furrowing of the earth, the new spring of a sweet and vigorous race. That is the logical outcome of Zola's attitude, the attitude of one who regards our present society as a thoroughly vicious circle. His pity for men and women is boundless; his disdain is equally boundless. It is only towards animals that his tenderness is untouched by contempts; some of his most memorable passages are concerned with the sufferings of animals. The New Jerusalem may be fitted up, but the Montsou miners will never reach it; they will fight for the first small, stuffy, middle-class villa they meet on the way. And Zola pours out the stream of his pitiful, pitiless irony on the weak, helpless, erring children of Men. [*Affirmation,* 1922]

But the hopeless vision above indicated could hardly have sustained Zola in the labors he imposed upon himself. I am disposed to consider him perfectly sincere in his suggestion, "Let us expose everything in order that everything may be healed." It is true, of course, that his hates become involved. "We naturalists are experimental moralists," Zola avowed. "We show through delineating a human experience how a passion works under certain circumstances. Whenever men understand the mechanism of this passion, they can reduce it or render it as inoffensive as possible. And thus the naturalistic novel is of practical moral value in that it takes the human mechanism apart piece by piece and then shows how the parts function under certain conditions. In time we can make generalizations and determine laws which have only to be applied if we wish to correct abuses and arrive at better social conditions."

Although Zola's theories cannot be neglected in forming an estimate of his work, we would do well not to apply all the theories to all the work. When taxed for his aberrations, Zola would reply, "Yes, I admit it. I am just an old-fashioned romantic." "Oh my God," he once expostulated, "I laugh just as you do at this word 'naturalism.' I repeat it because we must give things new names so people will think them new." And is not *Au bonheur des dames* a romance rather than an experimental novel? Nevertheless it may be said with all factors taken into account that Zola included the substance of life in his novels about as well as it could be done with due consideration given to interest and organic unity.

Zola's most enlightened critical utterance is that "art is a particular corner of existence seen through a temperament." His own temperament was, of course, largely a product of literary influences. The remarkable fact, however, is that he was a person of sufficient capacity to assimilate Hugo, Balzac, the Goncourts, and Charles Reade without imitating any one of them. Zola's temperament was a strangely homogeneous compound of three outstanding qualities:

That part of Zola's temperament which is socialist-reformer is indicated by the painstaking portrayal of the varied forms of human error and the details of these great Things which tend to create it.

That part of Zola's nature which is sensationalist is shown by his tendency to write exposés and by his stressing of physiological factors. As Arthur Symons points out, there is everywhere in Zola's novels the "savor of plebeian flesh." Zola shows a preference for the crude and animalistic qualities. But the suggestion that Zola had in mind the sale of his books cannot be overlooked. Zola might have been either a humanitarian or a sensationalist; as a matter of fact, he was both.

That part of Zola's nature which is romanticist is indicated by the zest and color of his narrative, his sensationalism, the exaggerated accounts of scenes of squalor, and the thumping of the tom-toms in the spectacular displays of mass action and mass force.

We have noted that only Zola among the naturalists was intent upon social change and the alteration of individual behavior. Flaubert, Maupassant, and the Goncourts by probing into motivation with scientific detachment felt only "a pathetic contemplation like that of the stars." Their despair, and the despair of scientific agnosticism, was aptly phrased by the Goncourts: "The telescopic and microscopic researches of the present day . . . lead . . . human thought to something far sadder to man than death—to a conviction of that nothing which is his lot even while alive." It was largely Zola's individual incitement to a general investigation of industrial civilization which was to affect the social impulses of both the nineties and the Edwardian period; but underlying the specific urge to explore the social framework was a conception of man developed in the works of all the naturalists. According to this conception mankind is, in the words of André Maurois,

> a confused crowd of poor human animals who think that they act freely, who suppose that they love, hate, judge, of their own responsibility, and who are in reality the toys of a few desperately simple physical and chemical laws. . . . Such a pessimistic theory leads to a tender sympathy for men. This is true in the first place because one cannot keep from pitying those unfortunate animals who are always the victims of illusions without remedy, always committing in vain tasks that lead to nothing except death; and, in the second place, scientific fatalism, by making all moral judgments absurd, imposes upon the writer an admirable impartiality in regard to his characters. [*Nouvelles Littéraires,* 6 March, 1926]

This view has been dominant in twentieth-century English fiction. It is needless to say, perhaps, that it has produced a revolution in moral and ethical values. It prepared the way for Freud and for fiction reflecting his ideas. (pp. 15-34)

> *William C. Frierson, "Naturalism in French Fiction," in his* The English Novel in Transition: 1885-1940, *University of Oklahoma Press, 1942, pp. 15-34.*

Lars Åhnebrink

[*Åhnebrink is a Swedish educator and critic who has written extensively on American literature. In the following essay, he discusses the inception and major proponents of Naturalism in France and the movement's manifestations throughout Europe.*]

Naturalism is a term somewhat loosely applied to the literary movement that may be said to have taken its inception from Flaubert's *Madame Bovary* (1857) and developed in the works of the brothers Goncourt, Zola, Daudet, Maupassant, and others. Zola became the champion of the new literary tendencies. After 1870 this movement took on the dignity of a naturalistic school of letters which greatly influenced French literature in the seventies and eighties. When in 1877 Zola achieved his success with *L'Assommoir,* naturalism was gaining rapid headway and the ten years between the publication of this novel about the lower classes and *La Terre* (1887) marked the climax of the movement in France. As early as 1884, however, a reaction set in, for in that year J.-K. Huysmans, Zola's friend and at first a faithful disciple of naturalism, published his famous *A Rebours,* in which he abjured his allegiance to the school. In 1887 there appeared the well-known *Manifeste des Cinq,* in which five of Zola's former disciples repudiated naturalism, or, more correctly, the Zolaism and bestiality of *La Terre.*

French naturalism, which exerted a certain influence on the literatures of other countries, developed out of the realism of the reign of Louis-Philippe and of the second Empire. It was a logical outgrowth of nineteenth century thought in the realm of letters. Great discoveries in the natural sciences affected the intellectual outlook of the century—the leading idea was evolution—and offered new visions and new prospects to mankind. The mid-century discoveries seemed revolutionary. Traditional thinking about man and the universe was challenged. The scientific tendencies of the period were characterized by a repudiation of previously accepted propositions and by a reliance on observation, experience, and facts; the century may be described as analytic, intellectual, and interrogative, in search of truth and exactness. Science put its imprint on it and became a sort of fetish which people worshiped for it seemed to offer a solution of the riddles of the universe. Nothing occult or transcendental existed; spiritual and organic phenomena were equally deduced from matter; natural laws were omnipotent and controlled everything; matter was the entire reality. Science invaded many fields of learning and rapid changes were effectuated through its impact on philosophy, religion, politics, belles-lettres, etc. In the field of religion, for instance, it threatened the supremacy of orthodoxy. The metaphysical school of philosophy was partly superseded by positivism, and realism received a new tenor, a new substance of ideas, which eventually led to naturalism. The basic philosophy of literary naturalism was deterministic and positivistic and consequently the naturalists focused their interests on the external reality. Darwin's interpretation of the mechanism of the universe, the positivism of Comte, and Marx's socialism were adopted by the naturalistic school. Mill, Spencer, Buckle, Huxley, Haeckel, and other scholars substantially influenced the new generation. The new scientific, philosophical, and social ideas were merged in the naturalistic novel and gave to it its specific character.

The scientific method of the natural sciences was applied to fields where emotion, speculation, and imagination predominated. For instance, Renan, an intimate friend of Berthelot, the chemist, used it in writing of religion. Claude Bernard's *Introduction à l'étude de la médecine expérimentale* (1865) did much to establish medicine as an exact science and he successfully advocated an experimental method. Upon this book Zola founded *Le Roman expérimental,* which demanded a literature governed by science and in which he used the same method as the scientist. By substituting for the word "doctor" the word "novelist," he could make his meaning clear and give to the work of art the rigidity of a scientific truth. He formulated the theory of naturalism and illustrated it in his gigantic study of degeneracy, *Les Rougon-Macquart.* To him literature, like medicine, was no longer an art; it was a science.

By applying the method of the scientist to literature, he hoped to raise the novel to the level of science, since to him and to others of his time the voice of science was ultimate truth. He based his ideas on the theories of Taine, who became the philosopher and theorist of naturalism. His theories about the causes of human actions and particularly his doctrines of *race, milieu,* and *moment* challenged traditional conceptions of man; these ideas were, of course, mainly derived from Darwin. Taine reduced psychology to physiology and the study of character to the study of temperament, and he applied his positivistic formula to literary criticism. He taught moreover that the physical milieu constantly affected the individual, who was subjected to the rigidity of determinism. Zola reduced Taine's doctrines to the study of heredity and milieu, the two basic factors which, to him, fundamentally transformed and reshaped human destinies.

Zola and other naturalists introduced into the novel a pseudo-scientific terminology. Many naturalistic novels were saturated with scientific terms and technical detail; the brothers Goncourt spoke of "la méthode anatomique," and the novel was nothing but "une analyse," "une étude," "un cas pathologique." In *Les Rougon-Macquart* Zola's intentions were purely scientific, for he stated explicitly in the preface to *La Fortune des Rougon* (1871) that he wanted to "expliquer" the development of a family through the "analyse" based upon "des documents" and that "l'hérédité" had its laws as "la pesanteur." The method of clinical dissection was successfully used in *Madame Bovary* by Flaubert, who, a doctor's son, said: "Je me suis moi-même franchement disséqué au vif en des moments peu drôles." Scientific methods and beliefs became of great importance to the contents and the technique of the naturalistic novel. It became "un roman documentaire," based solidly on physical reality and crammed with facts and data actually seen and experienced. The naturalistic writer was to seek the truth in the spirit of a scientist, for Zola and his followers did not admit of anything occult; reality, hard and brutal as it was, had to be described with exact minuteness of detail. The naturalist was to collect "human documents" and make a series of preliminary studies, sketches, etc., before he set about doing the real work. This involved careful preparation and endless toil; Zola was a great worker and his slogan was: "Travaillez, tout est là!" Imagination and plot were reduced to a minimum.

The result was both beneficial and detrimental to the novel. On the one hand it increased the sense of fidelity to reality and observed facts. Successful handling of the documents Zola exhibited, for instance, in *L'Assommoir* and *Germinal.* On the other hand he often went to extremes and created such distortions of reality as *La Faute de l'abbé Mouret* and *Le Ventre de Paris.* The naturalist had learnt from Taine that the milieu was of primary importance in the life of the individual and as a result much of the space was given to the description of setting. Furthermore, the French writers had a predilection for a certain kind of setting. Usually their stories took place in great industrial cities, preferably in the slums, which were exposed without mercy. Sometimes the descriptions expanded into accurate surveys of an epoch and became veritable documents of historical value. The naturalists liked to paint the ugly details of modern civilization. With scientific zeal they chose exact localities and used exact names, etc., for, according to Zola, the naturalistic novel was to be "la reproduction exacte de la vie." The study of the milieu was to be carried out methodically and objectively so that the novelist might reproduce it accurately.

Because of their scientific pretensions the naturalists felt free to choose for their study or analysis any subject however brutal or revolting. They excused their audacity and frankness and their lack of restraint and taste by resorting to the mystic word "science." As early as 1865 Taine had given the naturalistic writer certain fundamental doctrines:

> Du roman à la critique et de la critique au roman, la distance aujourd'hui n'est pas grande. Si le roman s'emploie à montrer ce que nous sommes, la critique s'emploie à montrer ce que nous avons été. L'un et l'autre sont maintenant une grande enquête sur l'homme, sur toutes les variétés, toutes les situations, toutes les floraisons, toutes les dégénérescences de la nature humaine. Par leur sérieux, par leur méthode, par leur exactitude rigoureuse, par leurs avenirs et leurs espérances, tous deux se rapprochent de la science.

In following this advice the novelists enlarged the scope and field of their work to embrace what seemed to them the entire man and the entire reality—that is, the entire natural and physical reality. The naturalists took up subjects earlier shunned or prohibited, such as prostitution, free love, social misery of many sorts, and burning questions of the day; they held the convenient belief that "La morale n'avait plus rien à faire avec la littérature, pas plus qu'avec la science" and that "Le vice et la vertu sont des produits comme le vitriol et le sucre." The lower classes, the masses became heroes and heroines of grim tales, and the new subject matter was treated of with a sincerity and brutality uncommon before.

While the novels of the brothers Goncourt may be labeled analytical monographs, describing single topics, the novels of Zola and Daudet portrayed society at large. Zola, for instance, chose large subjects; he wanted to present a vast tableau of French society during the second Empire and pictured the political world, the financial world, the world of pleasure, and groups such as laborers, peasants, soldiers, etc. This was exactly what Taine had suggested: "une grande enquête sur l'homme, sur toutes les variétés." Balzac's *La Comédie humaine* was of course Zola's immediate model. Occasionally he was inebriated by his descriptions and everything took on a gigantic, exaggerated form: ". . . il anime un des détails, pour en faire une sorte de symbole, et du coup tous les autres enflent, deviennent énormes; pendant une page, ou deux, l'auteur, obéissant à un emballement lyrique, oublie son dessein, si souvent répété, de n'écrire que des 'procès-verbaux.'" The mine in *Germinal,* for instance, became a living monster that devoured the miners.

Whereas in Flaubert, the brothers Goncourt, and some of their followers, the aim was fundamentally esthetic, in a naturalist like Zola the purpose was predominantly social and humanitarian. Flaubert and Maupassant were strictly objective, whereas Zola's objectivity was tinged with indignation. In this he deviated from strict naturalism, which claimed to be an objective study of life without any *Tendenz.* The naturalist was to be "as cold as a vivisectionist at a lecture," abstain from comment, never show his own personality, and never turn to the reader for sympathy. A classic illustration of this attitude was the description of the death scene in *Madame Bovary,* which Flaubert carried out with the detachment of a physician, for he believed that "le grand art est scientifique et impersonnel." The naturalistic novel should not satirize nor preach, but only describe human life objectively; the naturalist should draw no conclusions because the conclusions were implicit in the material. Despite its so-called objectivity naturalism was critical of society. Zola, especially, had a reformer's zeal. He believed that society was responsible for all the misfortunes that befell the French people; he criticized violently "ce régime politique détesté," and associated the doctrine of naturalism with the Republican idea. He was a moralist and depicted repulsive scenes in order to arouse disgust for vice. He wanted to know why there were drunkards and harlots. He aimed his most violent attacks at the French bourgeoisie, devoting whole books to the criticism of this class of society, but, in general, his criticism was leveled at society at large. He saw flagrant class-distinctions, fathomless corruption, intellectual ambiguity, and moral rottenness, all of which he wanted to disclose and hold up for opprobrium. At heart, he was an optimistic Utopian, whose temperament clashed with the naturalistic formula, while naturalists like Flaubert and Maupassant were misanthropists and pessimists who saw little hope for mankind.

Zola believed that, just as the animals were transformed by the surroundings to which they adapted themselves, the individual man was refashioned by the environment in which he lived. The individual could not be separated from the milieu that surrounded and molded him; it bound and enclosed him and he was unable to extricate himself. "Nous estimons," wrote Zola, "que l'homme ne peut être séparé de son milieu, qu'il est complété par son vêtement, par sa maison, par sa ville, et sa province; et, dès lors, nous ne noterons pas un seul phénomène de son cerveau ou de son cœur, sans en chercher les causes ou le contre-coup dans le milieu." In order to demonstrate their hypotheses, Zola and his disciples selected men and women on whom the influence of the environment easily put its imprint: weak and passive characters, who were afflicted by an hereditary taint and who submissively responded to, and were affected by, their milieu.

In the preface to *La Fortune des Rougon* Zola wrote:

> Je veux expliquer comment une famille, un petit groupe d'êtres, se comporte dans une société, en s'épanouissant pour donner naissance à dix, à vingt individus, qui paraissent, au premier coup d'œil, profondément dissemblables, mais que l'analyse montre intimement liés les uns aux autres. L'hérédité a ses lois, comme la pesanteur.
>
> Je tâcherai de trouver et de suivre, en résolvant la double question des tempéraments et des mi-

lieux, le fil qui conduit mathématiquement d'un homme à un autre homme.

These ideas concerning the influence of heredity and milieu, mainly derived from Taine, Claude Bernard, and Prosper Lucas, were basic pillars of Zola's naturalistic creed, and it was upon them that he built *Les Rougon-Macquart.* The fallacy of his arguments has been exposed by more than one critic, but to him, in the early seventies, they seemed true and unassailable. Man was a product generated by the struggle for life and was transformed by his surroundings. Thus, coal-miners grew crook-backed, heavy-built, anemic, brutal, wishing only to eat, to drink, and to sleep. The influence of heredity was of equal importance to the naturalistic writer and Zola founded *Les Rougon-Macquart* on "une mère affectée d'une tare nerveuse et un père alcoolique," and his novels show, like most naturalistic works, a process of dissolution and degeneration.

The naturalists extended the study of character to embrace the entire physical man with all his physical impulses and instincts and, in their emphasis on instincts and hidden, unconscious urges and the role these phenomena play in human life, they contributed to a deeper understanding of man. Too often, however, the novelists went to extremes. By stressing the Darwinian concept of man and his affinity with organic nature and the influence of heredity and environment on the individual, they identified him with the brute controlled by instincts, particularly sex.

The characters preferred by the French naturalists belonged to the lower classes. The heroes and heroines were workers, harlots, drunkards, servant-maids, forlorn creatures, and mass-individuals. They were generally portrayed as indolent and dull, devoid of free will and purpose, sensual, and often abnormal, the products of a certain milieu and a certain kind of work; but they were seldom pictured as evil. Usually they were depicted with shocking and sensual detail as creatures dominated by their instincts. Besides types with strong physiques the naturalists preferred characters of excitable and neurotic temperaments, and often these traits were merged into one character. The novelists' portraiture of character became superficial; they painted types instead of individuals, and since psychology was reduced to physiology, they were apt to view merely the animality and the primitiveness of man. Man was devoid of a soul and of higher ethical motives; he was a helpless creature determined by heredity and environment. Consequently the characters were not ethically responsible for their actions, they were pawns driven by outer forces or inner urges; moral checks were always lacking. The principle of free will was denied and man was the victim of forces beyond his control. The universe was controlled by the mechanistic laws of causation and the struggle for life was tragic in its hopelessness. The individual did not have confidence in religion or social government; everywhere vice, malice, wickedness, "les tares héréditaires, la misère" stared him in the face. The outcome of life was usually hopeless sorrow, sometimes stolid resignation; often there was no other end than annihilation.

The frank portrayal of sex was particularly characteristic of French naturalism. Love was generally depicted as a physical craving like hunger and thirst, irresistible, a natural force that blindly struck its victim. This was in conformity with the naturalists' belief in the importance of the instincts and desires of man and their denial of free will and the capacity of the individual to control natural urges. Love was no longer ethically or intellectually conditioned, but was reduced to sexual desire. The ideal concept of love was swept away before the naturalistic one.

The naturalistic conception of nature denounced the traditional, romantic, and symbolic view that conceived of nature as a living, incarnate entity. Nature should be studied and reproduced objectively and truthfully. The novelist chose phenomena which had an everyday, close-to-the-soil, and often repulsive effect on the reader; sounds became noises and odors bad smells. Climatic changes and the processes of nature were faithfully chronicled: heavy rains, supreme heat, growth, fructification, etc. The evolutionary doctrine placed man in a new and intimate affinity with the vegetative and the animal kingdom and in conformity with this concept the naturalist was apt to paint phenomena which directed one's attention toward the earth. Parallels between man, plant, and animal are often met with in naturalistic fiction. Take for instance the simultaneous births of a child and a calf in the opening chapter of *La Terre,* which illustrates the essence and quality of Zola's naturalism.

In spite of the fact that the naturalistic formula was both doctrinaire and extreme, and although the naturalistic school in France soon weakened, in the eighties naturalism as a literary movement, pregnant with the spirit and ideas of its age, and possessing an almost volcanic force, began to be felt in the literatures of other European countries, where it was adopted and transformed in conformity with tradition and prevailing taste. It opened up new paths to the delineation of man and nature and helped to break down prejudices and conventions.

In England it played a less significant role than in France and was adopted in a less extreme form probably because of the strong Victorian tradition of convention and decorum. Its chief exponents, George Moore and George Gissing, often softened the effect of their portrayals of slums and outcasts with sentiment and pity. Moore's most typically naturalistic novel in the manner of *L'Assommoir, A Mummer's Wife* (1885), carried the significant epigraph: "Change the surroundings in which man lives, and, in two or three generations, you will have changed his physical constitution, his habits of life, and a goodly number of his ideas." Another of Moore's powerful, naturalistic novels, *Esther Waters* (1894), is the depressing tale of a servant girl and her illegitimate child. Gissing's dismal novels of the slums and the lower classes, for instance *The Unclassed* (1884) and *The Nether World* (1889), treat of the sordid material typical of naturalism: viciousness, brutality, poverty, and prostitution. George Meredith transformed naturalism to an affirmation of life, whereas Thomas Hardy saw no hope for humanity and his somber work was a plea for the negation of life. His characters were helpless victims of deterministic forces, as well as subjects of chance or fate, doomed to inevitable catastrophe.

Georg Brandes helped to introduce naturalism to the Scandinavian countries, where it became aligned with social issues and ethical problems. In Denmark particularly J. P. Jacobsen—*Fru Marie Grubbe* (1876; Eng. tr., *Marie Grubbe,* 1917) and *Niels Lyhne* (1880; Eng. tr., 1896)—and Herman J. Bang were influenced by the movement. Such Norwegian writers as Hans Jæger, Christian Krohg, Arne Garborg, and Amalie Skram experimented with naturalistic techniques. Ibsen's *Gengangere* (1881; Eng. tr., *Ghosts,* 1885) may also be said to have been in part influenced by the movement. In Sweden especially some of the works of August Strindberg—*Röda rummet* (1879; Eng. tr., *The Red Room,* 1913) and *Fröken Julie* (1888; Eng. tr., *Miss Julia,* 1912)—exhibit naturalistic tendencies.

In Germany the impact of French naturalism was felt particularly after 1880. In the early years of the movement the lyric played a certain part through Arno Holz only to be superseded later by the drama. Gerhart Hauptmann wrote *Die Weber* (1892; Eng. tr., *The Weavers,* 1899) and Hermann Sudermann contributed several plays, among which the best known are *Die Ehre* (1889; Eng. tr., *Honor,* 1915) and *Heimat* (1893; Eng. tr., *Magda,* 1896).

Even before the emergence of French naturalism, Russia had produced three great writers who were destined to make valuable contributions to the world's literature: Turgenev, Dostoevsky, and Tolstoy. Russian realism has many points in common with French naturalism; practitioners of both aimed at an accurate and true portrayal of contemporary setting and character; but there are also striking differences, primarily in the attitude toward and the treatment of material. Whereas many French naturalists were like vivisectionists, cold and indifferent, the Russian realists viewed their characters with compassion and pity. The Russians were, in general, less—if at all—interested in the human animal and the theories of heredity and environment, stressing instead the significance of adverse fate. In *Le Roman expérimental* Zola stated explicitly that he was a determinist and not a fatalist. Both determinists and fatalists, of course, denied free will, but there was a vast difference between the two attitudes. "Le fatalisme," said Zola quoting Claude Bernard, "suppose la manifestation nécessaire d'un phénomène indépendant de ses conditions, tandis que le déterminisme est la condition nécessaire d'un phénomène dont la manifestation n'est pas forcée." On the whole, in the French naturalistic novel the action proceeded logically toward its inevitable ending, whereas in the Russian realistic novel, particularly in that of Turgenev and above all that of Dostoevsky, the action proceeded illogically through the influence of chance, fate, or circumstances.

The great Russian realistic novels were primarily psychological with a profound penetration into the human soul. Turgenev, a born aristocrat and an aesthete, was among the first to make Russian fiction of this sort known in Europe; he possessed a keen understanding of his country and its problems. He portrayed the culture of Russia before 1862 as that of a land of "superfluous men." He spent almost half of his life abroad and this helped him to view his material with detachment; he was no moralist, but a disinterested onlooker, an analyst, and above all a supreme artist. The theme on which he focused his interest was admirably synthesized by the character Potugin in *Smoke* (1867; Eng. tr., 1868): "Man is weak, woman is strong, opportunity all-powerful." This motif was repeated in practically all his novels: Rudin and Bazarov, the heroes of *Rudin* (1856; Eng. tr., 1873) and *Fathers and Sons* (1862; Eng. tr., 1867) are illustrations of failure. The strong woman is represented, for example, by Elena in the novel entitled *On the Eve* (1860; Eng. tr., 1871). Turgenev is also famous for his lyric pictures of the Russian countryside, his subtlety of touch, and the pictorial quality of his soft and sinuous prose.

There is a vast distance between the refined world of Turgenev and the chaotic one of Dostoevsky. Although both portrayed Russian life, the world of Dostoevsky was filled with misery, anguish, madness, and crime. He was a philosopher, a moralist, painter of the poor, the sick, the demented, whose souls he probed and analyzed with profound understanding; like Tolstoy he was a Slavophile and believed in Russia and her future. His fame rests chiefly on four novels: *Crime and Punishment* (1866; Eng. tr., 1886), *The Idiot* (1868; Eng. tr., 1887), *The Possessed* (1871-2; Eng. tr., 1914), and *The Brothers Karamazov* (1879-80; Eng. tr., 1912), and his characters may roughly be divided into three groups: the saint represented by Prince Myshkin in *The Idiot,* the culprit as portrayed by Stavrogin in *The Possessed,* the mixed type possessing both constructive and destructive elements, both noble and evil instincts as exemplified by Raskolnikov in *Crime and Punishment.* Unlike the slowly deteriorating characters of the French naturalists, those of Dostoevsky were usually ruined by sudden catastrophe. He viewed suffering humanity, humble souls struggling desperately for survival, with sympathy.

The third of the great Russians was Tolstoy, whose gradual evolution to a reformer and preacher was excellently drawn in his autobiographical works, *Childhood, Boyhood,* and *Youth* (1852-7; Eng. tr., 1886). His panoramic view of Russian society during the times of the Napoleonic wars in *War and Peace* (1865-9; Eng. tr., 1886) is classic. He was at heart a reformer endowed with a strong social sense and vast sympathy for the poor and the humble. He hated war and his descriptions of battles were filled with the moanings and lamentations of the wounded; his terrible scenes of blood and revolting detail swept away the glamour of war. In *Anna Karenina* (1875-7; Eng. tr., 1886) Tolstoy attacked adultery; he led Anna Karenina inevitably toward destruction, for he was a believer in the holiness of matrimony, in decent living and the sanctity of the family. Tolstoy began by viewing passion as something primitive, sensual, poetic even; he ended, however, by regarding it as something perverse, as for instance in *The Kreutzer Sonata* (1890; Eng. tr., 1890).

To sum up: Literary naturalism was an outgrowth of nineteenth century thought and involved the application of scientific methods to literary creation. The chief theorist of the movement was Taine who helped to formulate its underlying philosophy. Beginning with *Madame Bovary,* the new literary tendencies took on the dignity of a naturalistic school mainly through the works of such writers as the brothers Goncourt, Zola, Daudet, and Maupassant. Zola, by no means a consistent naturalist, advocated an experimental method in *Le Roman expérimental*. Particularly in the eighties creative writers in other European countries, for instance England, Denmark, Norway, Sweden, and Germany, became responsive to naturalism. Prior to the emergence of naturalism in France, Russia had produced three major realistic writers—Turgenev, Tolstoy, and Dostoevsky—who made lasting contributions to the world's literature.

Gradually during the latter part of the nineteenth century the rich and variegated literature of Europe began to be known and to enrich the cultural and intellectual life of the United States. When French naturalism eventually took root in America in the nineties, it was not an isolated cultural movement or wave, for it was accompanied and even preceded by other influences and forces, primarily from Russia and Scandinavia, that were to play decisive parts in the genesis, development, and general character of literary naturalism in the United States. (pp. 21-33)

> *Lars Åhnebrink, "Naturalism in France," in his* The Beginnings of Naturalism in American Fiction: A Study of the Works of Hamlin Garland, Stephen Crane, and Frank Norris with Special Reference to Some European Influences, 1891-1903, *Cambridge, Mass.: Harvard University Press, 1950, pp. 21-33.*

P. J. Keating

[*In the following excerpt, Keating explores the role of the urban working classes in French Naturalistic novels and illustrates the effect of Naturalism on the late-nineteenth-century working class novel in England.*]

During the last twenty years of the nineteenth century English novelists and critics were convinced that the art of fiction was at a critical stage of its development, and that French naturalism, as publicized and practised by Émile Zola, was mainly responsible for the crisis. In spite of the serious moral and aesthetic doubts raised by French naturalism, many people believed that under its influence a new era of the English novel was about to begin. Edmund Gosse wrote that naturalism 'has cleared the air of a thousand follies, has pricked a whole fleet of oratorical bubbles . . . the public has eaten of the apple of knowledge, and will not be satisfied with mere marionettes' [*Questions at Issue*, 1893]. Havelock Ellis made a similar point—that while Zola's own work was limited in scope, his courageous example had paved the way for others to follow:

> It has henceforth become possible for other novelists to find inspiration where before they could never have turned, to touch life with a vigour and audacity of phrase which, without Zola's example, they would have trembled to use, while they still remain free to bring to their work the simplicity, precision, and inner experience which he has never possessed. Zola has enlarged

the field of the novel. [*The Savoy* I, January 1896]

Hubert Crackanthorpe took the same point a step further, arguing that a change had taken place not only in the attitudes of novelists and critics but in the reading public as well:

> Heroism is at a discount; Mrs. Grundy is becoming mythological; a crowd of unsuspected supporters collect from all sides, and the deadly conflict of which we had been warned becomes but an interesting skirmish. Books are published, stories are printed, in old established reviews, which would never have been tolerated a few years ago. [*The Yellow Book* II, July 1894]

These quotations all come from articles written in the early nineties when the critical hostility that had first greeted the appearance of Zola's novels in England was rapidly disappearing. The recognizably exultant tone sounded by these critics was the result of release from tension, relief that the persecution of the eighties was not to be extended into the succeeding decade. But if the public debate on naturalism was brief it was also extremely bitter. The principal events are well known and can be quickly outlined.

The first serious attack came in 1879 from Swinburne whose denunciation of the French edition of *L'Assommoir* (1877) set the tone of hysterical indignation that was to dominate critical discussion of Zola's work throughout the eighties. The basic objection voiced by Swinburne and later by W. T. Stead and the National Vigilance Association was entirely moral. They argued that Zola's frank presentation of sex, violence, human cruelty, slang and swearing was indecent, liable to injure public morals and that therefore his novels should be banned from England. Until 1883 only the French editions of Zola's novels were available in England, but in that year the first translation appeared and in the following year Henry Vizetelly began systematically to publish English translations, beginning with *Nana, L'Assommoir, Germinal* and *Thérèse Raquin*. In 1886 further Zola translations were added to Vizetelly's list together with works by Flaubert and Edmond de Goncourt. Two years later Vizetelly was summoned for having published three obscene books (*Nana, La Terre* and *Pot Bouille*), fined, and placed on probation for twelve months, only to be rearrested in 1889 and charged with the same offence. This time the 'obscene' books mentioned, apart from those by Zola, included Bourget's *Un Crime d'Amour* and Maupassant's *Bel Ami*. Vizetelly was sent to prison for three months, a sentence which seems to have satisfied the retributive demands of the National Vigilance Association, as the public attack immediately began to fade away. In 1893 Zola was invited to London to address the Institute of Journalists. On this occasion and on his later visits to England, he was received with acclaim, there being hardly a dissenting voice. W. C. Frierson and Clarence R. Decker, in their detailed studies of the reception of French naturalism in England, agree that the controversy reached its climax with the jailing of Vizetelly in 1889, that from 1890 onwards the purely moral criticism of Zola's work was replaced 'in some quarters by tolerance, in others by curiosity, and in others by sympathetic understanding', and that by 1893 open hostility had almost disappeared.

Taken in its widest aspect, a discussion of the controversy over naturalism or 'realism' in late-nineteenth-century England should concern itself with issues such as the critical reception of Ibsen, the influence of French novelists other than Zola, the reading of Russian novels in England (at this time mainly in French translations), and the English conflict between the realist and the romantic schools. The relevance, however, of these various issues to the presentation of the working classes in English fiction is slight. Gissing had read Turgenev, Dostoyevsky and Tolstoy with great enthusiasm and in this respect seems to have been unique among the late-Victorian working-class novelists, but no specifically 'Russian' influence is discernible in his work. The influence of French novelists other than Zola also appears to be negligible. The short stories of Maupassant are very influential in the nineties (for both their form and content) but the urban working classes play only an incidental part in them. Huysman's early naturalistic novels written under the direct influence of Zola seem to have made no impact in England, though the novels of his later symbolist phase play an important part in the 'yellow' side of the nineties. Perhaps most surprising of all is Clarence R. Decker's finding that 'the literary reputation of the Goncourt Brothers in England was not, at this time, widespread, and had little connection with the naturalist controversy' [*PMLA* XLIII, June 1928]. In discussing the influence of French naturalism on English working-class fiction one always returns to Zola.

There are two main questions of special interest here. First, what part did the urban working classes play in French naturalistic novels? And secondly, to what extent were English working-class novelists influenced by the theory and practice of naturalism?

Both the urban and industrial traditions begin at a much later date in French than in English fiction. Balzac was fully aware of 'l'ouvrier, le prolétaire qui remue ses pieds, ses mains, sa langue, son dos, son seul bras, ces cinq doigts pour vivre', but such a man is entirely absent from *La Comédie humaine*. During the 1840s and 50s the romances of Eugène Sue, in which the Parisian workers play a significant role, were extremely popular both in France and England, but the first serious attempt to present the urban working classes in French fiction was made by the Goncourt brothers. In their preface to *Germinie Lacerteux* (1864) they claimed that the working classes had been unjustly ignored by French writers: a situation they were determined to put right:

> Vivant au dix-neuvième siècle, dans un temps de suffrage universel, de démocratie, de libéralisme, nous nous sommes demandé si ce qu'on appelle 'les basses-classes' n'avait pas droit au Roman; si ce monde sous un monde, le peuple, devait rester sous le coup de l'interdit littéraire et des dédains d'auteurs qui ont fait jusqu'ici le silence sur l'âme et le coeur qu'il peut avoir.

In the event their great claims were not really justified, for although there are several fine working-class scenes in the novel, it is primarily concerned with a maidservant's de-

cline from respectability and neither the psychological nor the sexual analysis deals with a specifically working-class situation. Zola, however, was much struck by *Germinie Lacerteux* and in a long article on the Goncourt brothers [in *Mes Haines,* 1866] praised them for having introduced a new social class into serious fiction. Even at this time Zola was planning to include in the *Rougon-Macquart* 'un roman qui aura pour cadre le monde ouvrier', but it was a task he continually postponed. When he did finally write *L'Assommoir* (1877) he seems to have temporarily forgotten his earlier remarks on *Germinie Lacerteux* and claimed his own work as 'une oeuvre de vérité, le premier roman sur le peuple, qui ne mente pas et qui ait l'odeur du peuple' [Preface to *L'Assommoir*]. *L'Assommoir* became immediately, both in France and in England, the archetypal late-nineteenth-century slum novel. The various artistic problems that . . . English working-class novelists were struggling with, are triumphantly solved in *L'Assommoir*. The direct influence of Zola upon the English slum novelists must be looked at a little later, here it can be said that *L'Assommoir* was the kind of novel that most of them were trying to integrate into the English tradition, although they were never to attain anything like Zola's degree of success. It is not necessary to discuss *L'Assommoir* in detail, but merely to indicate certain important aspects of it.

In the *ébauche* for *L'Assommoir* Zola wrote that 'le roman de Gervaise n'est pas le roman politique, mais le roman des moeurs du peuple', and his success in maintaining this distinction between two essentially different kinds of novel was something that had been achieved by no earlier English novelist. The rise and fall of Gervaise, unlike the decline of Germinie Lacerteux, is presented entirely within a working-class framework. By standing aside from the central action of the book, the author allows everything to be defined in terms of 'les moeurs du peuple', while he himself refuses to offer political, social or even humanitarian comment. Zola certainly possessed personal views on the Parisian working classes but these views are subordinated to the artistic demands of the novel:

> J'ai voulu peindre la déchéance fatale d'une famille ouvrière, dans le milieu empesté de nos faubourgs. Au bout de l'ivrognerie et de la fainéantise, il y a le relâchement des liens de la famille, les ordures de la promiscuité, l'oubli progressif des sentiments honnêtes, puis comme dénoûment la honte et la mort. C'est de la morale en action, simplement.

It is true, as has often been pointed out, that Zola's use of symbolism amounts to an implied comment by the author, but in *L'Assommoir* symbolism is employed to advance 'la morale en action', and rarely to superimpose a moral upon the action.

As a natural corollary of presenting everything through the minds of his characters, Zola felt it was essential not merely to show a familiarity with working-class speech patterns but to evolve a uniform colloquial tone so that there could be no discrepancy between the workers' and the author's response to any given situation. In answer to a critic of this method Zola wrote:

Front cover for Norris's second novel, begun during his student days at Harvard in 1895 and published in 1899.

Vous me concédez que je puis donner à mes personnages leur langue accoutumée. Faites encore un effort, comprenez que des raisons d'équilibre et d'harmonie générale m'ont seules décidé à adopter un style uniforme.

The early French criticism of *L'Assommoir* as a work vulgar in both style and subject was very similar to that which had greeted the appearance of *Oliver Twist* in England, and further recalled the claim made by the Goncourt brothers that the working classes were 'sous le coup de l'interdit littéraire et des dédains d'auteurs'. Zola answered such critics in the preface to *L'Assommoir:* 'Mon crime est d'avoir eu la curiosité littéraire de ramasser et de couler dans un moule très travaillé la langue du peuple'.

Zola's use of a central environmental symbol around which all the action of the novel revolves was a further important innovation in working-class fiction. In *L'Assommoir* he traces the history of the individual members of a particular family but constantly expands the significance of their story by a skilful, symbolic use of the dram shop itself, the tenement block and the wash-house. These environmental symbols are employed in such a way that the major characters are always seen in relation to a working-class community rather than to society as a whole. This technique is very different from that of Dickens and other earlier English novelists. In Dickens, for instance, Tom-All-Alone's in *Bleak House* and the river in *Our Mutual Friend* are used symbolically to link different sections of society; to point the moral of social responsibility. The view of society presented in all English novels of working-class life before Gissing's *The Nether World* (1889) is vertical; Zola's cuts into society were horizontal.

By these means Zola was able to explore aspects of working-class life hitherto ignored by novelists, and furthermore he could do this without passing moral judgement on the life he described. He demanded the authorial right of amorality and it was for this reason that English critics, accustomed to a policy of retribution and class comparison in fiction, denounced him as immoral. Viewed retrospectively the anger is understandable, for no previous author had so successfully demonstrated the way that a working-class environment breeds a culture of its own, the fictional presentation of which renders middle-class value judgements futile:

> Et il ne faut point conclure que le peuple tout entier est mauvais, car mes personnages ne sont pas mauvais, il ne sont qu'ignorants et gâtés par le milieu de rude besogne et de misère où ils vivent. [Preface to *L'Assommoir*]

Thus Gervaise's fight in the wash-house, her sexual relations with Lantier and Coupeau, Bijard's sadistic treatment of his daughter, the working-class wedding feast and the eventual moral and physical disintegration of the Coupeau family, are seen merely as manifestations of one particular way of life. It is the total picture rather than the individual scene with which Zola is concerned; his eyes are set upon the 'mould' into which he pours the material he has gathered.

Three years after the publication of *L'Assommoir* Zola advanced the famous rationalization of his artistic theories in *Le Roman Expérimental* (1880), in which he drew a series of analogies between his own attitude to the world around him and that of Claude Bernard. Many of Bernard's observations, Zola points out, required only the substitution of the word 'novelist' for 'doctor' to be applicable to the aims of the naturalist:

> From the moment that the result of the experiment is manifest, the experimenter confronts a true observation which he has induced, one which he must set down without preconceived ideas like any other observation.
>
> (Bernard)

> The naturalistic novelists observe and experiment, and . . . their whole task begins in the doubt which they hold concerning obscure traits, inexplicable phenomena, until an experimental idea suddenly arouses their genius and impels them to make an experiment, in order to analyze the facts and become master of them.
>
> (Zola)

For Zola, as scientist-novelist, the phenomena are people whose behaviour can be understood by analysing the twin forces of heredity and environment. Naturalism, he writes, is the 'literature of our scientific age', and the role of the scientist is to 'show the mechanism of the useful or the harmful; we disengage the determinism of human and social phenomena so that we may one day control and direct those phenomena'.

It is extremely important to note that what attracted English working-class novelists to naturalism was not Zola's scientific theories but the practical results of those theories. Today the scientific claims made for naturalism arouse little interest or enthusiasm. One of the most sympathetic of Zola's admirers can write: 'It had better be acknowledged at the outset that the concept of the "experimental novel", with most of what this concept involves, is infantile, and the manner of its presentation unbelievably naïve.' In the nineties English critics were often equally distrustful of scientific naturalism, and were quick to point out the long 'realistic' tradition in the English novel, invoking primarily the work of Defoe, Jane Austen, Dickens and George Eliot as examples of accurate and detailed observation of human behaviour. Edmund Gosse was by no means alone in arguing that if an Académie des Goncourts was to be built, then a statue of Jane Austen should be placed in the vestibule.

The continuing working-class tradition in English fiction has already been sufficiently stressed to show that Zola's work did not bring life to an unknown world, but show that with artistic courage that world could be faithfully presented in fiction.

Before looking at the attitudes of English working-class novelists towards naturalism, there is one further point that must be made. The scandalous success that surrounded *L'Assommoir* naturally associated naturalism with the portrayal of the working classes. Zola was annoyed that this should be so and pointed out that naturalism was merely an aesthetic theory, a literary method, applicable to all walks of life, and that the greater part of the *Rougon-Macquart* did not deal with the working classes. The only three novels of the series which did were *L'Assommoir*, *Germinal* (1885) which dealt with the industrial worker, and *La Terre* (1887), in which Zola portrayed the French peasantry; although urban workers do appear in other novels in the series. The whole emphasis of naturalism being upon the forces of heredity and environment, novelists were often attracted to 'sordid' or 'low life' aspects of society, in particular prostitution, drunkenness and marital incompatibility. These subjects are not necessarily connected with the working classes, and it should be remembered when we consider the limited impact French naturalism made upon the English working-class novel, that its influence was widespread in other areas of late-Victorian and Edwardian fiction.

George Moore, ever on the look-out for new artistic experiences, has recorded the profound impact that French naturalism had upon him:

> The idea of a new art based upon science, in opposition to the art of the old world that was based on imagination, an art that should explain all things and embrace modern life in its entirety, in its endless ramifications, be, as it were, a new creed in a new civilization, filled me with wonder, and I stood dumb before the vastness of

the conception, and the towering height of the ambition. [*Confessions of a Young Man,* 1928]

If we place beside this statement Morrison's defence of his 'realistic' position, we can clearly see the two critical poles within which late-Victorian working-class novelists moved:

> It seems to me that the man who is called a 'realist' is one who, seeing things with his own eyes, discards the conventions of the schools, and presents his matter in individual terms of art . . .
>
> If I had been a rich man I might have attempted to discharge my peculiar responsibility in one way; if I had been a statesman I might have tried another. Being neither of these things, but a simple writer of fiction, I endeavoured to do my duty by writing a tale wherein I hoped to bring the condition of this place within the comprehension of others. [*The New Review* XVI, March 1897]

This second statement might have been made by Defoe, or indeed by many other English novelists writing at any time during the previous century and a half. The former statement could only have been made by someone writing in the later years of the nineteenth century. So far as English working-class fiction is concerned, Moore's attitude is extremely rare, and Morrison's commonplace.

What excited Moore about naturalism was that it seemed to be an all-embracing philosophy of art. He was able to recognize not merely the isolated aspects of Zola's work which could be used to serve his own non-naturalistic purpose, but the imaginative genius of the total plan. The simple reason why most slum novelists of the nineties did not follow Zola more closely was that they did not possess the necessary imagination or technical ability. In their novels, and in Gissing's working-class novels of the eighties, 'realism' or 'naturalism' is employed to describe the more sordid or violent aspects of life, rather than to create an harmonious artistic pattern. Moore, on the other hand, had written several naturalistic novels before *Esther Waters* (his only working-class novel), the most successful of which was *A Mummer's Wife* (1885). In this novel every aspect of Zola's work is faithfully translated into English. The minutely detailed studies of the Potteries, seduction of a lower-middle-class provincial wife, careful analysis of marital incompatibility, as well as the naturalistic set pieces of Kate Eade's descent into drunkenness and her meticulously described death, show that Moore had completely absorbed the wider sweep of French naturalism from Flaubert, through the Goncourt brothers, to Zola. By the time he came to write *Esther Waters* Moore's early enthusiasm for Zola was on the wane and other influences are apparent. We thus have the odd situation that the only English working-class novel of this period that can be said to be profoundly influenced by French naturalism belongs in many ways to a purely English tradition. The conclusion that Brian Nicholas reaches in his exhaustive study of *Esther Waters* is perfectly sound:

> Moore's example reminds us that, though the English novel learnt much from the French in

terms of technical rigour and impersonality, their paths never really converged. Though he described his literary evolution in terms of allegiance to various French writers his very waverings of taste suggest a dissatisfaction, prompted in its turn by the weight of a completely different tradition. [*The Moral and the Story,* 1962]

Just as this is true of George Moore, so it is, to an even greater degree, true of the other working-class novelists in this period. The central fault of *Esther Waters* lies, as Brian Nicholas has so convincingly illustrated, in the character of the heroine. On one hand Moore presents her as the victim of forces she is unable to combat (the naturalistic tradition), and on the other, he allows her qualities of moral strength that enable her eventually to survive (the English tradition). The symbolic structure of *Esther Waters* owes everything to Zola. It centres upon the social disease of gambling which reaches out and strikes at all those who, for reasons of either character weakness or social expediency, cannot resist its temptations until, at the close of the novel, both masters and servants are ruined. Esther's personal story is determined by her contact with gambling. From the moment at the beginning of the novel when she innocently accepts a ticket for the sweepstake, her happiness ebbs away and reaches its lowest point when she fleetingly considers turning to prostitution as a way out of her troubles. Then she finds a post with Miss Rice and her fortunes begin to revive, reaching a climax with the prosperity of her husband's pub (the prosperity being founded on gambling) and the great dinner party that follows a joyous Derby Day at Epsom. From this moment her fortunes begin to decline once again until the final scene when she sits with Mrs Barfield in the now ruined Sussex mansion waiting for her soldier son to return home. This chart of Esther's fortunes is very similar to that of Gervaise, and the symbolic high spots of her life (the Latches' pub and the Derby Day scene) are taken directly from *L'Assommoir.* But there are other aspects of *Esther Waters,* apart from the incongruous psychology of the heroine, that rest uneasily within the naturalistic framework. Esther being saved at the last moment from prostitution by the appearance of Miss Rice and later being sheltered by the deeply religious Mrs Barfield, are Victorian solutions; the working-class issue is not resolved but merely postponed by Moore's recourse to the literary convention of middle-class paternalism. Moore, the reader feels, was always aware that *he* knew what was best for his characters. In spite of the supposedly inexorable forces at work upon her, Esther is finally rewarded for her 'virtue', and we are left wondering if this is to be the case then why should she be shown to suffer such terrible experiences. The answer is that she belongs to the working classes and such experiences are endemic in working-class life. Her family, consisting of a brutal stepfather, a gentle mother with religious leanings, and selfish sisters, is a classic example of the fictional working-class household as we find it throughout the Victorian period. It is not at all like the Coupeau family in *L'Assommoir* where all members of it (father, mother and daughter) are subject to the same effects brought about by heredity and environment. Esther is allowed to escape because of the qualities of moral strength, religious principles and maternal love she exhib-

its in moments of adversity; or to quote Brian Nicholas again, 'Esther is innocent because with two strings to her bow she has never been in a position to be guilty'. We can see from this that, in *Esther Waters,* Moore is in some respects as close to George Eliot, Mrs Gaskell or Dickens as to Zola. For all his claims of scientific objectivity Moore's only working-class novel is very much a work of class propaganda.

Enough has perhaps already been said about George Gissing to show that he was no mere disciple of Zola's, although his attitude towards French naturalism was always equivocal. When Frederick Harrison complained that *Workers in the Dawn* reminded him of the 'so called realism of Zola', Gissing could reply that he had never read anything by Zola. The discussions that take place on the art of fiction in *The Unclassed,* and especially the way that Waymark is praised for having written a novel that is 'hideous and revolting' yet absolutely true, show that Gissing had soon rectified this deficiency in his reading. What most attracted Gissing in French naturalism was the greater freedom it gave the novelist to deal with certain subjects (especially sex in this case) normally avoided or approached obliquely in English fiction. Unlike Moore, Gissing was not at all impressed by the scientific theories of naturalism which he dismissed quite contemptuously; nor did he ever speak of Zola with unqualified praise. Furthermore, his working-class novels show little formal influence that might have come from Zola. He maintains at all times the omniscient-author convention, and alternates between realism (for the working classes) and idealism (for the upper-class or classless characters) in a way that is nearer Kingsley than Zola. In Gissing's case this dichotomy epitomized his own persistent belief in the natural superiority of one code of behaviour above another. For Gissing the man who possessed a highly developed aesthetic sensibility, immaculate table manners and a standard English accent, was inevitably 'better' than other men. This belief was not merely a private quirk, but was frequently expressed in his novels, and rendered impossible the social impartiality theoretically essential to naturalism.

The case of the slum novelists is different from that of either Moore or Gissing. In the nineties one finds Zola's name everywhere, but at this time it was invoked whenever anything horrific or sordid required description. This metaphorical use of the words Zola, Zolaism or Zolaesque, does not, of course, necessarily signify even the faintest familiarity with the theory or practice of naturalism. The slum novelists did not make ambitious claims for their work, and there is little evidence that it was produced under the influence of any specific literary theory. Certainly the common critical view, expressed most definitely by W. C. Frierson, that the slum novelists were writing under the dual influence of admiration for Zola and reaction against Dickens is a gross over-simplification. This judgement can only be defended by looking closely at the slum novels, but several points can be made in the present context.

First, the most important single benefit the slum novelists derived from French naturalism was the change it brought about in the attitude of the English reading public towards realism in fiction. Dates are important here. As we have seen, the activities of the National Vigilance Association declined after the jailing of Vizetelly in 1889, and four years later Zola was being hailed in England as a great artist. This change of atmosphere was by no means absolute as the examples of Wilde and Hardy indicate, but in 1893-4 when slum life began to emerge as a popular fictional subject it no longer received the hostile press reception that Gissing, for example, writing just a few years earlier, expected as a matter of course. The special nature of this change has been noted by Kenneth Graham [in *English Criticism of the Novel 1865-1900,* 1965]: 'When a novel is attacked for not observing the moral code, the critic now takes it for granted that it could have been written *better,* instead of deducing that the whole genre is inferior.' Critics and reading public were now more willing to accept that the novelist should be allowed to explore subjects hitherto ignored in English fiction, so long as those subjects were treated with due artistic sincerity. The slum novelists, if they were big enough to rise to the occasion, were given advantages possessed by no earlier English working-class novelist.

Secondly, although it is easy enough to find theoretical statements by the slum novelists that appear to refer to lessons learnt from the French, they did not hail naturalism as a great liberating force, and what is most striking about their novels is their essential Englishness. They firmly believed in the novel as a vehicle for social propaganda, in the main expressed admiration for Dickens, referred slightingly to Zola, and often used contrived plot patterns. Furthermore, they called themselves 'realists' rather than 'naturalists', and in their interpretation of the term they once again showed greater affinity with the mid-Victorian novelists than with the French. Kenneth Graham has written that: 'Detailed verisimilitude is demanded, and any offences against it are considered fatal to the work: reviews abound with triumphant discoveries of minute inaccuracies' and Richard Stang has pointed out that the words 'copy' 'transcript' 'photograph' and 'daguerreotype' were the words most commonly used by both defenders and attackers of English realism. These two critics are both referring to mid-Victorian fiction; to Dickens, Thackeray and George Eliot and not to Morrison, Pugh or Pett Ridge; but they might well have been, for the same is true of both periods. The slum novelists, involved as they were with the 'discovery' of the East End, were concerned more with sociological than artistic truth.

There are two aspects of their work which they did share with the French naturalists, rather than their English predecessors; two qualities that firmly stamp them as *late*-Victorian writers—first, the widespread belief in and attempt to adhere to the doctrine of authorial objectivity; and secondly, the determination to present the working classes entirely within a working-class environment, to make horizontal rather than vertical cuts into society. Yet once again qualifications must be made, for given this adherence to two of the most important naturalistic tenets, it becomes all the more surprising that the work of the slum novelists should have been both firmly rooted in the English tradition and yet markedly different from the working-class fiction of the eighties. (pp. 125-38)

P. J. Keating, "French Naturalism and English Working-Class Fiction," in his The Working-Classes in Victorian Fiction, *Routledge & Kegan Paul, 1971, pp. 125-38.*

AMERICAN NATURALISM

Charles Child Walcutt

[*Walcutt is an American educator and critic who has written extensively on American literature. In the following excerpt, he describes the various forms and styles Naturalism assumed in the nineteenth-century novel. He also attempts to resolve critical debates over whether Naturalism is inherently pessimistic or optimistic in outlook.*]

Something extraordinary happened to the American novel about 1890, when what is called the Naturalistic Movement began to gather momentum. It was a wonder, a scandal, and a major force. Its effects appear everywhere today, both in fiction and in popular attitudes, for it reflects at once our faith in science and our doubts about the modern "scientific" world. And perhaps because the effects of science have been so disturbing and ambiguous, the true character of naturalism has not been determined. In one form it appears a shaggy, apelike monster; in another it appears a godlike giant. Shocking, bestial, scientific, messianic—no sooner does its outline seem to grow clear than, like Proteus, it slips through the fingers and reappears in another shape. The critics reflect its elusiveness. Whereas one authority describes it as an extreme form of romanticism, another counters that it is the rigorous application of scientific method to the novel. When others say it is desperate, pessimistic determinism, they are answered by those who insist that it is an optimistic affirmation of man's freedom and progress.

These authorities are not all mistaken. On the contrary, they are all correct. But each has reached his conclusion by looking at different aspects of naturalism, at different times between 1890 and about 1940, and having committed himself to a confining definition he has found it difficult to consider other areas and aspects of the subject. The Beast, which cannot be named until it is caught, is indeed of a Protean slipperiness. But if it may not be caught and held in a single form, it may be observed in enough of its forms so that we can finally mark the varieties and the limits of its changes. Only in this way can naturalism be explained and defined. (pp. 3-4)

Literary naturalism moves among three patterns of ideas: the religion of reason-nature, revealed in an enraptured contemplation of Process; the attack on the dualist (therefore unscientific) values of the past; the recognition and slowly growing fear of natural forces that man might study but apparently could not control.

Out of the never-resolved tension between the ideal of per-

Oscar Cargill on the American Naturalists:

It is important to note that the leaders in the American Naturalistic school are by no means *convinced* Naturalists—
they betray themselves by pet schemes for human betterment, schemes in which no genuine and thorough-going
pessimist has any legitimate interest. The volition to clutch
at a straw is yet a manifestation of the spirit and a sign of
hope. Since no accurate census is possible, we can merely
affirm our belief on this evidence that Naturalism has by no
means settled down as a dark cloud on this land and that
any brisk wind of controversy might quickly dissipate its vapors.

> *Oscar Cargill, in his* Intellectual America:
> Ideas on the March, *The MacMillan Co.,*
> *1948.*

---

fect unity and the brutal facts of experience come the
themes, motifs, forms, and styles through which naturalism found literary expression. These are all part of the picture of naturalism, although some are there more or less
by chance. To list them briefly is to suggest the rather dis-
orderly composition of this picture.

The major themes and motifs are *determinism, survival, violence,* and *taboo.* The theme of determinism, which is of
course basic, carries the idea that natural law and socio-
economic influences are more powerful than the human
will. The theme of survival grows out of the application
of determinism to biological competition; the notion that
survival is the supreme motive in animal life provides a
point of view from which all emotion, motivation, and
conflict may be approached; it fastens man to his physical
roots. The theme of violence grows with the transfer of
emphasis from tradition (ultimately supernatural tradition) to survival. Animal survival is a matter of violence,
of force against force; and with this theme there emerge
various motifs having to do with the expression of force
and violence and with the exploration of man's capacities
for such violence. "The lower nature of man," in short, is
revealed, explored, emphasized. It is also defiantly and triumphantly brandished; it may indeed be worshiped! A
generation later this theme will be found to have modulated into the discovery of psychic recesses—the acknowledgment of new kinds and qualities of emotional experience. The last link in this chain, dangling from survival
and violence, comes as an assault on taboo: a host of topics
that had been considered improper—sex, disease, bodily
functions, obscenity, depravity—were found to be in the
province of physical survival. In that province, where the
naturalists focused their attention, they could not be ignored. Nobody wanted to ignore them.

The forms which the naturalistic novel assumes are *clinical, panoramic, slice-of-life, stream of consciousness,* and
chronicle of despair. When the idea of the free, responsible
human will, making ethical choices that control its fate,
is set aside in favor of such concepts as determinism and
survival, a new notion of social process has appeared. It
is dramatized (or enacted) in these new kinds of novels.

Biological determinism can be set forth in a clinical study
of disease or deterioration, in which the course of the malady or mania is traced step by step as it destroys the individual. When these forces operate in or through the whole
body of society, a panoramic novel appears. Zola's *Germinal,* which "studies" a coal mining community and shows
the miners helplessly squeezed to the edge of starvation by
laissez-faire capitalism, is the classic of this form and the
archetype of the proletarian novel. The minute and faithful reproduction of some bit of reality, without selection,
organization, or judgment, every smallest detail presented
with "scientific" fidelity, is the formless form of a slice-of-
life novel. The same approach, but to the content of the
mind (all the data of experience) rather than to external
reality, gives a stream of consciousness novel, in which
every smallest detail of thought is presented without selection, organization, or judgment. And finally there is the
chronicle of despair, in which a whole life is depicted as
the weary protagonist trudges across the dreary wastes of
the modern world and finds, usually, an early death. *Studs
Lonigan* in 1930 or Motley's *Knock on Any Door* in 1950
have almost exactly the same form. (pp. 20-1)

Naturalistic styles cannot be defined in any exclusive
sense. They can be listed, perhaps, as *documentary, satiric,
impressionistic,* and *sensational;* but these are not very accurate terms for describing styles, and they are certainly
not exclusive. The ideal of a fact-freighted, uncolored, objective, "scientific" style can be stated, but it is not easy
to find an example of it in the novel. Frequently the most
superficially objective or restrained style is the most highly
charged with bitterness or indignation—as in the minute
and faithful reproductions of stupid conversations by, say,
James T. Farrell, or the vitriolic attacks on the middle
class by contemporaries of de Maupassant in France. At
the other extreme, the style of Zola, the fountainhead of
naturalism, is recognized as highly romantic by all the
critics, as is the style of his closest follower in America,
Frank Norris, who went to considerable pains in one of
his essays to explain that naturalism was romantic rather
than realistic. In a "naturalistic" novel, where the subject
matter is sensational, the style is likely to be restrained and
objective; where the subject matter is commonplace, the
style is likely to be turbulent or "romantic."

For these reasons, there cannot be a "naturalistic style."
When applied to a literary movement, the term *naturalism*
indicates [a] philosophical orientation. . . . The term *romantic,* in this connection, indicates an attitude or quality—an exuberance or intensity of approach, a sense of vitality or richness, a feeling that the demands of the human
spirit cannot be met by the commonplace or typical occasions of life. This romantic quality is frequently achieved
by naturalistic subject matter presented (because it is sensational) in a style that is restrained and objective; here the
effect would be called romantic, whereas the style would
be called realistic. Where the subject matter is typically romantic, as for example in Melville's *Typee,* the romantic
effect is rendered through a realistic style. Realism in style
is, as everyone knows, relative: the "realistic" Dickens
style has been turned by the passage of years into what
might today be called romantic. Even in our time, what
was the poignant, intense realism of Hemingway in 1927

has come to be considered romantic and even (God save the mark!) sentimental. When novels like Zola's *Germinal* and Norris's *McTeague* are considered naturalistic in philosophy, romantic in effect, and (though not consistently) realistic in style, it becomes very apparent that the three terms are not mutually exclusive; no one of them can characterize a novel to the exclusion of the other two. I use the term *naturalism* to indicate a philosophical orientation; *romanticism* to indicate extremes or intensities of effect; *realism* to indicate the apparent fidelity, through style, to details of objects, manners, or speech.

The word *naturalistic,* then, labels a philosophy fairly adequately, but by the time we have passed through the varieties of social and ethical application that have been drawn from it and listed the forms, styles, and motifs that it has evoked, we dare speak of the "naturalistic" novel only with the reservations implied by quotation marks. The significant form of a novel cannot be deduced from the fact that its writer is a philosophical naturalist, for naturalism does not account for spirit, imagination, and personality. A work that was perfectly controlled by the theory of materialistic determinism would not be a novel but a report. It is not surprising, therefore, that critics have run aground or afoul of each other when they have tried to characterize the naturalistic novel with sweeping generalizations. Current theories about the nature of naturalism disagree in general and in detail. They disagree so fundamentally that they give diametrically contrary statements about the matter. The focus of discord seems to be the question of whether the naturalistic novel is "optimistic" or "pessimistic." Some critics insist that the essence of naturalism is "pessimistic determinism," expressing resignation or even despair at the spectacle of man's impotence in a mechanistic universe; others claim that the naturalistic novel is informed with a bright, cheerful, and vigorous affirmation of progress—of man's ability through science to control his environment and achieve Utopia.

The hostility of such points of view might lead one to expect that their proponents were writing about entirely different groups of books, but they are not. It is true that one writer excludes Dreiser from the naturalistic movement, whereas another finds its epitome in his work; but on the whole these antipodal camps are dealing with the same works. The cause of the discord lies in the relation between science and literature: specifically, in the idea that scientific attitudes produce equivalent aesthetic effects. One group starts with the assumption that science is essentially optimistic and concludes that the naturalistic novel must therefore express an optimistic social purpose. Another group starts at the opposite end with the assumption that most novels of the naturalistic movement reveal a "pessimistic determinism" and concludes that the materialism of science must therefore be a philosophy of gloom and despair and that no novel written from its tenets can express any social purpose. A third set of critics, realizing that naturalistic novels embody "pessimistic determinism" and that scientists are generally idealists, innovators, and believers in progress, conclude that in the critical woodpile there is indeed a nigger, whom they cannot find.

The key to this puzzle (for it can be solved) lies in a distinction between what the socially minded man thinks and what the work of art is. The scientist who wants to improve the lot of man through knowledge and manipulation of the material world faces two obstacles: lethargy and unbelief. Some people think mankind is doing well enough. Others do not think that anything can be accomplished with "human nature" by scientific methods. The scientist-reformer therefore has to establish the validity of two assumptions: that the state of man needs to be improved, and that human conditions are determined by the operation of material causes which can be traced, recorded, understood, and, finally, controlled. The pieces of the puzzle fall into place when we understand that the best possible way to illustrate and validate these two assumptions is to write a "naturalistic" tragedy in which a human being is crushed and destroyed by the operation of forces which he has no power to resist or even understand. The more helpless the individual and the more clearly the links in an inexorable chain of causation are defined, the more effectively documented are the two assumptions which underlie the scientists' program of reform, for the destruction of an individual demonstrates the power of heredity and environment over human destinies. And if the victim's lot is sordid, the need for reform is "proved." The more helpless the character, the stronger the proof of determinism; and once such a thesis is established the scientist hopes and believes that men will set about trying to control the forces which now control men.

Advertisement for Dreiser's works, 1923.

Thus can the scientists' "optimistic" purpose be served by a "pessimistic" novel; and thus we see how the deduction that both must be either optimistic or pessimistic is untrue. In the works of Zola we frequently see pictures of degeneration and depravity flourished with the enthusiasm of a side-show barker describing a two-headed lady. The zeal is such that one imagines the author rubbing his hands in delight over his monsters. The most casual reading of *L'Assommoir* will identify this fusion of opposites—of sordid degeneracy and soaring enthusiasm—which troubles only the logical and abstracting critic.

The optimism of the scientist is undeniable; I shall not discuss here the formidable probability that it is not justified by his philosophy of naturalism. Nor do I mean to maintain that naturalistic novelists like Zola and Frank Norris grasped the distinction between a social policy, which proposes action, and a work of art, which is essentially self-contained. There is, on the contrary, a sharp discrepancy between what Zola announced in *Le Roman Expérimentale* and what he performed in his novels; it corresponds to the discrepancy between Theodore Dreiser's socialism and the inexorable fatality that controls *An American Tragedy.* Returning for a moment to our optimism-pessimism dilemma, we should not be surprised to find the critic who proceeds from social theory to literary practice affirming that *An American Tragedy* is authentic naturalism because Dreiser suggests that "radical social reforms are imperative"; whereas another might deduce, if he proceeded from the novel to the social theory, that the philosophy of naturalism is grimly pessimistic because the protagonist of the novel is utterly helpless to control his fate. But I should say that the novel is an almost ideal example of naturalism because within its framework Dreiser makes no proposals. He shows how, given certain hereditary and environmental conditions, what did happen had to happen; and he communicates this conviction because he is able to present so detailed an account of events that Clyde Griffiths is shown as powerless to choose at the very climax of the action and is never held morally responsible for his "crime."

Within its aesthetic frame the novel is completely deterministic and might be called pessimistic (though I should prefer merely to call it faithful to fact); it is for this reason that it can be considered an unusually consistent (and powerful) expression of the naturalistic philosophy. No novel, of course, can actually render the total context of an event. But it can create the *illusion* of doing so; and this is the fundamental aim, as well as the criterion, of this type of naturalistic novel. The writer's opinions about social justice cannot and will not interfere with the form of the work.

Observing the operation of determinism in *An American Tragedy,* the reader may well be led to conclude that something should be done to change the conditions that produce such tragedies. But this happens to the reader, not in the novel; and I believe it can be shown that it happens after and apart from the aesthetic experience of the novel, although of course it is an effect of the book and undoubtedly the author's intention. The force of this social conclusion depends, paradoxically, on the very inexorable

fatality of the action. The ultimate social implications of the action are doubtless with the reader as he reads, too, since no man can stay constantly within the framework or be constantly and exclusively controlled by the assumptions of the work he is reading; indeed his awareness of social conditioning and of the effect of social and financial ambition on Clyde Griffiths is an important element in his awareness that the work of art which he contemplates is unique and self-contained. The conditions as given are absolute for Clyde, although for America they can be improved. Reading a naturalistic tragedy in which the hero appears to have no freedom, one can know that one is performing an act of freedom in reading the book, and can sense that the author is by no means contained by the determinism which controls his novel, for he appeals to the reader's freedom and idealism as he shows that his hero is trapped. Thus the heightening of the reader's social consciousness (and any impulse to social action which he may subsequently experience) comes precisely because the movement of *An American Tragedy* is so perfectly "fatalistic," presenting in its massive and lumbering fashion a superb integration of structure and underlying philosophy. Observing this, the reader enjoys an access of wisdom that would not come if he were being systematically exhorted to action.

But *can* anything but despair emerge from such a spectacle? And by what right do we call a naturalistic novel tragic, when its premises strip the protagonist of will and ethical responsibility? The answer lies, surely, in the fact that will is not really absent from the naturalistic novel. It is, rather, taken away from the protagonist and the other characters and transferred to the reader and to society at large. The reader acknowledges his own will and responsibility even as he pities the helpless protagonist. But the protagonist is not an automaton: his fall is a tragic spectacle because the reader participates in it and feels that only by a failure of his will and the will of society could it have taken place. What appears as an error of choice or a weakness of character in the plays of Aeschylus and Shakespeare is thus transferred to society in the naturalistic tragedy; society has destroyed the hero and thus has destroyed a part of its immortal self—and pity and guilt result. It is guilt instead of terror, because the social forces which crush a hero are finally subject to man's will and do not have the fatal power and mystery of cosmic forces. This curious wrenching of the novel's enclosing frame, which permits the "guilty" reader to enter the action, explains, in part, why so much criticism of naturalism has dealt with the problem of social intent. It also shows that the Aristotelian definition of tragedy is so fundamentally true that even a writer who believes he denies its premises nevertheless contrives to fulfill its conditions. If we can admit that *An American Tragedy* is tragic in this quasi-Aristotelian sense, we can take a further step and conclude that it is irrelevant to ask whether it is optimistic or pessimistic. The question is whether it is true. And whatever its ultimate social intent, naturalistic fiction does not exhort the reader to action. If some of Zola's best novels are still read it is because of their logical, integrated, relentless movement toward disaster—not that *L'Assommoir* will discourage drunkenness, or *Germinal* usher in the Revolution, or *Nana* apprise us of the evils of sexual license in a decadent society.

When we grant that a novelist may promote his ideas on social reform by writing a novel in which he seeks to embody a thorough-going materialistic determinism, we evoke two formidable objections. First, carried through to perfection, such a work would be a report, uncolored by ideas of human personality or recognition of the freedom of the human spirit. Such a work does not exist as a novel, and one would be fairly safe in affirming that it could not exist and be a novel. Second, the conflict between confidence in progress-through-human-effort and a belief in scientific determinism is not reconciled by my showing that "tragic" novels can document social optimism. The conflict remains. It is the chief problem that any "naturalistic" novel presents to a thoughtful reader. . . . Like the critical controversy over optimism and pessimism, it is evidence of the divided stream—of a profound uncertainty as to whether science liberates the human spirit or destroys it. Novels, novelists, and critics consistently reflect this modern tension between science as god and science as devil, between progress and despair, between the hope of the future and the values of the past, between the two faces of human and physical nature.

A final observation on these contradictions: Naturalistic fiction which purports to receive its sanction from the scientific method and deterministic philosophy usually reveals, to the dispassionate observer, affiliations with several aspects of the aesthetic of ugliness, and these are apt to play a larger part in the novel's form than may appear to us if we keep our attention too closely on such concepts as science and reform. Art is anthropocentric. It is created by men whose dominant concern is to domesticate the physical universe to the uses of man's spirit. This aim is accomplished—or approached—by the artist's attempts to impose patterns of human thought upon the endless and eternal complexity of the physical universe. No matter how ardently he appears to be denying the worth or importance of man, the autonomy of the will, the permanence of life, the value of man's spirit, or the power of his knowledge, he is always in some fashion affirming these very things, for art is exercise and proof of them. The naturalistic novelist while he portrays with loathing and bitterness the folly and degradation of man is also affirming his hope and his faith, for his unspoken strictures imply an equally unspoken ideal which stimulates and justifies his pejorative attitude toward the world about him. The act of criticism, furthermore, is an exercise of creative intelligence which in itself denies what it may be saying about the futility of life and the folly of man.

This denial is a term in the dialectic of art; it is as much a part of the total effect of the work of art as its stated or implied scientific hypothesis. Hence all "naturalistic" novels exist in a tension between determinism and its antithesis. The reader is aware of the opposition between what the artist says about man's fate and what his saying it affirms about man's hope. Both of these polar terms are a part of the "meaning" of a naturalistic novel. (pp. 22-9)

> *Charles Child Walcutt, "New Ideas in the Novel," in his* American Literary Naturalism, a Divided Stream, *University of Minnesota Press, 1956, pp. 3-29.*

Willard Thorp

[*Thorp was an American educator, editor, and critic who was responsible for developing Princeton University's interdisciplinary program in American civilization. In the following excerpt, he examines the beginnings of American Naturalism, addressing particularly the works of Stephen Crane, Jack London, Frank Norris, and Theodore Dreiser.*]

Unlike the French, Americans are not much interested in critical wars. But we have endured one critical war which went on for years and was fought with the violence characteristic of civil strife. This was the war over literary naturalism. From the 1890's until the mid-twenties naturalism was for its partisans a battle cry; for its opponents a term of abuse. Both sides fought with deep conviction. At stake was the acceptance of a particular technique of presenting human life in fiction. The literary naturalists were also fighting for the right to tell the truth about American society, as they envisioned it. Their opponents believed that if the naturalistic novels came to be accepted as truthful accounts of American life, all aspiration for whatsoever things are pure, lovely, and of good report would disappear from the national consciousness.

This drawn-out war is supposed to have ended in the 1920's. When Paul Elmer More, the staunchest opponent of the literary naturalists, read Dreiser's *An American Tragedy* in 1925, he wrote with regret of the novelist's wasted talent. If only Dreiser had known the finer things of life as he did its shabby underside; if he had known the larger tradition of literature instead of relying for his standards on police court records and the dregs of science; if he had had a chance, in short, he might have produced "that fabulous thing, the great American novel." By implication, at least, More accepted the sad fact that Dreiser could no longer be fought off.

By this time, when the partisans of the two sides had effected their uneasy truce, the newer critics who were fixing their attention on the younger novelists—Fitzgerald, Dos Passos, and Hemingway in particular—found many more interesting things to discuss than such wornout concepts as heredity, environment, chance, determinism, and the slice-of-life theory of the novel. It was evident that these newer novelists were superior as craftsmen to the literary naturalists. Consequently the naturalistic elements in their writing were disregarded in order that their contributions to form and style might be sufficiently noted and praised.

From this time on literary naturalism was supposed to be a dead issue. Writers like Farrell and Steinbeck who were obviously in the tradition established by Norris and Dreiser had to be accepted, of course, because they were novelists of some stature. But the analytical critics rejoiced as they watched Farrell repeat himself in novel after novel, never attaining again the excellence of his Studs Lonigan trilogy, and as Steinbeck lapsed too often into patriotism and sentimentality. During the 1940's the gods of the critics were Henry James, Dostoevsky, and Kafka. Small wonder, therefore, that scant attention was paid to novelists who carried on in the naturalistic vein.

Though critics have grown weary of the term and have become petulant towards those who use it, a review of American fiction written since the second World War shows that the naturalistic tradition still persists. Literary naturalism is of course not now what it was in 1900; Norman Mailer's *The Naked and the Dead* differs as much from Norris' *McTeague* as the philosophical naturalism of John Dewey and his disciples differs from that of Herbert Spencer. But for more than fifty years there has been a persistent bias towards naturalism in American thought as well as in the novel. This bias has become deeply ingrained in the American mind. Events and ideas decade by decade have combined to strengthen it. (pp. 143-45)

It is time to turn back and look into the origins of this extraordinarily long-lived movement. How did it come about that great numbers of Americans became so convinced of the rightness of a view which permits no belief in supernaturalism, which may even, at times, deny man those rights which democratic idealists once asserted were inalienable? The question is all the more in need of an answer when one looks across the Atlantic and sees what has happened to the English novel during these past fifty years. English fiction had its naturalistic exponents—one numbers Hardy, Gissing, and George Moore among them—but the episode was of short duration. The same is true of France. Why is the story so different in America?

In the first place we must remember that Americans were ready and waiting for the influx of post-Darwinian concepts which poured in upon them. By 1880 the adherents of Jeffersonian democracy and of Transcendental idealism were having a rough time of it. Post-Civil War America was not the country the founders had dreamed of. Cyclic depressions, bloody strikes, the growing slums in the cities, social dislocations of many kinds made it impossible for thoughtful Americans to hold to older views of man's nature which were once dominant. What was needed, by those who were sensitive to these ills of the new age, was a philosophy which would account for them. As it turned out, the concepts of Social Darwinism, which flowed in to fill this intellectual vacuum, did more than explain. For those who embraced them, they supplied a justification, as well, for the ruthlessness of powerful leaders in business and politics who had transformed American society into a jungle. Paradoxically, the new ideas could be warped in opposite directions. Dreiser could meditate at the end of *Sister Carrie* on the pitiful "blind strivings of the human heart." But Andrew Carnegie, who like Dreiser had been illuminated by Spencer, could affirm that "man was not created with an instinct for his own degradation, but from the lower he had risen to the higher forms." Pessimism came in view at one end of the telescope; if the telescope were reversed, vistas of a boundless optimism opened out.

It was Herbert Spencer, of course, who was chiefly responsible for bringing the new views to America. It is recorded that the American sales of his various books, from their first publication in the sixties through 1903, amounted to 368,755 volumes. It may well be that no work save the Bible has had so much influence in America as Spencer's Synthetic Philosophy, which in its several parts carried his system upward from *First Principles* (1862) and *Principles of Biology* (1864-1867) to the capstone, the *Principles of Ethics,* in 1892-1893. The fact that he was a shoddy thinker, vulnerable in several of his doctrines, had no effect on his popularity. There was nothing he could not explain— from the origin of species (he was a Lamarckian) to the nature of evil. (It results simply and naturally from "the non-adaptation of constitution to conditions.") Evil tends to disappear—comforting thought to Americans then sadly perplexed by social evil—because the process of adaptation is rooted in the nature of the organism. It is true that man still has to cope with the vestiges of his animal heritage. That is why he is still predatory and brutal. But he will in time adapt himself to the needs of civilized life. Spencer's leading idea was the notion of the "survival of the fittest," a phrase which he invented. But the whole argument turned on the one word "fittest." In what sense "fittest"? Strict constructionists of Spencerian law doomed not only the stupid and the vicious but as well the idle and the poor. But no one need be poor if he were strong enough to compete.

If one were a thorough Spencerian, therefore, one must go the whole way with the master, ignoring the evil and suffering incidental to the ultimate working out of the great plan. Progress was not to be considered an accident, but a necessity. Civilization is a part of nature, "all of a piece with the development of the embryo or the unfolding of a flower." The human faculties will eventually be moulded into complete fitness for the social state. "So surely must evil and immorality disappear; so surely must man become perfect." Spencer fixed no date for this millennium. It would come to pass only in nature's good time.

If the Spencerian dogmas made glad the hearts of the Carnegies and Rockefellers, they had a very different effect on those who were too impatient to wait for nature to reach— how many thousands of years hence?—her grand conclusion. The social reformers, and certain critics of Spencer on whom they relied, wanted to help nature speed up the process, chiefly by calling in the state as the accelerator. Though the literary naturalists responded in diverse ways, they were most often humanitarians. Some were fascinated by the species which nature was discarding in her upward movement towards human perfection, the grotesque and malformed, who could not adapt themselves and so could not survive. These writers seized on the idea of evolutionary regression or devolution. Their fascination with its possibilities sometimes amounted to a delight which their detractors called morbid. Others, while subscribing to the conclusion that evolution is moving upward and that man will not forever balance between good and evil, chose to survey the human striving and suffering that still persisted in this time of transition. Essentially this is the theme of Dreiser's *Sister Carrie.* He pauses to tell us so directly in the eighth chapter of that novel. As an animal, man is still chiefly ruled by his instincts and desires. As a man he has not learned to align himself with nature. He is a wisp in the wind, "moved by every breath of passion, acting now by his will, and now by his instincts, erring with one, only to retrieve by the other, falling by one, only to rise by the other—a creature of incalculable variability." The spectacle fascinated Dreiser, but he could never hold fast for any length of time to a conviction of what it portended.

The early literary naturalists left abundant testimony, direct and indirect, of Spencer's fecundating influence in their work. Hamlin Garland states in *A Son of the Middle Border* that he grappled with the mighty masters of evolution—Darwin, Spencer, Fiske, Helmholtz, Haeckel—but for him Spencer was philosopher and master. "With eager haste I sought to compass the 'Synthetic Philosophy.' The universe took on order and harmony. . . . My mental diaphragm creaked with the pressure of inrushing ideas." Frank Norris concludes *The Octopus* with words which echo Spencer's optimism: "The individual suffers, but the race goes on. . . . The larger view always and through all shams, all wickednesses, discovers the Truth that will, in the end, prevail, and all things, surely, inevitably, resistlessly work together for good." Two years after his first reading of Spencer, Dreiser recommended him in an editorial because he could summon up the "whole universe in review . . . showing you how certain beautiful laws exist, and how, by these laws, all animate and inanimate things have developed and arranged themselves."

Spencer was the fountainhead but he was by no means the only source from which the new generation of novelists carried away ideas useful to them. As the battle of the books went on they could pick up the notion of "race suicide" from E. A. Ross, a pioneer in American sociology, who invented the term. They could follow Theodore Roosevelt's call for the "strenuous life." From the Reverend Josiah Strong's *Our Country: Its Possible Future and Its Present Crisis* (1885) they might come to believe in the nobility and unconquerable strength of Anglo-Saxon civilization. About the time Norris was imbibing academic evolutionism from Joseph Le Conte, a popular professor of geology and zoology at the University of California, Jack London was acquiring a more dubious Darwinism from Benjamin Kidd's *Social Evolution* (1894). This work by a British government clerk was so much in demand that it was translated into at least nine languages. One of Kidd's chief arguments, which accounts, incidentally, for his great popularity, was that religion performs a useful service by impelling man to be socially responsible. London conveniently ignored this notion, but was so much taken with Kidd's belief in Anglo-Saxon superiority that, on the basis of it, he could justify the ruthlessness of English and American imperialism. Beginning about 1905 the Nietzschean idea of the superman was added to this growing assortment of useful naturalistic concepts. Few writers took the doctrine straight. It was easily accessible in Shaw's *Man and Superman* (1903) and Huneker's *Egoists: A Book of Supermen* (1909).

From whatever widely scattered "authorities" the novelists selected the evolutionary ideas they needed, they agreed in calling Émile Zola the master of their craft. There are several reasons for this, the chief being the example he set them. In novel after novel he worked for twenty years at the vast canvas he was painting of the natural and social history of one family under the Second Empire. Through the twelve-hundred characters of the Rougon-Macquart novels he graphed a whole society. Zola's powerful example is responsible for the trilogies and tetralogies which American novelists, who sought his scope and massiveness, later produced: Norris' three-novel epic of wheat, of which only two parts were completed; Dreiser's trilogy on the career of the business titan Frank Cowperwood; Dos Passos' *U.S.A.* trilogy, and Farrell's compound novels grouped around Studs Lonigan and Danny O'Neill.

In spite of his declarations of scientific objectivity as a novelist, Zola was by nature a humanitarian for he had known "bread and oil" poverty himself. Zola the aesthetician might say "we are experimentalists without being practitioners; we ought to content ourselves with searching out the determinism of social phenomena," but it was Zola the hater of human injustice who defended Dreyfus and who cried out against his critics when they attacked *L'Assommoir:* "Educate the worker, take him out of the misery in which he lives, combat the crowding and the promiscuity of the workers' quarters where the air thickens and stinks; above all prevent drunkenness which decimates the people and kills mind and body." Zola's American disciples would attempt to follow his doctrine of the novelist's obligatory objectivity, but they were equally faithful to his humanity. They proposed to deny themselves the luxury of pity, but it often breaks through: Norris' frustrated sympathy for the wheat farmers in the toils of the railroad octopus; Dreiser's pity for Hurstwood as he sinks lower and lower till there is no exit except by the gas jet; Farrell's sympathy for Studs Lonigan who might have been the hero he longed to be if nature had given him a few more inches in his biceps and in his conscience.

Zola also taught his followers to amass in their files every document bearing on their subject. Because Zola knew all there was to know about peasant life and the city markets and the *ménage* of the courtesan, Dreiser was justified in pouring all he knew—and it was a great deal—about the methods and maneuvers of the American captain of industry into his Cowperwood trilogy. It was in the true Zola-esque spirit that Sinclair Lewis documented, down to the newest centrifuge and biological theory, the career of Dr. Martin Arrowsmith.

By 1880 Zola was prepared to set down his theory of the naturalistic novel. His *Le Roman Expérimental* became the textbook of his school. However outmoded it may seem to us now, it is surely one of the most important treatises in the not very extensive "poetic" of the novel form. And its influence has been immense.

Zola's premise is derived from science. He had been greatly impressed by *L'Introduction à l'Étude de la Medecine Expérimental,* written by a physiologist at the Collège de France, Claude Bernard. He insists, throughout his essay, that one may educate the theory of the experimental novel by substituting the word "novelist" wherever Bernard uses the word "doctor" in his treatise. Carrying Bernard's arguments over into the province of the naturalistic novelist, Zola arrived at this satisfying method of procedure.

> The problem is to know what such a passion [love], acting in a given surrounding and under

given conditions, will produce, from the point of view of an individual and of society. An experimental novel, Balzac's *Cousine Bette,* for example, is simply the report of the experiment that the novelist conducts before the eyes of the public. . . . In the end you will have knowledge of man, scientific knowledge, in both his individual and social relations.

In the course of his essay Zola set forth his ideas about the form and style appropriate to his new kind of novel. These ideas were to have considerable influence on his American followers. He declared that in the literature of his time form had been given an exaggerated emphasis. Form should depend on method alone. "We are actually rotten with lyricism; we are very much mistaken when we think that the characteristic of a good style is a sublime confusion with just a dash of madness." Zola's quarrel with the idealists in art was that they were content with verbal elaborations of the unknown and the unverifiable.

Partly in answer to his detractors, one supposes, Zola contends that novelists of his kind are really experimental moralists. The dream of the physiologist—to master maladies in order to cure without fail—is also the objective of the naturalistic novelist: "We also desire to master certain phenomena of an intellectual and personal order, to be able to direct them." To be thus the master of good and evil, to regulate life, to regulate society, to give justice a solid foundation by solving through experiment the questions of criminology—is a grand and noble work.

We are now in a position to ask how one may recognize the influence of naturalistic concepts in the work of the novelists who were writing at the turn of the century. What, in general, for the deviations were many, were the presuppositions about the nature of man which shaped the novels of Hamlin Garland, Stephen Crane, Frank Norris, Jack London, and Theodore Dreiser?

Almost without exception these American naturalistic novelists denied man's relation to any supernatural order. Even Herbert Spencer's "unknowable," which is manifested to man through the process of evolution, did not seem a very useful concept. Moreover, they agreed that the Idealists in literature had pictured man as far more capable of nobility and self-sacrifice and of the use of reason than the facts warranted. They proposed to turn their light on hitherto neglected aspects of human nature—on man frustrated, deprived, limited by atavistic regressions; man the victim of his own lusts and inadequacies as well as the brutal aggressions of his fellows. Here a vast area to be conquered by their art opened before them. Even if they followed Spencer in believing that human evolution was upward, they wished to study the stage on the evolutionary scale at which their characters had arrived. To do so required the scrutiny of what Zola named the "determining causes of phenomena." These causes were, of course, heredity and environment and the moment in history in which the characters lived. The proximate causes, the data of psychology and sociology being limited, were the only ones which could be ascertained with any degree of scientific certainty. This suggests the reason why the literary naturalists did not write historical novels. It was not possible to bring a Pericles or a Cotton Mather into the laboratory of the experimental novelist.

Fate was a word which they used in a special sense or avoided altogether. It could not mean any kind of theological predestination or any force operating on man which intervened in the natural order. The extent to which man possessed any freedom of will was arguable in the early years; he was generally permitted only a modicum of it. This issue was soon to be fought out by philosophers like William James and John Dewey in whose thought evolution played a large part. The decisions they arrived at helped to change the subsequent course of literary as well as philosophical naturalism.

Strangely enough there was less agreement on the nature of Nature than on any other problem that had to be faced. Nature could be viewed variously as hostile to man, or indifferent, or beneficent. These contradictions were possible because the hypothesis of natural evolution was the central argument. Nature could be seen as sublime and awe-inspiring in its universal dynamism if one were willing to take the waste of species and individuals as incidental to the grand upward movement. But as soon as one counted the cost in human terms, Nature must be viewed as Tennyson sees it: "careless of the single life" and of the thousand types now gone. Yet Nature was resorted to or appealed to inevitably by every literary naturalist. If it is not alluded to specifically, it appears in symbol and imagery.

Hamlin Garland (1860-1940) was the first novelist to domesticate literary naturalism in America, but he went only a short distance towards the naturalism of Norris and Dreiser. Having known as a boy the soul-destroying struggle of farm life in Wisconsin and Iowa, he produced his best work on this theme, in the stories collected in *Main-Travelled Roads* (1891) and *Prairie Folks* (1893), and his short novel, *Rose of Dutcher's Coolly* (1895). Herbert Spencer, he said, had given him a "measure of scientific peace," yet he did not read his master through to the end. His sympathies were too close to the farmers whose existence was unceasingly threatened by storms and droughts. He was not comforted by the idea that in some far-off time man and nature will be allies. He felt, rather, the force of Nature's forgetfulness of man.

Garland was one of the "discoverers" of Stephen Crane (1871-1900). Both Garland and Howells were quick to perceive the great talent evident in Crane's *Maggie: A Girl of the Streets* (1893) and were his champions in the difficult days before his *Red Badge of Courage* (1895) suddenly made him welcome in the publishing houses. In his honest depiction of the depths to which man can sink Crane was far more bold and searching than the two older novelists who were his champions, just as he excelled them greatly as an artist.

It is difficult to estimate just how much Crane owed to the increasing vogue of literary naturalism. He was frequently referred to as a follower of Zola, but he refused to acknowledge any discipleship. When he was living in England, he complained to Huneker that people at parties asked him how much money he made and from which French realist he planned to steal his next book. Yet Ford

Madox Ford observed that Crane's explosive denials that he had read the French naturalists were not to be believed. When the conversation got around to Flaubert or Maupassant his comments displayed a considerable acquaintance with their work.

Some scholars maintain that Crane pilfered scenes from *L'Assommoir* and *La Débâcle* for use in *Maggie* and *The Red Badge of Courage.* The evidence is too slight to justify the charge. The supposed resemblances to Zola in Crane's fiction would seem to be fortuitous. He was by nature a rebel, a hater of sham and gentility. He knew life in the Bowery at firsthand and he had befriended more than one Maggie. As for war and what it does to men, he thought and dreamed about it as a boy and listened avidly to what Civil War veterans could remember of their experiences. Nevertheless, in two respects Crane's work has close affinities with Zola's, although one does not have to predicate any direct influence in order to account for them. It might be said that he followed the ideal of the experimental novel in making "clinical" studies of particular passions—usually the passion of fear, as in *The Red Badge of Courage,* "The Open Boat," and "The Blue Hotel." Secondly he left nothing out when he was describing a "milieu" which was filthy and sordid. There are enough horrors of

this kind in "An Experiment in Misery" (a night in a New York flophouse) to satisfy any literary naturalist.

But these affinities are not strong enough to give a story by Crane any of the tone or texture of a novel by Zola. The distance between aspiration and outcome, between appearance and reality so fascinated Crane that in most of his work irony plays constantly over the surface and gives his fiction its characteristic tone. To the men in the open boat the safe shore is in sight, but the deadly surf lies between. The windmill tower (probably deserted) is in plain view on the beach, standing like a giant with its back to the plight of the ants. It represents ironically "the serenity of nature amid the struggles of the individual—nature in the mind, and nature in the vision of men." Here, explicitly, Crane connects the irony which is central to his vision with the indifference of nature, but this is one of the few places in which he attempts to explain it at all. It simply exists in human life as something to be encountered and recognized.

In contrast to Crane whose debt to literary naturalism is small, Frank Norris (1870-1902) was its avowed champion. His brother once remarked that "he was never without a yellow-covered novel of [Zola] in his hand." This corroborative evidence is hardly needed. Norris not only tried to follow the method and capture the spirit of Zola. Many of his scenes are borrowed and Americanized. Norris had to get up his naturalism. The son of a wealthy San Franciscan, he had the advantages of a Harvard education and of art study in London and Paris. His early enthusiasm for Froissart and the *Chanson de Roland* made him for the time a devoted romantic and accounts for the romantic lapses in his fiction. Indeed Norris, during his brief writing career—from *Moran of the Lady Letty* (1898) through *The Pit* (1903)—never sorted out his convictions. In the same work romantic episodes jostle Spencerian doctrine and socialistic theories.

While he was a student at Harvard, writing under the direction of a remarkable teacher, Lewis E. Gates, he began two novels in the naturalistic vein. *McTeague* is a study of a stupid brute of a man whom sexual passion and greed destroy. *Vandover and the Brute* (published posthumously in 1914) employs another favorite theme of the literary naturalists. Vandover is a man of refinement and an artist, but he starts on the backward path when the brute in him is aroused by lust and drink. In this novel Norris carried the idea of regression to the ultimate. Vandover is finally afflicted with lycanthropy and we leave him at the end growling like a beast, padding around his miserable room on all fours.

McTeague: A Story of San Francisco (1899) is the first avowedly naturalistic novel in American literature. Norris cut it carefully to pattern and was rewarded with the vituperation of the critics. (One reviewer said it should have been called *McTeague: A Study in Stinks.*) McTeague has come a certain distance up the evolutionary scale, having established himself with middle-class complacency as a dentist in San Francisco's Polk Street. But "the evil of an entire race flowed in his veins." By chance his best friend brings Trina Sieppe to his dentist's chair. He desires her and soon marries her. (The gross feeding at the wedding

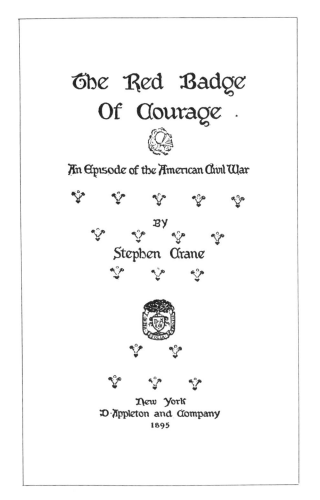

Title page for the Naturalistic novel that established Crane's reputation.

breakfast is worthy of Zola.) Then trouble begins. Trina has won $5,000 in a lottery and its possession turns her natural thriftiness into inordinate greed. Lust and greed grind out the horrible conclusion of the marriage, at the moment when McTeague murders her in the schoolhouse where she is working as a scrubwoman. The rest of the novel is a melodramatic manhunt, ending in death in the desert. Aside from the melodrama of the last sixty pages, there are some other deviations from strict naturalism. The subplots have more than a hint of Dickensian sentimentality in them. And though Norris skillfully describes the milieu of McTeague and Trina, the crowds below them in Polk Street actually serve no functional purpose in the story. But *McTeague* is no doubt an "experimental novel" in that it attempts to study what will happen when two such natures are brought together.

After *McTeague* Norris fell away from his professed creed. *Blix* (1899) is a slick success-story. In the Jack London manner, *A Man's Woman* (1900) mixes romance, love and honor, the struggle for existence in an Arctic expedition, and propaganda for the "new woman." At this point Norris returned to the fold. When he began on his epic of wheat, which was to require three novels in the telling, he wrote to a friend: "Now I think I know where I am and what game I play the best. The Wheat series will be straight naturalism with all the guts I can get into it."

As things turned out *The Pit,* the second novel in the series, was far from straight naturalism, and even in the first novel, *The Octopus* (1901), Norris did not observe all the rules of the game. *The Octopus* has the immense scope required of a Zolaesque novel and in it there are many big scenes full of the vitality characteristic of the genre: the ploughing of the fecund wheat-land in the spring; the gargantuan revels at Annixter's barn; Dyke's mad race, against capture or death, in the stolen locomotive; the bloody jack-rabbit hunt and the feast that follows. Yet the novel breaks apart because Norris was pulled in two directions. Until we come within a hundred pages of the end, we seem to be reading a novel about the class struggle, written in the naturalistic mode. All the elements are there, the hardworking but grasping wheat farmers, the wicked capitalists, and their hirelings who control the railroad Octopus which ruthlessly deprives them of their rights and of the results of their labor. There is even a "Red" who spells this all out for Presley, the young writer who is Norris' observer on the scene. But when Presley faces Shelgrim, the president of the railroad, he meekly listens and learns his lesson. Shelgrim informs him that Wheat is one force, the Railroad another, and the law of supply and demand govern them both. "Men have only little to do in the whole business."

Relying on Herbert Spencer to bring him through, Norris patches up an optimistic conclusion. The power of the Octopus and the maturing of the wheat reveal no malevolence in Nature; only a colossal indifference, a vast trend toward appointed goals. The agony of human defeat sends not the faintest tremor through her prodigious mechanism. Force only, exists, and men fall beside it, mere nothings, mere animalculae. The Wheat, wrapped in Nirvanic calm, grows steadily under the night, "alone with the stars and with God."

With Frank Norris naturalism was an acquired creed, the result of reading and thinking and, certainly, of a revolt, with some guilt in the process, against the gentility to which he had been born. The case was different with Jack London (1876-1916), likewise a son of San Francisco. London's life-story is perfect material for a naturalistic novel, as he himself proved when he transferred it, with few disguises, into his autobiographical *Martin Eden* (1909). As a boy he was forced to be a man. At the age of sixteen he was accepted among the outcast oyster pirates of San Francisco bay and had proved his virility by harboring on his boat the queen of the tribe. He knew all about sex before he had heard of the thing called love, a passion he deals with in his novels as if he had recently learned to kiss by the book. He was inordinately proud of his manhood, which he was constantly testing as a sailor, horseman, slugger, and drinker. At seventeen he was doing a man's work before the mast. During the panic of '93 he joined Coxey's army and saved his division by his power over men, though he deserted the cause at Hannibal, Missouri. In 1897, at the age of twenty, he was again a superman in the Alaska gold strike.

A few months at the University of California disgusted him, but he acquired there the habit of reading and he took down huge though adulterated doses of Darwin and Marx indiscriminately. Success as a writer came almost at once. Soon after the turn of the century he was making thousands a year, but he was always in debt. Two conflicts began to wrack him. He paraded as a Socialist and millions over the world were moved by his belligerent signature, "Yours for the Revolution." But Socialist doctrine cannot be reconciled with the kind of evolutionism which London was forcing on a friend in 1899: "The different families of man must yield to law—to LAW, inexorable, blind, unreasoning law, which has no knowledge of good or ill, right or wrong." A still more agonizing conflict developed in his career as a writer. Magazines were ready to buy any shoddy product from his workshop. Yet he knew that he possessed great talent and was ridden by the hope of producing a masterpiece. Add to these conflicts his disappointments as a lover and father (he begot no menchildren and his two daughters rejected him) and one has the clues to his suicide at forty.

What did Jack London make of all he assumed he knew about naturalistic doctrine? He was convinced, most of the time, that the strong survive because they have a drive that is irresistible. The struggle for survival is the theme of one story after another. The settings change from the sea, to the Klondike, to the prize-ring, to the class-war, but the theme is the same in *The Sea-Wolf* (1904), *The Game* (1905), and *Burning Daylight* (1910).

The kind of man who survives and leads is the blond beast, the superman for whom a mate equally scornful of convention usually waits in the next chapter. Sometimes his admirable brutishness sleeps beneath a veneer of civilization and has to be wakened. London's notion of reversion to the primitive is an interesting variation on the naturalistic idea of devolution, for to London it is a wholly admirable transformation. The dog who becomes a wolf in *The Call of the Wild* (1903) is still London's most popular hero. Socialist though he professed to be, London believed that the mass of men must be ruled by the few—because "most men are fools, and therefore must be taken care of by the few men who are wise." The "few" who were fit to rule were inevitably Anglo-Saxons.

Such was the "inexorable, blind, unreasoning" law which London professed to believe. Actually he compromised most of the time with the conventional morality of his age. His ruthless heroes do not sweep all before them; his mate-women are as chaste as his publishers required. This characteristic pulling back could be illustrated from a dozen stories but the autobiographical *Martin Eden* will serve best since there is so much of London's own life in it. Martin is a natural man, whose maleness attracts the refined and intellectual Ruth Morse. She yields to him because she can't help herself, being a mate-woman by nature. She rejects him when he turns Socialist, however, and then seeks him again when he becomes famous as a writer. What can the next stage be in Martin's struggle upward? An ending like London's own, a sense of futility and unfulfillment, and then suicide.

London's supermen have a habit of fizzling out. The lines of verse which he prefixed to *Martin Eden* are prophetic of his own end and a summary of much of his fiction.

> Let me live out my years in the heat of blood!
> Let me lie drunken with the dreamer's wine!
> Let me not see this soul-house built of mud
> Go toppling to the dust a vacant shrine!

Compared with the meteoric rise of Norris and Jack London, Dreiser's career moves at an elephant's gait. As a thinker Dreiser (1871-1945) was seldom to be found twice in the same place. Now that the facts of his life are known we begin to understand why he twisted and turned as he did, and why shortly before he died he became a Communist, and yet commented so oddly on what he had just done: "What the world needs is more spiritual character. The true religion is in Matthew."

The circumstances of his upbringing were decisive. His family was poor; his father's Catholicism ineffectual in teaching him the validity of moral ideas. When he broke away and was on his own in Chicago, he fumbled in business and in love. The pattern of his youthful years was similar to that of many second generation immigrants who tried to reject the culture of their parents. Thus far he resembled one of his own weak-willed heroes—groping, uncertain, unequal to live. The newspaper days that followed opened his eyes to the world of business and political power. Not all people, he discovered, are weak and submissive. Balanced against them are strong-willed individuals who get what they want. His pity went out to the weak; his admiration to the strong. Years later in a chapter of his *Hey Rub-A-Dub-Dub* (1920), "Equation Inevitable," he tried to make a formula out of what he had observed. He held (for the time, at least) that "there is, on the one hand, inherent in the chemic impulses and appetites of life (which man does not create), an instinct toward individuality which may be for good or for ill, plus, on the other hand, this law of balance or equation but over which nei-

ther the humanitarian nor the idealist, any more than the criminal or indifferent or self-seeking realist, has any control whatever." Nature desires equilibrium, and balances a St. Francis or a Buddha against an Alexander VI or a Morgan.

All his life Dreiser was a seeker. When he began to read in earnest, the Social Darwinists held sway over him. When he was working on *The Financier* (1912), he was fascinated by the explanation of human behavior in physiochemical terms which he found in Jacques Loeb's *The Mechanistic Conception of Life.* Towards the end he discovered Thoreau and thought he found an answer in the Thoreauvian fusion of science and intuition. He was also attracted to the quietism of the Friends.

There are several reasons why Dreiser's naturalistic beliefs helped him as a novelist and why they do not seem so antiquated as those which animated the fiction of Norris and London. In the first place they were always for Dreiser "tentatives," as Robert Frost would say. They did not pre-empt the mysteries of human existence. His predecessors shouted with Whitman "Hurrah for positive science! Long live exact demonstration." As the "scientific" tenets they used have been carried out with the rubbish, the actions or characters which they validated have also gone into the discard. Dreiser does not begin a novel with a flourish of hypotheses about his characters. Generalizations come later, when situations have been established from which they may be drawn.

Dreiser wrote his novels out of conviction and from the best knowledge of human nature with which his endless quest for answers could provide him. Thus when he wrote *Sister Carrie* (1900) he was spellbound by the Spencerian idea of the stage of civilization to which modern man (and woman) had attained. When he wrote *The Financier* he was not only calling on his memories of business leaders and his knowledge of the career of Charles T. Yerkes, who becomes the Cowperwood of the novel. He thought he had found some ideas in Jacques Loeb which helped to explain aggressive and ruthless American individuals of this type, and these ideas he used to buttress his novel. But he seldom made the mistake, as Norris and London did, of using mutually contradictory concepts in a single work. The ideas which inform *Sister Carrie* or *The Bulwark* (1946) work together in each instance and are sufficient for what they are required to do. The worlds they help to explain are wholly different. Dreiser seldom let his different worlds collide, though they did certainly once when he struggled, just before his death, to finish *The Stoic* (1947), the last novel of the trilogy of business. The mood in which he had conceived *The Financier* and *The Titan* (1914) had long since passed. The grand climax of Cowperwood's career, which ends in defeat and not victory, is missed and the novel drifts off into Berenice's conversion to oriental mysticism.

One is obliged to answer the question why Dreiser's fiction offended his fellow-Americans for so long a time. As Mencken observed, few writers have absorbed so much abuse and only a Dreiser could have persisted in the face of it. One can understand this opposition if one will consider how heretical a novel *Sister Carrie* was, a "banned book" that had to wait twelve years for public sale in this country.

Carrie Meeber comes to Chicago from Columbia City. She finds work but the pay is low and factory life intolerable. She drifts into a liaison with a drummer, then leaves him after a time for an older man, a saloon manager who deserts his wife for her and robs the safe in order that they may escape to New York. As her new lover drifts downward in the social scale, because he is too old to make a new life for himself, she drifts upward and becomes a successful actress. Without compunction she lets Hurstwood drop out of her existence. Too weak of will to struggle further, he turns on the gas in a shabby lodging house. Carrie sits by her window, dreaming of the happiness she may never feel.

What was so deeply shocking here? Though Carrie "sleeps" with two men to whom she is not married, the details of sexual intercourse are never mentioned. Hurstwood, it might seem, is duly punished for his moral lapse. But Dreiser implies that there are many—how many?—Carrie Meebers in America who use their sexuality for provender as naturally as they might use any other natural gift. She had, it is true, a few twinges of conscience and she thinks of herself, now and then, as a married woman. She is not even a courtesan in the grand manner, calculating, professional, and because she is damned, acceptable.

But this is not all. What offended most was the inevitability of Carrie's rise to fame and fortune. Braced by his naturalistic belief in Carrie's tropism, which draws her towards beauty and success, Dreiser lifts her to a higher point on the evolutionary scale than her lovers attained. But he leaves her there, because she can, in the nature of things, go no farther. She can see into the beautiful walled city where Ames, the man of culture, the man who really understands her, lives, but she cannot enter it. Nor can other Americans like her—Clyde Griffiths of *An American Tragedy* (1925) is such another—enter there. The happiness which pulsates within these walls they may dream of, but they can never know it. The "walled city" was Dreiser's discovery, and a very great one it was, for Americans have falsely believed anyone can get to the stars if only he struggles hard enough. Carrie is cheated of her starry victory in the end, but not because she chose to be a bad girl. Nature had interdicted her.

Though Dreiser had admirers in his early, difficult years, he did not have imitators. During the first twenty years of the new century novelists were little influenced by literary naturalism. Occasionally the muckrakers adopted naturalistic techniques in order to make more vivid the social evils they were trying to expose, but their novels were not shaped by any consistent naturalistic theory of life. The two leading novelists of the time, Edith Wharton and Willa Cather, had, of course, no alliances with literary naturalism. (pp. 147-68)

> *Willard Thorp, "The Persistence of Naturalism in the Novel," in his* American Writing in the Twentieth Century, *Cambridge, Mass.: Harvard University Press, 1960, pp. 143-95.*

An excerpt from Frank Norris's *The Octopus* (1901)

And as Presley looked there came to him strong and true the sense and the significance of all the enigma of growth. He seemed for one instant to touch the explanation of existence. Men were nothings, mere animalcules, mere ephemerides that fluttered and fell and were forgotten between dawn and dusk. Vanamee had said there was no death. But for one second Presley could go one step further. Men were naught, death was naught, life was naught; FORCE only existed—FORCE that brought men into the world, FORCE that crowded them out of it to make way for the succeeding generation, FORCE that made the wheat grow, FORCE that garnered it from the soil to give place to the succeeding crop.

Frank Norris, in his The Octopus, *Airmont Publishing Co., 1969.*

THE LEGACY OF NATURALISM

James T. Farrell

[*Farrell was an American novelist, short story writer, and critic who is best known for his grim Studs Lonigan trilogy, a series of novels depicting the life of a lower-middle-class man of Chicago. Influenced primarily by the author's own Irish Catholic upbringing on Chicago's South Side, and by the writings of Theodore Dreiser, Marcel Proust, and James Joyce, Farrell's fiction is a naturalistic, angry portrait of urban life. His writings explore—from a compassionate, moralistic viewpoint—the problems spawned of poverty, circumstance, and spiritual sterility. In the essay below, Farrell discusses the discrepancies between Zola's theories as defined in his essay "The Experimental Novel" and as implemented in his novels. He also asserts the widespread influence of the Naturalist movement on modern literature.*]

Emile Zola is usually characterized as the father of modern naturalism. And quite frequently Zola's "The Experimental Novel" is cited by critics as the gospel of literary naturalism. More than one critic has judged any number of books to be defective, and even dangerous, on the assumption that these books are illustrations of what Zola wrote in this particular essay in the year 1878.

Now, what did Zola really say in "The Experimental Novel"? He relied heavily on the writing of a French physiologist, Claude Bernard. In a time when it was argued that medicine was not a science but an art, Bernard claimed that it could become a science. Zola applied this and many other concepts of Bernard almost literally to the field of the novel. He equated art and science without making any clear distinction between them. Zola did not look upon the questions he raised in terms of the difference between problems in the laboratory and those in the writer's study.

What was paramount with Zola was determinism. Paraphrasing Bernard, he declared: "There is an absolute determinism in the existing conditions of natural phenomena, for the living and for inanimate bodies."

Zola conceived of determinism as "determining the conditions necessary for the manifestation of phenomena." Noting that Claude Bernard had found that there were fixed laws governing the human body, he wrote that it could be proclaimed without fear of error that the hour would come when the laws of thought and of passion would be formulated in a like manner. And he asserted that in terms of this determinism, the naturalistic novelist was a scientist who was analyzing man in both his individual and his social relations. Thus, he declared: " . . . We [novelists] operate on the characters, the passions, on the human and social data, in the same way that the chemist and the physicist operate on living beings. Determinism dominates everything."

A longer quotation will give a fuller sense of Zola's view:

> Man is not alone: he lives in society, in a social condition: and consequently, for us novelists, the social condition increasingly modifies the phenomenon. Indeed our great study is just there, a reciprocal effect of society upon the individual and the individual on society. . . . We are not able yet to prove that the social condition is . . . physical and chemical. . . . We can act upon the social condition, in acting upon the phenomena of which we have made ourselves masters of men. And this is what constitutes the experimental novel: to possess a knowledge of the mechanism of the phenomena inherent in man, to show the masking of the intellectual and sensory manifestations under the influence of heredity and environment, such as physiology shall give them to us, then finally to exhibit man living in a social condition produced by himself, which modifies daily, and in the heart of which he himself experiences a continual transformation. Thus, then, we lean on physiology: we take man from the hand of the physiologist solely in order to continue the solution of the problem, and to solve scientifically how men behave when they are in society.

Affirming these views, Zola looked forward to the day when the experimental novelist, the naturalist, would bring forth decisive results of a scientific character. He emphasized the word *experimental,* declaring that the novelist would show by experiments the ways that passion acts under certain given conditions, that these experiments would serve as a means of going from the known to the unknown, and that the experimental novelist would thus act as a scientist who went from the known to the unknown insofar as man was concerned. As such, he was to be contrasted with the "idealistic novelist" who deliberately remained in the unknown, and who clung to all sorts of religious and philosophical prejudices "under the extraordinary pretense that the unknown is nobler and more beautiful than the known."

In answer to the charge that the work of experimental novelists needed justification because it dealt with the ugly, Zola quoted Bernard as follows:

> You will never reach fully fruitful and luminous generalizations on the phenomena of life until you have experimented yourself and stirred up in hospital, the amphitheater, the laboratory, the fetid or palpitating source of life. If it were necessary for me to give a comparison which would explain my sentiments on the science of life, I should say that it is a superb salon, flooded with light, which you can only reach by passing through a long and nauseating kitchen.

Zola saw the experimental method as a means whereby scientific authority would be substituted for personal authority. With this, he also asserted that naturalism is not a school: " . . . it is nothing but a vast movement, a march forward in which everyone is a workman according to his genius. All theories are admitted and the theory which carries the most weight is the one which explains the most."

Zola was opposed to the supernatural. He believed that science had already demonstrated that the supernatural was not real or true. He saw in science the source of intellectual leadership in the nineteenth century, and he insisted that the novelist have a place in this scientific movement. Opposing scientists who would not give writers such a place, he declared:

> I have remarked that a great many of the most intelligent savants, jealous of the scientific authority which they enjoy, would very willingly confine literature to the ideal. They themselves seem to feel the need of taking a little recreation in the world of lies after the fatigue of their exact labor, and they are fond of amusing themselves with the most daring hypotheses, and with fictions which they know perfectly well to be false and ridiculous.

To Zola, romanticism and the ideal were lies—unreal and untrue and undemonstrable. Rather than trade in these "lies," as he styled them, the novelist should have equal place with the scientist, and should work as he does. Zola here established a conception of truth as the ideal, and he held that the artist must adhere to it. He believed that the feeling of the artist must "always be subject to the higher law of truth and nature." And he added that " . . . each time that a truth is established by the savants," the writers should immediately abandon their hypotheses to adopt this truth; otherwise they will remain deliberately in error without benefiting anyone. And in terms of these attitudes he also proclaimed the death of "metaphysical man" and the advent of the "physiological man."

In a lecture "From Poe to Valéry," delivered at the Library of Congress, T. S. Eliot made an excellent observation which can be applied to Zola's theory of the experimental novel. Speaking of the theory which Valéry held as a poet, Eliot said:

> Here I should like to point out the difference between a theory of poetry propounded by a student of aesthetics, and the same theory as held

by a poet. It is one thing when it is simply an account of how the poet writes without knowing it, and another thing when the poet himself writes consciously according to that theory. In affecting writing, the theory becomes a different thing from what it was merely as an explanation of how the poet writes.

Zola wrote consciously in terms of his theory. But if we wish to understand what has happened and what is still happening in literature, we must not test Zola, and a whole series of novels which have been written since Zola's time, by making a literal-minded effort to correlate and to judge specific works in terms of this theory. We must not forget that, up to the present time, no one has succeeded in creating a perfect theory of aesthetics.

Zola's attempt to embody scientific methods, procedures, and conclusions in the novel should be seen as an effort to incorporate in literature something of the developing mental climate of his own time. Today it is rather easy to make detailed criticisms of his theory, to formulate a clearer statement of scientific method, and to displace the copy theory of knowledge implied in his ideas with a better theory of epistemology.

The late V. F. Parrington, in *The Beginnings of Critical Realism in America* (Volume III of his *Main Currents in American Thought*), discussed the influence of science in American thought during the latter part of the nineteenth century. He observed:

> To speak exactly, it is not so much science that has taken possession of the mind, as certain postulates of science, certain philosophies presumably derived from science, and justified by science, which we have felt bound to incorporate in our thinking as a hundred years before the conclusions of the Enlightenment had been incorporated.

Parrington's observations can be applied to Zola. The novelist did set down a series of postulates, "presumably derived from science," which permitted him to widen the boundaries of that which was admissible in modern literature. He contributed to enlarging the area of human conduct which can be described by a novelist: he also changed and expanded the kind of theme which could be embodied in novels. He contributed to greater liberty of expression for the artist. His postulates, drawn from science, also gave him greater confidence, provided him with hypotheses which would help him look anew at the material of life, of characters and events. He risked hypotheses concerning heredity which, he recognized, were not completely established by science in his own time but which seemed plausible and for which there appeared to be some scientific evidence. Was he scientific or unscientific?

The American philosopher George Herbert Mead, in *The Philosophy of the Act,* made a pertinent distinction between scientific knowledge and information about science. Mead saw science as an evolving system of knowledge. In this evolving system, he contended that what remained of scientific endeavor were the facts discovered. And his theories indicated that, while he was a relativist, he more or less held that a fact had the character of factualness and

was valid within its proper frame of reference. But Mead pointed out that in this system of science the generalizations or conclusions change. We know this to be so. Mead further asserted that scientific knowledge was really gained only when you performed the experiments yourself, when you actually experienced the gaining of the knowledge, the finding out of the facts. Merely to read about this finding of the fact, as Mead properly noted, only gives us information. Zola, then, when he wrote about science, and when he stated his conclusions and hypotheses, was speaking largely in terms of information, the scientific information of his time. When he went out and gathered facts, and was proceeding with the scientific spirit and method, he was gaining knowledge. He was, then, trying to write with respect for the spirit of truth. This is part of what remains important in his legacy.

Zola's theory of naturalism is not so important today for its scientific as for its historical relevance. His theory should not be regarded simply as pessimistic determinism applied to literature. Nor has he been responsible for a school of novelists who have written books which only describe man as a "trapped animal," or, as the critics of naturalism have declared, as a rat in a cage. It should be obvious to us, in the present, that scientific advances, both theoretical and practical, have changed not only our mental universe but our way of life. Zola sensed that this was happening in his own day and attempted to deal with such a change as it might affect literature.

Just what has the problem of free will versus determinism to do with literature? Discussions of this problem are now usually of a piece with those concerning heredity versus environment, in which both elements appear to be solid forces in absolute conflict to one another. When we deal with such broad and all-inclusive categories it is more than well for us to recall an observation by Whitehead, who warned against committing the "fallacy of misplaced concretion." It is important here to observe that usually those who pose this question pose it in terms of a flat either/or. Is man free or is he not free? Does man have free will, or is he completely determined? To me, this is an unanswerable question.

What has this to do with a novel? How will the assumption that man has free will make someone a better writer? In what way does one or another answer to the question of free will versus determinism relate to the work of fiction? When a critic of naturalism logically demonstrates the existence of free will he is merely proving what he wants to prove. But you cannot prove that anything exists in the world with pure logic. If the question is put as an empirical one, then all that these literary critics can do is to build up a case on the basis of information. Their arguments have no more necessary scientific ground than do the assertions about heredity which Zola held and applied in his novels. As literary people, we are either reducing literature to a question of logic, or we are trying to resolve literary questions by talking in terms of sciences which we do not work in. The empirical answer to this question would demand scientific work in specialized fields, such as physiology and biology, as well as psychiatry. In addition, deterministic hypotheses, whether we call them true or false, have had a value in science. Those who dispute over literary naturalism in terms of free will versus determinism are generally opposing the scientific spirit. Zola's attitude was scientific, even though limited. That of many of his latter-day critics is antiscientific.

Zola denied that art was an expression of personal views. He insisted that scientific authority must be established in place of the personal authority of the artist. I think he was mistaken. Today we are inclined to be much less optimistic than Zola was. We are aware that we can know less than we would like to pretend to, and that the unknown is far vaster than many imagined it to be in the nineteenth century. We cannot proclaim, as Zola did, that the artist must abandon theories when science has disproved them. Proof is a much more complicated process than he thought it would be. Some scientific warrant can even be given, at least tentatively, to substantiate the possible validity of types of art which Zola might have described as unrealistic, idealistic, metaphysical, or romantic—as lies.

We can translate Zola's theories so that, with many qualifications, they can have one significant value at the present time. Zola insisted that the experimental novelist must apply methods of observation and analysis. He attempted to do this. Serious writers at the present time make a similar attempt. In some instances a writer will start with a metaphysical orientation. Or he may start with attitudes or postulates which have some ground in scientific discovery. Marcel Proust, for instance, organized his books in terms of metaphysical conceptions which had some correspondence with Bergson's theories of time and continuity. Was or was not Proust a realist? Was or was not Proust a naturalist? Whether we answer these questions yes or no, we will still face the question of what Proust means to us when we read him. Do we get any fresh insight? Do we feel anything? Do we learn anything? Are we excited? What happens to our emotions? When you read a book, the handling of your own emotions, the resolution of your own feelings is much more important than any kind of judgment you make about whether the book is good or bad, especially if that judgment is made in terms of questions which are pseudophilosophical and pseudoscientific.

Words such as *realism* and *naturalism* have been applied to many writers. Various definitions of these words have been given. One is that of Oscar Cargill, who, in *Intellectual America: Ideas on the March,* says that naturalistic writers have in common a theory of pessimistic determinism. Others, in attempting to establish a common meaning for naturalism, have come forth with definitions which are mutually exclusive. Some hold that naturalism is optimistic. Others believe it pessimistic, and will say that if a book has a hopeful ending it can't be naturalistic. I do not know all of the definitions of naturalism but I have come across enough to know they are many. I am reminded of the state of psychology fifty or sixty years ago, when a so-called instinct psychology was dominant. Apparently there was a competition among academic psychologists at that time for finding new phrases for new instincts, real or alleged. The same kind of competition must be going on among those who are attempting to get a definition of naturalism.

If you accept someone else's definition, you are not original.

I have been called a naturalist and I have never denied it. However, my own conception of naturalism is not that which is usually attributed to me. By naturalism I mean that whatever happens in this world must ultimately be explainable in terms of events in this world. I assume or believe that all events are explainable in terms of natural origins rather than of extranatural or supernatural origins. Although this assumption underlies what I have written, I do not write novels to prove or disprove this assumption. I write novels to try to reveal what life seems to me to be like. I write novels as part of an attempt to explore the nature of experience.

Another way of looking at these questions is in terms of necessity and of tragedy. Some contemporary criticism bases itself on the Aristotelian concept of tragedy. At its most banal level, this is not analysis at all, but often merely a kind of self-evident criticism to the effect that such and such a modern writer is not as great as Goethe or Euripides. When such criticism goes beyond the self-evident, certain points based upon Aristotle's conception of tragedy are applied.

Aristotle held that in order for a character to be a tragic figure that character must be superior. Of tragedy he said: "A tragedy . . . is the imitation of an action that is serious, and also, as having magnitude, complete in itself." And he added: "Tragedy is essentially an imitation not of persons, but of action and of life, of happiness and misery." The function of the poet was to describe not the thing that had happened, but "a kind of thing that might happen," i.e., what is possible is deemed "probable or necessary." When a play is truly tragic, it induces pity and terror in the audience: "pity is occasioned by undeserved misfortune, and fear [terror] by that of one like ourselves."

The tragic deeds of characters in the Aristotelian conception were necessary either to be done or not to be done, and the action could be undertaken either knowingly or unknowingly. This exhausted all of the possibilities. But for the character to be tragic he had to be "better than the ordinary man."

The two points to be stressed are the conception of the hero as a superior person, and the conception of Fate in the Greek drama. The Greek conception of Fate or of Nemesis involves the actions of a god who controlled human destinies. The tragic hero, superior to the ordinary man, a male rather than a female or a slave, met his fate and suffered; therein lies the essence of his tragedy. It well may be that writers today are far inferior to the Greek dramatists. However, this inferiority cannot be cured by adopting the attitudes of the Greeks to Fate or Nemesis, or the conception of a tragic character as a superior person. In modern life few people can be superior in the Greek sense. And the ordinary person today does not possess the freedom in circumstances necessary to a tragedy after the manner of Greek drama.

Quite frequently, tragedy in our society has a representational and a social character. Involved in modern tragic characters are such factors as powerlessness because of one's economic position; lack of experience because of social and economic position, or because of accidents at birth which are the result of the type of parents one has; suffering of consequences of an economic and political character which are far beyond a person's individual control. All of this is obvious, and yet the obvious is overlooked when a literal conception of tragedy based upon Aristotle's theory and the example of Greek drama is rigidly held. Today we assume, with some warrant, that social forces, social factors, social pressures and tendencies play a role similar to that played by the gods, by Fate and Nemesis, in ancient Greece. And this is not reducible to mere difference in postulates. It involves social and technological changes, and also what Whitehead styled "a mental climate."

We live in a different society and we live in a different mental climate from that of Aristotle. Man does not, today, believe himself to be the center of the world, as he once did. He does not now look upon his life as a drama of salvation in the way and to the extent that he did in the Middle Ages. Even the character and the nature of knowledge is different. This is to be seen in the scientific superseding of the Aristotelian world. Substantially, it is revealed in a conception of the world in terms of relationships rather than of essence. All of these changes have been and will continue to be registered in literature. We must take these developments into account when we concern ourselves with the reasons naturalism, so called, has developed. It has been an attempt to meet and to reveal and to explore the nature of experience in the modern world.

Many writers, strikingly different from one another, have been called naturalists; thus the brothers Goncourt, Flaubert, Zola in France, and in America Frank Norris, Stephen Crane, Theodore Dreiser, John Dos Passos. Those linked together as naturalists in terms of a definition like that of Professor Cargill are too often taken as representatives of a school. General similarities are stressed while significant differences are neglected. Within the framework of the naturalistic tradition there is an extraordinary variety of theme, subject matter, attitude, ideas expressed or implied, types of character. *Madame Bovary* by Flaubert, *Germinal* by Zola, *The Red Badge of Courage* by Stephen Crane, *Sister Carrie* by Dreiser, *U.S.A.* by Dos Passos, could be cited as naturalistic novels. But what insight do we gain by linking them together in terms of a watered-down generalization?

These and other books, linked together in this tradition, are all part of the effort by writers of the nineteenth and twentieth centuries to come to terms with experience. They have been written in the spirit of truth. If they are part of a tradition, that tradition has had more force and more impact, and has been able to nourish and give more energy to successive generations than any other tradition. This is especially so in America. The majority of critics of this tradition have been exponents of another, the genteel tradition in America. Speaking of the latter, Parrington aptly observed that its essence was to be found in "a refined aestheticism, that professed to discover the highest virtue in shutting one's eyes to disagreeable fact and the highest law in the law of convention." So-called American

realistic writers have grown up in a different American world from that of nineteenth-century New England. They have lived different kinds of lives. They have different origins.

But they are attacked in the name of nineteenth-century writers. In the light of this, I should like to quote from a long review, "The Deflowering of New England," by the critic Stanley Edgar Hyman in *The Hudson Review* (Winter, 1950). Mr. Hyman, who shares at least some of the attitudes to which I have alluded, criticizes a number of biographies of Hawthorne, Henry James, Thoreau, Emerson, and Henry Adams and Melville—all of whom I admire as writers. He writes:

> . . . there is the embarrassing and confusing question of the private domestic lives of these writers, that is, not to put too fine a point on it, sex. On a scale of healthy and normal domestic life, Thoreau, priggish, terrified of women, dependent on his mother, and frigidly ascetic, would be at the bottom, followed closely by the spinsterish James; and Hawthorne and Adams, both of them fortunate in storybook marriages (until the death of Marian Adams) would be somewhere at the top. And yet, dare we say that the latter lives were fuller, or rounder, or even happier? Wouldn't a scale of tough-mindedness, of living in ecological balance with the world and dying with a minimum of whining be just as apt to run the other way? If Emerson's first marriage was passionate, short-lived, and tragic, and his second cold, long-lived, fecund, contented, which one helped his work? What is the condition of health for the artist, is there any, and how would we know it if we saw it?

And then at the end of the review: " . . . we are all simmering: who will be the new Emerson, or even the exhumer of the old Emerson, to bring us to a boil?"

In this quotation, as in the writings of many critics of the so-called naturalistic tradition, I see an insecurity, a lack of sureness, a timidity, although it is often masked by an authoritative use of the hallowed names of the past and by an association with these hallowed names. I see a tendency to cling to stereotypes of what literature and the artist should be, to cling to these in times when literature is slowly being remade and changed in a world that is both changing and dangerous.

It is a curious fact that it is the writers of the so-called naturalistic tradition who constantly have had to bear the brunt of the struggle for freedom of literary expression. It is the writers of this tradition who constantly have been haled into court, who have had to defend their work at law, who have had to face the application of the police power. It is the writers of this tradition whose books have been excluded from libraries, from colleges, from bookstores, even excluded from being transported across the boundaries of democratic countries. The consequences of the best work in this tradition have been an increase in feeling and a desire for more freedom, more frankness, more understanding in the world.

The consequences of the obscurantist criticism of this tradition have been more or less in the direction of censorship, or narrowness, or tightness of feeling and thought. Today, much of this criticism seems strangely arrogant. It is today's advocates of the new gentility who are looking for something in the past which will steam them up to the boiling point.

I have always maintained that all artistic tendencies should have free play for expression, and that there should be a kind of free competition between them so that each may have its chance to attract those who may gain from it. I have always believed that there should be richness and variety and art in literature, in philosophy, and in thought. In speaking of naturalism, I do not want to establish it in any authoritative way over any other tendency. All I would state is that realism and naturalism have been in the forefront in the last century in shaping contemporary literature. These have encouraged a spirit of truth and free inquiry. The problems over which psychologists, sociologists, and many others today show great concern are the very problems that agitated, concerned, and provoked many of the realistic writers and stimulated the creation of their books, some of which became lasting works in world literature.

"It is only those," writes Alfred Kazin, in *On Native Grounds,* "who have no culture and no belief in culture who resent differences among men and the exploration of the human imagination." The naturalistic tradition, so called, has been one means of this exploration. (pp. 142-55)

> *James T. Farrell, "Some Observations on Naturalism, So Called, in Fiction," in his* Reflections at Fifty and Other Essays, *The Vanguard Press, Inc., 1954, pp. 142-55.*

Philip Rahv

[*A Russian-born American critic, Rahv was a prominent and influential member of the Marxist movement in American literary criticism. For thirty-five years he served as co-editor of* Partisan Review, *the prestigious literary journal T. S. Eliot once called "America's leading literary magazine." In the essay below, he discusses both the place of Naturalism in modern literary history and the reasons for its decline as a viable movement.*]

Quite a few protests have been aired in recent years against the sway of the naturalist method in fiction. It is charged that this method treats material in a manner so flat and external as to inhibit the search for value and meaning, and that in any case, whatever its past record, it is now exhausted. Dissimilar as they are, both the work of Franz Kafka and the works of the surrealist school are frequently cited as examples of release from the routines of naturalist realism, from its endless bookkeeping of existence. Supporting this indictment are mostly those writers of the younger group who are devoted to experimentation and who look to symbolism, the fable, and the myth.

The younger writers are stirred by the ambition to create a new type of imaginative prose into which the recognizably real enters as one component rather than as the total substance. They want to break the novel of its objective habits; some want to introduce into it philosophical ideas; others are not so much drawn to expressing ideas as to expressing the motley strivings of the inner self—dreams, visions, and fantasies. Manifestly the failure of the political movement in the literature of the past decade has resulted in a revival of religio-esthetic attitudes. The young men of letters are once again watching their own image in the mirror and listening to inner promptings. Theirs is a program calling for the adoption of techniques of planned derangement as a means of cracking open the certified structure of reality and turning loose its latent energies. And surely one cannot dispose of such a program merely by uncovering the element of mystification in it. For the truth is that the artist of the avant-garde has never hesitated to lay hold of the instruments of mystification when it suited his purpose, especially in an age such as ours, when the life about him belies more and more the rational ideals of the cultural tradition.

It has been remarked that in the long run the issue between naturalism and its opponents resolves itself into a philosophical dispute concerning the nature of reality. Obviously those who reject naturalism in philosophy will also object to its namesake in literature. But it seems to me that when faced with a problem such as that of naturalist fiction, the critic will do well not to mix in ontological maneuvers. From the standpoint of critical method it is impermissible to replace a concrete literary analysis with arguments derived from some general theory of the real. For it is plainly a case of the critic not being able to afford metaphysical commitments if he is to apply himself without preconceived ideas to the works of art that constitute his material. The art-object is from first to last the one certain datum at his disposal; and in succumbing to metaphysical leanings—either of the spiritualist or materialist variety—he runs the risk of freezing his insights in some kind of ideational schema the relevance of which to the task in hand is hardly more than speculative. The act of critical evaluation is best performed in a state of *ideal aloofness* from abstract systems. Its practitioner is not concerned with making up his mind about the ultimate character of reality but with observing and measuring its actual proportions and combinations within a given form. The presence of the real affects him directly, with an immediate force contingent upon the degree of interest, concreteness, and intensity in the impression of life conveyed by the literary artist. The philosopher can take such impressions or leave them, but luckily the critic has no such choice.

Imaginative writing cannot include fixed and systematic definitions of reality without violating its own existential character. Yet in any imaginative effort that which we mean by the real remains the basic criterion of viability, the crucial test of relevance, even if its specific features can hardly be determined in advance but must be *felt anew* in each given instance. And so far as the medium of fiction is concerned, one cannot but agree with Henry James that it gains its "air of reality"—which he considers to be its "supreme virtue"—through "its immense and exquisite correspondence with life." Note that James's formulation allows both for analogical and realistic techniques of representation. He speaks not of copies or reports or transcripts of life but of relations of equivalence, of a "correspondence" which he identifies with the "illusion of life." The ability to produce this illusion he regards as the storyteller's inalienable gift, "the merit on which all other merits . . . helplessly and submissively depend." This insight is of an elementary nature and scarcely peculiar to James alone, but it seems that its truth has been lost on some of our recent catch-as-catch-can innovators in the writing of fiction.

It is intrinsically from this point of view that one can criticize the imitations of Kafka that have been turning up of late as being one-sided and even inept. Perhaps Kafka is too idiosyncratic a genius to serve as a model for others, but still it is easy to see where his imitators go wrong. It is necessary to say to them: To know how to take apart the recognizable world is not enough, is in fact merely a way of letting oneself go and of striving for originality at all costs. But originality of this sort is nothing more than a professional mannerism of the avant-garde. The genuine innovator is always trying to make us actually experience his creative conflict. He therefore employs means that are subtler and more complex: *at the very same time that he takes the world apart he puts it together again.* For to proceed otherwise is to dissipate rather than alter our sense of reality, to weaken and compromise rather than change in any significant fashion our feeling of relatedness to the world. After all, what impressed us most in Kafka is precisely this power of his to achieve a simultaneity of contrary effects, to fit the known into the unknown, the actual into the mythic and vice versa, to combine within one framework a conscientiously empirical account of the visibly real with a magical decomposition of it. In this paradox lies the pathos of his approach to human existence.

A modern poetess has written that the power of the visible derives from the invisible; but the reverse of this formula is also true. Thus the visible and the invisible might be said to stand to each other in an ironic relation of inner dependence and of mutual skepticism mixed with solicitude. It is a superb form of doubletalk; and if we are accustomed to its exclusion from naturalistic writing, it is all the more disappointing to find that the newly evolved "fantastic" style of the experimentalists likewise excludes it. But there is another consideration, of a more formal nature. It seems to me a profound error to conceive of reality as merely a species of material that the fiction-writer can either use or dispense with as he sees fit. It is a species of material, of course, and something else besides: it also functions as the *discipline of fiction,* much in the same sense that syllabic structure functions as the discipline of verse. This seeming identity of the formal and substantial means of narrative prose is due, I think, to the altogether free and open character of the medium, which prevents it from developing such distinctly technical controls as poetry has acquired. Hence even the dream, when told in a story, must partake of some of the qualities of the real.

Whereas the surrealist represents man as immured in dreams, the naturalist represents him in a continuous waking state of prosaic daily living, in effect as never dreaming. But both the surrealist and the naturalist go to extremes in simplifying the human condition. J. M. Synge once said that the artist displays at once the difficulty and the triumph of his art when picturing the dreamer leaning out to reality or the man of real life lifted out of it. "In all the poets," he wrote, and this test is by no means limited to poetry alone, "the greatest have both these elements, that is they are supremely engrossed with life, and yet with the wildness of their fancy they are always passing out of what is simple and plain."

The old egocentric formula, "Man's fate is his character," has been altered by the novelists of the naturalist school to read, "Man's fate is his environment." (Zola, the organizer and champion of the school, drew his ideas from physiology and medicine, but in later years his disciples cast the natural sciences aside in favor of the social sciences.) To the naturalist, human behavior is a function of its social environment; the individual is the live register of its qualities; he exists in it as animals exist in nature. Due to this emphasis the naturalist mode has evolved historically in two main directions. On the one hand it has tended towards passive documentation (milieu-panoramas, local-color stories, reportorial studies of a given region or industry, etc.), and on the other towards the exposure of socio-economic conditions (muckraking). American fiction of the past decade teems with examples of both tendencies, usually in combination. The work of James T. Farrell, for instance, is mostly a genre-record, the material of which is in its very nature operative in producing social feeling, while such novels as *The Grapes of Wrath* and *Native Son* are exposure-literature, as is the greater part of the fiction of social protest. Dos Passos' trilogy, *U. S. A.,* is thoroughly political in intention but has the tone and gloss of the methodical genre-painter in the page by page texture of its prose.

I know of no hard and fast rules that can be used to distinguish the naturalist method from the methods of realism generally. It is certainly incorrect to say that the difference is marked by the relative density of detail. Henry James observes in his essay *The Art of Fiction* that it is above all "solidity of specification" that makes for the illusion of life—the air of reality in a novel; and the truth of this dictum is borne out by the practice of the foremost modern innovators in this medium, such as Proust, Joyce, and Kafka. It is not, then, primarily the means employed to establish verisimilitude that fix the naturalist imprint upon a work of fiction. A more conclusive test, to my mind, is its treatment of the relation of character to background. I would classify as naturalistic that type of realism in which the individual is portrayed not merely as subordinate to his background but as wholly determined by it—that type of realism, in other words, in which the environment displaces its inhabitants in the role of the hero. Theodore Dreiser, for example, comes as close as any American writer to plotting the careers of his characters strictly within a determinative process. The financier Frank Cowperwood masters his world and emerges as its hero, while the "little man" Clyde Griffiths is the victim whom it grinds to pieces; yet hero and victim alike are essentially implements of environmental force, the carriers of its contradictions upon whom it stamps success or failure—not entirely at will, to be sure, for people are marked biologically from birth—but with sufficient autonomy to shape their fate.

In such a closed world there is patently no room for the singular, the unique, for anything in fact which cannot be represented plausibly as the product of a particular social and historical complex. Of necessity the naturalist must deal with experience almost exclusively in terms of the broadly typical. He analyzes characters in such a way as to reduce them to standard types. His method of construction is that of accretion and enumeration rather than of analysis or storytelling; and this is so because the quantitative development of themes, the massing of detail and specification, serves his purpose best. He builds his structures out of literal fact and precisely documented circumstance, thus severely limiting the variety of creative means at the disposal of the artist.

This quasi-scientific approach not only permits but, in theory at least, actually prescribes a neutral attitude in the sphere of values. In practice, however, most naturalists are not sufficiently detached or logical to stay put in such an ultraobjective position. Their detractors are wrong in denying them a moral content; the most that can be said is that theirs is strictly functional morality, bare of any elements of gratuity or transcendence and devoid of the sense of personal freedom. Clearly such a perspective allows for very little self-awareness on the part of characters. It also removes the possibility of a tragic resolution of experience. The world of naturalist fiction is much too big, too inert, too hardened by social habit and material necessity, to allow for that tenacious self-assertion of the human by means of which tragedy justifies and ennobles its protagonists. The only grandeur naturalism knows is the grandeur of its own methodological achievement in making available a vast inventory of minutely described phenomena, in assembling an enormous quantity of data and arranging them in a rough figuration of reality. *Les Rougon-Macquart* stands to this day as the most imposing monument to this achievement.

But in the main it is the pure naturalist—that monstrous offspring of the logic of a method—that I have been describing here. Actually no such literary animal exists. Life always triumphs over methods, over formulas and theories. There is scarcely a single novelist of any importance wearing the badge of naturalism who is all of a piece, who fails to compensate in some way for what we miss in his fundamental conception. Let us call the roll of the leading names among the French and American naturalists and see wherein each is saved.

The Goncourts, it is true, come off rather badly, but even so, to quote a French critic, they manage "to escape from the crude painting of the naked truth by their impressionistic mobility" and, one might add, by their mobile intelligence. Zola's case does not rest solely on our judgment of his naturalist dogmas. There are entire volumes by him—the best, I think, is *Germinal*—and parts of volumes besides, in which his naturalism, fed by an epic imagination, takes on a mythic cast. Thomas Mann associates him with Wagner in a common drive toward an epic mythicism:

> They belong together. The kinship of spirit, method, and aims is most striking. This lies not only in the ambition to achieve size, the propensity to the grandiose and the lavish; nor is it the Homeric leitmotiv alone that is common to them; it is first and foremost a special kind of naturalism, which develops into the mythical. . . . In Zola's epic . . . the characters themselves are raised up to a plane above that of every day. And is that Astarte of the Second Empire, called Nana, not symbol and myth? (*The Sufferings and Greatness of Richard Wagner*)

Zola's prose, though not controlled by an artistic conscience, overcomes our resistance through sheer positiveness and expressive energy—qualities engendered by his novelistic ardor and avidity for recreating life in all its multiple forms. As for Huysmans, even in his naturalist period he was more concerned with style than with subject-matter. Maupassant is a naturalist mainly by alliance, i.e., by virtue of his official membership in the School of Médan; actually he follows a line of his own, which takes off from naturalism never to return to it. There are few militant naturalists among latter-day French writers. Jules Romains is sometimes spoken of as one, but the truth is that he is an epigone of all literary doctrines, including his own. Dreiser is still unsurpassed so far as American naturalism goes, though just at present he may well be the least readable. He has traits that make for survival—a Balzacian grip on the machinery of money and power; a prosiness so primary in texture that if taken in bulk it affects us as a kind of poetry of the commonplace and ill-favored; and an emphatic eroticism which is the real climate of existence in his fictions—Eros hovering over the shambles. Sinclair Lewis was never a novelist in the proper sense that Zola and Dreiser are novelists, and, given his gift for exhaustive reporting, naturalism did him more good than harm by providing him with a ready literary technique. In Farrell's chronicles there is an underlying moral code which, despite his explicit rejection of the Church, seems to me indisputably orthodox and Catholic; and his Studs Lonigan—a product of those unsightly urban neighborhoods where youth prowls and fights to live up to the folk-ideal of the "regular guy"—is no mere character but an archetype, an eponymous hero of the street-myths that prevail in our big cities. The naturalism of Dos Passos is most completely manifested in *U. S. A.*, tagged by the critics as a "collective" novel recording the "decline of our business civilization." But what distinguishes Dos Passos from other novelists of the same political animus is a sense of justice so pure as to be almost instinctive, as well as a deeply elegiac feeling for the intimate features of American life and for its precipitant moments. Also, *U. S. A.* is one of the very few naturalist novels in which there is a controlled use of language, in which a major effect is produced by the interplay between story and style. It is necessary to add, however, that the faults of Dos Passos' work have been obscured by its vivid contemporaneity and vital political appeal. In the future, I think, it will be seen more clearly than now that it dramatizes social symptoms rather than lives and that it fails to preserve the integrity of personal experience. As for Faulkner, Hemingway, and Caldwell, I do not quite see on what grounds some critics and literary historians include them in the naturalist school. I should think that Faulkner is exempted by his prodigious inventiveness and fantastic humor. Hemingway is a realist on one level, in his attempts to catch the "real thing, the sequence of motion and fact which made the emotion"; but he is also subjective, given to self-portraiture and to playing games with his ego; there is very little study of background in his work, a minimum of documentation. In his best novels Caldwell is a writer of rural abandon—and comedy. His Tobacco Road is a sociological area only in patches; most of it is exotic landscape.

It is not hard to demonstrate the weakness of the naturalist method by abstracting it, first, from the uses to which individual authors put it and, second, from its function in the history of modern literature. The traditionalist critics judge it much too one-sidedly in professing to see in its rise nothing but spiritual loss—an invasion of the arcanum of art by arid scientific ideas. The point is that this scientific bias of naturalism was historically productive of contradictory results. Its effect was certainly depressive insofar as it brought mechanistic notions and procedures into writing. But it should be kept in mind that it also enlivened and, in fact, revolutionized writing by liquidating the last assets of "romance" in fiction and by purging it once and for all of the idealism of the "beautiful lie"—of the long-standing inhibitions against dealing with the underside of life, with those inescapable day-by-day actualities traditionally regarded as too "sordid" and "ugly" for inclusion within an aesthetic framework. If it were not for the service thus rendered in vastly increasing the store of literary material, it is doubtful whether such works as *Ulysses* and even *Remembrance of Things Past* could have been written. This is not clearly understood in the English speaking countries, where naturalism, never quite forming itself into a "movement," was at most only an extreme emphasis in the general onset of realistic fiction and drama. One must study, rather, the Continental writers of the last quarter of the nineteenth century in order to grasp its historical role. In discussing the German naturalist school of the 1880's, the historian Hans Naumann has this to say, for instance:

> Generally it can be said that to its early exponents the doctrine of naturalism held quite as many diverse and confusing meanings as the doctrine of expressionism seemed to hold in the period just past. Imaginative writers who at bottom were pure idealists united with the dry-as-dust advocates of a philistine natural-scientific program on the one hand and with the shameless exploiters of erotic themes on the other. All met under the banner of naturalism—friends today and enemies tomorrow. . . . But there was an element of historical necessity in all this. The fact is that the time had come for an assault, executed with glowing enthusiasm, against the epigones . . . that it was finally possible to fling aside with disdain and anger the pretty falsehoods of life and art (*Die Deutsche Dichtung der Gegenwart, Stuttgart,* 1930).

And he adds that the naturalism of certain writers consisted simply in their "speaking honestly of things that had heretofore been suppressed."

But to establish the historical credit of naturalism is not to refute the charges that have been brought against it in recent years. For whatever its past accomplishments, it cannot be denied that its present condition is one of utter debility. What was once a means of treating material truthfully has been turned, through a long process of depreciation, into a mere convention of truthfulness, devoid of any significant or even clearly definable literary purpose or design. The spirit of discovery has withdrawn from naturalism; it has now become the common denominator of realism, available in like measure to the producers of literature and to the producers of kitsch. One might sum up the objections to it simply by saying that it is no longer possible to use this method *without taking reality for granted.* This means that it has lost the power to cope with the ever growing element of the problematical in modern life, which is precisely the element that is magnetizing the imagination of the true artists of our epoch. Such artists are no longer content merely to question particular habits or situations or even institutions; it is reality itself which they bring into question. Reality to them is like that "open wound" of which Kierkegaard speaks in his *Journals:* "A healthy open wound; sometimes it is healthier to keep a wound open; sometimes it is worse when it closes."

There are also certain long-range factors that make for the decline of naturalism. One such factor is the growth of psychological science and, particularly, of psychoanalysis. Through the influence of psychology literature recovers its inwardness, devising such forms as the interior monologue, which combines the naturalistic in its minute description of the mental process with the anti-naturalistic in its disclosure of the subjective and the irrational. Still another factor is the tendency of naturalism, as Thomas Mann observes in his remarks on Zola, to turn into the mythic through sheer immersion in the typical. This dialectical negation of the typical is apparent in a work like *Ulysses,* where "the myth of the *Odyssey,*" to quote from Harry Levin's study of Joyce, "is superimposed upon the map of Dublin" because only a myth could "lend shape or meaning to a slice of life so broad and banal." And from a social-historical point of view this much can be said, that naturalism cannot hope to survive the world of nineteenth-century science and industry of which it is the product. For what is the crisis of reality in contemporary art if not at bottom the crisis of the dissolution of this familiar world? Naturalism, which exhausted itself taking an inventory of this world while it was still relatively stable, cannot possibly do justice to the phenomena of its disruption.

One must protest, however, against the easy assumption of some avant-gardist writers that to finish with naturalism is the same as finishing with the principle of realism generally. It is one thing to dissect the real, to penetrate beneath its faceless surface and transpose it into terms of symbol and image; but the attempt to be done with it altogether is sheer regression or escape. Of the principle of realism it can be said that it is the most valuable acquisition of the modern mind. It has taught literature how to take in, how to grasp and encompass, the ordinary facts of human existence; and I mean this in the simplest sense conceivable. Least of all can the novelist dispense with it, as his medium knows of no other principle of coherence. In Gide's *Les Faux-Monnayeurs* there is a famous passage in which the novelist Edouard enumerates the faults of the naturalist school. "The great defect of that school is that it always cuts a slice of life in the same direction: in time, lengthwise. Why not in breadth? Or in depth? As for me, I should like not to cut at all. Please understand: I should like to put everything into my novel." "But I thought," his interlocutor remarks, "that you want to abandon reality." Yes, replies Edouard, "my novelist wants to abandon it; but I shall continually bring him back to it. In fact that will be the subject; the struggle between the facts presented by reality and the ideal reality." (pp. 141-54)

Philip Rahv, "Notes on the Decline of Naturalism," in his Image and Idea: Twenty Essays on Literary Themes, *revised edition, New Directions, 1957, pp. 141-54.*

FURTHER READING

Brandes, George. "The Beginnings of Naturalism." In his *Main Currents in Nineteenth Century Literature,* pp. 32-7. New York: Macmillan, 1905.
    Locates the source of Naturalism in William Wordsworth and Samuel Taylor Coleridge's rejection of eighteenth-century poetics.

Carter, Lawson A. *Zola and the Theater.* New Haven, Conn.: Yale University Press, 1963, 231 p.
    Includes discussions of Zola's plays and excerpts of his drama criticism in an attempt "to weave together the various strands of Zola's theatrical endeavors into a unified pattern."

Cowley, Malcolm. "Naturalism in American Literature." In *Evolutionary Thought in America,* edited by Stow Persons, pp. 300-33. Archon Books, 1968.
    Explores the basic tenets and major proponents of American literary Naturalism. Cowley concludes that, despite stylistic weaknesses, the Naturalists boldly introduced new subjects and themes to American literature.

Croyden, Margaret. "The Symbolists and the Naturalists." In her *Lunatics, Lovers and Poets: The Contemporary Experimental Theatre,* pp. 3-23. New York: McGraw-Hill Book Co., 1974.
    Chronicles the development of Naturalism and Symbolism in the latter half of the nineteenth century. Croyden asserts that "although they were sometimes viewed as irreconcilable opposites, in actuality aspects of each were to merge and interchange."

Davis, Gifford. "The Critical Reception of Naturalism in Spain before *La Cuestión Palpitante.*" *Hispanic Review* XXII, No. 2 (April 1954): 97-108.
    Discusses the Spanish reaction to French Naturalism and the development of the movement in Spain.

Decker, Clarence R. "'The Maiden in Tribute'—The Naturalists in England." In his *The Victorian Conscience,* pp. 79-114. New York: Twayne Publishers, 1952.
    Examines the changing English reception of French literature in the nineteenth century, focusing on the initial rejection and gradual acceptance of Zola.

De la Torre, Antonio M. "Naturalism and the Spanish American Novel." *Books Abroad* 26, No. 2 (Spring 1952): 147-50.
    Discusses the function of Naturalism in the Spanish-American novel, asserting that Naturalistic theories "may fairly be regarded as dominant forces of a widespread movement in contemporary art, which seeks in each of the Latin American nations to interpret the cultural factors that give its people a distinct character of their own."

Finney, Gail. "In the Naturalist Grain: Huysmans' *A Rebours* Viewed through the Lens of Zola's *Germinal.*" *Modern Language Studies* XVI, No. 2 (Spring 1986): 71-7.
    Analyzes *A Rebours* and *Germinal* as representative novels of Decadence and Naturalism, respectively, to uncover similarities between the two movements.

Frierson, William C. and Edwards, Herbert. "Impact of French Naturalism on American Critical Opinion, 1877-1892." *PMLA* LXIII, No. 3 (September 1948): 1007-16.
    Examines the controversy in the United States over French literary Naturalism, and discusses the difficulties faced by early American Naturalists.

Hatfield, Henry. "Art as Nature: Naturalism." In his *Modern German Literature: The Major Figures in Context,* pp. 1-16. Bloomington: Indiana University Press, 1966.
    Asserts that although the German Naturalists were "doctrinaire and often sentimental . . . they were obsessed with truth, and their obsession was a noble one."

Hewett-Thayer, Harvey W. "Naturalism and the German Zola." In his *The Modern German Novel: A Series of Studies and Appreciations,* pp. 67-102. Boston: Marshall Jones Co., 1924.
    Surveys German Naturalism, examining in particular the debt novelist Max Kretzer owed to Zola's theories.

Hill, Hamlin. "'There Ought to Be Clowns': American Humor and Literary Naturalism." *Prospect* 5 (1980): 413-22.
    Suggests that some American Naturalist writers used comically gross exaggeration to "insulate" the reading public from grotesque subject matter.

Hill, John S. "Trina Sieppe: First Lady of American Naturalism." *The University of Kansas City Review* XXIX, No. 1 (October 1962): 77-80.
    Discusses the wife of the title character in Frank Norris's novel *McTeague* as "the first well-created female character to be used to depict naturalism in American fiction."

Jelavich, Peter. "The Censorship of Literary Naturalism, 1890-1895: Bavaria." *Central European History* XVIII, No. 3-4 (September/December 1985): 344-59.
    Suggests that the conservative political tone of Bavaria in the early 1890s succeeded in "dividing and weakening the local naturalist movement."

Lehan, Richard. "American Literary Naturalism: The French Connection." *Nineteenth-Century Fiction* 38, No. 4 (March 1984): 529-57.
    Examines Frank Norris and Theodore Dreiser as fulfillments of Zola's definition of the novelist as a scientific observer of nature and society.

Lucas, John. "From Naturalism to Symbolism." *Renaissance and Modern Studies* XXI (1977): 124-39.

Discusses the brief existence of Naturalism in England and suggests that the movement resulted in the rise of Symbolism.

Peace, Richard. "The Nineteenth Century: The Natural School and its Aftermath, 1840-55." In *The Cambridge History of Russian Literature,* edited by Charles A. Moser, pp. 189-247. Cambridge: Cambridge University Press, 1989.

Studies the major figures of the Russian Naturalist movement, focusing on their sociological and psychological observations of peasant life.

Seltzer, Mark. "The Naturalist Machine." In *Sex, Politics, and Science in the Nineteenth-Century Novel,* edited by Ruth Bernard Yeazell, pp. 116-47. Baltimore: Johns Hopkins University Press, 1986.

Analyzes the Naturalist novel's reinvention of nineteenth-century technologies of power as evidenced in the work of Frank Norris.

Stark, Gary D. "The Censorship of Literary Naturalism, 1885-1895: Prussia and Saxony." *Central European History* XVIII, Nos. 3-4 (September/December 1985): 326-43.

Asserts that the censorship in Prussia and Saxony did not significantly thwart Naturalism, and in fact helped the movement to flourish.

Stewart, Mary E. "German Naturalism and the Novel." *The Modern Language Review* 71, No. 4 (October 1976): 846-56.

Discusses the elements of Zola's Naturalism that were employed in the works of minor nineteenth-century German novelists.

Stewart, Randall. "Dreiser and the Naturalistic Heresy." *The Virginia Quarterly Review* 34, No. 1 (Winter 1958): 100-16.

Suggests that Naturalism's deterministic philosophy is incompatible with the American belief in individual dignity and faith in human potential for heroic action.

Stromberg, Roland N. Introduction to *Realism, Naturalism, and Symbolism: Modes of Thought and Expression in Europe, 1848-1914,* edited by Roland N. Stromberg, pp. ix-xxxvi. New York: Walker and Company, 1968.

A comparison of Naturalism with Realism and Symbolism that emphasizes the continuity of the three movements.

Van Doren, Carl. "The Eighties and their Kin." In his *The American Novel,* pp. 221-45. New York: Macmillan, 1936.

Examines the novels of the 1880s, focusing on the artists' use of "local color" to create a definitively American genre.

West, Thomas G. "Schopenhauer, Huysmans and French Naturalism." *Journal of European Studies* 1, No. 4 (December 1971): 313-24.

Analyzes the Naturalists' attraction to Schopenhauer's pessimistic philosophy.

White, Lucien W. "Moral Aspects of Zola's Naturalism Judged by his Contemporaries and by Himself." *Modern Language Quarterly* 23 (December 1962): 360-72.

Surveys the criticism of the moral aspects of Zola's works, specifically their failure to consistently apply rewards for virtue and punishment for vice. White also discusses what Zola's contemporaries saw as his denial of the role of will in human action.

Yellow Journalism

INTRODUCTION

The term Yellow Journalism originally referred to the practices of many of the New York daily newspapers published during the 1880s and 1890s. Joseph Pulitzer, editor of the New York *World* and William Randolph Hearst, editor of the *New York Journal,* the dominant figures of the age, strove to increase circulation through a variety of aggressive tactics such as reporting sensational stories, setting headlines in extremely large type, making extensive use of pictures, and issuing Sunday supplements containing color comics. The most famous example of the last is Richard F. Outcault's "Hogan's Alley," which appeared in both the *World* and the *Journal;* this comic featured a character called the "Yellow Kid," from whom Yellow Journalism derived its name.

Best known for the journalistic and literary awards named after him, Pulitzer was a Hungarian immigrant who began his career in 1868 as a reporter in St. Louis for the German-language newspaper the *Westliche Post.* For several years, he maintained his journalistic endeavors alongside an active political life, serving on the Missouri legislature and campaigning for the Democratic presidential candidate Samuel J. Tilden. In 1878 he purchased the bankrupt *St. Louis Dispatch* and consolidated it with the *St. Louis Post,* to form the *St. Louis Post-Dispatch.* Crusading against inequities in the tax system, exposing government corruption, and advocating social reform, Pulitzer shaped the *Post-Dispatch* into a progressive and financially successful organization. Pulitzer felt compelled to leave St. Louis in 1882, however, when scandal erupted after John A. Cockerill, a journalist for the *Post-Dispatch,* shot and killed an attorney who challenged an editorial that he believed insulted his firm. Pulitzer relocated to New York City, where in 1883 he purchased the *World,* a financially unstable newspaper with a history of Democratic partisanship. Promising "a journal that is not only cheap but bright, not only bright but large, not only large but truly Democratic," he openly catered to a mass audience. The introduction of such eye-catching enhancements as two-column headlines and front-page illustrations enabled the *World* to surpass the circulation of its competitors, the *Times* and the *Herald,* from which Pulitzer had hired many key staff members, including managing editor Ballard Smith. In addition to presenting lurid and exaggerated news items, the *World* featured outright publicity stunts, such as sending famed reporter Nellie Bly around the world in an attempt to better the mark set by Phileas Fogg in Jules Verne's 1873 novel *La tour du monde en quatre-vingt jours (Around the World in Eighty Days).* (Bly, in fact, completed the trip in seventy-three days.) Under Pulitzer's direction, the *World* waged crusading editorial campaigns, promoting Grover Cleveland's election to the presidency and public funding for a pedestal for the Statue of Liberty, as well as fighting battles against the monopolizing efforts of Bell Telephone and Standard Oil. In 1890, Pulitzer, beset by blindness caused by long hours of proofreading, was forced to relinquish editorial control of the *World* to an executive board, though his guidance remained a powerful influence.

The ruthless and arrogant Charles Foster Kane, from Orson Welles's 1941 film *Citizen Kane,* endures for many as the definitive portrayal of William Randolph Hearst, considered by many one of the most notorious figures of the first half of the twentieth century. Hearst's editorial career began in 1887 when he took over the ailing San Francisco *Examiner* from his father, a mining tycoon and United States Senator. The younger Hearst doubled the newspaper's circulation in one year, utilizing many techniques borrowed from Pulitzer. Anxious to prove himself in New York, Hearst bought the *Journal,* a paper Pulitzer's brother Albert had founded, in 1891. Owing to a resourceful and iconoclastic vision of the daily newspaper, as well as the funds necessary to recruit such talented Pulitzer employees as Outcault, columnist Arthur Brisbane, and magazine-section editor Morrill Goddard, Hearst engineered a publication that exceeded even the sensationalism of the *World.* Piers Brendon has written of Hearst that "his stunts were more explosive, his self-puffery was more blatant and his crusades were more enterprising."

The rivalry between the *Journal* and the *World* reached its climax with the circumstances surrounding the Spanish-American War. According to many historians, America's intervention in the conflict between Cuban nationalists and the Spanish government might have been minimal without the relentless campaign by American newspapers on behalf of the Cubans. These critics argue that distortion of such events as the 1897 incarceration of Evangelina Cisneros—niece of the Cuban President—and the sinking of the battleship *Maine* in 1898 precipitated overwhelming public support for military action. Whether the newspapers incited, or merely reflected, war hysteria, war reporting was responsible for the soaring circulations of the newspapers. Many writers—including James Creelman, Richard Harding Davis, and Stephen Crane of the *Journal* and Frederick W. Lawrence and Honoré F. Lainé of the *World*—gained or enhanced their fame while working as war correspondents.

Witnessing the financial success of the *World* and the *Journal,* even the most traditional and conservative newspapers around the nation adopted aspects of the visual and editorial style of Yellow Journalism. With Pulitzer's continued ill health deterring him from setting policy at his newspapers and Hearst's entrance into the political arena, however, the phenomenon gradually abated. As historians began to scrutinize the effects of Yellow Journalism, most emphasized its irresponsibility and vulgarity; "Life, as it percolated through the *World* and *Journal*," wrote Will Irwin in 1911, "became melodrama, the song of the spheres a screech." Others, however, viewed Yellow Journalism as an effective vehicle for social change and as a useful component of urban living at the end of the nineteenth century. Carroll D. Clark determined: "The sensational news and human-interest material in which [Yellow Journalism] specialized was a response to urban needs, for it . . . enabled the city man to enter imaginatively into the thoughts and motives of the inscrutable throng."

OVERVIEWS

Will Irwin

[*Irwin was a highly respected journalist and the official biographer of President Herbert Hoover. In the following essay, originally published in* Collier's *magazine in 1911, he chronicles the rise of Yellow Journalism and highlights the tactics used to increase circulation.*]

The seeds of yellow journalism, so called for want of a better name, sprouted at St. Louis and San Francisco during the eighties; they came to fruition in New York, thrashing-floor for changes in journalism, during the early nineties. In the decade which preceded the full flowering of Hearst and Pulitzer, however, a change in the spirit of newspaper publication had crept in by way of the business office—a change which prepared the ground for this new seed. From a rather humble professional enterprise, the newspaper had become a great "business proposition," holding infinite possibilities of profit.

Dana, Medill, Greeley, Godkin, even Bennett, adopted their vocation from that mixture of motive and chance which leads a man into any profession; they certainly reckoned the chance of getting rich very slightly among possibilities. But the field for newspaper circulation grew, as I have shown; and with it grew the perfection of swift mechanical processes. By 1891 a quadruple Hoe press would print, fold, cut, paste, and count 72,000 eight-page papers an hour. The linotype, or mechanical typesetting machine, climax of delicate mechanism, was not yet perfected; that was to come just after the yellows made their start. Our publishers had facilities, therefore, to handle any imaginable increase in circulation. It was necessary only to enlarge basement spaces and increase the number of presses. And now big retail business discovered the newspaper as a salesman. Yankee advertising had been a jest of Europe for a half-century long, before experience proved that for most commodities advertisement in a regular and respectable periodical pays better, dollar for dollar, than advertisement by circular or sign-board.

In the same period the retail dry goods business, consistently an advertiser since the first newspapers, began to concentrate in department stores and to drag into these great emporiums other forms of retail business, such as hardware, jewelry, and groceries. With their bargain days,

their special offerings, designed to attract customers to the store, their advertising became a matter of news. They did not now announce, as in 1810: "We offer prints and calicoes at lowest prices," but: "Special today: A hundred dozen pairs of ladies' lisle hose, worth 75 cents, at 49 cents." For this form of publicity the newspaper was the only possible medium except privately distributed circulars; and a circular, as experience has shown, is usually thrown into the ash-can, while a newspaper notice, surrounded by matter which commands some respect, is kept and read. Newspaper and periodical advertising grew from tiny beginnings to a great force of distribution. Where the senior Bennett's old *Herald* got its advertising revenue by hundreds of dollars, the junior Bennett's *Herald* of the eighties got it by tens of thousands. There came, then, a gradual shift of power from the editorial rooms to the business office.

The stalwart old-time newspaper proprietor, who had entered the editorial game for love of it, still held his paper to editorial ideals, though he grew rich incidentally. McCullagh of the *St. Louis Globe-Democrat,* it is remembered now in these changed days, would not let a business office man come on to the editorial floor, lest his staff become commercialized. There remained, however, a multitude of lesser souls who yielded to the temptation of the flesh-pots and trained their eyes solely on commercial possibilities. Their advertising solicitors raked the city for copy; the less scrupulous coerced advertisers by a species of blackmail— "You advertise with us and we'll leave you alone." Above all—and this is where the commercial movement ties up with "yellow" journalism—they were ripe and ready for any method which would serve to extend circulation and therefore make their advertising space more valuable.

During the seventies, a young German-American, a pest to his fellows with his truculence, a blessing to his employers with his news sense and his vigorous writing, shuttled back and forth between the German and English newspapers of St. Louis. Joseph Pulitzer had been a soldier of bad fortune for some years before he entered journalism; he had served as coachman, as waiter, as common laborer, as private in the burial squad which laid away the dead after the St. Louis cholera epidemic; and he had learned the common man's attitude toward life and the news. His fellows of the police stations in his early journalistic days remember him as a restless, inquiring youth, ready to try almost any experiment with life, if he might learn thereby what was inside the sealed envelope: above all, as a man with his own opinions, ready to back them with fist and tongue. He rose; he did his turn at Washington, where his writing attracted the attention of Dana; and he might have taken service with the *New York Sun.* He preferred the power of the game to its art, however; and in 1878 he raised money to acquire the *St. Louis Post-Dispatch,* an obscure paper, dying of inanition.

It is not true, as some assume, that Pulitzer founded yellow journalism then and there. What he did discover— and that is only one element in yellow journalism—was the means of fighting popular causes by the news. The process was not wholly original with him; the *New York Times* had smashed the Tweed Ring by publishing plain accounts of their corrupt transactions. Perhaps, however, Pulitzer was first to go out systematically and find evil before evil obtruded itself on public notice. He had a conservative community to serve. In such an atmosphere certain set and old injustices always flourish for lack of popular opposition. Pulitzer scratched this surface and showed what lay beneath. He made himself the bugaboo of the big cinch; he made his organ such a champion of popular rights that to this day the humble citizen of St. Louis who has a grievance tends to write to the *P.-D.* before he employs a lawyer. That was the kind of journalism which Pulitzer brought to the hospitable-minded metropolis when, in the middle eighties, he bought the *New York World.*

The yellow streak was working from quite another beginning at the other end of the continent. William Randolph Hearst, only son of rich and able parents, had come out of Harvard. His father, Senator George Hearst, a rough, hustling mining millionaire and politician, had bought the *San Francisco Examiner* as a kind of a flyer in connection with his political and commercial schemes. The son had taken a fancy to journalism, and had his eye already on the *Examiner.* Even in college he made a daily study and comparison of the current newspapers. The *Examiner,* as he found it, was an old, conservative paper, weak in the spine through many changes of political ownership.

Unbiased and unblinded, as though this were the first and only publication in the world, Hearst set out to find how he could make it the greatest, the controlling newspaper of the Pacific Coast region. His father's old employees, and especially one "Petey" Bigelow, a wild genius of a reporter who flourished in San Francisco at that period, took him in hand and taught him all they knew. He listened to their advice—and rejected it, mainly. Not until he discovered that S. S. Chamberlain was willing to take a position on the far coast of the United States did Hearst find the man to show him the way.

Chamberlain had seen service with both Bennett and Pulitzer; for the former, he had edited the *Paris Herald;* and he had started *Le Matin.* He came to the *Examiner,* therefore, schooled in the most sensational journalism which had appeared up to that time. He was—and is—a master of popular psychology, a seer at perceiving the subtle values in public taste. Through all the subsequent years of the yellow craze he remained a rock of real news-journalism in the Hearst organization. To Hearst, experimenting blindly with what the public wanted, this exponent of sensationalism was a godsend. Under his tutelage the young millionaire began to make a noise. He attacked the Southern Pacific, the eternal corporation bugaboo of California—did it with such success that, during his first long absence from California, Collis P. Huntington compounded with his resident manager and bought the paper off for a thousand dollars a month. A schooner went ashore on Brandt Rock, a dangerous reef outside the harbor mouth. Hearst equipped a tug under command of "Petey" Bigelow and rescued the survivors—on behalf of the *Examiner.* He sent up balloons to distribute prizes to the populace—on behalf of the *Examiner.* Whenever, in all his radius of interest, occurred a disaster or a startling crime, he despatched to the scene a special train loaded to the

window with *Examiner* writers and illustrators. The public park of San Francisco wanted a specimen of the fast-dying Californian grizzly. Hearst set hunters to work; they trapped the biggest bear to be had; "Monarch, the *Examiner's* Grizzly," made space for weeks. This caught the fickle and unaccountable public fancy, and Hearst pushed the movement along by adopting the bear as the *Examiner* trademark. James Swinnerton, in the first flush of his powers as a rough-and-ready cartoonist, drew bears for a year, until people tired of the feature.

Whenever the other newspapers produced a man suited to his purposes, Hearst bought him over at his own figures. So he got E. H. Hamilton, one of the great American reporters; Homer Davenport, destined as a cartoonist to play his part in political history; Arthur McEwen, second only to Brisbane as a writer of editorials in the Hearst manner. Chamberlain conceived the idea that the city hospital was badly managed. He picked a little slip of a girl from among his cub reporters, and assigned her to the investigation. She invented her own method—she "fainted" on the street and was carried to the hospital for treatment. She turned out a story "with a sob for the unfortunate in every line." That was the professional beginning of "Annie Laurie" or Winifred Black, and of a departure in newspaper writing. For she came to have many imitators; but none other could ever so well stir up the primitive emotions of sympathy and pity; she was a "sob squad" all by herself. Indeed, in the discovery of this sympathetic "woman writing," Hearst broke through the crust into the thing he was after. His greatest single hit, before he left San Francisco for wider fields, was the "Little Jim Ward"—simply a movement to establish a ward for incurables in the local children's hospital. "Little Jim" was a helpless cripple whom Annie Laurie discovered and whom she used as an example. Every day for weeks the women of San Francisco exchanged tears across the back fences over "Little Jim."

Hearst was experimenting every week, every day; trying a hundred expensive departures, only to abandon ninety-nine for the sake of the one which "panned out." This week, he arranged the heads in certain symmetrical patterns—for "make-up" or the physical appearance of the paper, was always a hobby with him. Next week, he tried the effect of veiled salaciousness. Another, he got such sensation as he could out of Sunday's sermons to see if his readers "really cared for religion in the news." And he experimented always with one object in view—to find what the public wanted, how he might sell the greatest number of copies.

Consciously or unconsciously, Hearst and Chamberlain were working on a principle whose formation was as original to our Occidental journalism as Bennett's discovery of news. He who serves the intellectual and artistic demands of the populace must give them in some measure what they want. If he proceeds from the very highest ethical and artistic ideals, he must make concessions, or they will not listen. But having established a common ground with his public, he may give them a little better than they want, so leading them up by the slow process of education to his own better ideals; or he may give them a great deal worse.

The gentlemen who conduct our theatrical affairs, for example, have of late given the public worse than it wants, so that when some sound, sincere, and artistic piece of work like "The Three of Us," "The Great Divide," or "Paid in Full" slips past them to success, they stand amazed. When Hearst began, the spirit of the old-age editor still guided newspaper publication; the great majority of editors, no matter how strong their desire for circulation, still served news and editorial in fashion much more intellectual than the public wanted, still appealed to the mind rather than the heart. Hearst's task was to cheapen the product until it sold at the coin of the gutter and the streets.

So he came generally to reject all news stories which did not contain that thrill of sensation loved by the man on the street and the woman in the kitchen; no paper ever published fewer news items to the issue. He trained his men to look for the one sensational, picturesque fact in every occurrence which came to the desk, and to twist that fact to the fore. "What we're after," said Arthur McEwen, "is the 'gee-whiz' emotion." Pressed for further explanation, he said: "We run our paper so that when the reader opens it he says: 'Gee-whiz!' An issue is a failure which doesn't make him say that." The basic human passions— "Love for the woman, power for the man"—Hearst was after them. A story to be available for his purposes must have romance, sympathy, hate, gain, in the first sentence, the first line, the first paragraph.

Necessarily, since he was reaching out to grip and to hold the populace, his editorial policy leaned to the people's side. He began as a Democrat, that being then the party of the under dog. At once he ran clear beyond Democracy until he impinged on Socialism. He adopted the union labor cause, even at the cost of an expensive mechanical department in his own newspaper. For years, or until rows and bickerings over the political support of union labor broke the alliance, this was a foundation-stone of Hearst editorial policy. Here convenience wed sincerity, doubtless; those who knew Hearst best in this early era declare that under his cold exterior he kept a real sympathy for the submerged man and woman, a real feeling of his own mission to plead their cause.

When he took the *Examiner* it was dying. In 1888, when Chamberlain came, he had brought it to 30,000 circulation. By 1893 he had 72,000; and he held a secure lead over the other San Francisco newspapers. That lead he never lost; year in and year out, except for the set-back of the great disaster in 1906, the *Examiner* has returned its $30,000 to $40,000 a month to keep the other Hearst papers floating.

This journalism he brought to New York when he bought the *Journal* in 1895. It was not yet quite what we call yellow, though it approximated that happy condition. For real yellow journalism had beaten him by a few months. Joseph Pulitzer had been fighting his way on the *New York World* with the sensational, militant style which he perfected in St. Louis. He took personal charge of the *World* in 1884. Within two years he had attacked so many things which the other newspapers had not perceived as copy, or had not dared to touch, that he was disputing circulation

with Bennett the Younger and Dana. By the end of the decade the *World* was altogether the most reckless, the most sensational, and the most widely discussed newspaper in New York. He has been several men, all extraordinary, in the course of his career, this Pulitzer; nothing so impresses one who regards him in the light of a historic character as the manner in which his able, penetrating, highly energized mind has shifted its point of view. In that stage he was a creature of infinite recklessness and incredible suspicion. By mental habit he scratched every fair surface to find the inner corrupt motive. Journalism, it appears, bounded his ambition; that was one secret of his extraordinary freedom from control. Had he cared for political position, for pure financial power, the history of American journalism in the past twenty years might have been very different. Within that narrow limit he, like the silent, cold, light-eyed young man experimenting out on the Pacific Coast, had the passion for leadership. "If you should put Hearst in a monastery," said one of his early associates, "he would become abbot or die." The gods cut Pulitzer off the same stripe.

The Sunday supplement was by this time an integral part of metropolitan journalism. As early as the Civil War period, the newspapers had been giving space on Sunday mornings to entertaining matter bearing only indirect relation to the news. When, with the development of the rotary press, they were able to print large issues by eight-page sections, the most advanced journals began to add one of these sections on Sunday mornings as a kind of catch-all for routine semi-news matter, like notes of the fraternal orders and women's clubs, and mild write-ups of picturesque features of city life, together with such embellishment of fiction and beauty hints as they could afford. S. S. McClure, breaking into the world of print at about that time, made a fortune from his idea of selling the best current literature to newspapers for simultaneous publication on Sunday mornings, the famous McClure Syndicate.

Pulitzer, like the rest, published a supplement. Although by 1891 he had brought his Sunday circulation up to 300,000 copies, the *World* did not show so great a proportionate increase over daily circulation as the *Herald* or the *Sun;* and Pulitzer worried and tinkered over it. In 1891, H. H. Kohlsaat, then part owner of the *Chicago Inter Ocean,* saw in Paris the rotary color presses of the *Petit Journal.* Printing in colors, be it known to the layman, had hitherto been done almost exclusively on slow, flat-bed presses, fed by hand, not from a roll or web. It had been thought impossible to the swift rotary press. When Kohlsaat returned to Chicago, he had Scott build him a color rotary on the European model. This would not handle whole sections, but only small inserts; Kohlsaat used it mainly for premium World's Fair views and the like. Pulitzer, alert to anything new, sent a man to see this press. The report was favorable. He consulted the Hoes, who informed him that they were already manufacturing color rotaries for small sheets. As a costly experiment, he ordered a rotary, turning out full-size pages in three colors and black. With this the *World* printed colored cartoons and beauty pictures on the outside pages of one Sunday section.

The process was costly and infinitely troublesome; and the dash of color had no visible effect upon the Sunday circulation. At the end of the year the heads of the department sent a round-robin to Pulitzer, who was fighting blindness in Europe, begging him to drop it. "The very building groaned," says an old executive of the *World,* "when the boss cabled back ordering us to put a new man in charge of that section, and use the color pages for funny pictures, like *Puck* and *Judge.*"

Already, Pulitzer had found his editor for the Sunday supplement. Morrill Goddard, a young city editor "with a dynamo inside," had developed a faculty for getting "features" out of the news. Against his earnest protests, Pulitzer sent him over to the Sunday supplement. Once established at his new desk, Goddard, like Hearst, set out, naked-eyed, to find what the common mind wanted. An instinct quite extraordinary, considering that Goddard is a ripe scholar, led him to it; within the year he was running in that supplement what we now call "yellow journalism" as distinguished from "sensational journalism."

Pictures first—for ten grasp with the eye to one with the mind. He brought the size of pictures up from one column to two, to five; and, finally, the first "seven-column cut" made its appearance in his Sunday *World.* Then reading matter so easy, with the startling points so often emphasized, that the weariest mechanic, sitting in his socks on Sunday morning, could not fail to get a thrill of interest. "Economy of attention"—that, unconsciously to him probably, made up his whole formula. Nothing which called for any close attention; something which first caught the eye and then startled, tickled, and interested without wear on brain tissue. For subject-matter he clung close to the news, choosing and expanding the bizarre, the startling, the emotional, though the item occupied only a line in the daily paper. When such subject matter failed, he was capable of making history yellow. Did a treatise on *The Man in the Iron Mask* appear, Goddard, taking the publication of this book as an excuse, would rush into print a page of the *Iron Mask,* with nightmare pictures, three inches of "snappy" introduction "playing up" the mystery, and two or three "box freaks" distributed among the pictures, giving learned opinions by great historians. So he played on still another popular weakness; he made his readers believe that they were on the royal road to learning.

One of Goddard's old associates has given his formula for a page in a yellow Sunday supplement. "Suppose it's Halley's comet," he says. "Well, first you have a half-page of decoration showing the comet with historical pictures of previous appearances thrown in. If you can work a pretty girl into the decoration, so much the better. If not, get some good nightmare idea like the inhabitants of Mars watching it pass. Then you want a quarter of a page of big-type heads—snappy. Then four inches of story, written right off the bat. Then a picture of Professor Halley down here and another of Professor Lowell up there, and a two-column boxed freak containing a scientific opinion, which nobody will understand, just to give it class."

From the smallest opening, Goddard would develop a road to popular interest. He and Andrew E. Murphy, his assistant, used to walk home to their lodgings in Washington Square, talking newspaper as they went. "Have you noticed," said Murphy one night, "how the crowd stops to watch the picture in that drug-store window? It's nothing but a cheap chromo. What's the reason?" This was indeed the crudest kind of chromo—it represented "sponge fishing on the Florida coast." Goddard studied it a long time. "I have it," he said that night. "It's a sectional view. You can watch the ships above and the shark eating the diver below at the same time. Let's try it." And the Sunday magazine of the *New York World* had a "sectional view," first of its kind, in the next issue. This bit of prospecting opened a paying streak. A hundred others ended in blind pockets, and Goddard abandoned them at once.

And just when the comic section and the Sunday magazine of the *World* were beginning to bear fruit in increased circulation, Hearst bought the *New York Journal* and broke into the metropolis—"with all the discreet secrecy" some one has said, "of a wooden legged burglar having a fit on a tin roof." He brought his Chamberlains and McEwens, his Hamiltons and Winifred Blacks; brought his own sensational, ruthless style of journalism; brought also the Hearst millions and the steady profits of the *Examiner.* He began to win over the Pulitzer men by offers of increased salary; Goddard was one of the first whom he lured away. Forthwith, the yellow supplement burst out on the *Journal.* A carnival of bids and counter-bids for men followed. Newspaper salaries, in the sensational division, went up never to fall back to their old level; newspaper desks became tenancies of a day.

Some one met "Cosey" Noble, Hearst man, in a restaurant. "What are you doing now, Noble?" he asked. "When I left the office," Noble replied, "I was city editor."

Arthur Brisbane, a graduate of the *New York Sun,* was then a kind of factotum on the *World.* He admired the Goddard discoveries in journalism, and had maintained, against Pulitzer's own pride of invention, that the supplement, and not the colored comics, was responsible for the steady rise of Sunday circulation. When Goddard went over to Hearst, Pulitzer made Brisbane his Sunday editor. At once this section went still further in audacity, so that Goddard, to maintain the pace, had to outdo even himself. The Sunday *World* had 450,000 circulation when Hearst appeared. By 1897 Brisbane had raised it to 600,000. And now the yellow flood flowed over from the Sunday magazine to the daily paper. "What are you fellows doing?" asked Pulitzer and Hearst, in effect, of the managing editors and city editors. "The Sunday is going ahead; you are standing still." Having no great discovery of their own to stimulate circulation, the editors of the daily paper imitated the Sunday supplement. Into their own product they brought this fake, shallow, supersensational method, this predigested information, this striving for hitting effect at any cost.

Sensational newspapers tremble always with office politics. In 1897, after the club boycott on yellow journalism, Brisbane found his position on the *World* fading away from him. Hearst, meantime, had established a circulation for his morning *Journal* (later called the *American*), and was making inroads on the *World* with his Sunday paper;

but the evening paper lagged at little more than 100,000 a day. Brisbane, who had already received bids from across the street, approached Hearst with a proposition. "I'll take charge of your evening paper at a hundred dollars a week," he said, in effect. "But I'll expect a dollar a week raise for every thousand I add to the circulation." Hearst accepted.

Brisbane, with a free hand, started to make an evening newspaper on the plan of a yellow supplement. He invented the job-type head—half the front page devoted to two or three smashing words, blaring forth sensation. He went further and devised that trick headline wherein the first and third lines, in immense type, proclaim a sensation, while the interlarded second line, in small type, reduces the whole head to a commonplace meaning ("WAR Will Probably be DECLARED," for example). Then fortune filled his sails. He took the evening *Journal* late in 1897. On February 14, 1898, the *Maine* was blown up in Havana Harbor. There followed six months of rumors of war, preparation for war, and, finally, war. Never had sensational editor such an opportunity. In heads which occupied sometimes three-quarters of the page, the *Journal* blazoned forth the latest rumors. In smashing, one-sentence-to-the-paragraph Brisbane editorials, it bellowed at the Government the mob demand for vengeance on Spain. In one year the *Journal* touched the million mark; and Brisbane was earning, by his agreement, $50,000 per annum. It is said that the agreement was in form of a short note, and that Hearst might have broken it had he gone to law. But he paid gladly, personal liberality being one of his virtues. And liberality was wisdom, for Brisbane has been a gold-mine to his employer.

There followed the climax of the yellow craze, an episode in social history which we may yet come to regard with as much amazement as the tulip craze in Holland or the Mississippi Bubble. Now did the *World* and *Journal* go insane with violent scareheads, worded to get the last drop of sensation from the "story" and throw it to the fore; now did they make fact out of hint, history out of rumor; now did they create, for their believing readers, a picture of a world all flash and sensation; now did they change their bill day by day like a vaudeville house, striving always for some new and startling method of attracting a crowd. Now they hunted down the criminal with blaring horns, so playing on the mob weakness for the thief chase; now, with the criminal caught and condemned and sentenced, they howled for his reprieve, glorified him in hysterics, so availing themselves of the old mob sympathy for the victim of the law, mob hatred for the executioner. Now they dressed out the most silly and frivolous discussion of the day with symposiums of solemn opinion from prominent citizens; now they went a step further in audacity and headed an interview from Bishop Potter or Chauncey M. Depew "By Bishop Potter" or "By Chauncey M. Depew," as though these eminent citizens were real contributors. Now they discovered the snob in all humanity and turned reporters, artists, and—after the half-tones became possible—photographers loose on "Society." The Four Hundred of New York, largely a newspaper myth, was the target for this army. Their doings, with the follies emphasized, bedecked column after column, daily and Sunday,

of hysterical slush. Life, as it percolated through the *World* and *Journal,* became melodrama, the song of the spheres a screech.

Suddenly the *World* dropped the whole game; changed almost in a week from yellow to merely sensational. This came almost coincidentally with those three months in a dark room from which Pulitzer emerged almost totally blind. There are those who believe that Pulitzer, had he retained his sight, would have drawn a string of yellow newspapers across the country as Hearst has done. I prefer to think, as do his best old counselors, that Pulitzer perceived the end of this madness; that he came to one of his sudden transformations in point of view. This blind man sees further into his times than any other American journalist; he must have known that it could not last. Change he did in the spring of 1901, so that now the worst one can say of the evening *World* is to call it a little sensational and rather silly, while his morning *World* is possibly the freest and most truthful popular newspaper in New York.

Hearst went on; as he grew great in influence and money he spread out to Chicago, to Boston, to Los Angeles, carrying his journalism in a form modified for the environment. Only his *New York Journal* and his Chicago papers were ever supremely yellow; but in these, for a few years after Pulitzer dropped out, his office staffs, and especially the lesser reporters, went on to the very madness of journalism. At its best the form stretched truth to the bursting point; for it consisted in warping facts to suit a distorted,

THE OPEN-AIR SCHOOL IN HOGAN'S ALLEY.

Richard F. Outcault's "Hogan's Alley" cartoon, featuring the "yellow kid" (pictured in his nightshirt), from the New York World, *1896.*

melodramatic point of view. From this to outright false-hood was but a step, taken without perception by men no longer capable of seeing the truth. The fact became but a peg whereon to hang the lie. Did the police find a poor, tired, sodden servant girl dead by her own hand near the park lake?—"Mystery of the Park—Pretty Girl Richly Dressed—Believed to be Member of Prominent Family." Did the reporters need an interview to dress out any large general story? If the "prominent citizen" refused the inter-view, the reporter wrote it just the same. Often he did not even attempt to see the "prominent citizen." The method for avoiding the trouble which naturally followed was one of the Hearst arts.

After the *Slocum* disaster I, as reporter for a conservative New York newspaper, had the mournful assignment of watching that temporary morgue where the police and di-vers were laying out the bodies. A new consignment had just arrived when I started back for the office. The crowd outside, mainly relatives of the dead, had grown impatient with delay, and one little German shook his fist at the po-lice. For a minute the crowd pushed and jostled; then the doors flew open and they filed soberly in. When I reached the newspaper offices, an extra was pouring out from the *Journal* basement—"Riot at Morgue—Frantic Mob Charges Police!" This all over the front page in red letters three inches high. Later in that summer, the hypothetical Black Hand kidnapped one Tony Manino, six years old. Since this was an Italian case, the reporters could do no work of their own on it; we merely loitered about the po-lice station or the house, getting our news second-hand. Of course, with its appeal to emotion and mystery, this was a great yellow feature; the *Journal* went daft with it. And day by day the cubs and younglings of the *Journal* seized at every absurd rumor and shot it over the tele-phone as fact. "I heard a kid kind of yelling in one of the tenements and I followed it up. Nothing doing," a detec-tive would remark. A rush to the telephone by the *Journal* delegation; in an hour we would have it in an extra, some-thing like this: "Hears Tony Manino Weeping for His Mother." I mention these instances as typical, not excep-tional, in the height of the yellow insanity.

As for photographs—what offenses were committed in their name! For people who will yield up the news gladly are conservative about giving up pictures; and pictures the yellows must have, especially for "pretty girl stories." There was a time when they used the various poses of pho-tographic models for the "pretty girl" whose picture was unobtainable. This growing monotonous, they placed or-ders with photographic agencies for photographs of for-eign women in private life—people who would never know that their pictures were serving in America for the "Pretty Girl Who Whipped Burglar" or the "Prominent Society Leader of Evanston."

So much for its vices, of which its falsity was chief and its rowdy denial of the right of privacy in news-getting only second. Let me not omit its virtues, which loom larger now that the madness is over. Publishers, in relation to the public, may be divided roughly into two classes. On one side are the instinctive worshipers of wealth and money, the men hypnotized by success and its rewards. The other

and smaller class—which includes, it happens, most of our greatest editors—go just as far to the other extreme in sus-pecting the rich and great. To this class belonged both Pu-litzer and Hearst in their most active days. Question not too far the motives of great, strenuous spirits like these two. Such must find outlets for their energies without con-scious direction toward an end; "the job" itself is their ob-jective. Yet each—Hearst probably the more definitely—had somewhere down among his tangled motives a genu-ine sympathy for the under dog in the industrial fight. This sympathy, and the convenience which traveled parallel with it, made and kept them advocates of the common man at a period when he needed an advocate. Nothing made Pulitzer so indignant as "corporate iniquity"; and, as for Hearst, this may suffice to illustrate: the common schools have always been his hobby, and his editorial asso-ciates have seen him walking the floor with indignation at some injury to the system.

I have shown how Pulitzer brought to New York, as the nucleus of yellow journalism, the method of finding and fighting public evils through the news. This method the yellow newspapers perfected with their growth in general efficiency. They learned how to fight; they taught the method to other newspapers. Their period of greatest power was also the period of unchecked corporation abuses, of alliance between bad ward politics and bad high finance. The ten-cent magazine, with its healthful "muck-raking," had not yet arrived. These blatant voices, husky with much bawling, were almost the only voices raised, for a decade long, against such principles as Mark Hanna typ-ified.

Again, like the French philosopher, they "brought philos-ophy from the library and the cloister to dwell in the kitch-en and the workshop." A parade of learning, of scientific and philosophical knowledge, was always among their lit-tle tricks. They gave it to their readers predigested, the sensational detail to the fore, with an eye always on "econ-omy of attention"; but they did hammer the big principles home, I believe, to people who could have accepted them in no other form. Their "stories" were an edge of interest for the wedge of knowledge. So always philosophies first reach the bottom of popular intelligence. Had we an accu-rate and critical record of early Christianity, we should find, probably, that after its first pure flow the people in general accepted its picturesque superstitions before they grasped its spirit; and the Darwinian theories had been mentor to the laboratories for a quarter century before the mob believed that Darwin taught anything except the bi-zarre idea—which he never did teach—of man's descent from the monkey.

In this last activity of yellow journalism, Brisbane stands supreme. The country has forgotten, if it ever knew, his influence in making sensational journalism yellow journal-ism. We think of him as the writer of those "heart-to-heart" editorials which even the judicious sometimes ad-mire. With the hindsight so much better than foresight, the men who built with Hearst in his building days at San Francisco see what a chance they missed when they walked on the edge of Brisbane's methods. For Hearst said again and again: "I wish I could get the same 'snap' into my editorials that you fellows get into the news columns." Arthur McEwen tried the hardest and came nearest to grasping what Hearst wanted. The truth is, McEwen had too much of what the prize-ring calls "class." His talents as journalist and writer were basically too high and sound.

Now arrived Brisbane; he became the genius of the evening *Journal,* deepest yellow of all newspapers. He was a man after Hearst's own kidney. He, too, had a sympathy with popular causes underneath an amazing ruthlessness of method and a talent for insincere sincerities. He found how to get "snap" into the editorial page, how to talk politics and philosophy in the language of truckmen and lumbermen. Day by day for ten years he has shouted at the populace the moral philosophies of Kant and Hegel, the social and scientific philosophies of Spencer and Huxley, in lurid words of one syllable. On alternate days he has shouted, just as powerfully, the inconsistencies which suited Hearst's convenience of the day, the fallacies which would boost circulation, pull in advertising, kill rivals. No man can be so sincere or so plausibly insincere as Brisbane. To analyze his best flights, to show how artfully he conceals the one necessary flaw in an otherwise perfect chain of logic, is an exercise which I recommend to our university classes in forensics.

His violence of language and expression, which has led to so many assaults on the Hearst newspapers, is, in fact, a trick of method. At the risk of mental snobbery, it must be said that the comparatively uneducated class to which he appeals is weak in fine intellectual distinctions. Not only is black black and white white to them, but gray and cream and pearl are white, and brown and purple are black. "I've done hard work in the ditches," says one of the great, sane editorial writers of his time, "and let me tell you when a ditch-digger calls a man an unlimited whelp he doesn't mean what you and I mean. He may mean a slightly disagreeable person or a real scoundrel. In short, he has no language to express disapproval except the most violent. So, when Brisbane called McKinley 'the most hated creature on the American continent,' he shocked the educated, but he conveyed to his readers, in the only kind of language which they understood, merely general disapproval of McKinley."

As a writer, with these editorials, as an editor, with thorough grasp of what his kind of reader wanted, he came to typify yellow journalism in its last period of real power. The profession of journalism rightly calls him the one widely influential editorial writer in these declining days of the daily editorial page. Such Hearst newspapers as use his work publish a million and a half copies for at least five million readers. In the nature of Hearst circulation, he reaches that class least infused with the modern intellectual spirit of inquiry, least apt to study their facts before forming their theories—the class most ready to accept the powerfully expressed opinions of another and superior being. We cannot view American civilization without reckoning in this young exponent of means which justify ends, any more than we can view it without reckoning in his employer and discoverer—Hearst. (pp. 267-83)

Will Irwin, "Yellow Journalism," in Highlights in the History of the American Press:

A Book of Readings, *edited by Edwin H. Ford and Edwin Emery, University of Minnesota Press, 1954, pp. 267-83.*

Edwin Emery and Michael Emery

[Edwin Emery and his son Michael are American journalists and historians. Their The Press and America: An Interpretative History of the Mass Media *is a respected textbook for journalism students. In the following excerpt from that work, they provide an overview of the age of Yellow Journalism.]*

The American newspaper was making great strides by the mid-nineties, both as an instrument of society and as a business institution. Increased advertising and subscription revenues meant that conscientious publishers and editors could do a better job of telling the news honestly and fully and of demonstrating their community leadership, because they were better able to resist outside pressures. But there were obvious shortcomings. The financial bigness of metropolitan dailies brought a lessening of the personal element in editorial direction and sometimes muffled the voice of the newspaper and dulled its social conscience.

Because mass circulation was achieved by a popularizing of the product, the primary news function sometimes was overshadowed by efforts to entertain. It should be added, however, that corporate journalism did not need to speak in a timid voice. Popularization, while inevitable if mass readership was to be achieved, did not need to become mere sensationalism. Bigger headlines, more readable stories, pictures, and blobs of color might give the newspaper a new face, causing some readers to grimace and wish for the bygone days, but effectively used, these devices could be useful and desirable.

By the same token, these new techniques could be used to emphasize sensationalism at the expense of news. Some editors proceeded in the mid-nineties to do just this, as had been done in earlier periods when new audiences were available. But the difference was that now they had better tools with which to make their sensationalism distinctive and seemingly new—the degrading product of this effort became known as "yellow journalism."

Yellow journalism, at its worst, was the new journalism without a soul. Trumpeting their concern for "the people," yellow journalists at the same time choked up the news channels on which the common man depended with a shrieking, gaudy, sensation-loving, devil-may-care kind of journalism. This turned the high drama of life into a cheap melodrama and led to stories being twisted into the form best suited for sales by the howling newsboy. Worst of all, instead of giving effective leadership, yellow journalism offered a palliative of sin, sex, and violence.

Pulitzer's striking success had demonstrated once again the appeal of the age-old technique of sensation. Other papers, like the *Philadelphia Record* and *Boston Globe,* were playing the same game as the *World.* But it was a mistake to attribute the *World*'s circulation achievements to sensationalism alone, and those who saw the clever promotion and lighter side of the *World* did not see—or disregarded—the solid characteristics of its news coverage and the high qualities of the editorial page. The antics of those who did not make this attempt to balance information and entertainment paid off handsomely in dollars earned. Their competitors often were forced to take on the yellow hue, and although eventually most newspapers recovered from the disease, modern journalism has exhibited some of the effects of this age of yellow journalism ever since.

The man who more than anyone else brought about the era of yellow journalism was watching with sharp interest while Pulitzer was setting New York journalism on its ear in the mid-eighties. He was William Randolph Hearst, who was to become the most controversial figure in modern journalism before his 64-year publishing career was ended. The youthful Hearst was a calculating witness to Pulitzer's climb to glory, and when eventually he invaded New York to challenge the supremacy of the *World,* he came prepared to dazzle the city with a sensationalized and self-promoted kind of journalism that would put Pulitzer to shame. The resulting struggle brought repercussions whose effects are still being felt.

Hearst was a Californian, born in 1863, the son of a successful pioneer who struck it rich in the silver mines of the Comstock Lode and who later won more riches in Anaconda copper and western and Mexican ranch lands. The only child of George and Phoebe Hearst, he grew up in San Francisco under the guidance of a busy, ambitious father and a schoolteacher mother, who in later years became a noted philanthropist and able manager of the family fortune.

Having achieved wealth, George Hearst aspired to political power. In 1880 he acquired the *San Francisco Examiner,* a debt-ridden morning paper that lagged behind the *Chronicle,* and converted it into a Democratic party organ. Young Hearst showed an interest in the paper, but his father took a low view of the newspapermen who worked for him and packed his heir off to Harvard in 1883.

The Hearst career at Harvard was sensational, if not successful. He was a free-spending westerner who drank too much beer and listened to too much band music and who did his best job as business manager of the humor magazine, the *Lampoon.* He was suspended in his sophomore year for celebrating Grover Cleveland's election to the presidency with a noisy fireworks display and was expelled a few months later for perpetrating a practical joke on Harvard's professors. Distinguished faculty members like William James and Josiah Royce could see no humor, it seemed, in finding their likenesses decorating chamber pots.

But the eastern education had not been entirely wasted. Harvard may not have made its impression on Hearst's mind, but the *Boston Globe* and the *New York World* did. Hearst studied the somewhat sensational techniques of General Charles H. Taylor's successful *Globe* and visited its up-to-date mechanical plant. He was more interested in Pulitzer's *World,* however, and on one of his vacations he worked as a cub reporter for the newspaper he later was

to battle. After bowing out at Harvard, Hearst again spent some time in New York studying the *World*'s techniques and then returned to San Francisco.

William Randolph Hearst assumed the editorship of the *San Francisco Examiner* in 1887 when George Hearst was named senator from California. He was only 24 but the tall, blue-eyed, shy editor, whose high-pitched voice contrasted with a commanding physical presence, immediately began to staff the paper. Picked as managing editor was Sam S. Chamberlain, who had worked for both Bennett and Pulitzer, edited Bennett's Paris edition of the *Herald,* and in 1884 founded the Paris newspaper *Le Matin.* The brilliant Ambrose Bierce, later famous for his short stories, contributed his "Prattle" column. Star reporters like Edward H. Hamilton signed on, as did Arthur McEwen, an editorial writer who became a key figure in Hearst-style journalism. Homer Davenport began to draw his cartoons, James Swinnerton applied his artist's skill to the new field of comics, and literary flavor was added by Edwin Markham ("The Man With the Hoe," which first appeared in the paper) and E. L. (Phinney) Thayer, whose contribution was "Casey at the Bat."

Chamberlain's grasp of news techniques made him invaluable. He developed the career of Winifred Black—known as "Annie Laurie" to future generations of Hearst readers—who attracted San Francisco women readers with intense stories. Sent to investigate the city hospital's management, she fainted conveniently on the street, was carried to the hospital, and turned in a story "with a sob for the unfortunate in every line." The *Examiner* was ever experimenting with crusades, stunts, and devices to present the news in a yet more luring manner. A stalwart Democrat, Hearst attacked the Southern Pacific railroad, the bulwark of the Republican state machine, and attempted to present other types of serious stories. But news that was important but dull took a back seat as the paper strove for what McEwen called the "Gee-Whiz" emotion.

Hearst's experiments on the mechanical side were important and constructive contributions to the new journalism. Trying many new patterns of makeup, arranging headlines in symmetrical patterns, and using attractive type faces, Hearst eventually arrived at a distinctive formula that many another paper imitated. Hearst himself often worked on the page forms, but his mechanical genius was George Pancoast, who joined the *Examiner* staff in 1888 and for the next 50 years perfected the electric drive for presses, improved color printing, and designed 14 printing plants for the Hearst empire.

The *Examiner,* called by the ambitious Hearst "The Monarch of the Dailies," doubled its circulation in the first year, reaching 30,000, and by 1893 had pushed to 72,000. This was more than M. H. de Young's *Chronicle,* the recognized leading daily. Senator Hearst died in 1891 after watching his son turn a losing proposition into a paper averaging a $350,000 to $500,000 yearly profit. And with that success achieved, young Hearst was ready to tackle the challenge he saw in Joseph Pulitzer's city, New York.

The profits from the *Examiner* now were available for an invasion of New York. But Hearst needed more capital, and eventually he persuaded his mother to sell the family holdings in the Anaconda copper mines for $7.5 million and make the cash available for new publishing ventures. Later, when a friend told Mrs. Hearst that she had heard the *New York Journal* was losing a million dollars a year and expressed fear that the family fortune was being thrown away recklessly, Mrs. Hearst replied that, in such an event, her son could hold out for 30 years more.

Somewhat ironically, Hearst entered the New York field by buying the newspaper that Joseph Pulitzer's brother, Albert, had established in 1882. The *Morning Journal* had been a successful one-cent paper appealing to casual newspaper scanners. In 1894 its price was raised to two cents, and circulation fell off. Albert Pulitzer then sold the *Journal* for a million dollars to John R. McLean, ambitious publisher of the *Cincinnati Enquirer*. McLean was no stranger to sensational methods of publishing newspapers, but he was unable to break into the highly competitive New York field. In the fall of 1895, Hearst picked up the paper from the defeated McLean for $180,000.

Joseph Pulitzer had been busy during the 10 years since Hearst had left New York to launch his career in San Francisco. Particularly he had expanded the mechanical facilities available to his editors, and he had applied the new techniques to the development of the *Sunday World*.

It was Pulitzer who first demonstrated the full potentialities of the Sunday newspaper as a profitable news and entertainment medium. There had been weeklies issued as Sunday papers since 1796. The daily *Boston Globe* put out a Sunday edition briefly in 1833, but James Gordon Bennett's *Herald* was the first daily to print a Sunday edition steadily, starting in 1841. The demand for news during the Civil War stimulated Sunday publication, but even by the time Pulitzer invaded New York in 1883 only about 100 daily newspapers had Sunday editions. Most of them were appearing in eastern cities and a good share were printed in German and other foreign languages. Some carried a four-page supplement filled with entertaining features, fiction, and trivia.

Pulitzer's new *Sunday World* added many more pages of entertainment to the regular news section. Feature material for women, for young readers, and for sports enthusiasts appeared. Humorous drawings and other illustrations were concentrated in the Sunday pages. The offerings of the literary syndicates, such as that developed by S. S. McClure, added to the Sunday paper's appeal. Circulation of the *Sunday World* passed the 250,000 mark in 1887, and by the early 1890s the paper had reached 40 to 48 pages in size as retail advertisers realized the extent of its readership by families and by women. Other newspapers were quick to follow suit, and in 1890 there were 250 dailies with Sunday editions, crowding the metropolitan areas and driving the independent Sunday weeklies out of the picture.

Heading the Sunday staff in the early years was Morrill Goddard, a college graduate who as a young city editor had shown ability to spot the feature angle of news events. But in the Sunday section Goddard jazzed up his page spreads, exaggerating the factual information to the point

where serious news sources, particularly men of science and medicine, shield away. Sensationalism and pseudoscientific stories of this era greatly increased the credibility problem of newspapers, but the problem was ignored.

The installation of color presses in 1893 only gave Goddard another medium to exploit. As many as five colors could be used in the Sunday color supplement and included in it were the comic drawings that Goddard knew were most effective in spurring circulation. The *World* had started a regular comic section in 1889 and was the first to use color here (magazines had done so since the 1870s). The most successful of the artists was Richard F. Outcault, whose "Hogan's Alley" depicted life in the tenements. The central figure in each drawing was a toothless, grinning kid attired in a ballooning dress. When the *World*'s printers daubed a blob of yellow on the dress he became the immortal "Yellow Kid."

When William Randolph Hearst arrived on the New York scene he immediately set out to buy the men who were making the *Sunday World* a success. Using an office the *Examiner* had rented in the *World* building, he hired away Goddard and most of his staff of writers and artists. Hearst's lavish spending habits made Pulitzer's counter offers hopeless. Soon even the *World*'s publisher, S. S. Carvalho, was working at the *Journal* building. The battle on, Pulitzer turned to Arthur Brisbane, Socialist Albert Brisbane's brilliant young son who had broken into newspaper work on the *Sun* before joining Pulitzer's staff. As the new Sunday editor, Brisbane drove the circulation to the 600,000 mark, popularizing the news and pushing hard on Pulitzer's social concerns. Goddard had taken Outcault and the "Yellow Kid" with him, but Brisbane used George B. Luks, later a well-known painter, to continue the cartoon.

Circulation men for both papers used posters featuring the happy-go-lucky, grinning kid with his curiously vacant features. To opposition journalists the "Yellow Kid" seemed symbolic of the kind of sensational journalism that was being practiced, and the public agreed. The phrase "yellow journalism" soon became widely used and its techniques the object of hard scrutiny. Unfortunately for Pulitzer, Brisbane moved over to the *Evening Journal* as editor in 1897 and Luks also joined Hearst. At this Outcault moaned:

> When I die don't wear yellow crepe, don't let them put a Yellow Kid on my tombstone and don't let the Yellow Kid himself come to my funeral. Make him stay over on the east side, where he belongs.

Besides raiding Pulitzer's staff, Hearst moved in the best of his San Francisco staffers, including Chamberlain, McEwen, Davenport, and Annie Laurie. Dana's *Sun* lost its star reporters Julian Ralph, Richard Harding Davis, and Edward W. Townsend to Hearst's bankroll. Dorothy Dix joined the women's staff, and writers Stephen Crane, Alfred Henry Lewis, and Rudolph Block (Bruno Lessing) were signed, along with a host of other talented reporters, critics, and artists.

Two other events propelled Hearst into the thick of the

fight with Pulitzer. In 1896, when the *Journal* reached the 150,000 mark as a one-cent paper, Pulitzer cut his price to a penny, gaining circulation but allowing speculation that he was afraid of his challenger. More importantly, Pulitzer, while in sympathy with many of William Jennings Bryan's ideas, could not support his inflationary monetary policies. But Hearst, as a silver mine owner, had no problem in arguing against the gold standard. Political partisans were attracted by Hearst's stand for Bryan in the conservative East where Bryan was looked upon with horror.

Frankly adopting the sins of yellow journalism, the *Journal* continued its surge in circulation figures. One jump of 125,000 came in a single month in the fall of 1896 when the following headlines were typical: "Real American Monsters and Dragons"—over a story of the discovery of fossil remains by an archaeological expedition; "A Marvellous New Way of Giving Medicine: Wonderful Results from Merely Holding Tubes of Drugs Near Entranced Patients"—a headline that horrified medical researchers; and "Henry James' New Novel of Immorality and Crime; The Surprising Plunge of the Great Novelist in the Field of Sensational Fiction"—the *Journal's* way of announcing publication of *The Other House*. Other headlines were more routinely sensational: "The Mysterious Murder of Bessie Little," "One Mad Blow Kills Child," "What Made Him a Burglar? A Story of Real Life in New York by Edgar Saltus," "Startling Confession of a Wholesale Murderer Who Begs to Be Hanged." Annie Laurie wrote about "Why Young Girls Kill Themselves" and "Strange Things Women Do for Love."

The *Journal* was crusading, too, but it went beyond other New York newspapers in a manner that enabled it to shout, "While Others Talk the Journal Acts." The paper obtained a court injunction that balked the granting of a city franchise to a gas company and, pleased by its success, it took similar actions against alleged abuses in government. Hearst then solicited compliments from civic leaders across the country and printed them under such headings as, "Journalism that Acts; Men of Action in All Walks of Life Heartily Endorse the Journal's Fight in Behalf of the People" and "First Employed by the Journal, the Novel Concept Seems Likely to Become an Accepted Part of the Function of the Newspapers of This Country."

Before his first year in New York had ended, Hearst had installed large color presses at the *Journal*, added an eight-page colored comic section called *The American Humorist* and replaced that with a 16-page color supplement, *The Sunday American Magazine* (later, with Brisbane as editor, this was to become the famous *American Weekly*). In late 1896 the *Journal's* daily circulation was 437,000 and on Sunday it was 380,000. Within a year the Sunday figures had reached the *World's* 600,000. Circulation figures moved up and down, depending on the street sale appeal of the moment: on the day following the McKinley-Bryan election the *World* and *Journal* each sold approximately 1.5 million copies to break all records.

It was in this atmosphere that the leading papers scrambled for news around the nation and the world. And it was under these conditions that American papers approached the events that led to an international crisis and the Spanish-American War.

Of all the wars the United States has fought, the Spanish-American War was the most painless. But the results entirely changed the course of American foreign policy. In fewer than four months the Spanish government was forced to request an armistice, at an extraordinarily small cost in American lives, and the American flag floated over an empire stretching from Puerto Rico to the Philippines. Those who have sought to explain the causes of this unwarranted war often have centered the blame on William Randolph Hearst in particular and the newspapers of the country in general. Carefully documented studies made by Marcus M. Wilkerson and Joseph E. Wisan in the early 1930s gave ample proof that Hearst's *Journal*, Pulitzer's *World*, the *Chicago Tribune*, the *Sun*, and the *Herald* in New York (and as usually is ignored, many other American papers) so handled the news of events leading up to the crisis of the sinking of the *Maine* that a war psychosis was developed. It must not be forgotten, however, that the newspapers were cultivating public opinion in a favorable atmosphere.

The policies of expansion being advocated were in line with those pursued throughout the nineteenth century. Americans in general subscribed to the belief in "Manifest Destiny" that spurred the westward movement. The War of 1812 was forced on a reluctant New England by western expansionists who viewed the British in Canada as mortal enemies. The Mexican War and cries of "54-40 or Fight" brought the completion of the continental United States. Americans liked to buy the territory they wanted, but now, as in the past, they were ready to take it by force if necessary.

When viewed in the long perspective, the Spanish-American War was but one in a series of incidents that marked the arrival of the United States as a world and, in particular, a Pacific power. With newly acquired Alaskan territory protecting one flank, Americans moved to gain a foothold in the Samoan Islands. Agitation began in the 1880s for the annexation of Hawaii. Then, with a new modern navy at his disposal, President Grover Cleveland brought his country to the verge of war with Great Britain over a test of the Monroe Doctrine in the Venezuelan crisis of 1895. This was followed by the annexation of Hawaii, the Philippines, Guam, and Puerto Rico, and the building of the Panama Canal. Interest in the Asian mainland brought about John Hay's Open Door Policy in 1899 and President Roosevelt's negotiation of the peace treaty ending the 1904-5 Russo-Japanese War in a little New Hampshire town. Pan-Americanism became open American intervention in the affairs of Central American countries, and Roosevelt took the United States into European affairs as well by participating in the 1905 Moroccan crisis that had been precipitated by German expansionism.

This desire to be a powerful participant in world affairs was not the only driving force behind the American expansion of interest. There was pride felt by many Americans in the addition of new territories and there was keen interest in the expansion of trade and foreign investments. But Americans also felt they had a role to play in promot-

Portrait of Joseph Pulitzer by John Singer Sargent, painted in 1905.

ing the idea of peace and justice in the world. There was widespread sympathy for those Cubans, Armenians, and Greeks who were fighting for their freedoms in the 1890s. Both idealism and national pride came into play during the Spanish-American War. If later the advocates of imperialism and "dollar diplomacy" won out over the idealists, that was but one phase of America's coming of age in international affairs.

Newspapers reflected this conflict in goals, reporting both atrocities committed by Spanish troops against Cuban insurrectionists and the chance for the new American navy to prove itself against Spain. But mainly there was a strong desire to flex the nation's muscles. As the memory of the Civil War faded, many older Americans wondered if their country's military prowess was still secure. Younger citizens were eager to match the exploits of the boys in Blue and Grey. For them, war, 1898 style, still seemed to be an exciting personal adventure. John D. Hicks, an American historian of first-rank who was not unaware of the role of the newspaper as an organ of public opinion, summed up his discussion of the causes of the Spanish-American War [in his *A Short History of American Democracy,* 1943] by saying:

> Years later, Theodore Roosevelt recaptured the spirit of 1898 when he mourned apologetically, "It wasn't much of a war, but it was the best war

we had." America in the spring of 1898 was ripe for any war, and the country's mood was not to be denied.

From March 1895, when the Cuban insurrection began, until April 1898, when Spain and the United States went to war, there were fewer than a score of days in which a story about Cuba did not appear in one of the New York newspapers. This was due partly to the aggressive news policies of the big dailies, partly to the manufacturing of stories by some of the papers (notably the *Journal*), and partly to increasing reader interest in a controversial story. It was also the result of the activities of the Cuban junta that fed information and propaganda to American newsmen in New York and at the Florida news bases nearest the island.

A considerable number of Cubans had emigrated to the United States, settling in New York, Philadelphia, Baltimore, Boston, and several Florida cities. The junta had its headquarters in New York, where a Cuban newspaper was published. Through the Cuban residents in the eastern cities, a program of mass meetings was established. Money was raised, and several hundred volunteers were obtained in each city for service in running arms and taking part in filibustering expeditions. Cuban agents funneled information on the progress of the fighting in Cuba to the American newspapers. The work was well underway in 1895, and as the crisis intensified, the activities of the junta reached greater heights. Ministers, educators, civic leaders, and politicians were reached by the junta.

The Spanish decision in 1896 to use strong repressive measures in Cuba brought Captain-General Valeriano Weyler into the news. All loyal Cubans were ordered to congregate in small areas adjoining Spanish bases, and those who did not were considered enemies. But those huddled in the camps quickly fell victim to epidemics and many starved to death when food supplies became disrupted. Much of the newspaper copy centered about the effects of famine and pestilence (approximately 110,000 Cubans died in the three years, but newspaper estimates reached 400,000 as part of the exaggeration of these admittedly very serious conditions). Weyler was nicknamed the "Butcher" by American reporters and compared to the "bloodthirsty Cortez and Pizarro" of the days of the Conquistadors.

Competition for news became fierce. The Associated Press provided its own coverage and used information from stories printed by member papers. The *Journal* and *World* led the way as papers with correspondents in Cuba sold their stories to other papers. Papers in competing situations fought to sign up as soon as a rival announced it had obtained *World, Journal, Sun, Herald,* or other "big league" coverage. Striving to keep ahead in every way was Hearst, who persuaded star reporter James Creelman to stop reporting for the *World* in 1896 and sent Richard Harding Davis and artist Frederic Remington to join him in Cuba. The impact of pictorial journalism increased in 1897 when New York papers began to use halftone photographs that sometimes were accurate portrayals of Cuban misery and sometimes were fakes. It also was during this time that Remington, according to Creelman's 1901 reminiscences, cabled Hearst that there would be no war and that he was coming home. Whereupon Hearst was supposed to have cabled back: "Remington, Havana. Please remain. You furnish the pictures, and I'll furnish the war. W. R. Hearst." There is no evidence that Hearst actually sent this cable, so often quoted as conclusive evidence against him, but in a sense it reflected the situation. Of all the American papers, Hearst's *Journal* worked the hardest to create public sentiment for war. Episodes like this did much to tag him with "Hearst's war."

In the summer of 1897, after open advocacy of war for about a year and the sensationalizing of several minor incidents, the *Journal* built the story of Evangelina Cisneros into a daily chant for intervention. Miss Cisneros, a niece of the Cuban revolutionary president, had been sentenced to 20 years in prison for her rebellious activity. The *Journal* devoted an incredible number of news columns, 375, to the details of her condition and to her "rescue" by *Journal* reporter Karl Decker. Many notables congratulated the *Journal* on this achievement and Miss Cisneros was greeted by President McKinley on the White House lawn. Later it was discovered how other New York papers had treated this exciting but out-of-context story: *World,* twelve and one-half columns; *Times,* ten columns; *Tribune,* three and one-half columns; *Sun,* one column; *Herald,* one column. During the incident, when the *World* published Weyler's account of Miss Cisneros' treatment—which had been exaggerated—the *Journal* accused Pulitzer of unpatriotic motives.

The *Journal*'s most significant "scoop" came on February 9, 1898, when Hearst published a private letter written by Dupuy de Lome, the Spanish ambassador to the United States, to a Spanish newspaper editor visiting in Havana. The letter, stolen in Havana by a Cuban junta member, referred to President McKinley as "weak and catering to the rabble, and besides, a low politician." At the same moment Theodore Roosevelt was commenting that his chief had the backbone of a chocolate eclair, but to have the Spanish ambassador say the same thing, even in a private letter, was a different matter. American opinion of the Spanish government hit a new low and six days later the *Maine* blew up in Havana harbor. The impact of the two events proved to be the turning point in the diplomatic crisis.

No one has satisfactorily established the cause of the explosion that sank the *Maine,* with the loss of 266 American lives. But some American newspapers set about making it appear that the Spanish were indirectly responsible for the sinking. The *Journal* offered a $50,000 reward for information leading to the arrest and conviction of the criminals, and three days later that paper's streamer read "THE WHOLE COUNTRY THRILLS WITH WAR FEVER." Large headlines and striking illustrations became common in big city papers. Leading the way was Brisbane, who experimented with artist-drawn headlines that virtually filled the front page with two or three words. Later that year Brisbane wrote [in "The Modern Newspaper at War Time," *Cosmopolitan* XXV (September 1898)]:

> Before the type size reached its maximum, "War Sure" could be put in one line across a page, and it was put in one line and howled through the

streets by patriotic newsboys many and many a time. As war was sure, it did no harm.

Gradually the tide swung toward a declaration of war. Volunteer units such as the Rough Riders were formed, Congress passed a $50 million defense bill for war, and Secretary of State Sherman more than once made statements based on news reports from the *Journal.* In mid-March a leading Republican senator, Proctor of Vermont, made a speech based on his own trip to Cuba. He verified much of what had been published during the previous three years about deaths of Cubans, adding to the pressures on President McKinley to come out for war. The *World* at first urged caution in the handling of the *Maine* matter, but on April 10 Pulitzer published a signed editorial calling for a "short and sharp" war. Most of the nation agreed with this sentiment and Congress passed a war resolution on April 18.

The *New York Sun,* which under Dana's cynical editorship had been extremely jingoistic, stood with the *Journal* and *World* in demanding intervention. The *New York Herald,* while keeping up in sensational news coverage, opposed intervention in its editorial stands—an incongruity also true of the *Chicago Times-Herald, Boston Herald, San Francisco Chronicle,* and *Milwaukee Sentinel.* Strongly interventionist were such papers as the *Chicago Tribune, New Orleans Times-Democrat, Atlanta Constitution,* and *Indianapolis Journal.* Keeping calm were such papers as the *New York Tribune, New York Times, Chicago Daily News, Boston Transcript,* and other papers that reflected the thinking of the business community in their editorial columns. Wilkerson, in his study of the newspapers for the period [*Public Opinion and the Spanish-American War,* 1932], ranks the *Journal* as the leader in excessive journalism, and the *Chicago Tribune* and the *World* next in order. Joseph Medill's *Tribune,* strongly nationalistic in its editorial columns, did not originate sensational news stories as did the *Journal* and *World,* but it ran the cream of those collected by both papers.

It should be pointed out that the *World* was not a jingo newspaper. Pulitzer had opposed the annexation of Hawaii and did not support President Cleveland in the 1895 Venezuelan crisis, when most major papers warned the United States would fight to uphold Venezuela's boundary claims with British Guiana. During the Cuban crisis the *World* did not stand for the annexation of foreign lands and opposed the taking of the Philippine Islands. The *World* based its call for war on the issue of human liberty and in subsequent actions proved it was not merely jingoistic. Pulitzer later regretted the role the *World* played in preparing public opinion for killing and in 1907, when Theodore Roosevelt ordered the American fleet to the Pacific to impress Japan, Pulitzer requested that his editors "show that Spain had granted to Cuba all that we had demanded . . . Give further details of jingoism causing Cuban War after Spain had virtually granted everything."

But in 1898 only Godkin's *Evening Post,* among the New York dailies, held out to the end against yellow journalism and the decision to force Spain from Cuba. Lashing out against Hearst and Pulitzer, he bitterly attacked with statements like this:

A yellow journal office is probably the nearest approach, in atmosphere, to hell, existing in any Christian state. A better place in which to prepare a young man for eternal damnation than a yellow journal office does not exist.

The newspapers fought the war as determinedly as they had fostered it. Some 500 reporters, artists, and photographers flocked to Florida, where the American army was mobilizing, and to the Cuban and Puerto Rican fronts. Small fleets of press boats accompanied the Navy into action. Correspondents sailed with Dewey to Manila and with Schley to Havana. They covered every battle and skirmish in Cuba and more than once took part in the fighting itself. A *Journal* correspondent lost a leg during one fighting charge. Richard Harding Davis, then reporting for the *New York Herald* and the *Times* of London, led another charge and won the praise of Rough Rider Roosevelt.

Leading the *Journal*'s contingent was the publisher himself, who exuded enthusiasm as he directed the work of his staff of 20 men and women reporters, artists, and photographers, including a motion picture man. Creelman, who was wounded in one battle, records a picture of Hearst—wearing a beribboned straw hat on his head and a revolver at his belt—taking the story from his bleeding reporter and then galloping away on horseback to get to a *Journal* press boat.

American correspondents were learning how to use the boats and cables to speed their messages to the news offices. Stories from Cuba had to be brought to Key West for transmission to New York, with leading papers sending several thousand words a day. All this was expensive, but the race for news was an exciting one. The *World* scored the biggest single beat when Edward W. Harden, one of three correspondents to witness Dewey's amazing victory in Manila Bay, got his story off first by paying the "urgent" priority rate of $9.90 a word. Harden's beat arrived in New York too far into the dawn for the *World* to capitalize on it with a full-blown extra, but the *World*'s news client, the *Chicago Tribune,* had time to revamp its final edition and carry the most dramatic story of the war.

While Hearst said he did not care how much all of this cost (his paper spent $500,000 during the four months and put out as many as 40 extras in one day), Pulitzer began to view the situation with dismay. The *Journal* gleefully asked in its front-page ears, "How do you like the *Journal*'s war?" while Pulitzer began to retreat. In the end, Pulitzer withdrew from the competition in sensationalism at the turn of the century, while Hearst continued to exploit the news in a manner that seriously impeded the effectiveness of his role as a people's champion. By 1900, about one-third of metropolitan dailies were following the yellow trend, and it was another ten years before the wave of sensationalism subsided and journalists concentrated on the more intelligent use of headlines, pictures, and color printing. (pp. 243-55)

> *Edwin Emery and Michael Emery, "The Age of Yellow Journalism," in their* The Press and America: An Interpretative History of the

Mass Media, *fourth edition, Prentice-Hall, Inc., 1978, pp. 243-57.*

Joseph Pulitzer on journalism:

The entire WORLD newspaper property has been purchased by the undersigned, and will, from this day on, be under different management—different in men, measures and methods—different in purpose, policy and principle—different in objects and interests—different in sympathies and convictions—different in head and heart. . . .

There is room in this great and growing city for a journal that is not only cheap but bright, not only bright but large, not only large but truly Democratic—dedicated to the cause of the people rather than that of purse-potentates—devoted more to the news of the New than the Old World—that will expose all fraud and sham, fight all public evils and abuses—that will serve and battle for the people with earnest sincerity. . . . JOSEPH PULITZER.

Joseph Pulitzer, in the New York World, *11 May 1883.*

MAJOR FIGURES

Bernard A. Weisberger

[*Weisberger is an American historian. In the following excerpt, he details the changes in the American newspaper industry during the final decades of the nineteenth century, highlighting some of the important figures of the era.*]

In 1869 Henry Raymond, not yet fifty, died of a stroke. The next year saw the retirement of William Cullen Bryant, approaching his eightieth birthday, from the *Post.* In the summer of 1872 James Gordon Bennett was buried with pomp and ceremony. Horace Greeley was then campaigning for the Presidency on the Liberal Republican ticket, promising to drive the grafters from the government. In November, an avalanche of votes for Grant smothered him. A few weeks later Greeley was dead, too, his spirit finally broken by the frustration of his last political crusade. The passing of these four giants of the New York press signified the end of the era when modern journalism was founded.

A new cast took the boards. It was bigger and louder, but more disciplined, included fewer politicians and men of letters, and more millionaires. The drama it put on was a companion-piece to other spectacles on the national stage—the rise of the trust, the coming of the railroad barons, the conquest of the Far West. The stars of the new journalism shared the appetites, the successes, the laurels, and some of the catcalls which were the portion of their fellow magnates in rails, oil, steel, copper, lumber, meat, and grain. All of them profited by fantastic mechanical improvement and growth and stamped the institutions they managed into shapes which would endure into the oncoming twentieth century.

The marvels of mass production continued to transform the newspaper until the end of the nineties, when it assumed substantially its modern form. Web-perfecting and stereotyping presses were improved between 1870 and 1900 to the point where, by earlier standards, they were capable of prodigies. The cylinders grew wider to accommodate more pages simultaneously, and a series of clever devices for gathering and folding the pages made the four- and eight-page limits of the early days obsolete. By 1895 the Hoe firm was manufacturing an "octuple" press in which eight cylinders, each four pages wide, produced 24,000 thirty-two-page papers an hour. In 1902 a wealthy publisher could buy a "double octuple" Hoe which gave him 72,000 copies of a thirty-two-page journal in an hour, or lesser quantities of thicker papers. The problems of finding enough paper and type to feed these monsters were solved by methods as ingenious as they were important. Crude machines for making paper out of wood pulp had been patented before the Civil War, but in 1866 a Massachusetts firm, using equipment developed in Germany, began to produce pulp on a commercial scale. In another thirty years the production of newsprint had risen to something like half a million tons annually, the price had dropped from eight to two cents a pound, and the industry could count on the immense resources of the world's forests instead of an uncertain supply of rags for stock. In 1886, after various prototypes had tried and failed, Ottmar Mergenthaler's linotype machine had its first successful practical test. Operated by a keyboard, it arranged type matrices in a line automatically adjusted to the correct length, cast a solid slug, and reshuffled the matrices for the next line. It vastly increased the speed of composition, and permitted the used type to be recast again quickly and continuously.

These inventions broke down the last remaining barriers to the spread of cheap publications, with all their unbelievable power for mass organization, education, and propaganda. In the nineties the circulation leaders among American papers were reaching nearly 400,000 readers daily. Less than a hundred years after wooden hand presses were the only means of publication, it was possible to gather the material for fifty to eighty pages containing hundreds of thousands of words, set them in type, and distribute them by the quarter-to-half-millions of copies, all within twenty-four hours. The symbols of this new publishing power were the great newspaper buildings—factories, really—which the successful owners put up to house their behemoths. Thundering with the roar of the giant presses, surrounded by wagons (and later, trucks) delivering huge rolls of paper and carrying away bundles of finished copies in a frenzy of motion, rising dozens of stories above the streets, and showing lights in the windows of composing, engraving, teletype, and editing rooms which were never turned off, they represented the acme of controlled industrial energy.

The contents of the enlarged newspaper also blossomed in new forms under the sunshine of innovation. Stereotyping had broken the tyranny of column rules which held the

type in place, so that headlines could go marching across two, three, four, and even eight columns at the century's end. Color presses were introduced about 1892, and the comics and Sunday supplements appeared in their wake. Photo-engraving techniques were sharpened in the seventies, and more and more line cuts, after first being transferred to the curved stereotype plates, were printed. The effects of these changes were felt in two ways. More pictures made the newspaper even more desirable to semiliterate readers, and advertisers could display their wares with a variety of eye-catching type sizes and illustrations. Quarter-page, half-page, and even full-page advertisements demonstrated the splendors of washing machines, vegetable compounds, soap that floated, baking powders, new fashions in dress, bicycles, baby buggies, and a thousand other items in the mass-production cornucopia. Line cuts were supplemented in the eighties by halftone engravings, which allowed photographs to be reproduced, and by the time of the war with Spain news pictures were beginning to appear in small numbers, although problems of technique in taking, developing, and transmitting photos delayed the full impact of picture journalism until the second quarter of the twentieth century.

All this meant that the owners had more scope for experimenting with their papers—adding features and supplements, providing Sunday and evening editions, increasing the volume of wired news if they chose, and testing varieties of makeup and headlining in the relentless quest for super-marketability. In one sense they had no choice, for just as in other industries, the firm that did not adopt new techniques was likely to be driven from the field. But the costs of modernization were formidable, and the publisher glorying in a new four-color press soon found that his debts multiplied faster than the best and latest "Hoe double-octuple" could spew out copies. The answer was to solicit more advertising, which could be done successfully only by getting more circulation, and more circulation could only be achieved in a sharply competitive field by reducing the price of the paper (which reduced income) or by new features and additions (which were expensive). The boasted independence of the non-party newspaper seemed to be a freedom to run a neck-and-crop race with bankruptcy. Beginning in the nineties, some publishers began to form chains in efforts to cut overhead, and consolidations of older papers, always a feature of the American newspaper scene, increased in number. A landmark was reached in the twenties when, among the dailies, failures and consolidations finally exceeded new starts. The number of dailies in the nation reached some 2,400 in 1919 and then began the slow decline which is still in process.

Despite the financial hazards, the owners had more or less given the newspaper its contemporary look as early as 1914. To the modern reader an 1860 copy of the *New York Times* or the *Chicago Tribune* is clearly antiquarian, exuding a dusty air of mummification. But the edition of either paper announcing the outbreak of World War I, nearly half a century ago, leaves *its* reader with a comfortable feeling of being at home. The large department-store layouts, the illustrated come-ons for nationally advertised products, the photographs, the headlining, the women's and sports pages, the comics (in the case of the *Tribune,* at least) would scarcely seem out of place in 1961. Even the news, one reflects with discouragement, looks much the same.

The publishers who were responsible for incorporating these changes in format were a varied lot. The wealth which they commanded put them in the ranks of the mighty, although their incomes did not approach those of the railroad and industrial leaders of the day and they were often forced to borrow from the real titans of finance. Whitelaw Reid, a chief editor of the *New York Tribune* at the time Greeley died, bought a controlling share of the paper's stock with the assistance of Jay Gould, the unscrupulous stock-market and real-estate speculator whose feats had once included an attempt to corner the country's gold supply. The *New York World,* begun in 1861, was owned until 1876 by Manton Marble, a practicing newspaperman, but when he tired of it and sold it, the power behind the purchasing syndicate was that of Tom Scott, master of the Pennsylvania Railroad. Five years later, Henry Villard, who had made millions promoting railroads in the Pacific Northwest, bought out the venerable *New York Post.* Papers on the financial rocks, indeed, had a way of drifting into the portfolios of big-time investors, who recognized the utility of having press spokesmen on their side.

Yet the very greatest editors were not bought outright, as some owners of country papers were, simply by generous advertisements, printing contracts, or cash subsidies. Their alliance with captains of industry was a natural one, for they shared with them a common faith in the glories of business expansion, the divine right of the individual to be master of his own property, and the uplifting power of wealth. What they said and did in defense of these abstractions, they did in their own way, and, for all the hugeness of their journals, they still made their personalities felt in their pages. The day of the shoestring printer and promoter was gone, but the leadership of the daily press until the era of the first Roosevelt remained entertainingly full of curmudgeons, civic uplifters, and ballyhoo experts.

Chief among the curmudgeons, in some respects, was Charles A. Dana. In 1868, after serving in the War Department and trying his hand at editorship in Chicago, he returned to New York and organized a company which bought the *Sun.* Both Dana and the *Sun* had changed since the 1840's. The paper, once the forerunner of cheap, impudent, successful journalism, had slipped badly in circulation. As for Dana, the youthful ardors which had led him to Brook Farm and then the *Tribune* office had burned away, leaving a brittle residue of cynicism. Dana had the paper filled with local stories of high life and low, always with an eye to the piquant, the offbeat, the drily comic. A succession of good city editors drilled cub reporters in the exactitudes of polished writing. One of those editors, John Bogart, earned a kind of immortality by coining the famous maxim that a dog biting a man was not news, while a man biting a dog was. The point of the advice, that only the unusual is newsworthy, tells much about *Sun* policy. A man-biting dog was simply a problem of public health and safety; a dog-biting man was a curiosity from which a clever writer could extract a high yield of amusement.

Dana's favorite vent for sarcasm was his editorial page. He wrote much of it himself, staring critically over his eyeglasses at his own copy before sending it off to press, and exchanging comments with assistants and visitors as he sat at his desk, wearing a black skullcap on his bald head. Sometimes his temper was up and he hit hard at targets like New York's Boss William Tweed, or President Rutherford B. Hayes, whose crime, in Dana's eyes, was in accepting the "stolen" election of 1876. But more often he poked fun, sometimes with more devastating effect on friends than on enemies. He supported Greeley in 1872, with tongue in cheek, dubbing him the "Woodchopper of Chappaqua." In 1880 he was behind the Democratic candidate, Winfield Scott Hancock, but he did little for Hancock's cause by referring to him as "a good man, weighing 240 pounds." In 1884 he claimed to favor the presidential candidacy of the Greenback nominee, Benjamin F. Butler, a slippery politician who changed parties almost seasonally, but this advocacy was clearly Dana's way of showing his contempt for the more orthodox candidates on the Republican and Democratic tickets. He was a pillar of the new journalism which was proud of its independence of party, but his own attitude showed that at least one reason for this emancipation was something other than a pride in impartiality. Like many businessmen of the postwar generation, the editors took little interest in national politics. The parties had become machinelike organizations for winning elections and getting jobs, and there was little to dictate a choice between them except sentiment and habit. Dana was skeptical of politicians, but he also distrusted foreign nations, labor unions, Socialists, farmers, and reformers in general. This put him in step with both parties and enabled him to boast that he wore the coat of neither.

Even more of a cynic than the aging Dana was Chicago's unbelievable Wilbur F. Storey, who controlled the *Times* of that city from 1861 to 1878. White-bearded Storey raged through life, breaking things to see who would shout. During the war he was a violent Copperhead, crying daily that the war was a failure, Lincoln a tyrant, and the boys in blue dupes of the Republicans. The military authorities padlocked his office for a short period and mobs threatened him almost regularly, and neither experience hushed him for a moment. He drank as he argued and lived, extravagantly, brazenly, and noisily, and he kept Chicago courts busy with his libel suits. He was publicly horsewhipped by a lady entertainer who could not put up with the law's delays in avenging slander. He kept a female spirit medium at his side for counsel and solace when his wife died, and was finally adjudged insane, without ever having yielded any quarter in his war on propriety.

The Chicago *Times,* under Storey, was distinguished for its tales of seduction and scandal and its verbal raids on city fathers. It also achieved notoriety for its pun-filled and alliterative headlines—a story on Commodore Vanderbilt's will being captioned "The House that Vanderbilt," and accounts of hangings (a favorite *Times* topic) carrying such titles as "A Drop Too Much" and "Jerked to Jesus."

Storey's paper appealed to particularly urban groups—loafers and toughs who liked their news as they liked their whiskey, cheap and raw; clerks and laborers who found that the gossip and scandal of a great metropolis added spice to otherwise routine lives spent in its confines; and those who felt themselves sophisticated enough to enjoy flouting the conventional pieties, at least vicariously. All were drawn into a fraternity of *Times*-consumers, forming the kind of audience that sensational journalism could count on in the cities from that time forward.

In contrast to the Danas and Storeys who enjoyed the editorial prerogatives of puckishness, other prominent newspapermen chose to identify themselves with the promotion of municipal or sectional improvement. Henry Grady and Henry Watterson belonged to the latter camp. Grady was a poor boy from Georgia who worked his way up through the ranks of country journalism and in 1880 managed to buy an interest in the *Atlanta Constitution,* then fifteen years old. He became its managing editor and remained at that post until his death nine years later. Grady's own experience had been as a reporter, and some of his nationally reprinted stories gave him a reputation that went far beyond Atlanta. He filled the paper with a wide assortment of news, but his outstanding talent was as a spokesman for the industrialization of the South. He was one of the greatest southern editors to preach the gospel of saving that region from poverty by importing the factory, and his invocation of the spirit of progress endeared him to the business mind of North and South alike. Thus he was a potent figure in laying the ghosts of the Civil War.

Watterson was of a more peppery temperament, which he had room to exercise in the Louisville *Courier-Journal,* owned by Walter Haldeman. Watterson loved the excitement of politics and became a power among the Democrats of the upper South, eminently visible and important at a succession of conventions. Gifted also in playing the role of the traditional southern gentleman, he entertained businessmen and politicians with bourbon, chuckles, and white-moustached charm at his home outside the city and conveyed some of the emotional prestige of the old South of broad-brimmed hats and frock-coat oratory to the new South of cigarette factories and iron mines. He lived on until the 1920's. Both Watterson and Grady were throwbacks, in a sense, to the regional promoter-journalists of the Thomas Ritchie era. They inherited the job of guiding southern middle-class opinion, which had belonged mainly to preachers and politicians before the war, and they were possibly more effective leaders than their predecessors. Southern politicians had a diminished national prestige at the end of Reconstruction, and southern preachers, though they kept a strong hold on the local mind, were out of step with liberalizing and modernizing movements in their churches. The newspaper therefore had a strong civic function in the South.

In the larger towns, where the old-time role of the paper in public affairs was fading, a determined editor could revive it and keep up in the race for circulation as well. William Rockhill Nelson was just under forty when he founded the *Kansas City Star* in 1880. He had made money in building contracting, and came to the editorial desk with the handicap of inexperience but the asset of vast energy—"a big, laughing, fat, goodnatured, rollicking, haw-hawing person who loved a drink, a steak, a story, and a fight," in the words of William Allen White, who once worked for him as a reporter. The *Star* was at first an evening paper, an idea fast becoming popular. Brought home on the way from work, the evening paper was read by the whole family and was a better advertising medium for retail stores than the morning paper. Thanks to time differentials and transatlantic cables it could often beat the morning papers with wire news from Europe, which, when filed in the evening there, hit American headlines in mid-afternoon. And since it could be outstripped on local and national news which broke late in the day, it tended to make the best of circumstances by concentrating more on assessing the value of local stories and hunting out colorful feature material. This turned out to be Nelson's forte.

He took it on himself to make the *Star* "the mentor and monitor of Kansas City." He prodded the raw meatpacking and rail center into civic pride. He demanded that it light its streets, widen its avenues, clean up its parks, ride herd on its traction and utility magnates, fire its boodling officials whenever the *Star* uncovered their peculations, paint its houses, fine its grasping landlords, and behave as if it had a conscience. Exposing the sins of an unruly Kansas City kept the *Star*'s reporters busy and built for Nelson both a muckraking reputation and a big readership, touching 50,000 in 1893 and going past it soon after. Many of these crusades reflected simply the boosterism of the urban frontier, but they were something more, too. They gave the *Star* a personality and identified it with the "workingmen," whose two cents, in Nelson's view, entitled them to a friend and advocate as well as a newspaper. Nelson was trying to re-establish the organic link between the journal and the community which had existed in western towns a half-century before, when the editor was a political, social, and intellectual leader in the town as well as its gossip, raconteur, and advertiser. Hard as he fought the rings and bosses of his town, he was, like them, trying to win the loyalties of classes whose needs were ignored by more gentlemanly politicians and editors.

This kind of journalism was practiced elsewhere, too, a good example of it being the *Chicago Daily News,* founded by Melville Stone in 1875 and later carried on by Victor Lawson. It also specialized in crusades and deft local reporting, and its morning edition (issued as the *Chicago Record*) combined with the evening version to command over 200,000 readers by 1888. Lawson, like Nelson and like their imitators in many other cities, spelled out a worthy meaning for "independent journalism" by dedicating it to the service of the public at large. In such commitment lay the real power of the press. But it is noteworthy that this was not achieved, as the editors liked to suggest, by presenting "all the news" in nonpartisan fashion. The crusading editor had to catch his audience first. This required him not only to furnish plenty of the world-wide coverage that stamped a paper as one that kept up with the times, but also to provide a great many sporting, amusement, and advertising features having little to do with the news in any formal sense, as a record of momentous events. As for the local news, it was selected, shaped, and directed to a conscious end, just as it had been by the mercantile and party editors. The end might be more or less worthy than that served by political journalism, but it allowed editors to carry the serious, "objective" foreign and national news which could never hope to command mass circulation on its own.

There were, of course, papers which made the conventional kind of political and financial reporting the backbone of their offerings. The *New York Tribune* under Whitelaw Reid ran to politics, literature, and science, with an occasional dip into interesting scandal. The scandal could always be presented in the name of high moral purpose, if it happened to involve the saloon- and brothel-keepers who made up the rank and file of Tammany's voting platoons. Reid was only thirty-six in 1873 when he became the *Tribune*'s kingpin. A bright young graduate of Ohio's Miami College, with a good record as a war and Washington correspondent, he had come to the big city to make good, like Horace Greeley before him. Unlike Greeley, however, Reid did not aim to addle his readers by shouting their shortcomings in their ears. The *Tribune* stoutly defended all Republican candidates and every Republican policy. Reid himself was high in party circles, and its candidate for Vice-President in the unsuccessful year of 1892. He married wealth, served as minister to France for a time, and moved graciously and comfortably in an atmosphere of Anglo-Saxon friendship, banquets at Delmonico's, and a social milieu in which he could write easily of someone that he was "a liar as well as a trades unionist. In fact, the two things seem to go together." Reid could never be completely accepted as a high priest among the genteel, since he was running a daily newspaper instead of a literary monthly. But he came close.

The *Evening Post* also remained a paper for gentlemen and scholars. When Henry Villard bought it in 1881, he turned it over to a distinguished editorial triumvirate of Edwin L. Godkin, Carl Schurz, and Horace White. Godkin was the editor of the *Nation,* which Villard also purchased at that time. An English-born writer of laissez faire liberal persuasion, he had for years written distinguished, tart articles assailing the spoils system, the high tariff, monopolies, labor unions, and Socialists. He had at all times a high and firm sense of his own rectitude. Schurz was a reform politician of German background, and White was a former Washington correspondent and editor of the *Chicago Tribune.* All had taken some part in the Liberal Republican crusade which was in good part led by right-minded gentlemen-editors. They quarreled soon and often, and Schurz finally left the *Post* to White and Godkin, who used it to support hard-money policies nationally and to assail Tammany locally. Both the *Tribune* and the *Post,* holding to the three- and four-cent prices which had become common after the inflationary days of the Civil War, had modest circulations; both looked down on upstarts like the *New York Daily News* (the first of the city's papers so named), which sold, largely in the tenement house districts, for a penny, was loyal to Tammany, and reached between 100,000 and 200,000 people daily.

Municipal crusading, respectable reform, and sardonic

sensationalism were all variations on the theme of successful editorship in the seventies and eighties. Another variation was showmanship, a pioneer in which was, appropriately enough, James Gordon Bennett, Jr. He was not the pushful worker his father had been, and he ran the *Herald,* after it was handed on to him, by cables from Paris to his managing editors. He knew more of yachts, champagne, and polo ponies than of financial statements and pressroom problems, but he did inherit one Bennett instinct: he knew how to *make* news. He was particularly grateful when the American Indians, the French and Prussians, or the Russians and Turks furnished a war which enabled him to carry on the great tradition of battlefield correspondence at any cost established by his father during the Civil War. But when no war was forthcoming, the younger Bennett financed exploring and archeological expeditions, creating artificial wars against time and nature. The most celebrated of these manufactured stories was the search of *Herald* man Henry M. Stanley in 1871 for the "lost" missionary, David Livingstone, ending with the dramatic confrontation in Ujiji, Tanganyika, and the celebrated query, "Dr. Livingstone, I presume?" The expedition cost thousands but made royal copy and filled the need for popular press drama.

The newspaper "stunt" of this kind was to have a long and hardy life after the 1870's. In part it arose naturally out of the age which produced Barnum. In part it furnished second-hand color and excitement to city dwellers whose jobs and lives were becoming ever more routinized. But some of it was due to the natural dynamics of the new journalism. A paper achieved rank and readers by being first with the news. If the stories it furnished could be not only early but exclusive, that was even better. But "beats" and "exclusives" could not be furnished daily or weekly, particularly when the most important events were covered by the co-operative newsgathering agencies. Therefore, they had to be created by those who could afford to create them, which enhanced the lead of the already prospering sheets. The success of the spectacular report from the special correspondent, moreover, emphasized the degree to which the concept of news itself had come to embrace only the immediately exciting. No longer was there any pretense, as in early colonial papers, that the news should be a complete and continuous "history of the times." A general decline in crop prices in the West, an increase in bankruptcies in a given state, the emergence of new statesmen in European cabinets—these were not news but "background," possibly entitled to space only in the feature pages or Sunday editions of the more responsible papers. The craze for currency seemed to fit the accelerating tempo of city living, especially in the United States, where the present tense dominated almost all thought and the past was drawn on merely to justify, not retard, change. Yet the domination of the "hot" story gave the newspaper a May-fly character, with Monday's front-page earthshaker being Friday's ten-line filler at the end of the second section. It also gave the newspaper readers a distorted view of the world as a theater in which sudden, violent acts succeeded one another with convulsive speed. The stunt was journalism's shot in the arm of history, when history moved too slowly between editions.

Then, in 1883, the curious talent of Joseph Pulitzer entered the scene. Like the great figures in any field, Pulitzer was able to create new patterns by synthesizing old ones. Day and Bennett, a half-century before, had taken advantage of the new mass literacy created by public education, the widespread tract and pamphlet distributions of the reform and religious associations, and the comic and sporting weeklies, to build their popular newspapers. Pulitzer now combined the sensationalism, the wit, the crusades, the stunts, the features, the wide coverage, and the public conscientiousness of such diverse men as Dana, Nelson, the younger Bennett, Stone, and Godkin and created a dazzlingly successful amalgam of them in the *New York World.*

Pulitzer's was a Horatio Alger story with a foreign accent. He came to New York from Hungary in 1864 as a skinny recruit for the Union Army. Broke and footloose after his discharge, he drifted out to St. Louis and kept alive by odd jobs. Pulitzer was, however, full of ambition. He made influential friends among the German community in St. Louis, studied law, and finally was hired as a reporter on the German-language paper, the *Westliche Post.* He got a journeyman's education in newspaper fieldwork, went into politics as a Republican, and was sent to the state legislature. He next bought a share in the *Westliche Post,* sold it, bought another small German paper and sold that, and meanwhile continued his political life, moving through the Liberal Republican and into the Democratic party. In 1878, he bought and consolidated two young and sickly St. Louis journals, the *Post* and the *Dispatch,* combined them, and began to find his true vocation. Aided by a skilful assistant, John Cockerill, Pulitzer threw the *Post-Dispatch* into a succession of crusades, brightened up its format, multiplied its features, and made it a scrappy circulation rival for the *Globe-Democrat,* which was ably run by Joseph B. McCullagh, a one-time Civil War correspondent for the Cincinnati press.

In 1883 Pulitzer invaded New York. He bought the limping *World* from Jay Gould, who in turn had got it from Tom Scott as part of a parcel involved in a railroad transaction. Tall, big-nosed, and red-whiskered, Pulitzer made no secret of his intention to dominate his new arena. The *World,* he announced in a ringing salutation, would be "not only cheap, but bright, not only bright, but large, not only large but truly democratic." This final adjective was meant to be taken both politically and socially. Pulitzer was in fact a fairly unorthodox Democrat by the 1880's, and he not only supported Cleveland but advocated the governmental curbing of monopolies, the right of workers to unionize, and the imposition of stiff taxes on incomes and inheritances—all of them then somewhat heretical positions. It was Pulitzer's conviction that the paper should also appeal to the taste of New York's heterogeneous mass of immigrants and workers, and if that taste was coarse by patrician standards, patrician standards would have to go the way of the whale-oil lamp in the age of electricity.

The *World'*s pages, therefore, presented a curious, intellectually piebald appearance to the reader, as Pulitzer cast his net for both serious and light-minded buyers. Cockerill and his helpers had a genius for provocative headlining

that drew attention irresistibly to the story and made the paper hard to put down once it was begun. Here are the front-page items of a typical issue in 1884: "Ready To Visit Chicago" told of a meeting of Tammany to see how many members could attend the imminent Democratic convention. "A Boom for Cleveland," "The Illinois Democracy," "Carter Harrison's Candidacy," and "Blaine and Logan's Programme" were all straightforward political stories, but the makeup editor could not resist the sarcastic addition of "The Republicans Want Butler." It turned out that they did want the eccentric ex-general—as the Democratic candidate! Next came "Murdered on Shipboard," "Twenty-four Miners Killed," and "The Slugger Laureate," the last-named an interview with John L. Sullivan while he lay in his hotel room nursing a gargantuan hangover. "Proofs of By-gone Murders" dealt with skeletons unearthed in the process of digging a foundation trench for a new building on the site of a saloon in Illinois. "Accident to Alderman Kirk" was followed by "Fighting the Cholera," and foreign news re-entered the picture with "The Annexation of Cuba" (the subhead explained, "Spain Officially Assured That the United States Does Not Want Her White Elephant") and "Revising the Constitution" (of France). In the last two of the seven columns, the Tabasco sauce was poured on freely: "A Brother on the War-Path; He Attacks His Sister's Dentist and Then Tries To Shoot Him"; "Another Murderer To Hang"; "Love and Cigarettes Crazed Him" (an account of a suicide); "He Barked like a Dog" (the tale of a man seized with hydrophobia); and "Love Stronger Than Money" (in which a man remarried, forfeiting $12,000 left to him by his wife on condition that he remain a widower); and finally, "A Vice-Admiral's Son in Jail"; "He Pawned the Diamonds: How an Enterprising Broker Managed to Fail for $50,000"; and "Did She Take the Diamonds? A Hotel Maid Accused of Stealing Jewels Which Were Mysteriously Returned." All these were continued on inside pages. If, as a later journalistic truism had it, the requisites for big circulation were blood, money, and sex, then the *World* entered the readership wars with no lack of ammunition.

The *World'*s success was dazzling. In about a year it was selling 100,000 copies daily; a Sunday edition reached 250,000 before 1890, and an evening edition was begun in 1887, which, combined with the morning *World,* accounted for 374,000 copies daily by 1892. And Pulitzer continued to pour it on. The Sunday edition was a grab-bag of some forty-odd pages, half full of advertising, and half full of such diverse fare, according to one Saturday's promise, as "Lily Langtry's New Admirer," "Brooklyn Celebrities Illustrated," "Socialism and Its Meaning," "Monaco and Its Gambling," "A Sketch of Senator Bayard," and "Watering-Place Notes." When color presses appeared, the Sunday issue blossomed out with chromatic drawings, among them a cartoon illustrating the adventures of a group of ragamuffins from "Hogan's Alley." One of them, decked out in a wide, baby's nightshirt of brilliant yellow and nicknamed "The Yellow Kid," became a forerunner of comic-strip characters and the inspiration for the sobriquet "yellow journalism" applied to the Pulitzer (and later Hearst) formula.

Pulitzer's editorial column crackled with crusades—against aldermen who took bribes for favorable votes on a streetcar franchise that was a bad bargain for the city, against tenement contractors, against the Bell telephone monopoly and the Standard Oil trust, and against the conditions at Ellis Island, where hundreds of thousands of European newcomers were checked in by immigration authorities. When intellectual sympathy with popular causes was not enough to demonstrate the *World*'s love for the common man, Pulitzer went into open competition with the ward-heelers of Tammany (which, Democrat or no Democrat, he detested) and provided free ice, coal, picnics, and Christmas dinners for the needy. And when New York's citizens were not attending Pulitzer's civic parties or cheering his grapples with the "interests," they were paying wide-eyed attention to the *World*'s news, sporting, women's, and other feature sections (all plentifully illustrated) or laughing at its political cartoons or following some *World* reporter on a stunt in which he (or she) pretended to be a criminal or a lunatic or a contractor or an immigrant in order to write an inside account of conditions in the jail, the asylum, the legislature, or the sweatshop. One of Pulitzer's most celebrated coups was sending Elizabeth Cochran (who wrote over the byline "Nellie Bly") hurrying around the world on ships, trains, rickshas, sampans, and burros in seventy-three days, to beat the record of Jules Verne's fictitious hero, Phileas Fogg, who had turned the trick in eighty. Another was soliciting $100,000 from his readers, in nickels and dimes, to provide the money for the pedestal on which the Statue of Liberty was erected in the late eighties. In a sense, the familiar figure in New York's harbor is a monument to Pulitzer and the power of the new journalism as well as to freedom.

Pulitzer's triumphs and innovations successfully demonstrated the place of the popular paper in the United States. Despite the criticisms which rained about it, the *World* was not simply a lower-class scandal-sheet. In England, where sensational journalism was catching on in the eighties, and in France there was a wide and clear gap between the solid and informed journals of opinion or criticism and the lurid sheets aimed at the penny reader. But the *World,* together with its even more sensational imitators, was read by a population not so easily sorted out by class. Deacons and stockbrokers read it as well as their janitors and clerks, though a copy of it folded under the arm did not impart quite the tone of a copy of the *Post* or *Tribune.* The *World* sprinkled a good supply of the most respectable "hard" financial, political, and diplomatic information among its sordid vignettes, just as the most reverend and grave journals were not above reporting a murder trial or a particularly well-publicized sporting event. All the successful big-city journals embraced in themselves the many pasts of the American newspaper. Like fossils in the wall of a canyon the miscellany and advertising of the colonial gazette, the flamboyant editorials of the party and reform sheets, the special information of the business and mercantile papers, the stories and pictures of such popular quasi-magazines as *Harper's Weekly* and *Frank Leslie's Illustrated Newspaper* (both dating from the fifties) were all visible in the great newspapers of the Pulitzer heyday. The winning publisher learned that the laurels

went to the man who did not confine himself to one appeal, that in American society the inexorable market test was passed best by the journal that resisted categorization. The American conviction that a reader might be simultaneously informed, challenged, diverted, and relaxed by the same paper might be irritating, might even be part of a national illusion that opposites could be reconciled without cost, but it was there, and the big, bargain-basement, mass-circulation journal was obedient to it.

The hallmark of the Pulitzer type of journalism was not its novelty but its paternalism. The *World* might well be friend, counselor, jester, and advocate for the great public, but it took these roles only when and insofar as Joseph Pulitzer directed. Pulitzer's liberalism might be admirable, but what sold the *World* was not its antimonopoly crusades but the simple excitement of crusades no matter at whom directed, plus the spice of the features and the timeliness of the news. Pulitzer could change policies with no depressing effect on his circulation. On the contrary, when he became rattled by the competition of William Randolph Hearst in 1898 and temporarily dropped his normal opposition to jingoism in favor of preaching war with Spain, the *World*'s sales climbed over the million mark. Editorials seemed to have little to do with the acceptance of a paper. Moreover, in providing the easy delights of sensationalism, Pulitzer conditioned readers to expect handstands on the high wire and other acrobatic shows before they would concede their attention to the press. They became not so much members of a thinking public as consumers of peppy newsprint, waiting to be told by the providers of that newsprint what was good for them. Once the institution of the big-time daily had oriented itself to popular taste, it tended to take its direction increasingly from its owners alone. If they sought to enlarge their power by lowering the level of their papers still further, there was little to stand in their way. Pulitzer and his predecessors had released forces which might go out of control in less scrupulous hands, the perennial danger of paternalism.

Pulitzer learned this himself when William Randolph Hearst came into New York in 1895 to beat him at his own game. The son of a mining millionaire, Hearst was a dynamic, dictatorial, arrogant baron of journalism whose career spanned forty years of muckraking, reaction, scandal-mongering, empire-building, and fantastic spending. Although he liked to pose as the people's champion, he was never able to overcome his petulance when they voted against his wishes, and he made it clear in the editorial pages, whose contents he dictated, that he doubted their capacity to think in words of more than two syllables. He was initiated into the journalism of crusade and crime on the *San Francisco Examiner,* one of his father's incidental properties, which he took over at twenty-four after a wild and free-spending youth. New York was a prize he wanted badly, and he was accustomed to having enough money to gratify his desires. He bought the *New York Journal,* and then, with an inherited seven and a half million dollars at his disposal, bought the best talent in town to run it. He hired Pulitzer's entire Sunday staff, including the seasoned editors Morrill Goddard and his successor, Arthur Brisbane. He bought away such gifted reporters as Julian Ralph from the *Sun,* and he was able to engage

Richard Harding Davis and Stephen Crane to write war correspondence for him and Mark Twain to cover such special events as Queen Victoria's jubilee. *Journal* reporters on limitless expense accounts dug gold in the Klondike, bribed their way past bodyguards to hold interviews with celebrities, and even tried their hand at solving murder cases, at least once successfully.

The *Journal* really hit its stride, however, in 1897 and 1898 when Hearst appeared to take over personal management of the drive for United States intervention on behalf of the Cuban rebels against Spanish rule. Here was a field for yellow journalism at its gaudiest—a continuing crusade, with violence and brutality in the raging guerrilla warfare and the repressions of the Spanish authorities; sex in the persons of beauteous Cuban girls villainously maltreated by the cruel Spaniards; patriotism in the constant reminder that autocratic, Catholic Spain was an intruder in the Western Hemisphere reserved by destiny for Americans. The *Journal* lavishly paid reporters to steal alleged documents illustrative of Spanish perfidy, to get on-the-spot stories from the fighting fronts, and to rescue Cuban revolutionaries. Homer Davenport drew cartoons pointing up the message that only pusillanimity kept Americans from going to the relief of the Cubans. Illustrator Frederic Remington concocted sketches of Spanish atrocities, such as the imaginary episode in which Spanish policemen boarded an American vessel in pursuit of a young Cuban woman sailing for the United States and stripped her naked in a search for messages from the revolutionaries. When the battleship "Maine" was blown up in Havana harbor in February, 1898, the *Journal*'s headlines shouted, in type several inches high, that the Spaniards had been responsible (an allegation for which no proof has ever been discovered) and that war must be waged. The cry was taken up throughout the country, and President McKinley was swept along on an implacable tide toward a declaration of hostilities in April. When the American campaign in Cuba got under way, the newspapers, the *Journal* chief among them, had a gloriously expensive time covering it, and the *Journal,* not without reason, printed "ears" in the upper corners of its front pages asking, "How Do You Like the *Journal*'s War?"

Pulitzer, after initially holding back, had gone along with the jingo campaign, as the *Journal*'s circulation crept past the *World*'s, with each paper's morning and evening and extra editions selling over a million and a half copies on exciting days. By 1898, however, he was an absentee editor. Failing eyesight and poor health had driven him away from his desk in 1890. He spent twenty years thereafter cruising around the world in his yacht, issuing ukases from the Mediterranean or the South Atlantic to his editors in St. Louis and New York, being read to by a corps of secretaries, and contemplating in lonely magnificence what he had wrought. Hearst, too, eventually left New York and began to acquire more newspapers, so that the *Journal* became merely one child in the large family whose behavior Hearst supervised, finally, from a castle in California, surrounded by his purchased art treasures. Both men were among the last of the grandees of personal journalism, but both ended their lives (Pulitzer in 1911, Hearst in 1951) far from the direct, daily, shirt-sleeved participa-

tion in the papers which had lifted them to prominence. (pp. 121-45)

Bernard A. Weisberger, "Empires in Newsprint: The Century Closes," in his The American Newspaperman, *The University of Chicago Press, 1961, pp. 121-55.*

James Wyman Barrett

[*Barrett was an American editor and journalist who served as city editor for Joseph Pulitzer's New York* World. *In the following excerpt from his biography of Pulitzer, he provides a character sketch of the publisher in the form of a medical report.*]

For the sake of the medical record in JP's case, let us assume:

1. That the Subject was born in Hungary of ancestry unknown but believed to be partly Asiatic, his father being part Jewish, part Magyar, his mother, German; that he was the second of four children; that the oldest, Louis, died in youth, and the youngest, Irma, at the age of fifteen; that the third child, Albert, became insane at about the age of fifty and committed suicide at fifty-eight; and assume

2. That the father of the Subject died when the Subject was adolescent; that the mother, to whom the Subject was greatly devoted, married a second time; that the Subject, at seventeen, was overgrown, undernourished, awkward, possessed of weak eyes (no further information as to the original cause of trouble); delicate complexion, high forehead, prominent nose, and a short chin which the Subject regarded as "weak" and in later life sought to conceal under a beard; and assume

3. That the Subject, being anxious to get away from home, sought military service, but was rejected by the Austrian, the French, and the British armies because of defective eyesight and "unpromising physique"; that upon being accepted for the United States Army (Northern) during the American Civil War, the Subject enlisted in the Lincoln Cavalry; that he was the constant object of ridicule and practical joking on the part of his associates; that his persistent questions were met with evasive or false or humorous answers; that on one occasion when pestered by a petty officer, he struck his tormentor in the face, but was saved from military punishment through the intervention of a superior officer; and assume

4. That upon being mustered out of the army, the Subject sought in vain for employment in New York City and elsewhere; that he was refused the privilege of having his shoes polished in a certain hotel, being informed that its patrons objected to his poor appearance; that his overcoat was stolen; that upon inquiring where there was a city in the United States in which no German was spoken, he was informed by a practical joker that the city was St. Louis, Missouri; and assume

5. That upon arrival in St. Louis, by means of travel unknown, the Subject was forced to engage in the meanest sort of occupations, being variously deckhand on a ferryboat, gravedigger, stevedore, freight handler, coachman,

waiter, and man of all work; that the Subject employed all his spare time in a library in search of knowledge and constantly sought to learn the English language, and was addicted to reading in bed; and assume

6. That, upon becoming a reporter on a German newspaper, the Subject was treated to various kinds of teasing and practical joking on the part of English-speaking colleagues; that a certain cartoonist, when lacking in other material, often made caricatures of the Subject, featuring especially his prominent nose; that in spite of ridicule, the Subject attained proficiency in the newspaper art, and was appointed legislative correspondent at the State capital for the said German paper; and assume

7. That upon being nominated for a vacancy in the Missouri House of Representatives, as a practical jest on the part of a Republican minority in a strongly Democratic district, the Subject conducted a vigorous campaign and was elected; that upon taking his seat in the legislature he immediately started a fight against the so-called "county courthouse ring," and denounced a certain lobbyist; and assume

8. That the said lobbyist, a man of powerful build, publicly called the Subject a damned liar and other opprobrious epithets; that the Subject rushed to his lodgings, returning with a four-barreled pistol and fired two shots at the lobbyist, wounding the latter in the leg, and was struck down by him with the butt of a pistol; that the Subject pleaded guilty to assault and was fined about $400; and assume

9. That the Subject became intensely interested in national and state politics, finally leaving the Republican Party because of its notorious corruption, also, because of political differences, parting company with his German newspaper associates, by disposing of his interests for $30,000; that the Subject bought, for a nominal amount, another German newspaper and immediately sold it for $20,000; that thereafter the Subject enjoyed a brief period of comfort, during which time he fell in love and was married; and assume

10. That upon returning to St. Louis after his honeymoon, the Subject purchased a broken-down newspaper and built it up into a position of prosperity and influence, by arduous work and various editorial crusades designed to benefit the public and to remove special privileges of a wealthy few; that for about five years he worked eighteen, twenty, and often twenty-four hours a day, neglecting the bodily need of rest and recreation; having no regular mealtimes, and abusing his eyesight through editorial labors under open-flame gas lights; and assume

11. That through his unremitting efforts, the St. Louis newspaper was enjoying very large income, circulation, and prestige, until one day an editor shot and killed a prominent citizen of St. Louis in the offices of the newspaper, thereby causing great public indignation and also loss of influence to the newspaper; that as a result, the Subject suffered impairment of his health, the symptoms of which were nervousness, a cough accompanied by some loss of blood, sleeplessness, indigestion, and recurrent attacks of asthma, also some symptoms of diabetes; and assume

12. That the Subject, while bound for Europe with his wife in search of rest and recuperation, seized an opportunity to purchase a newspaper in New York for the sum of $346,000; and immediately plunged into new activities, involving long hours, irregular meals, loss of sleep, eyestrain, and constant nervous tension; the Subject being a perfectionist-idealist, forever unsatisfied either with his own labors or the work of those about him, but able to inspire his associates with the desire and the capacity for greater achievement; at the same time intolerant of injustice or corruption in public affairs; and assume

13. That the Subject, by reason of his perspicacity, energy, and unremitting study of national politics, his editorial vigor and warm devotion to a chosen cause, was largely responsible for the nomination and election of Grover Cleveland as President of the United States in 1884; that the same talent for arousing public opinion and for stimulating the nobler sort of sentiment in the American people was largely responsible for completing the base for the Statue of Liberty, a gift from the people of France to the people of America, this being accomplished through popular subscriptions to a fund in spite of indifference on the part of the wealthier classes; and assume

14. That the Subject, possessed of a burning hatred of incompetence, dishonesty, special privilege, and government favoritism toward predatory plutocracy as represented by certain groups in what is known as "Wall Street," labored and clamored relentlessly against a system of taxation falling largely on the poorer classes and the housewife and falling lightly upon the rich—in all of which efforts he received approval from the masses of the people and opposition from the wealthy groups and their newspaper mouthpieces, particularly one Charles Anderson Dana, editor of the (New York) *Sun,* a man learned in letters, but in politics eccentric—to put it mildly—a scholarly scamp if there ever was one; and assume

15. That the Subject, being convinced that a certain streetcar franchise for Broadway had been obtained through wholesale bribery to the tune of half a million dollars distributed among the New York Board of Aldermen by one Jacob Sharp, a promoter—the Subject, by means of news articles and editorials, was greatly instrumental in arousing public opinion and bringing about an investigation resulting in the Grand Jury indictment of all but two members of the said Board, indictment, trial, and conviction of the said Jakey Sharp, resulting directly or indirectly in such impairment to the health of the said Sharp that the said Sharp died from the results thereof, thereby causing much recrimination and blame to be hurled at the Subject; and assume

16. That the Subject, appreciative of the great public service rendered by De Lancey Nicoll, Assistant District Attorney, in the said boodle cases, proposed the nomination of Nicoll for District Attorney, a plan which was accepted by the Republican party in New York City, but rejected by the Democrats (although Nicoll was a Democrat and *The World* was regarded as the Democratic paper); and assume

17. That the aforesaid Charles Anderson Dana, then in his

sixty-ninth year and on his way out, journalistically speaking (politically he never amounted to anything)—that the said C.A.D. greatly alarmed over the growth of *The World's* circulation and the decline of the *Sun's* business and erstwhile prestige, infuriated as only an aged and pseudo-scholarly newspaper poseur can become when confronted with an up-and-coming editor-owner (especially one from the West) who habitually attacks the interests and sources from which C.A.D. and the *Sun* have been drawing large and often unexplained increments; and assume

18. That the said C.A.D., although he had previously endorsed Nicoll, proceeded to throw him overboard, and supported the Tammany candidate, at the same time publicly declaring that the one and only reason for the sudden switch (one of a series on Dana's part) was the alleged menace of the Subject and his newspaper; that the *Sun* continually and continuously for several weeks in the campaign attacked and denounced the Subject to the utmost resources of C.A.D.'s imagination and mastery of language (which was something)—applying to the Subject such epithets as

"Hungry Joe"

"Renegade Jew"

"Cringer for nickels in a barroom"

"Wandering Jew"

"Fugitive from unexecuted justice"

"Resorter to homicide"

"Choe Bulitzer."

And concluding, after the campaign had resulted in the defeat of Nicoll, in a torrent of abuse and denunciation, climaxing with the admonition, "Move on, Pulitzer, move on!"

And assume

19. That the Subject, by reason of the constant excitement and arduous work during the campaign, cast aside all thought of eating, sleeping, rest, recreation, and counter-actions to worry about the outcome of the election; and assume

20. That after absorbing the shock of defeat and the culminating invective of the aforesaid C.A.D., the Subject announced his intention of remaining in New York for good . . .

21. That shortly thereafter, the Subject, upon coming to his office and starting to examine editorials for the next day, found he could see nothing except the sheet of paper . . .

22. That medical examination showed that the Subject's eyesight was seriously impaired (one report says through the rupture of a blood vessel in one eye) and the prognosis indicated that he might never see again . . .

Which proved to be correct . . .

23. And that medical examination further indicated an acute nervous disorder which, according to physicians, could be remedied, if at all, only through prolonged absence from all work and all worry and complete rest, together with change of climate (California preferred) . . .

24. And assume, to make this quasi-hypothetical question no longer than necessary, that the Subject did not recover his eyesight; that it became progressively worse, resulting in almost complete loss of vision, except that in the late afternoon or early evenings he could dimly distinguish faint outlines of objects near by;

25. This nerve condition, although showing intermittent brief improvement, became steadily more acute, making the Subject so extremely sensitive to noise that the clink of a spoon, the closing of a door, the cracking of almonds by a guest at dinner, the rattle of a paper—anything in the nature of sniffling, or scratching, or scraping, or any kind of noise whatsoever except such as he could expect and identify and could enjoy, such as the rumble of surf, or the wind, or the galloping of horses—would react upon the Subject like a cannon shot, precipitating a paroxysm of pain and anger, and a certain degree (we must assume) of fright; the symptoms of which were violent cursing, shouting, shaking of the fist, stamping of feet, and culminating usually in weeping or sobbing, followed by long periods of extreme exhaustion, during which periods the Subject was an easy prey to colds, coughs, bronchitis, asthma, indigestion, inflammation of the lungs, certain indications of diabetes, and weakening of the heart;

26. That the series of nervous attacks and seizures continued for a period of twenty-four years, varied only occasionally with "good spells," during all which time the Subject's mind was continuously active; his curiosity insatiable; his demand for improvement on the part of his papers and their editors and reporters unrelenting; his thirst for knowledge unquenchable—for the latest or most authoritative information on politics, art, science, government, literature, drama, music, education, history . . . even to the extent, at one time, of commanding *The World* to find out if it was really true, as alleged by Guglielmo Ferrero in his *Greatness and Decline of Rome* (1907) that Marc Antony *did not* deliver a funeral oration (famous or otherwise) at Julius Caesar's funeral. . . .

[JP's equilibrium was gravely upset over Ferrero's "discovery"; he wanted to know: Where did Shakespeare get his information? He cabled orders from *The World* staff to interview scholars like Woodrow Wilson, James Ford Rhodes, John Bach McMaster, *et al.*—what did they think about it? Well, *The World's* reporters tried hard, but unfortunately were unable to locate anybody who had attended, or had any first- or second-hand knowledge of, the last rites for Caesar.]

And assume:

27. That the Subject had a multiple-track mind; that while one part or another of his stream of consciousness might be occupied with the reading of Monypenny's *Life of Disraeli*, or the description of a painting a secretary had seen in Munich, or the latest reports about his family, or the further advances in the art of soundproofing such as might be applied to the "town residence" at No. 7-15 East Seven-

ty-second Street, New York; or the summer home, "Chatwold" at Bar Harbor, Maine, or the yacht *Liberty;* or the "cottage" on Jekyl Island, Georgia, or a rented home at Lakewood, New Jersey; or various other homes, villas, hotel suites, steamship accommodations and special trains—the main track of the mind was occupied exclusively with *The World* and what it was doing to promote progress and reform, to combat injustice and corruption, to stimulate public opinion and public welfare; how to prevent *The World* from becoming satisfied with merely printing news, or coming to lack sympathy with the poor, or not marching ahead and always leading in the unfolding of the nation's history; and assume

28. That a cross section of the Subject's consciousness in what he called the period of "horrible invalidism and absenteeism," might be something like this:

"Take this cable to Cobb order the horses for eleven Ireland is to ride with me so he thinks he has a good memory does he editorial on Cortelyou weak very weak for God's sake how many times must I say *The World* must lead, lead, lead why wait two days before commenting tell Dunningham to remove the almonds entirely point out that Roosevelt denounces malefactors of great wealth while at the same time accepting their campaign contributions praise him for whatever good he does never fail to expose and denounce all acts of jingoism egoism blowing up the war scare Bryan must not be a candidate again reading for tonight is *Vanity Fair* no make it *Mill on the Floss*—but after all, no style like Jane Austen's—Thwaites was dull at dinner last night Ireland must be memorizing those figures on British income taxes Billing's analyses of Sunday papers very shrewd find out who wrote the editorial about Mrs. Rockefeller going to church it wasn't worth more than a paragraph what does Ralph say about his trip next summer who hit a glass with a spoon last night treat Hearst with restraint, almost respect, etc., etc."

And assume

29. That the inner battle between suffering and editing continued up to the end of the Subject's life; the physique gradually becoming less and less resistant to the aftereffects of the nervous attacks, finally ending in a heart attack at the age of sixty-four years, six months, and nineteen days, during which span of life there had never been the slightest diminution of the Subject's mental virility as expressed in curiosity, memory (copper plate), analysis and co-ordination, formulation of statement (although frequently repetitious and alliterative, always forceful and attention-compelling), appreciation, adequacy of reaction (sometimes over-reaction), ability to sift chaff from wheat at lightning speed; and during which time, barring the period of adolescence, the emotional life, barring the disturbances mentioned, was, generally speaking, adequate, normal, wholesome; the ideals noble and not at all egocentric; said ideals being concerned with honesty and efficiency in government and politics; the better education of youth; the establishment of a school and schools of journalism for the purpose of attracting into newspaper work men of superior ability and character . . . AND CHARACTER . . . the teaching of moral courage; the promotion of international peace; the lessening or removal of political, social,

and economic discriminations and all manner of special privilege; the spread of culture and knowledge; the encouragement of American drama, music, art, science, poetry, and other literature (including biographies of distinguished Americans), history of the United States, and fiction, emphatically and especially fiction reflecting "the wholesome character of American life and the highest standards of morals and manners"; and assume

30. That the Subject, in the last ten years of his life, devoted much time, thought, energy, and attention to a plan for perpetuating a newspaper which should always fight for progress and reform, never tolerate injustice or corruption, always fight demagogues of all parties, never belong to any party, always oppose privileged classes and public plunderers, never lack sympathy with the poor, always remain devoted to the public welfare, never be satisfied with merely printing news, always be drastically independent, never be afraid to attack wrong whether by predatory plutocracy or predatory poverty. . . .

31. And in the same plan, the Subject included a system of annual prizes for the encouragement of American drama and other literary types; prizes for high-school students desiring further education; for university or other students manifesting special talent or genius in journalism, music, and art . . . which prizes became known in time as "Pulitzer Prizes"; the system also including annual awards to newspapers and newspapermen for good work in exposing wrong and accomplishing public good; the keynote of the whole system being Sincerity, Nobility, Generosity (which keynote in recent years appears to have been forgotten or overlooked or misplaced, or, in some instances, entirely ignored)—all tending to show

32. That the Subject was a stiff-necked idealist as well as intellectually, politically, and sociologically the most incorrigible busybody of his day and age.

Assuming that the foregoing is truthful, that it is characterized by Accuracy, Accuracy, and Accuracy, if not Terseness . . .

What is the diagnosis?

From the medical standpoint, after consultation with qualified members of the neurological, psychological, and psychiatric specialization groups, the best explanation seems to be:

PSYCHO-NEUROSIS, resulting from a mental, emotional, neurological cataclysm, followed by a long period of exhaustion, out of which there developed a fear complex associated with noises.

The theory is that the early hardships and persecutions in JP's life; the abuses, the badgerings, the tormentings, goadings, and teasings inflicted in the Lincoln Cavalry; the frustrations of his natural curiosity and the blocking of his natural emotional outlets; the mistreatment experienced in New York after discharge from the army—i.e., inability to find work after fighting for the country, his exclusion from the shoe-shining department of French's Hotel, the practical joke perpetrated in sending him to St. Louis in search of an all-American city; the extreme difficulty of sustaining life and at the same time pursuing knowledge in a robust environment; the practical jokings of the St. Louis reporters; the abuse inflicted by Captain Augustine (resulting in "over-reaction" with a pistol); followed by the public outcry occasioned by the Cockerill-Slayback affair; followed later by the savage thrusts of Rapierist Dana, accompanied by the "Hungry Joe" and "Renegade Jew" excoriations. . . .

The theory is that the cumulative series of torments produced a storehouse of emotional conflicts which did not find outlet until after JP unfortunately had so neglected his health that the reservoirs of nervous energy became depleted; the reservoirs fell below the safety level and the complex began to scream and shout. Nature has a way of storing away memories of emotional disturbances. They seem to be forgotten, but they are not. When exhaustion sets in, they return in full force, often accompanied by other devils more deadly than themselves.

The blindness was something else. The progressive deterioration of the retina in one eye, gradually affecting the other, seems to be attributable to downright neglect and abuse of an eyesight never strong. At seventeen Joseph Pulitzer was rejected for military service because of defective vision—which should have been a warning, but turned out to be only an invitation to work, work, work because, as he seemed to sense, the night was coming.

And it finally caught up with him. (pp. 115-25)

James Wyman Barrett, "Tragedy," in his Joseph Pulitzer and His World, *The Vanguard Press, 1941, pp. 115-41.*

Theodore Roosevelt on Joseph Pulitzer:

While the criminal offense of which Mr. Pulitzer has been guilty is in form a libel upon individuals, the great injury done is in blackening the good name of the American people. It should not be left to a private citizen to sue Mr. Pulitzer for libel. He should be prosecuted for libel by the governmental authorities. In point of encouragement of iniquity, in point of infamy, or wrongdoing, there is nothing to choose between a public servant who betrays his trust . . . and a man as guilty as Mr. Joseph Pulitzer has been guilty in this instance. It is therefore a high national duty to bring to justice this vilifier of the American people, this man who wantonly and wickedly and without one shadow of justification seeks to blacken the character of reputable private citizens and to convict the Government of his own country in the eyes of the civilized world of wrongdoing of the basest and foulest kind, when he has not one shadow of justification of any sort of description for the charge he has made.

Theodore Roosevelt, in a special message to Congress dated 15 December 1908, regarding an inflammatory editorial published in the World.

Edwin Emery

[*In the following essay, Emery weighs arguments for*

and against William Randolph Hearst's journalistic ethos and concludes that his influence was almost wholly detrimental.]

The distinguished American historian Frederic Logan Paxson, of the Universities of Wisconsin and California, once told a graduate seminar that he willingly would abandon all his other work if William Randolph Hearst only would call him to San Simeon and tell him that the files were open for a legitimate historical study of the Hearst career.

Professor Paxson never was invited to San Simeon; nor in Hearst's lifetime was any other scholar permitted access to the publisher's private papers and the records of the Hearst empire. This didn't stop people from writing about Hearst. But either they wrote briefly after gleaning what they could from the public record—a necessarily fragmentary knowledge—or they patched together facts and rumors to produce book-length studies which fell far short of achieving either reasonable balance or real worth. Some persons, of course, attacked Hearst in vehement fashion without bothering to study the evidence at all.

As a result, the official Hearst biography released by International News Service when the publisher's 64-year newspaper career closed in mid-August 1951 noted in its second paragraph: "And as he fashioned his vast enterprises, there grew progressively in the public mind a picture of the builder himself. It was a strange portrait, obscured by myth and legend, confused by controversy and distortion."

The purpose of this brief essay is scarcely to clear away all those confusions and obscurities. It is only, first, to review the nature of what has been written about Hearst, and then to suggest some basic approaches to "the problem of Hearst" which should be borne in mind by those attempting to come to some judgments about him.

Hearst is not the only famous American newspaper publisher for whom no adequate biography exists. But considering the complex nature of the man's personality, the social and political impact of his many ventures, and the length and extent of his career, he probably is the most difficult man of journalism to study and to estimate. The lack of any successful attempts at definitive studies of the man and his newspapers, or of even easily accessible summary studies of any length, is therefore especially unfortunate.

Four biographers have tried their hand with Hearst. Mrs. Fremont Older's authorized account, *William Randolph Hearst: American* (1936), gets the student nowhere. John K. Winkler's *W. R. Hearst, An American Phenomenon* (1928) is generally favorable, but inconclusive and unsatisfying, and outdated. Ferdinand Lundberg's *Imperial Hearst* (1936) turns the spotlight on the publisher's financial affairs and sources of wealth, but gives Hearst the worst of it at every turn in unobjective fashion. Best of the lot (although also approaching the outdated label) is the book written by Oliver Carlson and Ernest Sutherland Bates, *Hearst, Lord of San Simeon* (1936), a strongly critical but better balanced study in contrast with the others.

From the biographies the student might turn to a collection of Hearst newspaper editorials published at the turn of the century, and to the voluminous selected writings of Hearst himself. He has the observations of Will Irwin, printed in *Collier's* in 1911; the comments of Oswald Garrison Villard and other press critics; the biographies and reminiscences of other newspapermen; and, of course, the accounts in the various journalism histories. For documentation of the sensationalism of Hearst's *New York Journal* in the nineties he has Willard G. Bleyer's painstaking analysis in *Main Currents in the History of American Journalism*. For documentation of the *Journal's* activity in the Spanish-American War period he has Marcus M. Wilkerson's *Public Opinion and the Spanish-American War* and Joseph E. Wisan's *The Cuban Crisis as Reflected in the New York Press*. Finally there are the magazine articles and newspaper stories, published at intervals during the long Hearst career and listed in journalism bibliographies. These are not as valuable in Hearst's case as they sometimes prove to be in journalism history, but the latest of them represent the only recently published sources of information available.

The mid-thirties brought several magazine pieces about Hearst. One, which turned out to be an overly-optimistic analysis of the Hearst financial picture, was published in *Fortune* in October 1935. *Editor & Publisher* recorded the fiftieth anniversary of Hearst's newspaper publishing career in March 1937. Forrest Davis did his "Mr. Hearst Steps Down" for the *Saturday Evening Post* in August 1938, summarizing the financial facts at a moment when the Hearst goose seemed cooked, and depicting life at San Simeon. *Collier's* added "Good That Hearst Did" in April 1939, and *Time* gleefully and bitterly wrote the publisher off in March 1939 with "Dusk at Santa Monica."

The facts were, Hearst was neither dead nor broke. But no one corrected the published record until August 1951 when at last "the Chief" was gone. Only occasional reports in *Editor & Publisher* testified to the Hearst empire's comeback and to the continued powerful, if diminished, position of the aging publisher.

What appeared in the first month after Hearst's death offers some updating and critical evaluation. The best work was done by two strongly contrasting publications. The *New York Times* for August 15 delved into the publisher's 88-year life and into the finances of the Hearst corporate maze in excellent fashion. The issue of *Life* for August 27 accompanied a pictorial story with a penetrating editorial analyzing the qualities of "Hearst Journalism." As an antidote for the flood of vaguely worded statements which appeared in the wake of Hearst's death, *Life*'s editorial was badly needed. A. J. Liebling, of course, dissected the New York newspapers' coverage of Hearst's death for the *New Yorker* of September 8. *Editor & Publisher*'s coverage, while voluminous, was disappointing. The newspaper world's trade journal no more came to grips with the problem of Hearst than did the Hearst organization's own official biography carried by INS and published in the chain's newspapers.

The result is that the student wishing to read beyond the journalism history book accounts of Hearst's career has a most difficult time obtaining even a balanced diet of factual information. He finds plenty of stories about Hearst's fabulous private life, his pre-capitalistic attitudes toward money and power, his incredible San Simeon. But interpretations of Hearst's journalism are less productive, and the student is hard pressed to come up with even some of the answers to the questions which present themselves when the name Hearst is mentioned.

These questions all revolve about the major one: Where does Hearst rank as a journalistic leader and as a contributor to the advancement of the newspaper profession? Many shades of answers might be obtained from the literature about Hearst, depending upon the weight given to one or another source.

The points most often listed in support of the thesis that Hearst made notable contributions to American journalism are these:

1. Hearst built the world's largest publishing empire, in terms of numbers of newspapers and their combined circulations. At the peak, in 1935, Hearst printed papers in 19 cities. They included 26 dailies, with 13.6 percent of the total daily newspaper circulation in the country, and 17 Sunday editions, with 24 percent of the country's Sunday circulation. In addition he controlled the King Features syndicate, largest of its kind; the money-coining *American Weekly;* International News Service, Universal Service, and International News Photos; 13 magazines, 8 radio stations, and 2 motion picture companies. This, then, spells a success which must be recognized.

2. Hearst's methods and innovations in newswriting and newshandling—particularly in makeup and headline and picture display—and his utilization of new mechanical processes were highly important. Hearst journalism changed the character of American journalism, and therefore it must be recognized.

3. Hearst newspapers were edited to appeal to the mass of readers, and encouraged millions to increase their reading habits. Because of this, and because of Hearst's editorial policies and his own political activities, Hearst newspapers exercised a powerful influence in American life which must be recognized.

4. Hearst was in many ways a constructive force—stalwart in his Americanism; a believer in popular education and in the extension of the power of the people; and during different phases of his long career an advocate of many progressive solutions to national problems. These included advocacy of popular election of senators, the initiative and referendum, a graduated income tax, widespread public ownership (in 1900 Hearst wanted to nationalize the coal mines, railroads and telegraph lines which were the symbols of the new industrial era), breaking up of monopolies and trusts, and strong encouragement of the economic and political powers of labor unions.

All this, the argument runs, cannot be washed out. It is in the record for all to see.

Counter-arguments to these points are also to be found in the record. They should be prefaced, however, with this general observation:

The building of a great publishing empire does not in itself assure Hearst a high standing in his profession. The newspapers which the craft recognizes as great are those which demonstrate their integrity and zealousness in the telling of the news, and which at the same time possess the social conscience which is acquired by their recognition of the needs of society, and by a proper and reasonable adjustment to society's desires. Honesty and comprehensive coverage of the news is of course the first essential. The second is a demonstration of what Professor Leon N. Flint so aptly called "The Conscience of the Newspaper." The great newspapers—whether conservative or liberal, Republican or Democrat in their political beliefs—are those which are aroused whenever basic principles of human liberty and progress are at stake in a given situation, and which are constantly on guard against intolerance and unfairness. Operating within a consistent social framework, they do their best to be the kind of progressive community leaders America expects.

Keeping these two tests of the greatness of a newspaper in mind, then, here are the rebuttals to the specific points listed in Hearst's favor:

1. The Hearst empire, for all its onetime size, was not the roaring success which the accumulated figures would indicate. Hearst began to borrow from banks as early as 1924. In the early 1930s he had his newspapers publicize and sell a 50-million-dollar stock issue to keep themselves afloat. Here, of course, the intricate nature of the Hearst corporate structures makes a clear answer to the causes of this economic decline impossible. The publisher had a very large income from inherited mining properties and other business investments which could be poured into his journalistic ventures—and was. He also spent fabulous sums—an estimated 40 million dollars on art treasures and oddities, untold millions for his personal life—and sank more than 50 million dollars in real estate holdings which by depression time became enormous liabilities. Some of this spending represents a drain on the journalistic properties; how much, no one knows. But it is known that great sums were lost, as well as made, in journalism. Hearst's efforts to win a foothold in Atlanta alone were calculated by him to have cost 21 million dollars before he gave up.

After the liquidation process had commenced in 1937, groups of trustees largely were responsible for the business decisions once made solely by the Chief. By 1951 Hearst papers were appearing in only a dozen cities, with 16 dailies and 13 Sunday editions on the list. Their combined circulations still were larger than those of the 26 dailies and 17 Sunday editions published in 19 cities in 1935. But Hearst had lost ground in his percentage of the country's total circulation. The average Hearst daily circulation at the time of his death was 5,264,420, or 9.8 percent of the total daily circulation; Sunday Hearst circulation was 8,357,795, or 18 percent of the national Sunday total. These represent substantial drops in Hearst circulation influence from the 1935 figures of 13.6 percent daily and 24 percent Sunday previously cited.

The remainder of the empire had melted, too. Universal Service was gone; only eight magazines and three radio

William Randolph Hearst.

stations remained; the *American Weekly* was being hard-pressed in the Sunday supplement field. On the non-journalism side, many of the art treasures had been auctioned off in Gimbel's basement; Hearst's 40 million dollars in New York real estate holdings had been largely liquidated; and even many of San Simeon's acres had been sold.

Despite the successful consolidation of the Hearst holdings and the regaining of some measure of the owner's power after 1947, danger signals continued to fly. Recent annual statements of Hearst newspaper operations show that they are earning less profit than the average for newspapers their size for which financial reports are available. In the first half of 1951, Hearst Consolidated, which controls the bigger newspapers in the chain, reported profits of but $1,322,700 as against $3,599,800 for the same period a year ago, and the corporation's Class A stock dividends went to $8.75 in arrears. This scarcely bears out the picture of success which is claimed for Hearst.

2. Undoubtedly Hearst editing and printing methods made their impress on American journalism. Particularly Hearst's sponsoring of mechanical innovations, and the Hearst format techniques, spurred others on. But these were contributions which are largely technical in their nature, and in the judgment of most newspapermen they were more than matched on the negative side by Hearst proclivities for sensational treatment of news.

3. Undoubtedly, too, Hearst drew many new readers of newspapers to his fold. But what was the end result? Pulitzer defended sensationalism in the *World* by arguing that it attracted readers who then would be exposed to the columns of his carefully-planned high-quality editorial page. The same could not be said of the Hearst newspapers, as will be explained later in detail.

Nor did Hearst exercise the powerful influence in American life which his great circulations might indicate. Among the men whom he wanted to see become president of the United States were William Jennings Bryan, Champ Clark, Hiram W. Johnson, William Gibbs McAdoo, John Nance Garner, Alf Landon, General Douglas MacArthur and William Randolph Hearst. Among the men whom he fought while they were in the White House were William McKinley, Theodore Roosevelt, William Howard Taft, Woodrow Wilson, Franklin D. Roosevelt and Harry Truman. Hearst got on the bandwagons of Warren Harding, Calvin Coolidge and Herbert Hoover in the 1920s largely because he disapproved of their Democratic opponents. He rode the Wilson bandwagon in 1912, and the Roosevelt bandwagon in 1932, but promptly got off in high dudgeon both times.

Hearst himself served two terms in Congress from a Democratic district in New York City from 1903 to 1907. His high point was the casting of 200 votes for him in the Democratic national convention of 1904 (Judge Alton B. Parker, the presidential nominee, got 658). In 1905, running as an independent for mayor of New York, he lost by some 3,500 votes as the result of Tammany's counting him out at the ballot boxes. The next year Charles Evans Hughes defeated him by 60,000 votes for the governorship of New York, and the Hearst political star had set. He lost decisively in the 1909 New York mayoralty race, and in 1922, when he wanted to run for senator, Al Smith refused to let him on the Democratic ticket, making a bitter speech attacking Hearst's isolationist record in World War I.

4. What then of Hearst as a constructive social force? Certainly he was an advocate of Americanism. But to many his continued espousal of nationalistic policies, in a time which demanded American cooperation in international security efforts, was the most distressing feature of his newspapers. Certainly, too, Hearst newspapers have given stalwart support to public education and to the idea of public ownership of utilities. But they have backslid on many of the other progressive features of the Hearst editorial platform as written before World War I.

Curiously enough, the official Hearst obituary contained several paragraphs describing the aid Hearst gave in swinging Garner delegates to the Franklin Roosevelt banner in the 1932 Democratic convention. Although this settled an old score with Al Smith, why anyone felt that Hearst still would want to receive credit in 1951 for helping to make Roosevelt president is not clear—unless perhaps there were some persons with long memories in the Hearst organization.

For the Hearst policy editorials, as published in the *San Francisco Examiner* in 1933, went like this:

Franklin Roosevelt's inauguration brings hope to the American people. . . . Curiously enough, though the G.O.P. in the last campaign sought to spread the propaganda that Roosevelt's election would be bad for business, business and financial leadership today are looking forward to receiving genuine stimulus from the new presidential program. (March 4)

President Roosevelt's remarkable skill in making up his mind quickly on critical problems and his ability to persuade his countrymen to follow under his banner are unseen assets which will go far toward turning the scales toward a new and more stable prosperity. (March 17)

President Roosevelt's message to Congress on unemployment relief (WPA) emphasizes the humane theme which dominates his entire reconstruction program. . . . (March 26)

Again in the crisis President Roosevelt has displayed courage and initiative. His decision to suspend exports of gold . . . is a victory for the Hearst newspapers. (April 20)

It is good news that the "New Deal" is drafting a so-called "National Industry Recovery Act," which embodies several basic policies long advocated by the Hearst newspapers. (May 6)

By 1935 the tune had changed. It was the "Raw Deal" and the "National Run Around" in both news and editorial columns. The Supreme Court decision outlawing NRA was greeted with an American flag and the headline, "Thank God for the Supreme Court!" And the Hearst editorial stand was now:

Which? American Democracy or Personal Dictatorship? The latest decisions of the Supreme Court should arouse all loyal American citizens to a full realization of how entirely this so-called Democratic administration at Washington has abandoned Democratic principles and how utterly it has discarded the fundamental Democratic policy, and the fundamental American constitutional principle of strict limitation of Federal powers. . . . (June 2)

There are other examples in the 1935 issues of the *Examiner* of the extent to which the earlier beliefs of Hearst had changed. The publisher who had once been perhaps the most aggressive in supporting the power of labor unions said now:

The Wagner Labor Bill . . . is one of the most vicious pieces of class legislation that could be conceived—un-American to the core, violative of every constitutional principle and contrary to the whole spirit of American life. Congress in passing it is betraying the country. (May 29)

The publisher who had fought so long against monopolies and trusts said now:

The Wheeler-Rayburn Bill, decreeing death to the holding companies, is PURE VENOM distilled by a PERSONAL and MALIGNANT OBSESSION, without a pretense of economic or legal justification. (June 21)

The publisher who believed that he understood the common people, and was understood by them, had extensive front-page coverage of WPA activities in 1936 with headlines like this one: "Taxpayers Feed 20,000 Reds on N.Y. Relief Rolls." And his newspapers warned that the Social Security Act was "A Pay Cut for You! . . . Governor Landon, when elected, will repeal this so-called security act."

What has happened since 1936 is familiar. Hearst newspapers have opposed the basic foreign policy adopted by the American people during and after World War II, and they have followed the 1935 line rather than that of 1933 in opposing domestic reform. Politically they descended to a ridiculously synthetic, but fully-publicized, boom for General Douglas MacArthur for president in 1948, giving every appearance that they believed he was a major contender for the Republican nomination that year (MacArthur received 11 votes in the convention, all from Wisconsin).

Hearst newspapers have used their news columns in behalf of their publisher's private beliefs, attaching labels to the ideas which he opposes, creating stories in behalf of their causes, and distorting the news picture in many ways. *Life* put it neatly when it said in its editorial on "Hearst Journalism": "Hearst Journalism never overburdened its readers with information of any kind—for information may sometimes be dull and dullness is a sin—but it was especially lean on any information from the other side of the fence."

On the modern record, then, Hearst newspapers have no claim—not even the superficial claim of success and power—to ranking as great newspapers. Their record in handling the news is bad, and their quick switches in thinking about basic social issues nullify their editorial leadership, to say the least.

In considering the place of their publisher, however, one must look back to the earlier years of the Hearst career to see whether or not historical perspective gives him a higher ranking among American journalistic leaders.

The crucial question for anyone seeking to evaluate Hearst's place in American journalism thus becomes: Was Hearst in his early days a sincere and effective champion of the common man? Upon the answer quite likely depends whatever measure of journalistic esteem Hearst might permanently retain, other than that won by his technical achievements in publishing. Yet in the literature about him the answers vary widely.

Will Irwin, writing about Hearst in 1911 [in *Collier's Weekly,* 18 February] says that his editorial policies might well represent a marriage of convenience and sincerity, but adds that "those who knew Hearst best in this early era declare that under his cold exterior he kept a real sympathy for the submerged man and woman, a real feeling of his own mission to plead their cause."

Time magazine said bitterly in 1939 [13 March]:

> No other press lord ever wielded his power with less sense of responsibility; no other press ever matched the Hearst press for flamboyance, per-

versity and incitement of mass hysteria. Hearst never believed in anything much, not even Hearst, and his appeal was not to men's minds but to those infantile emotions which he never conquered in himself: arrogance, hatred, frustration, fear.

To help avoid the dangers of hindsight coloring attitudes toward the early Hearst, the question might be put another way as a historical guessing exercise: If Hearst had died in 1915, rather than in 1951, what would have been the estimate of his contribution to journalism then?

Posing the question this way seems to be a means of getting at the problem. In many respects there do appear to be two Hearsts. One is the young publisher who invaded New York with his *Journal,* backed William Jennings Bryan for president in a year when the best people were terrified by the menace of populism, adopted a platform more radical than that of many progressives of his time, and centered his editorial appeal on a frank espousal of the gaining of political power by the working man.

The other Hearst is the older publisher of the past 30 years—thwarted in satisfying his own political ambitions; increasingly plagued with financial problems; consistently nationalist in his outlook and therefore increasingly isolationist in contrast to the changing currents of American thinking about world affairs; finally reviled as the enemy of the common people he had once sought to lead.

At once the question arises: Were there two Hearsts? Or is it simply that there were two social situations, in only one of which Hearst seemed to be a progressive force?

Unquestionably Hearst was profoundly affected by the bitter personal attacks made upon him during World War I, and by the consequent dashing of his lingering hopes of gaining political power. Like many another isolationist who stubbornly opposed the main trends of American foreign policy, he came to fight his enemies on domestic issues which the hated internationalists also happened to espouse. But basically it had to be the same Hearst for the entire 64 years. Whether for convenience's sake or in all sincerity, he traveled the main stream in the 1890s and early 1900s, seemingly accepting the necessity for social change, and recognizing the desirability of economic and political readjustments. Later, in many respects, Hearst was left behind in a new social situation to which he was unable or unwilling to adjust.

Nevertheless, judging solely on his socio-political record, a Hearst who had chanced to die in 1915 would seem to rank close to the Pulitzers and the Scrippses in his journalistic leadership. Yet there would be good reason not to accord him that position. Hearst journalism then was powerful; its master advocated progressive beliefs; his newspapers were widely read and were financially successful. But Hearst journalism then also was degrading in its use of techniques to reach the reader, no matter what; its master lacked in final analysis the responsible feeling a worthy publisher must have for his public mission; and, above all, Hearst journalism lacked depth.

Many things may be meant by the phrase, "Hearst journalism lacked depth": Depth of intellectual appeal; depth of sincerity; depth of understanding of social issues; depth of responsible conception of its public trust. No matter which of these objections was the one held by an individual, however, it would rule Hearst out as a journalistic leader of real force. And while Hearst had his loyal followers, there were many instinctive doubters.

The Norman Thomas of 1951 says (in the *Reporter* of September 18) that the Norman Thomas of 1905 admired Hearst's political stands but quite distrusted the publisher and believed him to be thoroughly cynical. Assuming that the Norman Thomas of 1951 can recall his opinions of 1905 objectively, why did he believe that Hearst lacked depth of character?

One answer lies in the kind of newspaper Hearst published. Its appeal was pitched to a low level, whether in the news columns or on the editorial page. Arthur Brisbane, writing in the *Cosmopolitan* in September 1898 about "The Modern Newspaper in War Time," unblushingly explained how the *Journal* went about its job of capitalizing on the just-ended Spanish-American War. Brisbane was so certain of his reading audience that he included this paragraph in his widely-circulated magazine piece: "Before the type size reached its maximum, 'War Sure' could be put in one line across a page, and it was put in one line and howled through the streets by patriotic newsboys many and many a time. As war was sure, it did no harm."

And of course there was the immortal explanation of the Hearst news technique given by Arthur McEwen, another Hearst stalwart: "News is anything that makes the reader say 'gee, whiz!' That is what we're after, the gee-whiz emotion."

The Hearst editorial page followed the same approaches. It spoke in one-syllable words. It talked about human virtues, religion, science and love more easily than it talked about significant current issues. It had no men of the intellectual caliber of William H. Merrill and Frank Cobb of the *World,* or Charles R. Miller of the *Times.* It did have Arthur Brisbane and Arthur McEwen, among others.

Hearst preferred the cartoonist and headline writer to the editorial thinker. As evidence of this, the testimony of Willis J. Abbot about life on the *New York Journal* of the late 1890s may be quoted. Abbot, who later became editor of the *Christian Science Monitor,* records the following in his autobiography [*Watching the World Go By,* 1933] about his introduction to Hearstian methods:

> Within an hour after meeting him [Hearst], I was engaged as "Editor-in-chief" of the *New York Journal.* The resonant title was most grateful to my still youthful and ingenuous mind. . . . It took months of cruel disillusionment to reveal to me the two facts that despite a liberal conferring of titles, Mr. Hearst was the only editor-in-chief of any of his papers, and that of all his newspaper pages the editorial page of which I had charge was the one on which he looked with most tolerant contempt.

Abbot continues by asserting that for three weeks he conducted the editorial page of the *Journal* without a single scrap of instructions from Hearst or any other editor. (Shades of Joseph Pulitzer and his rigorous training of Frank Cobb!) Abbot adds, however, that about 1910 Hearst took up the writing of editorials himself in earnest, and in good style, and thereafter held the page in slightly higher esteem. In Abbot's judgment, except for Hearst's own occasional contributions, the average Hearst editorial page in 1930 showed "no progress in quality or character from what it was in the 1890s."

W. A. Swanberg on William Randolph Hearst:

The external Hearst was a fraud, unintentional and therefore all the more deceiving. His inferiority complex manifested itself only in his outward manner. Inwardly he was Caesar, Charlemagne and Napoleon combined. He was the most megalomaniac of men, supremely sure of his own greatness. Megalomania, which is merely ridiculous in persons of small abilities, can be either dangerous or beneficient in a man of Hearst's superior, though uneven, endowments. Ever since college, he had read intensively about Napoleon, Caesar, Washington and other immortals. A painting of Napoleon hung over his desk. He owned busts or likenesses of Lincoln, Jefferson, Franklin and others of similar dimensions. He revered greatness and felt a kinship with the great. Behind his helpless disguise he thought and planned in large, lavish ways, uninhibited by the difficulties, obstacles and minor moral considerations that turned back normal men. This regal mode of thought was implemented by qualities of daring, determination, courage and ruthlessness that were hard to stop, particularly since they were backed by several millions of dollars.

W. A. Swanberg, in his Citizen Hearst, *Charles Scribner's Sons, 1961.*

Here then is the second major reason for Norman Thomas' instinctive distrust of Hearst. The editorial page lacked depth of intellectual appeal, and therefore to Thomas it lacked depth of sincerity and understanding. He was joined by many others in this judgment of Hearst the publisher in his early career. Hearst entertained, yes; he struck some high notes in popular appeal, yes; he performed some worthy services, yes; but in the end it all added up to a most disappointing performance.

Indeed, when one looks through the records of journalistic achievement, where does he find the name of Hearst, or of his newspapers? There are no high awards, no selections of Hearst papers on any lists of outstanding newspapers of the country; instead there are dead cats for the Hearst trophy shelf. There is no James Reston, no Bert Andrews, no James Pope coming to the front from Hearst papers. This is not to deny that there have been many competent newsmen among the thousands of Hearst staffers, but the high expression of leadership does not come from them.

It would not be right, however, to dismiss Hearst and his journalistic career as something to be buried and forgotten—nor could anyone do so if he wished. There is a final estimate to be agreed upon, whenever fresh studies of the man and his newspapers bring a better understanding of the complex "problem of Hearst." In the meantime, only tentative conclusions such as these can be advanced in the effort to interpret the impact of the Lord of San Simeon and to come to some judgments about him. (pp. 317-30)

> Edwin Emery, "William Randolph Hearst: A Tentative Appraisal," in Highlights in the History of the American Press: A Book of Readings, edited by Edwin H. Ford and Edwin Emery, University of Minnesota Press, 1954, pp. 317-30.

Charles Chaplin on William Randolph Hearst:

If I were asked what personality in my life has made the deepest impression on me, I would say the late William Randolph Hearst. I should explain that the impression was not always a pleasant one—although he had commendable qualities. It was the enigma of his personality that fascinated me, his boyishness, his shrewdness, his kindness, his ruthlessness, his immense power and wealth, and above all his genuine naturalness. In worldly values, he was the freest man I have ever known. His business empire was fabulous and diversified, consisting of hundreds of publications, large holdings in New York real estate, mining, and vast tracts of land in Mexico. His secretary told me that Hearst's enterprises were worth $400,000,000—a lot of money in those days.

There are conflicting opinions about Hearst. Some maintain that he was a sincere American patriot, others that he was an opportunist merely interested in the circulation of his newspapers and enlarging his fortune. But as a young man he was adventurous and liberal. Moreover, the parental exchequer was always at hand. The story goes that Russell Sage, the financier, met Hearst's mother, Phoebe Hearst, on Fifth Avenue. Said he: "If your son persists in attacking Wall Street his newspaper will lose a million dollars a year."

"At that rate, Mr. Sage, he can stay in business for another eighty years," said his mother.

> Charles Chaplin, in his My Autobiography, Simon and Schuster, 1964.

THE ROLE OF REPORTERS

Christopher P. Wilson

[*In the following excerpt, Wilson discusses the changing role of the newspaper reporter during the age of Yellow Journalism.*]

In the confident years of the Progressive era much of American writing would aspire to the ideal of *reportage*. In the 1870s and 1880s reporters like Julian Ralph, Jacob Riis, Richard Harding Davis, and Julius Chambers had launched American journalism on new urban and international exploits; then a younger generation—Vance Thompson, Lincoln Steffens, David Graham Phillips, Stephen Crane—gave reporting new intellectual credibility,

political status, even flamboyant celebrity. Gradually, American audiences adopted the reporter not only as a social and political pathfinder but indeed as a symbol of a burgeoning cultural aesthetic. The reporter became America's first public agent of exposure, the high priest of "experience," the expert on "real life"—all keywords emerging at the heart of American popular discourse. To the new way of thinking, reporters seemed less genteel than novelists or magazine writers: they were active participants in the city, knowledgeable about business and politics, deep in the muck of American life. Reporting was thus seen as the vital first step in a literary apprenticeship. In his early years, for instance, William Dean Howells had turned away from reporting, and he remained forever haunted by the experience of having witnessed a drunken woman raving in a police station where his "abhorred duties" had taken him. By 1916, however, Howells was calling journalism the "university of the streets and police stations, with its faculty of patrolmen and saloon keepers." It was, he now averred, the very "school of reality."

Within the trade, the reporter's new status was a direct byproduct of a gradual institutional transformation of metropolitan journalism after the Civil War. As newspapers shifted their loyalties from partisan affiliations and editorial opinion toward a professional attitude centering around a reputedly independent commercial function—"circulation," or the production and distribution of news (and advertising)—news gathering came to the fore. By now, the late nineteenth century's astounding advances in printing, distribution, advertising revenue, and format are commonplace items in textbook histories of American journalism. These were the days during which an individual press which cranked out hundreds of copies a day gave way to steam- and electric-powered presses capable of tens of thousands of (larger) papers per *hour,* when the grappling rivalries of individual circulations now multiplied by a factor of ten, when in the years in which the American population doubled (1870-1900) the number of papers tripled and aggregate national circulation jumped sixfold. Largely due to declining newsprint and telegraphic costs, these were also the years which sprouted evening editions galore, forty- and fifty-page Sunday extravaganzas, and which saw the introduction of color presses, photographs, and banner headlines. Marked by the adventurous careers of famous editors who prized investigative reporting— early on, James Gordon Bennett; later, Joseph Pulitzer and William Randolph Hearst—and their high-risk expenditures, large if inconsistent profits, and huge egos, metropolitan journalism was a dizzy and rapidly changing field. The reporter's new status was also reinforced by collective organizations like the American Newspaper Publisher's Association (founded in 1887) and the Associated Press (reorganized as a private consolidation in 1898), both of which seemed to augment the news emphasis of modern journalism at the expense of editorial writing. Today even our most revisionist histories tend to agree that the 1890s were the culmination of the "age of the reporter."

Within our textbook histories and in many a biography,

meanwhile, the reporter's new importance is usually credited to men like Pulitzer, Hearst, Melville Stone, and others—the presiding czars of American journalism during this pivotal modernizing phase. Even when technological and social factors are given their due, these figures remain as the patron saints of the modern reporter. In a banner headline appropriated from trade pronouncements to become the chestnut of the modern textbook, the late nineteenth century is often described as the era in which these editors and publishers freed the American reporter from the ills of "personal" and "partisan" journalism. Don Seitz, business manager of Pulitzer's *New York World* and active member of both the AP and ANPA, put the matter succinctly: Pulitzer was the "liberator" of journalism, severing it from bohemian and elitist pretensions and converting it to respectability and true democratic service. "In our earlier journalism of opinion and partisanship," Seitz wrote, "the reporter had but a small place," his role dwarfed by editors "imposing their views on the public mind." Thanks to Pulitzer and his followers, this older style had been replaced by a "powerful impersonality" of concrete facts and "organized intelligence" [Don Seitz, *Training for the Newspaper Trade,* 1916].

The new role of these editors is not to be denied. Yet it is important, nonetheless, that we begin to see them in another light: not just as editors but as modern news managers. As several historians have recently told us (Alfred Chandler, Jr., and Robert Wiebe in particular), the late nineteenth century witnessed an enormous revolution in the managerial and professional dimensions of an expanding and nationalizing economy. These were the years in which traditional individual or family partnerships in business commonly gave way to bureaucratic or "pyramid" structures, largely directed by middle managers and salaried professionals. The "visible hand" of managerial know-how, which stressed market anticipation and stability, replaced the traditional orientations of laissez-faire entrepreneurialism and craftsmanship. In these ways—with variations which must be acknowledged in the idiosyncratic realm of print—the re-making of the news marketplace only modeled itself on other industries. Likewise, metropolitan journalism only set a pattern to be repeated in other publishing fields in subsequent decades. Commonly, a new editor or publisher, characteristically an immigrant (like Pulitzer himself) or a regional "outsider" (like Hearst), trained outside the established gentry and literary circles of the Gilded Age, broke his way into the enterprise of words by introducing a new fascination for office rationalization, efficiency, and expertise—the values that became watchwords of the broader Progressive ethos after 1900. Although there were several successful individuals who straddled the older and newer persuasions, most were what historians commonly call "business progressives," and some even joined forces with the Progressive causes of the new century. The new editors, in short, were modernizers who inaugurated a newly professionalized vocation of reporting. The reporter's "rise," therefore, coincided with a broadly based restructuring of his social role, his work experience, even his literary habitat—in ways not always welcomed by audiences, or even by reporters themselves.

In fact, the reporter's rise towards public acceptance and professional status, a rise dependent upon an often-sensationalistic news orientation, succeeded only by overcoming considerable resistance from both within the trade and without. Reporters' search for the sensational news item, their growing disregard for privacy in favor of the public's right to know, and their exposure to crime all gradually became the hallmarks of their profession—and yet also the targets of their critics. The banner of Pulitzer's liberating army has only served to camouflage the contradictions emerging within the mass market itself. While there were signs of reporters' increasing social status—the appearance of by-lines, higher salaries, aggressive competition for their services, and seeming acceptance by public figures—reporters' daily routines were also enmeshed in the managerial and bureaucratic imperatives of the modern tabloid. The same forces that catapulted reporters to their public prominence also gave them quite a different "inside story." We might pause to consider that figures like Pulitzer *do* loom so large during a time in which the power of editors had supposedly been displaced. In actuality, many testimonials from the era indicate that editorial power had been transformed, not lost, and that the displacement of Gilded Age routines had actually cost reporters a good deal of diversified experience and autonomy. Even more fundamentally, it is not so clear that simple "facts" were their quarry at all, despite proclamations by men like Don Seitz. His metaphor "organized intelligence" was, in fact, rather ambiguous: as in the military, it hinted not at actual news campaigns but at advance scouting. As key figures in a public crusade for journalism's own acceptance, reporters were advanced to the front line. But rather than assaulting unobstructed "reality," they often became part of a system giving considerable ground to "invention."

That one could speak of "reporters" at all was a sign of changed times. Especially during the early national period, journalism had been conceived in more generalized and moralistic terms. Like the broader profession of authorship, of which it was part, journalism had been seen in traditionally republican terms—that is, as one version of a career as a "man of letters." Reflecting the initially wider and positive connotation of the term "literary," journalism was conceived by many as a vocation suitable for a man who desired to apply culture and book-learning to practical affairs. In the antebellum era, when editors first experimented with distancing themselves from party affiliations, journalism had been conceived as an agency of public cultivation comparable to schools, voluntary associations, or the church. In the post-Civil War decades, when journalists like E. L. Godkin and Charles Anderson Dana lengthened the distance of journalism from the often-scandalous politics of the Reconstruction years, journalism acquired an even more Arnoldian—and sometimes "Mugwumpish"—role. In the Progressive era, however, reporting remodeled the terms of this traditional vocation, chose specialization over a generalized literary role, and proclaimed itself a profession in its own right. The meaning of this transformation was especially visible in the era's sometimes-heated debate over the news gatherer's character, decorum, and education. As one observer put it, perhaps no other modern profession was so wept over.

In part this debate was the trade's response to external pressures, particularly to the recurrent charge of sensationalism. This charge, while as old as journalism itself, became especially intense in the Progressive era, taking on many forms. Even collective trade organization and partisan disaffiliation did not completely assure the new journalism's rise to public acceptance. In some eyes, business consolidation, coupled with the daily fare of sensationalistic news, only undercut the trade's claim to true professionalism. Critics often argued that newspapers were not truly "independent" because they had simply exchanged the dictates of personality and party for the prerogatives of irresponsible capital. For instance, when Dana of the *New York Sun* coined the term "yellow journalism" as a play upon Hearst's "yellow kid" comic strip and the compromised character of the new journalism, the phrase seemed to stick in the public mind. Meanwhile, on the legal front, men like Samuel Pennypacker (governor of Pennsylvania from 1903 to 1907), angered by the new invasions of privacy, sought stricter libel laws—a campaign which the ANPA opposed throughout the period. Predictably, conservative Americans tended to argue, rather continuously, that yellow journalism was simply a conscious ruse by irresponsible editors playing to what H. L. Mencken once called the "psychic tumescence" of the mob. A good deal of anger came from upper-class figures and intellectuals like William Morton Payne. Payne confidently cited a "consensus of intelligent and cultivated readers" who said that the only way to improve the press was to fund it through a public endowment. Within literary circles, notables like Arthur Reed Kimball and Julian Hawthorne—the latter having had a good deal of experience as a correspondent—drew much attention by writing that "high" literary ideals and journalistic practice were simply antithetical. Finally, clergyman Charles M. Sheldon, author of the best-selling *In His Steps,* chastised newspapers for their immorality, even calling the new genre of comic strips "unspeakable horrors . . . fit for nothing except a garbage pile and almost too bad to go in the crematory."

Some of these complaints were clearly irrelevant to the business of metropolitan reporting. But not all such attacks upon journalism were to be taken lightly; even Sheldon carried a certain amount of moral authority. More to the point, these anxieties pointed to the considerable obstacles reporters faced in doing their work and receiving recognition for it, especially among educated elites, the target of much newly popular society, political, and financial reporting. The slow acceptance by some public figures of the modern interview format, for example—gradually modified to reprint celebrities' actual words—was indicative. The policy received consensual acceptance among American presidents and Wall Street leaders only after 1900, a fact which testified to the reluctance of many Americans (and not all of them wealthy) to sacrifice a cherished right to privacy. Only when this reluctance was overcome—or, more accurately, when a new bargain was struck—could reporting develop into its modern form. Editors, moreover, had to think not only about audiences

and news sources but about potential recruits to the trade, who had to be convinced of the social legitimacy of the newspaper occupation. In sum, the new journalism's critics exposed the significance of the reporter to the larger battle engaging American journalism in this era: the campaign for public acceptance. It was not enough for the trade to shower the reporter with in-house recognition; to answer their critics, journalists were obliged to identify the character and integrity of the reporter with that of the trade itself. Trade leaders thus self-consciously formulated competing strategies for legitimizing the reporter's function: in so doing, their public debate reflected a developing change in the reporter's role which had serious consequences for journalism (and authorship) as a whole.

Well aware of the threat of commercial growth to journalism's image, trade luminaries like Dana, Godkin, Pulitzer, and Whitelaw Reid (of the *New York Tribune*) all participated in a broad debate over the "liberal arts" education of the journalist, his vocational training, his decorum on the job, and his future social role. In these frenetic times the pattern of advice was obviously mixed. But with some exceptions, the older and more conservative journalists, proud of their triumphant elevation of journalism from what Horace Greeley's generation had cherished as the "smell of ink," tended to emphasize a well-rounded man (the conceptions were always male) of gentlemanly de-

The Pulitzer Building, which at 309 feet was the tallest structure in New York City when it opened in December 1890.

meanor, "quiet and dignified in his behavior, considerate in his thoughts and ways"; he should also be essentially "literary" in orientation. According to Dana, the ideal journalist should be a devotee of the "wonderful resources" and "subtleties" of language, commonly a man of wit, a reader of the Bible, Shakespeare, Milton, Dr. Channing, and Nathaniel Hawthorne who could seize upon "human interest" in a literary way. Once in possession of this liberal arts tradition, he would be trained as an apprentice within the office, and learn that "all this culture" could be "brought into action." On the other side, the newer breed of editors—Hearst, Pulitzer, and others—tended to ridicule anything that smacked of elitism or "collegiate" affectation, favoring instead an unpretentious man of encyclopedic range capable of transposing active sleuthing into plain prose for a mass audience. This more modern conception was promoted in full polemical regalia by the *Journalist,* a professional publication founded in 1884. Long a supporter of the ANPA, *Journalist* editor Allan Forman praised the disappearance of "bohemians" whose slipshod work, fabled inebriety, and literary pretensions were being replaced, Forman said, by loyal, reliable, and efficient family men who saw journalism as a career. Rival editors, in other words, put forward a professional ideal but often divided over what they meant by "professional." Republican values argued for the virtues of a "cultured" man: the journalist's ability to write flexibly, edit a submitted manuscript, render his observations and opinions—something in the manner of an educated observer, or perhaps satirist. Those in Pulitzer's or Hearst's camp, on the other hand, stressed those traits which augmented, primarily, the collection and reporting of news: the ability to find a fact, acquire a new angle aggressively, and communicate to the reader the essential core of information.

The debate over the education of the reporter achieved a new form after 1900. The new breed pressed onward in favor of professional education, an idea endorsed by Pulitzer himself in 1904. But here again, the real differences about the *new* professionalism were pronounced. At first glance, it appeared that Pulitzer, like his Gilded Age counterparts, offered "professionalism" to offset the pressures of the profit motive. While many more eager mass-market advocates wanted to begin training candidates in the practical side of the trade—that is, in circulation, advertising, manufacture, and finance—Pulitzer actually argued for excluding such items from the reporter's training. It seemed, in other words, as if he dismissed commercial concerns in favor of a professional ideal of public service. Answering his critics in the *North American Review* in May of 1904 (still smarting from the backlash of 1898, no doubt), Pulitzer said he wanted "to begin a movement that [would] raise journalism to the rank of a learned profession." He said that the chief difficulty of newspapermaking was "to keep the news instinct from running rampant over the restraints of accuracy and conscience." But Pulitzer's professional ideal was, upon closer examination, inescapably editorial and managerial in design, and seemed only to contribute to a more intensified office life. He described the making of a newspaper, for instance, as a daily "battle for excellence," a military campaign in which the editor either defeated or was vanquished by his rivals. This, in fact, was where he thought professional education

would do the most good. The faster pace of modern news production, he lamented, had meant that newspaper offices no longer had the time to teach the young reporter necessary skills and ideals. Pulitzer asked the reader to "sympathize with the unfortunate editor who has to work with such incompetent instruments." His goal, therefore, was clear: to ease the *editorial* burden by creating what he called a "class feeling" among young journalists, and thereby promote canons of behavior as internal restraints upon overzealous subordinates. Although Pulitzer, like his Gilded Age counterparts, ostensibly offered professionalism to counter the trade's commercial pressures which gave rise to so much abuse in the first place, in fact his model ended up by legitimizing those commercial pressures. Even more to the point, Pulitzer's ideal actually was a force for office rationalization—a cause that hardly shifted power in the reporter's direction. Pulitzer even said his goal was to "make the soul of the editor the soul of the paper." So much for the decline of personal journalism.

Even though it would be years before his Columbia plan was in place, Pulitzer's notion of professional training betrayed a subtle equation of "education" and social control so prevalent in the progressive logic already at work in the trade. His military metaphor also proved especially indicative of the new pressures the reporter was now facing. The gradual displacement of Forman's "bohemian," or Dana's man of culture in action—so like the denigration of the "literary" in the plans of other mass-market wizards—articulated a new, hopeful professional faith. Yet as we move from this ideal portrait to its implication for practice—away from headline history to the nuts and bolts of reporters' routines—a rather different picture emerges.

The reporter's daily routine in the Progressive era, despite public proclamations about his new "independence," actually reflected tensions born of the modern specialization of labor that had accompanied the trade's expansion. Whereas in the 1840s a New York City newspaper *owner* might have researched, reported, written, and edited his own story, by the 1890s editorial functions alone were often divided among the (sometimes absent) owner; an editor-in-chief; one or more managing editors; a business, circulation, or advertising manager; a telegraphic editor; editorial page writers; and a city editor who supervised the local staff—that is, until the night editor took over. Reporters, barely in evidence on a large scale until after the Civil War, by 1900 were divided among departments—sports writers, political writers, financial reporters, some labor reporters, lots of society reporters, drama reviewers, police reporters, routine men—and even, in some cases, among editions (morning, evening, Sunday, and so forth). As papers grew more dependent on telephone and telegraphic coverage, reporting subdivided even further into "leg men" and "rewrite men," identifiable positions on major newspaper staffs after 1890. Illustrators, photographers, foreign correspondents, literary contributors, cub writers and more—all joined up; staffs in some cases even numbered over the thousand mark. This was an "army" indeed, and it was mobilized in different ways. The office of Pulitzer's *World,* for instance, was plastered with signs exhorting workers to seek accuracy, exhibit courtesy, and include "color."

A clue to these strategies of mobilization is to be found, first of all, in the increasingly nostalgic reputation accorded papers like Dana's *New York Sun.* For reporters of Pulitzer's era, the *Sun* seemed to be a touchstone of the world they had left behind. Despite its reputation among certain sections of the reading public for cantankerousness and no small amount of "human interest" sensationalizing, the *Sun* developed a rather different image among journalism's foot soldiers. Specifically, the *Sun* offices emerged as a symbol of a paper which, in contrast to newer establishments, had cherished individual autonomy and undifferentiated roles. The *Sun* was widely acknowledged as having been the "newspaperman's newspaper." Part of the reason for this seemed to be that Dana's office had struck a momentary balance between the thirst for news and the older "literary" style. But even more to the point, the *Sun*'s excellence, as reporters often recalled it, lay in its willing disregard of the imperatives of specialization, intra- and extra-office rivalry, and the endless hustle that characterized more progressively managed newspapers. Willis J. Abbot, a journalist who came to Whitelaw Reid's *New York Tribune* in 1886, recalled that he often spent an hour each night, after work, studying the *Sun* for his own education in journalistic technique; later he paid tribute to Dana's reign as a "golden age" of camaraderie and bohemianism, where "the reporter wrote his own stories, the malign day of the telephone and rewrite not having arrived." Likewise Julian Ralph, probably the leading reporter of his day, wrote whimsically that the *Sun* was "frequently likened to a club-house. No taint of caste poisons its atmosphere or forces its workers into cliques, and when its men have no work to do they play together, at cards or chess or gymnastics or whatever." Edward P. Mitchell, Dana's chief editorial writer, felt that the dominant personal element of this office was what gave it cohesion and character, not the restrictive atmosphere a Pulitzer trainee might have sensed. Like Ralph, Mitchell found the office more a "patriarchal family, or a club of good friends—all life members—working together, than an organized force for business enterprise. . . . Dana's personality inspired the almost perfect *esprit de corps.*"

Of course, these writers were offering partly a romanticized portrait, a modern journalist's *gemeinschaft.* After all, the elite atmosphere these men described reflected a constituency which could countenance low pay; lifelong membership had its advantages, but it could also mean little room for advancement. Nor was the *Sun* without its own sensationalistic tendencies, though they paled next to those of the *World* or Hearst's *Journal.* But these figures' allusion to the world of the gentleman's club was nonetheless revealing. For one thing, it suggested that the profession's boundaries, under men like Dana, were permeable—the office part of a larger literary culture. Second, under men like Dana, the world of reporting was not quite so distinct from that of "play," or "leisure" in its largest sense. That is, like workers in other industries, these reporters felt nostalgic for an older, less rationalized mode of business organization. Using an analogy which proves telling in light of the "visible hand" overtaking American

capitalism in these years, Mitchell pinpointed how the traditional sense of office routine differed. "Mr. Dana's editorial doctrine," he wrote, "was most peculiar to himself: it was *laissez-faire* in the case of most assistants in whom he had confidence. He depended little upon advance instruction as to what should be written by others. . . . Except on unusual occasions, he preferred to leave the choice to the initiative of contributors." (Mitchell himself continued this policy—in resistance to new ownership—until World War I.) Similarly, Jacob Riis recalled how this policy allowed him a free hand even when his reform activities had taken him far afield from the opinions presented on the editorial page. Another writer reported in the *Journalist* that Dana was not above giving advice to writers, but that he had no regular editorial counsels, mainly giving his staff free scope. Another reporter pointed out that, unlike in the offices of Pulitzer and Hearst, no signs decorated the walls with editorial boosting or cheerleading. The leading editors at the *Sun,* furthermore, sat in the same room with reporters; messages were passed by office boys; in general, everyone kept to his desk. Franklin Matthews, a *Sun* reporter and editor for twenty years, characterized the office as quiet and deliberate, without "undue splutter" or excitement, generally complying with Dana's adage regarding the successful newspaper: "never do anything in a hurry."

However literally we take these nostalgic sentiments pervading the *Sun*'s reputation, in other words, they underscore the fact that the advent of the evening dailies, multiple editions, and headline rushes, all of which narrowed the distance between the news event and its deadline, intensified the pace of office work immensely, especially in more "progressive" papers. News, in direct proportion to the speed at which it could be transmitted, became more and more a perishable commodity which lost its value if it was not harvested, processed, and delivered in a matter of hours. Colonel A. K. McClure, editor of the *Philadelphia Times,* was another of those who looked back to his days with the rural press, when there was "no rush or jostle about newspaper establishments . . . to get out an edition." John Addison Porter, editor of the *Hartford Post,* lamented in 1894 that "there is no leisure in a newspaper office nowadays, whether it be the editorial, the mechanical, or the business department. . . . Push and enterprise and executive ability, and sometimes 'cheek' and 'cussedness' have taken the place in large measure of literary skill and book knowledge." At the end of the day, Porter added, an editor was liable to be a physical wreck. The modern editor, he said, rarely had time left for vacations or for affiliated vocations. "Leisure," in other words, had once created space for the implementation of the republican ideal; hence all this nostalgia.

In more energetic offices the tone was different—in fact, the lament of these older journalists only described a condition that was welcomed by their mass-market counterparts. The shift in value was expressed in the positive tone of Don Seitz, who wrote buoyantly that there was "no place in journalism for the leisurely, reflective writer, carefully cultivating style. Speed governs." The condition bemoaned by a man like A. K. McClure or Porter could even be elevated to the stature of romance, as in Melville Phillips's whiz-bang "Getting Out the Paper." Here Phillips described a typical day at the office, replete with reporters coming and going, telephones ringing, and telegraph boys rushing messages to a night editor, who "lived at fever heat" and who returned to his den "adrip with perspiration," obviously a Promethean hero.

Of course, like the nostalgic portraits of Dana—including those often tediously anecdotal memoirs—such heroic accounts of the new journalism are probably laced with ideological exaggeration. But once again, the new portraits reflected a very real understructure: a specialized, hierarchical organization that was clearly no longer laissez-faire. In contrast to the warm colors of the Dana mythology, for instance, the mass-market office members characteristically described *their* camaraderie as that of a happy and extravagant sort, a world inhabited by talented, energetic, and often erratic young men. Melville Stone reported that at his *Chicago Morning News* "the rule of the office was to 'keep on movin'.' We were never idle." For Stone, news came first, and sleuthing was everyone's calling. Likewise, frenzy was not only ever-present in the Hearst shops, it was encouraged. A common trade folktale depicted S. S. Chamberlain, a Hearst lieutenant, storming into a quiet office and crying, "Get excited everybody. Everybody get excited." Frank Munsey, more famous in magazines but also a well-known (and widely disliked) newspaper czar in this era, prohibited smoking in his editorial and composing rooms—not for reasons we might expect, but because it wasted time. He also tended to roust out workers in short-sleeve shirts, or those whom he felt were overweight.

Naturally, the new office pace was translated into a more active, aggressive conception of the reporter which, as Porter correctly surmised, envisioned "literary" leanings, and republican connotations, as something to be overcome. As the front-line soldier in a publicity-minded editorial policy, the new reporter's style was characterized by the aggressive interview, by the crusade, and by the stunt. As one San Franciscan sardonically recalled of Hearst's reporters, "*Examiner* men go up in balloons. . . . *Examiner* young men jump off ferryboats to test the crews. *Examiner* young men swim to save fishermen marooned on rocks." "I am inclined to believe," this citizen wrote, "that many of their exploits are performed more for the love of adventure than for the love of advertising." In words that would recur in the language of mass marketers in other fields, Hearst once boasted: "The *Journal,* as usual, ACTS while the representatives of ancient journalism sit idly by and wait for something to turn up." Personifying the paper's new policy, the reporter was no longer expected to receive passively the daily course of events: he was to take a direct hand in making news, and if need be, in transcending the normal channels of news with a stunt. This last strategy was widely regarded as an increasingly effective means of making the grade. (In other words, the reporter succeeded when his work was intrinsically promotional.) Furthermore, it was felt by some analysts that *continuity* of readership—itself an often-overlooked prerequisite to those ever-expanding circulation figures—could be assured by taking advantage of the follow-up to a news event. As is so often the case today, the reporter's investi-

gation became news itself—coverage became news. The stunt and the follow-up only exemplified another of Hearst's dictums: "if news is wanted it often has to be sent for."

Such editorial dictums are certainly worth our attention. And yet they often obscure the fact that the activity of the reporter was insured in large part not by editorial will as much as by a modern principle of office organization, the assignment system. This practice, as it grew gradually in the post-Civil War era, clearly cut back on the autonomy of the reporter. As was pointed out by John L. Given, who had risen from reporter to special writer on the *New York Evening Sun,* modern business organization had taken the element of chance out of reporting, eliminating men who strolled haphazardly about the streets or who stood "idle at a street corner waiting for something to happen." This was accomplished by a top-down hierarchical system in which reporters would be sent by the city editor to cover certain assignments. Once the assignment had been covered, the reporter would usually "report in" (or later, phone in) his story to a rewrite man and receive another assignment. Novice reporters—known as "cubs" or "kindergartners"—would often be assigned to "space" writing, within which their salary was adjusted in accordance with how much column space an editor decided to give their stories. Specialized department or "routine" reporters would cover specific areas, day in and day out. "More and more," Given reflected, "are the employees of daily newspapers coming to be looked upon as part of the machinery." Given's metaphor was often literally applied. Frank Munsey, for example, often grouped the editorial room under the category of "equipment" in his public statements—hoping, he said, to make a newspaper into "one great big modern engine." The image of the engine fit nicely into the idea that the quest for news was an organized military campaign. Pulitzer, when searching for an analogy to the "class feeling" he envisioned arising out of his professional school, chose the example of West Point. (pp. 17-29)

Ultimately, the difference between the era's banner headline and its daily pressures might best be shown by one final look at the case of perhaps the era's most romantic figure, Richard Harding Davis. For his contemporaries, as for many journalism historians, Davis always sparked the image of romance in reporting on the metropolitan beat and the international front alike. But it was worthwhile to understand that Davis, like others of his generation, adhered to the notion of a reporter as a gentleman whose individual style was the key to his success, and whose real aspiration was to be a writer of books. Davis's sympathies were no clearer than in a story he wrote about the Spanish-American War entitled "A Derelict." Here Davis contrasted a heroic, old-style reporter—who was recurrently late to work, drank a fair amount, and was a bohemian—with a modern writer for what Davis called the "Consolidated Press." Though the latter has every resource at his command, his constant role as the "industrious collector of facts" at the expense of what "was dramatic, pathetic, or outrageous" has left him callous and indifferent, and a faker at that. Davis describes the new man's literary style by saying it was as picturesque as a ticker tape, and yet "consequently, he was dear to the heart of the Consolidated Press . . . as a 'safe' man." Davis's older hero, on the other hand, makes writing his act of heroism. The bohemian even goes so far as to give the younger man credit for the "beat" he has secured—as if to thumb his nose at the entire assignment system. Casual in the collection of data, heroic and serene in triumph, Davis's real hero seemed to be making a stand opposing, not exemplifying, the role called for by the rapid handling and packaging of the news. Given the choice, Davis apparently preferred not to be a loyal or "safe" man (pp. 32-3)

. . . . .

How a society defines "the real," and why writers feel compelled to write about it, of course, are very nearly imponderable historical questions. Yet we cannot overlook the strategic positioning of Progressive-era news reporting in not only providing a literary apprenticeship—that "school" Howells spoke of—but in charting out new terrain for literature as a whole. At one level, turn-of-the-century journalism was a major force in redefining the visible landscape of this nation, in pushing writers to explore these previously unseen areas and in testing the ability of older American values to explain those areas. Forecasting the new attractions of book and magazine work, journalism careers would continue to draw American literary apprentices for the relative surety of salary, the promise of adventure and public renown, and contact with social and political leaders. Writers thus flocked to reporting, compelled by a variety of cultural needs to explore and experiment with the American underside; reporting, in turn, set a tone for other writing. In subsequent years it became clear that metropolitan newspaper work, especially in New York, had become something of a cultural crucible, the principal medium within which the possibilities of the new mass market were first entertained. After 1900, in fact, a new chain of command would become visible: book publishers would keep their eye on events via the magazines, while magazine editors commonly would look to newspapers. Many a modern editor in books or magazines would apprentice in newspaper work, and typically would draft his staff from the offices of metropolitan papers. From the newspapers, the magazines would adopt modern methods of office organization, take on photographs, and copy subheads; some would consciously style themselves as monthly or weekly newspapers. A number of critics complained about a "tyranny of timeliness" which reflected the encroachment of the news ethic into different forms of American media; some would even argue that the entire culture had undergone a form of "journalization."

At the same time, it is also clear that the institutional imperatives thrusting journalists and other writers in this new direction provided an often perplexing context for a generation who looked to modern reporting for Don Seitz's "facts," for real "experience," and for contact with "real life." Occupationally, writers perhaps received more "real life" than they bargained for. But more important, those occupational pressures also had consequences for what reporters saw, how they reacted, what they wrote about. Rather than a sphere of philosophical or leisurely reflection, reporting had become a pressurized and unsta-

ble world; rather than an objective social laboratory, reporters now witnessed events in which their own presence and craft were implicated: events that were preplanned, promoted, or, in extreme cases, even fabricated. The endless pursuit of the stunt, for all its heroic potential, actually only pitted the reporter against any news ethic which might have called for sociological balance or even accuracy. Rather than approaching anything like a social average, the reporter's turf was preeminently antinormative: slums, Wall Street, police courts, White Houses. If an incident was commonplace—well, by definition, it was not news.

The new reporter's accommodation to the demands of professionalization will not be understood if, as in the complaints of his conservative critics, his compliance is portrayed as simply a moral failure. Reporters' adjustment was more complex. Not yet fully consolidated in the fashion foreseen by its chain-makers—Scripps, Hearst, Munsey—American newspapermaking remained an arena of tension and change, of idiosyncrasy and institutional imperatives. Yet the decidedly modern dilemma of the reporter cannot be overlooked, even given the variances of region, personality, and politics. In these years, reporters encountered the tensions of bureaucracy, the pressures of status and job security, the anxieties that came with being "radically institutionalized." The professional rhetoric of an "independent" journalism, despite its ideological power even today, actually obscured the pressures moving writers towards market needs. Journalism, in the mass tabloids, offered the ethos of work, yet it diminished the reporter's autonomy. It now offered journalism as a career, yet (even in deriding the bohemian) also cut the writer off from traditional literary networks and associations. Finally, it heralded the collection of "facts," and yet it immersed reporters in stunts and scenarios, and then often divided reporters among those who saw and those who wrote. This was a troubling backdrop for Howells's "school of reality." (pp. 38-9)

Christopher P. Wilson, "Metropolitan Newspapers and the Rise of the Reporter," in his The Labor of Words: Literary Professionalism in the Progressive Era, *The University of Georgia Press, 1985, pp. 17-39.*

Michael Schudson

[*Schudson is an American sociologist and educator. In the following excerpt, he analyzes journalists' conceptions of their jobs during the 1880s and 1890s, focusing on the tension between the obligation to report the facts and the desire to cultivate a lively writing style.*]

In December, 1896, William Randolph Hearst, a newcomer to New York journalism who had recently become owner and editor of the *New York Journal,* sent Richard Harding Davis and Frederic Remington to Havana to cover the conflict there between Spanish authorities and Cuban insurgents. Remington was a thirty-five-year-old artist whose drawings appeared frequently in newspapers and popular magazines. Davis, at thirty-two, was already a popular culture hero through his reporting, his fiction, and his stylish manner. Hearst offered him $3,000 for a month of reporting from Cuba; Davis counted as well on $600 from *Harper's* for an article on his travels, and he had promises that his dispatches would be collected with Remington's drawings and published in book form.

Like other reporters in Cuba, Davis and Remington were barred from the "war zone" by Spanish military authorities. News was hard to get. Rumors and minor incidents were generally the best the correspondents had to offer. This so discouraged Remington that he wired Hearst: "Everything is quiet. There is no trouble here. There will be no war. Wish to return." Hearst is supposed to have responded, "Please remain. You furnish the pictures and I'll furnish the war." Despite such encouragement, Remington left Cuba after a week.

Davis stayed in Cuba. On February 10, 1897, he wired a story to New York that Hearst splashed over the first and second pages on February 12. Davis described how Spanish police boarded an American ship bound for Key West to search three Cuban women passengers. The police claimed that the women were carrying messages to insurgent leaders in New York. The ship's captain protested, but the women were stripped in a search for the documents. The *Journal* paraded the story on page one under the headline: "Does Our Flag Protect Women? Indignities Practised By Spanish Officials on Board American Vessels. Richard Harding Davis describes Some Startling Phases of Cuban Situation. Refined Young Women Stripped and Searched by Brutal Spaniards While Under Our Flag on the Olivette." The story was accompanied on page two by a half-page drawing by Remington, imagining the scene from New York, showing one of the women naked and surrounded by Spanish officers going through her clothing.

It was good stuff for Hearst's purpose—building circulation. Nearly a million copies of the paper were sold. But the story was not quite true. The drawing, in particular, was not accurate. The leading paper in New York in 1897, Joseph Pulitzer's *New York World,* interviewed the Cuban women when they arrived in Tampa and discovered they had been searched by matrons, not by the Spanish officers. The *World,* whose leadership of New York journalism was threatened by the popular antics of Hearst, was delighted. It ran a front-page story headlined: " 'Tale of a Fair Exile.' Senorita Arango's Own Story of the Olivette 'Search Outrage.' A Statement to the World. She Loved Cuba for Whose Freedom All Her Brothers Are Now Fighting. Visited Them in Camp; Banished, She Denies Richard Harding Davis' Story That Men Saw Her Stripped and Searched. . . . "

The headline summarizes the story well. The important point was that Clemencia Arango denied being searched by Spanish officers. This popped the *Journal's* balloon of scandal and outrage. Richard Harding Davis considered the revelation a reflection on his integrity, and so he wrote to the *World* to defend himself. On February 17 the *World* featured on page two a story headlined, "Mr. Davis Explains." Davis argued that not he but Remington was responsible for any misrepresentations:

> I never wrote that she was searched by men . . . Mr. Frederic Remington, who was not present, and who drew an imaginary picture of the scene, is responsible for the idea that the search was conducted by men. Had I seen the picture before it appeared, I should never have allowed it to accompany my article . . .

Davis broke with Hearst over this incident and never again wrote for a Hearst paper.

This was an important moment in journalism, but its importance needs to be carefully defined. On the surface, it appears that the significance of the incident is that a reporter, proud of his professional standing and faithful to the norms of factual reporting, stood up to the evil influences of a circulation-building editor-publisher. Here, fidelity to facts is identified with reporters and threats to accuracy, with publishers, their eyes on the cash box. But this is not a fair picture of American journalism in the 1890s. For one thing, Hearst was the least scrupulous of all New York editors at the time, the most determined to build circulation, at any cost (and, indeed, he operated the *Journal* at huge losses for its first years). Other editors, even Pulitzer who vied with Hearst in the war for readership, were more concerned that their newspapers picture the world fairly.

If editors were not generally indifferent to accuracy in the news, neither were reporters generally devoted to it, and that included Richard Harding Davis. Davis wrote fiction as a kind of documentary journalism; his journalism was frequently a documentary fiction—the facts would be there, but their point was as often to entertain as to inform. Even in the incident in question, Davis cannot be absolved from blame for the misrepresentation. His report was ambiguous, as he admitted. He did not say that men searched the women, but he did not say that women had conducted the search. Given earlier reports in the *Journal* and other New York papers regarding Spanish mistreatment of Cuban women, it was possible, even likely, that any artist or headline writer would have made the interpretation the *Journal* made. True, Davis did feel an obligation to get the facts right and a willingness, at least in theory, to leave editorial judgment to the editors. He wrote in his report from Cuba on January 31, "I was taught in the days of 'old journalism' that reporters were meant to describe things they saw, and not to write editorials but to leave the drawing of conclusions to others. . . . " But in the story on the Olivette search, Davis clearly expressed his shock at the actions of the Spanish authorities and suggested that American intervention in Cuba would be justified. If Remington's drawing got the details of Davis' story wrong, it nonetheless caught the tone Davis expressed.

The incident, then, does not locate a devotion to facts in a particular echelon of the newspaper staff. It does not picture a typical editor. It does not feature a typical reporter. Nonetheless, it reveals one of the most important aspects of journalism in the 1890s: reporters were, for the first time, actors in the drama of the newspaper world. Davis felt himself independent of his employer, knew himself to have an authority with the reading public more valuable than his salary, and could with equanimity stand against his editor. Of course, Davis' fame was unusual, and it is

War correspondent Richard Harding Davis, 1890.

perhaps unique in the history of journalism that an editor and a reporter should play out their feud in the pages of a rival newspaper, but nothing could better indicate that this was, as one newspaperman [Irwin S. Cobb, in his *Exit Laughing*, 1941] remembered it, the "Age of the Reporter."

As news was more or less "invented" in the 1830s, the reporter was a social invention of the 1880s and 1890s. Early newspapers had been one-man bands: one man acted as printer, advertising agent, editor, and reporter. "Correspondents" for eighteenth-century and early nineteenth-century newspapers were generally travelers or friends of the editor in foreign ports who wrote letters back to their hometown newspapers. In the course of the nineteenth century, editors came to rely less on these informal sources of news and more on free-lance writers and hired reporters who wrote for pay. The penny papers were the first to employ reporters for local news. James Gordon Bennett pioneered . . . in making the "foreign correspondent" a paid staff member.

In the 1840s and 1850s, American journalism continued in the direction set by the penny papers. Political independence of newspapers, for instance, became a common feature of journalism. In 1847, the new *Boston Herald,* a

penny paper, had its morning edition edited by George Tyler, a Whig, and its afternoon edition managed by William Eaton, a Democrat. The arrangement did not last, but it is notable that the paper's proprietors could have supposed, as the *Herald's* historian wrote in 1878, that "a double-jointed paper like this ought to suit everybody" [Edwin A. Perry, *The "Boston Herald" and its History*]. When Lincoln broke from the policy of maintaining a semiofficial organ among the Washington newspapers, the traditional link between paper and party, at least on the national level, was conclusively broken.

If New York was the hub of journalistic enterprise in the 1830s, it was no less so by the time of the Civil War. By 1860, the *Tribune* and the *Herald* both had daily home delivery in Washington. In newspapers around the country the designation "From the HERALD" or "From the TRIBUNE" told all: everyone knew the reference was to the New York papers. The *Tribune,* the *Herald,* and the *Times,* a penny paper begun in 1851 by Henry J. Raymond, formerly managing editor at the *Tribune,* had grown from four pages to eight. Their competition for news continued, and they frequently emphasized the news-gathering process itself in headlines. The lead stories in one typical issue of the *Herald,* for instance, were headlined "News by Telegraph" and "Arrival of the Asia"; the former article included news from Washington, Albany, Buffalo, and elsewhere, while the latter included all the overseas news brought by the most recent steamer. A *New York Times* story which featured the texts of speeches by Victor Emmanuel and Count Cavour of Italy began: "The steamship *Fulton,* whose arrival off Cape Cod has been already announced, reached her dock at this port last evening."

In the *New York Herald* of the 1850s, one still can find several columns of advertising on page one—not every day, but not infrequently—and there sometimes was a serialized romance on the front page. Occasionally, there were "hoaxes"—stories of pure fiction presented as news—as there had been in the 1830s. Still, part of the delight of the hoax was its revelation as a literary invention. "Making news"—promoting or producing events one could then legitimately claim to report as news—was still unheard of. The most common and modest form of making news—interviewing a public figure—was a practice which did not make even its first tentative appearance in journalism until the 1860s. While the pursuit of news had grown more vigorous by the Civil War, the idea of news had not changed significantly since the first days of the penny press.

As for the Civil War itself, it is often taken to be a turning point in the history of the American press. It was not. It did not "turn" the direction of journalism; its impact was to intensify the direction in which journalism had been turning since the 1830s. As before, the leaders in this were the New York papers and, most of all, the *Herald.* Most striking was the sheer size of the news-gathering efforts of the leading papers. In the first years of the war, New York papers spent from $60,000 to $100,000 a year reporting the war, while papers in Boston, Philadelphia, and chief cities in the West spent between $10,000 and $30,000. In New York, only the *Herald* kept up its investment in news gathering throughout the conflict, although the *Times* and the *Tribune* maintained extensive reporting services, too. The number of reporters grew enormously; the *Herald* had more than forty correspondents covering the war at any one time. Newspaper circulation rose; extras appeared more often; newspapers printed more pages; and Bennett's Sunday *Herald,* published since the 1830s, found competition in the new Sunday papers published by the *Times* and the *Tribune.* Just days before the war began, the *Tribune* became the first paper to introduce "stereotyping," a process in which the paper is printed from curved stereotype plates cast from a mold taken from the original plates of type. This was a major step forward in printing technology; within four months the *Herald* and then the *Times* adopted stereotyping. The familiar pattern of the 1830s and 1840s was repeated: the penny papers set the pace of American journalism.

Journalism in the Civil War, then, was not so much different as bigger, more prominent, and, as people anxiously followed campaigns that involved their husbands and brothers and sons, more important to ordinary people. The war pushed the newspaper closer to the center of the national consciousness. Frederic Hudson, in his 1872 history of journalism [*Journalism in the United States*], paid tribute to the newspapers' coverage of the Civil War and the European wars of the next few years:

> No record of previous wars can surpass those of the years between 1861 and '71. Anterior to these events we spoke of Napier, Thiers, Gibbon, Bancroft. They were compilers from old documents. Now we speak of the TRIBUNE, TIMES, WORLD, HERALD. They have been eyewitnesses.

Indeed they were. But Hudson's language is good indication that, despite the courage of some Civil War reporters and the color of war correspondence, despite the temporary introduction of by-lines in 1863 (stipulated by General Joseph Hooker as a means of attributing responsibility and blame for the publication of material he found inaccurate or dangerous to the Army of the Potomac), and despite the great numbers of correspondents, the age of the reporter had not yet arrived. In the Spanish-American War, the names of Sylvester Scovel and Richard Harding Davis were as familiar as the names of the papers for which they wrote. This was not the case for correspondents in the Civil War.

It was only in the decades after the Civil War that reporting became a more highly esteemed and more highly rewarded occupation. The growing marketability of a college degree in journalism was an indicator of the reporter's new status. Horace Greeley, in the 1860s, would not hire a college graduate who did not show he could overcome the "handicap" of a college education. But times were already changing when Julius Chambers sought a job on the *Tribune* around 1870. Chambers told Greeley that he had just graduated from Cornell. Greeley replied, "I'd a damned sight rather you had graduated at a printer's case!" But Chambers got his *Tribune* job anyway by talking to managing editor Whitelaw Reid, who hired him when he discovered that they were both members of the same college fraternity. Charles Dana favored college

graduates on the *New York Sun* in the 1880s, and Lincoln Steffens, in his brief stint as editor of the *Commercial Advertiser* at the turn of the century, hired college graduates almost exclusively. *The Journalist,* a trade publication for journalism begun in 1883, declared in an editorial in 1900, "Today the college bred men are the rule." With more gentlemen and fewer Bohemians in the profession, *The Journalist* observed, newspaper writing improved, and the ethics and status of newspapermen rose.

Stereotypes of the old-time reporter and the new reporter quickly developed and pervade memoirs of editors and reporters, just as they do the pages of *The Journalist.* The "old reporter," according to the standard mythology, was a hack who wrote for his paycheck and no more. He was uneducated and proud of his ignorance; he was regularly drunk and proud of his alcoholism. Journalism, to him, was just a job. The "new reporter" was younger, more naïve, more energetic and ambitious, college-educated, and usually sober. He was passionately attached to his job and to the novels he felt his experience as a reporter would prepare him to write. David Graham Phillips exemplified the new spirit in saying, "I would rather be a reporter than President." [quoted by Isaac F. Marcosson in *David Graham Phillips and His Times,* 1932]

The reporter's rising status was marked and promoted by steadily rising income in the 1880s and 1890s. At the same time, reporting was becoming a more steady sort of employment. *The Journalist* repeatedly urged that newspapers give up the habit of relying on free-lance reporters who were paid "on space"—according to the number of column-inches their stories occupied in the paper. By 1898 *The Journalist* noted that not only did each of the large New York newspapers have at least ten college graduates on their staffs, but that the reporter working "on space," rather than on salary, was practically extinct.

Reporters in the 1880s and 1890s received popular acclaim. The popular appeal of Nelly Bly going around the world in eighty days, Henry Morton Stanley finding Livingstone in Africa, or the war correspondence of Richard Harding Davis added greatly to the esprit that attracted young men and more and more young women to the world of journalism and kept them there happily. Reporters were as eager to mythologize their work as the public was to read of their adventures. The Whitechapel Club in Chicago, founded in 1889 and named after the London site of some of the crimes of Jack the Ripper, was a gathering place for reporters. The club was decorated with mementos of crime—murder weapons, human skulls, and a coffin-shaped table; the reporters glamorized their familiarity with the rawness of city life while also creating the atmosphere of a college fraternity. But the Club had an important practical function, too, for reporters criticized one another's work there. Reporters became as sensitive to the reception of their stories at the Club as to the judgments of their city editors. In New York, the nightly gatherings of the newspaper fraternity for drink and talk at "Doc" Perry's Park Row pharmacy provided a similar forum for mutual criticism and collegiality. Formally organized press clubs had begun with the New York Press Club in 1873. In the 1880s, clubs were organized in Chicago, Minneapolis, Milwaukee, Boston, St. Paul, and San Francisco. In Washington, a socially exclusive Washington Correspondents' Club was organized in 1867, but most journalists shared a social and professional life simply because, in the late 1860s and 1870s, they almost all took offices in "Newspaper Row" on Fourteenth Street, between Pennsylvania and F Streets. Another exclusive club—the Gridiron Club—was established in 1885; the National Capital Press Club began in 1891 but folded within a few years on the bad credit of its members. The National Press Club we know today dates from 1908.

Whether the collegiality of journalism was formally organized or not, reporting in the 1880s and 1890s became a self-conscious and increasingly esteemed occupation in American cities. By 1890 E. L. Godkin could confidently write that news gathering had become "a new and important calling." There were even guides for aspiring young men and women on how to become a reporter; reporting was less strictly a job one drifted into, more and more a career one chose.

Reporters came to share a common world of work; they also shared common ideas about how to conduct their work. Competing with one another for circulation, newspapers tried to satisfy public standards of truth, public ideals of decency, and public taste in entertainment. That meant, on the one hand, that newspapers had to be lively, colorful, and entertaining. It meant, on the other hand, that they had to be factual. Reporters believed strongly that it was their job both to get the facts and to be colorful. In their allegiance to facts, reporters of the late nineteenth century breathed the same air that conditioned the rise of the expert in politics, the development of scientific management in industry, the triumph of realism in literature, and the "revolt against formalism" in philosophy, the social sciences, history, and law. But in their desire to tell stories, reporters were less interested in facts than in creating personally distinctive and popular styles of writing. This seems—and sometimes seemed to the reporters—to run counter to the zeal for facts. But they experienced the contradiction as conflict with their editors, not as ideological disharmony. It would be a mistake to read contemporary views of objectivity into the fact-mindedness of the 1890s. Objectivity is an ideology of the distrust of the self, something Richard Harding Davis and his colleagues did not feel. The Progressives' belief in facts was different from a modern conviction of objectivity; just what it was we shall now examine.

Reporters in the 1890s saw themselves, in part, as scientists uncovering the economic and political facts of industrial life more boldly, more clearly, and more "realistically" than anyone had done before. This was part of the broader Progressive drive to found political reform on "facts." At the turn of the century, state and federal labor bureaus began to gather better information on economic and social issues, as did private agencies like the Charity Organization Society of New York in its tenement house investigation of 1900. In the first decade of the twentieth century, systematic social investigation practically became a craze; it was a favorite project of the new Russell Sage Foundation, which sponsored social surveys in Pitts-

burgh, St. Paul, Scranton, Topeka, Ithaca, Atlanta, and Springfield, Illinois. There was a "public demand for facts," writes historian Robert Bremner, intentionally echoing the recollections of reporter and writer Ray Stannard Baker: "Facts, facts piled up to the point of dry certitude, was what the American people really wanted."

Many of the journalists of the 1890s and after were either trained in a scientific discipline or shared in the popular admiration for science. Ray Stannard Baker took special interest in his science courses at Michigan Agricultural College; Lincoln Steffens did graduate work in Wilhelm Wundt's world-famous psychological laboratory. The appeal of Herbert Spencer was strong among reporters, as it was among other educated Americans. Baker studied and imbibed Spencer's views on economy in literary style under Fred Newton Scott at Michigan Agricultural College; Theodore Dreiser read Spencer, as well as Darwin, Tyndall, and Huxley. Jack London, who, like Dreiser, began his literary career as a reporter, was influenced by Spencer. Abraham Cahan, a reporter who founded the *Jewish Daily Forward* in New York in 1897 and served as its editor for half a century, read Spencer avidly, especially his writings on art.

Whether reporters thought of themselves as scientists or as artists, they believed always that they should be realistic. Their ideal of literature, as of reporting, stressed factuality. Abraham Cahan championed realism in art in an essay printed in 1889; he argued that "the power of realistic art arises from the pleasure we derive from recognizing the truth as it is mirrored by art." Clarence Darrow, himself the author of one novel, expressed the dominant view of the time in an essay on realism in *The Arena* in 1893: "The world has grown tired of preachers and sermons; today it asks for facts. It has grown tired of fairies and angels, and asks for flesh and blood." The dean of American letters in the 1880s and 1890s, William Dean Howells, argued that a philosophy of art should be based on the laws of natural science; his own work, according to Everett Carter, was "dominated by the positivistic concern with the objective observation, analysis, and classification of human life." Reporters who turned to fiction followed him in this. Most of the turn-of-the-century writers whose novels we still read, wrote in a self-consciously realistic vein growing out of their experience as newspaper reporters—Theodore Dreiser, Jack London, Stephen Crane, Frank Norris, and Willa Cather, for instance. Other writers of fiction, enormously popular at the time, began as newspapermen—Richard Harding Davis, Lafcadio Hearn, David Graham Phillips, Ray Stannard Baker, Joel Chandler Harris, Harold Frederic, Ambrose Bierce, and George Ade. Ade, a Chicago reporter, wrote, in both his journalism and his fiction, a blend of sentiment and realistic detail which he generally subordinated to humor and to what Larzer Ziff terms "false geniality." Still, Ade shared in the literary ideology of his times and spoke for many others when he wrote that his ambition was to be known as a "realist" and a man with "the courage to observe human virtues and frailties as they showed on the lens."

The word "observe" was all-important to the reporters and realistic novelists of the 1890s; George Becker aptly notes that romantics praised a writer's powers of invention, while realists praised powers of observation. And Ade's word "lens," too, is well-chosen: it conveys the realists' sense that the newspaper story, the magazine article, and the novel could be, and should be, photographically true to life. What is important, however, is not that realists believed art to have a mimetic function—there was nothing new in that, and the term "realism," in the 1890s, was more a boast and an advertisement than a descriptive label. What is important is that realists identified "reality" with external phenomena which, they believed, were subject to laws of physical causality as natural science revealed them and as social science might reveal them. This *was* new. The world was disenchanted as never before, and the realists, embracing disenchantment to distinguish themselves from their literary fathers, were delighted.

Why this realism developed as and when it did is not easy to say. William Dean Howells wrote that nothing caused realism: it just "came" and it seemed "to have come everywhere at once." We can at least say a few things about what did not cause it. Autonomous developments in the arts did not cause it. Frank Norris followed the growth of a theory of realism in France, but most American realists were without knowledge of French intellectual life and came to their realism on their own. Nor did "the pervasive materialism of industrial capitalism," contrary to Alfred Kazin cause it. Writers in ante-bellum America also responded to what they experienced as "pervasive materialism," but they did so in a style called "romantic."

Nor was realism simply the inevitable consequence of the growing popularity of science. "Science" had long been a magical word in America. For instance, lawyers on both sides of the codification controversy in the 1830s defended themselves in terms of a "science of the law." There was, however, an important difference between the conservative tradition of "science" as the personal acquirement of learnedness and the idea of science invoked by middle-class reformers favoring codification of the law. The codifiers took science to be a body of knowledge necessarily clear, written, and public; in the law this meant that they favored legal rules legislatively enacted rather than judicially interpreted. They *externalized* the idea of science, making what conservative thinkers took to be a subtle and mysterious faculty of mind into an institution of democratic political life. This notion of science as only that body of knowledge constructed by the public and available to public view was especially congenial to a democratic market society. The idea of science as a process of data collecting open to all expressed a democratic epistemology and helped make the collecting and classifying activities of botany, zoology, and geology the models of natural science in Jacksonian America. By the late nineteenth century, under the influence of Darwin and Spencer, the meaning of science to the popular mind shifted. Evolutionary theory had become the model of science; it emphasized not just the collection, but the historical connections, of facts. Still more important, it included human beings as objects about which facts could be gathered and studied. The human mind externalized or objectified the human body, and, as psychologists and other social scientists worked

out the implications of Darwinian theory, human beings objectified themselves.

This changing concept of what science is, rather than simply the growing popularity of science, contributed to the rise of realism. But this begs a question: while science surely has some internal logic, it is also clearly shaped by social circumstances. What social circumstances promoted a fact-gathering and fact-connecting science which took human society as its subject?

My inclination is to argue that this idea of a science of human society would not have gained support without the advance of a market economy, the ideal and institutions of political democracy, and the emergence of an urban habitat. Such is the general theme of this study. But can it be stretched to cover the phenomenon I am now describing? The problem is not a simple one. Any explanation of the idea of science in the late nineteenth century as an expression of the culture of a democratic market society must handle the following puzzle. In the early nineteenth century, science was the darling of democrats, the open book of progress which anyone could write in and anyone could read. Empirical inquiry was a weapon of the middle class against the received wisdom of an established order. By the end of the nineteenth century, however, science was becoming an established institution in its own right, connected to the universities and professional associations and standing *against* popular democracy both in principle ("reason" and expert judgment versus the mob) and in actual class antagonism (the educated middle class against immigrants and workers). Science, at one time consonant with the culture of a democratic market society, seems, in retrospect, to have opposed it as the society matured.

While I feel tentative about this statement and uncertain about its implications, I believe that this general sociological approach to understanding the idea of science is sound. The history of science is not an autonomous intellectual history. It is, instead, a history of the interaction of a way of seeing the world, a set of ideas and institutions which promote the way of seeing, and the social conditions conducive or constraining to the way of seeing. In many areas of American life in the nineteenth century, people were ready to accept empirical sciences before science as an institution, or a set of workable ideas, appeared. Religion and religious explanations were not destroyed by science; they were in decline already. For instance, Charles Rosenberg shows, in his study of the American response to the cholera epidemics of 1832, 1849, and 1866, that by 1866 Americans, including religious leaders, were much more likely than they had been to think of cholera as a medical, rather than a moral, problem, even though the identification of the cholera vibrio was nearly two decades in the future. But by 1866 there was an "unashamed empiricism, not only in medical writings, but in sermons and editorials as well." A democratic age wanted a democratic vision, and empirical inquiry, not religion, fit most comfortably.

In journalism from the 1830s on, there was a growing emphasis on getting the facts. Still, in journalism, as in other fields, the idea of an empirical inquiry concerning human society did not triumph all at once. It is important to ask, in the case of journalism, not only why the journalists' belief in facts was so strong by the end of the nineteenth century, but why it was no stronger.

Reporters of the 1890s who later wrote memoirs recall, with grudging fondness, their first city editors. Julius Chambers, who served as managing editor of the *New York Herald* and the *New York World,* remembered his own apprenticeship in the 1870s under the *New York Tribune's* W. F. G. Shanks. Shanks forced Chambers to acquire "a form of composition very difficult to overcome in after years—a style accurately described by John Hay, then a paragraph writer on the *Tribune,* as 'The Grocer's Bill.' " That meant, Chambers recalled:

> Facts; facts; nothing but facts. So many peas at so much a peck; so much molasses at so much a quart. The index of forbidden words was very lengthy, and misuse of them, when they escaped the keen eye of a copy reader and got into print, was punishable by suspension without pay for a week, or immediate discharge. It was a rigid system, rigidly enforced.

Lincoln Steffens made a similar complaint about the training he received on E. L. Godkin's *Evening Post:*

> Reporters were to report the news as it happened, like machines, without prejudice, color, and without style; all alike. Humor or any sign of personality in our reports was caught, rebuked, and, in time, suppressed. As a writer, I was permanently hurt by my years on the *Post.*

Joseph Appel, later to be John Wanamaker's advertising manager and a pioneer in "journalizing" advertising copy, got his first job with Colonel McClure's *Philadelphia Times* in the 1890s. As he recalled, his first meeting with McClure was not auspicious. McClure waved a newspaper column at Appel and asked, "Young man, young man, did you write this?" Appel replied that he had. McClure then said: "Well, I want you to know and I don't want you ever to forget it, that when the *Times* expresses an editorial opinion I will express it and not you—go back to your work."

Young reporters were impressionable, and these sorts of encounters must have influenced them. Theodore Dreiser remembered Maxwell of the *Chicago Globe,* his editor when he first entered journalism in 1892. Maxwell told him that the first paragraph of a news story had to inform the reader of "who, what, how, when, and where." Maxwell noted, for emphasis, that there was a sign in the office of the *Chicago Tribune* which read "WHO OR WHAT? HOW? WHEN? WHERE?" When Dreiser would bring in a story, Maxwell would go at it with a blue pencil, advising as he went: "News is information. People want it quick, sharp, clear—do you hear?"

Dreiser was not surprised, then, when he moved to New York and walked into the city room of the *New York World:*

> I looked about the great room, as I waited patiently and delightedly, and saw pasted on the walls at intervals printed cards which read: Accuracy, Accuracy, Accuracy! Who? What? Where? When? How? The Facts—The Color—

The Facts! I knew what those signs meant: the proper order for beginning a newspaper story. Another sign insisted upon Promptness, Courtesy, Geniality! Most excellent traits, I thought, but not as easy to put into execution as comfortable publishers and managing editors might suppose.

The *World's* exhortation to accuracy took it for granted that there was no contradiction between "the facts" and "the color"—the good reporter should be alert to both. Edwin L. Shuman, in his handbook for aspiring journalists, *Steps into Journalism* (1894), wrote that a reporter with sparkle would be forgiven inaccuracy, just as a reliable reporter would be forgiven "a moderate degree of dullness" in style, but that the combination of "reliability and sparkle" was the recipe for professional success. This was the spirit of the times and it is remarkable how far even texts for journalists would go in promoting color, as well as facts. Shuman advocated the reporter's using his imagination to create images he had not witnessed and had no direct testimony about. This is, he wrote, "perhaps excusable as long as the imaginative writing is confined to non-essentials and is done by one who has in him at least the desire to represent the truth." Shuman cautioned that even this mild form of fakery is dangerous, but he acknowledged that it was practiced by all newspapers. Indeed, he went further:

> In spite of the fact that editors come to grief once in a while by its use, this trick of drawing upon the imagination for the non-essential parts of an article is certainly one of the most valuable secrets of the profession at its present stage of development. Truth in essentials, imagination in non-essentials, is considered a legitimate rule of action in every office. The paramount object is to make an interesting story.

If facts could not be championed to the exclusion of imaginative embellishment, neither could they be supported wholeheartedly to the exclusion of opinion. Here, of course, as is evident in the advice of editors to their young reporters, there was in principle a more rigid distinction: news and opinion should be kept apart. But even this distinction was not absolute. Shuman advised his readers:

> Opinions are the peculiar province of the editorial writer. The spirit of modern journalism demands that the news and the editorials be kept distinctly separate. The one deals with facts, the other with theoretical interpretations, and it is as harmful to mix the two in journalism as it is to combine church and state in government. *This, at least, is the only safe theory for the beginner.*

The last line is significant. It suggests that the separation of facts from opinion was more a principle of tutelage than an absolute ideal in journalism. Indeed, as Shuman would point out in a later edition of his book, it was customary for Washington and foreign correspondents to blend fact and opinion at will.

This, too, is a theme in the memoirs of reporters: that the rules one learned as a beginner one had to unlearn to stand out as a journalist. H. L. Mencken, as a young reporter in

Baltimore in the 1890s, found himself confronted, like Dreiser in New York at the same time, with the demands of editors for accuracy. He recalled later that there was "immense stress upon accuracy" at the *Baltimore Sun.* The *Sun* "fostered a sober, matter-of-fact style in its men." The *Herald,* where Mencken began in 1899, was looser. Mencken preferred it to the *Sun* where, he felt, reporters "were hobbled by their paper's craze for mathematical accuracy. . . . " The best *Sun* reporters overcame their paper's policies, "but the rank and file tended to write like bookkeepers." Much as Mencken tries in his recollections to distinguish his own early newspaper experience from that of the rival *Sun,* this must be weighed against his account of the advice the *Herald's* managing editor gave him in his first days as a staff member: never trust a copy; verify reports whenever possible; try to get copy in early; be careful about dates, names, ages, addresses, and figures; keep in mind the dangers of libel; and do not be discouraged by the *Sun's* monopoly on news.

What was true on newspapers was true for magazines as well. *McClure's,* founded in 1894 by Sam McClure, was the first of the new mass-circulation magazines which, as one contemporary regretfully observed, "journalized" magazine literature. While *McClure's* was designed to entertain, to be interesting, the editor and his staff "evinced an unusual preoccupation with facts and possessed a desire to let events and documents speak for themselves." McClure welcomed comparison of the magazine story to the news article of daily journalism: "I wish to go over the Pittsburgh article very carefully before it is published," he wrote to David Graham Phillips regarding an essay by Steffens. "I think that the article to begin with should be free from bias, just the same as a news article or newspaper. . . . " Facts and more facts: "If Turner has any defect in writing it is a defect that almost all writers lean towards," McClure wrote Willa Cather, "that is a certain distaste towards documentation."

These accounts suggest that reporters may have developed their attachment to facts despite themselves, forced into it by the organizational pressures of daily journalism. Young reporters came to the big-city dailies to make their reputations, to launch their literary careers. They had every reason to want to be colorful and enterprising, every reason to resent the dull discipline their editors tried to impose. The city editors, for their part, had to look in two directions: toward grooming reporters to get the news and write it with accuracy and verve; and toward satisfying the editor-publisher, which meant, at a minimum, keeping the paper free of the easily identifiable errors and excesses that would lead to libel, embarrassment, or public criticism for the newspaper. The city editor might well seek color in a news story, but he was likely to require factuality first of all. Besides, if he could hold reporters in conformity with rules and procedures he imposed, he could break them of some of their arrogance, make his own work easier, and make his own mark on the newspaper.

The conflict between editors and reporters is evident again in the recollections of Jacob Riis, a police reporter for the *New York Tribune* in the 1880s, who culled from his experience one of the important reform documents of the era,

How the Other Half Lives (1890). In his autobiography, Riis tried to explain how he took up photography as a tool for reporting. He confessed that he was not a good photographer, though he wanted to be. What kept him from his goal? According to Riis, it was his delight in the miracle, rather than in the technique, of photography:

> I do not want my butterfly stuck on a pin and put in a glass case. I want to see the sunlight on its wings as it flits from flower to flower, and I don't care a rap what its Latin name may be. Anyway, it is not its name. The sun and the flower and the butterfly know that. The man who sticks a pin in it does not, and never will, for he knows not its language. Only the poet does among men. So, you see, I am disqualified from being a photographer.

In his search for poetry, Riis felt the eyes of science derisively upon him. This is even more clear in his comments on his writing style. He complains that his editors told him his style was "altogether editorial and presuming, and not to be borne." They told him to give facts, not comments, to which he responded:

> By that I suppose they meant that I must write, not what I thought, but what they probably might think of the news. But, good or bad, I could write in no other way, and kept right on. Not that I think, by any manner of means, that it was the best way, but it was mine. And goodness knows I had no desire to be an editor. I have not now. I prefer to be a reporter and deal with the facts to being an editor and lying about them.

There may be some contradiction here in Riis' defending his mixture of facts and comments by appealing to his insistence on "dealing with facts"; it is interesting that his explanation of his own style is so defensive. He relies most of all on claiming his style as a fault of his own nature which he cannot change. Still, there are other passages in the autobiography where he offers a more positive account of the business of reporting as he practiced it. He took pride in reporting what he called the "great human drama." The reporter behind the scenes, he wrote, "sees the tumult of passions, and not rarely a human heroism that redeems all the rest. It is his task so to portray it that we can all see its meaning, or at all events catch the human drift of it, not merely the foulness and the reek of blood." He continued:

> If he can do that, he has performed a signal service, and his murder story may easily come to speak more eloquently to the minds of thousands than the sermon preached to a hundred in the church on Sunday.

In this passage, Riis distinguishes his teaching from the minister's, but the very idea of comparing his work to the preacher's and the religious language he uses ("a human heroism that redeems . . . ") contrasts sharply with reporters' usual borrowings from the language of science. Not surprisingly, other reporters were sometimes critical of Riis. Steffens criticized him for refusing to believe, or even to hear, some of the awful things going on in the world. Riis did not have the "scientific" interest in reporting Steffens boasted of himself; he cared, in Steffens' words, only for "the stories of people and the conditions in which they lived." Steffens recalled how Riis reacted when his assistant, Max Fischel, told him of a police raid on a party of homosexuals:

> "Fairies!" Riis shouted, suspicious. "What are fairies?" And when Max began to define the word Riis rose up in a rage. "Not so," he cried. "There are no such creatures in this world." He threw down his pencil and rushed out of the office. He would not report that raid, and Max had to telephone enough to his paper to protect his chief.

Steffens derided Riis' moralism, but he admired the personal style Riis cultivated. He must have, for that is exactly what he sought in his reporters when, in 1897, he became an editor himself, of the *Commercial Advertiser.* He recalled in his autobiography that he was inspired as an editor by little besides a love of New York. He inherited the politics of the paper from his apprenticeship on the *Evening Post;* he was self-conscious about literary ideals, not politics. He was determined to avoid the old "professional newspapermen" in creating a staff:

> I wanted fresh, young, enthusiastic writers who would see and make others see the life of the city. This meant individual styles, and old newspaper men wrote in the style of their paper, the *Sun* men in the *Sun* style, *Post* men in the Godkin manner.

So Steffens hired young graduates of Harvard, Yale, Princeton, and Columbia, men of literary ambition more hopeful of being writers than reporters. Steffens remembered himself as ruthlessly stressing freshness and individuality in his reporters. As soon as two staff members wrote alike, he would fire one of them.

While there are differences among all these recollections, there are strong similarities, too, almost more than seems reasonable. This may indicate that the occupational world of the big-city newspaper reporters was, indeed, a common one; it may also suggest, however, that the common experience was that of recalling and dramatizing one's past. Not all autobiography is as hearty and uncritical as the reminiscences of journalists; theirs seem to continue in the relatively unreflective, uncomplicated, and untragic sense of life they expressed as reporters. And their autobiographies, like their newspaper articles, seem to aim for an entertaining, lively tone without sacrificing a necessary factuality. The resulting contributions to the collective self-portrait of journalism standardize a mythic pattern. The myth centers on the struggle between a young eager reporter and a wizened, cynical editor. The reporter, a deracinated stranger in the big city, who has chosen not to follow in his father's footsteps, creates a father of the man whose footsteps he does follow. Then the myth is played out between editor and reporter as between father and son: the son dares to express himself and the father punishes; the son conforms to the father's demands and the father comes to trust him; the son rebels to express himself again, with more maturity this time, and triumphs over the father; the father grows old or dies, becomes a memory, and the son forgives, acknowledging that he had, after all, taken his father's admonitions to heart.

Steffens, Chambers, Mencken, Dreiser, Appel, and Riis all recalled the directives of their first editors for factual, impersonal reporting. Most of them remembered this emphasis on facts with some resentment, even though they claimed, after their own fashion, to be scrupulously faithful to reality. At the same time, they were happy to have incorporated into their own outlooks some of their editors' world-weary cynicism. They wanted their reports of the world to be lively, they wanted to speak in personal tones to a world growing impersonal about them, but they believed they could do that without interpretation, with complete mirrorlike accuracy. They had only contempt for the critical, and generally moralistic, efforts of editorial writers. In part, this was a contempt for the person who does not dirty his hands. The ideal of the Chicago journalist in the 1890s, as Hugh Dalziel Duncan puts it, was to dramatize the news, not as an impartial observer, but as "a participant who spits on his hands, rolls up his sleeves, and jumps into the fight." Thus, while turn-of-the-century reporters were unattuned to the ways in which their own values shaped their perception of "the facts," they were eager to accept the position that wishes should submit to facts, soft dreams to hard realities, moralism to practical politics, and religion to common sense. Dreiser was probably typical in being attracted to reporting by what he called its "pagan or unmoral character," which he contrasted to the "religionistic and moralistic point of view" of the editorial offices:

> While the editorial office might be preparing the most flowery moralistic or religionistic editorials regarding the worth of man, the value of progress, character, religion, morality, the sanctity of the home, charity and the like, the business office and news rooms were concerned with no such fine theories. The business office was all business, with little or no thought of anything save success, and in the city news room the mask was off and life was handled in a rough-and-ready manner, without gloves and in a catch-as-catch-can fashion. Pretense did not go here. Innate honesty on the part of any one was not probable. Charity was a business with something in it for somebody. Morality was in the main for public consumption only. "Get the news! Get the news!"—that was the great cry in the city editorial room. "Don't worry much over how you get it, but get it, and don't come back without it! Don't fall down! Don't let the other newspapers skin us—that is, if you value your job! And write—and write well. If any other paper writes it better than you do you're beaten and might as well resign." The public must be entertained by the writing of reporters.

Reporters were united in opposing moralism, sham, and hypocrisy. They thought little of clergymen, political orators, reform efforts to close saloons and brothels, and editorial writers. The city editors, with whom they were in constant contention, they felt kin to. Dreiser wrote admiringly that city editors were nearly all distrustful of conventional principles and "misdoubted the motives, professed or secret, of nearly every man." Reporters felt a close emotional bond to their hard-driving editors and, as well, to the tough and gritty men—both police and criminals—

they got to know on the police detail. They felt close, too, as Lincoln Steffens made clear in his autobiography, to the cynical and shrewd businessmen and politicians they interviewed and exposed. They struck a pose and saluted an ethic in which nonbelief was their pride. Dreiser summed up this posture of negatives: "One can always talk to a newspaper man, I think, with the full confidence that one is talking to a man who is at least free of moralistic mush."

And yet, the reporters themselves were full of a mush much the same. Richard Harding Davis was angry when the veracity of his report on the Olivette search was questioned in a *World* editorial. His letter to the *World* stressed the accuracy of his own report and the guilt of his friend Remington for the fabricated drawing. He then added, hoping to fully absolve himself from blame:

> My only object in writing the article was to try and show the people in the United States how little protection they may expect on one of their own vessels, under their own flag, in the harbor of Havana, where there should have been an American man-of-war stationed for the last six months.

For a contemporary journalist to make such a confession, and still contend that he or she had been scrupulously faithful to the facts, would be inconceivable; it would be a contradiction in terms. It was not so to Davis. The antagonism of journalists in the Progressive era to moralism may have been more a matter of style than of substance. McClure, for instance, told his writers to concentrate on telling an absorbing story, and the story, he believed, should have a moral—but the moral element was to be present "unconsciously." This was not difficult for writers of the Progressive era to accept, for they understood facts to provide moral direction of themselves and prided themselves that their own moral precepts grew naturally out of their association with the real world. They did not feel the moral declarations of the editorial writers to be subjective but to be dreamy; their own, of course, they took to be as irrefutable as the facts they uncovered. That assurance, already in question in some fields, would not last much longer, even in journalism. (pp. 61-87)

> *Michael Schudson, "Telling Stories: Journalism as a Vocation after 1880," in his* Discovering the News: A Social History of American Newspapers, *Basic Books, Inc., Publishers, 1978, pp. 61-87.*

THE SPANISH-AMERICAN WAR

Frank Luther Mott

[*Mott was an American historian, journalist, and educator whose four-volume* History of American Magazines *(1930-57) was awarded the Pulitzer Prize in history. In the following excerpt from his history of newspapers, he chronicles the jingoistic tendencies of American papers before and during the Spanish-American War.*]

Two phases of the history of American journalism are out-

standing in the period defined by the years 1892 and 1914. They are, first, the pyrotechnical outburst of yellow journalism, and second, the attainment by the leading papers of very large circulations, capitalizations, and profits. These two phenomena are by no means identical, yet they are curiously interrelated. We shall consider first the rise of yellow journalism. (p. 519)

The "ifs" of history are usually more amusing than profitable, but there seems to be great probability in the frequently reiterated statement that if Hearst had not challenged Pulitzer to a circulation contest at the time of the Cuban insurrection, there would have been no Spanish-American War. Certainly the most powerful and persistent jingo propaganda ever carried on by newspapers was led by the New York *Journal* and *World* in 1896-98, and the result was an irresistible popular fervor for war which at length overcame the long unwillingness of President McKinley and even swept blindly over the last-minute capitulation by Spain on all the points at issue.

This war passion was whipped up by news stories, headlines, pictures, and editorials in the yellow press. The news materials used in this great pre-war campaign were: Spanish atrocities in Cuba, Spanish actions against American citizens involved in the Cuban war for independence, the campaign for the recognition of the belligerence of the Cuban insurgents, incidents produced by newspaper intervention, the *Maine* disaster, and American preparations for war.

Although for nearly seventy-five years American newspa-

Front page of the New York Journal, *17 February 1898.*

pers had taken occasional notice of Cuban struggles against the Spanish rulers, it was not until General Valeriano Weyler was appointed Captain-General of the Spanish forces in Cuba early in 1896 that atrocity stories became prominent in American papers. At this time four New York papers—the *World, Journal, Herald,* and *Sun*—had correspondents in Cuba. Weyler was nicknamed "the Butcher," and sensational descriptions were sent home of the sufferings of the Cubans in the concentration camps into which all of them—men, women, and children—had been forced. Lurid pictures of mutilation of mothers and killing of babes, of the execution of suspects, of imprisonment in filthy and fever-charged stockades, were drawn both in words and by the pencils of artists. Doubtless many of the incidents reported were not witnessed by the correspondents, and too much reliance was placed on the exaggerated tales of the Cubans; there were cases then and later of correspondents who wrote "eye-witness" stories when they had approached no nearer to the scene than Key West.

"Butcher" Weyler attempted to deal with the American correspondents in his own way. One free-lance reporter was executed. Sylvester Scovel, of the *World,* was imprisoned by the Spanish, and released only after his paper had aroused the sympathy of the whole country in his behalf. The *Journal* made a similar case of the arrest of Ona Melton, a correspondent who had accompanied one of the many American filibustering expeditions which were complicating the situation, and secured his release through the intervention of the State Department.

Cuban atrocity stories proved to be good circulation pullers, and inevitably competition in this kind of matter developed between the *World* and the *Journal.* The *World*'s corps of correspondents in the island was at first superior to that of its rival, but early in 1897 Hearst bought a yacht, the *Vamoose,* and sent it to Cuba with Richard Harding Davis, famous as a writer of fiction and travel articles, and Frederic Remington, equally famous as an illustrator, to investigate conditions in the unhappy island and send back feature stories. Remington did not like the assignment, and the following interchange of cablegrams is said to have taken place:

> HEARST, JOURNAL, NEW YORK:
> EVERYTHING IS QUIET. THERE IS NO TROUBLE HERE. THERE WILL BE NO WAR. WISH TO RETURN. REMINGTON.
>
> REMINGTON, HAVANA:
> PLEASE REMAIN. YOU FURNISH THE PICTURES AND I'LL FURNISH THE WAR. HEARST.

Whether or not Hearst ever expressed himself in precisely these terms, the fact is that he pushed on vigorously with his war-making propaganda. The Davis-Remington articles put him out ahead, and he pressed the advantage. The Dr. Ruiz case, in which a naturalized American died in a Spanish prison, soon offered one opportunity; but a far greater sensation was developed a few months later on the basis that a paper should make as well as record news.

Evangelina Cisneros, niece of the president of the insurrectionist government, had loyally accompanied her fa-

ther to his prison home when he was banished to the Isle of Pines for sedition. There she was accused of having lured Colonel Berriz, military governor of the island, to her home, where hidden partisans leaped out and attempted to assassinate him. She was brought back to Havana for trial. It was then that Hearst, reading a short dispatch telling of the incident, realized the immense propaganda value of the situation and decided to build it up. The girl's story—that Berriz had attempted to assault her, and that fellow exiles, drawn by her cries for help, had beaten the brute—lent itself to the perfect propaganda story. "Miss Cisneros," said the *Journal,* "is, according to all who have seen her, the most beautiful girl in the island of Cuba. . . . She was reared in seclusion and, almost a child in years, is as ignorant of the world as a cloistered nun." Berriz was a "lecherous and foiled scoundrel." "This tenderly nurtured girl was imprisoned at 18 among the most depraved Negresses of Havana, and now she is to be sent in mockery to spend 20 years in a penal servitude that will kill her in a year." "The unspeakable fate to which Weyler has doomed an innocent girl whose only crime is that she has defended her honor against a beast in uniform has sent a shudder of horror through the American people."

The shudder was unmistakable. The *Journal* sent telegrams to prominent American women urging them to send appeals to the Pope and to the Queen Regent of Spain in the girl's behalf. Many of them responded. The *Journal* "played" the story all over its front page for weeks, but it was too big to be limited to one paper; others took it up, the Associated Press carried it, and the whole country was deeply stirred. Then Hearst played his ace. He sent Karl Decker, a resourceful correspondent, to Havana to rescue Miss Cisneros from her prison. Renting a house next the prison, Decker pulled off the iron bars from her windows, helped her out, dressed her in boy's clothes, and smuggled her out of Havana. In New York Hearst arranged a gigantic popular reception in Union Square for the pretty and rather dazed girl, and later took her to Washington to shake hands with President McKinley. The whole Hearst-built incident was a tremendous success, and did more to make the nation emotionally conscious of the Cuban struggle than anything else before the sinking of the *Maine.*

Another *Journal* beat was the printing of the stolen De Lome letter. The Spanish minister to Washington had written an incautious message to a friend in Havana in which he called the President of the United States a "low politician," and it had been somehow intercepted. The *Journal* predicted war as a result of this incident, though in trying to lash the reluctant McKinley into a belligerent attitude it had itself employed epithets quite as unkind as De Lome's.

The United States battleship *Maine* was blown up in Havana harbor on the night of February 15, 1898, by an agency which has never been ascertained. Next day came an answering explosion of black headings, display, and a diagram picture on the first page of the *Journal.* Hearst offered $50,000 for exclusive information which would "convict the person or persons who sank the *Maine.*" But the *Journal* needed no such information; its banner line read: "DESTRUCTION OF THE WAR SHIP MAINE WAS THE WORK OF AN ENEMY." It was soon claiming that the Spanish were guilty of the crime, regardless of the investigations of the regular court of inquiry. Immediately after the disaster, it began to set up a committee to raise funds for the building of a monument to the *Maine* victims. Famous men accepted membership, but ex-President Cleveland wrote: "I decline to allow my sorrow for those who died on the *Maine* to be perverted to an advertising scheme for the New York *Journal.*" Hearst also arranged for and financed a congressional commission which went to Cuba to investigate conditions. He printed an interview with Theodore Roosevelt, Secretary of the Navy, who was well known to be war-minded, congratulating the *Journal* on its attitude; but Roosevelt replied, "I never in public or private commended the New York *Journal.*" This rebuff the *World* printed on its first page, taking the occasion to describe its rival's war news as "written by fools for fools."

Nevertheless the *World* was not far behind the *Journal* in warmongering. Pulitzer, whose own military experience had given him a distaste for war, and who had strongly rebuked Cleveland's warlike attitude in the Venezuelan dispute, is said to have admitted that he liked the idea of a small war which might react on newspaper circulations. After the sinking of the *Maine,* the *World* hired a tug and engaged divers in order to investigate the wreck, but was refused permission to do so. It was soon claiming "discoveries," however, to show that the ship was sunk by a Spanish mine. The *World,* like the *Journal,* was trying its utmost to fan the flames of war. Both papers gave much space to stories of the war frenzy sweeping the country, discussed war resources and strategy, and urged the President and Congress not to delay.

The circulations of both papers again passed the million mark with the news of the destruction of the *Maine.* Only a war could now keep them on the upward curve. Of this dark chapter in our journalism, Godkin, *censor morum* of the press, wrote in the *Evening Post* a few days after the *Maine* disaster:

> Nothing so disgraceful as the behavior of two of these newspapers [the *Journal* and the *World*] this week has been known in the history of American journalism. Gross misrepresentation of the facts, deliberate invention of tales calculated to excite the public, and wanton recklessness in the construction of headlines which even outdid these inventions, have combined to make the issues of the most widely circulated newspapers firebrands scattered broadcast throughout the country. . . . It is a crying shame that men should work such mischief simply in order to sell more papers.

Journalistic jingoism was not limited to these two papers, however. The Chicago *Tribune,* which bought the New York *World*'s Cuban service in 1896, and later the *Journal*'s service also, was not far behind the leaders. The Chicago *Times-Herald* and the Boston *Herald* used the New York *Herald*'s Cuban service; and, though neither was consistently jingoistic editorially, they did their part in

stirring up war sentiment. Hearst's San Francisco *Examiner,* enjoying the *Journal* service, stimulated the warmongering of its rival, the San Francisco *Chronicle,* which took both the *Herald* and *Sun* reports. Certain southern papers at times had their own special services: the New Orleans *Times-Democrat* (which, with the rival *Item,* was jingoistic), the Atlanta *Constitution,* and the Charleston *News and Courier.* Other papers fell in line.

But on the other hand there were many papers which not only refused to join in the atrocity hunting but evidenced a sympathy with Spain in her attempts to pacify the island, condemned the sensational jingoism of the yellow press, and supported President McKinley in his efforts to avoid intervention. Such were the New York *Evening Post* and *Journal of Commerce* and the Boston *Transcript.* The New York *Tribune* and *Mail and Express,* strongly Republican, stood staunchly by McKinley. The *Times* and the Chicago *Daily News* were temperately pro-Cuban; the latter sent correspondents to the island in 1897, one of whom was killed by a Spanish bullet while with the insurrectionist forces.

The *Evening Post* was not the only paper which attacked "the hot gospellers of sensational jingoism," as the *Tribune* called the *Journal* and the *World.* Said the *Tribune* sarcastically a few weeks after the destruction of the *Maine:*

> Up to this point the war has been a glorious success, as will be seen by the billboard announcements of the increased circulation of the newspapers which have carried it on. If, as now seems probable, its ravages can be confined to Printing House Square, and Spain is "licked" right here with blood-red extras without resorting to shot and shell, it will be the greatest triumph ever achieved by large type and a liberty-loving press.

The Associated Press was also condemned [in the *Chicago Inter Ocean* 14 February 1898] for its warlike stories, and especially those released for Sunday papers:

> 'Tis then Field Marshall Melville Stone
>   Rides in his martial car,
> And makes, with genius all his own,
>   Our Sunday morning war.

The War with Spain was, as wars go, almost ideal for newspaper treatment. It was near at hand. American commanders allowed unusual freedom to correspondents. It was a small war, and thus not too difficult to cover. American arms on land and sea met with a series of successes which could be reported brilliantly. It was a short war, so that the public interest could be fully maintained until its end. Probably no greater army of correspondents had ever been mobilized for any war than that which covered the activities of the blockading fleet, gathered at the Florida camps, followed Shafter into Cuba, sent the news from Spain, and sailed with Dewey to Manila. Some observers estimated there were as many as 500 such writers, photographers, and artists, representing scores of newspapers and magazines. And that is more than were employed in reporting the four years' Civil War.

Some of these men were famous writers, such as Stephen

Crane, Richard Harding Davis, Frank Norris, John Fox, Stephen Bonsal, and Julian Hawthorne. Others were famous artists, as R. F. Zogbaum, Frederic Remington, W. A. Rogers, and John T. McCutcheon. But most of them were men recruited from all departments of the newspaper, who knew nothing whatever of military affairs. The drama editor of the *Evening Sun,* the humor editor of the *World,* and the owner of the *Journal* were among them. Some, however, were seasoned war reporters: Creelman, Davis, Scovel, Edward Marshall, Murat Halstead, and others.

In a charge at Las Guasimas, Edward Marshall, of the *Journal,* received two bullet wounds. Stephen Crane and others carried him miles to a field hospital, where he was told that he could not live. He insisted, however, on writing his dispatch; and late that night Dr. William S. Gorgas, later surgeon-general of the United States army, operated on him, amputating one leg. He lived to write novels and plays, and edit the Sunday supplement of the New York *Herald.* He seemed to bear a charmed life: after the Spanish War, he survived three train wrecks and two hotel fires, and was taken off a foundering lake steamer. He was aboard the British Sussex when it was sunk by a German torpedo in 1916; unable to swim, he clung to wreckage until he was rescued. He died in his bed at sixty-four.

Stephen Crane, of the *World,* though he displayed a courage near to recklessness when under fire, suffered from exhaustion and fever most of the time he was in Cuba. Picturesque though his signed articles were, he was far from a satisfactory correspondent.

Richard Harding Davis, on the other hand, was an excellent war reporter. Employed now by the New York *Herald,* the London *Times,* and *Scribner's Magazine,* he was resourceful enough always to be in the right place at the right time. He led a charge in the fighting at Las Guasimas and won the praise of Colonel Roosevelt.

James Creelman, of the New York *Journal,* led an attack on a small fort at El Caney. The place was taken, and Creelman seized the Spanish flag as a trophy for his paper, but he was struck by a Mauser bullet which smashed his arm and tore a hole in his back. He was carried, half delirious, to the rear. He later wrote [in *On the Great Highway,* 1901]:

> Some one knelt in the grass beside me and put his hand on my fevered head. Opening my eyes, I saw Mr. Hearst, the proprietor of the New York *Journal,* a straw hat with a bright ribbon on his head, a revolver at his belt, and a pencil and notebook in his hand. The man who had provoked the war had come to see the result with his own eyes, and, finding one of his correspondents prostrate, was doing the work himself. Slowly he took down my story of the fight. Again and again the tinging of Mauser bullets interrupted, but he seemed unmoved. The battle had to be reported somehow.
>
> "I'm sorry you're hurt, but"—and his face was radiant with enthusiasm—"wasn't it a splendid fight? We must beat every paper in the world!"

Hearst had asked for authority at the beginning of the war to organize and equip a regiment. McKinley had refused that offer, but had accepted the use of the Hearst yacht *Buccaneer* during the war. Commodore of a small fleet of purchased and hired steamers and tugs, Hearst himself led a force of twenty writers, artists, and photographers to the scene of the war. One of these was a pioneer motion-picture photographer. On board the flagship was a small printing plant, from which soon issued an edition of the *Journal* at Siboney, Cuba. When Admiral Cervera's fleet was attacked and destroyed by American battleships, Hearst's flagship edged in so close that a shot was fired across her bow to warn her out of the way. After the action, Hearst's correspondents, seeing a group of Spanish sailors huddled together on the beach, determined to capture them. A steam launch was lowered and run in to the shore. Hearst took off his trousers and leaped into the surf, brandishing a revolver. His party had no difficulty in forcing the twenty-six refugees to surrender; and a little later Hearst, properly clothed, ordered signals displayed, "We have prisoners for the fleet," and his yacht steamed proudly down the line of American battleships and delivered the bedraggled Spaniards to Admiral Schley amid the cheers of the bluejackets. It was a great moment, duly recorded the next day in the New York *Journal.* But however theatrical Hearst's personal record as a war correspondent may sound, he at least proved that he was vitally interested in reporting the conflict, even at personal risk.

The Associated Press, whose men were under the direction of Colonel Charles S. Diehl, obtained an advantage when it prevailed on President McKinley to issue permits which placed one of its men on each of the navy's flagships.

With Dewey's fleet when it sailed into Manila Bay were three reporters—Joseph L. Stickney, of the New York *Herald;* John T. McCutcheon, of the Chicago *Record;* and Edward W. Harden, of the New York *World.* Dewey had consented to take Stickney on the flagship, and later made him an aide so that he could view the battle of Manila Bay from the bridge. It was Harden, however, paying the "urgent" rate of $9.90 a word on his dispatch, who scored the beat on this biggest story of the war. Though the advantage of it was lost to the *World* because its circulation department was unprepared to handle a 4 a.m. extra to follow up the flash, the Chicago *Tribune* got the story through its *World* service in time for its final edition and scooped the town.

Few or no war correspondents really tried to preserve their proper status as noncombatants. They led charges and carried dispatches. Scovel was shown favors by American officers because of his work as a spy. The journalism which makes as well as records news must—occasionally, at least—do a brilliant bit in the actual fighting. General Blanco logically ruled that American correspondents should be treated as spies, and there were some narrow escapes from Spanish firing squads.

The leniency of the military censorship on the American side was extraordinary, and newspapers freely printed reports of the movements of the navy and army and such news and rumors of American plans as they could gather. Referring to the early months of the war, the *Journalist* observed: "We gave the Spaniards no use for spies, for our yellow journals became themselves the spies of Spain." In the early summer of 1898, however, Grant Squires, once a reporter on the New York *Tribune,* was appointed military censor at New York. He was only moderately effective, and soon earned the bitter dislike of most of the newspaper men. Military and naval officers occasionally attempted to curb the activities of correspondents at the scene of warfare, as when General Shafter banished all Hearst men from captured Santiago; but, on the whole, they were patient and coöperative.

Circulations of the *Journal* and *World* continued above a million copies a day during the mounting war fever after the sinking of the *Maine.* In the war weeks the *Journal* went to 1,500,000, and the *World* went almost as high. Even after the signing of the peace protocol in August, the circulations of these papers remained above the million mark for several months. Other papers gained in circulation, some more and some less.

Did this represent prosperity for the newspapers? Far from it. Few newspapers increased profits during the Spanish-American War, and many found their net incomes dwindling or disappearing. "Every newspaper of the first class has run far behind since the outbreak of the war," wrote Brisbane near its close. There were three reasons for this: advertising declined sharply, competition in extras was expensive (the *Journal* had issued as many as forty editions in one day), and the cost of war coverage was immense.

Immediately after the sinking of the *Maine,* the Havana cable was closed to reporters. This necessitated boats to carry dispatches to the Key West cable, and from this time on the chartering of steamships, sea-going yachts, tugs, and all such craft became a necessity for news coverage of the Cuban situation. The *Journal* at one time had no less than ten ships under charter at a cost of $1,500 a day. The Associated Press had five vessels in commission. The *World, Herald,* and *Sun* each had two to six ships in their respective fleets at one time or another during the war. And then the big newspapers each had form five to twenty-five correspondents covering the war news, and cable tolls were often very high. Single New York newspapers sometimes filed as much as 5,000 words in a day at the Key West cable office, which at the current rate of five cents a word made $250 per day for that item alone. Altogether, reporting the six months' war is said to have cost the New York *Journal* $3,000 a day, or more than half a million dollars; and while no other paper or news agency spent money so lavishly as that, the *Sun, Herald,* and A.P. each probably spent about a quarter of a million, and the *World* doubtless over that amount.

Hearst was not much concerned with money losses, so long as he "beat every paper in the world," and especially the *World* itself; but Pulitzer, his paper forced into the red for the first time since the beginning of its fight with the *Journal,* was inclined to cry quits. He lost his appetite for war and began to urge an early peace.

This was about the time of the famous "Reflipe W. Thenuz" incident. In the early months of the *Journal-World contest* Hearst had no A.P. franchise and had to take his news where he could get it. It was said that each day when the first edition of the *World* reached the *Journal* office, the staff would strike up the chorus:

> Sound the cymbals, beat the drum!
> The *World* is here, the news has come!

So the *World* men said then; but later, when the *Journal* was maintaining an expensive Cuban service, its editors began to suspect the *World* of stealing its news. Accordingly, the *Journal* planted the name "Colonel Reflipe W. Thenuz" as an artillery officer in a list of Spanish casualties at the bombardment of San Juan; and when the *World* published the name, the *Journal* pointed out that "Reflipe

---

William Randolph Hearst on the Spanish-American War:

Tonight, as I write, the ambulance trains are bringing in the wounded soldiers from the fierce battle around the little island village of Caney.

Siboney, the base of the army, is a hospital and nothing more. There is no saying when the slaughter will cease. The tents are crowded with wounded, and the hard-worked surgeons are busy with their mechanical work. There is an odor of anesthetics and the clatter of ambulances in the one narrow street.

Under the fierce firing of far-heavier artillery forces than it was supposed the Spaniards had, the American infantry and dismounted cavalry have done their work, and done it nobly.

I have been at the artillery positions all day to see what our guns could or could not do. There is no question of skill or courage of American gunners. Their work was as near perfect as gunnery gets to be, but there was no artillery to speak of.

The War Department has furnished the necessary heavy guns, but they remain in the rear because of the difficulty of transportation from the coast.

I set out before daybreak this morning on horseback with Honore Laine, who is a colonel in the Cuban Army, and has served for months as the *Journal*'s correspondent in Cuba. We rode over eight miles of difficult country which intervenes between the army based on the coast and the fighting line which is being driven forward toward Santiago. . . .

With a rush they swept up the slope, and the stone fort was ours.

Then you should have heard the yell that went up from the knoll on which our battery stood. Gunners, drivers, Cubans, correspondents, swung their hats and gave a mighty cheer. Immediately our battery stopped firing for fear we would hurt our own men, and dashing down into the valley hurried across to take up a position near the infantry, who were now firing on Caney from its new position before the musketry firing ceased and the Spaniards, broken into small bunches, fled from Caney in the direction of Santiago. . . .

William Randolph Hearst, acting as war correspondent in his own New York Journal, *4 July 1898.*

W." was "We pilfer" spelled backwards, and "Thenuz" was phonetic spelling of "the news." The *World* retaliated by planting in one of its dispatches the name "Lister A. Raah," and then revealing, after the *Journal* had lifted the name, that it was an anagram for "Hearst a liar." (pp. 527-38)

> *Frank Luther Mott, "Yellow Journalism and the War with Spain," in his* American Journalism: A History of Newspapers in the United States through 250 Years, 1690 to 1940, *The Macmillan Company, 1941, pp. 519-45.*

Charles H. Brown

[*Brown is an American historian, journalist, and educator. In the following excerpt, he focuses on three Spanish-American War correspondents: Ralph D. Paine, Stephen Crane, and Richard Harding Davis.*]

The last two months of 1896 marked a gathering of the forces for reportorial onslaughts on Spain. After Bradley T. Johnson left Cuba, the New York *Journal* was represented in Havana for a time by C. B. Pendleton, editor of the *Equator-Democrat* of Key West. He was arrested when he boarded a steamer to send dispatches to Florida. The charge was that his passport was not in order. But his employment had been just a stopgap. Hearst, to improve his news coverage, hired Creelman away from the *World* as his Madrid correspondent, and gave a young Philadelphia *Press* reporter, Ralph D. Paine, an assignment to go to Cuba, find Gómez, and give him in behalf of the *Journal* a jeweled sword. Charles Michelson on the *Vamoose* was in Florida waters ready for any daring reportorial enterprise. But Hearst's major effort was his employment of a reporter and an artist, two of the country's best-known, as a team to join the insurgents—Richard Harding Davis and Frederic Remington. The *Herald* was also planning expanded coverage. George Bronson Rea, who had spent the first nine months of the year in the interior with Generals Gómez and Maceo, was planning to return; Ernest W. McCready, a young and high-spirited reporter, was in Florida covering filibustering activities; and one of the period's best-known foreign correspondents, Stephen Bonsal, was to go to Cuba as a special commissioner to report on conditions. The *World's* Sylvester Scovel and *Harper's Weekly's* Thomas R. Dawley, Jr., were also planning to return to the island to join the insurgents. Victor Lawson, owner of the Chicago *Record* and *Daily News,* decided in December, on his return from a meeting of the Associated Press board of directors in New York, to set up his own organization at Havana and Key West to get the news of the insurrection. Other publishers were also thinking about establishing their own coverage.

In addition, adventuresome reporters were flocking to Florida, with and without assignments from newspapers, hoping to get to Cuba to join insurgents in the field. They thought the most feasible way was to land secretly on the coast from a filibuster boat, along with Cubans from the United States headed for the interior. The alternative was to go by passenger steamer to Havana and pass through Spanish military lines to the interior. This had major handicaps for many who wanted to be war correspondents. Unfamiliar with the countryside and unable to speak Spanish, they were almost sure to be captured. Moreover, if they got by the Spanish soldiers, they might be shot as suspected spies or robbed of their well-made American boots and clothing by the barefoot and ragged troops of the marauding bands of rebels if unaccompanied by junta representatives.

Although joining a filibuster expedition had its advantages it also had its dangers. Ona Melton discovered this when he and crew members of the *Competitor* were captured. There was also danger of arrest by the American government, as Ralph D. Paine and Ernest W. McCready soon learned. Naval vessels and revenue cutters were alerted to stop boats with arms shipments for Cuba, and arrest and conviction for neutrality law violations might mean fine and imprisonment. Paine, indicted as a filibuster, had to hide as a fugitive from justice in Florida for weeks. At that he was lucky, for a boat on which he and McCready had sailed barely escaped being sunk by Spanish gunboats. And there was the danger faced by all men who go to sea, as Stephen Crane found when the filibuster boat *Commodore* sank in a storm off the coast of Florida.

The peril facing reporters in Cuba was illustrated in the death of Charles Govin, twenty-three-year-old correspondent for the Key West *Equator-Democrat.* He was killed three days after landing from the filibuster boat *Three Friends* on July 6, 1896. The *World* gave the first details on August 18 in a story about an indignation meeting over his death held in Key West. The report was that Govin was captured in company with some insurgents. While he was being conveyed to prison, the officer in charge learned he was an American. Govin's only credential, in this version, was a notarized statement declaring him the correspondent of the *Equator-Democrat.* The officer, in his hatred of Americans, had Govin bound and hacked to pieces with machetes. Govin's death received wide publicity, for he was a member of a prominent Florida family, his father, a lawyer, for many years having been collector of customs at Key West.

The New York *Journal* on September 14 printed additional details obtained by Grover Flint from a Major Julio Rodriguez Baz of the Cuban army. Baz said Govin, unarmed and carrying a U.S. passport, was captured during a skirmish in Havana province. The rebel band he had joined was surrounded by Spaniards, and an order was given for the members to scatter. Govin, left without a guide, rode into an open area and was quickly captured. The officer in charge scornfully threw his papers to the ground after glancing at them. The young reporter was then bound to a tree and macheted to death.

The adventures of Paine and McCready as filibusters took place at the close of 1896 and the beginning of 1897. Two years out of Yale University and employed on the Philadelphia *Press,* Paine was enthralled by the derring-do of the filibusters. "As a newspaper reporter, life had not lacked flavor or variety," he recalled in his autobiography, "but now it seemed flat and unprofitable. The thing was to get afloat in one of those notorious steamers whose voyages had an air of mystery, whose departures and escapades were clouded in a baffling secrecy, and whose sailormen had the temper of the buccaneers who had cruised in those same seas long, long ago."

Paine's own managing editor was uninterested in sending him to Cuba—he called it "damfoolitis"—but the young reporter found a receptive ear when he called on William Randolph Hearst. Hearst had obtained the jeweled sword to send to Gómez in May, 1896, and had given it a great deal of publicity—it was exhibited at a fair held in Madison Square Garden to raise money for the Cubans and it was pictured almost full size in the *Journal* on May 13. A *Journal* writer described it ecstatically: "The exquisitely beautiful weapon is an ornament fit for a hero. In shape it is the regulation sword of the mounted army officer, straight and narrow. It is not designed for use in battle, though, but as an ornament, to be worn on gala days when the good fight is won." The sword handle was of pure ivory, "heavily corded with gold," and at the end was a huge solitaire diamond. On one side of the hilt, in brilliants, was the monogram "M. G." and on the other, in silver and enamel, the flag of the Republic of Cuba. Etched on one side of the blade was the inscription: "To General Máximo Gómez, Commander in Chief of the Cuban Republic from *Journal,* N.Y." and on the other: "With congratulations and best wishes 'Por Cuba Libre,' May 1896." Unhappily it still reposed in a mahogany case in Hearst's office. The publisher had found no way to get it presented, but in Paine he had a man quixotic enough to undertake the mission.

Paine had no trouble in getting the junta to aid the project. He was directed to seek out the head of the junta in Jacksonville, one Señor José Huau. At a meeting with the portly, cigar-smoking Cuban in a back room of his tobacco shop and soda fountain where, Paine imagined, many secret missions had been planned and set afoot, he was told to take a room in a hotel and he would be notified of the next filibuster expedition. The message was whispered to him one evening by a Cuban sauntering along the piazza: "Come to the freight yards at midnight and you will find friends."

Weighted down with the sword for Gómez, two revolvers, and a sheath knife, Paine made his way to the rendezvous. There in the darkness he found himself among a small crowd of men talking softly in musical Spanish. When they were boarding the freight cars, Paine stumbled over someone's leg in the blackness. He heard an oath with a distinctly American intonation and discovered there was another reporter aboard—Ernest W. McCready, of the New York *Herald.* At Fernandina the freight cars were detached at a wharf along which was moored the seagoing tug *Three Friends.* The skipper was the famous "Dynamite Johnny" O'Brien, hero of many a voyage in the delivery of arms to Latin-American revolutionaries. The cargo and the Cuban soldiers were quickly loaded and before daylight the *Three Friends* was racing southward. The expedition was unable to land, but on Christmas Day it made newspaper headlines: armed with a Hotchkiss gun,

the crew had fought off a Spanish gunboat—the first "naval" engagement of the Cuban war.

The *Three Friends* had sailed December 14 to land arms and a party of forty Cubans at the mouth of San Juan River in Puerto Príncipe province. After six days of dodging along the Florida coast and the southern coast of Cuba, the tug reached her destination on December 19. A boat was just about to be lowered—Paine was ready to go with his haversack over his shoulder, a saddle in one hand, and the sword for Gómez in the other—when under the shadow of a mountain at the river's mouth a Spanish vessel was discovered. Almost at the same moment a shot was heard and a shell came whizzing over the *Three Friends.* Other shots followed and the tug sped out to sea, only to run into more danger. Attracted by the gunfire, a second Spanish boat came up. This was when "Dynamite Johnny" gave the word to return fire. The explosion from the Hotchkiss gun spread consternation among the Cubans on the *Three Friends;* but the one shot must have been equally frightening to the Spaniards, for they gave up the chase.

On the tug's return to Florida waters, the Cuban filibusters and the munitions were landed on an isolated point of land called No Name Key. How much of the adventure could Paine and McCready tell in their news stories? "Dynamite Johnny" was somewhat proud of the exploit and rather wanted it publicized. McCready felt that there would be no legal involvements. "These newspaper stories of ours will not be accepted as legal evidence," he said. After expounding further on the law, McCready concluded: "The story will be played up on the front page and it is liable to raise a fuss, but in the eyes of the law all newspapermen are liars until proven to the contrary." They decided to tell the whole story, though later they were to regret doing so.

Their stories went off on the *Three Friends* when "Dynamite Johnny" sailed to port for coal and supplies. The correspondents and the Cubans spent a miserable week on No Name Key. It was hot, the drinking water was brackish, and the food was rationed. They received bad news when the junta sent out a schooner with a message that the *Three Friends* would not pick them up because they couldn't risk another landing, and no other filibuster boat was immediately available. Paine and McCready sailed on the schooner to Key West to find out the situation. The one-shot naval fight of the *Three Friends* was now being called a "battle royal" in the papers, but there was disconcerting news: the government might bring charges of piracy against the participants. There was also good news: the tug *Dauntless* was supposed to be on her way to pick up the expedition for another trip to Cuba.

Paine and McCready did not want to miss this, but they faced the problem of getting back to No Name Key. The solution was at hand, however; Hearst's yacht *Vamoose* was in the harbor and Charles Michelson was eager to cooperate with them to get the jeweled sword with its engraved felicitations on its way to Gómez. When the *Vamoose* sailed up to No Name Key, the two correspondents were cheered to see before them the *Dauntless* being loaded with ammunition by several small fishing craft. Then, to their surprise, the boats began scuttling away like beetles to hide in the coves and inlets and the *Dauntless* was left riding alone at anchor. They discovered the reason when they went on board: the *Vamoose* had been taken for a U.S. revenue cutter. Finally the sailing craft were rounded up and the task of loading resumed.

Before the *Dauntless* got away, another correspondent arrived, T. R. Dawley, Jr., who had chartered a schooner to locate the filibuster boat. In Key West, he related in a *Journal* article of January 2, it was well known that the cargo of the *Three Friends* would be transferred to another boat. Eager to get to Cuba, Dawley had cruised among the keys off the tip of Florida until he located the *Dauntless*. On the same day the *Journal* printed Paine's account of the departure of the expedition: "I am writing these last words as the steamer is weighing anchor to head for Cuba. I have been nearly a month en route for Cuba, ten days on the filibuster at sea, with the sea fight as a detail, and more than a week hidden in the swamps of the Florida keys. The *Journal* sword which I am bearing to General Gómez has had a baptism of fire and all sorts of other vicissitudes, but it will reach the commander safely in the end, I am sure."

But not on this trip of the *Dauntless*. The cargo was destined for Pinar del Río province, and General Emilio Nunez, commander of the expedition, persuaded Paine it would be hopeless for him to land there in the expectation of making his way to Gómez. "Pinar del Río is not a good place for you," Nunez told Paine. "Here you will be four hundred miles from Gómez. You will not get to him by land—impossible!" Reluctantly Paine and McCready agreed, heartened by a promise of Nunez, however, that there would be other expeditions. "We can send you soon in a ship that will carry arms and men to Gómez, to the coast where the *Three Friends* was driven away," Nunez said. "The *Commodore*, I expect, will be ready when you get back to Florida."

. . . . .

The *Commodore* was not ready for Paine and McCready when they got back to Florida. While the *Dauntless* was heading south from No Name Key, tossed by a heavy sea in a rainstorm, the *Commodore* had left Jacksonville on a filibuster expedition. It sank early in the morning of January 2 several miles off the coast near Daytona. Headlines on January 3 reported the ship had foundered at sea. Mentioned as one of the passengers was the well-known novelist Stephen Crane.

Crane had been in Jacksonville for a month and a half before the *Commodore* sailed for Cienfuegos with ten thousand dollars worth of cargo on the night of December 31, according to a New York *World* story of January 1 about this strangely well-publicized expedition. The *World* listed the munitions as 400 rifles, 1,000 pounds of dynamite, 200,000 rifle cartridges, 300 machetes, 1,000 rounds of cannon cartridges, and 2,000 rounds of ammunition for dynamite guns. Crane had been employed by the Bacheller Syndicate, which had serialized for newspapers his *The Red Badge of Courage,* to do a series on the Cuban revolution. While waiting for a chance to become a member of a filibuster expedition, Crane's companions had been Mc-

Cready, Paine, and, if a New York *Journal* story of the *Commodore* sinking is correct, Sylvester Scovel. The *Journal's* story of January 1 said the passengers included "Stephen Crane, the novelist, who had been in Jacksonville for some time past with Sylvester Scovel."

The *Commodore* sailed on the eve of the New Year. Its foundering was front-page news for several days after the first reports, sparse in detail, were printed on January 3. Fairly accurate and full stories were published on January 4. The *Journal's* story was a purported first-person account from Daytona by C. B. Montgomery, identified as a passenger but actually the *Commodore's* cook. He made it to shore in a dinghy that bore Crane, Edward Murphy, the captain, and William Higgins, an oiler. Montgomery said the *Commodore* was "sent to the bottom by the treacherous hand of an enemy to Cuba." The basis for this charge was that when the ship sprang a leak on the first night out the pumps would not work. On the same day the *World* carried a story, also attributed to Montgomery, that likewise alleged the sinking was due to sabotage. Montgomery related that the first lifeboat launched was taken over by twelve Cubans and the second by six. The third held nine Americans with the mate in charge. He said that he, Crane, and Higgins boarded the dinghy "to sink or swim with Captain Murphy." When the *Commodore* sank, Montgomery said, the mate's boat was discovered to have also sunk, and the nine Americans were "floating in a fearful sea." "We tried to save the doomed men," he continued, "but they were swept away by the waves and the heavy gale."

The cook's account was followed January 5 in the *World* by Murphy's narrative. To reporters' queries about sabotage, he replied that he "could not say" if the tug had been scuttled and that he did not think the pumps were "fixed." Murphy said nothing of the drowning of the men in the mate's boat, but he went into detail about the experiences of those with him in the dinghy and their rescue, with the exception of the oiler Higgins, when it was tossed by the surf onto the beach at Daytona. He praised Crane's calmness and fortitude during the dangerous hours in the rough sea: "And right here I want to say that Crane is a man, every inch of him, and he acted throughout with true grit."

Crane wrote his version of the adventure after reaching Jacksonville. It appeared January 7 in the New York *Press,* headlined "Stephen Crane's Own Story" and illustrated with a large portrait drawing of him. Crane began his narrative with a description of the loading of the *Commodore* in broad daylight with "a crowd of gleeful Cubans on the pier" singing "the strange patriotic ballads of their island." "There was none of that extreme modesty about the proceedings which had marked previous departures of the famous tug," Crane continued. "She loaded up as placidly as if she were going to carry oranges to New York instead of Remingtons to Cuba." The loading, Crane related, was completed by mid-afternoon, but, held up by customs, the tug did not depart until twilight, cheered on by the Cubans ashore. Two miles from Jacksonville she went aground, and the revenue cutter *Boutwell,* oddly, dragged her off the mudbank. The *Commodore* went aground again in the morning, New Year's Day, but was able to extricate herself.

Crane's account contained touches of his mannered literary style in the midst of commonplace prose and occasional unbelievably bad writing: "As darkness came upon the waters, the *Commodore* was a broad, flaming path of blue and silver phosphorescence, and as her stout bow lunged at the great black waves she threw flashing, roaring cascades to either side. And all that was to be heard was the rhythmical and mighty pounding of the engines. Being an inexperienced filibuster, the writer had undergone considerable mental excitement since the starting of the ship, and in consequence he had not yet been to sleep and so I went to the first mate's cabin to indulge myself in all the physical delight of holding one's-self in bed. Every time the ship lurched I expected to be fired through a bulkhead, and it was neither amusing nor instructive to see in the dim light a certain accursed valise aiming itself at the top of my stomach with every lurch of the vessel."

Finding it impossible to sleep, Crane went topside to the pilot house. Lying on the deck, he was drowsing when the chief engineer came up and told the captain the ship was leaking. Crane went below to join the bucket brigade of Cubans bailing out the engine room. "The engine room, by the way, represented a scene at this time taken from the middle kitchen of hades," he wrote. "In the first place, it was insufferably warm, and the lights burned faintly in a way to cause mystic and grewsome shadows. There was a quantity of soapish sea water swirling and sweeping and swishing among the machinery that roared and banged and clattered and steamed, and, in the second place, it was a devil of a ways down below."

Exhausted after awhile by the heat and exertion, Crane went topside again. His account of the hurried activity leading to the lowering of the boats and the abandonment of the ship is confused but it reports his sensitive impressions: "Now the whistle of the *Commodore* had been turned loose, and if there ever was a voice of despair and death, it was in the voice of this whistle. It had gained a new tone. It was as if its throat was already choked by the water, and this cry on the sea at night, with the wind blowing the spray over the ship, and the waves roaring over the bow, and swirling white along the decks, was to each of us probably a song of man's end."

When the lifeboats had shoved off, Crane jumped into the ten-foot dinghy, fending it off from the ship with an oar while the cook, the captain, and finally the oiler swung over the rail and dropped into the leaping little craft. The dinghy was tied to the *Commodore* with forty yards of lead line, and drifted back to leeward. "Boys, we will stay right near this ship till she goes down," the captain shouted to them. "When came the gray shade of dawn," Crane's narrative continued, "the form of the *Commodore* grew slowly clear to us as our little ten-foot boat rose over each swell. She was floating with such an air of buoyancy that we laughed when we had time, and said, 'What a gag it would be on those other fellows if she didn't sink at all.'"

Next happened a dramatic and tragic incident not recounted in other news reports. Those in the dinghy saw men aboard the *Commodore,* and as they rowed back to the ship the first mate cried out that his boat with six crewmen had foundered alongside the ship. They had made rafts, now floating astern, and wanted the dinghy to tow them. Crane's story continued: "There were five white men and two Negroes. This scene in the gray light of morning impressed one as would a view into some place where ghosts move slowly. These seven men on the stern of the sinking *Commodore* were silent. . . . Here was death but here also was a most singular and indefinable kind of fortitude."

Four men climbed over the railing and stood watching the steely water before leaping into the sea. First the chief engineer jumped and then a stoker; they swam to the raft and clung to it. "Then the first mate threw his hands over his head and plunged into the sea," Crane related. "He had no life belt and for my part, even when he did this horrible thing, I somehow felt that I could see in the expression of his hands, and in the very toss of his head as he leaped thus to death, that it was rage, rage, rage unspeakable that was in his heart at the time."

Then a fourth man leaped to a raft, leaving three men standing in silence on the *Commodore,* their faces turned toward the dinghy. Crane's story continued:

> The colored stoker on the first raft threw us a line and we began to tow. Of course, we perfectly understood the absolute impossibility of any such thing; our dinghy was within six inches of the water's edge, there was an enormous sea running, and I knew that under the circumstances a tugboat would have no light task in moving these rafts.
>
> But we tried it, and would have continued to try it indefinitely, but that something critical came to pass. I was at an oar and so faced the rafts. The cook controlled the line. Suddenly the boat began to go backward and then we saw this Negro on the first raft pulling on the line hand over hand and drawing us to him.
>
> He had turned into a demon. He was wild—wild as a tiger. He was crouched on this raft and ready to spring. Every muscle of him seemed to be turned into an elastic spring. His eyes were almost white. His face was the face of a lost man reaching upward, and we knew that the weight of his hand on our gunwale doomed us.
>
> The cook let go of the line. We rowed around to see if we could not get a line from the chief engineer, and all this time, mind you, there were no shrieks, no groans, but silence, silence and silence, and then the *Commodore* sank.
>
> She turned to windward, then swung afar back, righted and dove into the sea, and the rafts were suddenly swallowed by this frightful maw of the ocean. And then by the men on the ten-foot dinghy were words said that were still not words— something beyond words.
>
> The lighthouse at Mosquito Inlet stuck up above the horizon like the point of a pin. We turned our dinghy toward the shore.

A few weeks later when Crane was reliving his *Commodore* experience and putting it into words in a short story—published as "The Open Boat"—he omitted the horrifying scene of watching the crewmen swept beneath the waves to drown. When he wrote his newspaper account within a few hours after reaching shore, he composed an effective and graphic passage of description. But the day and night spent in an open boat afterward stood out as a more significant experience that he used for his short story. Immediately afterward this part of the adventure seemed to be an anticlimax and made two paragraphs tacked on to the newspaper article:

> The history of life in an open boat for thirty hours would no doubt be instructive for the young, but none is to be told here now. For my part I would prefer to tell the story at once, because from it would shine the splendid manhood of Captain Edward Murphy and of William Higgins, the oiler, but let it suffice at this time to say that when we were swamped in the surf and making the best of our way toward the shore the captain gave orders amid the wildness of the breakers as clearly as if he had been on the quarter deck of a battleship.
>
> John Kitchell of Daytona came running down the beach, and as he ran the air was filled with clothes. If he had pulled a single lever and undressed, even as the fire horses' harness, he could not seem to have stripped with more speed. He dashed into the water and grabbed the cook. Then he went after the captain, but the captain sent him to me, and then it was that he saw Billy Higgins lying with his forehead on sand that was clear of the water, and he was dead.

Returning to Jacksonville from the *Dauntless* expedition, Paine and McCready had gone into hiding to keep from being entangled in the legal proceedings that had been started against the owners of the *Three Friends*. With dirty, wrinkled clothes, straw hats cocked up in front in the Cuban fashion, and faces unshaved and hair unshorn, they did not think they would be welcome at a hotel and got a room for twenty-five cents a night above a saloon. Paine hardly dared to venture into the streets, for, having grown up in Jacksonville and being the son of the Presbyterian minister there, he feared he might be recognized. Señor Huau in response to a note sent them, among other things, a bundle of newspapers which brought them up to date: the *Commodore* had foundered and their friend Crane had been saved, the *Three Friends* had been seized by the government and members of the crew, as well as one named Ralph D. Paine, had been accused of piracy. Thus did Paine's byline in the *Journal* backfire on him. McCready, who had received no byline in the *Herald*, was happy for once that James Gordon Bennett preferred that his reporters remain anonymous. Paine was somewhat shaken to read in one paper that the penalty for piracy was death, but reassured to read in another that a conviction of those charged was unlikely because there would be no prosecution witnesses. The most interesting news in the papers, however, was that the two *Dauntless* correspondents—Paine and McCready—were reported to be in Cuba with the insurgents.

Front page of the New York Journal, *24 February 1898.*

Even though there was no real danger to life and liberty, Paine and McCready still had to live in retirement until they could join another filibuster expedition. One night, dining behind the drawn curtains of an alcove in a cafe, they heard a voice from an adjoining cubicle that was vaguely familiar. It seemed to come from someone who was reading. The regular pace of the reading was interrupted by a question:

"Listen, Ed, I want to have this right, from your point of view. How does it sound so far?"

"You've got it, Steve," came a reply. "That is just how it happened, and how we felt."

The voice continued reading—reading lines that years afterward Paine would turn to again and again in print: "The injured captain, lying in the bow, was at this time buried in that profound dejection and indifference which comes, temporarily at least, to even the bravest and most enduring, when willy-nilly, the firm fails, the army loses, the ship goes down. The mind of the master of a vessel is rooted deep in the timbers of her, though he commands for a day or a decade; and this captain had on him the stern impression of a scene in the grays of dawn, of seven turned faces and later a stump of a topmast with a white ball on it that slashed to and fro at the waves, and went lower and lower, and down. . . . "

Paine and McCready listened for awhile, and when there came a pause they broke into the next alcove. "Here were four of us, all in the same boat, as one might say, foregathered by a singular chance, and our combined experiences embraced all the vicissitudes of filibustering," Paine recalled. "And so we sat and wove together those recent voyages of the *Three Friends* and the *Dauntless* and the *Commodore.*"

There was no repetition of a filibuster experience for the three correspondents. McCready received a telegram from the *Herald* ordering him to return to New York; and the Bacheller Syndicate did not care to underwrite any more adventures for Crane—the gold he wore in a money belt to pay his way when he got to Cuba had been lost with the *Commodore*—and he too returned to New York. Paine, sought by government agents for his part in the *Three Friends'* naval "battle," remained in semiconcealment in Florida. His minister father arranged for him to hide out for a time at the home of an elder of the Presbyterian church, and later under an assumed name he stayed at a little hotel at Green Cove Springs twenty-five miles up the St. John's River from Jacksonville. After a month of this, with no prospects of getting to Cuba by a filibuster boat, Paine gave up and returned to his job on the Philadelphia *Press.* The sword he had been commissioned to bear to Gómez he turned over to Charles Michelson.

. . . . .

While Paine and McCready were rollicking about the Florida keys in the spirit of boys playing pirate and Crane was undergoing one of the great experiences of his short life, two other correspondents—both famous and talented—had arrived in Key West on their way to Cuba to join the insurgents. They were the newspaper writer and novelist Richard Harding Davis and the Western artist Frederic Remington. They found it no easier to get to the island clandestinely than their less well-known cohorts.

Davis then was not the famous war correspondent he later became—the Cuban rebellion was his first war—but he was a glamorous figure, the beau ideal of aspiring young reporters. He had joined the New York journalistic fraternity of Park Row in 1889 after several years' work in Philadelphia. There he had won only local fame because, as someone said of him, "To put a good newspaperman on a Philadelphia paper is like inviting a good musician to prove his skill on the jew's harp." In New York Davis got a job on the *Sun.* Within two years the Van Bibber stories he wrote at the suggestion of the managing editor, Arthur Brisbane, made him the talk of the city. Mr. Cortlandt Van Bibber was a young man about town, whose chivalrous adventures Davis narrated for the *Sun* every Saturday. Although a working member of the press, which was held to be a disreputable employment at the time, the suave, well-dressed Davis epitomized the gallant he had created and made famous. To New Yorkers, Davis was Van Bibber in the flesh. The artist Charles Dana Gibson chose Davis as the model for his male counterpart of the all-American sweetheart of the period—the high-pompadoured, clear-featured, swan-necked Gibson girl. The clean-cut, firm-jawed Gibson man was a somewhat romanticized version of Davis, who actually was rather heavy featured and solidly built—but no matter, he was the dream-hero of the sighing damsels of the time and exuded golden splendor wherever he went.

Remington lacked Davis' sophistication, his milieu not being the cafes and theaters of New York but the cattle ranches and Indian camps of the West. He had made his first trip there at the age of nineteen. His lively drawings of bronchobusters, cowboys riding herd, and Indian raiders were based on more than the imagination. He himself had been a cowboy and scout. But it had not all been adventure—he had run a sheep and mule ranch, made money and lost it. To recoup, he returned to the East with a portfolio of drawings he hoped to sell to magazines. Through his work for *Outing* magazine he got to know Poultney Bigelow, son of John Bigelow, former partner of William Cullen Bryant in publishing the New York *Evening Post* and former minister to France. In the 1880's the two were assigned by *Harper's Magazine* to do a travel series on Germany, Russia, and North Africa. By the 1890's Remington's drawings and paintings were popular magazine fare.

The *Journal* sent Davis and Remington to Key West early in December, 1896, to make their way to the Cuban coast and join Gómez in Santa Clara province. They were taken in tow by the *Journal's* Cuba veterans, Charles Michelson and Grover Flint. Davis wrote his mother, the novelist Rebecca Harding Davis, that their plan was to land from the *Vamoose;* they would spend a month with Gómez, their dispatches and sketches to be taken by courier to the coast each week and picked up by Michelson. Davis expected it would be a profitable month's work: the *Journal* was to pay him three thousand dollars plus expenses, *Harper's Magazine* had promised to buy one story for six hundred dollars, and a publisher planned to bring out a book of his articles, using Remington's drawings as illustrations.

The enterprise proved one of the most frustrating in Davis' career. On January 1 he wrote his mother that he was on his way, remarking that what he did not "know about the Fine Art of Filibustering now is unnecessary." But the next day he was forced to write disconsolately that the first quality needed by a filibuster was "patience." At sea, the *Vamoose* had run into heavy weather, and the captain refused to sail on to Cuba. As he continued to refuse in the days that followed, Davis and Remington after a month of idleness decided to give up their plan of joining the insurgents and to sail to Cuba on a regular passenger vessel. This they did on January 9.

The dispatch of Davis and Remington to Cuba was announced in the *Journal* with a front-page spread on January 17. They had reached the insurgents, the story said falsely, on an assignment "to present the true situation in the war-stricken island in more graphic and vivid style than it has yet been pictured to the American public." In Havana Davis was able to secure from Weyler a pass permitting him to travel in the western provinces. He knew he was unlikely to encounter any fighting, but he felt that since he had gone this far he might as well continue and see what developed. Remington, on the other hand, became bored within a week. James Creelman recorded in his reminiscences that Remington, discouraged by the prospect of seeing no action, wired Hearst: "Everything is quiet. There is no trouble. There will be no war. I wish to return." Hearst's reply made one of the notable quotations about the Cuban insurrection: "Please remain. You furnish the pictures and I'll furnish the war." But Remington did not choose to remain. Within a week he was on his way to New York with a portfolio of pictures.

Davis was not sorry to see Remington depart. "I am so relieved at getting old Remington to go [it's] as though I had won $5,000," he wrote his mother. "He was a splendid fellow but a perfect kid and had to be humored and petted all the time. I shall if I have luck be through with this in a few weeks but it has had such a setback at the start that I am afraid it can never make a book and I doubt if I can write a decent article even." The setback, of course, was the *Journal's* big splash of January 17 saying he and Remington were with the rebels. When copies of the paper reached Havana, Weyler had Davis followed by spies.

Davis did not agree with Remington that there was, or would be, no war. Writing his mother on January 15 after a rail trip up the coast to Matanzas, he observed: "There is a war here and no mistake and all the people in the fields have been ordered into the fortified towns where they are starving and dying of disease. Yesterday I saw the houses of these people burning on both sides of the track—they gave shelter to the insurgents and so very soon they found their houses gone."

Davis' next letter, written at Cárdenas on the north coast, reported a train ride of six hours through blazing fields of sugarcane. He was comfortably installed at a hotel and well taken care of by his interpreter, who also took pride in being his valet. "What would the new school of yellow kid journalists say if they knew that?" he asked. Although Davis was seeing Cuba from a train window, he began to comprehend what was happening on the island: "I always imagined that houses were destroyed during a war because they got in the way of cannon balls or they were burned because they might offer shelter to the enemy, but here they are destroyed with the purpose of making the war horrible and hurrying up the end. The insurgents began first by destroying the sugar mills, some of which were worth millions of dollars in machinery, and now the Spaniards are burning the homes of the people and herding them in around the towns to starve out the insurgents and to leave them without shelter or places to go for food or to hide the wounded. So all day long wherever you look you see great heavy columns of smoke rising into this beautiful sky above the magnificent palms. . . ."

A few days later, on January 24, the *Journal* printed the first sketches done on the scene by Remington. They took up all the first page and most of the second. The third page was devoted to a single drawing. It had the following caption written by Remington:

> The acts of the terrible savages, or irregular troops called 'guerrillas," employed by the Spanish, pass all understanding by civilized man. The American Indian was never guilty of the monstrous crimes that they commit.
>
> The treatment of women is unspeakable and as for the men captured by them alive, the blood curdles in my veins as I think of the atrocity, of the cruelty, practiced on these helpless victims.

> My picture illustrates one case where the guerrillas saw fit to bring their captives into the lines, trussed up at the elbows, after their fashion.

The first of the five articles Davis wrote for the *Journal* appeared January 31. It fitted in well with Hearst's campaign to get the United States to intervene in Cuba, carrying the headline: "Richard Harding Davis and the Horrors of the Cuban War. Weyler Wars, Not on Men, but Women. *Journal's* Special Commissioner Paints a Vivid Picture of the Butcher's Terrible Doings." The story dealt with Weyler's *reconcentrado* policy, which, Davis wrote, did not help the Spanish because it forced able-bodied men to join the insurgents and the old, the young, and the women to go into the towns. "So the order failed to distress those against whom it was aimed," Davis continued, "but brought swift and terrible suffering to those who are, and were, absolutely innocent of any intent against the government and to the adherents of the government as well."

The experience ended Davis' personal but not his professional neutrality toward Spain. He said in one article:

> I was taught in the days of 'old journalism' that reporters were meant to describe things they saw, and not to write editorials but to leave the drawing of conclusions to others; nor do I understand that it is any part of a reporter's work to discuss the political aspects of things and direct senators and congressmen and other men older than himself on the points of international law or to write 'open letters' to General Weyler from the safe distance of New York, or to attack the President of the United States. . . . I do not know that the President should interfere in the affairs of Cuba, but I do know that President Cleveland has better sources of information on the question than any other man can possibly have who studies it in the United States. But whatever may be the international difficulties of this matter now, this is what is likely to happen later, and it should have some weight in helping to decide the question with those whose proper business it is to determine it.

What Davis foresaw was mass sickness, starvation, and death.

Davis' next dispatch, written at Tampa February 10, was published February 12 on the first page. It was one of the most sensational of the war, though hardly because of any conscious effort on his part. It was preceded by the following series of excited headlines: "Does Our Flag Shield Women? Indignities Practiced by Spanish Officials on Board American Vessels. Richard Harding Davis Describes Some Startling Phases of the Cuban Situation. Refined Young Women Stripped and Searched by Brutal Spaniards While Under Our Flag on the *Olivette*." On page two was a five-column drawing by Remington showing a young woman with a bare backside standing among several Spanish officers who were searching her clothing.

Davis had learned of the search after the *Olivette* left port. Seated next to him at dinner was a Señorita Clemencia Arango, who told him she and two other young women were passengers—exiled from Cuba because they were thought to have aided the insurgents; her own brother was serving in the rebel forces. "I found that she was not an Amazon, or a Joan of Arc, or a woman of the people with a machete in one hand and a Cuban flag in the other," Davis wrote. "She was a well-bred, well-educated young person who spoke three languages and dressed as you see girls dress on Fifth Avenue after church on Sunday." His story continued:

> This is what the Spaniards did to these girls: After ordering them to leave the island on a certain day, they sent detectives to their houses on the morning of that day and had them undressed and searched to discover if they were carrying letters to the junta at Key West and Tampa. They then, an hour later, searched them at the custom house as they were leaving for the steamer. They searched them thoroughly, even to the length of taking off their shoes and stockings, and fifteen minutes later, when the young ladies stood at last on the deck of an American vessel with the American flag hanging from the stern, the Spanish officers followed them there and demanded that a cabin should be furnished them to which the girls might be taken, and they were then undressed and searched for the third time.

Nothing the chivalrous Davis had seen in Cuba so outraged him as this treatment of innocent maidenhood under Old Glory. In the past not a reporter to tell the President what he should do, now Davis wrote:

> Before I went to Cuba I was as much opposed to our interfering there as was any other person equally ignorant concerning the situation, but since I have seen for myself I feel ashamed that we should have stood so long idle. We have been too considerate, too fearful that as a younger nation we should appear to disregard the laws laid down by older nations. We have tolerated what no European power would have tolerated; we have been patient with men who have put back the hand of time for centuries, who lie to our representatives daily, who butcher innocent people, who gamble with the lives of their own soldiers in order to gain a few more stars and an extra stripe, who murder prisoners of war and who send American property to the air in flames.

He urged President Cleveland to listen to the correspondents—if not Davis himself, then to Stephen Bonsal, of the *Herald,* whom the President earlier had selected for two diplomatic missions, or C. E. Akers, of the London *Times* and *Harper's Weekly.*

None of the earlier stories of Spanish atrocities had so stirred the warlike instinct of American manhood as Davis' story and Remington's picture. None had been such a circulation booster either. The *World* at the time had a good story of its own—the arrest of Scovel—but his tribulations were not so titillating as those of the Spanish señoritas. Trying to salvage something from the *Journal's* scoop, the *World* sent reporters to the pier to interview Señorita Arango when she arrived at Tampa from Key West. Exultantly they discovered that the three women had not been stripped naked and searched by male officers. There had been a search, it was true, but by a woman and not

by men. The *World* printed this happy news under the headline: "Tale of a Fair Exile." Somehow in the controversy that followed two of the women searched were overlooked, the only one mentioned being Señorita Arango. Even Davis, in a letter to the *World* defending himself against the slur on his accuracy and blaming the misconception on Remington's drawing, mentioned only one. In the last paragraph of his letter Davis asked the *World:* "Please make this statement as conspicuous as you did your published interview with the young woman." The request was totally unnecessary; the opportunity to score off the *Journal* was not one the *World* would miss.

The exposure of the *Olivette* incident and Davis' letter to the *World* did not stop the *Journal* from printing three other articles he had written, although they were anticlimatic to the Arango story. In one, published on February 15, Davis reported a rail trip halfway along the Morón-Júcaro *trocha.* He claimed to be the first American *allowed* to visit it, which was true enough, but of course it had been crossed time and again by Scovel, Rea, and Flint, who did not do their traveling by train on passes signed by Weyler. An article of February 28 was devoted to Spanish atrocities. Davis admitted being skeptical of the atrocities he had read and heard about before going to Cuba, because he "had been kept sufficiently long in Key West to learn how large a proportion of Cuban war news is manufactured on the piazzas of the hotels of that town and of Tampa by utterly irresponsible newspapermen who accept every rumor that finds its way across the gulf to the excitable Cuban cigarmakers of Florida, and who pass these rumors on to some of the New York papers as facts and as coming direct from the field." On Davis' visit to Sagua la Grande, however, the testimony of Americans and Englishmen was such that he had to accept the fact of the frequent unprovoked slaying of *pacíficos.*

Although Davis himself did not go into the field in Cuba, he praised correspondents who did.

> They are taking chances that no war correspondents ever took in any war in any part of the world. For this is not a war—it is a state of lawless butchery, and the rights of correspondents, of soldiers, and of noncombatants are not recognized. . . . They [the correspondents] run the chance of being drowned before they even reach the shore; they risk capture at sea and death by the guns of a Spanish cruiser, and, escaping that, they face when they reach the island the greater danger of capture there and of being cut down by a guerrilla force and left to die in a road, or of being put in prison and left to die of fever, as Govin was cut down, as [José M.] Delgado [a naturalized American wounded by Spanish troops at his farm] died in prison, as Melton and Scovel are lying in prison now, where they will continue to lie until we have a secretary of state who recognizes the rights of the correspondent as a noncombatant, or at least as an American citizen.

A third article became one of the most famous of Davis' pieces on the revolution. It was "The Death of Rodriguez," which he reprinted in several compilations of his work. Davis' young Cuban rebel marching upright before the firing squad, smoking his last cigaret, and standing erect without a tremor to be shot down was the prototype for many such characters in later fiction and the motion pictures. The cigaret advertising slogan about being nonchalant while smoking a Murad may have been inspired by his account of the execution of Rodriguez. As the Cuban passed him, Davis wrote, "he held a cigaret between his lips, not arrogantly nor with bravado, but with the nonchalance of a man who meets his punishment fearlessly, and who will let his enemies see that they can kill but cannot frighten him."

There was one more echo in the *Journal* of the Davis-Remington trip to Cuba: an Easter supplement was issued on April 11 with four full pages of Remington's drawings showing Spanish atrocities. It had the somewhat unseasonal Christmas biblical sentiment: "Peace on Earth Good Will Toward Men As It Is in Cuba." (pp. 63-83)

> *Charles H. Brown, "The Romantic Adventurers," in his* The Correspondents' War: Journalists in the Spanish-American War, *Charles Scribner's Sons, 1967, pp. 63-83.*

Gerald F. Linderman

[*Linderman is an American historian and educator. In the following excerpt, he examines the popular press as an instrument of political action during the Spanish-American War.*]

William McKinley's administration would be the last to reflect an American public opinion that had remained throughout the nineteenth century fragmented and narrowly parochial. The president conceived of few of the problems reaching his desk as national problems. Until 1898 he devoted his work day to local issues, many similar in content, all susceptible to individualized solution but few central to local life: the appointment of a postmaster; a limited adjustment in a tariff schedule; the reception of a group from home; the granting of a pardon; the review of a decision handed down by the commissioner of pensions; the endorsement of relief measures, often private, to cushion the depredations of some natural disaster. (p. 148)

The executive was unequipped to register broad public sentiment, to temper it in response to data pertinent to situations overseas and to translate the result into a national policy and program incorporating both public opinion's claim to consideration and the administration's own informed sense of the national interest. The center's problem, as Bryce saw [in his *The American Commonwealth*, 1895], was that "[e]ach of . . . [the national government's] organs is too small to form opinion, too narrow to express it, too weak to give effect to it."

Illustrative of Washington's weakness was the difficulty of assembling basic information. Facts, especially in the increasingly important realm of foreign affairs, were elusive. The federal government's processes for gathering data on situations overseas were irregular and unreliable. American consuls abroad—the party faithful, the businessman intent on his own commercial ventures, the occasional writer like Nathaniel Hawthorne hoarding consular fees

against the day when they would suffice to support his art—only fitfully wrote dispatches home. The departments ordinarily lacked provision for the distribution of that intelligence which did arrive. There were few whose job it was to inform the public. Rarely did an official use information gathered by government to address the people on behalf of government.

William McKinley regularly revealed his own meager expectations of the executive branch as a source of information. The superintendent of the Coast and Geodetic Survey objected when he discovered the president following the movement of Dewey's fleet on a page torn from a school geography. McKinley was surprised, and pleased, to discover that someone in government could offer better maps. Falling within this assumption that government did not generate essential information was McKinley's frequent resort to the fact-finder, the old and trusted friend who would explore specific problems and report directly to the president. Symptomatic of this problem, the American peace commissioners would hold negotiating sessions with Spain's delegates concurrently with hearings designed to elicit the most elementary facts about the conquered Philippine archipelago.

In 1898 aroused Americans began demanding of the federal government a program of broad national action for which neither presidential will nor institutional equipment was available. The result was a variety of vacuum, an insistent need without the means to meet it.

The popular press possessed four assets that made its attempts to fill the political vacuum far less ludicrous than we might assume a similar effort today.

There was, first, the residual deference derived from the role that the newspaper had played within the older social consensus. Politicians who carried the locale's mandate to their seats in Washington were sensitive to the problem noted by another English visitor, Beatrice Webb: the absence of organic connection between elector and representative, between local and central authority. Even during the period of minimal local interest in, and pressure on, what transpired in Washington, there was tension rooted in their role. By what standard were office-holders to represent those who elected them? With no possibility of constant contact with constituency and with electors in any case reluctant to prescribe for problems without bearing on their own lives, how were representatives to judge each issue that came before them? A number apparently set for themselves the easy measure of personal enrichment. The majority, however, felt the need of another guide, one more frequent and comprehensive than the crossroads meeting at election time, one of direct help in measuring their actions against the ideal of public weal. Here the newspaper played an essential role.

Politicians showed deference to the press. Their attention seemed both a propitiation of, and an invitation to, public opinion—conciliating the priest in worshipping the deity, Bryce called it. The politician's interest, however, was of a special and limited kind. He viewed the newspaper less as a source of information on what was happening, less as a finger held to the public pulse, than as a support for the moral life. He wanted to know that men whom he respected thought as he did regarding the moral nature of the issues that confronted him. He looked first not to the news pages but to the editorials.

Joseph Pulitzer and William Randolph Hearst frequently risked their inheritance, this rooted assumption of the newspaper's morality and respectability. Both the *World* and the *Journal* gambled and partially lost their standing as reputable organs. In part this was a function of indelicate subject matter; in part a function of the yellow press' appeal to groups assumed not to share middle-class moral precepts; in part a function of the editors' backgrounds. Pulitzer, half-Jewish in a day when anti-Semitism incurred little onus, arrived in New York preceded by whispers condemning his role in a shooting that involved the editor of his St. Louis newspaper. Even more vulnerable was Hearst, whom West Coast society had censured for flaunting his mistress, a former waitress. To the respectable people of New York he appeared the dilettante-publisher lavishing momma's millions on crude pranks, the journalistic equivalent of the chamber-pot incident that had led to his expulsion from Harvard. Nevertheless, both publishers periodically courted respectability and thereby recouped some social standing: their journals remained at least the partial legatee of that older respect for the newspaper as the enunciator of moral concerns.

A second, more potent asset lay in the fact that Joseph Pulitzer had already begun, as government had not, to build an organization reflecting the shifting focus from individual to mass, from locale to nation.

In the 1870s and 1880s that which the politician found in the newspaper was not public opinion, though it called itself that. It was instead the sentiment of the eastern, urban educated, the group that Bryce called the "active class" and Edwin Lawrence Godkin labeled the "reading class." Editors thought it their principal function to reinforce standards of social conduct. In reality, they both shaped and reflected an "ethical likemindedness," a common outlook among small, often otherwise unrelated groups of subscribers. Acting in this capacity, editors seemed very powerful men. Before the extensive use of telephone, telegraph, and cable, newspapers were small and personalized. New Yorkers referred to their newspapers as "Dana's *Sun*" and "Bryant's *Post*." The appearance was that of giants of journalism creating private, powerful instruments of influence.

The reality, as Seymour Mandelbaum has shown [in his *Boss Tweed's New York*, 1965], was less flattering. In the New York City of the 1860s and 1870s tiny groups of readers supported numbers of small newspapers. Each journal's influence was ordinarily limited to a tight circle, with the location of its office pointing the center and the reach of local wagon transport, within perhaps a two-hour period, setting its circumference. If he moved too far beyond the reflection of local interests and moral sensibilities, the editor risked losing to numerous, nearby rivals that essential constituency.

Newspaper editors shared the common view that the thinking individual was the critical unit of American society. In presenting materials, they were kept within rather narrow bounds by their personal commitments to upper middle-class ethical standards and, equally, by their belief that the respectable individual, capable of discerning truth for himself, would recognize falsity in a paper's pages and, refusing to buy, would immediately go elsewhere. This focus on high ethical content, accurately and coolly reported, was manifest in page appearance: small type; single-column tombstone headlines; accounts framed as tales, with the important at the end.

Godkin spoke to the future when he asserted in 1898 that "the press is the nation talking about itself." The press of the 1870s, 1880s, and much of the 1890s was more accurately the locale talking about its own, largely self-contained interests or, on the only level even slightly to transcend locale, the urban educated talking among themselves of the way Americans should behave.

It was Joseph Pulitzer, perhaps the quickest mind in the history of American journalism, who smashed this mold. He refused to accept traditional limitations on subject matter. He set out to enlarge constituency by offering materials that, though abhorrent to respectables, were exciting to a new readership. He chose a strategic location and there applied a broad vision, that of a newspaper speaking "not to a select committee," not even to all the people of a single city, "but to the whole nation." An equally dramatic break with the past was his determination to realign the relationship of editor and reader. A childhood close to European poverty supplied both sympathy for those in the lower social ranges and immunity against the American middle-class conception of a society of discerning individuals. He would speak to the lower ranks, but not as respectable editors spoke to the urban educated. Instead of reflecting his readers' views, he would first catch their interest and then instruct them in his own views. His newspaper was to be a "daily schoolhouse" and a "daily teacher."

By 1883, the year of Pulitzer's arrival in New York City, it had become possible for an innovative editor to break the confines of small, single-type constituencies approachable only through the appeal to reason. Technological advance was making his vision practicable. The trolley car enlarged a paper's compass from nine or ten to perhaps fifty miles. The growth of regional advertising as corporate scale increased provided the essential alternative source of income. No longer need the editor remain chained to subscriptions. Reliance on advertising might at first appear to trade the rather diffuse control of class constituency for the tighter rein of the businessman, but advertisers, Pulitzer calculated, would be less interested than upper middle-class patrons in a paper's editorial policy and ethical content. Seeing in the larger public potential customers rather than threatening mob, they would look first to numbers. Pulitzer was the first to comprehend that a circulation large enough to attract and retain advertising opened the way to new influence.

Not only was there available a new source of funds, but by the mid-1880s a new and larger constituency—the immigrant masses—awaited tapping. With rapid increases in literacy came hunger for new reading materials. There would be in 1899 four times as many daily newspapers as in 1870. While population in cities of eight thousand or more would grow 52 percent between 1880 and 1899, daily newspaper circulation would rise 323 percent.

Pulitzer better than any other grasped the techniques necessary to win the loyalties of masses newly literate in English. In the twelve years between 1883 and Hearst's arrival in New York, Pulitzer, aided by Morrill Goddard and Arthur Brisbane, perfected his tactics: streamer headlines; huge line-cut illustrations; editorial cartoons; lead-sentence construction; simple words; short paragraphs.

His success no one would deny. Circulation rocketed. Half a continent away Jane Addams paid unknowing tribute to the swelling influence of Pulitzer's example:

> If one makes calls on a Sunday afternoon in the homes of the immigrant colonies near Hull-House, one finds the family absorbed in the Sunday edition of a sensational daily newspaper, even those who cannot read, quite easily following the comic adventures portrayed in the colored pictures of the supplement or tracing the clew of a murderer carefully depicted by a black line drawn through a plan of the house and street.

In 1900 Delos F. Wilcox concluded from measurements of illustrations, stories of crime and vice, and medicine and employment advertisements that forty-seven of one hundred and forty-seven newspapers were yellow. Frank Luther Mott, the foremost historian of American journalism, included in this category such papers as the Chicago *Tribune,* the Chicago *Times-Herald,* the New Orleans *Times-Democrat* and the Atlanta *Constitution.* Obviously many newspapers followed Pulitzer in striving to make the transition from class to mass audience.

The third asset available to the new journalism was its leaders' tactical flair in converting increased organizational and financial resources first into an enhanced power to influence the public and then into a new power of action.

William Randolph Hearst envied Pulitzer's success in declaring independence of a limited constituency by winning a mass audience. To the problem of securing for himself an equally strong circulation base he brought no new techniques. He did, however, possess a prankish and iconoclastic spirit that happily pushed to extremes those that Pulitzer had developed. In 1896-98, attempting to make himself the mobilizer of national sentiment, he applied this tactic to the situation in Cuba.

Hearst's particular genius lay in his ability to reduce abstractions to the personalized language of locale, to convert distant, complex problems to easily grasped and emotionally appealing personal predicaments. The *Journal* developed a major campaign around the fate of Doctor Ricardo Ruiz, a Cuban who had emigrated to this country, taken out citizenship papers, and then returned to join the insurrection. When the dentist died in a Spanish cell under mysterious circumstances, Hearst claimed without proof that prison officials had beaten Ruiz to death. In Hearst's rendering Ruiz became synonymous with Spanish persecution of American citizens.

By far the most successful of Hearst's case studies was that of Evangelina Cisneros, a young and attractive Cuban woman whom the editor alleged the authorities had imprisoned for resisting the advances of a Spanish officer. In fact, Miss Cisneros and her friends had assaulted a Spanish colonel in a futile attempt to escape the island to which she and her father, a ranking insurrectionist, were confined. Ignoring the episode's political ramifications and concentrating on the theme of a maiden's molestation, Hearst painted his story across the *Journal*'s front pages.

Another Hearst theme was that of patriots unjustly executed, plain people killed without cause. Not only did the *Journal* describe Spanish atrocities, it printed what it alleged to be the names and addresses of the Cuban dead. Each story, moreover, was lavishly illustrated to heighten the personal appeal of the victims and the sense of Spanish inhumanity. Willis Abbot later recalled a photograph of a Cuban beach scene; *Journal* artists drew in Spanish soldiers who appeared to be herding people into the water to drown.

Through the wires of the Associated Press the more remote corners of the country learned of such Hearst promotions. One can gain a rough measure of Hearst's success by noting his impress on those whose interests should have rendered them most resistant. Frequently moved by the misfortunes of others, William McKinley was unable to steel himself against the pitiable individual whose plight Hearst was exploiting. With greater sympathy than discretion, McKinley received Dr. Ruiz's widow at the White House. Following the liberation of Evangelina Cisneros, when the *Journal* quoted John Sherman as saying that "everyone would sympathize with the Journal's enterprise," the president was quoted as declaring that his secretary of state's words "correctly voiced the unofficial sentiment of the administration." No denial issued from McKinley's office. Indeed, Miss Cisneros was invited to talk with the president. Privately scorning the yellow press, banishing from the White House copies of both *World* and *Journal,* recognizing that Hearst was helping to set a collision course with Spain, McKinley nonetheless gave injury to Madrid, credence and respectability to Hearst by receiving a person he thought unjustly treated.

Such manifestations of influence failed to satisfy William Randolph Hearst. Neither he nor Joseph Pulitzer was content with the older precept that the journalist's job was simply to set out his position and wait for reason to prevail. The new journalism insisted on action, both as a reflection of already-mobilized support and as an inducement to further support. Attempting first to persuade government *not* to act, attempting subsequently to incite others, including the agencies of government, *to* act, in the end the popular press itself began to act in government's stead.

While big-city journalism remained the province of the urban educated, newspapers generally stood sentinel against any government's urge to meddle with what upper middle-class readers assumed a beneficent status quo. Editors monitored the executive branch with special care, for it was thought especially prone to deleterious initiatives.

During the Venezuelan crisis Joseph Pulitzer's role was this traditional one, the sentry alert to check executive encroachment. Angered by what he assumed administration bellicosity, he cabled British political and religious leaders, eliciting from almost all, including the Prince of Wales and former Prime Minister William E. Gladstone, gracious and conciliatory replies that were immediately printed in the *World* in the cause of peace. He cast his reading of the outcome in genteel fashion. "Publicity had done its work": the power of the press had compelled Cleveland and Olney to desist from government initiatives of a most dubious character.

This customary role, however, should not disguise Pulitzer's efforts to forge a new relationship for journalism vis-à-vis government. He wished to embody the popular will, and that required a conception far beyond the enforcement of laissez faire. He was not content with occasional chastisements of federal initiatives. Coveting recognition that the *World* spoke with the voice of the whole people, he demanded that Washington act in ways *he* thought reflected the popular will. If the federal government failed to respond, Pulitzer himself might mobilize resources to act in its place. He did so with an air of the nag, the person moving with a show of reluctance as if to shame another into accepting a clear responsibility.

Though his target seemed to be the rich rather than the government, Pulitzer as early as 1885 began to test his ability to mobilize action. When a private drive failed to collect sufficient funds to construct the pedestal for Frederic Auguste Bartholdi's Statue of Liberty, the *World* took the project in hand. "The World is the people's paper, and it now appeals to the people to come forward and raise the money. The $250,000 that the . . . statue cost was paid in by the masses of the French people—by the workingmen, the tradesmen, the shop girls, the artisans . . . Let us respond in like manner. Let us not wait for the millionaires to give money . . . Let us hear from the people." The crusade begun in March produced $101,091 by August: 120,000 people sent in sums ranging from five cents to Pulitzer's $250. A reporter caught his employer's spirit: "It is a grand thing to see a paper leading the sentiment of a nation. That is what the *World* is doing today."

During the Venezuelan dispute Pulitzer reached out beyond New York City and beyond the nation and, by enlisting the support of those figures important to English public life, brought undeniable pressure on what he deemed miscrreant government. Although Venezuela stole the drama, it was in an almost simultaneous confrontation—the debate over the sale of government bonds—that Pulitzer with great boldness pushed far beyond the concept of the newspaper as sentinel. Here Pulitzer disputed not the fact of federal action but the method. He castigated as "further costly dickers with a bond syndicate" negotiations between J. P. Morgan and a small group of government officials headed by the president. He insisted that the government offer its bonds directly to the public. "The World," he said, "offers in advance to take one million dollars of the new bonds at the highest market price. . . . It will *compel a public loan* . . . The voice of the country will be heard. . . ." The fact that a public sale had failed

two years earlier required action to establish the practicability of Pulitzer's alternative. The *World* sent telegrams and prepaid reply forms to 10,370 banks throughout the nation asking them to support a public issue. Fifty-three hundred replies, breaking Western Union's one-day record for messages sent to a single address, pledged purchases of $235,000,000.

As the *World* chided Washington, it became evident that the syndicate was only a secondary target. "The needless waste of ten or fifteen millions . . . [in brokers' commissions] is not the only or even the chief objection . . . [to this transaction]. It involves something of immeasurably greater worth than any number of millions. It involves popular confidence in the integrity of the Government . . . Secrecy of negotiation . . . awakens, unjustly, suspicions against the honor of the Government itself. . . . Trust the people, Mr. Cleveland!" On January 6, 1896, the secretary of the Treasury announced that he had authorized sale to the public. The issue was quickly oversubscribed. Attacking a government initiative, Pulitzer had moved on to prise open an alternative rejected by the executive, to mobilize opinion to compel government to abandon its preferred route.

William Randolph Hearst adopted Pulitzer's notion of the newspaper as an instrument of action vis-à-vis government. He quickly moved to persuade or, when necessary, to compel government to act in ways he urged. Again, however, there was the Hearst impulse to the extreme. Implicit in many of his actions was the portrayal of the newspaper as surrogate government. His was a journalism that in limited categories of action would rival and occasionally displace government.

Such a conception was not mere flatulence, for Pulitzer's innovative response to new technological capabilities permitted the newspaper to gather financial and organizational capacities that were, at certain points, superior to those of the federal government.

Information-gathering stands as a case in point. With government not yet providing an alternative source of information, political leaders accepted the newspaper as authoritative. Hearst's most famous reporter, James Creelman, claimed that the newspaper alone had access to the changing facts, and congressmen, who regularly cited newspaper stories in support of points made in debate, appeared to agree. Senator Mason called such articles "the only means of getting information." Senator Hoar employed his hometown newspaper as a private reference service, telegraphing for desired facts. As W. A. Swanberg concluded of the Cuban situation, "the United States administration . . . knew scarcely more than was printed in the newspapers."

To politicians watching Pulitzer and Hearst fling out their news networks, the *World* and the *Journal* seemed especially useful. While still one of the Senate's most powerful members, John Sherman quoted the *Journal* on the floor. The Senate's Foreign Relations Committee sought out *Journal* reporters Lawrence and Lainé for advice on the situation in Cuba.

Pulitzer and Hearst recognized the potential purchase in

sources of information superior to Washington's. Wagering that indispensability might scour some of sensationalism's tarnish, they raced to relay to office-holders news that was barely creeping through official channels. Ten days after the *Maine*'s destruction the *World* sent to the secretary of war a dispatch in which correspondent Sylvester Scovel described the progress of the official American inquiry then underway in Havana. Scovel's report, the *World* assured Alger, "contains information of the highest importance, and will prove useful to you." It would have, had the secretary paid it attention, for it told him, accurately in both cases, that "all the Board are now convinced that the *Maine* was blown up externally" and that Washington could not expect to receive the "secret" report before the following Wednesday. Alger and other administration officials, including the secretary of the Navy, first learned of Dewey's victory at Manila Bay when they opened telegrams from the *World*.

As the popular press moved to fill this information vacuum, so did Hearst exploit the void created by government's reluctance to act. Pulitzer's action tactics—urging the people to contribute money, to purchase government bonds, to sign petitions—did not encroach on government's sphere, but Hearst set for himself no such limit. In the Cisneros affair, for example, Hearst at first ordered more than two hundred reporters to knock on the doors of some of the nation's most respectable families. The widows of Ulysses Grant and Jefferson Davis, the wife of the secretary of state, even the mother of the president joined thousands of other women in signing petitions entreating the Pope's intervention and the Queen Regent's clemency. Lady Rothschild was prominent in the collection of two hundred thousand English signatures. Evangelina Cisneros, nonetheless, continued to languish in a Havana prison; in Hearst's reading, the government thereby revealed itself unwilling to meet its duty to translate public opinion into policy. Thus, before the popular frenzy had opportunity to subside or the Spanish had time to divest themselves of this acute embarrassment, Hearst sent reporter Karl Decker to Havana under orders to spirit the "Flower of Cuba" from her cell. Bribery rather than daring or ingenuity sufficed. Disguised as a sailor, Evangelina Cisneros was smuggled to New York for mammoth celebrations organized by Hearst to mark her deliverance.

Later, during the Spanish-American War, Hearst ordered Creelman to scuttle a vessel in midpassage of the Suez Canal in order to bar a Spanish fleet sailing for the Pacific. Though in the end of the outcome of the battle of Santiago Bay caused Madrid hastily to recall Admiral Manuel de la Carvara's squadron, Creelman was undismayed. Like Hearst, he had thought the United States government incapable of taking the essential step at Suez and, though his own aid had here proven unnecessary, he continued to uphold Hearst's belief in the indispensability of journalistic interjection: "There are times when public emergencies call for the sudden intervention of some power outside of governmental authority."

Equally as important as these actions was Hearst's constant resort to an imagery of surrogate government. As early as 1896, in a poll of the governors, he solicited opinion favorable to American intervention in Cuba and estimates of the numbers of volunteers each state would supply; he printed the results as if the *Journal* were an official organization whose capsulization of popular sentiment should lead automatically to its translation into government policy—specifically a war against Spain. Subsequent steps offered a picture of editor as powerful public servant. With no heed to Washington's possible diplomatic discomfiture, Hearst dispatched reporter Ralph Paine to deliver to the Cuban rebel general, Gomez, a diamond sword that, from its description, would seem a suitable gift from one potentate to another. He referred to his correspondents as "special commissioners." He designed a *Journal* flag to be flown from his buildings and vessels. He engaged a group of Congressmen to inspect conditions in Cuba under the *Journal*'s auspices. Speeches and articles issuing from this "Congressional Commission" were both fiercely interventionist and unabashedly laudatory of the accuracy of Hearst's reportage on Cuba.

Predictably, the *Journal*'s war organization was elaborate: between seventy and eighty correspondents; at least ten dispatch boats; extensive wire facilities and instrument depots. After offering the Navy his yacht and the Army a half-million dollar cavalry regiment—and securing no commission in return—Hearst entered the war zone as a journalist. Private Post, marching in column, noticed the editor at the roadside, drawn up as if to review the passing troops. Hearst later exposed himself to the enemy's fire and in his culminating adventure waded onto a beach to take as prisoners of war twenty-nine Spanish survivors of the naval battle of Santiago Bay.

Such activities must of course be weighed for serious substance against Hearst's penchant for self-advertisement. Whether he was moved by an aversion to discipline, by a particular form of social pretension, or by a truly radical vision is unclear, but there is evidence that he did see his own role as one of mobilizing power that would rival, and eventually supersede, the federal government's. The intent implicit in the pattern of his actions prior to and during the war was made explicit at the conflict's close. In a signed editorial appearing in the *Journal* on September 25, 1898, he wrote:

> The force of the newspaper is the greatest force in civilization.
>
> Under republican government, newspapers form and express public opinion.
>
> They suggest and control legislation.
>
> They declare wars.
>
> They punish criminals, especially the powerful.
>
> They reward with approving publicity the good deeds of citizens everywhere.
>
> The newspapers control the nation because THEY REPRESENT THE PEOPLE.

William Randolph Hearst alone could not have offered so comprehensive a challenge. Vital was the popular press' final asset, a cadre of reporters who shared his philosophy of expansive journalism.

The dynamic uniting in the popular press technology and circulation too often obscures the emotional dynamic that persuaded newspapermen that their actions on behalf of the people were at least as important as those of government. Many who worked for Pulitzer and Hearst, far from the stereotypical city-room cynic, were charged with an almost electric idealism. To them the old journalism had voiced only the interests of class or commercial constituencies. They brought to their battle to enlarge journalism a fervor that seemed to foreshadow that of the young settlement workers of the following decade. Their sense of journalism as a calling to public service was apparent in Arthur Brisbane of the *World* who, his friend Charles Edward Russell slyly and reluctantly conceded, "was willing to sacrifice himself for the cause of the common people." The leading motive of the yellow press, insisted James Creelman, was "moral responsibility." The newspaper would speak the needs of all the people, particularly the distressed. So heavily did enthusiasm armor these subalterns of the new journalism that one, the *Journal*'s Willis Abbot found selflessness even in his editor. Hearst, he reported, was entirely sincere in his sympathy for the masses. Even that supreme misanthrope Ambrose Bierce found excitement in the great numbers of people to whom the yellow press would carry his words.

These journalists of the second echelon were increasingly important for, in a result ironic to a movement undertaken to enlarge editors' influence, power was seeping from front offices. In December 1895 the circulation of the *World* stood at 583,000, an increase of almost 100,000 in twelve months. In the year following its purchase by Hearst, the *Journal*'s sales rose from 77,239 to 430,410. The defect concealed in such success was the passing of one-man management. No editor, however talented, could maintain control of such huge, multi-faceted operations.

Equally telling was the way in which the techniques of the new journalism, notably shouting headlines and magnetic illustrations, diminished the authority of the editor's own voice by drawing the reader from editorial to news pages. Despite his pivotal role in devising the new typography, Pulitzer retained an old-fashioned respect for the editorial page; he superintended editorial policy just as if careful reasoning continued to move his readership far more than those breathless and gaudy news columns. Hearst, more realistic, held the *Journal*'s editorial page in contempt.

A new kind of journalist waited to exploit these developments. As late as 1890 President Eliot of Harvard is reported to have denounced reporters as "drunkards, deadbeats and bummers"; five years later college graduates were already the rule in eastern newspaper offices. They were confident young men unwilling to assume that the editor's interests defined their own. They had a first glimpse of themselves as "professionals" whose standards would be rooted not in editorial dictation but in press clubs and in schools of journalism. Prizing the new typography, they discovered in the crusade and the human-interest story ideal vehicles both of their social idealism and its individualized expression. Again Hearst showed himself more adaptive than his rival. Pulitzer apparently overlooked the point that defections from the *World*'s staff

might hinge less on lavish salary increases than on Hearst's offer of by-lines denied Pulitzer employees. To characterize yellow-press correspondents solely in terms of a mock moralism intended to camouflage either cynicism, commercialism, or infantile adventurousness is to miss the wellspring of many of their actions.

Thus, in a James Creelman, the belief that he was serving others before self dictated a new relationship between newspaper and government. Professing to care about those whom he called "the distressed," he was at home with the notion of the newspaper as the appropriate agency to relieve victims, whether of Spaniards or politicians, criminals or rascals. When Spanish Premier Canovas noted during a conversation with the reporter that "the newspapers in your country seem to be more powerful than the government," Creelman offered no demurral on grounds of principle or practice. Yes, he replied, newspapers are "more in touch with the people."

Others shared this conception of the newspaper as an agency of action supplemental to, but at least commensurate with, the federal government. When General Shafter issued an order excluding correspondents from the ceremony marking Santiago's surrender, Sylvester Scovel announced himself from a rooftop overlooking the town square. Hauled down at Shafter's command, he insisted that he be included in official photographs of the surrender in recognition of the press' role in the war. When Shafter revealed that he found Scovel's proposition less than self-evident, the incensed reporter marred the dignity of the occasion by swinging at the general's nose.

Correspondents generally thought of themselves as full military participants, and the Army had no greater success in demarcating the line between soldier and newsman than between officer and enlisted volunteer. During the battle of El Caney, Creelman located a hidden route and then led General Chaffee's men in a bayonet charge against the Spanish position. Clambering atop the fort, he seized the Spanish flag—not for self, not for country, but as "a glorious prize for my newspaper." Those who have commented on the ensuing scene—Hearst arriving to tell the wounded Creelman, "I'm sorry you're hurt, but wasn't it a splendid fight? We must beat every paper in the world"—emphasize the editor's misplaced anxiety for the story rather than the survival of his correspondent. Overlooked is the fact that in relating the episode Creelman himself had no word of criticism for Hearst's reaction. He assumed, optimistically, that for Hearst too the cause transcended individual profit or puffery.

Because correspondents would act where government hesitated, because newspapers were "more in touch with the people," Creelman concluded that the newspaper must serve as their direct agent. Circulation rather than ballots would provide the measure of popular endorsement. To buy the newspaper was to vote its editor a "moral regency"; hence circulation figures would serve as referenda on a paper's specific actions "when it attempts to usurp the functions of the police, the courts, the legislature or even the President." It was to be—neither Hearst nor Creelman flinched from the ultimate logic of the argument—a system of "government by newspaper."

James Creelman was to be disappointed in his happy anticipation of the new journalism's assumption of power, and here Hearst and Pulitzer must bear partial responsibility. They delighted in exposing, denouncing, and demeaning one another, to the sole profit of an Associated Press whose ethics were not noticeably superior to their own. Hearst moreover drove on to the ultimate excess. When William McKinley was assassinated, many Americans connected the deed with the *Journal*'s earlier publication of Ambrose Bierce's quatrain

> The bullet that pierced Goebel's breast
> Can not be found in all the West;
> Good reason, it is speeding here
> To stretch McKinley on his bier

and an editorial suggesting that "If bad institutions and bad men can be got rid of only by killing, then the killing must be done." Many then concluded that Hearst was indeed a menace. Irate citizens burned bundles of the *Journal,* hanged the publisher in effigy, and forced advertisers to withdraw their patronage.

Hearst might have recouped the revenue and reputation lost in this setback, were not other developments revealing fundamental flaws in original yellow-press calculations. The gravest error lay in the basic economic assumption. While both *World* and *Journal* gained huge circulations, in neither case did advertising and revenue grow commensurately. Both newspapers lost money in 1898. Too many of the new readers either lacked purchasing power or were otherwise resistant to advertising; too many of the old, more prosperous readers defected to other dailies. The advertisers themselves began to organize, the better to resist rate increases by playing paper against paper. The Hearst-Pulitzer rivalry, in pursuing larger and larger numbers, had revealed unexpected limits to the circulation-advertising-profits equation.

The yellow press' thrust to power encountered yet another check. Both publishers had pressed the federal government to take various actions, but each was torn between urging government to act and acting as government. As Washington did respond to public pressure (most notably in mobilizing for war), it immediately reestablished itself as the focus of loyalty. The *Journal* and the *World,* with no claim on popular allegiances comparable to that of the state, found their area of maneuverability shrinking. A newspaper that conceded an identity between "the public interest" and administration policy invited eclipse, but to continue to court attention by championing the public interest *against* official policy and behavior in wartime required the most delicate calculations.

It was on this exposed flank that Hearst caught Pulitzer when the *World* printed a dispatch by Stephen Crane reporting that the 71st New York had wavered during the battle of San Juan. The *Journal* rushed into print a righteous denunciation of the *World*'s:

SLURS ON THE BRAVERY OF THE BOYS OF THE 71ST

Attempting to absolve itself, the *World* established a memorial fund for the regiment's dead, but so severe was public censure that it was compelled to return the money it had collected. Government rather than newspaper em-

bodied patriotism and though Hearst here invoked such sentiment to his tactical advantage, he at the same time reduced his own leverage vis-à-vis government.

To the first of these unforeseen problems Pulitzer and Hearst had no choice but to respond similarly. The cumulative effects of economic miscalculation so weakened the *World* and reduced the publisher's options that only a return to the status quo ante seemed feasible. Pulitzer opened negotiations with his rival, agreed to a truce and again admonished the *World*'s staff to practice journalism of only the highest character. Hearst, after probing with no success the possibilities of a newspaper cartel, was compelled by similar stringency to accept Pulitzer's armistice.

To the second problem Hearst and Pulitzer responded from very different ultimate aims. One cannot read Joseph Pulitzer's correspondence in the years 1896-98 without feeling shafts of sympathy. Those brilliantly innovative energies of the 1880s had cost him his health. He had lost his eyesight, and so fragile was his nervous system that a loud noise produced shattering pain. Traveling almost constantly in an unsuccessful quest for relief, Pulitzer visited the *World* office only three times after 1890. It was his greater misfortune that his nemesis appeared and, in pushing to its limits each of Pulitzer's propositions, revealed the unresolved tensions in his thought.

Pulitzer held initial impact essential. He prized format that seized readers' emotion, riveting their attention and rendering them receptive to his instruction. As he said of the *World:*

> It's read by, well, say a million people a day; and it's my duty to see they get the truth; but that's not enough. It's got to be put before them briefly so that they will read it; clearly so they will understand it; forcibly so they will appreciate it; picturesquely so they will remember it; and, above all, accurately so that they may be wisely guided by its light.

Pulitzer may have been wholly sincere, but the *World*'s pursuit of brevity, clarity, vividness, and especially force frequently terminated in gross simplification alien to accuracy. In large measure this grew from Pulitzer's inability to separate spheres of titillation and instruction. The basic concept, as Swanberg has noted, was that of a "hula dancer performing in front of a cathedral in order to attract the crowds," but Pulitzer never entirely purged himself of the temptation to summon those larger crowds that would flock to see the girl dance on the altar. The urge to attract readers often rendered the urge to instruct the victim of deferred purpose.

Nevertheless, his ultimate aims (however limping many of his efforts to achieve them) were essentially didactic. No longer nurturing the political ambitions of his youth—"I can never be president because I am a foreigner, but some day I am going to elect a president"—he still aspired to recognition as a moral force of national consequence. He assumed that whatever the day-to-day techniques employed to attract an expanding readership, he would be able to identify issues of moment to the nation and then, with the voice of reason, educate and mobilize the people to enlightened positions. He pursued power, but he never doubted that, when he chose, he could express that power as service to his fellow men. Never did he better approach this ideal than during the Venezuelan crisis: never did he move further from it than during the preliminaries to the Spanish-American War.

Hearst avoided the snare of Pulitzer's thought because he found it unnecessary to separate hula dancer and cathedral: Find out what your readers want and give it to them. The ultimate appeal, he thought, was to be found in what Arthur McEwen called "gee-whiz emotion." It followed that only through sensation could one speak to the entire nation, and Hearst too sought a national voice. His aims, however, lacked any pedagogical cast. They were purely manipulative. His goal in these years was specific, personal power. His method was that of fastening the *Journal* to any issue that would aid in forging a national political constituency.

Thus, with their efforts to establish a quasi-governmental power blocked by the intransigency of patriotism, it is not surprising that the two attempted to apply contrary solutions. Joseph Pulitzer retreated in some relief to that older role of sentinel: within a year he was denouncing that which he had helped to create, the "enormous expansion" of presidential power. Hearst, to the contrary, continued to press ahead. As the nation emerged from that extraordinary emotional climate of the 1890s, however, he was able to find no new way to bring mass circulation to bear on the political process. To hook the newspaper to still greater power only one route remained open: to unite newspaper, public interest, and government in the person of William Randolph Hearst. He stood for the nation's highest office and there his ultimate ambition met its defeat.

So disappeared the publishers' hopes for government by newspaper. The power of the yellow press was short-lived in part because economics and patriotism showed themselves less malleable than expected. In greater measure the transiency of its influence reflects the belated willingness of Washington itself to move into the political vacuum. Under Theodore Roosevelt the federal government began to respond to those entering and enlarging the center's political processes, those for whom only the *World* and the *Journal* had spoken. (pp. 151-73)

> *Gerald F. Linderman, "The Popular Press and the War," in his* The Mirror of War: American Society and the Spanish-American War, *The University of Michigan Press, 1974, pp. 148-73.*

YELLOW JOURNALISM AND SOCIETY

Arthur Brisbane

[*Brisbane was editor of the New York* Evening Journal *from 1897-1921. His editorials and columns for this and other newspapers owned by William Randolph Hearst were characterized by a fierce populism as well as an acute awareness of popular taste. In the following essay, he defends Yellow Journalism, specifically the Hearst*

papers, as responsible and aggressive agents of social change.]

> But be ye doers of the word, and not hearers only, deceiving your own selves.
>
> For if any be a hearer of the word, and not a doer, he is like unto a man beholding his natural face in a glass:
>
> For he beholdeth himself, and goeth his way, and straightway forgeteth what manner of man he was.
>
> But whoso looketh into the perfect law of liberty, and continueth therein, he being not a forgetful hearer, but a doer of the work, this man shall be blessed in his deed.—James I. 22-25.

From this text, every yellow journalist should preach.

It is the text of action, as opposed to inaction, of responsibility as opposed to indifference.

Yellow journalism is the journalism of action, and responsibility—whein it is the real and the right Yellow journalism.

Yellow journalism is simply Real journalism.

The other kind of journalism—that which barks as the Yellow Journal engine goes by, is the journalism of the past.

Each great newspaper in its turn is yellow. While it is in the ascendant, passing the others and setting new standards of action and of public spirit, it is yellow.

Success and prosperity combined dull the edge of the yellow editor. Then conservatism comes—"respectability" comes also, with a fine house, fine friends, social ambition, new interests, children that dread snubs.

Everybody knows that—in America especially—a man is largely what he owns.

The average American newspaper out much money. Then he is a real newspaper man, for it is a newspaper that he owns, and he works as a newspaper man, with his mind on nothing else.

Journalistic success brings money. The editor formerly has become a money man, he thinks and works as a money man. "Where your treasure is, there will your heart be also." When the treasure has been accumulated it is in Wall Street or that neighbourhood and there the editor's heart is also.

The editor with his heart in Wall Street ceases to be yellow. He takes on a superior dull golden hue—and that is reflected in the changed tone of his newspaper.

This is not meant as unkind criticism of the changing editors. The thin bird of the North changes into the fat rice bird when feeding among the Southern rice fields.

The thin, keen editorial bird, of real convictions and a desire to help other thin birds, changes into a morally fat and sleepy money bird when prosperity comes. He then thinks, acts and looks as the other fat birds do. He cannot help it, and he should not be blamed for it. Nature is stronger than man.

That editor was the sincere friend of other thin men when he was one of the thin. He is the sincere friend of other fat prosperous men now that he has become fat. He conscientiously adapts himself to the needs of his new class. But in doing so he betrays his thin readers and they find it out. Along comes another thin editor. He cries out that the people need saving. He makes a success which changes *him* into a fat editorial bird, and so it goes. The yellow newspaper of today becomes the conservative newspaper of to-morrow, and the DEAD newspaper of a little later, because money changes the editor's character, and with his character his newspaper changes.

William Randolph Hearst's appearance as an energetic, and consequently yellow editor, is interesting, because he began his work as a rich man. He did not enter journalism to make money. If he ever changes into a conservative "respectable" editor, with a newspaper slowly dying, it will be for some new reason.

It is impossible, of course, to discuss yellow journalism without discussing Hearst, the owner and editor of the New York *Journal,* and of eight other newspapers, ALL YELLOW.

Hearst is the yellow editor of the day. Nobody disputes his claim to the title, although not a few imitate him more or less ably, without ceasing to decry his objectionable activity.

Yellow journalism is perhaps yellower in Hearst's newspapers than it has been in any other. That is partly because he is the latest of the active editors—the "doers of the word." He makes himself especially offensive to the "hearers only," because he started out with unusual energy doing things, and had the means to do them.

Hearst's kind of yellow journalism is not entirely new.

Stanley died a few days ago. When James Gordon Bennett sent him into Africa to find Livingston, that was yellow journalism. Conservative, respectable journalism would have waited for Livingston to find himself. It would then have written mildly about him, or about his corpse, if he had been found dead.

There hasn't been any Livingston for Hearst to send after. If there were, he would send. He did send an expedition to get a Cuban girl out of prison. He got her out, and while that was not, perhaps, as important as the finding of Livingston, it was interesting, it was moral, and it was YELLOW.

A child named Marion Clarke was kidnapped in New York City. The case caused great excitement, and especially great apprehension among parents.

Yellow Journalism, represented by Hearst, offered and paid five thousand dollars reward for the recovery of the child. She was found through one of many thousand posters with which Yellow Journalism plastered the country. The kidnapper was convicted and sent to jail. The child returned to its mother. What was far more important, it was made evident to would-be kidnappers that they had

something more than the police to deal with. They learned that a yellow newspaper could set to work a million amateur detectives among its readers, and that even amateur detectives are to be dreaded when they number a million.

The New York *World,* which in its day was the leading yellow journal of America, and very useful, offered no reward for Marion Clarke and had nothing to do with finding her. But it did accuse Hearst of having caused the child to be stolen in order to create a sensation. That accusation was probably the last dying flicker of the old yellow enthusiasm gone wrong.

Dead or dying Yellow Journalism often shows traces of old activity in attacks on the yellow journal of the day.

Yellow Journalism attracts attention largely through deeds of active energy. The detection of crime, the sending of relief trains and relief boats at the editor's expense to flood victims at Galveston or elsewhere, the hiring of halls and organising of mass meetings to protest against franchise steals—such are the physical and externally visible good work of Yellow Journalism.

Far more important than anything else is the work that Yellow Journalism does in influencing the community in its *thought,* stimulating and supporting it in fighting the encroachments of class or of capital upon the popular rights.

The rich men, with their race tracks and their bookmakers, ignore public morality and the law because they want the pleasure and excitement of gambling. They debauch the public with their betting ring, that the public may pay for this pleasure. To denounce this, is to be a yellow journalist.

On the Stock Exchange, and in all sorts of Wall Street schemes, the respectable class rob the public respectably, while the little poolroom keeper, the petty swindler at the country fair must go to jail.

To criticise Wall Street gamblers, to bring criminal suits against Gas Trust extortion, against Ship Trust thieves, to fight the Coal Trust up to the Supreme Court and win—all that is Yellow Journalism.

Yellow Journalism is important to the great public because it does frighten, to some extent at least, the big public plunderers.

Yellow Journalism is important to the peaceful stability of society, BECAUSE IT ACTS AS A SAFETY VALVE FOR PUBLIC INDIGNATION..

There are among us perhaps ten millions of people very rich or fairly well to do, seventy millions who have not yet succeeded in entering the class of the rich, fat, human ricebirds.

While the great majority feel that they have a yellow journal to speak for them, while they see each other reading with approval the opinions of an editor who fights their battles, they know that their side is heard.

One of the greatest and ablest of railroad men in America—perhaps the ablest—told his counsel, a United States Senator, not long ago, that the social problems of this country could be settled only by a bloody revolution—the bloodiest in history—and declared it useless to hope for any other kind of a settlement.

That great railroad man was wrong.

There is no need of any bloody revolution, while the people realise that their side gets a hearing, while they are constantly reminded of the fact that with their votes they can do what they choose, that they don't deserve better conditions if they are not willing to vote for them.

What is Yellow Journalism?

It is the power of public opinion, the mental force of thousands or millions of readers utilised with more or less intelligence in the interest of those readers.

The yellow journal is the successor of the open spot where citizens of the Greek republic met to settle public affairs.

Those Greek citizens jostling each other's elbows were no more closely united in thought or purpose than the vastly greater crowd that makes up the power of the yellow journal.

I have no doubt that Hearst and his influence on public thought and action is the most powerful man in the United States to-day. That is because he owns the present meeting place of the people—the yellow journal—and he presides at all the meetings.

As to the faults of Yellow Journalism—they are numerous. But I think others can be trusted to point out these faults.

Let the mummies come out of the tombs of respectable journalism, and point their fingers at Yellow Journalism's defects. They can be trusted to do the work of criticism well and patiently.

Yellow journalists see the defects and deplore them. They remedy some of them, they neglect others in attending to more important matters.

Yellow Journalism is war, war on hypocrisy, war against class privilege, especially war against the foolishness of the crowd that will not think and will not use the weapon that it holds—the invincible ballot.

Henry L. Mencken on Yellow Journalism:

Look back a generation or two. Consider the history of our democracy since the Civil War. Our most serious problems, it must be plain, have been solved orgiastically, and to the tune of deafening newspaper urging and clamor. Men have been washed into office on waves of emotion, and washed out again in the same manner. Measures and policies have been determined by indignation far more often than by cold reason. But is the net result evil? Is there even any permanent damage from those debauches of sentiment in which the newspapers have acted insincerely, unintelligently, with no thought save for the show itself? I doubt it.

Henry L. Mencken, in his "Newspaper Morals," The Atlantic Monthly (March 1914).

All war is noisy, unpleasant, sensational. It often lacks taste, it does things rudely sometimes.

We may say the same of Yellow Journalism.

But war and Yellow Journalism are going to be necessary for some time to come. They will not die out until all the wrongs shall have been righted, all questions settled, all men filled with respect for justice, and the rights of others. (pp. 400-04)

Arthur Brisbane, "The American Newspaper," in The Bookman, *New York, Vol. XIX, June, 1904, pp. 400-04.*

Carroll D. Clark

[*In the following essay, Clark argues that Yellow Journalism fulfilled a social need created by the conditions of the American city at the end of the nineteenth century.*]

Among the cultural manifestations of recent times, yellow journalism holds a conspicuous, though by no means an honorific, position. Strange to say, considering the fact that the outstanding feature of "yellow" technique has always been to attract attention, the yellow press as a cultural phenomenon has largely escaped sociological scrutiny. Most of the few sociologists who have dealt with it have written not as sociologists but as moralists, adding their recriminations to the wholesale condemnation of religionists, *literati,* and welfare workers. As a natural consequence, little progress has been made toward an understanding of the "yellow" manifestation. Even today when most sociologists have learned to look with considerable objectivity at prostitution, crime, divorce, and race prejudice, there are those who still regard yellow journalism with moral abhorrence similar to that which King James I felt toward witchcraft.

One of the earliest, if not the first, of the attempts made by sociologists to get at the meaning of this type of journalism was essayed by W. I. Thomas [in his "The Psychology of Yellow Journalism," *American Magazine,* LXV (1908)]. While Thomas at that time joined the other critics in assuming an ethical attitude toward the yellow press, he felt the necessity of explaining it in social-psyhchological terms. "Of course the yellow journal is an immorality," he wrote, and "the most highly elaborated organ of untruth ever developed in the history of society." But the source of its badness lay "with the instinctive badness of human nature," the insatiable appetite of man for sensations in the form of horrors, crimes, disasters, and catastrophes.

> Whatever definition or characterization of the yellow journal we may finally determine upon, we must recognize first of all that in its sensational elements we have to do with something which, though it does not appeal to what we are accustomed to call the better part of ourselves, appeals nevertheless to something lying very deep down in us, something of the nature of impulse or appetite, and almost as blindly elemental as hunger itself. An appetite of this nature,

at once so powerful, so unanalyzable in consciousness, and so little amenable to intellectual oversight, may be assumed, from what we know of the laws of mental development to have a very early origin and to have been originally a trait of service to the species which it characterizes. . . .

A murder trial, a street or ring fight, a slanderous bit of gossip, a game in which you have a competitor to beat, and theatrical representations (which, whatever else may be said of them, are conspicuously reflections of conflict situations), are fascinating because they revive the elemental emotions. In the light of these facts it becomes plain that the yellow journal owes its existence to the persistence in men of primitive emotions of an essentially anti-social character, to the fact that emotions are pleasureable, no matter what their origin, and that people will pay to experience shock.

Thomas' article written twenty-three years ago shows a keener appreciation of the social significance of sensational news than much that is written today. However, he followed the bias of the day in explaining what was essentially a cultural phenomenon in terms of inborn tendencies of human nature. There is little in his discussion, or in that of later writers, to suggest that the sensational newspaper may be the product of a social situation. Professor Park was perhaps the first American sociologist to approach the newspaper from the latter standpoint ["The Natural History of the Newspaper," in Park and Burgess, *The City*]. The newspapers that today exist and are read, according to his view, are the product of social forces; the survivors of a long series of journalistic experiments in the struggle for circulation. It can be shown, I think, that yellow journalism was a type that sprang up spontaneously in a definite social milieu, and that its chief elements continue to flourish so long as the conditions that called them forth maintain.

First let us consider what are the chief characteristics of the type of journalism known as "yellow." Thomas singled out news of a highly sensational character as its quintessential trait. By sensational news he seems to have meant that which appeals to primitive passions and is shocking to certain moral or aesthetic sensibilities. Sensational news was indeed a trait of yellow journalism, but it likewise characterized the "penny-shockers" of the preceding generation. Inspection of famous yellow sheets shows that their outstanding features also included an appeal to romantic impulses, a great deal of "personal" details about celebrated or notorious individuals, muckraking crusades, and a variety of news stunts, special features, and typographical devices to compel attention. In short, they employed human-interest material, particularly the news that shocks or thrills, as a circulation bait. They did not follow the method of objective reporting, but dealt with their material much after the fashion of the dime novel, the "penny dreadful," and the Gothic romance. The muck-rakers, sob-writers, scandal-mongers, and other "shock" troops of the "yellow" forces were crude but effective artists who combined a romantic sense of popular desires and frustrations with a kind of grim re-

alism. The thesis to be set forth here is that yellow journalism was and, so far as it continues to exist, still is a phenomenon that arose as a response to the urban situation. True, the newspaper's entire development has been closely tied up with the growth of the city, since it is the latter which has forced the substitution of secondary for primary forms of association and has made reading a necessity. But the city in its present form is a very recent development. Early metropolises were merely aggregations of neighborhoods, drawn together for defense, rule, or commerce, and differing but little in fundamental organization from the country population around them. Even the population centers, like New York, Boston, and Philadelphia, where penny journalism flourished during the era of the elder Bennett, were for the most part concentrations of rural-minded communities within a small area.

The modern trend of urbanization began to gain momentum after the Civil War, and to modify rapidly traditional attitudes, culture complexes, and institutions. Economic specialization, social differentiation, and class segregation dissolved the old form of social solidarity based on informal and intimate relations in local areas. Gossip could no longer be purveyed from door to door until it became the property of the whole community. In proportion as the machine assumed the dominant place in widening fields of production, social life became mechanized and routinized, and the spontaneous desire for informal personal intercourse, for intimate participation in the thoughts and feelings of others, was thwarted. Experiences and interests became ever more divergent as specialization grew and mobility increased. Community of interest rather than community of residence became the basis of group organization, a fact that tended to fracture still further the fragmentary divisions of urban society.

Prior to 1880, newspapers had largely ignored news concerning the personal affairs of individuals. Such news was a matter for town talk or whisperings but not for printed publicity. While James Gordon Bennett had long before broken many traditions of privacy by brazenly publishing, in spite of horsewhippings and ostracism, news of bankruptcies, society balls, and religious meetings, his successors had made but little further headway in supplying spicy narratives of the personal doings of people. The new urban situation, however, made it inevitable that newspapers would sooner or later invade the realm of personal relationships and social transactions hitherto regarded as private. In the first place, city dwellers craved a substitute for the primary contacts and personal gossip which the social distance and the anonymous relations of the city had so largely undermined. Again, life in the city tended to become for great numbers a mechanical routine. Science and technology have rationalized the interests of life, but in so doing they have the effect of making them indirect instrumentalities rather than consummatory experiences. The specialized pursuits by means of which most city folk earn a livelihood become ever more remote from food, sex, shelter and other primitive needs of human beings. Shut in by walls of reticence and hedged about by depersonalized mechanisms, urban populations grow turgid with unsatisfied cravings. Yellow journalists discovered how to make news a surrogate for primary contacts and a romantic flight from the mechanized routine of workaday life. The manner in which this was accomplished is worth briefly noting.

Joseph Pulitzer, the first to introduce methods that were later to be known as "yellow," caught the fugitive attention of new masses of readers by muck-raking. He enlisted the public in a battle fought, avowedly, in its own interest. News, rather than editorial imprecations, became in his hands the chief weapon of assault upon graft, privilege, and political corruption. Damaging facts hitherto barred from the public were dug up and flung across the front page with little regard to the vested rights of institutions or the power of parties and prominent leaders implicated in the exposure. Muck-raking revived through the news columns the primitive passions of the manhunt. The "evil" attacked was hypostatized, or given some sort of tangible form, often through identifying it with a conspicuous malefactor. As the exposure of conditions filled the news columns day after day, aided by blasts from the editorial guns, common sentiments were aroused and public consciousness was focused ever more intently upon the issue. The result was to "organize" the crowd somewhat in the manner described by Gustav Le Bon. Employment of the newspaper in muck-raking induced the phenomena of orgiastic behavior rather than the orderly and purposeful responses of collective action. Its significance lies in the emotional release from the frustration and strain imposed by the conditions of urban existence.

In the hands of William Randolph Hearst, who shares with Pulitzer the somewhat doubtful honor of inventing yellow journalism, news became a bauble to distract and amuse, or a series of "stunts" to electrify a pleasure-seeking audience. It is the Hearst element in modern journalism that has led Waldo Frank to characterize news as a toy. He taught his reporters how to extract the ultimate heart throb out of every story, to trace imaginatively the human-interest details, to describe minutely the personal reactions of the actors. Thus, urban newspaper readers were enabled to find in the news a more or less authentic substitute for the variegated train of emotional responses that accompanies the more intimate and informal types of social intercourse.

Consciously or no, Hearst made the discovery that the inhabitants of the modern city retain essentially the same appetites, desires, and motives, and are swayed by many of the same beliefs, sentiments, and superstitions, as their unlettered ancestors who lived in caves and village huts. The sophistication of the city man, he perceived, was no more than skin deep. The human nature of the cave man has adapted itself to the urban habitat without being fundamentally remodelled. Hence, age-old credulities, antipathies, and passions may be played upon with profit through the necromancy of head lines and sensational news writing. In the great metropolis, where the whole gamut of human happenings is reënacted daily, there was no dearth of material. The problem faced by the yellow reporters was to portray events of human interest in the form of art; to make the oft-repeated but still unique episode symbolic of some phase of the common experience. Thus, Hearst's "sob-artists" would take the bare facts of

a penniless widow and her brood who had been ejected from a tenement, and produce a narrative summing up all the travail of the poor in the slums.

If Hearst was not an artist, he was at least a showman. His papers were designed for the masses who found their lives mechanically ordered and dull. For these masses his papers became a hippodromic exhibition providing vicarious thrills. The Hearst Sunday papers entered into lively competition with the various rising agencies of commercialized recreation, more than holding their own in the contest to provide emotional joyrides for cash. The New York Journal publicly boasted that its comic section contained "eight pages of iridescent polychromous effulgence that makes the rainbow look like a lead pipe." Jazz, with its florid tonal color, flashy syncopation, and giddy excitement, is perhaps the best metaphor for Hearst journalism.

The wave of journalistic "jazzmania" was less a product of the man Hearst than of the impersonal forces culminating in the social psychology of city life. The regard the man himself as the seducer of a virgin public, as many moralists have done, is to credit him with a power that could exist only in one of his own melodramas. Such power as he exerted came from the fact that he too was an offspring of the forces molding urban existence, and as a result could intuitively diagnose the strain, the monotony, and the drabness of life in slums, factories, and skyscrapers, and devise a stimulant and escape.

The yellow journalists did not invent sensationalism, but they carried it to new high levels. Sensational stories or news are found in folk-tales, in medieval chapbooks, in broadside ballads, in almanacs, and in many of the earlier newspapers. What is the meaning of "sensational?" Usually an experience is sensational when it shocks or startles us, or defies our capacity to assimilate it to our stereotypes or moral predilections. Examination of old and new forms of sensational material leads to the conclusion that almost invariably they deal with events that fall in domains where objective knowledge is lacking and where emotional attitudes and uncritical beliefs hold sway. Such events arouse strong subjective reactions unguided by rational adjustment techniques, with the result that they are deemed marvellous, startling, or shocking. Yet even though the untutored mind may be shocked and repulsed by such episodes, it finds a fascination in the emotional thrill they arouse, a fascination that may sometimes border upon morbid compulsion. Horrors, disasters, catastrophes, murders, executions, and supernatural terrors play a noteworthy part in folklore, classic and popular literature, and drama, as well as in journalism.

The significance of the extreme sensationalism of the yellow press appears when we examine the types of material treated. Where chapbooks, street ballads, and almanacs depended for source material chiefly upon natural catastrophes, freaks and monsters, ghost-fear, and the wiles of the Devil, the "yellow" news writers turned to the behavior of men in the new maze of social relations. In the urban habitat neighbors had become strangers, and conduct had become highly individuated. The break-down of custom and tradition had produced new and bewildering problems and brought about behavior that was frequently strange, violent and incomprehensible. Old crimes were committed in unprecedented ways, amours and scandals flourished, trusted leaders stooped to transactions of unbelievable corruption, and the Ten Commandments were broken in ways which, if not strictly novel, had at least never before been publicly broadcast. It was this weird and shocking social behavior within the gates rather than the external or supernatural forces of nature and the spirit world that aroused the orgies of sensationalism in the yellow sheets. Both the materials and the appetites for sensational news were autochthonous products of the urban environment. The morbid imaginations of profit-seeking publishers might devise techniques to satisfy the demand for such news, but they could not create that demand where it did not exist at least in latent form.

It was the city, then, with its disorganized areas and atomized personalities, its diversity of manners and morals, its conflicts of values and social definitions, and its confused involutions of human relations, that brought into existence the wave of extreme sensationalism. The experimenters in yellow journalism—Pulitzer, Hearst, Scripps, Bonfils, Goddard, and Brisbane—were merely brokers who speculated in a rising market. They hit on the news the public wanted to read and possessed the hardihood to publish it in the face of censure and contumely.

Yellow journalism, in the original sense of the term, may be said to have disappeared, except perhaps for its recent recrudescence in the tabloids. Its obsolescence did not come about so much from the abandonment of "yellow" methods as from a change in popular psychology. Sensationalism, jazz features, and other "yellow" techniques were standardized, diffused, and, with modifications based on practical experience, accepted as a part of modern urban journalism. Thereafter they gradually ceased to be regarded as "yellow" to the masses of readers. The early yellow sheets were primers for the marginally literate, and as times went on probably most of their readers graduated to a more substantial newspaper fare.

The front page and the Sunday edition remain as permanent contributions of the yellow period. The former is the specialized center of the news of universal appeal. Here are still gathered the "big" stories, the latest developments in "running news" like murder trials or sensational exposures, the juiciest bits of scandal; in short, the high lights of the news that shocks and thrills. The front page is an urban institution—it represents the focus of the mind of the heterogeneous urban crowd. In its columns are reflected the symptoms of our major social problems.

The Sunday edition still remains as Goddard and other yellow editors created it—a vast literary department store. In its sections are represented the diversified interests, fads, and foibles of the city's multitude. It is scanned by the semi-literate man and by the savant; probably no species of popular literature is so universal.

Yellow journalism was the first not to overrate the intelligence of the average reader and to appreciate how fugitive and transitory is the attention of the urban newspaper constituency. What statesmen, educators, religious leaders, welfare workers, and other uplifters had failed to do, it ac-

complished—it induced a "dull-minded and reluctant" public to read. The sensational news and human-interest material in which it specialized was a response to urban needs, for it served as a surrogate for primary contacts, and enabled the city man to enter imaginatively into the thoughts and motives of the inscrutable throng. In this way, perhaps, yellow journalism has helped to create a moral order within the urban habitat. (pp. 238-45)

Carroll D. Clark, "Yellow Journalism as a Mode of Urban Behavior," in The South Western Social Science Quarterly, *Vol. XIV, No. 3, December, 1933, pp. 238-45.*

E. L. Godkin

[*Godkin was a prominent figure in journalism in the late nineteenth century, founding the* Nation, *editing it from 1865 to 1899, and editing the* New York Evening Post *from 1883 to 1899. Both publications had reputations for intelligent writing and progressive views. In the following essay, Godkin lambastes Yellow Journalism for irresponsibly promoting the Spanish-American War.*]

The power of making war in a democracy must always, in the last resort, no matter what the constitutional arrangements may be, reside in the mass of the people. From them must come the demand which makes either war or peace inevitable. This, in a free state, there is no getting over. It is the popular will which puts armies in motion, or says there has been fighting enough. When war breaks out, therefore, it is really brought about by the influences which have acted most powerfully on the popular mind in its favor. When one sets about a minute examination of these influences, one is apt to be astonished by the number of them that are in some way irrelevant, such as misinformation about the causes of the war, about its cost, about its duration, about the character or doings of the enemy, about his motives in fighting, about the motives of our own public men, about international rights and duties, about the Government's state of preparation to fight. This can hardly be otherwise; it is so in every free country, when the war is an offensive one or is conducted at a distance from home. It is rare in any war, except a war of independence, that the public thoroughly understands what it is fighting about.

These influences are, in the main, the speaking and the writing which precede the war or bring it about. There is no other object ever submitted to a civilized human being for his decision so important as a proposal to go to war, or, in other words, to kill on a great scale the persons living in a certain country, and destroy their property. Our public men have long ceased to try to exercise this sort of influence. However much opposed to a war they may be, they dislike extremely to say so openly. They communicate their doubts or hesitations to their friends privately, but in public they shrink so much from the charge of want of "patriotism," which is the warrior's chief weapon, that their influence through speeches is almost always on the side of war, no matter what it is about. The days of Daniel Webster, and Calhoun, and Seward seem gone for ever. What the public man generally does now is to encourage war, if he speaks about it at all.

In default of other influences, the power of moulding opinion is passing—in fact, has long since passed—into the hands of the press. As a strange fate would have it, too, the subject on which the very worst portion of the press exerts most influence is war. The formenting of war and the publication of mendacious accounts of war have, in fact, become almost a special function of that portion of the press which is known as "yellow journals." The war increases their circulation immensely. They profit enormously by what inflicts sorrow and loss on the rest of the community. They talk incessantly of war, not in the way of instruction, but simply to excite by false news, and stimulate savage passions by atrocious suggestions. On some days they seem to have issued from an Iroquois village in war time, rather than from a Christian city. Read this, oh fighting parsons! clipped from a recent number of one of them, which claims a circulation of over a million copies every day:

> Occasionally we hear croaks from peace men. 'How sad to kill sons and fathers of sad-eyed women,' they say, etc. No sadder than to kill cousins and aunts of sad-eyed rattlesnakes. The man who would object to this war would object to the wholesale destruction of poisonous reptiles in India. And as for the American who has any feeling about the war other than a red-hot desire to hear of victories and Spanish ships sunk, all we can say is that he reminds us of the cannibal toad now on exhibition in the Paris Jardin d'Acclimatation.

Now the characteristic of these papers, which, as we have said, so powerfully influence opinion, is that they are, for the first time in American history, an irresponsible force, and the only one in the state. Every other influence in the community, not openly criminal, acknowledges some sort of restraint. The gamblers and policy-dealers live in fear of the police; the venders of obscene literature all have Anthony Comstock before their eyes; the dishonest business men live in dread of the loss of reputation or credit. Nearly every person prominent in any walk of life works under the control of something in the shape of a conscience. There are some things he does, or does not do, because his own heart tells him they would be wrong. Even our Congressmen stand in awe of their constituents. Statesmen recoil from violating the Constitution. Professional men dread the opinion of their professional brethren. In short, it would be difficult to name any body of men, pursuing a calling not openly criminal, who do not live and labor under some sort of discipline, seen or unseen, which constantly reminds them that they, too, have duties which they must perform, or suffer in some way.

From every such discipline or restraint, except libel suits, the yellow journalist is absolutely free. His one object is to circulate widely and make money. And he does circulate widely. He treats war as a prize-fight, and begets in hundreds of thousands of the class which enjoys prize-fights, an eager desire to hear about it or read about it. These hundreds of thousands write to their Congressmen clamoring for war, as the Romans used to clamor for *panem et circenses;* and as the timid and quiet are generally attending only too closely to their business, the Con-gressman concludes that if he, too, does not shout for war, he will lose his seat.

This is an absolutely new state of things. In none of our former wars did anything like the modern press play any part. In the Mexican war we even had a powerful anti-slavery press fighting vigorously for peace and justice, and, not to forget a great name, we had Lowell on the same side. The conservative, pro-slavery papers of that day, like the Washington *Intelligencer,* were gentlemanly, sober-minded sheets, still influenced by the old traditions of con-stitutional logic-chopping. In the civil war, too, the great newspapers were serious publications. Our cheap press today speaks in tones never before heard out of Paris. It urges upon ignorant people schemes more savage, disre-gard of either policy, or justice, or experience more com-plete, than the modern world has witnessed since the French Revolution. It is true it addresses the multitude mainly or only. The wise and learned and the pious and industrious do not read it. But it is the multitude mainly, and not the wise and learned and industrious, who now set fleets and armies in motion, who impose silence and ac-quiescence on all as soon as the word "war" is mentioned, and insist successfully that they shall not be interfered with, by either voice or vote, until they have had their fill of fighting. They have already established a régime in which a blackguard boy with several millions of dollars at his disposal has more influence on the use a great nation may make of its credit, of its army and navy, of its name and traditions, than all the statesmen and philosophers and professors in the country. If this does not supply food for reflection about the future of the nation to thoughtful men, it must be because the practice of reflection has ceased.

It is hardly possible to drop the subject without a word about the way in which men supposed to be thoughtful and far-seeing help these very agencies which are robbing them every year more and more of their legitimate influ-ence on the affairs of the nation. There appears to be hard-ly a clergyman, statesman, or lawyer in the country who does not denounce the yellow journals, and deplore their influence on the young and ignorant, and yet, whenever a yellow journal finds it desirable for advertising purposes to give itself a look of respectability, it does not find much difficulty in getting our prominent public teachers and moralists to comply with a request, fortified by a yellow check drawn on the proceeds of humbug and villany, to sanctify their columns with discourses on morality, patrio-tism, and religion. This is due partly to fear, and partly to vanity. The fear is that the yellow journal may, as it says, "alter its opinion about them"—that is, blackguard them vigorously and call them names for a week or two. The vanity comes from a delicious belief that anything which appears from their pens anywhere is sure to convince the yellow reader of his sin. It is very like a discourse to Marat from the Duc de la Rochefoucault, on "liberty, equality, and fraternity." (pp. 336-37)

E. L. Godkin, in an originally unsigned essay titled "The New Political Force," in The Na-tion, *New York, Vol. LXVI, No. 1714, May 5, 1898, pp. 336-37.*

FURTHER READING

Auxier, George W. "Middle Western Newspapers and the Spanish-American War, 1895-1898." *The Mississippi Valley Historical Review* XXVI, No. 4 (March 1940): 523-34.

Analyzes the wartime editorial policies of newspapers in Chicago, Detroit, Cleveland, and other cities and concludes that, unlike the sensationalist and jingoist papers in New York, Midwestern newspapers emphasized neutrality and arbitration.

Bent, Silas. "Changing Newspaper Morality." In his *Ballyhoo: The Voice of the Press,* pp. 150-79. New York: Boni and Liveright, 1927.

Focuses on the influence of Pulitzer, William Randolph Hearst, and Adolph S. Ochs.

———. "Roller Coaster Journalism." In his *Strange Bedfellows: A Review of Politics, Personalities, and the Press,* pp. 193-208. New York: Horace Liveright, 1928.

Attacks the newspapers of Hearst and Pulitzer as "journalism for juveniles."

———. *Newspaper Crusaders: A Neglected Story.* New York: Whittlesey House, 1939, 313 p.

Examines various social and political campaigns undertaken by newspapers in America since the colonial era.

Bleyer, Willard Grosvenor. *Main Currents in the History of American Journalism.* Boston: Houghton Mifflin, 1927, 464 p.

Historical survey including chapters on the newspapers of Pulitzer and Hearst and a list of sources for further study.

Brendon, Piers. *The Life and Death of the Press Barons.* New York: Atheneum, 1983, 288 p.

Contains sketches of British and American newspaper editors, including Charles Dana, Pulitzer, Hearst, and E. W. Scripps.

Budd, Louis J. "Color Him Curious about Yellow Journalism: Mark Twain and the New York City Press." *Journal of Popular Culture* 15, No. 2 (Fall 1981): 25-33.

Notes Twain's distrust of such newspapers as the *Sun,* the *World,* and the *Journal,* finding that only the *Evening Post* consistently avoided his wrathful remarks. Budd quotes Twain's reference to Hearst as the father of "Yellow Journalism—that calamity of calamities."

Coblentz, Edmond D., ed. *Newsmen Speak.* Berkeley and Los Angeles: University of California Press, 1954, 197 p.

Presents remarks on journalism by such prominent figures as Pulitzer, Hearst, Scripps, Ochs, James Gordon Bennett, Jr., Arthur Brisbane, and William Allen White.

Commager, Henry Steele. "Transition Years in Literature and Journalism." In his *The American Mind,* pp. 55-81. New Haven: Yale University Press, 1950.

Discusses the transition in American journalism at the end of the nineteenth century as "part of the transformation of America itself—of the process of mechanization, urbanization, and centralization, of the concentration of economic control, of the emancipation of women, the broadening of social interests, the standardization, democratization, and vulgarization of culture."

Creelman, James. *On the Great Highway: The Wanderings and Adventures of a Special Correspondent.* Boston: Lothrop, Lee & Shepard, 1901, 418 p.

Autobiography of the prominent wartime journalist. Creelman fiercely defends the editorial practices of Yellow Journalism.

Dana, Charles A. *The Art of Newspaper Making.* 1895. Reprint. New York: Arno & The New York Times, 1970, 114 p.

Contains three lectures: "The Modern American Newspaper," "The Profession of Journalism," and "The Making of a Newspaper Man."

Davis, Richard Harding. "Our War Correspondents in Cuba and Puerto Rico." *Harper's New Monthly Magazine* XCVIII, No. DLXXXVIII (May 1899): 938-48.

Profiles war correspondents including Howard N. Thompson, John F. Bass, and Stephen Crane.

Dreiser, Theodore. *Newspaper Days.* New York: Horace Liveright, 1931, 502 p.

Memoir of experiences as a newspaper reporter in several American cities. This work was originally published in 1922 as *A Book about Myself.*

Godkin, E. L. "Newspapers Here and Abroad." *The North American Review* CL, No. CCCXCIX (February 1890): 197-204.

Decries the state of American newspapers. Godkin claims, "It is not too much to say that they are . . . exerting more influence on the popular mind and the popular morals than either the pulpit or the book press has exerted in five hundred years."

Greene, Laurence, ed. *America Goes to Press: The News of Yesterday.* 1936. Reprint. St. Clair Shores, Mich.: Scholarly Press, n.d., 375 p.

Reprints newspaper articles covering historic events.

Irwin, Will. *The American Newspaper.* Ames: Iowa State University Press, 1969, 94 p.

Reprints a series of articles written for *Collier's* magazine in 1911, with commentary by Clifford F. Weigle and David G. Clark. "The Fourth Current," excerpted above, chronicles the rise of Yellow Journalism. "The Spread and Decline of Yellow Journalism" follows.

Lee, Alfred McClung. "The World's News" and "The World's News (Continued)." In his *The Daily Newspaper in America: The Evolution of a Social Instrument,* pp. 476-519, 520-75. New York: Macmillan Co., 1937.

Highlights technological innovations and the rise of news agencies.

"Hearst Journalism." *Life* 3, No. 9 (27 August 1951): 22.

Editorial accompanying an obituary feature on Hearst. The writer warns against praising Hearst's career too strongly, asserting, "Hearst Journalism never overburdened its readers with information of any kind—for information may sometimes be dull and dullness is a sin—but it was especially lean on any information from the other side of the fence."

Payne, George Henry. "The Melodrama in the News." In his

History of Journalism in the United States, pp. 360-69. New York: D. Appleton and Co., 1920.

Characterizes Pulitzer as an unappreciated genius.

Price, Warren C. *The Literature of Journalism: An Annotated Bibliography.* Minneapolis: University of Minnesota Press, 1959, 489 p.

Includes more than 3,000 citations of secondary sources related to journalism.

Rutland, Robert A. "Cross Currents" and "Rich Man, Poor Man." In his *The Newsmongers: Journalism in the Life of the Nation, 1690-1972,* pp. 240-62, 263-89. New York: Dial Press, 1973.

Accounts of newspaper journalism at the end of the nineteenth century, focusing especially upon the careers of Pulitzer and Hearst.

Wilcox, Delos F. "The American Newspaper: A Study in Social Psychology." *Annals of the American Academy of Political and Social Science* 16 (July 1900): 56-92.

Compares the amount of news, illustrations, literature, opinion, and advertisements in newspapers from different parts of the country, labelling some papers "yellow journalism" and others "conservative journalism." Wilcox concludes with a call for newspaper reform.

Wilkerson, Marcus M. *Public Opinion and the Spanish-American War: A Study in War Propaganda.* 1932. Reprint. New York: Russell & Russell, 1967, 141 p.

Argues that the American press was the strongest influence in bringing about the Spanish-American war.

Nineteenth-Century Literature Criticism

Topics Volume

Cumulative Indexes

Volumes 1-36

This Index Includes References to Entries in These Gale Series

Children's Literature Review includes excerpts from reviews, criticism, and commentary on works of authors and illustrators who create books for children.

Classical and Medieval Literature Criticism offers excerpts of criticism on the works of world authors from classical antiquity through the fourteenth century.

Contemporary Authors Series encompasses five related series. *Contemporary Authors* provides biographical and bibliographical information on more than 97,000 writers of fiction and nonfiction. *Contemporary Authors New Revision Series* provides completely updated information on authors covered in *CA. Contemporary Authors Permanent Series* consists of listings for deceased and inactive authors. *Contemporary Authors Autobiography Series* presents specially commissioned autobiographies by leading contemporary writers. *Contemporary Authors Bibliographical Series* contains primary and secondary bibliographies as well as analytical bibliographical essays by authorities on major modern authors.

Contemporary Literary Criticism presents excerpts of criticism on the works of novelists, poets, dramatists, short story writers, scriptwriters, and other creative writers who are now living or who have died since 1960.

Dictionary of Literary Biography encompasses four related series. *Dictionary of Literary Biography* furnishes illustrated overviews of authors' lives and works. *Dictionary of Literary Biography Documentary Series* illuminates the careers of major figures through a selection of literary documents, including letters, interviews, and photographs. *Dictionary of Literary Biography Yearbook* summarizes the past year's literary activity and includes updated entries on individual authors. *Concise Dictionary of American Literary Biography*, a six-volume series, collects revised and updated sketches on major American authors that were originally presented in *Dictionary of Literary Biography*.

Drama Criticism provides excerpts of criticism on the works of playwrights of all nationalities and periods of literary history.

Literature Criticism from 1400 to 1800 compiles significant passages from the most noteworthy criticism on authors of the fifteenth through eighteenth centuries.

Nineteenth-Century Literature Criticism offers significant passages from criticism on authors who died between 1800 and 1899.

Poetry Criticism presents excerpts of criticism on the works of poets from all eras, movements, and nationalities.

Short Story Criticism compiles excerpts of criticism on short fiction written by authors of all eras and nationalities.

Something about the Author Series encompasses three related series. *Something about the Author* contains well-illustrated biographical sketches on juvenile and young adult authors and illustrators from all eras. *Something about the Author Autobiography Series* presents specially commissioned autobiographies by prominent authors and illustrators of books for children and young adults. *Authors & Artists for Young Adults* provides high school and junior high school students with profiles of their favorite creative artists.

Twentieth-Century Literary Criticism contains critical excerpts by the most significant commentators on poets, novelists, short story writers, dramatists, and philosophers who died between 1900 and 1960.

Yesterday's Authors of Books for Children contains heavily illustrated entries on children's writers who died before 1961. Complete in two volumes.

Literary Criticism Series
Cumulative Author Index

This index lists all author entries in the Gale Literary Criticism Series and includes cross-references to other Gale sources. References in the index are identified as follows:

AAYA: *Authors & Artists for Young Adults,* Volumes 1-7
BLC: *Black Literature Criticism,* Volumes 1-3
CA: *Contemporary Authors* (original series), Volumes 1-136
CAAS: *Contemporary Authors Autobiography Series,* Volumes 1-15
CABS: *Contemporary Authors Bibliographical Series,* Volumes 1-3
CANR: *Contemporary Authors New Revision Series,* Volumes 1-35
CAP: *Contemporary Authors Permanent Series,* Volumes 1-2
CA-R: *Contemporary Authors* (first revision), Volumes 1-44
CDALB: *Concise Dictionary of American Literary Biography,* Volumes 1-6
CLC: *Contemporary Literary Criticism,* Volumes 1-71
CLR: *Children's Literature Review,* Volumes 1-25
CMLC: *Classical and Medieval Literature Criticism,* Volumes 1-9
DC: *Drama Criticism,* Volumes 1-2
DLB: *Dictionary of Literary Biography,* Volumes 1-114
DLB-DS: *Dictionary of Literary Biography Documentary Series,* Volumes 1-9
DLB-Y: *Dictionary of Literary Biography Yearbook,* Volumes 1980-1990
LC: *Literature Criticism from 1400 to 1800,* Volumes 1-19
NCLC: *Nineteenth-Century Literature Criticism,* Volumes 1-36
PC: *Poetry Criticism,* Volumes 1-4
SAAS: *Something about the Author Autobiography Series,* Volumes 1-14
SATA: *Something about the Author,* Volumes 1-68
SSC: *Short Story Criticism,* Volumes 1-10
TCLC: *Twentieth-Century Literary Criticism,* Volumes 1-45
WLC: *World Literature Criticism, 1500 to the Present,* Volumes 1-6
YABC: *Yesterday's Authors of Books for Children,* Volumes 1-2

Burroughs, William S(eward)
1914- . . . . **CLC 1, 2, 5, 15, 22, 42**
See also WLC 1; CANR 20; CA 9-12R;
DLB 2, 8, 16; DLB-Y 81

Busch, Frederick 1941- . . . **CLC 7, 10, 18, 47**
See also CAAS 1; CA 33-36R; DLB 6

Bush, Ronald 19??- . . . . **CLC 34**

Butler, Octavia E(stelle) 1947- . . . . . **CLC 38**
See also CANR 12, 24; CA 73-76; DLB 33

Butler, Samuel 1612-1680 . . . . **LC 16**
See also DLB 101

Butler, Samuel 1835-1902 . . . . . . **TCLC 1, 33**
See also WLC 1; CA 104; DLB 18, 57

Butor, Michel (Marie Francois)
1926- . . . . **CLC 1, 3, 8, 11, 15**
See also CA 9-12R

Buzo, Alexander 1944- . . . . **CLC 61**
See also CANR 17; CA 97-100

Buzzati, Dino 1906-1972 . . . . **CLC 36**
See also obituary CA 33-36R

Byars, Betsy 1928- . . . . **CLC 35**
See also CLR 1, 16; CANR 18; CA 33-36R;
SAAS 1; SATA 4, 46; DLB 52

Byatt, A(ntonia) S(usan Drabble)
1936- . . . . **CLC 19, 65**
See also CANR 13, 33; CA 13-16R;
DLB 14

Byrne, David 1953?- . . . . **CLC 26**

Byrne, John Keyes 1926-
See Leonard, Hugh
See also CA 102

Byron, George Gordon (Noel), Lord Byron
1788-1824 . . . . **NCLC 2, 12**
See also WLC 1

Caballero, Fernan 1796-1877 . . . . . **NCLC 10**

Cabell, James Branch 1879-1958 . . . **TCLC 6**
See also CA 105; DLB 9, 78

Cable, George Washington
1844-1925 . . . . **TCLC 4; SSC 4**
See also CA 104; DLB 12, 74

Cabrera Infante, G(uillermo)
1929- . . . . **CLC 5, 25, 45**
See also CANR 29; CA 85-88

Cade, Toni 1939-
See Bambara, Toni Cade

CAEdmon fl. 658-680 . . . . **CMLC 7**

Cage, John (Milton, Jr.) 1912- . . . . . **CLC 41**
See also CANR 9; CA 13-16R

Cain, G. 1929-
See Cabrera Infante, G(uillermo)

Cain, James M(allahan)
1892-1977 . . . . **CLC 3, 11, 28**
See also CANR 8; CA 17-20R;
obituary CA 73-76

Caldwell, Erskine (Preston)
1903-1987 . . . . **CLC 1, 8, 14, 50, 60**
See also CAAS 1; CANR 2; CA 1-4R;
obituary CA 121; DLB 9, 86

Caldwell, (Janet Miriam) Taylor (Holland)
1900-1985 . . . . **CLC 2, 28, 39**
See also CANR 5; CA 5-8R;
obituary CA 116

Calhoun, John Caldwell
1782-1850 . . . . **NCLC 15**
See also DLB 3

Calisher, Hortense 1911- . . . . **CLC 2, 4, 8, 38**
See also CANR 1, 22; CA 1-4R; DLB 2

Callaghan, Morley (Edward)
1903-1990 . . . . **CLC 3, 14, 41, 65**
See also CANR 33; CA 9-12R;
obituary CA 132; DLB 68

Calvino, Italo
1923-1985 . . . . **CLC 5, 8, 11, 22, 33, 39;**
SSC 3
See also CANR 23; CA 85-88;
obituary CA 116

Cameron, Carey 1952- . . . . **CLC 59**

Cameron, Peter 1959- . . . . **CLC 44**
See also CA 125

Campana, Dino 1885-1932 . . . . **TCLC 20**
See also CA 117

Campbell, John W(ood), Jr.
1910-1971 . . . . **CLC 32**
See also CAP 2; CA 21-22;
obituary CA 29-32R; DLB 8

Campbell, Joseph 1904-1987 . . . . . . **CLC 69**
See also CANR 3, 28; CA 4R;
obituary CA 124; AAYA 3

Campbell, (John) Ramsey 1946- . . . . **CLC 42**
See also CANR 7; CA 57-60

Campbell, (Ignatius) Roy (Dunnachie)
1901-1957 . . . . **TCLC 5**
See also CA 104; DLB 20

Campbell, Thomas 1777-1844 . . . . **NCLC 19**

Campbell, (William) Wilfred
1861-1918 . . . . **TCLC 9**
See also CA 106

Camus, Albert
1913-1960 . . . **CLC 1, 2, 4, 9, 11, 14, 32,**
63, 69; DC 2; SSC 9
See also WLC 1; CA 89-92; DLB 72

Canby, Vincent 1924- . . . . **CLC 13**
See also CA 81-84

Canetti, Elias 1905- . . . . **CLC 3, 14, 25**
See also CANR 23; CA 21-24R; DLB 85

Canin, Ethan 1960- . . . . **CLC 55**

Cape, Judith 1916-
See Page, P(atricia) K(athleen)

Capek, Karel
1890-1938 . . . . **TCLC 6, 37; DC 1**
See also WLC 1; CA 104

Capote, Truman
1924-1984 . . . . . **CLC 1, 3, 8, 13, 19, 34,**
38, 58; SSC 2
See also WLC 1; CANR 18; CA 5-8R;
obituary CA 113; DLB 2; DLB-Y 80, 84;
CDALB 1941-1968

Capra, Frank 1897- . . . . **CLC 16**
See also CA 61-64

Caputo, Philip 1941- . . . . **CLC 32**
See also CA 73-76

Card, Orson Scott 1951- . . . . **CLC 44, 47, 50**
See also CA 102

Cardenal, Ernesto 1925- . . . . **CLC 31**
See also CANR 2; CA 49-52

Carducci, Giosue 1835-1907 . . . . **TCLC 32**

Carew, Thomas 1595?-1640 . . . . **LC 13**

Carey, Ernestine Gilbreth 1908- . . . . **CLC 17**
See also CA 5-8R; SATA 2

Carey, Peter 1943- . . . . **CLC 40, 55**
See also CA 123, 127

Carleton, William 1794-1869 . . . . . **NCLC 3**

Carlisle, Henry (Coffin) 1926- . . . . . . **CLC 33**
See also CANR 15; CA 13-16R

Carlson, Ron(ald F.) 1947- . . . . **CLC 54**
See also CA 105

Carlyle, Thomas 1795-1881 . . . . . . **NCLC 22**
See also DLB 55

Carman, (William) Bliss
1861-1929 . . . . **TCLC 7**
See also CA 104

Carpenter, Don(ald Richard)
1931- . . . . **CLC 41**
See also CANR 1; CA 45-48

Carpentier (y Valmont), Alejo
1904-1980 . . . . **CLC 8, 11, 38**
See also CANR 11; CA 65-68;
obituary CA 97-100

Carr, Emily 1871-1945 . . . . **TCLC 32**
See also DLB 68

Carr, John Dickson 1906-1977 . . . . . . **CLC 3**
See also CANR 3; CA 49-52;
obituary CA 69-72

Carr, Virginia Spencer 1929- . . . . **CLC 34**
See also CA 61-64

Carrier, Roch 1937- . . . . **CLC 13**
See also DLB 53

Carroll, James (P.) 1943- . . . . **CLC 38**
See also CA 81-84

Carroll, Jim 1951- . . . . **CLC 35**
See also CA 45-48

Carroll, Lewis 1832-1898 . . . . **NCLC 2**
See also Dodgson, Charles Lutwidge
See also CLR 2; WLC 1; DLB 18

Carroll, Paul Vincent 1900-1968 . . . . **CLC 10**
See also CA 9-12R; obituary CA 25-28R;
DLB 10

Carruth, Hayden 1921- . . . . **CLC 4, 7, 10, 18**
See also CANR 4; CA 9-12R; SATA 47;
DLB 5

Carson, Rachel 1907-1964 . . . . **CLC 71**
See also CANR 35; CA 77-80; SATA 23

Carter, Angela (Olive) 1940- . . . . . **CLC 5, 41**
See also CANR 12; CA 53-56; DLB 14

Carver, Raymond
1938-1988 . . . **CLC 22, 36, 53, 55; SSC 8**
See also CANR 17; CA 33-36R;
obituary CA 126; DLB-Y 84, 88

Cary, (Arthur) Joyce (Lunel)
1888-1957 . . . . **TCLC 1, 29**
See also CA 104; DLB 15

Casanova de Seingalt, Giovanni Jacopo
1725-1798 . . . . **LC 13**

Casares, Adolfo Bioy 1914-
See Bioy Casares, Adolfo

Casely-Hayford, J(oseph) E(phraim)
1866-1930 . . . . **TCLC 24**
See also BLC 1; CA 123

Casey, John 1880-1964
See O'Casey, Sean

Francis, Robert (Churchill)
1901-1987 . . . . **CLC 15**
See also CANR 1; CA 1-4R;
obituary CA 123

Frank, Anne 1929-1945 . . . . **TCLC 17**
See also WLC 2; CA 113; SATA 42

Frank, Elizabeth 1945- . . . . **CLC 39**
See also CA 121, 126

Franklin, (Stella Maria Sarah) Miles
1879-1954 . . . . **TCLC 7**
See also CA 104

Fraser, Antonia (Pakenham)
1932- . . . . **CLC 32**
See also CA 85-88; SATA 32

Fraser, George MacDonald 1925- . . . . **CLC 7**
See also CANR 2; CA 45-48

Fraser, Sylvia 1935- . . . . **CLC 64**
See also CANR 1, 16; CA 45-48

Frayn, Michael 1933- . . . . . . **CLC 3, 7, 31, 47**
See also CA 5-8R; DLB 13, 14

Fraze, Candida 19??- . . . . **CLC 50**
See also CA 125

Frazer, Sir James George
1854-1941 . . . . **TCLC 32**
See also CA 118

Frazier, Ian 1951- . . . . **CLC 46**
See also CA 130

Frederic, Harold 1856-1898 . . . . . . **NCLC 10**
See also DLB 12, 23

Frederick the Great 1712-1786 . . . . . . **LC 14**

Fredman, Russell (Bruce) 1929-
See also CLR 20

Fredro, Aleksander 1793-1876 . . . . . **NCLC 8**

Freeling, Nicolas 1927- . . . . **CLC 38**
See also CANR 1, 17; CA 49-52; DLB 87

Freeman, Douglas Southall
1886-1953 . . . . **TCLC 11**
See also CA 109; DLB 17

Freeman, Judith 1946- . . . . **CLC 55**

Freeman, Mary (Eleanor) Wilkins
1852-1930 . . . . **TCLC 9; SSC 1**
See also CA 106; DLB 12, 78

Freeman, R(ichard) Austin
1862-1943 . . . . **TCLC 21**
See also CA 113; DLB 70

French, Marilyn 1929- . . . . . . **CLC 10, 18, 60**
See also CANR 3; CA 69-72

Freneau, Philip Morin 1752-1832 . . **NCLC 1**
See also DLB 37, 43

Friedman, B(ernard) H(arper)
1926- . . . . **CLC 7**
See also CANR 3; CA 1-4R

Friedman, Bruce Jay 1930- . . . . **CLC 3, 5, 56**
See also CANR 25; CA 9-12R; DLB 2, 28

Friel, Brian 1929- . . . . **CLC 5, 42, 59**
See also CA 21-24R; DLB 13

Friis-Baastad, Babbis (Ellinor)
1921-1970 . . . . **CLC 12**
See also CA 17-20R; SATA 7

Frisch, Max (Rudolf)
1911- . . . . **CLC 3, 9, 14, 18, 32, 44**
See also CA 85-88; DLB 69

Fromentin, Eugene (Samuel Auguste)
1820-1876 . . . . **NCLC 10**

Frost, Robert (Lee)
1874-1963 . . . **CLC 1, 3, 4, 9, 10, 13, 15,
26, 34, 44; PC 1**
See also WLC 2; CA 89-92; SATA 14;
DLB 54; DLB-DS 7; CDALB 1917-1929

Fry, Christopher 1907- . . . . **CLC 2, 10, 14**
See also CANR 9; CA 17-20R; DLB 13

Frye, (Herman) Northrop
1912-1991 . . . . **CLC 24, 70**
See also CANR 8; CA 5-8R;
obituary CA 133; DLB 67, 68

Fuchs, Daniel 1909- . . . . **CLC 8, 22**
See also CAAS 5; CA 81-84; DLB 9, 26, 28

Fuchs, Daniel 1934- . . . . **CLC 34**
See also CANR 14; CA 37-40R

Fuentes, Carlos
1928- . . . . . . **CLC 3, 8, 10, 13, 22, 41, 60**
See also WLC 2; CANR 10; CA 69-72

Fugard, Athol 1932- . . . **CLC 5, 9, 14, 25, 40**
See also CA 85-88

Fugard, Sheila 1932- . . . . **CLC 48**
See also CA 125

Fuller, Charles (H., Jr.)
1939- . . . . **CLC 25; DC 1**
See also BLC 2; CA 108, 112; DLB 38

Fuller, John (Leopold) 1937- . . . . **CLC 62**
See also CANR 9; CA 21-22R; DLB 40

Fuller, (Sarah) Margaret
1810-1850 . . . . **NCLC 5**
See also Ossoli, Sarah Margaret (Fuller
marchesa d')
See also DLB 1, 59, 73; CDALB 1640-1865

Fuller, Roy (Broadbent) 1912- . . . . **CLC 4, 28**
See also CA 5-8R; DLB 15, 20

Fulton, Alice 1952- . . . . **CLC 52**
See also CA 116

Furabo 1644-1694
See Basho, Matsuo

Furphy, Joseph 1843-1912 . . . . **TCLC 25**

Futabatei Shimei 1864-1909 . . . . . . **TCLC 44**

Futrelle, Jacques 1875-1912 . . . . . . **TCLC 19**
See also CA 113

Gaboriau, Emile 1835-1873 . . . . . . **NCLC 14**

Gadda, Carlo Emilio 1893-1973 . . . . **CLC 11**
See also CA 89-92

Gaddis, William
1922- . . . . . . **CLC 1, 3, 6, 8, 10, 19, 43**
See also CAAS 4; CANR 21; CA 17-20R;
DLB 2

Gaines, Ernest J. 1933- . . . . . . **CLC 3, 11, 18**
See also BLC 2; CANR 6, 24; CA 9-12R;
DLB 2, 33; DLB-Y 80;
CDALB 1968-1988

Gaitskill, Mary 1954- . . . . **CLC 69**
See also CA 128

Gale, Zona 1874-1938 . . . . **TCLC 7**
See also CA 105; DLB 9, 78

Gallagher, Tess 1943- . . . . **CLC 18, 63**
See also CA 106

Gallant, Mavis
1922- . . . . **CLC 7, 18, 38; SSC 5**
See also CA 69-72; DLB 53

Gallant, Roy A(rthur) 1924- . . . . **CLC 17**
See also CANR 4; CA 5-8R; SATA 4

Gallico, Paul (William) 1897-1976 . . . **CLC 2**
See also CA 5-8R; obituary CA 69-72;
SATA 13; DLB 9

Galsworthy, John 1867-1933 . . . . **TCLC 1, 45**
See also WLC 2; brief entry CA 104;
DLB 10, 34, 98

Galt, John 1779-1839 . . . . **NCLC 1**

Galvin, James 1951- . . . . **CLC 38**
See also CANR 26; CA 108

Gamboa, Frederico 1864-1939 . . . . . **TCLC 36**

Gann, Ernest K(ellogg) 1910- . . . . . . **CLC 23**
See also CANR 1; CA 1-4R

Garcia Lorca, Federico
1898-1936 . . . . . **TCLC 1, 7; DC 2; PC 3**
See also WLC 2; CA 131;
brief entry CA 104; DLB 108

Garcia Marquez, Gabriel (Jose)
1928- . . . **CLC 2, 3, 8, 10, 15, 27, 47, 55,
68; SSC 8**
See also WLC 3; CANR 10, 28;
CA 33-36R; AAYA 3

Gardam, Jane 1928- . . . . **CLC 43**
See also CLR 12; CANR 2, 18; CA 49-52;
SATA 28, 39; DLB 14

Gardner, Herb 1934- . . . . **CLC 44**

Gardner, John (Champlin, Jr.)
1933-1982 . . . . **CLC 2, 3, 5, 7, 8, 10, 18,
28, 34; SSC 7**
See also CA 65-68; obituary CA 107;
obituary SATA 31, 40; DLB 2; DLB-Y 82

Gardner, John (Edmund) 1926- . . . . . **CLC 30**
See also CANR 15; CA 103

Gardons, S. S. 1926-
See Snodgrass, W(illiam) D(e Witt)

Garfield, Leon 1921- . . . . **CLC 12**
See also CA 17-20R; SATA 1, 32

Garland, (Hannibal) Hamlin
1860-1940 . . . . **TCLC 3**
See also CA 104; DLB 12, 71, 78

Garneau, Hector (de) Saint Denys
1912-1943 . . . . **TCLC 13**
See also CA 111; DLB 88

Garner, Alan 1935- . . . . **CLC 17**
See also CLR 20; CANR 15; CA 73-76;
SATA 18

Garner, Hugh 1913-1979 . . . . **CLC 13**
See also CA 69-72; DLB 68

Garnett, David 1892-1981 . . . . **CLC 3**
See also CANR 17; CA 5-8R;
obituary CA 103; DLB 34

Garrett, George (Palmer, Jr.)
1929- . . . . **CLC 3, 11, 51**
See also CAAS 5; CANR 1; CA 1-4R;
DLB 2, 5; DLB-Y 83

Garrick, David 1717-1779 . . . . **LC 15**
See also DLB 84

Garrigue, Jean 1914-1972 . . . . **CLC 2, 8**
See also CANR 20; CA 5-8R;
obituary CA 37-40R

Garvey, Marcus 1887-1940 . . . . **TCLC 41**
See also BLC 2; CA 124; brief entry CA 120

Gary, Romain 1914-1980 .... CLC 25
See also Kacew, Romain

Gascar, Pierre 1916- .... CLC 11
See also Fournier, Pierre

Gascoyne, David (Emery) 1916- .... CLC 45
See also CANR 10; CA 65-68; DLB 20

Gaskell, Elizabeth Cleghorn
1810-1865 .... NCLC 5
See also DLB 21

Gass, William H(oward)
1924- .... CLC 1, 2, 8, 11, 15, 39
See also CA 17-20R; DLB 2

Gates, Henry Louis, Jr. 1950- ...... CLC 65
See also CANR 25; CA 109; DLB 67

Gautier, Theophile 1811-1872 ..... NCLC 1

Gaye, Marvin (Pentz) 1939-1984 ... CLC 26
See also obituary CA 112

Gebler, Carlo (Ernest) 1954- .... CLC 39
See also CA 119

Gee, Maggie 19??- .... CLC 57

Gee, Maurice (Gough) 1931- .... CLC 29
See also CA 97-100; SATA 46

Gelbart, Larry 1923?- .... CLC 21, 61
See also CA 73-76

Gelber, Jack 1932- .... CLC 1, 6, 14, 60
See also CANR 2; CA 1-4R; DLB 7

Gellhorn, Martha (Ellis) 1908- .. CLC 14, 60
See also CA 77-80; DLB-Y 82

Genet, Jean
1910-1986 ... CLC 1, 2, 5, 10, 14, 44, 46
See also CANR 18; CA 13-16R; DLB 72;
DLB-Y 86

Gent, Peter 1942- .... CLC 29
See also CA 89-92; DLB 72; DLB-Y 82

George, Jean Craighead 1919- ...... CLC 35
See also CLR 1; CA 5-8R; SATA 2;
DLB 52

George, Stefan (Anton)
1868-1933 .... TCLC 2, 14
See also CA 104

Gerhardi, William (Alexander) 1895-1977
See Gerhardie, William (Alexander)

Gerhardie, William (Alexander)
1895-1977 .... CLC 5
See also CANR 18; CA 25-28R;
obituary CA 73-76; DLB 36

Gerstler, Amy 1956- .... CLC 70

Gertler, T(rudy) 1946?- .... CLC 34
See also CA 116

Gessner, Friedrike Victoria 1910-1980
See Adamson, Joy(-Friederike Victoria)

Ghelderode, Michel de
1898-1962 .... CLC 6, 11
See also CA 85-88

Ghiselin, Brewster 1903- .... CLC 23
See also CANR 13; CA 13-16R

Ghose, Zulfikar 1935- .... CLC 42
See also CA 65-68

Ghosh, Amitav 1943- .... CLC 44

Giacosa, Giuseppe 1847-1906 ...... TCLC 7
See also CA 104

Gibbon, Lewis Grassic 1901-1935... TCLC 4
See also Mitchell, James Leslie

Gibbons, Kaye 1960- .... CLC 50

Gibran, (Gibran) Kahlil
1883-1931 .... TCLC 1, 9
See also CA 104

Gibson, William 1914- .... CLC 23
See also CANR 9; CA 9-12R; DLB 7

Gibson, William 1948- .... CLC 39, 63
See also CA 126

Gide, Andre (Paul Guillaume)
1869-1951 .... TCLC 5, 12, 36
See also WLC 3; CA 104, 124; DLB 65

Gifford, Barry (Colby) 1946- .... CLC 34
See also CANR 9; CA 65-68

Gilbert, (Sir) W(illiam) S(chwenck)
1836-1911 .... TCLC 3
See also CA 104; SATA 36

Gilbreth, Ernestine 1908-
See Carey, Ernestine Gilbreth

Gilbreth, Frank B(unker), Jr.
1911- .... CLC 17
See also CA 9-12R; SATA 2

Gilchrist, Ellen 1935- .... CLC 34, 48
See also CA 113, 116

Giles, Molly 1942- .... CLC 39
See also CA 126

Gilliam, Terry (Vance) 1940-
See Monty Python
See also CA 108, 113

Gilliatt, Penelope (Ann Douglass)
1932- .... CLC 2, 10, 13, 53
See also CA 13-16R; DLB 14

Gilman, Charlotte (Anna) Perkins (Stetson)
1860-1935 .... TCLC 9, 37
See also CA 106

Gilmour, David 1944-
See Pink Floyd

Gilpin, William 1724-1804 ...... NCLC 30

Gilroy, Frank D(aniel) 1925- .... CLC 2
See also CA 81-84; DLB 7

Ginsberg, Allen
1926- ..... CLC 1, 2, 3, 4, 6, 13, 36, 69;
PC 4
See also WLC 3; CANR 2; CA 1-4R;
DLB 5, 16; CDALB 1941-1968

Ginzburg, Natalia
1916-1991 .... CLC 5, 11, 54, 70
See also CANR 33; CA 85-88

Giono, Jean 1895-1970......... CLC 4, 11
See also CANR 2; CA 45-48;
obituary CA 29-32R; DLB 72

Giovanni, Nikki 1943- ..... CLC 2, 4, 19, 64
See also BLC 2; CLR 6; CAAS 6;
CANR 18; CA 29-32R; SATA 24;
DLB 5, 41

Giovene, Andrea 1904- .... CLC 7
See also CA 85-88

Gippius, Zinaida (Nikolayevna) 1869-1945
See Hippius, Zinaida
See also CA 106

Giraudoux, (Hippolyte) Jean
1882-1944 .... TCLC 2, 7
See also CA 104; DLB 65

Gironella, Jose Maria 1917- .... CLC 11
See also CA 101

Gissing, George (Robert)
1857-1903 .... TCLC 3, 24
See also CA 105; DLB 18

Gladkov, Fyodor (Vasilyevich)
1883-1958 .... TCLC 27

Glanville, Brian (Lester) 1931- ...... CLC 6
See also CANR 3; CA 5-8R; SATA 42;
DLB 15

Glasgow, Ellen (Anderson Gholson)
1873?-1945................ TCLC 2, 7
See also CA 104; DLB 9, 12

Glassco, John 1909-1981 .... CLC 9
See also CANR 15; CA 13-16R;
obituary CA 102; DLB 68

Glasser, Ronald J. 1940?- .... CLC 37

Glendinning, Victoria 1937- .... CLC 50
See also CA 120

Glissant, Edouard 1928- .... CLC 10, 68

Gloag, Julian 1930- .... CLC 40
See also CANR 10; CA 65-68

Gluck, Louise (Elisabeth)
1943- .... CLC 7, 22, 44
See also CA 33-36R; DLB 5

Gobineau, Joseph Arthur (Comte) de
1816-1882 .... NCLC 17

Godard, Jean-Luc 1930- .... CLC 20
See also CA 93-96

Godden, (Margaret) Rumer 1907- ... CLC 53
See also CLR 20; CANR 4, 27; CA 7-8R;
SATA 3, 36

Godwin, Gail 1937- .... CLC 5, 8, 22, 31, 69
See also CANR 15; CA 29-32R; DLB 6

Godwin, William 1756-1836...... NCLC 14
See also DLB 39

Goethe, Johann Wolfgang von
1749-1832 .... NCLC 4, 22, 34
See also WLC 3; DLB 94

Gogarty, Oliver St. John
1878-1957 .... TCLC 15
See also CA 109; DLB 15, 19

Gogol, Nikolai (Vasilyevich)
1809-1852 ..... NCLC 5, 15, 31; DC 1;
SSC 4
See also WLC 3

Goines, Donald 1937?-1974
See also BLC 2; CA 124; obituary CA 114;
DLB 33

Gokceli, Yasar Kemal 1923-
See Kemal, Yashar

Gold, Herbert 1924- .... CLC 4, 7, 14, 42
See also CANR 17; CA 9-12R; DLB 2;
DLB-Y 81

Goldbarth, Albert 1948- .... CLC 5, 38
See also CANR 6; CA 53-56

Goldberg, Anatol 1910-1982 .... CLC 34
See also obituary CA 117

Goldemberg, Isaac 1945- .... CLC 52
See also CANR 11; CA 69-72

Golding, William (Gerald)
1911- ..... CLC 1, 2, 3, 8, 10, 17, 27, 58
See also WLC 3; CANR 13; CA 5-8R;
DLB 15

Goldman, Emma 1869-1940....... TCLC 13
See also CA 110

Hentoff, Nat(han Irving) 1925- ..... **CLC 26**
See also CLR 1; CAAS 6; CANR 5, 25;
CA 1-4R; SATA 27, 42; AAYA 4

Heppenstall, (John) Rayner
1911-1981 .... **CLC 10**
See also CANR 29; CA 1-4R;
obituary CA 103

Herbert, Frank (Patrick)
1920-1986 .... **CLC 12, 23, 35, 44**
See also CANR 5; CA 53-56;
obituary CA 118; SATA 9, 37, 47; DLB 8

Herbert, George 1593-1633 .... **PC 4**

Herbert, Zbigniew 1924- .... **CLC 9, 43**
See also CA 89-92

Herbst, Josephine 1897-1969 .... **CLC 34**
See also CA 5-8R; obituary CA 25-28R;
DLB 9

Herder, Johann Gottfried von
1744-1803 .... **NCLC 8**

Hergesheimer, Joseph
1880-1954 .... **TCLC 11**
See also CA 109; DLB 9

Herlagnez, Pablo de 1844-1896
See Verlaine, Paul (Marie)

Herlihy, James Leo 1927- .... **CLC 6**
See also CANR 2; CA 1-4R

Hermogenes fl.c. 175- .... **CMLC 6**

Hernandez, Jose 1834-1886 ...... **NCLC 17**

Herrick, Robert 1591-1674 .... **LC 13**

Herriot, James 1916- .... **CLC 12**
See also Wight, James Alfred
See also AAYA 1

Herrmann, Dorothy 1941- .... **CLC 44**
See also CA 107

Hersey, John (Richard)
1914- .... **CLC 1, 2, 7, 9, 40**
See also CA 17-20R; SATA 25; DLB 6

Herzen, Aleksandr Ivanovich
1812-1870 .... **NCLC 10**

Herzl, Theodor 1860-1904 .... **TCLC 36**

Herzog, Werner 1942- .... **CLC 16**
See also CA 89-92

Hesiod c. 8th Century B.C.- ...... **CMLC 5**

Hesse, Hermann
1877-1962 ... **CLC 1, 2, 3, 6, 11, 17, 25,
69; SSC 9**
See also CAP 2; CA 17-18; SATA 50;
DLB 66

Heyen, William 1940- .... **CLC 13, 18**
See also CAAS 9; CA 33-36R; DLB 5

Heyerdahl, Thor 1914- .... **CLC 26**
See also CANR 5, 22; CA 5-8R; SATA 2,
52

Heym, Georg (Theodor Franz Arthur)
1887-1912 .... **TCLC 9**
See also CA 106

Heym, Stefan 1913- .... **CLC 41**
See also CANR 4; CA 9-12R; DLB 69

Heyse, Paul (Johann Ludwig von)
1830-1914 .... **TCLC 8**
See also CA 104

Hibbert, Eleanor (Burford) 1906- .... **CLC 7**
See also CANR 9, 28; CA 17-20R; SATA 2

Higgins, George V(incent)
1939- .... **CLC 4, 7, 10, 18**
See also CAAS 5; CANR 17; CA 77-80;
DLB 2; DLB-Y 81

Higginson, Thomas Wentworth
1823-1911 .... **TCLC 36**
See also DLB 1, 64

Highsmith, (Mary) Patricia
1921- .... **CLC 2, 4, 14, 42**
See also CANR 1, 20; CA 1-4R

Highwater, Jamake 1942- .... **CLC 12**
See also CLR 17; CAAS 7; CANR 10;
CA 65-68; SATA 30, 32; DLB 52;
DLB-Y 85

Hijuelos, Oscar 1951- .... **CLC 65**
See also CA 123

Hikmet (Ran), Nazim 1902-1963.... **CLC 40**
See also obituary CA 93-96

Hildesheimer, Wolfgang 1916- ..... **CLC 49**
See also CA 101; DLB 69

Hill, Geoffrey (William)
1932- .... **CLC 5, 8, 18, 45**
See also CANR 21; CA 81-84; DLB 40

Hill, George Roy 1922- .... **CLC 26**
See also CA 110, 122

Hill, Susan B. 1942- .... **CLC 4**
See also CANR 29; CA 33-36R; DLB 14

Hillerman, Tony 1925- .... **CLC 62**
See also CANR 21; CA 29-32R; SATA 6

Hilliard, Noel (Harvey) 1929- ...... **CLC 15**
See also CANR 7; CA 9-12R

Hillis, Richard Lyle 1956-
See Hillis, Rick

Hillis, Rick 1956- .... **CLC 66**
See also Hillis, Richard Lyle

Hilton, James 1900-1954 .... **TCLC 21**
See also CA 108; SATA 34; DLB 34, 77

Himes, Chester (Bomar)
1909-1984 .... **CLC 2, 4, 7, 18, 58**
See also BLC 2; CANR 22; CA 25-28R;
obituary CA 114; DLB 2, 76

Hinde, Thomas 1926- .... **CLC 6, 11**
See also Chitty, (Sir) Thomas Willes

Hine, (William) Daryl 1936- .... **CLC 15**
See also CANR 1, 20; CA 1-4R; DLB 60

Hinton, S(usan) E(loise) 1950- ..... **CLC 30**
See also CLR 3, 23; CA 81-84; SATA 19,
58; AAYA 2

**Hippius (Merezhkovsky), Zinaida
(Nikolayevna)** 1869-1945 ...... **TCLC 9**
See also Gippius, Zinaida (Nikolayevna)

Hiraoka, Kimitake 1925-1970
See Mishima, Yukio
See also CA 97-100; obituary CA 29-32R

Hirsch, Edward (Mark) 1950-... **CLC 31, 50**
See also CANR 20; CA 104

Hitchcock, (Sir) Alfred (Joseph)
1899-1980 .... **CLC 16**
See also obituary CA 97-100; SATA 27;
obituary SATA 24

Hoagland, Edward 1932- .... **CLC 28**
See also CANR 2; CA 1-4R; SATA 51;
DLB 6

Hoban, Russell C(onwell) 1925- .. **CLC 7, 25**
See also CLR 3; CANR 23; CA 5-8R;
SATA 1, 40; DLB 52

Hobson, Laura Z(ametkin)
1900-1986 .... **CLC 7, 25**
See also CA 17-20R; obituary CA 118;
SATA 52; DLB 28

Hochhuth, Rolf 1931- .... **CLC 4, 11, 18**
See also CA 5-8R

Hochman, Sandra 1936- .... **CLC 3, 8**
See also CA 5-8R; DLB 5

Hochwalder, Fritz 1911-1986 ...... **CLC 36**
See also CA 29-32R; obituary CA 120

Hocking, Mary (Eunice) 1921- ..... **CLC 13**
See also CANR 18; CA 101

Hodgins, Jack 1938- .... **CLC 23**
See also CA 93-96; DLB 60

Hodgson, William Hope
1877-1918 .... **TCLC 13**
See also CA 111; DLB 70

Hoffman, Alice 1952- .... **CLC 51**
See also CA 77-80

Hoffman, Daniel (Gerard)
1923- .... **CLC 6, 13, 23**
See also CANR 4; CA 1-4R; DLB 5

Hoffman, Stanley 1944- .... **CLC 5**
See also CA 77-80

Hoffman, William M(oses) 1939- ... **CLC 40**
See also CANR 11; CA 57-60

Hoffmann, E(rnst) T(heodor) A(madeus)
1776-1822 .... **NCLC 2**
See also SATA 27; DLB 90

Hoffmann, Gert 1932- .... **CLC 54**

**Hofmannsthal, Hugo (Laurenz August
Hofmann Edler) von**
1874-1929 .... **TCLC 11**
See also CA 106; DLB 81

Hogg, James 1770-1835 .... **NCLC 4**

Holbach, Paul Henri Thiry, Baron d'
1723-1789 .... **LC 14**

Holberg, Ludvig 1684-1754 .... **LC 6**

Holden, Ursula 1921- .... **CLC 18**
See also CAAS 8; CANR 22; CA 101

Holderlin, (Johann Christian) Friedrich
1770-1843 .... **NCLC 16; PC 4**

Holdstock, Robert (P.) 1948- .... **CLC 39**

Holland, Isabelle 1920- .... **CLC 21**
See also CANR 10, 25; CA 21-24R;
SATA 8

Holland, Marcus 1900-1985
See Caldwell, (Janet Miriam) Taylor
(Holland)

Hollander, John 1929- ...... **CLC 2, 5, 8, 14**
See also CANR 1; CA 1-4R; SATA 13;
DLB 5

Holleran, Andrew 1943?- .... **CLC 38**

Hollinghurst, Alan 1954- .... **CLC 55**
See also CA 114

Hollis, Jim 1916-
See Summers, Hollis (Spurgeon, Jr.)

Holmes, John Clellon 1926-1988.... **CLC 56**
See also CANR 4; CA 9-10R;
obituary CA 125; DLB 16

Holmes, Oliver Wendell
    1809-1894 .... **NCLC 14**
    See also SATA 34; DLB 1;
    CDALB 1640-1865

Holt, Victoria   1906-
    See Hibbert, Eleanor (Burford)

Holub, Miroslav   1923- .... **CLC 4**
    See also CANR 10; CA 21-24R

Homer   c. 8th century B.C.- .... **CMLC 1**

Honig, Edwin   1919- .... **CLC 33**
    See also CAAS 8; CANR 4; CA 5-8R;
    DLB 5

Hood, Hugh (John Blagdon)
    1928- .... **CLC 15, 28**
    See also CANR 1; CA 49-52; DLB 53

Hood, Thomas   1799-1845....... **NCLC 16**

Hooker, (Peter) Jeremy   1941-...... **CLC 43**
    See also CANR 22; CA 77-80; DLB 40

Hope, A(lec) D(erwent)   1907- .... **CLC 3, 51**
    See also CA 21-24R

Hope, Christopher (David Tully)
    1944- .... **CLC 52**
    See also CA 106

Hopkins, Gerard Manley
    1844-1889 .... **NCLC 17**
    See also DLB 35, 57

Hopkins, John (Richard)   1931-...... **CLC 4**
    See also CA 85-88

Hopkins, Pauline Elizabeth
    1859-1930 .... **TCLC 28**
    See also BLC 2; DLB 50

Horgan, Paul   1903- .... **CLC 9, 53**
    See also CANR 9; CA 13-16R; SATA 13;
    DLB-Y 85

Horovitz, Israel   1939- .... **CLC 56**
    See also CA 33-36R; DLB 7

Horvath, Odon von   1901-1938 .... **TCLC 45**
    See also brief entry CA 118; DLB 85

Horwitz, Julius   1920-1986........ **CLC 14**
    See also CANR 12; CA 9-12R;
    obituary CA 119

Hospital, Janette Turner   1942-..... **CLC 42**
    See also CA 108

Hostos (y Bonilla), Eugenio Maria de
    1893-1903 .... **TCLC 24**
    See also CA 123

Hougan, Carolyn   19??-............ **CLC 34**

Household, Geoffrey (Edward West)
    1900-1988 .... **CLC 11**
    See also CA 77-80; obituary CA 126;
    SATA 14, 59; DLB 87

Housman, A(lfred) E(dward)
    1859-1936 .... **TCLC 1, 10; PC 2**
    See also CA 104, 125; DLB 19

Housman, Laurence   1865-1959 ..... **TCLC 7**
    See also CA 106; SATA 25; DLB 10

Howard, Elizabeth Jane   1923- ... **CLC 7, 29**
    See also CANR 8; CA 5-8R

Howard, Maureen   1930- ..... **CLC 5, 14, 46**
    See also CA 53-56; DLB-Y 83

Howard, Richard   1929- ...... **CLC 7, 10, 47**
    See also CANR 25; CA 85-88; DLB 5

Howard, Robert E(rvin)
    1906-1936 .... **TCLC 8**
    See also CA 105

Howe, Fanny   1940- .... **CLC 47**
    See also CA 117; SATA 52

Howe, Julia Ward   1819-1910 ..... **TCLC 21**
    See also CA 117; DLB 1

Howe, Tina   1937- .... **CLC 48**
    See also CA 109

Howell, James   1594?-1666.......... **LC 13**

Howells, William Dean
    1837-1920 .... **TCLC 7, 17, 41**
    See also brief entry CA 104; DLB 12, 64,
    74, 79; CDALB 1865-1917

Howes, Barbara   1914- .... **CLC 15**
    See also CAAS 3; CA 9-12R; SATA 5

Hrabal, Bohumil   1914-......... **CLC 13, 67**
    See also CAAS 12; CA 106

Hubbard, L(afayette) Ron(ald)
    1911-1986 .... **CLC 43**
    See also CANR 22; CA 77-80;
    obituary CA 118

Huch, Ricarda (Octavia)
    1864-1947 .... **TCLC 13**
    See also CA 111; DLB 66

Huddle, David   1942- .... **CLC 49**
    See also CA 57-60

Hudson, W(illiam) H(enry)
    1841-1922 .... **TCLC 29**
    See also CA 115; SATA 35

Hueffer, Ford Madox   1873-1939
    See Ford, Ford Madox

Hughart, Barry   1934-............. **CLC 39**

Hughes, David (John)   1930- .... **CLC 48**
    See also CA 116, 129; DLB 14

Hughes, Edward James   1930-
    See Hughes, Ted

Hughes, (James) Langston
    1902-1967 .... **CLC 1, 5, 10, 15, 35, 44;**
                                    PC 1; SSC 6
    See also BLC 2; CLR 17; CANR 1;
    CA 1-4R; obituary CA 25-28R; SATA 4,
    33; DLB 4, 7, 48, 51, 86;
    CDALB 1929-1941

Hughes, Richard (Arthur Warren)
    1900-1976 .... **CLC 1, 11**
    See also CANR 4; CA 5-8R;
    obituary CA 65-68; SATA 8;
    obituary SATA 25; DLB 15

Hughes, Ted   1930-..... **CLC 2, 4, 9, 14, 37**
    See also CLR 3; CANR 1; CA 1-4R;
    SATA 27, 49; DLB 40

Hugo, Richard F(ranklin)
    1923-1982 .... **CLC 6, 18, 32**
    See also CANR 3; CA 49-52;
    obituary CA 108; DLB 5

Hugo, Victor Marie
    1802-1885 .... **NCLC 3, 10, 21**
    See also SATA 47

Huidobro, Vicente   1893-1948 ..... **TCLC 31**

Hulme, Keri   1947- .... **CLC 39**
    See also CA 125

Hulme, T(homas) E(rnest)
    1883-1917 .... **TCLC 21**
    See also CA 117; DLB 19

Hume, David   1711-1776. .... **LC 7**

Humphrey, William   1924-. .... **CLC 45**
    See also CA 77-80; DLB 6

Humphreys, Emyr (Owen)   1919-.... **CLC 47**
    See also CANR 3, 24; CA 5-8R; DLB 15

Humphreys, Josephine   1945-.... **CLC 34, 57**
    See also CA 121, 127

Hunt, E(verette) Howard (Jr.)
    1918- .... **CLC 3**
    See also CANR 2; CA 45-48

Hunt, (James Henry) Leigh
    1784-1859 .... **NCLC 1**

Hunt, Marsha   1946-.............. **CLC 70**

Hunter, Evan   1926- .... **CLC 11, 31**
    See also CANR 5; CA 5-8R; SATA 25;
    DLB-Y 82

Hunter, Kristin (Eggleston)   1931-... **CLC 35**
    See also CLR 3; CANR 13; CA 13-16R;
    SATA 12; DLB 33

Hunter, Mollie (Maureen McIlwraith)
    1922- .... **CLC 21**
    See also McIlwraith, Maureen Mollie
    Hunter

Hunter, Robert   ?-1734.............. **LC 7**

Hurston, Zora Neale
    1901?-1960....... **CLC 7, 30, 61; SSC 4**
    See also BLC 2; CA 85-88; DLB 51, 86

Huston, John (Marcellus)
    1906-1987 .... **CLC 20**
    See also CA 73-76; obituary CA 123;
    DLB 26

Hutten, Ulrich von   1488-1523....... **LC 16**

Huxley, Aldous (Leonard)
    1894-1963 .. **CLC 1, 3, 4, 5, 8, 11, 18, 35**
    See also CA 85-88; DLB 36

Huysmans, Charles Marie Georges
    1848-1907
    See Huysmans, Joris-Karl
    See also CA 104

Huysmans, Joris-Karl   1848-1907 ... **TCLC 7**
    See also Huysmans, Charles Marie Georges

Hwang, David Henry   1957-........ **CLC 55**
    See also CA 127

Hyde, Anthony   1946?-............ **CLC 42**

Hyde, Margaret O(ldroyd)   1917- ... **CLC 21**
    See also CLR 23; CANR 1; CA 1-4R;
    SAAS 8; SATA 1, 42

Hynes, James   1956?-............. **CLC 65**

Ian, Janis   1951- .... **CLC 21**
    See also CA 105

Ibarguengoitia, Jorge   1928-1983.... **CLC 37**
    See also obituary CA 113, 124

Ibsen, Henrik (Johan)
    1828-1906 ..... **TCLC 2, 8, 16, 37; DC 2**
    See also CA 104

Ibuse, Masuji   1898- .... **CLC 22**
    See also CA 127

Ichikawa, Kon   1915-.............. **CLC 20**
    See also CA 121

Idle, Eric   1943-................. **CLC 21**
    See also Monty Python
    See also CA 116

Ignatow, David 1914-...... CLC 4, 7, 14, 40
See also CAAS 3; CA 9-12R; DLB 5

Ihimaera, Witi (Tame) 1944-....... CLC 46
See also CA 77-80

Ilf, Ilya 1897-1937 .... TCLC 21

Immermann, Karl (Lebrecht)
1796-1840 .... NCLC 4

Ingalls, Rachel 19??-............. CLC 42
See also CA 123, 127

Ingamells, Rex 1913-1955 .... TCLC 35

Inge, William (Motter)
1913-1973 .... CLC 1, 8, 19
See also CA 9-12R; DLB 7;
CDALB 1941-1968

Innaurato, Albert 1948-........ CLC 21, 60
See also CA 115, 122

Innes, Michael 1906-
See Stewart, J(ohn) I(nnes) M(ackintosh)

Ionesco, Eugene
1912-........ CLC 1, 4, 6, 9, 11, 15, 41
See also CA 9-12R; SATA 7

Iqbal, Muhammad 1877-1938 ..... TCLC 28

Irving, John (Winslow)
1942-............... CLC 13, 23, 38
See also CANR 28; CA 25-28R; DLB 6;
DLB-Y 82

Irving, Washington
1783-1859 .... NCLC 2, 19; SSC 2
See also YABC 2; DLB 3, 11, 30, 59, 73,
74; CDALB 1640-1865

Isaacs, Susan 1943- .... CLC 32
See also CANR 20; CA 89-92

Isherwood, Christopher (William Bradshaw)
1904-1986 .... CLC 1, 9, 11, 14, 44
See also CA 13-16R; obituary CA 117;
DLB 15; DLB-Y 86

Ishiguro, Kazuo 1954- ...... CLC 27, 56, 59
See also CA 120

Ishikawa Takuboku 1885-1912 .... TCLC 15
See also CA 113

Iskander, Fazil (Abdulovich)
1929-...................... CLC 47
See also CA 102

Ivan IV 1530-1584 .... LC 17

Ivanov, Vyacheslav (Ivanovich)
1866-1949 .... TCLC 33
See also CA 122

Ivask, Ivar (Vidrik) 1927-...... CLC 14
See also CANR 24; CA 37-40R

Jackson, Jesse 1908-1983 .... CLC 12
See also CANR 27; CA 25-28R;
obituary CA 109; SATA 2, 29, 48

Jackson, Laura (Riding) 1901- ...... CLC 7
See also Riding, Laura
See also CANR 28; CA 65-68; DLB 48

Jackson, Shirley
1919-1965 .... CLC 11, 60; SSC 9
See also CANR 4; CA 1-4R;
obituary CA 25-28R; SATA 2; DLB 6;
CDALB 1941-1968

Jacob, (Cyprien) Max 1876-1944 ... TCLC 6
See also CA 104

Jacob, Piers A(nthony) D(illingham) 1934-
See Anthony (Jacob), Piers
See also CA 21-24R

Jacobs, Jim 1942- and Casey, Warren
1942-...................... CLC 12
See also CA 97-100

Jacobs, Jim 1942-
See Jacobs, Jim and Casey, Warren
See also CA 97-100

Jacobs, W(illiam) W(ymark)
1863-1943 .... TCLC 22
See also CA 121

Jacobsen, Jens Peter 1847-1885 .. NCLC 34

Jacobsen, Josephine 1908-......... CLC 48
See also CANR 23; CA 33-36R

Jacobson, Dan 1929- .... CLC 4, 14
See also CANR 2, 25; CA 1-4R; DLB 14

Jagger, Mick 1944-............... CLC 17

Jakes, John (William) 1932-....... CLC 29
See also CANR 10; CA 57-60; DLB-Y 83

James, C(yril) L(ionel) R(obert)
1901-1989 .... CLC 33
See also CA 117, 125; obituary CA 128

James, Daniel 1911-1988
See Santiago, Danny
See also obituary CA 125

James, Henry (Jr.)
1843-1916 ... TCLC 2, 11, 24, 40; SSC 8
See also CA 132; brief entry CA 104;
DLB 12, 71, 74; CDALB 1865-1917

James, M(ontague) R(hodes)
1862-1936 .... TCLC 6
See also CA 104

James, P(hyllis) D(orothy)
1920-................... CLC 18, 46
See also CANR 17; CA 21-24R

James, William 1842-1910..... TCLC 15, 32
See also CA 109

Jami, Nur al-Din 'Abd al-Rahman
1414-1492 .... LC 9

Jandl, Ernst 1925- .... CLC 34

Janowitz, Tama 1957-............ CLC 43
See also CA 106

Jarrell, Randall
1914-1965 .... CLC 1, 2, 6, 9, 13, 49
See also CLR 6; CANR 6; CA 5-8R;
obituary CA 25-28R; CABS 2; SATA 7;
DLB 48, 52; CDALB 1941-1968

Jarry, Alfred 1873-1907....... TCLC 2, 14
See also CA 104

Jeake, Samuel, Jr. 1889-1973
See Aiken, Conrad

Jean Paul 1763-1825 .... NCLC 7

Jeffers, (John) Robinson
1887-1962 .... CLC 2, 3, 11, 15, 54
See also CA 85-88; DLB 45;
CDALB 1917-1929

Jefferson, Thomas 1743-1826 .... NCLC 11
See also DLB 31; CDALB 1640-1865

Jeffrey, Francis 1773-1850....... NCLC 33

Jellicoe, (Patricia) Ann 1927-...... CLC 27
See also CA 85-88; DLB 13

Jen, Gish 1955-................. CLC 70

Jenkins, (John) Robin 1912-....... CLC 52
See also CANR 1; CA 4R; DLB 14

Jennings, Elizabeth (Joan)
1926-.................... CLC 5, 14
See also CAAS 5; CANR 8; CA 61-64;
DLB 27

Jennings, Waylon 1937-.......... CLC 21

Jensen, Johannes V. 1873-1950.... TCLC 41

Jensen, Laura (Linnea) 1948-...... CLC 37
See also CA 103

Jerome, Jerome K. 1859-1927..... TCLC 23
See also CA 119; DLB 10, 34

Jerrold, Douglas William
1803-1857 .... NCLC 2

Jewett, (Theodora) Sarah Orne
1849-1909 .... TCLC 1, 22; SSC 6
See also CA 108, 127; SATA 15; DLB 12,
74

Jewsbury, Geraldine (Endsor)
1812-1880 .... NCLC 22
See also DLB 21

Jhabvala, Ruth Prawer
1927-..................CLC 4, 8, 29
See also CANR 2, 29; CA 1-4R

Jiles, Paulette 1943-........... CLC 13, 58
See also CA 101

Jimenez (Mantecon), Juan Ramon
1881-1958 .... TCLC 4
See also CA 104

Joel, Billy 1949-................. CLC 26
See also Joel, William Martin

Joel, William Martin 1949-
See Joel, Billy
See also CA 108

John of the Cross, St. 1542-1591 .... LC 18

Johnson, B(ryan) S(tanley William)
1933-1973 .... CLC 6, 9
See also CANR 9; CA 9-12R;
obituary CA 53-56; DLB 14, 40

Johnson, Charles (Richard)
1948-.................. CLC 7, 51, 65
See also BLC 2; CA 116; DLB 33

Johnson, Denis 1949-............. CLC 52
See also CA 117, 121

Johnson, Diane 1934-........ CLC 5, 13, 48
See also CANR 17; CA 41-44R; DLB-Y 80

Johnson, Eyvind (Olof Verner)
1900-1976 .... CLC 14
See also CA 73-76; obituary CA 69-72

Johnson, Fenton 1888-1958
See also BLC 2; CA 124;
brief entry CA 118; DLB 45, 50

Johnson, James Weldon
1871-1938 .... TCLC 3, 19
See also Johnson, James William
See also BLC 2; CA 125;
brief entry CA 104; SATA 31; DLB 51;
CDALB 1917-1929

Johnson, James William 1871-1938
See Johnson, James Weldon
See also SATA 31

Johnson, Joyce 1935-............. CLC 58
See also CA 125, 129

Keene, Donald 1922- .... CLC 34
    See also CANR 5; CA 1-4R

Keillor, Garrison 1942- .... CLC 40
    See also Keillor, Gary (Edward)
    See also CA 111; SATA 58; DLB-Y 87;
    AAYA 2

Keillor, Gary (Edward)
    See Keillor, Garrison
    See also CA 111, 117

Kell, Joseph 1917-
    See Burgess (Wilson, John) Anthony

Keller, Gottfried 1819-1890 ...... NCLC 2

Kellerman, Jonathan (S.) 1949-..... CLC 44
    See also CANR 29; CA 106

Kelley, William Melvin 1937-...... CLC 22
    See also CANR 27; CA 77-80; DLB 33

Kellogg, Marjorie 1922-............ CLC 2
    See also CA 81-84

Kelly, M. T. 1947- .... CLC 55
    See also CANR 19; CA 97-100

Kelman, James 1946-............. CLC 58

Kemal, Yashar 1922- .... CLC 14, 29
    See also CA 89-92

Kemble, Fanny 1809-1893 .... NCLC 18
    See also DLB 32

Kemelman, Harry 1908-........... CLC 2
    See also CANR 6; CA 9-12R; DLB 28

Kempe, Margery 1373?-1440? .... LC 6

Kempis, Thomas á 1380-1471 .... LC 11

Kendall, Henry 1839-1882....... NCLC 12

Keneally, Thomas (Michael)
    1935- ...... CLC 5, 8, 10, 14, 19, 27, 43
    See also CANR 10; CA 85-88

Kennedy, Adrienne 1931-
    See also BLC 2; CANR 26; CA 103;
    CABS 3; DLB 38

Kennedy, Adrienne (Lita) 1931- .... CLC 66
    See also CANR 26; CA 103; CABS 3;
    DLB 38

Kennedy, John Pendleton
    1795-1870 .... NCLC 2
    See also DLB 3

Kennedy, Joseph Charles 1929-...... CLC 8
    See also Kennedy, X. J.
    See also CANR 4, 30; CA 1-4R; SATA 14

Kennedy, William (Joseph)
    1928- .... CLC 6, 28, 34, 53
    See also CANR 14; CA 85-88; SATA 57;
    DLB-Y 85; AAYA 1

Kennedy, X. J. 1929- .... CLC 8, 42
    See also Kennedy, Joseph Charles
    See also CAAS 9; DLB 5

Kerouac, Jack
    1922-1969 .... CLC 1, 2, 3, 5, 14, 29, 61
    See also Kerouac, Jean-Louis Lebris de
    See also DLB 2, 16; DLB-DS 3;
    CDALB 1941-1968

Kerouac, Jean-Louis Lebris de 1922-1969
    See Kerouac, Jack
    See also CANR 26; CA 5-8R;
    obituary CA 25-28R; CDALB 1941-1968

Kerr, Jean 1923-................. CLC 22
    See also CANR 7; CA 5-8R

Kerr, M. E. 1927-............. CLC 12, 35
    See also Meaker, Marijane
    See also SAAS 1; AAYA 2

Kerr, Robert 1970?-........... CLC 55, 59

Kerrigan, (Thomas) Anthony
    1918-..................... CLC 4, 6
    See also CAAS 11; CANR 4; CA 49-52

Kesey, Ken (Elton)
    1935- .... CLC 1, 3, 6, 11, 46, 64
    See also CANR 22; CA 1-4R; DLB 2, 16;
    CDALB 1968-1987

Kesselring, Joseph (Otto)
    1902-1967 .... CLC 45

Kessler, Jascha (Frederick) 1929-.... CLC 4
    See also CANR 8; CA 17-20R

Kettelkamp, Larry 1933-.......... CLC 12
    See also CANR 16; CA 29-32R; SAAS 3;
    SATA 2

Kherdian, David 1931-.......... CLC 6, 9
    See also CLR 24; CAAS 2; CA 21-24R;
    SATA 16

Khlebnikov, Velimir (Vladimirovich)
    1885-1922 ....TCLC 20
    See also CA 117

Khodasevich, Vladislav (Felitsianovich)
    1886-1939 ....TCLC 15
    See also CA 115

Kielland, Alexander (Lange)
    1849-1906 .... TCLC 5
    See also CA 104

Kiely, Benedict 1919-.......... CLC 23, 43
    See also CANR 2; CA 1-4R; DLB 15

Kienzle, William X(avier) 1928- .... CLC 25
    See also CAAS 1; CANR 9; CA 93-96

Kierkegaard, SOren 1813-1855... NCLC 34

Killens, John Oliver 1916-........ CLC 10
    See also CAAS 2; CANR 26; CA 77-80,
    123; DLB 33

Killigrew, Anne 1660-1685.......... LC 4

Kincaid, Jamaica 1949- .... CLC 43, 68
    See also BLC 2; CA 125

King, Francis (Henry) 1923- ..... CLC 8, 53
    See also CANR 1; CA 1-4R; DLB 15

King, Martin Luther, Jr. 1929-1968
    See also BLC 2; CANR 27; CAP 2;
    CA 25-28; SATA 14

King, Stephen (Edwin)
    1947- .... CLC 12, 26, 37, 61
    See also CANR 1, 30; CA 61-64; SATA 9,
    55; DLB-Y 80; AAYA 1

Kingman, (Mary) Lee 1919-....... CLC 17
    See also Natti, (Mary) Lee
    See also CA 5-8R; SAAS 3; SATA 1

Kingsley, Charles 1819-1875 ..... NCLC 35
    See also YABC 2; DLB 21, 32

Kingsley, Sidney 1906-............ CLC 44
    See also CA 85-88; DLB 7

Kingsolver, Barbara 1955-......... CLC 55
    See also CA 129

Kingston, Maxine Hong
    1940- .... CLC 12, 19, 58
    See also CANR 13; CA 69-72; SATA 53;
    DLB-Y 80

Kinnell, Galway
    1927- .... CLC 1, 2, 3, 5, 13, 29
    See also CANR 10; CA 9-12R; DLB 5;
    DLB-Y 87

Kinsella, Thomas 1928-...... CLC 4, 19, 43
    See also CANR 15; CA 17-20R; DLB 27

Kinsella, W(illiam) P(atrick)
    1935- .... CLC 27, 43
    See also CAAS 7; CANR 21; CA 97-100

Kipling, (Joseph) Rudyard
    1865-1936 .... TCLC 8, 17; PC 3; SSC 5
    See also YABC 2; CANR 33; CA 120;
    brief entry CA 105; DLB 19, 34

Kirkup, James 1918- .... CLC 1
    See also CAAS 4; CANR 2; CA 1-4R;
    SATA 12; DLB 27

Kirkwood, James 1930-1989 .... CLC 9
    See also CANR 6; CA 1-4R;
    obituary CA 128

Kis, Danilo 1935-1989 .... CLC 57
    See also CA 118, 129; brief entry CA 109

Kivi, Aleksis 1834-1872......... NCLC 30

Kizer, Carolyn (Ashley) 1925-... CLC 15, 39
    See also CAAS 5; CANR 24; CA 65-68;
    DLB 5

Klabund 1890-1928.............TCLC 44
    See also DLB 66

Klappert, Peter 1942-............. CLC 57
    See also CA 33-36R; DLB 5

Klausner, Amos 1939-
    See Oz, Amos

Klein, A(braham) M(oses)
    1909-1972 .... CLC 19
    See also CA 101; obituary CA 37-40R;
    DLB 68

Klein, Norma 1938-1989 .... CLC 30
    See also CLR 2, 19; CANR 15; CA 41-44R;
    obituary CA 128; SAAS 1; SATA 7, 57;
    AAYA 2

Klein, T.E.D. 19??-............... CLC 34
    See also CA 119

Kleist, Heinrich von 1777-1811.... NCLC 2
    See also DLB 90

Klima, Ivan 1931-................ CLC 56
    See also CANR 17; CA 25-28R

Klimentev, Andrei Platonovich 1899-1951
    See Platonov, Andrei (Platonovich)
    See also CA 108

Klinger, Friedrich Maximilian von
    1752-1831 .... NCLC 1

Klopstock, Friedrich Gottlieb
    1724-1803 .... NCLC 11

Knebel, Fletcher 1911-............ CLC 14
    See also CAAS 3; CANR 1; CA 1-4R;
    SATA 36

Knight, Etheridge 1931-1991....... CLC 40
    See also BLC 2; CANR 23; CA 21-24R;
    DLB 41

Knight, Sarah Kemble 1666-1727 ..... LC 7
    See also DLB 24

Knowles, John 1926- ......CLC 1, 4, 10, 26
    See also CA 17-20R; SATA 8; DLB 6;
    CDALB 1968-1987

Larkin, Philip (Arthur)
1922-1985 ... CLC 3, 5, 8, 9, 13, 18, 33, 39, 64
See also CANR 24; CA 5-8R; obituary CA 117; DLB 27

Larra (y Sanchez de Castro), Mariano Jose de
1809-1837 .... NCLC 17

Larsen, Eric 1941- .... CLC 55

Larsen, Nella 1891-1964 .... CLC 37
See also BLC 2; CA 125; DLB 51

Larson, Charles R(aymond) 1938-... CLC 31
See also CANR 4; CA 53-56

Latham, Jean Lee 1902- .... CLC 12
See also CANR 7; CA 5-8R; SATA 2

Lathen, Emma .... CLC 2
See also Hennissart, Martha; Latsis, Mary J(ane)

Latsis, Mary J(ane).............. CLC 2
See also Lathen, Emma
See also CA 85-88

Lattimore, Richmond (Alexander)
1906-1984 .... CLC 3
See also CANR 1; CA 1-4R; obituary CA 112

Laughlin, James 1914- .... CLC 49
See also CANR 9; CA 21-24R; DLB 48

Laurence, (Jean) Margaret (Wemyss)
1926-1987 .. CLC 3, 6, 13, 50, 62; SSC 7
See also CA 5-8R; obituary CA 121; SATA 50; DLB 53

Laurent, Antoine 1952- .... CLC 50

Lautreamont, Comte de
1846-1870 .... NCLC 12

Lavin, Mary 1912- ...... CLC 4, 18; SSC 4
See also CA 9-12R; DLB 15

Lawler, Raymond (Evenor) 1922-... CLC 58
See also CA 103

Lawrence, D(avid) H(erbert)
1885-1930 .... TCLC 2, 9, 16, 33; SSC 4
See also CA 104, 121; DLB 10, 19, 36

Lawrence, T(homas) E(dward)
1888-1935 .... TCLC 18
See also CA 115

Lawson, Henry (Archibald Hertzberg)
1867-1922 .... TCLC 27
See also CA 120

Laxness, Halldor (Kiljan) 1902- .... CLC 25
See also Gudjonsson, Halldor Kiljan

Laye, Camara 1928-1980 .... CLC 4, 38
See also BLC 2.; CANR 25; CA 85-88; obituary CA 97-100

Layton, Irving (Peter) 1912- ..... CLC 2, 15
See also CANR 2; CA 1-4R; DLB 88

Lazarus, Emma 1849-1887........ NCLC 8

Leacock, Stephen (Butler)
1869-1944 .... TCLC 2
See also CA 104; DLB 92

Lear, Edward 1812-1888 .... NCLC 3
See also CLR 1; SATA 18; DLB 32

Lear, Norman (Milton) 1922- ...... CLC 12
See also CA 73-76

Leavis, F(rank) R(aymond)
1895-1978 .... CLC 24
See also CA 21-24R; obituary CA 77-80

Leavitt, David 1961?-............. CLC 34
See also CA 116, 122

Lebowitz, Fran(ces Ann)
1951?- .... CLC 11, 36
See also CANR 14; CA 81-84

Le Carre, John 1931-... CLC 3, 5, 9, 15, 28
See also Cornwell, David (John Moore)
See also DLB 87

Le Clezio, J(ean) M(arie) G(ustave)
1940- .... CLC 31
See also CA 116, 128; DLB 83

Leconte de Lisle, Charles-Marie-Rene
1818-1894 .... NCLC 29

Leduc, Violette 1907-1972........ CLC 22
See also CAP 1; CA 13-14; obituary CA 33-36R

Ledwidge, Francis 1887-1917...... TCLC 23
See also CA 123; DLB 20

Lee, Andrea 1953- .... CLC 36
See also BLC 2; CA 125

Lee, Andrew 1917-
See Auchincloss, Louis (Stanton)

Lee, Don L. 1942-................ CLC 2
See also Madhubuti, Haki R.
See also CA 73-76

Lee, George Washington
1894-1976 .... CLC 52
See also BLC 2; CA 125; DLB 51

Lee, (Nelle) Harper 1926- ...... CLC 12, 60
See also CA 13-16R; SATA 11; DLB 6; CDALB 1941-1968

Lee, Lawrence 1903- .... CLC 34
See also CA 25-28R

Lee, Manfred B(ennington)
1905-1971 .... CLC 11
See also Queen, Ellery
See also CANR 2; CA 1-4R; obituary CA 29-32R

Lee, Stan 1922-................. CLC 17
See also CA 108, 111

Lee, Tanith 1947-............... CLC 46
See also CA 37-40R; SATA 8

Lee, Vernon 1856-1935 .... TCLC 5
See also Paget, Violet
See also DLB 57

Lee-Hamilton, Eugene (Jacob)
1845-1907 .... TCLC 22
See also CA 117

Leet, Judith 1935- .... CLC 11

Le Fanu, Joseph Sheridan
1814-1873 .... NCLC 9
See also DLB 21, 70

Leffland, Ella 1931- .... CLC 19
See also CA 29-32R; DLB-Y 84

Leger, (Marie-Rene) Alexis Saint-Leger
1887-1975 .... CLC 11
See also Perse, St.-John
See also CA 13-16R; obituary CA 61-64

Le Guin, Ursula K(roeber)
1929- .... CLC 8, 13, 22, 45, 71
See also CLR 3; CANR 9, 32; CA 21-24R; SATA 4, 52; DLB 8, 52; CDALB 1968-1987

Lehmann, Rosamond (Nina) 1901-... CLC 5
See also CANR 8; CA 77-80; DLB 15

Leiber, Fritz (Reuter, Jr.) 1910-.... CLC 25
See also CANR 2; CA 45-48; SATA 45; DLB 8

Leimbach, Marti 1963-........... CLC 65

Leino, Eino 1878-1926.......... TCLC 24

Leiris, Michel 1901-............. CLC 61
See also CA 119, 128

Leithauser, Brad 1953-........... CLC 27
See also CANR 27; CA 107

Lelchuk, Alan 1938-............. CLC 5
See also CANR 1; CA 45-48

Lem, Stanislaw 1921-........ CLC 8, 15, 40
See also CAAS 1; CA 105

Lemann, Nancy 1956-............ CLC 39
See also CA 118

Lemonnier, (Antoine Louis) Camille
1844-1913 .... TCLC 22
See also CA 121

Lenau, Nikolaus 1802-1850...... NCLC 16

L'Engle, Madeleine 1918- .... CLC 12
See also CLR 1, 14; CANR 3, 21; CA 1-4R; SATA 1, 27; DLB 52; AAYA 1

Lengyel, Jozsef 1896-1975......... CLC 7
See also CA 85-88; obituary CA 57-60

Lennon, John (Ono)
1940-1980 .... CLC 12, 35
See also CA 102

Lennon, John Winston 1940-1980
See Lennon, John (Ono)

Lennox, Charlotte Ramsay
1729?-1804................. NCLC 23
See also DLB 39

Lentricchia, Frank (Jr.) 1940-...... CLC 34
See also CANR 19; CA 25-28R

Lenz, Siegfried 1926-............ CLC 27
See also CA 89-92; DLB 75

Leonard, Elmore 1925-...... CLC 28, 34, 71
See also CANR 12, 28; CA 81-84

Leonard, Hugh 1926-............ CLC 19
See also Byrne, John Keyes
See also DLB 13

Leopardi, (Conte) Giacomo (Talegardo Francesco di Sales Saverio Pietro)
1798-1837 .... NCLC 22

Lerman, Eleanor 1952-............ CLC 9
See also CA 85-88

Lerman, Rhoda 1936-............ CLC 56
See also CA 49-52

Lermontov, Mikhail Yuryevich
1814-1841 .... NCLC 5

Leroux, Gaston 1868-1927........ TCLC 25
See also CA 108

Lesage, Alain-Rene 1668-1747....... LC 2

Leskov, Nikolai (Semyonovich)
1831-1895 .... NCLC 25

Lessing, Doris (May)
1919-.... CLC 1, 2, 3, 6, 10, 15, 22, 40; SSC 6
See also CA 9-12R; DLB 15; DLB-Y 85

Lessing, Gotthold Ephraim
1729-1781 .... LC 8

Lester, Richard 1932-............ CLC 20

Lowell, Robert (Traill Spence, Jr.)
    1917-1977 ... CLC **1, 2, 3, 4, 5, 8, 9, 11,
        15, 37; PC 3**
    See also CANR 26; CA 9-10R;
        obituary CA 73-76; CABS 2; DLB 5

Lowndes, Marie (Adelaide) Belloc
    1868-1947 .... TCLC **12**
    See also CA 107; DLB 70

Lowry, (Clarence) Malcolm
    1909-1957 .... TCLC **6, 40**
    See also CA 105, 131; DLB 15

Loy, Mina   1882-1966............. CLC **28**
    See also CA 113; DLB 4, 54

Lucas, Craig..................... CLC **64**

Lucas, George   1944-............. CLC **16**
    See also CANR 30; CA 77-80; SATA 56;
        AAYA 1

Lucas, Victoria   1932-1963
    See Plath, Sylvia

Ludlam, Charles   1943-1987..... CLC **46, 50**
    See also CA 85-88; obituary CA 122

Ludlum, Robert   1927- .... CLC **22, 43**
    See also CANR 25; CA 33-36R; DLB-Y 82

Ludwig, Ken   19??- .... CLC **60**

Ludwig, Otto   1813-1865......... NCLC **4**

Lugones, Leopoldo   1874-1938..... TCLC **15**
    See also CA 116

Lu Hsun   1881-1936 .... TCLC **3**

Lukacs, Georg   1885-1971......... CLC **24**
    See also Lukacs, Gyorgy

Lukacs, Gyorgy   1885-1971
    See Lukacs, Georg
    See also CA 101; obituary CA 29-32R

Luke, Peter (Ambrose Cyprian)
    1919- .... CLC **38**
    See also CA 81-84; DLB 13

Lurie (Bishop), Alison
    1926- ....CLC **4, 5, 18, 39**
    See also CANR 2, 17; CA 1-4R; SATA 46;
        DLB 2

Lustig, Arnost   1926-............. CLC **56**
    See also CA 69-72; SATA 56; AAYA 3

Luther, Martin   1483-1546.......... LC **9**

Luzi, Mario   1914-................ CLC **13**
    See also CANR 9; CA 61-64

Lynch, David   1946- .... CLC **66**
    See also CA 129; brief entry CA 124

Lynn, Kenneth S(chuyler)   1923-.... CLC **50**
    See also CANR 3, 27; CA 1-4R

Lytle, Andrew (Nelson)   1902-...... CLC **22**
    See also CA 9-12R; DLB 6

Lyttelton, George   1709-1773....... LC **10**

Lytton, Edward Bulwer   1803-1873
    See Bulwer-Lytton, (Lord) Edward (George
        Earle Lytton)
    See also SATA 23

Maas, Peter   1929- .... CLC **29**
    See also CA 93-96

Macaulay, (Dame Emilie) Rose
    1881-1958 .... TCLC **7, 44**
    See also CA 104; DLB 36

MacBeth, George (Mann)
    1932-.................... CLC **2, 5, 9**
    See also CA 25-28R; SATA 4; DLB 40

MacCaig, Norman (Alexander)
    1910-..................... CLC **36**
    See also CANR 3; CA 9-12R; DLB 27

MacCarthy, Desmond   1877-1952 .. TCLC **36**

MacDermot, Thomas H.   1870-1933
    See Redcam, Tom

MacDiarmid, Hugh
    1892-1978 .... CLC **2, 4, 11, 19, 63**
    See also Grieve, C(hristopher) M(urray)
    See also DLB 20

Macdonald, Cynthia   1928-...... CLC **13, 19**
    See also CANR 4; CA 49-52

MacDonald, George   1824-1905..... TCLC **9**
    See also CA 106; SATA 33; DLB 18

MacDonald, John D(ann)
    1916-1986 .... CLC **3, 27, 44**
    See also CANR 1, 19; CA 1-4R;
        obituary CA 121; DLB 8; DLB-Y 86

Macdonald, (John) Ross
    1915-1983 ...... CLC **1, 2, 3, 14, 34, 41**
    See also Millar, Kenneth
    See also DLB-DS 6

MacEwen, Gwendolyn (Margaret)
    1941-1987 .... CLC **13, 55**
    See also CANR 7, 22; CA 9-12R;
        obituary CA 124; SATA 50, 55; DLB 53

Machado (y Ruiz), Antonio
    1875-1939 .... TCLC **3**
    See also CA 104

Machado de Assis, (Joaquim Maria)
    1839-1908 ....TCLC **10**
    See also BLC 2; brief entry CA 107

Machen, Arthur (Llewellyn Jones)
    1863-1947 .... TCLC **4**
    See also CA 104; DLB 36

Machiavelli, Niccolo   1469-1527 ...... LC **8**

MacInnes, Colin   1914-1976...... CLC **4, 23**
    See also CANR 21; CA 69-72;
        obituary CA 65-68; DLB 14

MacInnes, Helen (Clark)
    1907-1985 .... CLC **27, 39**
    See also CANR 1, 28; CA 1-4R;
        obituary CA 65-68, 117; SATA 22, 44;
        DLB 87

Macintosh, Elizabeth   1897-1952
    See Tey, Josephine
    See also CA 110

Mackenzie, (Edward Montague) Compton
    1883-1972 .... CLC **18**
    See also CAP 2; CA 21-22;
        obituary CA 37-40R; DLB 34

Mac Laverty, Bernard   1942-....... CLC **31**
    See also CA 116, 118

MacLean, Alistair (Stuart)
    1922-1987 .... CLC **3, 13, 50, 63**
    See also CANR 28; CA 57-60;
        obituary CA 121; SATA 23, 50

MacLeish, Archibald
    1892-1982 .... CLC **3, 8, 14, 68**
    See also CANR 33; CA 9-12R;
        obituary CA 106; DLB 4, 7, 45;
        DLB-Y 82

MacLennan, (John) Hugh
    1907-.................... CLC **2, 14**
    See also CA 5-8R; DLB 68

MacLeod, Alistair   1936- .... CLC **56**
    See also CA 123; DLB 60

Macleod, Fiona   1855-1905
    See Sharp, William

MacNeice, (Frederick) Louis
    1907-1963 .... CLC **1, 4, 10, 53**
    See also CA 85-88; DLB 10, 20

Macpherson, (Jean) Jay   1931-...... CLC **14**
    See also CA 5-8R; DLB 53

MacShane, Frank   1927-.......... CLC **39**
    See also CANR 3; CA 11-12R

Macumber, Mari   1896-1966
    See Sandoz, Mari (Susette)

Madach, Imre   1823-1864........ NCLC **19**

Madden, (Jerry) David   1933- .... CLC **5, 15**
    See also CAAS 3; CANR 4; CA 1-4R;
        DLB 6

Madhubuti, Haki R.   1942-......... CLC **6**
    See also Lee, Don L.
    See also BLC 2; CANR 24; CA 73-76;
        DLB 5, 41; DLB-DS 8

Maeterlinck, Maurice   1862-1949 ... TCLC **3**
    See also CA 104

Mafouz, Naguib   1912-
    See Mahfuz, Najib

Maginn, William   1794-1842....... NCLC **8**

Mahapatra, Jayanta   1928-........ CLC **33**
    See also CAAS 9; CANR 15; CA 73-76

Mahfuz Najib   1912-........... CLC **52, 55**
    See also DLB-Y 88

Mahon, Derek   1941-.............. CLC **27**
    See also CA 113, 128; DLB 40

Mailer, Norman
    1923-...... CLC **1, 2, 3, 4, 5, 8, 11, 14,
        28, 39**
    See also CANR 28; CA 9-12R; CABS 1;
        DLB 2, 16, 28; DLB-Y 80, 83;
        DLB-DS 3; CDALB 1968-1987

Maillet, Antonine   1929-.......... CLC **54**
    See also CA 115, 120; DLB 60

Mais, Roger   1905-1955 .... TCLC **8**
    See also CA 105, 124

Maitland, Sara (Louise)   1950-...... CLC **49**
    See also CANR 13; CA 69-72

Major, Clarence   1936-....... CLC **3, 19, 48**
    See also BLC 2; CAAS 6; CANR 13, 25;
        CA 21-24R; DLB 33

Major, Kevin   1949- .... CLC **26**
    See also CLR 11; CANR 21; CA 97-100;
        SATA 32; DLB 60

Malamud, Bernard
    1914-1986 ..... CLC **1, 2, 3, 5, 8, 9, 11,
        18, 27, 44**
    See also CANR 28; CA 5-8R;
        obituary CA 118; CABS 1; DLB 2, 28;
        DLB-Y 80, 86; CDALB 1941-1968

Malcolm X   1925-1965
    See Little, Malcolm
    See also BLC 2

Malherbe, Francois de   1555-1628..... LC **5**

Mauriac, Francois (Charles)
1885-1970 . . . . CLC **4, 9, 56**
See also CAP 2; CA 25-28; DLB 65

Mavor, Osborne Henry 1888-1951
See Bridie, James
See also CA 104

Maxwell, William (Keepers, Jr.)
1908- . . . . CLC **19**
See also CA 93-96; DLB-Y 80

May, Elaine 1932- . . . . CLC **16**
See also CA 124; DLB 44

Mayakovsky, Vladimir (Vladimirovich)
1893-1930 . . . . TCLC **4, 18**
See also CA 104

Mayhew, Henry 1812-1887 . . . . . . NCLC **31**
See also DLB 18, 55

Maynard, Joyce 1953- . . . . CLC **23**
See also CA 111, 129

Mayne, William (James Carter)
1928- . . . . CLC **12**
See also CA 9-12R; SATA 6

Mayo, Jim 1908?-
See L'Amour, Louis (Dearborn)

Maysles, Albert 1926- and **Maysles, David**
1926- . . . . CLC **16**
See also CA 29-32R

Maysles, Albert 1926- . . . . CLC **16**
See also Maysles, Albert and Maysles,
David
See also CA 29-32R

Maysles, David 1932- . . . . CLC **16**
See also Maysles, Albert and Maysles,
David

Mazer, Norma Fox 1931- . . . . CLC **26**
See also CLR 23; CANR 12; CA 69-72;
SAAS 1; SATA 24

Mazzini, Guiseppe 1805-1872 . . . . NCLC **34**

McAuley, James (Phillip)
1917-1976 . . . . CLC **45**
See also CA 97-100

McBain, Ed 1926-
See Hunter, Evan

McBrien, William 1930- . . . . CLC **44**
See also CA 107

McCaffrey, Anne 1926- . . . . CLC **17**
See also CANR 15; CA 25-28R; SATA 8;
DLB 8

McCarthy, Cormac 1933- . . . . CLC **4, 57**
See also CANR 10; CA 13-16R; DLB 6

McCarthy, Mary (Therese)
1912-1989- . . . CLC **1, 3, 5, 14, 24, 39, 59**
See also CANR 16; CA 5-8R;
obituary CA 129; DLB 2; DLB-Y 81

McCartney, (James) Paul
1942- . . . . CLC **12, 35**

McCauley, Stephen 19??- . . . . CLC **50**

McClure, Michael 1932- . . . . CLC **6, 10**
See also CANR 17; CA 21-24R; DLB 16

McCorkle, Jill (Collins) 1958- . . . . . CLC **51**
See also CA 121; DLB-Y 87

McCourt, James 1941- . . . . CLC **5**
See also CA 57-60

McCoy, Horace 1897-1955 . . . . TCLC **28**
See also CA 108; DLB 9

McCrae, John 1872-1918 . . . . TCLC **12**
See also CA 109; DLB 92

McCullers, (Lula) Carson (Smith)
1917-1967 . . CLC **1, 4, 10, 12, 48; SSC 9**
See also CANR 18; CA 5-8R;
obituary CA 25-28R; CABS 1; SATA 27;
DLB 2, 7; CDALB 1941-1968

McCullough, Colleen 1938?- . . . . CLC **27**
See also CANR 17; CA 81-84

McElroy, Joseph (Prince)
1930- . . . . CLC **5, 47**
See also CA 17-20R

McEwan, Ian (Russell) 1948- . . . CLC **13, 66**
See also CANR 14; CA 61-64; DLB 14

McFadden, David 1940- . . . . CLC **48**
See also CA 104; DLB 60

McFarland, Dennis 1956- . . . . CLC **65**

McGahern, John 1934- . . . . CLC **5, 9, 48**
See also CANR 29; CA 17-20R; DLB 14

McGinley, Patrick 1937- . . . . CLC **41**
See also CA 120, 127

McGinley, Phyllis 1905-1978 . . . . . . CLC **14**
See also CANR 19; CA 9-12R;
obituary CA 77-80; SATA 2, 44;
obituary SATA 24; DLB 11, 48

McGinniss, Joe 1942- . . . . CLC **32**
See also CANR 26; CA 25-28R

McGivern, Maureen Daly 1921-
See Daly, Maureen
See also CA 9-12R

McGrath, Patrick 1950- . . . . CLC **55**

McGrath, Thomas 1916- . . . . . CLC **28, 59**
See also CANR 6; CA 9-12R, 130;
SATA 41

McGuane, Thomas (Francis III)
1939- . . . . CLC **3, 7, 18, 45**
See also CANR 5, 24; CA 49-52; DLB 2;
DLB-Y 80

McGuckian, Medbh 1950- . . . . CLC **48**
See also DLB 40

McHale, Tom 1941-1982 . . . . CLC **3, 5**
See also CA 77-80; obituary CA 106

McIlvanney, William 1936- . . . . CLC **42**
See also CA 25-28R; DLB 14

McIlwraith, Maureen Mollie Hunter 1922-
See Hunter, Mollie
See also CA 29-32R; SATA 2

McInerney, Jay 1955- . . . . CLC **34**
See also CA 116, 123

McIntyre, Vonda N(eel) 1948- . . . . . CLC **18**
See also CANR 17; CA 81-84

McKay, Claude
1889-1948 . . . . TCLC **7, 41; PC 2**
See also BLC 3; CA 104, 124; DLB 4, 45,
51

McKay, Claude 1889-1948
See McKay, Festus Claudius

McKay, Festus Claudius 1889-1948
See also BLC 2; CA 124; brief entry CA 104

McKuen, Rod 1933- . . . . CLC **1, 3**
See also CA 41-44R

McLuhan, (Herbert) Marshall
1911-1980 . . . . CLC **37**
See also CANR 12; CA 9-12R;
obituary CA 102; DLB 88

McManus, Declan Patrick 1955-
See Costello, Elvis

McMillan, Terry 1951- . . . . CLC **50, 61**

McMurtry, Larry (Jeff)
1936- . . . . CLC **2, 3, 7, 11, 27, 44**
See also CANR 19; CA 5-8R; DLB 2;
DLB-Y 80, 87; CDALB 1968-1987

McNally, Terrence 1939- . . . . . . CLC **4, 7, 41**
See also CANR 2; CA 45-48; DLB 7

McNamer, Deirdre 1950- . . . . CLC **70**

McNeile, Herman Cyril 1888-1937
See Sapper
See also DLB 77

McPhee, John 1931- . . . . CLC **36**
See also CANR 20; CA 65-68

McPherson, James Alan 1943- . . . . . CLC **19**
See also CANR 24; CA 25-28R; DLB 38

McPherson, William 1939- . . . . CLC **34**
See also CA 57-60

McSweeney, Kerry 19??- . . . . CLC **34**

Mead, Margaret 1901-1978 . . . . CLC **37**
See also CANR 4; CA 1-4R;
obituary CA 81-84; SATA 20

Meaker, M. J. 1927-
See Kerr, M. E.; Meaker, Marijane

Meaker, Marijane 1927-
See Kerr, M. E.
See also CA 107; SATA 20

Medoff, Mark (Howard) 1940- . . . CLC **6, 23**
See also CANR 5; CA 53-56; DLB 7

Megged, Aharon 1920- . . . . CLC **9**
See also CANR 1; CA 49-52

Mehta, Ved (Parkash) 1934- . . . . CLC **37**
See also CANR 2, 23; CA 1-4R

Mellor, John 1953?-
See The Clash

Meltzer, Milton 1915- . . . . CLC **26**
See also CLR 13; CA 13-16R; SAAS 1;
SATA 1, 50; DLB 61

Melville, Herman
1819-1891 . . . . . . NCLC **3, 12, 29; SSC 1**
See also SATA 59; DLB 3, 74;
CDALB 1640-1865

Membreno, Alejandro 1972- . . . . CLC **59**

Menander
c. 342 B.C.-c. 292 B.C. . . . . CMLC **9**

Mencken, H(enry) L(ouis)
1880-1956 . . . . TCLC **13**
See also CA 105, 125; DLB 11, 29, 63;
CDALB 1917-1929

Mercer, David 1928-1980 . . . . CLC **5**
See also CANR 23; CA 9-12R;
obituary CA 102; DLB 13

Meredith, George 1828-1909 . . . . . . TCLC **17**
See also CA 117; DLB 18, 35, 57

Meredith, George 1858-1924 . . . . . . TCLC **43**

Meredith, William (Morris)
1919- . . . . CLC **4, 13, 22, 55**
See also CANR 6; CA 9-12R; DLB 5

Moore, Lorrie 1957-........ CLC 39, 45, 68
See also Moore, Marie Lorena

Moore, Marianne (Craig)
1887-1972 ... CLC 1, 2, 4, 8, 10, 13, 19,
47; PC 4
See also CANR 3; CA 1-4R;
obituary CA 33-36R; SATA 20; DLB 45;
DLB-DS 7; CDALB 1929-1941

Moore, Marie Lorena 1957-
See Moore, Lorrie
See also CA 116

Moore, Thomas 1779-1852....... NCLC 6

Morand, Paul 1888-1976.......... CLC 41
See also obituary CA 69-72; DLB 65

Morante, Elsa 1918-1985....... CLC 8, 47
See also CA 85-88; obituary CA 117

Moravia, Alberto
1907-........ CLC 2, 7, 11, 18, 27, 46
See also Pincherle, Alberto

More, Hannah 1745-1833 .... NCLC 27

More, Henry 1614-1687............. LC 9

More, Sir Thomas 1478-1535 .... LC 10

Moreas, Jean 1856-1910 .... TCLC 18

Morgan, Berry 1919-............. CLC 6
See also CA 49-52; DLB 6

Morgan, Edwin (George) 1920-..... CLC 31
See also CANR 3; CA 7-8R; DLB 27

Morgan, (George) Frederick
1922-....................... CLC 23
See also CANR 21; CA 17-20R

Morgan, Janet 1945- .... CLC 39
See also CA 65-68

Morgan, Lady 1776?-1859....... NCLC 29

Morgan, Robin 1941-.............. CLC 2
See also CA 69-72

Morgan, Seth 1949-1990.......... CLC 65
See also CA 132

Morgenstern, Christian (Otto Josef Wolfgang)
1871-1914................... TCLC 8
See also CA 105

Moricz, Zsigmond 1879-1942 ..... TCLC 33

Morike, Eduard (Friedrich)
1804-1875 .... NCLC 10

Mori Ogai 1862-1922............ TCLC 14
See also Mori Rintaro

Mori Rintaro 1862-1922
See Mori Ogai
See also CA 110

Moritz, Karl Philipp 1756-1793 ...... LC 2

Morris, Julian 1916-
See West, Morris L.

Morris, Steveland Judkins 1950-
See Wonder, Stevie
See also CA 111

Morris, William 1834-1896 .... NCLC 4
See also DLB 18, 35, 57

Morris, Wright (Marion)
1910- .... CLC 1, 3, 7, 18, 37
See also CANR 21; CA 9-12R; DLB 2;
DLB-Y 81

Morrison, James Douglas 1943-1971
See Morrison, Jim
See also CA 73-76

Morrison, Jim 1943-1971.......... CLC 17
See also Morrison, James Douglas

Morrison, Toni 1931-..... CLC 4, 10, 22, 55
See also BLC 3; CANR 27; CA 29-32R;
SATA 57; DLB 6, 33; DLB-Y 81;
CDALB 1968-1987; AAYA 1

Morrison, Van 1945- .... CLC 21
See also CA 116

Mortimer, John (Clifford)
1923-.................... CLC 28, 43
See also CANR 21; CA 13-16R; DLB 13

Mortimer, Penelope (Ruth) 1918-.... CLC 5
See also CA 57-60

Mosher, Howard Frank 19??-....... CLC 62

Mosley, Nicholas 1923-....... CLC 43, 70
See also CA 69-72; DLB 14

Moss, Howard
1922-1987 .... CLC 7, 14, 45, 50
See also CANR 1; CA 1-4R;
obituary CA 123; DLB 5

Motion, Andrew (Peter) 1952-...... CLC 47
See also DLB 40

Motley, Willard (Francis)
1912-1965 .... CLC 18
See also CA 117; obituary CA 106; DLB 76

Mott, Michael (Charles Alston)
1930-.................... CLC 15, 34
See also CAAS 7; CANR 7, 29; CA 5-8R

Mowat, Farley (McGill) 1921-..... CLC 26
See also CLR 20; CANR 4, 24; CA 1-4R;
SATA 3, 55; DLB 68; AAYA 1

Mphahlele, Es'kia 1919-
See Mphahlele, Ezekiel

Mphahlele, Ezekiel 1919-.......... CLC 25
See also BLC 3; CANR 26; CA 81-84

Mqhayi, S(amuel) E(dward) K(rune Loliwe)
1875-1945 .... TCLC 25
See also BLC 3

Mrozek, Slawomir 1930-........ CLC 3, 13
See also CAAS 10; CANR 29; CA 13-16R

Mtwa, Percy 19??-............... CLC 47

Mueller, Lisel 1924-.......... CLC 13, 51
See also CA 93-96

Muir, Edwin 1887-1959........... TCLC 2
See also CA 104; DLB 20

Muir, John 1838-1914 .... TCLC 28

Mujica Lainez, Manuel
1910-1984 .... CLC 31
See also CA 81-84; obituary CA 112

Mukherjee, Bharati 1940-........ CLC 53
See also CA 107; DLB 60

Muldoon, Paul 1951-............. CLC 32
See also CA 113, 129; DLB 40

Mulisch, Harry (Kurt Victor)
1927-..................... CLC 42
See also CANR 6, 26; CA 9-12R

Mull, Martin 1943-............... CLC 17
See also CA 105

Munford, Robert 1737?-1783........ LC 5
See also DLB 31

Munro, Alice (Laidlaw)
1931- .... CLC 6, 10, 19, 50; SSC 3
See also CA 33-36R; SATA 29; DLB 53

Munro, H(ector) H(ugh) 1870-1916
See Saki
See also CA 104; DLB 34

Murasaki, Lady c. 11th century-... CMLC 1

Murdoch, (Jean) Iris
1919- ...... CLC 1, 2, 3, 4, 6, 8, 11, 15,
22, 31, 51
See also CANR 8; CA 13-16R; DLB 14

Murphy, Richard 1927-........... CLC 41
See also CA 29-32R; DLB 40

Murphy, Sylvia 19??-.............. CLC 34

Murphy, Thomas (Bernard) 1935-... CLC 51
See also CA 101

Murray, Les(lie) A(llan) 1938- ..... CLC 40
See also CANR 11, 27; CA 21-24R

Murry, John Middleton
1889-1957 .... TCLC 16
See also CA 118

Musgrave, Susan 1951-........ CLC 13, 54
See also CA 69-72

Musil, Robert (Edler von)
1880-1942 .... TCLC 12
See also CA 109; DLB 81

Musset, (Louis Charles) Alfred de
1810-1857 .... NCLC 7

Myers, Walter Dean 1937-........ CLC 35
See also BLC 3; CLR 4, 16; CANR 20;
CA 33-36R; SAAS 2; SATA 27, 41;
DLB 33; AAYA 4

Myers, Walter M. 1937-
See Myers, Walter Dean

Nabokov, Vladimir (Vladimirovich)
1899-1977 .... CLC 1, 2, 3, 6, 8, 11, 15,
23, 44, 46, 64
See also CANR 20; CA 5-8R;
obituary CA 69-72; DLB 2; DLB-Y 80;
DLB-DS 3; CDALB 1941-1968

Nagy, Laszlo 1925-1978............ CLC 7
See also CA 129; obituary CA 112

Naipaul, Shiva(dhar Srinivasa)
1945-1985 .... CLC 32, 39
See also CA 110, 112; obituary CA 116;
DLB-Y 85

Naipaul, V(idiadhar) S(urajprasad)
1932- .... CLC 4, 7, 9, 13, 18, 37
See also CANR 1; CA 1-4R; DLB-Y 85

Nakos, Ioulia 1899?-
See Nakos, Lilika

Nakos, Lilika 1899?- .... CLC 29

Nakou, Lilika 1899?-
See Nakos, Lilika

Narayan, R(asipuram) K(rishnaswami)
1906-................... CLC 7, 28, 47
See also CA 81-84

Nash, (Frediric) Ogden 1902-1971 .. CLC 23
See also CAP 1; CA 13-14;
obituary CA 29-32R; SATA 2, 46;
DLB 11

Nathan, George Jean 1882-1958 ... TCLC 18
See also CA 114

Natsume, Kinnosuke 1867-1916
See Natsume, Soseki
See also CA 104

Natsume, Soseki 1867-1916..... **TCLC 2, 10**
See also Natsume, Kinnosuke

Natti, (Mary) Lee 1919-
See Kingman, (Mary) Lee
See also CANR 2; CA 7-8R

Naylor, Gloria 1950- .... **CLC 28, 52**
See also BLC 3; CANR 27; CA 107;
AAYA 6

Neff, Debra 1972-.............. **CLC 59**

Neihardt, John G(neisenau)
1881-1973 .... **CLC 32**
See also CAP 1; CA 13-14; DLB 9, 54

Nekrasov, Nikolai Alekseevich
1821-1878 .... **NCLC 11**

Nelligan, Emile 1879-1941....... **TCLC 14**
See also CA 114; DLB 92

Nelson, Willie 1933-............. **CLC 17**
See also CA 107

Nemerov, Howard 1920- .... **CLC 2, 6, 9, 36**
See also CANR 1, 27; CA 1-4R; CABS 2;
DLB 5, 6; DLB-Y 83

Neruda, Pablo
1904-1973 .... **CLC 1, 2, 5, 7, 9, 28, 62;**
PC 4
See also CAP 2; CA 19-20;
obituary CA 45-48

Nerval, Gerard de 1808-1855...... **NCLC 1**

Nervo, (Jose) Amado (Ruiz de)
1870-1919 .... **TCLC 11**
See also CA 109

Neufeld, John (Arthur) 1938- ...... **CLC 17**
See also CANR 11; CA 25-28R; SAAS 3;
SATA 6

Neville, Emily Cheney 1919-....... **CLC 12**
See also CANR 3; CA 5-8R; SAAS 2;
SATA 1

Newbound, Bernard Slade 1930-
See Slade, Bernard
See also CA 81-84

Newby, P(ercy) H(oward)
1918- .... **CLC 2, 13**
See also CA 5-8R; DLB 15

Newlove, Donald 1928- .... **CLC 6**
See also CANR 25; CA 29-32R

Newlove, John (Herbert) 1938-..... **CLC 14**
See also CANR 9, 25; CA 21-24R

Newman, Charles 1938-.......... **CLC 2, 8**
See also CA 21-24R

Newman, Edwin (Harold) 1919- .... **CLC 14**
See also CANR 5; CA 69-72

Newton, Suzanne 1936-........... **CLC 35**
See also CANR 14; CA 41-44R; SATA 5

Nexo, Martin Andersen
1869-1954 .... **TCLC 43**

Nezval, Vitezslav 1900-1958 ...... **TCLC 44**
See also CA 123

Ngema, Mbongeni 1955- .... **CLC 57**

Ngugi, James Thiong'o 1938-
See Ngugi wa Thiong'o

Ngugi wa Thiong'o 1938-... **CLC 3, 7, 13, 36**
See also Ngugi, James (Thiong'o); Wa
Thiong'o, Ngugi
See also BLC 3

Nichol, B(arrie) P(hillip) 1944-..... **CLC 18**
See also CA 53-56; DLB 53

Nichols, John (Treadwell) 1940-.... **CLC 38**
See also CAAS 2; CANR 6; CA 9-12R;
DLB-Y 82

Nichols, Peter (Richard)
1927- .... **CLC 5, 36, 65**
See also CANR 33; CA 104; DLB 13

Nicolas, F.R.E. 1927-
See Freeling, Nicolas

Niedecker, Lorine 1903-1970.... **CLC 10, 42**
See also CAP 2; CA 25-28; DLB 48

Nietzsche, Friedrich (Wilhelm)
1844-1900 .... **TCLC 10, 18**
See also CA 107, 121

Nievo, Ippolito 1831-1861 .... **NCLC 22**

Nightingale, Anne Redmon 1943-
See Redmon (Nightingale), Anne
See also CA 103

Nin, Anais
1903-1977 ..... **CLC 1, 4, 8, 11, 14, 60;**
SSC 10
See also CANR 22; CA 13-16R;
obituary CA 69-72; DLB 2, 4

Nissenson, Hugh 1933-.......... **CLC 4, 9**
See also CANR 27; CA 17-20R; DLB 28

Niven, Larry 1938-............... **CLC 8**
See also Niven, Laurence Van Cott
See also DLB 8

Niven, Laurence Van Cott 1938-
See Niven, Larry
See also CANR 14; CA 21-24R

Nixon, Agnes Eckhardt 1927-...... **CLC 21**
See also CA 110

Nizan, Paul 1905-1940.......... **TCLC 40**
See also DLB 72

Nkosi, Lewis 1936-.............. **CLC 45**
See also BLC 3; CANR 27; CA 65-68

Nodier, (Jean) Charles (Emmanuel)
1780-1844 .... **NCLC 19**

Nolan, Christopher 1965-......... **CLC 58**
See also CA 111

Nordhoff, Charles 1887-1947...... **TCLC 23**
See also CA 108; SATA 23; DLB 9

Norman, Marsha 1947- .... **CLC 28**
See also CA 105; CABS 3; DLB-Y 84

Norris, (Benjamin) Frank(lin)
1870-1902 .... **TCLC 24**
See also CA 110; DLB 12, 71;
CDALB 1865-1917

Norris, Leslie 1921-.............. **CLC 14**
See also CANR 14; CAP 1; CA 11-12;
DLB 27

North, Andrew 1912-
See Norton, Andre

North, Christopher 1785-1854
See Wilson, John

Norton, Alice Mary 1912-
See Norton, Andre
See also CANR 2; CA 1-4R; SATA 1, 43

Norton, Andre 1912-............. **CLC 12**
See also Norton, Mary Alice
See also DLB 8, 52

Norway, Nevil Shute 1899-1960
See Shute (Norway), Nevil
See also CA 102; obituary CA 93-96

Norwid, Cyprian Kamil
1821-1883 .... **NCLC 17**

Nossack, Hans Erich 1901-1978..... **CLC 6**
See also CA 93-96; obituary CA 85-88;
DLB 69

Nova, Craig 1945-.............. **CLC 7, 31**
See also CANR 2; CA 45-48

Novak, Joseph 1933-
See Kosinski, Jerzy (Nikodem)

Novalis 1772-1801 .... **NCLC 13**

Nowlan, Alden (Albert) 1933-...... **CLC 15**
See also CANR 5; CA 9-12R; DLB 53

Noyes, Alfred 1880-1958 .... **TCLC 7**
See also CA 104; DLB 20

Nunn, Kem 19??-................ **CLC 34**

Nye, Robert 1939- .... **CLC 13, 42**
See also CANR 29; CA 33-36R; SATA 6;
DLB 14

Nyro, Laura 1947- .... **CLC 17**

Oates, Joyce Carol
1938- ..... **CLC 1, 2, 3, 6, 9, 11, 15, 19,**
33, 52; SSC 6
See also CANR 25; CA 5-8R; DLB 2, 5;
DLB-Y 81; CDALB 1968-1987

O'Brien, Darcy 1939-............ **CLC 11**
See also CANR 8; CA 21-24R

O'Brien, Edna
1932- ... **CLC 3, 5, 8, 13, 36, 65; SSC 10**
See also CANR 6; CA 1-4R; DLB 14

O'Brien, Fitz-James 1828?-1862.. **NCLC 21**
See also DLB 74

O'Brien, Flann
1911-1966 ...... **CLC 1, 4, 5, 7, 10, 47**
See also O Nuallain, Brian

O'Brien, Richard 19??-............ **CLC 17**
See also CA 124

O'Brien, (William) Tim(othy)
1946- .... **CLC 7, 19, 40**
See also CA 85-88; DLB-Y 80

Obstfelder, Sigbjorn 1866-1900.... **TCLC 23**
See also CA 123

O'Casey, Sean
1880-1964 .... **CLC 1, 5, 9, 11, 15**
See also CA 89-92; DLB 10

Ochs, Phil 1940-1976 .... **CLC 17**
See also obituary CA 65-68

O'Connor, Edwin (Greene)
1918-1968 .... **CLC 14**
See also CA 93-96; obituary CA 25-28R

O'Connor, (Mary) Flannery
1925-1964 ... **CLC 1, 2, 3, 6, 10, 13, 15,**
21, 66; SSC 1
See also CANR 3; CA 1-4R; DLB 2;
DLB-Y 80; CDALB 1941-1968

O'Connor, Frank
1903-1966 .... **CLC 14, 23; SSC 5**
See also O'Donovan, Michael (John)
See also CA 93-96

O'Dell, Scott 1903-.............. **CLC 30**
See also CLR 1, 16; CANR 12; CA 61-64;
SATA 12; DLB 52

Author Index

Parker, Dorothy (Rothschild)
1893-1967 . . . . **CLC 15, 68; SSC 2**
See also CAP 2; CA 19-20;
obituary CA 25-28R; DLB 11, 45. 86

Parker, Robert B(rown) 1932- . . . . . . **CLC 27**
See also CANR 1, 26; CA 49-52

Parkin, Frank 1940- . . . . **CLC 43**

Parkman, Francis 1823-1893 . . . . . **NCLC 12**
See also DLB 1, 30

Parks, Gordon (Alexander Buchanan)
1912- . . . . **CLC 1, 16**
See also BLC 3; CANR 26; CA 41-44R;
SATA 8; DLB 33

Parnell, Thomas 1679-1718 . . . . **LC 3**

Parra, Nicanor 1914- . . . . **CLC 2**
See also CA 85-88

Pascoli, Giovanni 1855-1912 . . . . . . **TCLC 45**

Pasolini, Pier Paolo
1922-1975 . . . . **CLC 20, 37**
See also CA 93-96; obituary CA 61-64

Pastan, Linda (Olenik) 1932- . . . . . . **CLC 27**
See also CANR 18; CA 61-64; DLB 5

Pasternak, Boris
1890-1960 . . . . **CLC 7, 10, 18, 63**
See also CA 127; obituary CA 116

Patchen, Kenneth 1911-1972 . . . **CLC 1, 2, 18**
See also CANR 3; CA 1-4R;
obituary CA 33-36R; DLB 16, 48

Pater, Walter (Horatio)
1839-1894 . . . . **NCLC 7**
See also DLB 57

Paterson, Andrew Barton
1864-1941 . . . . **TCLC 32**

Paterson, Katherine (Womeldorf)
1932- . . . . **CLC 12, 30**
See also CLR 7; CANR 28; CA 21-24R;
SATA 13, 53; DLB 52; AAYA 1

Patmore, Coventry Kersey Dighton
1823-1896 . . . . **NCLC 9**
See also DLB 35

Paton, Alan (Stewart)
1903-1988 . . . . **CLC 4, 10, 25, 55**
See also CANR 22; CAP 1; CA 15-16;
obituary CA 125; SATA 11

Paulding, James Kirke 1778-1860 . . **NCLC 2**
See also DLB 3, 59, 74

Paulin, Tom 1949- . . . . **CLC 37**
See also CA 123; DLB 40

Paustovsky, Konstantin (Georgievich)
1892-1968 . . . . **CLC 40**
See also CA 93-96; obituary CA 25-28R

Paustowsky, Konstantin (Georgievich)
1892-1968
See Paustovsky, Konstantin (Georgievich)

Pavese, Cesare 1908-1950 . . . . **TCLC 3**
See also CA 104

Pavic, Milorad 1929- . . . . **CLC 60**

Payne, Alan 1932-
See Jakes, John (William)

Paz, Octavio
1914- . . . . . . **CLC 3, 4, 6, 10, 19, 51, 65;**
PC 1
See also CANR 32; CA 73-76

p'Bitek, Okot 1931-1982
See also BLC 3; CA 124; obituary CA 107

Peacock, Molly 1947- . . . . **CLC 60**
See also CA 103

Peacock, Thomas Love
1785-1886 . . . . **NCLC 22**

Peake, Mervyn 1911-1968 . . . . . . **CLC 7, 54**
See also CANR 3; CA 5-8R;
obituary CA 25-28R; SATA 23; DLB 15

Pearce, (Ann) Philippa 1920- . . . . . . **CLC 21**
See also Christie, (Ann) Philippa
See also CLR 9; CA 5-8R; SATA 1

Pearl, Eric 1934-
See Elman, Richard

Pearson, T(homas) R(eid) 1956- . . . . **CLC 39**
See also CA 120, 130

Peck, John 1941- . . . . **CLC 3**
See also CANR 3; CA 49-52

Peck, Richard 1934- . . . . **CLC 21**
See also CLR 15; CANR 19; CA 85-88;
SAAS 2; SATA 18; AAYA 1

Peck, Robert Newton 1928- . . . . **CLC 17**
See also CA 81-84; SAAS 1; SATA 21;
AAYA 3

Peckinpah, (David) Sam(uel)
1925-1984 . . . . **CLC 20**
See also CA 109; obituary CA 114

Pedersen, Knut 1859-1952
See Hamsun, Knut
See also CA 104, 109, 119

Peguy, Charles (Pierre)
1873-1914 . . . . **TCLC 10**
See also CA 107

Pepys, Samuel 1633-1703 . . . . **LC 11**

Percy, Walker
1916-1990 . . . **CLC 2, 3, 6, 8, 14, 18, 47,**
65
See also CANR 1, 23; CA 1-4R;
obituary CA 131; DLB 2; DLB-Y 80

Perec, Georges 1936-1982 . . . . **CLC 56**
See also DLB 83

Pereda, Jose Maria de
1833-1906 . . . . **TCLC 16**

Perelman, S(idney) J(oseph)
1904-1979 . . . **CLC 3, 5, 9, 15, 23, 44, 49**
See also CANR 18; CA 73-76;
obituary CA 89-92; DLB 11, 44

Peret, Benjamin 1899-1959 . . . . **TCLC 20**
See also CA 117

Peretz, Isaac Leib 1852?-1915 . . . . . **TCLC 16**
See also CA 109

Perez, Galdos Benito 1853-1920 . . . **TCLC 27**
See also CA 125

Perrault, Charles 1628-1703 . . . . **LC 2**
See also SATA 25

Perse, St.-John 1887-1975 . . . . **CLC 4, 11, 46**
See also Leger, (Marie-Rene) Alexis
Saint-Leger

Pesetsky, Bette 1932- . . . . **CLC 28**

Peshkov, Alexei Maximovich 1868-1936
See Gorky, Maxim
See also CA 105

Pessoa, Fernando (Antonio Nogueira)
1888-1935 . . . . **TCLC 27**
See also CA 125

Peterkin, Julia (Mood) 1880-1961 . . . **CLC 31**
See also CA 102; DLB 9

Peters, Joan K. 1945- . . . . **CLC 39**

Peters, Robert L(ouis) 1924- . . . . **CLC 7**
See also CAAS 8; CA 13-16R

Petofi, Sandor 1823-1849 . . . . **NCLC 21**

Petrakis, Harry Mark 1923- . . . . **CLC 3**
See also CANR 4, 30; CA 9-12R

Petrov, Evgeny 1902-1942 . . . . **TCLC 21**

Petry, Ann (Lane) 1908- . . . . . . **CLC 1, 7, 18**
See also CLR 12; CAAS 6; CANR 4;
CA 5-8R; SATA 5; DLB 76

Petursson, Halligrimur 1614-1674 . . . . **LC 8**

Philipson, Morris (H.) 1926- . . . . **CLC 53**
See also CANR 4; CA 1-4R

Phillips, David Graham
1867-1911 . . . . **TCLC 44**
See also CA 108; DLB 9, 12

Phillips, Jayne Anne 1952- . . . . . **CLC 15, 33**
See also CANR 24; CA 101; DLB-Y 80

Phillips, Robert (Schaeffer) 1938- . . . **CLC 28**
See also CANR 8; CA 17-20R

Pica, Peter 1925-
See Aldiss, Brian W(ilson)

Piccolo, Lucio 1901-1969 . . . . **CLC 13**
See also CA 97-100

Pickthall, Marjorie (Lowry Christie)
1883-1922 . . . . **TCLC 21**
See also CA 107; DLB 92

Pico della Mirandola, Giovanni
1463-1494 . . . . **LC 15**

Piercy, Marge
1936- . . . . **CLC 3, 6, 14, 18, 27, 62**
See also CAAS 1; CANR 13; CA 21-24R

Pilnyak, Boris 1894-1937? . . . . **TCLC 23**

Pincherle, Alberto 1907- . . . . **CLC 11, 18**
See also Moravia, Alberto
See also CA 25-28R

Pineda, Cecile 1942- . . . . **CLC 39**
See also CA 118

Pinero, Miguel (Gomez)
1946-1988 . . . . **CLC 4, 55**
See also CANR 29; CA 61-64;
obituary CA 125

Pinero, Sir Arthur Wing
1855-1934 . . . . **TCLC 32**
See also CA 110; DLB 10

Pinget, Robert 1919- . . . . **CLC 7, 13, 37**
See also CA 85-88; DLB 83

Pink Floyd . . . . **CLC 35**

Pinkney, Edward 1802-1828 . . . . . **NCLC 31**

Pinkwater, D(aniel) M(anus)
1941- . . . . **CLC 35**
See also Pinkwater, Manus
See also CLR 4; CANR 12; CA 29-32R;
SAAS 3; SATA 46; AAYA 1

Pinkwater, Manus 1941-
See Pinkwater, D(aniel) M(anus)
See also SATA 8

Reyes y Basoalto, Ricardo Eliecer Neftali
1904-1973
See Neruda, Pablo

Reymont, Wladyslaw Stanislaw
1867-1925 .... **TCLC 5**
See also CA 104

Reynolds, Jonathan 1942?- ...... **CLC 6, 38**
See also CANR 28; CA 65-68

Reynolds, Michael (Shane) 1937- ... **CLC 44**
See also CANR 9; CA 65-68

Reynolds, Sir Joshua 1723-1792 ..... **LC 15**

Reznikoff, Charles 1894-1976 .... **CLC 9**
See also CAP 2; CA 33-36;
obituary CA 61-64; DLB 28, 45

Rezzori, Gregor von 1914-........ **CLC 25**
See also CA 122

Rhys, Jean
1890-1979 ...... **CLC 2, 4, 6, 14, 19, 51**
See also CA 25-28R; obituary CA 85-88;
DLB 36

Ribeiro, Darcy 1922- .... **CLC 34**
See also CA 33-36R

Ribeiro, Joao Ubaldo (Osorio Pimentel)
1941-............ **CLC 10, 67**
See also CA 81-84

Ribman, Ronald (Burt) 1932- .... **CLC 7**
See also CA 21-24R

Ricci, Nino 1959-................ **CLC 70**

Rice, Anne 1941-................. **CLC 41**
See also CANR 12; CA 65-68

Rice, Elmer 1892-1967......... **CLC 7, 49**
See also CAP 2; CA 21-22;
obituary CA 25-28R; DLB 4, 7

Rice, Tim 1944- .... **CLC 21**
See also CA 103

Rich, Adrienne (Cecile)
1929- .... **CLC 3, 6, 7, 11, 18, 36**
See also CANR 20; CA 9-12R; DLB 5, 67

Richard, Keith 1943- .... **CLC 17**
See also CA 107

Richards, David Adam 1950-...... **CLC 59**
See also CA 93-96; DLB 53

Richards, I(vor) A(rmstrong)
1893-1979 .... **CLC 14, 24**
See also CA 41-44R; obituary CA 89-92;
DLB 27

Richards, Keith 1943-
See Richard, Keith
See also CA 107

Richardson, Dorothy (Miller)
1873-1957 .... **TCLC 3**
See also CA 104; DLB 36

Richardson, Ethel 1870-1946
See Richardson, Henry Handel
See also CA 105

Richardson, Henry Handel
1870-1946 .... **TCLC 4**
See Richardson, Ethel

Richardson, Samuel 1689-1761 .... **LC 1**
See also DLB 39

Richler, Mordecai
1931- .... **CLC 3, 5, 9, 13, 18, 46, 70**
See also CLR 17; CANR 31; CA 65-68;
SATA 27, 44; DLB 53

Richter, Conrad (Michael)
1890-1968 .... **CLC 30**
See also CANR 23; CA 5-8R;
obituary CA 25-28R; SATA 3; DLB 9

Richter, Johann Paul Friedrich 1763-1825
See Jean Paul

Riddell, Mrs. J. H. 1832-1906..... **TCLC 40**

Riding, Laura 1901-............. **CLC 3, 7**
See also Jackson, Laura (Riding)

Riefenstahl, Berta Helene Amalia
1902-...................... **CLC 16**
See also Riefenstahl, Leni
See also CA 108

Riefenstahl, Leni 1902- .... **CLC 16**
See also Riefenstahl, Berta Helene Amalia
See also CA 108

Rilke, Rainer Maria
1875-1926 .... **TCLC 1, 6, 19; PC 2**
See also CA 104, 132; DLB 81

Rimbaud, (Jean Nicolas) Arthur
1854-1891 .... **NCLC 4, 35; PC 3**

Ringwood, Gwen(dolyn Margaret) Pharis
1910-1984 .... **CLC 48**
See also obituary CA 112

Rio, Michel 19??-................ **CLC 43**

Ritsos, Yannis 1909-........ **CLC 6, 13, 31**
See also CA 77-80

Ritter, Erika 1948?-.............. **CLC 52**

Rivera, Jose Eustasio 1889-1928... **TCLC 35**

Rivers, Conrad Kent 1933-1968...... **CLC 1**
See also CA 85-88; DLB 41

Rizal, Jose 1861-1896........... **NCLC 27**

Roa Bastos, Augusto 1917- .... **CLC 45**

Robbe-Grillet, Alain
1922- ...... **CLC 1, 2, 4, 6, 8, 10, 14, 43**
See also CA 9-12R; DLB 83

Robbins, Harold 1916-............. **CLC 5**
See also CANR 26; CA 73-76

Robbins, Thomas Eugene 1936-
See Robbins, Tom
See also CA 81-84

Robbins, Tom 1936-........ **CLC 9, 32, 64**
See also Robbins, Thomas Eugene
See also CANR 29; CA 81-84; DLB-Y 80

Robbins, Trina 1938- .... **CLC 21**

Roberts, (Sir) Charles G(eorge) D(ouglas)
1860-1943 .... **TCLC 8**
See also CA 105; SATA 29; DLB 92

Roberts, Kate 1891-1985 .... **CLC 15**
See also CA 107; obituary CA 116

Roberts, Keith (John Kingston)
1935-...................... **CLC 14**
See also CA 25-28R

Roberts, Kenneth 1885-1957 ..... **TCLC 23**
See also CA 109; DLB 9

Roberts, Michele (B.) 1949-........ **CLC 48**
See also CA 115

Robertson, Thomas William
1829-1871 .... **NCLC 35**

Robinson, Edwin Arlington
1869-1935 .... **TCLC 5; PC 1**
See also CA 104; DLB 54;
CDALB 1865-1917

Robinson, Henry Crabb
1775-1867 .... **NCLC 15**

Robinson, Jill 1936-............. **CLC 10**
See also CA 102

Robinson, Kim Stanley 19??-....... **CLC 34**
See also CA 126

Robinson, Marilynne 1944-........ **CLC 25**
See also CA 116

Robinson, Smokey 1940-.......... **CLC 21**

Robinson, William 1940-
See Robinson, Smokey
See also CA 116

Robison, Mary 1949-............. **CLC 42**
See also CA 113, 116

Roddenberry, Gene 1921-........ **CLC 17**
See also CANR 110; SATA 45

Rodgers, Mary 1931-............. **CLC 12**
See also CLR 20; CANR 8; CA 49-52;
SATA 8

Rodgers, W(illiam) R(obert)
1909-1969 .... **CLC 7**
See also CA 85-88; DLB 20

Rodman, Howard 19??- .... **CLC 65**

Rodriguez, Claudio 1934-......... **CLC 10**

Roethke, Theodore (Huebner)
1908-1963 ...... **CLC 1, 3, 8, 11, 19, 46**
See also CA 81-84; CABS 2; SAAS 1;
DLB 5; CDALB 1941-1968

Rogers, Sam 1943-
See Shepard, Sam

Rogers, Thomas (Hunton) 1931-..... **CLC 57**
See also CA 89-92

Rogers, Will(iam Penn Adair)
1879-1935 .... **TCLC 8**
See also CA 105; DLB 11

Rogin, Gilbert 1929-.............. **CLC 18**
See also CANR 15; CA 65-68

Rohan, Koda 1867-1947............ **TCLC 22**
See also CA 121

Rohmer, Eric 1920- .... **CLC 16**
See also Scherer, Jean-Marie Maurice

Rohmer, Sax 1883-1959.......... **TCLC 28**
See also Ward, Arthur Henry Sarsfield
See also CA 108; DLB 70

Roiphe, Anne (Richardson)
1935-...................... **CLC 3, 9**
See also CA 89-92; DLB-Y 80

Rolfe, Frederick (William Serafino Austin
Lewis Mary) 1860-1913...... **TCLC 12**
See also CA 107; DLB 34

Rolland, Romain 1866-1944....... **TCLC 23**
See also CA 118; DLB 65

Rolvaag, O(le) E(dvart)
1876-1931 .... **TCLC 17**
See also CA 117; DLB 9

Romains, Jules 1885-1972.......... **CLC 7**
See also CA 85-88

Romero, Jose Ruben 1890-1952 ... **TCLC 14**
See also CA 114

Ronsard, Pierre de 1524-1585........ **LC 6**

Rooke, Leon 1934-............ **CLC 25, 34**
See also CANR 23; CA 25-28R

Roper, William 1498-1578.......... **LC 10**

Rosa, Joao Guimaraes 1908-1967 . . . **CLC 23**
See also obituary CA 89-92

Rosen, Richard (Dean) 1949- . . . . . . **CLC 39**
See also CA 77-80

Rosenberg, Isaac 1890-1918 . . . . . . **TCLC 12**
See also CA 107; DLB 20

Rosenblatt, Joe 1933- . . . . **CLC 15**
See also Rosenblatt, Joseph

Rosenblatt, Joseph 1933-
See Rosenblatt, Joe
See also CA 89-92

Rosenfeld, Samuel 1896-1963
See Tzara, Tristan
See also obituary CA 89-92

Rosenthal, M(acha) L(ouis) 1917- . . . **CLC 28**
See also CAAS 6; CANR 4; CA 1-4R;
SATA 59; DLB 5

Ross, (James) Sinclair 1908- . . . . **CLC 13**
See also CA 73-76; DLB 88

Rossetti, Christina Georgina
1830-1894 . . . . **NCLC 2**
See also SATA 20; DLB 35

Rossetti, Dante Gabriel
1828-1882 . . . . **NCLC 4**
See also DLB 35

Rossetti, Gabriel Charles Dante 1828-1882
See Rossetti, Dante Gabriel

Rossner, Judith (Perelman)
1935- . . . . CLC 6, 9, 29
See also CANR 18; CA 17-20R; DLB 6

Rostand, Edmond (Eugene Alexis)
1868-1918 . . . . **TCLC 6, 37**
See also CA 104, 126

Roth, Henry 1906- . . . . **CLC 2, 6, 11**
See also CAP 1; CA 11-12; DLB 28

Roth, Joseph 1894-1939 . . . . **TCLC 33**
See also DLB 85

Roth, Philip (Milton)
1933- . . . . . . CLC 1, 2, 3, 4, 6, 9, 15, 22,
31, 47, 66
See also CANR 1, 22; CA 1-4R; DLB 2, 28;
DLB-Y 82; CDALB 1968-1988

Rothenberg, James 1931- . . . . **CLC 57**

Rothenberg, Jerome 1931- . . . . **CLC 6, 57**
See also CANR 1; CA 45-48; DLB 5

Roumain, Jacques 1907-1944 . . . . . . **TCLC 19**
See also BLC 3; CA 117, 125

Rourke, Constance (Mayfield)
1885-1941 . . . . **TCLC 12**
See also YABC 1; CA 107

Rousseau, Jean-Baptiste 1671-1741 . . . **LC 9**

Rousseau, Jean-Jacques 1712-1778 . . . **LC 14**

Roussel, Raymond 1877-1933 . . . . . **TCLC 20**
See also CA 117

Rovit, Earl (Herbert) 1927- . . . . **CLC 7**
See also CANR 12; CA 5-8R

Rowe, Nicholas 1674-1718 . . . . **LC 8**

Rowson, Susanna Haswell
1762-1824 . . . . **NCLC 5**
See also DLB 37

Roy, Gabrielle 1909-1983 . . . . **CLC 10, 14**
See also CANR 5; CA 53-56;
obituary CA 110; DLB 68

Rozewicz, Tadeusz 1921- . . . . **CLC 9, 23**
See also CA 108

Ruark, Gibbons 1941- . . . . **CLC 3**
See also CANR 14; CA 33-36R

Rubens, Bernice 192?- . . . . **CLC 19, 31**
See also CA 25-28R; DLB 14

Rubenstein, Gladys 1934-
See Swan, Gladys

Rudkin, (James) David 1936- . . . . . . **CLC 14**
See also CA 89-92; DLB 13

Rudnik, Raphael 1933- . . . . **CLC 7**
See also CA 29-32R

Ruiz, Jose Martinez 1874-1967
See Azorin

Rukeyser, Muriel
1913-1980 . . . . **CLC 6, 10, 15, 27**
See also CANR 26; CA 5-8R;
obituary CA 93-96; obituary SATA 22;
DLB 48

Rule, Jane (Vance) 1931- . . . . **CLC 27**
See also CANR 12; CA 25-28R; DLB 60

Rulfo, Juan 1918-1986 . . . . **CLC 8**
See also CANR 26; CA 85-88;
obituary CA 118

Runyon, (Alfred) Damon
1880-1946 . . . . **TCLC 10**
See also CA 107; DLB 11

Rush, Norman 1933- . . . . **CLC 44**
See also CA 121, 126

Rushdie, (Ahmed) Salman
1947- . . . . **CLC 23, 31, 55, 59**
See also CA 108, 111

Rushforth, Peter (Scott) 1945- . . . . . **CLC 19**
See also CA 101

Ruskin, John 1819-1900 . . . . **TCLC 20**
See also CA 114; SATA 24; DLB 55

Russ, Joanna 1937- . . . . **CLC 15**
See also CANR 11; CA 25-28R; DLB 8

Russell, George William 1867-1935
See A. E.
See also CA 104

Russell, (Henry) Ken(neth Alfred)
1927- . . . . **CLC 16**
See also CA 105

Russell, Mary Annette Beauchamp 1866-1941
See Elizabeth

Russell, Willy 1947- . . . . **CLC 60**

Rutherford, Mark 1831-1913 . . . . . **TCLC 25**
See also CA 121; DLB 18

Ruyslinck, Ward 1929- . . . . **CLC 14**

Ryan, Cornelius (John) 1920-1974 . . . **CLC 7**
See also CA 69-72; obituary CA 53-56

Ryan, Michael 1946- . . . . **CLC 65**
See also CA 49-52; DLB-Y 82

Rybakov, Anatoli 1911?- . . . . **CLC 23, 53**
See also CA 126

Ryder, Jonathan 1927-
See Ludlum, Robert

Ryga, George 1932- . . . . **CLC 14**
See also CA 101; obituary CA 124; DLB 60

**Séviné, Marquise de Marie de
Rabutin-Chantal** 1626-1696 . . . . . **LC 11**

Saba, Umberto 1883-1957 . . . . **TCLC 33**

Sabato, Ernesto 1911- . . . . **CLC 10, 23**
See also CA 97-100

Sacher-Masoch, Leopold von
1836?-1895 . . . . **NCLC 31**

Sachs, Marilyn (Stickle) 1927- . . . . . **CLC 35**
See also CLR 2; CANR 13; CA 17-20R;
SAAS 2; SATA 3, 52

Sachs, Nelly 1891-1970 . . . . **CLC 14**
See also CAP 2; CA 17-18;
obituary CA 25-28R

Sackler, Howard (Oliver)
1929-1982 . . . . **CLC 14**
See also CA 61-64; obituary CA 108; DLB 7

Sacks, Oliver 1933- . . . . **CLC 67**
See also CANR 28; CA 53-56

Sade, Donatien Alphonse Francois, Comte de
1740-1814 . . . . **NCLC 3**

Sadoff, Ira 1945- . . . . **CLC 9**
See also CANR 5, 21; CA 53-56

Safire, William 1929- . . . . **CLC 10**
See also CA 17-20R

Sagan, Carl (Edward) 1934- . . . . **CLC 30**
See also CANR 11; CA 25-28R; SATA 58

Sagan, Francoise
1935- . . . . **CLC 3, 6, 9, 17, 36**
See also Quoirez, Francoise
See also CANR 6; DLB 83

Sahgal, Nayantara (Pandit) 1927- . . . **CLC 41**
See also CANR 11; CA 9-12R

Saint, H(arry) F. 1941- . . . . **CLC 50**

Sainte-Beuve, Charles Augustin
1804-1869 . . . . **NCLC 5**

Sainte-Marie, Beverly 1941-1972?
See Sainte-Marie, Buffy
See also CA 107

Sainte-Marie, Buffy 1941- . . . . **CLC 17**
See also Sainte-Marie, Beverly

**Saint-Exupery, Antoine (Jean Baptiste Marie
Roger) de** 1900-1944 . . . . **TCLC 2**
See also CLR 10; CA 108; SATA 20;
DLB 72

Saintsbury, George 1845-1933 . . . . . **TCLC 31**
See also DLB 57

Sait Faik (Abasiyanik)
1906-1954 . . . . **TCLC 23**

Saki 1870-1916 . . . . **TCLC 3**
See also Munro, H(ector) H(ugh)
See also CA 104

Salama, Hannu 1936- . . . . **CLC 18**

Salamanca, J(ack) R(ichard)
1922- . . . . **CLC 4, 15**
See also CA 25-28R

Sale, Kirkpatrick 1937- . . . . **CLC 68**
See also CANR 10; CA 13-14R

Salinas, Pedro 1891-1951 . . . . **TCLC 17**
See also CA 117

Salinger, J(erome) D(avid)
1919- . . . . . . **CLC 1, 3, 8, 12, 56; SSC 2**
See also CA 5-8R; DLB 2;
CDALB 1941-1968

Salter, James 1925- . . . . **CLC 7, 52, 59**
See also CA 73-76

Author Index

Author Index

Walker, Edward Joseph   1934-
See Walker, Ted
See also CANR 12; CA 21-24R

Walker, George F.   1947- . . . . **CLC 44, 61**
See also CANR 21; CA 103; DLB 60

Walker, Joseph A.   1935- . . . . **CLC 19**
See also CANR 26; CA 89-92; DLB 38

Walker, Margaret (Abigail)
   1915- . . . . **CLC 1, 6**
See also BLC 3; CANR 26; CA 73-76;
   DLB 76

Walker, Ted   1934- . . . . **CLC 13**
See also Walker, Edward Joseph
See also DLB 40

Wallace, David Foster   1962- . . . . **CLC 50**

Wallace, Irving   1916- . . . . **CLC 7, 13**
See also CAAS 1; CANR 1; CA 1-4R

Wallant, Edward Lewis
   1926-1962 . . . . **CLC 5, 10**
See also CANR 22; CA 1-4R; DLB 2, 28

Walpole, Horace   1717-1797 . . . . **LC 2**
See also DLB 39

Walpole, (Sir) Hugh (Seymour)
   1884-1941 . . . . **TCLC 5**
See also CA 104; DLB 34

Walser, Martin   1927- . . . . **CLC 27**
See also CANR 8; CA 57-60; DLB 75

Walser, Robert   1878-1956 . . . . **TCLC 18**
See also CA 118; DLB 66

Walsh, Gillian Paton   1939-
See Walsh, Jill Paton
See also CA 37-40R; SATA 4

Walsh, Jill Paton   1939- . . . . **CLC 35**
See also CLR 2; SAAS 3

Wambaugh, Joseph (Aloysius, Jr.)
   1937- . . . . **CLC 3, 18**
See also CA 33-36R; DLB 6; DLB-Y 83

Ward, Arthur Henry Sarsfield   1883-1959
See Rohmer, Sax
See also CA 108

Ward, Douglas Turner   1930- . . . . **CLC 19**
See also CA 81-84; DLB 7, 38

Warhol, Andy   1928-1987 . . . . **CLC 20**
See also CA 89-92; obituary CA 121

Warner, Francis (Robert le Plastrier)
   1937- . . . . **CLC 14**
See also CANR 11; CA 53-56

Warner, Marina   1946- . . . . **CLC 59**
See also CANR 21; CA 65-68

Warner, Rex (Ernest)   1905-1986. . . . **CLC 45**
See also CA 89-92; obituary CA 119;
   DLB 15

Warner, Susan   1819-1885 . . . . **NCLC 31**
See also DLB 3, 42

Warner, Sylvia Townsend
   1893-1978 . . . . **CLC 7, 19**
See also CANR 16; CA 61-64;
   obituary CA 77-80; DLB 34

Warren, Mercy Otis   1728-1814. . . **NCLC 13**
See also DLB 31

Warren, Robert Penn
   1905-1989 . . . **CLC 1, 4, 6, 8, 10, 13, 18,
                              39, 53, 59; SSC 4**
See also CANR 10; CA 13-16R. 129. 130;
   SATA 46; DLB 2, 48; DLB-Y 80;
   CDALB 1968-1987

Warshofsky, Isaac   1904-1991
See Singer, Isaac Bashevis

Warton, Thomas   1728-1790. . . . . **LC 15**

Warung, Price   1855-1911. . . . . **TCLC 45**

Washington, Booker T(aliaferro)
   1856-1915 . . . . **TCLC 10**
See also BLC 3; CA 114, 125; SATA 28

Wassermann, Jakob   1873-1934 . . . . . **TCLC 6**
See also CA 104; DLB 66

Wasserstein, Wendy   1950- . . . . . . **CLC 32, 59**
See also CA 121; CABS 3

Waterhouse, Keith (Spencer)
   1929- . . . . **CLC 47**
See also CA 5-8R; DLB 13, 15

Waters, Roger   1944-
See Pink Floyd

Wa Thiong'o, Ngugi
   1938- . . . . **CLC 3, 7, 13, 36**
See also Ngugi, James (Thiong'o); Ngugi wa
   Thiong'o

Watkins, Paul   1964- . . . . **CLC 55**

Watkins, Vernon (Phillips)
   1906-1967 . . . . **CLC 43**
See also CAP 1; CA 9-10;
   obituary CA 25-28R; DLB 20

Waugh, Auberon (Alexander)   1939-. . **CLC 7**
See also CANR 6, 22; CA 45-48; DLB 14

Waugh, Evelyn (Arthur St. John)
   1903-1966 . . . **CLC 1, 3, 8, 13, 19, 27, 44**
See also CANR 22; CA 85-88;
   obituary CA 25-28R; DLB 15

Waugh, Harriet   1944- . . . . **CLC 6**
See also CANR 22; CA 85-88

Webb, Beatrice (Potter)
   1858-1943 . . . . **TCLC 22**
See also CA 117

Webb, Charles (Richard)   1939- . . . . . . **CLC 7**
See also CA 25-28R

Webb, James H(enry), Jr.   1946-. . . . **CLC 22**
See also CA 81-84

Webb, Mary (Gladys Meredith)
   1881-1927 . . . . **TCLC 24**
See also CA 123; DLB 34

Webb, Phyllis   1927- . . . . **CLC 18**
See also CANR 23; CA 104; DLB 53

Webb, Sidney (James)
   1859-1947 . . . . **TCLC 22**
See also CA 117

Webber, Andrew Lloyd   1948- . . . . . . **CLC 21**

Weber, Lenora Mattingly
   1895-1971 . . . . **CLC 12**
See also CAP 1; CA 19-20;
   obituary CA 29-32R; SATA 2;
   obituary SATA 26

Webster, John   1580?-1634? . . . . **DC 2**
See also DLB 58

Webster, Noah   1758-1843 . . . . **NCLC 30**
See also DLB 1, 37, 42, 43, 73

Wedekind, (Benjamin) Frank(lin)
   1864-1918 . . . . **TCLC 7**
See also CA 104

Weidman, Jerome   1913-. . . . . **CLC 7**
See also CANR 1; CA 1-4R; DLB 28

Weil, Simone   1909-1943. . . . . **TCLC 23**
See also CA 117

Weinstein, Nathan Wallenstein   1903-1940
See West, Nathanael

Weir, Peter   1944-. . . . . **CLC 20**
See also CA 113, 123

Weiss, Peter (Ulrich)
   1916-1982 . . . . **CLC 3, 15, 51**
See also CANR 3; CA 45-48;
   obituary CA 106; DLB 69

Weiss, Theodore (Russell)
   1916- . . . . **CLC 3, 8, 14**
See also CAAS 2; CA 9-12R; DLB 5

Welch, (Maurice) Denton
   1915-1948 . . . . **TCLC 22**
See also CA 121

Welch, James   1940- . . . . **CLC 6, 14, 52**
See also CA 85-88

Weldon, Fay
   1933- . . . . **CLC 6, 9, 11, 19, 36, 59**
See also CANR 16; CA 21-24R; DLB 14

Wellek, Rene   1903- . . . . **CLC 28**
See also CAAS 7; CANR 8; CA 5-8R;
   DLB 63

Weller, Michael   1942- . . . . **CLC 10, 53**
See also CA 85-88

Weller, Paul   1958- . . . . **CLC 26**

Wellershoff, Dieter   1925-. . . . . **CLC 46**
See also CANR 16; CA 89-92

Welles, (George) Orson
   1915-1985 . . . . **CLC 20**
See also CA 93-96; obituary CA 117

Wellman, Mac   1945- . . . . **CLC 65**

Wellman, Manly Wade   1903-1986 . . **CLC 49**
See also CANR 6, 16; CA 1-4R;
   obituary CA 118; SATA 6, 47

Wells, Carolyn   1862-1942 . . . . **TCLC 35**
See also CA 113; DLB 11

Wells, H(erbert) G(eorge)
   1866-1946 . . . . . . **TCLC 6, 12, 19; SSC 6**
See also CA 110, 121; SATA 20; DLB 34,
   70

Wells, Rosemary   1943-. . . . . **CLC 12**
See also CLR 16; CA 85-88; SAAS 1;
   SATA 18

Welty, Eudora (Alice)
   1909- . . . . **CLC 1, 2, 5, 14, 22, 33; SSC 1**
See also CA 9-12R; CABS 1; DLB 2;
   DLB-Y 87; CDALB 1941-1968

Wen I-to   1899-1946 . . . . **TCLC 28**

Werfel, Franz (V.)   1890-1945 . . . . . . **TCLC 8**
See also CA 104; DLB 81

Wergeland, Henrik Arnold
   1808-1845 . . . . **NCLC 5**

Wersba, Barbara   1932-. . . . . **CLC 30**
See also CLR 3; CANR 16; CA 29-32R;
   SAAS 2; SATA 1, 58; DLB 52

Wertmuller, Lina   1928- . . . . **CLC 16**
See also CA 97-100

Wescott, Glenway 1901-1987...... CLC 13
See also CANR 23; CA 13-16R;
obituary CA 121; DLB 4, 9

Wesker, Arnold 1932- .... CLC 3, 5, 42
See also CAAS 7; CANR 1; CA 1-4R;
DLB 13

Wesley, Richard (Errol) 1945-...... CLC 7
See also CA 57-60; DLB 38

Wessel, Johan Herman 1742-1785 .... LC 7

West, Anthony (Panther)
1914-1987 .... CLC 50
See also CANR 3, 19; CA 45-48; DLB 15

West, Jessamyn 1907-1984 ...... CLC 7, 17
See also CA 9-12R; obituary CA 112;
obituary SATA 37; DLB 6; DLB-Y 84

West, Morris L(anglo) 1916-..... CLC 6, 33
See also CA 5-8R; obituary CA 124

West, Nathanael
1903-1940 .... TCLC 1, 14, 44
See also CA 104, 125; DLB 4, 9, 28;
CDALB 1929-1941

West, Paul 1930- .... CLC 7, 14
See also CAAS 7; CANR 22; CA 13-16R;
DLB 14

West, Rebecca 1892-1983 .. CLC 7, 9, 31, 50
See also CANR 19; CA 5-8R;
obituary CA 109; DLB 36; DLB-Y 83

Westall, Robert (Atkinson) 1929-... CLC 17
See also CLR 13; CANR 18; CA 69-72;
SAAS 2; SATA 23

Westlake, Donald E(dwin)
1933- .... CLC 7, 33
See also CANR 16; CA 17-20R

Westmacott, Mary 1890-1976
See Christie, (Dame) Agatha (Mary
Clarissa)

Whalen, Philip 1923- .... CLC 6, 29
See also CANR 5; CA 9-12R; DLB 16

Wharton, Edith (Newbold Jones)
1862-1937 ...... TCLC 3, 9, 27; SSC 6
See also CA 104; DLB 4, 9, 12, 78;
CDALB 1865-1917

Wharton, William 1925-........ CLC 18, 37
See also CA 93-96; DLB-Y 80

Wheatley (Peters), Phillis
1753?-1784............... LC 3; PC 3
See also BLC 3; DLB 31, 50;
CDALB 1640-1865

Wheelock, John Hall 1886-1978.... CLC 14
See also CANR 14; CA 13-16R;
obituary CA 77-80; DLB 45

Whelan, John 1900-
See O'Faolain, Sean

Whitaker, Rodney 1925-
See Trevanian

White, E(lwyn) B(rooks)
1899-1985 .... CLC 10, 34, 39
See also CLR 1; CANR 16; CA 13-16R;
obituary CA 116; SATA 2, 29, 44;
obituary SATA 44; DLB 11, 22

White, Edmund III 1940-......... CLC 27
See also CANR 3, 19; CA 45-48

White, Patrick (Victor Martindale)
1912-1990 .. CLC 3, 4, 5, 7, 9, 18, 65, 69
See also CA 81-84; obituary CA 132

White, T(erence) H(anbury)
1906-1964 .... CLC 30
See also CA 73-76; SATA 12

White, Terence de Vere 1912-...... CLC 49
See also CANR 3; CA 49-52

White, Walter (Francis)
1893-1955 .... TCLC 15
See also BLC 3; CA 115, 124; DLB 51

White, William Hale 1831-1913
See Rutherford, Mark
See also CA 121

Whitehead, E(dward) A(nthony)
1933- .... CLC 5
See also CA 65-68

Whitemore, Hugh 1936-.......... CLC 37

Whitman, Sarah Helen
1803-1878 .... NCLC 19
See also DLB 1

Whitman, Walt
1819-1892 .... NCLC 4, 31; PC 3
See also SATA 20; DLB 3, 64;
CDALB 1640-1865

Whitney, Phyllis A(yame) 1903-.... CLC 42
See also CANR 3, 25; CA 1-4R; SATA 1,
30

Whittemore, (Edward) Reed (Jr.)
1919-...................... CLC 4
See also CAAS 8; CANR 4; CA 9-12R;
DLB 5

Whittier, John Greenleaf
1807-1892 .... NCLC 8
See also DLB 1; CDALB 1640-1865

Wicker, Thomas Grey 1926-
See Wicker, Tom
See also CANR 21; CA 65-68

Wicker, Tom 1926-................ CLC 7
See also Wicker, Thomas Grey

Wideman, John Edgar
1941- .... CLC 5, 34, 36, 67
See also BLC 3; CANR 14; CA 85-88;
DLB 33

Wiebe, Rudy (H.) 1934-...... CLC 6, 11, 14
See also CA 37-40R; DLB 60

Wieland, Christoph Martin
1733-1813 .... NCLC 17

Wieners, John 1934-............... CLC 7
See also CA 13-16R; DLB 16

Wiesel, Elie(zer) 1928-..... CLC 3, 5, 11, 37
See also CAAS 4; CANR 8; CA 5-8R;
SATA 56; DLB 83; DLB-Y 87

Wiggins, Marianne 1948-......... CLC 57

Wight, James Alfred 1916-
See Herriot, James
See also CA 77-80; SATA 44

Wilbur, Richard (Purdy)
1921- .... CLC 3, 6, 9, 14, 53
See also CANR 2; CA 1-4R; CABS 2;
SATA 9; DLB 5

Wild, Peter 1940-................ CLC 14
See also CA 37-40R; DLB 5

Wilde, Oscar (Fingal O'Flahertie Wills)
1854-1900 .... TCLC 1, 8, 23, 41
See also CA 119; brief entry CA 104;
SATA 24; DLB 10, 19, 34, 57

Wilder, Billy 1906-.............. CLC 20
See also Wilder, Samuel
See also DLB 26

Wilder, Samuel 1906-
See Wilder, Billy
See also CA 89-92

Wilder, Thornton (Niven)
1897-1975 ..... CLC 1, 5, 6, 10, 15, 35;
DC 1
See also CA 13-16R; obituary CA 61-64;
DLB 4, 7, 9

Wiley, Richard 1944-............. CLC 44
See also CA 121, 129

Wilhelm, Kate 1928-............. CLC 7
See also CAAS 5; CANR 17; CA 37-40R;
DLB 8

Willard, Nancy 1936-.......... CLC 7, 37
See also CLR 5; CANR 10; CA 89-92;
SATA 30, 37; DLB 5, 52

Williams, C(harles) K(enneth)
1936- .... CLC 33, 56
See also CA 37-40R; DLB 5

Williams, Charles (Walter Stansby)
1886-1945 .... TCLC 1, 11
See also CA 104

Williams, Ella Gwendolen Rees 1890-1979
See Rhys, Jean

Williams, (George) Emlyn
1905-1987 .... CLC 15
See also CA 104, 123; DLB 10, 77

Williams, Hugo 1942-............. CLC 42
See also CA 17-20R; DLB 40

Williams, John A(lfred) 1925-.... CLC 5, 13
See also BLC 3; CAAS 3; CANR 6, 26;
CA 53-56; DLB 2, 33

Williams, Jonathan (Chamberlain)
1929- .... CLC 13
See also CANR 8; CA 9-12R; DLB 5

Williams, Joy 1944-.............. CLC 31
See also CANR 22; CA 41-44R

Williams, Norman 1952- .... CLC 39
See also CA 118

Williams, Paulette 1948-
See Shange, Ntozake

Williams, Sherley Anne 1944-
See also BLC 3; CANR 25; CA 73-76;
DLB 41

Williams, Shirley 1944-
See Williams, Sherley Anne

Williams, Tennessee
1911-1983 .... CLC 1, 2, 5, 7, 8, 11, 15,
19, 30, 39, 45, 71
See also CANR 31; CA 5-8R;
obituary CA 108; CABS 3; DLB 7;
DLB-Y 83; DLB-DS 4;
CDALB 1941-1968

Williams, Thomas (Alonzo) 1926-... CLC 14
See also CANR 2; CA 1-4R

Williams, Thomas Lanier 1911-1983
See Williams, Tennessee

Williams, William Carlos
1883-1963 ... CLC 1, 2, 5, 9, 13, 22, 42,
67
See also CA 89-92; DLB 4, 16, 54, 86;
CDALB 1917-1929

Author Index

Literary Criticism Series
Cumulative Topic Index

This index lists all topic entries in the Gale Literary Criticism Series *Contemporary Literary Criticism, Literature Criticism from 1400 to 1800, Nineteenth-Century Literature Criticism,* and *Twentieth-Century Literary Criticism.*

Topic Index

NCLC Cumulative Nationality Index

Mickiewicz, Adam   **3**
Norwid, Cyprian Kamil   **17**
Słowacki, Juliusz   **15**

ROMANIAN
Eminescu, Mihail   **33**

RUSSIAN
Aksakov, Sergei Timofeyvich   **2**
Bakunin, Mikhail Alexandrovich   **25**
Bashkirtseff, Marie   **27**
Belinski, Vissarion Grigoryevich   **5**
Chernyshevsky, Nikolay Gavrilovich   **1**
Dobrolyubov, Nikolai Alexandrovich   **5**
Dostoevsky, Fyodor   **2, 7, 21, 33**
Gogol, Nikolai   **5, 15, 31**
Goncharov, Ivan Alexandrovich   **1**
Herzen, Aleksandr Ivanovich   **10**
Karamzin, Nikolai Mikhailovich   **3**
Krylov, Ivan Andreevich   **1**
Lermontov, Mikhail Yuryevich   **5**
Leskov, Nikolai Semyonovich   **25**
Nekrasov, Nikolai   **11**
Ostrovsky, Alexander   **30**
Pisarev, Dmitry Ivanovich   **25**
Pushkin, Alexander   **3, 27**
Saltykov, Mikhail Evgrafovich   **16**
Smolenskin, Peretz   **30**
Turgenev, Ivan   **21**
Tyutchev, Fyodor   **34**
Zhukovsky, Vasily   **35**

SCOTTISH
Baillie, Joanna   **2**
Beattie, James   **25**
Campbell, Thomas   **19**
Ferrier, Susan   **8**
Galt, John   **1**
Hogg, James   **4**
Jeffrey, Francis   **33**
Lockhart, John Gibson   **6**
Oliphant, Margaret   **11**
Scott, Sir Walter   **15**
Stevenson, Robert Louis   **5, 14**
Thomson, James   **18**
Wilson, John   **5**

SPANISH
Alarcón, Pedro Antonio de   **1**
Caballero, Fernán   **10**
Castro, Rosalía de   **3**
Larra, Mariano José de   **17**
Tamayo y Baus, Manuel   **1**
Zorrilla y Moral, José   **6**

SWEDISH
Bremer, Fredrika   **11**
Tegnér, Esias   **2**

SWISS
Amiel, Henri Frédéric   **4**
Keller, Gottfried   **2**
Wyss, Johann David   **10**

Nationality Index

ISBN 0-8103-5836-0